THE ENCYCLOPEDIA OF HASIDISM

Also by Tzvi M. Rabinowicz

The Will and Testament of the Biala Rabbi
A Guide to Hasidism
The Slave Who Saved the City
The Jewish Literary Treasures of England and America
The Legacy of Polish Jewry
The World of Hasidism
Treasures of Judaica
Hasidism and the State of Israel
Hasidism: The Movement and Its Masters
A Guide to Life
Hasidic Rebbes
A World Apart
The Prince Who Turned into a Rooster

THE ENCYCLOPEDIA OF HASIDISM

edited by

Tzvi M. Rabinowicz

JASON ARONSON INC.
Northvale, New Jersey
London

This book was set in 9.5 pt. Times Roman by AeroType, Inc., Amherst, New Hampshire.

10 9 8 7 6 5 4 3 2 1

Library of Congress Cataloging-in-Publication Data

The Encyclopedia of Hasidism / edited by Tzvi M. Rabinowicz.
p. cm.
Includes bibliographical references.
ISBN 1-56821-123-6
1. Hasidism—Encyclopedias, 2. Hasidim—Encyclopedias.
I. Rabinowicz, Tzvi, 1919-
BM198.E53 1996
296.8'332'03—dc20 94-3140

Manufactured in the United States of America. Jason Aronson Inc. offers books and cassettes. For information and catalog write to Jason Aronson Inc., 230 Livingston Street, Northvale, New Jersey 07647.

Dedicated to the revered memory
of my father,
Rabbi Nathan David Rabinowicz,
The Biala Rebbe, London

Contents

Introduction

Recent years have witnessed an upsurge of scholarly interest in Hasidism. Nearly four thousand works and innumerable essays have been written on the subject, and this vast amount of literature still awaits its bibliographers. This meteoric movement that flashed with such dazzling brilliance across the Jewish firmament has now attracted the attention of historians, writers, poets, sociologists, and philosophers. Many publications, ranging from the analytical works of J. G. Weiss to the recent discoveries of Murray J. Rosman, have illuminated much that was once obscure.

The lack of a concise and comprehensive encyclopedia of Hasidism has often been deplored and is long overdue. Despite the pioneering efforts in Hebrew of Shlomoh Hayyim Porush, Yitzhak Alfasi, and Meir Wunder, this work is the first of its kind in English. It is a historic event in Judaic publications. Never before has so much information been presented in such an accessible form.

Hasidism originated in Eastern Europe in the middle of the eighteenth century. It is the greatest revival movement in the history of the Jewish people. It is not a new form of Judaism, but a reaffirmation of Judaism's fundamental and mystical beliefs. It focuses on the principles of the joy of living, the love of God and man, sincerity, and dedication. Hasidism offers a form of otherworldly ecstasy to all Jews: equally to the untutored and destitute and to the learned and privileged. It is Judaism in its finest and most creative form. The movement stresses social justice and the hallowing of each day. It is more than a collection of ideals and noble purposes; it is a way of life, a civilization, a culture with a message that transcends the barriers of time and place.

Great leaders—outstanding and charismatic rebbes—guided the movement. During the past two centuries, Hasidism has produced more religious leaders than has any other period since talmudic times.

Between 1939 and 1945, almost one and a half million hasidim perished in the Nazi Holocaust, the most destructive genocide in human history. Yet out of the ashes, phoenix-like, Hasidism has made a remarkable reappearance in the United States, in Israel, in England, and in many other parts of the world. Its upsurge has confounded the prophets of its doom. Despite the pressures of modern life and the level of sophistication of the secular society all around it, hasidic life flourishes in Jerusalem, Bene Berak, New York, and many other cities throughout the world. Emissaries of the Lubavitch rebbe have established more than eleven hundred *Habad* houses in all six continents. "Lubavitch" has become a household name. It brings hasidic teachings to the Sephardim of Casablanca, Meknes, and Tunis and to the Jews in Moscow and St. Petersburg. Pietists in long *kapotes* and black hats, women in kerchiefs, and children with long sidelocks and speaking Yiddish add color to Jewish life everywhere. They have succeeded in transplanting the Eastern European *shtetl* to the West. They proudly describe themselves as hasidim of Lubavitch, Satmar, Belz, Bobov, and Ger—names that linger lovingly on their lips. They regard themselves as the contemporary defenders of the faith, continuing the traditions and mores of their ancestors, in the firm belief that the future is as important as the past.

Today there are probably no more than 400,000 hasidim throughout the world, but the movement's significance cannot be judged by numbers alone. Hasidim exert a discernible influence on Israeli politics and Diaspora writers. Their ideals have inspired Nobel prize winners, poet Nellie Sachs, storytellers Isaac Bashevis Singer, Elie Wiesel, Shlomoh

Joseph Agnon, and philosopher Abraham Joshua Heschel, and they can be detected in the works of their predecessors, Isaac Leib Peretz and Franz Kafka.

The work herein includes many biographies of hasidic leaders of the past two hundred years–from the founder of the movement, Rabbi Israel Baal Shem Tov, to the leaders of the different dynasties of the eighteenth, nineteenth, and twentieth centuries.

Limited cross-reference in the body of an article or at its end refers the reader to other entries containing essential supplementary material. At the end of each article the initials of its contributor are given. All unsigned articles are usually by the editor, who also updated most of the entries. The names of the contributors can be found at the beginning of the book. Many of the entries have a select bibliography attached to them, with preference given to books in English, but also listing books written in other languages. When there is no blibliography, the entries are either brief or based on interviews with contemporary rabbis and personalities who are well documented elsewhere.

The common forms of names appearing in the Bible have, with a few exceptions, been maintained. Names, particularly surnames, pose a serious problem in hasidic transliterations. Some of them have diverse spellings. Thus, names like Rabinowicz, Horowitz, and Shapira can be and have been spelled in a variety of ways. The dates of death (*yahrzeit*) of rebbes have been recorded in conformity with hasidic practice: according to the Jewish date–the day and month of the Hebrew calendar. Many of the tiny villages of Eastern Europe cannot be found in any gazetteer.

An encyclopedia is a difficult undertaking because of its sheer magnitude. Therefore, a work of such size must of necessity be selective, and it becomes inevitable that some rebbes and topics have been omitted.

As is natural with a work of this dimension, I have accumulated many debts of gratitude, which I cannot hope to repay. The work would have been impossible without the participation of a large and diverse team of collaborating scholars, a number of whom, alas, have not lived to see the fruits of their labor. I would like to single out the help given to me by my sister Rachel, a spirit that soared in wisdom, warmth, and wit. Her premature death, on 20 *Elul* 1987, left an irreparable void. In spite of her busy schedule, she read parts of the manuscript and gave much assistance and wise advice.

This work has had a somewhat prolonged period of gestation and a checkered history. It was David Olivestone, former manager of Hebrew Publishing Company, in New York, who first suggested the idea of an encyclopedia and who gave this work his full personal support. In November 1974, the editor was formally appointed. Three years later, a massive manuscript was in the publisher's hands. Due to financial problems and a change of ownership, Hebrew Publishing Company was no longer in a position to publish the work, and it was due to the efforts of Stephan J. Siegel, attorney-at-law in New York, that the Hebrew Publishing Company finally reassigned the rights to the editor. In May 1992, the work was taken up with enthusiasm by Arthur Kurzweil, of Jason Aronson Inc., to whom I am grateful for his vision, expertise, and valuable help. I am indebted to Muriel Jorgensen for her keen interest. She carefully and meticulously read the entire draft and provided me with constructive criticism and helpful suggestions.

A number of friends and colleagues carefully read and commented on my work. My profound thanks to Rabbis Efraim Gastwirth, Philip Ginsbury, Sidney Herman, Julian Jacobs, Joseph Shaw, Julian Shindler, and Messrs. Melvin Benjamin, Aaron Prijs, Jack Shamash, David Shepherd, and my sons Nathan David and Jacob Isaac.

I take this opportunity to express my appreciation to my friend Lord Max Rayne of the Rayne Foundation, to Clive M. Marks of the Lord Ashdowne Charitable Trust, and to J. Mark Kennedy for their encouragement. I am grateful to my wife, Bella, an unfailing guide, for her skill and devotion. Without her tireless efforts and extreme patience, this work would not have been brought up to date.

It is my fervent hope that this pioneering work will not only perpetuate the memory of the many hasidim who perished in the Holocaust, but will also be an invaluable and indispensable reference book. It should serve as a bridge between the world of the specialist and that of the general reader.

29 *Tishri* 5755

Ed.

Glossary

ADAR – twelfth month of the Jewish religious calendar, approximating February/March.

ADAR SHENI (lit. "Second *Adar*") – additional month occurring after *Adar* in a leap year; there are seven leap years in every nineteen years in the Jewish religious calendar.

ADDITIONAL PRAYER – see **Musaf**.

ADMOR – title given to a hasidic rebbe; acronym for *Adoneinu, moreinu, VeRabbeinu* (our master, teacher, and rabbi).

AFTERNOON PRAYER – see **Minhah**.

AGGADAH (pl. *Aggadot*) – name given to the section of rabbinic literature that contains the homiletic expositions of the Bible.

AGUDA (lit. "Union" or "Association") – world Jewish organization to preserve Orthodoxy founded in Kattowitz in 1912.

AGUNAH (lit. "a wife forsaken") – woman unable to remarry according to Jewish Law because of her husband's desertion.

AHAVAT HASHEM – love of God.

AHAVAT ISRAEL – love of Israel.

AHAVAT TORAH – love of the Torah.

ALEF – first letter of the Hebrew alphabet.

ALEF BET – Hebrew alphabet.

ALIYAH (lit. "going up") – term used in connection with being called on to read the Torah in the synagogue, also used to describe immigration to the Holy Land.

ALIYAH LEREGEL – visiting a rebbe at festival time.

ALMEMAR – raised platform in the center of a synagogue where the Scroll of the Law is placed for public reading.

ALTER REBBE (lit. "old rebbe") – refers to R. Shneur Zalman of Liady.

AM HAARETZ – ignorant man.

AMIDAH (lit. "standing") – name given to the main prayer at each of the statutory services, also known as *Shemoneh Esrei* or *Tefillah*; recited standing up.

AMORA (pl. *Amora'im*) – name given to the rabbinic authorities responsible for the *Gemara*.

ANSHEI SHLOMEINU (lit. "men of our fraternity") – term used by the hasidim when referring to their own group.

ARBA KANFOT – four-fringed garment worn by males under their outer garments during the day.

ARBA MINIM – four species of plant used during Sukkot, i.e., the palm branch, the myrtle, the willow, and the *etrog*.

ARI (lit. "lion") – acronym from the Hebrew words "Our master, Rabbi Yitzhak Luria" (1534–1572).

ASHKENAZ (pl. *Ashkenazim*) – Jews from central and eastern Europe.

ATZILUT (lit. "emanation") – highest of the four worlds described by the kabbalists.

AV – fifth month of the Jewish religious calendar, approximating July/August.

AV BET DIN – head of a Jewish court of law.

BAAL HANES – miracle worker.

BAAL KOREH (lit. "master of the reading") – person who reads from the Scroll of the Law in the synagogue.

BAAL MOFET – master of the miraculous deeds.

BAAL SHEM – master of the Name; title given to a man who works wonders through his piety and the employment of the Divine Name.

BAAL SHEM TOV – founder of Hasidism.

BAAL TEFILLAH (lit. "master of prayer") – leader of prayers during public worship.

BAAL TEKIYAH (lit. "master of the blowing") – one who blows the *shofar*.

BAAL TESHUVAH (lit. "penitent") – one who atones for his sins.

BAALEI BATIM–upright and respected people.
BABA KAMMA–talmudical tractate dealing with damage caused to property.
BADHAN–jester.
BAHIR–SEFER HABAHIR (lit. "book of brightness")–early kabbalistic work.
BAR–son of.
BAR MITZVAH (lit. "son of the Commandment")–ceremony that marks a boy's thirteenth birthday, when he becomes religiously responsible for his own conduct.
BEHELFER–assistant.
BEKESHE–long winter coat half-lined with fur.
BEN–son of.
BENIONI (lit. "the intermediate one")–kabbalistic term for one who is not a *tzaddik*.
BESHT–abbreviation of the Hebrew name *Baal Shem Tov*–"Master of the Good Name"–founder of Hasidism.
BET DIN–Jewish religious court.
BET HAKNESSET–synagogue, house of study.
BET HAMIDRASH–place where the study of the Torah is carried on.
BIMAH–reader's platform.
BINAH (lit. "understanding")–one of the three upper *Sefirot* corresponding to the faculty of the intellect.
BITTUL–to nullify, to be humble.
BREAKING OF THE VESSELS (*Shevirat Kelim*)–kabbalistic expression; see **Sparks**.
BRIT MILAH–circumcision.
BUND–Jewish Socialist Party, founded in Vilna in 1897.
CHEKA–All Russian Extraordinary Commission for Combatting Counterrevolutionary Activities and Sabotage.
CODES–systematic compilation of talmudic law.
DAAT (lit. "knowledge")–third *Sefirah*.
DAF YOMI–daily study of a page of the Talmud.
DAYAN–member of a rabbinic court.
DEVEKUT (lit. "devotion")–attachment or adhesion to God.
DIASPORA–Jews living outside the Holy Land.
DIN–judgment.
DIVREI TORAH (lit. "words of the Torah")–discourses delivered by a *rebbe*.
DREIDL–game played on Hanukkah.
DUNAM–unit of land area of 1,000 square meters, equal to approximately a quarter acre. Used in Israel.
DVAR TORAH–discourse.
DYBBUK–soul of a dead person that has invaded a living body.
EIN SOF (lit. "without an end")–(the Infinite) from which all forms in the universe are created.
EIN YAAKOV–popular aggadic work by R. Jacob Ibn Habib.
ELUL–sixth month of the Jewish religious calendar, approximating August/September.
ERETZ YISRAEL–Land of Israel.
ERUV (pl. *Eruvim*, lit. "blending")–method permitting the carrying of an object on the Sabbath.
ETHICAL WILL–ethical disposition made by the dying.
ETROG–citron, one of the four species used during Sukkot.
ETZAH–advice.
EVIL URGE–inclination to do evil.
EXILARCH (lit. "head of the exile")–title of the lay leader of Babylonian Jewry.
FARBRENGEN–gathering of *Habad* hasidim.
FRINGES–see **Tzitzit**.
GABBAI–rabbi's assistant.
GALUT–exile.
GAN EDEN–paradise.
GAON–genius; title given to an outstanding talmudic scholar.
GARTEL–prayer sash, belt worn by hasidim during prayer.
GEHINNOM–hell.
GELILAH (lit. "rolling")–after the Reading of the Law is completed, a member of the congregation is called upon to roll up the opened Scroll.
GEMARA–comments and discussions on the *Mishnah*; see **Talmud**.
GEMATRIA–numerical value of Hebrew letters, used as a basis for homiletic interpretations.
GEMILUT HASADIM–bestowal of loving-kindness.
GENIZAH (lit. "hiding")–storeroom for keeping the remains of sacred books.
GET–bill of divorce.
GEULAH–redemption.
GEVURAH–power; *Sefirah* signifying severity or fear.

GILGUL – transmigration of souls, reincarnation.
GLATT KOSHER (lit. "smooth Kosher") – indicates a meat product is kosher without any shadow of doubt.
GOLAH – Jewish Diaspora.
GOLEM – automaton, a human form created by magical means.
GOYIM (lit. "a nation") – non-Jews.
GUTER YID (lit. "good Jew") – title given to a hasidic rebbe.
HABAD – acronym of *Hokhmah, Binah, Daat* (wisdom, understanding, knowledge).
HADLAKAH – lighting of a bonfire on Lag BaOmer.
HAFSAKAH – interval.
HAFTARAH (lit. "conclusion) – selections from the prophetic books of the Bible read in the synagogue on the Sabbath, Festivals, and on afternoons of Fasts after the reading from the Pentateuch.
HAGGADAH – traditional text read on the first two nights of Passover.
HAKHAM (lit. a "wise man") – sage; title of a rabbi in the Sephardic congregation.
HAKKAFOT (lit. "circuits") – procession around the *bimah* with the Torah on Simhat Torah.
HALAKHAH (pl. *Halakhot*) – guidance; final decision by the rabbis; sections of rabbinic literature that deal with legal questions.
HALLAH (pl. *Hallot*) – specially prepared loaves for the Sabbath and Festivals.
HALLEL – additional Psalms (113–118) recited on the New Moon and Holy Days.
HALUKKAH – distribution of funds for indigent Jews in the Holy Land before 1948.
HALUTZIM – Zionist pioneer.
HAMETZ (lit. "leaven") – any fermented food or beverage that one is prohibited to consume or possess during Passover.
HANUKKAH – Festival of Lights, celebrated from 25 *Kislev* for eight days, to commemorate the rededication of the Temple in 165 B.C.E., after its desecration by Antiochus Epiphanes.
HAROSET – mixture of ground nuts and apples, part of the Passover *seder* table.
HASHEM (lit. "the Name") – alternative name for God.
HASID (pl. *Hasidim*) – member of the hasidic movement.
HASIDEI ASHKENAZ – adherents of the pietist movement of medieval Germany.
HASKALAH – Enlightenment, the movement that spread European culture into eastern Europe in the eighteenth and nineteenth centuries.
HAVDALAH – ceremony marking the end of the Sabbath or Festival.
HAVER – Hebrew for companion; title occasionally given to a scholar.
HAZAN – cantor.
HEDER – private Hebrew school, usually a room in the teacher's house.
HEIKHALOT (lit. "palaces") – traditional Jewish mysticism, centering on the mystical journey through the heavenly spheres.
HEREM – excommunication.
HESED (lit. "kindness") – *Sefirah* signifying love.
HESHVAN – see **Marheshvan**.
HETER MEAH RABBANIM – dispensation by one hundred rabbis, granted to one who may not ordinarily divorce his wife, in order to remarry.
HEVRAH (pl. *Hevrot*) – small congregation of traditional Jews.
HEVRAH KADDISHA (lit. "holy society") – organization that handles all the necessary rituals concerning preparations for burial.
HIBBAT ZION (lit. "Love of Zion") – Zionist movement that arose in Russia in the 1880s.
HIDDUSH (pl. *Hiddushim*) – novel insights into difficult Torah portions.
HINUKH – education.
HITBODEDUT – aloneness with God.
HITLAHAVUT – enthusiasm.
HITPAALUT – ecstasy.
HOIF – court, rebbe's residence.
HOKHMAH (lit. "Wisdom") – the second *Sefirah*, the primal point of emanation.
HOL HAMO'ED – intermediate days of a Festival.
HOLY SPARKS (*nitzotzot*) – kabbalistic concept; the unitary divine light was fragmented and sparks fell among the shells.
HOSHANAH RABBA – seventh day of Sukkot.
HOVEVEI ZION – pre-Herzl Zionist movement in Russia.
HOZEH – seer.
HUKKAT HAGOY – aping the ways of the Gentiles.
HUMASH – Pentateuch.

HUPPAH–canopy used for a marriage ceremony.

HURBAN–destruction.

IBBUR (lit. "pregnancy")–kabbalistic doctrine whereby the soul of one person may attach itself to the soul of another person.

IGGERET–letter.

ILLUI–outstanding scholar.

IYYAR–second month of the Jewish religious calendar, approximating April/May.

JUDENRAT–Jewish council, set up in Jewish communities under the Nazis.

JUDENREIN–free of Jews (German).

KABBALAH–Jewish mystical literature.

KADDISH–mourner's prayer.

KAFTAN–long coat.

KAHAL–Jewish community.

KAMAYOT–amulets.

KAPO–term used in Nazi concentration camps for an inmate appointed by the SS to supervise fellow prisoners.

KAPOTE–long-sleeved coat fastened by a sash and worn by the hasidim.

KASHER–ritually permitted food.

KASHRUT–Jewish dietary laws.

KAV HAKELI–palm string on which the soul rolls about after death.

KAVVANAH–intention, denoting spiritual concentration.

KEFAR–village.

KEHILLAH–community.

KELAL YISRAEL–congregation of Israel.

KETER (lit. "crown")–the most exalted of the *Sefirot*.

KIDDUSH–prayer of sanctification recited on the Sabbath and Festivals.

KIDDUSH HASHEM–martyrdom.

KINOT–lamentations recited on the 9th of *Av*.

KIPPAH–skullcap; see **Yarmulke**.

KISLEV–ninth month of the Jewish religious calendar, approximating November/December.

KITTEL–plain white overgarment, worn by some during prayers on the High Holy Days.

KLAUS (pl. *Klauslech*)–a small *Bet Ha-Midrash*.

KLIPPAH (pl. *klippot*)–husk; mystical term denoting force of evil.

KLOYZ–see Klaus.

KOHEN (pl. *kohanim*)–priest.

KOLLEL–community in the Holy Land, supported by its fellow countrymen in the Diaspora; also an institution for higher studies where men devote themselves to Torah study after marriage.

KOL NIDREI ("all vows")–opening words of the religious service on the eve of the Day of Atonement.

KOTEL MAARAVI–Western Wall. Part of the wall that enclosed Herod's Temple is still standing in the Old City of Jerusalem.

KUGEL–sweet baked pudding.

KUNTRES–tract.

KVITTEL (pl. *Kvittlech*)–short note or slip presented to a hasidic leader.

LAG BAOMER–thirty-third day of the *Omer* period, falling on 18 *Iyyar*, a semiholiday.

LAMDAN–scholar.

LANDESKANZLEI–council office.

LULAV–palm branch, one of the four species used during Sukkot.

LURIAN KABBALAH–the mysticism of R. Yitzhak Luria.

MAAMADOT–regular contributions from the *rebbe* for the upkeep of the court.

MAAMAR–discourse by a rebbe.

MAARIV–evening prayer.

MAASEI BERESHIT–Jewish mystical teachings pertaining to the creation of the world.

MAASIYOT–stories.

MAGGID–popular preacher.

MAHSHAVOT ZAROT–alien thoughts that are not related to prayer.

MAHZOR–festival prayer book.

MALKHUT–kingship; tenth of the *Sefirot*, administering the divine justice to the lower world.

MAOS HITTIN (Heb. "wheat money")–money distributed to the poor on the eve of Passover.

MARHESHVAN–also known as *Heshvan*, eighth month of the Jewish religious calendar, approximating October/November.

MASHGIAH–*Kashrut* supervisor.

MASHKEI–drink.

MASKIL (pl. *maskilim*)–adherent of the *Haskalah*.

MASMID–diligent student.

MATZAH–unleavened bread eaten on Passover.

MEGILLAH–term applied to the Book of Esther.

MEHUTAN–offspring's in-laws.

MELAMED—teacher of children.
MELAVEH MALKAH (lit. "escorting the queen")—last festive meal on Saturday night.
MENORAH—candelabrum.
MERKAVAH—divine chariot, mystical discipline associated with Ezekiel's vision of the divine throne.
MESHULAH (pl. *Meshulahim*)—emissaries sent to contact, propagate, and raise funds for charitable institutions.
MESIRAT NEFESH—self-sacrifice.
MESIVTA—talmudical college.
MEZUZAH (pl. *Mezuzot*)—parchment scroll containing selected Torah verses placed in a container and fixed to a doorpost.
MIDRASH (pl. *Midrashim*)—collection of rabbinic interpretation.
MIKVEH (pl. *Mikvaot*)—ritual bath.
MILAH or **BRIT MILAH**—circumcision.
MINHAG—local custom.
MINHAH—afternoon service.
MINYAN—quorum of ten men, required for congregational worship.
MISHNAH—collection of the statements edited by R. Judah the Prince (135–220 C.E.).
MITNAGGED (pl. *mitnaggedim*)—opponent of Hasidism.
MITTLER REBBE—*Middle Rebbe*, R. Dov Baer Schneersohn.
MITZVAH—religious obligation, good deed.
MO'ETZET GEDOLEI HATORAH—Council of Sages of the Aguda.
MOFET—miracle performed by a *rebbe*.
MOHEL—man who performs ritual circumcision.
MOKHIAH—chastiser, admonisher.
MOSHAV—small holding, cooperative settlement in Israel.
MUSAF—additional service on the Sabbath and Festivals.
MUSAR MOVEMENT—movement in Judaism devoted to the improvement of one's service to God by moral exhortation.
NEILAH—concluding prayer recited on the Day of Atonement.
NESHAMAH—soul.
NETUREI KARTA (lit. "watchers of the city")—ultra-Orthodox anti-Zionist sect.
NIGGUN—tune or melody, often without words, sung by the hasidim.
NISAN—first month of the Jewish religious calendar, approximating March/April.
NITZOTZOT—sparks.
NOTARIKON—method of abbreviating Hebrew words by acronym.
NOVELLA(E)—commentary on talmudic or rabbinic subjects.
NUSAH—rite or custom of prayer for religious service.
NUSAH ARI—rite arranged according to R. Yitzhak Luria.
NUSAH SEPHARD—rite according to the Sephardic tradition.
OHEL—sepulchre erected over the grave of a *tzaddik*, where candles can be lit and people stand in prayer.
OHEV YISRAEL—lover of the Jewish people.
OMER—first sheaf of barley harvested (Leviticus 23:9–14).
ONEG SHABBAT (lit. "Sabbath delight")—gathering held on Sabbath afternoon marked by the singing of *Zemirot* and the delivery of discourses on the biblical lesson of the day.
PALE OF SETTLEMENT—25 provinces of Czarist Russia where Jews were permitted to live.
PARNAS (pl. *parnassim*)—chief synagogue functionary.
PASSOVER—Festival commemorating the liberation of the Jews from bondage in Egypt, celebrated from 15 to 22 *Nisan*.
PELZ—fur coat.
PESAH—see **Passover**.
PEYOT—sidelocks worn by men.
PHYLACTERIES—see **Tefillin**.
PIDYON (pl. *pidyonot*)—money given to the rebbe.
PIDYON HABEN—redemption of the first-born, held on the 31st day after his birth.
PIDYON SHEVUYIM—redemption money collected to pay fines for those taken into captivity.
PILPUL—complex dialectical discourse.
PINKUS—communal minutes book.
PIYYUT (pl. *Piyyutim*)—liturgical poem.
PRAVE TISH—hasidic rebbe conducting the Sabbath meal.
PURIM—Festival held on 14 *Adar* in commemoration of the deliverance of the Jews of Persia at the time of Queen Esther.
RAV—rabbi.
REB—title of respect.
REBBE—spiritual leader of a hasidic sect.
REJOICING OF THE LAW—see **Simhat Torah**.

RESPONSA – collection of replies to questions addressed to rabbinic authorities.
RIKKUD – dance.
RISHONIM – codifiers of talmudic law, active during the period between the completion of the Talmud and R. Joseph Caro's compilation of the *Shulhan Arukh* in the sixteenth century.
ROSH HASHANAH – the Jewish New Year, a two-day holiday at the beginning of the month of *Tishri* (September/October).
ROSH HODESH – new moon, marking the beginning of a Hebrew month.
ROSH YESHIVAH – head of a talmudic college.
RUAH HAKODESH – holy spirit; the hasidim revered their leader, claiming that he possessed the holy spirit.
SANDEK – one who holds the infant during the circumcision ceremony.
SANHEDRIN – Assembly of 71 ordained scholars that functioned as a supreme council and as a legislature.
SEDER – service commemorating the Exodus, observed in Jewish homes on the first two nights of Passover.
SEFER – book of religious content.
SEFER TORAH – scroll of the Law.
SEFIROT (sing. *Sefirah*) – ten mystical terms denoting the ten emanations.
SEGULAH – charm or amulet.
SELIHOT – penitential prayers.
SEMIKHAH – rabbinic ordination.
SEPHARDI – Jew of Spanish or Middle Eastern extraction.
SEUDAH – festive meal.
SEYM – Polish parliament.
SHABBAT HAGADOL (lit. "the great Sabbath") – the Sabbath preceding Passover.
SHABBATEAN – adherent of the pseudo-Messiah Shabbetai Tzvi.
SHADKHAN – marriage broker.
SHAHARIT – morning prayer.
SHALOM BAYIT – domestic peace; harmony between husband and wife.
SHALOSH SEUDOT – third Sabbath meal, eaten after the afternoon service and accompanied by singing and discourses.
SHAMASH – synagogue beadle.
SHATNES – prohibition of wearing a garment of mixed wool and linen fibers.
SHAVUOT – Pentecost, the Festival of Weeks, second of the three annual Pilgrim Festivals, commemorating the Receiving of the Law on Mount Sinai.
SHEITEL – wig worn by married Orthodox Jewish women.
SHEHITAH – ritual slaughtering.
SHEKHINAH – divine presence.
SHELAH MANOT – sending of food to one another on Purim.
SHELITO – may he live for many good days.
SHEMA – central Jewish prayer, expressing the unity of God (Deuteronomy 6:4).
SHEMINI ATZERET – eighth day of the Sukkot Festival.
SHEMITAH – Sabbatical year. Every seventh year the land must lie fallow (Leviticus 25:2).
SHEMURAH MATZOT (lit. "guarded *Matzot*") – hand-baked *Matzot*. The flour of the *Matzot* is supervised from the time the wheat is harvested.
SHEVA BERAKHOT – seven blessings recited after the wedding ceremony.
SHEVAT – eleventh month of the Jewish religious calendar, approximating January/February.
SHEVIRAT KELIM – breaking of the vessels.
SHIDDUKH – arranged marriage.
SHIKKUN – housing project.
SHIMUSHE RABBA – type of *Tefillin* worn by the most saintly.
SHIRAYIM – remains of the food eaten by the rebbe and then distributed among the hasidim.
SHISHI – sixth portion of the Sabbath Torah reading reserved for the rebbe.
SHIUR – study session.
SHIVAH – weeklong mourning period.
SHOFAR – ram's horn, sounded during the month of *Elul*, on Rosh Hashanah, and at the end of Yom Kippur.
SHOHET – one who is qualified to perform ritual slaughter.
SHOMER SHABBAT – one who keeps the Sabbath.
SHTADLAN (lit. "persuader") – Jewish representative adroit in negotiating with dignitaries of state.
SHTETL – small town.
SHTIEBL (pl. *shtieblech*) – small house of prayer of the hasidim.
SHTREIMEL – wide-brimmed fur hat worn on the Sabbath by the hasidim.
SHULHAN ARUKH – authoritative Code of Jewish Law, consisting of four parts: *Orah Hayyim*, *Yoreh De'ah*, *Even HaEzer*, *Hoshen Mishpat*.

SHUSHAN PURIM–day after Purim.
SIAH (pl. *Sihot*)–hasidic teachings.
SIDDUR–Jewish prayer book.
SIMHAH–joyous occasion.
SIMHAT TORAH–Rejoicing of the Law, observed as a Festival immediately following Shemini Azeret, when the Pentateuch is completed and recommenced.
SITRA AHRA (lit. "the other side")–power of evil.
SIVAN–third month of the Jewish religious calendar, approximating May/June.
SIYYUM (lit. "completion")–marking the completion of either the study of a tractate of the Talmud or the writing of a *Sefer Torah*.
SOFER–scribe.
SPARKS (*Nitzotzot*)–during the "breaking of the vessels," i.e., the earlier chaotic world, the holy sparks fell into the shells. They fell in order to be lifted up again.
SUKKAH–booth or tabernacle erected for Sukkot, in which religious Jews dwell.
SUKKOT–one of the three religious Pilgrim Festivals, beginning on 15 *Tishri*.
TAHARAT HAMISHPAHAH–family purity.
TAKKANAH–ordinance promulgated for public welfare.
TALLIT–prayer shawl; a large, four-cornered shawl, with fringes at the corners, worn by men during the morning service.
TALLIT KATAN–garment with fringes worn during the day under the outer garments.
TALMID–student.
TALMUD–postbiblical rabbinic compendium, containing legal and moral teachings; the Babylonian and the Jerusalem Talmuds, both of which are written in Aramaic.
TALMUD TORAH–Hebrew elementary school, usually attached to a synagogue.
TAMMUZ–fourth month of the Jewish religious calendar, approximating June/July.
TANNA (lit. "one who repeats")–rabbi quoted in the *Mishnah*.
TANYA (lit. "it has been taught")–title of the work by R. Shneur Zalman.
TARGUM–Aramaic translation of the Bible.
TEFILLAH–prayer.
TEFILLIN–phylacteries, two small leather cases containing passages from the Pentateuch and affixed to the forehead and upper left arm during recital of the morning prayers on weekdays.
TEHILLIM–Psalms.
TEN DAYS OF PENITENCE–ten-day period from Rosh Hashanah to the Day of Atonement.
TESHUVAH–repentance.
TETRAGRAMMATON–four-letter name of God.
TEVET–tenth month of the Jewish religious calendar, approximating December/January.
TIFERET–beauty; sixth *Sefirah*.
TIKKUN–order of service for special occasions; also a mystical term denoting restoration of the right order and true unity after the spiritual "catastrophe" that occurred in the cosmos.
TIKKUN HATZOT–kabbalistic prayers recited at midnight, bewailing the destruction of the Temple.
TISH–communal meal conducted by the rebbe.
TISHAH B'AV–ninth day of the Hebrew month of *Av*, commemorating the destruction of the First and Second Temples.
TISHRI–seventh month of the Jewish religious calendar, approximating September/October.
TOHOROT–sixth and last order of the *Mishnah*.
TORAH–Hebrew for "teaching" or "guidance"; generally refers to the Five Books of Moses, to the Oral Law, and to the whole body of Jewish religious literature.
TOSAFOT–explanatory notes on the Talmud.
TREIFAH–food that is not *Kosher*.
TU B'SHEVAT–fifteenth day of the month of *Shevat*, the New Year for trees.
TZADDIK (pl. *tzaddikim*) (lit. "a just and righteous man")–hasidic rebbe.
TZANZER KLAUS–*shtiebl* of the hasidim of Zanz.
TZEDDAKAH–charity.
TZEMAH TZEDDEK (lit. "seed of the righteous")–refers to R. Menahem Mendel of Lubavitch, who was called after his book *Tzemah Tzeddek*.
TZIMMES–sweet carrot stew.
TZIMTZUM–contraction, a kabbalistic term; self-withdrawal of the Godhead to enable a finite world to come into being.

TZITZIT – fringes attached to a prayer shawl.

USHPIZIN (Aramaic for guests) – usually used to refer to the seven biblical personalities who are welcomed as spiritual guests to the Sukkah.

VIDDUI – confession.

YAHRZEIT – anniversary of a death.

YANUKKAH – child rebbe.

YARMULKE – skullcap.

YEHIDUT – hasidic private audience with the rebbe.

YERUSHALMI – Jerusalem Talmud.

YESHIVAH – traditional Jewish college, devoted primarily to the study of the Talmud and rabbinic literature.

YESHIVAH GEDOLAH – advanced college of learning.

YETZER HARA – evil inclination.

YETZER HATOV – good inclination.

YETZIRAH, SEFER (lit. the "Book of Creation") – mystical work dealing with cosmology.

YEVSEKTSIYA – Jewish branch of the Communist Party in Russia.

YID (pl. *Yidn*) – Jew.

YIDDISHKEIT – Jewishness; a term covering the traditional culture of the Jew.

YIDEL – little Jew, a diminutive term of affection.

YISHUV – Jewish community in the Holy Land prior to the establishment of the state of Israel.

YOM KIPPUR – Day of Atonement, on 10 *Tishri*.

YOM TOV – Jewish Festival.

YOREH DE'AH – second part of the Codes, dealing mainly with dietary and ritual laws.

YOSHEV – hasid who studies at a rabbi's *yeshivah*.

YUD TET KISLEV – fifteenth of *Kislev*, commemorating the release from prison of R. Shneur Zalman of Liady.

ZEMIROT – hymns sung at the Sabbath table.

ZOHAR – central work of Jewish mysticism, compiled by R. Simon ben Yohai in the second century, which first appeared in thirteenth-century Spain.

Contributors

A.E.	**Arnos Ehrman** (deceased), rabbi, editor of Talmud *El Am*, London
A.G.	**Arthur Green**, Ph.D., professor of Jewish theology, Brandeis University, Waltham, Massachusetts
A.I.K.	**Abraham I. Katsh**, Ph.D., president emeritus, Dropsie University, Philadelphia
A.Ka.	**Aryeh Kaplan** (deceased), author, editor, and translator, New York
A.L.	**Abraham Levy**, communal rabbi of the Spanish and Portuguese Congregation, London
Al.S.	**Alan Silverman**, scholar, New York
A.R.	**Alfred Rubens**, F.S.A., F.R.Hist.Soc., historian of Jewish art and costume, London
A.Ra.	**Ada Rapoport-Albert**, Ph.D., lecturer, University College, London
A.S.	**Abraham Schischa**, scholar, London
A.Shu.	**Avrom Shuchatowitz**, Yeshiva University Library, New York
A.T.	**Alexander Tobias**, Ph.D., New York
A.U.	**Alan Unterman**, Ph.D., rabbi, Yeshurun Synagogue, Gatley, Cheshire
A.W.	**Alfred Werner** (deceased), art critic and writer, New York
B.D.W.	**Bernard Dov Sucher Weinryb** (deceased), emeritus professor of history and of economics, Dropsie University, Philadelphia
C.U.L.	**Chaim U. Lipschitz**, editor, New York/Jerusalem
D.B.	**Dan Ben-Amos**, Ph.D., professor, University of Pennsylvania, Philadelphia
D.Be.	**Delphine Bechtel**, associate professor of German and Jewish Literature, University of Paris
D.G.	**David Goldstein** (deceased), Ph.D., assistant keeper, Department of Oriental Manuscripts and Printed Books, The British Library, London
D.M.F.	**David M. Feldman**, Ph.D., rabbi, Teaneck Jewish Center, Teaneck, New Jersey
Ed.	**Tzvi (Harry) Rabinowicz**, Ph.D., London
E.M.	**Emile Marmorstein** (deceased), writer, London
E.W.	**Ernest Wiesenberg**, Ph.D., former reader, Hebrew Department, University College, London
F.G.	**Frema Gottlieb**, Ph.D., former lecturer, Touro College, New York
G.H.	**Gertrude Hirschler** (deceased), editor, New York
G.K.	**Gershon Kranzler**, former professor of sociology, Towson State University, Baltimore
G.N.	**Gedaliah Nigal**, Ph.D., lecturer in Hebrew literature, Bar-Ilan University, Israel
H.W.	**Herbert Weiner**, emeritus rabbi, Temple Israel of the Oranges and Maplewood, New Jersey
I.F.	**Irving Finkel**, scholar, London
I.O.L.	**Israel O. Lehman**, D.Phil., former curator of Manuscripts and Special Collections, Hebrew Union College–Jewish Institute of Religion, Cincinnati

Is.F.	**Isidore Fishman** (deceased), Ph.D., former director of education of the London Board of Jewish Religious Education, London
J.A.	**J. Aloy**, former *Av Bet Din*, Johannesburg, South Africa
J.B.A.	**Jacob Bernard Agus** (deceased), Ph.D., rabbi, former adjunct professor of modern Jewish philosophy, Dropsie University, and professor of rabbinic Judaism, Reconstructionist Rabbinical College, Philadelphia
J.F.	**Josef Fraenkel** (deceased), former director of the Press Department of the World Jewish Congress, London
J.G.	**Jacques Gutwirth**, Ph.D., director of the Research Center of Scientific Research, Paris
J.I.	**Jona Indech**, emeritus rabbi, Bournemouth, England
J.I.D.	**Jacob I. Dienstag**, emeritus professor of bibliography, Yeshiva University, New York
J.K.	**Joseph Kitai** (deceased), scholar, Ramat Gan, Israel
J.Ku.	**Jeannette Kupferman**, M.A., sociologist, London
J.L.	**Joseph Leftwich** (deceased), poet and translator, London
J.M.	**Jeffrey M. Cohen**, Ph.D., minister of the Stanmore and Canons Park Synagogue, London
J.M.S.	**John M. Shaftesley** (deceased), former editor of *Jewish Chronicle*, London
J.N.	**Jacob Newman**, Ph.D., rabbi, educator, formerly professor of postbiblical literature, University of Pretoria, Jerusalem
J.R.M.	**Jerome R. Mintz**, professor of anthropology, Indiana University, Bloomington, Indiana
J.S.	**Jonathan Sacks**, Ph.D., chief rabbi of the United Hebrew Congregations of the British Commonwealth
J.Y.T.	**Jacob Yuroh Teshimo**, director of the Gilboa Institute, Fujisawa, Japan
L.D.S.	**Leon D. Stiskin** (deceased), emeritus professor of Jewish philosophy, Yeshiva University, New York
L.F.	**Lyle Fishman**, rabbi in Chevy Chase, Maryland
L.J.	**Louis Jacobs**, Ph.D., rabbi of New London Synagogue, London, and visiting professor at Lancaster University, Lancaster, England
L.K.	**Lionel Kochan**, formerly Bearstead reader in Jewish history, University of Warwick, England
Ma.F.	**Maurice Friedman**, emeritus professor of religious studies, philosophy and comparative literature, San Diego State University, San Diego, California
M.F.	**Mark Friedman**, scholar, Englewood, New Jersey
M.J.G.	**Markham J. Geller**, professor in Jewish studies, University College, London
M.K.	**Mark W. Kiel**, visiting professor of Jewish history, Jewish Theological Seminary of America, New York
M.Kr.	**Miles Krassen**, Department of Religion, Oberlin College, Oberlin, Ohio
M.M.B.	**Menahem M. Brayer**, Ph.D., professor of the Azrieli Graduate School of Jewish Education, Yeshiva University, New York
M.M.F.	**Maurice K. Faierstein**, assistant professor of history, University of Maryland
M.N.	**Mordecai Newman**, scholar, New York
M.S.	**Mosheh Sanders** (deceased), antiquarian and scholar, London
M.S.G.	**M. S. Geshuri** (deceased), authority on hasidic music, Tel Aviv
M.Sh.	**Moses Sherer**, rabbi, president of the Aguda, New York
M.W.	**Mordecai Wilensky**, former professor of Jewish literature, Hebrew College, Brookline, Massachusetts
M.Wa.	**Mosheh Waldock**, scholar, New York
M.Wu.	**Meir Wunder**, author of *Encyclopedia of Galician Rabbis and Scholars*, Jerusalem
N.L.	**Naftali Lowenthal**, honorary research fellow in the Department of Hebrew and Jewish Studies, University College, London

N.La. **Norman Lamm**, Ph.D., rabbi, president of Yeshiva University, New York
N.R. **Neil Rosenstein**, M.D., Elizabeth, New Jersey
P.S. **Pesach Schindler**, Ph.D., director of Center for Conservative Judaism in Jerusalem
R.P. **Ruth Rubin**, researcher, author, and singer, New York
S.A.B. **Solomon Asher Birnbaum** (deceased), D.Phil., former lecturer in Hebrew palaeography and epigraphy, School of Oriental and African Studies, University of London, London
S.C.R. **Stefan C. Reif**, Ph.D., director of the Taylor-Schechter Geniza Research Unit, Cambridge, England
S.F. **Salomon Faber**, D.H.L., emeritus rabbi, Kew Gardens, New York
S.H. **Simon Herman**, Ph.D., former rabbi and *dayan*, London
S.J.G. **Sam Joseph Goldsmith**, formerly London correspondent of *Haboker*, Tel Aviv, and European editor of the *Jewish Telegraphic Agency*, London
S.L. **Sydney Leperer**, Ph.D., lecturer in history, Talmud and Bible, Jews' College, London
S.L.B. **Seth L. Brody**, scholar, Philadelphia
S.Lev. **Schneier Zalman Levenberg**, Ph.D., former Jewish Agency representative, London
S.P. **Solomon Poll**, dean of the Faculty of Social Studies, Bar-Ilan University, Israel
S.R. **Sholom Rivkin**, head of the United Orthodox Jewish Community, St. Louis
S.T. **Steven Tyroler**, scholar, New York
S.T.K. **Steven T. Katz**, Ph.D., professor in the Department of Near Eastern Studies, Cornell University, Ithaca, New York
T.P. **Tovia Preschel**, rabbi, former professor of Talmud, Jewish Theological Seminary, New York
T.T. **Tsemah Tsamariyan** (deceased), Ph.D., educator, Haifa
V.D. **Vivian David Lipman** (deceased), Ph.D., historian, London
V.P. **Velvel Pasternak**, authority on Jewish music, New York
W.G. **Wolf Gottlieb** (deceased), *dayan* and *Av Bet Din*, Glasgow
W.S. **William Shaffir**, professor of sociology, McMaster University, Hamilton, Ontario, Canada
W.Z.R. **Wolf Zeev Rabinowitsch** (deceased), M.D., historian, Haifa
Y.A. **Yitzhak Alfasi**, Ph.D., historian, Tel Aviv
Y.E. **Yaffa Eliach**, professor of history and literature, Brooklyn College of the City University of New York, Brooklyn, New York
Z.A. **Zalman Alpert**, reference librarian, Yeshiva University, New York
Z.H. **Z. H. Telsner**, rabbi of Finchley Central Synagogue, London
Z.K. **Tzvi E. Kurzweil** (deceased), professor of education, Technion, Haifa
Z.M.S. **Zalman M. Schachter**, formerly professor of religion, Temple University, Philadelphia

THE ENCYCLOPEDIA OF HASIDISM

AARON of Chernobyl (1787–5 *Kislev* 1871) – The eldest son of R. Mordecai. "I have seven branches of the *menora*," said R. Mordecai, "and R. Aaron towers above them all." He studied under his grandfather R. Nahum and under his father. He married the daughter of R. Gedaliah of Linitz, and on her death, he married Sima Husha, the daughter of R. Aaron of Titov, a grandson of the Besht.

After the death of R. Mordecai, his sons established their own courts in different localities. R. Aaron succeeded his father in Chernobyl. He was the president of the *kollel* of the Ukraine in the Holy Land, and he financed the building in Safed of a *Bet HaMidrash* for the hasidim of Chernobyl.

His brother, R. Jacob Israel of Cherkasy, openly rebelled against him and sent out letters to the hasidim, requesting that all monies collected for the *kollel* in the Holy Land be sent to him. Two other brothers, R. Yitzhak and R. Yohanan, appealed in vain to his sense of family loyalty. However, when R. Jacob Israel realized that the hasidim were not responding to his appeal, he withdrew his claim.

R. Aaron had two daughters, Hayyah Sarah and Perl, and three sons, R. Menahem Nahum, R. Yeshaya Meshullam Zusya, and R. Barukh Asher.

A.D. Twersky, *Sefer HaYahas MiChernobyl*, pp. 31–36.

AARON of Starosselje (1766–22 *Tishri* 1828) – Son of R. Moses Horowitz, a descendant of R. Isaiah Horowitz, he was born in Orsha in the district of Moghilev. In his youth, Aaron became a disciple of R. Shneur Zalman of Liady, and he stated that he sat at R. Shneur Zalman's feet for a period of thirty years. He is indeed generally considered to be the favorite and most distinguished pupil of the master.

For a considerable period, R. Aaron and R. Dov Baer (R. Shneur Zalman's son) studied together as devoted friends and companions. When R. Shneur Zalman was arrested, R. Aaron collected vast sums of money to facilitate his liberation.

In the course of time, a serious quarrel appears to have broken out between R. Aaron and R. Dov Baer. Apart from the natural rivalry, which seemed to have developed between son and eventual successor of the master, and his favorite pupil, there is a good warrant for the opinion that the two men differed in their conception of the role of ecstasy in the mystical life. R. Dov Baer was exceedingly strict in his rejection of the slightest trace of sham emotion during Divine worship. Whereas R. Dov Baer is said to have recited his prayers in complete silence and immobility, the reports narrate that R. Aaron's prayers were of a frightening intensity and were an outpouring of religious fervor and enthusiasm, with R. Aaron's expressing himself in a mighty roar as his prayers were pronounced.

R. Aaron set up a rival hasidic court in Starosselje after the death of R. Shneur Zalman and R. Dov Baer's succession to the leadership of the *Habad* group. From the year 1813 until after his death, R. Aaron's followers were known as "Starosseljer hasidim." At one time, R. Aaron was arrested, but he was released on 10 *Kislev*.

R. Aaron died some ten months after the death of R. Dov Baer. Some of his followers then changed their allegiance to Lubavitch; others accepted R. Aaron's son, R. Hayyim Rafael, as their master in Starosselje. After a few years, when R. Hayyim Rafael died without leaving a successor in the Starosselje line, some of the diehards among the Starosselje hasidim preferred to remain without a master rather than to be led by a stranger, but the majority of them became followers of R. Menahem Mendel of Lubavitch.

He was the author of *Bad Kodesh* on *Megillat Ruth* (Warsaw, 1872); *Sod Kedoshim*, a commentary on the Passover *Haggadah*; *Avodat HaLevi* on the Pentateuch and festivals, printed in Lvov in 1842, and a second part, printed in Lvov in 1846; *Shaar HaTefillah* (Lvov, 1862); *Shaar HaYihud VeHaEmunah* (Gate of Unity and Faith), dealing with the theme of Divine unity (Shklov, 1806).

R. Aaron planned his work to correspond to R. Shneur Zalman's book, on which it is a commentary. Thus the first volume is an extended commentary on the second part of the *Tanya*, while the bulk of the second volume is a commentary on the first part of the *Tanya*. The fifth and final gate of Aaron's second volume is a commentary on the third part of the *Tanya*.

L. Jacobs, *Seeker of Unity*.

L.J.

AARON of Titov (d. 5 *Tevet* 1829)–Eldest son of R. Tzvi and a grandson of the Besht. He lived a life of extreme poverty in Staro Konstantinov and in Palvitch, where he died.

He was venerated as a miracle worker by a small but devoted coterie. His sons were R. Naftali Tzvi of Skvira, who emigrated to the Holy Land and died in Tiberias (27 *Elul* 1865), and R. Abraham, who succeeded him. His daughter, Sima Husha, was the wife of R. Aaron of Chernobyl.

A.D. Twersky, *Sefer HaYahas MiChernobyl*, p. 103.

AARON of Zhitomir (d. 26 *Tishri* 1816)–Son of R. Mordecai, he was a disciple of R. Levi Yitzhak of Berdichev. He was a fiery itinerant preacher who brought many into the hasidic fold. After the death of R. Zeev of Zhitomir, he succeeded him as preacher and stayed in Zhitomir for three years. He subsequently traveled as far as Hungary and spent some time in Nagykaroly and other towns.

His discourses on the weekly portions of the Law and on festivals were collected by his disciple R. Levi of Zhitomir and were published under the name *Toldot Aharon* (Berdichev, 1817). The book received the approval of R. Abraham Joshua Heschel and R. Mordecai of Chernobyl. Other discourses can be found in *Pisgamim Kaddishin* (Ostrog, 1891).

He stressed that the true understanding of God can be achieved only through the study of the Torah. One must constantly strive to improve oneself by overcoming egoistic and other negative tendencies.

Y. Alfasi, *Encyclopedia LeHasidut*, p. 156.

AARON THE GREAT of Karlin (1736–19 *Nisan* 1772)–Born in Yanova, near Pinsk, the son of R. Jacob, a synagogue beadle in Karlin, R. Aaron was persuaded by his uncle, R. Menele, to study under R. Dov Baer, the Maggid of Mezhirech. He became one of the pioneers of Hasidism in Lithuania, and he was deeply concerned with social problems.

In 1760, he helped to abolish in Neskhitz (Nieusochojeze) some of the heavy taxes that overburdened the poor. He inclined toward asceticism and fasted regularly. He advised his disciples to shut themselves up in a special room for one day every week, spending the time in fasting and repentance and in the study of the Torah. He cautioned his followers against pride and anger, urging them to divert to the worship of the Creator the time they otherwise spent in eating, drinking, sleeping, and sexual intercourse.

He urged his followers to study the *Mishnah* daily and to steep themselves in the Bible. "Sin and sadness," he maintained, "go together. But joy is Divine in origin. A Jew should rejoice in being a Jew, for in this way a Jew serves the Almighty best."

R. Aaron was the author of the hymn *Yoh Ekhsof Noam Shabbat* (Lord, I yearn for the Sabbath delight), which is sung every Sabbath by the hasidim of Karlin and for which there are twenty different melodies. He died in Karlin, and some of his discourses are to be found in his grandson's book, *Bet Aharon*. His son R. Jacob and his son-in-law, R. Abraham, settled in the Holy Land. His other son, R. Asher, who was only nine years old when his father died, succeeded him as rebbe.

M.H. Kleinman, *Zikhron LaRishonim*, pp. 22–45.

AARON THE SECOND of Karlin (1802–17 *Sivan* 1872)–Son of R. Asher the First of Stolin, he was born on *Rosh Hodesh Sivan*. He married the daughter of R. Mordecai of Kremenetz. Expelled by the czarist government from Karlin in 1808, he settled in Stolin.

In 1866, he urged his followers to fix regular times for the study of the *Mishnah*, the Talmud and *Tosafot*, and the works of R. Shmuel Edels, "each according to his abilities." His teachings are recorded in *Bet Aharon* (Brody, 1875), which contains discourses on the portions of the Law for weekdays and festivals, a number of letters written by R. Aaron before the penitential days, and letters to his son, R. Asher. He attached great significance to joyfulness, which became the hallmark of the hasidim of Karlin. He stressed the importance of sincerity and believed that prayer should be followed by study. He introduced instrumental music into his house and had two orchestras at a *melaveh malkah*.

In his *Olam KeMinhago* and *Aharit Simhah Tugah* (Vilna, 1873), the poet Y.L. Gordon graphically describes the court of Karlin. R. Aaron supported the hasidic settlers in the Holy Land and repeatedly urged his followers to contribute money promptly and generously.

After being rebbe for forty-five years, he died in Mlynov, near Dubno, where he was buried. He was succeeded by his son, R. Asher the Second, who died one year after his father's death. The sons-in-law of R. Aaron were R. Abraham Jacob of Sadgora and R. David Twersky of Zlotopolye.

W.Z. Rabinowitsch, *Lithuanian Hasidism*, pp. 80–103.

ABRAHAM DOV BAER of Ovruch

ABRAHAM DOV BAER of Ovruch (1765–12 *Kislev* 1841)—Son of R. David Auerbach, the Maggid of Chmelnick. At the age of nine, he lost both his parents and was brought up by his grandmother. He married the daughter of R. Nathan Nata, who lived in Ovruch, a town near Zhitomir. He was befriended by R. Zusya of Annopol and R. Levi Yitzchak of Berdichev. His main hasidic mentors were R. Nahum of Chernobyl and his son Mordecai.

At the age of twenty, Abraham Dov became rabbi of Chmelnick. When his father-in-law died in 1785, he succeeded him as rabbi of Ovruch. There he attracted as his disciple R. Hillel of Poryck.

In 1830 Abraham Dov settled in Safed, and he soon became the spiritual leader of the hasidic community. R. Menachem Mendel of Kamienic-Podolsk records that he was a faithful shepherd who served the community in a spirit of self-sacrifice. He had to marshal all his spiritual resources to cope with manifold problems. On June 15, 1834, the Jewish community was attacked, and many had to escape to nearby villages. In 1837 there was an earthquake in Safed, which killed two thousand Jews, and the community dwindled to four hundred souls. Abraham Dov appealed to Sir Moses Montefiore for help "to enable the poor of Safed to till the soil and to become shepherds." In spite of the dangers, he refused categorically to leave Safed. "We remain here, no matter what befalls us, in order to maintain this settlement and to protect our sacred places."

He welcomed Sir Moses Montefiore on his arrival in Safed on May 17, 1839. He kept in touch with his followers in the Diaspora and spent a year visiting them in Russia.

In 1841 he fell victim to a plague that was ravaging Safed and was buried near the grave of R. David Solomon Eibeschutz. He left no children. His great literary legacy was his book *Bat Ayin* (Jerusalem, 1847), based on discourses he delivered. It is replete with lyrical hymns in praise of the Holy Land. "As long as one is in exile," he maintained, "one cannot develop one's full potential. The highest spiritual rungs can be attained only in the Holy Land. The redemption will not come haphazardly. One is obliged to pray and strive for it continuously. Even an ordinary person is capable of achieving great spirituality in the Holy Land." This book is highly venerated by the hasidim. "Our rabbi," the hasidim used to say, "was a living *Shulhan Arukh*."

ABRAHAM GERSHON of Kutov

ABRAHAM GERSHON of Kutov (d. 25 *Adar I* 1761)—Son of R. Hayyim of Kutov, he was the brother-in-law of the Besht. He was a learned talmudist and kabbalist. He was probably born in Kutov (Kuty), Ukraine, where his father, R. Efraim, was rabbi. R. Jonathan Eibeschutz (1690–1764) of Prague called him the "pious rabbi." R. Ezekiel Landau described him as the "perfect sage and holy saint."

He was a member of one of the four *Batei Din* in Brody and also served for a time as synagogue cantor. He did not, at first, recognize the hidden greatness of his sister's husband but later became a devoted follower of the Besht, who entrusted him with the education of his only son, Tzvi. He was affiliated with the hasidic association in Brody and prayed according to the Lurian liturgy.

Accompanied by his second wife, Blumah, and his two young sons, Hayyim Aaron and Yakir, he traveled to Istanbul, where he became acquainted with R. Moses Soncino. He arrived in Jerusalem on the eve of the New Year, 1747, and was warmly welcomed by the Sephardim, especially those who were students of the Kabbalah. He lived in Hebron for six years, until 1753, visiting Jerusalem from time to time. In 1753, he moved to Jerusalem and was associated with the *yeshivah Bet El*. The Besht often wrote to him and occasionally sent him funds. It is, however, difficult to prove the authenticity of the many letters that are ascribed to the Besht.

There is no factual basis for the view that R. Abraham Gershon met R. Hayyim Ibn Atar, unless we accept the theory that he went to the Holy Land before 1747. In *Iyyar* 1752, R. Abraham Gershon was among the signatories of an appeal to the community of Mainz, asking for support of the Holy Land.

He was buried on the Mount of Olives. For more than two hundred years, his grave could not be found. Only after the Six-Day War (1967) were his grave and that of his wife Blumah (d. 1757) discovered.

He had two daughters and six sons. Two of his sons, R. Hayyim Aaron and R. Yakir, were concerned about the welfare of their fellow Jews, and they, too, appealed to the community of Mainz. R. Hayyim Aaron went on a fund-raising tour, visiting Bamberg and other cities in Germany. He died in Tiberias. The other four sons of R. Gershon–R. Moses, R. Yitzhak, R. Efraim Fishel, and R. Yehudah Leib–remained in the Diaspora.

A.J. Heschel, "Rabbi Gershon Kitover."

ABRAHAM HAKOHEN of Kalisk (1741–4 *Shevat* 1810)–Son of R. Alexander, Abraham was born in Kalisk (Kalinsky), White Russia. He became a disciple of R. Dov Baer, the Maggid of Mezhirech. For a time he lived in Vilna, where he exasperated the *mitnaggedim* by his exuberance and extrovert behavior during prayers. His nonconformist conduct caused a great deal of criticism and was one of the factors that led to the issuance of the ban against the hasidim in 1772.

Together with R. Menahem Mendel of Vitebsk, R. Abraham emigrated to the Holy Land in 1777, and after the death of R. Menahem Mendel, R. Abraham became the undisputed leader of the hasidim in the Holy Land. He was a superlative letter writer, and his letters reveal a hard-core pragmatism: "One who arrives in the Holy Land," he wrote, "must accustom oneself to the new way of living. One must often be content with a humble cottage. If we try, however, to live in the style to which we were previously accustomed, we may become distraught and blame the land for our misfortunes."

With the publication of the *Tanya* in 1796, the relationship between him and R. Shneur Zalman rapidly deteriorated. R. Abraham felt that R. Shneur Zalman was deviating from the teachings of the Maggid of Mezhirech. In a letter to R. Shneur Zalman, he wrote, "I am not at all pleased by your attempt to 'enclose the sun in its cover,' meaning to dress up the words of our teachers, R. Dov Baer, the Besht, and R. Yitzhak Luria." A relentless antirationalist, R. Abraham believed in simple, unquestioned faith. Theological differences were compounded by the clash of personalities. R. Abraham felt that residing in the Holy Land entitled him to precedence, and he wanted R. Shneur Zalman to relinquish his stewardship of the funds.

There were unedifying exchanges. For two years, R. Shneur Zalman refused to hand over the administration of the charity funds. Eventually, the two parties were reconciled, but the dispute had lasting repercussions. There was no longer a united hasidic front, and henceforth *Habad* hasidim took care of their own finances. Meanwhile, R. Abraham experienced more problems even closer to home. In the Holy Land, he had to face the active antagonism of R. Eliezer Disna, formerly of Vilna, who had begun a campaign to discredit him.

R. Abraham's discourses were printed in *Hesed LeAvraham* (Czernowitz, 1851) and in *Iggerot Hasidim Me'Eretz Yisrael* (Jerusalem, 1980).

To R. Abraham the essence of Hasidism was unquestioned faith, and any attempt to base faith on reason would lead to diverse heresies. Very little is known about his personal life.

I. Halpern, *HaAliyot HaRishonim shel HaHasidim LeEretz Yisrael*.

ABRAHAM HAMALAKH (1741–12 *Tishri* 1776) – Son of R. Dov Baer, the Maggid of Mezhirech, he married the daughter of R. Meshullam Feivish of Kremenetz. Already in his youth, he studied Kabbalah. He taught his friend and colleague, R. Shneur Zalman of Liady.

Unlike his father, R. Abraham chose the path of seclusion and extreme asceticism. He became preacher in Fastov, where he lived until his death. He barely partook of food, which earned him the name of *Malakh* (angel). The hasidim of *Habad* called him *HaKadosh* (the holy one). His father, R. Dov Baer, disapproved of his son's ascetic lifestyle, begging him not to ignore his fragile body, to which his son replied, "You are only my physical father, and not the heavenly one."

His work *Hesed LeAvraham* was published by his grandson in Czernowitz in 1851. His hasidic interpretations are independent and original. He maintained that the only vehicle to redemption is to be found in the persona of the *tzaddik*. Due to the continued suffering in the Diaspora, the great fire of Kabbalah became dimmed, causing the true Torah to be obscured by materialism.

He died at the early age of thirty-five and was buried in Fastov. His young widow, who never remarried, emigrated to the Holy Land and lived there until her death. He was succeeded by his son R. Shalom Shakhnah. His other son was R. Israel Hayyim of Ludomir.

S. Dubnow, *Toldot HaHasidut*, p. 213.

M.M.B.

ABRAHAM HAYYIM of Zloczov (1750–26 *Tevet* 1816) – Son of R. Gedaliah, he studied under his father, who was the rabbi of Zolkiev. He was a disciple of R. Dov Baer, the Maggid of Mezhirech; R. Yehiel Michael of Zloczov; and R. Samuel (Shmelke) Horowitz of Nikolsburg.

When his first wife, the daughter of R. Pinhas Horowitz, died, he married the daughter of R. Issachar Dov of Zloczov. When his father-in-law emigrated to the Holy Land, R. Abraham Hayyim succeeded him as rabbi of Zloczov.

He is described by R. Efraim Zalman Margulies as "a learned talmudist and a hasid who spends almost the whole day in prayer and good deeds and whose acts of charity have brought back many people from sin."

He was the author of *Orah LeHayyim* (Berdichev, 1817), a commentary on the Bible published by his stepson, R. Joseph Azriel. He was also the author of *Pri Hayyim* (Lvov, 1873) on *Avot* and on the Passover *Haggadah* (Lvov, 1873).

Y. Raphael, *Sefer HaHasidut*, p. 331.

ABRAHAM JOSHUA HESCHEL of Opatov (1748–5 *Nisan* 1825) – He was born in Zmigrod, near Rzeszov, the son of R. Shmuel of Neustadt. His family can be traced to Maharam Padwa and to Saul Wahl.

He married Hayyah Sarah, the daughter of R. Jacob of Titkin, in 1763. In 1788, he became rabbi of Kolbuszov, where he lived in dire poverty. It was in this town that R. Moses Leib of Sasov introduced him to Hasidism and to his mentor, R. Elimelekh of Lejask.

In 1800, he became rabbi of Opatov. In 1809, he assumed the rabbinate of Iasi, Moldavia. Among his staunch supporters was the wealthy Daniel of Iasi. This town proved to be an unhappy place for him. Thereafter, he moved to Medziborz, where he lived for twelve years, but there is no evidence that he was the official rabbi there. He was looked upon as an arbiter in matters affecting the hasidic movement. He defended the hasidim of Bratzlav against the onslaught of R. Moses Tzvi of Savran. He acted as conciliator at the hasidic wedding at Ustilug, where the Przysucha way of life was attacked.

Toward the end of 1823, in the wake of a decree by Czar Alexander I, which dispossessed the Jews of the villages in the districts of Vitebsk and Mohilev, he ordered a public fast. He was very active in securing financial support for the hasidim in the Holy Land, and he acted as treasurer of the funds.

He was survived by two sons, R. Yitzhak Meir (d. 2 *Adar* 1855), who succeeded him and settled in Zinkov, and R. Yosef Moses, who remained in Medziborz. His three daughters were Yohebed, Dinah, and Rachel. His grandson R. Meshullam Zusya of Zinkov published his work *Ohev Yisrael* in Zhitomir in 1863. This work was acclaimed by R. Mordecai Twersky of Chernobyl and by R. Abraham Jacob of Sadgora. R. Joseph Saul Natanson of Lvov gave a *haskamah* to the Lvov edition of 1872. So far, twelve editions have appeared. R.

Issachar Dov of Radoszyce published his second book, *Torat Emet*, in Lvov in 1854. Many of his homilies are quoted in books by other hasidic authors, such as *Siftei Tzaddikim*, by R. Joshua Heschel of Rymanov and by R. Pinhas of Dinowitz.

The rebbe of Opatov himself gave over sixty *haskamot* to printed books, covering a wide range of topics, but he did not endorse any work dealing with Kabbalah. He was opposed to asceticism, and he maintained that it is a positive command to love every Jew. Love of the Jewish people is bound up with the love of the Almighty.

He stressed that it was the purpose of people to seek the nearness of God by sanctifying all their thoughts and activities. We should all help our fellows to do this, but it was the task of the *tzaddik* to lift up ordinary mortals toward God and to cause the Divine blessing to descend upon them.

He believed that he had lived before, that he had been a high priest, a king of Israel, and an exilarch, and he maintained that he had to go through these various incarnations because his love of Israel had not been perfected.

M.E. Gutman, *Migdolei HaHasidut*, pp. 172–233.

T.P.

ABRAHAM MOSES of Przysucha (1800–1 *Tevet* 1829)–Son of R. Simhah Bunem of Przysucha, Abraham Moses married the daughter of R. Shmuel Rafael, a son-in-law of the Holy Jew of Przysucha.

After the death of his father in 1827, most of the notable disciples followed R. Menahem Mendel of Kotzk, but R. Yitzhak of Warka, R. Jacob Aryeh of Radzymin, and R. Shragai Feivel of Grica gave their allegiance to R. Abraham Moses. It was a brief reign, as he died two years after becoming rebbe.

His sons were R. Tzvi Mordecai and R. Jacob. His daughter married R. Fishel of Makov.

Z.M. Rabinowitsch, *R. Simhah Bunem MiPrzysucha*, p. 43.

ABRAMOVITCH, Hayyim Zanvil (b. 1900), Ribnitzer rebbe–Born in Botosani, Romania, he served as rabbi of Burduzhen until the beginning of World War II. He was a hasid of R. Abraham Mattityahu Friedman of Stefanesti.

He spent the war in a labor camp in Transnistria, and after the liberation he returned to Ribnitz and acted as *shohet* and *mohel* for the district of Moldavia. In 1972, he settled in Brooklyn, New York, and became active in the *Rav Tov* organization of Satmar. He now lives in Monsey.

A.Z.

ADAM BAAL SHEM–The identity of this kabbalist cannot be ascertained with any degree of certainty. Adam was a name rarely used by Jews.

The *Shivhei HaBesht* records that a "R. Adam instructed his son to hand over his kabbalistic writings to the Besht." We are also told that these writings were found by R. Adam in a cave and that they contained secrets of the Torah.

Gershom Scholem identifies R. Adam as a follower of Hershel Zoref, who died in Cracow in the beginning of the eighteenth century. On the other hand, Ch. Shmeruk identifies him with R. Adam of Bingen, who is reputed to have performed miracles before the Emperor Maximilian II. The hasidim of Chernobyl believed that he was identical with R. Nahum Shustok, the brother of R. Tzvi, and the father of R. Nahum of Chernobyl. The *Habad* hasidim claim that he is identical with R. Adam of Ropczyce, a disciple of R. Elijah Baal Shem Tov of Worms.

Ch. Shmeruk, "Tales about R. Adam Baal Shem," pp. 86–105.

ADAM KADMON–Primordial man. The early mystics inferred from Genesis 1:26–"Let us make man in our image"–that the physical Adam was created on the pattern of a spiritual Adam that existed in the celestial world (cf. also Ezekiel 1:26–"the likeness as the appearance of a man"). This became part of the later mystical view of the cosmos in which everything on earth had its counterpart in the realm of the Godhead.

In Kabbalah we find other names for this phenomenon: *adam elyon*, or *adam ila'ah*. "*Adam Kadmon*" does not occur until the thirteenth century.

Sometimes it represents the totality of the ten *Sefirot*, at others just one *Sefirah*. Since, from one point of view, the whole sefirotic system is a manifestation of the unknow able God, symbolized by the tetragrammaton YHWH, *Adam Kadmon* was itself thought to be a symbol of this manifestation. (Both *Yod-Heh-Vav-Heh* and *Adam* have the same value in *Gematria*, viz. 45.) This was represented in more detail by the separate *Sefirot*, which were seen as parts of the body of *Adam Kadmon*: the upper three *Sefirot* (*Keter*, *Binah*, and *Hokhmah*) represent the head (in the *Zohar* the three cavities of the brain); *Din* and *Hesed*, the arms; *Tiferet*, the torso; *Hod* and *Netzah*, the arms; *Yesod*, the penis; and *Malkhut* being regarded variously as the totality of the whole image or as the female element. In later Kabbalah, particularly in Hasidism, the performance of the *mitzvot* by any of the physical limbs had a beneficial influence on the *Sefirah* that corresponded to that limb, and all human activity influenced for good or evil *Adam Kadmon* in the upper world.

The wearing of *tefillin* is of particular significance because according to Lurianic Kabbalah, the primeval light, which was the starting point of Divine emanation, emerged first from that part of the head of *Adam Kadmon*, where in man the *tefillin shel rosh* is placed.

D.G.

ADEL (ca. 1720–ca.1787)–Only daughter of R. Israel Baal Shem Tov and his wife, Hannah. The Baal Shem Tov said that he took his daughter's soul from the Torah, *Esh Dat Lamo*–"a fiery Law unto them." The word "Edel" is formed from the three first letters (*In Praise*, p. 137). She was a bright woman and her father's favorite. She accompanied him on his attempted voyage to Israel in 1739–40.

After the death of his wife, Adel took care of her father. During his illness, she was his nurse and was beside him at the time of his death.

Adel was involved in the activities of her father's close circle of followers, and she has a prominent place in hasidic tradition and folklore. She married R. Yehiel Ashkenazi, and they owned a store. She was the mother of two prominent hasidic personalities–R. Moses Hayyim Efraim of Sudzilkov and R. Barukh of Medziborz. Her daughter, Feige, possessed the "holy spirit" and was the mother of R. Nahman of Bratzlav.

D. Ben-Amos and J.R. Mintz, *In Praise of the Baal Shem Tov*, pp. 136–137, 223–224.

Y.E.

ADLER, Naftali Hayyim, of Netanya (1914–9 *Adar I* 1995)–Born in Jerusalem, his father, Mordecai Yehudah, died when he was very young. His mother remarried R. Barukh Hager of Seret Vishnitz. R. Naftali Hayyim married Hinda, the daughter of R. Hayyim Meir Hager of Vishnitz, in 1938. In 1964, he established a *Bet Ha-Midrash* in Netanya. At one time he was planning to establish an agricultural settlement in the Negev. He died in Netanya.

ADLER, Nathan HaKohen (1741–27 *Elul* 1800), kabbalist–He was a disciple of R. Tevele David Schiff (who later became rabbi in London) and of R. Jacob Joshua Falk, author of *Penei Yehoshua*. Among his disciples were R. Seckel Loeb Wormser, the Baal Shem of Michelstadt, and R. Moses Sofer.

Although Adler was not affiliated to the hasidic movement, he wrote *kamayot* for the sick, adopted the Lurian liturgy, used the Sephardic pronunciation, and recited the priestly benediction every day, as is the custom in the Holy Land.

Paradoxically, in 1779 R. Pinhas Horowitz, the head of the *Bet Din* of Frankfurt, himself a hasid, threatened to excommunicate him for holding religious services in his home. In 1782, Adler became rabbi in Boskowitz, Moravia, but after three years returned to Frankfurt. It was R. Horowitz who delivered the eulogy on his death.

J. Unna, "Nathan HaCohen Adler," pp. 167–185.

ADMOR (plural, Admorim)–An abbreviation of the words *Adoneinu, Moreinu, V'Rabbeinu* (Our Lord, teacher, and master). A title given by the hasidim to their rebbes.

AFIKOMAN–The piece of *matzah*, broken off from the middle one of the three *matzot*, at the *seder* service on the first two nights of Passover. It became customary among the hasidim to preserve a piece of the *afikoman* as a charm for protection against the evil eye.

AFTERLIFE–Whereas Orthodox Judaism is committed to the belief in an afterlife, Hasidism takes this belief and refines it along the lines of kabbalistic doctrine.

The biblical references to afterlife are few. Manasseh ben Israel of Amsterdam, in his *Nishmat Hayyim*, maintained that it is because in the biblical period, belief in the afterlife was so strong that faith in the soul's survival after bodily death needed no specific emphasis.

In the *Zohar*, we find descriptions that tell us about the pleasures of the righteous and the agonies of the sinners. The statements of the *Zohar* are later systematized in *Reishit Hokhmah*, by R. Elijah ben Moses de Vidas (sixteenth century), and in *Shevet Musar*, by R. Elijah ben Solomon Abraham HaKohen of Smyrna (d. 1789).

The doctrine of reincarnation, first mentioned by Saadia Gaon, is reinstated by the *Zohar*, which teaches that in most cases there are only three or four such incarnations. But in *Shaar HaGilgulim*, by R. Hayyim Vital, this doctrine is further amplified.

The call for the soul's return goes out about a month before death. Even a *tzaddik* becomes powerless. This world begins to fade, and the other realm takes on a greater significance and reality. From the Besht's own deathbed to those of many of his disciples, most inspiring tales are told of the clarity of mind with which *tzaddikim* die.

The Angel of Death comes to take the soul. The soul separates from the body, and the body suffers the pangs of death. At the time of death, a person sees Adam, on account of whose sin we suffer death, and also sees God: "Thou canst not see My face, for man shall not see Me and live" (Exodus 33:20). In other words, one cannot see God in life but only in death. At the time of our death, we are vouchsafed to see our dead relatives and companions from the other world (*Zohar*, *Vayehi*, 218b). The summons to appear before the Heavenly Court is sounded by the Angel Duma, who also asks what our name was on earth. The shock of death is so great that many do not remember their name. This can be remedied if a person were to recite a verse from the Torah at the end of the *Amidah* each day.

If the soul does not hear the summons, it wanders in the Universe of Chaos, *Olam HaTohu*. Eventually, judgment takes place, and all the good deeds, performed with proper intentions, have become good angels, each pleading for the soul. Angels created by *mitzvot*, performed without intention, are defective. Evil deeds become accusers, and those who were overindulgent in physical pleasures undergo *Hibbut HaKever* (the beating of the grave).

The next stage is called *Kaf HaKela* (the catapult). Two angels—one stationed at one end of the world and the other at the other end—toss the soul back and forth. By this method they cleanse the soul from the dust of empty words and thoughts, and only then can the true purgation of the *Gehenna* take place.

G. Scholem, *Major Trends in Jewish Mysticism*, chap. 6.

Z.S.

AGNON, Shmuel Joseph (1888–1970)

Leading Hebrew author and winner of the Nobel prize for literature in 1966. He was born in Buczacz, Galicia, into a hasidic family associated with the hasidim of the rebbe of Chortkov. As a child, Agnon was given a traditional Jewish and hasidic education and in addition became acquainted with the literature of the *Haskalah* and then later with the secular world of German and European culture. From his own autobiographical reminiscences, we learn that the first book he bought at the age of eleven was the *Shivhei HaAri*, and that at thirteen or fourteen, he read and was deeply impressed by the tales about R. Nahman of Bratzlav recorded in the *Shivhei HaRan*. Agnon's later writings constantly reveal the influence of these youthful readings.

His first work, a Yiddish poem, was published in 1903, and from then on he continued to write prolifically. (For a full list of his writings and English translations, see A. J. Band's *Nostalgia and Nightmare* [1968]). Because of his early interest in Zionism, Agnon emigrated to *Eretz Yisrael*, settling first in Jaffa in 1907 and then in Jerusalem, the latter becoming his permanent home, except for a period of residence in Germany between 1913 and 1924, during which he worked on an anthology of hasidic tales with Martin Buber. It was with the first work of his Jaffa period (1908) that he adopted the name Agnon. It was also during this period that he became associated with the hasidim of Jerusalem, being especially close to the Bratzlaver hasidim, and these groups reinforced the influences of his childhood, making Hasidism a constant theme in his work.

Agnon's genius has been recognized in his twice having been awarded the Bialik prize (1934 and 1951) as well as a variety of honorary degrees and awards by some of the great universities of the world. His career reached its high water mark in 1966, when he was awarded the Nobel prize for literature.

The deep connection between Agnon's literary works and his autobiography is unmistakable, and acknowledgment of this is essential for an understanding of his writings. He constantly uses the traditional and hasidic images of his youth to present both the general background and the particular characters of his fiction. It must also be recognized, however, that his use of this material is extremely complex. At one and the same time, his work reflects profound ambivalence and spiritual disquietude, as well as deep piety and religious sensitivity, casting light and shade on the traditional values of Judaism-Hasidism and the meaning of Jewishness in the modern world.

We witness these alternating characteristics in such immature and unoriginal works as *Aliyat Neshamah* (The Ascent of a Soul), which deals with the struggle between hasidim and *mitnaggedim* and with the dialectic of tragedy and ecstasy that Agnon saw in the hasidic search for God; *Mitokh Sin* (Out of Hatred), which is a poem satirizing the intense hasidic dislike of the *maskilim*; and *Ir HaMetim* (City of the Dead), which is a literary-historical reflection on his hometown of Buczacz. These themes and characteristics reappear in his more mature works, written in Jaffa, such as *VeHayah HeAkov LeMishor* (And the Crooked Shall Become Straight [1912]); *The Nidah* (The Banished One [1919]), which again deals with the conflict of hasid and *mitnagged*; and *Hakhnasat Kallah* (The Bridal Canopy [1931]), perhaps his most famous work.

The centrality of the hasidic weltanschauung is especially in evidence in this last work, as indicated by its subtitle, which reads as follows: "The wonders of the hasid Reb Yudel of Brody and his three modest daughters." The entire tale is permeated with hasidic images, concepts, and symbols. The same concerns, issues, symbols, and tensions continue to reverberate through Agnon's later work, especially *Ore'ah Nata Lalun* (A Guest for the Night [1939]), which is his most poignant prewar work and which most adequately captures the sense of struggle inherent in the meaning of Jewish existence.

In his postwar writings, for example, *Temol Shilshom* ("In Yester Year" [1945]), which tells of the struggle between modernity and tradition in the life of one Hershel, who is the descendent of Reb Yudel, the central figure of *Hakhnasat Kallah*, we see a continued working out of the same concerns that had dominated the earlier compositions. The hasidic element continues to be of significance in many of the tales collected in two of Agnon's more recont collections of stories: *HaEsh VehaEtzim* (The Fire and the Trees [1962]) and *Ad Hena* (Thus Far [1957]). In summary, it is fair to note that Hasidism provides Agnon with more material on which to exercise his creative imagination than any other single source.

B. Kurzweil, *Essays on the Fiction of S. Y. Agnon*.

S.K.

AGUDAT ISRAEL, World Organization of Orthodox Jewry–It was the urgent need to find the "solution of contemporary problems in the spirit of the Torah" that led to the Kattowitz conference and the birth of the *Agudat Israel* (Union of Israel). In the gathering of Kattowitz, in Upper Silesia, on May 27, 1912, were three hundred communal leaders, laymen and rabbis, and *mitnaggedim* and hasidim.

Many and differing reasons had brought the delegates together. Jacob Rosenheim, vice president of the Free Union of the Interests of Orthodox Judaism (founded by R. Samson Raphael Hirsch in 1883), yearned to integrate the unorganized Orthodox masses of Eastern Europe. A number of Mizrachists had been driven to seek new pastures by the adoption of the Syrkin Cultural Committee Report by the Tenth Zionist Congress, which urged "to intensify cultural work in Palestine and the East." Others felt that only a strong, Torah-entrenched citadel could hold back the tidal waves of heresy and militant antireligious ideology of the secularists and the arid nationalism of the Zionists.

Although Rosenheim, the movement's founder and lifelong guide, maintained that they were not establishing "an organization at the side of other organizations," the Aguda ultimately adopted the whole familiar complex of organizational accoutrements: a constitution, a general council, an executive committee, an acting committee, a *Mo'etzet Gedolei HaTorah* (rabbinical council) with an executive of eleven members, a Torah fund, and even a press bureau. There were soon sizable Aguda groups in Budapest, Amsterdam, Vienna, and many other parts of the world. Nominally, the headquarters remained in Frankfurt until 1935, but Aguda's heart and soul were lodged in Poland. The organization had the support of R. Israel Meir HaKohen (Kagan), the *Hafetz Hayyim*, R. Hayyim Soloveitchik of Brest-Litovsk, R. Hayyim Ozer Grodzensky of Vilna, and R. Abraham Mordecai Alter of Ger. In the interwar years, nearly one-third of Polish Jewry was associated with the Aguda, by then an intricately organized and widespread structure. It maintained its own schools, published daily newspapers, and set up its own publishing house, two youth organizations (*Tzeirei Aguda* and *Pirchei Aguda*), and even a women's division (*B'not Aguda*), which, by 1939, had 25,000 members. For the first time in the history of Polish Jewry, religious women and girls assembled in 1931 to discuss their problems at an all women's conference.

The Aguda formed its Workers' Branch, the *Po'alei Aguda*, and the *Bund* was no longer the sole protector of the working class. When, by 1936, the Aguda controlled 115 cooperatives, it wrested communal leadership from the assimilationists and participated in municipal and parliamentary elections.

Isaac Breuer (1883–1946), its ideologist, believed that "political Zionism seeks to exchange the *Galut* of Israel for the *Galut* of the nations. The goal of the Aguda," he maintained, "should be to prepare and bring together the people of God and the Land of God, in order to create a new kingdom of God under the rule of God." This belief colored the attitude of the Aguda. Consequently, it collaborated with the assimilationists rather than the Zionists. It rarely cooperated with the Club of Jewish Deputies in Poland, and never with the Jewish Agency. It supported the Polish pro-government block, and its parliamentary representatives were thereby forced to accept the discipline of a government whose avowed objective was the economic strangulation of the Jews.

Admittedly, the Aguda was anti-Zionist, yet in a poignant paradox it was also passionately pro-Zionist. In 1922, resolving to support "the Jewish people spiritually and physically in the Holy Land and abroad," it established a Palestine office and a settlement fund to provide training camps in Poland and to acquire land in Palestine. It established a special agricultural school (Hirschhof) near Falkengesass, Germany, and two colonization societies in Poland (*Givat Yehudah* and *Nahlat Lublin*). In the Holy Land, it founded the settlement of *Mahaneh Yisrael* and established schools in Jerusalem, Tel Aviv, and Safed.

There were various nuances between the branches of the Aguda in Germany, Hungary, Eastern Europe, and the Old City of Jerusalem, but they were all united in their struggle against the World Zionist Organization. In the Holy Land, a branch of the Aguda movement was set up in 1912, guided by R. Moses Blau and R. Hayyim Joseph Sonnenfeld. It refused to join other sections of the Jewish community, organized in the *Vaad Leumi*, nor did it recognize the chief rabbinate. The Aguda demanded that (1) the National Council should acknowledge the authority of the Holy Torah, (2) no person desecrating the Sabbath be eligible for membership, (3) women should not have the right to participate in the election of members, and (4) it should not subsidize such enterprises as workers' kitchens that served forbidden foods.

Nonetheless, a number of the members of the *Po'alei Aguda* had established fourteen settlements by 1993 and took part in the work of self-defense, especially after the murder of Orthodox Jews in Hebron, Safed, and Jerusalem in 1929. The two first Great Assemblies of the Aguda were held in Vienna in 1923 and 1929.

The Aguda did not join "the enlarged Jewish Agency" founded in 1929. It made its own representations to the British administration and the Mandate Commission of the League of Nations, challenging the "monopoly" of the agency to deal with matters affecting the development of the Jewish National Home.

In 1937, the publication of the Report of the Peel Commission (set up by the British government under Viscount Peel), recommending that the Holy Land be partitioned into two sovereign states—one Jewish and the other Arab—with historic and strategic sites remaining under British jurisdiction, led to deep divisions within the Aguda. The internal conflicts reached a peak at the third *Knessiyah Gedolah*, which was held in Marienbad in 1937. There was, however, complete unanimity that a Jewish state, not founded on or governed by Torah principles, could not possibly call itself a Jewish state.

It was during this period that Vladimir Jabotinsky (1880–1940), the leader of the New Zionist Organization, managed to enlist the cooperation of the Aguda. A joint letter was sent to Dr. Chaim Weitzmann on July 22, 1937, suggesting a roundtable conference under a neutral chairman. Nothing came out of that initiative. The Aguda took part, however, in the St. James conference, convened by the British government in 1939. It was at this fateful gathering that the Aguda agreed to coordinate its policy with that of the Jewish Agency. A number of Agudists and hasidim were among the 280,000 Jews who emigrated to Palestine between 1918 and 1936.

During the war years, there was still a great deal of friction between the Aguda, led by Harry A. Goodman, and the Zionist movement. By the end of 1945, Goodman had given evidence before the Anglo-American Committee of Enquiry when it held a session in London.

Prior to the establishment of the state of Israel, an agreement was reached between the Aguda and David Ben Gurion, then chairman of the Jewish Agency, whereby assurances were given that the status quo on questions of religion would be maintained, and the Orthodox movement undertook to join the struggle for the state. The Aguda joined the provisional council of state, took part in Israel's coalition government, and participated in the *Knesset* elections. R. Yitzhak Meir Levin (d. 1971) served in the Israel provisional government as minister of social welfare (1949–1952).

In the first *Knesset* elections of 1949, the Aguda and the *Po'alei Aguda* joined with the Mizrachi. In the election for the second *Knesset* (1951), the Aguda and the *Po'alei Aguda* together obtained 2.01 percent of the vote. In the third and fourth *Knesset* elections, of 1953 and 1959, the Aguda joined the *Po'alei Aguda* and obtained 3.01 percent and 3.69 percent, respectively, with six seats. In the fifth (in 1961), the sixth (in 1965), and the seventh (in 1969) elections, they obtained four seats. The Aguda representation in the *Knesset* varied from 4 to 6 percent.

In May 1977, the Aguda did not join the government of Menahem Begin, but it was granted the chairmanship of two major *Knesset* committees—Finance and Labor. The anatomy and pathology law, the abortion law, and the women and service in the army law were amended in accordance with the demands of the Aguda. The 1981 coalition agreement awarded vast sums to the independent schools of the Aguda and to various *yeshivot*. R. Eliezer Schach, head of the Lithuanian-style Ponovezh *yeshivah* of Bene Berak, demanded the expulsion of Lubavitch from the Aguda. When this was not forthcoming, he sponsored, together with R. Ovadia Yosef, former Israeli Sefardic chief rabbi, his own party—*Degel HaTorah*—which had the allegiance of the *Po'alei Aguda*.

The Aguda, however, in 1988, received for the first time the support of R. Menahem Mendel Schneerson, who was mainly responsible for the Aguda's increased representation in the *Knesset* from two seats in 1984 to five seats in 1988.

In 1992, the *Degel HaTorah* and the *Agudat Israel* agreed to join together. Under this agreement the *Degel HaTorah* would receive the second and fifth slots on a unified list, with the fourth and fifth members of the *Knesset* to rotate midway through the *Knesset* term. In addition, the two sides have agreed to set up one council of Torah sages.

The Aguda established its own school system. *Hinukh Atzmai* supports the *Bet Yaakov* movement, *yeshivot*, and *kollelim*. Among the active Agudists are Shlomoh Lorentz, Menahem Porush, and Abraham Hirsch. The Aguda controls two settlements—*Komamiyot* and *Kefar Gideon*. It issues a daily paper—*Hamodia*—and a monthly periodical—*Bet Yaakov*—and has *shikkunim* (settlements) in Jerusalem, Petah Tikva, and Bene Berak.

The American branch of the Aguda was established in 1922 and from 1941 was guided by R. Aaron Kotler, R. Moses Feinstein, and R. Eliezer Silver. There are branches for women, girls, and young men.

The Aguda in the United States is the preeminent movement of organized Torah Jewry. Its constituency includes most of the major hasidic groups, with Satmar and Lubavitch being the prime exceptions. It fosters Torah study among all levels of the population through *Daf Yomi*, *Reshet Shiurei Torah*, and *Halakhah* seminars for laymen in various professions.

It advocates on behalf of Orthodox Jewish rights before government, advancing laws that safeguard the Orthodox way of life. It represents the *yeshivot* and secures large government grants for education. It oversees rescue and relief. It provides help in training and sponsoring senior citizen programs and offers help to widows and divorcées.

It has always been deeply influenced by its hasidic members. In 1921, on a visit to the United States, R. Meir Dan Plotzky helped to establish the American Aguda. Among the American delegates to the second *Knessiyah Gedolah* was R. Gedaliah Schorr, a hasid of Sadgora, who became the head of the *Mesivta Torah Vodaat*. Among the early supporters were R. Pinhas Horowitz of Boston and R. Moses Lipshitz of Philadelphia, who had settled in the United States before World War I. During the interwar years, R. Moses Yehiel Halevi Epstein, who arrived in 1926; R. Nahum Mordecai Perlow of Novominsk; R. Mordecai Shlomoh Friedman of Boyan; R. Abraham Joshua Heschel; and R. Benjamin Hendeles played important parts in the establishment of the Aguda.

During World War II, R. Saul Yedidiah Taub, who lived in New York prior to settling in Israel, was one of its staunch supporters. The many refugees who arrived after the war and a number of hasidic rabbis, such as R. Shimon Shalom Kalish of Amshinov and R. Israel Shapira of Blazowa, became members of the American *Mo'etzet Gedolei HaTorah*. It was the Aguda that helped R. Shlomoh Halberstam and R. Yehudah Horowitz, the Stetchiner rebbe, to settle in the United States.

Among the rebbes who maintained cordial ties with the Aguda were R. Yekutiel Judah Halberstam, Zanz-Klausenberger rebbe; R. Eliezer Zusya Portugal; R. Jacob Joseph Twersky of Skver; and R. Yitzhak Twersky of Rotmastrivka.

R. Moses Horowitz of Boston and R. Levi Yitzhak Horowitz are members of the *Mo'etzet Gedolei HaTorah*, and R. Jacob Perlow of Novominsk is a member of the *Nesiut*. The *rosh kollel* of Ger in New York, R. Elya Fisher; R. Ezekiel Besser, a hasid of Radomsk; and R. Moses Sherer, president of the Aguda today, are all deeply involved in its work.

It has published *Dos Yiddishe Vort*, America's foremost Yiddish monthly, which is edited by R. Joseph Friedenson, a hasid of Ger, and which includes a broad range of articles on hasidic life since 1952. Since 1963, it has published an English language monthly, the *Jewish Observer*.

The founder of the Aguda in England in 1917 was R. Meir Jung, chief minister of the Federation of Synagogues, who urged the British government, in 1917, to issue the Balfour Declaration.

The first Aguda conference took place in London in March 1921, when Harry Goodman was elected secretary. Among the leaders were R. Abraham Babad, R. Z. Semiaticki, *Dayan* D. Schneebalg, and R. J. H. Cymerman. The Aguda was well served by lay leaders such as E. Liff and S. B. Unsdorfer. Today there are an Israel Community Service, a *Keren HaTorah* Committee, a Russian Immigrant Aid Fund, a Society of Friends of the Torah, and a *Beth Jacob* Council of Great Britain.

J. Rosenheim, *Agudistische Schriffen*.

E.D., S.L., M.Sh.

AGUS, Jacob Bernard (1911–1986), philosopher and rabbi—Born in Poland and received his education in Israel and the United States. He was the author of many books in the field of Jewish thought, among them *Modern Philosophy of Judaism* (1941) and *Dialogue and Tradition* (1969). He was a consulting editor to the *Encyclopaedia Britannica*. He was professor of religion at Temple University and rabbi of the Beth El Synagogue in Baltimore, Maryland. His interest in Hasidism was expressed in his essays *Ish HaMistorim* (Talpiyot, 1946), *LeHeiker Hagyon HaKabbalah* (*Sefer HaShanah* [1947]), *Torot Habad* (*Sefer HaShanah* [1949]), and *HaHidush BeTorot shel HaBesht* (special issue of *Hadoar*).

AHAD HA-AM (Asher Hirsch Ginsberg, 1856–1927)—Ahad Ha-Am was a leading figure in the history of modern Zionism, a leader of the Hibbat Zion movement, and an important contributor to the revival of the Hebrew language. He was born in Skvira, near Kiev, Russia (which he later described as "one of the most benighted spots in the hasidic sector of Russia"), into a well-to-do hasidic family. His father was a hasid of the rebbe of Ruzhyn. In addition to the traditional Jewish education he received from private tutors, he acquired a broad secular education through his own wide reading in *Haskalah* literature, secular philosophy, history, and science. During his youth, he visited R. Abraham Jacob of Sadgora, only once, just before his *bar mitzvah*. Unfortunately, this one meeting made an unfavorable impression on the sensitive boy, and thereafter he felt estranged from Hasidism, though he did later marry into an important hasidic family.

In 1884, Ginsberg settled in Odessa and there became involved in the Zionist activity that was to be his consuming interest for the remainder of his life. He began to publish articles on Zionist and Jewish issues and in 1896 succeeded to the editorship of the monthly journal *HaShiloah*, which was the most important Hebrew-Jewish periodical of its day in Eastern Europe. It was during this period that he thought through his own Zionist program, which stressed the rebirth of a creative spiritual-cultural center in *Eretz Yisrael*. From 1907 to 1922, he resided in London, visiting *Eretz Yisrael* several times before finally settling there in 1922. A prolific author of essays, his collected Hebrew papers have been published under the title *Al Parashat Derakhim*; a full edition of his correspondence, *Iggerot Ahad Ha-Am* (1957–1960), has been published under the editorship of L. Simon and Y. Pogravinsky. Three volumes of selected essays have also been translated into English by Leon Simon and have appeared as *Selected Essays of Ahad Ha-Am* (1912 and subsequently reissued), *Ten Essays on Zionism and Judaism* (1922), and *Ahad Ha-Am: Essays, Letters, Memoirs* (1946).

As his own thought matured, Ahad Ha-Am grew increasingly distant from his hasidic origins. His late work, for the most part, presents a negative estimation of religion in general and of Judaism and Hasidism in particular. Although valuing religion for its national and cultural contribution to Judaism's "will to survive" or revaluing it in terms of his own German idealist philosophy, he expresses himself skeptically regarding its specific metaphysical claims and theological beliefs. Despite that skepticism, however, he saw the value of tradition and *Halakhah*, not only as these phenomena reveal the historic forces that shape our own self-consciousness, but also insofar as they are the means for the continuing development of the spiritual energies of the Jewish people. In his view, the resettlement of *Eretz Yisrael* would provide new opportunities for the development of the *Halakhah* in the direction of modern needs and concerns.

In trying to evaluate the direct significance of Hasidism to Ahad Ha-Am's thought, one must be cautious not to completely dissociate his later views on cultural Zionism and the central value of *Kelal Yisrael* (Community of Israel) from his youthful environment and early inspirations. His biographer, Leon Simon, has described this relation in the following way: "Despite the completeness of his later revulsion from hasidism and its beliefs . . . the intense piety and patriotism of the hasid reappear, however transmuted, in his almost mystical faith in the Jewish people, its unique character, and its indissoluble connection with its ancient homeland" (L. Simon, *Ahad Ha'Am: A Biography* [1960], p. 14). Moreover, even though Ahad Ha-Am felt estranged from Hasidism, he saw the need to recognize and call attention to Hasidism's profound genius. In discussing the nature and history of modern Hebrew thought and literature, he wrote, "We must admit that if today we want to find even a shadow of original Hebrew literature, we must turn to the literature of Hasidism; there, rather than in the literature of the *Haskalah*, one occasionally encounters . . . true profundity of thought which bears the mark of the original Jewish genius" ("Tehiyat HaRuach," in *Parshat Derakhim*, vol. 2, p. 129).

S. J. Zipperstein, *Elusive Prophet: Ahad Ha'Am and the Origins of Zionism*.

S.K.

AHIJAH THE SHILONITE–Israelite prophet during the reign of King Solomon.

According to R. Jacob Joseph of Polonnoye, Ahijah was the "teacher of my teacher," in other words, the teacher of the Besht. Writing to his brother-in-law, the Besht refers to Ahijah as his mentor. When the ship on which the Besht took the legendary journey to the Holy Land was wrecked, Ahijah comforted him and taught him the way of moderating Heavenly judgments.

Ahijah was one of the transmitters of the Oral Law, and it is possible that he was introduced into hasidic mythology to enhance the reputation of the Besht, stressing that this fabled prophet of antiquity revealed the inner secrets of the Torah to him.

J. Nigal, "Moro V'Rabbo Shel R. Israel Baal Shem Tov," pp. 150–159.

N.G.

AKSENFELD, Israel (1787–1866), Yiddish writer–Originally a hasid of Bratzlav, Israel became a *maskil* and a vehement opponent of Hasidism. In October 1841, writing to S. Uvarov, minister of education of Russia, he stated that Hasidism is "a sect which conceals grave moral defects under the mask of piety, and undermines morality and interferes with education."

In August 1860, while applying to the mayor of Odessa for permission to open a printing press, he wrote, "Hasidism is a plague which spread among the Jews—a plague against which the government as well as the better circles of Jews have been fighting without success."

S. Ginsburg, *Yivo Annual of Jewish Social Sciences*, 1950, pp. 172–184.

ALCOHOL—The practice of drinking alcoholic beverages at hasidic gatherings was a natural development of the conviction that joy belongs to the realm of the Divine and a depressed or melancholic mood is derived from the "other side." It was regarded as a *mitzvah* to bring joy to other people by offering them a drink. This was called *tikkun*. R. Naftali of Ropczyce, commenting on the verse "Drink not wine nor strong drink, thou nor thy sons with thee" (Leviticus 10:9), stated that the verse implied that "one may drink when celebrating a marriage, dedicating a home, at a circumcision, on Purim, and at the conclusion of a tractate."

The Besht's famous principle that "God wishes to be served in all ways" was also an important factor. God could be served through conversation about mundane matters and festive gathering, which may be of help to people to overcome their anxieties and to rescue them from the grip of melancholy. When people wish each other all kinds of blessings, they pray in effect on behalf of each other, and "he who prays for his friend, being himself in need, is answered first" (*Baba Kamma* 92a).

However, R. Menahem Mendel of Vitebsk warned his family not to drink alcohol during the week, not even on Purim or Simhat Torah. Only on the Sabbath did he permit a drink or two (*Torat HaAretz*, chap. 6). Similarly, R. Elimelekh of Lejask and R. Nahman of Bratzlav warned their followers against drinking in excess and against drinking alone (*Tzetal Katan*). The *mitnaggedim*, however, complained that the rebbes allowed their hasidim to transform every day into a holiday.

A. Wertheim, *Halakhot VeHalikhot*, pp. 223–224.

J.B.A.

ALEKSANDROV LODZKI, a town in central Poland—"Alexander," as the hasidim called it, a little townlet near Lodz, occupied a unique position in Hasidism. No other hasidic dynasty in Poland, apart from Ger, attracted so vast a multitude. Ger lured the scholars, but Alexander drew the *baalei batim*, the merchants, and the masses. Just as Warsaw was the stronghold of Ger, so Lodz was the capital of the Alexander hasidim. Lodz alone had no fewer than thirty-five Alexander *shtieblech*, and there were few towns in Poland that did not have such a *shtiebl*. Considerable rivalry existed between the followers of Ger and Alexander. Alexander stood aloof from political parties, associating neither with the *Mahzikei HaDat* of Belz nor with the Aguda of Ger.

It was R. Hanokh Heinokh HaKohen Levin who brought Hasidism to Alexander, and the town became the home of R. Shragai Feivel Danziger and his successors: R. Yehiel, R. Shmuel Tzvi, and R. Yitzhak Menahem Mendel.

All three thousand five hundred Jews were transported by the Nazis to Glowno on December 27, 1939. In Israel, the spiritual leader of the Alexander hasidim was R. Judah Moses Teihberg of Bene Berak.

A. Y. Bromberg, *Migdolei HaHasidut*, vol. 4, *Admorei Alexander*.

ALFANDARI, Solomon Eliezer (c. 1829–1930), kabbalist—Known as the *Maharsha* (*Moreinu HaRav Shlomoh Eliezer*) or *Saba Kaddisha* (the "holy elder"), he served as rabbi first in Damascus and Safed (1904–18), then settled in Jerusalem in 1926.

He was befriended by R. Hayyim Elazar Shapira of Munkacz, who regarded him as the *Tzaddik HaDor* (the most righteous man of his generation) and visited him before his death. It was the "holy elder" to whom the hasidim of Munkacz dedicated the book *Massot Yerushalayim* (1931).

M. D. Gaon, *Yehudei HaMizrach BeEretz Yisrael*, p. 85f.

ALFAS, Moses Simhah, of Opoczno (1801–3 *Heshvan* 1864)—Son of R. Jacob, he was born in Opoczno, where his father and grandfather served as rabbis. He married the sister of Tamarel Bergson. He was befriended by R. Abraham Moses of Przysucha and R. Yitzhak Kalish of Warka.

He left an "ethical will," in which he recorded his communal activities, including his supervision of repairs made to the fences of the cemetery and the floor of the synagogue. "I have never asked people for money," he wrote. "I have never complained that they gave me too little. Often I insisted that they take back the money they had given me. I never wanted gifts that were not given with a perfect heart."

Y. Alfasi, *HaHasidut*, p. 149.

ALFASI, Yitzchak (b. 1929), hasidic writer–Born in Tel Aviv on October 13, the son of Israel, a hasid of Ger. He studied in the Hebron *yeshivah* and is honorary executive vice president of B'nai B'rith and head of the Hasidic Institute in Jerusalem. He is one of Israel's most prolific writers on Hasidism.

He is the author of *Rabbi Menahem Mendel of Kotzk* (1952), *Nahum of Bratslav* (1953), *The Grandfather of Shpole* (1957), *Toldot HaHasidut* (1959), *Rabbi of Gur* (1954), *Sefer HaAdmorim* (1961), *Tiferet ShebeMalkut* on Vishnitz (1961), and *HaHasidut* (1969).

His style is clear and concise.

ALTER, Abraham Issachar Benjamin Elijah, of Pabianice (1896–14 *Shevat* 1943)–Son of R. Menahem Mendel and Esther, daughter of R. Abraham Issachar Hakohen of Radomsko, he was born in Radomsko. He was brought up in his grandfather's home in Ger and married his cousin, the daughter of R. Moses Bezalel. He studied under R. Meir Dan Plotzki.

After World War I, he lived in Pabianice and supervised the publication of *Likkutei Sefat Emet* on the Pentateuch, *Sefat Emet* on the Psalms, and the Ethics of the Fathers. He was the author of *Meir Enei HaGolah*, of which part one was published in Piotrokov in 1928 and part two in Tel Aviv in 1954.

When his father became rabbi in Kalish, he succeeded him in Pabianice.

At the outbreak of the Second World War, he lived in Warsaw. He, his wife Leah, his sons R. Judah Leib and R. Solomon Yitzhak Meir, and his daughter, Esther Rebecca, were murdered in Treblinka.

ALTER, Abraham Mordecai, of Ger (1866–Shavuot 1948), third rabbi of Ger–Eldest son of R. Yehudah Aryeh Leib, the *Sefat Emet*, he was born in Ger on 7 *Tevet*. He married *Hayyah* Yehudit, the daughter of R. Noah Shahor of Biala. He spent one year in the home of his father-in-law, where he came into contact with R. Gershon Heinokh Leiner of Radzyn and R. Nahum Zeev Bornstein.

On 5 *Shevat* 1905, at the age of thirty-nine, he succeeded his father as rebbe. His succession marked a return to meticulous observance of the *Shulhan Arukh* and an emphasis on Torah study. On Friday evenings between *Minhah* and *Maariv* and on the Sabbath, between *Shaharit* and *Musaf*, time was set aside for study. Following the traditions of Ger, he refused to accept *pidyonot* from his followers. He did not sit at the head of the table, but in the middle. An unassertive, diffident man, he could act with courage and resolution in times of crisis. He cultivated the quality of *zerizut* (diligence), and time to him was more precious than gold.

During World War I, he lived in Warsaw, Lodz, and Otwock.

Like his grandfather, he had a deep sense of communal responsibility. At the Bad Homburg conference in 1909, he helped prepare the way for the founding of the Aguda. He attended three Agudist conferences: in 1923, 1929, and 1937. He supported Orthodox publications and gave great encouragement to the *Bet Yaakov* school movement. He favored the establishment of the *Yeshivat Hakhmei Lublin* and the *Daf HaYomi*.

He visited the Holy Land five times (1921, 1923, 1927, 1932, and 1935). In a letter dated 7 *Iyyar* 1921, he wrote, "I am pleased to note that it is possible to observe Judaism here without any hindrance." He visited High Commissioner Herbert (later Viscount) Samuel, who assured him that he would help religious settlers. He also met R. Abraham Yitzhak Kook, the chief rabbi. Yet, he discouraged his hasidim from contributing to the Jewish National Fund (JNF), because Sabbath observance was not mandatory on JNF holdings. In 1925, he encouraged the establishment of Bene Berak and of the *yeshivah Sefat Emet* in Jerusalem. In 1937, he opposed the partitioning of Palestine as envisaged by the Peel Commission.

A dedicated bibliophile, he had a library of over five thousand books, among them incunabula. He urged the publication of the unpublished manuscripts of R. Menahem ben Shlomoh Meiri of Perpignan, as well as the works of R. Hayyim Vital and R. Mordecai Galanti. He made extensive comments and glosses on Yitzhak ben Yaakov's *Otzar HaSefarim*. In 1907, when R. Shlomoh Yehudah Friedlander published *Seder Kodashim* of the Jerusalem Talmud, the rabbi of Ger maintained that his texts were literary forgeries.

With the outbreak of the Second World War, the rebbe urged his followers to subscribe generously to the Polish air defense fund. He moved to Warsaw, constantly changing his residence to elude the Nazis, who spared no effort to locate the "wonder rabbi." An energetic committee in the United States managed to obtain an entry visa for the rabbi. He, together with his wife, Feige Mintze, the daughter of R. Jacob Meir Biderman (whom he married after his first wife died on 13 *Shevat* 1922), his sons—R. Israel, R. Simhah Bunem, and R. Pinhas Menahem—left Warsaw via Cracow and Trieste in *Adar* 1940. They arrived in *Eretz Yisrael* after Passover and settled in Jerusalem. One son, R. Yitzhak, died on 17 *Heshvan* 1937. Another son, R. Meir Alter, perished in the Holocaust. His daughter, Feiga, the wife of R. Yitzhak Meir Alter, also perished. Other daughters were Breindel, the wife of R. Shlomoh Yoskowitz; Esther, the wife of R. Yitzhak Aaron Efraim Fischel Heine; and Devorah Matel, the wife of R. Yitzhak Meir Levin.

The rebbe of Ger participated in special prayers for Polish Jewry held in the *Hurva* synagogue on 29 *Kislev* 1942.

When he died on the first day of Shavuot 1948, R. Dr. Yitzhak Herzog, then chief rabbi of the Holy Land, proclaimed in eulogy, "On Shavuot the Torah was given, and on Shavuot the Torah was taken away." As the Mount of Olives was then in Arab hands, the rebbe was buried in the courtyard of the *yeshivah Sefat Emet* in Jerusalem.

Sixty members of his family perished in the Holocaust. In his will and testament, dated 7 *Tevet* 1936, he nominated his brother, R. Moses Bezalel, as his successor. When his brother perished in the Holocaust, he nominated his son, R. Israel, as his successor. His other surviving sons were R. Simhah Bunem and Pinhas Menahem.

His letters—*Mikhtavim* (Lodz, 1925), *Osef Mikhtavim* (Warsaw, 1937), *Osef Mikhtavim U'Devarim* (Augsburg, 1947), *Peninim Yekarim* (Tel Aviv, 1955), and *Likkutei Yehudah* (Jerusalem, 1963)—and a number of his discourses were printed in *Mikhtevei Torah* (Tel Aviv, 1967). R. Benjamin Alter, his grandson, has published more of his discourses on the Pentateuch under *Imrei Emet* (Bene Berak, 1978, 1980, and 1983).

A. Y. Bromberg, *Migdolei HaHasidut*, vol. 26, *R. Abraham Mordecai Alter*.

ALTER, Abraham Mordecai, of Zychlin (1872–1940)—Son of R. Solomon, who was the younger brother of R. Yehudah Aryeh Leib, the *Sefat Emet*. He was born in Warsaw. He married the daughter of the rabbi of Zychlin. He was a devoted follower of his uncle, the *Sefat Emet*, whom he visited regularly.

After the death of his father-in-law, he succeeded him as rabbi in Zychlin. A man of exemplary character, he was known for his forbearance. "Once upon a time," he would say, "there were hardened heretics. These days, all we have is nonbelievers." He was active in the work of the Aguda.

ALTER, Israel (24 *Tishri 1885–2 Adar* 1977), Ger/Jerusalem—Son of R. Abraham Mordecai, he was born in Ger. His mother was Radda Yehudit. He married his first cousin, Hayyah Sarah, the daughter of Rabbi Jacob Meir Biderman, on 4 *Nisan* 1910. After his marriage, he lived in Warsaw. During World War II, he lost his wife and his son, Aryeh Leib. He left Poland together with his father for the Holy Land. There, in 1948, he married Perl, a widow, the daughter of R. David Wiedenfeld and sister-in-law of R. Abraham Weinberg of Slonim. There was no issue of that marriage. In accordance with the last will and testament of his brother, R. Israel succeeded him as rabbi of Ger on Shavuot 1948.

Although time was precious to him, he had time for everybody. Twice daily he would receive people in private audience. With almost lightning speed he could solve the most complicated problems. The material and spiritual problems of every one of his followers were familiar to him. His discourses were economical, rarely lasting longer than a few minutes. The brevity did not diminish his depth, and there was an original thought in every discourse.

He took an active interest in the work of the Aguda, whom he endearingly called the "*Agudath Israel* of my father." He was also a leader of the *Mo'etzet Gedolei HaTorah*. He expanded the *yeshivah Sefat Emet* in Jerusalem and encouraged the building of the *yeshivah Hidushei Harim* in Tel Aviv and other hasidic educational institutions.

He was buried on the Mount of Olives in *Helkah Polin*, near the grave of Yehiel Fishel Heine. He was succeeded by his brother, R. Simhah Bunem.

ALTER, Meir (1883–1942)–Eldest son of R. Abraham Mordecai of Ger. He studied under his grandfather, R. Yehudah Aryeh Leib, the *Sefat Emet*. He married the daughter of R. Leibish Berliner of Warsaw and was able to combine study with mercantile activities.

Though his father was permitted to leave Poland during the Second World War, he was refused an exit visa. He, his two sons, R. Hayyim Elazar and R. Naftali, and his two sons-in-law were murdered by the Nazis.

ALTER, Menachem Mendel, of Kalish (1877–1943)–The fourth and youngest son of R. Yehudah Aryeh Leib, the *Sefat Emet*, he married Esther Leah, the daughter of R. Abraham Issachar HaKohen of Radomsko on 3 *Elul* 1893. She died in childbirth, and he subsequently married the daughter of R. Moses Privas of Warsaw, a hasid of Ger. He had three sons and three daughters.

He supported the Orthodox newspaper *Hakol* and the weekly *Hakol Kol Yaakov*, and established a *yeshivah, Darkhei Noam*, in Ger. During World War I he lived in Vitebsk.

In 1921, he became rabbi in Pabianice and was active in the *Mo'etzet Gedolei HaTorah*. In 1934 he succeeded R. Ezekiel Lipshitz as rabbi of Kalish.

He visited the Holy Land in 1938 and fought strenuously against *shehitah* restrictions in Poland.

He and his family, with the exception of one son, R. Hayyim Eliezer, perished in Treblinka.

J. Silberberg, *Malkhut Bet Radomsk*, pp. 474–476.

ALTER, Moses Bezalel (1861–22 *Elul 1942)*–Second son of R. Yehudah Aryeh Leib, the Sefat Emet, he married his cousin, Hayyah Sarah, the daughter of R. Shimon, in 1886. When his father died, his elder brother became the rebbe, and R. Moses Bezalel remained at his brother's side for the next thirty-five years. His brother designated him his successor, "for he is bound to me with his heart and soul." He would act as *baal tekiyah* in Ger.

In 1925, he and his wife visited the Holy Land.

His son, R. Yitzhak Meir, was killed during the Second World War. R. Moses Bezalel had the opportunity to leave Poland, but he gave his exit permit to his grandson, R. Benjamin. For a time, R. Moses Bezalel worked in the Shultz factory in the Warsaw ghetto. He was murdered in Treblinka.

ALTER, Nehemiah (1875–22 *Tammuz* 1941)–The fourth son of the *Sefat Emet*, Nehemiah was born in Ger. In the month of *Elul* 1900, he married Esther Glicka, the daughter of R. Tzvi Morgenstern of Lamaz, in Radzymin, where he stayed for a number of years. He was known for his great diligence, and all year round, he would rise at three in the morning to pursue his studies.

In 1925, he visited the Holy Land and lived first in Safed and then in Jerusalem, where he spent five years supervising the development of the *yeshivah Sefat Emet* in Jerusalem, whose foundation stone was laid on 15 *Tammuz* 1926.

In 1931, he returned to Otwock and later lived in Lodz. Three years later he was appointed a member of the Lodz rabbinate. During the Second World War, he violently opposed the activities of the *Judenrat* under the chairmanship of Mordecai Hayyim Rumkowski. He died in Lodz.

He had three sons and five daughters, one of whom married R. Simhah Bunem Alter. He was the author of *Hiddushei R. Nehemiah*, which was published in 1983.

A. Surasky, *Marbitzei Torah*, vol. 3, pp. 48–71.

ALTER, Pinhas Menahem, of Ger (b. 1923)–Son of R. Abraham Mordecai Alter by his second wife, Feige Minze, daughter of R. Jacob Meir Biderman. R. Pinhas Menahem emigrated with his father to the Holy Land in 1940. He studied in the *Hayyei Olam yeshivah*. In 1948, he married the granddaughter of R. Moses Bezalel Alter.

He is very active in the Aguda and wrote frequently for its paper, *HaModia*. He was the principal of the *yeshivah Sefat Emet* in Jerusalem. His twenty-seven-year-old son, R. Yehudah Aryeh Leib, married the daughter of R. Manasseh Klein of Ungvar, New York;

stayed in New York for three years; and gave *shiurim* at the Ungvar *yeshivah* after being ordained by R. Moses Feinstein. On his return to Israel, he was appointed to the *Bet Din* of the *hasidei Ger* and was also rabbi in the Romema district of Jerusalem. He was injured by a car as he emerged from a ritual bath and died from his injuries on 15 *Tishri* 1969.

His surviving sons are R. Jacob Meir; R. Saul, who is the *rosh yeshivah* of the *Sefat Emet yeshivah*; R. Yitzhak David; and R. Daniel Aaron.

R. Pinhas Menahem succeeded his brother, R. Simhah Bunem, as rebbe of Ger in 1992. He dedicated the new *yeshivah* of Ger in London on November 22, 1992.

The rebbe is the spiritual head of forty-five centers in thirty-two towns in Israel, as well as of five centers in England and the United States. They include *kollelim*, *yeshivot gedolot*, *yeshivot ketanot*, and *Talmud Torah* schools. Between four thousand and forty-five hundred people study in these institutions. There are also many *shtieblech*; in Bene Berak alone there are over fifteen.

He maintains contact with all the principals and occasionally visits the institutions. Up to ten thousand hasidim attend the Ger place of worship in Jerusalem on the High Holy Days.

He strongly disapproves of the Israel/PLO accord of September 1993. "Just as a *Sefer Torah* becomes invalid if one letter is missing," stated the rebbe, "so is it wrong to deprive the Holy Land of any of its territory."

The Rebbe conducts *tish* every other Sabbath and often delivers discourses after *Shaharit* on Sabbath morning. He still lives in his former residence above the *yeshivah Sefat Emet*.

J.N.

ALTER, Pinhas Menahem, of Pilice (d. 10 *Kislev* 1921) – Son of R. Benjamin Eliezer Justman, he married the daughter of R. Abraham Mordecai Alter. He held rabbinical positions in Pilice, Virshov, and Czestochova. He was the author of *Siftei Tzaddik* (Pioktrokov/Bilgoraj, 1924).

His son, Hanokh Gad, born in 1884 and his successor in Czestochova, was murdered in Treblinka.

ALTER REBBE (lit., "Old Rebbe") – A term by which the Lubavitch hasidim refer to R. Shneur Zalman of Liady.

ALTER, Simhah Bunem (23 *Nisan* 1888–7 *Tammuz* 1992), Ger/Jerusalem Fourth son of R. Mordecai Alter, he was born in Gora Kalwaria and was named after R. Simhah Bunem of Przysucha. His mother was Yehudit Rada, the daughter of Noah Shahor of Biala. His father called him the "wise one."

In 1915 in Warsaw, he married his cousin, Yuta Henni (d. 1983), the daughter of R. Nehemiah Alter, the third son of the *Sefat Emet*, and *dayan* in Lodz. The couple waited ten years for a first child, and that baby daughter, Hayyah Roda Yehudit, died at six months. After another four years, they eventually had two more children – a daughter followed by a son. R. Simhah Bunem's life was full of troubles, but he never uttered a word of complaint. Together with his father-in-law, he visited the Holy Land in 1927 and stayed there for a few years. In 1934, he settled in the *Mekor Barukh* district of Jerusalem. On returning to Poland in 1939, he lived in Lodz and then in Warsaw. As a Palestinian citizen, he was able, together with his family, to leave for the Holy Land on *Hol HaMo'ed* Passover 1940.

For twenty-nine years he gave his allegiance to his brother, R. Israel, and kept out of the limelight. When his brother died intestate on 8 *Adar* 1977, he acceded to the request of ten senior hasidim to become the fifth rebbe of Ger. He was renowned for his modesty and remained in his original small apartment. He pioneered the setting up of cost-price stores for the hasidim. The size of an apartment, its furnishing, the money spent on a *bar mitzvah* – even the cost of *etrogim* for Sukkot – all these were subject to detailed regulations. He was against lavish wedding celebrations. No more than 150 in addition to the family should be invited to the wedding meal. Others may be invited to the reception after the *huppah*.

He encouraged young religious couples to live outside the two main Orthodox centers of Jerusalem and Bene Berak, and instead to settle in Arad, Ashdod, and Hazor, where there were opportunities for apartments at lower rentals. He led the campaign to stop El Al airlines from flying on the Sabbath, and he fought against the establishment of the Mormon University on the Mount of Olives. He encouraged the Aguda to join and support the coalition government.

At the sixth *Knessiyah Gedolah*, the rebbe instituted the study of a daily page of the *Yerushalmi* side by side with the Babylonian Talmud. He visited London in 1954 and 1977. He was active in the leadership of the Aguda and was a member of the *Mo'etzet Gedolei HaTorah*. He supported Torah institutions and expanded the hasidic *yeshivot* of Ger in the Holy Land. He combined an unworldly manner with worldly interests, and he was renowned for his entrepreneurial skills. In 1986, his health deteriorated, and he ceased holding *tishen*, the festive Sabbath meals. He was buried on the Mount of Olives.

He was survived by his daughter, Rebecca, who was married to Meir Mandel of London but is now divorced, and by his son, R. Jacob Aryeh, who, in *Kislev* 1960, married the daughter of R. Menahem Mendel Weitz, the *rosh yeshivah* of Tel Aviv, and lives in Bene Berak.

R. Simhah Bunem was succeeded by his half-brother, R. Pinhas Menahem.

ALTER, Yehudah Aryeh Leib (28 *Nisan* 1847–5 *Shevat* 1905), the *Sefat Emet*—R. Leibele, the son of R. Abraham Mordecai (d. 1855), is known as the *Sefat Emet*, which became his literary pseudonym. He was born in Warsaw, and when his father died, he was barely eight years old. To his grandfather's delight, he studied with phenomenal diligence.

On 3 *Adar* 1862, he married Yocheved Rifka, the daughter of R. Yudel Kaminer of Chechiny. After the wedding he returned to Ger. He was nineteen years old when his grandfather, R. Yitzhak Meir, died in 1866. For the next four years, he was a devoted disciple of R. Heinokh HaKohen of Alexander. When the rebbe of Alexander died in 1870, he reluctantly assumed the leadership of the Gerer hasidim.

His wife kept a tobacco shop, which enabled him to decline *pidyonot*. Not one minute of his life was wasted. He rose at dawn and spent the entire day in study and prayer. Even when he received visitors, he would hold a volume of the *Shulhan Arukh* in his hands. He prayed in his own rooms, and only on the Sabbath and festivals did he attend the *Bet HaMidrash*. After the reading of the Law, he would return to his room, where he would recite *Musaf* privately.

In a letter to R. Hayyim Morgenstern of Pulava, the rebbe wrote, "Certainly, it will be reckoned as a *mitzvah* to settle in *Eretz Yisrael*." He urged his hasidim to import Palestinian *etrogim*. Dr. Theodor Herzl pleaded passionately for his cooperation in the Zionist endeavor, but the rebbe did not reply to his letter.

On 18 *Elul* 1901, his wife died. He then married the widowed daughter of R. Barukh Halberstamm of Gorlice. There were ten children from his first marriage, four of whom died in their infancy.

He left four sons and two daughters and such monumental works as *Sefat Emet*, a commentary on the Torah and festivals in five parts (Piotrokov/Cracow, 1905–1908); *Likkutim* on the Torah in two parts (Piotrokov, 1934–1936), and *Hiddushim* on *Seder Moed* (Warsaw, 1925–1931), on *Pirkei Avot* (Piotrokov and Landsberg, 1948), on the Passover *Haggadah* (Warsaw, 1930), on the *Scroll of Esther* (Jerusalem, 1952), on *Ecclesiastes* (Jerusalem, 1952–1953), on *Psalms* (London, 1952); and on *Proverbs* (Jerusalem, 1951).

He corresponded on halakhic matters with R. Shlomoh Abraham of Ozorkov and R. Abraham Hayyim Elazar Waks of Kalish. One halakhic responsum appeared in the rabbinical periodical *Shaarei Torah* (Warsaw, 1933), addressed to R. Joshua David Banin.

In the lifetime of the rebbe, Ger grew great and powerful. Not without reason did R. Elimelekh Shapira of Grodzisk call his illustrious contemporary "King of Israel."

A. Y. Bromberg, *Migdolei HaHasidut*, vol. 2, *R. Yehudah Leib Alter MiGur, The Sefat Emet*.

ALTER, Yitzhak Meir (1789–23 *Adar* 1866), founder of the Ger dynasty—Yitzhak Meir Rothenburg (Alter), better known as the *Hiddushei HaRim*, after the title of his works, was born in Magnuszev, near Radom, where his father, R. Israel, was rabbi. He traced his ancestry as far back as R. Meir of Rothenburg (1215–1293). His mother, Hayyah Sarah (d. 1852), was a descendant of R. Nathan Nata Spiro of Cracow.

At an early age, he became betrothed to Feigele, the daughter of the wealthy banker Moses ben Yitzhak Isaac Lipshitz, known as R. Mosheh Halfan. The wedding took place in Warsaw in 1812. After living in Kozienice for three months, he settled in Warsaw.

He studied in the *yeshivah* of his relative, R. Aryeh Leib Zinz, known as R. Leibish Harif, formerly rabbi of Plotsk, together with R. Abraham Landau of Czestochowa and R. Jacob Gezundheit. With single-minded passion, he devoted himself to his studies, spending some eighteen hours a day at his books. R. Yitzhak Meir, or "Itche Meir," as he was popularly called, attracted a group of young men of exceptional talent to study with him. Like his father, he was a devoted follower of R. Israel, the Maggid of Kozienice. He also visited the "Seer" of Lublin and the son of the Maggid of Kozienice, R. Moses Eliakum Beria. Loyalty to the Maggid's successor kept him for a while in Kozienice, but he soon became a follower of R. Simhah Bunem, the spiritual heir of the "Holy Jew," whom he visited no fewer than seventeen times. When R. Simhah Bunem died, he transferred his allegiance to R. Menahem Mendel of Kotzk, and his devotion to him never waned.

The Polish insurrection of 1830–1831 impoverished his father-in-law. For the first time, he was beset with financial worries and faced the urgent need to earn a living. He opened a workshop for the manufacture of *tallitim*, sold books, and turned printer. He prized his independence and refused to present himself as a candidate for the rabbinate. It was not until 1852 that he was officially appointed *dayan* of Warsaw with a fixed salary.

His personal life was beset by tragedies. He had thirteen children and outlived them all. In 1834, his sole surviving son, R. Abraham Mordecai, died on 27 *Av* 1855 at the age of forty. When R. Menahem Mendel of Kotzk died in 1859, R. Yitzhak Meir reluctantly became a hasidic rebbe, first at Krochmalna in Warsaw, then at Eisengass 57, and later in Ger (Gora Kalwaria), a small town near Warsaw, which became the "Jerusalem" of the most influential hasidic dynasty in Poland. "R. Simhah Bunem led with love, R. Menahem Mendel of Kotzk led with fear," he said. "I will lead them with Torah."

In 1841, he associated himself with R. Hayyim Dawidsohn of Warsaw and was one of the signatories to a manifesto urging Jews to settle on the land. When Sir Moses Montefiore visited Warsaw in May 1846, R. Yitzhak Meir and R. Yitzhak of Warka called upon the distinguished visitor.

R. Yitzhak Meir was against the teaching of secular subjects in the *heder*. Undaunted in his struggle against compulsory education, he took a firm stand on the issue of the dinstinctive garments worn by the hasidim and was duly imprisoned by Governor Paskevitch for his defiance. So great was the indignation of the entire Jewish community that he was soon released and lived for a time in Nowy Dwor. He returned to Warsaw before Passover 1851.

During the Crimean war (1853–1856), he prayed for the victory of the Allies (the French and British forces) but remained aloof when on June 22, 1863, the Poles rose in revolt against their Russian masters.

The doctrines of Przysucha and Kotzk were combined in Ger. There was neither emphasis on miracles nor acceptance of *pidyonot*. On 12 *Shevat* 1866, a door that fell off its hinges caused him serious injury and increasing pain. He died in the same year. His last words, "Leibele, *Kaddish*," were interpreted to mean that his grandson R. Yehudah Aryeh Leib should recite *Kaddish* after him and should be his successor.

R. Yitzhak Meir was a prolific author. Published posthumously were *Hiddushei HaRim* on tractate *Hullin*; *Teshuvot HaRim*, responsa on the four parts of the *Shulhan Arukh* (Yozefov, 1867, and Warsaw, 1882); *Hiddushei HaRim* on *Shulhan Arukh, Hoshen Mishpat* (Warsaw, 1870); *Hiddushei HaRim* on tractates *Ketubot* and *Kiddushin* (Warsaw, 1875); *Sefer HaZekhut* on the Pentateuch (Warsaw, 1876); *Hiddushei HaRim* on tractate *Shevuot* and *Shulhan Arukh*, *Even HaEzer* (Warsaw, 1881); and *Torat Hiddushei HaRim* on the Pentateuch and Festivals, edited by R. Yehudah Leib Levin (Jerusalem, 1950). His responsa pinpoint some of the day-to-day problems that Jewry faced in the mid-nineteenth century. For instance, scholars of the time debated the permissibility of baking *matzot* by machine. He endorsed the view of R. Shlomoh Kluger and forbade the use of machine-made *matzot*.

Y. Alfasi, *Gur*.

AMDUR – A hasidic dynasty in the northwestern part of Lithuania, founded by R. Hayyim Heikel. The dynasty was maintained by R. Samuel and his two sons, R. Moses Aaron and R. Hayyim Heikel II.

AMULETS – The use of amulets among Jews reflects an early and well-established tradition of amulet use throughout the Middle East. Amulets were used to protect the bearer against both physical and psychic diseases embodied in the form of malevolent demons.

Although already well attested to in the talmudic period, the Talmud makes only passing reference to amulets. The rabbis considered amulets to be an acceptable form of magic, since "anything in which there is healing contains no superstition" (*Shabbat* 67a), although one must use only proven amulets from an expert (*Shabbat* 60a–61a). The talmudic amulets offered protection by invoking the Ineffable Name, as in an amulet described in *Yoma* 84a against a dog bite. Such use of the Divine Name was permitted because amulets themselves did not heal but merely protected the wearer against disease (*Shabbat* 15b).

Not all amulets were worn, but many were inscribed on bowls and buried around the precincts of the house, as in the case of the Aramaic incantation bowls written by Jews in Babylonia in the talmudic period. These Jewish incantation bowls, together with talmudic discussions of amulets, became the primary sources from which later hasidic amulets were derived.

Amulets proliferated among Jews in later periods, although attitudes toward amulets varied. Maimonides, for instance, strongly condemned the use of amulets, but Menasseh ben Israel defended their effectiveness, because amulets contain holy names and excerpts from Psalms, which have authority against demons (*Nishmat Hayyim* III, 25). Amulets were used particularly by hasidic Jews, and the *Sefer Hasidim* permitted the use of amulets inscribed by both Jews and non-Jews (*Sefer Hasidim* 1114).

These hasidic amulets, like early predecessors, usually contained many forms of the Divine Name, the names of a host of archangels and heavenly beings, and references to biblical verses. Because the alphabet itself acquired prophylactic powers, such names often appear in the form of cryptograms, anagrams, and especially *gematria*—the substitution of words with numerical equivalents. Such names were often inscribed within triangles, rectangles, hexagrams, pentagrams, and circles, so as to contain or ensnare malevolent agents. Such diagrams are frequently illustrated in the *Sefer Raziel*; diagrams of magical letters or characters also appear in the earlier *Sefer HaRazim* (cf. *Sefer Raziel* 40ff.).

A great many hasidic amulets are intended to protect women and children during childbirth. Like the Babylonian *lamashtu* amulets and the Jewish incantation bowls, hasidic amulets were employed against Lilith, who was ousted as Adam's first wife and hence avenges herself upon infants (*Erubin* 18b). Childbirth amulets thus mention Adam, Eve, and Lilith together, seeking the protection of Eve against her rival (cf. *Sefer Raziel* 43a). Other amulets offer protection against the fearful Evil Eye, which could be imposed by either hostile demons or jealous humans. Most amulets, however, offer general protection against ill health, although one unusual amulet offers to protect a sea voyager from all mishaps and enemies and includes a drawing of a ship in the center (H. Gollancz, *Sefer Mafteah Shlomoh*, 58b).

Of those who fostered the spread of Jewish amulets, most prominent is Eleazar of Worms, whose thirteenth-century manuscript, the *Sefer Raziel*, remains the primary source for the study of Jewish amulets. The work of Rabbi Moses Zacuto, the *Sefer Shoreshei HaShemot*, collected and explained the cryptic formulas and names that appeared on amulets. Further impetus for the production of amulets was provided by Shabbetai Tzvi, the false Messiah who wrote numerous amulets, although both the man and his amulets were eventually discredited. Amulets continued to be used, however, and in the eighteenth century the amulets of R. Hayyim Azulai, the kabbalist and scholar, were particularly prized.

L. Blau, *Das altjudische Zauberwesen*.

T. Schrire, *Hebrew Amulets*.

I. Shachar, "Catalogue of Amulets," pp. 227–304.

M.J.G.

ANGELS AND ANGELOLOGY–

The concept of angels is fully developed in the Bible, Talmud, Midrash, and kabbalistic literature and is extensively discussed by the hasidic masters. The Besht taught that the angels are sustained only through our prayers. Even though both the Talmud and *Zohar* teach that angels must carry our prayers up to God, this is really only an illusion, since the angels themselves are nothing more than garments of God.

The Mezhiricher Maggid taught that even though angels constantly worship God, He has more delight in the praise that comes from humans, because humans must elevate themselves above their lowly physical state. Whereas the angels are primarily in the Universe of Speech, humans can ascend much higher–to the Universe of Thought, and even to the Universe of Nothingness.

In the *Habad* system, great emphasis is placed on the fact that the angels do not have free will, this being a quality found only in humans. Angels dwell in the Universe of Formation (*Yetzirah*), where the supernal Attributes are revealed, but the human soul is rooted in the Universe of Creation (*Beriyah*)–a higher level–where even the supernal Thought is revealed. (These correspond to the Universes of Speech and Thought mentioned earlier.)

An important teaching by R. Nahman of Bratzlav is that angels descended to the physical world, only to be overcome by its evil. Therefore people should learn a lesson from them and never lower their vigilance. When we study the Torah, we can literally create angels. Before we do anything, we should first praise God, since even the angels cannot function until they first praise God.

An important debate among the earlier Jewish philosophers involved the question of who is greater–a human being or an angel. The consensus of hasidic opinion is that the angel is greater than the physical being, whereas the human soul is much higher than the angels. R. Levi Yitzhak of Berdichev adds a new twist, teaching that although angels are normally greater than physical beings, when God expresses His love for the people Israel, they are greater than the angels. Only when an angel acts kindly toward Israel is it permitted to sing praise before God.

Although this is also a point debated by earlier Jewish theologians, R. Levi Yitzhak teaches that when one prays, one should be seeking help from the angels. One should meditate on the great awe that the angels experience before God and, at the very least, attempt to emulate it.

R. Israel, the Maggid of Kozienice, taught that the universe of angels was created with only one saying, and therefore angels do not have free will. It was so that human beings should be given free will, as well as reward and punishment, for their deeds, that the human world was created with ten sayings.

An important concept in angelology is that of the Angel of Death, whom the Talmud identifies with the Evil Urge (*Yetzer HaRa*) and the Accuser (*Satan*). The Talmud also teaches that the Angel of Death will eventually be slaughtered by God. The Besht interpreted this to mean that the Angel of Death will ultimately be made into a good angel. The angels of evil ultimately fulfill God's purpose when they tempt us, and therefore, instead of listening to them, we should emulate them and also strive to fulfill God's purpose.

One of the most important hasidic studies in angelology, *Sikhat Malakhei HaSharet*, (Lublin, 1927), was written by the hasidic master, R. Tzadok HaKohen Rabinowicz, in which he probes the reason why angels were created.

A.K.

ANGER–The avoidance of anger is stressed in midrashic, medieval, and *Musar* literature. The *Zohar* affirms that whoever rages in anger is like one who serves an idol (Genesis 27b). R. Shlomoh of Karlin used to say that "anger and sadness are rooted in arrogance." R. Nahman of Bratzlav stressed that "you must break the force of your anger with love. If you feel yourself becoming angry, make sure that you do nothing unkind because of your anger. You must make a special effort to be kind to the very person you are angry with. The remedy for anger is to fast. Anger can make a person lose his money. When a person fights his anger and breaks it, the spirit of the Messiah is drawn into the world."

In general, Hasidism stressed the importance of "shunning evil" and not permitting the "other side" to hold on to a person who performs a *mitzvah*. At the same time, the Talmud praises a scholar who is angered by the irreverence of the people (*Taanit* 4a), so when the *tzaddik* bursts into rage, it must be regarded as an expression of his supreme piety. R. Shneur Zalman maintained that on occasion it is indeed meritorious to hate a transgressor, but he advises that those who are remote from Torah and *mitzvot* should be attracted by the ropes of love. It is truly a *mitzvah* to hate them, but also a *mitzvah* to love them (*Tanya*, chap. 32).

According to A. J. Heschel, one of the differences between R. Menahem Mendel of Kotzk and R. Mordecai Joseph of Izbice turned on that point concerning whether or not the feelings of anger should be utilized in the training of hasidim.

We find many references to the theurgic potency of the anger of a *tzaddik*. Hasidic legend tells us that the reason for the deaths of the thirteen sons of R. Yitzhak Meir Alter was that he had offended his former rebbe by transferring his allegiance to the rebbe of Kotzk.

J.B.A.

ANIMALS–Belief in the transmigration of souls impelled the hasidim to be extremely careful in dealing with animals. R. Hayyim Vital, in his *Sefer HaGilgulim*, asserts that the souls of the deceased enter into animals, plants, and stones, as well as other humans. He maintained that "most of the people of our generation were incarnated in beasts and cattle" (*Sefer HaGilgulim* [Przemysl, 1975], chap. 66).

The Besht, according to legend, encountered a frog that contained the soul of a learned Jew, who was compelled to be incarnated in that form because he had been careless about the *mitzvah* of washing his hands before the partaking of bread (*Shivhei HaBesht*, p. 49). His disciple, R. Jacob Joseph of Polonnoye, was prevented for two weeks from praying properly, because he had declared a correctly slaughtered goose to be *treifah* when that goose had the soul of a Jew (*Meirat Einayim*, p. 279). We are also told of the incarnation of a person into a horse in order to repay an old debt to a creditor (Ibid., p. 142).

The Besht, according to hasidic legend, was familiar with the language of birds and beasts. He taught his disciple, R. Aryeh Leib, to understand this language. As human beings are divided into categories of Jews and gentiles, so animals, too, are divided into *kosher* and *treifah* categories. The former draw their vital power from the "shell of radiance" (*nogah*), but the latter are held fast by the "other side" (*Tanya*, chap. 7). This distinction between *kosher* and *treifah* is generalized into a perpetual contest between the forces of God and Satan. In the course of the partaking of food, especially the flesh of living things, the *tzaddik* selects the holy sparks, which are captured by the shells and thereby reinforce the powers of holiness.

In his *Tzetil Katan*, R. Elimelekh of Lejask includes the following exhortation to his followers: "Before washing one's hands in preparation for eating, one should pray, that no sin or strange thought prevent the unifications . . . that the taste one feels in the mouth when chewing the food is the holy essence and the holy spark. . . ."

R. Wolf of Zbarazh would not permit his driver to beat the horses. R. Moses Leib of Sasov, when he noticed that some cattle breeders had left their animals standing in the marketplace unattended, took a bucket of water and gave it to the calves to drink. "God commanded us," he admonished the owners, "to be merciful to His creatures."

"From the cat, we can learn modesty," a hasidic rabbi said. "From the ant, honesty; from the tiger, courage; from the lion, bravery; and from the eagle, diligence."

L. I. Newman and S. Spitzer, eds., *Hasidic Anthology*, pp. 12–14.

J.B.A.

AN-SKI, S. (1862–1920), Russian and Yiddish publicist–Born in Chashnik, White Russia, as Solomon Zanvil Rapaport, he was a writer of Yiddish and hasidic stories and an avid collector of Jewish folklore. He is best known for his play, *The Dybbuk*.

An-ski saw in Hasidism a great factor that contributed to the vitality and the exuberance of the Jewish spirit.

See DYBBUK.

APTA, Meir (1767–28 *Tammuz* 1831)–A disciple of R. Yitzhak of Pinczov and of R. Jacob Yitzhak, the "Seer" of Lublin. He was rabbi of Opatov. After the death of the Seer, many of the Seer's disciples followed R. Meir.

He urged meticulous observance of the doctrines of the Besht and opposed the variations introduced by the school of Przysucha. He was the author of *Or LaShamayim* (1850) on the Pentateuch, as well as novellas and responsa. He was succeeded by his son, R. Pinhas, who died in 1837.

R. Mahler, *HaHasidut VeHaHaskalah*, pp. 293–297.

ARIK, Meir (1856–15 *Tishri* 1926), halakhic authority–Son of R. Aaron Yehudah of Jaslowice, he studied under R. Jacob Wiedenfeld. In 1912, he became rabbi in Buczacz. He was a devoted hasid of Chortkov and the author of a great halakhic work, *Imrei Yosher*, part 1 (Munkacz, 1913) and part 2 (Cracow, 1925).

ARYEH (JUDAH) LEIB of Polonnoye (d. 21 *Tevet* 1769)—Son of R. Yehiel Michael, R. Aryeh Leib was popularly known as the *Mokhiah* of Polonnoye. He was closely associated with the Besht, who urged him to use his remarkable powers to spread Hasidism throughout the Ukraine and Galicia.

The *Mokhiah* spent his whole life in his native town of Polonnoye, where he served as reader and preacher. He was no respecter of persons and spoke out fearlessly on all subjects. His discourses on the Pentateuch and Prophets were printed in *Kol Aryeh* (Korzec, 1798). R. Levi Yitzhak of Berdichev and R. Asher Tzvi of Ostrog wrote letters of approval. R. Jacob Joseph of Polonnoye quotes many of his sayings in his work *Toldot Yaakov Yosef.*

He was critical of the philosophical approach and stressed the importance of faith and prayers. "The greater the *tzaddik*," he maintained, "the more he loves sinners and the more he strives to bring them back and restore them to the path of righteousness."

S. A. Horodezki, in *HaHasidut VeHaHasidim*, vol. 1, pp. 133ff.

ARYEH LEIB of Ozarov (d. 13 *Tevet* 1837)—Son of R. Yehiel Michael Epstein, he was a disciple of R. Jacob Yitzhak, the "Seer" of Lublin, and a colleague of the "Holy Jew" of Przysucha. He married the daughter of R. Reuben Halevi of Dzierzgovice. After the death of the Seer, he became an adherent of R. Abraham Joshua Heschel of Opatov and of R. Meir of Opatov. In 1812, he became rabbi of Ozarov but later moved to Opole. His grandson quotes his discourses in *Birkat Tov* (Bilgoraj, 1938).

He was succeeded by his son, R. Yehiel Hayyim (1820–8 *Tammuz* 1888), the son-in-law of R. Abraham Shlomoh of Wlodowa. The dynasty was maintained by R. Aryeh Yehudah Leib of Ozarov.

Y. Alfasi, *HaHozeh MiLublin*, p. 248.

ARYEH LEIB of Shpola (1725–6 *Tishri* 1811)—Aryeh Leib, popularly known as the *Shpola Zeide* (grandfather from Shpola), was the son of R. Barukh Gerundi, a native of Bohemia who settled near Uman on the estate of Count Potocki. Aryeh Leib was a disciple of R. Pinhas of Korzec.

For a number of years, he lived with his in-laws at Medvedovka. He visited the Besht, who told him that he had been sent to redeem souls. "There are many outcasts whom you alone can redeem."

The Besht attributed to him the lofty soul of R. Judah Low ben Bezalel, known as "Der Hohe Rabbi Low" or the *Maharal*. He instructed his new disciple to go into exile, and at the age of thirty, R. Aryeh Leib obeyed. He wandered for seven years from town to town, helping people in distress and converting many to the hasidic way of life. He became known as a miracle worker.

At first he was a beadle, then a teacher and slaughterer in Zlatopolye, where he lived for eight years. He then moved to Shpola.

When he became rebbe, he aroused the antagonism of R. Barukh of Medziborz and R. Nahman of Bratzlav. R. Aryeh Leib felt that R. Nahman's way of life was dangerous, because he was deviating from the teachings of the Besht. The friendly "Lion of the *Tzaddikim*," as R. Aryeh Leib was called, continued his antagonism of R. Nahman. Not even the intervention of R. Levi Yitzhak of Berdichev could halt the conflict.

R. Aryeh Leib reproached the rabbis who had calculated the year of the advent of the Messiah. He agreed, however, that 1840 seemed to be a propitious time according to the *Zohar*. His deeds are recorded in *Tiferet Maharal*, by Yudel Rosenberg (1812).

His three sons—R. Abraham, R. Pesah, and R. Jacob—did not become rebbes but were buried next their father.

I. Halpern, *Tarbiz* (1958–1959), pp. 90–98.

ARYEH LEIB of Szydlowiec (d. 1826)—He was one of the disciples of R. Elimelekh of Lejask and R. Jacob Yitzhak, the "Seer" of Lublin, as well as a close associate of R. Jacob Yitzhak, the "Holy Jew" of Przysucha. After the death of the Holy Jew in 1814, he became rebbe in Szydlowiec, and even R. Menahem Mendel Morgenstern of Kotzk gave him his allegiance for a time.

ARYEH (YEHUDAH) LEIB SARAH'S (17 *Tammuz* 1730–4 *Adar* II 1791)—Born in Rovno, he was the son of a Hebrew teacher named Joseph. He is known as "Leib Sarah's," after his mother. Hasidic legend has it that his mother, Sarah, fell victim to the advances of the son of the local squire. She was, at that time, a young unmarried girl, and in order to avoid his further advances, she married, of her own free will, an elderly widower who was known for his extreme piety.

At the age of twelve, R. Leib is said to have visited the Besht. He was a disciple of R. Dov Baer, the Maggid of Mezhirech. "I did not go to the Maggid of Mezhirech to study Torah," he declared, "but to watch him tie his bootlaces."

He founded no dynasty of *tzaddikim* and held no court, but was an itinerant *tzaddik*, wandering from place to place, helping the poor, the pious, and the needy. He frequently visited fairs and collected money for the redemption of prisoners.

R. Leib's name became associated with that of the Austrian Emperor Joseph II, who planned secular education for the Jews, many detecting ultimate assimilation by way of this measure. Expulsion of Jewish mendicants, compulsory attendance by Jews at German schools, a tax on kosher meat, and obligatory military service were among the measures introduced by the emperor. Hasidic legend has it that R. Leib visited the emperor on a number of occasions, endeavoring to achieve retraction of these insidious enactments.

According to his own instructions, R. Aryeh Leib was buried in Yaltushkov, Podolia, with only a simple stone above his grave bearing his name. It was eventually encircled by an enclosure with a thatched covering. Every effort to erect a more handsome structure over the grave has brought tragic results to the builder. His deeds are recorded in *Gevurat Ari* (1911).

Y. Raphael, *Sefer HaHasidut*, pp. 146–150.

A.T.

ASCETICISM–The early hasidic masters claim that the Besht taught a new way in the service of God–one in which the asceticism prominent in the Lurianic Kabbalah was abandoned in favor of *avodah begashmiut*, (worship through corporeality). The basic argument says that the ascetic way is perilous in that it can easily lead to spiritual pride if successfully pursued, and, if unsuccessful–as it is virtually bound to be among these "inferior generations"–can result in total despair of ever leading a disciplined religious life. Moreover, the duty of the hasid is to release the holy sparks inherent in food and drink and all material things so that the ascetic flees the spiritual battlefield in which, "nowadays," the real struggle is to take place.

A typical hasidic observation in this connection is that by R. Barukh of Medziborz (1757–1810), the grandson of the Besht, that the latter introduced a new way, without mortification of the flesh, in which the three essentials are love of God, love of Israel, and love of the Torah. The two wives–one beloved, the other hated (Deuteronomy 21: 15–17)–are two different ways of worship. The beloved wife represents the ascetic way, which the common people love and admire for its heroic qualities. The hated wife represents engagement in worldly things in order to elevate the holy sparks.

The common people dislike this *tzaddik* who follows this way because he seems to be no better than they are. Yet, in reality, it is through this way that the *tzaddik* acquires a "double portion" of spiritual grace. This idea is repeated in many a hasidic text and was one of the reasons why the *mitnaggedim* ridiculed the new movement, which, for them, simply panders to worldly appetites and ambitions. Undeterred, the hasidim introduced such institutions as the *tish*–the sacred meal blessed by the participation of the *tzaddik*. The hasidim thought of their way as a more rigorous form of self-discipline. As it was frequently put, it is more difficult to eat and drink for the sake of Heaven than not to eat or drink at all.

Yet there is not total rejection of asceticism in hasidic doctrine. The moralistic ideal of sanctification of the licit, for instance, to abstain from food for which one has a longing, was generally followed so that it can fairly be said that although the hasidim were not normally ascetics, they did have a puritanical attitude toward worldly pleasures, especially in sexual matters. Nor is it true that none of the hasidic masters were ascetics. R. Elimelekh of Lejask, R. Nahman of Bratzlav, and others lived a life of severe self-torment. As late as the twentieth century, R. Aaron of Belz could say that one who serves God through eating serves Him only when eating, but one who serves God by fasting serves Him all the time.

Shimon Menahem Mendel of Garvatshov, *Sefer Baal Shem Tov*, vol. 2, *Mishpatim*, end, pp. 68–70.

L.J.

ASCH, Sholem (1880–1957), novelist–Born in Kutno, Poland, into an Orthodox family, Asch received a traditional Jewish education. At the age of sixteen, he began to study secular literature and slowly became familiar with the broad spectrum of European culture. He was the first Yiddish novelist to gain international recognition. Always struggling between the fascination of the *shtiebl* of his youth and his repulsion of the *shtetl* culture of Eastern Europe, he came under the influence of Peretz.

In his short stories and in his novels, especially in *Der Tillim Yid* (Salvation) (1934), Asch describes Hasidism at its best.

M. Waxman, *A History of Jewish Literature*, vol. 4, pp. 526–543.

ASHER THE FIRST of Karlin

(1760–20 *Tishri* 1828)–R. Asher, known as the "old Man of Stolin," was the son of R. Aaron the Great of Karlin. He was a disciple of R. Barukh of Medziborz and of R. Israel, the Maggid of Kozienice. For a short time, he served as rabbi in Zelechov and then settled in Stolin, near Pinsk. Thereafter, the Karliner hasidim were known as the Stoliner hasidim.

R. Asher made many public appeals on behalf of the hasidim in the Holy Land: "Strengthen the hands of those engaged in these important works by donating money to the house of the Lord." He supported R. Abraham of Kalisk against R. Shneur Zalman of Liady. He was among the leading hasidim who were imprisoned in 1798. The day of his release, the fifth day of Hanukkah, became a day of rejoicing for his followers. In his rules of conduct (*Hanhagot Yesharot*), which were printed together with the "will" of his father in Czernowitz in 1855, he urges every hasid "to divide the days and years between the study of the Bible, the *Mishnah*, the *Gemara*, and *Aggadah*. . . . All must devote themselves to the study of the *Gemara* and *Posekim* and must learn according to their needs. . . . A little studying done with our whole heart will be of benefit to us alike in sharpening our wits, improving our memory, and increasing our piety."

Other writings attributed to him are to be found in *Bet Aharon* (Brody, 1875). In 1810, he returned to Karlin, where he died and was buried. He was succeeded by his son, R. Aaron. His daughter, Perl, was the wife of R. Aaron of Lachowicze.

W. Z. Rabinowitsch, *Lithuanian Hasidism*, pp. 62–80.

ASHER THE SECOND of Stolin

(1827–15 *Av* 1873)–Son of R. Aaron the Second of Karlin, he married the daughter of R. Nahum Twersky of Makarov, and when she died, he married the daughter of R. Elimelekh Shapira of Grodzisk. He succeeded his father and died only one year after R. Aaron the Second, in the town of Drohobycze, where he was buried. Hence, he became known as the "man of Drohobycze" or the "young rebbe," so as to distinguish him from the "old man of Stolin"–R. Asher the First.

He was greatly influenced by mystical doctrines and laid great stress on the importance of the *mikveh*. He himself would remain immersed in the *mikveh* for hours on end. In his "Rules of Daily Conduct," he stressed the importance of humility.

He was succeeded by his son, R. Israel, who was then four and a half years old and was known as *HaYenukah*. (See entries under PERLOW.)

W. Z. Rabinowitsch, *Lithuanian Hasidism*, pp. 100–101.

ASHKENAZI, Asher Anshil, of Stanislav

(1832–21 *Heshvan* 1897)–Son of R. Joel, the rabbi of Zloczov, he married the daughter of R. Hanokh Heinokh of Olesk, who greatly influenced him. He settled in Stanislav and was known as the rebbe of Olesk. He wrote an introduction to his father's work, *Responsa of Mahari Ashkenazi*, which was printed in Munkacs in 1893. He was succeeded by his son-in-law, R. Yitzhak Vilitzker Ashkenazi.

His sons were R. Moses David, R. Abraham Naftali, R. Tzvi Hirsch, and R. Israel.

ASHKENAZI, Jacob Tzvi

(d. 20 *Tevet* 1889)–Son of R. Asher, grandson of R. Jacob Yitzhak, the "Holy Jew," R. Jacob Tzvi married Sarah Yutta, the daughter of R. Shlomoh Halperin of Pinczov. He was greatly influenced by his uncle R. Nehemiah of Bichov and by R. Yitzhak Baer of Radoszyce.

He was an ascetic and for more than twenty years slept on a wooden bench, saving the luxury of a bed for the Sabbath. He visited the ritual bath twice a day. A volume of his discourses, *Attarah LeRosh Tzaddik*, was printed in Warsaw in 1898.

He had twelve daughters and one son, R. Uri Joshua Asher, who succeeded him.

ASHKENAZI, Meshullam Issachar, of Stanislav/London (4 *Tammuz* 1904–3 *Kislev* 1994)–He was born in Stanislav, Ukraine, where his father, R. Tzvi Hirsch, was rabbi. During the First World War, the family took refuge in Kolomyja, in Satmar, and in Budapest, eventually settling in Vienna, where Meshullam studied under Rabbi Abraham Menahem Steinberg of Brody and Rabbi Benjamin Katz of Braszov. In 1937 he married Esther, a descendant of Rabbi Uri Hakohen Yolles of Sambor. He lived in Vienna until 1939, when he settled in Manchester and established a *minyan*. He moved to London in 1943 and founded a *Bet HaMidrash* in North London.

"Not with fire and brimstone" did he convey his message, but with gentle persuasion. Though a great friend and a blood relation of the late Rabbi Joel Teitelbaum of Satmar, who stayed twice in his home when he visited London, Rabbi Ashkenazi was not heir to his temperament.

He was the doyen of the post-war hasidic rebbes in London, and no hasidic gathering was complete without his presence. Despite physical handicaps he endeavored not to change his way of life.

He is survived by three daughters and two sons: R. Uri, a leading *mohel*, succeeded him, and R. Herschel is a teacher at the Klausenburg Yeshiva in Borough Park, New York.

ASHKENAZI, Tzvi Hirsch, of Stanislav (1870–1942)–Son of R. Asher Anshel, the rabbi of Olesk in Stanislav, he married Hayyah Sarah, the daughter of R. Yitzhak Yehoshua Kliger. At the outbreak of the First World War, he went to live in Vienna but returned to Stanislav, where he, his wife, his two daughters–Reizel and Frieda Malkah–his son R. Asher, and his son's family perished in the Holocaust.

His one surviving son, R. Meshullam Issachar, lived in London.

ASHKENAZI, Uri Joshua Asher (1865–1941)–Son of R. Jacob Tzvi, Uri married Berachah Reizel, the daughter of R. Shmelke Rokeah. He delivered four discourses every Sabbath: on Friday evening, after the morning service, after *Kiddush*, and at *seudah shlishit*. He moved from Porisov to Kaluszyn, then to Kolbiel, and finally to Warsaw.

Five of his eight children died at birth. His sixth son, R. Israel Eliezer, rabbi of Sabin and author of *Migdanot Eliezer* (Piotrokov, 1931), died on 20 *Tevet* 1930.

R. Uri died in the Warsaw ghetto. His wife and their other children were murdered by the Nazis. The only surviving member of the family is R. Shlomoh Ashkenazi, author of *Dorot BeYisrael* (Tel Aviv, 1975).

ASHKENAZI, Yehiel (d. 1783)–He originated from Germany and married Adel, the daughter of the Besht. He visited R. Dov Baer, the Maggid of Mezhirech. His son, R. Moses Hayyim Efraim of Sudzilkov, quotes him in his work *Degel Mahanei Efraim* (Korzec, 1810).

ASHLAG, Barukh Shalom Halevi, of Bene Berak (1905–1991) Eldest son of R. Yehudah Leib Ashlag, he was born in Warsaw. In 1920, he and his father arrived in Jerusalem. There he studied in the *yeshivah Torah Temimah*. At an early age, he knew the complete book of *Tanya* by heart. At the age of seventeen, he was ordained by R. Joseph Hayyim Sonnenfeld. He also studied under R. Elimelekh Rubinstein.

When his father died, he succeeded him. Every night of the year, including the Day of Atonement, he would give a discourse starting one hour after midnight and lasting until daybreak. He had a *yeshivah* and *kollel* in Kfar Saba.

ASHLAG, Yehudah Leib Halevi (1886–10 *Tishri* 1955), kabbalist–A native of Warsaw, he was a disciple of R. Meir Shalom Rabinowicz of Kaluszyn and of his son, R. Joshua Asher of Parysov. He also visited R. Issachar Dov of Belz. In his youth, he wrote a number of esoteric religious poems, which have never been published. He also composed songs on the Psalms. He was so poor that his compositions were written on scraps of paper.

In 1920, he emigrated to the Holy Land and then lived in London for two years–first in the home of R. Joseph Lew and then in the home of Joseph Margulies. During that time, he studied the kabbalist manuscripts in the British Library.

On his return to the Holy Land, he settled in Jerusalem, where he established a *yeshivah, Bet Ulpana LeRabbanim*. He published a rabbinical periodical, *Kuntres Matan Torah*. He became rabbi in Givat Shaul, a suburb of Jerusalem, where he established a small circle of kabbalists.

R. Ashlag felt that Kabbalah was a neglected subject and believed that the survival of Israel depended on the study of the *Zohar*. He finished his twenty-one-volume magnum opus, *HaSullam* (The Ladder), in 1954. His work is a running commentary as well as a translation of the *Zohar*. It received high praise from R. Joseph Hayyim Sonnenfeld, R. Abraham Mordecai Alter of Ger, and Abraham Yitzhak Kook. He was also the author of *Panim Meirot* and *Panim Masbirot*, a commentary on the *Etz Hayyim*. His works have been printed in Israel and in England.

He was buried on *Har HaMenuhot* in Jerusalem.

He was survived by two sons—R. Benjamin, who established a *kollel* in Bene Berak, and R. Barukh Shlomoh, who also lived in Bene Berak and died in 1983.

ATTAR, Hayyim (1696–15 *Tammuz* 1743), kabbalist—A native of Sale, Morocco, he became a celebrated kabbalist. After living for a time in Meknes, he arrived in Leghorn in 1739. His commentary on the Pentateuch, *Or HaHayyim*, was printed in Venice in 1741.

In 1741, he and his two wives (as an oriental he was not bound by the monogamist enactment of Rabbeinu Gershon) settled in Jerusalem, where he established the *Midrash Knesset Yisrael yeshivah*, where a great deal of time was devoted to the study of the *Zohar*.

According to the Besht, the soul of R. Hayyim was that of King David. When R. Hayyim died, the Besht exclaimed, "The western light has been extinguished." The Besht was eager for his brother-in-law, R. Abraham Gershon, to meet R. Hayyim. But by the time the former arrived in the Holy Land, the latter was dead. R. Abraham Gershon reported the disappointing news to the Besht.

R. Hayyim became a figure greatly venerated by the hasidim, and his work on the Pentateuch—*Or HaHayyim*, or *Or HaHayyim HaKadosh*—was highly regarded. R. Hayyim Halberstam of Zanz was convinced that this work was divinely inspired, and the hasidim believed that studying this work was equal to studying the *Zohar*.

R. Hayyim Joseph Azulai maintained that R. Hayyim learned the Torah from the Almighty Himself. When R. Yerahmiel Israel Yitzhak Danziger of Alexander died, soil from the grave of R. Hayyim was placed in his grave. R. Meir Dan Plotzki wrote novellas, printed by R. Margulies in 1925, on the work of R. Hayyim.

This commentary is in no way similar to the general run of Pentateuch commentaries by hasidic authors in Eastern Europe. It is, in some respects, akin to the rabbinical exegetical literature, favored, at that time, by the Jews of Italy. His treatment of authors—as quoted in his work, specifically, his references to R. Abraham Ibn Ezra—and his somewhat curt dismissal of comments by Nachmanides differ from the attitude of the hasidim in Eastern Europe.

He defines his methods as based on the four traditional ideas of *Peshat*, *Derash*, *Remez*, and *Sod*. He adheres to those ideas throughout his work. Yet, *Peshat* and *Derash* are not easily kept apart, since a great deal on what passes as plain exegesis in the literary style—in vogue in one country or in one generation—is apt to appear as somewhat extravagant homiletics in another.

He combines, for homiletical purposes, halakhic and aggadic reasoning, which had been used with consummate skill by an older contemporary, R. Judah Rosanes. He is no mere imitator of Rosanes. He displays considerable originality of thought.

E.J.W.

AUERBACH, Abraham Benjamin (1897–22 *Adar I* 1976)—Born in Jerusalem, Rabbi Abraham Benjamin Auerbach studied at the *Etz Hayim yeshivah* and was an accomplished Torah scholar. His father, R. Isaac Auerbach (1878–1 *Adar* 1951), son-in-law of R. Hayyim Naftali Zilberberg, a noted hasid of Ger in Warsaw, was rabbi of the Ruchama section of Jerusalem and the author of *Otzar Halachah* (two vols., Jerusalem, 1909–46) on the Talmud: *Baba Kamma*, *Baba Metzia*, *Baba Batra*.

Although he was descended from a long line of rabbis that originated in Germany and extended into Poland, he was not heir to a hasidic dynasty, nor did he start his own. He became attracted to Hasidism through his father-in-law, R. Abraham Joseph Gottesman of Ozhiran-Iasi. He wore hasidic garb and practiced certain hasidic customs but did not hold public table gatherings or accept *kvitlech*.

He spent his time in Torah study and had a small following, which came to him for advice. He arrived in the United States in 1921 and lived first in Williamsburg and later in Crown Heights, where he was known as the "Yerushalayimer Rebbe" and was a member of the *Agudat HaAdmorim*.

A.Shu.

AUSCHWITZ (Pol Oswiecin) – The largest Nazi concentration camp, thirty-seven miles (sixty kilometers) from Cracow. In March 1941, Himmler ordered the erection of a second, larger section of the camp. It was called Auschwitz II, or Birkenau. More than one and a half million Jews – men, women, and children – were murdered in the gas chambers there, amounting to almost one quarter of all the Jews killed during World War II.

Among the hasidic rabbis who perished there were R. Solomon Halberstam, R. Ezekiel Fish, R. Shalom Eliezer of Ratzfield, R. Alter Menahem Mendel Hager, R. Barukh Hager, R. Benjamin Morgenstern, R. Joshua Aaron Morgenstern of Lukov, and R. Isaac Weiss of Spinka.

The camp was liberated by Soviet troops on January 27, 1945.

AUSTRALIA – Organized hasidic life in Australia is only four decades old. It was originally limited to a few individuals who clung to the hasidic lifestyle. With the influx of Eastern European immigrants after World War II came a number of Jews of hasidic stock. But most of them became assimilated into Jewish communal life.

In 1948, an organized hasidic group of about eight Russian families settled in the Shepparton area in the state of Victoria. Subsequently, in the early 1950s, this Lubavitch group moved to Melbourne, eventually establishing its own community. Their synagogue in East St. Kilda, a Melbourne suburb, now has several hundred regular members. There are also additional *Habad* houses in the suburbs of Brighton, South Caulfield, Malvern, and Doncaster.

The Lubavitch Yeshiva College for boys and the *Bet Rivkah* Ladies' College cater to boys and girls from kindergarten to high school. In 1966, the Rabbinical College of Australia and New Zealand, also known as the *Yeshivah Gedolah*, was established. The year 1970 saw the establishment of a tertiary institution for girls, known as *Ohel Hannah*. The spiritual leader of Lubavitch is R. I. D. Groner.

Lubavitch organizes various *Mitzvah* Campaigns and gatherings, where, on special occasions, the rebbe's speeches were broadcast live from New York. The Jewish community in Melbourne consists predominantly of post-Second World War Polish and Hungarian immigrants. The *Adat Yisrael* congregation was founded in the late 1940s and is now guided by R. A. Z. Beck. It has a hasidic *Bet HaMidrash*, and there are other small groups – followers of Belz, Ger, and other hasidic sects. There is also a full-time *kollel*.

Though organized hasidic life was confined until recently to Melbourne, a small, active hasidic community exists in Sydney, Australia's largest city. A number of Sydney's Orthodox rabbis belong to Lubavitch. A small Hungarian hasidic community also exists.

M.G.

AUTOGRAPH – Handwriting itself is the raw material upon which scientific graphology is founded. It was R. Nahman of Bratzlav who said, "By means of looking at the handwriting of a *tzaddik*, one is able to fathom the soul of the writer."

Letters were used widely as a means of disseminating ideas between the *tzaddik* and his followers. The letters of R. Shneur Zalman of Liady and R. Elimelekh of Lejask are classics of their genre. Rebbes realized that letters written in their own hand and signed by them were greatly appreciated by their followers. R. Abraham of Kalisk and R. Menahem Mendel of Vitebsk were superb letter writers.

Letters by the rebbes were always hard to come by, and they were kept by the hasidim as relics and venerated almost as charms. R. Wolf Goldberger relates that his grandfather, R. Hershele Lisker, was presented with an autograph by R. Meir of Premyshlan. "R. Hershele would show it to us [his children and grandchildren], and he kept it as a much treasured charm" (*Derekh HaYashar VeHaTov* [Munkacs, 1910], 11b).

R. Mendel Halberstam, in one of his letters to the editor of his father's work *Divrei Shalom* (Jerusalem, 1955), urged that one of the volumes that bears marginal notes in his father's hand should be kept by the printer in his house as a memento of his saintly father.

The greatest collector of Jewish autographs, Abraham Schwadron, states that he had great difficulty in obtaining specimens of the handwriting of persons of prominence in Eastern Europe. He found that the hasidim would not part with them. They were convinced of their therapeutic properties. The letters were kept between the leaves of sacred writings (Talmud and *Zohar*) – not ideal places for their safekeeping.

Forgeries of letters abound. There is not a single authentic autograph known to exist of the Besht. The vast cache of forgeries, known as the Herson *Genizah*, is replete with such specimens. Collections of letters by hasidic personalities have been published, such as *Igrot HaKodesh* (Kopys, 1814), *Igrot Baal HaTanya* (a critical edition of all the genuine letters of the founder of *Habad*, edited by R. D. Z. Hellman [Jerusalem, 1953]), *Alim LeTerufah* (Berdichev, 1896, and New York, 1955), *She'erit Yisrael* (Bene Berak, ca. 1970), *Osef Mikhtavim* (of R. Abraham Mordecai Alter of Ger, 2nd ed. [Augsburg, 1947]), an enlarged edition called *Mikhtvei Torah* (Tel Aviv, 1967), and *Kuntres Kitvei Kodesh* of Slonim (Windelsheim, 1948).

Some of the hasidic dynasties had large collections of autographs. The *Genizah* of Stolin existed until the destruction of Eastern European Jewry. It was fully utilized by Dr. W. Rabinowitsch in his *History of Lithuanian Hasidism*. The rebbe of Lubavitch has a fine collection of hasidic material in New York.

Abraham Schwadron (later Sharon) presented his collection of autographs to the National Library in Jerusalem in 1926. It contained letters by R. Dov Baer, the Maggid of Mezhirech; R. Shneur Zalman of Liady; R. Abraham Joshua Heschel of Opatov; R. Hershele Rymanover; R. Meir of Premyshlan; R. Hayyim Halberstam of Zanz; R. Israel of Ruzhyn; and R. David Twersky of Talanoye and his son, R. Aaron, as well items on the Ger and Munkacz.

A.S.

AVIGDOR BEN JOSEPH HAYYIM

AVIGDOR BEN JOSEPH HAYYIM (eighteenth century–beginning nineteenth century) – R. Avigdor ben Joseph Hayyim was one of the main opponents of Beshtian Hasidism at the end of the eighteenth century.

He was rabbi of Lithuanian Pinsk from 1786, after R. Levi Yitzhak left Pinsk for the rabbinate of Berdichev. R. Avigdor's ideological opposition to Hasidism, in addition to his personal pique at being fired from the rabbinate of Pinsk in 1794 through the intercession of the local hasidim, turned him into a zealous combatant of Hasidism. There is substance to the view that through his influence the book *Tzavaat HaRibash* (The Ethical Will of the Besht) was burned in Vilna at the directives of the Vilna Gaon.

In the spring of 1800, R. Avigdor arrived in St. Petersburg and submitted a petition – in reality a calumny against Hasidism – to Czar Paul I. This derogatory document included, as well, excerpts from *Tzavaat HaRibash* to prove that the hasidic philosophy is harmful. He also argued that Hasidism is a continuation of the Sabbatean and Frankist sects, known as rebels against government authority. The "petition" was considered by Russia's high government officials. The hasidim had already made a strong impact in the courts of the Russian government, and the officials' report favored the hasidim.

However, R. Avigdor did not refrain from his vendetta, as a result of which R. Shneur Zalman of Liady was reimprisoned in November 1800 at St. Petersburg. R. Avigdor submitted nineteen questions to R. Shneur Zalman, in which he argued that Hasidism constitutes a danger to the welfare of the state. He also presented to the government a new calumny including passages from the *Tanya*, in which the gentiles are dealt with disgracefully. R. Shneur Zalman was released from prison in December 1800 and permitted to return home in March 1801.

Moreover, R. Avigdor's request that the Russian authorities support his financial claim against the *kahal* of Pinsk was rejected.

H. M. Heilman, *Bet Rabbi*, pp. 54–68.

M.W.

AVODAH BEGASHMIYUT–The belief that one can serve God through physical acts, such as eating, drinking, manual labor, and sexual relations, is based on the Lurian doctrine of the "shattering of the vessels." A *tzaddik*, by using the proper *kavvanot*, can restore these "sparks" to their original source.

R. Dov Baer, the Maggid of Mezhirech, believed that one's main purpose on earth is to restore the holy sparks.

In Hasidism, *avodah begashmiyut* is intrinsically related to *devekut*, as a hasid is commanded to know God "in all His ways." Such communion can be achieved through all forms of human activity. While eating, the hasid should reflect upon the spiritual forces animating the food. Upon seeing a beautiful woman, one should contemplate the Divine beauty of which she is a reflection. Thus, *avodah begashmiyut* leads to *hitpashtut begashmiyut*–the stripping away of the material world in order to commune with the Divine. This is to R. Jacob Joseph of Polonnoye the true meaning of the phrase "in all your ways, know Him."

In the writings of R. Elimelekh of Lejask, the *avodah begashmiyut* takes on an important function in the work of the *tzaddik*, who labors in the material world to elevate the sparks of his follower's soul. It also reverses the sin of Adam, so by clinging to the holy sparks, one can again become a spiritual being.

R. Schatz-Uffenheimer, *HaHasidut KeMistikah*, pp. 14–18.

S.L.B.

B

BAAL SHEM–*Baal Shem* (Heb., "master of the Divine Name"; lit., "Possessor of the Name"). In hasidic literature, the most common title for Israel ben Eliezer, founder of the movement. *Baal Shem* is a name given to one who possessed the secret knowledge of the tetragrammaton and other Holy Names and who worked miracles by utilizing those names. The term *baalei shem* was already mentioned by Hai Gaon (939–1038) and Judah Halevi (1075–1141), who were critical of the activities of *baalei shem* (*Kuzari* 3:53).

In medieval Ashkenazic hasidic tradition, the title *baal shem* was given to several liturgical poets. The Spanish kabbalists used the term *baalei shem* from the middle of the thirteenth century onward. From the end of the thirteenth century, the term *baal shem* was used for writers of amulets based on Holy Names. From the sixteenth century onward, there were a large number of *baalei shem*, especially in Germany and Poland. Some were prominent rabbis and talmudic scholars.

In the seventeenth and eighteenth centuries there was an increase in the number of *baalei shem* who were not at all talmudic scholars. They attracted a following by the services they performed. Such *baalei shem* were a combination of a practical kabbalist and a popular healer. They cared for the sick, exorcised demons, prayed for rain, and prevented fires. They performed these various acts by means of prayers and amulets and by concocting various remedies from animal, vegetable, and mineral matter.

Y.E.

BABAD, Abraham Moses (27 *Kislev* 1908–11 *Nisan* 1966), leader of the Aguda–Born in Mikulnice, Galicia, the son of R. Joseph Baer Abraham, he studied under his uncle, R. David Menahem Munish Babad. In 1936, he accompanied his uncle to Switzerland for medical attention. He then settled in London, where he married his second cousin, *Hayyah*, the eldest daughter of R. Israel Aryeh Margulies, the rebbe of Premyshlan. In 1937, he was appointed principal of *Or Yisrael yeshivah*, which catered to refugee boys rescued from Nazi-dominated Europe.

In 1943, he became rabbi of the Edgware *Adat Yisrael* and also acted as the official spokesman of Orthodox Jewry in the Polish government in exile in London. In 1946, he was appointed rabbi of Sunderland, and in 1962, he became chairman of the European Executive of the Aguda. He was also a member of the *Mo'etzet Gedolei HaTorah* and chairman of the *Vaad HaRabbanim* of the Aguda.

He was opposed to the Reform and Liberal movements and declared that "a marriage in a Reform temple is tantamount to a marriage in a Catholic church." Throughout his life he remained a devoted follower of Belz. His son, R. Joseph Dov, born in 1949, is the *dayan* of the London New Belz community.

BABAD, David Menahem Munish (1865–1938), halakhic authority–The son of R. Joshua Heshel, rabbi of Strzysov, he was born in Brody. He married Leah, the daughter of R. Joel Moses Segal Landau, the rabbi of Jaworov, where he lived for ten years. After succeeding his father as rabbi of Strzysov, he became rabbi of Tarnopol in 1911. He participated in the Rabbinical Conferences of 1925 and 1928. He was the author of responsa *Havatzelet HaSharon* (1931–1938) on the four parts of the *Shulhan Arukh*. He was a devoted hasid of R. Issachar Dov and his son R. Aaron of Belz.

BAK, Israel (1797–1 *Kislev* 1874), printer–Son of a bookseller, Israel traced his lineage to printers in Prague and Livorno. One of his ancestors died a martyr's death, and the family adopted the surname Bak, which stands for the first letters of the phrase *Ben Kedoshim* (son of martyrs). Israel acquired his printing skills at the hasidic printing press of Slavuta.

After printing twenty-six books in Berdichev (1815–1821), he settled in Safed in 1831. The first book he printed was *Siddur Sefat Emet*, a prayer book for the Safed rabbinate. After two years, he was joined by his wife, his five daughters, and his son Nisan, as well as other families from Berdichev and Odessa. His printing press grew, and he soon had a staff of thirty.

During the peasant revolt against Muhammad Ali in 1834, his press was destroyed. He acquired land on Mount Yarmak, near Safed, and farmed it. After the earthquake of 1837 and the Druze revolt of 1838, he moved to Jerusalem in 1841. He became friendly with Sir Moses Montefiore, who, in 1843, sent him a new printing press. Sir Moses also acted as *sandek* to Bak's grandson Samuel.

Bak enjoyed a monopoly in the printing of Hebrew books. By 1873, one hundred and thirty-nine Hebrew books had been printed by him. The first Hebrew book printed in Jerusalem in 1841 was *Avodat HaKodesh*, by the kabbalist R. Hayyim Joseph David Azulai. From 1844 to 1846, Bak printed the *Zohar*, with a frontispiece of an engraving of the Western Wall, the Temple Mount, and the Mount of Olives. It became the traditional printer's mark for all of Bak's books printed in Jerusalem.

When competitors published a Hebrew periodical, *HaLevanon*, in March 1863, Bak, five months later, with the help of his son-in-law Israel Dov Frumkin, began to publish a monthly periodical, *Havatzelet*. The last page carried the words "Printed by the Printing Press of Sir Moses Montefiore and his wife, Judith." After six or seven issues, the Turkish authorities closed both journals, and Bak went to Istanbul to appeal the ban. In 1870, *Havatzelet* resumed publication, but five years later, his son Nisan sold the printing press to Samuel ben Jacob Halevi Zuckerman and his brother-in-law, Israel Dov Frumkin, who became editor in chief and continued in that position for forty years.

Bak also inspired Montefiore and other European philanthropists to found agricultural colonies. Throughout his life, he was a hasid of R. Israel of Ruzhyn.

M. Benayahu, "The Printing Press of R. Israel Bak in Safed," pp. 271–295.

BAK, Nisan (1815–10 *Kislev* 1889), printer – Son of Israel and a hasid of R. Israel of Ruzhyn. It was the rebbe who sent him to London to urge Sir Moses Montefiore to persuade the czar to permit fund-raising in Russia for the Holy Land.

In 1845, Sir Moses sent Nisan together with Mordecai Zalman and Yitzhak Rosenthal to Caterham, near Preston, to study the art of weaving. When Sir Moses subsequently opened a weaving workshop in Jerusalem, there was friction between the gentile expert and the local Jewish workmen. In 1858, the venture came to an end.

In 1843, Nisan told R. Israel of Ruzhyn about an available site near the Western Wall. Quickly, the rebbe raised the money that enabled him to acquire this strategic piece of land for the building of a synagogue. The completion of the *Hurvah* synagogue in 1864 inspired Bak to persevere in his efforts to erect a hasidic synagogue. He was backed by R. Abraham Jacob of Sadgora and by the family of Ezekiel Reuben Sassoon. Even the emperor of Austria gave a donation. The beautiful synagogue, with thirty windows facing the Temple Mount, was consecrated in 1870 and was known as *Tiferet Yisrael* or *Bet HaKnesset Nisan Bak*, for Nisan was its first *gabbai*. In 1883, Nisan sold his printing press and became active in the hasidic community. Together with Mordecai Warshavsky, he helped to build the quarter *Kiryah Ne'emanah*, also known as *Ohelei Mosheh VeYehudit* or *Batei Nisan Bak*. In 1884, he founded *Ezrat Niddahim*, a society to combat the activities of the missionaries.

D. Tidhar, *Encyclopedia LeHalutzei HaYishuv* vol. 1, p. 64ff.

BALABAN, Meir (1877–1942), historian – Meir came from a mitnaggedic background. In 1772, his ancestor Alexander was a cosignatory of a *herem* against the hasidim. His grandfather Meir was known for his opposition to Hasidism.

He studied law at Lvov University and subsequently became director of the rabbinical academy *Tachkemoni* in Warsaw and a lecturer at the University of Warsaw, where he taught Jewish history. His numerous publications made him one of the founders of Jewish historiography. He was particularly interested in studying the communal life of Polish Jewry, for which purpose he utilized a wide variety of archival material, both Jewish and non-Jewish.

He retained a lack of sympathy for Hasidism throughout his scholarly life. He saw the movement in negative terms—as an obstacle to secular education and enlightenment. He maintained, furthermore, that hasidic influence in the Jewish school distorted the study of the Bible, Hebrew grammar, and the Talmud. He also argued that Hasidism had led to a deterioration in the position of women in the Jewish community by reserving for the men spiritual and scholarly concerns, leaving to women the pursuit of practical matters alone.

In the two short studies that Balaban devoted specifically to Hasidism—a review of S. Setzer's *R. Israel Baal Shem Tov* (*Bicher-Velt* I, 4–5, pp. 406–407 [Warsaw, 1922]) and the bibliographical article "Hasidut" (*Hatekufah* 18 [1923], pp. 487–504), he took issue with the authenticity of the letters attributed to the Besht and also argued that no reliable evidence existed as to the Besht's activities. Balaban would accept hasidic tales and lore only at the levels of poetic allegory and legend.

I. M. Biderman, *Mayer Balaban.*

L.K.

BARANOVICHI—Polish, Baranowicze, now part of Belorussia, and from 1921 to 1939, part of Poland and the home of the hasidic dynasties of Koidanov and Slonim. After the Russian revolution, R. Nehemiah Perlow settled there. On the eve of World War II, 12,000 Jews were living there. Very few Jews survived the Holocaust.

Baranowicze: Sefer Zikharon.

BAR-ILAN UNIVERSITY—The Orthodox university in Ramat Gan houses the Margalioth Collection, consisting of many books and seven hundred manuscripts. Many of the manuscripts deal with mysticism and the writings of R. Hayyim Vital and R. Samson Ostropoler. Bar-Ilan has endowed a chair in hasidic studies, and Dr. Abraham Rubinstein, who was the editor of the hasidic section of the *Encyclopaedia Judaica*, was its first incumbent.

BARRENNESS AND CHILDREN—To be barren is to be dead. To have no one to recite the *Kaddish* after one is to lack even the assurance of ultimately being released from eternal torment after death. Who can help the barren? Did not Sarah conceive by miraculous Divine intervention, and did not the Shunamite woman conceive when Elisha promised her an offspring? For the hasid, there is only one who can help, and that is the rebbe. So hasidim travel to the rebbe to receive his blessing and his counsel. But his blessing alone is not enough. Rebbes compare the blessing to the watering of a plant, but first the seed must bc sown. To obtain the "seed" for planting requires an *etzah* from the rebbe.

All of the *etzot* that the rebbe prescribes in order to overcome barrenness are of the *segulah* variety. The rebbe does not enter into the whole problem of biological fertility with the hasid, and there is no question of medical prescription. The rebbe may, however, ask the hasid whether he abides by the talmudic prescription to eat fish, for it increases semen, and garlic, for it causes greater stimulation. Questions concerning the regularity of the wife's period or any intimate questions concerning such matters as the timing of the male's ejaculation are usually not raised by the rebbe.

R. Naftali of Ropczyce suggested that for irregular menstruation, the husband keep his wife in mind when he recited the words "They shall not change their appointed times" at the ritual of the renewal of the sanctification of the New Moon. For this same reason, R. Elimelekh of Lejask suggested that the husband study the "order of women" in the *Mishnah*.

Thus, rather than dealing with the biological determinants of sterility or infertility, the rebbe concerns himself with the magical, religious determinants.

Perhaps the chief counsel offered for barrenness was the *mitzvah* of hospitality. The great test of the Besht's father was held up as an example: how Elijah first came to test him to see how he fulfilled the commandment of hospitality.

In order to ensure that the wife would conceive, the rebbe might suggest various measures to bring husband and wife into the proper kind of harmony. At times, the couple's inability to have children was related to the fact that there was a lack of peace, *shalom bayit*, in the household.

Other *segulot* for barrenness were to be careful in adding additional time before and after the Sabbath, Torah study before congress, a woman's going to the *mikveh* after the Sabbath, giving charity, husband's and wife's not cursing one another, reciting Psalms before the rising of the morning star, and praying with exertion.

Z. M. Schachter, *The Yehidut*, pp. 456ff.

Z.S.

BARUKH BEN ABRAHAM of Kosov (1725–13 *Heshvan* 1781)–Very little is known about his antecedents. The family name of Kosov is a derivation from the place name where he officiated for many years as Maggid. He was a renowned preacher. His oratory was based on a profound understanding of human psychology. He was known to seize upon dramatic effects to underscore his teachings.

He was a disciple of R. Menahem Mendel of Vitebsk and was a prolific author. In 1761, he submitted his writings to a number of contemporary rabbis for their approval. He died, however, before publication. His son R. Joseph, who was preacher in Botosani, made another attempt to obtain further approvals in 1795. A third attempt was made by the latter's son, R. Simel. The works were finally published in Czernowitz in 1854: *Yesod HaEmunah* offers comments on Rashi, on the prophets, and on the Talmud and had the approval of R. Menahem Mendel of Premyshlan and many other scholars; a second part, *Amud HaAvodah*, was reprinted in Jerusalem in 1968.

He urges every learned Jew to study Kabbalah. He is fully aware of the pitfalls that this may cause, in view of the results of the Shabbatai Tzvi movement and its misuse of mysticism. He counsels that no one should undertake the study of the *Zohar* before mastering the works of R. Yitzhak Luria and R. Hayyim Vital. The second part of the work is in the form of a dialogue between a propagator of popular Kabbalah and an opponent of mysticism. His work follows the pattern of an earlier work in the same style as *Shomrei Emunim* (Amsterdam, 1736) by R. Joseph Ergas (1685–1730) of Livorno. He quotes extensively from the work *Mishnat Hasidim* (Amsterdam, 1727) by Immanuel Hai Ricchi.

In addition to R. Joseph, he had another son, R. Abraham, and a son-in-law, R. Abraham Katz, who was preacher in Butchan.

Y. Raphael, *Sefer HaHasidut*, p. 141.

A.S.

BARUKH BEN YEHIEL of Medziborz (1753–18 *Kislev* 1811), hasidic rabbi–Barukh was the son of Adel, the daughter of the Besht, and of R. Yehiel Ashkenazi, and he was the younger brother of R. Moses Hayyim Efraim of Sudlykov. His brother was heir to their father's retiring disposition, whereas Barukh inherited his mother's fiery temperament. Conciliation and compromise were not part of his character. For a short time, he studied under R. Dov Baer, the Maggid of Mezhirech, and under R. Pinhas Shapira of Koretz. After marrying the daughter of the wealthy R. Tuvia of Ostrova, he settled in Tulchin in the Ukraine.

When his wife died, he married the daughter of his relative, R. Aaron of Titov, and moved to Medziborz, the former home of his grandfather. There he built a spacious residence and had a coach and horses in his stable. He lived in a luxurious and regal fashion. He was the first rebbe to stress the concept of *malkhut* (royalty). Throughout his life he remained faithful to the teachings of the Besht, and any deviation aroused his bitter antagonism. The publication of the *Tanya* and the views expressed by R. Shneur Zalman of Liady angered him a great deal.

He had a low opinion of his contemporaries. When R. Shneur Zalman visited Podolia in 1808 to raise funds for the Jews who had been evicted from their homes, R. Barukh felt that the visiting fund-raiser was trespassing on his territory. R. Shneur Zalman tried to appease the contentious rabbi: "What cause is there for any misunderstanding between us? Have I not suffered martyrdom and twice been dragged in chains to St. Petersburg, so that the name of your grandfather might be vindicated? Might I not have said, 'There is his grandson, R. Barukh, in Medziborz. Send for him that he may come and answer for his grandfather!' "

R. Barukh did not suffer fools gladly. He was always aware of his great background. "My soul," he once said, "knows its way to the Torah, and all its gates are open to me." He often suffered fits of melancholy and depression, and the hasidim employed the Yiddish jester Hershel Ostropoler to cheer up the rabbi. He dearly loved *Shir HaShirim* (the Song of Songs), which expresses the Almighty's love for His people in the mystical allegory of the Divine and His people.

He had no sons and was survived by three daughters. His sons-in-law were R. Yaakov Pinhas Orbach, R. Yitzhak of Kalish, and R. Dov Baer of Tulchin. His discourses are to be found in *Butzino Dinhora*, first printed in Lvov in 1879. An edition printed in Bilgoraj in 1927 has the *haskamah* of R. Abraham Yaakov Friedman of Sadgora. It has since been reprinted seven times. Other discourses are to be found in *Imrot Tehorot* (Lvov, 1891).

BASHEVIS SINGER, Isaac (1904–1991), Yiddish writer–Born in Leoncin, Poland. His father was rabbi in Krochmalna Street, Warsaw. He came from a hasidic background and early in life began to probe into hasidic and kabbalistic lore. He studied for a time at the *Tachkemoni* rabbinical seminary in Warsaw and was proofreader and translator of the *Literarische Bletter* in Warsaw. In 1935, he emigrated to New York, where he worked as a journalist at the Yiddish daily *Forward*. In 1978, he was awarded the Nobel prize for literature for Yiddish language, novels, and short stories.

Buber writes of Hasidism as an assimilated Jew; Singer's Hasidism is rooted in the *shtetl*. He is a gnostic writer. In literature as in our dreams, death does not exist. In Singer's own words, "While I hope and pray for the Redemption and the Resurrection, I dare say that, for me, these people [the Jews of Eastern Europe, especially the Yiddish-speaking Jews who perished in Poland] are all living right now."

The societies Singer depicted range from the Warsaw bohemia, to the New York literary circles, to the Polish hasidim in Bilgoraj and Warsaw. Although his is philosophical fiction, his narrative technique contains very little commentary or interpretation but is highly dramatic.

To him the *Haskalah* lacked warmth and the exultation to really lift up the spirit. It could promise nothing but worldly gains. Willingly or unwillingly, he maintained that Judaism's finest writers and painters had to return to the life of the ghetto that *Haskalah* despised, to its pious ancestors, and to the joys that only Hasidism in its early stages could bring to the Jews. When the *Haskalah* came to Eastern Europe, fervor of Hasidism was a powerful antidote against its cold rationalism. The hasidim maintained that one touch of joy in the service of God was worth more than all secular accomplishments or even the diligent study of Jewish Law carried out with fervor. A spiritual leader could only be one who was able to establish soul-to-soul rapport with his followers. And since the needs of a soul differed from individual to individual, each hasid had to find a *tzaddik* or rebbe whose guidance he would feel able to follow, because he would sense that this man's soul responded to the most profound yearnings of his soul.

Among his publications were *The Family Moskat* (1950), *Satan in Goray* (1955), *Gimpel the Fool and other Stories* (1957), *The Magician of Lublin* (1959), *The Spinoza of Market Street* (1961), *The Slave* (1962), *In My Father's Court* (1966), *The Manor* (1967), *The Séance* (1968), and *The Hasidim*, text by Bashevis Singer, illustrated by Ira Moskovitz (1973).

M. Allentuck, ed., *The Achievements of Isaac Bashevis Singer*.

F.G.

BAT YAM–City on the seashore south of Tel Aviv and home of the hasidic *Kiryat Bobov*. The foundation stone was laid on 20 *Kislev* 1958, and today there are many families living in the *kiryah*'s modern apartments. The magnificent *yeshivah Kedushat Zion* and the *Bet HaMidrash Bet Yehoshua*, the gift of the rebbe's brother-in-law, Osias Freshwater of London, were founded in 1963.

The *yeshivah* has excellent accommodation, and efficient medical services are provided for the students. The *Talmud Torah Kol Aryeh* is named after R. Aryeh Leib Rubin, the martyred father of the wife of the rebbe of Bobov. Forty-eight elderly people live in a home *segulah*, which was opened in 1963. The development of the *kiryah* has been hindered by technical and financial problems.

BEARD–The prohibition in the Torah (Leviticus 19:27 and 21:5) against shaving off one's beard and sidelocks was variously interpreted in premodern times. The *halakhah* prohibits the shaving of the beard and the sidelocks by a razor, scissors, electric shaver, or chemical means (depilatory powder).

The kabbalists, however, ascribed a high degree of sanctity to the beard and sidelocks on the grounds that a man's beard reflected and symbolized the outflow of Divine energy (*Zeir Anpin*) of the Supreme Being.

In the *Zohar* (Numbers, p. 61), we read of the mysterious roots of man's hair. Each hair has its own "fountain, deriving from the hidden brain." R. Yitzhak Luria kept his hands from his beard, lest they should cause some of the hair to fall out. R. Moses Cordovero speaks of the "mystery of the beard" (*sod diknah*).

The hasidim stressed the supreme importance of wearing beard and *peyot*. In 1845, when Nicholas I attempted to force the Jews to cut their beards and wear Western European garments, the hasidim, led by R. Yitzhak Meir Alter of Ger, defied the decree, preferring to pay fines or even go to jail. The rabbis of Kotzk and Ruzhyn, however, did not agree that this was part of *Kiddush HaShem*.

Some hasidim would put into holy books the hair that fell out of their beard. Others would not comb their beard, so as not to pluck out some hairs. R. Tzvi Ezekiel Michelson stated that "the beard was an adornment for the pious Jew." In the course of time, very long sidelocks and untrimmed beards became characteristic of pious hasidim, especially in Eastern Europe. The rabbi of Lubavitch forbade shaving on the grounds of transvestism.

A. Wertheim, *Halakhot VeHalikhot BeHasidut*, pp. 1934–200.

J.B.A.

BELGIUM–Today 40,000 Jews live in Belgium. Of the 17,000 Jews living in Antwerp, more than 3,000 are hasidim.

From the beginning of the century, the harbor city of Antwerp served as a transit center for the many thousands of Jews who were en route to the United States and other countries. On the eve of the Second World War, some 50,000 of the 100,000 Jews who were living in Belgium lived in Antwerp, where there were then thirty-four synagogues and houses of prayer.

A number of charitable and philanthropic agencies were founded to aid refugees. Many who settled in Antwerp began to play a leading role as craftsmen and merchants in the growing diamond industry. At first the hasidim worshiped in the local synagogues, but soon separate *shtieblech* were founded for the hasidim of Belz, Grodzisk, Chortkov, Vishnitz, Ger, Alexander, and Zanz. The hasidim settled in the poorer areas of Kievit, Leeuwerik, and Somerstreet.

Outstanding among the prewar rabbis was the spiritual leader of the *Mahzikei HaDat* community, R. Mordecai Rothenberg (1872–1943), a disciple of the rabbi of Bobov. Another congregation, *Shomrei HaDat*, was headed by R. Samuel Brodt (1886–1963), a well-known preacher. For a time, a *yeshivah* in Heide (20 km from Antwerp) was guided by R. S. Shapira. R. Joseph Fucksman was the headmaster of the *Yesodei HaTorah* boys' school. *Tachkemoni* was another Jewish boys' school.

Most of the hasidim shared the fate of their fellow Jews and perished during the Nazi occupation. They were deported to Auschwitz and to labor camps in northern France. Only 3,000 Jews went into hiding. Following the liberation of Antwerp on September 4, 1944, and after the end of World War II, a fresh wave of immigrants from Poland, Hungary, and Romania settled in Antwerp, which is now regarded as the "Jerusalem of Europe." More than 3,000 Jews are hasidim. There are now many *shtieblech*, the largest group being that of Belz, who, in 1947, established the first *Talmud Torah* in Antwerp. In spite of a recent split, the hasidim of Belz still represent the major segment of Antwerp hasidic life, with a *heder* for boys and *Benot Yerushalayim* for girls.

Other hasidim are followers of Ger, Vishnitz, Alexander, Bobov, Chortkov, and Lubavitch and maintain their own *shtieblech*. In 1957 Satmar established a *Talmud Torah* and a *Bet Rochel* school for girls, *Torah Veyirah* school, as well as a summer camp. There are also a *Bet Yaakov* primary and secondary school, a Jewish Teachers' Seminary for girls, a *yeshivah Etz Hayyim*, and a *kollel*. An *Agudat Israel* youth center is under the auspices of the *Mahzikei Hadat*.

The hasidic leader of Antwerp was R. Yitzhak (Itzikel) Gewircman (d. 1976), who was visited by many hasidim from other European countries. He was known as a miracle worker. He was succeeded by his son-in-law, R. Jankale, a native of Jaslice, Poland (a descendant of the rebbes Teitelbaum), who had spent the war years in Siberia. After the war, he lived for a short time in Poland, France, and the United States, and he is now the most charismatic rebbe in Europe. His son, R. Aryeh Leib, is a great help to him.

The majority of Antwerp Jews used to work in the diamond industry as cleavers, brokers, or traders, but current technical changes in the industry and poor economic conditions have forced many to change to other jobs or trades. Many are engaged in religious occupations, such as slaughterers, teachers, and *kashrut* supervisors, as well as retailers of religious requisites.

The number of hasidim is growing, not only due to the high birth rate but also to the influx of hasidim from other parts of the world. One of the attractions for the newcomers is the favorable housing situation, with property being cheaper than in the rest of western Europe. The hasidim live mostly in the inner city, whereas the less religious Jews are moving to the suburbs.

The rabbinate under R. H. Kreiswirth is helped by Dayan E. Sternbuch, the son-in-law of R. Hager of Seret-Vishnitz, and by Dayan Tuviah Weiss. The majority of the hasidim work in the diamond industry as cleavers and brokers. They have a strong spiritual solidarity, and they are always able to find support for the less fortunate among them. In general, the community enjoys a certain degree of affluence. The wearing of *peyot* and *streimlech* are commonplace.

J. Gutwirth, "Antwerp Jewry Today," pp. 14–137.

J.G.

BELZ, a town in Galicia, near Lvov—It was the home of the Belz dynasty, which was founded by R. Shalom Rokeah. His successors were R. Joshua, R. Issachar Dov, and R. Aaron. The rebbes of Belz were actively engaged in politics, and they established the *Mahzikei Hadat*, set up to counteract the doctrines of Enlightenment. They opposed political Zionism and did not associate with the Aguda.

BELZEC—A Polish town near Lvov, which was the site of a Nazi concentration and extermination camp. From March 17 to mid-April 1942, a total of about 80,000 Jews (of which many were hasidim) were murdered there: 30,000 from the Lublin ghetto, 15,000 from Lvov, and the rest from other ghettos in the Lublin district and eastern Galicia. The camp functioned until the end of 1942.

BENDERY—City in Bessarabia, the home of the hasidic dynasty of R. Aryeh Leib Wertheim of Savran.

BENE BERAK, a town five miles northeast of Tel Aviv—The greatest concentration of hasidim in Israel is to be found in Bene Berak, a Torah-state in miniature. In addition to *Kiryat Vishnitz* and *Shikkun Yoel*, it houses many hasidic rebbes and their *shtieblech*. This is one of the few towns in Israel where all roads are closed to traffic on the Sabbath and Holy Days.

Apart from the *yeshivah* of Ponovetz, where many hasidic students study, there are many other *yeshivot* and *kollelim*, schools of the *Hinukh Atzmai* and a *Bet Yaakov* seminary, and over two hundred places of worship.

The town was founded in 1924 by thirteen Orthodox Polish families, led by R. Yitzhak Gerstenkorn (1891–1976). He was encouraged by R. Menahem Mendel Guterman of Radzymin and by R. Abraham Mordecai Alter of Ger. At the invitation of Gerstenkorn, R. Joseph Tzvi Kalish (1885–1957) became the spiritual leader. Gerstenkorn was succeeded as mayor by Reuben Aaronowitz (1903–1975), a hasid of Ger, and by Simon Siroka of the Aguda. The rabbi of Bene Berak was R. Jacob Landau, a hasid of Lubavitch.

Bene Berak is the home of the rebbes of Alexander and of the rebbes of Biala: R. David Mattityahu has a *yeshivah*, *Or Kedoshim*, and a *Bet HaMidrash*, *Nahlat Yehoshua*, and his brother, R. Jacob Yitzhak, also has a *Bet HaMidrash*. It was also the home of the dynasty of Alexander (R. Abraham Menahem Danziger), Beregszasz (R. Abraham Hayyim Roth), Bohush (R. Yitzhak Friedman), Chernobyl (R. Nahum Twersky), Eger (R. Abraham Eger), Kalev (R. Menahem Mendel Taub), Kasan (R. Tzvi Elimelekh Panet), Komarno (R. Menahem Monish Safrin), Machanovka (R. Joshua

Rokeah), Nadvorna (R. Jacob Issachar Baer Rosenbaum), Narol (R. Hayyim Meir Shapira), Ottynia (R. Moses Hayyim Hager), Radzyn (R. Abraham Issachar Engelhardt), Shatz (R. Jacob Moskovitz), Slonim (R. Abraham Weinberg), Spinka (R. Israel Hayyim Weiss and R. Moses Kahana), Zutzke (R. Yitzhak Eizig Rosenbaum). It was also the home of the Trisker rebbe, R. Aryeh Leib Twersky and, until recently, that of R. Simon Nathan Nata Biderman of Lelov. It has many *shtieblech*, *yeshivot*, and *kollelim*. R. Jacob Aryeh Alter, the son of R. Simhah Bunem of Ger, lives there.

M. H. Rabinowicz, *Hasidism and the State of Israel*, pp. 199–208.

BENJAMIN of Zalocze (d. 25 *Tishri* 1791)—Son of R. Aaron, who was the preacher of Zalocze for many years. There is no evidence that he ever met the Besht, but he quotes the Besht, R. Dov Baer the Maggid of Mezhirech, R. Jacob Joseph of Polonnoye, R. Yehiel Michael of Zloczov, R. Nahman of Kossov, and many other hasidic leaders.

He was the author of *Ahavat Dodim*, a commentary on the Song of Songs (Lvov, 1793), which received the approval of R. Levi Yitzhak of Berdichev. He also wrote *Amtahat Binyamin* on Ecclesiastes (Minkoce, 1796); *Helkat Binyamin*, a commentary on the Passover *Haggadah* (Lvov, 1794); and *Turei Zahav* (Mohilev, 1816) on the Pentateuch, Lamentations, and the Book of Esther. All his works were published posthumously by his son, R. Asher Zelig. Another son was R. Jacob.

He maintained that a *tzaddik* is like Moses and that those who doubt him are like Korach. One must pray for personal redemption and the ability to overcome wickedness. God shares the sufferings of Israel. We should realize that our sins cause the Creator to grieve, and we should remember that the *Shekhinah*, too, is in exile.

Y. Raphael, *HaHasidut VeEretz Yisrael*, pp. 39–40.

BERDICHEV, a city in Volhynia—Renowned in Hasidism as the hometown of R. Levi Yitzhak.

From 1807 to 1820, Samuel ben Eliezer Baer Segal, popularly known as Samuel *Hamadfis*, printed twenty-eight works on Hasidism, Kabbalah, and *Halakhah*, with the endorsement of either R. Levi Yitzhak himself or one of his children. It was there that Israel Bak printed his first twenty-six books.

Prior to World War II, Berdichev had a Jewish population of 30,000 out of a total population of 66,000. When Berdichev was liberated on January 15, 1944, only fifteen Jews were found in the town.

H. D. Friedberg, *History of Hebrew Typography in Poland*, p. 133.

BERDYCZEWSKI, Micha Joseph (1865–1921), Hebrew writer—Born in Medziborz, Podolia, the son of a rabbi and a descendant of R. Shmelke of Nikolsburg. Micha Joseph was brought up in a hasidic atmosphere. After studying in the Volozhin *yeshivah*, he spent many years at Breslau and Berlin universities and was awarded a Ph.D. in 1897. The vitality and aesthetic beauty of Hasidism appealed to him. Between 1896 and 1900, he collected hasidic legends, which he published in 1900.

He greatly admired the Besht, and his hasidic stories are the best in modern Hebrew literature. In his essay *Divrei Hazon* (Words of Vision), Hasidism is glorified. He regarded the hasidim as revolutionary spirits in their struggle against static Orthodoxy. The qualities of enthusiasm, communal spirit, and holiness especially appealed to him. He admired those hasidic rabbis who sought seclusion from the masses and communed with nature. Only in later life, in his essay *Lekorot HaKabbalah VeHaHasidut*, does he give a more realistic appreciation of the movement.

His collected essays, *Kol Kitvei*, were published in twenty volumes between 1921 and 1925.

BEREZNA DYNASTY—This hasidic dynasty was founded in Volhynia by R. Yehiel Mikhal, known as "R. Mikhele" (Pichenik). He succeeded his father as rebbe in 1809 and made his home in Berezna, not far from Stepan (between Sarny and Rovno). He died in 1848 and was succeeded by his son, R. Yitzhak. When R. Yitzhak died in 1865, the dynasty split into two. One group followed R. Yitzhak's son, R. Joseph, and another group chose R. Yitzhak's son-in-law, R. Hayyim (Taubman). When R. Joseph died in 1870, he was succeeded by his son, R. Abraham Samuel, who died in 1917.

This dynasty left no books or written records. Most of the hasidim were simple people who had unquestioned belief in their leader.

W. Z. Rabinowitsch, *Lithuanian Hasidism*, pp. 207–209.

BERGEN-BELSEN – The concentration camp near Celle, in Lower Saxony, North Germany, was established in April 1943 as an *Aufenthaltslager* (transit camp). It had five satellite camps: a prison camp, a special camp, a neutral camp, a star camp, and a Hungarian camp. About 5,000 "exchange Jews" with foreign passports were deported to this camp between 1943 and 1945. Only 351 were actually exchanged. Among the many hasidic rabbis imprisoned there were the rabbi of Blaszov and R. Joseph Perlow of Novominsk. On April 15, 1945, the camp was liberated by the British army, which found 60,000 famished prisoners.

BERGER, Getzel (1895–1977), London – The main supporter of Satmar institutions in London was born in Toporov, Galicia, into a family of devoted hasidim of Alesk. He studied under R. Judah Greenwald and R. Yekutiel Aryeh Kamelhauer. He lived for a time in Simleni, Romania, where, in 1920, he married Brachah, the daughter of Issachar Berish Laufer.

In 1923, he arrived in London and attended the Dzikover *shtiebl*. At the age of fifty, Getzel became a property tycoon, and at the same time, a devoted follower of Satmar. He supported wholeheartedly the rebbe's institutions in London, New York, and Israel. He was also a supporter of the *Mesivta yeshivah* and *Yesodey HaTorah* schools, London, and was from 1943 to 1947 the president of the Union of Orthodox Hebrew Congregations.

He was survived by two sons, Shalom Tzvi and Menachem Mendel, and two daughters.

BERGER, Israel (d. 21 *Adar* 1911) – Son of R. Yitzhak Shlomoh, he was a disciple of R. Yekutiel Judah Teitelbaum. He occupied rabbinical positions in Bukovina and in Bucharest.

He was the author of *Esser Kedushot* (Warsaw, 1902), *Esser Orot* (Warsaw, 1912), *Esser Atarot* (Piotrokov, 1914), and *Esser Zahkarot* (Piotrokov, 1910), all dealing with the lives of hasidic rebbes and of importance in the study of Hasidism.

BERLIN, Israel (1880–1944), historian – Descended from a hasidic family, he studied in the Lithuanian *yeshivot*. He was a member of the editorial board of the *Russian Jewish Encyclopedia* and contributed many articles on mysticism and Hasidism.

BERNARD, Hayyim David (1782–20 *Shevat* 1858), hasidic physician – Son of R. Issachar Baer of Dzialoszyn, he studied medicine at Erfurt. After qualifying, he joined the medical corps of the Prussian army and later served in the court of Frederick William III. As an army doctor, he accompanied the Prussian army to Poland.

He married the daughter of Samuel Segal Landau of Bratslav. He was, at first, one of the founders of the Polish-speaking Jewish school and associated with the *maskilim*.

It was R. David of Lelov who converted him to Hasidism. He grew a long beard and *peyot* and settled in Piotrokov. He became devoted to R. Jacob Yitzhak, the "Seer" of Lublin, and befriended R. Simhah Bunem of Przysucha. He looked after the Seer during his last illness. His wife, too, became a penitent and was called Helena, "the rebbetsin."

When his wife died in 1848, he married Feiga Viner. He studied Kabbalah and became known as a miracle worker. He was highly regarded by R. Issachar Dov of Radoszyce and by R. Shlomoh of Radomsk. Hasidim would give him petitions, and a sepulcher was erected over his grave in Piotrokov.

His son, R. Jacob Yitzhak, named after the Seer, was a devoted hasid.

A. Bornstein, *HaAdmor HaRofeh*.

BESSARABIA – An area in southeastern Europe, between the rivers Dniester and Prut. In 1812, it was ceded to Russia. In 1918, it was incorporated into Romania, but it reverted to Russia after World War II. Its present name is Moldova.

The hasidic movement took roots in Bessarabia in the lifetime of the Besht. A number of his followers came from Bessarabia. Among them were R. Abba of Dubossary, R. Menahem Mendel, and R. Zalmina of Sazgorod, who was the first hasidic rabbi in Kishinev.

Among the disciples of R. Dov Baer, the Maggid of Mezhirech, who came from Bessarabia, were R. Abraham Joseph of Soroki, the founder of the Luboshov (Weingarten) dynasty, and R. Yitzhak of Kishinev.

The hasidic movement in Bessarabia flourished in five centers as follows.

Kishinev: Many of its rabbis were hasidim. The best-known were R. Hayyim of Czernowitz and R. Aryeh Leib of Lancut (d. 1823), author of *Homat Ariel* (Lvov, 1886) and *Gevurat Ari* (Lublin, 1870).

Rashkov: A hasidic dynasty was established there by R. Shabbetai and his son R. Joseph, who died in 1800. Notable rebbes of the dynasty were R. Shlomoh Zalmina (d. 1852); his son, Shabbetai II; and R. Yehiel Joseph (d. 1896). The last member of the dynasty was R. Shlomoh Zalmina II, who died in 1920.

Bendery: R. Aryeh Leib Wertheim, who settled in Bendery in 1814, established a dynasty that was maintained by his son, R. Shimshon Shlomoh, and his grandson, R. Yitzhak (d. 1911).

Dubossary: It was R. Mordecai Margaliot, the son-in-law of R. Nahum Twersky, who established a hasidic dynasty there.

Soroka: The town was known for its great hasidic scholars, such as R. David Solomon Eibeschutz, author of *Levushei Serad* (Moghilev, 1812) and *Neot Deshe* (Lvov, 1861).

Among the hasidic rebbes who lived for some time in Bessarabia were R. Dov Baer Friedman of Leove, R. Meir of Premyshlan, R. Jacob Joseph Spivak, R. Aaron Twersky, R. Mordecai Israel of Hotin, and R. Jacob Joseph Twersky.

The hasidim controlled the educational system, which consisted of 520 *hadarim* with 10,000 male pupils. The emergence of the *Hibat Zion* movement and the establishment of the Zionist movement weakened this dominance, especially after the Russian revolution. The Holocaust destroyed the last remnant of Hasidism in Bessarabia. Today there are no hasidic rebbes in Bessarabia.

H. Huberman, "Hasidism and Hasidut in Bessarabia."

Y.A.

BET YAAKOV SCHOOLS–Orthodox educational establishments.

In the nineteenth century, religious instruction was unavailable to women. Private teachers were in great demand. Women were often the breadwinners, and a knowledge of the Polish language stood them in good stead in their dealings with peasants and squires.

Already in 1912, at the Kattowice Aguda conference, Aaron Marcus brought this problem to the fore. But it was Sarah Schenierer, a dressmaker turned educationalist, who established, in *Heshvan* 1918, the first *Bet Yaakov* School in Cracow. The school started with twenty-five girls. It received the approval of the rebbes of Bobov and of Belz.

This school in Cracow became the model to which large and small Orthodox communities turned for advice and guidance. By 1927, there were 87 schools with 12,000 pupils; by 1929, the number had increased to 147 schools with 16,149 pupils; and by 1937, there were 250 schools catering to 38,000 pupils.

The curriculum included (1) the Pentateuch–the study of the Torah with explanations by Rashi; (2) the Prophets–a study of the Hebrew text and translation of thirty chapters of Isaiah and Jeremiah; (3) the Psalms–fifty psalms committed to memory; (4) prayers–daily, Sabbath, and holiday–with explanations; (5) Jewish laws and customs governing daily, Sabbath, and holiday conduct, as well as duties governing the relationships between man and God, man and man, in the home, and in the family life of the Jewish woman; (6) Hebrew language and grammar–a reading knowledge of the "sacred tongue," needed for an understanding of the Jewish religious past; (7) Polish language, literature, history, and geography, as prescribed by state educational laws; and (8) such readings on Jewish themes as Luzzatto's *Way of the Pious*, Hirsch's *Gesammelte Schriften*, and Breuer's *Judenproblem*.

To supply the teachers for this mushrooming movement, the *Bet Yaakov* Teachers' Seminary was established in Cracow in 1925. The budget for the upkeep of the network was met by students' fees, aid from the Joint Distribution Committee of America, and subsidies from the *Agudat Yisrael* of Poland, Germany, Holland, England, and the United States.

In 1931, a new *Bet Yaakov* Teachers' Seminary and Boarding School was built in Cracow at a cost of $60,000.

Sarah Schenierer was fortunate in her associates. One of them was Judah Leib Orleans (1900–1943), a hasid of Ger, and Leo Deutschlander. The *Bet Yaakov* movement was supported by rabbinical groups all over the world. "It is our sacred duty nowadays," wrote the rabbi of Ger, "to work for the *Bet Yaakov* movement." In this he was supported by the *Hafetz Hayyim*. The movement also gained the support of Chief Rabbi Dr. J. H. Hertz, Dr. M. Gaster, and the society for the protection of girls and women. It was also aided by Dr. Leo Jung and R. Tobias Horowitz of the United States.

In the Holy Land, the first Orthodox school was established by R. Benzion Yadler. In 1931, the first *Bet Yaakov* school was established in Jerusalem, and three years later, schools were opened in Tiberias and Tel Aviv. By 1975, there were ninety-two *Bet Yaakov* institutions in Israel.

In the United States there are *Bet Yaakov* schools under the auspices of the *Bet Yaakov* national council. There are also *Bet Yaakov* schools in England, Switzerland, Belgium, France, and South America.

M. Eisenstein, *Jewish Schools in Poland, 1919–1939*.

BIALYSTOK – A city in northeastern Poland, which had a prewar Jewish population that represented 75 percent of the total population of 48,000.

Bialystok in many ways was a model community, with many synagogues large and small, a Jewish hospital and a home for the aged, a *Talmud Torah*, and many benevolent organizations. When R. Yom Tov Lipman Heilprin was called to the rabbinate of Bialystok in 1860 and became involved in a quarrel with the hasidim, clear evidence of the existence of a virile hasidic faction in the town was revealed.

The closeness of Kobryn and Slonim to Bialystok made the latter a great center of Lithuanian Hasidism, where hasidic synagogues and *yeshivot* functioned. Instrumental in their development was R. Menahem Nahum Epstein (1846–1918), a disciple of R. Abraham Weinberg of Slonim. R. Meir Shalom Schzedrubitzky officiated as rabbi before he became rebbe. Also active was R. Hillel Moses Meshel Glubstein (1833–1907), who lived there until 1869.

During the years 1939–1941, the Soviets destroyed the Jewish institutions and evacuated many Jews to Siberia. With the coming of the Nazis, the community was liquidated, and only 200 Jews from Bialystok survived.

I. Schmulewitz, *The Bialystoker Memorial Book*.

BICHOVSKY, Hayyim Eliezer Hakohen (d. 1926) – He began his literary career shortly before the outbreak of the First World War, with the publication of the first volume of the *Tzemach Tzedek*'s commentary on the Pentateuch, entitled *Or Ha-Torah*. It involved collating a number of hasidic manuscripts. He also published a prayer book and a festival prayer book, according to the liturgical uses of *Habad*. After the First World War, he published the works of R. Yitzhak of Homel and of R. Hillel of Poryck.

He emigrated to the Holy Land, where he continued his literary activities. He published *Bonei Yerusahalayim* (Jerusalem, 1926) and a collection of letters by the Besht, the Maggid of Mezhirech, and R. Shneur Zalman of Liady. At the time of his death, he was compiling a collection of commentaries on the Torah. He was the author of notes on the *Tanya* (New York, 1975).

Z.T.

BIDERMAN, Alter Abraham Bezalel Nathan Nata, of Sosnowiec (1862–25 *Elul* 1933) – Son of R. Eleazar Menahem Biderman of Lelov, he was born in Jerusalem. In 1894, he left the Holy Land and returned in 1898. He married Rebecca Rachel, the daughter of his relative, R. Benjamin Bernstein of Jerusalem.

At the beginning of World War I, he returned to Poland and lived in Sosnowiec, where he was popularly known as the "rebbe of the Land of Israel." He died in Sosnowiec, but a year and a half after his death, he was reinterred on the Mount of Olives, on 20 *Kislev* 1935.

He was succeeded in Sosnowiec by his son-in-law and nephew, R. Mordecai, the son of R. Yerahmiel Joseph Biderman.

M. Y. Weinstock, *Tiferet Banim Avotam*. *Tiferet Bet David*. p. 262.

BIDERMAN, David, of Lelov (1746–7 *Shevat* 1813) – Son of R. Shlomoh, David was probably born in Biala. He married Hannah, the daughter of R. Jacob. R. David was an ascetic who fasted from Sabbath to Sabbath. He was a diligent student and went over the Talmud many times. According to hasidic legend, he was endowed with the soul of King David. He was a disciple of R. Elimelekh of Lejask and of R.

Jacob Isaac, the "Seer of Lublin." He was known for his compassion. He would say, "Would that I loved the greatest *tzaddik* as much as God loves the greatest sinner. How can anyone call me a *tzaddik* when I love my own son more than another's son?"

He loved children and was concerned with the welfare of animals. At country fairs, he himself would bring water to thirsty horses neglected by their owners. He rarely delivered any discourses, and he was very modest. When asked why so many hasidim followed him, he replied, "All rivers flow into the sea, because the level of the sea is low."

His son Moses married the daughter of the "Holy Jew" of Przysucha, who expressed his high esteem for R. David: "On every word R. David utters, one could make a hundred commentaries."

Among his many disciples were R. Yitzhak of Warka and Dr. Hayyim David Bernard of Piotrokov. His discourses are to be found in the works of many of his followers, in *Migdal David* (Piotrokov, 1930), and in *Likkutei Divrei David* (Jerusalem, 1968). He was survived by three sons: R. Avigdor, R. Moses, and R. Nehemiah. The initial letters of their Hebrew names form the Hebrew word *amen*.

BIDERMAN, David Tzvi Shlomoh (1844–5 *Elul* 1918) – Son of R. Eleazar Menahem, he accompanied his grandfather to the Holy Land in 1851. In 1865 he visited R. Aaron of Karlin. He succeeded his father in 1883. He was one of the founders of the *Talmud Torah Hayyei Olam* and of the *Batei Warshaw* for the *Kollel Warshaw* in Jerusalem.

He was at one time imprisoned for a short while by the Turkish authorities, and it was due to the efforts of the *Sefat Emet* of Ger and R. Abraham of Sochaczev that he was released.

He was buried on the Mount of Olives. His son R. Shimon Nathan Nata succeeded him. His other sons were R. Jacob Joseph and R. Pinhas Uri. His daughters were Rivkah Rachel, who married R. Abraham Adler; Malkah Eksa, who married R. Mordecai David Weinstock; Nehamah Rickel, who married R. Aaron Joshua Eliakh; and Sarah Leah, who married R. Abraham Horowitz.

M. Y. Weinstock, *Tiferet Bet David. Tiferet Banim Avotam*, pp. 255–257.

BIDERMAN, Eleazar Menahem Mendel, of Jerusalem (1827–16 *Adar* II 1883) – Son of R. Moses of Lelov and of Rebecca Rachel, the daughter of the "Holy Jew" of Przysucha. For thirty-two years he lived a life of poverty and deprivation in Jerusalem. Every day, regardless of the weather and of the constant risk of attack by marauding Arabs, he made his way to the Western Wall to spend three hours reciting the Afternoon and Evening prayers. Four times a year he made a pilgrimage to Hebron. It was he who introduced the white kaftan that the Jerusalem hasidim now wear. He was highly esteemed by his contemporaries. R. Hayyim Halberstam of Zanz said, "The Passover *seder* of R. Eleazar is superior to the *sedarim* of all the *tzaddikim*."

He married Matel Feige, the daughter of R. Tzvi, a grandson of R. Jacob Isaac, the "Seer of Lublin." Some of his discourses are to be found in *Likutei Divrei David* (Jerusalem, 1968). His last words were: "May it be Thy will that I may be worthy to behold the Coming of the Messiah."

His son R. David Tzvi Shlomoh succeeded him. His other sons were R. Yerahmiel Joseph, R. Alter Abraham Bezalel, and R. Nathan Nata. His daughters were Deborah Golda and Sheina Elka.

M. Y. Weinstock, *Tiferet Bet David. Tiferet Banim Avotam*, p. 254.

BIDERMAN, Jacob, of Opatov (1806–18 *Tevet* 1858) – Son of R. Nehemiah and of Rebecca, he was the grandson of R. David of Lelov. His teacher, R. Leib of Ozarov, called him "holy of holies." He married Feiga, the daughter of R. Jacob Kopel. He was a disciple of R. Meir of Opatov and R. Leibish of Opole, and of the rabbi of Radoszyce, who ordained him. He became known as a miracle worker.

He firmly believed in the efficacy of the *tzaddik*, because the *tzaddik* is a partner in the work of Creation. He was survived by his sons – R. Meir, R. Shlomoh Tzvi, and R. Alter Joseph Yehiel – and by his daughters – Zirrel and Mattel.

M. Y. Weinstock, *Tiferet Bet David*, pp. 269–270.

BIDERMAN, Jacob Meir (1870–15 *Sivan* 1941) – Son of R. Nathan Solomon, he married Esther, the daughter of R. Yehudah Aryeh Alter, the *Sefat Emet*. He declined to become a rebbe, and his wife kept a tobacco shop.

During the First World War, he settled in Warsaw and participated in the *Mo'etzet Gedolei HaTorah*. He attended rabbinical and Agudist conventions held in interwar Poland. In 1929 he visited the Holy Land, and six years later he was appointed member of the Warsaw rabbinate.

His discourses were published in the periodical *Degel HaTorah*. His grandson, R. Pinhas Menahem Alter, published some of his responsa in Jerusalem. Only one daughter, the wife of R. Abraham Mordecai Alter of Ger, survived the Holocaust.

BIDERMAN, Joseph David, of Lelov (1827–15 *Av* 1897)–Son of R. Solomon Yehiel, he was brought up by his grandfather, R. Moses, and from the age of nine, by his uncle, R. Menahem Nahum Twersky of Makarov. At the age of twelve, he returned to Poland, where he married Leah, the daughter of R. Eleazar of Kozienice. When R. Moses left for the Holy Land in 1851, he succeeded him as rabbi in Lelov.

When his wife Leah died, he married Malkah Nehamah, the daughter of R. Simhah Bunem Posner. His third wife was the daughter of R. Nahum Reisher.

His sons were R. Moses Solomon Yehiel and R. Alter Eleazar Elikum Beriah of Lelov.

M. Y. Weinstock, *Tiferet Bet David*, p. 245.

BIDERMAN, Moses, of Lelov/Jerusalem (1777–13 *Tevet* 1851)–Son of R. David of Lelov, he was born in Lelov in Kielce province. His mother, Hannah, was the daughter of R. Jacob of Negviene. He studied under his father and only very much later came under the influence of his father-in-law, the "Holy Jew" of Przysucha. His father imbued him from his early youth with a great love for the Holy Land. He told his son, "I am not worthy to settle in the Holy Land. You, however, will go there and hasten the coming of the Messiah."

His father died in 1814, and in 1843 R. Moses settled in Przedborz. His disciples were R. Solomon of Radomsk and R. Hillel of Radoszyce. His desire to settle in the Holy Land was ever present in his mind. Personal and financial problems stood in his way. He was bereaved of his son, Shlomoh Yehiel, who died on Yom Kippur 1835 at the age of twenty-two. His wife, Rebecca Rachel, was opposed to the journey. She was reluctant for him to leave his ever-growing following. Though R. Moses was the most unmaterialistic of men, he appealed for funds to finance his journey. During *Elul* 1851, accompanied by two sons–R. Eliezer Menahem Mendel and R. Yitzhak David–and ten disciples (his wife remained in Poland), he embarked in Galati for the Holy Land.

On the eve of *Rosh Hodesh Heshvan*, he arrived in Acre. By the time he arrived in Jerusalem, he was exhausted and in failing health. Since the rebbe no longer had the strength to walk to the Western Wall, he begged his sons to carry him there. Arabs attacked the little group of pilgrims, and they were unable to reach the Wall. He died at the age of seventy-four, seventy-four days after arriving in the Holy Land. He was buried on the Mount of Olives, near the grave of the prophet Zechariah.

The prophetic words of R. Israel of Ruzhyn were fulfilled: "Rabbi Menahem Mendel of Vitebsk and Rabbi Abraham of Kalisk settled in the Holy Land, but they did not establish roots there. Rabbi Moses' traditions will, however, be continued and maintained in the Holy Land."

BIDERMAN, Moses Mordecai, of Lvov/Bene Berak (1904–1987)–Son of R. Shimon, he was born in Jerusalem. Though his father left the Holy Land before the First World War, Moses Mordecai remained there with his grandfather. For two decades he lived in Tel Aviv, before settling in Jerusalem, finally making his home in Bene Berak. A descendant of the "Holy Jew," he followed the Przysucha custom of praying late in the day. The morning service did not finish before evening. On 13 *Heshvan* (the traditional anniversary of the death of Rachel), he visited her grave in Bethlehem and then the graves of the Patriarchs in Hebron. "When one is in trouble," he used to say, "one first goes to the mother and then to the father." He spent most of his day preparing himself for prayer, praying that he should be able to pray.

He was the target of criticism by the followers of Karlin. When R. Yohanan Perlow of Karlin died in New York in 1955, many hasidim persuaded R. Biderman to assume the role of rebbe of the Lvov-Karlin hasidim, though a large section pledged their allegiance to the *Yanukkah* (child), Barukh Meir Jacob Shochet, the only male survivor of Karlin.

BIDERMAN, Shimon Nathan Nata (1870–3 *Tishri* 1930)–Second son of R. David Tzvi, he was born in Safed on *Lag BaOmer* and studied in the *yeshivah Shaar HaShamayim*, together with his uncle, R. Alter. His father called him a "perfect Jew." He visited Poland in 1893, in 1906, and in 1913. He became the friend of R. Israel Perlow, the *Yanukkah*, of R. Yerahmiel Moses of Kozienice, and of the rebbe of Radomsk.

After fifteen years in Poland, he returned to Jerusalem in 1926. He married Hannah Reizah, the daughter of R. Joseph Zeinwert of Cracow, a descendant of R. Joel Sirkes. His son R. Moses Mordecai succeeded him as rebbe. His other sons were R. Pinhas Hayyim and R. Jacob Yitzhak. His daughters were Elisheva, Rifkah Rachel, and Mattel.

M. Y. Weinstock, *Tiferet Bet David*, pp. 139–141.

BIDERMAN, Yitzhak David (1815–3 *Tishri* 1887)–Son of R. Moses, he accompanied his father to the Holy Land in 1851. He was known for his piety, integrity, and humility. After the death of his father, he returned to Poland for a time, but returned to the Holy Land. He died in Jerusalem and was buried on the Mount of Olives.

His daughter Deborah Hannah married R. Abraham Eliezer Mintzberg, the rabbi of Yosefov. His other daughter, Rachel Elka, married R. Benjamin Judah Leib Berenstein.

M. Y. Weinstock, *Tiferet Bet David*, pp. 246–247.

BIRNBAUM, Abraham Baer (1865–1922), cantor–Born into a hasidic family in Pultusk, he accompanied his father, R. Moses Leib, to Kotzk and Ger. He played the violin at hasidic gatherings, wrote numerous settings for synagogue liturgy, and composed folk songs. He was the author of *Hamanut HaHazanut* (vol. 1, 1908; vol. 2, 1912). He also wrote articles for the *HaTzefirah* and *HaOlam*.

BIRNBAUM, Nathan (1864–1937) Son of R. Menahem Mendel, he was of hasidic stock. His maternal grandfather, Zanvil, was the *gabbai* of R. Naftali of Ropcycze. Nathan's first acquaintance with Hasidism occurred in 1907, when he spent some months in Galicia as a candidate for the Austrian parliament. His paean to Galician Jews, *Wie eine strahlende Welt*! (*Die Welt*, vol. 11, no. 23, 1907), reflected their hasidic fervor. Hasidic youth turned to him. Tobias Horowitz, a scion of hasidic dynasties, became a contributor to his publication *Words of Those Who Strive to Ascend* (1917), and it was due to him that Nathan adopted the hasidic liturgy.

Nathan's attitude toward Hasidism can be seen in his admiration of R. Nahman of Bratzlav. "The tales of R. Nahman . . . are only for those who crowd around the storyteller, thirsting for salvation and passionately longing for revelation, with no wish to be entertained or to be lulled into a beautiful dream world–who seek salvation, who yearn to be led into a higher reality."

He stated that never had he read holier polemics against the world of money than in the story called "Master of Prayer." Hasidism to him was never a protest against Phariseeism. It was never a rebellion against discipline in religion. Never was that undeniably hasidic characteristic–the struggle of the heart within the individual toward closeness to God–in opposition to hasidic discipline. On the contrary, Hasidism represents the first practical attempt at asserting the principle of religious discipline for the community (*Gottes Volk* [1918], pp. 33–34).

After World War I, Birnbaum became intensely religious and for a time acted as secretary of the Aguda.

S. Birnbaum, *Men of the Spirit*, pp. 519–549.

S.A.B.

BIRNBAUM, Solomon Asher (1891–1990), Yiddish philologist–Son of Nathan. Taught Yiddish and Hebrew paleography at the London School of Oriental Studies (1936–1956). From the *Shivhei HaBesht* he adapted *Leben und Worte des Baalshem* (1920) and wrote an English version, *The Life and Sayings of the Baal Shem Tov* (1933).

BIRTH CONTROL–On religious grounds, Hasidism is opposed to birth control and to any contraceptive acts or devices that restrict procreation.

The birth rate among the hasidim is higher than among the non-hasidim. The average young family in Israel has three or four children; the number of families with six children decreased from 20.7 percent in 1961 to 18 percent in 1990.

The birth rate among the hasidim is higher than that among the general Jewish population. In Williamsburg (Brooklyn), New York, the median in hasidic families is 6.3 children, as opposed to the average Jewish family, which has 2 children.

D. M. Feldman, *Birth Control in Jewish Law*.

BITTUL HAYESH–Annihilation of selfhood: the hasidic ideal of self-transcendence. In hasidic theory a person's ego interposes a barrier between the real self and God. A saying attributed to R. Uri of Strelisk, for example, interprets the passage "I stood between the Lord and you" (Deuteronomy 5:5) to mean that a person's "I" stands between that person and that person's God. For this reason some of the hasidic teachers would never use the personal pronoun "I."

The practice of the hasidim of R. Hayyim Heikel of Amdur of turning somersaults during their prayers was in obedience to the *bittul hayesh* doctrine–the complete overturning of self. One of the reasons given for the need of the hasidim to journey to the *tzaddik* was that through their association with others in a common enterprise and through their appreciation of their insignificance when they appeared before the holy man, they would attain to *bittul hayesh*. A text frequently quoted in hasidic literature for the doctrine is, "What are we?" (Exodus 16:8), said by Moses and Aaron. Our true greatness consists in our ability to say "What am I?" to ourselves.

The theory behind this doctrine is the hasidic view that God alone is the true Reality, so that the created universe and those who inhabit it do not enjoy ultimate being. Consequently, people's grasping ego, calling as it does our attention to the world of the senses, causes our life to be invaded by illusion, and we fail to see the power of God infusing all. The early hasidic text *Tzavaat HaRibash* (Jerusalem, 1948, p. 2) states:

> In what way is a man better than a worm? For the worm serves God with all its might and mind, and man, too, is a worm, as it is written: "But I am a worm, and no man" (Psalms 22:7). If God had not endowed man with intellect, he could only have worshipped Him as does a worm. Consequently, he has no more worth up on high than does a worm and certainly not more than other men. He should think to himself that he and the worm and all minute creatures are all companions in this world, for all are God's creatures and have no power except that which the Creator, blessed be He, gives them.

This is the hasidic basis for the ideal of humility, but it is not incompatible with a high degree of self-regard and self-fulfillment. Before he can attain to self-annihilation, man must develop the self to be annihilated.

The doctrine of *bittul hayesh* is clearly at variance with Martin Buber's attempt to read his "I and Thou" philosophy into Hasidism. As a mystical movement, Hasidism may begin with the "I" and its enjoyment of the world in a spirit of consecration, but the ultimate aim of the hasid is to peer beneath the veil and see only the divine vitality, which infuses all things. Instead of the encounter between the hasid's "I" and God's "Thou," the hasid seeks to arrive at that stage at which, lost to the divine, the "I" is completely negated.

G. Scholem, *The Messianic Idea in Judaism*, pp. 227–250.

L.J.

BLAU, Amram (1894–1975), Neturei Karta–Born in Jerusalem, Amram was at first a leading member of the Aguda youth movement. In 1935, he broke away and founded the fanatically anti-Zionist group *Hevrat Hayyim*, which later became the *Neturei Karta*. He was jailed several times for leading his sect in often violent demonstrations against the desecration of the Sabbath in the Holy City.

He refused to recognize the state of Israel. In 1965, after the death of his first wife, he defied the *Bet Din* of his own sect in order to marry a forty-five-year old convert from Roman Catholicism and a French divorcée–Ruth. He was, for a time, "exiled" to Bene Berak.

His son, one of his ten children, was the leader of the *Neturei Karta*.

BLAU, Moses (1885–1945), Agudist leader–Brother of R. Amram Blau, Moses was the head of the Aguda office in Israel and was the leader of the *Eda Haredit*. He cooperated with the hasidic rebbes and represented the Aguda at international conferences.

BLESSINGS–"The *tzaddik* decrees, and God fulfils," states the Talmud (*Moed Kattan* 16a). The decree is given with the blessing, and no interview with a rebbe is complete without it. Like the closing prayer, the *Neilah*, on the Day of Atonement, the blessing is the time of the seal. By granting the blessing, the rebbe recharges the energy source within himself. It is obvious, therefore, that the power of the blessing is not absolute: it requires the hasid's collaboration. Just as a handshake finalizes a completed business deal, so the blessing of the rebbe finalizes an interview. The hasid need only say "Amen" to the rebbe's blessing. He need not even hear it fully. God has heard the blessing, and this is what counts.

In most cases, the blessing follows the formulas of liturgical devices for intercession. However, each rebbe uses a different formula. Most of them begin with "*Der Eibishter zoll helfen*," and some rebbes recite the blessing by holding the hasid's hand. Others place their hands on the hasid's head.

Z. M. Schachter, *The Yehidut*, p. 469.

BLOCH, Hayyim (1881-1973), writer–He was a descendant of R. Moses Hayyim Efraim of Sudzilkov. He studied rabbinics under R. Moses Grunwald of Huszt, R. Mordecai Shalom Schwadron of Brzezany, and R. Aryeh Leibish Horowitz of Stanislav. At the outbreak of World War I, he left his native Dolyatin and settled in Vienna. He was drafted into the Austrian-Hungarian army and spent the war years as a chaplain to Jewish prisoners of war.

Most of his literary work was of hasidic and kabbalistic content. He was the author of *Die Gemeinde der Chassidim* (Vienna, 1917), *Der Prager Golem* (Vienna, 1919), *Israel der Gotteskampfer* (Berlin/Vienna, 1920), *Kovetz Mikhtavim Me'Koriyim MeHa-Besht Ve'Talmidov* (Vienna, 1923), *Lebenserinnerungen des Kabbalisten Vital* (Vienna, 1926), and *Priester der Liebe/Die Welt der Chasidim* (Vienna/Leipzig, 1930).

Bloch's objective was to popularize hasidic and kabbalistic folklore. Most of his works have been reprinted many times and translated into different languages.

He left Austria and lived for a time in Amsterdam and in London. He settled in New York in 1939. Of particular hasidic interest is his three-volume edition of *Dovev Sifsei Yeshenim* (Brooklyn, 1959, 1960, 1965), which contained 329 letters written by hasidic rabbis against political Zionism. Some serious doubts have been cast on the authenticity of these epistles.

G. Kressel, *Leksikon HaSifrut HaIvrit BeDorot HaAharonim*, vol. 1, col. 247.

A.S.

BLOOD LIBELS (1700–1914)–The allegation that Jews murdered Christians in order to obtain blood for Passover or other rituals was one aspect of the general degradation of the Jew in the Middle Ages, particularly in Western and Central Europe. In Eastern Europe, a frenzy of blood accusations occurred at the end of the seventeenth century and led not only to the imprisonment and death of innocent Jews, but often to the destruction of synagogues and cemeteries and to the expulsion of entire communities.

The most important of these trials took place at Sandomierz (1698–1710), Posen (1736), and Zaslow (1747). All of these judicial inquiries were conducted in inquisitorial fashion and were accompanied by the most hideous forms of torture. Only the large, and therefore influential, community of Posen was able to secure the release of the prisoners through the Jewish banking house of Wertheimer and by arousing public opinion in Western Europe. The Zaslow trial was followed by a succession of ritual-murder accusations, such as those at Yampol (1756); Stopnica, near Przemysl (1759); and Woislawize (1760).

These indictments led the Jewish communities of Poland to send Jacob Selek to Rome in order to seek the mediation of Pope Benedict XIV. Ultimately, a thorough investigation was carried out by Cardinal Ganganelli (subsequently Clement XIV), whose memorandum demonstrated the falsehood of ritual-murder charges. Despite Ganganelli's efforts, however, cases of blood libel continued into the nineteenth century, by which time they had spread to Russia. One of the most notorious examples was the incident at

Velizh (1823), which led to the closure of all synagogues in the locality.

It was not until 1835 that Czar Nicholas I endorsed the verdict of the Council of State, which exonerated the accused of all blame. Nevertheless, ritual-murder trials continued in Lithuania and Volhynia and provoked the "Russian Mendelssohn," Isaac Baer Levinson to write his *Efes Damim* (Vilna, 1837), in which he refuted this horrible libel. Before the close of Nicholas I's reign, yet another trial took place, this time at Saratov in Central Russia (1852). Four years passed before a judicial commission freed the accused Jews. By 1878, the intensification of anti-Semitism in Russia gave rise to a case of blood libel at Kutais in the Caucasus and subsequently to a new series of pogroms, which began in South Russia (1883). Again accusations of ritual murder were leveled against the Jews by the perpetrators of these massacres, such as at Kishinev (1903).

The following year saw the formation of the notorious Black Hundreds in Russia. Led by prominent government and local officials, this organization comprised, in the main, a large number of the lower-middle classes, which aimed to destroy the emergent liberal middle classes that were identified with the "Jewish class." This union was employed by Peter Stolypin, the minister of the interior, to undermine the fabric of Jewish communal life throughout Russia. In addition to pogroms, these nationalist reactionaries revived the old canard of blood libel.

In March 1911, the dead body of a boy, Andrei Yushchinsky, was discovered in the outskirts of Kiev. Stolypin encouraged the local authorities to accuse a Jew, Mendel Beilis, of the crime of ritual murder. For over two years, liberal-minded Russian intellectuals joined with their counterparts in the West in agitating against this false accusation, and finally Beilis was acquitted (October 1913). Czar Nicholas II distributed honors and promotions to those who had participated in the prosecution, since they had helped "alert Russia to the Jewish menace."

C. Roth, *Ritual Murder Libel and the Jews*.

M. Samuel, *Blood Accusation: The Strange History of the Beiliss Case*.

S.B.L.

BOBRUISK–A town on the river Beresina. It was the home of many hasidic rebbes, such as R. Mordecai Hayyim Ettinger, R. Hillel of Poryck, and R. Shemaryah Noah Schneersohn.

BODEK, Menahem Mendel (1825–17 *Tishri* 1874), author–The son of R. Reuben Shragai, he was born in Lvov and studied under R. Joseph Saul Nathanson. He was acquainted with R. Shalom of Belz and R. Yitzhak Eizig of Zydaczov.

His wife, Rosa, was the breadwinner, thus enabling Bodek to devote himself to study.

He was the author of *Seder HaDorot MiTalmidei HaBesht*, also known as *Seder HaDorot HeHadash*, probably printed in Lvov in 1865, a chronicle of the disciples of the Besht; *Maasei Tzaddikim* (Lvov, 1864); *Peer Mikdoshim* (Lvov, 1865); *Nifalot HaTzaddikim* (Lvov, 1867); and *Kehal Kedoshim* (Lvov, 1865). According to H. D. Friedberg, *Kehal Kedoshim* was written by Frumkin Rodkinson.

He did not complete his commentary on the *Tikkunei Zohar*, but the work was published after his death by his wife, Rosa, and his son, Shragai Feivish, under the title *Zikhron Menahem* in Lvov in 1875. The book, *Sippurei Kedoshim*, published in 1886, was attributed to him.

His close collaborator was Aaron Walden, and many tales in *Kehal Hasidim* were written by Bodek. Israel Berger, Abraham Hayyim Simhah Bunem Michelson, Shmuel Joseph Agnon, Martin Buber, and Micha Josef Berdyczewski are all indebted to Bodek's work.

A critical edition of his hasidic tales was published by Gedaliah Nigal in 1990.

G.N.

BORNSTEIN, Abraham, of Sochaczev (1839–11 *Adar* 1910)–Son of R. Zeev Nahum Bornstein, the rabbi of Biala. His mother was a descendant of R. Moses Isserles. A child prodigy, he became known as the "*Illui* of Lekish" or the "Torah Jew." He married Sarah Zenah, the daughter of R. Menahem Mendel Morgenstern of Kotzk. His father-in-law became his guide and mentor, and he spent seven years with him in Kotzk.

Four years after R. Mendel's death, R. Abraham became rabbi in Parczev (1863–1866). Subsequently, he became rabbi of Krosiewice (1866–1876) and of Nasielsk (1876–1883), but, because he forgot to invoke a blessing on the new czar, he had to leave the town. He then settled in Sochaczev, where he lived for thirty years.

His *yeshivah* was renowned for its high standards. The students had to provide for themselves financially, and no emissaries were sent out for funds. His discourses would last between six and eight hours. He was uncompromising in his insistence on integrity and on obedience to the authority of the *Bet Din*.

In 1884, he issued a proclamation denouncing "heretical works, published in Hebrew or Yiddish, that tend to lead young people astray." He equivocally opposed and roundly condemned the practice of purchasing rabbinical posts. He was one of the 300 signatories, as were the rebbes of Alexander and Ger.

In every situation, he tended to take the traditional point of view. He concurred with R. Joshua of Kutno and R. Hayyim Halberstam of Zanz in forbidding the use of machine-made *matzot*. He decreed that when *etrogim* from the Holy Land were available, *etrogim* from Corfu should not be utilized.

He corresponded with R. Joshua of Kutno, R. Hayyim Eleazar Waks of Kalish, and R. Shneur Zalman of Lublin. When asked a question concerning a woman whose life was in danger when giving birth, he ruled that there was no prohibition against sterilization drugs. He agreed that she was permitted to take medication that would render her sterile (*Even HaEzer* 1:1).

He complimented R. Israel Morgenstern of Pulawy on his tract *Shaali Shelom Yerushalayim*: "I have examined the contents of your work," he wrote, "and have derived much pleasure from it."

He was steadfast in his support of the Holy Land and urged his followers to settle there, provided they were able to earn their living and would not have to depend on charity. In 1898 he sent his son and his son-in-law to purchase land from the Turkish authorities.

Though he was not a *Kohen*, he avoided cemeteries, and he did not even visit, on the day of his father's *yahrzeit*, the cemetery where his father was buried. "It is better to study one page of the Talmud, or the *Zohar*," he would say, "than to visit graves." It was in 1870, only after the death of R. Heinokh Danziger of Alexander, that he became a rebbe.

In *Adar* 1908, he urged the rabbis to arrange *shiurim* every day between *Minhah* and *Maariv* for those who worked all day long. In *Sivan* 1909, he participated in a rabbinical conference in Vilna, which had the aim of establishing a *Knesset Yisrael* organization, the forerunner of the Aguda. His wife died on 24 *Kislev* 1910.

He was the author of responsa *Avnei Nezer*, a seven-part scholarly work on the *Shulhan Arukh* (*Orah Hayyim*, two parts; *Yoreh De'ah*, two parts, *Even HaEzer*, two parts; and *Hoshen Mishpat*, one part). Six parts were published by his son and the seventh part by his grandson in Piotrokov between 1912 and 1934, and they were reprinted in Jerusalem in 1961 and 1968. He was one of the great codifiers and halakhic authorities of Polish Jewry. His work *Eglei Tal*, on work that is forbidden on the Sabbath, was first published in his lifetime in Piotrokov in 1905 and was reprinted in Piotrokov in 1939, in Jerusalem in 1960, and in New York in 1968.

His grandson, R. Aaron Israel Bornstein, published *Neot Hadeshe* on Torah and Festivals in Tel Aviv in 1974.

He was succeeded by his son, R. Shmuel Bornstein. His daughter married her uncle, R. Meir Bornstein.

A. Y. Bromberg, *Migdolei HaHasidut*, vol. 5, *R. Abraham Bornstein MiSochaczev*.

BORNSTEIN, David, of Sochaczev (1 *Elul* 1877–5 *Kislev* 1942) – Son of R. Shmuel of Sochaczev, he was born on *Rosh Hodesh Elul* in Nasielsk. He was a disciple of his grandfather and of R. Joab Joshua Weingarten, who ordained him. His first rabbinic post was in Visgorod in 1907, where he established a *yeshivah*. During World War I, he lived first in Lodz, then in Visgorod; later, in 1918, he became rabbi in Tomaszov. In 1926, he succeeded his father as rebbe and lived in Otwock, Pabianice, and Lodz.

He established a *yeshivah*, *Bet Avraham*, in memory of his grandfather. He took an interest in the life of the community and was active in the Aguda. He participated in the *Knessiyah Gedolah* conferences, held in 1929 and 1937. Together with R. Aryeh Leib Frummer, he made plans to settle in the Holy Land, and he visited it in 1924 and in 1935.

But his plans came to nothing due to the outbreak of the Second World War.

During the Nazi occupation, he moved to Warsaw, where, for a time, he worked in the shoe factory of Abraham Hendel on Novolipka Street. He constantly reminded his followers of the dangers that were threatening them. In *Tammuz* 1942, he convened a conference of rabbis, urging them to take action. He died in the ghetto and was buried near the grave of R. Solomon Zalman Lipshitz, the first chief rabbi of Warsaw.

His wife, sons, daughters, and daughters-in-law were all murdered by the Nazis. Only one son, R. Abraham, survived in the Holy Land. All his manuscripts were destroyed. His commentary on the Passover *Haggadah*, *Hasdei David*, was published posthumously in the Holy Land.

M. Unger, *Admorim SheNisfu BaShoa*, pp. 77–80.

BORNSTEIN, Hanokh Heinokh (14 *Heshvan* 1896–26 *Elul* 1965) – Son of R. Shmuel, he married Freida, the daughter of R. Nathan Nahum Rabinowicz of Krimlov. In 1925, he emigrated to the Holy Land, worked for a time for the *Keren Kayemet*, and was one of the editors of *HaHod*.

When his father died on 24 *Tevet* 1924, his brother R. David became rebbe. It was only when his brother perished in 1943 that he reluctantly became rebbe of Sochaczev and lived in Bayit VeGan, Jerusalem, for twenty-two years.

He was buried on *Har HaMenuhot* in Jerusalem. His younger son, R. Menahem Shlomoh, succeeded him.

BORNSTEIN, Menahem Shlomoh, of Sochaczev (1935–26 *Av* 1969) Son of R. Hanokh Heinokh, he studied in the *yeshivah Knesset Hiskiyahu* in *Kefar Habad* and in the Hebron *yeshivah*. He married the daughter of Daniel Halevi Mubshowitz. When his father died in 1965, he became rebbe in Yad Eliyahu, Tel Aviv.

He was killed in a car accident on his way to visit a sick hasid in Tel Hashomer Hospital. He left five young children. A *kollel* in Bene Berak is named after him.

One son, R. Shmuel, is now rebbe of Sochaczev, and another, R. Abraham, is rebbe in Bene Berak.

BORNSTEIN, Shmuel, of Sochaczev (4 *Heshvan* 1855–24 *Tevet* 1926) – Son of R. Abraham, he married Yuta Leah, the daughter of Lipman Litmanowicz of Radomsk. When his wife died, he married the daughter of R. Nathan Nata Shapira.

He was a member of the *Mo'etzet Gedolei HaTorah* and an active member of the Aguda, and he participated in the Aguda conferences in Vienna in 1929 and in Marienbad in 1937. He fought strenuously against the *shehitah* restrictions made by the Polish government.

He succeeded his father as rebbe in 1910. He held festive meals for his hasidim, not only on the Sabbath and festivals, but also on the eve of the New Year, on the eve of the Day of Atonement, on every *Rosh Hodesh*, on *Purim Katan*, on *Pesah Sheni*, and on *Lag BaOmer*. In 1914, while visiting a spa in Germany, he was detained by the German authorities as a Russian citizen.

On returning to Poland, he lived for five years in Lodz, where he established a *yeshivah*. He then moved to Zgierz near Lodz.

He welcomed the Balfour Declaration in 1917. Like his father, he was concerned about the welfare of the hasidim living in the Holy Land, and he sent his two sons to acquire land there.

On 4 *Kislev* 1923, he wrote a circular urging his fellow Jews to observe the Sabbath, and like his father, he denounced the reading of secular newspapers.

He was the author of a commentary on the Passover *Haggadah* (Piotrokov, 1927) and of an eight-volume work – *Shem MiShmuel* (Piotrokov, 1927–1932) – containing discourses on the Pentateuch and festivals.

Heir to his father's great erudition, he was well versed in the art of homiletics. He died in the spa Otwock, where he was recuperating from a lung ailment. He died at the same age as his father and was buried in Sochaczev. He was succeeded by his son, R. David.

J. U. Zilberberg, *Malkhut Bet David*.

BORNSTEIN, Zeev Nahum, of Biala (1821–19 *Elul* 1885) – Son of R. Aaron of Skutshin, a hasid of R. David of Lelov. His mother, Feiga, the daughter of R. David Katz of Chenchin, was a descendant of R. Mosheh Isserles.

In 1837 he married Dobrish, the daughter of R. Mordecai Tzvi Erlich of Bendin, where he lived for a number of years. He became rabbi in Elkish, and when R. Moses Michael died in 1856, he became rabbi of Biala, where he lived for almost thirty years. Among his disciples was R. Yeheskel Tzvi Michelson, later rabbi of Warsaw.

He was the author of *Agudat Ezov* on the Codes and Tractates, published in Bilgoraj in 1909.

His sons were R. Abraham of Sochaczev and R. Meir.

BOSTON–Capital and principal city of Massachusetts. The founding center of the *Bostoner* hasidic dynasty and the only hasidic movement to originate within, and to be named after, a North American city. The dynasty was established by R. Pinhas David Horowitz (1876–1941) and continued by his son, R. Levi Yitzhak Horowitz, who is the only hasidic rebbe whose native tongue and major mode of communication are English.

His concern for young people resulted in the establishment of a Torah institute in New England. He has translated his hasidic role into uniquely Western terms, most notably through his service as a source for medical liaison and diagnostic referrals and through his role as an adviser and therapist to those who seek personal counsel.

BOTOSHANSKY, Jacob (1895–1964), writer–A native of Bessarabia, he studied in the *yeshivot* of Kishinev and Odessa. He emigrated to Buenos Aires in 1926. He was the author of two plays, *Hershele Ostropoler* and *Reb Baer of Leove* (1928), which have been staged in Argentina and the Soviet Union.

BOYAN DYNASTY–The founder of the Boyan dynasty was R. Yitzhak Friedman (1850–1917), who settled in Boyan, near Chernowitz, in 1883. The town became a hasidic center with a grandiose court, which was destroyed by the Russians in 1914. The entire family then settled in Vienna. The dynasty of Boyan was renowned for its original style of worship and prayer. Hasidic *hazanim* composed *niggunim* that were sung with a choir at the rebbe's *tish*. Hasidim used to endanger their lives crossing the Russian border in order to be with the rebbe.

The Boyan dynasty traditionally inherited the privilege to light the *hadlakah* on *Lag BaOmer* at the grave of R. Shimon bar Yohai at Meron. R. Yitzhak, like his father, was the *nasi* of the *kollel* Volhynia, coordinating all welfare funds for the support of the *yishuv* in Israel.

The sons of R. Yitzhak settled in different localities, R. Menahem Nahum in Czernowitz, R. Mosheh in Cracow, R. Israel in Leipzig, R. Abraham Jacob in Lvov, and R. Mordecai Shlomoh in New York.

M.M.B.

BRANDSTAEDTER, Mordecai David (1844–1928), writer–A native of Tarnov, he lived in Vienna during the years of the First World War. He was the author of short stories, such as *Eliyahu HaNavi*, *Mordecai Kizovitz*, and *Zalman Goi*. He dealt with the struggle between the hasidim and the *mitnaggedim*, ridiculing hasidic rabbis and portraying the movement in a very unfavorable light.

BRANDWEIN, Abraham, of Stretyn (1795–3 *Tevet* 1865)–Elder son of R. Yehudah Tzvi of Stretyn, he was a disciple of R. Uri of Strelisk, R. Dov Berish of Olesk, and R. Israel Friedman of Ruzhyn. He became rebbe in 1844 and among his disciples were R. Uri of Zambor and R. Shlomoh Meir of Sasov.

He was survived by four daughters–Sarah, Esther, Leah, and Bluma. His son-in-law, R. Uri Langer of Rohatyn, succeeded him.

BRANDWEIN, Eliezer, of Stanislav (1869–*Shevat* 1943)–Son of R. Nahum of Bursztyn, he was born in Stretyn and married Beila, the daughter of R. Shmuel Shmelke Rubin of Seret, a descendant of Ropczyce. In 1918, he succeeded his father as rebbe of Bursztyn in Stanislav. He miraculously escaped the pogrom that took place in Stanislav on *Hoshanah Rabba* 1943 but died soon after. His son, R. Moses, was murdered by the Nazis in Stanislav.

M. Unger, *Admorim SheNisfu BaShoa*, pp. 150–151.

BRANDWEIN, Israel, of Brzezany (1875–1943)–Son of R. Pinhas of Stretyn, he succeeded his father as rebbe. He married the daughter of R. Hayyim Tzvi Langer. He, his son R. Yehudah Tzvi and his daughter perished on the Day of Atonement 1943.

His son R. Jacob Mordecai emigrated to the Holy Land in 1912, and his sons were R. Pinhas, R. Hayyim Joseph, R. Yehudah Tzvi, and R. Abraham.

BRANDWEIN, Nahum, of Bursztyn (1847–15 *Elul* 1915) – Son of R. Eliezer of Jesupol, he was born in Stretyn. He married Bluma, the daughter of R. Tzvi Hirsh Hager, and he studied under his father and his uncle, R. Abraham.

In 1865 he succeeded his father as rebbe in Bursztyn, where he lived for forty years. In 1914, a fire burned down the town, and he moved to Stanislav.

He was the author of *Imrei Tov* on the Torah (Lvov, 1891), *Imrei Hayyim* on the 613 Commandments (Lvov, 1893), *Imrei Berakhah* on the *Aggadot* in the tractates of *Berakhot* and *Shabbat* (Lvov, 1898), and *Imrei Ratzon* on the Book of Genesis (Lvov, 1909).

He was succeeded by his only son, R. Eliezer. His daughters were Miriam, Sheindel, Yohebed, and Peshe.

BRANDWEIN, Yehudah Tzvi, of Stretyn (1780–11 *Iyyar* 1830) – Son of R. Samuel Zanvil, he was born in Zawalov, Galicia, where his father served as a rabbi. He was the favored disciple of R. Uri of Strelisk. He married the daughter of R. Eleazar Kahana of Rozdol.

On the suggestion of the "Seer" of Lublin, he gave up his position as slaughterer and established a hasidic dynasty of his own while R. Uri was still alive. After R. Uri's death, many of R. Uri's hasidim followed him.

Like his teacher, he prayed with great ecstasy. He had a reputation as a healer, and he prescribed popular remedies as well as *segulot*. During the last three years of his life, he was afflicted with a terrible disease, and his body was covered with sores.

Three of his sons – R. Abraham, R. Samuel Zanvil, and R. Eliezer – and their descendants were all hasidic rebbes. R. Abraham succeeded his father in Stretyn.

He was the author of *Sheerit Yehudah Derekh Hayyim Tokhahat Musar* (Brooklyn, 1971) and *Degel Mahaneh Yehudah*, a collection of tales and homilies (Jerusalem, 1957).

R. Mahler, *HaHasidut VeHaHaskalah*.

T.P.

BRANDWEIN, Yehudah Tzvi, of Tel Aviv (11 *Adar* 1903–18 *Nisan* 1969) – Son of R. Abraham, he was born in Safed. His mother, Hannah, was the daughter of R. Meshullam Weisblum, a descendant of R. Elimelekh of Lejask and R. Levi Yitzhak of Berdichev.

Yehudah Tzvi studied in the *yeshivah Hatam Sofer* in Safed and also at the *yeshivah Hayyei Olam* in Jerusalem. He was ordained by Rabbis Kook and Sonnenfeld. He married Miriam Hadassah, the daughter of R. Shlomoh Wexler, and on her death, he married Leah, the daughter of R. Meir Joseph Abramovitch, whose sister was the wife of R. Ashlag.

In 1957, he began to work in the religious department of the *Histadrut* and was known as the "rabbi of *Histadrut*." He made notable contributions to Kabbalah and completed the work of his brother-in-law, *Maalot HaSulam* (Tel Aviv, 1960).

His children were R. Mosheh Hayyim, Esther Miriam, Alta Rachel, Zipporah Devorah, Tubah, Menuhah, and Bat Sheva.

BRATZLAV – A town in Podolia on the river Bug. It was the home of R. Nahman of Bratzlav and of his disciple, R. Nathan Sternharz, who set up a printing press in 1819. Among the books printed were *Likkutei MoHaran*, *Likkutei Tefillot*, and *Kitzur Likkutei MoHaran*. On the eve of the Second World War, there were 2,500 Jews living there. The community was destroyed by the Nazis between July and September 1941.

BRATZLAV CONTROVERSY – The controversy concerning the Bratzlav group was one of the most bitter in the history of the hasidic movement, yet its origins and precise causes have not been ascertained. The Bratzlav sources, while openly acknowledging its existence and, moreover, presenting it as a positive and essential constituent of the Bratzlav way, suppress much of the evidence relating to its contents. Other hasidic circles directly involved in the controversy have not produced literary records that might shed light on the affair.

Two distinct stages may be observed in the course of the controversy, and it is not yet clear what degree of continuity there was

BRATZLAV CONTROVERSY

between them. The first stage was the clash between R. Nahman and R. Aryeh Loeb of Shpole (the Shpole *Zeide*), which began shortly after R. Nahman's move from Medvedevka to Zlatopol in 1800 and appears to have subsided with the death of R. Nahman in 1810. The second stage was the campaign against the Bratzlav circle and the man who had become its leader after the death of R. Nahman–R. Nathan Sternharz of Nemirov. The campaign was initiated and organized by R. Mosheh Tzvi of Savran. It began early in 1835 and had died out by the beginning of 1839.

In his biographical work *Hayyei Moharan* (*Life of R. Nahman*), R. Nathan traces the start of the controversy between R. Nahman and the Shpole *Zeide* to an incident that occurred almost immediately after R. Nahman's move to Zlatopol and involved a certain follower of R. Aryeh Loeb in that town, who had been offended by R. Nahman. The incident could, perhaps, be understood as an initial territorial clash, resulting from R. Nahman's sudden move to Zlatopol, a town that lay close to Shpole and must have been regarded as part of the *Zeide*'s domain. R. Nathan stresses that R. Aryeh Loeb was at first most hospitable to R. Nahman. If his account of the beginning of the controversy is to be accepted, it would seem that R. Nahman's tactless interference in local affairs so soon after his arrival in the town must have first provoked the *Zeide*'s hostility. As a result, R. Nahman was persecuted in Zlatopol to such an extent that two years later he fled the town and moved to Bratzlav. Although the opposition to him and his followers did not abate, he gained sufficient local support to establish his headquarters there.

The nature of the allegations against R. Nahman by R. Aryeh Loeb and his supporters is not quite clear. However, there is reason to believe that the Bratzlav circle was accused of Shabbatean-Frankist tendencies. This suggestion is based on a few guarded allusions in the Bratzlav literature, as well as a document (published by M. Litinsky, *Korot Podolia* . . . [Odessa, 1895], pp. 62–63) purported to have been written by R. Nathan, which refers to this allegation quite explicitly. Although the authenticity of the document has been questioned, its contents are considered to be based on historical fact.

The Bratzlav group remained unpopular even after the deaths in 1810 and 1811 of R. Nahman and the Shpole *Zeide*, respectively–before the start of the second campaign against them in the 1830s. The Hebrew term "*mitnaggedim*, opponents," usually denoting the rabbinic campaigners against the hasidic movement as a whole, was applied in Bratzlav to the enemies of the circle–both hasidic and nonhasidic.

The identity of Bratzlav's opponents during those years is unknown, but their accusations can sometimes be reconstructed from the refutations that occur in the Bratzlav sources. According to R. Nathan, for example, as soon as his unique collection of prayers, based on the teachings of R. Nahman, began to circulate within the Bratzlav group and became known outside it, the controversy became more acute. His composition of original prayers was, apparently, proclaimed as blasphemous on the grounds that R. Nathan was devoid of Divine Inspiration, a quality that, it was argued, was a precondition for the legitimate composition of new prayers but had ceased existing in Israel after biblical times. A number of obscure references to subsequent, mostly localized, outbursts of the controversy occur in R. Nathan's letters to his son from 1832 on.

The second distinct phase of the controversy began at the start of 1835, when, according to the official Bratzlav account, a certain member of a dissident faction within Bratzlav, which did not recognize R. Nathan's leadership, offended the followers of R. Moses Tzvi of Savran in the town of Bratzlav. Ironically, through their ignorance of internal Bratzlav affairs, they directed their indignation at R. Nathan and his followers. A bitter campaign was launched against them. R. Moses Tzvi and his hasidim resorted to extreme verbal and, indeed, physical abuse, denunciation to the authorities, economic pressures that robbed many Bratzlav hasidim of their means of livelihood, mutilation of Bratzlav books, and even conspiracies to murder R. Nathan. R. Moses Tzvi circulated a letter in several communities calling on all his supporters to boycott the Bratzlav hasidim and to persecute them by all means available. As a result of one of the denunciations to the regional governor of Bratzlav, R. Nathan was imprisoned and later exiled to his native town of Nemirov, where he remained until–after the death in 1837 of R. Moses Tzvi of Savran–the controversy finally subsided at the start of 1839.

Once again, the nature of the arguments against R. Nathan and his followers is not clear. However, it seems that a certain passage in R. Nahman's *Book of the Alef Bet* was interpreted by the opponents of Bratzlav as calling for the understanding of nature's mysteries by heretical resort to philosophy and science. Such an allegation might well have been inspired by the knowledge of R. Nahman's, and, later, R. Nathan's, close contacts with *maskilim* in Uman, but it is not known whether the same allegation had been laid against R. Nahman at the time of his controversy with the Shpole *Zeide*. Another accusation that, on the other hand, suggests the possibility of continuity of content between the two stages of the controversy was the alleged Sabbatean-Frankist inclination of R. Nathan and his followers. This can be construed from reports to the effect that R. Nathan was seen eating meat on the fast day of the 9th of Av, as well as from the allegation that the Bratzlav group did not uphold the validity of the Oral Law. Some aspects of R. Nahman's teachings, as well as rumors concerning his bizarre behavior on certain occasions, may have given rise to these allegations. But it is clear that, whereas he was concerned with "repairing" the messianic heresy, neither R. Nahman nor any of his followers had any direct links with Sabbateanism.

The fact that the leader of Bratzlav was a controversial figure was incorporated into the ideology of the group by R. Nahman himself, as proof of his unique greatness and as one of the essential qualifications for his role.

M. Piekarz, *Studies in Bratzlav Hasidism* (Hebrew), pp. 68–76, 209–211.

N. Sternharz, *Alim LiTerufah–Mikhtevei Moharnat*.

A.R.A.

BRAYER, Nahum Dov, of Boyan

(b. 1936)–Born in New York, he is the son of R. Menahem Mendel, professor of psychology at the Yeshiva University, New York.

He studied in the *yeshivah* of Ruzhyn in Jerusalem and married the daughter of R. Zusya Heshel (son of R. Mordecai Heshel), the rabbi of Kopyczynice. When his maternal grandfather, R. Mordecai Shlomoh Friedman, died in 1971, his father was reluctant to become rebbe. In December 1984, R. Nahum Dov was persuaded to become the rabbi of Boyan in Israel. He frequently visits New York.

BREAKING OF THE VESSELS

(shevirat kelim)–The concept of *shevirat kelim* is alluded to in the *Zohar* and developed in depth in the Lurianic Kabbalah. The idea is given new meaning by the hasidic masters.

The ten Emanations (*Sefirot*) parallel the *Ten Sayings* with which the universe was created, and these were first brought into existence in the form of undifferentiated points, as *vessels* to contain the Infinite Light. The vessels could not hold the Infinite Light, and they were overwhelmed by it, hence they were shattered.

The broken pieces of these vessels fell to a lower spiritual level, becoming the source of all evil. Sparks of the light that was contained in them also fell, and these sparks became the means by which evil can be rectified. The broken vessels themselves became the source of the evil husks (*klippot*). After the vessels were shattered, the Emanations (*Sefirot*) were again reformed and were known as Personifications (*Partzufim*), each having 613 parts, as counterparts of the 613 parts of the body, as well as the 613 Commandments of the Torah.

The vessels were originally created without the ability to hold the Infinite Light. The breaking of the vessels is alluded to in the Torah in the account of the Kings of Edom, mentioned at the end of Genesis, chapter 36. The death of each of these kings is said to imply the shattering of a particular vessel and its fall to a lower level. They are called "kings" because a king only takes from his subjects and does not give. Similarly, the original vessels could only receive the Light but could not give any of their own. The Besht taught that the enjoyment of sin comes from the sparks of holiness that exist in these broken vessels. He also emphasized that those sparks could inspire repentance and redemption.

R. Elimelekh of Lejask wrote that all the suffering in the world is the result of the breaking of the vessels. Just as the vessels must be shattered before they can be rectified, so the righteous must suffer before they can attain their rectified state.

In the teachings of R. Nahman of Bratzlav, all godlessness comes either from the broken vessels or from the vacated space that resulted from the original Constriction (*Tzimtzum*).

The *Habad* system took the concept even further. The original vessels are seen as words that contain an idea. When a word is shattered, the idea can no longer be contained. Furthermore, before the vessels were broken, they were part of the divine perfection, *Ein Sof*. The breaking of the vessels was then the beginning of the concept of separation and plurality. One's task is then to elevate the shattered vessels through the sparks of holiness contained in them, thus restoring all things to the original Unity.

A.R.K.

BREST-LITOVSK–In Yiddish, *Brisk*. It was a city of learning, famed throughout the Jewish world. Its rabbinate was the most important of all the communities in Poland and on par with those of Cracow, Lvov, and Lublin.

It was at first a fortress of *mitnaggedim*, and disputations between hasidim and their opponents took place there. During the formative period of Hasidism, Brest was in the forefront of the battle against the movement, and a *herem* signed by the rabbi, R. Abraham Katzenellenbogen, was issued against them. Nevertheless, in the course of time, the town contained a sizable and active hasidic community with several *shtieblech* belonging to Kobrin and Karlin. In 1931 the Jewish population numbered 21,000. When it was liberated on July 28, 1944, only ten Jews, who had hidden, had survived.

M.S.

BREUER, Isaac (1883–1946)–Son of R. Salomon, a grandson of R. Samson Raphael Hirsch on his mother's side, he practiced as a lawyer in Frankfurt and then took an active part in the work of the Aguda, in which he was a member of the World Executive and drafted the Aguda constitution. He visited Israel in 1926 and 1933, settling there in 1936. He worked for the *Po'alei Agudat Yisrael* and collaborated with the hasidic rebbes. He was also the director of the *Keren HaYishuv* (Palestine fund) of the Aguda.

"My aim," he said, "is to make our people turn to the Land, and the Land turn to our people, and both to turn to the God of the people and of the Land."

S. Ehrmann, *Guardians of our Heritage*, pp. 617–646.

BRODY–A city in Galicia, fifty miles northeast of Lvov.

Brody can claim the earliest contact with Hasidism through R. Abraham Gershon, the brother-in-law of the Besht, who acted as cantor of a synagogue. He was, however, unsuccessful in his endeavors, since the scholars of Brody were not inclined to accept the new teachings of the Besht.

Brody had a *klaus* of early kabbalists. Among them were R. Hayyim Zanzer (1720–1783), who was a great opponent, R. Jonathan Eibeschutz, and R. Mosheh Ostrer.

One of the first communities to which R. Elijah, the Gaon of Vilna, sent his *herem* against the hasidim, in the year 1772, was Brody. The *herem* was copied there and distributed, together with another antihasidic tract, entitled *Musar Evilim*, by the secretary of the community, R. Aryeh Yehudah Leib ben Mordecai. In order to make it more effective, the document received the endorsement of all the leading rabbis of the district, with the exception of R. Shmuel (Shmelke) Horowitz, who refused to support the *herem*.

In a letter to the communal leaders, he pleaded for peace and tolerance. In 1781, the work of R. Jacob Joseph of Polonnoye was destroyed by fire there.

It was R. Yehiel Michael of Zloczov, a native of Brody, who established the first hasidic *shtiebl* there. Although friction between the hasidim and their opponents continued, it did not lead to violence, as it did in other communities.

It was in Brody that the hasidic rabbi R. Mosheh Leib of Sasov was born. Among its rabbis were R. Abraham Noah Halevi Heller, a disciple of the Maggid, and R. Efraim Zalman Margulies (1760–1829).

Brody was also the home of many opponents of Hasidism, such as Nahman Krochmal, Dov Baer Blumenfeld, and Isaac Erter. The *mitnaggedim*, however, soon joined forces with the hasidim to combat the common foe–the Enlightenment–and gradually, the hasidim infiltrated the ranks of the leaders of the community. This phenomenon continued until the Nazis' destruction of this great center of Jewry.

N. M. Gelber, *History of the Jews of Brody*.

M.S.

BROMBERG, Abraham Yitzhak (1898–1975), writer–Born in Ostrova, Poland, he was a descendant of R. Abraham Landau of Ciechanov. He studied in the rabbinical seminary in Warsaw, where he was ordained by R. Samuel Abraham Poznanski. Bromberg was a regular contributor to the Polish Jewish newspaper *Nasz Pzeglad* and later acted as chaplain to the Polish forces under General Anders.

After the Second World War, he settled in Jerusalem and published twenty-four monographs on the major hasidic rebbes. He made good use of original sources, but his personal involvement with the subject matter invariably colored his judgment.

BUBER, Martin (1878–1965)–More than any other single person, Martin Buber was the writer who brought Hasidism to the Western world in a meaningful form. Until Buber, Hasidism had been largely regarded as a form of crude, popular superstition, perhaps of interest as a revival movement but of no intrinsic value within the stream of Judaism and positively at odds with the whole spirit of the *Haskalah*, or Jewish enlightenment, and of the modern science of Judaism. Here and there a storyteller such as Yitzhak Leib Peretz had given an insight into this strange world, but otherwise it represented the very things the Western, Europeanized Jew was most eager to get away from.

Buber first encountered Hasidism in his childhood when his grandfather, the Midrash scholar Solomon Buber, took him to Sadgora, the seat of a dynasty of "rebbes," to pray in a hasidic *klaus*. Here, Buber reported in his 1917 essay "My Way to Hasidism," was–debased yet uninjured–the living double kernel of humanity:

> The palace of the rebbe, in its showy splendor, repelled me. The prayer house of the hasidim with its enraptured worshippers seemed strange to me. But when I saw the rebbe striding through the rows of the waiting, I felt, "leader," and when I saw the hasidim dance with the Torah, I felt, "community."

When Buber became active in Zionism as a young man, he saw Hasidism at first as one of the elements, along with the *Haskalah*, that had to be integrated into the new Judaism for the "Jewish Renaissance" movement to finds its way forward. After coming back to Judaism through Zionism, Buber realized that he did not really know Judaism, so he began to return to the Hebrew of his childhood. It was a passage about fervor in *The Praises of the Baal Shem Tov* (*Shivhei HaBesht*) that won Buber's soul for Hasidism and created in him the mission to proclaim it to the world as "a primal human reality, the content of human religiousness."

At twenty-six, Buber withdrew himself for five years from all Zionist-party activities and devoted himself to the study of Hasidism. "I gathered, not without difficulty, the scattered, partly missing literature," he wrote, "and I immersed myself in it, discovering mysterious land after mysterious land."

Buber's first book was *The Tales of Rabbi Nachman* (1906). When he began to translate the allegorical and even fairy-tale-like stories in which the Bratzlaver rebbe clothed his teaching, he discovered that mere translation left them even more paltry and impure than did the distortions of form and the insertions of vulgar rationalistic and utilitarian motifs portrayed by Nachman's disciples. Rejecting his first attempts, Buber proceeded to the far harder task of real artistic creation, interweaving new material into the old but also occasionally leaving out sections that his Western readers would find too alien.

His second book, *The Legend of the Baal Shem* (1908), was a similar re-creation and elaboration. The largest part of *The Legend of the Baal Shem* is autonomous fiction, composed, with the active cooperation of Buber's wife, Paula, from traditional motifs. "I bear in me the blood and the spirit of those who created this legend," Buber wrote in his Introduction, "and out of my blood and spirit it has become new." What Buber received from the spoken word stammered by "awkward lips" he transformed into artistic and urbane literature not destined for "the ears of anxious listeners" but for the sophisticated appraisal of readers attuned to the highest in German culture at the time.

Buber saw himself as an honest artisan carrying out the commission to reveal to the world something hidden in Hasidism, even against the wishes of Hasidism itself. Yet fifty years later, he recognized that he was then still subject to the spirit of the times, which led him to mix genuine testimony to a great reality of faith with the desire to display the contents of foreign religions to curious readers seeking "culture."

> I did not, to be sure, bring in any alien motifs; still I did not listen attentively enough to the crude and ungainly but living folktone which could be heard from this material. . . . The need, in the face of . . . misunderstanding, to point out the purity and loftiness of Hasidism, led me to pay all too little attention to its popular vitality. ("Jewish Mysticism," pp. 12–13)

The essay, called "Jewish Mysticism," with which Buber opened *The Tales of Rabbi Nachman*, set forth many motifs that were later to become central to both his interpretation of Hasidism and his own philosophy: the central importance of *kavvanah*; the strength of inner intention; the possibility of apprehending God in each thing if every action, no matter how lowly, is dedicated; and the notion that one's urges, far from being evil, are the very things that make greatness possible. But the exalted tone of this essay and of "The Life of the Hasidim"—the famous introductory section of *The Legend of the Baal Shem*—is very different from Buber's later interpretation of Hasidism as a "messianism of the everyday" persevering in an *unexalted* life.

Yet it is in the Introduction to *The Legend of the Baal Shem* that Buber first makes his own the mutual relationship of I and Thou: "The legend is the myth of I and Thou, of the caller and the called, the finite which enters into the infinite and the infinite which has need of the finite." "The Life of the Hasidim," moreover, stresses *kavvanah*, the dedication of the whole being, as opposed to *kavvanot*, conscious mystical and magical intentions, an emphasis Buber persevered in throughout his lifetime of work on Hasidism.

Later, however, the emphasis on ecstasy, which dominated the opening section of "The Life of the Hasidim," gave way to the hallowing of the everyday in ordinary life: "Where the mystic vortex circled, now stretches the way of man." On the other hand, his understanding of "the true *tzaddik* . . . who hourly measures the depth of responsibility with the sounding lead of his words" deepened throughout the years, as his remarkable characterizations of the early and later masters in the introductions to his two-volume *Tales of the Hasidim* bear witness.

Although recognizing that Hasidism derived its formal teaching entirely from the *Zohar* and the Lurian Kabbalah, Buber contrasted that kabbalistic gnosis that attempts to see through the contradiction of existence by schematizing the mystery with the "holy insecurity" of Hasidism, which stops short and cowers before the reality that outstrips all ready-made knowledge and acquired truth. The passion, alien thoughts, and evil urges that seek to take possession of us must be transformed by our giving them direction in genuine dialogue with the world into the substance of real life. Only thus can the contradictions that distress us be endured and redeemed.

The project that Buber and S. Y. Agnon embarked on in the early 1920s—the publication of the six-volume *Corpus Hassidicorum*, made up of the formal teachings of the hasidic masters—was cut short when a fire in Agnon's house burned all his papers, including the manuscript of the first volume. The third volume of Buber's *Werke* (1963) is a 1,270-page compilation of all of his retellings and interpretations of Hasidism.

In addition to his tales of Nachman and legends of the Besht, Buber is best known in the English-speaking world for the two-volume *Tales of the Hasidim*; for *Ten Rungs*, a small collection of hasidic sayings; for two volumes of interpretation—*Hasidism and Modern Man* and *The Origin and Meaning of Hasidism*; and for his hasidic chronicle-novel, *For the Sake of Heaven*, in which Buber learned to combine the right faithfulness with the right freedom, producing, in Karl Kerényi's words, a "breathtaking combination of insights into the phenomena of the spirit with perfection of style, which has won for Buber a secure place among the ranks of classical writers."

In *For the Sake of Heaven*, Buber contrasted the apocalyptic attempts by the "Seer" of Lublin to hasten the coming of the Messiah with the prophetic demand for redemption of just this world with all its contradictions, through turning back to God, that characterized his disciple, the "Holy Yehudi," who made justice visible in the communal existence of Pshysha. This novel demonstrates that Buber was well aware of the double strain that continued and interacted in the succession of *tzaddikim*—the Baal Shem's emphasis on hallowing the everyday and sanctifying the profane and the Maggid of Mezhirech's mystical teaching of nullifying the particular in order to reach the spiritual essence. It is precisely the lack of this later emphasis in his discursive interpretations of Hasidism that Gershom Scholem condemns in his essay on Buber's interpretation of Hasidism (*The Messianic Idea in Judaism*). Where Scholem sees only the gnostic and neoplatonic elements as essential to Hasidism, Buber recognizes two streams, one of which he emphasizes in his role, not as a historian, but as a "filter" for the needs of faith of today. To Scholem the formal teachings of the masters represent the true heart of Hasidism, whereas Buber sees that true heart in the "legendary anecdotes" told by inspired but stammering witnesses, which give us insight into the actual communal life of the hasidim as well as into the host of unique *tzaddikim* who led them.

That these tales and legends were not written down until fifty years after the formal teachings contributes to Scholem's assertion that Hasidism did not want to hallow the everyday but to nullify it. Buber, on the contrary, wants to retain just this oral quality of the crude and rough originals as they were handed down, for in Hasidism, as in Zen Buddhism and Sufi mysticism, tales were preserved orally long before being written, and they are the truer witnesses to the life of the hasidim.

Buber points to Hasidism as a living antidote to the modern Western crisis that has split the world into spiritual ideals that have no binding power or connection with everyday life. This "concentrated degree of inauthenticity" Buber counters with the hasidic recognition that the wretchedness of present-day living is founded on the fact that we do not become "humanly holy" in the measure and manner of our personal resources and in the structures of community. Therefore, far from simply reading his existential philosophy into his interpretation of Hasidism, Buber formed his existentialism of dialogue in no small part through his deep life-relationship to Hasidism.

For a far more complete account of the development and significance of Buber's retelling and interpretation of Hasidism, see the contributor's 1976 book *Encounter on the Narrow Ridge: A Biography of Martin Buber* (Maurice Friedman, Ph.D., Professor of Religious Studies, Philosophy, and Comparative Literature, San Diego State University).

M.F.

BUCHAREST—Capital city of Romania.

It was some time before Hasidism gained a foothold in Bucharest. When the biblical exegete R. Meir Malbim (1809–1879), left Bucharest in 1864, he was succeeded by R. Shimshon Weiser and R. Jacob Meir Spiro (1813–1888), a disciple of R. Solomon Zalman of Wiepoli.

R. Jacob was born in Ropczyce and served as rabbi in Craiova. In 1849 he settled in Bucharest. Apart from his knowledge of Kabbalah, he was a great halakhic authority and an author of many important works, such as *Nahlat Yaakov* on the thirteen principles of faith (Salonika, 1856), *Avnei Gazit* on the first twenty-five sections of the *Shulhan Arukh* (Bucharest, 1865), and *Tal Orot* on Kabbalah (Lvov, 1876–1883).

He was succeeded by another hasid, R. Yitzhak Eizig Shor (d. 1894), the son-in-law of R. Aaron Moses Taubes. He, too, was a prolific writer, and among his works were *Mashmi'ei Yeshua* (Bucharest, 1886), *Toldot Adam* (Zolkiev, 1873), and *Meorei Or* (Lvov, 1892).

Another renowned rabbi was R. Israel Berger (1855–1919), a descendant of the Hager dynasty and a prolific author of hasidic works.

After World War I, many hasidic rebbes lived in Bucharest. Among them were R. Asher Isaiah, the son of R. Ittamar Rosenbaum of Nadvorna; R. Samuel Deutsch of Kretshnoff; R. Moses Lupovitz, a descendant of R. Hayyim of Czernowitz; R. David Landman, a descendant of R. Uri of Strelisk; R. Shlomoh Ingerleib; R. Shmuel Lieberman; R. Abraham Joseph Gottesman; and R. Eleazar Yolles, who served as vice president of the hasidic rabbis' organization of Romania. Most of these rabbis survived the Holocaust and settled in the United States, Canada, and Israel.

During the Second World War, many Jewish refugees streamed into Bucharest. It was a haven, for a time, for many of the rebbes escaping from Hungary and Galicia. The entry into the city by the Soviet army on August 30, 1944, prevented a disaster.

Today, there are no hasidic rebbes in Bucharest. The chief rabbi, R. David Moses Rosen, was a descendant of Ruzhyn. The communal paper *Revista Cultului Moizaic*, published by the Federation of the Jewish Religious Communities, regularly publishes hasidic material.

Pinkas HaKehillot, ed. T. Lavi, vol. 1.

Y.A.

BUHUSI–A town in eastern Romania, the home of R. Yitzhak Friedman (died in 1866) and of his son, R. Israel Friedman (died in 1943).

In 1906 R. Mendel Friedman and R. David Twersky opened a hasidic *yeshivah* there. R. Mattathias Ezekiel Gutman was rabbi there from 1914 to 1927.

BUKOVINA–A region covering the northeastern Carpathians that, until 1774, was under Ottoman suzerainty. From 1774 until 1918, it was ruled by Austria; it was then incorporated into Romania.

It was in Bukovina that Hasidism originated. Okopy, the village in which the Besht was born, was on the border between Bukovina and Galicia.

It was, however, R. Nahman of Kosov and, later, R. Hayyim Tyrer of Czernowitz who spread Hasidism throughout Romania.

With the departure of R. Hayyim Tyrer for the Holy Land, R. Menahem Mendel Hager of Kosov became the undisputed leader of Hasidism in Bukovina. His descendant, R. Menahem Mendel Hager of Vishnitz, settled there. Many members of the family established their courts there: R. Hayyim Hager in Ottinia, R. Moses Hager in Suceava, R. Yitzhak Jacob in Storojineti and Csudin, R. Yehiel Michael in Czernowitz, R. Joseph Alter in Radauti, R. Israel and his son, Eliezer, in Vishnitz, and R. Barukh in Cozmeni and Seret. Other members of the family lived for a time in Maldbanila, Costesti, Novslitsa, Nepoleauti, and Berhomete.

The arrival of R. Israel Friedman in Ruzhyn increased the influence of the dynasty. Sadgora became the home of his successor, R. Abraham Jacob.

H. Gold, *Geschichte der Juden in Bukovina*, 2 vols.

A. Schmelzer, "Toldot Yehudei Bukovina," p. 55.

Y.A.

BUNIM, Hayyim Yitzhak (1875–1943), writer–Born in Gomel, he studied in the Mir Yeshivah and lived for a time in Vilna, Lodz, Warsaw, and Otwock, where he was befriended by R. Joseph Yitzhak Schneersohn.

An itinerant teacher, Bunim devoted himself to research into the *Habad* movement and published a series of articles in the Hebrew periodicals *HaOlam* (1913) and *HaTzfirah* (1919). He was the author of *Mishnat Habad* (Warsaw, 1932).

He perished in Treblinka.

Z. Raisen, *Lexicon*, 1.

BURNING OF BOOKS–Hasidic books were burned for the first time in Vilna before Passover 1772. It occurred on a Friday afternoon as worshipers were gathering for the Sabbath eve service, near the so-called *kunia*, a ring in which the neck of a pilloried person was enclosed. The order to burn the books was given by R. Elijah, the Gaon of Vilna. He instructed that *Tzavaat HaRibash*, the will of R. Israel Baal Shem Tov, should be burned. The same fate was meted out later to a collection of sayings, attributed to R. Dov Baer, the Maggid of Mezhirech, and to *Toldot Yaakov Yosef* by R. Jacob Joseph of Polonnoye, which were burned in Cracow.

The hasidim retaliated by burning in Grodno a collection of documents written by the leaders of the *mitnaggedim*. In a letter by R. Abraham of Kalisk, we read that he was instrumental in the burning in Tiberias of a collection of mitnaggedic testimonies concerning the alleged misdeeds of the hasidim.

When books of the *Haskalah* began to appear at the end of the eighteenth century, hasidim and *mitnaggedim* joined forces in burning some of them. The translation of the Pentateuch into German, with a commentary *(biur)* by Moses Mendelssohn and his associates, and the circular letter by Naftali Herz Weisel, *Divrei Shalom VeEmet*, were condemned to be burned by leading Orthodox rabbis.

M. Wilensky, *Hasidim U'Mitnaggedim*, vol. 1, pp. 42, 66, 202, 252; vol. 2, pp. 93, 135.

J.B.A.

BUSINESS AND LIVELIHOOD

–Economic and social forces were involved in the emergence and spread of the hasidic movement. The hasidim in every community did not belong to a clearly different social economic caste, though it appears that teachers, preachers, and kosher slaughterers tended to favor the new movement. Essentially, the controlling organs of the Jewish community were the prize for which the hasidim and their opponents contended. The "outs" blamed the "ins" for the various evils of the day. The hasidic movement tended to favor the "outs" in most communities.

In every community there were regulations that limited the range of competition. For instance, if a Jew had been renting a mill or an inn from a gentile landlord, another Jew was not allowed to underbid him. Such claims were enforced by the Jewish authorities, but when the hasidim split the Jewish community, such regulations were violated by both sides.

The Maggid of Mezhirech endeavored to amend communal regulations, when, in his judgment, the regulations favored the rich against the poor. R. Aaron the Great of Karlin succeeded in introducing new regulations, which greatly improved the lot of the poor and freed the teachers from the "sales tax" (*koropke*).

R. Dov Baer of Lubavitch encouraged the settlement of Jews in the "new lands" of Russia in the hope of improving the lot of the impoverished people in the small towns.

Hasidism did not encourage the competitive spirit. A person was expected to achieve success in the ways of piety, not in the financial world. Hasidic businessmen could undertake long journeys because the Besht taught that they could worship God in all ways. On the other hand, the hasidim were opposed to the acquisition of secular culture, so they were therefore unable to compete on an equal basis with enlightened Jews and educated gentiles. "Five things," said R. Pinhas of Koretz, "can help achieve a livelihood: regular and earnest study, strict honesty, regular prayers for sustenance, devotion of a tithe to charity, and not to be extravagant or a reckless spender."

J.B.A.

C

CAHANA, Joseph Meir, of Jerusalem (1910–8 *Shevat* 1978)–Son of R. Tzvi Hirsch of Spinka, he studied under his grandfather, R. Barukh Rubin of Gerela, and was ordained by R. Joseph Elimelekh Cahana of Ungvar, R. Joel Wolf Glattstein of Kiralyhelmecz, and R. Joab Adler of Hanusfalva.

In 1930, he married the daughter of R. Yitzhak Teitelbaum of Husakov, and for the next three years he lived in the house of his father-in-law.

He became rabbi in Seredna, near Munkacs, and two years later moved to Radwanka, a suburb of Ungvar, where he became known as the Spinka rebbe. He was the first of the Spinka dynasty to reach the Holy Land, and from 1941 he made his home in Jerusalem, where he established a *kollel, Imrei Yosef.*

His aim was to reconcile the teachings of Zydaczov with the doctrines of the Kabbalah. He was survived by five sons and four daughters. He was succeeded by his son R. Mordecai David. His other sons are R. Alter, the rebbe of Zydaczov in Jerusalem; R. Tzvi, rebbe in Los Angeles; and R. Tzvi Hirsch, the rebbe of Spinka in Williamsburg. His son R. Barukh married the daughter of R. Itzikel of Antwerp.

CAHANA, Nahman, of Spinka/Bene Berak (1905–17 *Tishri* 1976)–Son of R. Tzvi Hirsch, the head of the *Bet Din* of Spinka, and the son-in-law of R. Joseph Meir Weiss of Spinka. R. Nahman married the daughter of R. Jacob Israel Viyishurin Rubin, the rebbe of Szaszregen, a descendant of R. Naftali of Ropczyce. R. Nahman received his rabbinical diploma from R. Jacob Gottlieb of Miskolc and R. Hirsch Kunstlicher. In 1929 R. Nahman became the rabbi of Gyulafehervar.

During the Second World War he lived in the Romanian ghettos, and after the war he became the rabbi of Cluj. He emigrated to Israel in 1951 and lived for a time in Bene Ram, the first *moshav* of the *Po'alei Agudat Israel.* He settled in 1957 in Bene Berak, where he established a *bet midrash* and a *kollel.* He followed the traditions of Zydaczov and was ideologically inclined to Satmar. He was renowned as a halakhic authority.

He was buried on the Mount of Olives and was survived by two daughters and five sons: his successor R. Moses Eliakim Briah, R. Mendel (Manchester), R. Barukh, R. Elimelekh, and R. Asher Isaiah. One son-in-law, R. Moses Halevi Rotenberg of Brooklyn, is publishing his works.

CANADA–There are more than 300,000 Jews living in fifty communities in Canada. Very few hasidim settled there before World War II. There are now *Habad* houses in Vancouver, British Columbia; Winnipeg, Manitoba; and Ottowa, Ontario.

In Montreal, there are more than 100,000 Jews. In 1941, a Lubavitch center was established there. After the Second World War, new immigrants, survivors of the Holocaust, gave a boost to Hasidism. R. David Flaum and R. David Eliezer Zanzer lived there. With the patronage of R. Halberstam of Klausenburg, a *yeshivah* was established under R. Samuel Unsdorfer (formerly of London). There are now a large Jewish day school, a *Bet Yaakov* school, and *shtieblech* of Vishnitz, Bobov, Satmar, Zanz, and Klausenburg. R. David Rokeah, R. Joel Moskovitch and R. Yolles, the Tosher rebbe, have established hasidic centers there.

Toronto, with a Jewish population of more than 90,000, has a *Yesodey HaTorah* school and a large *Bet Yaakov* school. Among the active hasidic Aguda leaders were Dr. Ochs, Herschel Rubinstein, and B. Urman.

Recently, a film on Hasidism, *Moise,* written by Michelle Allen, was produced for the National Film Board and Radio Quebec by producer Ina Fichman and director Howard Goldberg. A documentary, *Bonjour, Shalom,* directed by Gary Beitel, portrays scenes of hasidic life in Canada.

J. Gutwirth, "The Structure of a Hasidic Community in Montreal," pp. 43–62.

J.G.

CANTONISTS—Cantonists are children taken into military service in Russia. By a decree of August 26, 1827, Jews were made liable to military service and could be called up between the ages of twelve and twenty-five. Every year, the Jewish community had to supply ten recruits per thousand of the population. Among the non-Jews the proportion was seven per thousand. Recruits, aged twelve to eighteen, were placed in establishments for military training. The Jewish community (the *Kahal*) was instructed to appoint three to six persons to be responsible for selecting the recruits.

These recruits, mostly the children of poor families, had to serve for a period of twenty-six years, a term that began when the recruit reached the age of eighteen. Bitter indeed was the life of such young boys, often snatched away from their mothers' arms when they were but eight or nine years old and sent to distant and remote provinces. Unscrupulous agents, known as *khappers* (hunters or snatchers), roamed the streets looking for prospects.

R. Menahem Mendel Schneersohn of Lubavitch set up a *Hevrah Tehiat HaMetim* (Society for the Revival of the Dead), which ransomed as many children as possible. Special Lubavitch delegates visited army camps to bring comfort and moral support to the child-soldiers and to lessen the likelihood of conversion.

It was not until 1855 that the discriminatory system of Jewish conscription was abolished by Alexander II and the recruitment of Jews to the armed forces placed on the same basis as that for other subjects of the empire.

L. Greenberg, *The Jews in Russia,* pp. 48–53.

CARLEBACH, Eli Hayyim (25 *Tevet* 1925–1990)—He was born in Berlin, scion of an illustrious family of German rabbis, twin son of R. Naftali, who served as rabbi in Berlin and in Baden near Vienna until the family left Europe in 1939.

He studied under R. Nathan Ordman in Berlin, and later in the United States under R. Aaron Kotler. He married Hadassah, a first cousin of R. Menachem Mendel Schneerson of Lubavitch, but subsequently became a hasid of Bobov.

In 1969 he founded the Hasidic Research Center, *Zekher Naftali,* in Israel, which was established to publish works on major concepts of Hasidism and cognate teachings. He was supported in this project by R. Moses Solomon Kasher and R. Eliyahu Ki-Tov.

Among the books published were the works of R. Judah Low ben Bezalel and R. Hayyim Attar, *Toafot HaRim,* on R. Yehiel Michael of Zloczow, and on the *Shpoler Zeide*.

He was survived by five daughters.

CARLEBACH, Shlomoh (25 *Tevet* 1925–15 *Tishri* 1994), folk singer—A twin brother of R. Eli Hayyim, he left Vienna with his family for Switzerland in 1933 and settled in New York in 1939.

After studying at *yeshivot* in Brooklyn and at Lakewood Yeshivah under R. Solomon Hyman, Shlomoh turned toward Hasidism, and then studied from 1951 at the Lubavitch Yeshivah in Brooklyn.

For four years he worked in the court of R. Menahem Mendel Schneerson. As his fame as a hasidic folksinger spread, Shlomoh began to combine his singing with the teaching of Hasidism. In 1966, he helped to establish a center where he held *Shabbos Love and Prayer* sessions in San Francisco, in an attempt at reaching estranged, radical American youth. By way of *havurah* groups he influenced many to return to their roots.

In 1972 he married Neilah Gluck of Toronto and had two daughters.

He was the rabbi of a synagogue on West 79th Street in Manhattan, New York, in succession to his father.

In the 1980s he started a *Moshav MeOr Modi'in* outside Lod in Israel, where he was known as the "dancing rabbi."

He was a consummate artist and composed many songs that became classics of hasidic music. His most familiar melodies are *Am Yisrael Hai* ("The people of Israel lives") and *Pithu Li* ("Open to me the gates of righteousness"). His tunes can be described as *neshamah niggunim* (soul melodies), expressing the yearning and passion for the Maker.

He was buried in Israel.

N.W.

CEMETERY–The Jewish cemetery is known by many euphemistic names, such as "House of Eternity," "House of the Living," and "Good Place."

Hasidim believe that the stone over the grave should be simple so as to indicate that in death, rich and poor meet together (Proverbs 22:2). Ostentatious tombstones have always been considered in poor taste. It was felt that they did not reflect the belief in the coming of the Messiah and the resurrection.

It was customary to erect an *ohel* over the grave of a rebbe. This became a place of pilgrimage on *yahrzeits* and other occasions. A number of hasidic rabbis instructed that no *ohel* be erected.

Hasidim would rend their garments when their rebbe died. Those who participated in the *Taharah* would first go to the *mikveh,* and *hakkafot* (circuits) would take place around the coffin.

CENTRAL ARCHIVES AND RESEARCH INSTITUTE FOR THE HISTORY OF GEDOLEI ISRAEL, Jerusalem–The archive was founded in 1973 by Samuel Gorr, who was born in 1931 in Melbourne, Australia. He studied at the Scotch College, Melbourne; at the Telshe Yeshivah in Cleveland, Ohio; and at the Gateshead Talmudical Seminary in England. He was the founder and director of the Jewish Art Museum of Australia. He researched and drew up the eight pages of Hasidic Family Trees published in the Index volume of the *Encyclopaedia Judaica*.

The archive contains photographs of hasidic rebbes, as well as their family trees. A card-index system that contains geographical data on each rebbe is kept up-to-date. The archive is also engaged in a Judeo-geographic project to identify all place names in hasidic history on a formal gazeteer basis.

CHAIKIN, Moses Avigdor (1852–1928), *Habad* hasid–This fervent hasid of *Habad* was born in Shklov, Russia, and was educated in St. Petersburg. Ordained by R. Yitzhak Elhanan Spector of Kovno, he was, from 1884 to 1887, the spiritual head of the Russian and Polish Jews in Paris. He then returned to Russia and became rabbi in Rostov-on-the-Don until his appointment as minister and chief *shohet* in Sheffield, England, in 1892.

In December 1901 he was appointed chief minister of the Federation of Synagogues, later becoming *dayan* of the London Beth Din. He was the author of *The Celebrities of the Jews: A Glance at the Historical Circumstances of the Jewish People from the Destruction of Jerusalem to the Present Day* (Sheffield, 1899) and of *Sefer Kelalei Ha-Posekim* (Rules of the Codifiers) (London, 1923). He was one of the early personalities who established hasidic roots in England.

CHARITY–The practice of charity was powerfully promoted within the hasidic community. Before the emergence of Hasidism, every Jewish community had a variety of organizations (*hevrot*) for the purpose of helping the sick, the poor, widows, orphans, itinerant beggars, and needy brides. Several weeks before Passover, a special campaign would be launched to help the poor obtain the food for the holidays, *maot hittin*.

In its diversion of pietistic energy from the practices of asceticism, Hasidism focused attention on deeds of charity. The Besht used to say, "If you do a good deed but have an ulterior motive, it is better not to do it at all. The only exception is charity. Even though there may be an ulterior motive, it is still a good deed, since you sustain the poor, no matter what your motive is."

Hasidism sought to supplement Torah study and ritualistic observances with the ardor of mystical piety and the practice of charity.

R. Nahman of Bratzlav used to say that one should give charity before one prays. This is the way to avoid the extraneous thoughts that come to a person while praying. Giving charity expands and elevates the mind. Charity for the Land of Israel can save one from distracting thoughts. Acts of charity bring blessings of love to the world. Charity saves from sin, and through charity comes wisdom. Charity is also a remedy for immorality, and zealousness for the Lord of Hosts is seen as an act of charity.

Many hasidic leaders, such as R. Moses Leib of Sasov, R. Zusya of Anopol, and R. Leib Sarah's, spent a lifetime helping Jewish tenants and lessees who had been imprisoned by their landlords for the nonpayment of rents.

The movement, moreover, brought into being a fellowship in which rich and poor considered themselves brothers. The movement was cemented by the mortar of personal friendship as well as by loyalty to the rebbe.

In the court of the rebbe, they would share their food and pay jointly for their lodgings. Money given to the rebbe was often used to help the poor.

Often, the rebbes were able to mobilize the resources of their hasidim on behalf of worthy causes. R. Shneur Zalman of Liady organized support for the hasidim who lived in the Holy Land. So great was his success that his opponent, R. Avigdor of Pinsk, jealously lodged a complaint against him with the Russian government.

Later, when many Jews were expelled from their villages, R. Shneur Zalman organized a nationwide effort for the resettlement of the refugees. For that purpose, he demanded from his followers 20 percent of their income. He also introduced the practice of dropping some coins into a charity box for the poor of the Holy Land, before daily prayers.

A. Wertheim, *Halakhot VeHalikhot BeHasidut*, pp. 78–80.

J.B.A.

CHELM, Nata (d. 1 *Shevat* 1812) – Son of R. Abraham and Malka, he was a descendant of Saul Wahl, who, according to legend, was appointed king of Poland for one day.

R. Nata was a disciple of R. Barukh of Medziborz, R. Elimelekh of Lejask, and R. Mordecai of Neskhiz, who encouraged him to become a rebbe.

Motionless and in silence, R. Nata recited his prayers. It was said of him: "R. Nata does not sway to and fro during the Day of Atonement, because his fear of God is so great that he is too terrified to move." He stressed that business should be conducted according to ethical standards.

Most of his manuscripts were destroyed in a fire. He was the author of *Neta Shashuim* on the Pentateuch, published in Warsaw in 1891. His son, R. Tzvi, succeeded him, and the dynasty was continued by his grandson, R. Todres, who died in 1887.

M. Y. Weinstock *Tiferet Banim Avotam*, pp. 231–234.

CHELMNO (in German, Kulmhof) – Chelmno was the first Nazi death camp established for the specific purpose of mass killing by means of gas. It was located in the Polish village of Chelmno, forty-seven miles (seventy-five km) west of Lodz. It was put into operation on December 8, 1941, and it functioned until April 1943. Killing operations were resumed in April 1944. From June 23 to July 14, 1944, more than 70,000 Jews from the Lodz ghetto were put to death. In all, over a quarter of a million people were murdered in the camp, mostly Jews and hasidim from the Lodz ghetto.

CHERNOBYL – A city on the river Pripet in the Ukraine. R. Menahem Nahum established a hasidic dynasty there.

See TWERSKY.

CHILDREN – One of the most important functions of the hasidic family is procreation, which is a commandment of God. Birth control is rarely practiced by hasidic women, so hasidic families are noted for their large number of children. Having children is of such prime importance to the hasidic family that lack of children is considered one of the major grounds for divorce, though in actual fact this rarely happens, as the childless couple lives in hope that, through faith, prayer, and the rebbe's blessing, the Almighty will yet bless them with children. Thus it is rare, too, to find adoption of children by the childless in hasidic communities, as this would be tantamount to a public admission of lack of faith.

The socialization process of hasidic children begins practically at birth, when in some hasidic families, a *kapel* (skullcap) is placed on the boy baby's head at the breast. Ritual hand washing and blessings are taught as soon as the child can say a few words. Children are very conspicuous at all gatherings, and they participate in festivals to a much greater extent than is common among other Jewish groups. For example, at Simhat Torah, even toddlers and babes in arms stay up all night to take part in the *hakaffot*. Often indulged on one level (one common complaint by outsiders is their lack of "manners" and "discipline"), enormous self-control and discipline are expected of them on another level–the ritualistic one. Discipline is usually totally authoritarian and may involve the use of corporal punishment, such as a quick slap or boxing of ears. The children early on acquire the gestures and mannerisms of their elders as reflected in their gait and their fervent movements of praying. Yiddish is often expressly taught as their first language because it is regarded as the proper embodiment of *Yiddishkeit* (i.e., Jewish values).

The children are expected to respect their parents, and they are trained to be observant Jews. Although the mother is largely responsible for instilling hasidic norms into the child at home, the community and community schools play an active part in child rearing from the time the child is able to talk. *Hinukh* (education) is of overriding concern to hasidic parents, for it is only by exposing the child to the "right" influences that hasidic values can be maintained. It is the school system to a large extent that is responsible for perpetuating hasidic values–from the *heder* to the *yeshivah*.

The boy is taught to become a religious man observing all the laws and rituals prescribed by Jewish law. He is initiated into participation in observance of the Jewish laws at an early age, when he accompanies his father to the house of worship, and he is formally initiated at the age of thirteen, when he becomes *bar mitzvah*. After that he continues with his talmudic studies and becomes a recognized man in the society at eighteen, when he is of age for marriage. He becomes a full-fledged member of the community, however, only after marriage.

Although *bar mitzvah* and marriage are the two formal stages of initiation, there are a number of other rites of passage, reflected in the changing garb and appearance of children over the years. In some hasidic groups (e.g., Belzer), the boy has his first haircut at the age of three; this is, too, when he first enters *heder* and dons his first *tzitzit*. Until the age of five or six, he is still allowed some leeway with his clothes (e.g., wearing bright colors); after six or seven, however, he puts on the darker, more somber clothing of his elders and adopts a cap or hat. From thirteen he is entitled to put in the satin-edged *bekishe* and a larger hat, and after marriage itself, he can wear a *shtreimel* (fur-edged hat).

There is no official puberty ceremonial for girls. Girls do not receive any social recognition while young. At the age of three they are considered females according to the Law and are subject to all the restrictions applicable to women. As they grow and mature physically, they wear clothing that covers them (i.e., long-sleeved, high-necked garments with modest hemlines; thick stockings). Some groups, such as the Satmarer, restrict women's clothing to the darker hues too, but many allow greater variation. The education of girls is largely restricted to learning the "roles expected of women." Though many do go on to seminary after the age of sixteen–to learn religious teaching, for example–often they have more exposure to secular education. For example, some learn to play musical instruments.

Before marriage, girls are allowed to display their femininity within the limitations of group norms. This is the only time, for example, that hair can be worn long. At festivals and gatherings, they sing and dance among themselves, but at no time are they allowed joint activity with the boys.

The youthful exuberance of both sexes is channeled into the singing and dancing that the hasidim are so noted for. There is no socially recognized period of adolescence, and because the role of youth is to obey their elders and behave in a way appropriate for hasidic people, there are few of the ambiguities and conflicts in this period, in contrast to those encountered in the wider society.

J. A. Kupfermann, "The Lubavitch Hasidim of Stamford Hill."

J.K.

CHMIELNICKI MASSACRES

(1648–1649)–Described by contemporary historians as the Third Hurban, these massacres initially affected the western Ukraine, Volhynia, and Podolia in the west, and Chernigov and Poltava in the east, namely, the areas that had become Polish territory during the preceding century. Politically, these regions were ruled by the absolute kings of Poland; economically, they were controlled by the Polish nobility, who regarded the inhabitants as serfs.

The Jews living in these areas had to suffer the tension between the nobles and the serfs, the Polish Catholics and the Russian Orthodox Christians, and the townspeople and the small peasants. Moreover, for long the Jews had proved an important factor in the Polish economy in their capacity as stewards of the Polish absentee landlords. In this way they helped in the management and exploitation of the nobles' estates. But to the oppressed Ukrainians, the Jews appeared to be the real possessors of power. Earlier, in 1637, the military wing of the Ukrainians—the Cossacks—spurred on by the battle cry "Down with the Pans and the Jews"—had invaded the district of Poltava but were finally repelled by the Polish army. That the Jews failed to heed the warning of that uprising has been attributed to the influence of kabbalistic teachings, which permeated many communities in southern Russia and which led them to believe that 1648 would witness the advent of the Messiah.

By 1648, the Cossacks and the peasants were better organized and, led by Hetman Bogdan Chmielnicki, they entered into an alliance with the Crimean Tartars. The aims of Chmielnicki were the spread of the true faith, the freedom of the Cossacks, and the extirpation of Pans and Jews. In the early stages of the revolt, many Jewish communities east of the Dnieper were destroyed. Those Jews who escaped either converted to Christianity or were sold into slavery. During the summer of 1648, the massacres spread to the west bank of the Dnieper. In June of that year, the community of Nemirov suffered a cruel fate at the hands of the rebel hordes, and more than 6,000 Jews were either massacred or drowned.

In his "Scroll of Darkness," Shabbatai ben Meir haKohen, an eyewitness of the carnage, described the horrible scenes: "They [the Cossacks] drowned several hundreds in the water and by all kinds of cruel torments. Before the holy ark in the synagogue they slaughtered with butchers' knives, after which they destroyed the synagogue and took out all the scrolls of the Torah. These they tore up and laid them out for men and animals to trample on. They also made sandals from them."

At the end of June, the fortress town of Tulchin suffered a similar fate, as did the communities of Polonnoye and Narol. In September, Chmielnicki himself led a Cossack army into Galicia and, failing to penetrate the inner fortress of Lemberg (Lvov), proceeded toward Warsaw. The newly elected Polish king, John Casimir, entered into peace negotiations with the rebels, but these efforts failed owing to the excessive demands of the Cossacks. Consequently, the massacres resumed in the spring of 1649, and many Jewish communities were almost annihilated. Finally, a peace treaty was concluded between John Casimir and Chmielnicki at Zbarov. The peace treaty included a clause that forbade Jewish residence in those areas of the Ukraine inhabited by the Cossacks. However, the Treaty of Zbarov proved abortive, and civil war broke out again in 1651 and continued intermittently until 1658.

In that final period, the Jews living in White Russia and Lithuania suffered at the hands of the Cossacks and Muscovites, particularly the communities of Moghilev, Vitebsk, and Vilna.

When Sweden invaded Poland in 1665, the Jews enjoyed a short respite, but because the Jews were friendly toward the Swedes, the Poles charged them with disloyalty. The result was the massacre of Jews in Great and Little Poland by bands of Polish irregulars. According to conservative estimates, nearly 100,000 Jews lost their lives in the decade 1648–1658, and over 300 communities were completely or partially destroyed. Yet despite its terrible sufferings, Polish Jewry showed remarkable resilience, and by the end of the century, the Jewish population of Poland exceeded that of the whole of Western European Jewry. Nevertheless, the memory of the Chmielnicki massacres remained, particularly in the period immediately following 1648–1649. Supercommunal organizations such as the Councils of Lithuania and the Four Lands instituted a period of three years of mourning while at the same time involving themselves in the redemption of captives and the salvation of converts.

The Nemirov massacre (20 *Sivan* 1648) was appointed as a day of mourning, and special *kinot* (dirges) were composed for recitation throughout Poland. The wider efforts of the Cossack holocaust were especially felt in the southwestern regions of Poland, which were so economically reduced that they yielded their former supremacy to the northwest (i.e., Lithuania and White Russia), which had, on the whole, suffered comparatively little. The latter areas also became the cultural centers of Judaism in Eastern Europe. In the following century, it was southwestern Poland that witnessed the rise of Frankism and subsequently the rapid expansion of Hasidism.

S. M. Dubnov, *A History of the Jews in Russia and Poland,* pp. 144–153.

N. Hannover, *Yeven Metzulah,* pp. 54, 63, 80.

S.B.L.

CHOLENT (Yiddish, tsholent)–A Sabbath overnight casserole. Cholent, first mentioned in Italy 500 years ago, is still a favorite hasidic dish. Prepared on the eve of the Sabbath, it is placed in a slow oven and served for lunch on the Sabbath.

CHORTKOV (Polish, Chortkov), city in Tarnopol Oblast, Ukraine–Until 1918, Chortkov belonged to Austria, then, in the interwar years, to Poland. In September 1939 it was annexed by Russia. In the nineteenth century, it was a great center of Hasidism and the home of the hasidic rabbi, R. Friedman. In April 1942 a ghetto was established from which the Jews were deported to the Belzac concentration camp.

CIECHANOV, Abraham Landau (1784–5 *Adar* 1875)–Son of Rafael Dubrzinsky, Abraham was a disciple of R. Fishel of Strykov and of R. Simhah Bunem of Przysucha. He married the daughter of Don Landau of Plotzk and in tribute to his father-in-law adopted Landau as his surname. He became the rabbi of Ciechanov in 1820 and remained there until his death.

Contrary to hasidic practices, he did not adopt the Lurian liturgy in his prayers, nor did he accept petitions from his followers. He distributed *shirayim* and chanted the melodies of R. Isaac Luria, however. Whenever he visited his widowed mother, Rada, he would don fresh garments in her honor. At the conclusion of the Fast of *Av,* he would discard his copy of the *kinot,* because by the following year the Messiah would have come and there would be no need for lamentations. He was known for his donations to charity but stressed that the mere act of giving was not enough and that it was important to give joyfully.

He was communally minded and participated in many communal activities. Together with R. Isaac Meir of Ger he strongly opposed any change in hasidic garments. Among the many halakhic authorities with whom he corresponded was R. Elijah Guttmacher. He was highly esteemed by his contemporaries. "He has the appearance of an angel of God," commented R. Menahem Mendel of Kotzk. All his writings originated from his youth; he wrote nothing for the last forty years of his life. He was the author of *Zekhutei DeAvraham,* novellas on Talmud (Warsaw, 1865); *Ahavat Hesed* on *Nashim* and *Tohorot* (Pietrokov, 1897); *Bet Avraham* on the Talmud and Maimonides (Warsaw, 1899); a commentary on the Passover *Haggadah* (Lodz, 1939); and *Tzelutei DeAvraham,* on his liturgical customs (Tel Aviv, 1962).

R. Abraham's eldest son, R. Zeev Wolf Landau of Strykov (1807–11 *Elul* 1891), succeeded him. His other sons were R. Dov Berish of Biala (1840–25 *Sivan* 1876); R. Rafael, a rabbi in Warsaw; and R. Jacob, rabbi of Yezov (1834–19 *Tevet* 1894). His widowed daughter, Breindel, was married to R. Samuel Shinover, the author of *Ramatayim Tzofim.*

CLUJ (Kolozsavar or Klausenburg)–A town in central Romania, 210 miles northwest of Bucharest. In 1921, the hasidim established a separate community, and R. Halberstam was rabbi there until May 1944. In 1941, it had a Jewish population of 17,000, all of whom were deported to Auschwitz between May 25 and June 9, 1941.

CONFESSION–Whereas confession in Judaism generally is made directly to God and forms part of the formal liturgy, in early Hasidism individual confession was sometimes addressed to the *tzaddik,* who, in his capacity as intermediary between God and man, could secure the expiation of all sins confessed before him. The evidence for the practice of confession in Hasidism is sparse, and this, as well as its very failure to become widely established within the movement, may be accounted for by the traditionally negative attitude in Judaism toward the institution, which had been associated with Christianity since medieval times.

In an antihasidic petition to the czar, directed against R. Shneur Zalman of Liady, R. Avigdor, the deposed rabbi of Pinsk, included an account of confession among the "Karliners" who, upon joining the "sect," must each hand to the rebbe a signed list of all sins committed to date, accompanied by a sum of money fixed by the rebbe. R. David of Makov, in his attack on Hasidism, similarly wrote of the followers of Hayyim Heikel of Amdura that, after enticing innocent people to sin, they invite them to join the sect by confessing before the rebbe, who, for a certain *pidyon* (redemption money), would grant them instant absolution. (See M. Wilenski, *Hasidim U'Mitnaggedim* [Jerusalem 1970], part I, p. 276, and part II, p. 161.)

Against these hostile accounts by outsiders, the literature of the hasidic circle of Bratzlav offers detailed descriptions of confession before R. Nahman, as well as a theoretical exposition of its significance, from which it emerges clearly that, despite the superficial similarity between this type of confession and the Catholic institution of confession before a priest, the idea of confession in Bratzlav was a natural extension of traditional Jewish mystical, particularly Lurianic, notions.

R. Nahman heard confessions of the most intimate details in the lives of his followers already during his period of residence in Medvediovka, both before and immediately after his journey to the Holy Land in 1798. But he did not make the practice obligatory on all his disciples until after his move to Zlatopol in 1800. It would appear that, as in the two previously mentioned reports, confession formed part of the initiation into the circle of new recruits. Refusal to confess prevented admission.

Although details of the contents of these confessions have not survived, as they were held in strict privacy, it is clear that confession before R. Nahman was a taxing emotional experience, culminating almost invariably with temporary mental collapse. R. Nahman had the power to uplift, at the time of confession, each evil combination of letters in the alphabet constituting the verbal expression of each sin confessed, and to convert it to holiness, thus annulling the effect of the sin on the *Sefirah* of *Malkhut* and atoning for it on behalf of the confessing disciple. He also used to prescribe various *tikkunim* (remedial measures) tailored to combat the individual weaknesses of each disciple who had confessed his sins.

The hasidic opponents of R. Nahman and his followers nicknamed them contemptuously the "Vidduynikkes" ("Confessors"), thus indicating that, although evidently not unique, Bratzlaver hasidim were distinguished by this practice within the hasidic camp. For reasons that are never stated in the sources, R. Nahman abandoned the practice of confession shortly after his move from Zlatopol to Bratzlav in 1802, and it was never resumed.

A. Rapoport-Albert, "Confession in the Circle of R. Nachman of Braslav," pp. 65–97. *Likkutei Moharan*, part I, Torah 4, "*Anohi*."

A.R.

CONTROVERSY BETWEEN THE HASIDIM AND THE MITNAGGEDIM–Polish Hasidism, whose founder was Rabbi Israel Baal Shem Tov (Besht), encountered strong opposition on the part of the organized Jewish community as early as the second half of the eighteenth century. The conflict between the hasidim and *mitnaggedim* was confined at first to the Jewish community and manifested itself in the imposition of bans and sanctions, libelous writings, and economic and social deprivations. As the conflict continued, each of the opposing camps resorted to bringing the issue before the non-Jewish authorities.

Criticism against the first hasidic groups was voiced already during the lifetime of the Besht. But as long as these groups operated in Podolia and the Ukraine, backward provinces in terms of Torah learning, they aroused no organized opposition. Soon the center of the movement moved northward to Volhynia, White Russia, Polesie, and even to Vilna, the center and stronghold of Lithuanian Torah study. It was then that organized war against the new movement began. The leaders of the Vilna community, led by the Gaon, R. Elijah, began their overt war against Beshtian Hasidism in 1772, and they continued their aggressive opposition to the movement up to the beginning of the nineteenth century. The communities of Lithuania, White Russia, and Galicia soon followed Vilna.

Three waves of controversy arose during the approximately forty years of the dispute. The first was in 1772, the second was in 1781, and the third began in 1796 and extended into the early nineteenth century. All three originated in Vilna, each starting with the imposition of bans and sanctions on the new sect.

The first phase of the controversy started in the spring of 1772, after the hasidim succeeded in infiltrating Vilna and establishing their own prayer house (*minyan*). Some hasidic leaders of Vilna, including the local Maggid, were severely punished and humiliated. The Vilna *kahal* excommunicated the hasidim and issued proclamations in which were enumerated its indictment of the new sect. The communities of Lithuania, White Russia, and Galicia (Brody) were asked to follow the steps of Vilna's *mitnaggedim*. The antihasidic writings of 1772 were collected in the pamphlet *Zemir Aritzim VeHarevot Tzurim* (The Song of the Terrible Ones and Knives of Flint). That pamphlet, published in 1772, includes the first bans imposed on the hasidim, and it voices most of the objections made, during the entire conflict, against the hasidim, except the one about the "elevation of strange thoughts" during prayer.

The accusations against the hasidim can be summarized: their separation from the established prayer houses and the founding of their own *minyanim,* in which they introduced changes in liturgy; their changes in the set times of prayer according to the Halakhah; their changes in the method of prayer; their changes in ritual slaughter (*shehitah*), using sharply honed knives; their neglect of Torah study and their disrespect for Torah scholars; much merrymaking and partying; suspicion of Shabbateanism; bizarre actions; and miracle working by hasidic *tzaddikim.* It was claimed that the greediness of hasidic *tzaddikim* caused waste of Jewish money. And there were other accusations, such as changes in their dress, a great deal of pipe smoking, and so on. It should be noted that the allegation against the hasidic *shehitah* was neither included in the Vilna ban of 1772 nor, consequently, in Vilna's later antihasidic bans. This charge is absent because, according to the Gaon of Vilna, it does not violate Jewish law.

The second phase of the conflict started in 1781, one year after the appearance in print of the first hasidic book, *Toldot Yaakov Yosef,* a commentary on the Pentateuch. That book, by R. Jacob Joseph of Polonnoye, an ardent disciple of the Besht, forced severe criticisms against contemporary rabbis and communal leaders and in turn aroused Vilna's *mitnaggedim* from their relative inaction.

The ban of 1781 was threatening the hasidim also with economic and social sanctions. Following Vilna's precedent, the representatives of the four Lithuanian communities–Grodno, Brest, Pinsk, and Slutzk–issued proclamations against the hasidim at their meeting in Zelva (*Elul* 1781). During that second phase, bans consisting of excommunications against the hasidim were issued also by the communities of Cracow (1785) and Shklov (1787).

The third phase of the controversy started in the mid-1790s, after the Gaon formally denied hasidic rumors that he regretted his opposition to them. The printing of *Tanya,* by R. Shneur Zalman of Liady, was another major cause of the renewal of hostility. The Gaon's most bitter attack on the hasidim appeared in his epistle written on the day following Yom Kippur in 1796.

Also written during the 1790s were the most vitriolic antihasidic pamphlets, by the two zealous opponents of Hasidism, R. David of Makov and R. Israel Loebel.

In contrast to the prolific writings of the mitnaggedic camp, there is a paucity of written reaction on the part of the hasidim to the conflict. Presumably, the reason for this is that few of their number had the literary ability to express their reactions in writing.

In defense of Hasidism rose R. Samuel Horovitz and R. Elimelekh of Lejask, but the primary hasidic spokesman was R. Shneur Zalman, who from 1772 to the abatement of the controversy continually attempted to reconcile the two camps. In his letters, Shneur Zalman of Liady turned to his adversaries, at times pleadingly and at times resolutely, in order to make them see the error of their way and stop their war with the hasidim. Initially, he wrote letters to his followers, in which he prevailed upon them not to antagonize the *mitnaggedim* and to be sure to respect the Gaon of Vilna. However, when his hasidim at Vilna suggested, in the mid-1790s, that he come to Vilna to debate the Gaon so as to thereby make peace between the two parties, R. Shneur Zalman answered that his previous attempts to meet with the Gaon had failed utterly. "He closed the door in our face twice," he said, and the Vilna Gaon's views had not changed since then. Even arbitration between the two rival parties would not help, for the arbiter of the *mitnaggedim,* even should he recognize the rightness of the hasidim, would be afraid to express his opinion because "there is no one in the region of Lithuania who would dare not to annul his own view in the face of the saintly Gaon's and say wholeheartedly that he [the Gaon] does not speak rightly."

With the death of the Gaon in October 1797, a change was introduced in the war methods of the two hostile parties. The conflict moved beyond the confines of the Jewish community. The hasidim were the first who turned to the Russian authorities to interfere in the inner conflict. The complaint submitted by them (Spring 1798) to the Russian government included also slanderous information about the organization of the *kahal*. The Vilna *kahal* did not sit idle either and turned to the government with slander about the hasidim. As a result, R. Shneur Zalman was imprisoned in St. Petersburg in October 1798. His release in November 1798 has been celebrated as a holiday by *Habad* hasidim to this very day.

In spite of R. Shneur Zalman's intercession with the hasidim of Vilna to discontinue their war on the *kahal,* they succeeded, with the assistance of the Russian authorities, in dismissing the board of the *kahal* and choosing a new board in its place (February 1799), composed mainly of members of the hasidic camp, which constituted only a minority in the community. All efforts of the *kahal* to return to power failed; the Russian authorities supported the hasidim.

The authorities supported the hasidim not only on the local plane–the conflict of the Vilna *kahal* and the hasidim–but also on the more comprehensive plane that R. Avigdor, the former rabbi of Pinsk, directed against the hasidim. R. Shneur Zalman, who was imprisoned a second time in the fall of 1800 at St. Petersburg prison as a result of R. Avigdor's slanderous information submitted to Czar Paul I, was again released.

The Russian government's position favoring the hasidim, which was expressed both by the exoneration of R. Shneur Zalman and by the promulgation of the "Statute of 1804" by Alexander I, in which the hasidim were given legitimate status, was one of the causes of the abatement of the conflict between the two hostile camps.

But internal causes worked as well toward the abatement of the dispute. The hasidim, at that time, at the beginning of the nineteenth century, had been turned from a minority into a recognized power and, in many places, into an overwhelming majority in many regions of Poland and even of White Russia. Moreover, at the beginning of the nineteenth century, *tzaddikim* arose in Hasidism who preached erudition and called for a return to the study of *Gemara* and *Tosafot*. In any case, a bridge was built between the two rival forces. Finally, the rise of the *Haskalah* movement, a common enemy for the *mitnaggedim* and the hasidim, caused the rivals to cease their war and mobilize their forces for the war on the *Haskalah*.

Although the dispute continued for many more years and its traces are discernible throughout the nineteenth century, by the first decade of the nineteenth century both sides had reached a point of peaceful coexistence in Vilna, and the rest of the communities of White Russia and Lithuania soon followed in their footsteps.

M. Wilensky, *Hasidim U'Mitnaggedim,* vol. 1, p. 2.

M.L.W.

CORDOVERO, Moses ben Jacob (1522–1570)–Moses, known as the *Remak,* was one of the most profound and systematic exponents of the teachings of the *Zohar* and a leading figure in the circle of mystics for which sixteenth-century Safed in Palestine was renowned. Few details of his life are known with certainty. Little, for instance, is known of his wife beyond that he predeceased her, leaving her with a child of eight, named Gedaliah, who later made himself responsible for printing some of his father's works.

He was undoubtedly one of the most prolific writers in the history of Jewish literature. No less than about thirty works, some of them extant only in manuscript, poured from his pen during his comparatively short life. Among his printed works were *Pardes Rimonim,* a detailed exposition of kabbalistic doctrines, consisting of thirteen "gates" and subdivided into chapters, published in Cracow in 1591; *Elimah Rabbati,* a detailed work of exposition on the main kabbalistic themes, published in Brody in 1881; *Shiur Komah* (measurements of height), an exposition of the doctrine of the *Sefirot* (Warsaw, 1883); and *Tomar Deborah,* an ethical treatise devoted to the kabbalistic significance and application of the doctrine of the Imitation of God, published in Venice in 1558.

Moses' brother-in-law was R. Solomon Alkabetz. R. Yitzhak Luria refers to Cordovero as his "master and teacher." Among his disciples were Elijah ben Moses de Vidas, Abraham ben Mordecai Galante, and Samuel Gallico.

L. Jacobs, *Rabbi Moses Cordovero: The Palm Tree of Deborah.*

L.J.

COUNCIL OF THE FOUR LANDS–The Council of the Four Lands in Poland, in the sixteenth to eighteenth centuries, was one of the most famous representative organizations in Jewish history. It had originally emerged from the meetings of local councils of Polish Jewry going back to the fifteenth century. These dealt with such matters as relations with central and local government officials, protection of Jewish merchants, and defense of Jewish rights, which were the topics that continued to engage the Council of the Four Lands as it evolved in the course of the second half of the sixteenth century.

The council was formed of representatives from the smaller councils in Lesser Poland (Cracow/Lublin), Greater Poland (Poznan), Red Russia (Lvov), and Lithuania (Brest). In 1623, Lithuania withdrew, on fiscal grounds, to form a council of its own, known as Council of the Province–*Vaad HaMedinah.* But the former name persisted with the accession of Volhynia to the Polish council. The latter enjoyed its heyday in the sixteenth century and the early part of the seventeenth century, but it was not actually dissolved until 1764. In addition to the matters that had always engaged the attention of the local councils, the Council of the Four Lands also dealt with the regulation of intercommunal disputes, maintenance of relations with Jewish communities outside Poland, and supervision of educational, philanthropic, and book-publishing facilities.

Ever-increasing attention had to be devoted to fiscal and financial matters, for the council was responsible for the implementation of the fiscal policy of the Polish Crown so far as the Jews were concerned. This was achieved by way of distribution of the tax burden among the lesser individual communities.

The records of the council are not by any means complete, but they do show that it usually consisted of some thirty members elected by provincial councils within the jurisdiction of the Four Lands. The members of the council came from leading families throughout Polish Jewry, and the resulting oligarchic structure was extended by the practice of also employing members of those families as the staff of the council (secretaries, treasurers, etc.).

The council held its meetings twice yearly–at the great fairs of Lublin and Yaroslav in the spring and summer, respectively. The activities of the council suffered irreparably from the Chmielnicki massacres and the Swedish and Muscovite invasions (1648–1657). However, it was the growing fiscal burden that ultimately undermined the council's existence. Increased taxation and the need to provide supplementary payments for officials of the state, clergy, and so forth, brought the councils of the communities, at both the local and the national levels, into ever-deeper indebtedness.

A default by the provincial council of Greater Poland (Poznan) at the end of the 1680s led to a revision of the system of revenue collection and tax apportionment, but this did not prevent a later and more serious general financial collapse of the council. The situation encouraged the enemies of Jewish autonomy in the Polish Seym, and in 1764 they were successful in securing the dissolution of both central and provincial councils in Poland.

Despite the abuses inseparable from its oligarchic structure, the Council of the Four Lands stands out as an example of Jewish autonomous rule in the Diaspora and was, for example, the inspiration of Dubnow's historiography.

I. Halpern, *Yehudim VeYahadut BeMizrach Eiropa,* pp. 37–107.

S. W. Baron, *The Jewish Community,* vol. 1, pp. 323–327, vol. 3, pp. 81–85.

S.L.

CRACOW–One hundred and fifty-eight miles southwest of Warsaw, Cracow is the former capital city of Poland. The third partition of Poland of 1795 assigned Cracow to the Austrian empire. In the interwar years, it was part of the Polish state.

Cracow was the home of notable kabbalists, such as R. Samson of Ostropole and R. Nathan Nata Shapira, the author of the *Baal Amukot*. Hasidism, as a movement in its infancy, did not encounter strong opposition. It was, however, in the year 1783 that the first pioneer of Hasidism, in the person of R. Simon Matlis, planted the seeds of the movement, which soon began to bear fruit. Matlis was acquainted with R. Abraham Joshua Heschel of Opatov. His uncle even knew the Besht, and his father, Leibish, met R. Elimelekh of Lejask and the Maggid of Mezhirech.

The religious and lay leaders of the community issued a *herem* against the hasidim on 25 *Tishri* 1786, which was attested by the *Av Bet Din,* R. Yitzhak Halevi.

In 1799, Israel Loebel, an itinerant preacher and the author of two antihasidic tracts—*Sefer Avikuah* and *Tzavaat Tzaddikim* (Warsaw, 1798)—influenced the communal leaders to enter a complaint against the hasidim to the city council. The city council directed, however, that the issue be settled by agreement, which gave the hasidim permission to have their own synagogue outside the ancient Jewish quarter. Thus the movement was firmly established in the city, but friction still continued until the appointment of R. Saul Rafael Landau (d. 29 *Sivan* 1854).

Hasidim of diverse dynasties flourished in the city. It was the home of R. Kalonymus Kalman Epstein of Neustadt, the author of the classical work *Meor VeShemesh*. It had many followers of R. Solomon Rabinowicz of Radomsk. It had *shtieblech* of Zanz, Bobov, and Sianiawa, as well as three *shtieblech* of Ger. R. Shimon Sofer, one of the organizers of the *Mahzikei Hadat,* enlisted the hasidim to combat new trends he considered dangerous to Judaism.

Another distinguished member of the hasidic community, held in esteem by many hasidic masters, was R. Aaron Marcus (d. 1916), the author of a classical history book on Hasidism.

Among the active workers of the Aguda was Alter David Kurtzman (1865–1943), a hasid of Chortkov, at whose home all hasidic rebbes were given hospitality. Other active workers were Zeev Wolf Friedman, Rafael Landsman, and Yitzhak Bauminger. Active in communal life was Feivel Stempel, the in-law of the rebbe of Bobov, who was deputy for the Polish Seym in 1923 and president of the community. He was ably supported by the printer and hasid of Ger, Moses Deutscher (1880–1941), who served as a senator in the Polish Seym. There was also an active *Zeire Agudat Yisrael* group, under David Rosenfeld, as well as the *Po'ale Aguda,* under Judah Leib Orleans.

It was in Cracow that Sara Schenierer, in 1918, established a *Bet Yaakov* school, which revolutionized education for Orthodox women in Poland. There was a *Talmud Torah* for 1,500 children, as well as a *yeshivah, Bet Meir*. In the interwar years, it was the home of R. Moses Friedman.

Hasidism flourished until the Nazis deported the Jews to Belzec concentration camp.

Sefer Cracow, Ir VeEm BeYisrael, pp. 167–179.

M.S.

CREATOR AND CREATION–

Hasidic thought follows the kabbalistic understanding of *creatio ex nihilo* (creation out of nothing, *yesh me'ayin*) in terms of the emanation of the *Sefirot* and the universe (of *yesh,* that which is) from *Ein Sof* (the Limitless, the Ground of Being), known as *ayin* (nothingness), because this aspect of deity is utterly beyond all comprehension.

In some versions of Hasidism, notably in *Habad,* this doctrine sometimes results in a thoroughgoing "acosmism." That is, from the point of view of God, as it were, there is no created universe at all. Since the universe emerges out of nothingness, its nature is to revert to nothingness so that its continued existence is possible only through the supernatural act of God that keeps it in being. Suspended over the void, the universe has to be created anew at every moment of time (*Tanya,* part II, chap. 1–7). Because creation involves the emergence of "somethingness" (*yesh*) from the divine nothingness (*ayin*), it is the task of the *tzaddik* to reverse the process by acknowledging God in all he does and thinks, thus restoring the somethingness of things to the nothingness whence they come (Menehem Mendel of Vitebsk, *Pri HaAretz,* pp. 3–4, commentary to Genesis 1:16).

To the old question about why God decided to create the world at the time when He did rather than beforehand, Pinhas of Koretz replies that the question is meaningless because God can be known only through

His manifestations in Creation (*Midrash Pinhas,* no. 51, pp. 30–31). Not only that question but any other as well cannot be asked about the Deity before the stage of Creation since here no thought has any grasp at all. Similarly, the tremendous mystery behind Creation, concerning how the Infinite could have produced the finite, is stressed by Israel of Kozienice, who remarks that all that can be said has been said by Maimonides in connection with the nature of God (*Avodat Yisrael,* beg., commentary to Genesis 1:1). The human mind is utterly incapable of grasping the marvelous wisdom of the Creator.

Levi Yitzhak of Berdichev begins his *Kedushat Levi* (commentary to Genesis 1:1) with the following typical hasidic understanding of the doctrine of Creation:

> The principle is that the Creator, blessed be He, created all and He is all and His flow of grace is unceasing. For at every moment He allows His grace to flow to His creatures and to all worlds, all heavenly halls, all angels and all Holy *Hayyot*. That is why we refer in our prayers to God as: "He who creates" (*yotzer*), not: "He who has created" (*yatzar*). For at every moment He infuses vitality into all. All is from Him, blessed be He. He is perfect and His Being embraces all.

The hasidic teachers refused to accept Maimonides' idea that God's providence extends only over the species of animals. All things are created by the divine wisdom, and by that wisdom every blade of grass lies exactly where it is.

I. Stern, Introduction to *Shomer Emunim,* by Joseph Ergas, pp. 31–34.

L.J.

CZECHOSLOVAKIA, HASIDISM IN

IN – (Note: Prior to 1918, the territory comprising the Czechoslovak Republic was within the Austro-Hungarian monarchy; hence, additional information about the early history of Hasidism in Czechoslovakia may be found in the articles on Hasidism in Austria and Hungary.)

Geographical distribution. There were no hasidic communities in the western provinces of Czechoslovakia (Bohemia, Moravia, and Czech Silesia) that belonged to Austria prior to 1918. The center of Hasidism in Czechoslovakia was Subcarpathian Ruthenia, the easternmost sector of Slovakia, which bordered on Hungary, Romania, and Poland. This region was part of Hungary until 1919 and again during World War II, after which it was annexed by the Soviet Union. From Subcarpathian Ruthenia, Hasidism spread into other parts of Slovakia (including Bratislava, or Pressburg, the Slovak capital), which were strongholds of Hungarian Orthodoxy, as typified by the spiritual heirs of R. Moses Sofer (Schreiber; known as *Hatam Sofer* [1763–1839]). But the history of Hasidism in Czechoslovakia is basically that of Hasidism in Subcarpathian Ruthenia.

Historical background. Between the end of the eighteenth century and the period immediately following World War I, hasidim from neighboring Galicia migrated in a fairly constant stream to Subcarpathian Ruthenia as refugees from persecution in Poland. They perpetuated Galician-type Hasidism in their new homes, and many of them (and their descendants) remained adherents of rabbinic dynasties in Galicia (for example, Kosov, Vizhnitz, Zydaczov, and Belz).

Among the earliest hasidic rebbes from Galicia to move to sub-Carpathian Ruthenia was R. Mordecai of Nadvorna, a progenitor of the rabbinic dynasties of Ungvár (Uzhorod) and Huszt (see later). These two cities and Mukacevo (Munkacs) became major centers of Hasidism in Czechoslovakia. However, the majority of the hasidim lived in smaller towns and remote hamlets amid a gentile peasant population, which, until World War I, was overwhelmingly illiterate. Most of the rural hasidim were poor, eking out their existence as artisans or small shopkeepers; some obtained additional income from a small plot of land, a cow, or a couple of horses or sheep.

The hasidim of sub-Carpathian Ruthenia were known for their unquestioning devotion to their rebbes and their uncompromising opposition to such phenomena in modern Jewish life as secular education and Zionism. During the years when sub-Carpathian Ruthenia was part of the Czechoslovak Republic, the hasidim exerted a considerable influence upon the nonHasidic Orthodox and even helped revive the interest of assimilated Jews in the customs and traditions of Judaism.

Hasidic communities in Czechoslovakia.

1. Mukacevo (Munkacs). The most important hasidic community in Czechoslovakia,

Mukacevo, on the eve of World War II, had thirty synagogues, most of which were hasidic. The community was led by the Shapira (Spira) dynasty. The first hasidic rebbe in Mukacevo, R. Tzvi Elimelekh of Dynov (d. 1841), who came to the city in 1825, was a close kinsman of R. Elimelekh of Lejask. His grandson, R. Solomon Shapira (1832–1893) was the founder of the Munkacser dynasty. Solomon's son, R. Tzvi Elimelekh Shapira (1850–1913), first made the city an important hasidic center. His son and successor, R. Hayyim Elazar Shapira (1872–1937), was widely known not only for his halakhic and kabbalist erudition but also for his zealotry and for his frequent use of the *herem* (ban, anathema) against individuals and movements holding views opposed to his own. He fiercely fought against the establishment of the Hebrew high school in Mukacevo during the 1920s and violently opposed Zionism, which gained a substantial following in Subcarpathian Ruthenia during the period between the two world wars. R. Shapira forbade his adherents to vote for the Zionist "Jewish Party," which represented Czechoslovak Jewry as a "nationality group" in the country's parliament during the period of the republic; indeed, he gave active political support to the party in power at the time. He considered the members of the then anti-Zionist Agudat Israel as little better than Zionists.

When the rebbe of Belz, R. Issachar Dov Rokeah (1854–1927), and many of his followers came to Mukacevo in 1918 as refugees from war-torn Galicia, R. Shapira fought him bitterly, even appealing to the Czechoslovak government to have him expelled on the grounds that Mukacevo was not in need of two "chief rabbis." Rabbi Rokeah left the city of his own accord in 1921, but a large number of Belzer hasidim remained behind.

In 1927, the hasidim in Mukacevo launched a Yiddish-language weekly, *Yidishe Tzeitung*. Listed on the paper's masthead as editor was one Tzvi Elimelekh Kalish, but the real editorial work for some time was done by Leib Kanner, who, beginning in 1929, served also as ghost editor of the *Yidishe Shtime*, the city's Zionist weekly, whose official editor was one Tzvi Sternbuch.

The last rebbe of Mukacevo before the Holocaust was R. Hayyim Elazar Shapira's son-in-law, R. Barukh Joshua Yerahmiel Rabinowicz (b. 1913), a son of R. Nathan David of Parczew, who was of more conciliatory temperament than his predecessor. R. Rabbinowicz survived the Holocaust and is now living in Petach Tikva, Israel.

2. Ungvár (Uzhogorod). The first hasidic rebbe of Ungvár, capital of Subcarpathian Ruthenia, was R. Bercze Leifer (c. 1857–1923). His three sons—Meir, Hayyim Leb, and Reuben Menahem—had their own *bet midrashim*.

The great hasidic *klojz* built in 1908–1909 was considered a bulwark against the spread of Reform Judaism and as such enjoyed the support of R. Eleazar Loew (d. 1917), the city's Orthodox chief rabbi, who was himself not a hasid.

Among the hasidic leaders who lived in Ungvár at various times were R. Yaakov Tzvi Hirsch Waldmann and R. Itzhak Teitelbaum (son of R. Mordecai David of Sticzin), who eventually settled in Palestine and died in Safed.

The last rebbe of Ungvár before the Holocaust was R. Bercze Leifer's successor, Issachar Dov Lipschutz (c. 1879–1944), son of R. Aryeh (Leib) of Apt (Opatov) and grandson of R. Aryeh Leibusch Lipschutz (d. 1849). R. Lipschutz combined strict religious observance with concern for peace in all sectors of the Jewish community. He died in Auschwitz.

3. Huszt. The first Huszter rebbe was R. Jacob of Zydaczov, who came to Huszt in 1812. A later rebbe, R. Israel Jacob Leifer (d. 1929), was widely known as a miracle worker to whom even nonhasidim turned for advice. He was succeeded by his son, Shmuel Shmelke Leifer (d. 1934), who was admired for his fine singing voice and his fervor at worship. His successor, the last rebbe of Huszt before the Holocaust, was his brother, Issachar Berl, who was killed in Auschwitz.

Among the other well-known hasidic figures who lived in Huszt during the period between the two world wars was R. Mosheh Grunzweig from the nearby village of Lipsch, who settled in Huszt in the late 1930s. Grunzweig was known as an orator and as the composer of many *niggunim* and marches. He had his own *bet midrash* in Huszt but frequently visited remote mountain communities. He died in Auschwitz.

4. Bardejov. Situated near the Polish border, this town had a spa that was patronized by many hasidim. The rebbes of Bardejov were descendants of R. Hayyim Halberstam (1793–1876).

5. Sevljus (Nagyszöllös, Vinogradov). SW1For a period of fourteen years between the two world wars, this town was the home of R. Itzhak Eizik Weiss of Spinka (1875–1944), who had left Spinka (Szaplonca, Sapinka), a small town near the Polish border, after the outbreak of World War I and stayed for some time in Mukacevo before settling in Sevljus. In Sevljus, R. Weiss established a *yeshivah,* which he named *Imre Yosef,* after the major work written by R. Joseph Meir Weiss (1838–1909), the first Spinker rebbe. This *yeshivah* was attended by hundreds of students from all over Czechoslovakia as well as foreign countries.

R. Itzhak Eizik Weiss maintained a large court in Sevljus and was so greatly admired by the local populace that even Gentiles would ask his blessing. He had a fine voice and prayed with unusual fervor. It was said that whoever had not observed the rebbe of Spinka at worship during the High Holidays had never really seen a religious service. R. Weiss was deported to Auschwitz in the spring of 1944.

Influence of hasidim and their leaders. During the period between the two world wars, many young men from sub-Carpathian Ruthenia left home to study at *yeshivot* in other parts of Slovakia and in Hungary (for example, Bratislava, Trnava, Hunovice, Kosice, Dunajska Streda, Galanta). There they taught hasidic ideas and customs to nonhasidic fellow students from Hungary, Austria, and even Germany. As a result, a large number of "Westernized" Orthodox students returned to their homes from these *yeshivot* with a new respect for Hasidism and for the single-mindedness of its followers. The heads of the *yeshivot* found it necessary to modify their own attitudes and policies to meet the spiritual needs of their hasidic students.

The most successful results in this respect were achieved by R. Samuel David Ungar, head of the *yeshivah* of Trnava (Tyrnau), who later (in 1932) became chief rabbi of Nitra. He was able to satisfy the religious proclivities of hasidic as well as nonhasidic students in an exemplary fashion. The hasidic opposition to secular studies brought about a change in attitude at the famous *yeshivah* of Bratislava (Pressburg), which at times had shown a certain amount of permissiveness regarding the desire of students to obtain secular learning.

The external trappings of Hasidism (beard, *peyot, bekeshe,* and *shtreimel*) were increasingly adopted even by nonhasidic Orthodox Jews, who came to view them as a protection of sorts against the temptations of assimilation.

Large numbers of Jews not only from Czechoslovakia but also from other European countries were first brought into contact with Hasidism at the Bohemian spa of Marienbad (Marianské Lázne), which was favored as a health resort by many hasidic rebbes. The rebbes, who would arrive in state, escorted by dozens and at times even hundreds of followers, to "take the cure," would receive visits from hasidim and other Jews in need of advice on personal and business problems. Many visitors, including non-Orthodox Jews, were profoundly impressed with the hasidim and the rebbes they encountered in Marienbad.

By the 1930s Hasidism had begun to draw the interest also of young Jewish students from assimilated homes. Troubled by the rise of anti-Semitism throughout Europe, they sought to gain a better understanding of the "Jewish problem"; their search led a goodly number of them to a study of Orthodoxy and Hasidism. Many of them were greatly inspired by the writings of Jiri Langer (1894–1943), who had been raised in an assimilated Prague family and who, a year before the outbreak of World War I, had traveled to Galicia to live for a time among the hasidim there.

The Holocaust and the postwar world. The occupation of Subcarpathian Ruthenia and part of Slovakia by Hungary (1938–1939), the Nazi occupation of Czechoslovakia, the outbreak of World War II, and the Nazi occupation of Hungary brought the history of Hasidism in Czechoslovakia to a tragic end. Most of the Jews in the hasidic areas of Czechoslovakia were herded into ghettos and subsequently deported to the death camps. A number of hasidic leaders, notably R. Barukh Y. Y. Rabinowicz of Mukacevo, were active in rescue work.

During the Holocaust period, a legendary hasidic figure in sub-Carpathian Ruthenia was R. Samuel Moskowitz, who hailed from a village near Huszt and was known as the "hasidic partisan" because of his passive resistance to the German occupation. After Passover 1944, when the Jews of Huszt were herded into a ghetto for deportation, Moskowitz, his wife, and his children fled into the mountains. At night, they would make contact with peasants and gentile former neighbors to obtain food and to learn the latest news. Moskowitz died shortly after the liberation of sub-Carpathian Ruthenia, late in 1944. His widow, Eta, did what she could to help survivors secure food and shelter and to care for orphans whose parents had perished in the Holocaust. She eventually settled in Israel.

Following the annexation of sub-Carpathian Ruthenia by the Soviet Union in 1945, several thousand Jewish survivors–mostly hasidim–from the region fled into the western sector of Czechoslovakia. There, many of them were resettled temporarily in the Sudetenland region, from which the German inhabitants had been expelled. Many other hasidim fled to Hungary and Romania. Still others joined transports put together by *Berihah,* the underground organization that helped move Holocaust survivors from Europe to Palestine during the final years of the British mandate.

The hasidic communities of Czechoslovakia no longer exist, but remnants have settled in other countries, notably in the United States (largely in Brooklyn, New York) and Israel. Many Munkacser hasidim settled in Brooklyn's Borough Park section, where they founded Yeshivat Minhat Elazar (named after R. Hayyim Elazar Shapira). The *yeshivah* was headed (1976) by R. Moser Perlstein, whose father, Ezekiel, had been president of the Orthodox community in Mukacevo. Before coming to the United States, R. Perlstein had lived in Tel Aviv (where he was a leader of Tz'ire Agudat Israel) and in Montreal, Canada.

R. Aaron Moses Leifer, a survivor of the rabbinic dynasty of Huszt, lived (1976) in Brooklyn. R. Joseph Leifer, a grandson of R. Bercze Leifer, was in the United States, as were the grandsons of R. Itzhak Eizik Weiss of Spinka: Samuel Tzvi Horowitz (b. 1920) and Joseph Jacob Weiss (b. 1917). The hasidic community of Bardejov is memorialized in the *Divre Hayyim* synagogue in Jerusalem. The name of the synagogue commemorates the famous book written by R. Hayyim Halberstam, whose descendants had included the spiritual leaders of the hasidim of Bardejov.

G.H.

CZERNOWITZ (Romanian, Cernauti or Chernovtsy)–Czernowitz is the capital city of Bukovina, which, until 1918, was under Austrian rule, and from 1918 to 1940 was part of Romania.

Hasidism began to penetrate into Czernowitz at the end of the eighteenth century and was intensified with the appointment, in 1789, of R. Hayyim Tyrer (1770–1816), known as "R. Hayyim of Czernowitz," a disciple of R. Yehiel Michael of Zloczov, whose books are venerated by the hasidim.

R. Mendel of Kosov and his son, R. Hayyim, wielded great influence there, and one of the twelve sons of R. Barukh Hager settled there. It was also the home of R. Yehiel Michael Hager, the son of R. David of Zablatov, R. Feivish, son of R. Barukh of Vishnitz, R. Menahem Mendel of Horodov, and R. Menahem Nahum Friedman. R. Mosheh Leib Moskovitch and R. Ittamar Rosenbaum of Nadvorna, too, lived there.

The establishment of a printing press, and eventually of nine printing presses, led to the appearance of many hasidic works. Among the works printed there were *Beer Mayyim Hayyim* (1861), *Tzemach Tzaddik* (1892), and the last hasidic work printed there, *Or Yitzhak,* by R. Yitzhak Eizig Rosenbaum (1939).

There was a *yeshivah* there–*Beer Mayyim Hayyim*–established in 1923 by R. Alexander Zusya Portugal.

The community contained a rich variety of religious elements. By 1930 there were 46,000 Jews, 40 percent of the total population. The Jews were deported to Transnistria. Among the deportees were R. Mordecai Friedman of Boyan and R. Eliezer Hager. By April 1945, only 2,000 Jews remained alive.

Pinkas HaKehillot Romania, vol. 2, pp. 487–511.

M.S.

CZESTOCHOWA–A town, 125 miles southwest of Warsaw. It had a large hasidic community.

R. Issachar Wingot (d. 1789), who visited R. Israel, the Maggid of Kozienice, was the rabbi of the town. R. Avigdor Shapira (b.

1880) settled there in 1900. It was also the home of R. Pinhas Menahem Eliezer Justman (d. 10 *Kislev* 1921), a relative of the rabbi of Ger, and the home of R. Hanokh Heinokh Gad, the rabbi of Pilice.

In Czestochowa there were four *shtieblech* of Ger and a *shtiebl* of Alexander. Before World War II, 28,000 Jews lived there. When the Soviet army liberated the city, only 500 Jews were in the area.

D

DACHAU – One of the first Nazi concentration camps, ten miles (sixteen km) northwest of Munich. It was established on March 22, 1933. After Kristallnacht (November 9, 1938) more than 10,000 Jewish citizens and many hasidim living in Vienna were imprisoned there. The camp files reveal that more than 206,000 prisoners were held there in the years up to 1945. An experimental station under Dr. S. Rascher was set up in Block 5, where high-pressure and high-exposure experiments were practiced on defenseless prisoners. On April 29, 1945, the camp was liberated by the Seventh U.S. Army.

DAN, Joseph (b. 1935), professor of Kabbalah at Hebrew University – Born in Bratislava, he emigrated to Jerusalem in 1935, and from 1974 he has taught mysticism at the university. He is the author of approximately one hundred scholarly articles and nine books, including *The Hasidic Novel* (1966), *The Hasidic Story* (1975), *The Emergence of Mystical Prayer* in *Studies in Jewish Mysticism* (Cambridge, Ma: 1982, pp. 85–120), *Jewish Mysticism and Jewish Ethics* (University of Washington Press, 1986), and *Gershom Scholem and the Mystical Dimensions of Jewish History* (New York, 1988).

His doctoral thesis was on the theological thoughts of the German hasidim.

DANCE – From time immemorial, music and dance as religious ritual have been important in Judaism. The Bible records numerous examples, including a passage from Psalm 149:3: "Praise Him with psaltery and harp; praise Him with timbrel and dance." But it was with the birth of Hasidism in Eastern Europe that the real spirit of the Jewish dance was revived. As exemplified in their oral tradition and contemporary culture, to "serve the Lord with joy" is a vital aspect of hasidic worship. What better way to lift the soul toward the highest Heavens and to receive God's spirit than through the joyous expression of song and dance?

From the swaying of the head and trunk to the bouncing, shuffling steps of the feet, the hasidim hold on to each other's shoulders or *gartels* with a warm enthusiasm and communal bond characteristic of common folk. So unlike the graceful gliding and pretty poses of the elegant European court ballets, hasidic dance rings and processionals are no social diversion, but a form of prayer. As such, neither mixed dancing nor mixed praying is permitted, since it is said in Orthodox Jewish Law that men and women shall neither rejoice nor mourn together.

Hasidic literature is filled with proof of prohibitions and parables indicating the great role that dance has played in Hasidism's historical development. Legend has it that the Besht worshiped with fiery intensity, dancing ecstatically. The highest form of prayer, said he, is that which not only moves the soul but sets all the limbs in motion, as it is written: "All my bones shall say, Lord, who is like unto thee?" (Psalm 35:10). This manner of praying became the distinguishing outward feature of the Besht and his followers. Soon hundreds of occasions in the religious life of the people were accompanied by some form of dance or ritual movement, especially on Sabbath around the *tish* and on festivals after prayer.

Many a tale revolves around R. Aryeh Leib, the "Grandfather" of Shpola, who turned dance on the Sabbath into the most ecstatic of rituals. He was as light on his feet as a little child, it is told, and all who saw him were moved to tears and joy. But among all the disciples there was no one like R. Nahman of Bratzlav, the great-grandson of the Besht. He held that every limb of the body contained its own rhythm corresponding to the rhythm of a given melody. To this day, many dances are defined by the melodies and texts of the accompanying hasidic *niggunim*.

Indeed, life among the Jewish masses under the Polish and Russian dominations was full of suffering and sadness. But at weddings and gatherings, and even on the anniversaries of a rebbe's death, the hasidim made dancing an outlet for the downtrodden. Enthusiasm and enkindlement in worship, often achieved through frenzied body motions, singing, and dancing rather than strict talmudic learning, were welcomed as a foil for the austere, formalistic traits of much of the traditional Jewish observance associated with the rabbinic ideal of the day. From the crudest gesture to its purest form, this exaggerated manner of praying was considered a disgrace by the opponents of the hasidim, who looked upon the Besht with contempt and laughed at the actions of his following. Denounced as heretics, the hasidim were accused of threatening the stability of the old Jewish community and dishonoring the Sabbath with singing and dancing.

During 1771, in Shklov, the first anti-hasidic proclamation was formulated, condemning one rabbi–Abraham of Kalisk–for his undisciplined manner of worship, which consisted of swaying and dancing, singing, sighing and laughing, and, particularly, turning repeated somersaults before the ark as the mood seized him. That "they turn over like wheels, with the head below and the legs above . . ." was a practice repeatedly attacked in many of the anti-hasidic documents that followed. As stated in the *herem* of Brody in 1772, the hasidim were not allowed to dance and leap about, indulging in all sorts of acrobatics at weddings and circumcisions.

In this desperately critical time, R. Shneur Zalman of Liady, founder of *Habad* (Lubavitch) Hasidism, succeeded in developing a kind of compromise, an attempt to reconcile Rabbinism with Hasidism by incorporating both reason and feeling into the movement. Although his hasidim worshiped with fervor and joyous devotion, they did not exhibit the frantic boisterousness that made the hasidic synagogue ridiculous in the eyes of its critics. His system, which spread mainly in the north (Russia), met with strenuous opposition from the hasidim of southern Galicia, who held fast to the extreme emotionalism of the Besht. Shneur Zalman taught his hasidim to master their emotions–a discipline that penetrated to their tunes and their dances, emphasizing in them a more profound introspective quality in contrast to the outwardly frenzied characteristics of the south. Due, in part, to Shneur Zalman's struggle for reforms, Hasidism was officially sanctioned throughout Eastern Europe. Thus, the dance developed in direct relationship to the history of the movement, extending from its birth–in those times of great stress and struggle–through times of peace and acceptance as a part of the religious establishment.

Even today, differences between the philosophy and practices of the northern hasidim and their southern counterparts have served to distinguish the particular form and style of their movements. Influenced greatly by their respective masters, as well as the geographical environments from which they have come, each dynasty has developed its own repertoire of dances. In contemporary America, one may observe the meeting of Occident and Orient as variations of the Russian *kazatske* and the Romanian *horah*–the most common circle dance form among the hasidim–fuse with Israeli-Arabic influences and native American folk dances to produce a unique American-hasidic style. At weddings and *farbrengens*, on Purim, on Lag BaOmer, and especially on Simhat Torah, American hasidim dance with renewed vigor as a means of reflecting, reaffirming, and strengthening a "hasidic identity" within their society and with their Lord.

J. Gellerman, "The Ecstatic Dance of Prayer as Exemplified in the Oral Tradition, of Hasidism," pp. 1–24.

M. S. Geshuri, *HaNiggun VehaRikud BeHasidut* (Music and Dance in Hasidism).

J.G.

DANZIGER, Bezalel Yair, of Lodz

(1865–28 *Adar* 1924)–Third son of R. Yehiel, he studied under his father and his brother, R. Yerahmiel Israel Yitzhak. In 1914, he became rabbi in Lodz. He was buried in Alexandrov.

He was succeeded by his son, R. Abraham Yehudah, who was murdered by the Nazis on Rosh Hashanah 1943.

His son-in-law, R. Yitzhak Dombinsky, the rabbi of Makov, also perished in the Holocaust. R. Yehudah Moses Teihberg became rebbe of Alexander in Bene Berak in 1973 and changed his name to Danziger. An opposing group, however, appointed R. Yehiel Menahem Singer of New York as their rebbe of Alexander.

DANZIGER, Samuel Tzvi, of Alexander (d. on the eve of *Rosh Hodesh Heshvan* 1924) – Second son of R. Yehiel, he succeeded his brother, R. Yerahmiel Israel Yitzhak, in 1910. He was the author of *Tiferet Shmuel*, in which he stressed the importance of Torah, *tefillah*, and service to one's fellowmen. He declined to participate in the work of the Aguda.

He was survived by his son, Yehiel Menahem, who lived in New York.

DANZIGER, Shragai Feivel, of Alexander (d. Shemini Atzeret 1849), founder of the Alexander dynasty – Fourth and youngest son of Tzvi Hirsch (d. 1823), he was a staunch *mitnagged* who was related by marriage to R. Levi Yitzhak of Berdichev. Shragai Feivel was very young when he first met R. Levi Yitzhak, who prophesied a great future for the diligent young student. At the age of thirteen he was sent to study under R. Jacob ben Jacob Moses of Lissa, who had the highest regard for the new student, whom he entrusted with the copying of the manuscript of the second part of his *Nesivot HaMishpot*, a commentary on the *Shulhan Arukh*. On returning home to Warsaw, Shragai Feivel married Malkah. Subsequently he went to study under the "Seer of Lublin," R. Simhah Bunem of Przysucha, and under R. Isaac of Warka.

He was gifted with a beautiful handwriting and consequently became a scribe. The "Seer" was very impressed with the phylacteries written by Shragai Feivel and commented, "This young man has correctly divined the real meaning of this section." He eventually obtained rabbinical positions in Gombyn, Grice, and Makova. His first post lasted only four weeks, for his authority was challenged by hostile *mitnaggedim*. He was among the five distinguished disciples whom R. Simhah Bunem sent to Ostilla to the wedding of the son of R. Don ben Isaac of Radzvillov and the daughter of R. Joseph ben Mordecai of Neskhiz, to defend him against his opponents.

Shragai Feivel's son, Levi Yitzhak, married the daughter of R. Simhah Bunem. To fund the dowry, Tamarel Bergson paid him one thousand rubles to write a *Sefer Torah*. When Simhah Bunem died, Shragai Feivel became a disciple of his son, Abraham Moses.

Shragai Feivel's personal life was beset by tragedy. Apart from one son who became his successor, all his children died young. When R. Yitzhak of Warka died in 1848, he became Rebbe of Alexander, his reign lasting only six months. "The hardest task," he would say, "is to help people to become God-fearing." He interpreted the adage of Hillel (*Sukkah* 53a), "If I am here, everyone is here," to mean that it was not sufficient for a leader to serve God in seclusion. A leader must take care that "everybone is here" and that all the people are reaching out to their Father in heaven.

He died on Shemini Atzeret 1849. His wife died the following Hoshanah Rabba. He was buried in Makova. Several of his responsa were published in *Pri Hadash* by R. Hayyim Leib Halevi of Kaluszyn and in *Kobetz Bet Shmuel* (1932). Most of his discourses are quoted in the work *Yismah Yisrael* by R. Yerahmiel Israel Yitzhak Danziger (Lodz, 1911).

A. I. Bromberg, *Migdolei HaHasidut*, vol. 4, *Admorei Alexander*, pp. 7–30.

DANZIGER, Yehiel, of Alexander (1848–14 *Shevat* 1894) – He was the only surviving son of R. Shragai Feivel. He married Rosa Mindel of Przysucha.

He was a frail child whose health caused great concern. "Leave him in my hands," R. Yitzhak of Warka told his worried parents, "and I will convert him into a precious vessel." Yehiel spent his boyhood in the home of the rebbe of Warka, a memorable experience for the susceptible boy. He was an assiduous student. To keep himself awake he would place his feet in icy cold water. For a time he studied in the *Bet HaMidrash* that was formerly used by the "Holy Jew" of Przysucha. He visited R. Leib Eger of Lublin and R. Yehudah Aryeh Alter, the *Sefat Emet*. Yehiel became rabbi first in Torshin and then in Grice (where his father was rabbi for a time). He inherited his father's mild disposition. Despite constant provocation by his opponents, he remained serene, refusing to retaliate. For the sake of harmony and peace he would bear all indignities.

He was, however, unyielding and uncompromising when religious matters were involved. He was no respecter of persons. He lived in a state of perpetual poverty. Every day he distributed among the poor all the money that came into his house. At Warka he learned the virtue of brevity. He delivered few discourses and spoke in a concise and forceful manner.

After the death of R. Mendel of Warka, Yehiel became a disciple of R. Dov Berish of Biala, and it was only after the death of his master on 25 *Sivan* 1870 that he reluctantly became rebbe of Alexander. He acquired the *Bet HaMidrash* originally used by R. Heinokh Levine, and his home remained the headquarters of all Alexander rebbes until it was destroyed in the Holocaust.

Like the rebbe of Warka, he believed in joy (*simhah*) and urged his hasidim not to brood over their misfortunes, for joy drives away evil urges. He lived on the stipend he received as the rabbi of the town. In his last will and testament, printed in his work *Tiferet Yisrael* and covering four pages, he stressed that honoring father and mother is a precept that applies even after the death of one's parents. He exempted his children from fasting on the day of his *yahrzeit*. He forbade them to put the title of "Rabbi" or "Rebbe" on his tombstone, and he requested that no sepulcher be erected over his grave. Instead, he requested his hasidim to study *Mishnah* or recite Psalms.

R. Yehiel left three daughters and three sons. His sons were: R. Yerahmiel Israel Yitzhak, the author of *Tiferet Yisrael*; R. Samuel Tzvi, the *Tiferet Shmuel*; and R. Bezalel Yair of Lodz. He never wrote down any of his discourses, but his sayings were quoted in the work *Yismah Yisrael* (Lodz, 1911). R. Abraham Bornstein of Sochaszev called R. Yehiel "King of the Tzaddikim."

A. I. Bromberg, *Migdolei HaHasidut*, vol. 4, *Admorei Alexander*, pp. 32–64.

DANZIGER, Yerahmiel Israel Yitzhak, of Alexander (1853–*Rosh Hodesh Shevat* 1910) – Son of R. Yehiel, he was born in Torshin. His mother, Rosa Mindel, was the daughter of a hasid of Przysucha. He married Deborah, the daughter of R. Dov (Berke) Cheitschke, a hasid of Parysov. The marriage was not blessed with children. R. Jacob Aryeh Guterman of Radzymin told him that his soul was the reincarnation of R. Hayyim Attar, who had also been childless.

He was renowned for his mastery of the Talmud and rabbinic lore, and it was said that he knew the whole *Zohar* by heart. He corresponded with halakhic authorities, such as R. Jacob Ridbaz of Safed. The rebbe visited R. Sholem Rokeah of Belz, R. Hayyim Halberstam of Zanz, R. Abraham Jacob Friedman of Sadgora, and R. Abraham Twersky of Turiysk.

On 14 *Shevat* 1894, he succeeded his father. At first he was reluctant to become rebbe, for he yearned to settle in the Holy Land. "To visit the rebbe for one Sabbath," hasidim used to say, "provides inspiration for a whole year." The rebbe was greatly troubled by the many personal, social, and political problems that beset his flock. People entered his study with heavy hearts but left his presence comforted. He stressed the need for continual striving to achieve perfection. He also taught that modesty and humility are the most important attributes, since they are conducive to the fear of God and to the love of one's neighbor.

In a letter dated 6 *Elul* 1907, he urged his followers neither to read heretical works nor to engage teachers who were not imbued with the fear of God. The rebbe, in a letter to his followers, urged them to study diligently and make progress in the Torah. "Concentrate on the *Rishonim* [the early medieval authorities] and do not go in for *pilpul*. The Hebrew word *besimhah* [with joy] is equivalent to *mahshavah* [thought]."

The gentle, mild-mannered rebbe never became embroiled in controversies. When R. Gershon Heinokh Leiner reintroduced the "Cord of Blue" into the ritual fringes, the innovation caused considerable acrimony among the sages. The rebbe of Alexander refused to take sides.

However, when Dr. J. Jung (1891–1960) proposed to establish a secular school in Galicia, the rebbe expressed strong disapproval. In a lengthy letter, he asked his followers not to be led astray by Dr. Jung. "Bring up your children in the ways of the Torah and do not try new paths."

He was known for his phenomenal memory. He not only remembered everything he read but also the names of the thousands of his followers and the names of their children. He refused to take *pidyonot*. He sent money to Jerusalem for the restoration of the grave of R. Hayyim Attar on the Mount of Olives. His brother and brother-in-law published his discourses on the Torah under the title *Yismah Yisrael* (Lodz, 1913).

A. I. Bromberg, *Migdolei HaHasidut*, vol. 4, *Admorei Alexander*.

DANZIGER, Yitzhak Menahem Mendel, of Alexander (1880–1943) Son of R. Samuel Tzvi – For sixteen years he studied under his father and under his uncle. When his father died in 1924, he succeeded him as rebbe and served for eighteen years. He encouraged the development of the Alexander *yeshivot Yismah Yisrael* in Alexander and Lodz. His followers were required to make regular contributions toward the maintenance of the *yeshivot*. In Lodz alone there were twenty-five *shtieblech* of Alexander. The rebbe stressed the significance of congregational worship and urged his followers to attend regularly for study as well as prayer. He encouraged them to establish *Gemilat Hasadim* societies to help the needy hasidim. He visited his *yeshivot* regularly. Unlike his father, he merely functioned as the rebbe and not as the rabbi of Alexander. His son-in-law, R. Isaac Meir Singer, was the rabbi. Neutral in politics, he did not associate with the Aguda, but he supported the *Beis Yaakov* movement. His discourses were published in *Akedat Yitzhak* (1953).

At the outbreak of World War II, he and his ten children lived in Warsaw. He refused to leave for the Holy Land, since it would have meant abandoning his followers. For a time he worked in Abraham Handel Shultz's shoe factory in the ghetto. He was murdered in Treblinka together with his six sons-in-law: R. Alter Hayyim Baumgarten of Lodz; R. Elimelekh Shapira; R. Jacob, the son of the rabbi of Krimlov; R. Menahem, the grandson of the rabbi of Komarno; R. Hayyim; and R. Solomon David Joshua of Slonim. His grandson was R. Judah Moses Teihberg, the rebbe of Alexander in Bene Berak.

A. I. Bromberg, *Migdolei HaHasidut*, vol. 4, *Admorei Alexander*.

DAVID OF MAKOV (ca. 1741–1814), critic of Hasidism – Son of Ben Zion Yehezkel, he was born in Rovno, and from 1772 until his death he was *dayan* of Makov, Poland. He was probably a disciple of R. Menahem Mendel of Vitebsk. David became not only a *mitnagged* but also a fierce opponent of Hasidism. He gained renown for his zealous opposition to Beshtian Hasidism, which he accused of neglecting Torah study, disparaging scholars and *mitzvot*, and even nurturing pagan and Shabbatean elements. He sharply criticized the hasidic masters, including the Baal Shem Tov himself. "I remember that he was not known as a scholar (*lamdan*) but only as a Baal Shem who wrote amulets."

His anti-hasidic writings are *Zemir Aritzim*, a rhyming satire (Warsaw, 1798), and *Shever Posh'im*, known also under the titles *Zimrat Am HaAretz* (manuscript, Friedland Collection, Leningrad) and *Zot Torat HaKena'ot* (manuscript, Oxford, Bodleian Library). The Turberg manuscript without its title page is in the National Library, Jerusalem. *Shever Posh'im* was published in its entirety in 1970 (M. Wilensky, in *Hasidim U'Mitnaggedim*, vol. 2, pp. 51–188).

The treatise, one of the most important in the polemical literature of hasidim and *mitnaggedim*, is of two parts: Part one is a collection of excommunication bans, proclamations, testimonies, and letters against the hasidim, accompanied by the author's own negative comments. The second part is primarily a critical evaluation of hasidic philosophy, especially attacking the "Elevation of Strange Thoughts" during prayer. This part also contains a negative description of the courts of the hasidic *tzaddikim*, particularly the court of R. Hayyim Heikel of Amdur.

In his bitter critique, David makes the following points:

1. The warnings by Elijah, Gaon of Vilna, against the "idolatrous" tendencies of Hasidism should be heeded by rabbis and communal leaders.

2. The innovations of the hasidim should be resisted.

3. The journeys by the hasidim to the "courts" of the *tzaddikim* involve great expense, which adds to the heavy financial burdens of the impoverished masses.

He also criticized R. Levi Yitzhak of Berdichev, R. Hayyim Heikel of Amdur, R.

Israel of Kozienice, and R. Jacob Isaac of Lublin. His campaign against the hasidic leaders was intensified when R. Hayyim Heikel left Amdur and settled in Makov, where the latter's son was an influential personality.

Two letters by R. David and his *Ethical Will* constitute a significant source for the history of the controversy. R. David was the likely author of an additional anti-hasidic pamphlet, *Masah U'Merivah*, which was destroyed by the hasidim.

He was hated by the hasidim. After his death, the hasidim of Makov desecrated his grave. His son, Ezekiel, the rabbi of Radzymin, who assisted him in his war on the hasidim, died a few months after the death of his father.

R. David's unpublished commentaries on the Bible and the *Mishnah* were destroyed in a fire in Serock in 1893.

A. R. Malachi, *Jubilee Volume of Hadoar*, pp. 286–300.

M. Wilensky, *Tarbitz*, pp. 396–404.

——, *Hasidim U'Mitnaggedim*, vol. 2, pp. 9–250, 350–360.

M.W.

DAVID OF MIKOLEYEV (d. 25 *Shevat* 1800) – One of the early disciples of the Besht, who called him "a *tzaddik*, very saintly and very revered." He is also mentioned in *Hesed LeAvraham* by Abraham of Polotsk and in *Turei Zahav* by Benjamin of Zalocze.

DAVID of Talnoye (1808–10 *Iyyar* 1882) – Son of R. Mordecai of Chernobyl, he married the daughter of R. Israel of Ostrog-Czarni. After living for five years in Vasilkov, where all his children died in infancy, he settled in Talna (Talnoye), Ukraine.

Like the rebbes of Ruzhyn and Sadgora, he lived in luxury, with servants to attend to his palatial residence. He had a golden chair with the inscription "*David Melekh Yisrael, Hai Vekayam*." He was a great lover of music, and musicians, such as Nisan Belzer, were among his entourage.

His son, Mordecai, died in his father's lifetime, and he was succeeded by his grandson, R. Nahum, who celebrated his *bar mitzvah* seven days after the death of his grandfather.

He was the author of *Magen David*, on the Pentateuch (Zhitomir, 1852); *Birkhat David* (Zhitomir, 1862); and *Kehillat David* (Lublin, 1882).

D. L. Meckler, *Fun Chernobyl bis Talna*.

DEATH – In Judaism the emphasis is on life and on the fact that there is life after death. Life and death are different aspects of the same reality, and the hasidim endorse the view of R. Meir that the biblical verse "And it was good" applied to death as much as to life. To the hasidim, the world to come is not an unknown country but a well-charted territory. In their "second life," man will be compensated for his sufferings in his brief earthly existence.

Belief in the resurrection of the dead is a fundamental principle in Judaism as a whole, as it is in Hasidism. In the hour of his death, the Besht said, "Now I know the purpose for which I was created." When his son wept, the Besht told him, "Do not cry, my son, for I am passing through one door in order to enter through another." The Besht maintained that "a *tzaddik*'s soul does not at first ascend to the upper regions of paradise. At first, it resides in the lower Eden. Only by stages is it conducted to higher realms."

The rebbe of Kotzk said that death "is merely moving from one home to another. If we are wise, we will make the latter the more beautiful home." When R. Simhah Bunem of Przysucha was on his deathbed, his wife wept bitterly. "Why do you weep?" he asked her. "The purpose of my whole life was to learn to die."

Similarly, R. Moses Leib of Sasov said, "If you believe that this world is the roadway to eternal joy, how can you grieve over the prospect of dying? Bitter is death to the sinner, but sweet to the Godly."

"Why should I not rejoice?" asked R. Elimelekh of Lejask before he died. "I am now allowed to leave this world below, in order to enter the higher worlds of eternity."

"Why does a man fear to die?" asked the rebbe of Ger. "Is he not returning to his Father in heaven?" According to many rebbes, death is a *mitzvah* and thus desirable when it comes.

When R. Nahman of Bratzlav visited a dying hasid, he said, "What? Worries over death? There is a much nicer world there." In assuring him of a better world beyond the grave, he was preparing the hasid to accept his death with serenity.

After a hasid's death, it was the rebbe's duty to console the bereaved, and it was also his duty to purify the soul of the deceased. A man once told the rebbe of Belz that he wished to die like a good Jew. The rebbe replied that such a wish was wrong: "It is like Bilaam praying: 'May my soul die the death of the righteous.' It is far more important to concentrate on living like a good Jew, and the rest will follow naturally."

L. I. Newman, *The Hasidic Anthology*, pp. 68–73.

DEPRESSION AND DESPAIR–

R. Nahman's counsel to his hasidim, "For Heaven's sake, do not despair," is simple and to the point. He stressed that depression weakens one, that it presages illness, that it leads to heartache, that it brings many afflictions to a man, and that God does not abide with a man of sadness.

Yet in the *shtetl*, sadness and melancholy were far from rare. It was the appearance of joy that was difficult to explain. Powerlessness, inadequacy, and hopelessness easily become chronic and pathological. To live for a long time under conditions that would bring on grief, if they were to occur suddenly, soon causes one's mental condition to become chronic.

The Besht is quoted as saying: "There is a great rule in the service of the Creator: guard yourself from sadness in every possible way. Weeping is very bad. A person must serve in joy, but if the weeping is occasioned by joy, it is very good. Sadness is a great frustrator of divine service. It is much better to serve His blessed name with joy and without austere means. For they cause sadness."

There are many more statements of this nature in hasidic literature. Because of Hasidism's preoccupation with joy, rebbes were concerned when hasidim were brought before them suffering from deep depression and sadness.

Hasidism distinguishes between *atzvut* and *merirut*–sadness and bitterness. *Atzvut* was occasioned by the same misapplied inertia that characterized the evil aspect of the element of earth. *Merirut* was seen as the bitterness that resulted from grief over a reality that, when faced, tended to move one to do something about it.

The rebbe of Koretz used to say that "a person of melancholy may be known by these signs: a lack of desire to visit the Holy Land, a lack of interest in holy studies, an inability to serve God through everything he hears and knows, and an inability to shed tears."

Z. M. Schachter, *The Yehidut–A Study of Counselling in Hasidism*, p. 411.

Z.M.S.

DER NISTER,

pseudonym of Pinhas Kaganovich (1884–1950), Yiddish writer, was born in Berdichev (Volhynia). His father was a Korshever hasid, and his brother Aaron, who joined the Bratzlaver hasidim, exerted a great influence on him and served as a model for the character of Luzi in Der Nister's only novel, *Di Mishpokhe Mashber* (The Mashber Family) (Moscow, 1939 and 1948).

To escape military service, Der Nister moved to Zhitomir, where he lived for twelve years under an assumed name. This was the occasion for choosing his literary pseudonym, "Der Nister," meaning "the concealed, the hidden one." The choice of this pen name also reflects his mystical inclinations, the Hebrew word *nistar* being closely associated with the kabbalistic interpretation of the Bible. His early works *Hekher fun der Erd* (Higher than the Earth) (Warsaw, 1910) and *Gezang un Gebet* (Song and Prayer) (Kiev, 1912), on the borderline between prose and poetry, use motifs from the Book of Genesis, *Sefer Yetzirah*, the *Zohar*, and Christian and Greek mythology. The hasidic influence is also discernible in his writing *Gedanken un Motiven* (Thoughts and Motives) (Vilna, 1906) and *Di Yiddishe Welt* (Vilna, 1939).

In 1912, Der Nister joined the Kiev group of modernist Yiddish writers, with David Bergelson, David Hofshteyn, and others. The Russian Revolution supported Yiddish culture and literature, and Der Nister started publishing his symbolist tales. However, the civil war and the pogroms in the Ukraine forced the Yiddish writers into exile, and Der Nister moved to Berlin in 1920. There, he was the coeditor of the journal *Milgroym* (1922–1924), devoted to Jewish literature, art, and folklore, and he published the two volumes of his collected tales, *Gedakht* (Imagined) (1922–1923). His tales are much influenced by the folktale and the hasidic tale, in particular the tales of R. Nahman of Bratzlav. Other influences were old Yiddish literature (the *Bove-bukh* and the *Kav Ha-*

Yasher) and Russian symbolism. The trend in Jewish and European literature at the beginning of this century involved a return to national traditions, folklore, and primitivism: Berdyczewski, Bialik, and Rawnitzki collected *aggadot*; Buber rewrote hasidic tales. Following the Yiddish writer Y. L. Peretz, Der Nister used the form of the hasidic tale, creating modernist kabbalistic allegories with a haunting incantatory style. His heroes are often hermits pursuing undefined research, who are tempted by demons and witches.

In 1926, Der Nister returned to the Soviet Union, which then seemed to be the only state that guaranteed the survival of Yiddish culture. He continued publishing his tales in the journals available to political fellow travelers. They were collected in *Fun mayne Giter* (from My Estates) (Kharkov, 1928) and in a second edition of *Gedakht* (Kiev, 1929).

He was a leading Yiddish literary figure in the Soviet Union before the Second World War, but he was sharply criticized by the Soviet censors, who vilified his "poor-*yeshivah*-boy moralizing, reeking of green mold of decaying remnants of sacred books" and disparaged his ideas as "empty metaphysics, mysticism, and idealism."

His last tales describe his renunciation of the elitist aesthetics of symbolism. After several years of silence, he began working secretly on his great novel, *Di Mishpokhe Mashber*, in which he describes the world of the Bratzlaver hasidim in Berdichev around 1870. This apparently realistic novel bears witness to his fascination for the lost world of the seekers and hermits of his former tales.

Together with all of the major Yiddish writers, Der Nister was jailed in 1948. He died in prison, thus escaping the fate of his fellow writers, who were executed in 1952.

Dalphine Bechtel, *Der Nister, Sortilèges Contes*.

D.B.

DEUTSCH, Hananiah Yom Tov Lipa (1908–1990), Helmetzer rebbe, Williamsburg – Son of R. Samuel Aaron Deutsch of Keresztur, he studied under R. David Dov Meisels of Ujhely, R. Hayyim Mordecai Jacob of Miskolc, and R. Joseph Tzvi Duschinsky of Huszt. He married the daughter of R. Joseph Abeles of Shalui. He became the rabbi of Dabshina, and after World War II settled in Cleveland, Ohio, and then moved to Williamsburg, where he established a *Bet HaMidrash*. He had a keen interest in *mikvaot*, maintaining that the cause of the Holocaust had been the neglect and laxity of the strict observance of family purity. He devoted his energies to the establishment of *mikvaot* and traveled throughout the United States, Canada, and South America for this purpose. He also visited Europe and Israel, setting up a *kollel taharat yom tov* in Jerusalem for the study of the Laws of Family Purity.

His magnum opus is *Taharat Yom Tov*, in ten volumes (Brooklyn, New York, 1948 and 1963–1971), dealing with family purity. He published *Yesod Yosef*, by R. Joseph ben Solomon HaDarshan of Posen, an ethical treatise on sexual purity, with his own commentary, and a commentary on the *Mishnah, Zera Yitzhak*, by R. Isaac Chajes (Brooklyn, New York, 1960), with the genealogical details of the author.

He was survived by seven daughters and was succeeded by his son-in-law R. Aaron Isaiah Pekter.

R. Isaac Tzvi Deutsch, a brother of the Helmetzer rebbe, was rabbi in Sendre in Hungary and later in Vienna, and he is now in Detroit, Michigan.

A.S.

DEUTSCH, Samuel Aaron (1882–26 *Sivan* 1944) – Son-in-law of R. Shalom Joseph Weinberger, a descendant of Zydaszov. He studied under R. Hananiah Yom Tov Lipa of Sighet and R. Tzvi Hirsch Spira of Munkacz. He was a *shohet* in Keresztur and was known as a great talmudist. All his writings, including a description of the customs and rituals of Munkacz, were destroyed in the Holocaust. One complete work, *Shem Aharon* on the Pentateuch, has been preserved and now awaits publication.

A.S.

DEUTSCHLAENDER, Leo (1885–9 *Av* 1935), educationist – His father, Nathan, died when Leo was five years old, and he was brought up by Dr. E. C. Beberfeld, formerly rabbi of Karlsruhe.

After Lithuania attained independence, Leo became the head of its Jewish educational institutions. In 1922 he was appointed director of the *Keren HaTorah* by the Aguda. He helped Sarah Schenierer to expand the *Bet Yaakov* schools and to establish the *Bet Yaakov* Seminary in Cracow.

J. Grunfeld-Rosenbaum, "Sarah Schenierer," in *Jewish Leaders*, p. 426ff.

DEVEKUT – Attachment to God, cleaving to Him in thought at all times, having God in the mind constantly – this idea is found in the work of a number of medieval authors, especially in Nahmanides' comment: "To love the Lord your God, to walk in all His ways, and to cleave unto Him" (Deuteronomy 11:22), and in Maimonides' description of what it means to be with God (*Guide for the Perplexed*, III, 51).

In the earlier sources, however, *devekut* is an ideal capable of realization only by the greatest of saints after arduous training. In Hasidism, it is an ideal to be striven for by the average Jew, though the hasidic thinkers generally add that it is only the *tzaddik* who can maintain life always at this level and that his followers can be led to its approximation only through their attachment to the *tzaddik*. The hasidic emphasis is a direct result from the hasidic idea (see PANTHEISM) that the only true reality is God, which is implied in monotheism, so that a failure to achieve *devekut* is really a kind of idolatry.

The hasidic teachers urged people to have this state of attachment even when studying the Torah, to which the *mitnaggedim* retorted that it is impossible to have God always in mind when studying adequately the difficult talmudic arguments that demand complete concentration.

It is by virtue of the doctrine of *devekut* that Hasidism urges man to engage in worldly things, that is, to use these as steppingstones toward the realization of his aim. The true hasid sees only the divine element in all things. Even when hasidim partake of the world, their thought is not on the material delights and pleasures but on the holy sparks by which they are nourished. In many a hasidic tale of the saints, the *tzaddikim* engage in what appears to be childish, worldly, or frivolous conduct, but in reality their minds are on the *yihudim* (unifications), the source of all these things in the upper world. In an oft-quoted hasidic saying, attributed to a Midrash, Enoch was a cobbler, and whenever he stitched the upper part of the shoes he was repairing to the lower part, he performed unifications.

The hasidic masters appreciated that there is an ebb and flow in the life of *devekut* and that there are bound to be times of "littleness of soul," when all is dry, when God is far from present in the mind. The hasid must not be deterred by such a fall from *devekut*. On the contrary, it is only through this descent that the hasid can later rise to even closer degrees of attachment.

R. Moses Hayyim Efraim of Sudzilkov (d. 1800), the grandson of the Besht, reads this idea into the narrative of Jacob's dream in Genesis 28:10–12 ("*Va-yetzei*," in *Degel Mahanei Efraim* [Jerusalem, 1963], pp. 40–41). He quotes his grandfather as commenting: "The living creatures (*hayyot*) run to and fro" (Ezekiel 1:14), which he reads as "vitality" (*hiyyut*). Man's vital nearness to God is not possible all the time. The angels on Jacob's ladder are, in fact, the *tzaddikim*, and even these ascend and descend. Yet the purpose of their descent is for an even more elevated rise.

A saying quoted by a number of early hasidic teachers in the name of the Baal Shem Tov is on the verse "Lest you turn aside and serve other gods" (Deuteronomy 11:16). This is interpreted as meaning that whenever one turns aside from *devekut*, one is, in fact, guilty of idolatry. It further means that the ideal of *devekut* was held up for emulation even by the ordinary folk. There is much evidence that even those who were among the early hasidim at least tried to cultivate the ideal, using – since they were incapable of attaining it by purely spiritual exercises – such aids as tobacco and alcohol.

G. Scholem, "*Devekut*, or Communion with God," in *The Messianic Idea in Judaism*, pp. 203–227.

L.J.

DEVOTIONAL LITERATURE – Hasidism generated renewed interest in popular devotional literature, such as *Mesillat Yesharim*, by R. M. H. Luzzatto, and *Menorat HaMaor*, by Yitzhak Aboab.

The Besht directed his followers to engage in the study of books of *Musar*: "The evil desire (*Yetzer HaRa*) does not attempt to persuade man not to study at all, knowing that people would not listen to him, but the evil desire induces people not to study the kinds of works that teach piety, like the books of *Musar*. . . . It is essential to study *Musar* every day, be it much or little."

The pietistic works the hasidim preferred were not those that expatiated on the horrors of hell, like *Shevet Musar*, *Reshit Hokhmah*, and *Kav HaYashar*, but those that breed the spirit of yearning for the love of God. In addition to the emphasis on joyousness, the hasidim introduced the practice of telling stories concerning the *tzaddikim*. R. Nahman of Bratzlav even composed a special prayer for his hasidim, in which they petition God so as to be able to tell stories of the *tzaddikim*.

R. Yitzhak of Neskhiz used to read every day the Besht's letter describing "ascents of the soul." He regarded it as of equal importance to the *mitzvah* of putting on *tefillin*. The Besht is reported to have said that he who engages in relating the praises of the *tzaddikim* is like one who describes the wonders of the divine chariot (*maasei merkavah*). Some rebbes, like R. Nahman of Bratzlav and R. Elimelekh of Lejask, composed brief meditations and prayers for their followers. The hasidim of Przysucha and Kotzk used to study the works of R. Judah ben Bezalel, the *Maharal*. Many of the old books of *Musar* were reprinted in Slavuta by the Shapira brothers.

S. A. Horodetsky, *HaHasidut VeHaHasidim*, pp. 8–34.

J.B.A.

DIN TORAH MIT GOTT – A Hebrew/Yiddish folk song, also subtitled "R. Levi Yitzhak Berdichever's Kaddish" or the "Rebbe's Kaddish."

It is attributed to R. Levi Yitzhak of Berdichev, who, on a Rosh Hashanah before the recitation of *Kaddish*, chanted this personal prayer. The popular melody is based on the *Neilah Kaddish* theme as well as on the concluding motive of the Festival *Amidah*. A version has been notated by N. Kipnis in his *140 Folks-Lieder*.

DINUR, Benzion (1884–1973), historian – Benzion Dinur (formerly Dinaburg) specialized in the study of East European Jewry in the late medieval and early modern period. In his research for his book *BeMifnei HaDorot* (Jerusalem, 1955), he made a notable contribution to the understanding of the rise of Hasidism.

He demonstrated that the social roots of Hasidism derived from the deep discontent of the masses with the establishment. In the middle of the eighteenth century, the structure of Jewish self-government had broken down. In the local *kehillot*, power was vested in small cliques. The rules of elections were so indirect that the ruling circles were rarely upset. Frequently, the rabbi made common cause with the rich *parnassim*. The office of rabbi was often obtained by bribing the leading *parnassim*. The mass of the people was exploited.

The hasidic movement spread so rapidly because it provided an alternative organizational pattern for the religious communal life of the disaffected masses. Instead of the local rabbi, the rebbe became the supervisor and the protector of the community. It was the rabbi's aides who became the distributors of charity.

Dinur emphasized the role played by the small pre-Beshtian groups of kabbalistic hasidim in Brody and Medziborz. They busied themselves with the study of the *Zohar* and Kabbalah, rather than the Talmud and the Codes. They adopted certain patterns of conduct, such as chanting midnight lamentations, doing frequent ablutions in *mikvaot*, wearing white garments on the Sabbath, eating common meals on festive occasions, instituting impassioned modes of prayer, and fasting from Sabbath to Sabbath.

Dinur believed in letting source material speak for itself. Much of his work consisted in the collation of sources.

Sefer Dinuburg, ed. Y. Baer, J. Guttman, and M. Shur, pp. 447–483.

J.B.S.

DISHONESTY AND DECEPTION – Deception and dishonesty are condemned by Hasidism, as by all Jews. "He who cheats in even a single matter," said the rabbi of Warka, "is far from all righteousness. But he who is truthful is near to all goodness."

A special kind of deception was practiced by the hasidim of the dynasties of Przysucha and Kotzk. They would pretend to neglect their religious duties in order to hide their piety. The more their fellow Jews scorned them, the more pleased they were. In this spirit, they interpreted the command "Thou shalt not steal" to mean "Thou shalt not steal from yourself, let alone from your fellowmen."

Some hasidic dynasties made a special point to prod their followers to search their souls for any shred of untruth. R. Menahem Mendel of Kotzk was noted for his analytic probing of the psyches of his followers. He recognized that conscious honesty is not enough. He insisted that his followers should not recite their morning prayers before they reached that degree of piety that the psalmist had in mind when he wrote, "All my bones will say, 'who is like Thee, O Lord' " (Psalms 35:10).

The hasidim of Kotzk were trained to question themselves again and again (*sich iberfregen*). To a rabbi who was troubled by dissension in his community, the rebbe said, "It is because you are not at peace with yourself that the community is in uproar. The true leader is always in search of deeper levels of truth, and his community responds to his leadership."

A. J. Heschel, *Kotzk*, vol. 1.

J.B.A.

DIVINE PROVIDENCE–The concept of a personal God is fundamental to religion. God not only created the world but remains continuously involved with all His creatures. Indeed, the Divine involvement and attentiveness sustains all that exists: if it were to cease even momentarily, the world would revert to its original naught.

The Midrash thus interprets the verse "For ever, God, Your word stands fast in heaven" (Psalms 119:89) to refer to the ten utterances by means of which God created the world. They "stand for ever," that is, they are constantly proclaimed even as when originally stated, thereby sustaining the existence of heaven and earth.

Creatio ex nihilo, therefore, implies of itself the principle of Divine Providence. This principle is much discussed by religious philosophers. They distinguish between *hashgahah kelalit* (general Providence) and *hashgahah peratit* (individual Providence). *Hashgachah kelalit* relates basically to the preservation of species, their role and their purpose in the overall plan for creation, which involves the species but not necessarily any of its particular members. *Hashgahah peratit* relates to the specific events of individual entities.

The general concensus in Jewish thought, of both rationalists and mystics, is that *hashgahah peratit* applies only to humans; for all others there is but *hashgahah kelalit*. Moreover, even with humans (each of which is, in effect, a species on his own), the *hashgahah peratit* is relative or proportional to the individual's human perfection. The greater one's moral virtues and merits, the closer one is to God, thus benefiting from a more individualized watching and protection of the specific events and affectations in one's life.

The hasidic view differs. R. Israel Baal Shem Tov taught that *hashgahah peratit* relates to all beings. Proportionate *hashgahah* is not rejected but applied essentially to the qualitative and manifest aspects of Providence. Every created entity, however, whether human or nonhuman, is guided and directed by *hashgahah peratit*. The hasidic view may be summarized as follows:

All the specific motions of the various species occur by individual Providence of the Creator. This Providence is in fact the very vitality and sustaining force of each being. Moreover, the specific motions of each being has a bearing upon the general purpose of the total creation. For example, any motion of a blade of grass growing in the depth of a forest where no man may ever have trodden is directed by Divine Providence, which determines that blade's life span and all its occurrences. Each of these particular occurrences, in conjunction with all those of the uncountable other creatures (of the mineral, vegetative, animal, and human strata), contributes to the ultimate Divine intent for the creation of the universe.

Every human, from the greatest to the smallest, must realize that everything happening to him, from seemingly chance meetings to whatever he happens to see or hear, is by *hashgahah peratit*. There is no such thing as coincidence. Everything is a Divinely guided event that one is to ponder in order to discover and extract its meaning and purpose: it is a message from Above to improve or sublimate everyone and everything involved in that event.

To perceive anything negative or sinful is an indication that this evil is present in oneself, like looking into a mirror and seeing oneself. The perceiver need not have committed that wrong in the same way or fashion that it is observed, but is at least guilty of an analogous transgression. Even a saintly person may see or hear about a serious offense to indicate some personal defect. Thus it is said of the Baal Shem Tov himself that he heard that someone had violated the Sabbath: thus he examined himself and found that he had once made use of a Torah scholar. (Torah scholars are compared to *Shabbat*: to use them, therefore, is analogous to violating the *Shabbat*.)

Likewise, one may go on a trip for personal or business reasons. In truth, however, such motives are a Divine ruse to cause him to go there for a higher, Divine purpose. Thus it is said, "The ways of man are ordered by God, and He delights in his way" (Psalms 37:23): God leads a person to a certain place by means of his seeking there something of his own, but the real intent is for him to be mended or to carry out a Divine mission in that place (performing some *mitzvah* or good deed). The traveler, therefore, should try to figure out and fulfill the ultimate intent of the trip, to "delight in *His* (God's) way."

Needless to say, this concept of *hashgahah peratit* governing all details and particulars, does not contradict the fundamental principle of freedom of choice. Divine Providence does not interfere with man's moral option to obey or disobey the Divine Will, any more than God's foreknowledge impedes that freedom.

Rather interestingly, the hasidic concept of *hashgahah peratit* has very much become the normative Jewish perspective throughout. Numerous works cite many talmudic-midrashic passages to support it, not realizing that this concept is an innovation of the Baal Shem Tov without precedent among the earlier Jewish authorities. This is one more hasidic contribution that has revolutionized Jewish thought and life.

Y. Halevi, *Kuzari* 3:11.
Shneur Zalman of Liady, *Tanya* 2.

J.I.S.

DOCTORS–The attitude of talmudic teachers toward the art of medicine was ambivalent. On the one hand, doctors are specifically permitted to practice their profession (*Baba Kamma* 85a). On the other hand, King Hezekiah is praised for having hidden a book of cures in order that the sick should pray to God and not rely on the doctors.

This ambivalence was carried over into the hasidic movement, in which there were two prevailing attitudes concerning the use of medical means: Some rebbes felt that the hasid need not place faith in the empirical workings of medical prescriptions. All that was necessary was to remember "I, the Lord, am your Healer." Other rebbes themselves prescribed medicines or used the services of a physician for this purpose. In the *Shivhei HaBesht*, we read of the confrontations between the Besht and doctors. On one occasion, the Besht explained to a physician the difference between their respective methods: while the former sought the sin that corresponded to the particular illness, the latter could examine only the physical condition.

Prayer, herbal recipes, and use of magical amulets were some of the rebbe's methods.

The great-grandson of the Besht, R. Nahman of Bratzlav, urged his followers not to consult doctors. In his view, a doctor was a new type of sorcerer. He used to say, "The angel of death found it hard to fulfill his role all by himself, so he hired some helpers–the doctors." It is not quite certain whether he intended his advice to be taken literally. He himself did consult doctors: first, for his dying wife in 1807, and then, in that same year, for treatment of his own illness. His journey to Lvov in 1807 was for the purpose of visiting physicians in that city. We may assume that R. Nahman counseled his followers not against asking the help of physicians but against putting their trust in doctors alone.

There were many rebbes who prescribed medicines. One man, Dr. Bernard of Piotrokov, himself became a rebbe. Although few rebbes studied medicine or pharmacology, they wrote prescriptions. R. Simhah Bunem of Przysucha was a qualified chemist. Dr. Aaron Gardia was the physician of R. Dov Baer, the Maggid of Mezhirech. R. Issachar Baer of Radoszyce ran a pharmacy. Among the rabbis of the twentieth century who prescribed remedies were R. Israel Shalom Joseph of Bohusi, the rebbes of Radzyn, and R. Yitzhak Zelig Morgenstern of Sokolov. The rebbe of Piaseczno, R. K. Shapira, prescribed, and his prescriptions were honored by Warsaw druggists.

The courts of the rebbes were frequently filled with sick people hoping to become cured by the prayers of the rebbes. Nervous diseases were, for the most part, attributed to demonic seizures by ghosts, and the exorcism was a common occurrence among the Ukrainian *tzaddikim* of the nineteenth century.

For various circulatory diseases and diseases involving fever, rebbes prescribed bloodletting and cupping.

In the hasidic world, to be healthy was a *mitzvah* and to be sick a sin. The main purpose of the rebbe's work was to bring his hasidim to repentance. The formula recited in the night prayer indicates the intrinsic connection between health and morality: "May it be Thy will that I sin no more, and that which I incurred by sin, please erase in Thy great mercies, and not through suffering and painful diseases."

A. Green, *Tormented Master*, p. 234.

J.B.A., Z.M.S.

DONNER, Nathan Nute HaKohen

(c. 1850–1926)—Son of a middle-class family steeped in Hasidism, he was ordained by R. Hayyim Eleazar Waks of Kalish. In 1864, he became rabbi of Rahishitz, and in 1894, of Kolbiel.

He became closely associated with R. Yehiel Meir Lipshitz, the rabbi of Gostynin, and he ultimately published the homiletical sayings of the rebbe in his biography *Mey HaYam* (Lodz, 1910). He also was the author of *Mayim Rabim* (Warsaw, 1899) and *Rishpei Esh HaShalom* (Piotrokov, 1908). His work *Tiferet Hayyim* (Warsaw, 1905) is dedicated to the memory of R. Hayyim Meir Yehiel of Moglienice, and his work *Menorat Zahav* (Warsaw, 1902) is the biography of R. Zusya of Annopol.

He was greatly assisted by his friend R. Simon Menahem Mendel of Gowarczov.

His son, Jacob Shalom (1875–1960), was the son-in-law of R. Joseph Lewenstein. He published *Derekh Emunah U'Maasei Rav* (Warsaw, 1899), a hasidic anthology. He settled in the United States.

Y. Alfasi, *Kiryat Sefer*, vol. 49, pp. 659–660.

A.S.

DOV BAER (the Maggid) of Mezhirech

(1704–19 *Kislev* 1772)—Son of a poor Hebrew teacher, Dov Baer was born in Lukatz, Volhynia. The boy showed great aptitude for learning, and he studied under R. Shlomoh Dov Baer, the rebbe of Lukatz. Later he was sent to a *yeshivah* under R. Jacob Joshua Falk (1680–1756), author of *Penei Yehoshua*. Dov Baer married the daughter of R. Shalom Shakhna of Torchin. He was at first a teacher and then a preacher in Koretz and Dubno and in Rovno. He became renowned as a maggid using graphic parables to illuminate abstruse texts, which he made meaningful and relevant. He was a diligent student of the Kabbalah, adhering rigidly to the ascetic Lurian practices, which gravely undermined his health.

From the Besht, Dov Baer sought healing for his stricken body but instead received an elixir for his soul. His first visit was brief, but his second visit lasted six months. "He taught me the language of the birds, and the secrets of the sages, and the mystical meanings of many things," recorded Dov Baer. There is no basis for the view expressed by Dubnow that Dov Baer did not regard himself as a disciple of the Besht. Nor is there any foundation for the view expressed by Schipper that Dov Baer was a disciple of R. Joel Baal Shem. The Besht perceived Dov Baer to be a suitable successor, and after the former's death, Dov Baer settled in Mezhirech in the Ukraine.

Failing health restricted R. Dov Baer's travel, but what he was unable to do in person, he achieved through his disciples. His court was the center of an enclave of remarkable personages, who later became the founders of distinguished dynasties. The Maggid's court was a college and the spiritual training ground for future hasidic leaders. From the Ukraine came R. Levi Yitzhak of Berdichev, R. Menahem Mendel of Vitebsk, R. Nahum of Chernobyl, and R. Zeev Wolf of Zhitomir and from Lithuania came R. Aaron of Karlin, R. Shneur Zalman of Liady, and R. Hayyim Heikel of Amdur.

For a short time the Maggid lived in Annopol, where he died twelve years after the death of the Besht. In his last will and testament, he wrote to his son:

> For heaven's sake, do not seclude yourself for solitary meditations more than once a month, but on that one day do not speak even with members of your household. On the anniversary of my death, do not fast. On the contrary, you are to make a festive meal and give charity beyond the norm. When opponents provoke strife, remain silent and let God requite them.

There are conflicting figures regarding the numbers of the Maggid's disciples. Estimates range from 39 to 300. By the time he died there were hasidim in many parts of the country, even in Vilna, the *mitnaggidic* stronghold.

What the Besht had achieved through parables, the Maggid achieved through discourses. Like the Besht, he himself did not write books. His discourses were published by his disciple R. Solomon of Lutzk (d. 1813): *Maggid Devarav LeYaakov*, or *Likkutei Amarim*, was first printed in Koretz in 1871 and has subsequently been reprinted thirteen times; *Or Torah* on Torah, prophets, and Aggadot was printed in Koretz in 1804 and reprinted eleven times; and *Or HaEmet*, printed in Husiatyn in 1899, has been reprinted five times. A critical edition of *Maggid Devarav LeYaakov* was published by Rifka Schatz-Uffenheimer in Jerusalem in 1955. His letters *Iggrot Kodesh* were printed in Jerusalem in 1933 and his parables in Tel Aviv in 1959.

These works explain the Maggid's concept of God, cosmology, and the role of the *tzaddik*. If the Besht was the soul of Hasidism, the Maggid was its body. He created the hasidic court, and like the Besht he taught that in our every act or thought there is the Creator, for no move can be made without His power. There is, therefore, a divine manifestation in all human actions, even in evil ones. We should be self-critical, and even when performing good deeds, we should scrutinize our actions to determine if they are tinged with any ulterior motive. We can attain communion with God when we endeavor to rise to the upper worlds by raising our thoughts and aspirations. When praying, one should not pray merely for one's own material needs but should pray that the *Shekhinah* should no longer remain in exile.

R. Dov Baer inherited not only the mantle of the Besht but also his master's love for the Holy Land. For R. Dov Baer, *Eretz Yisrael* was the spiritual center of the world. The *Shekhinah*, which had accompanied the Jews into exile after the destruction of the Temple, had shared the tribulations of the children of Israel. He taught that though we are concerned mainly with our own sufferings, we should remember that the *Shekhinah*, too, yearns for redemption. The role of the *tzaddik* is to help restore the *Shekhinah* to its original glory. The freeing from the bondage of Egypt did not signify the end of bondage. As long as we are in exile, we are in Egypt. Spiritual redemption and physical redemption are interwoven. We are all responsible for the exile and for the reasons it has lasted so long. By purifying ourselves and overcoming our faults, we can hasten the redemption.

The Maggid was survived by a son, R. Abraham, the *Malakh*.

A. J. Heschel, in *Sefer HaYovel HaDoar*, pp. 86–95.

R. Schatz-Uffenheimer, *HaHasidut KeMistikah*.

DREAMS – It is to be expected that hasidim are more preoccupied with dreams and their interpretation than other Jews are. Rationalists tend to disregard the shadowy realms of dreams; mystics are likely to brood over the intimations received in dreams.

At the time of the Talmud, the dream mystique received a great deal of attention. In the *Zohar* (Genesis 83), the righteous are assured that the Lord will communicate with them in their dreams. R. Hayyim Vital recorded a great number of dreams.

We are told that Dov Baer, the Maggid of Mezhirech, appeared to his daughter-in-law in a dream, advising her what to do in various contingencies. R. Abraham, the "Angel," appeared to his son, asking him not to permit his mother to remarry. Several of the disciples of the Besht were persuaded of the authenticity of his teachings when they heard him, in their dreams, reciting Torah in the heavenly academy. After the Besht's death, his son, R. Tzvi, called upon him for help, and he appeared promptly.

When the Besht required interpretation of a dream, he called upon his disciple R. Jacob Joseph of Polonnoye. The grandson of the Besht, R. Moses Hayyim Efraim of Sudzilkov, recorded some of his own dreams, especially those relating to his grandfather. Typical of them is his dream in the summer 1781 when he dreamt of performing the rite of circumcision on an infant and saw the Besht sitting in the chair of Elijah.

There is a good deal of dream material in Hasidism, but that which is recorded is generally the rebbe's dream material and not that of his hasidim.

R. Yitzhak Judah Yehiel, in his *Megillat Setarim*, writes, "From the age of two until I was five years old, I had marvelous visions. The holy spirit filled me and I spoke words of prophecy. I saw from one end of the world to the other."

When a hasid came to the rebbe to relate a dream, it was usually because of the disturbing nature of the dream. The hasid did not consider it folly to worry about a dream. Hasidim knew that dreams may have a message for them. It may be a premonition or a warning. The hasid whose dream has been troubling needs the rebbe's reassurance of its innocuous nature; if a dream is a foreshadowing of unfortunate events to come, the hasid will need the rebbe's help in taking countermeasures.

Erotic dreams, for example, are not brought to the rebbe, unless they are recurrent. According to R. Nahman of Bratzlav, a dream in which there has been no fantasy content, but that, nevertheless, brings on pollution (i.e., loss of semen), needs no reparation. It is merely a bodily release that does not involve the imagination, and for this reason, according to R. Nahman, it is as innocent as any other bodily excretion.

Hasidim often dream of encounters with their rebbe.

J.B.A., Z.M.S.

DRESNER, Samuel Harold (b. 1923), author – A native of Chicago, he received a Bachelor of Arts degree at the University of Cincinnati and was ordained by the Jewish Theological Seminary, where he later received the degree of Doctor of Hebrew Literature. He served as a director of the Hillel Foundation at City College of New York and was rabbi in Highland Park, Illinois. He is the author of two works on Hasidism.

His first book, *The Zaddik* (London, 1960), deals with the *Toldot Yaakov Yosef*, by R. Jacob Joseph of Polonnoye, the first hasidic book published in 1780. He deals with the concept of the *tzaddik*, who is the cornerstone upon which the whole world is built. The *tzaddik* brings together the transcendence of God and the humanity of people. He deals with the concept of *devekut* (the clinging to God), which comes about through our inner yearnings. A great deal of thought is given to the "descent of the *tzaddik*" and his suffering, joy, and leadership. It was the *tzaddik*'s task to reunite the imprisoned sparks of the divine light in Creation with their source, thus bringing back the now shattered harmony of the universe and the return of the exiled *Shekhinah*.

The second book, *R. Levi Yitzhak of Berdichev* (New York, 1974), deals with a personality who made a tremendous impact on Hasidism.

Dresner presents the theosophy of Hasidism in terms of modern research.

I.O.L.

DRESS – When the hasidic movement emerged during the eighteenth century, a distinctive type of Jewish dress in Poland had already been firmly established. It had developed during the previous two or three centuries by the adoption of various pieces of regional items of dress, the design of which, particularly that of headgear such as the *streimel* and *spodek*, was largely influenced by climatic conditions.

By the middle of the nineteenth century, as we see from Hollaenderski's *Israélites de Pologne* (1846), the everyday dress of the hasidic Jews could clearly be distinguished from that of other Jews by their white knee-length smock with *tzitzit* attached to the corners and their white hose. There was also a difference in the way the girdle was worn tied round the smock with the outer caftan left open. The wives, like other Jewish women, wore the typical bodice, or *brüsttuch*, and had their hair completely covered.

The only known rules with regard to hasidic dress are those laid down by R. Menahem Mendel Rymanov (b. 1815), of which the following is a summary from *Ateret Menahem* (Lvov, 5637, p. 12):

1. Women should not go out wearing *stern tüchlech* (forehead bands), *grund* (headdress), or head scarves.
2. Unmarried women should not keep their hair in curls nor should they wear *kreindlech* (lace caps) or German blouses.
3. New fashions are forbidden for both men and women, and tailors who break this rule should be fined the first time and expelled from the tailors' guild if they repeat the offense.
4. Tailors must make *arba kanfot* knee length.
5. Men should not wear collars but only *kreis* (ruffs [?]) as in former times.

A. Rubens, *A History of Jewish Customs*, pp. 104–115.

A.R.

DROHOBYCZ, Yitzhak, of Drohobycz (c. 1700–1768) – He was a descendant of R. Yitzhak Hayon, the author of *Apei Ravrani* (Cracow, 1591). His father, Joseph Virnick, was known as "R. Yosef, the man of truth." Gentiles called him *Prawdziwi* (truth). The mother of R. Yitzhak was known as "Yente, the Prophetess." Once, while she was sweeping the house, she recited the *Kedushah*: "I heard the angels reciting the *Kedushah* so I had to respond." The Besht testified that she had "seeing eyes and hearing ears."

We know very little about the personal life of R. Yitzhak. He was known as the Maggid of Drohobycz, where he lived for a number of years. An itinerant maggid, he often took up his wanderer's staff, traveling to Galicia, Volhynia, and even Slutzk in Lithuania. For a time he lived in Brody and also in Ostrog.

He was often involved in controversy. He maintained that before delivering a discourse, a preacher should consider three things: first, that the spirit of the Torah should permeate the soul of every listener; second, that the discourse should be for the benefit of the whole community; and third, that it should not be delivered unless the preacher has heard it from the Almighty Himself. He once remarked, "People usually become reconciled on the eve of the Day of Atonement. This is not right. How can we bear a grudge against a fellow Jew for a whole year? How can we wait a whole year before making peace? Reconciliation should take place every day and not just on the eve of the Day of Atonement."

He was highly esteemed by his contemporaries. The Besht said of him, "R. Yitzhak has a saintly soul. They gave him a tiny soul, the tiniest soul in existence, but he stretched and expanded it to such an extent that it is almost tantamount to the soul of R. Shimon bar Yohai."

His son was R. Yehiel Michel of Zloczov, the author of *Mayyim Rabim*.

A. J. Heschel, "Rabbi Yitzhak of Drohobycz," pp. 152–153.

DROPSIE UNIVERSITY – Formerly Dropsie College, Dropsie University is an academic graduate institution in Philadelphia, Pennsylvania, founded by Moses Dropsie in 1909. The library contains microfilms of the Baron Joseph Yozel Guenzburg (1812–1873) collection at the Lenin Library in Moscow. In 1957, Dr. A. Katsh published in New York a catalog of the manuscripts he had microfilmed in Russia, the microfilm at first deposited at New York University and now at Dropsie University.

The microfilm contains an exceedingly large number of items dealing with mysticism. There are seven different codices of *Sefer Bahir*, the earliest work of kabbalistic literature, and five copies of *Shiur Komah*, the kabbalistic book describing the appearance of God. There are several copies of *Otzrot Hayyim*, by R. Hayyim Vital, and five copies of Joseph Gikatila's *Shaarei Tzedek*.

An interesting codex is *Shaar HaKedushah*, its fourth chapter dealing with the methods by which one may acquire the holy spirit and prophetic wisdom. That chapter does not appear in the printed editions of the work. There are also works by Moses Cordevero, Moses de Leon, Menahem Azariah da Fano, and Abraham Abulafia.

The *Zohar* itself is not found complete; there are only parts of the *Zohar* on *Noah* and *Lech Lecha*, which are not found in the printed edition.

The largest number of kabbalistic texts are those by Isaac Luria. There is a commentary on Sabbath melodies transmitted by his student Israel Sarug. Other works by Luria are transcribed by anonymous disciples. Some of these works also contain commentaries and notes by Nathan Shapiro, Moses Zakuta, and Benjamin Cohen.

Dropsie University has recently acquired the library of Moses Sanders of London, which contains many valuable hasidic works.

A.K.

DUBIN, Mordecai (1889–1956), Agudist leader – Son of Shneur Zalman, a hasid of Lubavitch, who settled in Latvia in 1882. Mordecai received a traditional Jewish education. From an early age, he worked in the lumber trade and devoted most of his life to helping the Latvian Jewish community.

From 1919 to 1934, he was a member of the Latvian senate, representing the Aguda. From 1920 to 1940, he was the head of Riga's Jewish community and became an effective *shtadlan*. He played a key role in achieving the release of R. Joseph Yitzhak Shneersohn from a Soviet prison in 1927. After the annexation of Latvia by the Soviet Union, Dubin was arrested by the communist authorities but subsequently released. He spent the

Second World War years in Moscow. In 1946, he returned to Riga but was once again arrested. He died in a Soviet labor camp.

Elleh Ezkerah, vol. 7, pp. 141–162.

Z.A.

DUBNOW, Simon (1860–1941), father of Jewish historiography – Born in Mstislavl, Belorussia, he was the son of Meir Jacob (1833–1887), a talmudical scholar, merchant, and descendant of the MaHaRal of Prague. He inherited his great love of the Jewish past from his great-great-grandfather R. Joseph Yoske of Dubno. Simon was self-educated. From 1908 he taught Jewish history at the Institute of Jewish Studies at St. Petersburg. In 1922, he left Russia and lived in Berlin. When the Nazis came to power in 1933, he moved to Riga. He was one of the founders of autonomism, the movement that advocated Jewish national autonomy in the Diaspora. His major work was the ten-volume *Weltgeschichte des Judischen Volkes* (World History of the Jewish People) (1925–1929). He was shot dead in the Riga ghetto on December 7, 1941.

From 1888 to 1893, Dubnow published in the Russian periodical *Voshkod* his studies on Hasidism. He also published essays on Hasidism in *Pardes* (1897) and *HaHasidim HaRishonim VeEretz Yisrael* (*Hashiloah*, 1901), and he then devoted years of research to an understanding of the hasidic movement. His *History of Hasidism* (in Hebrew, 1930–1932) is divided into three parts: the first one deals with the period of the emergence of the movement (1740–1782); the second describes its spread among the Jewish community (1782–1815); the third part contains the sources of his original study. He gives a factual account of the life of the Besht and of his leading disciples such as the Maggid Dov Baer of Mezhirech and Shneur Zalman of Liady. He presents Hasidism as a philosophical movement, a kind of pantheism. His pantheism has, however, little in common with the pantheism of Spinoza (1632–1677), who died thirty-two years before the Besht was born and of whose previous existence the Besht was probably unaware.

Though Dubnow was critical of the reactionary policies of some of the hasidic dynasties in his own lifetime, he was far more appreciative of the religious vitality of the movement than was Heinrich Graetz, who condemned the movement as a sect "born in darkness and continuing to flourish in darkness." To Graetz Hasidism was essentially a popularization of Kabbalah, and Kabbalah in turn amounted to an invasion of mythology, an incursion of "Catholicism within Judaism."

To Dubnow, Hasidism was an attempt to deflect away from the pseudomessianic endeavors the impassioned longing for redemption aiming to liberate the entire people and toward the more modest ambition of bringing salvation to the individual.

Dubnow did not ignore the emphasis on saving *Kelal Yisrael* as found in hasidic writings, but in Dubnow's view the movement was impelled by revulsion and despair over the failures of Shabbatai Tzvi and Jacob Frank. The pseudomessianists drew their inspiration from Kabbalah, stressing the redemption of the people. Hasidism, however, stressed the sanctification of the life of the individual. Dubnow believed that Hasidism responded to the religious needs of the common person. The rabbis could offer only a religious regimen, not a living faith, and the kabbalists only asceticism and frustration. The average Jew was religiously starved by the dry formalism of Torah learning. The messianic frustrations and feverish expectations weakened the Jew's power. Jews were hungry for a faith that would let them escape from reality. Hasidism responded to this need of the people.

Whereas the authentic exponents of Judaism ranked the unity and survival of the Jewish people above all other considerations, the sectarians of ancient and medieval times stressed the religious feelings and convictions of the individual. In keeping with this view, Dubnow categorized the emergence of Hasidism as a would-be sectarian outburst, which, however, was kept by historical forces from leaving the besieged Jewish community. As a movement of popular mysticism, Hasidism generated at first "light in the heart" but "darkness in the mind." Dubnow's interpretation of Hasidism was criticized by Raphael Mahler, Myer Waxman, and others on the following grounds: he did not take account of the conflicts and rivalries between different socioeconomic classes; he ignored the impassioned messianism of the Hasidic movement, which saw in the *tzaddik* an embodiment of the companions of the Messiah; he exaggerated the role of national unity in the Jewish "nomocracy."

Dubnow exaggerated the so-called formalism of rabbinic Judaism and the smoothness of the historical curve from growth to decline. *Tzaddikism*, with all its aspects, good and bad, was of the essence of Hasidism from its very inception. He asserts that the Besht in his youth fought with himself as he was drawn to Shabbataism. He cites the libelous story about R. Hirsh of Rymanov (part 4, p. 114) and dismisses the tales of R. Nahman of Bratzlav as the product of a man sick in body and in mind.

Unlike Graetz, he displays great objectivity in his treatment of the subject. Though imbued with a spirit of rationality, he showed understanding of the basic elements of Hasidism, and he aimed throughout at a scientific analysis. He wrote with clarity and insight. He saw in Hasidism a fresh manifestation of Jewish creativity and a source for the rejuvenation of East European Jewry. Dubnow's work is still the most indispensable for the study of Hasidism.

Toldot HaHasidut, 2 vols.

Sefer Shimon Dubnow, ed. S. Ravidowicz.

J.B.A.

DUDELE (also known as Du-Du)–This tune is attributed to R. Levi Yitzhak of Berdichev, who refers to God as *Du* (Thou). The text is probably based on the morning prayer *Kah anah emtza'akhah* (Lord, where shall I find Thee?) by Judah HaLevi (1075–1141).

M. Nulman, *Concise Encyclopedia of Jewish Music*, pp. 66–67.

DYBBUK (Hebrew, meaning "affixing")–A disembodied soul that is unable to find a resting place after death and seeks shelter in the body of a living person in order to escape the attacks of the demons.

The doctrines of evil spirits, reincarnation, demonic power, and exorcism are of remote antiquity, dating back to the Greek philosopher Pythagoras. They are found in neoplatonism, in the teachings of Buddha and Zoroaster, and in the popular beliefs in India, Tibet, and Egypt.

An illuminating passage from the writings of the first-century historian Josephus states that King Solomon possessed a recipe for driving out demons and that Josephus himself witnessed a rite of exorcism by a certain R. Eliezer in the presence of the Emperor Vespasian.

There is no paucity of material on evil spirits and demons in rabbinic literature. The belief in reincarnation was propounded by Anan ben David, founder of the Karaite movement, but was categorically rejected by Saadia Gaon in the tenth century and by Leone da Modina seven centuries later.

In the twelfth century, an age of universal credulity, the *Sefer HaBahir* took literally the verse of Ecclesiastes "One generation passeth and another generation cometh." It was believed that reincarnation could carry on for a thousand generations and that by assuming a new bodily existence, one could rectify shortcomings and fulfill destiny. By similar means, sins could be expiated after death.

The *Zohar* maintains that "all souls are subject to transmigration" (*gilgul*). This soon became a major doctrine of Jewish mysticism, which suggests that Cain's soul entered Jethro's body, that Abel's soul entered Moses' body, and that King David, Bathsheba, and Uriah had the souls of Adam, Eve, and the serpent.

R. Abraham Joshua Heschel of Opatov (d. 1825), although not a *kohen* (hereditary priest), believed that he had been a High Priest in an earlier existence. He would change the prescribed text in the order of service of the High Priests–the *Avodah*, recited on the Day of Atonement–from "Thus did he say" (i.e., the High Priest) to "Thus did I say."

The actual term *dybbuk*, an abbreviation of *Dybbuk MiRuah Ra* (a cleaving of an evil spirit), first occurs in *Sefer HaBrit*, by R. Pinhas Elijah (1743–1821). Unlike *gilgul*, which occurs at the birth of an infant, the *dybbuk* possesses a fully grown person already endowed with a soul, creating a person with two souls–souls at war with one another.

A variety of formulas emerged for the exorcism of a *dybbuk*. It had to be performed by a charismatic scholar known as a *baal shem* (a master of the divine name). Psalm 91, the use of the *shofar*, the display of seven Holy Scrolls, black candles, *kittles*, incantations, and, above all, the promise of salvation for the *dybbuk*, were the most effective methods of exorcism.

There were a number of *baalei shem*—itinerant preachers who claimed to be able to drive out *dybbukim*. Even eighteenth-century London could boast of a *baal shem*. Hayyim Samuel Jacob, also known as "Dr. Falk," achieved considerable prominence among Jews and non-Jews, and many miraculous tales were told of his achievements.

In *Shivhei HaBesht*, the Besht himself exorcised a dybbuk from a madwoman (Tale 20) and from a house (Tale 23).

G. Scholem, *Kabbalah*, pp. 348–350.

DYNASTIES—The history of the hasidic dynasties is enmeshed in a bewildering context of names, dates, lineages, and intermarriages.

Rabbinic leadership was controlled mostly by certain families in one city or country. With the rise of Hasidism, this dynastic approach was no exception. Indeed, it was strengthened for a number of reasons, both internal and external. Hasidic leaders strengthened their position by close family ties through intermarriage, although, when the Besht died, he was not succeeded by his son, R. Tzvi, but by the Maggid, Dov Baer of Mezhirech. Similarly, R. Tzvi Hirsch of Rymanov (d. 1846), a tailor's apprentice, succeeded his master, R. Menahem Mendel. As a rule, however, son followed father, and thus the dynasties were perpetuated. Inevitably, quarrels occasionally arose between the followers of different rebbes, to the amusement of the *mitnaggedim* and the *maskilim* alike, and these controversies sometimes degenerated into unseemly squabbles.

A number of hasidic rebbes did not establish lasting dynasties: R. Jacob Joseph of Polonnoye, R. Menahem Mendel of Vitebsk, R. Levi Yitzhak of Berdichev, R. Nahman of Bratzlav, R. Zusya of Annopol, and R. Shmelke of Nikolsburg.

Other dynasties, such as the Tluste dynasty, whose rebbe, R. Baer (d. 1931) was the last of the line, came to an end in the twentieth century. Similarly, R. Mordecai of Kamenka (d. 1947) was the last of the Slavuta/Shepetovka dynasty. R. Eliezer (d. 1898) was the last of the Radzvillov dynasty. R. Israel Elimelekh, who died in 1954, was the last of Galina/Zborov. R. Yitzhak (d. 1908) was the last of the Gorodok dynasty.

Over a period of five generations, after R. Mordecai Twersky of Chernobyl had established the Chernobyl dynasty, there were over fifty cousin marriages in the families. The same applied to the families of Heschel, Friedman, Horowitz, Teitelbaum, Sufrin, and Rabinowicz.

The great dynasties that are still going today are the descendants of Alexander, Biala, Chernobyl, Eichenstein, Hager, Satmar, Ruzhyn, Ger, Przysucha, Lelov, Sighet, Teitelbaum, Vishnitz, Zydaczov, Zanz, and Belz, Sasov, Sqvira, Nadvorna, Novominsk, Amshinov, Talnoy, and Trisk.

In a number of dynasties, the succession came through sons-in-law. R. Naftali Tzvi Horowitz, the first rebbi of Ropczyce, was succeeded by his son-in-law, R. Asher Isaiah Rubin, in 1827. The third rebbe of Ropczyce, R. Manasseh, was succeeded by his son-in-law, R. Yitzhak Mariles.

In the Lubavitch dynasty, the second rebbe was succeeded by his nephew and his son-in-law, R. Menahem Mendel Schneersohn. He himself was succeeded by his younger son, R. Shmuel, and R. Joseph Yitzhak was succeeded by his son-in-law, R. Menahem Mendel Schneerson. When R. Itzikel Gewirzman of Antwerp died, he was succeeded by his son-in-law, R. Leizer.

The rebbe of Ger, R. Yitzhak Meir, who died in 1866, was succeeded by his grandson, R. Yehudah Aryeh, who died in 1905. The son of R. Mordecai Alter, R. Israel, was succeeded first by his brother R. Simhah Bunem, then by his younger brother, R. Pinhas Menahem Alter. Similarly, when the rebbe of Munkacz, R. Hayyim Elazar, died in 1936, his successor was his son-in-law, R. Barukh Rabinowicz. When the rebbe R. Aaron of Belz died, his nephew, the present rebbe of Belz, R. Berele, succeeded him.

When R. Abraham of Slonim died in 1884, his son R. Michael Aaron encouraged his grandson, R. Shmuel (d. 1916), to become rebbe. Today, R. Shalom Noah Brozovsky, his son-in-law, is the rebbe of Slonim. When the rebbe of Ozarov, R. Moses Yehiel Epstein, died, he was succeeded by his grandson, R. Tanhum Becker. The dynasty of Alexander was maintained by R. Yehudah Moses Danziger, who was the son-in-law of R. Bezalel Yair Danziger. R. Yoel of Satmar was succeeded by his nephew, R. Moses Teitelbaum.

N.R., S.K.

E

EATING—Eating as an act of devotion occupies a prominent place in hasidic life and thought. In addition to the sacred meal in which the hasidim gather round the *tzaddik* (the *tish*, "table") and eat of the food he has consecrated (*shirayyim*), the act of eating is repeatedly mentioned in hasidic literature as a means of evaluating the holy sparks (see KABBALAH), which are in the food. Furthermore, the taste of food is produced by the spiritual vitality that is its source on high. Consequently, hasidim are urged to let their mind soar above the more physical enjoyment of the taste, allowing it to become associated with the spiritual worlds by means of which the lower world is nourished. A favorite quotation of the hasidic masters in this connection is the verse "And they saw God and they ate and drank" (Exodus 24:10–11), which the kabbalist Elijah of Smyrna (d. 1729) applies in his *Midrash Talpiot* (ed. Warsaw, 1875, pp. 50b–51a, from Bahya Ibn Asher): "When man needs to eat he should free his mind from other thoughts so that it can soar to think on God while each mouthful is being swallowed."

R. Jacob Joseph of Polonnoye (*Toldot Yaakov Yosef*, p. 225) remarks that there are two kinds of intention while eating. The simple intention is to eat in order to have strength to serve God. The higher and more difficult intention is to eat in order to elevate the holy sparks and raise in thought all the spiritual forces inherent in the food. This is why God makes the *tzaddik* experience hunger and thirst. The desire for food and drink is an inducement to people to eat and drink so that they might elevate the holy sparks in that which they consume. The spiritual aspect is concealed by the physical pleasure in the way that an honest woman whose face is veiled may be mistaken for a harlot, but the *tzaddik* knows how to see the reality, and his thoughts are only on the holy sparks to be elevated. Rabbi Nahum of Chernobyl (*Meor Enayyim* [Jerusalem, 1968], *mattot*, pp. 168–170) states that the holy spark in the food one eats becomes united with one's own essential being, providing energy and vitality. This spark is in reality spiritual food because therein is contained the divine nature, albeit covered as with a garment. We should have this in mind when we eat and we should use in God's service the fresh energy the food has given us, once the spark has become assimilated. By so doing, we unite the spark to its source in God. Fasting is, consequently, sinful (*Taanit* 11a) because it constitutes a refusal by people to engage in their allotted task. It is true that there is also a talmudic saying (*Taanit* 11a–b) that one who fasts is called a holy one, but very few can serve God by fasting. The easier way is to serve God while enjoying food. R. Levi Isaac of Berditchev (*Kedushat Levi* [Jerusalem, 1964], *Likkutim*, p. 288) similarly states that we can have the intention of eating in order to have strength to serve God or in order to release the holy sparks, but in the first instance, our eating is only a means to God's service, whereas in the second instance, our eating is itself an act of divine worship.

Further ideas mentioned in the hasidic sources regarding eating and drinking are the great value in one's breaking off in the middle of a meal one is enjoying as an act of penance or sheer devotion to God; that the very word for food—*okhel*—has the same numerical value as the tetragrammaton and the name El; that a wandering soul may have been punished for its sins by being condemned to exile in food until that food is eaten by a saint in a spirit of holiness by which the saint releases the lost soul from its bitter lot.

Leshon Hasidim, *s.v.* "*akhilah*," pp. 18–19.

A. Roth, *Shulhan HaTahor*.

Tzaddok HaKohen of Lublin, *Kunteros Et HaOkhel* in *Pri Tzaddik*, pp. 235–240.

L.J.

ECSTASY—The term generally used in Hasidism for burning enthusiasm in prayer and worship is *hitlahavut*, from *lahav*, a flame. The term used for the raptures that result from the nearness of God in prayer and worship is *hitpaalut*, from *paal*, to do, to be effected, or to be in a state of ecstasy. From the beginnings of the hasidic movement appears the idea of ecstatic prayer during which the worshiper's corporeal nature is stripped off, as the hasidic masters put it—*hitpashtut hagashmiyut*. A number of the *tzaddikim* were especially noted for their ecstatic prayers. Of Levi Yitzhak of Berdichev it was said that after he had led the congregation in prayer on the Day of Atonement, he would cry out aloud, "My heart is on fire." Of the Maggid of Kozienice it is reported that, sick though he was, he would leap to the prayer desk "as if he were flying through the air" and that when he recited the verse "Sing unto the Lord a new song" (Psalm 149:1), his weakness would leave him and he would sing in joy "like a little girl." Of the grandson of the Besht, R. Barukh of Medziborz, it was told by Tzvi Hirsch of Zhydaczov that when he recited the Song of Songs on the eve of the Sabbath, those who heard him singing "For love is as strong as death . . . the flashes thereof are flashes of fire, a very flame of the Lord" (Song of Songs 8:6) and who had secreted themselves in the room were obliged to run from the room in terror, having almost lost their reason "because of the great attachment and longing."

The *Habad* movement in particular considers at length the role of ecstasy (*hitpaalut*) in prayer. The basic contention of R. Shneur Zalman, the founder of the *Habad* movement, is that religious emotion is suspect unless it is the fruit of profound contemplation—*hitbonanut*. After the death of R. Shneur Zalman, his son, R. Dov Baer, and his favorite disciple, R. Aaron of Starosselje, were divided on the question of how far the master had rejected ecstasy in prayer that was not entirely spontaneous and uncontrived, R. Dov Baer taking the stricter view that every type of ecstasy is spurious unless it comes without any awareness whatsoever and is solely the result of the divine's confronting human beings through the latter's deep contemplation on the kabbalistic mysteries. R. Dov Baer is the author of two tracts—one on contemplation (*Kunteros HaHitbonanut*) and one on ecstasy (*Kunteros HaHitpaalut*). The latter is an acute analysis of the stages in ecstatic prayer.

Habad tradition describes the difference between R. Dov Baer and R. Aaron in their personal religious life, reflecting their differing views on ecstasy. On one hand, R. Aaron used to pray with a great shouting so that all who observed him at prayer were themselves moved to ecstasy. Of R. Dov Baer, on the other hand, it was said that he would stand immobile in prayer for as long as three hours at a time and that at the end of his prayer his hat and shirt would be soaked in perspiration.

This whole debate is peculiar to *Habad*. There is surprisingly little reference to *hitpaalut* among the other hasidic groups among which ecstasy is always considered under the heading of *hitlahavut*.

L.J.

EDUCATION—In Judaism the purpose of education is not merely to provide the necessary skills for the practice of faith but also to foster the habit of lifelong Torah study for all the men in the community. The commandment "and you shall medidate on it by both day and night" was interpreted literally, as an exhortation to devote to Torah learning every minute that could be spared from the harsh necessities of one's livelihood. Failure to do so was considered to be a grave sin—*bittul Torah*—wasting the time that belonged to the Torah.

It is this extreme zeal for the utilization of every minute for Torah study that in the view of the *Mitnaggedim* was endangered by the hasidic movement.

The gathering of hasidim for the purpose of storytelling, drinking together, conviviality, and singing and dancing appeared to the *Mitnaggedim* as a deliberate conspiracy against the ideal and practice of Torah study. The fact that many hasidim traveled long distances to the courts of the *tzaddikim* was also regarded by their opponents as *bittul Torah*.

Much of the argument between the two sects centred on the definition of the term "*Torah lishmo*"—Torah for its own sake.

To the hasidim *lishmo* meant for the sake of clinging to the *Shekhinah*, the lowest *Sefirah*, represented as female. To the *Mitnaggedim, lishmo* meant for the sake of understanding the Torah itself. It has been well said that the hasidim directed their love and fear to God, seeking to cling to Him, whereas the *Mitnaggedim* directed all their energies to the study of the Torah.

To the hasidim the discourses of the *tzaddik* would be repeated and interpreted. In the great *yeshivot* of their opponents, the emphasis was on the understanding of the intricacies of the Talmud and the codes. R. Shneur Zalman sought to effect a synthesis between Torah learning and hasidic meditation. Students would alternate periods of study with periods of meditation. "For through Torah study, man calls the Holy One, blessed be He, to come to him, like a person calls a friend or like a little boy calls his father to come to him" (*Tanya*, chap. 37).

Every system of education upholds an ideal that determines the character of the various steps reaching up to it. Among the hasidim the ideal was the *tzaddik*, the one who has overcome all the "shells within his own person" and has become an embodiment of holiness. Among the *Mitnaggedim* the ideal was a Gaon, a preeminent scholar and sage who had mastered the entire sacred literature of Judaism.

In fact, Hasidism followed the established educational patterns. At a very early age, boys were sent to the *heder*. Secular subjects had no place in the curriculum, and Hebrew grammar and the Bible were neglected. "Verily, grammar is useful," admits R. Menahem Mendel of Vitebsk. "I know that our great ones studied it, but what can we do, now that the godless have taken possession of it?" At first, the hasidim would not send their sons to the *yeshivah*, and the young men would study in the *Bet HaMidrash*, but gradually hasidim established their own *yeshivot*, such as the *Mesivta* set up in 1919 under R. Meir Dan Plotzky, rabbi of Ostrowiec. Hasidic youngsters, reluctant to travel to far-off institutions, converged on this local fountainhead of scholarship.

In the interwar years, many hasidic *yeshivot* sprang up, and today they flourish in Israel, England, and the United States. A famous hasidic *yeshivah* was *Yeshivat Hakhmei Lublin*, established by R. Meir Shapira. "Nowadays, *yeshivah* students should not live in shacks and eat like beggars. I will build a palace for them." And the *yeshivah* of Lublin was one of the finest prewar buildings in Poland. Only the most promising candidates were admitted, and they were required to know by heart 200 pages of the Talmud. R. Solomon Hanokh HaKohen Rabinowicz of Radomsk directed thirty-six hasidic *yeshivot Keter Torah* in Poland and Galicia. By 1937, there were seventy-eight *yeshivot* in Poland, half of which were hasidic.

In Israel today, the establishment of *yeshivot* is part of the hasidic way of life. Almost every rebbe has his own academy. Of the educational institutions enumerated in the *Directory of Recognized Agencies*, published by the Ministry of Social Welfare, nearly one-third are hasidic. Of the 150 hasidic *yeshivot*, half are associated with the *Vaad HaYeshivot*, and the Ministry of Religious Affairs provides for them and their students. The hasidic *yeshivot* in Israel, like their forerunners in Eastern Europe, are not training schools for professional rabbis, and students have no immediate vocational objectives. Apart from Lubavitch, hasidic *yeshivot* frown upon yeshivah-cum-technical-college institutions.

The *kollel* that subsidizes the studies of married students was hardly known in Poland. In the past three decades there has been an extensive growth in the number of *kollelim* in Israel and in the Diaspora, where students continue their studies to a higher level, for five to ten years after marriage.

Both hasidim and *Mitnaggedim* made no provisions for the education of women before the twentieth century. Parents would arrange for the private tuition of their daughters. Women were often the breadwinners, and a knowledge of the Polish language stood them in good stead in their business dealings. It was Sarah Schenierer, dressmaker turned educator, who provided a new approach. A school for girls, the first *Bet Jacob* Institute, was founded in Cracow in 1917. The *Bet Jacob* schools, acknowledged by the *Knessiyyah Gedolah* of the Aguda, "are the best solution for the education of girls." In 1937, there were in Poland 250 *Bet Jacob* schools with an enrollment of 38,000. To supply the teachers for this mushrooming movement, a seminary was built in Cracow in 1925. Moral support came from the rebbe of Belz and other hasidic rabbis.

In the Holy Land, the first Orthodox girls' school was established by Benzion Yedler and named *Bet Hinukh Livnot al Yedei Darkhei Yisrael Saba*, popularly called *Benzion Yedler's Heder*. In 1921, the first *Bet Jacob* school was established in Jerusalem. Another was founded in Tiberias three years later. By 1972, there were 83 *Bet Jacob* institutions in Israel.

Most hasidic children in Israel attend the schools of the *Hinukh Atzmai*, which was founded in 1953. In these schools, a thorough study of Jewish studies goes hand in hand with a secular curriculum. The language of instruction is Hebrew and the sexes are segregated. Though nominally *Hinukh Atzmai* is independent and free from party influence, it is guided by the Aguda and the hasidic rebbes of Ger, Vishnitz, and Sadgora.

Today, the survivors of the Holocaust group themselves round the hasidic dynasties, using all modern technical means to develop their own specific networks of education. *Hedarim*, *yeshivot*, and *kollelim* in Israel, the United States, and other countries still maintain a negative attitude toward secular studies. Of the hasidic dynasties of today – Satmar, Lubavitch, Ger, Bobov, and Vishnitz – all have their own educational establishments, from kindergarten to *kollel*, where the ideals of Hasidism are implanted in the young.

J.B.A., Ed.

EGER, Abraham, of Lublin (1846–22 *Tevet* 1914), hasidic rebbe

– Elder son of R. Judah Leib, who, after the death of his father, at first declined to succeed him as rebbe. He continued as a disciple of R. Tzaddok HaKohen Rabinowicz of Lublin. When R. Tzaddok died, he became rebbe and lived at Siroka 40.

He was an ascetic and ate only at night. In his will and testament, written in 1906, he instructed his hasidim not to put *kvittlekh* on his grave.

He was the author of *Shevet MiYehudah* on Genesis, the first part of which was published in Lublin in 1922, and the latter part before the Second World War. He was succeeded by his son R. Alter Azriel Meir. His other sons, R. Noah Yisrael and R. David, did not become rebbes. His daughter, Kale, married R. Saul Yedidyah Eliezer Taub. On their divorce, she married R. Jeremiah Kalish of Opole.

Y. Alfasi, *Toldot HaHasidut*, p. 74.

EGER, Abraham, of Bene Berak (b.1916)

– Son of R. Solomon, he became rebbe in 1945 and established *shtieblech* in Tel Aviv, Jerusalem, and Antwerp. He also established a Talmud Torah *Shevet Yehudah* in Bene Berak. He is a man without affectation or pomposity, who is wise and warmhearted, and to whom his followers take their problems.

EGER, Alter Azriel Meir (1873–5 *Tammuz* 1941)

– Second son of R. Abraham, he was brought up by his grandfather R. Judah Leib. He was successful in his business dealings and was able to devote his time to study. After the death of his father, the hasidim were divided. Some followed R. Solomon of Lublin, others followed R. Alter Azriel Meir, who settled in Pulawy.

In 1929, he published a tract, *Hazaot Tekuna Nehuza*, on usury and devised a formula that would obviate transgression of the biblical law. He was supported by R. Meir Arik and R. Ezekiel Lipshitz.

He had three sons and two daughters. His son R. Leibish married the daughter of the rabbi of Sokolov. Another son, R. Yitzhak Jacob Moses, married the daughter of the rabbi of Yaroslav. His third son, R. Akiva, was the son-in-law of the rebbe of Alexander and served as a *dayan* in Lodz. His daughter Yehudit married R. David Alter, the son of R. Moses Bezalel Alter, the brother of the rebbe of Ger. The Eger dynasty is today represented in New York by R. Abraham Eger.

Y. Alfasi, *Toldot HaHasidut*, pp. 76–77.

EGER, Judah Leib, of Warsaw (1816–11 *Shevat* 1888)

– Son of R. Solomon Eger and grandson of R. Akiva Eger of Poznan. R. Leibele was born in Warsaw and was the youngest of five sons. Among his teachers was R. Mordka Grunbaum, later the rabbi of Neustadt. He joined a small circle of gifted young men who clustered around R. Yitzhak Meir of Ger. He married Bathsheba, the daughter of R. Azriel Meir Grunstein, and became a hasid of R. Menahem Mendel of Kotzk. Later he became a follower of R. Mordecai Joseph Leiner of Izbice. "When we hear Torah from R. Leiner," he remarked, "it is as if we heard it from Sinai." He studied regularly the works of the "Seer of Lublin," and he regarded him as his spiritual teacher.

When his father died in 1852, R. Leibele first refused to succeed his father as rabbi of Poznan. He could not tear himself away from Lublin, or from his great disciple, R. Tzdaddok HaKohen Rabinowitz of Lublin, who eventually persuaded him to become a rebbe. However, he did not deliver any discourses until after the death of R. Mendel of Kotzk.

R. Leibele would prolong every service, even the Day of Atonement liturgy. *Neilah* was rarely recited before midnight. "How can I let go of such a sacred day," he said. He prayed aloud, and his prayers were accompanied by bitter tears. He believed in elaborate preparations for prayer and for the performance of any *mitzvah*. "It would be inappropriate," he would say, "to welcome the Prophet Elijah without due preparations." He did not, however, conform entirely to hasidic practices. He refused to accept *pidyonot* and lived on the income derived from a small business carried on by his wife. His life was austere, and he ate only one meal each day. He acted as both the *mohel* and the *sandek* at circumcisions. On his death, his colleague R. Israel Mordecai wrote a eulogy with the title *Eivel Gadol* (Warsaw, 1909).

He wrote encomiums on many books, such as *Etz HaDaat Tov* (1863), *Hinukh Bet Yehudah*, and *Bet Yaakov* (Warsaw, 1870). Two of R. Leibele's manuscripts were published posthumously: *Torat Emet* in three volumes on the Pentateuch and Festivals (Lublin, 1889) and *Imrei Avot* in two volumes (Lublin, 1902).

A. I. Bromberg, *Migdolei HaTorah*, vol. 13, *Mishpahat Eiger*, pp. 91-160.

EGER, Solomon (1871-5 *Tammuz* 1942), hasidic rebbe—He was the eldest son of R. Abraham and succeeded his father as rebbe in Lublin in 1914. After the death of R. Meir Shapira he became one of the spiritual guides of the *Yeshivat Hakhmei Lublin*. He introduced the diploma *Tzubra MiRabbanan*, a special award for students who achieved high academic distinction.

He was a bibliophile and collected an important library of Hebraica. "I am not concerned with printed books, but with fine bindings," he said. "But I have a great love for books and what they contain."

He died in the Warsaw Ghetto.

His brother Azriel, who was also a rabbi in Lublin, published his father's works, *Shevet MiYehudah* on Genesis in 1922 and on Exodus in 1938.

Y. Alfasi, *Toldot HaHasidut*, p. 76.

EGER, Solomon, of Lissa (1786-11 *Tevet* 1852)—Second son of R. Akiva Eger, Solomon was born in Lissa and married the daughter of R. Israel Hirschensohn of Warsaw, where he lived for thirty-five years.

He participated in the communal activities of the community and frequently came in contact with the hasidic rebbes, especially R. Yitzhak Meir Alter of Ger and R. Simhah Bunem of Przysucha. He became rabbi first in Kalish in 1831, and in 1839, in Poznan.

He appealed to the Emperor Frederick William IV to sponsor Jewish agricultural settlements. He opposed both the missionaries and the *Haskalah*. He tried to enlist R. Nathan Marcus Adler, chief rabbi of Britain, whom he met in Hannover, to help him fight the Reform movement.

EHRMAN, Berl (1860-1944), communal leader and hasidic writer—Born in Bodrog-Keresztur, Hungary. His background was of militant Orthodoxy of the nonhasidic type. Berl attended the *yeshivah* of his uncle Maharam Schick in Huszt. While still a *yeshivah* student, Berl took a positive interest in Hasidism, which was rapidly spreading through the northeastern regions of Hungary. He paid several visits to the main centers of Hasidism in Galicia. He mentions particularly his visit to R. Joshua Rokeah of Belz.

Berl married Miriam Schwartz, whose family was closely associated with R. Isaac Taub of Kalev. Berl's interest in Hasidism was an "ecumenical" one. He carefully avoided becoming the devotee of any of the rivaling dynasties. He tried in his works to do justice to all the leading hasidic rebbes of his time. His presentation of hasidic stories has both originality and authenticity. His aim is to put on record stories he himself had heard from reliable authorities who had some personal connection with the events recorded.

He meticulously gives the names of the sources and describes the way a story was handed down to him.

Berl's publications (all printed in Munkacs) include *Devarim Arevim* in two parts, which appeared in 1903 and 1905, respectively; *Pe'er VeKhavod* (1911); and *Zokhrenu LeHayyim* (1937). The first part of *Devarim Arevim* and *Pe'er VeKhavod* were reprinted several times. A consolidated edition was published in Tel Aviv in 1972. Berl's works are widely quoted even by modern writers, by M. Buber in his *Or HaGanuz*, by Shai Agnon in his *Yamim Noraim*, and by L. I. Newman in his *Hasidic Anthology*.

The most active part of Berl's life was spent in Kisvarda, Hungary, where he was one of the foremost leaders of the large hasidic community. Only during the Second World War did he move to Ungvár, where he died in the ghetto shortly before the deportation of the whole community.

Among Berl's numerous descendants was R. Dr. A. Herman, the editor of the *Talmud El Am*.

A.E.

EIBESCHUTZ, David Solomon of Soroka (1755–22 *Heshvan* 1813) – The son of R. Yerahmiel, he was born in Lacriowicze and was the disciple of R. Zeev Wolf of Ostrog and of R. Meshullam Feivish of Zbarozh. He married the daughter of Yehiel Michael Seidman. In 1780, he became head of a *yeshivah* in Nadvorno, and in 1803, he became rabbi of Soroka, where he lived for sixteen years. In 1809, he settled in Safed, where he was buried near R. Abraham David of Ovruch.

He was the author of *Eshed HaNehalim* (Livorno, 1821), *Bigdei Serod* (Breslau, 1822), *Kad HaKemah* (Przemysl, 1899), *Levushei Serod* on *Yoreh De'ah* (Mohilev, 1812), *Megillat Sesarim* (Lvov, 1863), *Neot Desheh* (Lvov, 1861), and *Arvei Nahal* (Sudzilkov, 1822).

EIBESCHUTZ, Jonathan (ca. 1690–1764), kabbalist – Hasidim held in great esteem the writings of Eibeschutz. When he was writing his *Scroll of the Law*, R. Shragai Feivel Danziger of Alexander would study his work *Urim VeTumim*. "To study the works of R. Jonathan," said R. Shragai, "is to cleanse one's mind of impure thought."

EICHENSTEIN, Aaron Menahem Mendel, of Olesk (1860–19 *Av* 1923) – He was the third son of R. Alexander Sender Yomtov Lippa. He married Sarah Shlomze, the daughter of R. Yitzhak. He then moved to Olesk, where he was the rabbi from 1904.

When his wife died, he married Chavah, the daughter of R. Hayyim Yehiel Meir of Glogov. During World War I, he lived in Lvov, where he died.

His son, R. Shimon, who succeeded him, perished in the Holocaust.

EICHENSTEIN, Alexander Sender, of Komarno (1770–1818) – The third son of Yitzhak Eizig and a disciple of the "Seer" and also of R. Tzvi Wolf of Zbarazh. He was the rabbi of Zydaczov and became the rabbi of Komarno in 1812.

He suffered poverty all his life. He became so absorbed in his studies that he went without food for days.

He was the author of *Zikhron Devarim* on the Pentateuch, the first part of which was printed in Lvov in 1871, and the second part in Przemysl in 1879.

He died in Ujhely.

EICHENSTEIN, Elijah, of Zydaczov (1837–5 *Sivan* 1878) – Fourth son of R. Yitzhak Eizig of Zydaczov. He married Hinda, the daughter of R. Yehiel Leibish Erlich of Rozdol. When his father died, Elijah succeeded him, remaining in Zydaczov, where his brother Sender Lippa was already the established rabbi. This was the cause of great controversy.

He died at the age of forty-one, and in his last will and testament he urged his followers to give their allegiance to his other brother, Issachar Berish. His daughter, Sarah Hannah, married the son of R. Joshua Rokeah of Belz. Some of his discourses are published in *Zikhron Eliyahu* (Lvov, 1880).

EICHENSTEIN, Issachar Berish, of Dolina (1839–2 *Shevat* 1886) – He was the third son of R. Yitzhak Eizig of Zydaczov. He married the daughter of R. Abraham of Stretyn. He became *dayan* of Zydaczov in 1856, and, after his father's death, rebbe of Dolina. He was reluctant to publish any work and would say, "Would that I be worthy to be among those rebbes who did not write books."

However, his discourses were noted by his follower Yehudah Yitzhak Segal Stern, who published them in Lvov in 1886 under the title *Likkutei: Torah Mahari*, which was reprinted in Brooklyn, New York, in 1973.

He was succeeded by his only son, R. Yehudah Tzvi Hirsch. His daughters married R. Pinhas Rokeah of Karov and R. Jacob Yitzhak Dov of Vienna.

EICHENSTEIN, Issachar Berish, of Zydaczov (1849–21 *Nisan* 1924) – He was born in Zydaczov, the son of Alexander Sender Yomtov Lippa of Zydaczov. He married Sheindel, the daughter of R. Manasseh of Ropczyce. He was a disciple of his grandfather R. Yitzhak Eizig of Zydaczov. He served as rabbi in Zydaczov for one year and then in Alsoverczki.

During the First World War, he lived for a time in Grosswardein and later in Munkacs. He was the author of *Malbush LeShabbat VeYom Tov* on Deuteronomy, which was printed in Munkacs in 1927; the part on Genesis to Numbers was printed in Bilgoraj in 1937. He was survived by his sons, R. Manasseh, R. Moses, and R. Asher Yeshaya.

EICHENSTEIN, Issachar Berish, of Zydaczov/Petah Tikvah (1928–1989) – Son of Joseph of Grosswardein. After the death of his uncle, Yitzhak Meir, he succeeded him as rebbe. He studied at the Ponevezh Yeshivah, Bene Berak, and in the *kollel* of Volozhin of Tel Aviv. He married Miriam Reisel, the daughter of R. Ezekiel Samuel of Bene Berak.

He published a *Haggadah* for Passover, according to the custom of Zydaczov, and a second edition of *Malbush LeShabbat VeYom Tov*. He was succeeded by his son, R. Joshua, who married Beila, the daughter of R. Benzion Jakobovits of Bene Berak.

EICHENSTEIN, Issachar Dov, of Zydaczov (1768–7 *Sivan* 1832) – Fourth son of Yitzhak Eizig of Safrin. He was the disciple of the "Seer" and of his own brother R. Tzvi Hirsch. He married Elya, the sister of R. Joseph of Strelisk.

He became rebbe in 1831 but died a year later. He was succeeded by his son, R. Yitzhak Eizig of Zydaczov.

EICHENSTEIN, Joseph, of Tarnopol (1855–1920) – Son of Alexander Joseph Lippa, he married Sheindel, the daughter of R. Nahum Brandwein, rabbi in Tarnopol. His son, R. Alexander Lippa, was rabbi in Strykov.

EICHENSTEIN, Joshua, of Grosswardein (1896–16 *Sivan* 1945) – He was the son of R. Asher Yeshaya and a grandson of R. Issachar Berish. He was born in Pruchnic Miasto and he studied under R. Hayyim Yeruchem of Altstadt, whose daughter Berachah Freide he married in *Kislev* 1912.

During World War I, he lived in Vienna and in 1922 settled in Grosswardein. During World War II, he urged Jews to escape to Romania and hide in the mountains. He was transported to Auschwitz and died in Huldhausen camp. He was reburied in Safed in 1952.

All his children survived the Holocaust. His son R. Nathan (1928–30 *Adar* 1976) was the rabbi in the hasidic synagogue of Zydaczov *Ateret Tzvi* in Tel Aviv.

EICHENSTEIN, Joshua Heschel, of Chicago (1882–11 *Adar* II 1940) – Son of Issachar Dov, he succeeded his father as rabbi in Chodorov. He married Berachah Gitel (d. 1930), the daughter of R. Alter Zeev Horowitz of Strzyzov. On the death of his father, he succeeded him as rabbi of Chodorov. He had three sons and one daughter: R. Abraham, who succeeded him; R. Menahem Tzvi, rabbi of St. Louis; R. Moses (b. 1912) of Chicago; and his daughter Minche, who married R. Abraham Mordecai Hershberg of Mexico. In 1924, R. Joshua Heschel and his family left Poland. He was one of the very first rebbes to arrive in the United States.

His son and successor, R. Abraham, was born in Strzyzov in 1908 and accompanied his father to the United States. He studied at the *yeshivah* Givat Shaul in Jerusalem, and then in New Haven, Connecticut. In 1932, he married Babche, daughter of R. Pinhas Shalom Rothenberg. They had six children, one son and five daughters. He died on 22 *Tammuz* 1967 and his son, R. Joshua Heschel, who married Sarah Rivkah Horowitz of Strasbourg, succeeded him as rebbe.

His daughter Yehudit married R. Jacob Perlow of Novominsk; Miriam Etel married

R. Jacob Zeev Landinsky, formerly of Gateshead; Rachel Perel married R. Hayyim Pinter of London; Rivkah Leah married R. Moses Meiselman of Jerusalem; and Hayyah Libah married R. Barukh Benzion Twersky, now of Monsey.

EICHENSTEIN, Manasseh, of Rzeszov (1865–16 *Tammuz* 1935) – Son of Issachar Berish of Alsoverczke. He married the daughter of R. Joshua Horowitz of Dzikov in 1880, and it was there that he published his first work, *Alfei Manasseh* on *Shulhan Arukh, Hoshen Mishpat* (Przemysl, 1895), which had an encomium of his father-in-law. He returned to Alsoverczke in 1898. When Joshua Heschel, the rabbi of Rzeszov, died, R. Manasseh succeeded him in 1904. He was a devoted hasid of Zanz.

He was the author of *Torat HaAsham* on purity and uncleanliness, which was printed in Podogorze in 1904. After the First World War, he lived in Munkacs, and in 1927, he became rebbe of Alsoverczke. He was also the author of *Mateh Manasseh* on the Sabbath, New Moons, and Festivals (Munkacs, 1927), and *Alfei Manasseh* on the Pentateuch (Munkacs, 1935). His son, R. Mattathias, was the rebbe of Dzikov in New York, and his daughter, Hayyah Devorah, married R. Simhah Rubin of Sasov in London.

EICHENSTEIN, Manasseh Yitzhak Meir, of Petah Tikvah (1894–27 *Tevet* 1971) – Born in Pruhnik Miasto, the son of R. Asher Yeshaya, he studied under R. Issachar Berish of Alsoverczke and was closely associated with R. Issachar Dov of Belz. He married Hayyah Sheindel, the daughter of R. Shimon Schiff, the rebbe of Lejask, who lived in Cluj. He first became the rebbe in Zydaczov and later lived in Petroseni, Romania.

After the Second World War, he emigrated to the Holy Land and settled in Haifa. He was renowned for his musical aptitude and was an active supporter of the Poale Agudat Yisrael.

He died without issue and was succeeded by his nephew, R. Joshua. R. Joshua was succeeded by R. Dov Berish Eichenstein in 1990.

EICHENSTEIN, Mattathias, of Dzikov (1886–5 *Elul* 1970) – Born in Dzikov, the son of R. Manasseh. In 1904, he married Bina, the daughter of R. Abraham Jacob Silverstein of Halicz. He emigrated to the United States in 1924 and participated in the work of the *Admorim* (Rebbes) Association. He was known as the rebbe of Dzikov.

EICHENSTEIN, Menahem Mendel, of Zydaczov (1840–11 *Adar* 1901) – The fifth son of R. Isaac of Zydaczov. He was named after R. Menahem Mendel of Rymanov. He married Friah, the daughter of his teacher R. Hayyim Abraham of Mikolayev, a descendant of Przemyshlan, whom he succeeded as rabbi. From 1884 he was rabbi in Zydaczov.

He was a prolific writer who wrote on Talmud, Midrash, and Kabbalah. His work *Adam VeHavah VeToldoteihem U'Menahem Tzedek*, a kabbalistic commentary, was published in Lvov in 1881. Another work, *Menahem Tzedek*, a commentary on *Sefer Yetzirah*, was published in Lvov in 1887.

His only son was R. Abraham Hayyim.

EICHENSTEIN, Menahem Tzvi, of St. Louis (1910–1981) – Born in Stryzov, the son of R. Joshua Heschel and Berachah Gitel, the daughter of R. Alter Zeev Horowitz. Soon after his birth, his father became rabbi of Chodorov. In 1923, the family emigrated to the United States and settled in Chicago. Menahem Tzvi was sent to study in Pressburg under R. Akiva Sofer and to Lublin to R. Moses of Boyan. He was ordained by R. Shalom David Kahane and R. David Halevi Ish Horowitz. He married Rikel Sarah, the daughter of R. Moses Mordecai Twersky of Lublin.

In 1938, he returned to the United States, and on the death of R. Hayyim Fishel Epstein, he became chief rabbi of the United Orthodox Congregations of St. Louis; he lived in St. Louis for forty years.

He was the author of *Pri Yehoshua* (St. Louis, 1949) and *Iturei Tzvi*. Dr. Norman Paris edited *Berachah Menahem* (St. Louis, 1955) in his honor.

He is survived by two sons and one daughter, Miriam Deborah. His son R. Dov Berish Alter is the rabbi of the *Agudat Yisrael* in Belle Harbor; his son, R. Moses Mordecai, with the encouragement of the rebbe of Belz, became, in February 1993, the Trisker rebbe in Jerusalem. His other son, R. Joshua

Heschel, is the principal of a Jerusalem *yeshivah*.

Jewish Tribune, February 11, 1993, p. 3.

EICHENSTEIN, Moses, of Sambor (1765–6 *Iyyar* 1840)–The second son of Yitzhak Isaac of Safrin. He was a disciple of his brother, R. Tzvi Hirsch. He visited R. Eleazar of Lejask, R. Menahem Mendel of Rymanov, and the "Seer of Lublin." He married the daughter of R. Yudel Harif. He lived on the proceeds of a small shop his wife kept in Sambor. In 1832, he became rebbe.

After his death, R. Joseph Rappaport printed his book *Tefillah LeMosheh* on the Pentateuch in 1856. A second edition was published in Lvov in 1893. His children were R. Yehudah Tzvi Hirsch of Rozdol; R. Jacob Kopul, rabbi of Rudick; R. Yeshaya, and R. Yehiel Michel.

EICHENSTEIN, Moses, of Zydaczov (1874–3 *Sivan* 1944)–Son of R. Issachar Berish of Alsoverczke. He studied under R. Issachar Spiegel, the *dayan* of Zydaczov. He married the daughter of R. Tzvi Hirsch Erlich, and when she died, he married his cousin, Sarah Hannah. In 1892, he became rabbi in Zydaczov, and he suffered much from controversies. He moved to Munkacs.

He was renowned as an outstanding scholar with a photographic memory. He knew whole tractates of the Talmud by heart. He perished in Auschwitz.

His sons were Elijah and Sender Lippa.

EICHENSTEIN, Moses Mordecai, of Chicago (b. 1913–)–Born in Chodorov, and in 1942 married Sarah, the daughter of R. Alter Israel Simon Perlow of Novominsk. He was the rabbi of the Galician Synagogue, in Chicago.

EICHENSTEIN, Nathan, of Tel Aviv (1921–*Rosh Hodesh Adar* II 1976)–Son of R. Joshua Eichenstein of Grosswardein. His mother was the daughter of R. Hayyim Isaac Yerucham, rabbi of Stary Sambor. He married Hannah, the daughter of Shemaryahu Gurrary of Tel Aviv. He studied in the Hungarian *yeshivot* and served as rabbi in Tetrush, Romania, and then in Grosswardein.

After the Second World War, he settled in Tel Aviv. He was buried in Safed near the grave of his father.

He was survived by five daughters.

EICHENSTEIN, Shlomoh Jacob Zeide, of Podhajce (1899–9 *Heshvan* 1964)–Son of R. Yitzhak Eizig Menahem of Podhajce. He was brought up by his grandfather R. Nahum Brandwein of Bursztyn. He married his cousin Hannah, the daughter of his uncle, R. Tuvye Horowitz, the rabbi of Sendziszov.

He was very active in education. He established a school for girls and a *kollel* for young men in Podhajce.

When he settled in the United States in 1936 and became the rebbe of Bursztin in a synagogue called *Massat Binyamin Anshei Podhajce*, his wife and children stayed in Europe. She perished in the Holocaust together with their four sons and four daughters.

After the Second World War he married Reisel, the daughter of R. Eleazar Weinberger of Huszt.

He was survived by two sons: his successor, R. Yitzhak Eizig, and R. David, who married Hayyah Sarah, the daughter of R. Moses Elikum Cahana, the rebbe of Spinka in Bene Berak. He left a manuscript, *Shema Yaakov*, on the Pentateuch.

EICHENSTEIN, Tzvi Hirsch, of Zydaczov (1763–11 *Tammuz* 1831)–Eldest son of R. Yitzhak Eizig of Safrin. He was a disciple of R. Yitzhak Harif of Sambor and R. David Jacob, the rabbi of Bolechov. He married Rachel Perl, the daughter of an innkeeper of Ruda, and when his wife died, he married Perl. He was tremendously diligent, and he concluded the whole Talmud seven times in a single year. He would study and revise seven pages of the Talmud every single day. He visited R. Moses of Przeworsk, R. Moses Leib of Sasov, and R. Israel of Kozienice.

At the age of twenty he became intrigued by mysticism, and from then on he devoted himself to its study. He showed a very practical concern for the poor and friendless. In the course of his life, he arranged the marriages of forty orphans. He would never sit down to his meal without a guest at his table.

His only son, R. Yehiel Michael, died in his lifetime, and he was survived by four daughters. He was a prolific and meticulous writer. He would go over his manuscript one hundred and one times.

His work *Sur Mera VeAssei Tov* was published in Lvov in 1832, and it was reprinted many times. *Pri-Kodesh Hillulim* on *Etz Hayyim* by R. Hayyim Vital was printed in Lvov in 1833. *Beth Yisrael*—hasidic homilies on the Torah—was printed in Lvov in 1834, and *Ateret Tzvi*, a commentary on the *Zohar* in two parts, was published in Lvov in 1834. *Kuntres HaShemot*, a lengthy commentary on the *Zohar* in two parts, was printed in Lvov in 1849. *Haggaot* on *Pri Etz Hayyim* was printed in Munkacs in 1928. His *Sefer Tzvi LeTzaddik* on *Tikkunei Zohar* was printed in Jerusalem in 1959. In 1931, to mark the centenary of his death, a book was published in Vienna with the title *Toldot Tzvi LeTzaddik*, by Michael Brawer.

EICHENSTEIN, Yehudah Tzvi Hirsch, of Dolina (1858–12 *Iyyar* 1909)—The only son of R. Issachar Berish. In 1873, he married the daughter of R. Mosheh Ungar of Zanz, where he stayed for three years. In 1876, when R. Hayyim of Zanz died, he returned to Dolina, where he eventually succeeded his father.

Most of his works have not seen the light of day, as only the prefaces to *Tefillah LeMosheh* and *Likkutei Torah* were published.

He was succeeded by his son-in-law, R. Joshua Halberstam.

EICHENSTEIN, Yehudah Tzvi Hirsch, of Rodzol (1791–7 *Heshvan* 1848)—Son of R. Moses of Sambor, he was a disciple of his uncle R. Tzvi Hirsch, whose daughter Sarah he married. He was an outstanding scholar, who revised, seventy times, the code *Yoreh De'ah*, dealing with the dietary laws. He was renowned for the manner in which he prayed, and the hasidim would throng to listen to him. He was particularly attached to R. Tzvi Hirsch of Liska.

He had no sons but was survived by three daughters. His son-in-law R. Ezekiel Shragai published his kabbalistic work *Daat Kedoshim* in Lvov in 1849 and, in 1853, published *Amud HaTorah* on Kabbalah. In 1889, his work *Taalumot Hokhmah* on *Midrash Rabbah* was published in Kolomyja.

EICHENSTEIN, Yitzhak Eizig, of Zydaczov (1795–9 *Sivan* 1873)—He was the only son of R. Issachar Berish. He studied under his uncles—R. Tzvi Hirsch and R. Moses. He was immersed in the study of Kabbalah, and he testified that he went over Luria's *Sefer Etz Hayyim* one hundred times. He was an ascetic and lived a life of poverty. He visited his contemporary rebbes of Strelisk, Zanz, Dzikov, Nadvorna, and Ropczyce. He was highly regarded by them. R. Aaron of Chernobyl called him a "mirror without blemish." Among the rebbes who visited him were Abraham of Stretyn and Joshua of Kaminka.

Among his works published posthumously were a two-volume commentary on *Midrash Rabbah* (Lvov, 1874). His work *Likkutei Torah VeHaShas*, the first part on Genesis, was printed in Lvov in 1877, the part on Exodus in Munkacz in 1883, the third and fourth parts on Leviticus and Numbers in Lvov in 1889, and the fifth part on Deuteronomy in Sighet in 1892. His work, in two parts, on the prophets and writings—*Likkutei Mahari* on *Yalkut Shimoni*—was printed in Lvov in 1890 and reprinted in Jerusalem in 1972.

He was survived by five children: R. Alexander Sender Lippa, R. Shlomoh Jacob, R. Issachar Berish, R. Eliyahu, and R. Menahem Mendel. None of them survived their father for long.

EIDELBAUM, Meir (d. 30 *Nisan* 1991), writer—Son of Yehiel, a descendant of R. Yehiel Halpern of Minsk, he was born in Mezhirech. He studied under R. Zeev Soloveitchik of Brest-Litovsk and then at the Tachkemoni Seminary in Warsaw.

He emigrated to Belgium in 1926 and soon after, settled in London, where he studied for a time at Jews' College under A. Buchler and also in the *Etz Hayyim Yeshivah*. He became a journalist and worked for many years on the Yiddish paper *Die Zeit*. His first hasidic work was published in *Ha-Olam*, edited by M. Kleinman. A number of hasidic themes on the hasidic rebbes in London appeared in *Die Zeit*.

In 1941, he left for the United States of America and twenty years later settled in Tel Aviv. He wrote on Israel Baal Shem Tov, the Maggid of Mezhirech, R. Elimelech of Lejask, and the *Hozeh* of Lublin.

EIN SOF—A kabbalistic term meaning "endless" or "infinite." All the names of God in the Bible refer to the various manifestations of the Deity, whereas *Ein Sof*, the kabbalists tell us, cannot even be named, let alone conceived. The kabbalists never tire of affirming the essential unit of *Ein Sof* and the *Sefirot*.

The term was first used by R. Azriel of Gerona (1160–1238) in his *Perush Esser Sefirot*: "That which has no limit is called *Ein Sof*." R. Yitzhak Luria describes it as the "supernal light," a term for the infinite.

EINHORN, Efraim Tzvi, of Mosty-Wielkie (1854–24 *Tammuz* 1901)—He was born in Brzesko in Galicia, son of a wheat merchant, Zeev Wolf. He married Debora Freidel, the daughter of R. Zelig Ritman of Cracow. He studied under R. Joshua Trunk of Kutno.

At the age of twenty-four he became principal of the *yeshivah* in Mosty-Wielkie, where he attracted outstanding students. His daily *Shiur*, which lasted five hours, began at dawn and was rarely concluded before ten o'clock in the morning. His studies were conducted in great depth, as he barely covered one page of the Talmud per session.

He was succeeded by his son, R. Dov Berish (1877–1942), who married the daughter of R. Pinhas Menahem Justman of Pilice and who perished in the Holocaust.

ELIEZER FISCHEL, of Strzyzov (eighteenth century)—Son of R. Yitzhak, he was born and lived in Strzyzov, near Tarnopol. Though a great exponent and follower of the Lurian doctrines, he was very critical of Hasidism.

He was the author of *Sefer Olam HaGadol* (Zolkiev, 1800), *Sefer Olam Ehad* (1802), *Sefer Olam Barur* (1800), and *Sefer Olam Hafukh* (1800).

ELIEZER HALEVI, of Pinsk (second half of the eighteenth century)—He was formerly *Av Bet Din* in Homsk (a small town near Pinsk) and afterward, rabbi of Pinsk. He was one of the first to persecute hasidim. R. Aaron the Great was his special target.

In vain did R. Dov Baer, the Maggid of Mezhirech, urge him to "live together in peace and harmony with R. Aaron." His homiletical work *Siah HaSadeh* (Shklov, 1795) received high praise from R. Avigdor, another antagonist of Hasidism.

W. Z. Rabinowitsch, *Lithuanian Hasidism*, pp. 13, 24, 43.

ELIJAH BEN SOLOMON ZALMAN, Gaon of Vilna (1720–1797) Popularly known as the "Vilner Gaon," he wielded extraordinary power as the greatest rabbinic authority of East European Jewry. Venerated by his contemporaries, he became a legend in his lifetime. By reason of his intellect and personality, he loomed like a colossus over the great ones of his generation. He was born on the first day of Passover, on April 23, 1720, in Vilna or nearby Seltz. A descendant of Moses Kramer (d. 1688) and R. Moses Rivkes, he was already known in his early childhood as a prodigy. One of his early teachers was probably R. Moses Margolies, the rabbi of Kaidan. At a very early age, Elijah married Hannah, the daughter of R. Yehudah Leib of Kaidan, and she bore him two sons, Aryeh Leib and Abraham.

When Elijah was about twenty years old, he began an incognito journey through Poland that lasted eight years. It was part of a self-afflicted penance, known as "going into exile." His capacity for study was almost superhuman, and to the study of the Torah he dedicated his mind, his heart, and his soul. Unswervingly, without any deviation, he followed the path of the Torah. His general knowledge, too, was encyclopedic, and his range of interests wide. In addition to Hebrew grammar, he studied biology and astronomy. He encouraged Barukh of Shklov (1740–1810) to translate into Hebrew the six books of Euclid's *Geometry*. He is himself credited to be the author of many books, among them commentaries on the Bible, the *Mishnah*, the Palestinian Talmud, *Sefer Yetzirah*, the *Zohar*, and the *Shulhan Arukh*. Not all his works have seen the light of day, and many have been lost.

He declined a position as rabbi and lived on a small legacy from his great-great-grandfather. The Gaon reflected the intolerance of his generation.

It is one of the ironies of history that he, who was called the "hasid" and who was the author of works on mysticism, became one of the most bitter antagonists of Hasidism. Even though he held no public office in the community, the heads of the Vilna *Kahal* consulted him on important problems that confronted them. At that time, small hasidic groups had been established in Brest-Litovsk, Grodno, and Lutsk, and the fiery activities of R. Aaron of Karlin near Pinsk sent sparks flying far and wide. And when a hasidic house of prayer was established in Vilna, the *Kahal* began to wage war against the new sect and sought the Gaon's advice on how to direct their attacks.

Hasidism to him was a rival movement, and his opposition to it was derived from his suspicion that it had been infected with Shabbatean heresy. He was of the opinion that hasidic doctrines had absorbed Shabbatean views. To the Vilner Gaon, so dedicated to scholarship, and for whom no amount of Torah study was adequate, let alone excessive, the hasidic advice that "one must not pass all one's time in study" was intolerable. The fear that the sect wanted to introduce changes in the scales of value focal to Judaism, wherein the study of Torah is of supreme importance and the scholar (*lamdan*) is preeminent, led to the Gaon's zealous opposition to Hasidism. He strongly opposed the adoption by the hasidim of the *Nusah Ari*, the liturgy of the kabbalist Isaac Luria, in preference to *Minhag Ashkenaz*, the Polish-German liturgy. The Gaon feared that separatist tendencies would disrupt and demoralize the house of Israel.

To him it was intolerable that some of the hasidim disregarded the prescribed hours of worship. He was moreover deeply concerned with the conduct of the hasidim in the synagogue. He abhorred the undisciplined way in which many hasidim worshiped—by swaying and dancing, singing, and sighing or laughing as the mood seized them. The cult of the *tzaddik*, too, was alien to him, for it produced a new type of teacher whose power stemmed from the heart rather than from the mind. Mystic though he was, he failed to discern in Hasidism a new and momentous phase in the evolution of Jewish mysticism.

In 1771, an epidemic broke out in Vilna and many children died. A scapegoat had to be found, and the community chose the hasidim for the role. With the consent of the Gaon, they issued a *herem* against the heretical sect. Even this mass excommunication did not satisfy the Gaon: "Had I the power," he declared, "I would have punished the infidels as the worshipers of Baal were punished of old." A month after the proclamation of the *herem*, a letter was sent to the communities of Lithuania and White Russia in which it was stated that "so long as they do not make full atonement, the hasidim should be scattered and driven away so that no two heretics remain together."

The Vilna authorities urged the Brody community to follow their example, and the response was immediate. On 20 *Sivan*, the Brody leadership, too, excommunicated the hasidim. Similar steps were taken by other communities. In 1775, two of the finest hasidic scholars, R. Shneur Zalman of Liady and R. Menahem Mendel of Vitebsk, came to Vilna and sought a personal interview with the Gaon, but he refused to see them. In 1781, Vilna proclaimed a second *herem* against the hasidim. Once again, the Gaon was in the forefront. "Although it was not my custom to trespass beyond my province," wrote the Gaon, "yet here I give my approval, being mindful of the saying that 'when the Torah is being annulled, it is time to act.' " Two envoys, R. David and R. Joshua Siegel, were sent from Vilna to warn people throughout Lithuania against the hasidim. On 3 *Elul* 1781, the rabbinical assembly of Zelva (near Grodno) endorsed the *herem*. In Shklov and in Moghilev in White Russia, a circular was issued condemning the hasidim in the most severe terms: "For they tread a path which our fathers did not tread." In 1794, the hasidic works *Toldot Yaakov Yosef* and the *Testament of the Besht* were burned in public in front of the Great Synagogue in Vilna. Hitherto peaceful communities were rent by hatred and bitterness. Even acts of physical violence were not uncommon.

In May 1796, it was related in Vilna that a hasid was journeying through the country purporting to be the son of the Gaon, publicly proclaiming that his father deeply regretted his harshness toward the hasidim and was now making atonement for his grievous error. This led to the Gaon's most bitter utterance toward them. In letters dated June 22 and October 14, 1796, the Gaon thundered, "No one should have pity upon them and take their part, but rather they should be cast out from all the tribes of Israel as evildoers." He saw himself in the role of his namesake, the Prophet Elijah.

On the third day of Sukkot (October 9, 1797), the Gaon died. Some of the hasidim in Vilna would not allow his death to diminish the "Season of Rejoicing." The *Kahal*, incensed by what they considered to be the unseemly behavior of the hasidim, set up a special committee to deal with them, and the conflict moved beyond the confines of the Jewish community. The Russian authorities became involved and took advantage of the opportunity to reduce Jewish communal authority.

Two decades of relentless warfare by the Gaon had failed to destroy or even weaken the movement.

S. J. Fuenn, *Kirya Ne'emanah* Vilna, pp. 144–156.

J. Klausner, *Vilna BeTekufat HaGaon*, pp. 16–49.

M. Wilensky, *Bitzaron* (1968), pp. 143–148.

M.W. and T.R.

ELIMELEKH of Lejask (1717–21 *Adar* 1786), hasidic rabbi–Elimelekh, the son of wealthy landowner Eliezer Lippa, was born in Lapacha near Titkin. He studied, together with his brother Zusya, in Titkin, where they came in contact with R. Shmelke Horowitz, from whom he and his brother learned to study with single-minded diligence. They practiced asceticism and went into "exile." Wandering incognito from town to town for three years, they suffered the rigors of the road, often weary and hungry. They traveled through Poland as far as Auschwitz.

R. Elimelekh married the daughter of R. Jacob Margulies, a descendant of R. Eliezer Rokeah of Amsterdam. When the Besht died, Elimelekh's brother Zusya urged him to visit R. Dov Baer of Mezhirech, whom he regarded as his teacher. It was there that he met R. Levi Isaac of Berdichev and R. Yehiel Michael of Zloczov. After the death of the Maggid in 1772, Elimelekh was the uncrowned head of Hasidism for the next thirty years. He was loyally supported by most of the Maggid's disciples, among them R. Jacob Isaac, the "Seer of Lublin"; R. Israel, the Maggid of Kozienice; R. Menahem Mendel of Rymanov; and R. Kalonymus Kalman Epstein.

He first settled in Sianiawa and then in Lyzhansk (Lejask), which became the Jerusalem of Hasidism. Like the Besht, R. Elimelekh took up the wanderer's staff and visited many villages and distant hamlets. He was deeply concerned with the fate of orphans, and it was his particular pleasure to arrange marriages for them. There was never any money in his house, for all monies were promptly distributed among the poor.

R. Elimelekh himself composed a special prayer to be recited before every service. He counseled moderation in all things. Under his influence, Torah study was intensified. His hasidim were exhorted to apply themselves, each according to ability, to the study of the Pentateuch, *Mishnah*, and Talmud with all their commentaries.

When the Vilna authorities excommunicated the hasidim, R. Elimelekh advised restraint. Even when one time he was physically assaulted by an overzealous *Mitnagged*, his reaction was mild. Two letters written at the time and included in R. Elimelekh's book *Noam Elimelekh* throw some light on the "civil war" that was raging so fiercely in Galicia between the hasidim and the *mitnaggedim*. In one letter, his son refutes accusations by R. Abraham Katzenellenbogen of Brest-Litovsk and justifies the adoption by the hasidim of *Nusah Ari*. The other letter stresses the high caliber of the *tzaddikim*: "They serve God in truth and without pride."

The grave of R. Elimelekh in Lejask has become a place of pilgrimage, and in recent years, regular annual excursions to Lejask have been organized by the hasidim, who had his *Ohel* renovated in 1960. He was survived by two daughters, Merish and Ettel, and by three sons–R. Eleazar, his successor in Lejask; R. Eliezer Lippa of Chmielnik, the author of *Orah LeTzaddik*; and R. Jacob, the rabbi of Moglienice.

R. Elimelekh's work *Noam Elimelekh*, a commentary on the weekly Torah readings, is one of the classics of hasidic literature. It was first printed in Lvov two years after his death by his son and successor, and it underwent fifty editions until 1952. The book was instantly acclaimed for its power and profundity. The name of the author was omitted in the first edition, and R. Hayyim of Kosov declared that "only a person who is able to revive the dead is able to understand this book." There is also an epilogue–*Tzetel Katan* (small paragraph)–which advises the reader to repeat it at least twice a day and to translate every word into Yiddish. Among his other works were *Igeret HaKodesh* (Zolkiev, 1799) and *Or Elimelekh* (Jerusalem, 1988). In 1978, Dr. G. Nigal published in Jerusalem a critical edition of *Noam Elimelekh*.

Among R. Elimelekh's rules were: Jews should guard themselves against hating any fellow Jew, except the wicked, who are unrepentant; Jews should not engage in any conversation at all before prayers, not even a single word, because it is a hindrance to concentration during prayer; Jews should speak gently to all; and they should see to it that their clothes are always clean.

The major concerns of Elimelekh's theology are the nature of the spiritual life, the problem of evil, and the function of the *tzaddik*. Human life is a pilgrimage from duality to union (*Ahdut*). Evil inclination and materialistic urges drive us away from God, yet if these undesirable instincts are sanctified by the rediscovery and rekindling of the inner sparks, they become a vehicle for the service of God. The purification of earthly desires in conjunction with the control of such negative qualities as anger opens the soul to divine graces.

A *tzaddik* is one who has attained a high standard through spiritual purification and the subjugation of the ego. The *tzaddikim* are called *serafim* and rank higher than the angels. The *tzaddik* is often compelled to descend in order to raise fellowmen to the former's own level. Such a descent entails personal sacrifices as it lessens the *tzaddik's* communion with God. Having descended, the *tzaddik* works through both example and precept. The *tzaddik's* sacrifices and lifestyle awaken followers to their proper destiny. R. Elimelekh believed that a sympathetic relationship exists between rebbes and the souls of their followers. Thus rebbes could mystically bind themselves to their hasidim and purify their souls.

He emphasized the theurgic nature of the *tzaddik's* prayer, teaching that such prayer could annul evil decrees, heal the sick, and even ensure financial well-being. This great power stemmed from the *tzaddik's* overflowing love for God and all people. Coupled with this love is the *tzaddik's* realization that a *tzaddik* is the people's servant, rather than their leader. All Elimelekh's writings reflect his great personal humility before God and Israel.

B. Landau, *R. Elimelekh MiLejansk*.

T.R. and S.L.B.

ELIOR, RACHEL (b. 1949) – Leading Israeli professor and scholar of Kabbalah and Hasidism in the Institute of Jewish Studies, Hebrew University of Jerusalem. In 1976, Elior was awarded a Ph.D., summa cum laude, for her dissertation, *Theology and Divine Worship in the Second Generation of Habad Hasidism* (Hebrew), written under the direction of Rivkah Schatz-Uffenheimer. A version of the work was published in 1982. With that work, Elior established herself as one of the foremost authorities on *Habad* Hasidism, a field to which she has continued to contribute.

Her work in the area has focused especially on the systematic structure of *Habad* theology in the writings of its originator, R. Shneur Zalman of Liady, and his two principal interpreters – his son and successor – R. Dov Baer of Lubavitch and R. Aaron Halevi Horowitz of Starosseljie, respectively. Particular emphasis is given to the articulation of R. Aaron's teachings and the basis for the controversy concerning his interpretation and that of R. Dov Baer, especially regarding the meaning and place of *hitpaalut* (ecstasy) in *Habad* worship. Elior's work on *Habad* is summed up in her English publication *The Paradoxical Ascent to God*, which was published in 1993. Here Elior not only clarifies dialectical tensions in *Habad* kabbalistic theosophy but also places it within the history of religion and mysticism.

In addition to her writings on *Habad*, Elior has published important studies on other aspects of early Hasidism. These include essays on the relationship between Hasidism and Kabbalah; on R. Jacob Isaac, the "Seer of Lublin"; on spiritual reality and social verification in early Hasidism; and on R. Nathan Adler of Frankfurt, as well as a major article on the teachings of R. Jacob Isaac of Lublin and R. Mordecai Joseph Leiner of Izbica. In the summer of 1993, Elior was writing a comprehensive work on the founder of Hasidism – *R. Israel Ba'al Shem Tov and the Beginning of Hasidism: Spiritual Image and Cultural Influence*.

R. Elior, *The Paradoxical Ascent to God: The Kabbalistic Theosophy of Habad*.

M.KR.

ELOHIM – A biblical name of God. Early rabbinic sources already regarded it as indicating the stern nature of the deity, particularly the aspect of divine Judgment, in contrast to the tetragrammaton, which was thought to indicate God's love and mercy.

This tendency was continued in kabbalah. The name symbolized the fifth *Sefirah*, *Gevurah* (Power), or *Din* (Judgment), occupying a position on the left side of the sefirotic tree. It is counterbalanced on the right side by *Hesed* (Love), the intermediary link between them being *Rahamim* (Mercy), sometimes called *Tiferet* (Beauty).

The word "*Elohim*" was also considered in the *Zohar* to be a representation of the union of *Mi* (Who?) with *Eleh* (These). It "guarantees the continued existence of creation insofar as it represents the union of the hidden subject *Mi* and the hidden object *Eleh*" (Scholem).

The recital of both names together (*YHVH Elohenu*) in the benediction unifies the opposing aspects of the deity.

D.G.

EMANCIPATION – The movement for Jewish emancipation grew gradually in Europe from the mid-seventeenth century on. In the eighteenth century, as part of the general movement toward civil libertarianism and the breakdown of medieval institutions and disabilities, the issue of Jewish emancipation proceeded apace. Assisted by liberal non-Jews and encouraged by the growing number of "emancipated" modern Jews, such as Moses Mendelssohn, the debate gave way to practical expressions in the late eighteenth century. Political rights and full emancipation first came to Jews in the United States, then in France as a result of the French Revolution, and thereafter throughout Europe wherever Napoléon's armies carried it.

In Eastern Europe, Jewish subjects of the Hapsburg Empire were granted a certain degree of emancipation through the Edict of Toleration, issued in January 1782 by Emperor Joseph II. This political progress was accompanied by and gave rise to movements aimed at Jewish secularism, Jewish religious reform, and a broad movement of "Jewish Enlightenment," known as the *Haskalah*. Though many mixed motives were present in these movements, they all aimed at bringing the Jews into the mainstream of European culture and breaking down the barriers of separatism that had kept them apart from the large, non-Jewish environment.

Among the favorite targets of the *maskilim* (disciples of the *Haskalah*) was Hasidism, which was constantly satirized and caricatured as a paradigm of all that was wrong with traditional Judaism and its insular ways. (See, e.g., Solomon Helma's early anti-hasidic polemic *Mirkevet HaMishneh* [1751] or the unflattering view of Hasidism presented in Solomon Maimon's *Autobiography* [1792]). In addition to the positive benefits of emancipation, there was also a less well understood yet equally powerful motive operating in many of its advocates: the Jews need a twofold emancipation: they need both to be emancipated from civil disabilities and to be liberated from their Jewishness if they are really to become full citizens of the modern European state. Emancipation was thus not an unadulterated blessing, and it certainly was not seen as such by the traditionalist Jewish camp, both mitnaggedic and hasidic.

Hasidic opposition to emancipation was profound. The *tzaddikim* viewed emancipation as a false promise that would undermine Torah-true Judaism and lead to the eventual breakdown of the Jewish way of life. This instinctual suspicion was supported on the one hand by the results of the liberal religious tendencies that were beginning to gain the upper hand in Western Europe and on the other hand by a seeming connection between apostasy and emancipation witnessed not only in Western Europe but also among supporters of emancipation and *Haskalah* in Eastern Europe.

The practical forms that the hasidic opposition took were twofold: the first was to fight against the increasing Westernizing tendencies in the general society, and the second was a steady battle against all liberal and *Haskalah* elements within the Jewish community. With regard to the issue of liberalism, the reaction to what was perceived as the liberal forces of Napoléon can be taken as paradigmatic of the hasidic attitude. Shneur Zalman of Liady, an ardent opponent of emancipation and liberalism, wrote, "If Bonaparte (representing the liberal forces) wins, the wealthy among Israel would increase and the greatness of Israel would be raised, but they would leave and take the heart of Israel far from their Father in Heaven" (*Iggrot Baal HaTanya*, p. 238).

Again, we know that R. Levi Yitzhak of Berditchev was the leading Jewish contributor to the czar's war effort (1807) against the

French. Likewise, the Polish *tzaddikim*–R. Yaacov Yitzhak of Lublin (the "Seer"), R. Israel of Kozienice, and R. Naftali of Ropczyce–all worked for the defeat of Napoléon. With regard to emancipation and enlightenment in Russia and Poland, perhaps the surest evidence of the intensity of hasidic opposition consists in the fierce antihasidic polemics one finds among the liberal groups. For example, Joseph Perl's work in the form of an *Epistolae Obscurorum Virorum* (*Megalleh Temirim*, "The Revealer of the Hidden") paints the darkest picture of the hasidim as opponents of emancipation and enlightenment. Moreover, Perl felt so strongly about the negative attitude of the hasidim that he invoked government aid against the *tzaddik* Hersh Elchenstein, saying, "[All progressive influences] are being annihilated on one Sabbath by a hasidic *tzaddik*." Somewhat later, the same views are expressed, less emotionally, by Max Lilienthal, a leader of the movement for Jewish school reform in Russia, among others.

The hasidic reaction to these internal liberal forces was vigorous. For example, R. Menahem Mendel of Vitebsk laments, "Verily, grammar [knowledge of Hebrew] is useful . . . but what is to be done since the wicked and sinful [*maskilim*] have taken possession of it." A broader indictment expressing similar sentiments is found in the teachings of R. Nahman of Bratzlav; R. Shalom Rokeah, the founder of the Belzer dynasty; and R. Shneur Zalman of Liady, the founder of the *Habad* (Lubavitch) dynasty, and his heirs R. Dov Baer of Lubavitch, the second Lubavitcher rebbe, and R. Menahem Mendel, the third Lubavitcher rebbe, also known as the *Tzemah Tzedek* ("Offspring of Righteousness"). The Polish *tzaddikim* also generally shared these views, among them being R. Jacob Yitzhak of Lublin and the "Holy Yehudi," Jacob Yitzhak of Przysucha, and their disciples, notably Simcha Bunam of Przysucha, and Yitzhak Meir of Ger. R. Nahman Bratzlav stated very succinctly the hasidic view on the matter: "Heresies are spreading. . . ." (*Sihot v'sippurim moharan* (1910, p. 23f.).

R. Mahler, *HaHasidut VeHaskalah*.

S.K.

ENGEL, Samuel, of Radomysl (13 *Nisan* 1853–19 *Adar* 1935)–He was born in Tarnov, Galicia. His father was Zeev Wolf, who died when Samuel was only six years old. At the age of sixteen, he was renowned as the *Illui of Tarnov*. He married the daughter of R. Isaac of Bilgoraj, and he remained in the home of his father-in-law for twelve years. In 1872, he became the rabbi of Bilgoraj, having received his ordination from R. Shneur Zalman Ashkenazi.

After being rabbi for seven years, he had to escape the Russian authorities. He stayed and studied Kabbalah with R. Barukh of Gorlice in Rudnik for two years. In 1886, he became the rabbi of Radomysl, where he stayed until the outbreak of the First World War. In 1917, he settled in Kosice, Hungary (later, Czechoslovakia), where, as *Av Bet Din*, he spent eighteen years. Every day, before his prayers, he would recite eighteen chapters of Psalms. Then he would study the *Shulhan Arukh*, by R. Shneur Zalman of Liady, which he regarded as an indispensable guide to the intricate laws of Passover. Daily he would study the hasidic works of *Noam Elimelekh*, *Bnei Yissachar*, and *Tiferet Shlomoh*. Not a day would pass without his mentioning the name of R. Hayyim Halberstam.

He was a prolific writer. In Yaroslav, in 1905, he published part one of a work consisting of 99 responsa. Part two, another 72 responsa, appeared in 1908. Part three, with 124 responsa, was printed in 1925. Part four, with 104 responsa, was published in 1929. In 1936, his son-in-law R. David Halperin published part five, with 110 responsa, and in 1938, part six, with 130 responsa.

His grandson, R. Elhonon Halpern of London, resumed publication of the literary legacy of his grandfather, and he printed *Shem Shmuel* in 1941, part seven of the responsa in 1957, and part eight in 1958. He also printed *Sifsei Maharash* on Torah and *Hiddushei Maharash* on *Kiddushin* (Jerusalem, 1965), as well as a complete edition of R. Samuel's work, which was printed in Jerusalem in 1981.

R. Samuel was survived by two sons and five daughters. His son R. Hayyim succeeded him as rabbi of Radomysl.

A. Surasky, *Marbitzei Torah*, vol. 4, pp. 63–68.

ENGELHARDT, Abraham Issachar, of Bene Berak (b. 1919)–Son of R. Israel, the rabbi of Sosnowiec, he was a partisan during the Second World War. After the war, having lived for a number of years in the United States, he settled in Bene Berak in 1968. He married the daughter of R. Mordeccai Eliezer Leiner and is the present representative of the Radzyn dynasty in the Holy Land.

ENGELHARDT, Isaiah, of Sosnowiec (1885–1943)–Son of R. Yitzhak Nahum, a descendant of R. Dov Baer Meisels of Warsaw, he studied under his uncle, R. Isaiah Kazunzer, a brother-in-law of the *Sefat Emet*. In 1901 he married Esther Frimet, the daughter of R. Nathan Nahum HaKohen Rabinowicz of Krimlov. He became rabbi in Mondszev near Sosnowiec, and then in Sosnowiec.

He participated in the founding conference of the Aguda in 1912. He was a prolific writer, but all his manuscripts perished in the Holocaust.

He was strongly opposed to the collaborationist activities of the *Judenrat*, such as the preparation of lists for the Germans. He, together with his two sons–R. Solomon Meir and R. Shapsai Ezekiel–three daughters, and one grandson, perished in the Holocaust.

He was survived by one daughter, Gitel, married to R. Simon Ezekiel Frankel Teumim of *Kiryat Ono*, and two sons, R. Jacob Elimelech (29 *Shevat* 1992) and R. Abraham Issachar of Bene Berak.

J. Silberberg, *Malkhut Bet Radomsk*, pp. 404–407.

ENGLISH LANGUAGE/LITERATURE–The accumulated literature on Hasidism is staggering. A number of authors, both academic and popular, have written on it. It took some time before a favorable picture was presented. It was Solomon Schechter who pioneered a revisionist picture. Unlike his contemporary Franzos, author of the *Jews of Baranow* and who wrote as an outsider, Schechter in his essay *The Hasidim* (1896) confessed that he learned to love in Hasidism that "which is ideal and noble and to hate what is bad and pernicious." What Buber achieved in Germany, Schechter achieved in England. He stressed the genius of Hasidism's founder and appreciated the strong bond that the hasidim created among themselves.

Israel Zangwill in his *Children of the Ghetto* and his *Dreamers of the Ghetto* was the first English writer who brought Hasidism into his works. He described a hasidic synagogue in London where "they prayed metaphysics, angelology, Kabbalah" and described the Besht as "ever-glorious and luminous." He admired the Besht's quality of humility.

In 1904, Helena Frank translated into English Peretz's hasidic story *If Not Higher*, and it was incorporated into his *Book of Jewish Thoughts* by Chief Rabbi Hertz.

Dr. Moses Gaster (1856–1939) in his introduction to the English translation of Horodezky's *Leaders of Hasidism* stated that "Hasidism brought hope and joy to the downtrodden, to the weak and the ignorant."

Similarly, R. Dr. J. Abelson in his *Jewish Mysticism* (London, 1913) describes Hasidism as a "force that deserves an abiding place in the history of Jewish theology."

Unlike Buber, "the self-appointed apostle to the Gentiles, carrying to them a metamorphosed message of Hasidism," the Yiddish writers Sholem Asch in *Salvation* (*Tehillim Yid*) and in *Three Cities*, Zalman Schneur in his *Emperor and the Rabbi* and in *Noah Pandre*, and Joseph Opatoshu in *Polish Woods* all deal sympathetically with Hasidism. The influence of Hasidism is clearly discernible in the writings of Franz Kafka, who was influenced not only by Buber but also by Dora Dymant, who came from a hasidic Polish background.

Nor can one minimize the impact of the production of Ansky's *Dybbuk* by the *Vilna Troupe* and the *Habimah*. R. Azriel's speech from the play was incorporated into Victor Gollancz's *Anthology*. Israel Singer's *Joshe Kalb* and Wolf Mankowitz and Sam Wanamaker in the *World of Sholom Aleichem* are all flavored with Hasidism.

Louis Golding in his *Day of Atonement* portrays a hasid, Eli of Manchester, who prayed "with fervor typical of the hasidim." He also portrays a hasidic rabbi in the *Glory of Elsie Silver* who urged his followers to fight against the Nazis. In his book *The Wall*, the American author John Hersey describes a hasidic rabbi, clad in *tallit* and *tefillin*, dying a martyr's death. Izaak Goller in his novel *Moses* graphically describes R. Zalman, a hasidic rabbi of Whitechapel, who influenced a Mr. Moses, an English-born Jew, to convert to Hasidism.

Meyer Levin, who wrote a book of hasidic tales, *The Golden Mountain*, even stated that "had I been born near Vilna, I might have become a hasid."

The artist Alfred Wolmark went to Cracow to paint hasidim, and Sir William Rothenstein painted hasidim of the *Mahzikei Hadas* and *Hevrah Shass* in London.

Joseph Leftwich, "Hasidic Influence in Imaginative English Literature," pp. 3–11.

ENVY–As a quietistic movement, Hasidism stressed the concept of prenatal determination: one's fate on earth was determined to some extent by the kind of soul (*neshamah*) one inherited. Was it "rooted" in the highest realm of *Atzilut*? In that case, one was virtually incapable of sinning or being envious. "Whoever possesses a soul deriving from *Atzilut* is incapable of sin" (*Toldot Yaakov Yosef*, *Tetzaveh*).

The commandment "Thou shalt not covet" (Exodus 20:14), said the rebbe of Radzvillov,

> . . . is placed at the end of the Decalogue, because he who has observed this commandment is certain to have observed all those which precede. But he who has not sufficient self-discipline, to fulfill this prohibition against coveting, must recommence anew with the first commandment: belief in the justice of God. For had he sincerely believed in God, he would not be covetous of that which God had allotted to the share of others.

"When envy will cease," said R. Nahman of Bratzlav, "redemption will come. Envy is often the cause of destruction and murder. Envy of another man's property may cause derangement of mind."

A hasid was less likely than others to experience the pangs of envy. Hasidim were encouraged to try to obtain that which belongs to them in the heavenly perspective, not to be envious of others. The famous saying of the rabbi of Kotzk illustrates the thought that each of us must be true to our own self. "If I am I, because you are you, then I am not I, and you are not you; but if I am I because I am I, and you are you, because you are you, then I am I, and you are you" (M. Buber, *Tales of Hasidim*, vol. 2, p. 283).

In addition, envy, like anger, was one of the expressions of the evil desire that needed to be transmuted through the threefold process of subjugation (*hahanah*), analysis (*havdalah*), and sweetening (*hamtakah*), i.e., the hasid was bidden to transfer the feelings of envy from the goods of this world to that of excelling in Divine service, in accordance with the character of his soul.

J.B.A.

EPSTEIN, Abraham Meir, of Liskiava (1726–1772), talmudist–Son of R. Aryeh Leib, he was also known as "Meir Harif" (the sharp-witted). He was first rabbi in Liskiava and then in Nowy Mysz. He was the author of novellas to the Talmud and to Maimonides. He favored Hasidism and befriended R. Israel of Plotsk, a disciple of R. Dov Baer, the Maggid of Mezhirech.

EPSTEIN, Abraham Solomon, of Ozarov (1865–11 *Heshvan* 1917)–He was born in Tarlo or Chmielnik on the 25th day of *Tishri*, the son of R. Aryeh Leibish, the second rebbe of Ozarov. On 15 *Heshvan* 1880, he married Reize Mirrel (d. 21 *Iyyar* 1918), the daughter of R. Hayyim Samuel of Chenchin, a descendant of the "Seer of Lublin." He lived in Chenchin for eight years. He was known as R. Solomon "Harif." Ordained by R. Joshua Trunk of Kutno, he became rabbi first in Josefov, and then in 1888 in Ozarov, where he lived for twenty-seven years.

He was a follower of R. Ezekiel of Sianiawa, R. Abraham Twersky, the Maggid of Turiysk, and the rebbes of Chortkov, Husyatin, and Boyan.

He was renowned for his tearful prayers. During the first World War, when the Jews were expelled from Ozarov by the Russian authorities, he went to live in Opatov. Many of his manuscripts were lost during this period.

His son, R. Eliezer Joshua, published his works in Warsaw in 1938 under the title *Sheerit Berakhah*. His other son, R. Moses Yehiel, was rabbi of Ozarov.

A. Surasky, *BeLahavat Esh*, pp. 152–267.

EPSTEIN, Aryeh Judah Leib (1837–7 *Nisan* 1914), the third rebbe of Ozarov–Son of Yehiel Hayyim and son-in-law of Eliezer Shalom, the rabbi of Siedlice and Piotrokov. He studied under Eleazar of Kozienice, R. Yitzhak of Neshkhiz, R. Abraham of Turiysk and R. Hayyim David of Piotrokov, known as "Dr. Bernard." He married Reizel, the daughter of R. Eliezer Shalom Morgenstern of Piotrokov and Siedlice, and when she died, he married the daughter of R. Efraim Fischel Hakohen.

At the age of twenty he became rabbi of Tarlo and then held rabbinical positions in Josefov, Chmielnik, Opole, and Ozarov, where he succeeded his father in 1888.

He was the author of *Birkhat Tov* on Genesis, published in Bilgoraj in 1938. Many of his discourses are mentioned in his son's work, *Sheerit Berakhah*, and by his grandson, R. Moses Yehiel in his *Esh Dat* and *Beer Mosheh*.

He had five sons: R. Eliezer Shalom of Parczev, R. Joseph of Josefov, R. Alter Moses David of Tarlo, R. Jacob and R. Abraham Shlomoh who succeeded him. His daughter Havah married R. Yerahmiel Tzvi Rabinowicz of Siedlice. His other daughter, Feige, married R. Jacob Yerahmiel Taub of Radom.

A. Surasky, *BeLahavat Esh*, pp. 90–151.

EPSTEIN, Barukh Halevi, of Bobruisk (1860–1942), talmudical scholar–Born in Bobruisk, son of Yehiel Michael Epstein, the author of *Arukh Hashulhan*. He was ordained by R. Menahem Mendel Schneersohn of Lubavitch, with whom he spent a whole month. Throughout his life he was sympathetic to Hasidism. He was the author of *Torah Temimah* (1902), a compilation of quotations from the Oral Law.

EPSTEIN, Joseph Barukh, of Neustadt (1792–10 *Adar* 1867)–Son of R. Kalonymus Kalman Halevi of Cracow. His humility earned him the title "*Der guter Yid*" (the good Jew). He venerated the Psalms and would recite the entire book every day. "His recital of the Psalm," said R. Hayyim Halberstam, "is more important in heaven than my study of the Talmud."

He became known as a miracle worker and gave to the *Meir Baal Haness* fund the money he received from his followers. He died while preparing to emigrate to the Holy Land.

He was succeeded by his son, R. Kalonymus Kalman of Neustadt (d. 9 *Tevet* 1903).

EPSTEIN, Kalonymus Kalman Halevi, of Cracow (1754–1 *Tammuz* 1823)–Son of R. Aaron Halevi, Kalonymus was a disciple of R. Elimelekh of Lejask; R. Jacob Yitzhak, the "Seer of Lublin"; R. Menahem Mendel of Rymanov; and R. Yehiel Michal of Zloczov. In 1785, he established a hasidic *shtiebl* in Cracow, a step that aroused strong opposition.

His major work, *Ma'Or VaShemesh* (Breslau, 1842), is a fundamental work of Hasidism, which was reprinted many times. In this work he describes the court of the *tzaddik* as "a holy group" consisting of old and young, rich and poor. The climax of the spiritual experience of the hasid is the rebbe's discourse. In the hours of intense devotion (*devekut*), the *tzaddik* almost ceases to exist. He survives only because God wishes him to continue his work on earth. He must slightly descend from his great spiritual height in order to understand the need of the community. The *tzaddik* worships God not only through Torah study, prayer, and religious duty but also through material needs. The prayers of the *tzaddik* can mitigate harsh decrees. The *tzaddik's* power of *hamtakat dinim* (softening the heavenly Judgment) does not alter the laws of nature but becomes part of the law of nature. It does not nullify God's will but, rather, supplements it. He attributes great importance to repentance.

By his exemplary conduct, the *tzaddik* should encourage his followers to repent. He opposes fasting and self-affliction.

His son R. Aaron (d. 7 *Kislev* 1882) married the daughter of R. Israel Horowitz of Lublin. He was attached to R. Shlomoh HaKohen of Radomsk. He died childless. His other son was R. Joseph Barukh, known as "the good Jew of Neustadt."

G. Nigal, in *Sinai* 75 (1974): 144–168.

G.N.

EPSTEIN, Moses Yehiel Halevi, of Ozarov/New York/Tel Aviv (6 *Tevet* 1890–1 *Shevat* 1971)–Son of R. Abraham Shlomoh and a grandson of R. Aryeh Leib. Moses Yehiel was born in Ozarov. His mother was Reize Mirrel of Chenchin. At the age of seventeen he married Hannah, the daughter of R. Emanuel Weltfried of Pabianice. In 1912, he became rabbi of Ozarov, and during the First World War, he lived for a time in Cologne. He was bereaved of his son and one daughter, and his wife died of typhus, leaving him with two small daughters, Beile and Miriam. In 1920, he married Keila, daughter of R. Menahem Mendel Tennenbaum, and returned to Ozarov.

In 1921, he was part of the Aguda delegation visiting the United States, which included R. Asher Lemel Spitzer, R. Meir Hildesheimer, R. Dan Plotzki, Nathan Birnbaum, and R. Joseph Lew. They visited Belgium and England and spent six months in the United States. Returning to Poland, he made his home for the next five years in Otwock, where he wrote his commentary on Psalms *Likkutei Orot* and *Panim Yafot*.

In 1927, he emigrated to the United States and settled in the Bronx, New York. In 1949, he visited Israel for the first time. At that time, his son of twenty-one, R. Alter Abraham Shlomoh, drowned at a summer camp in the United States. His wife died four years later. In 1954, he married Sheindel Yocheved Landau and settled in Tel Aviv, where he lived for the last seventeen years of his life. He was communally minded, participated in the work of the Aguda and *Hinukh Atzmai*, and was a member of the *Mo'ezet Gedolei HaTorah*. He established a *kollel*, *Barukh Taam*, in Tel Aviv.

He visited his followers in the United States, Canada, and Belgium in 1956, 1957, and 1961.

The most prolific writer of modern hasidic rabbis, he produced voluminous works: *Esh Dat* (11 volumes) and *Beer Mosheh* (1965, 6 volumes), and commentaries on *Tractate Avot* and on the Passover *Haggadah*, edited by Shalom Hayyim Porush.

He was buried in Zikhron Meir in Bene Berak. He was survived by one daughter, Hayyah, and was succeeded by his grandson, R. Tanhum Benjamin Becker.

A. Surasky, *BeLahavat Esh*, 2 vols.

EPSTEIN, Samuel Elijah Halevi, (1892–1984) – Son of R. Nathan David of Neustadt and a grandson of R. Joseph Barukh, "the good Jew" of Neustadt, Samuel Elijah was born in Zwolin. He became rabbi in Kielce. In 1928, he emigrated to the United States, settling in New York, where he was known as the rebbe of Neustadt.

EPSTEIN, Yehiel Hayyim, second rebbe of Ozarov (1820–8 *Tammuz* 1888) – Son of Yehudah Aryeh Leibish, he frequently visited R. Issachar Baer of Radocyce and R. Abraham Twersky of Turiysk. He married Hayyah Rachel, the daughter of R. Abraham Shlomoh of Wlodowa, where he lived for several years.

At the age of seventeen, he became rabbi of Opole and eventually settled in Ozarov. He was renowned as a great hasidic storyteller. He died in Cracow, where he was buried.

His son, R. Aryeh Leibish, succeeded him.

EPSTEIN, Yehiel Michael (1829–1908), halakhic scholar – Born in Bobruisk, Belorussia, he studied under R. Yitzhak of Volozhin and received *semikhah* from R. Menahem Mendel Schneersohn of Lubavitch. For a time he was rabbi in Novosybkov, where he was befriended by the *Habad* hasidim.

In 1874 he was appointed rabbi of Novocrudok, where he remained until his death.

He was the author of the authoritative work *Arukh HaShulhan* on the four parts of the *Shulhan Arukh*, *Orah Hayyim* (1903–1907), *Yoreh De'ah* (1894–1898), *Even HaEzer* (1905–1906), and *Hoshen Mishpat* (1884–1893).

EPSTEIN, Yehudah Aryeh Leib, first rebbe of Ozarov (d. 23 *Tevet* 1837) – Son of R. Yehiel Michal. He married Malkah, the daughter of R. Uziel of Ostrowiec, and when his wife died, he married Miriam Leah, the daughter of R. Reuben Halevi Horowitz. He was popularly known as R. Leibish Opole. He was a disciple of R. Jacob Isaac, the "Seer of Lublin" and the "Holy Jew" of Przysucha, as well as of R. Abraham Joshua Heschel of Opatov and R. Meir of Opatov.

In 1812, he became the rabbi of Ozarov. It was believed that he had the soul of R. Nissim Gerondi, who had died in 1380, and R. Meir of Opatov used to say, "Whenever I reach the heavenly spheres, I always meet R. Aryeh Leib." In 1827, he became rebbe and moved to Opole.

His discourses are to be found in *Birkhat Tov*, published in Bilgoraj in 1928.

His son, R. Yehiel Hayyim, succeeded him.

EPSTEIN, Yitzhak (ca. 1780–26 *Iyar* 1857), *Habad* scholar – Son of R. Mordecai, he was a disciple of R. Shneur Zalman of Liady and of R. Dov Baer Schneersohn. He declined to become rebbe, but he was rabbi of Gomel. He defended R. Dov Baer against attacks by R. Aaron of Starosselje. He was the author of *Maamar HaShiflut VeHaSimhah* (1864) and *Maamar Yetziat Mitzrayim* (1877).

I. Hillman, *Bet Rabbi* vol. 1.

ERTER, Isaac (1791–1851), Hebrew writer and satirist–Born in Koniuszek, near Przemysl, he was the son of an innkeeper. He married at the age of thirteen and was at first attached to Hasidism. At the age of thirty-five, he began the study of medicine. He became a *maskil* and was associated with a circle of young intellectuals in Lvov. He subsequently lived in Tarnopol, Brody, and Budapest, where he died.

He was the first satirist of modern Hebrew literature. Social and national aspirations were his subjects. His essays were published posthumously under the title *HaTzofeh LeBet Yisrael* (1858). Unlike Perl, Erter was not only concerned with Hasidism, but with every section of the population. His satiric style is directed against the superstitious hasidic masses, the unholy zeal of some *tzaddikim*, the casuistic and arrogant scholasticism of certain talmudists, as well as the self-seeking and the arrogance of the alienated Jews. His satire is thus directed against spiritual and moral rather than economic defects. He felt himself to be a *tzofeh* (watchman), concerned with the problems of Jewry. Visions and dreams provide his literary forum. He derides the doctrine of the transmigration of souls. Religious reforms, a revival of Hebrew, and Jewish education, he believed, would alleviate the lot of the Jewish people.

Erter made his debut in the annual *Bikkurei HaIttim*. He was cofounder of the Hebrew periodical *HeHalutz* (Lvov, 1852–1889). M. Letteris edited his satires, which were published in Vienna in 1858, and the ninth edition was published in Tel Aviv in 1945.

J. Klausner, *Sifrut*, 1952, pp. 321–349.

I.O.L.

ESH KODESH (Holy Fire)–A rare collection of discourses written in the Warsaw ghetto by R. Kalmish Kalonymus Shapira, this work was discovered by workers digging a foundation for a new apartment building in Warsaw. The documents were published in 1960 by the *Vaad Hasidei Piazesna* in Israel under the title *Esh Kodesh*.

The discourses cover the period from New Year's 1939 to the summer of 1942. Though the material follows the traditional style of hasidic homiletics, there is an attempt here to explain the unfolding catastrophe in the Warsaw ghetto. R. Shapira maintains that the Holocaust presents the Jewish people with the opportunity to fulfill the uncompleted task of Abraham at the binding of Isaac. Quoting R. Menahem Mendel of Rymanov, he underscores the self-defeating consequences of excess suffering. If the living may not be worthy of redemption, should not the aimless murder of the innocent martyrs call forth God's redemptive response? How can the world continue to exist in the wake of the protesting cries of innocent children?

Undoubtedly, the most intense passages in his discourses are aimed at strengthening the Jews during ordeals and trials. Repeatedly, the Jews are reminded of their royal heritage and that it is imperative to prevent the enemy from destroying their divine image. The Jew is not alone. God experiences the tragedy with each Jew–feels with the Jews and cries with the Jews. If the Jews capitulate to despair, they remove God from the experience, which is an ultimate tragedy. The heroic passages of faith mark this book as one of the epic works that have emerged from the Holocaust. The rebbe perished on 4 *Heshvan* 1942.

P. Schindler, "The Holocaust and Kiddush Hashem in Hassidic Thought," pp. 88–104.

P.S.

ETROG–One of the four species used on the Festival of Sukkot.

Up to the end of the nineteenth century, Corfu and Genoa were the centers of *etrog* supply. In 1874, R. Joshua Trunk of Kutno urged people to purchase *etrogim* from the Holy Land because they were making their first appearance in Eastern Europe. A number of hasidic rebbes followed his lead. Among the halakhic and hasidic authorities who supported him were R. Yitzhak Elkhanan of Kovno, R. Hayyim Eliezer Waks, and R. Judah Alter, the *Sefat Emet*, who wrote, "It is a religious obligation to acquire an *etrog* from the Holy Land." And R. Abraham Bornstein of Sochaczov stated that "it is even forbidden to make a benediction over *etrogim* from Corfu when Palestinian *etrogim* are available."

In 1905, a society for the supervision of the *Kashrut* of the Palestinian *etrogim* was established with the encouragement of R. A. Y. Kook, and the demand gradually increased among the hasidim. R. Johanan Twersky of Rachmastrivka said, "I am convinced that when the Torah commanded us to take the fruit of the 'goodly tree' (Leviticus 23:40), this precept referred to the produce of the Holy Land." R. Yitzhak Friedman of Bohusi spoke in similar terms.

It is traditional among Lubavitch, dating back to R. Shneur Zalman of Liady, to use *etrogim* from Janova (Genoa). The present rebbe of Lubavitch, R. Menahem Mendel Schneerson, has an *etrog* from the Holy Land as well as one from Genoa.

In 1903, Solomon Marcus, the son of R. Aaron Marcus, published a booklet in Cracow, in which he criticized the use of *etrogim* from Corfu. R. Ezekiel Halberstam of Sianiawa and the rebbes of Sadgora would use *etrogim* from the Holy Land in addition to those from Corfu.

ETTINGER, Abraham Halevy (ca. 1870–ca. 1925) – Son of R. Jonah, a descendant of Polish rabbinical families, he was born in Brody. His mother was the daughter of R. Hayyim Yehudah Kluger. Abraham was educated by his father and his maternal uncle, R. Abraham Benjamin Kluger. In 1902, he was appointed head of the *yeshivah Kovey Itim LeTorah* in Dukla, where he died twenty-three years later.

He was the author of a biographical dictionary, *Shem HaGedolim HaShlishi*, which contained nearly 20,000 entries. In 1909, he published *Sihat Hullin Shel Talmidei Hahamim HeHadash*, and within three years an enlarged edition appeared (Sanok, 1912). He also published *Daat Zekenim* (Sanok, 1912). These works contain much hasidic lore, biographical notes, genealogical details, and homiletical ideas. They bear testimony to discerning scholarship. His other publications are *Yikre Dehaya*, a funerary oration on the death of his mother (Lvov, 1900), and *Imrei Tzaddikim*, which was published posthumously by R. Reuben Margulies (Lvov, 1927).

He was in correspondence with scholars such as R. Z. J. Michelson, R. Y. A. Kamelhar, and R. J. J. Greenwald.

A.S.

EVIL – "Evil is the chair for the good." This is the recurrent theme of the Besht. Not that evil is either rare or illusory, but it is powerful, subtle, drenching the world in blood, and lurking in wait to trip the unwary. In a larger sense, the world is controlled by God, Who is good. And all things and events that appear evil to us really serve God's purpose. When the pious overcome temptation, their reward in heaven is much greater. The evil demons have no power of their own. Whatever power they possess at any moment is lent to them by God for good purposes. Hence, they disappear when they are faced by persons of resolute faith.

The capacity of the Besht to find some good even in the worst catastrophe is illustrated in his ascent of the soul: "I prayed there and asked, 'Why has the Lord permitted such horrors? Why are so many Jewish people killed?' I was given permission to inquire from the Satan why he had arranged that many Jews were first converted and then murdered. He told me that his intention was for the sake of Heaven" (end of *Ben Porat Yosef*).

The Besht maintained that absolute evil does not exist. When the good person perceives evildoers, that good one rejoices in goodness. "One cannot be consciously good," said the rabbi of Koretz, "unless one knows evil. No one can appreciate pleasure, unless one has tasted bitterness. Good is only the reverse of evil, and pleasure is merely the opposite of anxiety. Without the evil impulse, we could do no evil, but neither could we do good."

Commenting on the verse "It is not good that a man should be alone; I will make a helpmeet for him" (Genesis 2:18), he said that God was saying, "There can be no goodness in man while he is alone, without an evil impulse within him; I will endow him with the ability to do evil, and it will be as a helpmeet to him, to enable him to do good, if he masters the evil nature within him."

L. I. Newman, *The Hasidic Anthology*, pp. 95–97.

J.B.A.

EVIL EYE–A belief in the evil eye is a folk superstition shared by many cultures of both the ancient and modern worlds. As early as the second millennium B.C.E., Sumerian and Akkadian incantations from Mesopotamia mention the evil eye, and it is well known that in Judaism, the evil eye has played a significant role. In the Bible, the expression means only "stinginess" or "meanness" (although cf. the denominative verb "to look at anxiously"), but later rabbinic tradition considered it at work as a destructive force among people.

In a Jewish context, the term applies to two essentially different phenomena: First, the capacity to harm, or even kill, merely by the glance of a baleful eye (cf. the later *jettatura*) is often referred to in the Talmud. In the Babylonian tradition of Rab and Hiyya the elder, for example, 99 out of every 100 persons die through the workings of the evil eye, and it is recorded of several rabbis that their glance could change people into a "heap of bones" or that they could make an object burst into flames just by looking at it. The second is a more general form of evil waiting to attack people whenever they might become vulnerable. A further illuminating source for the talmudic period lies in the Jewish Aramaic incantation bowls, where the evil eye is named as a personified demon, *yn'bšt*.

Fear of the evil eye persisted well after the talmudic period, remaining a cardinal element of superstition among hasidic Jews. In the writings of the period, a more analytical approach sought to clarify the causes of the evil eye: in the *Nishmat Hayyim* of R. Manasseh ben Israel, for example, three possible causes are distinguished (3:27):

1. The most common–a person brings the Evil Eye to bear on others by praising them or otherwise drawing attention to them, thus stimulating the envy of the demons. A practical precaution against this was the practice of keeping young children dirty or ill clad or giving them unattractive names (see Rashi on Numbers 1:2).

2. Specific groups of people can impose the evil eye on a person, notably old or menstruating women, or a *ba'al nefešh hara'* (one with an evil soul).

3. Demons can bring it of their own accord, since they are constantly jealous of human beings, being on a lower plane of existence (*madregah*), and their jealousy is likened to that of the cripple toward the healthy.

It was necessary, therefore, not to provoke the demons: see the strictures of the *Sefer Hasidim* (1182) to ensure a peaceful life. To combat the dangers of the evil eye, hasidic Jews resorted to various devices, prominent among which were amulets. These were usually inscribed with a passage from the Bible, traditionally deemed to be effective against the evil eye. A common example is Numbers 6:24–26, the "priestly blessing." A late medieval manuscript in Maghribi script (Hebrew and Arabic) in the library of Jews' College, London (Mont. 438, no. 26), prescribes the use of Genesis 6:8, "But Noah found grace in the eyes of the Lord." Clearly the reference to these holy and benevolent eyes was felt to be a strong protection. Other devices in use among the hasidic Jews survived from the Talmud, as the use of the "fig" gesture described in *Berakhot* 55b. Still others were influenced by non-Jewish sources and included the suspension of herbs, plants, and stones, as well as even the use of the *Havdalah* candle for fumigation.

Since the Middle Ages, and particularly since the seventeenth century, the widespread popularity of the evil eye in folk superstition has increased, especially among East European Jews (see R. LILIENTHAL), until expressions to forbid its presence have become an "automatic accompaniment on Jewish lips of the slightest compliment" (*J. Trachtenberg* 283), in order not to excite that malicious envy.

J. Trachtenberg, *Jewish Magic and Superstition*.

I.F.

EXEGESIS–The principle behind hasidic exegesis of the Bible, as evidenced in the classical hasidic works, is that of the *Zohar* (III,152a), according to which, in addition to the plain meaning, Scripture has an esoteric meaning, the "soul of the Torah." Once this is accepted it follows, according to the hasidic teachers, that the Torah (and this includes the rabbinic literature) seeks to inculcate the hasidic ideals–*devekut* (attachment to God), the role of the *tzaddik*, the life of holiness, joy in God's service, humility and self-annihilation–and these can legitimately be read out of the biblical verses and sayings of the rabbis.

For its method, hasidic exegesis owes much to the Midrash. Like the midrashic preachers, the hasidic exegetes consciously rely on novel and startling reinterpretations of familiar verses, giving them a new turn and applying them to the contemporary situation. The sometimes very far-fetched nature of these interpretations is acknowledged by the hasidic masters themselves when they speak of the Torah "hinting" at this or that, though it is obvious that normally they really believed that the hasidic understanding of the texts was perfectly authentic.

Very revealing in this connection is the comment of R. Barukh of Medziborz, grandson of Besht, on the verse "And the spirit of God hovered over the face of the waters" (Genesis 1:2). The waters referred to are the waters of the Torah. The *tzaddikim* often derive valid teachings from biblical verses, but these have only a tenuous association with the verses. Yet although the spirit of God only "hovers" over the text, barely touching its essence, it is the holy spirit that is at work and is close to the truth (*Botzina De-Nehora*, Lemberg, 1930, p. 27a).

The *torot* of the hasidic masters were delivered at the third meal of the Sabbath and on the festivals and so naturally drew chiefly on the weekly *sidrot*, the five *Megillot*, the *Haggadah* of Passover, *Ethics of the Fathers*, and the weekly *haftarot*. Because of hasidic familiarity with the Book of Psalms this, too, became a popular hunting ground for hasidic ideas. The other biblical books are almost totally neglected, except for the rare instances when an oft-quoted verse can be made to yield a typical hasidic doctrine.

A good example of hasidic exegesis is the famous comment of the Maggid of Mezhirech reported by Solomon Maimon (*Lebensgeschichte*, ed. J. Fromer [Munich, 1911], p. 200) and found, too, in early hasidic books (see J. G. Weiss in *Zion* 20 [1955]: 107–108). The comment is on the verse: "And it came to pass, when the minstrel played, that the hand of the Lord came upon him" (2 Kings 3:15). The Maggid reads this as "And it came to pass that when the minstrel was like his instrument (*ke-naggen hamenaggen*) the hand of the Lord came upon him," that is, that when the *tzaddik* is devoid of selfhood and is a purely passive instrument, the spirit of God rests upon him.

As in the Midrash, punning on words is resorted to by the hasidim in their exposition of the Bible. On the verse "A light shalt thou make to the ark" (Genesis 6:16), a comment, attributed to the Besht, takes *tevah* (ark) as meaning a "word." When man utters the *word*, of prayer and devotion, he must illumine that word by the intensity of his contemplation, dwelling on its spiritual significance in all its details. And the word for light (*tzohar*) has the same letters as the word for sorrow (*tzarah*), only in a different order. By the power of his prayers with holy concentration, it is possible for the saint to avert the evil decree, converting darkness and sorrow into brilliant light. Thus an otherwise unpromising text, dealing with the remote past, becomes a vehicle for hasidic teachings on the value of prayer. The *Sefer Baal Shem Tov* (Lodz, 1938, vol. I, pp. 118–195) contains, as a comment on this verse, a whole treatise on prayer culled from the writings of the *tzaddikim*.

The biblical heroes are seen in hasidic exegesis as paradigms for the conduct of the *tzaddik* and of hasidic life in general. Abraham is ordered to leave his land, his birthplace, and his father's house (Genesis 12:1). In our pursuit of holy living, we must first relinquish our natural desire for worldly, material pleasures (our "land"); then we have to conquer the evil traits with which we were born (our "birthplace"); and, finally, we have to rise above the shallow pride of belonging to a good family (our "father's house") to take pride only in being a servant of God (*Noam Elimelekh*, *lekh lekha*). Jacob prayed to be delivered from the hand of his brother Esau (Genesis 32:12).

The evil inclination seeks to get the better of us by persuading us that an evil act we contemplate is not really evil at all but good. It is when Esau poses as Jacob's "brother," as pursuing the same aims as he, that the danger is particularly acute (*Kedushat Levi*, *vayishlah*). The angels of God whom Jacob saw in his dream ascending and descending on the ladder reaching to heaven (Genesis 28:12) are the *tzaddikim*, who have their periods of spiritual darkness and descent but who, as a result, encourage themselves to rise even higher toward God (*Degel Mahanei Efraim*, *vayetzei*).

Frequently, in hasidic exegesis, biblical verses are taken completely out of their context to be laid under tribute for the ideas that can be read out of the Hebrew words, even if the latter are taken without regard to form or syntax. For example, R. Uziel Meizels, disciple of the Maggid of Mezhirech, comments (*Tiferet Uziel* [Jerusalem, 1952], *VaYakel*) on the verse "the son of Uri, the son of Hur, of the tribe (*lematteh*) of Judah (*yehudah*)" (Exodus 38:30). *Uri* is from *or*, "light"; *hur* means a "crevice"; *lematteh* is read as *lemattah*, "downward"; and *Yehudah* is read as *hodaah*, "praise." If one who was once a "son of light," of high spiritual elevation, illuminating the world, falls into the depths of degradation, all the praises of God one uttered while in the state of grace are rejected by heaven and cast downward. The *mitnaggedim* seized on this kind of fanciful exegesis as a target for their ridicule.

R. Meir of Peremyshlyany (d. 1850) was especially noted for his playful treatment of scriptural verses (S. A. Horodezky, *HaHasidut VeHaHasidim* [Tel Aviv, 1951], vol. IV, pp. 113–115). In his comment to Exodus 14:14–"The Lord will fight (*yillahem*) for you, but ye shall hold your peace" (*taharishun*)–this master takes *yillahem* as if it were connected with *lehem*, "bread," and *taharishun* as if it were from *harash*, "to plough," yielding the thought that God helps those who help themselves: "God will give you bread, but you must do your share by ploughing the field."

Mention should be made of the *Habad* school, in which there is a return to the classical kabbalistic methods of scriptural exegesis, the biblical narratives seen as referring chiefly to the mystery of the divine nature and the complex relationships between the forces on high. Reference must also be made to the remarkable approach, for which he was severely criticized, of R. Mordecai Joseph of Izbica (d. 1854) in his *Mei HaShiloah* (New York, 1975), who see not only the biblical heroes but also its villains as great men with the noblest ideals.

I. Jacobs, *Jewish Teachings of the Hasidic Masters*.

L.J.

EXILE–"Exile," said the rebbe of Ger, "contains redemption within itself, as seed contains the fruit. Good works and real diligence will bring out the hidden reward." For just as the Jews are in exile, the hasidim believed that the *Shekhinah*, too, is in exile.

"The real exile of Israel in Egypt," maintained the rebbe of Alexander, "was that they had learned to endure slavery."

"There are three kinds of exile," said the rebbe of Belz: "exile among the nations, exile among Jews, and exile among one's own desire."

Voluntary exile, *galus abrichten*, was to serve as an atonement for sin. "Exile atones for half of our sins," states the Talmud (*Sanhedrin* 37b). Elijah, the Gaon of Vilna, went into exile, as did R. David of Mikolayev, a disciple of the Besht; R. Elimelekh of Lejask; and his brother, R. Zusya of Annopol.

Wandering incognito for three years, they suffered the rigors of the road, often weary and hungry, often in danger of their lives. R. Elimelekh and his brother traversed Poland, reaching as far as Auschwitz and spreading hasidic teachings wherever they went. In the words of R. Noah of Kobrin: "You will find hasidim up to the point that the brother, R. Zusya and R. Elimelekh, reached in their long wanderings. Beyond that you will not find hasidim."

"He who voluntarily leaves his home and wanders as a beggar, living a life of discomfort but trusting always in the Lord, becomes a partner in the exile of the *Shekhinah*," said the rebbe of Komarno (d. 1874). "His sins are forgiven, and he understands the secrets of the Torah. Happy is the lot of those who go into exile."

Not many rebbes in the latter half of the nineteenth century engaged in a life of wandering. Yoshe Kalb, in L. J. Singer's novel, travels about as a wanderer to do penance for his sins.

L. I. Newman, *Hasidic Anthology*, pp. 97–102.

EXISTENTIALISM–Atheistic existentialism, in which nothing is given, not even God, is obviously at variance with Hasidism. Religious existentialism, with its preference for involvement over detachment, its mistrust of rationalism or attempts at "proving" the existence of God, its recognition of the importance of the individual, its stress on direct encounter, and its demand for the spontaneity that brings the whole of human beings into play, does have close affinities with a movement of rebellion against the established order and mere conformity such as Hasidism. Yet the similarities should not obscure the many differences between

Hasidism and any existentialist philosophy. For all its personalistic and individualistic thrust, Hasidism is a mystical movement, which shares the mystic's quest through self-negation (see *Bittul HaYesh*). Moreover, the hasidic masters, despite the rich variety of religious expression among them, were Orthodox Jews, who claimed no real originality of approach and who would have considered it to be rank heresy to believe that the traditional pattern, as God given, could be improved upon.

It is, consequently, more accurate to speak of certain existentialist trends in some branches of Hasidism than to attempt any closer identification between the thought of the movement and existentialism. These trends are to be discerned in many of the tales the hasidim tell about their saints, and some of the hasidic masters emphasize both the leap of faith and the sense of religious crisis and tension reminiscent of Kierkegaard, the founder of religious existentialism. Of these teachers, the closest to the thought of the Danish thinker are Nahman of Bratzlav and Menahem Mendel of Kotzk.

J. G. Weiss, *Mekharim BeHasidut Bratzlav*.

L.J.

EXORCISM – Ansky's very popular play *The Dybbuk* has, as a central theme, an exorcism practiced by a hasidic *tzaddik*. There are, in fact, numerous tales of *tzaddikim* being called upon to use their magical powers to drive out a *dybbuk* (lit., "attachment"). The *dybbuk* is not an instance of demonic possession but the soul of a dead sinner pursued by demons, which has obtained relief from its persecuters by lodging temporarily in the body of a living person, generally one who has invited the invasion by committing a sin, albeit of a minor nature such as drinking water without reciting the holy words of the benediction.

The whole idea of the *dybbuk*, derived from the Lurianic Kabbalah, came very late in Jewish folklore. There is no official order of exorcism, but the reports usually speak of the blowing of a *shofar*, the recitation of Psalm 91, and the holy man's ordering the oppressed spirit to depart. It must be appreciated that tales of exorcism in Eastern Europe are by no means confined to the circles of the hasidim, yet the miracle-working *tzaddik*, with his profound knowledge of the unseen world, is the personage around whom such tales tend to gather.

There is to be observed among contemporary hasidim in the Western world a decline in the belief in *dybbukim* and consequently in the need for exorcism. Hasidic rebbes have been known, nowadays, to refer to a psychiatrist a person said to be afflicted by a *dybbuk*, though here and there one still hears of hasidic rebbes practicing exorcism.

The skeptism is never extended to any outright denial of the *dybbuk* notion because that would be to cast doubts on the "reliable witnesses" who testified that famous *tzaddikim* had driven out *dybbukim*. The rationale for current skepticism among the hasidim is either that the saints of old have succeeded in driving away all evil spirits from the hauntings of humans or that if the *dybbukim* were still able to enter the bodies of humans, the *tzaddikim* would be obliged to drive them out, which would be in the nature of the kind of miracle of which our poor generation is unworthy.

J. Trachtenberg, *Jewish Magic and Superstition*, p. 50 and note.

L.J.

F

FALK, Samuel Jacob Hayyim (1710–1772), kabbalist–Probably born in Podolia, the area in which Hasidism originated, he came in about 1742 to London via Germany, where he was banished from Cologne as a sorcerer. In London, he achieved notoriety as a miracle worker and was known as the *Baal Shem* of London.

His relationship with the London Jewish community was ambivalent. He was at first denounced by R. Jacob Emden as a Shabbetean and for having sheltered Moses David Podheizer of Podhajce, an associate of R. Jonathan Eibeschutz. He subsequently enjoyed good relations with the community and left a considerable bequest to the Great Synagogue, which is now administered by the United Synagogue.

His portrait painted by J. S. Copley between 1775 and 1782 was previously confused with that of the Besht.

C. Roth, *Essays and Portraits in Anglo-Jewish History*, pp. 139–164.

L.K.

FARBRENGEN (Yiddish, time spent together)–Term used by the hasidim of Lubavitch to denote gatherings at which there are eating, drinking, singing, and discussion of hasidic teachings. The Hebrew expression for *farbrengen* is *Hitvaadut*.

There are two kinds of *farbrengen*: the *farbrengen* at the *yeshivah*, in which the *mashpia* (instructor in Hasidism) is surrounded by students and is the only speaker, and the *farbrengen* of older hasidim, in which an old hasid presides over a number of speakers.

A special *farbrengen* is one that is presided over by the rebbe. In Russia, in the days of R. Shalom Dov Baer, *farbrengen* with the rebbe took place on rare occasions only: on *Simhat Torah* and on 19 *Kislev*, the anniversary of the release from prison of R. Shneur Zalman of Liady. There were also minor *farbrengen* on Purim, on Lag BaOmer, and on 12 *Tammuz*, the anniversary of the release of R. Joseph Yitzhak Schneersohn from prison.

The immediate past rebbe, R. Menahem Mendel Schneerson, held numerous *farbrengen*: on the second day of *Rosh Hashanah*, the final day of the three pilgrim festivals, the Sabbath preceding a New Moon, on 19 *Kislev*, on 12 *Tammuz*, and on the anniversaries of the deaths of the rebbe's parents. Since 1970, until the rebbe's illness in 1991, the major *farbrengens* that did not fall on a Sabbath or Festival were broadcast live to Lubavitch groups around the world.

T.P.

FAST OF THE FIRSTBORN (*Taanit Behorim*)–This fast is observed on the eve of Passover, on 14 *Nisan*. The firstborn fasts to commemorate the deliverance in Egypt of the firstborn of the children of Israel. This is the only fast that is permitted during the month of *Nisan*.

The first reference to the fast appears in Tractate *Soferim* (chap. 12). R. Tzvi Hirsch of Zydaczov in his work *Pri LeTzaddik* maintains that the text of the Talmud should read "the firstborn enjoy themselves on the eve of Passover" instead of "the firstborn fast." R. Moses Teitelbaum, however, actually fasted and would not avail himself of the *siyum* (the conclusion of the study of a tractate of the Talmud that exempts participants from fasting).

FEAR OF GOD–The term "fear of God" is employed in Scripture to designate piety in general, in addition to awareness of dependence on and reverence for God.

In medieval literature, a distinction is drawn between the fear of punishment (*Yirat HaOnesh*) and the fear of exultation (*Yirat*

HaRomemut), the overpowering awe felt by pietists when they contemplate the majesty of the Creator.

Fear of God is the elementary component of piety. On a higher level, it is supplemented by the love of God, when love and fear are blended together. The hasidic movement stressed the ideal of serving God in love and not in fear. The fear of God is inseparable from the realization of the immanence of the divine presence in worship. We are told that the Besht would tremble so powerfully when he was deeply engaged in prayer that the grains of wheat in a barrel or the water in a pail would visibly tremble, echoing his uncontrollable shaking. As the Besht once said, "I wonder at you, O physical body, that you do not crumble to pieces out of fear of your Creator."

Generally, the rebbes would instruct the hasidim to alternate in experiencing joy and experiencing fear, in keeping with the psalmist's injunction: "Serve the Lord in joy and rejoice with trembling."

R. Nahman of Bratzlav stressed that the fear of God is in itself an earthly reflection of God's presence, the lowest link in an infinite chain reaching up to God Himself. The only way to begin serving God is through fear of divine retribution.

Without such fear it is impossible even to take the first step. Even the righteous must have such fear, "for very few people can devote themselves to God out of love alone." A person can serve God only out of a sense of awe, because He is great and powerful. This is a higher level of fear, but it is also one that is very difficult to attain. For the average individual, the path to true devotion is the simple fear of divine punishment. Even though the *Zohar* belittles the mere fear of punishment, our great moral classics indicate that this is still the main gateway to true devotion (*Sihot HaRan* 5).

R. Menahem Mendel of Kotzk was especially noted for his great emphasis on fear as the pathway to God. His motto was the verse of Proverbs 28:14: "Happy is the man who is always fearful." The feeling of holiness contains the elements of fear, mystery, and fascination. And fear is the indispensable first step.

A. J. Heschel, *A Passion for Truth*. (Tel Aviv, 1973).

J.B.A.

FEDER, Tobias (pseudonym of Tobias Gutman, ca. 1760–1817), writer – Born near Przedborz, near Cracow, he was a writer, poet, teacher, proofreader, and grammarian. In his new *Zohar* for Purim, written in the style of the *Zohar*, he satirized the hasidim.

He was the author of an anti-Yiddish polemic work in Hebrew, *Kol Mehatzetzim* (Berdichev, 1816), which was aimed against Mendel Levin's Yiddish translation of the Book of Proverbs.

FEDERBUSH, Simon (1892–1969), rabbi and author – A native of Narol, Galicia, he studied in the rabbinical seminary of Vienna under Samuel Krauss and Avigdor Aptowitzer. In 1913, he became chief rabbi of Finland, and in 1940, he settled in New York, where he was rabbi and principal of the *Yeshivah Rabbi Israel Salanter* (Bronx).

Under the auspices of *Mokad HaRav Kook*, he edited *Hazon Torah VeTziyon* (Jerusalem, 1960) and *HaHasidut VeTziyon* (Jerusalem, 1963), a collection of popular and scholarly articles.

Y. L. Maimon, ed., *Sefer HaYovel Shimon Federbusch*, pp. 9–40.

FEIGENBAUM, Yitzhak, of Warsaw (1828–24 *Iyyar* 1911), rabbi – Son of R. Israel Isar, Yitzhak studied under R. Yitzhak Meir Alter and under his son, R. Abraham Mordecai. He visited R. Menahem Mendel Morgenstern of Kotzk, whom he greatly venerated.

In 1868, he succeeded R. Leibish Kodesh as *dayan* of Warsaw. He supported the *Hovevei Zion* movement and acquired a plot of land in the Holy Land. He founded the monthly *Shaarei Torah* (1893), a journal of rabbinical studies.

For forty years he was a hasid of R. Abraham Bornstein of Sochaczov. He had a large antiquarian library.

He was survived by three sons, R. Jacob Solomon, R. Israel Isar, and R. Moses, and five daughters.

Of all his family only R. Israel Isar survived the Holocaust.

A. Y. Bromberg, *Migdolei HaHasidut*, vol. 23, *HaAdmorim MiPraga*, pp. 118–152.

FEIRBERG, Mordecai Zeev (1874–1899), Hebrew writer – He came of a hasidic family from Novograd Volhynsk. He was the son of a pious *shohet*, and he studied Talmud, Kabbalah, and *Musar*. His mother, too, came from a hasidic background, and he imbibed from her many hasidic tales of the Besht and R. Leib Sarah's. He was later very much influenced by R. Nahman Krochmal's *Guide to the Perplexed of the Time*.

He married the daughter of a *shohet* and died of tuberculosis in his twenty-fifth year.

His literary output, mainly autobiographical, consists of short stories, *Sippurim* (Warsaw, Ahiasaf, nd). Stories like *Ba'Erev* ("In the Evening"), *The Shadows*, *The Calf*, *The Charm*, *The First Story*, *Nahman the Madman*, and *Hophni the Dreamer* portray the bitter struggle between Hasidism and the *Haskalah* and paint a glowing picture of the legendary activities of R. Leib Sarah's. He is a forerunner of Peretz, Berdichevsky, and Yehudah Steinberg.

I. Rabinowich, *Major Trends of Modern Hebrew Fiction*, pp. 43–55.

FILMS–Hasidism has figured prominently in only a few feature films in the sixty or so years that film has been a popular medium. The earliest movies to deal with hasidic subject matter were the two silent German versions of *The Golem*, both made by director Paul Wegener and released respectively in 1914 and 1919. These films pertain to Hasidism insofar as the "Golem of Prague" legend comes out of the kabbalistic tradition. The Jewish characters, however, are not specified as followers of the Besht or his successors, nor do they exhibit, apart from R. Loew's explorations into kabbalistic mysteries, specifically hasidic concerns.

The 1919 version, which Wegener codirected with Henrik Galeen, was released for English-speaking audiences in 1921 and is still considered a major work of the silent Expressionist cinema. A French version of *The Golem* appeared in 1936, this one with sound, directed by Julien Duvivier and starring French classical actor Harry Bauer. With its Marxist overtones as the Golem leads oppressed masses in revolt, this version strayed from the hasidic roots of the story even farther than Wegener's did. Its most impressive feature was Harry Bauer's performance as mad King Rudoph II, who tries to discover the Golem's secret.

Kabbalistic Hasidism is central to the two film versions of *The Dybbuk*, both based on S. Anski's classic Yiddish play. The earlier version, spoken in Yiddish and generally thought to be the superior of the two, was released in 1938, directed by Michael Waszinski from a screenplay by S. A. Kacyzna and Marek Arenstein. Despite its technical crudity, the film captures the supernatural oppressiveness of Ansky's world and is an interesting example of the highly emotional, if sometimes attitudinized, acting style common in the Yiddish theater. The later film of *The Dybbuk*, a 1968 Israeli-German coproduction performed in Hebrew, was released in commemoration of the original Habimah stage production's fiftieth anniversary. Many have felt that the direction (by Ilan Eldad) and acting of this version are uneven and lack the force of the Yiddish film.

The Flying Matchmaker and *The Mad Adventures of Rabbi Jacob* are two relatively recent movies that treat hasidic characters as subjects for comedy. *The Flying Matchmaker* (the title given the film upon international release) is a 1966 Israeli musical comedy, originally entitled *The Two Kouny Lemels*, the name of the Goldfaden play from which the film was adapted. Kouny Lemel, a fatuous hasidic youth, is the look-alike of a dapper young man who is in love with Lemel's prospective bride. The comedy grows mostly from situations of mistaken identity and Mike Burstyn's characterization of a cretinous Kouny Lemel. The film never addresses Hasidism explicitly as a topic (we gather Lemel is a hasid from his dress and sidecurls), but there is implied satire of the Mea Shearim sort of mentality. *The Flying Matchmaker* was popular in Israel but not equally so abroad, where it struck audiences as unsophisticated.

Accorded a much better international reception was *The Mad Adventures of Rabbi Jacob*, a 1973 French farce directed by Gerard Oury. French comic Luis de Funes plays a bigoted industrialist who, through a series of mishaps, is forced to impersonate a hasidic rebbe from Brooklyn visiting France for a family *bar mitzvah*. Although the movie suffers from ignorance of certain Orthodox Jewish practices, it is affectionate toward its hasidic characters and overtly ecumenical in general.

The preceding are the only widely distributed films in which hasidim have been major characters. Presumably because of their parochialism and apparent incongruity in modern society, hasidic characters have also been the basis for short, comic vignettes in several recent films. Woody Allen has gags featuring them in *Take the Money and Run*. A comic moment in *Serpico* shows Al Pacino as a policeman disguised for undercover purposes as a Williamsburg-type hasid. In the 1975 Canadian film *Lies My Father Told Me* there is a circumcision scene in which a hasid debates a Marxist, drawing on homilies from the Besht. In this instance, the tone of the sequence is comic but affectionate.

(See also John Schlesinger's *The Marathon Man* [1976] and Sidney Lumet's *Stranger Among Us* [1992].)

M.N.

FINKELSTEIN, Issachar Dov (d. 1977) – Born in Radom, the son of Alexander Ziskind, a hasid of Radzyn. He became rabbi in Novozivkov, Russia, and for nine years he was on the city council of Chelm, later holding the presidency of the Jewish community as well as being the head of the *yeshivah* for many years. He was a disciple of R. Shmuel Solomon Leiner and was one of the very few men in England to wear *Teckhelet* (the Cord of Blue).

He came to England in 1935. After living for some time in Leeds, he settled in London in 1947 and opened a *shtiebl*, *Keser Torah*, in Cricklewood. He made an impact on the area. His knowledge of Hasidism soon manifested itself. He was instrumental in setting up the *yeshivah Keser Torah* in Willesden, London. His many writings have not yet been published.

FINKLER, Eliezer, of Pinczov (1860–10 *Shevat* 1936) – Son of R. Hayyim Meir, he studied under his father and Abraham Twersky of Turiysk. In 1917, he became rebbe and was known as a miracle worker. Most of his life he lived in Kielce, where his father lived, but he was known as the rabbi of Pinczov because it was his birthplace. In 1929, he moved to Sosnowiec, where he died. He was succeeded by his son, Pinhas Issachar.

FINKLER, Eliezer David, of Radoszyce (d. 22 *Adar* 1926) – Son of R. Hillel. He succeeded his father in 1901. He would immerse himself in the ritual bath at least ten times each day, and no one could visit him unless he first visited the ritual bath. Toward the end of his life, he became blind. He died in Lodz, where he was buried. His son, R. Hayyim, succeeded him.

FINKLER, Hayyim Asher, of Radoszyce (d. 24 *Adar* 1941) – Son of R. Eliezer David of Radoszyce, he married his cousin, the daughter of R. Meir Menahem of Radoszyce. He was brought up by his grandfather, R. Hillel, and was ordained by R. Joav Joshua Weingarten of Kinsk. He corresponded with R. Abraham Bornstein of Sochaczev and other halakhic authorities. His *melavah malkah* rarely finished before Sunday morning. On the Day of Atonement, he officiated at the reader's desk throughout the day. The petitions given to him by the hasidim were studied by him in the *mikveh*, where he would immerse himself ten times each day.

He established *yeshivot* in Lodz and Radoszyce, instructing senior students himself and preparing them for the rabbinical diploma. He was a great supporter of the *yishuv* in the Holy Land.

In 1927, he became rabbi of Radoczyce in succession to his father. Six years later, in 1933, he became rabbi of Wloszclawa. Like his father, he was an ascetic. He would sleep at his desk, fully dressed, and ate only one meal a day.

During the war, he lived in Lodz, then in Radoszyce, and later in Kielce. He died of acute diabetes in the ghetto of Kielce, where he was buried. His son, R. Jacob Finkler, the son-in-law of R. Yitzhak Kalish of Skierniewice, perished in the Holocaust.

Y. Alfasi, *HaSaba HaKadosh*, pp. 148–152.

FINKLER, Hayyim Meir, of Pinczov (d. 29 *Adar* 1919) – Son of R. Yitzhak of Radoszyce, he studied under R. Solomon HaKohen Rabinowicz of Radomsk and under his uncle, R. Israel Yitzhak of Radoszyce. He married the daughter of R. Mordecai Nathanson. In 1866, he became rebbe and settled in Pinczov. He was an ascetic, and for nearly forty years, he fasted every day, partaking of a sparse meal late at night.

He was the author of *Imrei Hayyim* for the month of *Adar* (Piotrokov, 1913); *Imrei Hayyim* on talmudical problems, which appeared anonymously and was printed in Warsaw in 1899; and *Minhat Yehudah* on the Torah (Piotrokov, 1910). He also left manuscripts on Maimonides, on liturgy, and on Hanukkah, which were never published.

In 1914, he moved to Kielce, where he died. His son was R. Eliezer of Sosnowiec and Kielce. He also had four daughters.

FINKLER, Hillel, of Radoszyce (d. 23 *Tevet* 1901)–Son of R. Yitzhak, the rabbi of Radoszyce, his mother was drowned while he was very young, and he was brought up by his grandfather and by his uncle, R. Yisrael Yitzhak of Radoszyce. He was a disciple of R. Moses Biderman of Lelov, R. Solomon Rabinowicz of Radomsk, and R. Hayyim Meir Yehiel of Moglienice.

He married the daughter of R. Yissachar Baer of Radoszyce. In 1846, he became rebbe and was known as a miracle worker. He immersed himself in the ritual bath several times each day and prolonged his prayers. He ate only one meal each day, a dairy meal. He was a great supporter of the Holy Land and raised large sums of money. He spoke mainly Hebrew, only rarely using Yiddish.

His sons were R. Eliezer David and R. Meir Menahem. He had two daughters.

FINKLER, Israel Joseph, of Radoszyce (d. 22 *Tammuz* 1937)–Son of R. Eliezer David. In 1927, he succeeded his father as rabbi of Radoszyce. His services were very melodious and his *Musaf Amidah* on the Day of Atonement took many hours. He was well versed in secular subjects and spoke Russian fluently.

His son R. Kalmish was murdered in the Holocaust, and another son, R. Yitzhak, was a partisan during the war.

FINKLER, Pinhas Issachar, of Pinczov (1887–18 *Kislev* 1943)–Son of R. Eliezer, he married the daughter of R. Moses Solomon Yehiel Biderman. He lived in Kielce and was active in the work of the Aguda and its educational institutions *Yesodei HaTorah*, *Bet Yaakov*, and *Yeshivat Torat Hesed*. In 1921, he moved to Sosnowiece, and in 1937, he succeeded his father as rebbe.

During the Second World War, he warned his followers not be deluded by the German propaganda about the so-called resettlement. He urged them to resist and not to allow themselves to be deported. He and a number of his followers were captured as they tried to escape to Cracow. They all perished in the Holocaust.

FINKLER, Yitzhak, of Pinczov (1898–1942)–Son of R. Eliezer of Pinczov, he was communally minded and was a member of the Mizrachi. He was among the founders of the *Yavne* school in Kielce. When his father died, his brother, R. Pinhas, succeeded him. He perished in Chelm.

FINKLER, Yitzhak Samuel Elijah, of Piotrokov (1892–1942)–Son of R. Meir Menahem, he married the daughter of R. David Taub of Kazimierz. In 1912, he became rabbi in Piotrokov.

During the High Holy Days, in the absence of a Festival prayer book, he wrote down the entire liturgy from memory.

At the outbreak of the Second World War, he was deported to a series of infamous death camps, including Buchenwald, where he died. His two daughters survived: Malkah married the writer Yehiel Greenstein, and Sarah married R. Abraham Joshua Heschel Eichenstein.

FISH, Aaron Isaiah, of Hodasz (1859–6 *Tevet* 1928)–Son of R. Tzvi Avigdor Fish, a descendant of R. Yaakov Fish of Kalev. He was a disciple of R. Eliezer Tzvi Safrin of Komarno. He became rabbi and rebbe in Hodasz. He left many manuscripts on *Halakhah* and *Zohar*. His only published work was *Kedushat Aharon* on the Festivals, the first part printed in Debrecyn in 1938, and the second part in Mateszalka in 1940.

His son, R. Hezkeyahu, succeeded him. His sons-in-law were R. Yehezkel Roter, the rebbe of Klausenburg, and R. Hayyim Uri Jakobovitz.

FISH, Eliezer, of Bikszad (1880–20 *Sivan* 1944)–Son of R. Mosheh, he was born in Moiseu, Hungary. He married the daughter of R. Mosheh Zeev Kohn of Epdoszentyorgy, studied in Sighet, and was known as the rebbe of Bikszad. He was a renowned scholar and is reputed to have known the works of R. Samuel Eliezer Edels (the Maharsha) by heart. During the war, he escaped to Klausenburg but was caught by the Nazis and then perished in Auschwitz.

His work *Shem Eliezer*, on Torah and Talmud, was printed in New York in 1954.
Sefer Marmoros, p. 135.

FISH, Hayyim Mosheh of Bikszad (1918–1944) – Son of Eliezer, he studied under his father in Satmar. In 1940, he married the daughter of Benjamin Zeev Schwartz, the rabbi of Kapolnokmonostor, where he became rabbi. He perished in the Holocaust.

FLAUM, David, of Montreal (1896–12 *Nisan* 1971) – Son of Isaac David, he was born in Krotchin and was a descendant of Ropczyce, Belz, and Olesko. In 1922, he married Sarah, the daughter of R. Moses Langer of Stretyn. After living in Galicia, he emigrated to Canada and established *Ahavat David Bet HaMidrash* in Montreal. His son Shalom lives in New York.

A. Shu.

FOLKLORE – Hasidism was not so much the teaching of any one person or by a specific school as it is a tide of feeling that inundated the Pale of Settlement and transformed the character of its life. The most basic quality of hasidic piety is reflected in its legends concerning its *tzaddikim*, rather than in the changes it introduced within the existing *Halakhah* or in the collections of sermons by its masters. On this point, Buber, with all his modernistic distortions, is more correct than his detractors.

The "tales" of the hasidim, Buber points out, are the immediate creations of the pietistic conventicles (*klauslach*). They are not polished works of art, nor are they clearly folk creations, but they hover between the two categories. Like the folktales of the Grimm brothers, which were instrumental in generating the folkloric movement in Germany, the hasidic tales were transmitted orally for generations, changing in nuance and coloration as they were repeated. They all aimed to make a point – that the righteous triumph over evil, that God is near and redemption is at hand.

As Buber put it,

> Everything the true hasid does or does not do mirrors his belief that, in spite of the intolerable suffering men must endure, the heartbeat of life is holy joy, and that always and everywhere, one can force a way through to that joy – provided one devotes oneself entirely to his deed. (M. Buber, *Tales of the Hasidim*, vol. 1, p. 10)

We might add that, as in all folktales, it is the common people who win as against the sophisticated and the mighty ones of this world. In hasidic stories, simple piety and humility are exalted, sometimes even to the point of antinomianism. For what matters in the sight of God are the purity of intention and the fervor of devotion, not the subtle complexities of the learned.

Because the hasidim were taught that it was a supreme *mitzvah* to tell tales of wondrous miracles concerning the *tzaddikim*, we can understand how such tales originated. What the eyes of piety can see as an overwhelming reality, those of flesh and blood will never perceive. So the natural artistic faculties of the hasidim were encouraged to create an ideal reality. At the same time, there was a general reluctance to fix the oral tradition into a written form. The way in which the tale was told made it either true or false. We are told that the Besht saw a demon walking among his disciples. After an inquiry, he determined that the demon was generated by his own words as they were being set down in a notebook kept by one of his disciples. He then glanced through the pages of the notebook, remarking that not a word in it was true (ibid., p. 66).

To be sure, the Besht's grandson R. Nahman of Bratzlav consciously composed long and symbolic tales, which his disciple R. Nathan of Nemirov set down faithfully. But, then, those didactic allegories were in a class by themselves. Generally, the tales of the hasidim were more folktales than either gnomic, aphoristic wisdom or literary creations, so they incorporate the usual products of the popular imagination – the scheming of witches, the exorcism of devils, and the secret triumphs of *tzaddikim* in their perpetual struggle against the manifold evils of this world.

The legends in *Shivhei HaBesht*, the earliest collection of stories about the founder, contain (1) the folkmotifs of the sage who becomes a viceroy and who is given the hand of a highborn lady in marriage but refuses to touch her, forsakes his high position, and runs away to rejoin his Jewish wife; (2) the motif of Satan's taking the shape of a gentile warlock who turns into a wild beast; (3) the opposing motif of a kabbalist who conjures up a wonderful palace, replete with wondrous drinks and gourmet dishes, by means of the theurgic powers of secret formulas; (4) the motifs of witches, spells, and the battle against them; (5) the motif of journeys to heaven; and (6) the motif of generating great heat through the fervor of piety—a common enough trait in the legendry of shamanism (*Shivhei HaBesht*, ed. Talpiot, pp. 43, 55, 95, 98, 109).

We encounter reflections of popular piety: the Besht's parents were 100 years old when he was born. So noble a soul could not have been brought down to earth by natural lust. The dead reappear among the living in diverse guises (ibid., p. 80, 93, 142). Magical devices work on the principle of mimicry—"like leads to like" (ibid., p. 87). Demons are created by the lustful thoughts of men and women, even in a synagogue (ibid., p. 88). Devils are driven out of a haunted house by means of exorcism (ibid., p. 124). The common people journey to Tartar shamans in quest of magical cures (ibid., p. 73). The Besht knows the "conversation of animals and birds," who are often privy to heavenly secrets (ibid., p. 154).

Animals are treated with cautious reverence. They might contain the souls of departed sinners. Furthermore, they "derive" from a high spiritual realm. As R. Shneur Zalman wrote, "The category of cattle fell way down, at the time of the breaking of the vessels, but in their source, they are extremely high; therefore the love that is awakened in man's animal soul is very, very high . . ." (Shneur Zalman, *Torah Or*, Noah).

The early hasidim wore white garments, because white in Kabbalah is the color of compassion. But this belief is far older than Kabbalah.

Some of the *tzaddikim* employed certain dramatic gestures and hand clappings in order to effect changes in government policy. So, we read in the biography of R. Nahman of Bratzlav, "and I heard from his holy mouth that he said, 'in this year (1803) I danced a great deal, because it was then reported that the government would issue new decrees, called "punkten" against Jewry, for by means of dances and hand-clappings it is possible to sweeten severe laws and annul decrees' " (*Hayyei Moharan*, vol. 2 [Jerusalem, 1947], p. 11).

To achieve the same result, the Apter Rav put on a dramatized debate with the czar, in which the latter's role was played by a hasid, who was born on the same day as the czar (*Tarbitz*, vol. 17). To heal the sick, the *tzaddikim* sometimes made use of whatever was employed in a *mitzvah*, such as apples and honey left over from Rosh Hashanah or an afikoman from the Passover *seder*.

The hasidic movement was, sociologically speaking, a rebellion against the "establishment," so it was bound to dredge up popular practices, which the rationalistic tradition condemned. Among them, was the disregard of civility and decency. For instance, the practice of turning somersaults in the synagogue and in the street, "for the sake of God and the sake of the rebbe," was particularly widespread in the year 1770.

To be close to the people, the *tzaddikim* would include prayers in the vernacular—Yiddish. In their gatherings, gentile melodies were adopted and infused with fresh fervor. The songs were generally in Yiddish, but sometimes in Hungarian and other dialects.

J.B.A.

FOREKNOWLEDGE—Hasidism follows Jewish tradition in its belief in God's foreknowledge and in belief in human beings' free will.

"The Lord is deliberately sparing in the nonmanifestation of miracles," said R. Barukh of Medziborz, "in order to give people the opportunity to exercise free will. Were miracles common, our fear of God's power would overcome our free will to choose for ourselves between evil and good" (*Buzine Dinehora*, p. 21). R. Abraham Joshua Heschel in his work *Ohev Yisrael* (*Ki Tisa*) devotes much thought to this problem.

God's knowledge (of the future) is absolute and imperative. Therefore, if God knows that an individual will be righteous, it is impossible for that individual to be otherwise. The same is true of the opposite case, in which God knows that a person will be wicked.

The question then arises: How is it possible that people be given absolute free will to do as they choose? This is the essence of the paradox as expressed by Maimonides.

Maimonides himself actually answers this paradox. It is well known that we have absolutely no conception of God's true nature and unity. God, His name, and His knowledge are all one true absolute unity. God's knowledge is not at all like that of human beings, since human beings and their knowledge are two separate and separable entities. God's essence and knowledge comprise a single unity. Therefore, just as we have absolutely no conception of God's own essence, we have no understanding of his knowledge. It is thus written: "My thoughts are not your thoughts" (Isaiah 55:8).

R. Nahman of Bratzlav maintains that in the ultimate future, free will shall cease to exist. The Talmud, therefore, says that "the righteous will sit." Sitting alludes to the absence of free will.

A. Kaplan, *The Light Beyond*, pp. 130–134.

A.K.

FRANCE–France has a Jewish population estimated at 700,000, of which 380,000 live in Paris. It has never been a propitious soil for Hasidism, and today, there are only about 1,000 hasidim in France–less than 0.25 percent of all French Jewry.

In the interwar years, a number of hasidim lived in Paris, especially in the fourth district, in the neighborhood of the so-called *Pletzel* (the place), where there were several hasidic *shtieblech*. From 1933 to 1940, R. Eliezer Israel Hofstein of Kozienice lived in Paris. After World War II, a number of hasidim settled in Paris under the leadership of R. Yitzhak Gewirzman, popularly known as "R. Itzikel," who arrived there in 1946, later moving to Antwerp.

A central Lubavitch office was established there in 1945 under R. Benjamin Gorodetszky. It has been instrumental in establishing, with the help of the American Joint, a Lubavitch *yeshivah*, *Tomhei Temimim* in Brunoy, 17 miles (twenty-seven kilometers) from Paris. A traditional girls' school, *Bet Rifka*, was established in Montmorency; it is now in Yerres, near Brunoy. That school, which follows the French education curriculum, contributes to the spread of Lubavitch in France. Provisions are also made for the Sephardic Jews from North Africa.

Lubavitch have taken over an old prayer house in the Rue de Rosiers, where services are held for more than a hundred families. They have also set up first-grade schools, which provide religious instruction and have many Sunday schools all over the city. There is another prayer house on Rue Lamartine in the ninth district.

There are *Habad* houses in Lyons, Marseilles, Strasbourg, and Toulouse.

Hasidism in France has been revitalized thanks to the immigration of North African Jewry.

M. Gurfinkel, "Les Lubavitcher," pp. 58–63.

J.G.

FRANKEL, Abraham, of Wielopole (1842–3 *Shevat* 1891)–Son of R. Shlomoh Zalman Yosef. He became rebbe and was renowned as a miracle worker. He was survived by two sons, Shlomoh Zalman and Yosef Hayyim.

FRANKEL, Asher Yeshaya (1879–1942), Strelisk–Son of R. Israel Aryeh Leib, the rebbe of Premishlany, he married Batsheva, the daughter of R. Levi Yitzhak Klinkop of Strelisk. He succeeded his father-in-law as rebbe and in 1914, settled in Stryj.

He had four daughters and two sons. He and some of his family perished in the Holocaust. His son Levi Yitzhak was a writer, and another son, Dr. Israel, served as a librarian of the Jewish Library of Toronto.

FRANKEL, Issar (b. 1933), writer–Son of R. Yitzhak Yedidiah, he emigrated to the Holy Land in 1935. He is the author of a biography, *R. Meir of Lublin* (Tel Aviv, 1915), and of *Yehidei Segulah*, biographies of hasidic rebbes.

FRANKEL, Samuel (1814–15 *Heshvan* 1883), Haidudorog–Son of R. Shragai Feivel, he was orphaned when he was very young and was brought up by his uncle, R. Isaiah Frankel. He was a disciple of R. Hayyim Halberstam of Zanz.

In 1874, he became rabbi in Haidudorog.

A modest man, he declined to set himself apart from other men by wearing rabbinical garb. He was the author of *Imrei Shefer* on the Pentateuch (Munkacz, 1887).

His son-in-law, R. Zeev Citron (d. 9 *Nisan* 1927), son of R. Abraham Eliezer Citron, succeeded him. He was a disciple of R. Abraham Yitzhak Weinberger of Kleinwardein and of R. Menahem Mendel Panet of Des. He was the author of *Aggadot Mahazaz* on the Pentateuch, which was printed in Miskolc in 1938.

FRANKEL, Solomon Zalman Joseph (1804–13 *Kislev* 1891), Wielopole–Son of R. Abraham of Pinczov, he was a follower of R. Tzvi Hirsch of Rymanov. He became rabbi of Wielopole near Ropczyce and was also the rebbe for fourteen years. He was renowned as a miracle worker. He was an ascetic and lived a life of poverty, refusing to accept any financial support from his followers. He was so weak that he had to lie down all day and rose only for prayers. He instructed that all his writings be buried with him. He nonetheless aroused the antagonism of R. Hayyim of Zanz but enjoyed the friendship of the rebbe of Belz.

He was survived by his sons–R. Abraham, who succeeded him, and R. Yitzhak Tzvi Hirsch Schiff, the rebbe of Wielopole. He also had two daughters.

FRANKEL, Tzvi Hirsch (d. 1 *Tevet* 1856)–Son of R. David Frankel Teumim. His mother, Feiga, was a descendant of the Baal Shem. He was a disciple of Uri of Strelisk. In 1829, he married Esther Zina, the daughter of R. Meir Premyshlan, who lived to the age of ninety-five, as did his mother.

After the death of his father-in-law, he succeeded him as rebbe of Premyshlan. He was survived by his sons, R. Benjamin of Lvov and R. Israel Aryeh Leib, who became rebbe of Premyshlan, and by a daughter, Yentl, who married R. Joshua, rebbe of Premyshlan.

FRANKISTS–The group was a radical wing of the Sabbateans named after its founder and leader, Jacob Frank (1726–1791), who was an imposter and trickster. Frank saw himself as the incarnation of Sabbetai Tzvi, and by perverting the Kabbalah to suit his purpose, he expounded a doctrine akin to Christianity. His followers were consequently initiated into a mystic worship highlighted by sexual orgies and other debaucheries.

When the contemporary rabbinic authorities denounced the sect, Frank sought vengeance by inciting the Polish clergy against his rabbinic opponents. Several of the latter were involved in religious disputations with the Frankists, and, according to legend, one of the participants in the public debate in Kamanetz-Podolsk (1757) was the Besht himself. Following one of these disputations, Frank, together with the extremist section of his followers, converted to Christianity.

The anarchism of the Frankists drew them closer to the spirit of *Haskalah* so that Jonas Wehle, a leading Shabbatean ideologue of Prague at the end of the eighteenth century, found little difficulty in reconciling the essential teachings of Moses Mendelssohn and Sabbetai Tzvi. Moreover, the deviationism of the Frankists was probably an important factor in the opposition that Hasidism provoked in Poland-Lithuania.

S.B.L.

FRANZOS, Karl Emil (1848-1904), Austrian writer–Born in Podolia of Jewish parents, he spent his early years in Chortkov. His themes and settings were taken from Galicia, the Bukovina, Southern Russia, and Romania. His novels contain vivid pictures of life among hasidic Jews. In his *Die Juden von Barnow* (1877), *Aus Halb-Asien* (1876–1883), *Ein Kampf ums Recht* (1882), and *Der Pojas* (1905), he criticized the insularity of Hasidism and its unassimilated Jewish figures.

FREE WILL–It cannot be maintained that there is a special hasidic doctrine of free will. The hasidic sources, when referring, as they do frequently, to human freedom, generally content themselves with simply repeating the standard Jewish teaching that man is free; otherwise there would be no meaning to the constant appeals in the Torah for man to do God's will. Philosophical speculations on this theme are rare in hasidic literature.

When such masters as R. Barukh of Kossov and Tzvi Elimelekh of Dynov do examine the old theological problem of how human freedom can be reconciled with God's foreknowledge, they do so only in order to stress the impotence of the human mind when confronted with the tremendous mystery of the divine nature. This most stubborn intellectual problem is, in fact, used to reject intellectualism in favor of simple, unsophisticated faith, of belief in the absurd, because it is absurd.

Following the Kabbalah, a number of hasidic masters point to the freely choosing will (*ratzon*) as reflecting the highest of the *Sefirot* in the divine realm, that of *Keter* (Crown), which is placed above the head, more elevated than *Hokhmah* (Wisdom) and *Binah* (Understanding). Man's free choice is said to come from a deeper level of his being than his reason. There is thus no reasonable explanation of either God's free choice of Israel or of Israel's response to God. Israel's martyrdom for its faith affronts common sense, but it stems from the free, selfless love that defies logic.

In spite of its constant emphasis on God as the All, Hasidism is normally completely faithful to the traditional Jewish belief in free will. How human autonomy is compatible with God's omnipotence is a great mystery, but that it is compatible is accepted by virtually all the teachers of Hasidism, as it was for their rabbinic predecessors.

The sole exception is the *tzaddik* of Izbica, R. Mordecai Joseph, author of *Mei HaShiloah*, in whose scheme religious determinism has a definite place. For this thinker the talmudic saying "All is in the hands of Heaven except the fear of Heaven" is only true of life as humans see it before the messianic redemption. With the advent of the Messiah, the truth will become revealed that all along man's religious and ethical deeds were ordained by God, that, in reality, "All is in the hands of Heaven, *even* the fear of Heaven." Obedient to his views, this thinker's interpretations of some of the biblical characters as spurred on to commit their sins by a kind of divine destiny for them was a source of grave offence to his contemporaries.

J. G. Weiss, "The Religious Determinism of Joseph Mordecai of Izbica" (Hebrew), pp. 447–453.

L.J.

FREED, Joshua Heschel HaKohen, of Nagykapos (1824–21 *Sivan* 1921) – A disciple of R. Hayyim Halberstam of Zanz, R. Tzvi Hirsch of Liszka, and R. Yitzhak Eisig of Zydaczov.

He became rebbe in 1870 and established a *yeshivah*. He was known for his fiery and enthusiastic prayers and was the author of *Zikhron Yehoshua* (Bilgoraj, 1929).

In 1900, he handed over the rabbinate to his son, R. Jacob Meir (1855–1935).

FRESHWATER, Joshua Meir (1896–15 *Tammuz* 1976) – Born in Sasov, the son of Raphael, he came to London in 1939. In 1947, he married Nehamah Golda Halberstam, the daughter of R. Benzion of Bobov. By 1970, he was one of London's biggest private landlords. He was also one of the founders of the *Beis Yaakov* and *Pardes* house schools in London and a very generous supporter of the Bobov institutions in London, Israel, and the United States.

FRIEDLANDER, Hayyim, of Liszka (d. 9 *Iyyar* 1904) – Son of R. Moses, the *dayan* of Kisvarda, R. Hayyim succeeded his father-in-law as the rabbi of Liszka, where he served for thirty years. He claimed descent from R. Samuel Edels (d. 1632).

He established a *yeshivah* and would regularly wake his pupils at 3 A.M. saying: "Let's go and study! It is already late!" He only slept in a bed on the Sabbath.

He was the author of *Tal Hayyim VeHa-Brakhah*, a pilpulistic discussion on talmudical themes (Przemysl, 1898) and *Tal Hayyim*, hasidic homilies on the Torah (Bethlen, 1909). His elder son, R. Tzvi Hirsch, was murdered in Auschwitz.

Elleh Ezkerah, vol. 5, p. 158

A.S.

FRIEDLANDER, Tzvi Hirsch, of Liszka (1808–1874) – His father died when he was six years old, and his mother, who was known as "Sorel die Bekern" or "Sorel die Tzedakes," entrusted him to R. Moses Teitelbaum of Ujhely. He studied in the *yeshivah* of R. Hirsh Harif of Bonyhad and spent his early married life with his parents-in-law in Olasz-Liszka, where he became the spiritual leader of the community.

It was R. Moses Teitelbaum who imbued him with a love of Hasidism. To widen his hasidic experience, he visited R. Israel of Ruzhyn, R. Shalom Rokeah, and R. Menahem Mendel of Rymanov. He was reluctant to become rabbi and for a time had a shop while his wife was the breadwinner. He eventually agreed to become the rabbi of Liszka. It was with the encouragement of R. Meir of Przemyshlan that R. Tzvi Hirsch, or "R. Hershele," became rebbe. He attracted many followers. He continued his ties with R. Hayyim Halberstam and continued to visit many rebbes. He corresponded with his colleagues on many halakhic problems.

In his later years, he entrusted the care of the rabbinate to his son-in-law R. Hayyim Friedlander. He was survived by two sons-in-law: R. Hayyim and R. Joseph Goldberger, whose son, R. Wolf, edited and published the literary legacy of his grandfather: *Av Pri Tevua* (Munkacs, 1875–1876) and *HaYashar VeHaTov* in two parts (Munkacs, 1880–1889). R. Wolf also wrote a biography of his grandfather.

A.S.

FRIEDLANDER, Tzvi Hirsch, of Liszka (1874–27 *Iyyar* 1944)–Eldest son of R. Hayyim. He was ordained by R. Tzvi Hirsch Shapira of Munkacs and by R. Yitzhak Shmelke of Lvov. He married the daughter of R. Yitzhak Isaac of Hegyalja-Mad, where he became *dayan* and founded a *yeshivah* that was transferred to Gava, and later to Liszka, where he succeeded his father as rabbi in 1904. He was a renowned scholar who was appointed to a committee of ten rabbis whose function it was to ordain rabbis and ecclesiastical officials.

During World War I, he did his utmost to ease the plight of the *agunot*, and frequently corresponded with Rabbis S. Engel, M. Y. Halstock of Ostrowiec, and Mordecai Hakohen of Brzezany. He wrote glosses on the *Shulhan Arukh*, on *Mikvaot*, on *Agunot*, commentaries on *Pri Etz Hayyim* and on the Song of Songs, but only *Shaar HaYashar*, a commentary on the Psalms, was published in his lifetime (Budapest, 1934).

In 1925, he was accused of complicity in a financial scandal that shook the national economy of Hungary. He was arrested and taken to Budapest, where he had to endure the indignities of a long, drawn-out investigation and public pilloring by the press. However, the judicial investigation proved his complete innocence.

In later years, after the death of R. Abraham Steiner in 1928, a small number of Liszka and Kereszturer hasidim gathered around him.

He, his three sons–R. Simon, R. Hayyim, and R. Abraham–and another twenty-four members of his family were murdered by the Nazis in Auschwitz.

Elleh Ezkerah, vol. 5, p. 158.

A.S.

FRIEDMAN, Aaron, of Czernowitz (1900–14 *Heshvan* 1942)–Son of Menahem Nahum, the rebbe of Boyan-Czernowitz. In 1914, the whole family took refuge in Vienna. In 1907, he married Henia, the daughter of R. Hayyim Hager of Ottynia. On the death of his father in 1936, he succeeded him as rebbe. His only daughter died in 1937. He and his wife were transported to Transnistria, in western Ukraine, where they perished.

His discourses are mentioned in *Toldot Aaron* (Jerusalem, 1944).

FRIEDMAN, Aaron, of Sadgora (1877–19 *Tishri* 1913)–Son of R. Israel. In 1896, he married Sarah Sheindel Rosa, the daughter of R. Sholom Yosef of Husyatin. When his father died in 1907, he succeeded him as rebbe of Sadgora. He was a gifted musician and played the violin. He was the author of *Kedushat Aharon* on the Pentateuch (Warsaw, 1913). His son Sholom Yosef succeeded him.

FRIEDMAN, Abraham Jacob, of Boyan/Lvov (24 *Nisan* 1884–2 *Elul* 1942)–Third son of Isaac of Boyan, he was born in Sadgora. He married Reizel, the daughter of Aaron Shur of Berdichev, and when he divorced her, he married Hannah, the daughter of Mordecai Twersky, the rabbi of Leovo.

During the First World War, he lived in Vienna, where he was known for his hospitality to the war refugees. After the war, he settled in Lvov and became known as the Boyaner rebbe. He actively encouraged his followers to settle in the Holy Land, and he himself visited in 1933, when he was honored with the kindling of the lights at Meron on the thirty-third day of the Omer.

He and his wife were killed in Stryj in 1942.

Some of his discourses are recorded in *Nahalat Yaakov* (Jerusalem, 1973).

FRIEDMAN, Abraham Jacob, of Sadgora (20 *Heshvan* 1820–11 *Elul* 1883)–The second son of Israel of Ruzhyn. He married Miriam, the daughter of R. Aaron of Karlin. His father described him as a "pillar of Torah and wisdom" and applied to him the verse of Micah, "Thou givest truth to Jacob." When his elder brother, R. Sholom Joseph, died, he succeeded his father as rebbe of Sadgora.

In 1856, a few days after Passover, he was arrested by the czarist authorities on trumped-up charges of forging passports and of currency irregularities. He was in prison for fifteen months and was released on 23 *Tammuz* 1857. He sent emissaries to Sir Moses Montefiore to intervene with the czarist authorities on behalf of Russian Jewry. In 1882, Laurence Oliphant visited him to enlist his help in the resettlement of a million Jews in the Holy Land.

He was succeeded by his son, Shlomoh. His discourses are recorded in *Irin Kaddishin* and *Emet LeYaakov* (Piotrokov, 1912) and *Bet HaHayyim* (Przemysl, 1898).

FRIEDMAN, Abraham Jacob, of Sadgora/Tel Aviv (8 *Av* 1884–5 *Tevet* 1961)–Son of R. Israel of Sadgora. In 1902, he married Bluma Reizel, the daughter of R. Isaac Meir of Kopyczynice. In 1907, he became rebbe of Sadgora, where he established a *yeshivah*. During the First World War, he lived in Vienna, but at the end of the war, he decided not to return to Poland. "I believe," he said, "that Vienna is the gateway to the Holy Land." However, he regularly visited his hasidim in Galicia.

After the *Anschluss*, the Nazis forced him to sweep the streets of Vienna, and he vowed that he would one day sweep the streets of the Holy Land. In 1938, he settled in Tel Aviv and faithfully carried out his vow. Every morning, broom in hand, he would sweep the street outside his home. He was active in the work of the Aguda, in the *Hinukh Hatzmai*, and in the *yeshivah* of Ruzhyn in Jerusalem.

At the fourth *Knessiyyah* in 1954, he urged religious Jews to settle in the Holy Land and not to heed leaders who discouraged *aliyah*. "I can study tractate *Zeraim* only here," he would say. "And only those who are actively engaged in agriculture can fulfill the agricultural laws." He enjoyed visiting Haifa, which he called the "mountain of Elijah." He supported the establishment of diplomatic relations between Israel and Germany.

His discourses *Abir Yaakov* on the Pentateuch and Festivals were published in Jerusalem in 1964.

He was buried in *Nahlat Yitzhak* in Tel Aviv near his wife.

FRIEDMAN, Abraham Jacob, of Tel Aviv (b. 5 *Elul* 1928)–Son of Mordecai Shalom Yosef. In 1953 he married Zipporah, the daughter of R. Joseph Aryeh Feldman of Brooklyn. In 1979, he succeeded his father as rebbe in Tel Aviv. He established educational institutions and was a member of *Mo'etzet Gedolei HaTorah*.

His son, Yisrael Mosheh (b. 1957), married the daughter of Hayyim Mosheh Feldman of London.

His discourses are printed in the Sadgora periodical *Mesilot* and *Keser Torah*.

FRIEDMAN, Alexander Zusya (1897–1943), writer–A hasid of Amshinov, he was active in Orthodox Jewish life as a speaker, writer, administrator, and educationist.

He was the author of *Die Torah Kvall* (Warsaw, 1938), originally published in Yiddish and later translated into Hebrew, as *Mayenei shel Torah*, and into English, as *The Wellsprings of Torah*. He was also the editor of *Diglenu* (1919–24) and *Darkenu* (1930–31 and 1936–38).

He was murdered by the Nazis.

FRIEDMAN, David Moses, of Chortkov (7 *Sivan* 1827–*Hoshanah Rabba* 1904)–Fifth son of R. Israel, he was born in Ruzhyn. When he was a child, his father predicted that "this great soul will bring the hearts of Israel near to their Father in heaven." He was known as the *Tzitzit Yid* because he cried bitterly if he forgot to put on his *tzitzit*. He married Feigele, the daughter of R. Aaron of Chernobyl, and after her death, he married his niece, Rachel Leah, the daughter of his elder brother, Sholom Yosef.

After the death of his father, he lived in Potok, and in 1895, he settled in Chortkov, where he established a palatial residence. He was renowned for his love of every Jew. He even refused to curse Jew-baiters. "I pray constantly," the rabbi said, "that the children of the House of Israel be uplifted, and that no gentile should harm them."

He reacted with silent fortitude to the onslaught launched against the house of Ruzhyn by R. Hayyim Halberstam of Zanz. He greatly supported the establishment of the *Ahavat Zion* organization, which encouraged the settling of Jews in the Holy Land. Dr. Herzl corresponded with R. Yehudah Menahem Halevi of Przemysl, who offered to negotiate with the rebbe. Dr. Herzl noted in his diary, "I sent a letter in which I invited Friedman to send me his son." Herzl met the rabbi's son, and the writer Aaron Marcus joined them in trying to persuade the rebbe to convene a conference of rabbis to gain support for Zionism. The conference never took place.

His son Nahum Mordecai died in his father's lifetime, in 1870, and his other son, Israel, succeeded him. His discourses are found in *Divrei David* (Husiatyn, 1904), in *Bet Yisrael* (Piotrokov, 1913), and in *Knesset Yisrael* (Warsaw, 1906).

FRIEDMAN, Dov Baer, of Chortkov/Vienna (1882–24 *Elul* 1936) – Younger son of R. Israel, Dov Baer was born in Chortkov. He married Miriam, his cousin, the daughter of R. Isaac of Boyan, in 1899. When his father died in Vienna in 1934, he declined to become rebbe. He was active in the Aguda and was highly respected for his wisdom and penetrating intelligence. His son, David Mosheh, died in London in 1988.

FRIEDMAN, Dov Baer, of Leove (1817–13 *Kislev* 1876) – Son of Israel of Ruzhyn. "Dov" or "Berenui," as he was called, was educated by private tutors in almost princely style. At the age of fourteen, he married Sheindel, the daughter of R. Mordecai Twersky of Chernobyl. It was not a happy marriage. After his father's death in 1851, he first settled in Husi, Romania, then in Sureni, and finally in Leove. He was of a sensitive and brooding disposition and tended to keep his hasidim at a distance, seeking the company of the enlightened local apothecary and physician.

Concerned about his mental health, his brother, especially after the death of his brother R. Menahem Nahum in 1869, took him to his house in Sadgora. This gave rise to the rumor that he was being held a prisoner by his brother. A lawyer, Dr. Judah Leib Reitman, invoked the help of the civil authorities. As a result, R. Dov Baer came to live in Czernowitz for six weeks. In a manifesto that appeared in *HaMelitz* (no. 7, 14 *Adar* 1869), Dov Baer declared that he wished "to eliminate the foolish customs that have no basis in Judaism and to remove the thorns from the vineyard of the House of Israel."

Dov Baer's brother-in-law, R. Mendel, and his nephew, R. Sholom Yosef, were among those who attempted to reason with the renegade rebbe. On *Shushan Purim*, he returned to Sadgora. There, four months later, he issued a public statement expressing his desire to return to the rock "from which I was hewn" and promising to observe scrupulously "our laws and customs."

For six years, until the day of his death, he lived in Sadgora, deserted by his wife, shunned by his brothers, and ignored by his former followers.

He was buried in the sepulcher of his father, but not adjacent to him. He was one of Hasidism's most tragic and enigmatic characters.

Some of his discourses are to be found in M. E. Gutman's *R. Dov of Leove* (Cluj, 1926).

FRIEDMAN, Israel, of Chortkov (10 *Iyyar* 1854–13 *Kislev* 1934) – Son of David Mosheh. He was one of the first hasidic rabbis to advocate the establishment of vocational schools. He married his cousin, Rechumah Shevah, the daughter of R. Abraham Israel of Sadgora.

Prior to the establishment of the Aguda, he proposed the founding of an organization called *Histadrut HaHaredim* to safeguard the interests of Orthodox Jewry. The Aguda received his full support, and he urged his followers to settle in the Holy Land. Among his ardent supporters was R. Meir Shapira of Lublin, who said, "I am fully convinced that were the Messiah to come now, he would appoint the rebbe of Chortkov to be the king of Israel."

His discourses are to be found in *Ateret Yisrael* (Husiatyn, 1904), *Tiferet Yisrael* (Vienna, 1933), *Yismah Yisrael* (Vienna, 1933), *Ginzei Yisrael* (Brooklyn, New York, 1965), and *Nezer Yisrael* (Jerusalem, 1981).

His elder son, Hayyim Aaron, died in his youth. His other son, R. Nahum Mordecai, succeeded him.

FRIEDMAN, Israel, of Husiatyn/Tel Aviv (16 *Kislev* 1858–29 *Kislev* 1949) – Son of R. Mordecai Shragai, he was born in Husyatin. He married Gitel, the daughter of Avi Ezra Selig Shapira of Moglienice, and when she died, he married the daughter of R. Hayyim Hager of Ottynia. He succeeded his father in 1894 and during the First World War moved to Vienna. He supported religious Zionism, especially the Mizrachi, and constantly urged his followers to settle in the Holy Land.

In 1937, he settled in Rehov Bialik in Tel Aviv. He frequently visited religious *kibbutzim* and opposed religious extremists. When Rommel reached Egypt, R. Israel prayed at the grave of R. Hayyim Ibn Attar, assuring his followers that Rommel would not advance any further. In his last will and testament, dated 23 *Nisan* 1939, he wrote, "I would like to be buried on the Mount of Olives in Jerusalem. If this is not possible, bury me in either Safed or Tiberias." He was buried in Tiberias. His son-in-law R. Jacob of Bohusi succeeded him in Tel Aviv.

FRIEDMAN, Israel, of Leipzig/Boyan (24 *Elul* 1878–30 *Av* 1951) – Second son of R. Yitzhak of Bohusi. In 1896, he married Duba Miriam, the daughter of R. Shlomoh of Sadgora. After the death of his father in 1917, he settled in Leipzig, and he visited the Holy Land in 1934. In 1939, after first finding refuge in Switzerland, he settled in Tel Aviv. He was known for his integrity and impartiality. He was survived by two daughters, Gittel Leah and Havah *Hayyah*.

FRIEDMAN, Israel, of Ruzhyn (3 *Tishri* 1797–3 *Heshvan* 1851) – The founder of the Ruzhyn and Sadgora dynasty, he was the son of Sholem Shakhna. His mother, Havah, was a granddaughter of R. Nahman of Chernobyl. Israel was six years old when he was orphaned; he was brought up by his elder brother, R. Abraham. At thirteen, Israel married Sarah, the daughter of R. Moses Halevi Efrati of Berdichev.

When Israel's brother, Abraham, died childless in 1813, the sixteen-year-old Israel succeeded him. He first settled in Skvira and then in Ruzhyn, where he established his court. Ruzhyn spelled royalty, and the rabbi was virtually the exilarch of Hasidism. He dressed elegantly and lived in a style that befitted descendants of the house of David. He rode in a splendid carriage with silver buckles that harnessed his four horses. "What can I do?" asked the rebbe. "It is not my choice. I am forced from above to take the road of honor and glory, and it is impossible for me to deviate from it." So demanding were the claims on his time that he slept for only a few hours each day. "One must not waste the hours of the kingdom," he said. He would rise at dawn and spend many hours in prayer and study.

In the winter of 1838, two notorious Jewish informers (*malshinim*) were assassinated in Novaya Ushitsa in Podolia. As a result, many Jews were arrested, including R. Israel, whom the governor of Kiev, General Bibikov, regarded as "wielding almost the power of a czar." R. Israel languished in the prisons of Kiev and Kamenets-Podolsk for twenty-two months. In 1840, on Shushan Purim, he was released and allowed to live in Kishinev. He was under strict surveillance and in order to forestall banishment to Siberia, he escaped to Jassy, then later to Shatsk, Kompling, and Skola. The Russian government demanded his extradition, but R. Isaac Noah Mannheimer (1793–1865) and Solomon Mayer Rothschild (1774–1855) interceded with Count Metternich and Ferdinand I of Austria so as to refuse to accede to the Russian demands.

The rabbi acquired an estate (Zoloti-Potok) in Sadgora, near Czernowitz, and there the glory of Ruzhyn was revived. His family joined him in 1842. On the last day of Passover 1847, his wife died. He subsequently married the widow of R. Tzvi Hirsch of Rymanov. He became a Turkish citizen, and on his passport, his place of birth was shown as "Jerusalem." He sent Israel Bak, his hasid, to visit Sir Moses Montefiore to urge him to persuade the czarist government to permit fund-raising in Russia for the Holy Land. He helped Nisan Bak to acquire a site near the Western Wall for the building of a synagogue, which became known as *Tiferet Yisrael* or *Bet HaKnesset Nisan Bak*.

"Everyone leaves behind books," he mused. "I leave sons." Each one of his sons established his own dynasty: R. Sholom Joseph, R. Abraham Jacob, R. Menahem Nahum, R. Dov Baer, R. David Moses, and R. Mordecai Shragai. There were also three daughters: *Hayyah* Malkah, Leah, and Gittel Tobah.

R. Israel's discourses are found in *Irin Kaddishin* (Warsaw, 1887), *Knesset Yisrael* (Warsaw, 1906), *Bet Yisrael* (Piotrokov, 1913), *Nahlat Yisrael* (New York, 1951), and *Orot Yisrael* (Jerusalem, 1973).

FRIEDMAN, Israel, of Sadgora (20 *Shevat* 1852–13 *Tishri* 1907) – The son of Abraham Jacob of Sadgora. In 1868, he married Esther, the elder daughter of Yitzhak of

Bohusi, and when she died, he married his cousin, Bathsheba, the daughter of Sholom Joseph of Sadgora. When his father died in 1883, he succeeded him as rebbe. His younger son, Aaron, succeeded him.

FRIEDMAN, Israel Shalom Joseph, of Bohusi (13 *Tishri* 1853–3 *Nisan* 1923) – The elder son of Yitzhak of Bohusi. He married Malkah, the daughter of R. Mosheh Abraham Zuckerman of Rashkov. In 1896, he succeeded his father as rebbe. He was known for his great medical knowledge and wrote prescriptions for his followers. He established a *yeshivah* in Bohusi and was president of the *kollel* of Romania in the Holy Land. During the First World War, he spent some time in Hungary and Galicia. His discourses are to be found in *Peer Yisrael* (Jerusalem, 1971).

FRIEDMAN, Jacob (b. 1910), poet – A descendant of the hasidic dynasty of Ruzhyn, Jacob began his literary activities with the poem *Adam*. He spent the war years in Transnistria and attained his maturity in Israel with the poems *Titians* (1963) and *Love* (1967).

FRIEDMAN, Jacob, of Husiatyn (25 *Heshvan* 1878–18 *Heshvan* 1957) – The youngest son of R. Yitzhak of Bohusi, he was born in Bohusi. In 1895, he married his cousin, *Hayyah* Sarah, the daughter of R. Israel of Husyatin, where he lived for a number of years. At the outbreak of the First World War, after living for some time in Frankfurt, like other members of the family, he settled in Vienna.

He was a staunch supporter of the *Hevrat Yishuv Eretz Yisrael* and acted as chairman of the Mizrachi. In 1920, he represented the Mizrachi at the *Keren HaYesod* conference in London. In 1937, together with his father-in-law, he settled in Tel Aviv and succeeded him as rebbe in 1949. He led protest demonstrations in Tel Aviv against the desecration of the Sabbath. Apart from such rare demonstrations, he lived very quietly, "because," he said, "Hasidism does not spread by means of publicity. The leaders of Hasidism are not speech makers. So long as there are *tzaddikim* who maintain a high standard, there will be hasidim."

He was buried next to his father-in-law in Tiberias.

His discourses are to be found in *Oholei Yaakov* (Jerusalem, 1962). He was succeeded by his son, R. Yitzhak.

FRIEDMAN, Jacob David, of Pascani (1892–22 *Av* 1956) – He was the son of R. Moses Judah Leib of Pascani and married his cousin, *Hayyah* Sarah Simah, the daughter of R. Pinhas. He succeeded his father in 1947 and was the president of the Rabbinical Association of Romania. In 1950 he settled in Jaffa.

He was buried in Nahlat Yitzhak.

He was survived by a son, R. Israel Shalom Joseph.

FRIEDMAN, Menahem Nahum, of Czernowitz (21 *Kislev* 1869–19 *Av* 1936) – He was born in Sadgora, the eldest son of Yitzhak of Bohusi. He married his second cousin, Havah, the daughter of R. Mordecai Shragai of Husiatyn, where he lived for three years. At the outbreak of the First World War, he and his father lived in Vienna. After Boyan was destroyed during the war, he settled in Czernowitz.

In 1927, he visited the Holy Land, where he kindled the bonfire *Hadlakah* in Meron on the thirty-third day of the Omer. Every Lag BaOmer, he sent his silk scarf to Meron to be used in the *Hadlakah* ceremony. He was the author of *Zeh Yenahameinu* (Czernowitz, 1937), *Devarim Nihmudim* (Czernowitz, 1937), and *Tiferet Menahem* (Jerusalem, 1953).

He died and was buried in Vienna. He was succeeded by his son R. Aaron.

FRIEDMAN, Menahem Nahum, of Itcani (8 *Heshvan* 1879–21 *Sivan* 1933) – Son of Abraham Joshua Heschel of Adjud, he was brought up in Bohusi and Chortkov. He married Miriam, the daughter of R. Israel of Chortkov, and spent the war years in Vienna. From 1925, he was rabbi in Stefanesti. In addition to rabbinics, he was well versed in philosophy and other secular subjects.

He was the author of *Divrei Menahem* on Pentateuch (Cracow, 1912); a commentary, *Man* on the *Ethics of the Fathers* (Vienna, 1920); *HaHalom U'Pitrono* (Czernowitz, 1925); *Al HaEmet VeHaSheker* (Kishinev,

1927); *Al HaYofi* (1929); and *Al HaAdam* (1932).

He supported the settlements in the Holy Land and was one of the founders of the *Histadrut Yishuv Eretz Yisrael*. He contributed articles to periodicals, and in his commentary to the *Ethics of the Fathers*, he describes his visits to Italy and Switzerland. He died in a sanatorium near Vienna.

FRIEDMAN, Menahem Nahum, of Lvov (18 *Tevet* 1880–10 *Kislev* 1943)–Son of R. Sholom Yosef, he was born in Husyatin. In 1898, he married his cousin, Havah, the daughter of R. Israel of Husiatyn, and he spent the years of the First World War in Vienna. When his father-in-law settled in the Holy Land in 1937, he became the rebbe of Husyatin in Lvov. During the Second World War, under Soviet occupation, he worked for the refugees in Siberia, to whom he sent parcels of food. When the Nazis occupied Lvov, he was deported to Belzec, where he perished.

FRIEDMAN, Menahem Nahum, of Sadgora (1843–27 *Av* 1883)–He was the son of Shalom Yosef of Sadgora, and when his father died in 1861, he was brought up by his brother, R. Yitzhak of Bohusi. He married his cousin, Pearl, the daughter of R. Abraham Yaakov of Sadgora. He had one of the largest Hebrew private libraries in Eastern Europe. His books were beautifully bound and fully cataloged. One quarter of the library was eventually sold to the Jewish community of Vienna. A catalog, *Minhat Shlomoh*, was published in Vienna in 1912.

On his return from the Gleichenberg spa, he died suddenly in Vienna and was buried there. He was survived by a son and two daughters.

FRIEDMAN, Menahem Nahum, of Stefanesti (1827–14 *Kislev* 1869)–He was the fourth son of R. Israel of Ruzhyn and married the daughter of R. Eleazar Kushansky of Linitz. In 1852, he settled in Stefanesti, where he was rebbe. One of the rooms in his palatial home was called the "room of the Messiah." "Take off your shoes," the rebbe told his followers, "for this is holy ground. When the Messiah comes, he will dwell here." He prepared a golden crown in readiness for the long-awaited visitor. He died in Iasi, and he was reinterred in Israel on 5 *Heshvan* 1969.

His son, R. Abraham Mattathias, succeeded him.

FRIEDMAN, Mordecai Shalom Yosef, of Sadgora/Przemysl (17 *Kislev* 1897–29 *Sivan* 1979)–Son of R. Aaron, his mother was Sarah Sheindel. At the age of sixteen, he became rebbe. He married Mirel Mirah, the daughter of R. Yisrael Sholom Yosef Heschel of Medziborz. To keep in touch with his scattered followers, he regularly traveled from Vienna to Przemysl, and in 1922, he settled there.

In 1939, he emigrated to the Holy Land. He was very active in the Aguda, the *Mo'etzet Gedolei HaTorah*, and the *Hinukh Atzmai*. It was his hope to establish a hasidic settlement in the Land of Israel to perpetuate the Sadgora dynasty.

His discourses are to be found in *Knesset Mordecai* (Przemysl, 1938).

He had two sons–Israel Aaron, who lives in New York, and R. Abraham Yaakov, who succeeded him as rebbe.

FRIEDMAN, Mordecai Shlomoh, of Boyan/New York (13 *Tishri* 1891–5 *Adar* 1971)–Youngest son of R. Isaac of Boyan, his mother was Malkah, the daughter of R. Yohanan of Rotmistrowke. At the age of seventeen, he married Havah Sarah, the daughter of R. Yisrael Sholom Yosef Heschel of Medziborz. In 1917, he succeeded his father as rebbe in Boyan, where he lived a total of twenty years.

In 1927, he settled on the West Side of Manhattan, New York. He was active in the Aguda and visited the Holy Land four times. He was buried on the Mount of Olives. He was survived by two sons and a daughter, and his grandson, R. Nahum Dov, is the rabbi of Boyan in Jerusalem.

FRIEDMAN, Mordecai Shragai Feivish, of Husiatyn (1834–22 *Iyyar* 1894)–The sixth and youngest son of R. Israel of Ruzhyn. In 1850, he married his cousin, Brakhah Dinah, the daughter of R. David Tzvi Kublansky of Berdichev.

After living for a short time in Strzyzov, he established his court in Husiatyn. He lived in regal style and attracted many wealthy hasidim from eastern Galicia. Merchants and industrialists came to him for guidance and advice. He encouraged his wealthy hasidim to support the poor and to subsidize impoverished scholars. He was a staunch opponent of *Haskalah* and an equally staunch supporter of the counter-*Haskalah* activities of R. Simon Sofer. His son Sholom Yosef died in his lifetime, and he was succeeded by his son Israel. He also had two daughters, Gittel and Havah.

FRIEDMAN, Moses, of Boyan/Cracow (14 *Adar* 1881–3 *Elul* 1943) – Son of R. Sholom Yosef, he was born in Husyatin. When he was barely two years old, his father died and he was brought up by his grandfather and his uncle, R. Israel of Husyatin. In 1901, he married Miriam, the daughter of R. Isaac of Boyan. He spent the war years in Vienna, and his valuable library in Boyan was destroyed by Russian troops. In the summer of 1925, he settled in Cracow and was popularly known as "R. Moishenu of Cracow." He was renowned as a great talmudical scholar but rarely delivered discourses; nor did he officiate at the reader's desk.

According to the custom of Ruzhyn, he prayed in a room adjoining the synagogue, where he could be heard but not seen. He was active in the Aguda and in 1923 was elected as a member of the *Mo'etzet Gedolei HaTorah*. He supported the *Yesodei Hatorah* and *Beis Yaakov* school movements. When R. Meir Shapira died in 1934, R. Moses became the spiritual head of the *Yeshivat Hakhmei Lublin*. He corresponded with R. Meir Arak and R. Abraham Menahem Steinberg of Brody.

When the Nazis entered Cracow in the winter of 1941, he escaped to the ghetto of Tarnov, where he lived in the home of Israel Marcus, son of R. Aaron Marcus. He was deported to Bochnia, where he was murdered.

He was the author of responsa *Daat Mosheh* (Jerusalem, 1947). A number of his responsa were published in *Mareh Yehezkel* (Bilgoraj, 1929).

FRIEDMAN, Moses Yehudah Leib, of Pascani (15 *Shevat* 1855–10 *Elul* 1947) – Son of Yitzhak of Bohusi. He lived in Sadgora and Bohusi, and in 1897, settled in Pascani. Many of the hasidim of Stefanesti rallied around him. His celebration of Simhat Torah drew great crowds. He miraculously survived the Holocaust and was buried in Bohusi. He was succeeded by his son Jacob David. His discourses are to be found in *Birkhat Mosheh* (Jerusalem, 1986).

FRIEDMAN, Nahum Mordecai, of Chortkov (17 *Shevat* 1874–18 *Adar* II, 1946) – He was born in Chortkov, the son of R. Israel. He married Havah Leah, the daughter of R. Shlomoh of Sadgora. R. Nahum Mordecai was reluctant to become rebbe but succumbed to his mother's persuasion. He was closely associated with the work of his brother, R. Dov Baer. He emigrated from Vienna to the Holy Land in 1939.

He was buried on the Mount of Olives. His son, R. Shlomoh, succeeded him. His discourses are to be found in *Doresh Tov* (Jerusalem, 1964).

FRIEDMAN, Shalom Joseph, of Czernowitz (13 *Tevet* 1879–28 *Shevat* 1936) – Son of R. Israel of Sadgora. He married Sheindel, the daughter of R. Barukh Hager of Vishnitz. His wife and his son perished in the Holocaust. He is survived by one son, Dr. Hayyim Barukh of Haifa.

FRIEDMAN, Shalom Joseph, of Sadgora (1813–11 *Elul* 1851) – The eldest of R. Israel of Ruzhyn. He married Bluma Reizel, the daughter of R. Don Yungerleit of Radzwilov. He was very frail and died in Leipzig, where he had gone for a cure. He was survived by two sons, Yitzhak and Menahem Dov, and by two daughters.

FRIEDMAN, Shalom Joseph, of Spikov (1878–14 *Adar* 1920) – Son of R. David of Bohusi. He married Feige, the daughter of R. Mordecai Twersky of Spikov. In 1897, he succeeded his father-in-law as rebbe. He was the only hasidic rebbe of the Ruzhyn dynasty to remain in the Soviet Union. His son, R. Yitzhak, is the rebbe of Bohusi of Tel Aviv.

FRIEDMAN, Shlomoh Hayyim, of Sadgora/Tel Aviv (*Rosh Hodesh Sivan* 1887–26 *Av* 1972) – Son of R. Israel of Sadgora. At the age of fourteen, he wrote articles for the *Mahzikei Hadath*, a Zionist

Orthodox weekly. He married Breindel, the daughter of R. Shmuel HaKohen Hornstein of Radomysl. During World War I, together with his family he found refuge in Vienna, where together with R. Hayyim Meir Shapira of Drohobycz, he formed an association *Yishuv Eretz Yisrael*.

He was also active in the Mizrachi. He attended a Zionist conference in London in 1920, as well as the Zionist congresses in Carlsbad in 1923 and in Lucerne in 1935. In 1938, he settled in Tel Aviv, but only when his brother Abraham Jacob died did he become rebbe. In 1949, he went to Switzerland to organize efforts to rescue Jewish children who were still in monasteries. He made few public appearances, but on special occasions, such as the anniversary of his father's death, he would deliver a discourse.

After the Six-Day War, he asked to meet Zalman Shazar, the president of Israel. He generally spent the summer months in London, where he died. He was buried in Nachlat Yitzhak, Tel Aviv. He was survived by three daughters. His discourses are to be found in *Imrei Kodesh* (Jerusalem, 1972)..

FRIEDMAN, Shlomonui, of Chortkov/Tel Aviv (14 *Nisan* 1884–15 *Heshvan* 1859)–Son of R. Nahum Mordecai. He married his cousin, Rachel, the daughter of Israel of Sadgora. After the death of his father in 1946, he became rebbe. He took part in communal life and when the leaders of the *Neturei Karta* urged him to withdraw his support of the Aguda and the *Hinukh Atzmai*, "since they receive financial support from the Zionists," he retorted, "I never listen to libel."

He survived his eighty-four-year-old mother Havah by two days. His son, Abraham Jacob, died in Vienna in 1926. He was survived by an only daughter, Zipporah Feige. His discourses are recorded in *Divrei Shlomoh* (Jerusalem, 1961).

FRIEDMAN, Yitzhak, of Bohusi (5 *Kislev* 1825–10 *Elul* 1896)–Son of Shalom Joseph. He married Sheine Rachel, the daughter of R. David Hager of Zablotov. After the death of his father and grandfather, he became rebbe first in Potok and then in Izmail, Bessarabia, finally establishing his court in Bohusi, where he also established a *yeshivah*, *Bet Yisrael*.

The rabbi gave limited support to the *Hovevei Zion*. In 1880, he was invited by the communal leaders of Galati to participate in a conference at Iasi. His reply was noncommittal. He felt that the proposed gathering might prejudice the struggle for Jewish civil rights. When he passed through Czernowitz in *Elul* 1888, a delegation that included Aaron Marcus urged him to back the movement.

On 7 *Iyyar*, Abraham Mordecai, the rabbi's secretary, informed the *Hovevei Zion* that the rabbi was willing to encourage the purchase of *etrogim* from the Holy Land. In 1887, R. Yitzhak made it clear that he did not oppose agricultural settlement in the Holy Land. He advocated gradual settlement and slow integration. He even sent one of his followers to explore the possibility of settling fifty Romanian families in the Holy Land. He was succeeded by his son R. Israel Shalom Joseph. His other sons all established hasidic dynasties.

FRIEDMAN, Yitzhak, of Bohusi/Bene Berak (26 *Iyyar* 1903–13 *Av* 1992)–He was born in Spikov, the son of R. Sholom Yosef. In 1926, he married his cousin, Yoheved Feige, the daughter of R. Menahem Mendel of Bohusi. He was ordained by R. Bezalel Safran and R. Judah Leib Zirelson. After the Russian revolution, he and his family endured the pogroms of Petlura. His father and his mother died from typhus, and in 1920, he succeeded his father.

In 1930, he settled in Bucharest, where he opened his own *Bet HaMidrash*. He devoted all his energies, particularly during the Second World War, to helping the refugees from Poland. In 1951, he settled in Tel Aviv, and in 1988, he moved to Bene Berak, where he opened the Bohusi-Puscan *Bet HaMidrash* and established *yeshivah Or Shragai Yitzhak* for young people. He also maintained a small *kollel* and was very popular, especially with the large contingent of Romanian Jews. He was a people's rebbe rather than a scholar's rebbe. He was survived by an only daughter, Shoshanah Sheindel Sarah, who married R. Israel Joseph Friedman.

The rebbe died in Arosa, Switzerland, and was interred in the Ruzhyner plot in *Nahlat Yitzhak*, Tel Aviv. He was succeeded by his grandson, R. Jacob Mendel.

FRIEDMAN, Yitzhak, of Boyan (2 *Tishri* 1850–17 *Adar* 1917)–Son of R. Abraham Jacob of Sadgora. He married Malkah, the third daughter of R. Yohanan of Rotmistrovka. After the death of his father in 1883, he became rebbe in Sadgora, where his brother Israel also resided. In 1887, he established his court in Boyan and became the president of the *kollel* of Volhynia. He was known among the hasidim as *Pahad Yitzhak* (fear of Jacob) due to his great reverence of the Almighty.

Commenting on the verse in Deuteronomy 18:13–"Be perfect with the Lord, your God"–the rabbi stressed the importance of simple, unquestioning faith and of the need for the hasidim to live together in harmony. At the outbreak of the First World War, he moved to Vienna, where he died. All of his four sons (R. Menahem Nahum, R. Israel, R. Abraham Jacob, and R. Mordecai Solomon) became rebbes. His daughter Miriam married R. Israel of Chortkov.

A number of his discourses are printed in *Urian Talisai* (Jerusalem, 1980).

A. D. Twersky, *Sefer HaYahas MiChernobyl VeRuzhin*, p. 142.

FRIEDMAN, Yitzhak, of Rymanov (2 *Heshvan* 1889–11 *Kislev* 1928)–Son of R. Yisrael of Sadgora. In 1903, he married Sarah Devorah, the daughter of R. Asher Yeshaya Horowitz. In 1907, he became rebbe in Rymanov. During the First World War, he stayed for a short time in Budapest and then settled in Vienna.

In 1924, he emigrated to the United States and lived in New York, where he died at the age of thirty-nine. He was survived by two sons and two daughters.

FRIEDMAN, Yitzhak Eizik, of Nyiardehaz/Boyom (d. 17 *Tishri* 1894)–Son of R. Moses Joseph, who, after serving as rabbi in Potok, Poland, settled in Hungary in 1829. He was attracted to Hasidism by R. Halberstam of Zanz. He served as rabbi in the towns of Nyiardehaz and Boyom in Hungary. He was the author of *Emek HaMishpat*, included in *Milhemet Mitzvah* (Sighet, 1898; New York, 1890), which describes the controversy over the rabbinate of Sighet.

A.Shu.

FRIEND, Abraham Joshua, of Naszod (1855–11 *Elul* 1932)–Son of R. Mosheh Aryeh, the head of the Jewish community of Sighet. He married the daughter of R. Mordecai Yehudah Lew. He was a disciple of R. Hayyim Halberstam. After the death of his father-in-law, he succeeded him as rabbi of Naszod in 1905. He was the author of responsa *Maor Yehoshua* (Jerusalem, 1967). He was survived by two sons, R. Israel and R. Hanokh Heinokh.

FRIENDS AND FRIENDSHIP–From the time of the Besht, the love of friends and the close attachment of friends marked the hasidic *shtieblech*. Hasidism stressed the marvelous friendship that united David and Jonathan in a spontaneous effusion that endured to death (2 Samuel 1:25).

The reason the movement thrived and expanded so rapidly was due, in a large measure, to its emphasis on developing close personal ties among its followers. New hasidim were welcomed with open arms. They came to feel that they were part of one family. They could enter the homes of other hasidim as "brothers." They could share the most intimate concerns with older hasidim, who would act as their "big brothers." They could confess their innermost secrets to the rebbe.

This theme permeates hasidic literature. The Besht, commenting on the verse "The Lord is your shade" (Psalm 121:5) stated, "As you conduct yourself toward others, so does the Lord conduct Himself toward you. If you are kind and merciful, the Lord will be kind and merciful toward you." Similarly, R. Simhah Bunem of Przysucha advised all hasids to endeavor to gain a true friend to whom they could unburden their heart and disclose even their transgressions.

R. Nahman of Bratzlav maintained that where there is no love among people, there are slander, mockery, and false accusation. When the "Holy Jew" of Przysucha was once asked, "How does the commandment 'Love thy neighbor as yourself' (Leviticus 19:18) harmonize with the command to 'love one's rabbi more than any other man,' " he replied, "The verse teaches us to love our fellowmen in the same degree as we love ourselves. But as a person loves the head more than the other limbs, so may one love one's rabbi more than any other person."

At the same time, the hasidim would tend to withdraw from any association with those who did not belong to their particular sect. The hasidim favored their own—at the expense of other Jews—acting at times as if the nonhasidim had no claim at all on their generosity and fellow feelings. R. Shneur Zalman, however, called upon his followers to love all Jews.

M. Wilensky, *Hasidim U'Mitnaggedim*, vol. 1, p. 306.

J.B.A.

FRISHERMAN, Joseph, of Narol/Tomaszov (1787–25 *Nisan* 1839)—One of six children and the son of R. Simon Green. He married the daughter of R. Aaron of Stryj. He visited many hasidic rabbis, especially the "Seer." He became rabbi in Narol and later moved to Tomaszov. He was bitterly opposed to the teachings of R. Mendel of Kotzk. He had five sons. His son R. Joshua succeeded him.

FRISHERMAN, Moses, of Tomaszov/Brooklyn (1914–8 *Adar* 1974)—Son of R. Joseph Aryeh Leib, he was brought up by his uncle, R. Asher Rubin. In 1933, he married Nehamah Mindel, the daughter of R. Barukh Rubin in Transylvania. After the death of his father-in-law, he succeeded him as rebbe. He survived the Holocaust and settled in New York, where he published *Tefillah LeMosheh* (New York, 1950).

FRUMER, Aryeh Tzvi, of Koziglov (1884–1943)—Son of a humble tailor, Hanokh Hendel. His mother, Miriam Keila, died when he was only nine years old. He was educated in the *yeshivot* of Wolbrum, Amstov, and Sochaszev, where he spent five years. In 1902, he married Esther, the daughter of R. Judah Shragai Schwitzer of Milavich and became principal of the great hasidic *yeshivah* of Sochaszev, where he remained until the outbreak of World War I.

After the war, he held rabbinic positions in Koziglov, Zwierzyniec, and Sosnowiec, and on the death of R. Meir Shapira, he became the spiritual leader of the *Yeshivat Hakhmei Lublin*. He visited the Holy Land in 1934. During the Second World War, he worked in the shoe factory in the Warsaw ghetto, and he and his entire family were murdered in Maidanek.

He was the author of a 298-page work, *Eretz Tzvi* (Lublin, 1939, reprinted in the United States in 1964).

G

GABBAI–The word originally denoted a collector of taxes for charitable contributions. In the centuries following the dispersion, *Gabbai* was the title given to the congregation's treasurer and general administrator. A synagogue frequently had two *gabbaim*–one in charge of the funds, used for synagogal purposes, and the other to administer the charity funds (*gabbai tzedakah*).

In hasidic circles, the *gabbai* was the rebbe's right-hand man, secretary, and attendant.

GALICIA–An area in western Ukraine, it belonged to Austria from 1772 to 1918 and was part of Poland in the interwar years. It was annexed by Russia in 1939.

Southern Galicia was the cradle of Hasidism. The paths of the Carpathian Mountains felt the first footsteps of the Besht, and the inhabitants of the region could point to the hidden places where he meditated, where he prayed, and where he immersed himself in the pools. His active dissemination of Hasidism began in the cities of Galicia: Kuty, Kosov, Tlust, Kolomyja, and Horodenka. The Besht visited Drohobycz, Lvov, and Brody.

The disciples of the Besht, especially R. Dov Baer, the Maggid of Mezhirech, extended the hasidic influence. Additional hasidic centers were established in the lifetime of R. Elimelekh of Lejask in Lancut, Przeworsk, and Zbarazh, where R. Issachar Dov Baer of Zloczov, his son-in-law R. Abraham Hayyim, R. Moses of Dolina, R. Moses of Przeworsk, and R. Feivish of Zbarazh were active. Entire communities enthusiastically embraced Hasidism.

After the death of R. Elimelekh of Lejask, despite the *herem* pronounced in Cracow in 1786 and the burning of *Toldot Yaakov Yosef* in Brody, a number of his disciples settled in Cracow, Rymanov, Ropczyce, and Sokal. In the period from 1815 to 1848, six-sevenths of Galician Jewry were hasidim. They violently opposed the activities of Joseph Perl and the *maskilim* and the efforts of the Austrian authorities to make secular education compulsory. Hasidic rebbes were active in Zydaczov, Yaroslav, Dynov, Nadvorna, Strelisk, Kosov, and Premyshlany.

The spread of *Haskalah* and Reform Judaism brought hasidim and *mitnaggedim* together. Many hasidim and rebbes participated in the formation of the *Shomer Yisrael* organization and of its weekly paper, *Mahzikei Hadas*, which helped to cement Orthodox Judaism. The hasidim were able to circumvent legislation against printing and disseminating of kabbalistic and hasidic literature and the restriction on establishing new *minyanim*. In Galicia, Hasidism became the focal point of Orthodoxy.

The hasidic rebbes were opposed to the mass immigration of hasidim to the United States and other countries. Nor did they approve of the emerging nationalist movements, such as *Hibbat Zion*, Zionism, and the Mizrachi. It is true that a number of Galician rebbes, such as R. Nahman of Horodenka and R. Issachar Dov Baer of Zloczov, settled in the Holy Land and that hasidic rebbes, such as the rebbes of Rymanov, Ropczyce, Kosov, and Zanz, were indefatigable in raising sums of money for the Galician *kollel* in the Holy Land. But they all opposed secular Zionism.

The Russian invasion of Galicia during the First World War brought about an exodus of many hasidim to Czechoslovakia, Austria, and Hungary.

Galicia's annexation by Poland in the interwar years strengthened the ties between the hasidic rebbes. They were all united in fighting against the anti-Semitic legislation and the economic discrimination by the Polish government.

Outstanding hasidic leaders were R. Issachar Dov and his son, R. Aaron Rekeah of Belz; R. Benzion Halberstam of Bobov; and R. Moses Friedman of Cracow.

Very few hasidim survived the Holocaust. But many of the descendants of the Galician rebbes have established dynasties in the United States and in Israel.

Y. Alfasi, *Toldot HaHasidut*, pp. 32–34.

M.W.

GALUT–Hasidic literature abounds in rich and varied treatments of the motif of *galut*, or exile, as the spiritual situation of the Jew. *Galut* is perceived as a reality on the national, historical, cosmic, and personal planes of religious truth; it is most particularly on the last of those three planes, however, that Hasidism makes an original contribution.

Living wholly within the religious world of posttalmudic Orthodoxy, Hasidism accepts the classical rabbinic notion that the destruction of Jerusalem and the dispersion of Israel serve as punishments for the nation's sins. Following well-known motifs from aggadic literature and particularly from the *Zohar*, hasidic authors frequently speak of postexilic Israel as the king's beloved firstborn son who has transgressed against his father and has therefore been exiled from the father's palace. Neither son nor father is content with this situation; indeed, the longings and regrets of the father may be even greater than those of his wayward offspring. This notion of the mutuality of exile, often symbolized by the participation of the *Shekhinah* (the bride of God and the mother of Israel) in Israel's sufferings, undoubtedly serves to provide a measure of comfort for the tribulations of life in historical exile.

The Dov Baer Maggid of Mezhirech went an important step further in asserting the participation of God in the situation of exile. He claims that revelation or the "holy spirit" is more readily accessible in *galut* than it was in the days when the prophets flourished in the Holy Land. "When the king is at home in his palace," says the Maggid, "not everyone may approach him," but when he is traveling on the way, he is not so carefully guarded, and then even commoners may come near to him (*Tiferet Uziel* 137a; *No'am Elimelekh*, *vayeshev*). Here and elsewhere in hasidic literature one seems to find a certain glorification of *galut*, or at least the notion that God's presence is as readily discoverable here in the present Diaspora as it will be in the restored Land of Israel.

This indeed seems to be the central point in hasidic discussions of the exile: *galut* is a state of mind. The historical situation of Israel is a symbolic embodiment of the human conditions; it is man's *daat*, or awareness of God, that is most truly in exile. The most basic task of man's religious life is the discovery that God is present with him in all places and at all moments. In a motif reminiscent of ancient gnostic literature, the hasidic masters will speak of the discovery as an awakening from spiritual sleep. Jacob's words upon awakening from his dream, "Behold the Lord is present in this place, and I had not known it" (Genesis 28:16) are taken as a paradigm of this experience (*Degel Mahaneh Efraim*, *vayetzei*).

Hasidic schools diverge as to the best means of achieving this experience of the ever-presence of the divine. The Besht and his immediate disciples seem to have viewed it as a moment of instantaneous transformation: when a person realizes that God is hidden in all things, that hiding has come to an end (*Toledot*, Intro.). In *Habad* Hasidism it is rather by means of complex metaphysical speculation that one comes to realize that *galut* is but a veil of illusion and that in truth God alone is everywhere present. The disciples of R. Nahman of Bratslav, joined in the twentieth century by the followers of R. Aaron ("Arele") Roth, seek rather to confront the full depth and bitterness of the exilic situation and to promulgate a path of longing and heartrending supplication as the proper way to restore God's presence to the world.

A.G.

GAN EDEN–The Garden of Eden, the place of reward for the souls of the righteous after death. The location of *Gan Eden* on earth was the object of much speculation in rabbinic literature, Mesopotamia and the Arabian peninsula being the most popular sites.

In the *Zohar* little attention is paid to the exact location. It emphasizes rather the older view that there is a *Gan Eden* in the upper world to match that in the lower world. The terrestrial *Gan Eden* was thought to be the home of the souls of the dead before final judgment was passed. It was also contrasted with the celestial *Gan Eden* in that the latter received the souls of those who observed the *mitzvot* with correct *kavvanah*, whereas the terrestrial *Gan Eden* was the final resting place of the souls of those who performed the *mitzvot* without *kavvanah*.

In *Gan Eden* the souls of the dead received new "garments." The souls of the righteous in particular were clothed with light in the celestial *Gan Eden* so that they could ascend subsequently as far as *Ein Sof*.

D.G.

GARTEL (Yiddish, "girdle")–A belt, made of black wool or black silk. The Talmud (*Shabbat* 10a) advocates the wearing of a girdle during prayers. Many authorities maintain that this applied only in countries where *kaftans* are worn. The Code (*Shulhan Arukh* 92:2) rules that one should wear a girdle during prayers.

The hasidim wear a girdle over their *kaftan*, to mark the division between the lower and upper parts of the body.

GASTER, Moses, Haham (1856–1939)–Rabbi, scholar, and Zionist, his writings cover a wide field. In his introduction to the English translation of Horodezky's *Leaders of Hasidism*, he wrote, "It [Hasidism] came from the lowly, the poor, the ignorant, but it spoke with a tongue of fiery conviction, and deep enthusiasm. It brought hope and joy to the downtrodden."

He had a large number of manuscripts on mysticism, which are now part of the British Library.

GEDALIAH, of Luniniec (1738-29 *Kislev* 1804)–Son of R. Yitzhak, the *dayan* of Luniniec, he knew the Besht in his youth and was a disciple of R. Dov Baer of Mezhirech and R. Jacob Joseph of Polonnoye. He was one of the early hasidic pioneers and was renowned for his eloquent discourses. He married the daughter of R. Moses, the brother of R. Tzvi of Kaminka.

From the age of eighteen he served as rabbi in Ostropol, Mariepol, and Luniniec, where he also acted as rebbe. Among his disciples was R. Sholom, the father of R. Israel of Ruzhyn. His discourses were recorded in *Teshuot Hen* (Berdichev, 1817). They had the approval of R. Levi Yitzhak of Berdichev and were reprinted many times.

He was survived by two sons: R. Yitzhak Yoel and R. Shmuel Leib.

GEDALIAH, of Siemiatycze (18th century)–He accompanied R. Judah Hasid on his journey to the Holy Land in 1700. In his book *Shaalu Shelom Yerushalayim* (Berlin, 1716), he gives a graphic description of the fate of R. Judah and his group and of the conditions in the Holy Land at the beginning of the eighteenth century.

GEHINNOM–The teachers of Hasidism were masters of positive thinking, stressing the duty to serve God in love, not in fear; in joy and faith, not in sorrow, bitterness, or despair. They nevertheless called upon their followers to read regularly the works of *Musar*, such as *Reshit Hokhmah*, *Shevet Musar*, and *Kav HaYashar*, which pictured the horrors of hell in vivid and frightening terms.

The Besht used to say that the greatest hell for the wicked is paradise. The delights of paradise are spiritual ones, such as the study of the Torah and prayer. The wicked are not accustomed to these occupations and therefore experience them as hell (*Ketonet Pasim* 6d).

R. Nahman of Bratzlav would say that in this world one has the burden of livelihood and many other concerns, and therefore one is not aware of minor annoyances. "A mosquito can bite you, and because of your many concerns, you will not even notice. In the grave, however, there are no other distractions. You can even hear the sound of the maggots, crawling toward you, and feel the pain of their every bite into your flesh. There is nothing that can then take your mind off this suffering" (*Sihot HaRan* 84).

The Besht maintained that in the ultimate future there will be no *Gehinnom*. The wicked will merely be brought into paradise, and this will be their punishment. They will see people praying with joy, dancing in worship, and studying Torah with diligence, and this will cause them to suffer, because they are not used to it. Therefore, through the very things that delight the righteous, the wicked will be judged (*Tzofnat Paneah*, *Beshalah*, 59b).

The ordinary hasid felt sure that his rebbe would save him from the torments of hell and help him enter paradise. The hasid did not stand alone on judgment day and, like R. Yitzhak Luria, the Besht and other rebbes were preoccupied on the eve of the Sabbath with saving the souls (*tikkun*) of the dead that came to them for help. The torments of hell were described to the Besht by departed souls as being so excruciating that all other agonies were as nothing by comparison.

A. Kaplan, *The Light Beyond*, p. 350.

J.B.A.

GEMATRIOT (sing. *Gematria*, from the Greek geqmetria)–The complex hermeneutical system whereby the meaning of a word is calculated in terms of its numerical value, according to a standard mathematical value that is assigned to each letter of the Hebrew alphabet (i.e., א (alef) = 1, ב (bet) = 2, ג (gimmel) = 3, etc.). In rabbinic sources it is associated with the thirty-two hermeneutical rules (of which it is the twenty-ninth) attributed to the second-century C.E. sage R. Eliezer ben Jose. There are also more complex systems of *Gematriot*, wherein not only are words evaluated and understood in terms of their numerical value, but also various substitutions of letters, on a set pattern, are permitted, or the Hebrew vowels are either omitted or added to a word, or entire parts of a word are disregarded in order to attain the required mathematical symmetry.

In biblical and rabbinic literature, the use of *Gematria* is infrequent. It is, however, only in the hermeneutic works of the kabbalists and, to a lesser degree, the hasidim that *Gematria* become a primary methodological tool. In these mystical circles, *Gematria* first became prominent among the Hasidei Ashkenaz in the twelfth to thirteenth centuries, especially in the works of Eliezer of Worms; then slightly later in the kabbalistic system of Abraham Abulafia; and then again in the works of Joseph Gikatilla and the kabbalistic works *Raaya Meheimna* and *Tikkunei Zohar*. Its classic kabbalistic expression is found in the seventeenth-century kabbalistic work *Megalleh Amukot* (Lvov, 1975), by seventeenth-century scholar Nathan Nata ben Solomon Shapira. In these later kabbalistic circles, the entire theory of *Gematria* became even more complex, with new forms and permutations and means of arriving at numerical values and equivalents being introduced (e.g., squaring the value of letters and giving values in terms of arithmetical series).

In hasidic literature the kabbalistic enthusiasm for *Gematria* was somewhat sublimated, although its use can be found throughout hasidic literature. In the earliest strata (e.g., in the important early works of R. Jacob Joseph of Polonnoye; R. Dov Baer, the Maggid of Mezhirech; and R. Shneur Zalman of Liady) there is only incidental use of *Gematria*. This is probably to be explained by the somewhat more practical, homiletical, and polemical concerns of these works compared to the more strictly theosophical and mystical purposes of the older, late kabbalistic writings in which *Gematriot* abound. This same reserve is in evidence in the early collections of hasidic tales (e.g., *Shivhei HaBesht*, *Keter Shem Tov*, and *Tzavaat HaRibash*), in which the use of *Gematriot* was out of character with their style and purpose. The same can also be said of the body of early hasidic homiletic and pedagogical works.

In the nineteenth century, from the third and especially the fourth generation of hasidic authors, there is evidence of a renewed interest in *Gematria*. Even here, however, this interest is not universal, being of little importance for example in the *Habad* tradition and of little significance in all the more popular forms of hasidic literature. It is only in the latter part of the nineteenth century–that period that produced the greatest outpouring of hasidic writings of all types, such as tales, biblical exegesis, and theoretical works, that we find works heavily favoring the detailed use of *Gematria*. Among the body of hasidic texts of this sort, mention should be made of the work of R. Tzvi Elimelekh Shapira of Dynow, *Igra DeKallah* (1868); R. Meir Horowitz of Dzikow, *Sefer Imrei No'am* (1877); and R. Abraham Twerski of Turiysk, *Magen Avraham* (1886). *Gematriot* can also be found to be employed in, for example, the prayer book *Harei Besamim*, based on the thoughts of R. Isaiah Mushkat of Praga, and the *Kehillat Yaakov* of R. Jacob Tzvi Yolles.

W. Bacher, *Exegetische Terminologie der Judischen Tradition und Literatur*, vol. 1.

S.K.

GENTILES–R. Hayyim Vital in his *Shaarei Kedushah* stated that "I call heaven and earth to witness that any individual, man or woman, Jew or gentile, freeman or slave, can have *Ruah HaKodesh* [the holy spirit] come upon him and that it all depends on his deeds" (Seventh Gate).

Similarly, R. Hillel of Paritch, in the name of R. Dov Baer of Lubavitch, stated that "the righteous gentile achieves an inner spiritual transformation."

The Talmud teaches us that Israel was exiled in order that it should receive proselytes (*Pesahim* 87b).

At first this is difficult to understand. "Is it fitting," asked R. Elimelekh of Lejask, "that Israel should be exiled in order to accept converts? It would seem more appropriate that the nations should come to the Land of Israel by themselves and be converted there."

The concept is this: "The thing that motivates gentiles to become a proselyte is the holy spark that is in them. The spark is very weak, however, and it does not have the power to lift their heart and bring them to the land of Israel to convert of their own accord. But when they see the Jews and gaze upon them, the holiness of Israel gives strength, power, and motivation to that holy spark in them, and this motivates them to become a proselyte. It is for this reason that Israel had to be exiled" (*Noam Elimelekh, Yitro* 41a).

As popularized by R. Shneur Zalman in his *Tanya*, the souls of the gentiles were derived from two sources—the unclean "shells" and the "shell" of radiance *Nogah*, which contains an admixture of light and darkness, good and evil. Because of this metaphysical difference, even the secular wisdom of gentiles is a snare and a delusion.

R. Shneur Zalman was convinced that Jews and gentiles are alike only in appearance. Nevertheless, the basic belief of Jews that God seeks to redeem all of humankind is not given up by R. Shneur Zalman. It is the function of Jews to play a crucial role in the redemption of humankind. Jews cannot fulfill their destiny without also saving the gentiles.

L. Jacobs, *Seeker of Unity*, p. 68.

J.B.A.

GER (Hebrew, Gur; Polish, Gura Kalwaria)—The small town near Warsaw was the home of the most influential hasidic dynasty in Poland. It was founded by R. Yitzhak Meir Alter and continued under his grandson R. Judah Leib and then under R. Abraham Mordecai Alter.

At one time, more than 100,000 Jews owed their allegiance to the rebbe of Ger, and there was no town in Poland without a *shtiebl* of Ger.

The dynasty of Ger is now maintained in Israel by R. Pinhas Menahem Alter, whose brother, R. Abraham Mordecai Alter, came to the Holy Land during World War II. Today, the rebbe's synagogue in Ger, Poland, is a warehouse, and the rebbe's apartments are used as a school.

The graves of the rebbes have been restored in Ger. Also buried there were Feiga (d. 1870), the wife of R. Yitzhak Meir; Yoheved Rebecca (d. 1911), the wife of R. Judah Leib; Yehudit (d. 1922), the wife of R. Abraham Mordecai; and R. Yitzhak (d. 1935), the son of R. Abraham Mordecai.

GERSTENKORN, Yitzhak, founder of Bene Berak (d. 1967)—A native of Warsaw, Gerstenkorn formed a society *Bet Hanahalah* with the aim of establishing a hasidic settlement in the Holy Land. Encouraged by R. Menahem Mendel Guterman of Radzymin and R. Abraham Mordecai Alter of Ger, he bought land in Bene Berak. He was the first mayor of the town and was the author of an eight-volume work on Psalms, *Neim Zemirot Yisrael*.

GESHURI, Meir Shimon (1897–1977), writer and researcher of Jewish music—Born into a hasidic family in Upper Silesia, he accompanied his father to hasidic courts, where he heard hasidic melodies. He studied in *yeshivot* and later in Berlin at the Stern Conservatory. In 1920, he emigrated to the Holy Land and was instrumental in collecting many hasidic melodies and classifying them according to their place of origin.

He was the author of *LaHasidim Mizmor* (1936); the three-volume *Encyclopedia of Hasidism*; *The Song and Dance* (1955–1959); *Kol Yisrael*, vols. 1 and 2 (1964); *Jerusalem the Musical City* (1968); and *Music and Hasidism in the House Kuzmir and Its Affiliations* (Jerusalem, 1952).

GESUNDHEIT, Jacob (1815–1878)—A native of Praga, he studied under R. Leib Zinz of Plotsk. He succeeded R. Dov Beirish Meisels as rabbi of Warsaw. He was opposed to Hasidism and after four years had to resign from the rabbinate.

He was the author of *Tiferet Yaakov* and of novellas on the *Shulhan Arukh* (1842), on the tractate *Gittin* (1858), and on *Hullin* (1867).

GEVURAH (lit., power)–The name given to the fifth *Sefirah*. It is situated on the left side of the sefirotic tree, is symbolized by the divine name *Elohim*, and signifies God's strict Judgment (*Din*). This identification goes back to early rabbinic sources, but it assumed great importance in kabbalah.

The force of *Gevurah* is basically destructive, and in Lurianic kabbalah the midrashic idea that God created other worlds and destroyed them before He created the present one was interpreted to mean that the previous worlds were created solely by *Gevurah* and therefore could not survive. The present world exists only because *Gevurah* (or *Din*) is tempered or "sweetened" by the contrasting force of *Hesed* (Love).

Gevurah was also thought by some kabbalists to be the source of the power of evil (*sitra ahra*), which in their view arose through the superfluity of *Gevurah* after its encounter with the force of love. Human beings through their own sins fortify the power of *Gevurah* and hence also strengthen the force of evil.

D.G.

GEWIRCMAN, Moses Yitzhak (12 *Tevet* 1882–10 *Tishri* 1977), Antwerp–Son of R. Naftali Elimelekh (d. 1916) and Hannah Breindel, he was born in Przeworsk, near Gorlice, and was popularly known as R. Itzikel or the rabbi of Przeworsk. He was a descendant of R. Elimelekh of Lejask. When R. Abraham Hayyim of Plantsh (father-in-law of R. Joel of Satmar) saw R. Itzikel in Sianiawa, he stated that "the *Shekhinah* accompanies this young man." He was a disciple of R. Moses Apter of Tarnov and of R. Simhah Issachar Baer of Cieszanov (d. 1914) and R. Honah Halberstam of Kalaszyce. He was also a follower of R. Yoel Teitelbaum of Satmar, to whose anti-Zionist ideology he subscribed. In *Nisan* 1899 he married Rachel, the daughter of R. Yissachar Dov HaKohen Glantz of Sianiawa, known as R. Berele Glantz. During World War One, when Sianiawa was ravaged, he lived in Przeworsk near Lvov, where he prayed in the *Bet HaMidrash* of the hasidim of Cieszanov and became rebbe there.

During the Second World War he stayed for seven months in Holitch, and then in Talamenko in Siberia. He was bereaved of his only son, Joseph Hayyim, and two daughters, Miriam Hannah and Beilah.

After the war he returned for a while to Poland, living in Breslau and Cracow, and then moved to Paris in 1949, where he stayed until 20 *Adar* 1957, when, on the advice of the rabbi of Belz, he moved to Antwerp and established a *Bet HaMidrash* at Mercator Street 56. He became the undisputed rebbe of postwar Europe with many people thronging to him for advice and practical assistance. He was known as a "heiliger Yid," a holy Jew.

He was buried in the *Mahzikei Hadat* cemetery in Holland. He was succeeded by his son-in-law, R. Jacob Leizer.

A. Z. Schneebalg, *Rosh Even Yisrael.*

GILGUL–The transmigration of souls was an important doctrine in the formative period of Hasidism. The idea goes back to the books of *Bahir* and *Galli Razaya*, written in 1552, and referred to by David Kimhi in his commentary to Psalm 104. Hasidism took over this idea from the Lurian Kabbalah, where it played a major role. "Looking at the forehead of a man, R. Yitzhak Luria could tell at a glance from what particular source his soul was derived, and the process of transmigration through which it had passed, and what its present mission was on earth" (*Sefer HaGilgulim*, Przemysl, 1875).

A soul may have to be reborn several times in order to fulfill all 613 commandments. It may also be reborn in order to atone for one or more sins committed during a previous incarnation. Those who were guilty of grave transgressions might be incarnated in animals, plants, or even stones.

In the hasidic biography of the Besht, we encounter many instances of *gilgul*. One story tells of a scholar who was reincarnated as a frog because he scorned the precept of washing one's hands before a meal. In another instance a sinner was incarnated first in a dog and then in a fish, which was eventually redeemed when it was eaten by a holy man.

We also read how a sinner was saved from incarnation in a dog by a preacher who defamed his memory at his funeral. That humiliation was accepted by the heavenly court in lieu of reincarnation.

The doctrine of transmigration of souls is associated in the Hindu and Buddhist worlds with pessimism–the feeling that to be reborn is to be punished. Hasidism was imbued with an optimistic temper, yet it included the idea of reincarnation as punishment, even if one were incarnated into another Jewish person. The danger of committing even a minor sin and atoning for it in hell was too great even for the "holy souls" to risk.

S. A. Horodezky, *Torat HaKabbalah shel Ari VeHayyim Vital*, pp. 245–252.

J.B.A.

GLASGOW–The Jewish community in Glasgow is the largest in Scotland. Its members are mainly of Lithuanian origin. However, in 1913 a small synagogue *Nusah Ari* was set up over a public house on Oxford Street, later moving to 14 Main Street. After World War II, the *shtiebl* moved to Nicolson Street. It eventually amalgamated with the *Bet Jacob* synagogue under the name *Poale Zedek*.

Among the hasidic personalities who lived there was R. J. D. Siroka (1870–1957), rabbi of the *Hevrah Kadisha* and *Av Bet Din* of the Glasgow *Bet Din*. His son-in-law, R. S. D. Morgenstern, who stayed in Glasgow some time, headed the *Shtiebl Bet Jacob* in Abbotsford Place. R. Dr. Wolf Gottlieb, who came from hasidic background, was appointed *Rosh Bet Din* of Glasgow in 1955.

In 1969, R. Jeremy Rosen invited R. Hayyim Jacobs to assist with the education and the communal needs of the 10,000-strong Jewish community, where R. Jacobs later established a Lubavitch center, which is a beehive of activity.

GOD–The spirit of Hasidism is radically different from the prevailing mood in kabbalah–the immanence of God, or His "nearness" is more stressed than His transcendence; the joy and zest of life are emphasized as against the asceticism of the kabbalists, and the attempt to restructure the entire life of the Jewish people takes the place of withdrawal from communal involvements for the sake of attaining high states of mystical ecstasy. As a leading hasidic authority put it,

> Our Master, the Besht, followed up the work of Luria, to reveal the Deity in the lowly depths of this world in every detail, for Luria dealt with the upper worlds and upper lights . . . and Besht revealed divinity here on earth, in earthly man, whose organs and faculties are garments for the divine power . . . and he taught how to bind oneself in unification with His Holy Name even while engaging in idle conversations. (*Sefer Seder HaDorot MiTalmidei HaBesht*, p. 3, Jerusalem, 1965)

An interpretation of the act of creation lies at the heart of the change from kabbalah to Hasidism. Luria had proclaimed the doctrine of *tzimtzum*, contraction, which asserted that God contracted Himself before creation, in order to allow room for the world to come into being. The emergence of the space-time continuum was due to a prior withdrawal, on the part of the divine Being. Thereupon, the light of God entered into the space that was now empty, apart from some traces of the divine Being (*reshimu*). As a result, the cosmos is surrounded by the light of God (*makif*), and some things contain sparks of light (*penimi*). Unification (*yihudim*) between the outer and inner lights is brought about in various ways–traditionally and kabbalistically. But the vastness of the universe is neutral.

The hasidim, beginning with Besht, interpreted this doctrine in a subtler way. The "contraction" was only mental, as when a father restricts his thought to the things that his infant son can grasp. In reality, there is no world, and God is "all in all." Every thing as well as every event is an embodiment of God through many and diverse "garments." "Holy sparks" are scattered in all things and it is the *tzaddik*'s role to redeem them from the power of the "shells" (*klippot*).

Those shells are also incarnations of the divine Being, save that they are more removed from Him in the chain of being. There is no absolute wickedness. Satan, or the "other side" (*sitra ahra*), is but the extension of the left side of God Himself. Besht was fond of saying "evil is a chair for the good."

The famed rabbi of Berdichev put it simply: "When a person is seized by physical lusts, the brightness [of God] is contained in two vessels, one within the other, but when a person feels the love of the blessed Name, the brightness is contained in one vessel" (*Kedushat Levi*, Noah).

This pantheistic interpretation of *tzimtzum* generated an intense feeling of God's immediate presence. Instead of seeking Him in books or in solitary meditations, the hasid could find Him in convivial gatherings, in eating and drinking, in the manifold glories of nature–even in feminine beauty. For the mark of God's presence is joy.

A famous parable of Besht is an excellent illustration of this feeling of divine immediacy.

> A wise and great king contrived to make it appear that there were walls, towers and gates and he commanded that people should come to see him through these gates and towers, scattering some of his treasures at the various gates. Most people went through one gate or another, contenting themselves with the rewards they found. But his beloved son tried very hard to come directly to his father, the king. Then he realized that no partitions separated him from his father. It was all appearance and make-believe. (*Keter Shem Tov*)

In keeping with this conviction, the rebbes taught themselves to feel the immediate presence of God, at all times. As the son of R. Elimelekh of Lejask writes, "The Name of God (YHUH) actually does not move away from their eyes at all; they see the letters in fire . . . and if on occasion the Tetragrammaton does not face them or another Name takes its place, they know immediately that 'severe laws' are increasing. . . ." (*Iggeret HaKodesh*, by R. Eliezer of Lejask, printed at end of *Noam Elimelekh*, New York, 1942, p. 229).

Since the world revealed by our senses is only the veil of appearance, the hasidim were urged to put away materiality (*hitpashtut Hagashmiut*) and think of themselves as naught (*ayin*), corresponding to the naught of God, since He cannot be grasped by any human concepts or feelings.

" 'Wisdom comes from the naught (*ayin*)'–this means that those who turn themselves into naught and cling to it, the Naught bestows upon them true being (*yesh*), which is wisdom" (saying attributed to R. Dov Baer of Mezhirech, quoted by Rivkah Schatz-Uffenheimer in *HaHasidut KeMistikah*, Jerusalem, 1968, p. 29, n. 36).

In hasidic folklore, the feeling of God's loving presence was expressed in many songs and in exclamations during prayer such as "*tate zisser*" (dear father) or "*tateniu*" (lovely father) or as the rabbi of Berdichev used to shout every few minutes, "*derbaremdiger*" (the merciful One). The use of Yiddish phrases in prayer was intended to emphasize the feelings of intimacy.

In this mood, the feeling of being led by Providence was greatly intensified. Not only in respect of the big crises in life, but even in regard to the clothes one wears, the food one eats, and the minor mishaps of life, the wise guidance of God was seen. There are no accidents. We are constantly tested and directed.

> The people who travel in distant places with merchandise believe that they do so for commercial purposes, to increase their wealth . . . but His thoughts are not our thoughts, for He knows better what we need. At times, there is a loaf of bread in that distant land, which relates to his soul and that he has to eat, or a drink of water. At times, it is the soul of one of his servants that requires that journey, and Providence arranged the journey of the merchant for the sake of his servant, who could not otherwise get there . . . ." (R. Zev Wolf of Zbaraz, *Or Hameir*, Tzav)

The liberation of "holy sparks" from food consumed by a holy man played a very important role in the early generations of Beshtian Hasidism. In the biography of Besht, we read how he planned to associate two persons with him in eating together the third meal of the Sabbath in order to redeem certain sparks that were related to their souls (*Shivhei HaBesht*, Talpiot edition, p. 97).

At times, the soul of a person, incarnated in a fish or a kosher animal, might be ready for redemption through the festive meal of a holy man (ibid, p. 162). R. Elimelekh of Lejask asked his followers to imagine the Hebrew letters of food (*maakhal*) and keep them steadily before their eyes while they eat, bearing in mind that the numerical value of those letters equals those of two Names of God (*Adonai* and YHUH) (*Tzetel Katan*, in *No'am Elimelekh*, p. 15).

In many of the first generation hasidic works, we encounter the same reference to the beauty of women as being derived from God. The variations are significant, of course, but the core of the advice is the same:

"For example, when you see a beautiful woman, you should think, whence does she derive this beauty? Had she been dead, the same features would have been not attractive, but ugly. So, her beauty comes from a divine power that is manifest in her. By leading all things to their 'roots,' we come to see God everywhere" (R. Dov Baer from Mezhirech, *Or Torah*, Vayehi) (cf. *Tzavaat Haribash*, in *Shivhei HaBesht*, p. 229).

In this way, a person can obtain glimpses of God on every occasion. Even when Satan puts temptation in our way, we should recall that Satan is a messenger of God, whose task it is to tempt us. If on the other hand, good thoughts come to us, we should regard them as messages from on high.

"When he clings to the Creator, and a thought occurs to him, he should know that it corresponds to the truth – this is indeed a measure of the Holy Spirit" (*Keter Shem Tov*).

In contrast to the complex symbolism of Kabbalah, Hasidism taught that our immediate feeling is sufficient to bring us close to God. "Whenever a person performs a *mitzvah* with more fear and love, he enters into a more inward chamber of the King . . . ." (R. Levi Yitzhak, *Kedushat Levi*, *Vayera*).

In brief, the hasidim were taught to feel that God comes at them from all directions – through temptations they must overcome, through good thoughts outlining their tasks, and through the food they eat, the garments they wear, the business they do, and the children they raise. As Besht put it, in a comment on Psalm 16:8, "all things are equal to me, since the Lord is before me at all times" (*Tzavaat Harivash*).

J.B.A.

GOLDBERG, Abraham Shalom, of Zelechov (d. 1942) – Son of R. Joshua Asher Goldberg, a descendant of Zloczov. He was for many years rabbi of Zelechov. When the Nazis occupied the town, he refused to hide in a bunker and requested that he should be taken to the cemetery together with the community. He, his wife, Hannah, and daughters, Reizel and Rivele, were all murdered by the Nazis and buried in a mass grave. His two sons, Shlomoh and Joshua, were also captured by the Nazis; Shlomoh jumped off the train on the way to Treblinka and was killed. Joshua, who escaped, was betrayed by a Pole and was shot near a concentration camp.

GOLDMAN, Gedaliah Mosheh, of Zevil/Jerusalem (26 *Iyyar* 1907–24 *Heshvan* 1950) – Son of R. Shlomoh. At the age of twenty-two he was ordained by R. Hayyim Soloveitchik of Brest-Litovsk. He became rabbi of Zevil. The communist authorities exiled him to Siberia for seven years, and in 1937 he settled in Jerusalem but refused to become rebbe. It was not until 1945 that he succeeded his father.

He married Feiga, the daughter of R. David Shlomoh of Kobrin.

D. Werner, *Tzaddik Yesod Olam*.

GOLDMAN, Mordecai (1825–14 *Tishri* 1901) – Son of R. Yehiel Michael, he married the daughter of R. Shalom of Linz. He had twenty-one children, of whom only a few survived. Throughout his life, he supported the poor and was engaged in the redemption of the captives. He was especially concerned with the fate of the Cantonists, to whom he distributed books of Psalms and *tzitzits*. He had a great love for the Holy Land, and he named a daughter *Bat Zion*. Although a special synagogue was built for him, on the High Holy Days he prayed in the communal synagogue, where the liturgy was Ashkenazi.

One son, R. Michael, became rebbe in Koretz, and the youngest son, R. Shlomoh, succeeded him.

GOLDMAN, Mordecai, of Jerusalem (1906–28 *Shevat* 1979) – Son of R. Gedaliah Mosheh, he married Esther Shapira, the daughter of R. Samuel Mordecai of Zablotov. After being rebbe in Zevil, he emigrated to the Holy Land in 1926. He became rebbe in 1950 and established a *yeshivah Bet Mordecai* in Jerusalem.

His views and opinions were voiced with rigor and forthrightness. He never used electricity, not even on weekdays. He was buried on the Mount of Olives and succeeded by his son, R. Abraham.

GOLDMAN, Mosheh (1770–10 *Iyyar* 1837) – Son of R. Yehiel Michael of Zloczov, he married the daughter of R. David, the rabbi of Gravitz. He was an itinerant preacher, who traveled through the villages to disseminate Hasidism. He was greatly venerated by R. Pinhas of Koretz. It was R. Mordecai of Nesvish who persuaded him to become rebbe.

He gave approval to the *Kezot Hahoshen*, by R. Aryeh Lob, which was printed in Lvov in 1788. He was succeeded by his son, R. Yehiel Michael.

GOLDMAN, Shlomoh (1861–26 *Iyyar* 1945)–He was the youngest and eighth son of R. Mordecai. He succeeded his father as rebbe in 1901 and established a *yeshivah*. In 1919, the town of Zevil was burned down.

He emigrated to the Holy Land in 1926. For three years he lived incognito in the home of R. Israel Shohet, who was the *gabbai* of the *Tiferet Yisrael* synagogue.

He would walk to the *kotel* every day and would recite the whole book of Psalms on the eve of the Sabbath and on the eve of *Rosh Hodesh*.

His son, R. Gedaliah Mosheh, succeeded him.

GOLDMAN, Yehiel Michael (1788–12 *Tishri* 1856)–Son of R. Mordecai, he married Deborah, the daughter of R. Israel of Ludomir. He had three sons and three daughters.

GOLEM (shapeless matter)–A popular designation for a body formed by magic or by kabbalistic means. The term "golem" appears only once in the Bible (Psalm 139: 16). Adam for the first twelve hours of his existence is called a golem (*Sanhedrin* 38b). In the Talmud we read of the creation by the third-century rabbi Rava of a golem who looked like a human being but could not speak. Rava's colleague Zera returned him to dust (*Sanhedrin* 65b). Two amoraim on the eve of every Sabbath made a calf for themselves and ate it. There is, furthermore, a legend of the creation of a golem by the Prophet Jeremiah. R. Moses Cordovera even believed that the mystics by means of *Sefer Yetzirah* or *Hilkhot Yetzirah* had the power to give vitality (*hiyyut*) but could not give a golem a proper soul (*neshamah*).

A chain of legends regarding the golem was formed around the personality of R. Low ben Bezalel, known as the *Maharal* (1525–1609). The rabbi and his two disciples fashioned out of clay a golem to be used to defend the Jewish community. The rabbi was forced, however, to return him to dust in the attic of the Altneuschul synagogue in Prague.

R. Tzvi Hirsch Ashkenazi and his son, R. Jacob Emden, discuss in their responsa whether or not it is permitted to include a golem in a *minyan*. The books of the *Maharal* were especially popular with the Przysucha school of Hasidism, but a study of the *Maharal's* work gives no clue of the creation of the golem. The hasidic movement is in no way related to the golem folklore except that it believes in the efficacy of practical kabbalah.

Even the arch opponent of Hasidism, R. Elijah, the Gaon of Vilna, was a believer in practical kabbalah. He told his disciple R. Hayyim of Volozhin that in his youth he, too, attempted to create a golem but was prevented from doing this by a vision.

In general, the hasidic movement absorbed the basic use of kabbalah, but it eschewed the attempt to achieve miracles by the use of sacred letters. The golem legend has received literary treatment by many writers, especially by Judah Rosenberg in his book *Nifla'ot Maharal im HaGolem* (1909). The Yiddish writer H. Leivick (1888–1962) wrote a dramatic poem in eight parts on the subject of the golem.

C. Bloch, *Der Prager Golem*.

J.B.A. and Ed.

GOOD AND EVIL–The messages of the Besht were a joyous proclamation: "Serve God in joy" and "Evil is a chair for goodness." The Besht used to say that at the end of the account of creation, the Torah states, "And God saw all that He had made, and, behold, it was very good" (Genesis 1:31). Throughout the story of creation, this is repeated many times. In the book of Deuteronomy, however, it is written, "Behold, I have set before you life and good, death and evil" (Deuteronomy 30:15). This would tend to indicate that evil also comes from God. The question then arises, "Where did evil originate?"

The truth is that evil is also (actually) good. It is merely the lowest level of good. Therefore, when it is used for good, evil also becomes good. When it is involved in a sin, however, then it becomes true evil.

The idea compares to a broom. When a broom is used to sweep the dirt out of a house, it is somewhat good. Even though it is on the lowest level, it is still serving a good purpose. But when that broom is used to beat a child who has done wrong, then it becomes truly evil (*Tzavaat HaRibash*, p. 233).

R. Jacob Joseph of Polonnoye maintained that in the ultimate future, God will slaughter the angel of death, and the slaughtering of the angel of death means that God will remove the evil from it, and it will become a holy good angel (*Toldot Yaakov Yosef, Kedoshim*).

A. Kaplan, *The Light Beyond*, pp. 94–105.

A.K.

GOSTYNIN–A town in central Poland (see LIPSHITZ, Yehiel Meir).

GOTT FUN AVRAHAM (lit., God of Abraham)–A meditation recited by women at the end of the Sabbath. It is attributed to R. Levi Yitzhak of Berdichev, who intoned it at the third meal on the Sabbath. There are several textual and musical variations to it. The text reads:

God of Abraham, Isaac, and Jacob,
Guard your beloved people from every evil,
Now that the cherished Sabbath departs.
This week, this month, this year, let us gain in perfect belief,
In faith in our sages, in love for our fellow beings,
In devotion to the blessed Creator.
Our Sovereign ruler of the world,
You give strength to the weary.
Then grant Your beloved Jewish children strength to praise You.
This week, this month, this year, let us gain in health, good fortune, blessing, and success–to be granted kindness, good children, long life with bountiful provision, and heavenly help for us and for all Jewry.
And let us say Amen.

GOTTESMAN, Aaron Aryeh Leib (d. 1942)–He married Rebecca, the daughter of R. Hayyim Greenberg of Gliniany. At the time of the German occupation, he and his family were deported to the ghetto of Przemysl, where they perished.

GOTTESMAN, Abraham Joseph (Yosko) (1877–10 *Adar* 1948)–He was born in Jeriezany, the son of R. Meir. He studied in Ulaszkowcze and under his uncle in Jeriezany, by whom he was ordained. He was rabbi in Bohusi in Romania, and in 1898 he married Feiga, the daughter of R. Pinhas Landman. From 1916 he was rebbe in Iasi and Bucharest, and from 1922 he lived in the United States.

He was the author of *Emunah Shelemah*, on the thirteen articles of faith, published in Brooklyn in 1924.

He was survived by his sons, R. Aaron Aryeh, R. Tzvi Dov, Binyamin Wolf, and Meshullam Feivish.

GOTTESMAN, Abraham Joshua Heschel, of Stanislav (1888–19 *Heshvan* 1943)–Son of Naftali Meshullam Feivish, he was born in Ulaszkowze. He was ordained by R. Horowitz. He married Shifhah, a descendant of R. Sholom Yolles, the rabbi of Stryj. He became rebbe in Stanislav in 1906, and he and his wife perished in Drohobycz.

GOTTESMAN, Shimshon Efraim, of Sniatyn (1880–1942)–Son of R. Naftali Meshullam Feivish, the rabbi of Ulaszkowcze in Sniatyn. He married the daughter of R. Eliezer Zeev Merellis. During the Second World War he was caught by the Nazis and, together with his children, murdered.

GOTTESMAN, Shmuel, of Ribashov/New York (1902–1970)–He was born in Ulaszkowcze, the son of Abraham Yosef Yosko. In 1925, he married Rachel, the daughter of R. Hayyim Yosef Teitelbaum. He succeeded his father in 1933 and in 1940 settled in the United States, where he established a community on the East Side of New York. His aim was to establish a *kiryah* near Bene Berak in Israel in the memory of the Besht. This never materialized.

GOTTLIEB, Hayyim Joseph, of Stropkov (1790–4 *Adar* 1867)–Born in Bercel, Hungary, the son of R. Yehudah Aryeh, and on his mother's side, a descendant of R. Isaiah Horowitz. Hayyim Joseph studied in the *yeshivah* in Kroly under R. Moses Aryeh Oestreicher and R. Yekutiel Wolf. It was there that he was influenced by the hasidic R. Yitzhak Isaac Taub of Kalev, who made a tremendous impact on him. After

Taub's death, he would, when he encountered a difficult problem, go to pray at Taub's grave.

In 1813, he married his first wife, Breindel, the daughter of R. Meir Lichtstein of Tarcal, and lived there for several years while studying in the *yeshivah* of R. Yehezkel Panet, the author of *Mareh Yehezkel*. He then became attached to R. Menahem Mendel of Rymanov, R. Naftali Tzvi of Ropczyce, and R. Hayyim Halberstam of Nowy Sacz, whom he visited every year on Sabbath Hannukah, and who affectionately called him the "Hungarian wise man."

When R. Panet left Tertzal, Gottlieb was appointed *dayan*, and in 1841, he became the rabbi of Stropkov, where he became known as a miracle worker. He even drove out *dybbukim*. He enjoyed an affectionate relationship with R. Menahem Esh, the rabbi of Chush and Ungvar; R. Shimon Barukh Tennenbaum; and R. M. Schick.

He strengthened Orthodox Judaism in Kosice, where he established its first Orthodox *minyan*. He remained neutral in the 1848–1849 rebellion by L. Kossuth against Austrian rule. He participated in the rabbinical assembly in Michalvitz in 1866. He was a talented violinist, and, particularly on Purim, he played his melodies for his congregation.

When his wife died in 1848, he married Peril, a descendant of R. Abraham of Bohuslav. He was survived by five sons and one daughter. He was the author of *Tiv Gittin VeKiddushin* (Ungvar, 1868).

GOTTLIEB, Maurycy (1856–1879), painter—He was sixteen years old when he left his home in Drohobycz, in eastern Galicia, for Vienna, where he received wide recognition. His major work, *Jews Praying on the Day of Atonement*, was his only hasidic painting.

GOTTLIEB, Moses, of Ludomir (d. 18 *Shevat* 1821)—Son of R. Solomon Halevi of Karlin, he married the daughter of R. Leib, the author of *Or Haganuz*. He became rebbe in Ludomir (Vladimir Volynski) in 1792. His son, R. Solomon, was the son-in-law of R. Aaron of Chernobyl.

GOTTLIEB, Moses, of Stanislav (d. 13 *Adar* 1943)—Son of R. Gedaliah of Ludomir, he was born in Sambor. He was active in strengthening religious life in Galicia. He was murdered by the Nazis in Drohobycz.

GOTTLIEB, Uri Aaron, of Kalish (d. in *Av* 1942)—Son of R. Gedaliah of Ludomir, a descendant of R. Shlomoh of Karlin, he married the daughter of R. Shalom HaKohen of Sambor. He was rebbe in Kalish, Galicia, and was murdered by the Nazis.

GOURARY, Shemaryahu (1898–1 *Adar* I 1989)—Son of R. Menahem Mendel Schneersohn, he studied in the *yeshivah Tomhei Temimim* in Lubavitch. On 11 *Iyyar* 1921, he married Hannah, the elder daughter of R. Joseph Yitzhak Schneersohn. In 1929, he accompanied his father-in-law to the Holy Land and to the United States.

In 1940, together with the rebbe R. Menahem Mendel Schneerson, he settled in New York. He was the executive director of United Lubavitch Yeshivot. He was indefatigable in consolidating the network of *yeshivot* in the United States and Canada.

He had one son, Barry (b. 1922), of Montclair, New Jersey, and a managerial consultant in Manhattan, who took 400 books of the rabbi's library and sold them for $186,000. On January 6, 1987, Judge Charles P. Sifton of the eastern district of Brooklyn, in a twenty-nine-page report, awarded the library to the Lubavitch community.

Z.T.

GRAETZ, Heinrich (1817–1891)—The foremost historian of the Jewish people. He was the author of the eleven-volume *Geschichte der Juden* (1853–1876), in which he illuminated many an obscure period in Jewish history. He was, however, groping in the dark when he dealt with the hasidic movement that was making such headway in his own lifetime.

According to him, "the new sect, a daughter of darkness, was born in gloom, and even today, proceeds stealthily on its mysterious way."

His views on Hasidism amount to a denunciation of the movement. He relied entirely on the account given by Solomon Maimon. He adopted the view that Hasidism was a revolt against talmudic law and rabbinic dogmatism. This has no historical basis, for the movement not only attracted many leading scholars but also encouraged and sponsored many halakhic works. He further overlooked the existence of a positive element in the rise of Hasidism, and he refused to acknowledge, or did not detect in it, a philosophy and theology. To him it was mere obscurantism.

Graetz exploits for his own purposes the antagonism of Elijah, the Gaon of Vilna. He blamed the dissolution of the Council of the Four Lands on Hasidism. It can only be said that he was out of touch with the masses of Russian and Polish Jewry, among whom he might have witnessed the synthesis of learning and piety, which became the strong feature of Hasidism. This prejudice of Graetz antagonized his Hebrew translator Saul Pinhas Rabinowitz (1845–1911), who abandoned his translation into Hebrew of *The History of the Jews*, by Graetz, when he reached the hasidic epoch.

H. Graetz, *Geschichte der Juden von den Altesten Zeiten bis auf die Gegenwart*, vol. 11, chap. 3. English translation (Jewish Publication Society), vol. 5, chap. 9.

A.T.

GREENBERG, Hayyim of Gliniany (1890–1943) – The eldest son of R. Yitzhak Eliezer of Gliniany. He married Bathsheva, a granddaughter of R. Nahum Widerman, a descendant of R. Uri of Strelisk. After living in Gliniany for many years, he settled in Lvov. In the month of *Elul* 1942, he and his wife were deported to Belzec, where they died.

GREENBERG, Uri Tzvi (1894–1981), Hebrew poet – Born in Bialykamien, eastern Galicia, he was a descendant of R. Meir of Premyshlan and of R. Uri of Strelisk. Between 1931 and 1934 he lived in Warsaw. In 1936 he settled in the Holy Land and was awarded the Israel prize for Hebrew literature in 1957.

In many of his poems he stresses the religious mystical view of Zionism and the Jewish longing for messianic redemption. He frequently utilizes biblical devices and kabbalistic concepts.

GROSS, Hayyim Issachar Baer, of Petrova (1875–1938) – Son of poor parents, he studied under R. Moses Grunwald in Huszt and under R. Tzvi Hirsch Spira of Munkacz. He married the only daughter of a rich innkeeper in Petrova (Marmaros district). His father-in-law provided him with the means to establish a *yeshivah*. He became known as the "Petrova *Illui*." In 1904 he was appointed honorary *dayan* there. In 1908 he moved to Munkacz, where he was referred to as the "Petrova *dayan*." When he lost all his fortune in the First World War, he eked out a meager living as an arbitrator of disputes in which members of the community were involved.

When the hasidim of Belz set up a *Bet HaMidrash* of their own, he accepted the position of *dayan* with that dissident organization. This rendered him persona non grata with the establishment. He corresponded widely with halakhic scholars and with the Sefardic scholar R. Hayyim Hezkiyahu Medini. He published many articles in the learned periodicals.

His knowledge of the details and wide-ranging genealogical ramifications of the rabbinic and hasidic dynasties was all-embracing. He edited three works of great hasidic interest: *Even Shetiyah*, the genealogy of the Kosov dynasty (Munkacz, 1930), a work based on R. Hayyim Kahan; *Haggadah Shel Pesach*, with the commentary *Helkat Binyamin* (Munkacs, 1930), by R. Binyamin of Salzhin, which was first published in Lvov in 1794, but Gross, in his edition, provided references, corrected the text, and added a biography of the author; and *Torat Shimon*, by R. Shimon of Yaroslav (Munkacz, 1932), to which Gross added new material and corrected the text. His genealogical work contains among others the genealogies of R. Simhah Bunem of Przysucha (*Hedvat Simhah*, Warsaw, 1930); the Komarner dynasty (*Ben Bayeti*, Ungvar, 1927); and *Migdal David*, being additions to the biography of R. Barukh of Medziborz (*Mekor Hayyim*, Szamosujvar, 1931).

His only son, R. Jacob, and his family perished in the Holocaust.

P. Z. Schwartz, *Shem HaGedolim MeEretz Hagar*.

A.S.

GRUNWALD, Leopold (1889–1955), writer – Son of Yekutiel Zalman Leib, a Hebrew bookseller and author. Leopold studied in the *yeshivot* of Hunsdorf, Bonyhad, Huszt, Satmar, Pressburg, and Frankfurt. When the First World War broke out, he saw active service on the southeastern front in Dalmatia, Greece, and Bulgaria.

He was a prolific author, and among his works were *Pe'erey Hahmei Medinatenu* (Sighet, 1911), a biographical dictionary of Hungarian rabbis, and *HaYehudim BeHungaria*, Part 1 (Vacz, 1913). He published articles in the *Egyenloseg* on *A Chasidizmus Magyaraoraszagon*, which were reprinted in Hebrew in *HaTzofeh* (Budapest, 1922). The publication of these articles in the non-Orthodox press gave Hasidism much publicity. In 1924 he settled in the United States, and after serving as a rabbi in Borough Park, in Brooklyn, New York, he became the rabbi of the Bet Jacob synagogue in Columbus, Ohio.

Apart from his work *LeKorot HaHasidut BeUngaria* (Budapest, 1922), all his other works, such as *Tausend Yor Iddish lebn in Ungarn* (New York, 1945) and *Matzevat Kodesh*, the history of Sighet (New York, 1952), are replete with hasidic personalities. In his *HaShohet VeHaShehitah BeSifrut HaRabanit* (New York, 1955), he describes the hasidic controversy around the Shohet of Berdichev. His vast archives, containing his unpublished work and correspondence covering half a century, were destroyed.

N. Gordon, *Der Morgen Journal*, New York, January 26, 1956.

J. H. Zupnik, *Hamaor*, New York, *Tishri* and *Kislev* 1955.

A.S.

GUTERMAN, Aaron Menahem Mendel, of Radzymin (22 *Shevat* 1860–9 *Adar* 1934)—Son of R. Shlomoh Joshua David, he received his education from his father and grandfather. He was further influenced by R. Abraham Bornstein of Sochaczev and R. Shlomoh Zalman of Kapust. In 1882 he married Matale, the daughter of R. Yitzhak Jacob Rabinowicz of Biala. He remained in the house of his father-in-law for several years. He succeeded his father as rebbe in Radzymin in 1903. Much of his life was lived in the glare of publicity.

He set up a *Shomer Shabbos* organization and became a familiar figure on Friday afternoons, urging Warsaw Jewish shopkeepers to close their shops on the Sabbath. He established *Tomhei Assirim* (Prisoners' Aid Committee) to supply kosher food for Jews in Polish prisons and to provide kosher facilities for Jewish students who lived in Praga. During the Russo-Japanese war, he arranged for five railway-wagon loads of matzot to be sent to Jewish soldiers serving in the Far East, particularly in Port Arthur.

In 1912 he founded *yeshivah Orhot Hayyim* in Radzymin and despite his many preoccupations, rarely missed giving his students their daily *shiur*. From 1914 he lived in Warsaw, where his advice was sought by Polish ministers; he was even received by the Polish ruler Josef Pilsudski. When Sir Stuart Montagu Samuel, the president of the Board of Deputies of British Jews, visited Poland on a British government mission, the rebbe attended the farewell banquet. He appealed to the Bundist leader Victor Erlich to refrain from producing nonkosher kitchens during Passover, and he offered from his own funds to defray all the expenses involved.

Like his father before him, he was president of the *Meir Baal Haness* foundation, which distributed funds for the needy in the Holy Land. In *Elul* 1928, when he visited the Holy Land, he became involved in a cause célèbre: At his own expense, without prior consultation, he set up a simple canvas screen at the Western Wall to separate male and female worshipers. This affair became the subject of a British White Paper issued on November 9, 1928, and in 1930 the League of Nations set up an International Commission to resolve the problem of the wall. It decided that the use of benches, chairs, and screens was strictly forbidden.

His childless marriage of forty years ended in divorce. In 1922 he married the daughter of R. Jacob Moses Safrin of Komarno. This marriage, too, remained childless. He died in Warsaw, and a special *Bet Din* ruled that he should be interred in Warsaw near his grandfather and not in Radzymin next to his father.

The dynasty was continued by his nephews, R. Jacob Aryeh Morgenstern and R. Abraham Pinhas Morgenstern of Siedlice.

He was the author of *Hinukh Habonim* (Warsaw, 1913, reprinted in Israel in 1968); *Hiddushei Torah* (Jerusalem, 1972); *Alim Litrufah*, novella on page 21a of the Tractate *Betzah* (Warsaw, 1936); *Tzemah Menahem*, on the Passover *Haggadah* (Warsaw, 1930, reprinted in Jerusalem in 1973); and *Toafot Rom* (Warsaw, 1936).

GUTERMAN, Jacob Aryeh, first rebbe of Radzymin (1792–18 *Tammuz* 1877)—He was born in Warka, the son of a businessman, R. Shlomoh. He was a disciple of the "Seer" of Lublin, the Maggid of Kozienice, the "Holy Jew," and R. Simhah Bunem of Przysucha. In 1810 he married Hayyah, the daughter of R. Berish of Rychyval, where he lived for many years.

When his father-in-law lost his money, Jacob became for a time a teacher in the house of R. Jacob of Przysucha, eventually becoming rabbi of Rychyval. To supplement his meager income, his wife peddled merchandise to the nearby villages.

At the recommendation of R. Yitzhak Meir Alter, R. Jacob Aryeh became the rabbi of Radzymin in 1848. Only when R. Yitzhak of Warka died did R. Jacob Aryeh become rebbe, at the age of fifty-six, and ironically, the disciple of Przysucha became known as a miracle worker. "R. Yankele," as he was popularly known, soon attracted a large following—particularly childless women and even non-Jewish ones came for his blessings. Every petitioner was asked to give a few coins of silver or gold, which were promptly distributed to the poor.

He did not hesitate to write stern letters to the gentile squires who refused to renew the leases of their hasidic tenant-innkeepers. He warned the former that such inhuman conduct might have dire consequences. He frequently visited Warsaw on communal matters and kept in touch with R. Yitzhak Meir Alter. R. Israel Yitzhak Danziger of Alexander said of him, "The rebbe of Radzymin has the soul of R. Hayyim Attar."

Among his disciples were R. Yehiel Meir of Gostynin and R. Yehiel Isaac Danziger of Alexander. In 1857 he dismissed his domineering beadle, and, in revenge, the beadle's wife poisoned his food, which affected his health. She was arrested and imprisoned. The rebbe himself appeared in court and pleaded for the mitigation of her sentence. She was sentenced to only five months' imprisonment.

He was the author of *Divrei Aviv*, on *Midrash Rabbah* (Warsaw, 1924) and *Bikkurei Aviv*, on Genesis, Exodus, and Leviticus (Piotrokov, 1936, and reprinted in London in 1948).

He was succeeded by his son R. Shlomoh, who died on 15 *Shevat* 1903. His other sons were R. Israel and R. Abraham Hayyim.

Moving eulogies on him were delivered by R. David Dov Meisels, printed in his *Hiddushei HaRid* on *Pesahim*, and by R. Aaron Simhah Pilitzer, in *Imrei Esh* (Warsaw, 1937).

GUTERMAN, Solomon Joshua David, of Radzymin (d. 15 *Shevat* 1903)—Second son of R. Jacob Aryeh of Radzymin. In 1870, in the lifetime of his father, he became president of the *Meir Baal Haness* fund. Four years later, he succeeded his father as rebbe and served for thirty years. He was forthright and uncompromising. He was indefatigable in his efforts to help the poor and underprivileged.

His daughter married R. Tzvi Hirsch, the son of R. David Morgenstern of Kotzk.

His discourses are to be found in *Hinukh Banim* (Warsaw, 1913) and *Bikkurei Aviv* (Piotrokov, 1937). He was buried in Radzymin and was succeeded by his son, R. Aaron Menahem Mendel.

GUTMAN, Menahem Nahum, of Iasi/Jerusalem (1902–7 *Tevet* 1989)—Born in Iasi, the third son of R. Sholom of Iasi. After studying in the *yeshivot*, he was active in the Mizrachi and became rabbi in Iasi. In 1964 he settled in Jerusalem and contributed many articles on Hasidism to various periodicals.

Among his published works are *Hayyei HaBaal Shem Tov*, *VeAvotenu Mesaprim*, *Mishnat Hasidim* on Tractate *Avot*, *Torah U'Maasim Tovim* on the weekly *Sidra*, and *Yalkut Hasidim* on the Festivals. In his later years he regularly published in *Hazofeh* hasidic stories and biographies of rabbis. Among his unpublished manuscripts are a biography of the Baal Shem Tov and works on Bratzlav Hasidut, on Ruzhyn, and on the "Seer" of Lublin.

GUTSCHECHTER, Hayyim Joshua, of Vlozhin/Warsaw (1860–13 *Nisan* 1942)—He was born in Warsaw, the son of Manasseh Simhah Bunem, a follower of R. Yitzhak Meir Alter of Ger. At the age of sixteen he married the daughter of Shlomoh Gutrad. After his marriage he spent twelve years in Volozhin under R. Joseph Baer Soloveitchik and R. Naftali Tzvi Yehudah Berlin.

When the *yeshivah* of Volozhin closed in 1891, he settled in Warsaw, where he became a member of the rabbinate. It was there that he became attached to Hasidism, and he often visited R. Aryeh Leib of Ger. He wore a *streimel* and prayed according to the Lurian liturgy.

He died in Warsaw, where he was buried.

GUTTMACHER, Elijah, of Grodzisk-Wielpolski (1796–24 *Tishri* 1874)–Born in Borek, near Poznan, he studied from the age of nineteen under R. Akiva Eger in Poznan. He was a diligent student of mysticism. From 1822 he was rabbi in Pleschen, where he established a large *yeshivah*. From 1841 until his death he was the rabbi of Grodzisk-Wielpolski. He acted as a hasidic rabbi. He distributed amulets, and wrote *kamayot*, and was renowned for his miracles. In vain did he beg people not to come to him, even printing such entreaty in the Hebrew periodical *HaMaggid* (1874, No. 12).

The appearance of *Derishat Zion*, by R. Z. H. Kalischer, made a tremendous impact on him, and he enlisted the help of R. Abraham Landau of Ciechanov, to whom he wrote, "It is important to acquire land fromthe Arabs, and to fulfill those *mitzvot* that can be fulfilled these days." Together with R. Kalischer he issued a proclamation in both Hebrew and German in which he wrote that he had the backing of Adolphe Cremieux (1796–1880) and Sir Moses Montefiore.

Elijah was eager to set up Torah institutions in the Holy Land, and in a letter dated 1860 he and R. Jacob Etlinger of Altona implored Jews to support those institutions. In the same year, he attended a conference of rabbis convened by Kalischer in Thorn to consider practical steps for the establishment of settlements in the Holy Land. He supported Jacob Mordecai Hirschenson (1821–1888), who settled in Safed in 1848 and established *Sukkat Shalom U'Meor Yaakov*. A site was acquired near the Yeshurun synagogue in Jerusalem and in 1870 was renamed *Shenot Eliyahu* in honor of R. Elijah. *Kibbutz S'de Eliyahu* in Bet Sharon also bears his name.

He was a prolific writer, and many of his unpublished manuscripts are in the Hebrew University Library in Jerusalem. Among his works are novellas on Mishnayot and Talmud published in Vilna, *Tzofnat Paneah* (1875), and *Shenot Eliyahu* (1879). In 1979, two volumes of novellas on Talmud were printed in Jerusalem.

He was survived by four sons.

R. Tzvi Hirsch became his successor in Pleschen.

A. Y. Bromberg, *HaRav Eliyahu Guttmacher*.

H

HABAD–A school of hasidic thought, founded by Rabbi Shneur Zalman of Liady (1747–1812) and usually, though not exclusively, identified with the Lubavitch movement.

Habad is an acronym formed of the initial letters of *Hokhmah*, *Binah*, and *Daat*, literally "wisdom," "understanding," and "knowledge." However, these terms, within the system of *Habad*, bear a precise and special significance. *Hokhmah*, *Binah*, and *Daat* are the first triad in the kabbalistic scheme of the ten *Sefirot*, the creative instruments or emanations of God. *Hokhmah* represents the creation in its earliest potentiality: the idea of a finite world as it is first born in the divine mind. *Binah* is the idea conceived in its details, the result of contemplation. *Daat* is, as it were, the commitment to creation, the stage in which the idea becomes an active intention.

In the kabbalistic setting these are therefore progressive stages in the unfolding of the world from possibility to actuality, and they are descriptive primarily of God and the universe. In *Habad* they take on an additional connotation, for they are also regarded as descriptive of a human being's inner life. The human soul is a microcosm of the universe, and its workings reflect the process of cosmic creation. In that context, *Hokhmah* represents the birth of an idea in the human mind; *Binah*, its working out in thought; and *Daat*, the first step in personal commitment to the idea, the beginning of motivation, whose end point is action. This dual aspect of the *Sefirot* in *Habad* thought has had two important consequences: First, it provided a kind of psychology of the soul in terms of which the Jews' spiritual life could be described, in particular, the process by which Jews could translate an awareness of God, which lay higher than thought, into thought, reflection, emotion, and, ultimately, action. This was an important advance, because bridging the gap between spiritual insight and daily behavior had always been a problem for Jewish mysticism.

Second, the human soul could now stand as a precise analogue in terms of which cosmic processes, hitherto regarded as esoteric and remote from human understanding, could be explained. The words of Job, "From my flesh I shall see God," are here developed to the full: man, by searching himself, is able to glimpse the sublimest aspects of the divine.

Habad, as its name implies, represents an emphasis on the intellectual powers of the soul, and it stands in contrast with the emotionalist, or *Hagat*, school of Hasidism. Underlying the divergence between these two movements are two different attitudes toward the emotions. All hasidic thought shares a preoccupation with the emotions: the love and fear of God and the polarities of kindness (*Hesed*) and severity (*Gevurah*) in spiritual relationships. It is possible, however, to view the emotions as an autonomous realm, excited by physical stimuli–by singing, dancing, exaggerated gestures in prayer, and so on. This tends to characterize the *Hagat* movement. Alternatively, the emotions can be seen as intimately dependent on the mind–on perception and contemplation. This is the view of *Habad*. It therefore tends to stress study and meditation as central to the proper performance of the *mitzvot*: the head as ruler of the heart. While conceding that the emotions have alternative and more immediate origins, it argues that those that are the result of careful contemplation are more stable, enduring, and inward.

A number of distinctive features of the *Habad* movement followed from this initial premise. The first concerns the relationship between the hasidim and their rebbe. Other hasidic movements had tended to conceive a marked division of functions between the leader–the rebbe or *tzaddik*–and the followers. Initiated by the Besht and articulated by his successor, the Maggid of Mezhirech, the idea of the *tzaddik* was that of a charismatic leader, possessed of spiritual powers different in kind from those of his disciples. He was blessed by a special relationship with God; his prayers were effective beyond the hope of the average person; he was the bridge between the upper and lower worlds. This had tangible manifestations in the life of the hasidim.

The *tzaddik* was often the leader of prayer, raising up his disciples' devotions by the intensity of his own. He was, in the minutiae of his life, a living textbook of perfection, and his slightest habits were accordingly imitated. In general, the life of the intellect fell to him, whereas his followers enacted the life of the emotions. In their attachment to him they were made whole.

In contrast, *Habad* stressed the need for every Jew to develop individual powers of understanding, through study and meditation. Jews were to use their own resources in reaching self-fulfillment. A heavier personal burden was therefore laid upon them. The rebbe, still the nerve center of the movement, became more a teacher and adviser, recognizing the vocation of each of his followers, guiding them toward it, uncovering their strengths, and rejoicing in their achievements.

The second consequence of the emphasis on individual study was that hasidic thought was more thoroughly and systematically expounded in the *Habad* movement than elsewhere. This was evident from its beginning when, in the *Tanya*, R. Shneur Zalman produced the first schematic treatment of hasidic moral philosophy and its metaphysical foundations. The same disposition has been evident in each of his successors to the present day: to render the difficult concepts of the Kabbalah intelligible to rational thought by demonstrating their interconnections and illustrating their meaning by analogues taken from human experience. One striking instance of this is an analysis, given by the Lubavitcher rebbe R. Menahem Mendel Schneerson, of the place of hasidic thought in Judaism as a whole.

Each of the four traditional levels of biblical interpretation–*p'shat* (literal), *remez* (allegorical), *drush* (homiletical), and *sod* (esoteric)–corresponds to a level of the individual soul and to a level of reality in the universe as a whole. Each dimension of the Torah, therefore, discloses a particular order of reality and evokes a response from the appropriate realm of the soul.

Hasidut represents the fifth level, corresponding to the essence of the Torah, the universe, and the soul. It is thus not merely one approach to Judaism among many; rather, it is the inner truth of each, illuminating them all and demonstrating their essential unity. As a result, a recent emphasis has been discernible in *Habad* thinking–to treat Hasidut not as a self-contained discipline but as a means of shedding light on all levels of Judaism, from the mysteries of the *Zohar* to the apparent simplicities of Rashi's commentary to the Torah.

Related to this sense of the unity of all branches of Judaism has been a parallel stress on the unity of the Jewish people. In *Tanya* the principle is established that individuals, in discovering the source of their identity, come at the same time to recognize the real unity and community of all Jewish souls. This has combined with the relatively informal nature of the contact between hasid and rebbe in *Habad*, to make it an open-ended movement, active in promoting religious awareness throughout the Jewish world. The Lubavitch movement today is particularly noted for its outgoing efforts to draw back the alienated into the circle of Judaism. In this, it is pursuing a famous axiom of the vocation of Hasidism, stated by the Besht: "When will the Messiah come? When the wellsprings (of your teachings) spread abroad."

A. H. Glitzenstein, *Or HaHasidut*.

N. Mindel, *Philosophy of Chabad*.

J.S.

HAGER, Alter Menahem Mendel, of Borsa (4 *Kislev* 1895–29 *Iyyar* 1944)–Son of R. Pinhas, he was born in Vishnitz. He married his cousin Deborah, the daughter of Israel of Vishnitz. In 1924 he became rabbi of Borsa, where he established a large *yeshivah*. When the entire Jewish quarter was burned down on July 4, 1930, he moved to Nagyazollos. Before the Second World War he visited the Holy Land. He succeeded his father as rebbe in 1941.

During the war, he escaped to Seret but returned to Nagyazollos in an attempt to rescue his son Yitzhak. He and his other son, Hayyim, were deported to Auschwitz, where they perished.

HAGER, Barukh (1898-1985), Yiddish writer–Born in Tshudi, North Bukovina, where his father, Yitzhak Jacob David, was rabbi. From 1913 to 1923 he studied in Vienna. He married the daughter of the writer R. Israel Berger of Bucharest. He lived in Bucharest from 1933 to 1940, when he was transported to Transnistria. He found refuge in France and lived in Paris from 1947 to 1951.

In 1952 he settled in Buenos Aires, where he was employed in the cultural department of the Jewish community. He wrote many articles in the *Ikuf* (Bucharest), *Kiyyum* (Paris), *Zukunft* (New York), and *Goldene Keit* (Tel Aviv). He is the author of *Malkhut Hasidut* (Buenos Aires, 1953), for which he was awarded the Mordecai Stolier prize in 1956.

He died in Buenos Aires.

HAGER, Barukh, of Czernowitz (1899–13 *Kislev* 1942)–Son of Yehiel Michael of Horodenka and a grandson of R. Barukh Hager of Vishnitz. In 1922 he married his cousin Miriam, the daughter of R. Shragai Feivish Hager. In 1936 he became rabbi of Cozmeni, Bukovina, and then was *dayan* in Czernowitz. He was very active in the Mizrachi and the Zeire Mizrachi and was president of the Torah V'Avodah.

He was deported to Transnistra, where he died of typhus. He was survived by four sons–R. Mosheh, R. Barukh, R. Aryeh, and R. Eliezer–and two daughters.

HAGER, Barukh, of Seret/Haifa (1895–2 *Heshvan* 1964)–The fourth son of R. Israel, he was born in Vishnitz. His father called him the "wise one." He was ordained by R. Meir Arak of Buczacz and R. Abraham Menahem Steinberg of Brody. He married Henia, the daughter of R. Issachar Dov Rokeah of Belz, a union that ended in divorce. He remarried to Tsyril, the daughter of Naftali Hayyim Horowitz. From 1923, he occupied a rabbinical position first in Erzecse-Batvaros, Kutzman, and then in Seret, where he established a *yeshivah*.

Together with his father he visited the Holy Land in 1935. He became rebbe in 1936. He was active in the Aguda and advocated the establishment of agricultural centers for the training of religious pioneers. He was transported to Transnistra, where he spent two and a half years in hiding. His brother Eliezer rescued him and took him to Czernowitz and Braszov.

In 1947 he arrived in Haifa, where he established the hasidic settlement *Ramat Vishnitz*. He was active in the *Mo'etzet Gedolei HaTorah* and *Hinukh Atzmai*. He was buried in Bene Berak.

His son Eliezer succeeded him as rebbe, and another son, R. Moses, is the principal of the *yeshivah Yahel Yisrael* in Haifa.

HAGER, Barukh, of Vishiva (29 *Nisan* 1908–20 *Kislev* 1945)–Son of R. Menahem Mendel. He married Sheindel, the daughter of Tzvi Hirsch Leib Rubin. He succeeded his father in 1941. He was arrested by the Hungarian authorities on trumped-up charges of forging passports for refugees. He was taken to Budapest and then to Grosswardein from which he was deported. He was survived by his son Naftali Tzvi of Bene Berak, and by a daughter, Zipporah.

HAGER, Barukh Asher, of Vishnitz (1845–20 *Kislev* 1893)–Son of R. Menahem Mendel of Vishnitz. He married Zipporah, the daughter of R. Aryeh Leib Shapira of Korets. He was involved in a bitter controversy with R. Yomtov Lippa Teitelbaum over the status of a ritual slaughterer. He was backed by R. Aaron of Lvov and R. Meshullam Issachar Horowitz. In the Austrian parliamentary elections, he strongly supported the candidacy of Dr. Joseph Samuel Bloch (1850–1923). His discourses are to be found in *Imrei Barukh* (Kolomyja, 1912).

He had nine sons and three daughters, and seven of his sons became hasidic rabbis.

HAGER, David, of Zablotov (1797–16 *Shevat* 1848)–Popularly known as "Rab Dubke," he was the son of R. Menahem Mendel of Kosov. He married Pessia Leah, the only daughter of R. Mosheh Leib of Sasov. She was renowned for her scholarship and piety and even took petitions from the hasidim who came to her for help. In

1826, to avoid dispute with his brother Hayyim, he settled in Zablotov, where he established a great hasidic dynasty. He was known for his wisdom, and R. Israel of Ruzhyn described him as "worldly wise." He was succeeded by his son Jacob. He was the author of *Tzemah David* (Kolomyja, 1893).

HAGER, Eliezer, of Haifa (b. 1924)–He was born in Grosswardein, the son of R. Barukh, under whom he studied. He was deported to Transnistria, where he continued his studies under his uncle R. Abraham Moses Babad. He arrived as an illegal immigrant in the Holy Land in 1946 and was detained in the Atlit Camp. When his father died in 1964, he became rebbe. In 1950 he married Hayyah, the daughter of Sholom Ozer Brown of Kiryat Ata. His son Jacob married Havah, the daughter of David Mattathias Rabinowicz of Bene Berak.

HAGER, Eliezer, of Vishnitz (22 *Shevat* 1891-2 *Elul* 1946)–He was the second and favorite son of R. Israel of Vishnitz. "When they ask me in the hereafter 'Who I am?' " said his proud father, "I will reply, 'I am the father of R. Eliezer.' " He was ordained by R. Abraham Menahem Steinberg of Brody. In 1907 he married Havah, the daughter of R. Yitzhak Meir Heschel of Kopyczynce. The marriage was childless. After staying with his father-in-law in Vienna during the First World War, he became rabbi of Vishnitz in 1922 and established a large *yeshivah, Bet Yisrael VeDamesek Eliezer*. He participated in the work of the Aguda and the *Mo'etzet Gedolei HaTorah*.

During the Second World War he helped with the rehabilitation of refugees in Transnistria. He arrived in the Holy Land on 27 *Nisan* 1944 and set up a *Bet HaMidrash* and a *yeshivah* in Tel Aviv. Two years later he became ill. Although he was in great pain, he would not permit his doctors to hush the hasidim who were singing and dancing in the nearby *Bet HaMidrash* in Rehov Feiberg. "Their joy gives me consolation," he murmured.

His discourses are to be found in *Damesek Eliezer*, on the Bible and Festivals (Jerusalem, 1949); *Damesek Eliezer*, on the Pentateuch (Bene Berak, 1970); and a commentary on Psalms (Jerusalem, 1955, and reprinted in Bene Berak, 1972).

HAGER, Gershon, of Touste (1884-1954)–Son of R. Menahem Mendel of Zablotov, he married Hayyah Sarah, the daughter of R. Zeev Horn in 1902. In 1912 he became rabbi of Touste. During the First World War he lived in Vienna, where, for twenty-five years, he was a member of the *Bet Din* and the principal of the *yeshivah Tomhei Torah*.

After the Anschluss, he found refuge in New York. He was the author of *Minhat HaGershuni* (New York, 1949).

He was survived by an only daughter, Nehia, the wife of R. Israel Mordecai Friedman.

HAGER, Hayyim, of Kosov (1795-25 *Iyyar* 1854)–He was the elder son of R. Menahem Mendel of Kosov. He married Zipporah, the daughter of R. Yehudah Meir Shapira of Shepetova. She was renowned for her piety. R. Israel of Ruzhyn maintained that she was "the most righteous person in the world."

Hayyim visited many rabbis, especially R. Abraham Joshua Heschel of Opatov, his uncle R. Jacob Shimon Spira of Zaslov, and R. Aryeh Leib of Shpole. In 1826 he became rabbi of Kosov. He was renowned for his scholarship. He attached a great deal of importance to R. Abraham Ibn Ezra's commentary on the Pentateuch. "The words of Ibn Ezra," he said, "are as sacred as the Scroll of the Law." He was respected for his kindness, hospitality, and compassion. He maintained that the function of a *tzaddik* was to be a faithful shepherd, ministering to his flock with love and rarely with discipline.

Among the hasidic personalities who visited him were R. Yitzhak Isaak of Zydaszov, R. Joseph Shmuel Gelernter of Yablonov, and R. Joseph Mordecai Kahane of Sighet. He was the president of the *kollel* for the support of the poor in the Holy Land.

His son R. Aaron Shimshon succeeded him.

His discourses are to be found in *Torat Hayyim*, on the Pentateuch, published first in Lvov in 1857, and since reprinted six times. Another small tractate under the name *Torat Hayyim Taninah* was printed in Sighet in 1906.

HAGER, Hayyim, of Kosov (1900-19 *Heshvan* 1943)–He was the only son of

R. Moses and was brought up in his grandfather's house. He was ordained by R. Abraham Menahem Steinberg of Brody and by R. Jacob Shur of Kuty. In 1928, he succeeded his father as rabbi of Kosov. In 1935, he visited the Holy Land and was anxious to settle there. He was a melodious officiant and a proficient violinist.

During the Nazi invasion, he lived in the Kolomyja ghetto, where his wife, Heniah Rivkah, and his daughter, Havah, perished. He tried to escape to Hungary but did not succeed. He and the rest of his family were murdered. His son R. Alter was later murdered in Lvov.

HAGER, Hayyim, of Ottynia (1863–25 *Kislev* 1932)–Second son of R. Barukh of Vishnitz, he was ordained by R. Yitzhak Aaron of Lvov, and R. Jacob Wiedenfeld. He married Pessia Leah, the daughter of R. Yitzhak Friedman of Bohusi. In 1893 he became rebbe in Ottynia, near Stanislav, and in 1895, the president of the Rabbi Meir Baal Haness Fund and of the *kollel* of Volhynia. It was through his influence that a home for the poor was bought in Jerusalem.

During the First World War, he spent four years in Vienna, and as Ottynia was almost completely destroyed, he lived for a time in Czernowitz. In 1924 he settled in Stanislav, where he established a *yeshivah*. He died in Cracow but was buried in Stanislav.

Many of his manuscripts–on the Codes, Talmud and Kabbalah–were lost during the war. Only his work *Nimukei Hayyim* on the Talmud was printed in Tel Aviv in 1954.

He was succeeded by his son Shalom Joseph of Stanislav.

HAGER, Hayyim, of Zablotov (1893–1 *Heshvan* 1942)–The son of R. Moses, he succeeded his father as rebbe. He married Reizel, the daughter of R. Tzvi Hirsch Ashkenazi of Stanislav. He lived in Vienna during the First World War. After the war he returned to Zablotov. He visited the Holy Land in 1930.

During the Nazi occupation, he worked on road construction in Kosov and Kolomyja. He, his wife, his younger son, Moses, and his twin girls perished.

One of his discourses appeared in the periodical *Be'er*, published in Poland.

HAGER, Hayyim Judah Meir, of Vishiva (17 *Elul* 1912–11 *Iyyar* 1969)–Son of Menahem Mendel, he was born in Vishnitz. He was ordained by R. Pinhas Zimtbaum of Grosswardein and R. David Weiss of Vishiva. In 1935 he married Ritzah, the daughter of Eleazar Reiman of Karassonfaly Marmaros. He assisted his father in the *yeshivah*.

In 1940, Vishiva became part of Hungary, and he and the students at the *yeshivah* were all deported to Auschwitz. From there he was taken to Dachau and Bergen-Belsen. Miraculously, he survived, and in 1947 spent some time in Sweden, from which he emigrated to the United States. He became the rabbi of *Menahem Yisrael Shtiebl* in Williamsburg, Brooklyn, and later moved to Crown Heights. In 1960 he settled in Tel Aviv and was buried in *Zikhron Meir*.

He had no children.

HAGER, Hayyim Meir (15 *Kislev* 1888–9 *Nisan* 1972), founder of *Kiryat Vishnitz*–Second son of R. Israel, he was born in Vishnitz. He was ordained by R. Shalom Mordecai of Brzezany. He assisted his father in the *yeshivah*. In 1905 he married Margalit, the daughter of Zeev Twersky of Rotmistrovka. He divided his time between Vishnitz and Wilhowitz. In 1935 he visited the Holy Land, accompanied by his brothers, R. Barukh and Eliezer.

The *yeshivah* at Vishnitz was closed in 1940 when the Russians occupied the Bukovina. In September 1940 Grosswardein was overrun by the Hungarians, and a ghetto was established. Hayyim Meir worked in a labor camp. After the war he returned to Grosswardein and tried to rebuild the shattered community. Frustrated by Communist rule, he left Romania in 1947 and after a short stay in Antwerp, settled in Tel Aviv.

Acquiring thirty dunams of land in Bene Berak in 1949, he established the very first hasidic *shikkun* since the establishment of the State of Israel. He encouraged his followers to support the Six-Day War, which he called the beginning of the redemption. He was a staunch Agudist and one of the leaders of the *Mo'etzet Gedolei HaTorah*. He led the way to the polling station at election time. He and his brother R. Barukh issued a proclamation in 1961 urging their followers to vote for the Aguda.

He was buried in *Zikhron Meir*.

His discourses are to be found in *Imrei Hayyim*, published in Bene Berak in 1973. His son R. Moses Joshua succeeded him in Bene Berak, and his other son, R. Mordecai, is the rebbe of Vishnitz in Monsey in New York. His daughter, Hinda, married R. Naftali Hayyim Adler of Netanya.

HAGER, Israel, of Vishnitz (2 *Elul* 1860–2 *Sivan* 1937) – Eldest son of R. Barukh, he was known as the "*Ahavat Yisrael*." He was ordained by R. Berish Wiedenfeld and R. Ezekiel, the rebbe of Sianiawa. In 1975 he married Hinda, the daughter of R. Meir of Dzikov, and when she died, he married Miriam, the daughter of R. Jacob Kahana. In 1885 he became rabbi in Bidvall. The authorities accused him of opposing secular studies, and he barely escaped arrest. He settled in Vishnitz, where he established a *yeshivah*, *Bet Yisrael* for older students. He paid close attention to the curriculum and set a high standard. His son R. Menahem Mendel was one of the administrators of the *yeshivah*.

At the outbreak of the First World War, he found refuge first in Kutov and then in 1915 in Grosswardein, where he attended the communal synagogue and even listened to the German discourses of R. M. Fuchs. At the end of the war he did not return to his native Vishnitz, where his son Eliezer was rabbi. R. Israel was involved in a controversy with R. Hayyim Tzvi Teitelbaum over the presidency of the *kollel* Marmaros and Sighet.

He was unassuming and friendly to everyone, greeting every follower with the words "A sweet life to you." Often, he embraced his visitors. His memory was phenomenal. He gave encomiums to many books, and every day he would recite the whole Book of Psalms before prayers.

Twelve years after his death, on 13 *Adar* 1949, he was reinterred, in *Zikhron Meir*, Bene Berak, to the singing of the Vishnitz melody *Shalom Aleikhem* (Welcome, ye ministering angels) by his sons. This was made possible through the intervention of the Romanian Jewish foreign minister Anna Pauker.

He was survived by five sons: R. Menahem Mendel, R. Eliezer, R. Barukh, R. Samuel Abba, and R. Hayyim Meir, who became rebbe of *Kiryat Vishnitz* in Bene Berak. His discourses are published in *Ahavat Yisrael* on Genesis (Grosswardein, 1943) and reprinted in Bene Berak in 1976.

Roshei Golat Ariel, pp. 70–76.

HAGER, Israel Shalom Joseph, of Ottynia (1884–24 *Iyyar* 1944) – Son of R. Hayyim, he married his cousin, the daughter of Samuel Abraham Abba of Horodenka. When his wife died, he married the daughter of R. Yehiel, son of R. Meir of Dzikov.

He succeeded his father as rebbe in Stanislav in 1932. For nearly four years he found refuge in a bunker in Stanislav, but he, his wife, their son Barukh, and daughters Zipporah and Pesiah Leah were killed by the Nazis.

All of his writings were lost, except eighteen of his discourses, which are printed in *Nimukei Hayyim* (pp. 307–316).

Y. Alfasi, *Tiferet SheBeMalkhut*, p. 219.

HAGER, Issachar Dov (1877–20 *Kislev* 1967) – Elder son of R. Jacob Yitzhak David of Strozynets, Bukovina. He married his cousin Sheine Rachel of Peczenizyn, Galicia. After finding refuge in Vienna during the First World War, he came to London in 1938, where he established the first hasidic *shtiebl* in Golders Green. He avoided the limelight and spent his years in London in prayer and study.

His son, R. Mendel (b. 1910) and his grandsons R. Gershon (b. 1945) and R. Jacob (b. 1949) maintain the Hager *Bet HaMidrash* in London, which is named after the founder, *Bet HaMidrash Yisokhor Dov*.

HAGER, Jacob Yitzhak David, of Storojineti (1866–13 *Adar* 1932) – The fifth son of Barukh of Vishnitz, he married the daughter of R. Issachar Dov Eichenstein of Dolina. From 1893, he was rabbi first in Tshuain, Bukovina, then in Storojineti. He took refuge in Vienna during the First World War, where he died.

He was survived by his son R. Issachar Dov Berish, who succeeded him. Another son, Barukh, became a writer of hasidic books.

HAGER, Joseph, of Tysmenitsa (1878–1942) – Son of R. Menahem Mendel, he was born in Zablotov. He married Yohebed, the daughter of R. Yitzhak, the rebbe of Tysmienica, whom he succeeded as rebbe in 1904. After taking refuge in Vienna in the First World War, he returned to Tysmienica, where he 1926 he was appointed rabbi. He was in sympathy with Zionism and the Mizrachi.

He, his wife, and their younger son, Yitzhak, were deported to Stanislav, where they perished. His elder son, R. Leibish, married the daughter of R. Shapira of Grodsisk, and died in Warsaw.

HAGER, Menahem Mendel, of Kosov (1769–17 *Heshvan* 1826)–Son of Jacob Kopul, he was born in Kolomyja and married his cousin Sheine Rachel, the daughter of Shmuel Simhah of Kosov, where he lived for a number of years. When his father-in-law died in 1786, he moved to Tysmienica and then to Kolomyja, where his wife kept a small shop. Unsuccessful in business, he returned to Kosov.

He was a disciple of R. Elimelekh of Lejask, R. Tzvi Hirsch of Nadvorna, and R. Moses Leib of Sasov. In 1890 he succeeded his father as rebbe of Kosov. He was highly venerated by his contemporaries, but his succession was troubled. Many of his father's followers gave their allegiance to his brother R. David. His disciples included R. Eliezer Horowitz of Dzikov and R. Shmuel Sianover.

R. Menahem Mendel believed that his message could be communicated through music and melody, and his melodious tunes resounded through Romania, Hungary, and Czechoslovakia. His discourses, which are full of *Gematriyot*, are to be found in *Ahavat Shalom* (Lvov, 1802, reprinted in 1850 and 1859). He was also the author of *Ahavat Shalom Tanina* (Czernowitz, 1888).

His son R. Hayyim succeeded him in Kosov and another son, R. David, became rabbi of Zablotov.

Roshei Golat Ariel, pp. 65–66.

HAGER, Menahem Mendel, of Vishiva (1886–13 *Tevet* 1941)–He was the son of R. Israel of Vishnitz. His father described him as "Holy Ark full of books." He was ordained by R. Shalom Mordecai of Brzezany and R. Benjamin Aryeh Weiss of Czernowitz. In 1902 he married his first cousin, Yente Miriam, the daughter of R. Mordecai Chodrov of Kolomyja. From 1908 he was the rabbi of Vishnitz and the principal of the *yeshivah Bet Yisrael*.

During the First World War he lived in Grosswardein, and in 1922, he became the rabbi of Vishiva (Felsoviso), known as the "Jerusalem of Marmaros." There, too, he established a *yeshivah*, which provided accommodation and food for the students.

In 1928, he traveled to Western Europe and the United States to raise funds for his educational establishments. He also set up a Talmud Torah for younger boys and issued a monthly periodical, *Degel HaTorah*.

In 1936, he succeeded his father as rebbe and was active in the *Mo'ezet Gedolei HaTorah*. His writings were preserved during the Holocaust and were published under the title *Torat Menahem* (Bene Berak, 1972) and *Sheerit Menahem* (Bene Berak, 1974).

His son Barukh succeeded him in Vishiva but was murdered by the Nazis on 29 *Kislev* 1944. His other son, R. Hayyim Yehudah Meir, was rebbe in the United States and in Israel and died on 11 *Adar* 1969. On 29 *Kislev* 1966, R. Menahem Mendel was reinterred in Bene Berak. His grandson, R. Naftali Tzvi (son of R. Barukh), established a *Bet HaMidrash Tiferet Menahem* in Bene Berak.

A. Surasky, *Marbitzei Torah U'Mussar M'Olam HaHasidut*, vol. 5, pp. 31–48.

HAGER, Menahem Mendel, of Vishnitz (24 *Iyyar* 1810–29 *Tishri* 1895)–Third son of R. Hayyim Hager of Kosov. In 1844 he married Miriam Manya, the daughter of R. Israel of Ruzhyn. He became rebbe of Vishnitz in 1854 and was the head of the *kollel* Vishnitz and Marmaros. His contemporaries held him in high esteem. "A fire rages in his soul," remarked R. Isaac of Warka.

He was an ascetic and eschewed luxuries. He was renowned for his hospitality, and he would make arrangements prior to the Sabbath to have money available on Sunday for distribution to the poor.

He was the author of *Tzemah Tzaddik* (Czernowitz, 1855).

His son, R. Barukh, succeeded him.

HAGER, Menahem Mendel, of Zablotov (1889–29 *Kislev* 1954)–Son of R. David Eliezer, he married Sprinze, the daughter of R. Eliezer Rokeah, in 1907. He served successively as rabbi of Halicz, Newstadt, and Sosnowiec. During the First World War he was chaplain to the Austrian forces. He was a member of the executive of the Mizrachi Rabbinical Organization and a delegate to the Zionist congresses from 1912 to 1939.

In 1943 he settled in Tel Aviv, where he established a *yeshivah Ateret Zekenim* in Yad Eliyahu. He was the author of *Menahem Avelim* on the laws of mourning (Tel Aviv, 1950). None of his three sons became rebbe.

HAGER, Mordecai, of Vishnitz/ Monsey, New York (b. 1922) – Son of R. Hayyim Meir of Vishnitz, he studied in the *yeshivot* of Satmar and Papa. After the Second World War he settled in New York, where he was rabbi of the *Torat Hayyim* community in Brooklyn. He was the founder of *Kiryat Vishnitz* in Monsey. He married Feige Malkah, the daughter of R. Jacob Joseph Twersky of Sqvira. When she died a year later, he married her sister, Seima Mirel. He recently built a new *shikkun* in Montclair, New Jersey, to which he transferred his *yeshivah*.

He has eight sons and six daughters. All his sons are rebbes of Monsey: R. Pinhas Shalom in Borough Park, R. Israel in Monsey, R. Menahem Mendel in Monticello, R. Yitzhak Yohanan in Williamsburg, R. Eliezer Zeev in Jerusalem, R. David in London, R. Aaron in Montreal, and R. Barukh Shimshon in Bene Berak.

His daughters all married rabbis: Zipporah married R. Abraham Dov Twersky of Rotmistrovka; Hannah Rachel, R. Israel Eliezer Fish of Williamsburg; Hinda, R. Joseph Benzion Rothenberg of Borough Park; Havvah Reizel, R. Aaron Mendel Twersky of Sqvira, New York; Golda, R. Yitzhak Michael Moskowitch of Flatbush; and Brachah, R. Nahman Joseph Twersky of Rotmistrovka, New York.

HAGER, Moses, of Shatz (1863–9 *Iyyar* 1926) – Son of R. Barukh of Vishnitz, he married the daughter of R. Abraham Joshua Heschel of Medziborz. He settled in Shatz in 1899. His life was beset by personal tragedies, with three of his children dying in early infancy. He expressed his faith in melodies that became famous throughout the land. His son R. Hayyim succeeded him.

HAGER, Moses Joshua, of Vishnitz/Bene Berak (b. 13 *Sivan* 1916) – Son of R. Hayyim Meir. He studied under his uncle R. Eliezer of Vishnitz. As a young man, in 1937, he became rabbi of Vilchowitz, and later, of Grosswardein. In 1942, he married Leah Esther (1921–1993), the daughter of R. Hayyim Menahem Mendel Panet of Des.

In 1945, he settled in the Holy Land and lived in Tel Aviv. When his father arrived in Israel in 1947, he helped him set up *Kiryat Vishnitz* in Bene Berak. He is the head of *Mo'etzet Gedolei HaTorah* of the Aguda. His brother, R. Mordecai, lives in Monsey.

He has two sons. His four daughters married the rebbe of Sqvira, the rebbe of Belz, R. Aaron Teitelbaum of Monroe, and R. Menahem Mendel Ernster, the head of the *yeshivah*, *Bet Yisrael and Damesek Eliezer*.

HAGER, Pinhas, of Borsa (1867–12 *Adar* 1941) – Son of R. Barukh, he married the daughter of R. Samuel Rokeah of Sokal. In 1899 he became rabbi of Borsa. During the First World War and thereafter he lived in Vishiva and Sighet.

His son, Alter Menahem Mendel, succeeded him in Borsa.

HAGER, Samuel Abraham Abba, of Horodenka (1865–30 *Shevat* 1895) – Son of R. Barukh of Vishnitz, he married Hinda Matel, daughter of R. Moses Mordecai Twersky of Makarov. In 1893 he became rabbi in Horodenka. He was the author of *Sifsei Tzaddik* (Kolomyja, 1906).

He was survived by two daughters.

HAGER, Yehiel Michal, of Horodenka (1872–13 *Kislev* 1942) – The youngest son of R. Barukh of Vishnitz, he was the rebbe of Horodenka from 1895. He married his niece Bluma Reisel, the daughter of his brother R. Hayyim of Ottynia.

During the First World War, he lived first in Vienna and then in Czernowitz. He was deported by the Germans to Transnistria, where he was murdered a few hours after his son had died of typhus, his wife dying four days later.

He was survived by one son, R. Barukh, and one daughter.

HAGER, Yehiel Michal, of Storojineti (1824–14 *Nisan* 1905) – Fourth son of R. David of Zablotov, he succeeded his father as rebbe in 1848. In 1854 he settled in Storojineti. He was survived by one son, R. Shalom, and three daughters.

HAKKAFOT (lit., circuits) Processional circuits on ceremonial occasions. Hasidim outside Israel make such circuits around the *Almemar* on Shemini Atzeret, the eighth day of Sukkot.

There is a reference to this custom in the *Zohar* (Pinhas, 256b) and in the kabbalistic work *Hemdat HaYamim*. During the *Hakkafot*, the participants sing, dance, and celebrate. In hasidic circles, circuits are made under the wedding canopy when the bride goes around the bridegroom three or seven times. Circuits are also made around the coffin of a rebbe.

There is no uniform liturgy for Simhat Torah. R. Uri of Strelisk recited the Song of Songs before *Hakkafot*.

HALAKHAH – The legal side of Judaism, the practice and study of the rules, customs, and observances. There is no doubt, despite occasional accusations to the contrary on the part of the *Mitnaggedim*, that the hasidim always accepted the complete authority of the *halakhah*. The hasidim were observant Jews who adhered strictly to the rules laid down in the Talmud and the Codes except in a very few instances. Where Hasidism differed was in interpreting the *halakhah* not as a supreme end in itself but as a means to an end, that of attachment to God in love and fear (see DEVEKUT).

Typical of the hasidic approach is R. Jacob Joseph of Polonoye's understanding (*Toldot Yaakov Yosef, shelah*, ed. Warsaw, 1881, p. 141c) of the term *halakhah*. Two meanings are given to the term: The first connects it with the root *halakh*, "to go." We are expected to progress spiritually in the study and practice of the *halakhah* so that we proceed from observance based on self-seeking motives to observance based on pure motive.

The second meaning of *halakhah* is derived, following the Lurianic Kabbalah, from the observation that the letters of the word, when transposed, form the word *hakallah*, "the bride," meaning the Shekhinah. The observances ordained by the Torah are the adornments of the celestial bride, rendering her attractive to those who love her. But the ultimate purpose is the consummation of the "marriage," in which the adornments are removed, having fulfilled their purpose.

Because of that attitude, the hasidim preferred to perform the *mitzvot* in a spirit of mystical fervor, influenced very strongly by the ideas read into the performances by the Kabbalah. Moreover, certain of the *mitzvot* – the *seder* on Passover, the Sabbath, *tefillin*, the wearing of the *tallit*, the blowing of the *shofar* on Rosh HaShanah, and the *sukkah* and *lulav* on Tabernacles – which lend themselves more readily to mystical interpretation, were stressed more than others. Again the emphasis on mystical fervor led the hasidim to conclude that in some ways the preparations for the performance of the *mitzvot* are more important than the actual performance.

Only in rare instances did the hasidic approach result in deviations from the standard *halakhah*, but it did have such a result in the following instances.

1. Believing that the prayer book compiled by the great kabbalist R. Isaac Luria was based on the Sefirotic map on high – its very letters and their order corresponding to the various combinations of divine names – the hasidim, to the consternation of the *mitnaggedim*, departed from the Ashkenazic custom and adopted that prayer book. The antihasidic polemics on this question accuse the hasidim of halakhic offense in that it is forbidden, according to the *halakhah*, for an Ashkenazi to follow the Sephardic rite or one based on it. Some of the hasidic masters tried to defend the departure on halakhic grounds, but it is clear that the halakhic justification here is extremely dubious. When the *halakhah* came into conflict with the hasidic preference, it was the former that had to yield. (For a fuller discussion of the question from the hasidic point of view, see R. Hayyim Eleazar Shapira's Responsa *Minhat Eleazar*, Part I, no. 11, and the same author's *Hamishah Maamarot* (Jerusalem, 1962), pp. 159–186.

2. The Talmud and the Codes lay down strict rules regarding the times of prayer. Many hasidim, however, from the earliest times, tended to disregard those rules, offering various defenses of their deviation, for example, that the preparations for prayer

precluded strict attention to the rules or that the essence of prayer was its spontaneity. Awareness that this was a departure from the Halakhah is expressed in the oft-repeated hasidic tale of the *tzaddik* who said that he knew he would have to go to hell for disobeying the *halakhah* about the times of prayer but he preferred to be in hell with the *tzaddikim* than to be in heaven with the ordinary folk who did keep the rules but had no fervor in their prayers.

A further justification, obviously non-halakhic, was that the times of prayer were only for those bound by time, not for the *tzaddikim* and their followers, who endeavored to reach in their prayers the world of eternity beyond time. Nevertheless, some hasidic groups in a later period did revert to the tradition and observed scrupulously the laws regarding the proper times of prayer.

3. As an aid to spiritual progress, the hasidim introduced the practice of regular immersion in the *mikveh*, especially before prayer. That this is not demanded by the *halakhah* cannot be construed as a departure from the law, but the hasidim went further and immersed themselves in the *mikveh* even on the Sabbath, a practice that is halakhically questionable.

4. According to the *Shulhan Arukh* (*Orah Hayyim* 136), when the Torah is read, it is the third *aliyah* that is especially significant and that should be allotted to the most scholarly and pious member of the congregation. Following the Kabbalah, the hasidim attached greater significance to *shishi*, the sixth *aliyah* (according to the Kabbalah the sixth of the lower *Sefirot* is called the *tzaddik*!).

5. Once *matzah* has been adequately baked, it cannot become leaven and there is consequently no halakhic objection to soaking or boiling this *matzah*. But the hasidim—in their fear of offending against the most remote possibility of the laws of leaven, since the Kabbalah is similarly strict—universally refuse to eat "soaked *matzah*" (*sheruyyah*) except on the last day of Passover.

6. According to the Talmud (*Nedarim* 12a) and the Codes (*Shulhan Arukh*, *Yoreh De'ah* 402:2), the anniversary of the death of a parent (*yahrzeit*) is a period of mourning. Hasidism, on the contrary, sees it as a time for rejoicing, because each year, on the anniversary, the soul of the departed is said to rise to ever-greater heights. Consequently, the hasidim gather together on such an occasion and drink a toast, praying for the soul's ascent. Especially the anniversary of the death of a famous *tzaddik* is an occasion for rejoicing (*hillula*). The *tahanun* prayers of supplication are not recited on this day by the hasidim. Reuben Margaliout has published a booklet that lists for this purpose the dates on which the saints died (*Hillula DeTzaddikayya*, Lemberg, 1939).

7. Although the *halakhah* frowns on dancing and clapping the hands on Sabbaths and Festivals (*Shulhan Arukh*, *Orah Hayyim* 339:3, *Magen Avraham* 669), the hasidim could not easily forgo the demands of mystical joy expressed by dancing on the sacred days. Consequently, it is the universal custom of the hasidim to permit this (see the attempt at halakhic justification in *Minhat Eleazar*, I, 29).

In addition to the general practices binding upon all Jews, the customs developed among the various hasidic dynasties were adopted by their followers so that a kind of hasidic *halakhah* developed, even a *halakhah* of particular dynasties. The conduct of the *tzaddikim* was closely studied, and when it seemed intended to set the pattern for all the hasidim of the particular group, it was recorded as a guide to practice. All this resulted in what virtually amounted to a totally different way of life for the hasidim. The earlist sources produced by the *mitnaggedim* refer, in fact, to the hasidim as a *kat* (sect). It is fairly obvious that it was their adherence to the *halakhah* that kept the hasidim within the traditional fold and prevented Hasidism from becoming the victim of sectarianism.

Some of the hasidic masters were themselves halakhic authorities, although it is perhaps significant that the two roles they fulfilled generally existed independently so that there is little indication that the halakhic works they produced were compiled by hasidic *tzaddikim* rather than by pure halakhists. R. Shneur Zalman of Liady compiled a code of Jewish law (*Shulhan Arukh HaRav*).

Halakhic responsa enjoying widespread authority were compiled by R. Moses Teitelbaum (*Heshiv Mosheh*), R. Abraham of Sochaczev (*Avnei Nezer*), R. Hayyim of Zans (*Divrei Hayyim*), R. Menahem Mendel of Lubavitch (*Tzemah Tzedek*), R. Hayyim Eleazar of Munkacs (*Minhat Eleazar*), and R. Yitzhak Meir of Ger (*Teshuvot HaRim*).

R. Tzvi Hirsch of Munkacs wrote a widely used compendium of responsa to the *Yoreh De'ah* (*Darkhei Teshuvah*).

Outstanding halakhic commentaries were written by hasidic masters: R. Yitzhak Meir of Ger, *Hiddushei HaRim*; R. Abraham of Sochaczev, *Eglei Tal*, on the thirty-nine types of work forbidden on the Sabbath; and R. Gershon Henoch of Radzyn, *Sidrei Tohorot*.

Works by hasidic masters that attempt to combine the *halakhah* with kabbalistic and hasidic themes, are R. Tzvi Elimelekh of Dynov's *Derekh Pikkudekha* and R. Yitzhak Eizik of Komarno's code of law–*Shulhan HaTahor*.

A number of distinguished halakhists were hasidim, for example, R. Menahem Munish Babad, author of responsa *Havvatzellet HaSharon*, a hasid of Belz; and R. Menahem Zemba, a hasid of Gur.

Y. M. Gold, *Darkhei Hayyim VeShalom* (The Customs and Observances of Rabbi Hayyim Eleazar of Munkacs).

I. Z. Kahana, *Mehkarim BeSifrut HaTeshuvot*, pp. 408–420.

A. Wertheim, *Halakhot VeHalikhot BaHasidut*.

L.J.

HALBERSTAM, Aaron, of Biala/Bielsk (1865–26 *Sivan* 1942)–Son of R. Joseph Zeev of Cieszanov and a grandson of R. Hayyim of Zanz, he studied under his uncle R. David and was ordained by R. Dov Berish of Rava. In 1879 he married his relative Rebecca Rachel, the daughter of R. Alter Meir David Halevi Rothenberg, the rabbi of Wolbrum. He was renowned for his scholarship.

In 1889, he became rabbi in Biala, near Bielsk, where he served until the Holocaust. During the Second World War he escaped to Zanz and then to Tarnov, where he was murdered.

He was the author of *Megged Eretz* on *Orah Hayyim* (Munkacz, 1907); *Pri Noah*, an abridged code on *Yoreh De'ah* (Bilgoraj, 1939); and *Muzzal M'Hesh* on Hasidism and Talmud (New York, 1942).

His son, R. Menahem Binyamin Benzion, was rabbi of Wodzislov in Brooklyn.

HALBERSTAM, Aaron, of Zanz (1826–*Rosh Hodesh Av* 1903)–Third son of R. Hayyim Halberstam and popularly known as the "Kreizer Rav," he was born in Rudnik. He accompanied his father on visits to various hasidic rebbes. He married Hannah Elka, the daughter of Jacob Weinberger of Dukla. In 1857 he was appointed rabbi of Zanz and its district.

After the death of his father, he moved to Zanz, where he succeeded him as rabbi. He was reluctant to become rebbe. He and his colleagues languished in prison for six weeks because he had excommunicated a man who would not attend a summons of the *Bet Din*.

He was survived by his sons–R. Shmuel Shmelke, R. Shalom, and R. Aryeh Leibish–and one daughter.

His discourses were not published because he left specific instructions that all his manuscripts be burned.

HALBERSTAM, Abraham Shalom, of Sztrapko (1854–first day of Pentecost 1942)–Son of R. Ezekiel of Sianiawa by his fourth wife. In 1898 he became rabbi of Sztrapko and then rebbe. He later settled in Ungvar and Kassa. He married Yehudit, the daughter of R. Abraham Hayyim Horowitz. He was a modest and self-effacing man who would often say to petitioners: "Who am I to intercede for you?"

He was the author of *Divrei Shalom* on Torah and Festivals, which was printed in Miskolc in 1944, with a second edition printed by his grandson in Jerusalem in 1955.

His son, R. Menahem Mendel, succeeded him.

HALBERSTAM, Avigdor Tzvi, of Zanz/Bardiev (1884–1943)–Eldest son of R. Yehiel Nathan, rabbi of Bardiev, he married his cousin, the daughter of R. Aryeh Leibish of Grybov. He succeeded his father as rabbi of Old Zanz, and when his father died, he succeeded him in Bardiev. At the beginning of the Second World War, he lived in Zanz and then in the ghetto of Piekiely. All of the inhabitants of the ghetto were deported to Belzec, where they perished.

HALBERSTAM, Barukh, of Gorlice (1829–1 *Adar* 1906)–Fifth son of R. Hayyim of Zanz, he married Pessel, the daughter of R. Yekutiel Judah Teitelbaum of Sighet, in 1848. In 1856 he became rabbi of Gorlice and then Rudnik. He corresponded with his father on halakhic matters, and he is quoted four times in *Divrei Hayyim*.

When mass immigration to the United States began in 1881, he planned to be among the emigrants but was discouraged by his brother, R. Ezekiel. He opposed the Zionist movement. He rarely delivered discourses. He published his father's works.

He had five sons and three daughters. He was succeeded by his son R. Moses.

HALBERSTAM, Benzion, of Bobov (10 *Iyyar* 1874–4 *Av* 1941) – The only son of R. Shlomoh, he was born in Bokovsk. He married Tirzah, the daughter of R. Naftali Horowitz of Mielec, and when the marriage ended in divorce, he married, in 1899, Hayyah Fradel, the daughter of R. Shalom Eliezer Halberstam. They had four sons and seven daughters. While his father was rebbe in Vishnitz, he acted as the head of the *yeshivah*, and when they moved to Bobov, he became the junior rabbi of the town. He succeeded his father in 1905, and during World War I took refuge in Vienna and Marienbad. In 1919 he lived for a time in Cracow, where he established a *yeshivah*, *Etz Hayyim*. Two years later he returned to Bobov and established a network of sixty *yeshivot* throughout Galicia.

A melodious singer as well as a noted scholar, he combined the erudition of Zanz with the music of Ropczyce. Simple folk melodies became the vehicle for awesome concepts. He was renowned for his musical creativity, and hasidim flocked to listen to the compositions of this untutored genius.

Apart from establishing *yeshivot*, he set up a special organization called *Tomhei Oraita* (supporters of learning), which cared for the material needs of the students. He was one of the first hasidic rabbis to pay special attention to the young, whom he treated with tenderness and consideration. He urged his followers to live in harmony and to avoid controversy and dissension. He urged them to refrain from talking during prayers and during the reading of the Law. He also advised them to always avail themselves of the best medical treatment available.

He strongly objected to the establishment of the Hebrew University in Jerusalem in 1925 and was against the introduction of modern Hebrew in schools. He was against the placing of the *bimah* near the ark.

He participated in communal affairs, often intervening successfully with government departments on behalf of his followers. When on February 7, 1936 a bill of so-called "humane slaughter" was introduced into the Polish Seym, requiring among other things that animals be stunned before slaughter – a measure designed to outlaw *shehitah* – he participated in a meeting of 300 rabbis held in Warsaw, at which "a fortnight without meat" was proclaimed. From March 14 to March 30, Jews were required to refrain from eating meat, even on the Sabbath. Yielding to pressure from the Jewish community, the government rescinded the bill.

When on October 28, 1938, 15,000 Polish Jews were kept as virtual prisoners in a camp at Zbanszyn on the Polish-German border, the rebbe of Bobov supported the organization of relief measures. "We must be mindful of the plight of those of our brethren who have been expelled from their native soil."

His charity was legendary. He was particularly concerned with the plight of orphans.

At the outbreak of World War Two, on 14 *Elul* (September 1,) 1939, he escaped first to Tarnov and then to Lvov. He and his younger son, R. Moses Aaron, together with his three sons-in-law – Ezekiel Shragai Halberstam, Moses Stempel of Cracow, and Shlomoh Rubin – were murdered in Lvov on 4 *Av* (July 25) 1941.

His discourses in *Kedushat Zion*, Part One on Torah, were published in Brooklyn in 1967; Part Two on Bible and Talmud, in New York in 1976. His son R. Shlomoh succeeded him as the rabbi of Bobov.

A. Surasky, *Marbitzei Torah U'Musar M'Olam HaHasidut*, vol. 5, pp. 71–133.

HALBERSTAM, David, of Cieszanov (1818–25 *Elul* 1893) – Third son of R. Hayyim, he was born in Rudnik. He became rabbi in Cieszanov in 1851. At the death of his father, he became rebbe. He married Echse Gitel, the daughter of R. Joseph Zeev of Tarnogrod. She died after giving birth to their second child. He then married Leah Zissel Zinz.

He corresponded with his contemporaries, and R. Yitzhak Shmelkes quotes him in his works.

He had four sons and five daughters. His son R. Naftali succeeded him.

HALBERSTAM, Hayyim, of Czechov/New York (1882–17 *Nisan* 1956) – Born in Belz, the only son of R. Yitzhak Yeshayahu of Czechov, he was brought up in the home of his grandfather R. Issachar Rokeah of Belz. In 1899, he married Mirrel, daughter of R. Menasseh Merilles, the rabbi of Ropczyce and Dubienka.

In 1924, he settled in New York and was active in the establishment of *mikvaot*. He participated in the work of the rabbinical association. Both of his sons, R. David Joshua of Sosnowiec and R. Shimon of Ropczyce, and their families perished in the Holocaust.

HALBERSTAM, Hayyim, of Nowy Zanz (17 *Iyyar* 1797–25 *Nisan* 1876) – Son of R. Aryeh Leibish, a descendant of R. Solomon Luria and R. Tzvi Hirsch Ashkenazi, he was born in either Tarnogrod or Brody. He was educated by his father and by R. Joseph Horowitz and R. Moses Joshua Heschel Orenstein and was known as the *Illui* of Tarnogrod. He was a delicate child with a deformed leg, which caused him constant pain. His memory, however, was phenomenal, and his zeal to learn and to absorb was boundless.

It was his teacher R. Joseph Horowitz who influenced the young Hayyim to visit his brother, R. Jacob Isaac the "Seer" of Lublin. The "Seer" was very much taken with Hayyim. He endearingly called him "my Hayyimel," and he predicted that he would be the leader of his generation.

At the age of seventeen, he married Feige Rachel, the daughter of R. Barukh Teumim Frankel of Leipnik, Moravia. "*Er hat a krimmen fees*" (He has a deformed leg), protested the bride. "Yes," replied her father, "*a krummen fees ober a groisen kop*" (a deformed leg but a brilliant mind). After the marriage, he stayed on and studied with his father-in-law in Leipnik for one year, eventually being ordained by him. He also received ordination from R. Jacob of Lissa.

In 1817 he became rabbi in Rudnik, near Rzeszov, in Galicia, a town where many hasidim of Ropczyce lived. R. Hayyim became a follower of R. Naftali of Ropczyce. He also visited a number of hasidic rabbis, among them R. Meir of Opatov, R. Tzvi Hirsch of Zydaczov, R. Israel of Ruzhyn, and R. Shalom Rokeah of Belz. To supplement his meager income, his wife had a concession to sell salt.

From the rabbi of Ropczyce R. Hayyim acquired an appreciation of song and melody. "Through music," he maintained, "one can unlock all heavenly gates." After a short stay at Zalin and Kalev (Nagy-Kallo), R. Hayyim, in 1830, succeeded R. Berish Moses David Landau as the rabbi of Zanz (Nowy Cacz). The hasidim spelled Cacz with a Z to indicate that a *tzaddik*, a righteous person, resides there.

The three main principles he adopted and taught throughout his life were (1) that Hasidism and scholarship were complementary and that a synthesis of both was essential, (2) that extreme generosity and self-sacrifice in order to alleviate poverty were vital to religious conduct, and (3) that sincerity in prayer combined with song and dance stimulate religious fervor.

He was the principal and founder of a *yeshivah*, and under his influence Zanz became a focal point of Hasidism and a fortress of learning. He attracted many scholars who were anxious to imbibe his knowledge and his spirit of saintliness. As an acknowledged authority on halakhic problems and because of his great insight into human nature, his decisions, often based also on the book of the *Zohar*, were widely accepted. Though humble in his personal demeanor, he was unswerving in his decisions. He possessed a remarkable sense of humor, which gave rise to many of the hasidic witticisms still quoted to this very day. In Zanz the *Shulhan Arukh* ruled supreme, and every one of his actions was based strictly on the Codes. He was loath to allow the omission of *Tahanun* on a *yahrzeit*. He did not allow the gabbling of the massed *Kaddish* in the synagogue. *Piyyutim* were regularly recited, and he was meticulous with his prayer text.

Charity was practiced in Zanz in an unprecedented manner. His followers showered on him *pidyonot* and *maamadot*, but the rabbi gave everything away.

"I love the poor," he would say, "for God loves them too." Perhaps it was because the royal life-style of the Sadgora dynasty was so alien to him that he fought so violently against the Hasidism and the rabbi of Sadgora. It became one of the great internal controversies in the life of the hasidim. He publicly deprecated the acquisition and display of wealth as well as the deviation from traditional dress by the dynasty of Sadgora. The rift between them developed to an extent that even in the Holy Land the followers of Sadgora were accused by the hasidim of Zanz as being the disciples of Shabbatai Tzvi, the false Messiah. It was not until after R. Hayyim's death that there was a reconciliation between the two hasidic sects.

When the "Light of Exile," as R. Hayyim was called, stood in prayer, light seemed to radiate from him. He forgot the world around him; he even forgot the pain in his leg, stamping it until it bled, as he poured out his heart before his Father in heaven. He spent almost the whole day in prayer and study, allowing very little time for sleep, especially on the Sabbath. "One must not sleep away the Sabbath," he observed.

In 1864, he published anonymously in Zolkiev his first work in two parts: *Divrei Hayyim* Part One, containing the laws of divorce, with particular stress on the proper spelling of names and towns used in the drafting of the divorce bills, and Part Two, dealing with the laws and tractate of *mikvaot* (ritual baths).

His great work, *Divrei Hayyim*, on the four parts of the *Shulhan Arukh*, consisting of 831 responsa, was printed in Lvov in 1875. There is hardly a halakhic problem that is not dealt with. His responsa reflect the social and religious life of the Jews in the nineteenth century. He was an uncompromising opponent of the growing practices of mechanical production of religious accoutrements, such as *tzizit*, and of the manufacture of *matzot* with the aid of machines he considered *hametz*. The introduction of machine-made *matzot* in the nineteenth century sparked a violent halakhic controversy. It was maintained by detractors, with R. Hayyim among them, that milling by heavy machines caused the wheat to exude a moisture that resulted in fermentation, thus rendering the *matzot* unfit for use.

He also deemed contrary to Jewish law the use of wigs as head covers by women. He also opposed the introduction of a choir into the synagogue service.

In other matters he was more lenient than many of his contemporaries. R. Hayyim found no valid reason why the Cochin chickens, introduced into Europe a little earlier, should not be permitted to be eaten. The custom, based on early kabbalistic thought, that no marriage should be arranged when the prospective mother-in-law and the prospective daughter-in-law bore the same name, was, in his opinion, to be ignored. He had no sympathy for *Haskalah* and ruled that the editions of Maimonides' *Milot HaHigayyon* that contained Moses Mendelssohn's commentary be burned.

In addition to his responsa *Divrei Hayyim*, a commentary on Torah and Festivals on Tractate *Baba Metzia* and published in two parts in Munkacs posthumously in 1877 by his sons, he was the author of *Sefer Darkhei Hayyim*, first published in Lvov in 1831 and reprinted several times; a commentary on the Passover *Haggadah* (Lublin, 1936); *Hiddushei Torah* (Munkacs, 1938); *Mekor Hayyim* (Bilgoraj, 1912); *Totzaot Hayyim* (Podgorze, 1899); *Kol HaKatuv L'Hayyim* (Jerusalem, 1962); and *Nusah HaKorbanot* (Lvov, 1875).

He married four times. When his first wife died, he married her sister. On her death he married Rachel Deborah, the daughter of R. Tzvi Hirsch Unger of Tarnov. His fourth marriage was to the daughter of R. Elimelekh of Gorlice. He had fifteen children—eight sons and seven daughters. Most of his sons established hasidic dynasties.

A. Y. Bromberg, *Migdolei HaHasidut*.

R. Mahler, *Sefer Zanz*.

T. Moskovitz, *Kol HaKatuv LeHayyim on Rabbi Hayyim Halberstam*.

A.S. and Ed.

HALBERSTAM, Hayyim Dov Berish, of Bardiev/New York (1891–1972)—He was the son of R. Shmuel, the rabbi of Bardiev, where he was born. He married Sarah, the daughter of R. Joseph Shapira of Bircza.

He was survived by two sons, R. Tzvi Elimelekh and R. Israel Meir, and one daughter, *Hayyah* Freidah.

HALBERSTAM, Honah, of Kalusz (6 *Tammuz* 1884–18 *Tishri* 1943) Son of R. Menahem Mendel, the rabbi of Frysztak. His mother, Gena Beila, was a daughter of R. Ezekiel Shragai of Sianiawa. R. Hona lived in Kosice for seven years and married Pessel, the daughter of R. Moses Halberstam of Bardiev. In 1923, he settled in Rzeszov, where he established a *yeshivah*, *Zera Kodesh*.

He was nonpolitical. He did not even participate in the activities of the Aguda. He was a great collector of funds for the poor of the Holy Land. "I am not afraid of anything," he used to say, "not even of an angel. I am only afraid to see a poor Jew."

At the outbreak of the Second World War, he escaped to Frysztak. His sons were killed in his presence. After hiding for many months in a bunker in a potato field outside Jaslo, he was arrested and imprisoned in Jaslo. He was shot together with his wife.

He was the author of *Binah VeDaat* (Cracow, 1927) and *Divrei Honah* (New York, 1952).

HALBERSTAM, Jacob, of Szczakowa/New York (1902–3 *Heshvan* 1967) – Son of R. Sinai, the rabbi of Zemigrod Nowy, and a grandson of R. Hayyim of Zanz, he studied in Ungvar and was ordained by R. Meir Arak. He married Edel Hannah, the daughter of R. Shalom Moskovitz. He stayed with his father-in-law in Tarnov and in Cologne. In 1923, he became rabbi of Szczakowa. In 1935, he settled in Jerusalem, where he established a *yeshivah*, *Divrei Hayyim*.

At the outbreak of the Second World War, he went to the United States to raise funds for the *yeshivah* and remained there. After the war, he established a synagogue *Tiferet Yaakov* on the East Side of New York.

He had four daughters and four sons: R. Meir of Kiryat Zanz; R. Naftali of Jerusalem; R. Moses, the head of *Divrei Hayyim*, Jerusalem; and R. Haham Tzvi of Bene Berak.

He was the author of *Tefillah*, a prayer in Yiddish, to be recited by a sick person. It was printed in New York in 1951.

Panim el Panim, November 17, 1967.

HALBERSTAM, Joshua, of Dolina (1878–1943) – Son of R. Moses of Bardiev, he married Rebecca, the only daughter of R. Yehudah Tzvi Hirsch Eichenstein, the rabbi of Dolina. After the death of his father-in-law in 1909, he succeeded him as rabbi. During World War I he lived in Hungary, and in 1922, he returned to Dolina.

At the outbreak of the Second World War, he tried to smuggle his family into Hungary, but they were murdered by the Nazis at the frontier. None of his family survived.

HALBERSTAM, Menahem Binyamin Benzion, of Wodzislav/Brooklyn (1881–22 *Nisan* 1957) – The son of R. Aaron, the rabbi of Biala Bielsk, he was brought up by his grandfather and also by R. Hirsch Leib of Wolbrum. He had a phenomenal memory. He knew by heart the works of the German talmudist R. Meir Schiff. In 1899, he married Berakhah, the daughter of R. Mordecai Zeev Halevi Sternfeld-Horowitz, who was the rabbi of Bielsk.

In 1903, after the death of his wife, he married Henne Rachel, the daughter of R. Abraham Hayyim Reuben Rothenberg of Wodzislav. He was a devoted follower of Belz and also of R. Meir Shalom of Kaluszyn. In 1922, he settled in Brooklyn and became one of the leaders of the Aguda and of the rabbinical association. He left many manuscripts, which remain unpublished.

He had four sons and three daughters.

HALBERSTAM, Menahem Mendel, of Sztrapko (1873–6 *Iyyar* 1954) – Son of Abraham Shalom of Sztrapko, he was ordained by R. Shmuel Engel. He married Esther, the daughter of R. Jacob Kopul Parnes, and they had eight children – four sons and four daughters. He was the head of the *yeshivah* and the rabbi of Sztrapko while his father was still alive. After his father's death, he succeeded him as rebbe.

During the Second World War he lived in Budapest and later in Bratislava. One *seder* night, he was able to escape to Switzerland. He settled in Brooklyn in 1947, and Israel Zupnik established for him a *Bet HaMidrash*, *Divrei Yehezkel*. He was the author of *Divrei Menahem*, which was published in Jerusalem in 1957. He was buried on *Har HaMenuhot* in Jerusalem.

His son R. Ezekiel Shragai Lipshitz Halberstam succeeded him. A *kollel* and *yeshivah*, *Divrei Menahem* was established in his memory in Meah Shearim in Jerusalem.

HALBERSTAM, Moses, of Sianiawa (1843–12 *Heshvan* 1919) – Son of R. Ezekiel Shragai of Sianiawa, his mother died when he was very young, and he was brought up by his uncle R. Moses Unger. He married the daughter of R. Meir Tzvi Hirsch

Tennenebaum of Brzesko. He was ailing most of his life and spent lengthy periods of hospitalization in Vienna. Until 1912, he was rabbi in Sianiawa.

He participated in the rabbinical conferences in Cracow in 1903 and Sandowa-Wisznia Miasto, as well as in the rabbinical conference in Vienna at which the Austrian government wished the rabbis to oppose the Balfour Declaration.

He had seven daughters and one son, R. Aryeh Leibish Mordecai, who succeeded him in Sianiawa.

HALBERSTAM, Naftali, of Grybov/New York (b.1926) – Son of R. Barukh of Grybov who miraculously survived the Holocaust and reached New York in the middle of the war. He studied and was ordained at the Lubavitch *yeshivah* in New York.

In 1950, he became the proprietor of a printing press *Hadar* and the publishing house *Menorah*. He is the rebbe of Grybov and Zanz in Brooklyn. He has nine sons and four daughters.

HALBERSTAM, Shalom Eliezer, of Ujfeherto (1862–16 *Sivan* 1944) – Son of R. Hayyim of Zanz, he was born on *Hol HaMo'ed* Passover when his father was sixty-five years old, and fourteen when his father died. He was brought up by his brothers. In 1876 he married Miriam Sarah, the daughter of R. Mordecai David Twersky of Hornistopol, where he lived for ten years after the marriage. He then lived for a time with his brother in Sieniawa and in Tarnov. In 1898, on the death of R. Naftali Hirtzke Zilberman, he succeeded him as rabbi of Ujfeherto.

His Friday night *Tish* lasted until dawn. At the conclusion of the first session he conducted a second session, at which he told hasidic tales as was customary in Zanz. He had four daughters and two sons. His son R. Hayyim was *dayan* in Satmar, and his second son, R. Meshullam Zusya, was *dayan* in Ujfeherto. Dressed in *kittels*, he and his son R. Meshullam Zusya were murdered by the Nazis in Auschwitz.

HALBERSTAM, Simhah Issachar Baer, of Cieszanov (1870–20 *Tevet* 1914) – Son of R. Ezekiel Shragai of Sianiawa, he was born in Sztropkov. In 1886 he married Frieda, the daughter of R. Yehoshua Rokeah of Belz. He was the author of *Divrei Simhah* – discourses on Pentateuch and Festivals – which was published in two parts in Cracow in 1932 and reprinted in New York in 1960.

He was an outspoken opponent of Zionism and of the Mizrachi. He participated in the rabbinical conference that was held in Sandowa-Wisznia Miasto. The rabbis who followed him were R. Izzikel Gewirczman of Przeworsk-Antwerp and R. Shalom Noah Landau. He was succeeded in Cieszanov by his son-in-law, R. Aryeh Leibish Rubin. His son, R. Yehezkel Shragai, was the last rebbe there.

HALBERSTAM, Solomon, of Bobov (1847–2 *Tammuz* 1905) – Son of R. Meir Nathan and a grandson of R. Hayyim Halberstam, his mother, Beila, was the daughter of R. Eliezer of Dzikov. His father died when he was eight years old, and he was brought up by his grandfathers, the rebbes of Zanz and Dzikov. He helped his grandfather, R. Hayyim, prepare his responsa, *Divrei Hayyim*, for the press.

In 1861 he married Rivkah Henieh, the daughter of R. Joshua Halevi Rosenfeld of Kamenka, and after living in Kamenka for two years, he returned to Zanz. He became rabbi first in Bokovsk, where he stayed ten years, then in Auschwitz, and later, in 1880, in Vishnitz, where he stayed for fourteen years. He established a *yeshivah*, and among his disciples were R. Bezalel Isaiah Bornstein, later of Jerusalem; R. Mordecai Rothenberg, later of Antwerp; R. Dov Berish Meisels, later of Ujhely; and R. Eliezer David Grunwald, later of Satmar.

He was against secular education, and was, together with R. Joshua Rokeah of Belz, part of a delegation on behalf of the *Mahzikei Hadas* to the minister of education of Austria, urging upon him to rescind the rule that rabbis should receive a secular education. He similarly opposed secular education that was being introduced in Jewish orphanages in Galicia. In *Elul* 1889, he met the Emperor Franz Joseph in Bochnia.

His entire library and all his manuscripts were burned in a fire on 25 *Tishri* 1889.

He suffered ill health and regularly visited the spas in Austria and Germany. He died at the age of fifty-eight in a spa in Germany and was buried in Bobov. His grave was restored in 1945.

He was survived by a daughter, *Hayyah*, who married R. Hayyim Jacob Teitelbaum of Limanov, and by a son, R. Benzion, who succeeded him. Some of his discourses are to be found in *Kedushat Tziyyon*, published by his son.

A. Surasky, *Marbitzei Torah U'Mussar M'Olam HaHasidut*, vol. 2, pp. 111–156.

HALBERSTAM, Solomon, of Bobov/Brooklyn (b. *Rosh Hodesh Kislev* 1908) – Son of R. Benzion, he was born in Bobov. He studied under his father and under R. Hayyim Hakohen Friedman of Frysztak. He was ordained by R. Samuel Fuhrer and R. Yehiel Nebenzahl of Stanislav. At the age of eighteen he married his cousin, Bluma Rachel, daughter of R. Hayyim Jacob Teitelbaum of Leminova. From 1931, while his father was away in Trzebinia for five years, R. Solomon was acting rabbi in Bobov and principal of the *yeshivah Etz Hayyim*.

At the outbreak of World War Two he lived with his parents in Lvov, which was under Russian domination. After the German invasion of Russia, R. Solomon and his family returned to Bobov. He was soon confined to the labor camp of Bochnia near Cracow. He escaped the massive Nazi purges and organized an underground escape route that enabled many people to get away to Hungary and to Czechoslovakia. His wife and two of their children were caught by the Gestapo and were taken to Auschwitz, where they were murdered in 1944. His Hungarian citizenship stood him in good stead as he was permitted to return to Bochnia. He, his mother, and his son Naftali Tzvi then escaped to Grosswardein and later to Romania.

After the war he made his way to Italy and then to New York, where he first settled in Crown Heights and then, in 1967, in Borough Park, Brooklyn. In 1947 he married his second wife, Freidel, daughter of R. Aryeh Leib Rubin of Cieszanov, by whom he had five daughters and one son. He founded a network of educational establishments, from elementary schools to *kollelim*. His *yeshivah* in Borough Park is one of the largest in New York. He did not hesitate to break new ground by introducing a scheme where courses leading to jobs in industry are taught in *yeshivah* trade schools.

At one time he planned to build a $20-million-dollar housing project for 200 families on Parsons Boulevard, in Queens, New York, but because of opposition by local residents, the scheme was abandoned.

In 1959 he laid the foundations of *Kiryat Bobov* in Bat Yam, where a magnificent *yeshivah*, *Kedushat Zion*, and a synagogue, *Bet Yehoshua*, the gift of the rebbe's brother-in-law, Osias Freshwater, were opened in 1963. A Bobov *yeshivah* was also established in London in 1966, and there are Bobov *shtieblech* in Bene Berak, Jerusalem, Antwerp, Toronto, and Montreal.

His discourses are to be found in the monthly periodical *Shaarei Zion* (New York, 1960), *Etz Hayyim* (New York, 1965), and *Kerem Shlomoh* (New York, 1978).

HALBERSTAM, Tzvi Hirsch, of Rudnik (1851–15 *Av* 1918) – Son of R. Barukh of Gorlice, he studied in Sighet under his grandfather who ordained him. In 1865 he married the daughter of R. Yisrael Horowitz of Baranov. For ten years he was rabbi of Nisko, and in 1887 he became *dayan* in Rudnik. He was always known as the "rabbi of Nisko." In 1902, after his wife died, he married *Hayyah* Mindel, the daughter of R. Meir Meshullam Shapira of Lancut.

During the First World War he lived in Hungary and in Kleinwardein, where he lost all his manuscripts.

He died in Vienna and was buried in Gorlice next to his father. None of the children of his first marriage survived. He was succeeded by his son from his second marriage, R. Yekutiel Yehudah.

HALBERSTAM, Yehezkel Shragai, of Cieszanov (1901–3 *Shevat* 1942) – Only son of R. Simhah Issachar Dov of Cieszanov, who died in 1914, before his son's *bar mitzvah*. During the First World War Yehezkel Shragai lived with his uncle in Belz and in Munkacs. In 1917 he married Rosa Bluma, the daughter of R. Tzvi Hayyim Teitelbaum, in whose house he lived for six years following the marriage. In 1923 he became rebbe in Tarnov. He was befriended by R. Meir Arik.

During the Second World War he lived in Belz, Munkacs, and Zborov, and to escape the Nazis, he lived for a time in Lubaczov. He, his wife, his children, and his son-in-law were taken by the Nazis to a village–Dachanov, near Cieszanov–where they were murdered.

HALBERSTAM, Yehezkel Shragai, of Sianiawa (1815-6 *Tevet* 1898)–Elder son of R. Hayyim, he was born in Tarnogrod. He studied under R. Moses Teitelbaum and under R. Tzvi Hirsch Eichenstein. At an early age he married Tauba, the daughter of R. Aryeh Leib Lipshitz of Ujhely. Within a few years of his marriage, his wife died and he was left with an infant son, Naftali. He then, in 1833, married his first wife's niece, Dreizel, the granddaughter of R. Teitelbaum. His second wife died without issue. His third wife was Breindel, the widowed daughter of R. Tzvi Hirsch Eichenstein of Rozdol.

He was a man of strong physique whose presence immediately created respect. He was utterly fearless and forthright in speech but gave advice and practical help with sympathy and understanding. He was venerated for his vigour, his subtlety of mind, and, above all, his love and pursuit of truth. Already early in life he showed the qualities of intellect, diligence, and utter dedication that characterized him throughout his life.

His father took him on visits to various contemporary rebbes: to R. Naftali Horowitz of Ropczyce, R. Tzvi Hirsch of Rymanov, and R. Shalom of Belz. He lived in Ujhely for ten years, and then, at the age of thirty-four, began his rabbinical career in Rudnik, moving in 1849 to Rozdol. In 1856 he established himself in Sianiawa, where he founded a *yeshivah*. In 1868 he succeeded R. Hayyim Joseph Gotlieb as rabbi of Sztrapko, and after his father's death in 1876, he lived in Zanz for a year, before finally returning to Sianiawa, where he lived until his death and became known as the "Shinaver Rav." He became rebbe in his father's lifetime.

He visited the Holy Land in 1869. He was anxious to visit the grave of R. Shimon Bar Yohai on Lag BaOmer but refrained after being told that the highlight of the occasion was a bonfire (*hadlakah*), which was fueled by usable garments. Such unnecessary waste was repugnant to him. Nor did he visit the grave of R. Meir Baal HaNess in Tiberias, because men and women were not segregated there. He established a *Zanzer klaus* in Safed, which is still in existence today. To the end of his life he was a great supporter of the Old Yishuv.

In the Holy Land he acquired a number of manuscripts he subsequently published: *Sefer HaGilgulim*, by R. Hayyim Vital (Przemysl, 1875), and the works of R. Mordecai Azulai, *Or HaHamah*, commentary on the *Zohar*, of which the parts on Genesis, Exodus, and Leviticus were edited by R. Yitzhak Boehm in collaboration with Shneur Zalman Schneersohn and printed in Jerusalem between 1876 and 1879. A smaller work by the same author, edited by R. Boehm, *Mahzei Avraham*, was printed in Jerusalem in 1880. In his old age he saw the same works through the press for a second time, adding to them volumes containing the commentaries on the *Zohar*, Numbers, and Deuteronomy (Podgorze, 1896–1898). He eagerly inspired others to publish neglected manuscripts, such as the commentary to *Tohorot*, *Mishnah Aharonah* (Przemysl, 1882).

"The rebbe of Sianiawa," hasidim used to say, "knows every letter of the *Shulhan Arukh* by heart. The *Shulhan Arukh* is part of his very being." The rebbe was uncompromising and unbending regarding the minutiae of the Law. He maintained throughout his life that "whoever contravenes one of the laws of the *Shulhan Arukh* inherits *Gehinnom*." He was an acknowledged Gaon, dispensing *halakhah* with an independent mind. Many a time his views differed even from his father's, and this caused some erudite and occasionally heated disputes between father and son. His father lovingly referred to him as *Ish HaEmet*, and it was a fact that nothing could move him when attempts were made to tamper with the truth. When, by means of a *shtar mehirah* (bill of sale), his father permitted gentiles to work in a Jewish concern on a Sabbath, he strongly opposed it. Whereas his father interpreted the Law leniently, he took a more stringent attitude. Nor did he support his father in his controversy with the rebbe of Sadgora, which lasted for seven years.

He was reluctant to deliver discourses, and it was only after his father's death that he began to expound his views. His work *Divrei Yehezkel*, containing comments on the Torah and Festivals, was printed in Podgorze in 1901 and has since been reprinted eight times. It is one of the great classics of Hasidism. It is based on the notes taken by one of his hasidim, R. Akiva HaKohen Lieber of Yasienice. Though his responsa have never been collected and printed in a single volume, thirteen of his letters are printed in *Divrei Yehezkel*, and others are to be found in his father's work *Divrei Hayyim*; in the responsa *Tosafot Re'em* (Zolkiev, 1856), by R. Aaron Moses of Jassy; and the works of R. Shmuel Engel.

R. Yehezkel was not only a rebbe for his hasidim but was also involved in the management of communal matters. He fought innovations introduced by the *maskilim*. In a letter to the hasidim of Klasno in 1886, he urged them not to allow the opening of a "reading room," where people would be able to read newspapers. He strongly objected to *Kohanim* (priests) visiting the graves of *tzaddikim*. He would not permit a *mitzvah tenzel* (a handkerchief dance with a bride).

Among his great disciples were R. Shmuel Engel of Radomysl and R. Yehiel Halstock of Ostrowiece. Leading Hungarian heads of *yeshivot* like the Unsdorfer rabbi used to advise their pupils to visit Sianiawa and not to miss listening to the rabbi's daybreak recitation of Psalms. To those who listened to him it remained an unforgettable experience. Every day he would recite *tahanun* even on the *yahrzeit* of a *tzaddik*. He was against rabbis' studying secular subjects, and he was equally opposed to any changes in the traditional manner of dress, especially for women. He opposed the modern *yishuv* and wrote critical letters against the Zionist movement. However, he supported the *Mahzikei HaDat* and Joseph Shmuel Bloch (1850–1923), who was elected to the Austrian parliament in 1881, 1885, and 1888.

He left five daughters and four sons, of whom three, in due course, became leaders of hasidim. His eldest son, R. Naftali, was the exception, who died at the age of twenty-six in Cherkasy on 21 *Kislev* 1864. R. Naftali's literary legacy was edited by his father under the title *Ayalah Sheluhah* (Przemysl, 1895). His son, R. Moses, succeeded him in Sianiawa, and later settled in Zanz.

A. Y. Bromberg, *Migdolei HaHasidut*, vol. 9, *Admorei LeBet Zanz*, pp. 9–85.

A.S. and Ed.

HALBERSTAM, Yekutiel Judah, of Klausenburg/New York (1904–10 *Tammuz* 1994) – The son of R. Tzvi Hirsch, he was born in Rudnik. When his father died in Kleinwardein at the age of forty-four, the fourteen-year-old Yekutiel Judah delivered the eulogy. He was brought up by his great-uncle, R. Shalom Eliezer of Ujfeherto. He studied under R. David Tzvi Zehman. He was ordained by R. Yehiel Meir Halstock of Ostrowiece, R. Samuel Engel, and R. Meir Arik. He married Hannah, the daughter of R. Hayyim Tzvi Teitelbaum of Sighet, in 1921. After living with his father-in-law for five years, he accepted the position of rabbi of the hasidic community of Klausenburg (Cluj). He was firm and uncompromising when it came to challenging the nascent reform community of Klausenburg.

After the Nazi occupation of Romania in 1940, anti-Jewish measures were imposed, and in 1944 the Jews of Cluj were confined to a ghetto. He himself was interned in a number of labor camps in Hungary and transferred to the ghetto of Nagy Banya. For a time he was forced to work in the ruins of the Warsaw Ghetto, and in 1944 he was taken to Auschwitz, where his wife and his ten children were murdered and the eleventh child died of typhus.

He was interned in the camps of Mildorf and Feldafing, Germany. Immediately after the liberation, he traveled from camp to camp, nourishing the broken shards of humanity with the teachings of their fathers. He established kosher kitchens, *yeshivot*, and religious schools for girls. Working in the Friedenwald displaced persons' camp, he soon gained wide reputation as a wonder rabbi.

In order to mobilize the conscience of Jewry, he traveled to the United States and in 1947 settled in the Williamsburg section of Brooklyn. Later he moved to Union City, New Jersey, founding the *yeshivah She'erit HaPletah*, branches of which were soon established in Montreal and Mexico.

Shortly after his arrival in New York, he married *Hayyah* Nehamah, daughter of R. Samuel David Halevi Unger, formerly of Nitra. They had two daughters and five sons. He was one of the very few rabbis to work with Dr. Nahum Goldman to establish the Conference on Material Claims Against Germany in 1951.

In 1954 he visited Israel and met David Ben-Gurion. His travels finally led him to Netanya, where he acquired three hundred dunam of land on which he established *Kiryat Zanz*. The foundation stone was laid on March 4, 1956. A year later the rabbi arrived in Israel with a Scroll of the Law and a nucleus of fifty American immigrants. Under his expert direction, his dream was rapidly translated into reality. The most impressive building in the *kiryah* is the Great Synagogue, and its centerpiece is a three-hundred-year-old Italian ark.

In the *kiryah* diverse Torah institutions cater for every age. There is a Talmud Torah, a *yeshivah ketanah*, and a main *yeshivah*, as well as a *kollel*. As he was particularly concerned with the status of Israel's Yemenite and North African citizens and became incensed when he heard of discrimination and intolerance toward them, he established an orphanage for Sephardic children and a synagogue where they could follow their own traditional liturgy. The most interesting building in the settlement is the Laniado Hospital, the first religious hospital to be built. His life in Israel was not devoid of problems, technical as well as spiritual.

Encouraged by the success of the *kiryah*, the rebbe established a *shikkun* of fifty dunam to the northwest of Jerusalem, near *Shikkun Habad* at Tel Arza. Other Zanz groups in Israel are to be found in Bene Berak, Petah Tikvah, Tiberias, and Safed, and a large tract of land has been acquired in Beer Sheva.

The rabbi did not believe in courting publicity. Owing to ill health, he lived in Kiryat Zanz, but maintained close links with his followers in New York.

He followed the traditions of R. Hayyim Halberstam of Zanz, who published very little during his life but wrote many responsa and discourses. A number of R. Yekutiel Judah's discourses are to be found in *Divrei Torah* (Bene Berak, 1956), *Daat Torah* (Brooklyn, 1957), *Kovetz Iggrot Kodesh* (Bene Berak, 1958), the monthly *Yisrael Saba*, published by the *kiryah* in 1962, and *Yehudit* (Brooklyn, 1964).

His son, R. Tzvi Elimelech, succeeded him as rebbe of *Kiryat Zanz*, and the other son, R. Shmuel David, is rebbe in Union City, New Jersey. His daughters married R. Shlomoh Goldman, head of the *yeshivah* of Zanz in Union City; R. Dov Weiss, rabbi of Zanz in Jerusalem; R. Efraim Fishel Mutzan, rabbi in Monsey; R. Saul Yehudah Prizent; and R. Eliezer David Shapira.

HALBERSTAM, Yitzhak Isaiah, of Czechov (1864–3 *Elul* 1943)–The youngest son of R. Hayyim of Zanz, he was twelve years old when his father died. He was brought up by his brothers, R. David and R. Barukh of Gorlice. He first married Freide, the daughter of R. Yehiel Heschel, the rabbi of Krylowitz, but his wife died very young, leaving him with one son and two daughters. He remarried Esther, the widowed daughter of R. Jacob Tzvi of Parysov. He was appointed rabbi of Czechov at the age of nineteen.

He was renowned for his acts of charity, and on Purim he refused to read the *Megillah* until a large sum was collected for distribution to the poor. Like his father, he forbade the use of machine-made *matzot* as late as 1930. At the beginning of 1940 he lived in Lvov and urged everyone to escape to the villages and not to remain in the ghetto. The Nazis imprisoned him in Bochnia, where he, three daughters, and two of his sons were murdered. His son R. Hayyim is the rebbe of Czechov in New York.

HALBERSTAM-LIPSHITZ, Ezekiel Shragai, of Jerusalem (4 *Nisan* 1907–6 *Kislev* 1994)–Son of R. Issachar Dov Lipshitz, he was born in Sztrapko. He was brought up in Ungvar, Hungary, and studied under R. Abraham Joseph Grunwald and R. Joseph Elimelech Kahana. In 1930 he married his cousin, Miriam Leah, the daughter of his uncle, R. Yitzhak Reuben Lipshitz. Before the Second World War he was rabbi in Jablonka Nizna and later *dayan* in Bergszasz.

During the war he stayed in Ungvar. From there he and his family were deported to Auschwitz, where he miraculously survived, but his wife and children perished.

After the liberation he was a rabbi in Bamberg and Frankonia, and he helped the rabbis of Munich with the rehabilitation of the survivors. In 1949 he settled in Ramla, and in 1953 he moved to Jerusalem. He succeeded his uncle, R. Menachem Mendel Halberstam, and was known as the rebbe of Sztrapko. He established educational institutions in Meah Shearim, Jerusalem, and was a member of the *Sefardi Bet Din* of the *Edah Haharedit*.

After the Second World War, in Budapest, he married Miriam Taba, the daughter of R.

Yehiel Michal Schlager, and they had five children—four daughters and one son. R. Abraham Shalom Issachar Dov succeeded him.

He was a prolific author. In 1944 he published in Miskolc his grandfather's book *Divrei Shalom*. In 1948 he brought out in Bamberg his book *Taharat HaMishpahah*. He also published *Divrei Yehezkel Shragai* (Jerusalem, 1956), a commentary on the Passover *Haggadah* (1957), and *Divrei Yehezkel Shragai* on the laws of *Shemittah* (Jerusalem, 1959).

HALPERN, Alexander Samuel, of Lvov (22 *Kislev* 1828–26 *Tevet* 1904)—Born in Brody, he was the son of R. Pinhas David. He studied under R. Meshullam Yissachar Horowitz of Stanislav and became attracted to Hasidism under the influence of R. Meir of Przemyslany. In 1848, after marrying Esther Beila, the daughter of R. Eliezer Zeev Yaar of Brody, he became the rabbi of Galigor, Galicia, until he became rabbi of Lvov in 1886. He was the author of *Rosh HaMizbeah* (Lvov, 1883) on the tractate *Zevahim* and responsa *She'elot U'Teshuvot Maharash* (Lvov, 1896).

He had one daughter, Leah, and two sons, R. Hayyim Jonah, rabbi of Rzeszov, and R. Mordecai.

A.Shu.

HALPERN, David, of Ostrog (d. 16 *Tammuz* 1765)—Son of R. Israel Harif of Ostrog, he was one of the earliest followers of the Besht. He is mentioned in *Degel Mahanei Efraim* and *Shivhei HaBesht*. In 1737 he became rabbi in Ostrog, and later in Zaslav.

He wrote an ethical will, *Darkhei Zion*, which was printed in Polonnoye in 1796, an edition no longer extant. It was reprinted in Bartfeld in 1899.

He was extremely wealthy. He left his estate to the poor and to a number of hasidic rabbis: R. Dov Baer of Mezhirech, R. Yehiel Michael of Zloczov, and R. Menahem Mendel of Przemyslany.

HALPERN, Elhanan, of London (b. 1922)—Born in Kosice, the son of R. David, the rabbi of Drohobycz. In 1939 "R. Hune," as he is generally known, came to London and in 1942 married Henau *Hayyah* Lidzbarsky. He is one of the founders of Pardes House School in London and honorary president of the Union of Orthodox Hebrew Congregations.

He himself has written extensively for the rabbinical annual *Yagdil Torah* and has reprinted the responsa of R. Samuel Engel.

He has nine children. Two of his sons have established their own *batei midrash* within walking distance of his *Bet HaMidrash*, R. David in Brent Street, Hendon, and R. Hayyim in Bridge Lane, Golders Green, London. One of his daughters, Nehamah Miriam, married R. Menahem Nahum Twersky of Bene Berak.

HALPERN, Hayyim Dov, of Vaslui (1876–22 *Sivan* 1957)—Son of R. Shalom of Vaslui, he married the daughter of R. David Safrin. He succeeded his father as rebbe in 1940. During the Second World War he lived in Bucharest, and in 1950 he settled in Haifa. He was buried in Tiberias and was succeeded by his son, Jacob Joseph Shlomoh.

HALPERN, Issachar Dov Berish, of Biecz (1889–29 *Iyyar* 1986)—Son of R. Hayyim Yonah, he was born in Rzeszov. He studied under R. Nathan Levin and was ordained by R. Meir Arak and R. David Horowitz of Stanislav. He married Deborah, the daughter of R. Aaron Horowitz of Biecz. When his father-in-law moved to Kosice, he succeeded him as rabbi of Biecz.

He was very active in the *Agudat Harabbanim* in Poland and in the *Agudat Yisrael*. During World War II he was incarcerated in various concentration camps and was released by the American army from the Austrian camp Ebensee. After living for a time in Rome, he came to the United States in 1946 and established a congregation *Zikhron Eliezer* in the Bronx. During the war he lost his wife and four children. He remarried to Sarah Shlimze, the daughter of R. Tuvia Yehiel Michael Halpern of Sasov.

He republished the work of his grandfather—*Nahalat Reuven* (Rzeszov, 1924)—and *Mishneh LeMelekh* (New York, 1952)—the sermons of R. Eliezer Weissblum of Rzeszov.

A.Shu.

HALPERN, Issachar Yisrael Aryeh, of Sokolovka (1900–9 *Iyyar* 1962)—

Son of R. Barukh, a descendant of R. Meir of Przemyslany. He married Shevah, the daughter of R. Leibish Stikler of Kulikov. In 1931 he emigrated to the United States and established a congregation, *Yismah Yisrael*, in New York.

HALPERN, Jacob Joseph Shlomoh, of Vaslui/Tel Aviv (1902–11 *Tevet* 1985) – Son of R. Hayyim Dov, he was brought up by his grandfather R. Shalom and by R. Mendel of Vishivi. He married the daughter of R. Jacob Samson Kanar of Czechov. He emigrated to Israel in 1950 and after living in Nahariyyah for some time, settled in Tel Aviv.

HALPERN, Menahem Mendel, of Dukla (1870–*Av* 1943) – Son of R. Hananyah Joseph of Brzezany, he lived for many years in Dukla but would visit his followers in Brzezany twice a year. He settled in Jaslo in 1930. He and his family were murdered by the Nazis.

HALPERN, Meshullam Shragai Feivish, of Brzezany (1810–19 *Elul* 1874) – Son of R. Naftali Hirsch, the rabbi of Brzezany, he studied under R. Shimon of Yaroslav. He married the daughter of R. Simhah, the rabbi of Bobarka, and when she died leaving him with small children, he remarried to Hannah, the only daughter of R. Asher Yeshayah of Ropczyce, who had ordained him. He became rebbe in Brzezany and was the author of *Sefat Emet* on the Pentateuch (Lvov, 1874). After his death he was succeeded by his son, R. Abraham Zerach Aryeh Yehudah Leibish, in Brzezany.

HALPERN, Mordecai (7 *Adar* II 1883–29 *Kislev* 1971) – Son of R. Yehezkel, he was much influenced by Meir Balaban and Dr. Hayyim David Lipa. He studied secular subjects and began to publish essays on Hasidism in the periodical *Hashiloah* (1908). He studied philosophy in the universities of Berne, Berlin, and Vienna, where he stayed during the First World War. In 1921 he became a teacher in Jaffa/Tel Aviv. His book *Sefer HaMasiyot* (Hasidic Tales) was published in Berlin between 1927 and 1928 and has gone through several editions.

HALPERN, Shalom, of Vaslui (1856–24 *Av* 1940) – Son of R. David, he married the daughter of R. Yitzhak Friedman of Bohusi. In 1906, he moved to Vaslui.

A scholar of exceptional diligence, he would study for eighteen hours each day. He was knowledgeable, too, in secular subjects, history, geography, and philosophy.

His son, R. Hayyim Dov (1876–1957), emigrated to the Holy Land in 1950 and lived in Haifa.

HALPERN, Tzvi Hirsch, of Sasov/New York (1890–24 *Nisan* 1971) – Son of Tuviah Yehiel Michael, he was brought up by his grandfather R. Shlomoh Meir of Sasov. He was rebbe of Brzezany, then in Sasov, and finally in New York. He married Hannah, the daughter of R. Jacob Shlomoh, who, together with their children, perished in the Holocaust.

HALPERN, Yoel, of Zilin (1887–*Hoshanah Rabba* 1954) – Son of R. Abraham Zerach Aryeh Yehudah Leibish, he was born in Brzezany. In 1905 he married Rachel, the daughter of Eliyahu Horowitz of Zilin. After the First World War he lived in Rzeszov and settled in 1930 in New York, where he was active in the *Vaad Hatzalah*. His children perished in the Holocaust.

HALSTOCK, Ezekiel, of Ostrowiece (1887–10 *Tevet* 1943) – Only son of R. Meir Yehiel Halevi, he was born in Skerniewice. He studied under R. Immanuel, *dayan* of Bendin, and R. Yudel Levin or Yudel Lipsker, who was later *dayan* in Cracow. He was soon recognized as an outstanding halakhic authority. He married Beila Miriam, the daughter of R. Naftali Horowitz of Mielec. At the age of twenty-three he accepted his first rabbinical position, in Invalodoz, near Tomaszov, where he served for ten years. In 1916 he also became rabbi of Nasielsk.

After the death of his father in *Adar* 1928, he succeeded him as rabbi of Ostrowiece, where he established a *yeshivah*, *Bet Meir*, in his memory. Even the followers of other dynasties would regularly visit him, and he himself visited R. David Moses Friedman of Chortkov. He was the author of *Kodshei Yehezkel* on *Kodashim*, a tractate of the

Mishnah, and *Meir Enei Hakhamim*, edited by Reuben Mandelbaum (New York, 1950).

At the outbreak of the Second World War he lived in Warsaw and then returned to Ostrowiece, where he lived in the house of his eldest son, R. Jacob. He refused to have any contact with the *Judenrat* of Ostrowiece. He, his wife, and sons were all murdered by the Nazis outside the synagogue in Sandormiez.

HALSTOCK, Meir Yehiel Halevi, of Ostrowiece (1852–9 *Adar* 1928)– Born in Sabin, near Warsaw, the son of Abraham Itsche, a baker who was very pious and very poor. At the age of ten, he was taken to R. Elimelekh Shapira of Grodzisk, who advised his father to entrust the boy to the scholarly R. Berel Goldfarb. When he was seventeen years old, he married the daughter of R. Abraham of Warka. He lived a very ascetic life, spending the whole week in the *Bet HaMidrash* and returning to his family only on the Sabbath. His diligence was phenomenal. He could go through the whole of the Talmud between Purim and Passover. On the eve of Passover he would make a *siyyum* of the entire Talmud.

At the age of twenty-seven he became the rabbi of Skerniewice and received ordination from R. Yehoshua Trunk of Kutno and from his son-in-law R. Eliezer Waks of Kalish. His rabbinate in Skerniewice lasted for ten years, and in 1889 he became rabbi of Ostrowiece, where he spent almost the next forty years. When his spiritual guide, R. Elimelekh, died in 1892, he became rebbe and won the support of many hasidim of Grodzisk. He still visited R. Joshua Rokeah of Belz, R. David Moses of Chortkov, and R. Yehezkel of Sianiawa.

He was the great ascetic of Hasidism, who fasted every day for forty years, eating only a very frugal meal at night. Even the Sabbath was no exception. "On the Sabbath," he would say, "I can rejoice in the knowledge that I can fast easily." He was proud of his humble origins. "My father, of blessed memory, said that the best thing in the world is a freshly baked bread." He was also interested in astronomy and mathematics.

His health was exceedingly precarious. R. Abraham Mordecai Alter of Ger was one of his many colleagues who begged him to forgo such hazardous extremes as fasting. But the rabbi refused to alter his life-style.

Despite his physical frailty, he was wholeheartedly involved in communal affairs. When he heard that the Poles of Ostrowiece were preparing a pogrom, he instructed the Jewish authorities to organize a self-defense group. As soon as the cowardly hoodlums appreciated that they were not dealing with defenseless victims, they dispersed. The Kishinev disorders were not reenacted in Ostrowiece.

During World War I, when a local Jewish teacher was accused of espionage, the rebbe pleaded with the military authorities that the man be released from jail.

In 1921 his disciple R. Yehudah Joseph Leibish Rosenberg published his work *Or Torah* (Piotrokov, 1921), on Genesis. The rebbe was versed in *Gematria*, the method of exegesis based on the interpretation of a word or words according to the value of its Hebrew letters. In his talmudic studies, however, he was a follower of R. Jacob Pollack, the father of the *pilpul*.

In the last years of his life he was so weak from fasting that he could hardly walk. He was, however, strong enough to fight passionately for his community. He was succeeded by his son, R. Yehezkel, and it was R. Reuben Mandelbaum who recently published in two volumes *Meir Einei Hakhamim*, containing many of the discourses of the rabbi of Ostrowiece. His whole life was a lesson in the triumph of mind over matter.

HALUKKAH–Organized collection in the Diaspora of funds for distribution in the Holy Land.

Supporting the *yishuv* was tantamount to ransoming prisoners (*pidyon shevuim*), a sacred duty that took precedence over all other obligations. The unstable political conditions in the Holy Land put the Jewish settlers in a very precarious position and made them virtually hostages to fortune.

Money from the Polish communities was collected by the Council of Four Lands. In 1754, the council issued a special appeal on behalf of the inhabitants of Safed. During the 1750s and 1760s, the main office for the collection of funds was situated in Brody. *Shelihei Tziyyon* (emissaries of Zion) frequently visited Jewish communities, not only in Europe but also in North Africa.

Until 1777, the Sephardim had control over the monies collected, but the arrival of the hasidim and other immigrants put an end to the Sephardic monopoly. Though the hasidic movement was splintered by then, support for the *yishuv* was an issue that united the various groups. R. Barukh of Medziborz and R. Levi Yitzhak of Berdichev, worlds apart in temperament, character, and outlook, found common ground here. Supported by R. Jacob Samson of Sheptovka and R. Yitzhak of Neshkiz, R. Levi Yitzhak endorsed the ruling that it was wrong to divert to any other charity the money collected for the poor of the Holy Land. Support for the Holy Land became one of the unwritten articles of Hasidism.

R. Abraham of Kalisk, like R. Menahem Mendel of Vitebsk, repeatedly appealed for help. It was R. Shneur Zalman who urged his followers to make weekly or at least monthly contributions to sustain people in the Holy Land who were literally without food. He was denounced to the Russian authorities by his opponents, who accused him of smuggling money for Turkey, meaning, funds for the Jews in Palestine in support of the *yishuv*.

The harmony among the hasidim was marred by the undignified clashes between R. Shneur Zalman and R. Abraham of Kalisk as to who would collect, control, and distribute the funds. It was the first of many such controversies in the nineteenth century.

Many *kollelim* (groups that supported their own hometowns) came into being. The immigrants from Germany and Holland formed their own *kollel*, *kollel Hod* (the abbreviation for "Holland and Deutschland"). There was also the *kollel Perushim* (the disciples of the Gaon of Vilna), *kollel Habad*, *kollel Hungaria*, Bukovina, Galicia, Grodno, Karlin, Koidanov, Kosov, and Vishnitz. By the middle of the nineteenth century, the *kollelim* were split into twenty-five sections, each with its own president as well as its own patron in Eastern Europe, usually the rebbe. There were different modes of distribution, and different amounts were distributed.

In 1866, R. Meir ben Yitzhak Auerbach (1815–1878), the rabbi of the Ashkenazic community of Jerusalem, sponsored the establishment of *Vaad Klali*, a central committee of all Ashkenazic *kollelim*. The records of the *kollelim* provide a storehouse of information about the settlers. Unlike the Sefardim, who gave most of their financial aid to scholars, the Ashkenazic *kollelim* supported all who needed help. The committee arranged for each *kollel* to receive a fixed sum for deserving cases. There were the *Great Halukkah*—the money collected in Eastern Europe—and the *Minor Halukkah*—the money collected in Western Europe and the United States. In all, the funds collected amounted to £40,000 per annum and supported 23,616 people, of which 2,000 were hasidim.

After the second *aliyah* in 1904, and the extension of Jewish colonization, only the residents of the *old yishuv* had to rely on *halukkah*. In 1913, 80 percent of the Ashkenazim still depended on *halukkah*.

M. M. Rothschild, *HaHalukah*.

HAMETZ, sale of—R. Shneur Zalman of Liady objected to the "legal fiction" involved in the sale of *hametz* to a non-Jew. He proposed the idea of a general sale through an agent acting on behalf of the vendor.

Hametz was deposited in ten separate places in the house prior to the symbolic search (*bedikat hametz*). The number ten represented the ten *Sefirot*.

"How wonderful are your people Israel," R. Levi Yitzhak of Berdichev once explained. "Were the czar to issue an order forbidding the import of certain goods into his realm, his subjects would seek means to smuggle them across the borders. But You, God, declared that *hametz* should be 'neither seen nor found,' and every Jew religiously removes even the last crumbs of leaven from the household."

Moreover, the evil impulse, *yetzer hara*, is called leaven (*Berakhot* 17a). *Matzah*, on the other hand, is called by the *Zohar* "celestial bread," for it serves as an antidote to Egyptian bondage.

HANNAH (d. ca. 1750), wife of the Besht—The Besht was often asked to settle local disputes, and it was in the course of such an arbitration that he met R. Efraim of Brody, who happened to be passing through Horodenka. A shrewd judge of character, R. Efraim offered his daughter in marriage to the youthful adjudicator. The Besht readily accepted the proposal. R. Efraim died before he reached home, and the betrothal documents baffled the family.

Later, when the Besht arrived to claim his bride, her brother, R. Abraham Gershon, tried in vain to persuade his sister to annul the betrothal. But Hannah resisted all persuasion, and they were married.

She gave birth to a son, R. Tzvi, and a daughter, Adel. When she died, the Besht said, "I had hoped that a whirlwind would sweep me up to heaven like the prophet Elijah. But now that I am merely half a person, this is no longer possible." The Besht did not remarry.

HANOKH HEINOKH HAKOHEN of Alexander (1798–18 *Adar* II 1870)—Son of R. Pinhas Hakohen Levin, a descendant of R. Shapsei ben Meir Hakohen the Shach, Alexander was born in Lutormisk. He married Hannah Feiga, the daughter of Jacob Yockel of Przysucha, where he lived after his marriage and met R. Jacob Yitzhak, the "Yehudi."

He studied under R. Jacob Aryeh Guterman and the "Yehudi." He was also a disciple of the "Seer" of Lublin and R. Yitzhak Meir Alter of Ger, as well R. Menahem Mendel Morgenstern of Kotzk. He served a long apprenticeship and did not become rebbe until the age of sixty-eight. He was reluctant to take on the responsibility, and it was only after the death of R. Yitzhak Meir of Ger that he could no longer refuse. Having for so long subordinated his will to others, he found the crown of leadership weighty and burdensome. Yet, he proved to be a conscientious and dedicated rebbe who became close to each one of his followers. Underlining those individual relationships, he established the custom of handing each hasid a goblet of wine during the *Kiddush* on the Sabbath. Another innovation was the acceptance of petitions from women, which had not been the custom in Ger or Kotzk. Nor did he follow the custom of having twelve loaves on the Sabbath.

Prior to becoming rebbe, he served as rabbi first, in Alexandrov Lodzki, or "Alexander," as it was called by the hasidim. Then he served in Nowydwor Proshnitz, eventually returning to Alexander. He urged his hasidim to maintain high moral standards when away from home. "When one is on a journey," he explained, "one sometimes conducts oneself according to a *Shulhan Arukh* different from the Code one follows at home."

After the death of his first wife, the rabbi married the daughter of R. Asher of Parysov. He had two daughters and one son, R. Yehiel Fishel, who did not succeed him. The dynasty of Alexander was continued by the Danziger family.

Throughout his life he was an ardent supporter of the poor in the Holy Land. He raised 12,000 rubles for charitable institutions there. Among his disciples were R. Abraham of Parysov, R. Dov Zeev Hakohen Rapoport of Kotzk, and R. Zeev Nahum of Biala.

Apart from a number of responsa and discourses, he did not put his thoughts on paper. Later his discourses were printed under the name *Hashavah LeTovah* (Piotrokov, 1929).

He was survived by one son, R. Samuel, and one daughter, Sarah Hannah.

HANUKKAH—The festival of lights, celebrated for eight days, beginning on 25 *Kislev*.

To the hasidim, Hanukkah was not a minor festival. They regarded it as the completion or climax of the Day of Atonement, the time when a person's fate was determined, a time when great things could be achieved.

The numerical value of the Hebrew word *Matathiahu* was equal to the Hebrew words of *Rosh Hashanah*, that is, 861. Hasidim carried numerological analogies further, pointing out that Adam enjoyed the divine light for thirty-six hours before it was extinguished. On Hanukkah, too, thirty-six lights are lit. "The hidden lights of the Messiah," declared R. Pinhas of Koretz, "are revealed on Hanukkah."

Purim meant the danger of physical annihilation, whereas Hanukkah represented spiritual extinction. "Hence, on Hanukkah," said R. Yitzhak Meir Alter of Ger, "we celebrate by the recitation of *Hallel*, whereas on Purim, we indulge in physical delights."

R. Hayyim Halberstam of Zanz played with a *dreidel*, because the Hebrew words engraved on it have the same value as the word "Messiah" (358). R. Tzvi Hirsch of Dynov, however, forbade hasidim to play cards on Hanukkah, for the word for cards has the same numerical value as "Satan."

In Ropczyce, hasidim recited *Ono Bekoah* (we beseech You), a prayer that was a favorite of the kabbalists. In the court of Chernobyl, Ruzhin, and Talnoye, the rebbes used ornate golden *menorot* and always used oil and not candles. The last day of Hanukkah, *Zot Hanukkah*, had a deep significance for the hasidim. A special *seudah* was held, and the rebbes delivered discourses. R. Alter Yisrael Shimon Perlow of Novominsk used to recite the *Eshet Hayil* (who can find a valiant wife) from the Book of Proverbs (31:10–31) before the recitation of the benedictions.

HASID (pl., hasidim) – The general term *hasid* was in use long before the advent of the hasidic movement in the eighteenth century. Its general connotation is "pious one." There was a movement in the third century B.C.E. whose members were known as *hasidim* and who were important in the history leading up to and including the Hasmonean rebellion (167 B.C.E.). We also find the term in rabbinic material with regard to a special type of extremely pious Jews who are identified especially by their going beyond the requirements of the Law. That characterization continues throughout the medieval period and is discussed in many medieval literary-philosophical works. Also during that period the term became associated with a popular mystical movement originating among the Jews of medieval Germany known as the *Hasidei Ashkenaz*. The leading figure of the movement was R. Judah HeHasid, the author of the popular *Sefer Hasidim*. The movement bears no direct relation to Beshtian (eighteenth-century) Hasidism; what influence it did exert was as part of the general Jewish world, which Beshtian Hasidism was heir to.

The unique modern use of the term *hasid* as applied to a member of the movement started by R. Israel Baal Shem Tov has its origins in small groups of East European ascetic mystics (hasidim), which formed the background milieu of the Besht and many of whose members became associates or disciples of the Besht. Through the impact of the Besht, these other hasidic groups either were absorbed into his movement or lost their influence and disappeared. In the specific context of Beshtian Hasidism, the term *hasid* has three basic meanings: (1) it retains its traditional meaning of piety and total devotion to God; (2) it usually and broadly means living a life dedicated to the new/old values of joy (*simhah*), ecstasy (*hitlahavut*), service (*avodah*), intention (*kavanah*, i.e., inwardly committed action), and humility (*shiflut*), as stressed in the new weltanschauung of the Besht and his disciples; and (3) it takes on a new connotation of "adherence to," that is, commitment to a *tzaddik*. Hence, to be a hasid means to be a hasid of a specific *tzaddik*, and one cannot be a hasid independently of that interpersonal relation, which lies at the center of Hasidism. The implications of the commitment were understood in a variety of different ways during the earliest period of the history of Hasidism, but from that complex picture the following basic requirements emerge as constant. The *tzaddik*, being uniquely blessed by God and being especially close to God, serves to assist his hasidim in their struggle for *teshuvah* (repentance), *yihud* (unity), and personal and universal *tikkun* (reunification with the divine), acting to bring his hasidim closer to God and God closer to his hasidim. In addition, he is generally thought to intercede with God in order to provide his hasidim with three things: children, health and long life, and a livelihood. In return the hasidim provide their *tzaddik* with three things: total faith in his judgment and authority, their best efforts to avoid sin and to seek redemption, and financial support, which is a sign of love, gratitude, and the attachment between them. As the institution of the *tzaddik* grew, it came to be seen in the broadest possible way, attributing to the *tzaddik* all sorts of miraculous and theological powers that could be and were invoked by the *tzaddik* in aid of his hasidim. The *tzaddik* was, in this sense, rightly called "the cornerstone upon which the world (at least of his hasidim) is built" (Yaakov Yosef, *Ben Porat Yosef* 67a), and it is more than a metaphor when it is said that for the hasid the *tzaddik* was a "living Torah."

This basic structure gave rise to certain established patterns of behavior vis-à-vis the hasidim to their *tzaddik* and to certain uniquely hasidic institutions. The hasid sought to spend as much time as possible with the *tzaddik*, especially on the Sabbath during the *seudah shleshit* (third meal), when it was customary for the *tzaddik* to give his "Torah teaching" for the week. This became the most important weekly occasion for the hasidim and the hasidic court. If some hasidim did not live close by and if more regular visits were impossible, they would at least make yearly pilgrimages to the *tzaddik*, usually on the High Holy Days and, to a lesser degree, on other holy days. This at least yearly pilgrimage served to renew the cement on which the hasidic community was built: the personal, dynamic relation of hasid and *tzaddik*. And it served both to spiritually energize the hasid and to reinforce the larger social community, of which the *tzaddik* was the pivotal center. In addition to this physical pilgrimage, the hasid would also seek the *tzaddik*'s advice on all the major decisions and aspects of life, either in person or through written communication. This was usually done through a set pattern that included the hasid's sending a written request, known as a *kvitl*, accompanied by a monetary gift known as a *pidyon* (redemption) for the financial support of the *tzaddik* and his charitable activities. The request and the gift were sent to the *tzaddik*'s *gabbai* (administrative assistant), who would pass it on to the *tzaddik*. If the hasid were at the *tzaddik*'s court, he would also, after attending to the described preliminaries, come to the *tzaddik* for his blessing, known as the *birkat hapridah* (parting blessing) before leaving. There was also a more intimate and complex counseling situation that existed between the *tzaddik* and the hasid, known as, among other terms, the *yehidut* (as this meeting is called in *Habad* Hasidism). It consisted of the preliminary formalities of *kvitl* and *pidyon* and then a direct meeting in which the hasid petitioned the *tzaddik*—handing him the *kvitl*—for assistance and advice, and the *tzaddik* offered his counsel—called the *Etzah*—after which the hasid was dismissed with a parting blessing.

The development of these practices, and, indeed, of the entire theory of the role and nature of the hasid and *tzaddik*, was gradual. The most important sources in this development, in which the meaning and ramifications of the theory are discussed, are the four works of Yaakov Yosef of Polonnoye; the teachings of the Maggid of Mezhirech; the various writings of R. Shneur Zalman of Liady, especially the *Tanya*; and, above all, Elimelekh of Lejask's *NoAm Elimelekh*, perhaps the locus classicus of the doctrine of the hasidim and their obligations to the *tzaddik*, who is presented in a truly imperial fashion.

A wide variety of more general homiletic explanations of the term *hasid* are also found in hasidic literature. They do not compete or conflict with the technical outline described but complete it and provide its richness and appeal. As a sample of these views, we note the following: "A hasid is one who loves Hasidism." The Baal Shem Tov said, "A hasid is one who prevents others from stumbling, even if it entails injury to oneself. Hasidism is altruism far . . . above the love of oneself." Pinhas of Koretz said, "The hasid is not like the *mitnagged*. The *mitnagged* fears Gehenna, but the hasid fears sin." R. Pinhas of Koretz taught, "The *mitnagged* fears the *Shulhan Arukh*; the hasid fears the Holy One, blessed be He." R. Mendel of Kotzk said, "A hasid is he who gives an account to himself for every utterance and every deed, for what he desires to say and what he intends to do."

S. Dresner, *The Zaddik*.

S.K.

HASIDEI ASHKENAZ (the pious men of Germany)—The leading German mystics of the twelfth and thirteenth centuries were R. Judah ben Samuel HeHasid of Regensburg (d. 1217) and R. Eliezer ben Judah of Worms (d. 1230). Their beliefs are elaborated in the book *Sefer Hasidim*.

They waited six hours between eating dishes of meat or fowl and eating dishes of dairy products. They refrained from eating meat from 17 *Tammuz* until 9 *Av*. They would stand up the whole day and night on the Day of Atonement. They kept the *lulav* and the willow until Passover, using them as fuel for the baking of the *matzot*. They slept in the *sukkah*. They fasted on the eleventh day of *Tishri*, thus observing the Day of Atonement on two days. They lit two candles on Friday night, at a time when this custom was not practiced. They used for the baking of *matzot* only wheat that had been under supervision from the time of harvesting.

They maintained that all human beings are equal; that one should not beat dogs or any other animal; that it was utterly wrong to do injustice to either Jew or gentile; and that a father should not kiss a son in a public place, because it might offend or sadden Jewish onlookers who have no children of their own or who were orphaned of their father.

HASIDIC TALE DURING THE HOLOCAUST—The hasidic tale and

anecdote of the Holocaust and post-Holocaust periods are very much in evidence. This genre of hasidic literature–storytelling–follows its traditional structure but is changing contentwise. From its very inception, the hasidic tale was flexible and adaptable, suiting the needs and moods of the movement. Both Holocaust and post-Holocaust tales follow this tradition.

The hasidic tale during the Holocaust belongs to the period when the *tzaddik* was the central figure of the tale. The hasidim tell stories in order to enhance the personality of the *tzaddik*, to sanctify his name and those of his ancestors, and to reveal his miraculous powers.

In most hasidic Holocaust-related tales, the *tzaddik* remains the central figure; however, the environment changes. The East European countryside gives way to replacement by the ghetto, labor camp, and concentration camp. Demons and sorcerers are replaced by gestapo agents and German dogs. The *tzaddik* faces these forces of evil and works his wonders in the valleys of death during World War II. Like in the pre-Holocaust tale, he brings comfort to his believers and offers glimmers of hope to those on the threshold of death.

Today the Holocaust-related hasidic tale is gaining popularity. Tales about the rebbe's liberation from Bergen Belsen may at times overshadow the traditional stories about a *tzaddik*'s deliverance from a czarist Russian prison. It is natural to hear a story told about a *tzaddik* who was saved from the crematorium due to the protective merit of the shirt of R. Barukh of Medziborz–a shirt he wore under his striped camp uniform. Or the tale about an aging hasidic rabbi in Yanovska who jumped over a huge pit filled with bodies and landed safely on the other side while younger people fell into the pit and perished; at the time, he felt as if he were being carried to safety by his hasidic ancestor. And there's the story about the huge German shepherd dog trained to attack Jews. The dog carried out the instruction with great zeal. However, when facing the Belzer rabbi, the dog retreated in fear. R. Aaron Perlow of Karlin jumped from the safety of his attic in ghetto Warsaw to the aid of a pregnant woman being attacked by a Ukrainian guard. He wrestled for the gun and failed. His body was found in a puddle of blood. Nearby were his broken violin and his *tefillin*.

The hasidic anecdote likewise retained its traditional structure and hasidic wit. Emmanuel Ringelblum records on May 5–6, 1942 the following anecdote circulated in ghetto Warsaw:

> They tell this story: [Winston] Churchill invited the hasidic rabbi of Ger to come to see and advise him how to bring about Germany's downfall. The rabbi gave the following reply: "There are two possible ways–one involving natural means, the other supernatural. The natural means would be if a million angels with flaming swords were to descend on Germany and destroy it. The supernatural would be if a million Englishmen parachuted down on Germany and destroyed it.

The hasidic tale and anecdote during the Holocaust reflect the spirit of Hasidism, its optimism, its hope, its unwavering belief in God, and the unlimited powers of God's chosen *tzaddikim*.

J. Dan, *The Hasidic Novella* (Hebrew), pp. 7–22.
E. Ringleblum, *Notes from the Warsaw Ghetto*, p. 265.
M. Unger, *Admorim SheNisfu BaShoah*, p. 209.

Y.E.

HASIDISM–The followers of the Besht did not coin the term *hasidim* with which to describe themselves but found it ready to hand among the early eighteenth-century ascetics and pneumatics, groups of whom existed in Eastern Europe and some of whose forms together with the name itself the new hasidic movement adopted. Nevertheless, the use of the name *hasidim* was bound to suggest to the Besht's followers and probably to the Besht himself that ideas associated with *Hasidut* (saintliness) in the rabbinic literature should provide guidelines for the new way that was being advocated. For instance, the *Mishnah* (*Berakhot* 5:1) states that the saints of old (*Hasidim HaRishonim*) would spend much time in attuning their heart to prayer so that prayer itself and the preparations (*hakhanot*) for it are high on the scale of hasidic values. Or when the Talmud (*Baba Kamma* 30a) quotes three different opinions as to what one must do in order to become a hasid–namely, to take care never to cause any harm to others, to engage in God's praises, and to carry out the ethical precepts contained in "Ethics of the

Fathers"—the hasidim took upon themselves the implications of all three opinions. Attributed in hasidic lore to the Besht is a definition of what it means to be a hasid based on the Talmudic definition. The Talmud (*Mo'ed Katan* 18a) observes that if a pregnant woman steps on fingernails, she may suffer a miscarriage. The wicked, it is said, having no care for others, simply throw their nail parings away. The righteous bury them. But the hasidim, anxious to avoid even the remotest possibility that anything of theirs might be a source of danger to others, are not content with burying the nail parings; they burn them in fire so as to destroy them completely.

In addition to their reliance on rabbinic descriptions of *Hasidut*, the hasidim made much use of accounts of saintly conduct in the standard moralistic works, especially those of a mystical nature such as the thirteenth-century *Sefer Hasidim* and the devotional works published as a result of the influence of the Safed circle of kabbalists in the sixteenth century, for example, Elijah de Vidas's *Reshit Hokhmah*, Eliezer Azikri's *Sefer Haredim*, and Isaiah Horowitz's voluminous compendium the *Shelah*, popularly spoken of by the hasidim as "fat with holiness." The ethical and religious ideals of the *Zohar* and the other kabbalistic works were familiar to the hasidim, even among those who did not study the works themselves (see KABBALAH).

The major concepts of Hasidism were thus based on earlier formulations in the classical Jewish sources. Even the hasidic doctrine of the *tzaddik*, the gurulike master, clearly a startling innovation so far as Judaism is concerned, was held by the hasidim to be based entirely on the traditional sources. Since the term *hasid* was now applied to the follower of a master, a different term was required for the master himself. The name "*tzaddik*" was adopted with a consequent reversal of the rabbinic scheme in which the *tzaddik* is the ordinary good person and the hasid the person of extraordinary goodness and piety. Once, however, the name "*tzaddik*" was used for the saint, it was possible for Hasidism to adapt all the rabbinic sayings about the *tzaddikim* to their own situation. In hasidic works describing the role of the *tzaddik* there are frequent references, for instance, to the talmudic saying (*Mo'ed Katan* 16b) that even when God has issued a baneful decree, the *tzaddik* can render it null and void, with the radical corollary that when the *tzaddik* issues an order, God must obey it. The biblical heroes, particularly those who interceded for the people, performed miracles on their behalf and healed the sick. Moses, Elijah, and Elisha, together with the miracle-working saints mentioned in the Talmud—Hanina ben Dosa, Honi the Circle-Drawer, and Nahum Ish Gamzu—became the models for the hasidic *tzaddikim*, the prototype of the holy man as the channel through which the divine grace flows. The talmudic saying (*Berakhot* 17b) that the whole world is provided with sustenance because of (*bishvil*) Hanina ben Dosa is read as meaning that both material and spiritual well-being flow down into the world through the channel (*bashevil*) of the *tzaddik* (*Toldot Yaakov Yosef*, *Naso*, ed. Warsaw, 1881, p. 261b). Similarly, many of the references in the Talmud to the conduct of scholars (*talmidei hakhamim*) are interpreted as applying to the *tzaddikim*.

It follows that the hasidim did not see themselves as real innovators. The originality of hasidic thought lies mainly in the fresh emphasis it gave to conventional Jewish ideas and its selectivity among those ideas. Hasidism sees itself as a revivalist movement with no new ideas but with new ways (*derakhim*) and fresh techniques for the realization of the old ideas and their revitalization.

In the well-known early anthology of hasidic ideas known as *Leshon Hasidim* (Lemberg, 1876), the hasidic compiler remarks in his Introduction concerning the Besht:

> God sent us a savior, a holy and tremendous teacher, a holy angel who came down from Heaven to illumine the eyes of all the holy people of Israel who desire to fear God's name and take upon themselves the yoke of the Torah and the *mitzvot* and the yoke of the Kingdom of Heaven in love and true fear from the depths of the heart, and with powerful attachment (*devekut*) to God, and with the great burning enthusiasm (*hitlahavut*) of holiness.

Hasidism chose to emphasize those ideas in the classical sources hospitable to the hasidic immanentist philosophy (see PANTHEISM).

Prominent among the hasidic virtues is *simhah*, (joy, cheerfulness). To serve the Lord with gladness is no new idea in Judaism, but the hasidic understanding of *simhah* is based on hasidic views regarding the essential unreality of the finite world and its sorrows, the hasid being expected to gaze always beyond the veils of ignorance, imperfection, and evil to see only the divine energy sustaining all, the only true reality. Very revealing is the comment by R. Nahum of Chernobyl (*Yismah Lev*, end of *Meor Enayyim*, Jerusalem, 1968, pp. 300–301) that although the Talmud (*Berakhot* 31a) forbids us to fill our mouth with laughter in this world, the *tzaddikim* do frequently fill their mouth with laughter, because, in their constant attachment to God, the *tzaddikim* do not really inhabit this world at all. For the same reason, *atzvut* (melancholia) is, for Hasidism, one of the worst vices. A popular hasidic saying has it that this is not because melancholia is a technical sin but because it detaches one from the appreciation of the divine as all-pervading and is thus the main cause of all sin. The hasid is not unaware of life's tragic dimension but is confident that ultimately all is for the best and that one can assist in the task of sweetening the judgments (see KABBALAH) by acknowledging that these severities also come from God and are really the divine mercy in disguise.

Since God is always so near and His goodness ever present, as Hasidism teaches, the mystical love of God is seen not as a remote ideal to be attained only by the greatest of saints but as a normal emotion for the ordinary hasid. Yet as an antidote to religious sentimentalism, self-delusion, and sheer wallowing in naive religiosity, the love of God requires to be tempered by the fear of God. That fear rarely means for the hasidic masters the fear of punishment for transgression. Hell-fire preaching is conspicuously absent from hasidic sermonizing. Fear is usually conceived of in terms of the numinous, the awe one experiences when confronted by the *mysterium tremendum*. R. Hayyim of Czernowitz (*Shaar HaTefillah*, Sudylkov, 1813, p. 7b) writes:

> And how much more so the dread and fear, the terror and trembling, which fall upon such a man when he performs a *mitzvah*, knowing as he does with certainty that he stands before the name of the Holy One, blessed be He, the great and terrible King before whom "all the inhabitants of the earth are reputed as nothing; and He doeth according to His will in the host of Heaven" (Daniel 4:32), who stands over him always, seeing his deeds, for His glory fills the earth. Such a man is ever in a state of shame and lowliness so intense that the world cannot contain it, especially when he carries out the *mitzvot*. Such a man's *mitzvot* are those which fly upward in joy and satisfaction to draw down from there every kind of blessing and the flow of grace into all worlds.

This fear of God, without which the love of God has no permanence, is far from easy to attain. The hasid requires the inspiration provided by the example of the *tzaddik*. Those close to the *tzaddik* are alone capable of catching, as it were, the tremendous sense of awe that is the fruit of the *tzaddik*'s sustained reflection on the majesty of the Creator. Adapting a talmudic saying (*Berakhot* 33b), the hasidic maxim is, "Yes, for those close to Moses the fear of God is a small thing" (*Toldot*, end, p. 208c).

The love and fear of God are to be given expression in the practice of the *mitzvot* and the study of the Torah. But for the hasidim, *Torah lishmah* – the study of the Torah for its own sake – means for the sake of God, meaning, as a devotional exercise of the highest magnitude. Although the Talmud (*Pesahim* 50b) permits Torah study even when the motive is impure, the tendency in Hasidism is to decry such self-seeking as, at best, a very inadequate means to an end, hence the general hasidic preference for the ignorant but sincere worshiper to the learned but arrogant scholar who studies in order to acquire wealth or fame.

During the nineteenth century, partly in response to criticisms of alleged hasidic denigration of Torah studies, many of the hasidic masters adopted a more lenient attitude, stressing that the question of motive should not be allowed to discourage study. Typical is the observation by R. Yitzhak Eisik of Kormarno (*Notzer Hesed*, commentary to the *Mishnah*, *Avot* 1:13):

> The fools try to grasp at once the inner light but since they have not as yet reached such a stage they leave aside entirely the study of the Torah. Since they

are *hasidim* they feel it to be wrong to study with an unworthy motive and, on the other hand, they have not yet reached the stage of study for its own sake. The main thing is to study the Torah (i.e., and not be deterred by inadequacy of motive), for nothing in the whole world is more precious than the Torah.

The worship of God is not confined to purely spiritual pursuits. All created things are aglow with the divine; in all there are holy sparks (see KABBALAH) waiting to be rescued for the holy. Normally, therefore, Hasidism is opposed to asceticism. Numerous hasidic tales tell of masters warning their disciples against leading a too self-denying life. Those who reject worldly things overlook the opportunities those things can provide for elevating the creation to its Creator. Yet, obliged though the hasidim may be to use the things of the world, they must not dwell on the physical pleasure they afford but beyond that to the spiritual source of all delight. The hasid who sees a thing of beauty should be led on by it to reflect on the source of all beauty on high. Those who experience pride should remind themselves that God alone is to be exalted, for all pride comes from Him.

Pride (*gaavah*), precisely because it calls attention to the self, acts as the greatest barrier to awareness of God. The hasidic ideal is that of *shiflut* (lowliness), a somewhat different ideal from that of conventional humility. Although Hasidism, naturally, knows of the need of the good person to think little of self in relation to other human beings, *shiflut* represents much more a religious than a social or ethical value. It involves the realization that all creatures are as naught before the tremendous majesty of the Creator, so that the more of selfhood there is in us, the more remote are we from any true apprehension of the divine (see BITTUL HAYESH).

> Among *tzaddikim* themselves we find distinctions. Abraham said, "I am but dust and ashes" (Genesis 18:27). David said, "I am a worm, not a man" (Psalms 22:7). These things enjoy some existence. But Moses our Teacher, on whom be peace, said, "What are we?" (Exodus 16:7), and he was as nothing, as Scripture says: "But the man Moses was exceedingly humble" (Numbers 12:3). That is why he was able to apprehend God's essence, but it was otherwise with regard to the other prophets who came before him and after him. (*Maggid Devarav Le-Yaakov*, ed. Jerusalem, 1962, p. 88)

Hasidism does not believe that the ideals it seeks to foster can be realized by the individual who seeks salvation unaided by the *tzaddik* or by companions who follow the same path. From its beginnings the movement stressed the social aspects of the religious life. From the days of the "holy brotherhood" of the Baal Shem Tov there were companies of hasidim whose members assisted one another materially and spiritually, meeting together in a convivial atmosphere, telling and retelling the marvelous tales of the *tzaddikim*. Arele Roth, a latter-day *tzaddik*, writes in this connection:

> "See, my brother, that which I have explained in some small measure of the important idea that associates convene in order to discuss topics which have to do with the fear of Heaven, provided their intention is for the sake of Heaven." This was virtually the main technique introduced by the disciples of the Besht. I refer to the simple technique, not to the more secret techniques they had. I have seen it recorded from one of the great *tzaddikim* that before the coming of the Messiah all the energies of the wicked Amelek and all his strategy will be directed toward preventing the holy people of Israel from having meetings of this kind and to see, even when they do manage to meet, that their conversation is mingled with stupidities, vanities and gossip. (*Shomer Emunim*, Jerusalem, 1964, vol. II, p. 376)

Once the various dynasties of the *tzaddikim* had begun to proliferate, this spirit of fraternity began to be expressed in a more limited way and confined to the members of a particular group, often with intense rivalry between the various groups. The hasidim tend to think of their own rebbe as superior to all the others, and they feel intensely proud of belonging to their own particular fellowship.

The Karliner hasidim used to sing: "*Happy are we*, for we are Jews, not gentiles; *how goodly is our portion*, for we are hasidim, not *mitnaggedim*; *and how beautiful is our lot*, for we are Karliner hasidim, and not hasidim of other dynasties."

There are hasidic stories of disciples going from master to master until they found the teacher to whom they belonged by virtue of their "soul-root"; having found such a master, they would rarely forsake him for another. There are, nonetheless, a few instances of controversy not alone among the hasidim of rival groups but also between a master and his disciples.

I. Tishby and J. Dan, *Torat HaHasidut VeSifrutah*, pp. 769–822.

L.J.

HASIDISM: POLITICAL, SOCIAL, AND RELIGIOUS BACKGROUND – The term "*hasid*" in the sense of "pious one" or "devotee" is found in the Bible (Deuteronomy 33:8; Psalms 149:9) and throughout the ages reappears in most Jewish writings including the Talmud and later works. At times it acquires additional connotations. In Poland, *hasid* may have meant simply "pious" or may have echoed some other definition, because in the first half of the eighteenth century, an Orthodox anti-Shabbatean group of hasidim in the *Close* (*Klaus*) of Brody was involved in Kabbalah and its members were strict followers of normative Judaism. There were also other hasidim in Poland at that time: some practiced extreme ascetism; others, according to Prof. Gershom Scholem, may have evolved a species of crypto-Shabbateanism.

The new hasidim of Israel Baal Shem Tov (Master of the Holy Name; ca. 1700–1760), emerging as a group in 1740, were, or became, generally antiascetic and developed a new sort of Jewish piety and a distinctive way of life. As a Jewish revivalist or pietist group striving to make the Jewish religion "a religion of love" or "a religion of the heart," they, like non-Jewish pietists (though apparently not necessarily in imitation), opposed some aspects of Orthodox beliefs and practices, rejected rigidity and formalism, and challenged certain forms of the established institutional framework. They tempered their views on evil, sin, and punishment in hell, and they modified some of the stringent requirements for fulfilling the numerous prescriptions.

Like the non-Jewish revivalist trends of the time, Hasidism appealed to the lower classes by making religion intensely enthusiastic and personal. By advocating social betterment, Hasidism brought religion nearer to certain groups, especially those less learned in Torah or those whose status in the Jewish society of the period was a low one.

Topography

At first, the topography of Hasidism seems to have been closely connected with Volhynia and Podolia. Of the fifty places mentioned in *Shivhei HaBesht*, which deals with Israel Baal Shem Tov's (the Besht's) life and travels and his pupils, sixteen were in Podolia, seventeen in Volynia, and about ten in neighboring eastern Galicia. The Frankists, a dissident group that developed about a decade later, were also concentrated in the same geographical area. Jewish life in that region of the then Polish Ukraine developed differently from Jewish life in ethnic Poland.

Settlement and Resettlement

The region of the Ukraine that, in 1569, passed administratively to Poland became an area of rapid settlement encouraged by the nobles and magnates who had been granted vast tracts of land to colonize. In their desire to gain an income from these lands, they endeavored to bring in settlers, to found towns and rural settlements, and to build up agricultural and similar undertakings. The Jews, under pressure at that time in ethnic Poland, or as new immigrants from the West, found here relatively open doors and the opportunity to employ their organizational talents or at any rate to make a living.

During the first eighty years, the number of Jews rose about five times. The massacres, wars, invasions, and epidemics, which began with the Chmielnicki uprising of 1648 and lasted about two decades – until the Peace of Andrusov of 1667 – brought death, devastation, and exile to the Ukraine generally, with Podolia and Volhynia apparently suffering most heavily. These two regions belonged to Western Ukraine, which remained in Polish hands until the end of the eighteenth century. The Polish officials, the landowners, and the magnates promulgated a reconstruction of the region (in Podolia after 1699, when it was returned to Poland after having been occupied by Turkey since 1672). They favored settlement of Jews, apparently considering them more loyal than the Ukrainians. The Jewish population of

Volynia-Podolia, greatly reduced by the catastrophe of 1648 when the people were killed by or fled before the Cossacks, now not only replenished itself but grew five or six times by 1764, amounting to roughly 90,000–110,000 people living in 167 urban settlements and 2,616 villages.

Character of Jewish Life

Jewish life in the Ukraine generally, including Volynia and Podolia, developed somewhat differently from the way it did in ethnic Poland. There was less of a concentration of Jews in royal cities and/or segregation in "ghettos" and special Jewish streets. The Jews lived for the most part in villages, rural places, towns, and cities belonging to the gentry, and intermingled with the non-Jewish population. In some towns they even had a limited voice in the local government.

Their occupations, too, differed greatly. Here the Jews were to a large extent engaged in a wide range of occupations associated with leaseholding of estates (sometimes of whole towns), such as tax farming, revenue and toll collecting, innkeeping, ownership of pubs, and the buying, collecting, processing, and exporting of a variety of agricultural products (grain, animals, forest products and by-products, beeswax, honey, furs, and liquor and other beverages). On the other hand, at least some of them played a role in supplying the local population, the gentry, and/or their officials as well as the peasants with industrial and artisan goods produced locally by Jews or non-Jews or brought in from other parts of Poland or from abroad. The economic base was here generally much broader than in the rest of Poland.

At the same time, the frontier conditions of the region, the unsafe roads, and the lurking danger of repeated Tartar attacks had a few other consequences. The Polish authorities, who did not have enough of a standing army to fully defend the region against attackers, organized local defense militia detachments, for which the residents were obliged to undergo training, to possess arms and cannonballs, and the like. Jews participated in that defense enterprise, as evidenced by both general and Jewish sources. Individual Jews were trained by Polish officials to use arms, and Jewish groups were made responsible for defending specific points (e.g., turreted synagogues with cannon built for that purpose, or portions of the city walls) at times under Jewish commanders who shared the responsibility with others. A Jew bearing arms and using them presented a somewhat different image from that of the stereotypical timid Jew "afraid of his own shadow" (Nathan Hanover, chronicler of the Chmielnicki massacres, tells about the courage of such Jewish detachments).

Social Stratification

For large numbers of Jews to settle and resettle in these regions, to put down roots, and to find a way to integrate into the economy of the country—on the downgrade following the seventeenth-century wars must have been a tremendous undertaking—the more so since the region did not remain entirely peaceful. There was no agency to lighten the burden; each person or family had to fend for itself so that competition was stimulated between individuals and groups. Combined with economic and social mobility—both upward and downward—this tended to create clusters (or "classes") of nouveaux riches and nouveaux pauvres, which in turn led to social tension.

The situation was aggravated in Jewish Poland, where the local community organization (the *Kehillah*) controlled settlement rights (*hezkat yishuv*) and some sources of income (*hazakah*) but was itself controlled mostly by the rich and powerful who were in good relations with the authorities and upon whom the rabbis were usually dependent.

The many shifts and changes tended to increase the number of the disaffected and alienated, among whom were, on the one hand, the lower ranks of the "religious intelligentsia"—itinerant preachers, slaughterers (*shohetim*), rabbis without a permanent position, healers, medicine men, and "miracle workers"—and, on the other hand, those to whom the lower ranks ministered: the tens of thousands of village Jews, innkeepers, owners of pubs in town and village, and all manner of brokers and jobbers who were dependent on the "Jewish establishment."

An anonymous Hebrew authority—not a sociologist but a wandering preacher—characterized the "class structure" at the end of

HASIDISM: POLITICAL

the seventeenth century and the beginning of the eighteenth as follows:

> . . . the great hatred of today's aliens—the expellees from the Ukraine . . . in time their Jewish friends in the new places will revolt and become their foes and persecutors. . . . Those who can pay "ransom" have a hope . . . the rest must wander around . . . remain at the bottom of the [social] ladder . . . become woodcutters and water drawers, and the middlings are suspended in shame and there is no one to show compassion for them.

The Jewish religious literature of that time reflects both the disaffection of the authors and apparently also the climate of opinion among the readers or those who listened to the sermons.

Religion

Jewish religious life in Poland in the seventeenth to eighteenth century—patterned on modified Franco-German ideas—generally pursued the ideal of strict observance of the Torah precepts, study, and asceticism, allied with mystic—magic—kabbalistic tendencies, some of which were enforced, and others of which were modified. The rabbi and the communities sought to enforce the mores, but in practice individuals or small clusters of their members were lax about fulfilling the precepts of the Law. Preachers and other authors wrote fiery diatribes against the wicked, whom they threatened with punishment in hell and with hordes of vengeful demons. They demanded that the sinners repent, devising harsh penalties for them. These writings reiterated the standard age-old themes of wickedness (usury, avarice, pride, injustice, cheating, corruption, oppression of the poor); mentioned various ways in which adherence to the Law was being neglected; and indicated strained relations between the scholars and rabbis and the unlearned.

Jews in the south who were, to a great extent, "not living in seclusion" could and did acquire some of the non-Jewish behavior patterns. In the villages, one or two Jewish families living among a whole villageful of peasants fraternized with their neighbors and tended to emulate some of their neighbors' life-styles. In that way they became alienated from the urban Jewish community, though they usually returned to it for the High Holy Days. (The type of *Yishuvnik*—the "strange," uncouth, illiterate village Jew familiar through the folklore and literature of the nineteenth century—existed earlier.)

Urban Jews, sharing with non-Jews in the defense enterprises and in training and fighting together, acquired in the process certain secular traits. This happened to some of the wealthy Jews, too, through their contact with the gentry. Add to this that some of the enterprises run by Jews to serve the general population (innkeeping, leaseholding, and management of estates) created special religious problems for the Jews, such as observance of the Sabbath, use of leaven on Passover, hybridization of animals, feeding nonkosher food to gentiles, and raising nonkosher animals. The rabbis and community organizations devised some new, and for the most part symbolic, regulations designed to keep up appearances, some of which were observed more in the breach than in fact.

Briefly, some proof exists of the veracity of the accusations contained in the Jewish religious literature that at least some Jews were failing to fulfill the religious precepts properly, that they missed synagogue services, that they frequented inns where they danced or drank in the company of non-Jews with whom they fraternized or whom they imitated, that they indulged in illicit sexual relations, or that they strayed far from the ascetic ideal.

The emphasis on sin and sinners in the literature and in the sermons preached may have created guilt feelings among some, led others to repent, and still others to doubt or deny sin altogether. The same literature that threatened the sinful with demons and the fires of hell also indicates the existence of some tendency to doubt hell's existence—"It is impossible that hell should be as bad as it is pictured"—or to justify nonascetic life-styles and to equate the value of worldly matters with otherworldly hopes.

Early hasidic leaders, generally from the lower levels of the religious intelligentsia, who ministered to the lower strata of Jewish society, mostly accepted existentially prevailing practice including the remissions and the permissiveness. They justified their attitude by means of selected appropriately meliorating passages in older Jewish writings and in kabbalistic or semikabbalistic images and metaphors, which they used either in the original or in a changed meaning. They endowed profane matters with a certain holiness (as having been created by the omnipresent loving God) and in this way were able to minimize existing "sin," laxity, and secularization. Other "innovations" they picked up from existing, albeit not widespread, usages, for instance, fostering adoption of the Sephardic (Lurianic) prayer book that had been used sporadically by individual Jews in Poland already at the end of the seventeenth century.

Some, mostly external, behavior traits of Hasidism could be found among Christian sectarians in the area. It is not clear, however, whether these were imitations or simply characteristic of sects generally.

B. D. Weinryb, *The Jews of Poland: A Social and Economic History of the Jewish Community in Poland.*

B.D.W.

HAVAZZELET, Hebrew newspaper, Jerusalem – This first hasidic publication in the Holy Land was published by Israel Bak from July 13, 1863 until 1864. Banned by the Turks, it resumed publication on September 16, 1870, first as a biweekly, and, after a year, as a weekly.

The dominant personality of the paper was Bak's son-in-law, Israel Dov Frumkin (1850–1914), and later, A. M. Lunz. The paper's news coverage was extensive. It reported on the Montefiore and Rothschild activities and supported secular studies and vocational training in schools, as well as the educational activities of the *Alliance Israelite* schools. A special section was devoted to literature under the name "*Pirhei Havazzelet.*"

Havazzelet denounced Ben Yehudah's paper, *Hazevi*, which was established in 1884. It criticized the administration of the *Halukkah* fund and the ideologies of Ahad HaAm, *Hovevei Zion*, Zionism, the non-Orthodox immigrants, the *maskilim*, and the Christian missionaries. It ceased publication in 1911.

T. Tsamriyon, *Die Hebraische Presse in Europa*, vol. 1, pp. 255–264.

Z.Z.

HAYYIM of Krasnoye (d. 5 *Av* 1793) – He was among the close associates of the Besht who highly regarded him. It was said that he never lifted up his eyelids unless it was in the service of the Almighty. He was befriended by R. Pinhas of Koretz and R. Menahem Mendel of Vitebsk.

He was shipwrecked en route to the Holy Land. He interpreted his misfortune as a mark of divine displeasure. Accordingly he requested that there should be no inscription on his gravestone, "for I have not been worthy of visiting the Holy Land."

He is quoted in *Teshuot Hen* (Berdichev, 1816) by R. Gedaliah of Luniets, in *Bat Ayyin* by R. Abraham Dov Ovruch, and by R. Pinhas of Dinowitz in *Siftei Tzaddikim.* His sons, R. Joseph Moses and R. Israel Judah Leib, settled in the Holy Land.

Y. Raphael, *HaHasidut VeEretz Yisrael*, p. 19.

HAYYIM HEIKEL of Amdur (d. 23 *Adar* 1787) – Son of R. Shmuel, Hayyim Heikel (or Heiki) was the disciple of R. Dov Baer, the Maggid of Mezhirech, and R. Aaron the Great of Karlin. He was an ascetic who fasted, mortified his body, and stayed awake for one thousand nights to study the Torah. After the death of the Maggid, he settled in Amdur, near Grodno.

David of Makov, the antagonist of Hasidism, records that R. Hayyim sent emissaries to many communities to "ensnare" souls for Hasidism. Unlike R. Levi Yitzhak of Berdichev and R. Shlomoh of Karlin, who had to leave their posts due to the persecution by the *mitnaggedim*, Hayyim Heikel remained in Amdur until his death. He advocated restraint. He raised his voice in protest against the distortion by the *mitnaggedim* of the true character of the hasidim. Writing to his son R. Shmuel, he advised him that a hasid should not become involved in disputes: "When a man rises up in the morning, he should dedicate every organ, his eyes, his ears, and his mouth, all to the service of God."

R. Hayyim's discourses are to be found in *Hayyim VeHesed*, printed by Bezalel Levin (Warsaw, 1891), and in *Igeret HaKodesh* (Mezyrow, 1794). His son R. Dov settled in Siedlice, and his son R. Shmuel, who died in 1798, succeeded him as rabbi in Amdur.

W. Rabinowitsch, *Lithuanian Hasidism*, pp. 121–140.

HAYYIM JOSHUA of Glogow (1790–1877) – Son of R. Abraham Israel, he was a disciple of R. Menahem Mendel Schneersohn, who sent him on many special missions. One such mission was intended to improve the situation of the Cantonists.

These activities led to his arrest by the czarist authorities in 1845. He was released after three months through the intervention of the rebbe who described him as "my dear friend who is as dear to me as my brother."

He settled in Glogow.

HAYYIM TYRER of Czernowitz (1760–7 *Kislev* 1818)–Son of R. Shlomoh, a descendant of R. Joel Sirkes, he was born in Buczacz. He studied under R. Tzvi Hirsch Kara and under R. Yehiel Michael of Zloczov. He was also influenced by R. Abraham Joshua Heschel of Opatov, R. Aaron Aryeh of Przemyslany, and R. Mordecai of Neshkhiz. His first rabbinical post was in Kosova in Galicia, and between 1798 and 1807 he was rabbi in Czernowitz. He then held rabbinical appointments in Butchan, Mohilev, and Kishinev. In 1796 he was fined fifty florins by the Russian authorities for permitting a private *minyan* in a house of mourning. To fulfill a long-held dream of return to Zion, R. Hayyim made his home in Safed in 1814.

He was known as the "man of the Sabbath" and derived his greatest joy from the sanctity of the Sabbath. He wrote, "One cannot compare the countenance of a human being on a weekday with that on the Sabbath." In accordance with hasidic legend, he appeared to be a head taller on the Sabbath.

The only work of his that was published in his lifetime was *Siddurei Shel Shabbat* (Mohilev, 1813), which has gone through twenty-four editions so far and is regarded as one of the great classics of hasidic literature. His other works, published posthumously, were *Beer Mayyim Hayyim* (Sudzilkov, 1820) on the Pentateuch, which has been reprinted twenty times; *Eretz Hayyim*, comments on the Bible (Czernowitz, 1861); and *Shaar Tefillah* (Sudzilkov, 1825).

His son Kalman Kalonymus, the son-in-law of R. Abraham Joshua Heschel, caused his father great grief when he became a *maskil* and divorced his wife. R. Hayyim, nevertheless, treated him with understanding and affection. The moral of it was that even an errant child should be shown compassion and tolerance. His other son, R. Yaakov Yosef, was rabbi in Mohilev.

R. Hayyim was buried in Safed.

Y. Raphael, *Sefer HaHasidut*, pp. 206–210.

HAZAN, Nahman, of Tulcin (d. 1884)–He helped R. Nathan of Nemirov print R. Nahman's work *Likkutei Halakhot*, the last volume of which appeared in Lvov in 1861. He smuggled out of Russia a number of his own manuscripts, which he printed in Galicia and Romania.

His son, Abraham Hazan (d. 1917), was the author of *Yemei HaTelaot* (Jerusalem, 1933), *Hokhmah U'Tevunah* (Bene Berak, 1962), and *Beur HaLikkutim* (Bene Berak, 1967).

HAZANIM–The *hazan*, or cantor, who conducted services with the help of *meshororim* (singers), was generally not favored by the hasidim. "A *hazan* is a fool," R. Pinhas of Koretz was fond of saying. "He is so close to the gates of *teshuvah* but does not enter, for the gates of song and *teshuvah* are adjacent."

Very few rebbes showed any understanding of the work of the *hazan*. They felt that the purpose of prayer was surrender to God and that the vocation of the *hazan*, which called attention to his own very prominent part in the service, made such surrender extremely difficult. The hasidim believed in a *baal tefillah*. However, R. David of Talnoye was known for his fondness for artistic cantorials. Other rebbes tolerated *hazanim* but would not allow them to conduct services. The Besht conducted his own services, establishing a precedent.

The court *hazanim* of the Ruzhyn dynasty were greatly honored. Yossele Rosenblatt was said to have been blessed by the rebbe of Radomsk. The late rebbe of Lubavitch had one of his students, Cantor Shmuel Kantrowitz, assist at public functions but would not allow him to lead the services. R. Joshua of Belz asked R. Itchele Krakowitzer to sing at a *melaveh malkah*.

In general, it seems, that while most rebbes did not favor *hazanim*, they were not averse to counseling a hasid to become a *hazan* when they felt that this could be his particular life-style.

When a professional *hazan* was appointed, R. Hayyim Halberstam wrote, "I have heard that in the hasidic synagogue in your community, a *hazan* with a choir has been appointed, and I am greatly surprised. . . . Our forefathers struggled hard until they succeeded in removing this scab from the children of Israel. . . . How then could your heart have changed, so as to bring an idol into the House of God?" (*Divrei Hayyim, Orah Hayyim*, Part 2, no. 1, pp. 17 and 18, Lvov, 1875).

He merely reiterated the words of R. Jacob Joseph of Polonnoye, who wrote, "Our souls are weary of listening to the *hazanim*, for this plague has spread in every worthy and pious community. . . . They sin and cause others to sin. . . . They prolong their melodies without end, and the people gossip in the synagogues, interrupting the prayers at times when such interruptions are forbidden" (*Toldot* 100).

Hasidic *shtieblech* did not engage professional cantors. Any man with a good voice was qualified to act as a reader.

Z. Schachter, *The Yehidut*, p. 427.

Z.M.S.

HEBRON–A town southwest of Jerusalem. A number of hasidim settled there in the eighteenth century. R. Abraham Gershon, the brother-in-law of the Besht, lived there for a time and had high praise for his Arab neighbors. In a letter to the Besht, in 1748, he wrote, "The most distinguished of the gentiles are very cordial toward us. When festivities take place they come to share our rejoicing and they entertain us."

By 1820, a group of *Habad* hasidim, under R. Benjamin Beinush and R. Menahem Aryeh Simeon Smerling, settled there. They were encouraged by R. Dov Baer of Lubavitch, who quoted rabbinic authorities to the effect that "one who owns land in Hebron was saved from the tribulations of the grave." He urged the hasidim of Safed and Tiberias to move there. In an appeal dated 1823, he pleaded for the support of Hebron, "the city of our Patriarchs." He advised his followers to secure land there, and he himself bought some land there. Among the early settlers was R. Jacob Slonim, the son-in-law of the rebbe of Lubavitch.

Kollel Habad dispatched R. Yitzhak Ashkenazi to Iran in 1839 to raise funds for the community. Sir Moses Montefiore visited Hebron in the same year and made a census of the inhabitants. He generously supported them throughout his visit in the Holy Land.

The inventory made for Sir Moses Montefiore in 1875 lists various *Habad* institutions in Hebron: a *bikkur holim* society, a *hevrah kaddisha*, a *hahnassat kallah* (aiding orphan girls with their marriage preparations), *olei regalim* (arranging for ten members of the community to represent *Habad* in Jerusalem on the Festivals), *hahnassat orkhim* (providing hospitality for visitors), and *hevrat gemilut hasadim* (granting loans to the poor in time of need).

In 1895, there were about 1,400 Jews in Hebron. Among the rabbis of *Habad* were R. Samuel Segal, R. Simon Menahem Chaikin (1812–1893), and R. Dov Baer Efraim Elitserow. There were two *Habad* synagogues–*Avraham Avinu* and *Bet Menahem*–which were supported by David Sassoon. In 1900, R. Shalom Dov of Lubavitch established a *yeshivah*, *Torat Emet*. In 1929, when R. Joseph Yitzhak Schneersohn visited Hebron, a special permit was granted allowing the rebbe and his party to enter the cave of Machpela by way of Jacob's gate.

The hasidic community suffered severe casualties in the Arab massacre of 1929. The survivors were evacuated from the town. From 1948 to 1967, Hebron was in Arab hands. In 1967, Hebron was liberated by the Israeli forces, and today a number of hasidim are once again living in the 250 housing units in *Kiryat Arba*.

HEDER–The *heder* was a fee-paying, privately owned elementary school for boys, in contrast to the Talmud Torah, which was maintained by the local Jewish community mainly for poor children. The frequent charges of incompetence and ignorance brought against the *melamed* or rebbe (as the *heder* teacher was often styled) placed the institution in a very unfavorable light.

The *heder* was usually accommodated in one small room in the teacher's house, under the most unsatisfactory conditions. Pupils of various grades sat on long benches; the teacher sat at a table facing them, with a cane at his side. The presence of the teacher's wife and family in the same house or room caused distractions, and the lessons were often disrupted by the *melamed*'s carrying on certain other business, such as the writing of *mezuzot*, to augment his meager income.

There were three types of *heder*. The first was the *heder dardeke* for the three- to five-year-old age group–and the only one that occasionally admitted girls. This was the largest, attended by about eighty youngsters, who were divided into three sections: aleph bet; reading from the *Siddur*; and *Humash* in Yiddish translation. The teacher was assisted by two *behelfers*, or helpers, who for a mere pittance not only helped in giving instruction but, inter alia, also brought the youngsters to and from school, played games with them, and relied on private hospitality for their maintenance.

The second category was the *Humash heder*, for some thirty boys between the ages of six and eight, who were soon introduced to Rashi's commentary as a preliminary to the study of *Gemara*. Generally, one *behelfer* sufficed.

Last came the *Talmud heder*, for about twelve boys between the ages of nine and thirteen. The students were invariably at different stages, some even learning *Tosafot*. The rebbe was the sole teacher.

Weekday instruction lasted from early morning until late at night, and on Shabbat there was a regular examination at home in the presence of the teacher and the father. The pressure of conceited parents, on whom the *melamed* relied for his salary, often resulted in the boy's being promoted far too rapidly and led to constant rivalry among teachers to obtain each other's pupils. Moreover, the poverty of most teachers made them mercenary so that they favored the rich pupil.

It must be emphasized that this account of the *heder* system was recorded by educational reformers of the seventeenth to twentieth centuries who concentrated on the faults rather than on the merits. There were more positive aspects such as the warm affection between rebbe and talmid and the fact that many a *heder* pupil graduated to the *yeshivah*, several becoming leading figures in the rabbinic hierarchy.

The *Haskalah* movement, fortified by the Edict of Toleration issued by Joseph II of Austria in 1782, provided the impetus for a revolutionary revision of the *heder* curriculum. Strenuous efforts were made to introduce the "improved" *heder* (*heder metukkan*), which was nationalistic in aim, combining religious education with secular culture and insisting on the revival of Hebrew as a living language. These proved more successful in the communal-run Talmud Torahs, but only here and there were the *hadarim* influenced by the new ideas. By the early decades of the twentieth century, the number of *hadarim* had diminished considerably, largely due to the massive East European exodus to the West. The emigrants brought their traditions with them, and, to the present day, almost exact replicas of the old style of *heder* are to be found in the Jewish communities of Western Europe and the United States.

I. Fishman, *History of Jewish Education in Central Europe*.

I.F.

HEIKHAL HANEGINAH–The kabbalists believed that there is a heavenly palace known as the Temple of Song, into which entrance could be gained only by melody.

R. Nahman of Bratzlav maintained that all melodies are derived from the Temple of Music. Hasidic legend has it that many hasidic rebbes entered the Temple of Music and gained inspiration for melodies. The Besht used even secular melodies as a vehicle for sacred texts.

HEIKHALOT–"Halls" or "palaces." A term used by the *Merkavah* mystics to signify the seven stages through which the initiate must pass on the spiritual ecstatic journey toward a contemplation of the heavenly chariot and the divine glory. This journey was fraught with difficulty and danger. Each hall was guarded by awesome celestial beings, and access could be gained only by the recital of magical formulas, which became more complex as the journey proceeded.

There are many texts extant dealing with the *heikhalot*, but most of them are fragmentary in character, and a critical examination of the whole material is still awaited. The three main sources are *Heikhalot Zutrati* (Lesser Heikhalot); *Heikhalot Rabbati* (Greater Heikhalot), also called *Pirkei Heikhalot*; and *Sefer Heikhalot*, known also as *Third Enoch* or *The Hebrew Book of Enoch*. This source literature represents an early phase in the development of Jewish mysticism. Some of the texts can be dated to the third century and appear to represent authentic traditions going back to tannaitic times. They contain elaborate hymns of glory, said to emanate from the ministering angels and other attendants of the divine chariot. They also give detailed instructions concerning the preparations that the mystic has to make before beginning the ascent to the heavenly realm.

There was little significant development of the *heikhalot* theme in later Kabbalah, since it tended to become intertwined with medieval astronomical and philosophical ideas concerning the nature of the heavenly spheres.

G. Scholem, *Major Trends in Jewish Mysticism* (Second Lecture), *Encyclopaedia Judaica*, vol. 11, col. 1387–1388.

D.G.

HELLER, Meshullam Feivish Halevi, of Zawierce (1740–20 *Kislev* 1795)–Son of R. Aaron Moses, rabbi of Sniatyn, a descendant of R. Yom Tov Lipman Heller. He married the daughter of R. Mordecai Halpern of Brzezany. He was a disciple of R. Dov Baer, the Maggid of Mezhirech; R. Menahem Mendel of Przemyslany; and, above all, R. Michael Yehiel of Zloczov.

He stressed purity of thoughts and strove for the truth with no ulterior motives. He held the teachings of R. Yitzhak Luria in great esteem and maintained that the *Zohar* was a valuable source of knowledge and truth.

He was the author of *Derekh Emet* (Lvov, 1830), *Darkhei Tzeddek* (Lvov, 1857), *Har HaShem* (Lvov, 1840), and *Yosher Divrei Emet* (Munkacs, 1905). Many of his sayings have been published in *Kitvei Kodesh* (Des, 1933) and in *Likkutei Yekarim* (Lvov, 1792).

A.Shu.

HELLER, Samson (1782–19 *Heshvan* 1840)–Son of R. Meshullam Feivish Halevi, he married the daughter of R. Joseph Yoska Halevi Horowitz of Voltchisk-Iasi. He was rabbi of Jezerizany. He was the author of *Nezirat Shimshon* on Pentateuch, Prophets, and Talmud, which was printed together with his father's book *Yosher Divrei Emet* (Munkacz, 1905). He was succeeded by his son R. Yosef Yoske, who was the son-in-law of R. Meir of Przemyslany.

A.Shu.

HEREM–As Hasidism became a widespread movement in the latter part of the eighteenth century, it aroused fierce opposition on the part of rabbis and lay leaders in various communities, notably in White Russia and Lithuania. This opposition culminated in the proclamation of a *herem*, or ban, against the hasidim and their leaders. First issued in 1772 by the communities of Vilna and Brody, the bans were renewed several times, most significantly by the authorities centered in Vilna in 1781 and 1797.

The reasons for the rabbinic opposition to Hasidism are manifold and complex. On one hand, the bans themselves mention various alleged infractions of the law, most of them of a rather minor nature, such as the tendency of hasidim to prefer the Sephardic version of the liturgy to the generally accepted version of the Ashkenazim, laxness as to the hour of prayer, interruptions in the service, and a slight change in the preparation of knives for ritual slaughter. They also speak of wild or unruly behavior on the part of the hasidim and recount with particular horror the report that hasidim are said to have made light of scholars and the study of Torah. On the other hand, hasidic sources attribute the bans to a possible misunderstanding of Hasidism on the part of the rabbis, based on "false reports" they had received from "wicked persons." *Habad* sources admit that there were certain excesses in enthusiasm during the early days of the movement but assert that these were soon corrected.

It is undoubtedly true that certain of the early hasidic leaders showed less than the traditional high measure of respect for scholarship. The Jewish community of Eastern Europe had long been ruled by an oligarchy consisting of the wealthy and the learned. As a popular pietistic movement, Hasidism often chose to contrast the ideal of simple faith and devotion with the irrelevant edifice of abstruse Talmudic learning. Hasidism taught that it was not through intellectuality but rather by way of joyous and wholehearted prayer that human beings could come close to God.

Historians have further noted that Hasidism came about in part as a reaction to the breakdown of communal leadership in the eighteenth century. The *tzaddik* became the rallying point for a new type of community organization; rather than viewing the local rabbi and Jewish civil authorities as their leaders, Jews now began to identify themselves as followers of a given *tzaddik*. Thus political, economic, and religious factors combined to set the stage for the anti-hasidic *herem*.

The most important personage of the anti-hasidic forces was R. Elijah, the Gaon of Vilna. Although himself a leading kabbalist, the Gaon was an elitist when it came to mystical teachings; it seems that he foresaw dangers in the popular promulgation of mysticism, perhaps recalling the Sabbatarian and Frankist debacles.

The latter two *haramim* were proclaimed in particular response to the publication of two of the classics of hasidic literature—the *Toldot Yaakov Yosef* (published 1780) and the *Tanya* (1796). Here it would seem that the implicit theological radicalism and near pantheism of hasidic thought further contributed to the conflict. In a world thoroughly permeated with divinity and in which all human actions can serve as paths to God, Hasidism's opponents felt there lay a danger that the specific *mitzvot* of Judaism would lose their centrality.

The conflict tended to die down at the turn of the nineteenth century. Hasidism in practice had shown itself to remain fully within the Law, and both the rabbis and the *tzaddikim* saw a greater common enemy in the new *Haskalah* movement, which was moving eastward from Berlin. The Russian constitution of 1804 forbade the use of the *herem* by rabbis within the czarist realm, and no more was heard of bans against the hasidim.

There were several occasions within the history of Hasidism when internecine strife raised the threat of *herem* by one hasidic group against another. In 1803 the supporters of R. Nahman of Bratzlav sought to proclaim a ban against Aryeh Leib (the "Zeide") of Shpola for publicly disgracing Nahman. Levi Yitzhak of Berdichev managed to dissuade them from taking so radical a step. The denunciations of the Bratzlav hasidim by R. Moses Tzvi of Savran in the middle 1830s were tantamount to a *herem*, although an official ban was not permitted by the authorities. The opponents of R. Simhah Bunem of Przysucha, suspecting him of modernizing tendencies, also unsuccessfully sought to issue a *herem* against him at the famous wedding in Ostila (Ustilug). The only incident in which a *herem* actually was pronounced by one hasidic group against another, however, was in the context of the controversy between Zanz and Sadgora in 1869–1870, when the hasidim of Sadgora in Jerusalem formally issued a ban against R. Hayyim Halberstam of Zanz.

A.G.

HERSCHBERG, Abraham Mordecai (1916–1985)—He was born in Kadnic, near Biala, and educated in the *yeshivot* of Brest-Litovsk and Lublin by R. Meir Shapira. He was ordained by R. E. Michelson of the Warsaw *Bet Din*.

After living in Vilna and Japan, he became rabbi of the *Tzeire Daat*, in Montreal, and then at the *Shaarei Tefilah Bene Reuven*, in Chicago. He married Minche, the daughter of R. Eichenstein. For the last years of his life he was rabbi in Mexico.

He was survived by a son, Joshua Heschel of Square Town, and a daughter, Hannah Rachel of Jerusalem.

HERZL, Theodor (1860–1904)—Herzl, the father of political Zionism, did not succeed in enlisting the sympathies of Hasidism for the restoration of the Jewish homeland in Palestine through political means.

The battle was then raging between Hasidism and *Haskalah*. The hasidim associated *Haskalah* with assimilation and even apostasy. Many of the *maskilim* carried the flag of Zionism. Moreover, repossession of the promised land at this stage was regarded by many hasidic rabbis as tantamount to interference with the divine order of things.

Herzl was anxious to enlist the support of the hasidim. His intermediary was Aaron Marcus, who had been a disciple of R. Shlomoh HaKohen of Radomsk. On April 27, 1896, Marcus wrote to Herzl, "Your wonderful pamphlet *The Jewish State* held me enthralled for hours. . . . It came like a lightning bolt in the dark of night to both the assimilationists and the hasidim, who are so bitterly opposed to each other."

In his diary, under May 8, 1896, Herzl noted, "The hasid Aaron Marcus again writes to me a fine letter in which he holds out the possibility that the three million hasidim of Poland will join my movement. I assured him that the participation of the Orthodox will be welcome, but no theocracy will be created" (*Diaries*, vol. 1, p. 347).

In a letter dated May 7, 1896, Marcus gives Herzl an illuminating account of Hasidism in Eastern Europe. "These masses are under the guidance of some fifty to sixty rabbis, on whom the propaganda will have to be concentrated."

The Zionist leader kept in touch with R. Leibish Mendel Halevi Landau of Przemysl, who offered to negotiate with R. Moses David Friedman of Chortkov. A letter to the rebbe of Chortkov dated November 28, 1896 was drafted by Michael Berkovitz, Herzl's Hebrew secretary, but it is not clear whether it was ever delivered.

An entry in Herzl's diary for November 10, 1896 records, "A man from Jerusalem named Bak came to see me. . . . He claims to be under the patronage of the Galician wonder rabbi Friedman."

In December 1897, Herzl met R. Israel Friedman, the rabbi's son; Marcus joined them in trying to persuade the rabbi to convene a conference of rabbis to promote the aims of Zionism. In January 1900, Marcus once again traveled to Chortkov, where he stayed for three weeks. The rabbi had asked him to contact R. Benjamin Aryeh Weisz of Czernowitz, with the suggestion that he summon rabbis to negotiate with the Zionist executive. However, the conference never took place.

The rabbi of Chortkov was not Herzl's only contact with the world of Hasidism. Herzl reports on yet another encounter: "One of the most curious figures I have yet met is Rabbi Horowitz, the son-in-law of the wonder rabbi. . . . He promised to arouse the interest of all the wonder rabbis."

Herzl also strove for the attention of the hasidim of Poland. Writing to R. Yehudah Aryeh Alter of Ger in 1899, Herzl insisted that Zionism was not opposed to religion. Herzl's moving appeal remained unanswered. To the Polish hasidim, Herzl, who had been brought up in an assimilationist milieu, was not the ideal founder for a homeland in Palestine. The rebbe of Ger could not be persuaded that Zionism would not weaken Orthodoxy, and such was the attitude of the overwhelming majority of hasidic leaders until the outbreak of World War I.

J. Rapoport, "A Letter from Dr. Herzl to the Rabbi of Chortkov," pp. 351–352.

HESCHEL, Abraham Joshua (1907–1972)—One of the most loved and greatest thinkers of the twentieth century, he was the son of R. Moses Mordecai, the rabbi of Medziborz, and Rivkah Reizel (Perlow). Heschel, one of six children, was orphaned when nine years old. Of his four sisters, the eldest, Sarah, married the Kopyczynicer rebbe; the others, Devorah Miriam, Ester Simah, and Gittel, perished in the Holocaust. His brother Jacob was rabbi in London.

In addition to being, on his father's side, a descendant of R. Israel of Ruzhyn, R. Abraham Joshua Heschel of Opatov, and R. Dov Baer of Mezhirech, Heschel was related on his mother's side to R. Levi Yitzchak of Berdichev and R. Pinhas of Korzec. It was the Novominsker rebbe, R. Alter Yisrael Shimon, who, after the untimely death of his father, became the spiritual guide of the young family.

Heschel spent two years studying in Vilna where he associated with a group of young poets, the "Jung Vilna," and published a volume of poems in Yiddish, *Der Shem Hameforash-Mensch*.

At the age of twenty-two he moved to Berlin and studied at the Humboldt University and at the Hochschule fur die Wissenschaft des Judentums. In 1937, he succeeded Martin Buber as director of the Lehrhaus in Frankfurt. In 1938, he was deported to Poland and fled to England in July 1939.

Arriving in the United States in 1940, he taught at the Hebrew Union College, Cincinnati, until 1943, then at the Jewish Theological Seminary of New York. In 1946, he married Sylvia Strauss, a talented pianist, and their only child, Hannah Shoshanah, follows her father's footsteps.

He rejected conventional conceptual analysis in the field of religious philosophy and mysticism. Instead, he proposed an existentialist approach characterized by depth theology and situational thinking to explore "the total situation of humanity," which is God's stake in human history.

Among his numerous works of Judaica and religious philosophy, three books provide substantial information for study of the area of Hasidism: *The Earth Is the Lord's* (Yiddish, 1946; English, 1950) describes the inner world of the East European Jewry significantly influenced by Hasidism; *KOTZK, the Struggle for Integrity* (Yiddish, 1973) discusses the problem of hasidic doctrine and its practice revolving around the life and teaching of R. Mendel of Kotzk; *A Passion for Truth* (English, 1973) is a comparison of the Kotzker rebbe and Soren Kierkegaard. Anxious to preserve the exact meaning and precise nuance of hasidic dialogue and discourses originally expressed in Yiddish, Heschel, who was uniquely sensitive to the function and limit of language, wrote *Kotzk* in Yiddish. This contribution to

Yiddish culture is highly appreciated by students of Yiddish as well as Hasidism.

Unlike other contemporary existentialists for whom philosophic ideas are more important than acts, Heschel was concerned with prayer, education, and civil rights, and he undertook a special mission to the Vatican in an effort to revise its prejudice against the Jews. These acts represented silent attempts in the hasidic tradition of emphasis upon *maasim* (practice, deeds) to stir the conscience of human beings. Indeed, many central ideas of Heschelian philosophy developed from hasidic ones: wonder (*peleh*), awe (*yira*), faith (*emunah*), ultimacy (*takhlis*), and more.

Sensitive to the problems of contemporary life, Heschel gives not only an answer but also a profound insight to comprehend "the holy dimension," which is given with and within experience, and he urges people to return to God, for God is in search of them. Religion, according to him, consists of God's question and man's answer: Where art thou? (Genesis 3:9). God is the subject "I," and man is the object "thou," or even "it."

The indebtedness of human existence to God for its life and holiness, which stands in the center of Heschel's consciousness, thus encourages us to celebrate life, to sanctify time, and to share the continuing efforts of creation as God's partners. By recognizing the value of deed in which the divine will is planted, Heschel succeeded in penetrating the veil of mystery and made deed, furthermore, the source of human commitment. He founded the Yivo Hasidic Archives Department in New York.

He did not endorse the Scholem-Weiss hypothesis of the origin of Hasidism. He regarded the Besht as a revivalist rather than a revolutionary. His hasidic essays on R. Pinhas of Korzec, R. Gershon Kutover, R. Nahman of Kosov, and R. Isaac of Drohobycz have been collected in a book entitled *The Circle of the Baal Shem Tov*, which was edited by Samuel H. Dresner and published by the University of Chicago Press in 1985.

J.Y.T.

HESCHEL, Abraham Joshua, of Berdichev (d. 25 *Shevat* 1909) – Son of R. Mordecai and son-in-law of R. Eleazar Shapira of Polonnoye. He succeeded his grandfather as rabbi of Polonnoye and Berdichev. He was renowned for his charity and began each day by distributing money to the poor.

HESCHEL, Abraham Joshua, of Kaminka (1832–19 *Tishri* 1880) – Son of R. Meshullam Zuzya of Zinkov. In *Adar* 1849 he married Leah Rachel, the daughter of R. Shalom Joseph of Sadgora. In 1864 he succeeded his father as rebbe of Medziborz. He was the author of *Or Yehoshua*, a manuscript published in Jerusalem in 1982.

He was survived by seven children: His sons were R. Israel Shalom Joseph, R. Yitzhak Meir, R. Mordecai, and R. Meshullam Zusya. His daughters were Gitel, Havvah, and Deborah. His widow remarried to R. David Moses of Chortkov.

HESCHEL, Abraham Joshua, of Kopyczynice/New York (4 *Iyyar* 1888–16 *Tammuz* 1967) – Son of R. Yitzhak Meir. His mother was the daughter of R. Mordecai Feivish Friedman of Husyatin. In *Elul* 1909 he married his cousin Sarah Berachah, the daughter of R. Moses Mordecai Heschel of Medziborz. After his marriage he stayed with his father-in-law for a time and then returned to Kopyczynice.

During the First World War, he, together with many of his relatives, lived in Vienna, where on Rosh Hashanah 1936, he succeeded his father as rebbe in Vienna. He established an orphanage in Baden, near Vienna. At the Nazi Anschluss, he was imprisoned and in 1939 emigrated to the United States, where he established his synagogue *Bet Avraham* on the East Side of New York; in 1965 he moved to Borough Park.

On one of his frequent visits to the Holy Land, he established an orphanage in Petah Tikvah. He helped financially the *Hinukh Atzmai* and other Torah institutions in Israel and in the United States. He died in Monsey, New York, but was interred in Tiberias.

He left three sons: R. Moses Mordecai (1937–1975), who succeeded him but was rebbe for only seven years; R. Meshullam Suzya, who declined to succeed his brother; and R. Israel (d. 1993), who lived in London during World War II and also declined to succeed his brother. He later established a Kopyczynice *Bet HaMidrash* on the East Side.

HESCHEL, Abraham Joshua, of Tarnopol (1892–4 *Nisan* 1943) – Son of R.

Israel Shalom Joseph of Medziborz. In *Adar* 1912 he married his first cousin, Miriam, the daughter of R. Yitzhak Meir of Kopyczynice. In 1911 he succeeded his father as rebbe in Medziborz and suffered under communist oppression for six years. In 1925 he left Russia and settled in Tarnopol.

The Nazis offered to free him on condition that twenty-five Jews be delivered into their hands. The rebbe steadfastly refused. He, his wife, and his only daughter, Berachah Dinah, were murdered in the village of Piotrokov, near Tarnopol.

HESCHEL, Israel Shalom Joseph, of Medziborz (1853–29 *Av* 1911) – Son of R. Abraham Joshua Heschel, whom he succeeded as rebbe in 1881, a position he held for thirty years. In *Elul* 1866 he married his cousin Sarah Rebeccah, who died six years later without issue. He remarried to Batsheba Treina, the daughter of R. Shimshon Hordov. He was succeeded by his son, R. Abraham Joshua Heschel.

HESCHEL, Meshullam Zuzya, of Zinkov (1813–3 *Elul* 1864) – Son of R. Yitzhak Meir of Zinkov, he succeeded his father as rebbe of Zinkov. He married Simah, the daughter of R. Israel of Savran. He published the work *Ohev Yisrael* in 1863 and *Nishmat Adam*, by R. Aaron Shmuel of Kramnitz (Warsaw, 1863).

He had seven children, three daughters and four sons, R. Hayyim Menahem, R. Samuel, R. Yehiel, and R. Abraham Joshua Heschel of Medziborz, who succeeded him.

Y. Alfasi, *HaRav MiApta*, pp. 162–164.

HESCHEL, Moses Mordecai, of Medziborz (1873–27 *Heshvan* 1917) – Son of R. Abraham Joshua Heschel of Medziborz. He was orphaned very young and was brought up by his uncle the rabbi of Chortkov, who married his mother, Rachel Leah. He married Rebecca Reizel, the daughter of R. Jacob Perlow of Novominsk (a twin sister of R. Alter Yisrael Shimon Perlow of Novominsk), where he lived for ten years. In 1900 he became rabbi of Pelcovizna, near Warsaw. He was very concerned about the welfare of the Jewish conscripts and provided meals for them during the Festivals.

His daughter, Sarah, married R. Abraham Joshua Heschel of Kopyczynice. His sons were R. Jacob Heshel of London and Prof. Abraham Joshua Heschel of New York.

HESCHEL, Moses Mordecai (17 *Sivan* 1927–17 *Nisan* 1976) – Son of R. Abraham Joshua Heschel of Kopyczynice, he was born in Vienna. He studied in American yeshivot. He married Hannah, the daughter of R. Tzvi Hirsch Brendler.

Like his father he was a great supporter of the Aguda and a member of the world executive. In 1969 he succeeded his father as rebbe. He died suddenly and was buried in Tiberias. He is survived by four children – two sons and two daughters.

HESCHEL, Yehiel, of Krilivits (1843–9 *Tammuz* 1916) – Son of R. Meshullam Zuzya of Zinkov, he married Merel, the daughter of R. Joshua Rokeah of Belz. He succeeded his brother R. Shmuel as rabbi of Morava-Krilivits in Podolia. He visited his hasidim in the outlying villages of Podolia and Bessarabia.

He died in Kishinev. His only son, R. Meshullam Zuzya, died in his lifetime. He was survived by five daughters.

HESCHEL, Yitzhak Meir, of Kopyczynice (1862–1 *Tishri* 1936) – Son of Abraham Joshua Heschel, he was born in Medziborz on 21 *Kislev*. In 1881 he married Gitel, daughter of R. Mordecai Shragai of Husyatin. In 1894 he settled in Kopyczynice, where he had a large following.

In *Adar* 1912 he participated in the rabbinical conference convened by R. Israel of Chortkov in Czernowitz when the *Histadrut HaHaredim* was established. He also attended the *Knessiyyah Gedolah* in Vienna.

During World War I he and his family found refuge in Vienna. His home in Vienna was a haven for the needy. He would visit his followers in Galicia and Bukovina annually.

He died in Vienna and was succeeded by his son, R. Abraham Joshua Heschel. His other sons were R. Moses Heschel, R. Shalom Joseph, and R. Mordecai Shragai.

Y. Alfasi, *HaRav MiApta*, pp. 180–185.

HESCHEL, Yitzhak Meir, of Medziborz/Haifa (11 *Av* 1904–1 *Av* 1985) – Son of R. Yisrael Shalom Joseph. In 1929 he married Sarah, the daughter of R. Nahum

Yoel Rabinowicz of Kantikoziba. He succeeded his father as rebbe of Medziborz. From 1931 he served as rabbi of Odessa under the oppression of Soviet rule.

In 1936 he settled in Haifa, and from 1941 he lived in New York. In 1968, he returned to Haifa, where he established a synagogue, *kollel*, and kindergarten. He left three daughters.

HESCHEL, Yitzhak Meir, of Zinkov (1776–1 *Adar* 1855) – Son of R. Abraham Joshua Heschel of Opatov, he married Mirel, the daughter of R. Hayyim Jacob Strum of Dukla. From 1800 he succeeded his father as rabbi of Kolbuszov and later became rabbi of Zmygrod Nowy and Zinkov.

He eventually succeeded his father as rebbe of Medziborz. He was also active as a preacher in nearby Zinkov. Hence, he was known as the rebbe of Zinkov. He loved Zinkov, because it was the only village with no church. He had many followers in Podolia, Volhynia, and Bessarabia. His son, R. Meshullam Zuzya, succeeded him in Zinkov.

HESHEL, Jacob (1903–3 *Tevet* 1971) – Son of R. Moses Mordecai of Pelcovizna, he was born in Minsk-Mazowiesk. On the death of his father when he was fourteen, he moved to Warsaw with his widowed mother and was greatly influenced by R. Alter Israel Shimon of Novominsk. He studied at the Mesifta *Yeshivah* in Warsaw. He subsequently lived in Vienna where, in 1931, he married his relative, Sarah, the daughter of R. Nahum Mordecai Friedman of Chortkov.

In 1939 he came to London. In 1947 he was appointed rabbi of the Edgware *Adat Yisrael* congregation. He helped to edit the homiletical book *Tov Doresh*, by R. Nahum Mordecai of Chortkov, and contributed an essay entitled "History of Hasidism in Austria."

He was buried in Enfield Cemetery, London. He is survived by one daughter, Thena, a program director at the British Broadcasting Corporation.

HESS, MOSES (1812–1875) – Born in Bonn, Germany, Hess became one of the ideological founders of the socialist movement and a coworker of Karl Marx. Unlike the latter, however, he was a romantic, with a healthy regard for the unique differentiae of nations and races. In fact, he asserted that the struggle between races constituted the basic motif of world history. Modern society, in his view, was shaped by the Aryans and the Semites, the former stressing aesthetics and logic, and the latter, ethics and holiness. The freedom and self-determination of all nationalities, he believed, will bring about the age of universal peace.

His little book *Rome and Jerusalem* developed the basic ideas of Zionist socialism. He believed that the national spirit of Judaism was socialistic in essence, as demonstrated by the laws regarding allotment of land and the Jubilee year and that egoism was foreign to the Jews in their own native habitat but that the Western Jews were bent on assimilation.

His plans for the rebuilding of a socialist Jewish society in Palestine were based on what he heard regarding the Jews of the Pale of Settlement in Russia and the province of Galicia in Austria. He believed that hasidic fellowships represented the principles of fraternity and mutual concern and that they demonstrated that the social idealism of Jewish people was still alive and vigorous. Hence, a political renaissance of world Jewry is possible.

Hess was an ardent disciple of Spinoza. From Solomon Maimon's autobiography, he learned that the philosophy of Hasidism was a religious-mystical version of Spinozistic pantheism. He might also have heard of the interest R. Dov Baer, son of R. Shneur Zalman ("Der Mitteler Rav" in *Habad* Hasidism), expressed in the settlement of Jews on newly conquered land in southern Russia. He was also familiar with the efforts of R. Tzvi Hirsch Kalisher to establish colonies of religious Jews in the Holy Land.

J. Frankel, *Prophets and Prophecy*, pp. 6–28, 183, 257, 288.

M. Hess, *Rom und Jerusalem*.

J.B.A.

HEVRAT YISHUV ERETZ YISRAEL – A society established by a number of hasidim in Vienna to work for the rebuilding of the Holy Land. The founder members were R. Hayyim Meir Yehiel Shapira of Drohobycz, R. Solomon Friedman, and R. Moses Reich (secretary).

The initial announcement appeared in the *Hazphirah* on 13 *Nisan* 1918. "Our program is that of Ezra and Nehemiah, to establish the people in the land of Israel, in the spirit of the Torah and Jewish tradition," asserted the signatories, among whom were R. Hayyim Meir Yehiel Shapira, R. Yitzhak Mordecai, R. Jacob Joseph Twersky of Stanislav, and R. Solomon Hayyim Friedman of Sadgora.

Branches were set up in Drohobycz and Stryj. The society eventually merged with the Mizrachi, and its delegates participated in the twelfth Zionist Congress held in Karlsbad.

S. Federbusch, *HaHasidut VeZion*, p. 270.

HILLEL of Poryck (1795–11 *Av* 1864)–Son of R. Meir Halevi of Brahin, he was a disciple of R. Abraham Dov of Ovruch and of R. Mordecai of Chernobyl. He then became a devoted follower of R. Dov Baer of Lubavitch and R. Menahem Mendel. He was rabbi first in Poryck, then in Brobruisk.

He died in Herson. He was the author of *Likkutei Biurim* on Torah (Warsaw, 1868), *Pelah Harimon* on Genesis (Vilna, 1887), *Imrei Noam* on Rosh Hashanah (Vilna, 1836), and *Pelah Harimon* on the Song of Songs (Pultava, 1918), and many of his discourses are printed in the periodical *Yagdil Torah* of Lubavitch.

His son, R. Zalman, died in his father's lifetime, and he brought up his grandson, R. Pinhas. His son-in-law was R. Rafael Mordecai, a grandson of R. Shneur Zalman of Liady.

HILLEL MOSES MESHEL of Bialystok (1883–24 *Heshvan* 1907)–Son of R. Tzvi Hirsch, the head of the community of Bialystok, he was a descendant of R. Isaiah Horowitz. For ten years he was a disciple of R. Menahem Mendel of Kotzk, R. Menahem Mendel Schneersohn of Lubavitch, R. Yitzhak Meir Alter of Ger, and R. Yitzhak of Neshkhiz. He married the daughter of R. Eliyahu of Sokolovka, a hasid of Kotzk.

It was R. Jacob Aryeh Guterman of Radzymin who encouraged him to settle in Jerusalem. He refused to be a rebbe, and his wife ran a bakery to maintain them.

He kept in close touch with the kabbalist R. Simon Tzvi Horowitz and R. Jacob Orenstein. He was particularly concerned with safeguarding the sanctity of the Temple Mount. He would not permit people to even touch the Western Wall, and he strongly advocated the reintroduction of *mishmarot*, the watchmen who in Temple times guarded the Temple in Jerusalem. In 1888 he proposed the building of a *Bet HaMidrash* near the Western Wall and enlisted the support of the philanthropist Mendel Rand. A site was acquired but the scheme never materialized.

He was a prolific writer and the author of *Or LaYesharim* on tractate *Pesahim* (Jerusalem, 1889); *Or LaYesharim*, novellas on the tractate *Pesahim* (Jerusalem, 1891); *Hosen Yeshuot*, novellas on the tractate *Baba Kamma* (Jerusalem, 1879); *Tefillah LeMosheh*, a commentary on the prayer book (Jerusalem, 1898); and *Mishkenot L'Abir Yaakov* on tractate *Tamid* (Jerusalem, 1875). All his books were reprinted in Jerusalem in 1972 by Bezalel Landau.

HINUKH ATZMAI–The education branch of the Aguda, which was established in Israel in 1953 with an enrollment of 16,000. By 1995, there were 60,000 students. In these schools a thorough study of Jewish subjects goes hand in hand with a secular curriculum.

It has extended the school day in order to cover a comprehensive syllabus. Preparation for *yeshivah* is the goal of its educational activities. It operates a widespread network of kindergartens and has teachers' seminaries. The language of instruction is Hebrew, and boys and girls are segregated. It is guided by the ideology of the Aguda and is supported by the hasidic rebbes of Ger, Vizhnitz, and Sadgora.

In 1993, 3,000 children from Russia were enrolled in the *Hinukh Atzmai*, which established special schools and *ulpanim* for those children.

Among the active leaders are Shlomoh Grossbart, Samuel Weinberg, and Meir Luria.

HIRSCH, Samson Raphael (1808–1888)–German leader of Jewish Orthodoxy who, from 1851, was the rabbi of the separatist Orthodox community of Frankfurt-am-Main.

He was highly esteemed by the hasidim. R. Israel Friedman of Ruzhyn was eager for Hirsch's work–especially his commentary on the Pentateuch–to be translated into Hebrew. R. Abraham Mordecai Alter of Ger called Hirsch the "*tzaddik* of Frankfurt" and described him as a living "*Musar* book."

HISTORY AND HISTORIOGRAPHY–From its very beginning, the

history of the hasidic movement was recorded by its most ardent opponents and its staunchest supporters. These polarized attitudes are gradually diminishing.

One of the first recorded statements on Hasidism was made by Moses ben Jacob of Satanov (*Mishmeret HaKodesh* [Zolkiev, 1746], p. 2/a); it was a negative comment. In the 1770s, some adverse testimonies against Hasidism followed, Israel Loebel and David of Makow being the most outspoken (M. Wilensky, *Hasidim U'Mitnaggedim*, 1970). The polemic literature included a wide range of accusations leveled against Hasidism, dealing mainly with the hasidic changes in traditional practices, eccentric hasidic behavior, and separatist tendencies.

Hasidic literature began to appear in print in 1780; the first published work was by Jacob Joseph of Polonnoye—*Toldot Yaakov Yosef* (1780). It was followed by an ever-increasing number of books compiled in the manner of homiletic discourses (*derashot*) on selected weekly readings from the Torah. Another type of hasidic literature consisted of expository pamphlets and epistles. Among the most known ones are *Tanya* (1796); *Iggeret HaKodesh* (1787), by R. Shneur Zalman of Liady, and similar works by R. Menahem Mendel of Vitebsk, R. Hayyim Heikel of Amdur, R. Elimelekh of Lejask, and *Kuntres HaHitpaalut* (1876) by R. Dov Baer.

This literature represented both a reply to contemporary problems and an indirect reply to the opponents of Hasidism. Despite the highly inflammatory tone of the polemic literature, the writings of R. Shneur Zalman of Liady are restrained in tone and are written in a better Hebrew and a more lucid style than his opponents'. Kabbalistic and halakhic writings, liturgy, vision literature, and narrative literature helped to mold the movement.

The literature of the movement, best known through tales and anecdotes, was first committed to book form in 1814. *Shivhei HaBesht* (Kopys, 1814) is the indispensable "chronicle" of the Besht's life. The tradition of collecting and publishing hasidic tales continues to the present. Some question the reliability of oral history as a valid historical source. Nevertheless, every one of the various forms of hasidic literature serve as the main sources for the movement's history—by those who were attracted to Hasidism and by those who rejected it.

With the abatement of the polemic literature and the death of David of Makow in 1814, the Enlightenment represented the most formidable opponent to Hasidism. The *maskilim* saw in Hasidism a manifestation of primitive Judaism and an obstacle to the modernization of Jewish life. The most ardent opponent was Joseph Perl of Tarnopol. Attracted to Hasidism in his youth, he acquired knowledge of the movement's way of life. In his German manuscript *Uber das wesen der Sekte Chassidim* (1816), he condemned Hasidism, claiming it misled innocent believers. In his principal work, *Megaleh Temirin* (Revealer of Secrets) (Vienna, 1819), he wrote satirical stories in the form of letters.

Isaac Erter, a maskil, continued in the same vein. Hypocrisy, ignorance, and superstition characterized in his views the world of Hasidism. Those views are expressed in his book *HaZofeh LeBet Yisrael* (Watchman of the House of Israel [1858]).

Eliezer Zweifel (1815–1888) was the first writer of the *Haskalah* to view Hasidism sympathetically. His father was a follower of *Habad*, and by nature, Zweifel was a moderate. In his work *Shalom al Yisrael* (Peace to Israel 1868–1873 [Jerusalem, 1972]), he defended Hasidism. The books included numerous hasidic sources and their analysis. The work sparked a reevaluation of Hasidism and eventually led to a historical appraisal of the movement by M. J. Berdyczewski, S. A. Horodezky, S. Dubnow, M. Buber, and others.

The writings of Heinrich Graetz, on Hasidism, presented a setback to the favorable climate created by Zweifel. In his *History*, Graetz showed no understanding for mystical forces and movements such as Kabbalah and Hasidism. He saw Hasidism as a "daughter of darkness" (*History of the Jews*, vol. 5 [1956], p. 375) and the founder of the movement as a man whom "the graces did not sit by his cradle." He intensely disliked Hasidism and considered it a malignant growth in the body of Judaism. His dislike for this East European sect was extended to the "fossilized Polish talmudists."

Micha Josef Berdyczewski (later Bin Gorion) was a native of Medziborz and a descendant of hasidic rabbis. He found in Hasidism vitality and individuality and viewed the movement as a Jewish renaissance, an antithesis of rabbinic Judaism, and an attempt to

HISTORY AND HISTORIOGRAPHY

break down the barriers between humanity and God.

Martin Buber was influenced by Berdyczewski. In principle Buber adopted Berdyczewski's opinions, but Buber's thesis was more profound. At first his interest in Hasidism was essentially aesthetic. He translated *The Tales of Rabbi Nachman* into German: *Die Geschichten des Rabbi Nachman* (1906) (*The Tales of Rabbi Nahman* [1956]) and *Die Legende des Baalschem* (1908) (*The Legend of the Baal Shem* [1955]). Later his interest turned from the aesthetic aspect in Hasidism to its content. Among others, Buber particularly emphasized the concrete and historical importance of Hasidism. It led him to place a greater emphasis on the movement's literature, tales, and anecdotes rather than on its theoretical writings.

Buber saw the essence of Hasidism as the direct encounter between human beings and the world around them. It is best reflected in his work *BePardes HaHasidut* ([1945], *Hasidism and Modern Man* [1958], and *The Origin and Meaning of Hasidism* [1960]).

The new approach to Hasidism by Berdyczewski, Buber, Y. L. Peretz, and A. J. Heschel helped to mold neo-Hasidism. The Zionist *maskil* Samuel Joseph Ish Horowitz (1862–1922) attacked the neo-Hasidism of Berdyczewski and Buber in a series of articles, later published under the title *HaHasidut VeHaHaskalah* (Berlin, 1909). He dismissed the view that Hasidism has unique qualities of authenticity, encourages activism, and is of a revolutionary nature. He saw in the hasidic movement the continuity of traditions rather than a break in them. The harsh statements by S. J. Ish Horowitz were the exception rather than the norm for history and historiography of Hasidism in the twentieth century.

Aaron Marcus, a native of Germany, joined the hasidic movement in Poland in 1862. A major part of his work was devoted to the defense of Hasidism and explanation of hasidic doctrine. Yet despite Marcus's great erudition, his book on Hasidism, *Der Chassidismus* (under the pseudonym of Verus, 1901), does not withstand modern critical scholarship.

Samuel Abba Horodezky studied in the courts of *tzaddikim* in Malin and Chernobyl and was the founder of the hasidic archives of the Schocken Publishing House (1935). His major books on Hasidism are entitled *HaHasidut VeHaHasidim* (Hasidism and hasidim) (1922–1923) and are basically monographs on the great hasidic personalities and their doctrines, including a few brief sketches of women. He is informative and nonargumentative in his presentation, and he helped to some extent to break the boycott by the *maskilim* against the hasidim. He is accused by his critics of presenting Hasidism in a romantic light, namely, the overemphasis of personality at the expense of ideology and lack of consideration of the literature of opposition. He edited *Shivhei HaBesht* (1922) in a fashion detrimental to the original structure of the book.

Simon Dubnow, at the age of 70, summarized his lifelong study of Hasidism, producing thereby the most comprehensive history of Hasidism. His *Toldot HaHasidut* (History of Hasidism) (1930–32) still serves as the most basic book for the study of Hasidism. It is a combination of source material, critical analysis, and interpretation of both the history and the theory of the movement. Dubnow saw in Hasidism a fresh manifestation of Jewish creativity, a source of rejuvenation for East European Jewry, and a new Jewish center that had preserved its tradition but had not yet entered an era of cooperation with other nations. His work is still the single most indispensable book in the research of Hasidism. Dubnow's was the last major attempt to write an all-inclusive history of Hasidism. The trend in historiography of Hasidism is to deal with specific aspects of the movement rather than with its totality.

Gershom Scholem, a pioneer and leading authority in the field of Jewish mysticism, had as his main interest the theoretical writings of the movement and the significance of the messianic idea in Hasidism. Scholem views the Lurianic Kabbalah, Shabbateanism, and Hasidism as three stages of the same process, Hasidism being the latest phase and the one to popularize kabbalistic thought (*Major Trends in Jewish Mysticism* [1972], pp. 324–330). According to Scholem, redemption in hasidic thought lost its urgency. The movement survived, however, for it was able to neutralize the messianic elements (*Messianic Idea in Judaism* [1971], pp. 176–202).

Although Scholem shares Buber's views on some aspects of Hasidism–the spiritual regeneration of Judaism through Hasidism and its being more original than the *maskilim* and the centrality of the hasidic *tzaddik* in which personality takes place of a doctrine—he is critical of Buber's views of the centrality of hasidic literature in the understanding of the movement. Scholem locates the essence of the movement in its theoretical writings.

One other problem in the research of Hasidism is that in an evaluation of the novelty of the movement, the innovations may be located in a shift of emphasis rather than in revolutionary changes. According to Scholem, Hasidism appeared in Podolia because Podolia was a Shabbatean stronghold. Y. Eliach suggests that the local Russian pietistic and various sectarian groups in the vicinity were also an important and influential factor.

Opinion is also divided on the messianic significance of Hasidism. Benzion Dinur and I. Tisby see Hasidism as a manifestation of active messianism; Scholem and Joseph Weiss (1918–1969) see the messianic element as a dormant one. Rivka Schatz, like Joseph Weiss and Scholem, focuses exclusively on understanding the spiritual aims of Hasidism. Her book *HaHasidut KeMistikah* (Hasidism as Mysticism [1968]) is a phenomenological analysis of quietistic elements in Hasidism based on available hasidic texts.

Louis Jacobs, in *Hasidic Prayer* (1973), also deals with a central idea in Hasidism and its application.

Another group of scholars is preoccupied with the social aspects of Hasidism. Jacob Katz (b. 1904), in *Tradition and Crisis*, notes changes in the internal structure of the Jewish society mode of organization, in the source of authority, in the weakening of leadership of the *kehillah*, and in the coexistence of two institutions—Rabbanism and Tzaddikism. Shmeruk points out the social significance of the hasidic *shehitah* and the *arrendah* (*Zion*, vol. 20 [1957], pp. 94–99; *Zion*, vol. 35 [1970], pp. 182–192) in the founding of the movement.

S. Ettinger comments on aspects of early hasidic leadership (*Dat veHevrah*, 1964).

Israel Halpern (1910–1971), in his meticulous studies on isolated events in Hasidism, exposed new sources that opened new vistas in the research on Hasidism. In the most recent years, a new trend is visible in studies in Hasidism—the Holocaust and American Hasidism. Hasidism during the Holocaust and Hasidism's theological and social response are best reflected in studies by P. Schindler, M. Unger, S. Rosman, and others. With the destruction of the hasidic community in Eastern Europe, the majority of the hasidic survivors settled in the United States; lesser numbers settled in Israel.

The hasidic community of Williamsburg in Brooklyn, New York, was singled out as a focal point of attention. The community of Williamsburg fascinates sociologists, not as a hasidic experience but primarily as a community that did not succumb to the American urban realities and that maintains its Old World traditions. Studies by Poll, Kranzler, and Rubin belong in this category.

The prime source for all studies on Hasidism remains mainly within the hasidic literature, which first began to appear in print in 1780 and which has produced 3,000 volumes of literature. Hasidism as a movement has not as yet produced its own chronicler for an all-inclusive history of the movement.

Y.E.

HODEROV, Menahem Mendel David (1887–11 *Adar* 1980)—Born in Vizhnitz, son of R. Mordecai, he was ordained by R. Leibish Horowitz of Stanislav. From 1912, he served as a member of the rabbinate in Kolomyja and then in Czernowitz. He emigrated to New York in 1921 and was very active in the rabbinical association and in the work of the Aguda.

In 1905, he married the daughter of R. Samuel Abba of Horodenka and lived in the Bronx.

HODEROV, Mordecai (1867–2 *Kislev* 1938)—Son of R. Hayyim Judah Meir, he was born in Talnoye and was brought up in the home of R. David of Talnoye. In 1884, he married the daughter of R. Barukh Hager of Vizhnitz.

He served as rebbe in Talnoye, Kolomyja, and Budapest. He published the work of his father-in-law, *Imrei Barukh*, and founded the association of rebbes of America and Canada.

HOFSTEIN, Aaron Yehiel, of Kozienice (1889–Eve of the Day of Atonement 1942)—Son of R. Yerahmiel Moses of

Kozienice. After the death of his father in 1908, the hasidim of Kozienice were divided: some chose R. Aaron as their leader; others followed R. Kalonymus Kalman of Piasczeno.

"R. Aarele," as he was popularly known, discouraged the scholars and the wealthy hasidim and welcomed the workers and the wagoners. He married the daughter of R. Elimelekh of Grodzisk but divorced her and left Kozienice. Residing in Lodz and Warsaw and finally settling in Otwock, his home was a lodging place for the poor and the underprivileged, who were attracted to him in large numbers.

He died of typhus. "I have no desire to live any longer" were his last words.

HOFSTEIN, Eleazar, of Kozienice

(1806–26 *Kislev* 1862) – Son of R. Moses Elikum Briah, he married the daughter of R. Jacob Horowitz of Mielec, a descendant of R. Naftali of Ropczyce. He studied under his father; R. Issachar Dov of Radosczyce; and R. Hayyim Meir Yehiel Shapira of Moglienice. He visited R. Israel of Ruzhyn and R. Naftali Tzvi of Ropczyce.

In 1848, he succeeded his father as rebbe. He was the author of *Likkutei Mahara* on Torah and Psalms (Lvov, 1872), reprinted in Warsaw in 1894 and in Jerusalem in 1967. Some of his discourses can also be found in *Vayakel Shlomoh* (Piotrokov, 1909).

He was succeeded by his son, R. Yehiel Jacob.

HOFSTEIN, Moses Elikum Bria, of Kozienice

(1757–12 *Elul* 1828) – Second son of R. Israel of Kozienice, he accompanied his father on visits to R. Elimelekh of Lejask and was impressed by his ascetic lifestyle. He married the daughter of R. Yehudah Leib HaKohen of Annapol. R. Moses believed that a *tzaddik*, to achieve perfection, should actively minister to his followers rather than isolate himself. He differentiated between a *tzaddik* who is also the son of a *tzaddik* and those whose ancestors were not *tzaddikim*. The former are liable to boast about their ancestry, which is most improper. Unless a *tzaddik* is truly humble, he will achieve very little – neither in the upper world nor on earth.

The duty of the *tzaddik* is to raise his followers from their low spiritual level and lead them to repentance. If people have faith in him, he will surely help them. His followers must cling to him, travel to him, and have great faith in him. Lack of faith diminishes the *tzaddik*'s power. His followers should study him, gaze at him, and regard him not as an accuser, but as a defender of the House of Israel. The *tzaddik*, to achieve his goal, must practice *devekut* (ecstasy). Only then will he be able to annul the harsh decrees of the Almighty.

R. Moses was a prolific author. Among his works are *Beer Mosheh* (Lvov, 1858); *VeYahal Mosheh* (Lvov, 1868); *Tefillah Le-Mosheh* (Lvov, 1864); a commentary on the *Haggadah* (Lvov, 1864); *Matei Mosheh*, a commentary on the Song of Songs (Lvov, 1868); *Daat Mosheh* (Lvov, 1879); *Binat Mosheh* (Cracow, 1889); *Kohelet Mosheh* (Lublin, 1895); and a commentary on *Pirkei Avot* (Lvov, 1866).

HOFSTEIN, Yehiel Jacob, of Kozienice

(d. 30 *Sivan* 1866) – Son of R. Eleazar, he was fourteen years old when his father died. He married Sarah Devorah, the daughter of R. Eliezer of Grodzisk. It was only thanks to the persuasion of R. Hayyim Halberstam of Zanz that he became rebbe. He was an ascetic. Both in the winter and in the summer he would regularly immerse himself either in the cold *mikveh* or in the river of Kozienice.

He suffered from a heart condition and died on the eve of the Sabbath while immersing himself in the *mikveh*. He was succeeded by his son, R. Yerahmiel Moses.

He was survived by five daughters and two sons, R. Issachar and R. Eliezer.

A. Y. Bromberg, *Bet Kozienice*, pp. 52–81.

HOFSTEIN, Yerahmiel Moses, of Kozienice

(10 *Elul* 1860–13 *Elul* 1909) – Son of R. Yehiel Jacob, he was born in Grodzisk. His father died when he was six years old. In 1867 his mother remarried to R. Asher Perlow of Stolin, who brought him up. Among his teachers were R. Barukh, the rabbi of Tarnov, and R. Jacob Nathan Weisman, the author of *Mahshavot Bezah* (Berdichev, 1902).

He married Rachel Zipporah, the daughter of R. Mordecai Twersky of Chernobyl. When his grandfather R. Aaron died in 1872 and his stepfather in 1873, he returned to

Kozienice, where he became rebbe. He rarely delivered discourses, but it was his custom to tell hasidic stories. Every Saturday night, he would play the violin. He attached great value to R. Isaiah Horowitz's book *Shenei Luhot HaBrit*, which the Besht described as "God's inheritance."

He was particularly concerned with the fate of the Old Yishuv, and every petitioner was required to make a contribution toward the upkeep of the poor of the Holy Land. He encouraged the use of products of the Holy Land, such as olive oil, wine, and *etrogim*. When he was urged to consult physicians in Germany on his kidney troubles, he refused to go there, remarking prophetically: "Germany is a polluted country. Even the air there is unclean."

He died at the age of forty-nine on his return from Krenice, and he was buried in Kozienice. He left four daughters and three sons. He was succeeded by his son R. Aaron Yehiel. Three of his children were murdered by the Nazis.

His son, R. Israel Eliezer, was one of the founders of *Kefar Hasidim*, and his daughter, Malkah Shapira, was the well-known writer on Hasidism.

The second son of R. Yehiel Moses, R. Asher Elimelekh, the Maggid of Ryki, and his daughters, Hannah Goldah and Rachel *Hayyah* Miriam (the wife of the rebbe of Piascezno) perished in the Holocaust.

A. Y. Bromberg, *Bet Kozienice*, pp. 142–180.

HOKHMAH – Wisdom, identified in early rabbinic literature with the Torah, which God "consulted" before creating the world. This was deduced from Proverbs 8:22: "The Lord created me [i.e., wisdom] at the beginning of His way." Hence *Hokhmah* is also called *Reshit* (beginning) and is regarded in Kabbalah as the absolute divine wisdom, containing within itself the potentiality for all later divine emanative or creative activity.

The first words of the Torah were interpreted to refer to the beginning of this activity: "through *Hokhmah* (= *reshit*) the first *Sefirah* (*Keter*) created *Elohim* (a name for the third *Sefirah*, *Binah*)." *Hokhmah* is the second of the three upper *Sefirot*, occupying an intermediate place between *Keter* and *Binah*, and is the highest point that human beings can reach in mystical contemplation.

Hokhmah is represented by the divine name *Yah* and also by the first letter, *yod*, of the tetragrammaton.

D.G.

HOL HAMO'ED (the weekdays of the Festival) – The hasidim do not put on *tefillin* on the intermediate days of the Festivals of Passover and Tabernacles.

The practice of not wearing *tefillin* on *Hol HaMo'ed* became prevalent in the fifteenth century. "Nowadays," wrote R. Joseph Karo, "it has become customary among all the Sephardim not to put on *tefillin on Hol HaMo'ed*." R. Moses Isserlis, on the other hand, wrote, "In these regions it is customary to wear them." The hasidim thus adopted the old Sephardic custom.

HOLINESS – The purpose of the hasidic way was to help its followers attain the goals of holiness. From its inception, the movement wavered between policies of easing the pathway to holiness and of increasing the requirements of piety.

The former policy was stressed by the Besht. He pointed out that simple piety was the key to holiness, that all occasions could be utilized in the service of God, that all *mitzvot* must be performed in joy and with enthusiasm, and that immersion in the *mikveh* could be substituted for fasting and other ascetic practices. According to R. Yehiel Michal of Zloczov, the Besht said, "I attained the consent of God to the proposition that to dip every morning in the *mikveh* shall be counted as a fast day by the Holy One, blessed be He" (*Meirat Einayim*, in *Shivhei HaBesht*, ed. Talpiot, p. 269).

But there was also another side to the Besht's teaching, which was developed by his successor, the Maggid, R. Dov Baer of Mezhirech. The achievement of "unifications" (*yihudim*) in accordance with the Lurianic tradition; the attainment of the mystical ecstasy of clinging to the divine Being (*devekut*) and ultimately of the Holy Spirit; and the perpetual exercise of self-criticism and self-purification, whereby the various levels of holiness (*madregot*) might be attained (from a letter by the Besht concerning his ascent of the soul, printed in R. Jacob Joseph's *Ben Porat Yoseph*).

With the rapid growth of the movement, the two approaches to holiness were referred to the disciples and the *tzaddikim*, respectively. For the masses of the *hasidim*, the pathway to holiness was made easily accessible. All they had to do was to "attach" themselves to a *tzaddik* (*hitkashrut*) and to follow his instructions.

In some of the early groups, the hasidim were actually told "to surrender their thoughts to the *tzaddik*" (*Mesirat mahshavah*), with the understanding that the *tzaddik* would elevate their prayers and petitions to the heavenly throne. This practice was especially characteristic of the regimen established by R. Hayyim Heikel in Amdur. It was singled out for criticism by R. David of Makov in the name of Elijah, Gaon of Vilna (M. Wilensky, *Hasidim U'Mitnaggdim* [Jerusalem, 1970] vol. II, p. 44).

In the first printed work of the hasidic movement, the author asserted that the *tzaddik* needed to go down from his high level in order to maintain contact with the coarse and vulgar sentiments of his followers. Then, as he would rise back to his own proper level, he would uplift the prayers of the entire community (R. Jacob Joseph, *Toldot Yaakov Yoseph* [Vayetse, Warsaw ed., 1841], p. 51).

In the *Habad* movement, this division between two pathways to holiness is clearly marked out. The classic manual of piety—the so-called *Tanya*—was designed for the average person (*beinuni*), whereas the deeper philosophy of the movement was expounded in other works. On one hand, ordinary *hasidim* were warned against attempting to purify the "strange thoughts" (*mahshavot zarot*) that intruded in their consciousness during prayer (*Tanya*, ch. 28). On the other hand, this task was left to the *tzaddikim*, whose own evil desire had already been overcome, and the "strange thoughts" that floated into their consciousness were those of their followers.

The unity of the *tzaddik* and the populace reached a fantastic intensity in hasidic thought, "for the *tzaddik* is the inwardness of society; he is called man (adam) and the other people of the generation are called the flesh of man" (*Toldot Yaakov Yoseph*, *Shemini*, p. 176).

The demand for pitiless self-criticism as a way of reaching ever higher levels of holiness was particularly stressed in the schools of Przysucha and Kotzk (A. J. Heschel, *Kotzk* [Yiddish], 2 vols.).

J.B.A.

HOLOCAUST (1939–1945)—With very few exceptions and not unlike most segments of European Jewry, the rabbis and the hasidic communities neither anticipated the pending tragedy nor responded to those minority forces inside the Jewish communities who may have sounded the alarm. As a rule, the closed, self-contained character of the hasidic groupings provided an insular screen from post–World War I events. Anti-Jewish activity had always been part of the East European landscape, so that its overt manifestation in distant Germany may not have been considered unusual.

Neither the increased pace of Zionist ferment, the revolution in Russia, the demographic and economic upheavals following World War I, nor the emergence of the Nazi totalitarian regime seemed to suggest a significant change in the hasidic life-style or pace. Group *aliyah* to *Eretz Yisrael* was the exception rather than the rule, such as the founding of Moshav *Avodat Yisrael* (later known as *Kefar hasidim*) in 1924. In the same year, hasidic elements from Warsaw founded Bene Berak. In the main, however, East European Hasidism between the wars either ignored or was hostile to political Zionism, though it continued to espouse its traditional spiritual ties to *Eretz Yisrael* and maintained its support of hasidic institutions in the *Yishuv*. No major hasidic dynasty relocated its center from Eastern Europe, and the plans of the third Gerer rebbe, Rabbi Abraham Mordehai, to transfer his court to *Eretz Yisrael* in 1936 were rejected by his supporters in Poland.

In summary, the hasidic communities did not seem to anticipate the gravity of the pre-Holocaust period. In this respect, though for different reasons, they differed little from most of East European Jewry and, indeed, the world at large. Once the Holocaust trap was set, however, one may speak of a unique hasidic response. Authenticated hasidic responses generally fall into two major categories: behavioral responses and conceptual responses. In the latter are included written or verbal statements that respond to Holocaust events and are posited within hasidic-mystical categories of thought. The former refers to uniquely hasidic behavior in the face of an enemy who sought to destroy both the hasidim and their value system.

Clearly, among the consistent responses was the refusal of many rabbis to abandon their communities during the crisis. Opportunities for exclusive escape were rejected on the grounds of "I am no better than they [other Jews]." Not atypical was the telephone response by the *Radomsker rebbe* in Poland to his hasid Abba Bornstein in London in August 1939: "*Un wie ahin zol ich iberlossen die Yidden*?" Others, in the context of *imitatio Dei*, supported their decision to remain with their fellow Jews by echoing the psalmist's "*Imo anohi*, *Ve'zarah*" ("I will be with him in trouble") (Psalm 91:15). These were interpreted by hasidim as radical acts of *Ahavat Yisrael* within the snakepit of *Sin'at Yisrael*. The comforting, yet agonizing presence of the rebbe during the initial shock of Nazi occupation, during the creation of the ghettos, during the death marches, on the freight trains, in the camps, and during the final stages of *kiddush Hashem* (sanctification of God's name), is described both in the Holocaust literature and by eyewitnesses.

Like other religious and communal leaders, the rebbe was often singled out for ridicule, for beatings, and, as in the case of the Ostrowtzer rebbe, to be shot in public in efforts to break the morale of the community and deprive it of its spiritual leadership. Until the rebbe's own death, however, he inevitably provided a source of encouragement for hasidim and nonhasidim alike. He served as a model for *kiddush hahayyim* (sanctifying life) with dignity while confronting the enemy, who sought to obliterate any semblance of the *Tzelem Elokim*. Thus, the rabbis led the difficult battle and the classic hasidic struggle against *yi'ush* (despair). Precisely in a time of suffering, teaches the rabbi of Piacezno in the Warsaw ghetto, it is the duty of the Jews to remember that they are yet "*b'nei*-Melech" (children of God) and to beware being dragged down to the bestial level of the enemy.

The rabbis exploited their networks of hasidim for assistance and rescue operations. When the protective zeal of the hasidim on behalf of their *tzaddik* prevailed over the inclination of the rebbe not to abandon his community, rescue operations were employed on his behalf. The complex operations that spared the lives of the rabbis of Belz, Bobov, Gur, Klausenburg, and Satmar have been documented, with various degrees of authenticity.

The dedication of the hasidim to their rebbe could reach the ultimate. Twenty Jews offered to die so that the Ostrowtzer rebbe could be spared. The Germans accepted their offer and murdered the rebbe as well. The heroism of hasidic decoys who were prepared to sacrifice themselves in order to protect the rebbe is recorded in a number of eyewitness reports related to the rebbes of Belz and Radzyn. A young hasid exposed himself to danger in order to bury valuable volumes from the library of the Gerer.

Whenever possible, and more often when impossible, attempts were made to continue with the hasidic way of life. The hasidic "shabbas *tish*" is depicted in the ghettos, where the Zabner, Zichliner, Belzer, Karliner, and Dzikover continued to conduct hasidic life. The significant collection of hasidic teachings—*Esh Kodesh*—discovered in the Warsaw ghetto represented the "Torah" material of the rabbi of Piacezno on the Shabbat and Festivals. The Radomsker rebbe's "*tish*" is depicted in Auschwitz. The Bobover rebbe described a "*tish*" conducted together with his son in a gestapo jail on the Friday night before their planned execution. Possibly the most remarkable of the "hurban *tishen*" is described in *Sefer Krako*. The Melizer rebbe, R. Elimelekh Horowitz, is depicted as follows:

> When R. Elimelekh realized that his end was near, he requested a piece of bread for his final meal. He reclined and ate with his hasidim in front of the open pit. Following the blessing over the piece of bread, he said "torah" and entered into a state of great *hitlahabut*. He began to sing a new melody with his hasidim, "Nishmat Kol Hai," and together [they] danced their final dance. He then approached the German in command and said, "We have done our part. Now you do yours."

The *kvittel* served as a source of comfort and hope throughout the Holocaust. The memorial volume *Hurban Czenstochov* contains an eyewitness account of an unidentified rebbe petitioned with *kvittlech* by fellow hostages at a critical stage during their ordeal. The rebbe's efforts at comfort immeasurably strengthened the frightened victims.

Paradoxically, the hasidic *niggun* and dance emanated from within the ghettos and camps. Three eyewitnesses record the saga of the Gerer hasid Shlomoh Zelichovsky, who sang hasidic melodies on the way to the gallows. The epic incident inspired the Holocaust poet Yitzhak Katzenelson to write the poem "Dos Lied wegen Shlomoh Zelichovsky."

Research after five decades has ripened to the degree whereby definitions of "resistance" and "courage" are no longer routinely and exclusively linked with counterforce and violence. Holocaust responses seem to be more objectively evaluated depending upon the given circumstances and within the context of the realities of the persecuted rather than by the standards of resistance dictated by the enemy. Thus the refusal to alter hasidic dress and appearance; the continued use of the *mikveh*; conducting daily services and Torah study; observance of the dietary laws; birth, marriage, and burial practices; and the minutiae of observances related to the Jewish calendar, the Sabbath, and the Festivals represented for the hasidim actions of resistance within their own frame of reference and their own value system. These activities were conducted illegally, literally with *mesirat nefesh*, since they were often punishable by death. Yaakov Steinberg chronicles one such operation in the ghetto of Cracow:

> One also recalls the passive type of rebels in the ghetto of Cracow. These were young people who fought with spiritual weapons. They sat day and night in a cellar without ever seeing the light of day, absorbed in study. This group consisted of an amalgamation of various hasidic schools (Belz, Gur, Bobov, Radomsk, etc.). This youth was fortified with *mesirat nefesh* in the service of the Creator. Following the liquidation of the ghetto, these young *tzaddikim* were forced to emerge from the cellar by the defiled gestapo. All were murdered with the name of God on their lips. (*Sefer Krako* 412)

No evidence has emerged from documents to indicate any form of hasidic cooperation with the enemy, nor is there evidence of hasidim who agreed to be recruited into the role of the dreaded and despised *kapo*, or Jewish ghetto police enforcers.

Huberband, however, depicts an unusual, militant group of young Gerer hasidim, bordering on the nihilistic, which operated in the Warsaw ghetto. They aroused strong opposition by the Gerer elders, the rebbe's brother, and neighbors in the ghetto to their bizarre behavior, which included the severance of ties with their parents, indulgence in alcoholic drink, and petty theft and extortion, claiming loyalty only to the Gerer rebbe.

Forms of armed resistance were alien to Hasidism, born as it was on the foundation of the Besht's *Ahavat Hashem*, *Yisrael*, and *Torah*. Hasidic tradition tended to spiritualize the passages in scripture that demanded armed violence. Thus the commandment of waging war against Amalek is transformed into the imperative to battle with one's own *yetzer hara*, according to *Toldot Yaakov Yosef*. Nevertheless, there is evidence of some who broke through their own tradition. The son of the rebbe of Radoczyce led a partisan unit in the Lazisker forests, and the Rivner rebbe fought together with partisan groups. Among the most militant of the hasidic leaders was the Radziner rebbe immortalized in Katzenelson's poem ("Dos Lied wegen Radziner"), who called for armed revolt in Vlodave, assisted the partisans, and was hanged for his activities. Leib Scheransky, in hasidic garb, is described by some as a participant in Mordechai Anilewitz's headquarters command during the Warsaw ghetto rebellion. (Yitzhak Zuckerman, Anilewitz's deputy in the revolt, denies this, an instance of the delicate path of Holocaust studies documentation.)

Two significant documents that emerged from the Holocaust represent the major authenticated hasidic conceptual reaction: The "Torot" of R. Kalmish Kalonymos Shapiro, the Piaczezno rebbe, was presented on the Shabbat and Festivals between September 1940 and Summer 1942 in the Warsaw ghetto and was subsequently titled *Esh Kodesh*. *Em HaBanim Semehah*, a volume by R. Yissachar Shlomoh Teichthal, a leading hasid of the Munkacher rebbe, was written in Budapest three months prior to the formal German occupation of Hungary in March 1944. Both attempt to probe into the meaning of the calamity; both confront the eternal questions of theodicy, *galut* and *geulah*, and the quality and type of the desired Jewish response amidst *Hurban*.

Whereas *Esh Kodesh* emerges as a personal hasidic theology, *Em HaBanim Semehah* represents a powerful and shocking accusation of religious European Jewry for having deluded itself into a passive, helpless position and for rejecting the option of building the *Yishuv* in *Eretz Yisrael*. Whereas *Esh Kodesh* views the Holocaust from the perspective of deep faith, even to the degree of engaging in theological protest, *Em Habanim* reflects the classic activist anti-*galut* stance. Both authors have in common their hasidic tradition, upon which they significantly draw in order to support their respective positions.

Conceptual responses that emerged following the Holocaust have not yet been adequately treated and deserve greater attention. According to observers, the Holocaust directly influenced the establishment of key hasidic centers in *Eretz Yisrael* (Belz, Gur, Zanz, Viznitz). In the vehement "Eretz Yisrael Hashlemah" stance of Lubavitch, enunciated from their center in the Crown Heights section of Brooklyn, New York, one notes not only the arguments of *halakhah* but also the lessons of the Holocaust in the spirit of "*Al Tivtehu Bindivim*" ("Put not your trust in princes") (Psalm 146:2). These include the plea to reject once and for all the overused crutch of "*Mah Yumru Hagoyim*" ("What will the Gentiles say?") (Psalm 115:2), those who totally abandoned the Jews during their hour of need.

At the other end of the spectrum, the radical and isolated views of Satmer Hasidism tie the Holocaust to post-Holocaust events. The Zionists antagonized Hitler; thus, the Holocaust (*Al HaGeulah Ve'al HaTemurah*). If the Hitler Holocaust is not heeded, claims the Satmer, the Zionists will incite another catastrophe. The bulk of hasidic movements, however, do not engage in Holocaust theodicic inquiry. They prefer to rebuild their communities, painfully aware of their depleted ranks. Rather than speculate, the emphasis (especially among *Habad* documents) is on understanding Holocaust lessons as a basis for future action.

Inherent hasidic optimism remains. In the words of the Bobover rebbe, in a personal interview (New York, July 30, 1969), "Were it not for the *lahav* (flame) of *Hasidus*, I would not have survived the fires of the *Hurban*." Hasidism during the post-Holocaust period seeks to nourish that flame, as a means to pay homage to the martyred and to transmit it to the emerging generation.

P. Schindler, "Responses of Hasidic Leaders and Hasidim during the Holocaust in Europe, 1939–1945."

P.S.

HOLY SPARKS–It has already been clearly demonstrated that Hasidism is not merely an emotional philosophy but also a teaching based on an intellectual approach, which was instrumental in rejuvenating the fallen House of Israel in the post-Chmielnicki era of 1648–1649.

In prayer and study, in *mitzvot* and mundane activities, hasidic philosophy found and utilized new and profound ways of explaining Judaism to the Jew of exile, within exile. Its teachings are based firmly on Lurianic Kabbalah and succeed in painting a lucid picture, adding deep insight into the intricate teachings of that famous sixteenth-century kabbalist. Among the numerous ideas expounded by the Besht was the concept of *nitzutzim*, translated freely as "sparks." The concept added a new dimension to the understanding of the pluralistic world around us and to the role of humanity within it.

Everything is the creation of God. The entire garment of worlds and galaxies is God's domain, yet to the human eye He is concealed. Looking at the gross mundane universe, we perceive a physical and materialistic entity, which in no way lends itself to the revelation of the original source–God. In truth the very opposite idea is gained: that the majority of creation appears static, with no visible sign of life; human beings, who are the ultimate of created life, are quite removed from the pristine spiritual source of their existence. Adding to our confusion, we look to the static and dormant material not only for our growth and perfection but also for our survival–a total paradox in itself.

To clarify the unfocused picture in our eye, the idea of holy sparks is introduced. The oft-quoted verse "Not by bread alone liveth man, but by the word of God" is the root of the concept of *nitzutzim*. Yet do we in fact see or even sense the word of God in our bread or water? The Kabbalah answers our question and says that every created entity has the "word" of God within it, the soul of everything that keeps it in existence. To quote the kabbalistic term, "Koach HaPoel

BeHanifal" is the creative force within the created thing.

But the crux of the matter is not as simple as we have stated. As a result of *shevirat hakelim* (the breaking of the vessels), fragmentation took place and gave rise to sparks, or particles. Tracing this process a step backward, when God created the worlds, He used a system known as *orot* and *kelim* (light and vessels). Allegorically speaking, these refer to the light, or life force, that issues from God, entering a vessel or *Sefirah*. The light, being a simple ray, enters a vessel, according the composition of that vessel; so is the light emitted.

These *Sefirot*, which were created to channel God's light ever downward in order to create a multifarious and mundane world, were of an individualistic nature. Each had its own character and was totally independent of the other *Sefirot*. Thus, when the light passed into the *Sefirah Hesed*, whose nature is unbounded benevolence, the resultant emission of light was an uncontrolled outflow. This passed from *Hesed* to the next *Sefirah Gevurah*, sternness, whose nature is to control and withhold. The flow was of such a magnitude that *Gevurah* was unable to contain it and thus "broke"; a similar effect occurred among the subsequent *Sefirot* or vessels. The fragmentation is called *shevirat hakelim*, and the particles are called *nitzutzim*.

Utilizing the principle that whatever was higher fell lower, we come to realize that our own lowly world contains the end result of fragmented lofty entities. The sparks are contained within everything physical, so it is for that reason that most *mitzvot* are directly connected with the realm of physicality. By using the physical for a holy purpose, we release the spark contained within it and cause an elevation of that spark to its source. By wearing *tzitzis* (wool) and *tefillin* (skin) and taking the vegetation of the four species, we liberate these sparks from their captivity. Just as the soul of a Jew yearns constantly to be freed from its captivity within the body, so these sparks yearn for the act that will liberate them from their place of internment.

If, God forbid, one fails in one's duty and commits sins, then the bondage is strengthened. Only true repentance and remorse can relieve the sparks. Each Jew is given a certain number of sparks to liberate, which may be scattered in many parts of the world, hence the reason for exile. The purpose of exile and the length of exile are for the ingathering of the sparks wherever they may be embedded. As the Talmud (*Pesahim* 87b) states, exile was given to the Jews in order that proselytes should be added to the fold. As explained, this means that even proselytes—who before they convert are the furthest removed from Judaism, so with all things that are removed from their source—must ultimately be returned to their original source, hence the purpose of reciting a blessing before eating, before performance of a *mitzvah*, and so forth. We reunite the spark with God, Who is *Melekh HaOlam*, Sovereign of the Universe.

Z.T.

HORODEZKY, Samuel Abba (1871–1957)—Descendant of hasidim, explorer of Jewish mysticism and rabbinics. He wrote in Hebrew, Yiddish, German, and Russian. Born in Malin (Kiev region) in the Ukraine, he studied with the *tzaddikim* in Malin and Chernobyl. At the age of twenty, he settled in Berdichev, in the eighteenth century the "Jerusalem of Volhynia," where R. Levi Isaac had stormed the heavens with his prayers. The hasidic leaders there followed the *tzaddikim* of Chernobyl and Sadgora. But Horodezky was attracted by *Haskalah* too.

Being made a delegate to the eighth Zionist Congress (1907), he remained for thirty years abroad, largely in Germany and Switzerland. In 1938 he emigrated to Palestine, settling in Tel Aviv, where he died and where his library is preserved in the Bet Faitlovitch.

Like many of his contemporaries from the East European "shtetl," he was largely self-educated and so his views of historical developments (e.g., the antilegalism of the prophets, the ancient mystical basis of the aggadah) as well as his dates repeatedly lack true perspective and precision, not to mention the hasidic traditions of *gilgul* (the transfer by metempsychosis) of the soul of Moses into Samuel, that of Abimelech into Herod, and of Essenism into Hasidism in spite of some superficial historical parallels.

But, unlike many writers on Hasidism, he still knew hasidic traditions at firsthand. No wonder that the scholar in him should have been attracted to the "Wissenschaft des

Judentums." He began with writing novellas with halakhic-homiletic content, but many of his best contributions before his Israeli period appeared in his journal *HaGoren*, (the bundle of sheaves) devoted to New Jewish Learning (vols. I–VIII published in Berdichev, vols. IX–X in Berlin), and the German *Encyclopaedia Judaica* (1928–1934).

He became widely known for his biographical studies and monographs, besides those on rabbinic scholars largely in Poland and not treated by I. H. Weiss (in his *Dor Dor weDoreshaw*), then collected in *Le-Korot HaRabbanut* (Warsaw, 1914), in particular those studies on Hasidism: R. Nahum of Chernobyl (d. 1797; Berdichev, 1902); R. Jacob Joseph of Polonnoye (d. ca. 1782; Berdichev, 1906); R. Nahman of Bratzlav (d. 1811; Berdichev, 1906); R. Baer, the maggid of Mezhirech (d. 1772; Berlin, 1923); the kabbalist R. Moses Cordovero (d. 1570; Berlin, 1924); and R. Hayyim Vital (d. 1620).

Various studies are collected in *Ha-Hasiduth we-ha-hasidim* from the Besht (R. Israel Friedman of Ruzhyn, founder of the Sadgora dynasty, [d. 1851]). The work presents a glorification of Hasidism rather than critical analyses. Horodezky was always more occupied with individual personalities rather than with the description of movements in their own setting.

Where Martin Buber achieved literary fame by his renderings of hasidic lore, Horodezky made solid contributions by combining as he did the approaches of Hasidism, *Haskalah*, and Western scholarship. More than that, he could depict the soul of Hasidism—the grain with the chaff—as he had known, nay, felt, its brighter side to be: Hasidism with its perfection and its humility, its thirst for God, and its weakness in theory, and Hasidism with its holy joy and its ear for the needy in the hour of their distress, when even the occasional miracle story would serve only to transcend the narrow confines of humanity upon earth.

F. Lachower, *Rishonim VeAharonim*, pp. 290–293.

M. Waxman, *A History of Jewish Literature*, vol. 4, pp. 457, 793 ff., 840 ff., 952 ff.

I.O.L.

HORODOK DYNASTY—A small hasidic group that flourished in David-Horodok, near Pinsk. The founder of the dynasty was R. Wolf, or Wolfche (Ginsburg), the son of R. Samuel Halevi of Koshivka.

He was succeeded by his son, R. David, and he, by his son, R. Israel Joseph Halevi, who was a personal friend of R. Yitzhak of Neskhizh. When he died in 1899, an *Ohel* was erected over his grave. The dynasty left no written records apart from some letters.

W. Rabinowitsch, *Lithuanian Hasidism*, pp. 209–210.

HOROWITZ, Aaron Halevy, of Starosselje (1766–29 *Tishri* 1829)—He was born in Orsha, in the district of Mohilev. His father, R. Moses, was a direct descendant of R. Isaiah Horowitz, the author of *Shenei Luhot HaBerit*. He studied Talmud and Kabbalah. At the age of seventeen he became a disciple of R. Shneur Zalman of Liady, with whom he studied for thirty years. For a considerable time, R. Aaron and R. Dov Baer (Shneur Zalman's son) studied together and were devoted friends and companions. R. Dov Baer used to say that whenever he recited the words of the mystical prayer "Guard the seekers of Thy unity as the apple of Thine eye," he had Aaron in mind.

R. Aaron is generally acknowledged as the most outstanding systematic exponent of the *Habad* theory of Hasidism. He established his own school and was critical of R. Dov Baer's tract on *Ecstasy*. He established a rival court in Starosselje and he regarded himself as the spiritual heir of *Habad*. His works form a clear and a most systematic treatment of pantheism or acosmism. He had a lucid style, great originality, and profundity of thought. From 1813 until his death, R. Aaron's followers were known as the Starosseljer hasidim. After his death, many of his followers transferred their allegiance to Lubavitch; others accepted his son, R. Hayyim Rafael, as their teacher, but when the son died without an heir, the Starosseljer dynasty came to an end.

R. Aaron was the author of *Bad Kodesh* on the Book of Ruth (Warsaw, 1872); *Sod Kedoshim*, a commentary on the Passover *Haggadah* (Konigsberg, 1866); *Avodat HaLevi* in two volumes: the first part, printed in Lvov in 1842, containing homilies on the three books of the Pentateuch and Festivals as well as letters to his followers, and the second part, printed in Lvov in 1846, containing discourses on the last two books of the Pentateuch and the festivals; *Shaar HaTefillah* on prayer (Lvov, 1842); *Shaar HaYihud VeEmunah* in two parts, the first being a commentary on the second part of the *Tanya* and the second part being a commentary on the first part of the *Tanya* (Shklov, 1820); and *Shaar Avodah* (Shklov, 1821).

L. Jacobs, *Seeker of Unity*, pp. 11–12.

HOROWITZ, Abraham Abba (Abish), of Krolle (1897–2 *Sivan* 1944)—Son of R. Naftali of Mielec, he was ordained by R. Shmuel Engel and R. Meir Yehiel Halstock of Ostrowiec. He married the only daughter of R. Yitzhak Weiss of Spinka, where he stayed for many years. When his father-in-law settled in Munkacz in the First World War, he succeeded him as rebbe of Spinka and established a *yeshivah* for fifty students. In 1924 he became rabbi of Krolle, where he also set up a *yeshivah Bet Avraham*.

He was the author of *Barukh Matir Assurim* (Siena, 1935).

He was deported to Auschwitz, where he and two of his children were murdered. His son, R. Shmuel Tzvi Hirsch, is the rebbe of Spinka in New York.

HOROWITZ, Abraham Hayyim, of Linsk (1789–25 *Av* 1831)—The eldest son of R. Naftali Tzvi of Ropczyce, he married his cousin, the daughter of R. Shmuel Shmelke Horowitz. Succeeding his father, he was rabbi of Linsk for only four years.

He had seven children, six daughters and one son, R. Menahem Mendel, who succeeded him.

A. Stern, *Melitzei Eish*.

HOROWITZ, Abraham Hayyim, of Plansh (1850–29 *Tishri* 1919)—Son of R. Moses of Rozwadov, he studied under his brother-in-law, R. Shalom David Unger. He married the daughter of R. Bezalel Weinberger of Gorlice. When his father died, he first became rabbi in Plansh and then at Radomysl. He was renowned for his melodies and learned discourses.

During the First World War he lived for a time in Budapest, then settled in Rzeszov, where he died. He was survived by three sons—R. Solomon, R. David, and R. Eliezer—and three daughters.

HOROWITZ, Abraham Simhah, of Baranov (1846–15 *Adar* 1916)—He was the only son of R. Israel of Baranov. He married the daughter of R. Mordecai Tzvi Hirsch Weinberger of Dukla. In his youth he visited R. Hayyim of Zanz and the rebbes of Ropczyce and Dzikov. When his father died in 1870, he became rabbi of Baranov, where he served for forty years.

In 1909, he traveled to Turkey, Syria, and the Holy Land, where he became closely associated with the kabbalist R. Hayyim Saul Hakohen Dwik.

He was the author of *Magdil Yeshuot Malko* (Jerusalem, 1956); *Hamrah Tovah*, a commentary on the Torah and *Targum* (Jerusalem, 1965); and *Orah VeSimhah*, a homiletical work (Jerusalem, 1975).

He died in Jerusalem and was buried on the Mount of Olives. His eldest son, R. Yitzhak, succeeded him as rebbe in Baranov.

HOROWITZ, Abraham Tzvi, of Biec (1887–17 *Adar* 1961)—Son of R. Aaron of Biec, he was born in Dzikov. He married Beila, the daughter of R. Aryeh Leibel Rokeah of Bukovsk. He was, for a time, rabbi in Tarnov, and in 1913 he emigrated to New York, where he was known as the rabbi of Biec. He was buried in *Kiryat Zanz*, Netanya. His son R. Shalom succeeded him as rabbi of Biec, New York.

His other sons, R. Moses and R. Hayyim Joseph and their families, perished in the Holocaust.

HOROWITZ, Alter Ezekiel Eliyahu, of Dzikov (3 *Heshvan* 1885–7 *Adar* II 1943)—Son of R. Joshua of Dzikov. He married his cousin Havah Hager, the daughter of R. Israel of Vishnitz in 1900. In 1909 he became rabbi of Dzikov. At the outbreak of the First World War, to escape the fury of the Russian invaders, he found refuge first in Vishnitz, then in Grosswardein. After the war he settled to Tarnov but maintained links with Dzikov, visiting twice annually, on the *yahrzeits* of his father and his grandfather.

Prayers in his synagogue were conducted by gifted officiants, accompanied by a choir. His discourses were replete with Kabbalah and *gematriyot*. On *Hoshanah Rabba* he would deliver discourses between the *Hoshanot*, and the service never finished before midday. His *hakkafot* did not commence until midnight.

In the winter of 1936 the rabbi visited Antwerp and London, where he officiated at the Dzikower *shtiebl* at 30 Dunk Street, the most influential *shtiebl* in interwar London. On his return to Poland, he foresaw the impending German attack and urged his followers to leave Poland.

At the outbreak of the Second World War, the rebbe took refuge in Pukshivnitz and lived for a time in the Cracow ghetto, where he was registered as a factory worker. He was almost blinded by an accident to his eyes, and subsequent surgery in the ghetto was unsuccessful. He died a martyr's death in Plaszov, near Cracow. He was survived by one daughter and four sons. His second son, R. Yudele, died in London.

Twelve of his discourses appear in *Zikhron Yehezkel* (Jerusalem, 1936).

HOROWITZ, Alter Zeev, of Strzyzov (d. on the Eve of Passover 1930) – Son of R. Abraham Horowitz of Sendiszov, he became rabbi of Stryszov in 1882. His prolonged morning services lasted until three o'clock in the afternoon. He was a great musician and composed many melodies. During World War I he lived in Vienna.

His son, R. Hayyim Yehudah, was the rebbe in Rzeszov, and his daughter, Tirzah, married R. Yehiel Epstein.

HOROWITZ, Aryeh Leib Halevi, of Stanislav (15 *Av* 1847–21 *Sivan* 1909) – Only son of R. Yitzhak, the rabbi of Ottynia and Stanislav, he was born in Krystonopol. His mother was Tobah Miriam, daughter of R. Efraim Teumim. He was ordained by R. Hayyim Halberstam of Nowy Zanz and R. Joseph Saul Nathanson. He occupied rabbinical positions in Zalozce, in Strij for twenty-six years, and in Stanislav, where he succeeded his father and established a *yeshivah*, *Or HaTorah*, and appointed R. Yekutiel Aryeh Kamelhar as principal.

In 1865 he married Zlata Rachel, daughter of R. Moses Waks of Seret. When she died in 1883, he married her sister Pesil, widow of R. Solomon of Lublin.

He was the author of authoritative responsa *Harei Besamim* (Part 1 – Lvov, 1882; Part 2 – 1897), which have gone through four editions. Another volume was edited by S. Federbusch and published by Mosad HaRav Kook in 1957.

Despite his mitnaggedic background, he befriended hasidic rabbis R. David Moses of Chortkov and R. Hayyim Halberstam. He opposed secular studies, which were imposed on rabbis by the Austrian authorities.

He was survived by two sons, R. Saul and R. Pinhas. His grandson is the well-known bibliographer Dr. L. Prijs of London.

N. M. Gelber, *Arim VeImahot BeYisrael*, p. 27.

HOROWITZ, Asher Joshua, of Rymanov (1860–27 *Heshvan* 1934) – Younger son of R. Meir of Dzikov. His father died when he was very young, and he was brought up by his brother R. Joshua. He married Malkah, the daughter of R. Joseph Friedman of Rymanov, and in 1896 succeeded his father-in-law as rebbe in Rymanov. He moved to Cracow in 1905 and in 1914 went to live in Vienna, but he kept in touch with his followers in Galicia and Poland. He was a musician of note and composed many hasidic melodies.

He died in Vienna and was buried in Cracow. He was the author of *Maadanei Melekh* on the Pentateuch (Bartfeld, 1913) and a commentary on the Passover *Haggadah* (Vienna, 1934). He was succeeded by his son, Tzvi Hayyim.

HOROWITZ, Eleazar, of Grodzisk (1881–6 *Kislev* 1943) – Son of Abraham Hayyim of Plansh. At the age of sixteen he married the daughter of R. Meir Yehudah Shapira of Bukovsk, with whom he studied. In 1909 he became rabbi of Grodzisk.

During World War I he lived in Tarnov, and after the death of his father in 1919, he succeeded him as rebbe. He established a *yeshivah* and delivered daily discourses. He would regularly travel throughout Galicia to visit his followers.

He was murdered by the Nazis. His last wish was that he should be wrapped in his father's prayer shawl before he died. He had two sons and three daughters.

HOROWITZ, Eliezer, of Dzikov (1790–3 *Heshvan* 1861) – The third son of R. Naftali Tzvi of Ropczyce, he was born in Dukla. He studied under his father and under R. Aryeh Leibish Lipshitz of Wisnicz Nowy. He accompanied his father on his visits to the

"Seer" of Lublin and the Maggid of Kozienice. He married the daughter of R. Yehiel Michael Rosenfeld of Rawa-Ruska, where he lived. When his father-in-law lost all his money, he returned to his father in Ropczyce, eventually becoming the rabbi of Dzikov.

He continued visiting contemporary rebbes, and he strongly opposed the doctrines of the school of Przysucha. Every New Year it was his custom to bestow his blessing on his fellow rebbes. He himself prepared the list with great care, giving priority to the descendants of Ruzhyn.

Many people believed that the Messiah would come in 1860, a belief based on a reference in the *Zohar*. In 1860, during the Festival of Tabernacles, R. Eliezer publicly affirmed that the Messiah would not come. Later he explained the motive for his negative statement: "Better that people should lose faith in me and accuse me of telling lies than that they should lose faith in the Messiah." He wrote down his discourses but would not allow them to be printed, saying that "on a Sabbath after the meal many hasidim will take my book with them. Assuredly, they will fall asleep, and I do not want to sleep with them!" A number of his stories were printed in Yiddish under the title *Kedushat Eliezer* (Warsaw, 1930).

He was survived by two daughters and four sons, R. Israel, R. Reuben, R. Moses, and R. Meir who succeeded him.

HOROWITZ, Eliezer, of Tarnogrod (1740–1806) – Son of R. Yaakov Halevi, rabbi of Sianiawa. He was a disciple of R. Yehiel Michael of Zloczov, R. Elimelekh of Lejask, and R. Mordecai Meshullam Feivish of Zbaraz. He was the author of *Noam Maggidim U'Kvod HaTorah* (Lvov, 1806) and *Imrot Tehorot* on Psalms (Warsaw, 1839). His works reflect his wide-ranging knowledge of halakhic literature: Kabbalah and *Mussar*. He describes the *tzaddikim* as "possessors of divine inspiration who know the secrets of men."

He believed that *tzaddikim* are in a state of perpetual devoutness, spiritually soaring in the upper worlds and practicing *devekut* (devoutness) all week long, whereas the common people achieve it only on the Sabbath. He maintained that abundance flows to the world thanks to the influence of the *tzaddik*, who should, therefore, be supported materially by his followers. In his view, the *tzaddik* should endeavor to cause people to repent. The ordinary person cannot return to the right path without the advice of the *tzaddik*. The *tzaddik* should utilize stories and legends to convey his message to his followers and to capture their hearts.

Y. I. Levin, "The Holy Rabbi, R. Eliezer of Tarnogrod."

E.N.

HOROWITZ, Elimelekh, of Mielec (1881–1942) – Eldest son of R. Naftali of Mielec, he married the daughter of R. Tzvi Hirsch Horowitz of Rozwadov. While his father was still alive, he acted as junior rabbi in Mielec and after his death, succeeded him as rebbe. After World War I he stayed for some time in the United States; on his return he lived in Cracow. He was one of the very few hasidic rabbis who could read and write music.

When the Nazis deported him to Radomysl and he realized that his end was near, he requested a piece of bread for his final meal. He reclined and ate with his hasidim in front of the open pit, delivered a discourse, and sang "Nishmat Kol Hai," a melody he had specially composed for the occasion. He then approached the Nazi commandant and said to him "We have done our part. Now you do yours!"

His son R. Naftali also died in a concentration camp in Proskurov near Tarnov.

Sefer Cracow, Ir VeEm BeYisrael, pp. 167, 175.

HOROWITZ, Hayyim Menahem Mendel, of Dzikov (1904–23 *Tishri* 1944) – Son of R. Alter Ezekiel Elijahu, he was born in Dzikov and was brought up by his grandfather R. Joshua. During the First World War he stayed with his grandfather R. Israel of Vishnitz and then studied in Tarnov under R. Meir Arak, who ordained him. He married his cousin Rebecca, the daughter of R. Emanuel Weltfried of Pabianice. Her mastery of the Polish language enabled her to intervene with government departments on behalf of her husband's followers. In 1924, he became rabbi of Dzikov.

He suffered much during the Second World War when he was incarcerated in Cracow, in Plaszov, and in Mauthausen, where he was a laborer in the granite works and where he died of typhus on Simhat Torah. His wife was deported to a concentration camp at Studthof near Danzig, where she perished.

Some of his discourses can be found in *Hemdah Genizah*, published in Jerusalem in 1954. His son, R. Joshua, and his daughter, Perele, survived the Holocaust.

HOROWITZ, Hayyim Shlomoh, of Strzyzov/New York (1905–27 *Kislev* 1969) – Son of R. Alter Eliezer of Biece. He married the daughter of R. Rafael Gross. He served as a rabbi in Selicz near Munkacz. He survived the Holocaust and settled in Brooklyn, New York, where he was known as the rabbi of Strzyzov.

He was buried on *Har HaMenuhot*, Jerusalem. He was survived by four sons. The eldest, R. Israel Jacob Joel, succeeded him.

HOROWITZ, Isaiah (ca. 1556–1630), kabbalist – Son of R. Abraham Halevi, he was popularly known as *HaShelah HaKadosh* (the Holy *Shelah*). Isaiah studied under his father; under R. Meir ben Gedaliah, the Maharam; and under R. Joshua Falk. He lived in Dubno, Ostrog, Frankfurt-am-Main, and Prague before he settled in the Holy Land in 1621. He was the author of *Emek Berachah* (Cracow, 1597) – glosses on his father's work – and *Bigdei Yesha* (Amsterdam, 1577); his magnum opus was the 422-folio work *Shnei Luhot HaBrit* (Amsterdam, 1649).

He was a noted kabbalist and believed that "those who do not study the wisdom of the Kabbalah separate themselves from the eternal spiritual light." However, students who devote themselves to mysticism needed three important prerequisites: "an understanding heart filled with the love of God; great diligence and the ability to study the *Zohar*; and intense concentration on the subject." He was responsible for the popularizing of the Kabbalah in Poland, thus paving the way to Hasidism. All hasidic masters quoted him. R. Solomon HaKohen of Radomsk knew the whole of the *Shelah* by heart.

E. Newman, *Life and Teachings of Isaiah Horowitz*.

HOROWITZ, Israel, of Lublin (d. 27 *Nisan* 1828) – Son of R. Jacob Yitzhak, the "Seer" of Lublin, he married the daughter of R. David, the brother of R. Moses of Przeworsk. After the death of his father, most of his father's disciples and followers deserted Lublin.

R. Israel had a very tiny following, and he suffered great hardship. His contemporaries venerated him. R. Yitzhak Meir Alter said, "He is not in need of his father's pedigree, he is a worthy tractate by himself."

His son, R. Kalonymus Kalman, the son-in-law of R. Noah of Poryck, died in Jerusalem on 24 *Av* 1885.

Y. Alfasi, *HaHasidut*, pp. 66–67.

HOROWITZ, Israel David, of Sedziszov (1899–1967) – Son of R. Tuviah, the rabbi of Sedziszov, he married Yentel, the daughter of R. Meir Moskovitch of Shatz in 1921. In 1932 he emigrated to the United States, where he established a *Bet HaMidrash, Sendziszov-Shatz*, in New York.

He was succeeded by his son, R. Meir.

HOROWITZ, Jacob, of Mielec (1792–19 *Tevet* 1839) – Second son of R. Naftali of Ropczyce, he first became rabbi of Kolbuszowa, then in 1810 the rabbi of Mielec, where he established a dynasty. He was known as the "Minor Baal Shem Tov." He married the daughter of R. Abraham Mordecai of Pinczev.

He had three sons and three daughters and was succeeded by his son R. Yehudah.

HOROWITZ, Joshua, of Dzikov (1848–11 *Tevet* 1913) – Third son of R. Meir, he was born on Shushan Purim in Dzikov. By the age of twenty he is reputed to have mastered the *Zohar*. He married the daughter of Leibush Reich of Rzeszov. In 1877 he succeeded his father as rebbe. Under his leadership, Dzikov became the great force in Galicia, second only to Belz and Bobov. He participated in the *Mahzikei Hadat* conference that was held in Lvov in 1879. He was a noted composer of hasidic melodies, and even the renowned cantor Zeidel Rovner spent many weeks with the rabbi listening to his music.

He predicted the outbreak of the First World War and did not discourage mass emigration to the United States.

He was succeeded by his only son, R. Alter Ezekiel Eliyahu.

He was a prolific author. In 1870, at the age of eighteen he published in Lvov his first work, *Emek Halakhah* on the Talmud. His other works were *Ateret Yehoshua*, hasidic discourses (Cracow, 1919); responsa *Ateret Yehoshua*, part one (Cracow, 1932); *Derekh Melakhim* (Munkacs, 1900); and *Kedushah Meshuleshet* (Podgorze, 1905). In 1977 the *kollel* of Dzikov in Jerusalem published a selection of his responsa under the title *Ateret Yehoshua*.

HOROWITZ, Joshua Heschel Halevi, of Chenciny (1856–3 *Av* 1943)–Son of R. Hayyim Samuel Halevi, he married the daughter of R. Joshua Heschel Frankel of Komarno. He was brought up by his grandfather R. Joseph Barukh, the "good Jew of Neustadt." He made his home in Chenciny.

During the Nazi occupation, he refused to cut off his beard. He was shot by the Nazis in Sosnowiec.

HOROWITZ, Levi Yitzhak, of Boston/Israel (b. 1921)–Second son of R. Pinhas David, he was born in Boston and educated in Jerusalem and in the *yeshivah Torah Va'Daat* in New York, where he received his ordination. In 1943 he married Rechel, the daughter of R. Naftali Unger. In 1944 he became rebbe first in Dorchester, Massachusetts, and from 1966 in Brookline, Massachusetts, where he established a community center, *Bet Pinhas*. He has a mastery of English as well as Yiddish and is famed for attracting college-educated young people to Orthodoxy and Hasidism.

Among the projects under his leadership are the *Mahzikei HaTorah* Institute for men and the Lionel Goldman Seminary of Judaic studies for women. He was active in the areas of *Kashrut*, *Taharat HaMishpahah*, and *Hevrah Kadisha*. He also acted as a medical liaison aid and counselor. He is one of the very few hasidic rabbis who delivers his discourses in English. He is a member of the presidium of the American Aguda. He now commutes between the United States and Israel, where he is establishing a *kiryah*.

His son, R. Pinhas David, is the Huszter rebbe in Brooklyn, New York.

Z.A. and S.P.

HOROWITZ, Meir, of Dzikov (1819–8 *Tammuz* 1877)–The fourth son of R. Eliezer, he was born in Rawa-Ruska and was educated under his father, his grandfather, and his uncle, R. Asher Yeshaya, as well as under R. Tzvi Hirsch of Rymanov. He married Deborah, the daughter of R. Kalman Pitzelis of Cracow. He became rabbi of Dzikov in his father's lifetime. He lived in great style in a palatial residence surrounded by gardens, with an integral *sukkah*, *mikveh*, and special kitchen for Passover.

He corresponded with the halakhic authorities of his day–R. Saul Nathanson of Lvov and R. Shlomoh Kluger.

He died while in Karlsbad and was buried in Dzikov.

He was the author of *Imrei Noam* on the Pentateuch (Przemysl, 1877); *Imrei Noam* on the Festivals (Cracow, 1866), which has gone through several editions; and responsa *Imrei Noam* (Cracow, 1848).

He had ten children, four daughters and six sons: R. Naftali Hayyim, R. Tuviah, R. Yehiel, R. Aaron, R. Asher Isaiah, and R. Joshua, who succeeded him.

M. Wunder, *Meorei Galicia–Enzyklopedia LeHakhmei Galicia, vol.* 2, pp. 254–256.

HOROWITZ, Moses, of Rozwardov (1824–10 *Sivan* 1894)–Son of R. Eliezer of Dzikov, and son-in-law of R. Moses Teitelbaum, he established the dynasty of Rozwardov, which endured until the Holocaust. He was known as a miracle worker. He often visited R. Hayyim Halberstam and R. Barukh of Gorlice.

He was survived by three sons and five daughters. His son R. Tzvi Hirsch succeeded him.

HOROWITZ, Moses Halevi, of Boston/New York (1909–13 *Sivan* 1985)–Eldest son of R. Pinhas David, he was born in Jerusalem and, with his mother, joined his father in Boston. He was educated in the *yeshivot* of the Holy Land, under R. Asher Lemel Spitzer of Kirschdorf, and under R. Moses Kliers of Tiberias. He married Leah Freidel, the daughter of R. Hayyim Abraham Eichenstein of Zydaszov in New York in 1919. In 1941 he succeeded his father as the rebbe of "Boston" in the Borough Park section of Brooklyn, New York, where he established a *yeshivah*, *Darkhei Noam*.

He was a leading spokesman of the Aguda and a member of *Mo'etzet Gedolei HaTorah*. He was active in rescue operations during the Holocaust and helped many refugees to establish themselves in the United States. He was also active in glatt kosher meat production in the United States. He was a noted composer, and a record of his melodies was issued by his son in 1966.

He was survived by his brother R. Levi Yitzhak of Boston and two sons, R. Hayyim Abraham and R. Pinhas David.

Z.A.

HOROWITZ, Naftali, of Mielec (4 *Tevet* 1845–18 *Tishri* 1916)—Son of R. Yehudah, the rebbe of Mielec. He was a disciple of R. Hayyim Halberstam of Zanz and of the "good Jew of Neustadt." He married the daughter of R. Meir Nathan Halberstam of Zanz.

In 1879, he succeeded his father as rebbe. During World War I he took refuge in Vienna, where he died, but he was buried in Mielec.

He had fifteen children, and his son, R. Menahem Mendel, succeeded him in Mielec.

He was the author of *Kedushat Naftali* (New York, 1950).

HOROWITZ, Naftali Hayyim, of Dzikov/Jerusalem (1840–10 *Tishri* 1895)—The eldest son of R. Meir of Dzikov, he married Yoheved Rebecca, the daughter of R. Moses Unger, and lived for a time in Nowy Zanz. He refused to accept rabbinical posts. Leaving his wife and children behind, he emigrated to the Holy Land, settling first in Safed, then in Jerusalem. He visited Nowy Zanz for a short time, then returned to the Holy Land. He observed *Tikkun Hatzot* at the *Kotel*.

He was the author of a commentary on the Passover, *Haggadah Minhah Hadashah* (Jerusalem, 1879) and of *Minhah Hadashah*, comments and novellas on the Jerusalem and Palestinian Talmud (Jerusalem, 1880).

He was survived by three sons—R. Elijah, R. Bezalel, and R. Eliezer Nissan—and one daughter, Frimet.

HOROWITZ, Pinhas, of Frankfurt (1730–4 *Tammuz* 1805)—Son of R. Tzvi Hirsch of Chortkov and the younger brother of R. Shmelke. He, like his brother, was a disciple of R. Dov Baer, the Maggid of Mezhirech. He married Rachel Devorah, the daughter of R. Joel Halpern, the rabbi of Lesznov. He was at first the rabbi in Vitkova and then in Lachowiece; in 1772 he became rabbi of Frankfurt. His halakhic works gained him a reputation as an outstanding talmudical scholar. He became known as the *Baal Haflaah*, which was the title of his work consisting of three parts: *Sefer Ketubah* (Offenbach, 1877), *Sefer HaMakneh* on *Kiddushim* (Offenbach, 1801), and *Panim Yafot* (Ostrog, 1824).

Though R. Pinhas followed the Lurian rite, he opposed an attempt to organize a hasidic group in Frankfurt. He never mentioned the *Zohar* or Kabbalah in his discourses.

When his friend R. Nathan Adler headed a group in the 1770s that was influenced by Polish Hasidism, R. Pinhas Horowitz joined the signatories of the excommunication proclamation issued by the Frankfurt community against R. Adler in *Elul* 1779.

He had two sons—R. Meir Jacob, who died in his youth, and R. Tzvi Hirsch, who succeeded him as rabbi in Frankfurt.

E. Steinman, *Shaar HaHasidut*, pp. 121–125.

N.W.

HOROWITZ, Pinhas David, of Boston (*Elul* 1876–7 *Kislev* 1942)—Son of R. Shmuel Shmelke, he was born in the Old City of Jerusalem and studied in Safed under his uncle. At age of twenty he married the daughter of R. Aaron Brandwein. In 1913, he went to Europe to collect funds for Torah institutions and remained for some time in Belz.

When World War I broke out, as he was an Austrian citizen, he was not allowed to return to the Holy Land. He then traveled via Britain to New York. He first lived in the Brownsville section of Brooklyn, where he established a hasidic community *Reim Hahuvim*. In 1916, he moved to Boston, where he became known as the Bostoner rebbe. He was one of the very first hasidic rebbes to settle in the United States, and his was the only hasidic dynasty to bear the name of an American city. He was known as *Baal Hesed* (the compassionate one), who dedicated himself to fostering Sabbath observance and kashrut.

In 1940, he moved to Williamsburg and was instrumental in saving many lives during the Holocaust. He had specialized knowledge of *mikvaot* and was consulted by many contractors on the subject.

He was survived by his sons, R. Moses of New York and R. Levi Yitzhak of Boston.

Z.A.

HOROWITZ, Reuben, of Debica (1820–1885)–The youngest son of R. Eliezer of Dzikov, he became rabbi in Dembice, where he established a dynasty. He married the daughter of R. Isar, the rabbi of Rozwardov. He would never sleep on the Sabbath but would all day long dance with his hasidim. A special rota of hasidim participated in the dancing.

He was succeeded by his son, R. Alter Yeshaya.

HOROWITZ, Samuel (Shmelke), of Nikolsburg (1726–1 *Iyyar* 1778)–Son of R. Tzvi Hirsch, rabbi of Chortkov, he studied under R. Yitzhak Harif and became a disciple of R. Dov Baer, the Maggid of Mezhirech. He married the daughter of R. Joshua, the head of the Jewish community of Rzeszov. He was rabbi in Rychwal and Sianiawa. In 1772, he became rabbi of Nikolsburg in Moravia, and the Empress Maria Theresa confirmed his appointment.

He came out in defense of Hasidism when it was excommunicated in Vilna and Brody in 1782. In his letter to the community of Brody, he refuted the arguments brought by the *mitnaggedim* against Hasidism. He repudiated the accusations of the *mitnaggedim* about the hasidic changes in the liturgy, stating that the *mitnaggedim* "spoke ill of God and caused a desecration of God's name and His Torah."

This letter, first published by M. Bieber in *Yalkut Menahem* (1903), constitutes one of the most important apologetics on Hasidism at that time. During his residence in Nikolsburg, he did not act as a hasidic rebbe, but he continued to preach hasidic doctrines, thereby arousing the opposition of the leaders of the community.

Among his disciples were R. Levi Yitzhak of Berdichev, R. Moses Leib of Sasov, and R. Israel of Ruzhyn.

He was the author of *Divrei Shmuel* on the Pentateuch (Lvov, 1862), *Nezir HaShem* on the Codes (Lvov, 1869), *Shemen HaTov* (Piotrokov, 1905), and two commentaries on the Psalms (Piotrokov, 1924).

Like the Prophet Samuel he lived for fifty-two years. His son was R. Tzvi Joshua, the rabbi of Tarnov.

M. Wilensky, *Hasidim U'Mitnaggedim*, pp. 84–85.

M.W.

HOROWITZ, Samuel Joseph (1862–1922), writer–He was a Zionist *maskil* and attacked the neo-Hasidism of Berdyczewski and Buber in a series of articles he later published in book form under the title *HaHasidut VeHasidim* (Berlin, 1909).

He dismissed the views that Hasidism had unique qualities of authenticity and a revolutionary nature. He saw in Hasidism a continuity of traditions.

HOROWITZ, Yehiel, of Tarnov (1850–14 *Shevat* 1928)–Son of R. Meir of Dzikov, he married Miriam, the daughter of R. David Halberstam. In 1880 he became rabbi of Czarazanov, where he stayed for ten years. He then returned to Galicia and two years later, in 1892, he settled in Tarnov, where he lived in great poverty.

His son R. Naftali succeeded him as rabbi in Czarazanov. His other two sons, R. Alterel and R. Abraham, perished in the Holocaust.

HOROWITZ, Yitzhak, of Mielec/New York (1902–22 *Tammuz* 1978)–Son of R. Naftali, he married Havah Perel, the daughter of R. Shmuel Horowitz of Dembice. He officiated as rabbi in a number of towns in Volhynia, and after World War I emigrated to the United States, where he first lived in New York, then in Cleveland, and, later, in Manhattan, where he was renowned for his melodies. His recordings enjoyed wide acclaim. He was the author of *Kevod Shabbat* (New York, 1942).

He was survived by a son, Samuel Aaron, and two daughters, Reizel Sarah and Beila.

HOROWITZ, Yudele, of Dzikov/London (18 *Elul* 1905–11 *Sivan* 1989)–R. Yehudah, or "Reb Yudele," as he was popularly known, was born in Dzikov. His mother was Havah, the daughter of R. Israel Hager of Vishnitz, and his father was R. Alter Ezekiel Eliyahu. He studied for five years under R. Meir Arak, and, in 1918, he married his cousin Hannah Miriam Simah, the daughter of R. Hayyim Meir Hager. After ten childless years he divorced her, but they then remarried and again divorced. She subsequently married R. Yitzhak Weiss of Manchester.

R. Yudele was a great admirer of R. Moses Sofer (1762–1839), and he knew almost by heart the *Hatam Sofer*'s seven-volume responsa, as well as his sermons and novellas on the Talmud. At the age of thirty, he was appointed *dayan* first in Klausenburg and then, in 1939, after living in the Dzikov ghetto, in Cracow, in Arad, in Bucharest, and in Klausenburg. Miraculously, he survived the Holocaust.

In 1947 he settled in Israel, first in Tel Aviv and then in Jerusalem. He was urged to become rebbe, but he emphatically refused. For a time, he acted as *rosh yeshivah* in *kollel Tarbitza* in Jerusalem. His *shiurim* lasted three to four hours. He would concentrate on just two or three pages of the Talmud, studying them in great depth.

From 1985, he lived in London. He hardly ever spoke, nor did he deliver any discourses but spent his days in study and prayer. He was an ascetic and lived a very frugal life. He would eat meat only on the Sabbath; throughout the week he never ate bread.

He died in London and was interred at the Enfield *Adat Yisrael* cemetery in London. An elaborate *ohel* was erected over his grave, which is frequently visited by all sections of the hasidic community.

He left many unpublished writings—glosses on the works of R. Moses Sofer, on *Toldot Yaakov Yosef*, and on the works of R. Hayyim Joseph David Azulai.

HOROWITZ-STERNFELD, Hayyim Shmuel, of Chenciny (1843–18 *Tevet* 1916)—Son of R. Eliezer of Neustadt, he married Sarah, the daughter of R. Joshua Heschel Frankel Teumim of Komarno. A diligent student, he concluded the study of the *Mishnah* every month, and once a year he completed the study of the Talmud.

He lived in great splendor, surrounding himself with selected students. Before his prayers he devoted many hours to study, and a special *minyan* worshiped with him. On the Sabbath he spoke only Hebrew, and the clocks in his house kept Palestinian time.

He was probably the only rebbe who subscribed to the Hebrew periodical *HaZephirah*, which appeared in Warsaw and supported Zionism. In the betrothal documents of his children, he used the formula of R. Levi Yitzhak of Berdichev: "The wedding will take place in Jerusalem. If, God forbid, the Messiah does not come, it will be held in Chenciny." He was critical of those who found fault with the Holy Land, calling them the "descendants of the twelve spies."

During the First World War he was exiled from Chenciny by the Russians and settled in Kielce, where he died. He was survived by three sons, R. Eliezer, R. Shalom, and R. Joshua Heschel, who all became rebbes. His grandson R. Yeshaya Shapira was one of the founders of *Hapoel Mizrachi*.

Sefer Kielce.

HOSPITALITY—Hasidism added new dimensions to the traditional view of hospitality. Hasidic legend tells of the hospitality of the father of the Besht, who followed the example of Abraham in receiving all—including the destitute, the unlearned, and the sinful—with the same warmth with which he greeted scholars.

One day, bearing a staff and a bundle, a man appeared at his father's door on the Sabbath day. Although such desecration of the holy Sabbath must have grieved him, he did not betray his displeasure. On the contrary, he took special care to make his guest feel at home.

Throughout his life, the Besht both preached and practiced hospitality. "Let your home be open, and let the poor frequent it" (*Avot* 1:5) was the motto of Hasidism. R. Jacob Joseph of Polonnoye, in his *Toldot Yaakov Yosef*, insisted that few qualities ranked higher than hospitality.

R. Levi Yitzhak of Berdichev insisted upon serving his guests himself. He would bring in food and prepare their beds for them. When asked why he did not leave these duties to his servant, he responded, "Hospitality is an excellent deed when performed without payment. The servant would do it for pay, and the intrinsic kindness of the good deed would be lost."

R. Nahman of Bratzlav stated, "An inhospitable person strengthened the hand of evildoers, and a city where hospitality is not practiced will turn to immoral behavior, [which] would bring murder into their midst." He stressed that "hospitality is even greater than arriving early at the house of Torah study."

Hasidic rebbes repeatedly detailed the duties of a host. "When a guest comes," advised R. Simhah Bunem of Przysucha, "the master of the house should show the guest that a bed has been prepared in advance. He should do this even before he invites the newcomer for a meal, for the guest will enjoy the food without anxiety by knowing there is a place to rest the head."

R. Barukh of Medziborz suggested that the householder should eat with the guest as a sign of courtesy, even when the host has already eaten.

When the community of Berdichev wanted to discourage the poor from begging door-to-door, by its organizing a central fund for the distribution of alms, R. Levi Yitzhak vetoed the proposal. He told them that they were trying to institute the practices of Sodom and Gomorrah.

L. Newman, *The Hasidic Anthology*, pp. 181, 184.

J.B.A.

HUMILITY–The virtue of humility (*anivut*) was given a new metaphysical twist in Hasidism. To walk in true humility is the first duty of every hasid. "For humility," said the Besht, "leadeth forth to love man and God."

"Only the lowly," said R. Simhah Bunem of Przysucha, "are able to comprehend the highness of God. We read (Psalm 138:6), 'Though the Lord is high, yet hath He respect unto the lowly.' "

R. Nahman of Bratzlav never tired of stressing the quality of humility and humbleness. He stated, "Faith leadeth to humbleness, humility brings one long life, humility eliminates dispute and suffering. It causes a person to advance and keeps him from falling from his high level. For the world exists only because of a person who makes himself as naught, and that humility is the foundation of true repentance. . . . The Torah can be acquired only with meekness. Humility protects against sexual temptation, and therefore we must pray and plead with God to make us worthy of true humility and lowliness."

The greatest *tzaddik* is worthless if the slightest taint of pride affects him. "But the *Shekhinah*," said R. Pinhas of Koretz, "rests upon a person who attains the level of naught."

Hasidic literature is replete with legends regarding the paradoxical nature of humility and its supreme importance. The Besht told his disciples that his successor should be the one who can guide them in the ways to overcome pride. Why is the first page of the printed tractate of the Talmud not numbered? To teach us that no matter how much we have learned, we are still at the beginning.

The soul of the pseudo-Messiah, Shabbetai Tzvi, came to the Besht to be saved. The latter tried but discovered that Shabbetai Tzvi's soul was trying to get the better of him. The Besht then rejected him and said, "A holy spark it certainly has, but pride and anger overcame it" (*Shivhei HaBesht*, p. 77).

R. Nahum of Chernobyl stressed that humility does not mean that one should imagine oneself to be inferior. The more we are spiritually endowed, the more conscious we should be of our unworthiness.

R. Menahem Mendel of Kotzk maintained that all *mitzvot* should be performed with proper intentions. There is only one exception: humility.

R. Schatz-Uffenheimer, *HaHasidut KeMistikah*.

J.B.A.

HUMOR–The hasidim emphasized the principles that God must be served with a joyous heart and that it is Satan who causes us to feel sad and depressed. To the kabbalists and the hasidim, joy was a sign of nearness to God. Every gathering for prayer must be marked by rejoicing and happiness.

The Besht spoke of the concept of engaging in humor before serious study. It is written, "As for the likeness of the living creatures, their appearance was like coals of fire, burning like the appearance of torches; it flashed up and down among the living creatures; and there was brightness to the fire, and out of the fire went forth lightning." (Ezekiel 1:13). In human beings this refers to greatness and smallness. Through joy and humor we can make the transition from smallness to greatness. We can then study and attach ourselves to God.

R. Jacob Joseph of Polonnoye quoted the Besht as saying that "this was the task of the two humorists mentioned in the Talmud" (*Taanit* 22a). Through their humor they were able to remove humanity's anguish. They could then draw people close to God and elevate them (*Ben Porat Yosef* 49b).

Some of the rebbes encouraged one or more of their followers to entertain visiting hasidim with humorous tales and jokes. Hershele Ostropoler, famous for his jokes and pranks, was a favorite in the court of R. David of Talnoye. In the school of Przysucha, humor was enlisted to hide sincere piety. A truly pious person would want to appear as an ordinary human being, and the ideal hasid should be "good within and evil without." The protean wit and acute perception of the common people were articulated in the various tales that circulated in the hasidic courts. Renowned were the aphorisms and witticisms of R. Naftali Horowitz of Ropczyce.

Sefer Emunat Tzaddikim.

J.B.A.

HUNGARY – Tradition has it that, in the mid-eighteenth century, the Besht visited the eastern parts of Hungary, gaining many adherents to his ideals. He is reputed to have visited Szerencs (com Zemplen), Nagyszollos, and Asvar. It is noteworthy that these areas had at that time only a sparse Jewish community. Szerencs was the home of R. Ezekiel Taub, whose son was R. Yitzhak of Kalev.

Folklore has it that R. Leib Sarah's visited Kalev, where he discovered and influenced R. Yitzhak Taub. R. Barukh, the father of R. Shneur Zalman of Liady, lived for a time in Selis, which has been identified with Nagy Szollos. R. J. J. Greenwald even discovered the gravestone of R. Barukh. *Habad* hasidim, however, do not identify Selis with Nagy Szollos and deny the authenticity of R. Barukh's grave.

R. Levi Yitzhak of Berdichev and R. Aaron of Zhitomir were among those leaders of Hasidism who journeyed to Hungary to spread the teachings of Hasidism. R. Meir Eisenstadt (d. 1744) even left Poland to settle in Hungary. Moreover, there are instances of local rabbis who acknowledged their hasidic colleagues, calling upon them to help them in halakhic matters. It is known that a mitnaggedic rabbi of Nagy Karoly referred the case of an *agunah* to a hasidic rabbi.

However, it was not until the appointment of R. Eizig Taub as rabbi of Nagy Kallo that Hasidism began to take deep roots in Hungary. Over the next three decades many prominent hasidic rebbes accepted rabbinical positions in Hungary. Among them were R. Moses Teitelbaum of Uhjely in 1808 and R. Ezekiel Panet in Tarczal in 1813, both determined to "gain souls" for Hasidism. In Nagyalja (com Emplen) R. Hayyim Tzvi, a pupil of R. Menahem Mendel of Rymanov, became rabbi. R. Menahem Tzvi, who continued to visit his master, was murdered in 1797 while on such a journey. R. Joseph Harif (d. 1857), a disciple of Jacob Yitzhak of Lublin, was rabbi in Zborov (com Saros). Other rabbis in Munkacs included R. Hirsch Melech Shapira.

A dominant influence in the densely populated Jewish areas of eastern Hungary, the Marmaros, was the hasidic dynasty of Kosov. Frequent visitors were rebbes of Galicia; in 1840, a grandson of R. Zusya Twersky, R. Michele, settled in Kurima, Hungary.

The growth of Hasidism did not silence the hasidic critics. R. Moses Teitelbaum was criticized for the dispensing of *kamayot*, and his grandson R. Zalman Leib Teitelbaum left the rabbinic post of Uhjely for Galicia. Later, however, he settled in Marmaros-Sighet, where he established the Sighet dynasty. The most outspoken opponent of Hasidism was Solomon Rosenthal-Moor, the lay leader of Hungarian Jewry in the nineteenth century.

It is noteworthy that the early hasidic rebbes did not impose the Lurian liturgy. Even in centers where Hasidism predominated, the *Nusah Ashkenaz* remained the norm in the main synagogues. It was only in the *shtieblech* that the Lurian liturgy was used. The first major place of worship to introduce the Lurian liturgy was Nagyalia in about 1840, in a synagogue founded by R. Hayyim Zartle, a learned layman who had left a sum of money for the maintenance of the synagogue with the stipulation that the Lurian liturgy be used.

Liturgical differences were not the only cause of friction. At Sarospatak (com Zemolen), the hasidim insisted that only those who wore garments containing no wool would be permitted to officiate. Both the hasidic rebbe, R. Moses Teitelbaum, and the mitnaggedic authority, R. Moses Sofer, dealt with the matter in their responsa.

The collection of money for the poor of the Holy Land constituted another source of contention between the hasidim and the *mitnaggedim*. The hasidim demanded an equitable share of the proceeds for their own institutions, and it was as a result of efforts by R. Moses Sofer that agreement was reached.

Unlike the situation in Lithuania, opposition to hasidim never assumed serious proportions. Hasidic leaders in Hungary were highly regarded by R. Moses Sofer and his followers, for, in addition to the major hasidic luminaries like R. Moses Teitelbaum and R. Zalman Leib, there were also R. Ezekiel Panet and R. Hershele Friedman, better known as "Hershele Lisker"; R. Meir of Premyshlany; and the rebbes of Belz, Rymanov, and Ruzhyn.

Most of the hasidic rebbes were ranking talmudical authorities and were accepted by the schools of the Hatam Sofer. One popular rebbe was R. Mordecai of Nadvorna, who had a large following in the mountainous villages.

During the great constitutional controversies of Hungarian Jewry, the struggle for emancipation led to a bitter schism in Hungary. The liberal Jews wanted to reform the ritual, which the Orthodox resisted. R. Hershele Lisker aligned himself on the side of the Orthodoxy. He had the full support of the Galician rebbes, such as R. Hayyim Halberstam. The hasidic rebbes were invited to sign the *Tekkanot of Michalovce* (Nagy-Mihaly) of 1866, but R. Zalman Leib could not persuade the lay learship to join the organization.

The influence of Galician hasidic leaders was felt in Hungary. Many hasidim in Hungary were followers of R. Hayyim Halberstam, and many students from Hungary studied in the *yeshivot* of R. Hayyim and his son, R. Ezekiel, who for sixteen years was rabbi in Stropkov.

R. Moses Grunwald visited the rabbi of Belz, and R. Hirsch Melech Shapira lived in Munkacz. It was his grandson R. Solomon who founded the dynasty that was maintained for three generations.

After some of the earlier dynasties, like Kalev, lost ground, they were soon replaced by others, such as those of R. Mordecai of Nadvorna, R. Joseph Meir Weisz of Spinka, and R. Asher Anshel Jungreis of Csenger.

One interesting personality was R. Meshullam Feivish Levi (d. 1871). He visited the leading hasidic rebbes and became rabbi of Nyir Tas. Two other rebbes who made their home in Hungary were R. Pinhas Aaron Taub of Rozdol, who lived for more than a decade in Margitta, Transylvania, and R. Israel Hager, the rebbe of Vishnitz, who during the First World War lived in Grosswardein.

Most of the native hasidic rebbes in Hungary were talmudical scholars who frequently combined the dual role of practicing rabbi with the leadership of Hasidism. They were heads of *yeshivot* and exerted themselves to imbue into their students the tenets of Torah and Hasidism. They were authors of learned works and made contributions to Jewish scholarship.

In 1941, Hungary had a Jewish population of 725,000, a quarter of whom were hasidim. During the war, the Jewish community lost 564,500 lives. There are hardly any hasidim left in Hungary today.

J. J. Grunwald, "Lekorot HaHasidut BeHungaria," in *HaZofeh LeHohmat Yisrael*, vol. 5, part 4.

A.S.

I

IBN EZRA, Abraham (1089–1164), biblical commentator and poet—A number of hasidic rebbes rallied to the defense of the biblical exegete whose acute observations, esoteric language, and veiled suggestions have been the cause of scholarly controversy through the ages. Ibn Ezra's criticisms of the liturgical poet Eleazar Kalir (seventh century), for his intricate linguistic constructions, were defended by R. Pinhas of Koretz. "He lived a long time after the destruction of the Temple," wrote R. Pinhas, "and could not appreciate the qualities of Kalir. Ibn Ezra, moreover, was an incarnation of the Tannaim, and he had every right to express a dissenting view" (*Midrash Pinhas* 28).

After he had made some disparaging comments, R. Jacob Samson of Sheptovka had a vision in which his father told him, "All the words of Ibn Ezra are as sacred as a Scroll of the Law." Henceforth, whenever R. Samson mentioned Ibn Ezra, he called him "the holy one." R. Eliezer Halevi Horowitz of Tarnogrod praised Ibn Ezra, calling him "the sage and holy one" (*Noam Megadim*, p. 31a).

R. Simhah Bunem of Przysucha studied Ibn Ezra regularly, because "such study was conducive to the fear of God." In his *Yismah Yisrael*, R. Moses Teitelbaum frequently quoted Ibn Ezra's commentary on the Pentateuch. R. Joseph Meir Weiss used the phrase "the holy book of Ibn Ezra" (*Imrei Yosef*, *Bereshit*).

N. Ben Menahem, "Yahas Shel Gedolei HaHasidut el Abraham Ibn Ezra," pp. 107–112.

IDEL, Moses (b. January 19, 1947)—Leading Israeli scholar of Kabbalah and Hasidism, born in Tirgu Neamtz, Rumania, who emigrated to Israel in 1963. After several years of study at Haifa University, Idel began to study Jewish philosophy and Kabbalah at Hebrew University in Jerusalem, under the supervision of Shlomoh Pines. He was awarded a Ph.D. in 1976 for his dissertation, *The Doctrine and Works of R. Abraham Abulafia* (Hebrew). Material from this dissertation and further studies concerning the work and school of the thirteenth-century Spanish kabbalist Abulafia would later appear in three English volumes.

Idel's research into early Kabbalah has been wide-ranging, dealing with its origins in early rabbinic sources and its relationship to ancient and medieval philosophical systems, but one of its principal objectives was to clarify the nature and significance of ecstatic Kabbalah within the history of Jewish mysticism. The results of his efforts lead Idel to challenge several of Gershom Scholem's theories, particularly the claim that *unio mystica* was not an important feature of Jewish mysticism. Idel's theories appeared in English in his book *Kabbalah: New Perspectives*, in which substantial evidence was produced for the importance of a nondual mystical experience, from the time of Abulafia and continuing in the writings of early hasidic masters.

Idel has further argued that Abulafian influence can be detected in Hasidism as a result of the hasidic masters' interest in Moses Cordovero's *Pardes Rimmonim*, which contains unattributed Abulafian writings. More recently, Idel has criticized Gershom Scholem's interpretation of Hasidism, which attributes its rise to proximate historical traumas, especially Shabbateanism. Idel has argued that Hasidism can be better understood as a further development of phenomenological models that are typical of Jewish mysticism, namely, theosophy, magic, and ecstasy. In Idel's view, Hasidism, in its fundamental teachings, emphasized the magical and ecstatic models, which served to form the basis of the concept and experience of the hasidic *tzaddik*.

M. Idel, *Hasidism: Between Ecstasy and Magic*. M. Idel and B. McGinn, *Mystical Union and Monotheistic Faith: An Ecumenical Dialogue*.

M.KR.

IMITATION OF GOD–The ideal of *imitatio Dei* is praised by Philo as common to the teaching of both Moses and Plato. Yet it is somewhat problematic in rabbinic Judaism–it can only mean "to walk in His ways–as He is merciful, so you must be merciful."

Yet, not in all His ways. So, one must not imitate His "jealousy."

In Maimonides' Code, *imitatio Dei* is given a characteristic twist. God is totally transcendent and ineffable, but the prophets have ascribed to Him the kind of attributes that human beings ought to emulate. The form of piety that Maimonides urges is not to imitate God but to seek His nearness, so as to be worthy of receiving flashes of insight from the Holy Spirit (*Guide of the Perplexed*, III, 51; "*Yad HaHazakah*," *Hilkhot Deot*, chap. 1).

In speculative Kabbalah, which portrayed God in anthropomorphic terms, it was natural for pietists to model themselves after the Divine Being. Yet, Kabbalah, as a version of Judaism, had to insist that God in Himself (*Ein Sof*) is totally without any qualities, absolutely beyond all the categories of space and time. So, whereas the Divine Being radiates His light into Primal Man (*Adam Kadmon*), the ultimate goal of prayer is to reach the Holy Ancient One (*Atika Kadisha*), Who transcends all human concepts.

Hence, in the Kabbalah of Cordovero, the *imitatio Dei* takes the form of transforming one's personality in such a manner as to become a fit "dwelling place for the *Shekhinah*" (*maon laShekhinah*). This ideal, which occurs in tannaitic sources, is spelled out by Cordovero in concrete detail, organ by organ and limb by limb. (See Louis Jacobs's translation of *Tomer Devorah*.)

In Hasidism, only the *tzaddik* is deemed worthy of becoming a "dwelling place for the Shekhinah," since by definition, the *tzaddik* has overcome the drives of the material "shells." He no longer shares "the lusts of the flesh for food, drink, and sex." He fulfills the obligation of raising a family by means of a special act of divine assistance that is granted to him for this purpose (Sh. Dubnow, *Toldot HaHasidut*, vol. II, chap. 5, p. 186). The parents of the Besht were 100 years old when he was born, so that they were completely devoid of physical lust (*Shivhei HaBesht*, beginning).

As for the common people, their ideal could only be to "adhere to God" (*devekut*), to serve Him with passion and zeal (*hitlahavut*), and to attempt to rise momentarily and occasionally to the level of immateriality (*hitpashtut hagashmiut*).

The endeavor to "see God in all things" was actually so revolutionary that it had to be curbed by the insistence that the hasidim shall imitate the *tzaddik*, not set out on their own to find ways of imitating God. So, the great *tzaddikim* did dare to develop unique and original patterns of piety. But the hasidim were cautioned to stay within the beaten paths and follow closely the examples set by their respective *tzaddikim*.

J.B.A.

INDECH, Judah Leib (1871-1944)–Born in Praga, he was a disciple of R. Judah Leib Alter of Ger. Declining rabbinical posts, he moved to Antwerp in 1910 and settled in London in 1914.

Though engaged in business, he devoted his time to kabbalistic and rabbinic studies. In his work *Zoharei HaShass*, published in London in 1974, by his son, R. Jonah Indech of Bournemouth, England, he records a number of passages from the *Zohar* that have a relevance to *Halakhah*, demonstrating the impact of the *Zohar* on talmudic studies.

J.I.

INFORMERS–From time to time, informers (*malshinim* or *moserim*) made their unwelcome appearance in Jewish life.

Avigdor ben Joseph Hayyim of Pinsk and the *kahal* of Vilna denounced the hasidim as a "pernicious sect," and as a consequence, R. Shneur Zalman of Liady was arrested. In counteraction, the hasidim accused the *kahal* of Vilna of diverting to other purposes certain money collected for taxes. As a result, the community's leaders were arrested in February 1799.

In 1838, two notorious Jewish informers, Isaac Oksman and Samuel Schwartzman, were assassinated in Ushitso, Podolia, as a result of which many Jews, including R. Israel Friedman of Ruzhyn, were arrested.

On October 24, 1823, Judah Leib Mieser denounced the hasidim in a memorandum to the district officer of Lvov. As a result of this denunciation, a number were arrested.

Isaac Baer Levenson, too, submitted information to the authorities in 1823, urging them to close all Jewish printing presses.

Joseph Perl, in his struggle against Hasidism, tendered to the Austrian authorities denunciations against Hasidism. Similarly, Jacob Silberstein of Oleszyce denounced the rebbe of Zydaczov.

R. Mahler, *Hasidism and the Jewish Englightenment*, pp. 123, 366.

ISAAC THE BLIND (ca. 1160–1235), father of Kabbalah – Son of R. Abraham of Posquieres (southern France), Isaac is generally held to have been the founder of medieval mysticism.

The date of his birth cannot be determined with any degree of certainty, but we know that the period of his activities covered the end of the twelfth and the beginning of the thirteenth centuries.

He is generally referred to as *Yitzhak Sagi Nahor* (Aramaic euphemism for "blind"). There is reason to believe that he was not born blind, since he is known to have been able to distinguish colors. No written work is attributed to him. Bahya ben Asher refers to him as the "godly teacher, the father of Kabbalah."

Menahem Rekanati refers to him: "I have heard that R. Yitzhak was able to distinguish by the presence of a person whether he was a new soul or an old one" (*Beur al HaTorah al Derekh HaEmet* [Venice, 1545], p. 209a).

A. Neubauer names Isaac as the author of an obscure commentary on the *Sefer Yetzirah* (Catalog Bodleiana Mss. 2546:12). It is doubtful whether he was the author of the *Sefer HaBahir*. He was, however, the first to introduce the idea of metempsychosis.

G. Scholem, *Reshit HaKabbalah* (1948), pp. 99–126.

A.T.

ISRAEL, LAND OF – The Land of Israel occupies a pivotal role in Hasidism. According to the Besht, exile from the Holy Land was the cause of Jewish spiritual degeneration. The Besht yearned to fulfill the commandment to "live in the Land of Israel" and to plant the seed of Hasidism in the hallowed soil, a fusion that could speed the messianic era. According to tradition, the Besht set out three times for the Holy Land.

"God knows," writes the Besht in a letter to his brother-in-law, "that I have not given up hope of traveling to the Land of Israel." A number of his disciples and associates did make the journey successfully, however, and one such emigrant was R. Abraham Gershon, his brother-in-law.

Four years after the death of the Besht, two of his associates, R. Nahman of Horodenka and R. Menahem Mendel of Premyshlany, settled there in 1764.

In *Adar* 1777, 300 hasidim left Eastern Europe for the Holy Land under the leadership of R. Menahem Mendel of Vitebsk, R. Abraham of Kalisk, and R. Israel of Poltusk.

Not since Juda Halevi had Zion such a lover as R. Nahman of Bratzlav. The emotions that Juda Halevi expressed in his "Odes to Zion" were voiced by R. Nahman in the pitty aphorism for which he was renowned. He maintained that by settling in the Land of Israel, a person gained insight into God's providence over the world. The yearning one feels for settling there brings one great blessing in one's livelihood.

Prayers are more acceptable when offered in the Holy Land. No one can go there except through sufferings. One who goes there to attain holiness will achieve that aspiration. The Holy Land is the center of Israel. Each one has a share in it, as long as one honors the Lord. If one desecrates God's name, one loses association with the Holy Land. We should always pray that we may yearn for the Holy Land.

At the age of twenty-seven, R. Nahman visited the Holy Land, and when he returned, he stated, "My place is in the Land of Israel. If I travel anywhere, I shall travel there. The air I breathe and my very being and whatever holiness I possess come from the Holy Land." Throughout his life, he relived every detail of his journey.

The primary themes in hasidic literature are the Land of Israel, exile, and the redemption. R. Dov Baer, the Maggid of Mezhirech, inherited his master's love of Zion. For him, Zion was the spiritual center of the world. R. Solomon, the rabbi of Lutzk, stressed that it is essential that the people living in the Holy Land use the Holy tongue –

the language in which the universe was created.

R. Jacob Joseph of Polonnoye, too, made careful preparations for his pilgrimage to the Holy Land, but for reasons unknown to us, the journey was never made. He stated, however, that "the Land of Israel is an exalted land, and the Holy One, Blessed be He, gave it to Israel as a perpetual gift. It is reserved for them and belongs exclusively to them."

In 1791, R. Pinhas Shapira of Koretz, too, set out on the pilgrimage. He died, however, in mid-journey. He, too, felt that anyone who is able should settle in the Holy Land.

Like many hasidic leaders, R. Elimelekh of Lejask wanted to settle in the Holy Land but was dissuaded by his followers. R. Levi Yitzhak of Berdichev stressed that Israel is a holy nation and God's peculiar treasure, and when the people cease to sin, they will be worthy of returning home. Only if they meticulously observe the Torah will the Land be restored to the children of Israel.

R. Simhah Bunem of Przysucha compared the love of the Jews for the Land of Israel to the love of a bride for her bridegroom. When the Messiah came, the marriage would be consummated. He expressed surprise that Moses Montefiore did not attempt to purchase the Holy Land from the Turks.

In the nineteenth century, hasidim came to the Holy Land as individual settlers or in groups of two and three. Among the settlers were R. Tzvi of Kaminka and his brother R. Benzion, R. Issachar Dov Baer of Zloczov, and R. Abraham Dov Baer of Ovruch, who so much impressed Sir Moses Montefiore.

Having denied himself the privilege of living in the Holy Land, R. Shneur Zalman was indefatigable in supporting those who settled there. They received the support of all the rebbes of Lubavitch, who encouraged settlements in Safed, Hebron, Jerusalem, and Tiberias.

Throughout the nineteenth century, the hasidim contributed regularly to the *kollelim* and to the *halukkah*. A small number were associated with the *Hovevei Zion* movement, but they did not participate in the work of Zionism.

The first hasidic attempt to establish an agricultural settlement between the wars was made by R. Ezekiel Taub of Yablona and by R. Isaiah Shapira of Grodzisk, who established *Kefar hasidim*.

Notable among the hasidic settlements are *Kefar Habad*, *Kiryat Vishnitz*, *Ramat Vishnitz*, *Kiryat Zanz*, *Kiryat Bobov*, *Kiryat Yismah Mosheh*, and *Kiryat Hazor*, established in the Galilee in 1976. The state of Israel now has the second-largest hasidic community in the world (the United States has the largest). Today, there are many hasidic rebbes, *yeshivot*, and *kollelim* in Israel. In no other country are there so many prolific writers on the history of Hasidism. Hundreds of volumes have been printed in the past decades, and interest in the subject appears to be growing.

M. H. Rabinowicz, *Hasidism and the State of Israel*.

ISRAEL, LOVE OF – "Israel is a good and holy nation," said the Besht, "a people versed in the Torah, gracious and upright." His great-grandson, R. Nahman of Bratzlav, stressed that "all the world was created only for the sake of Israel and that every single Jew has some element from which God has particular pride. This is even true of the lowliest Jew—even the sinners of Israel. Such a person is called a sinner of Israel, and therefore, the name Israel still applies to him. Even he is included in God's pride."

The title "lover of Israel" was bestowed on R. Levi Yitzhak of Berdichev, R. Zusya of Annopol, R. Abraham Joshua Heschel of Opatov, R. Moses Leib of Sasov, R. David Biderman of Lelov, and R. Israel Hager of Vishnitz. Virtually all of the hasidic rebbes were accustomed to gaze on the House of Israel with an almost magic benevolence. Their love for their fellow Jews was pure, passionate, and boundless, lavished on the godly and the ungodly alike, for they believed that righteousness lay dormant in the heart of even the most drastic sinner.

No one had a better right to be called a "lover of Israel" than R. Levi Yitzhak of Berdichev. He regarded every Jew as a letter in a *Sefer Torah* and above reproach. Even the most blatant transgressor was given the benefit of the doubt. To one individual sinner, he once confided, "I envy you, for if you only repented and returned wholeheartedly to the Almighty, a ray of light would stream forth for every one of your transgressions, and you would be altogether luminous."

Fiercely, he defended people against the itinerant *maggidim* who harassed and harrowed them. Yet even this wrath was muted by compassion. "God of the Universe," he exclaimed, "this poor *maggid* reviles and rebukes your people, for that is how he earns his livelihood. Give him, therefore, his daily bread, so that it will no longer be necessary for him to defame your people."

"It is a grave sin," said R. Abraham Joshua Heschel of Opatov, "to speak evil of the most wicked Jew. Such abuse grieves the *Shekhinah*." These views were echoed by other hasidic masters. "What evidence do we have that we have made such progress in the service of God?" asked R. Jacob Yitzhak of Przysucha. "We can judge this by the depth of our love for Israel."

R. David of Lelov called every Jew "my brother." R. Kalonymus Kalman of Piasczeno used to say, "Children, precious children, just remember that the greatest thing in the world is to do someone else a favor."

A. Kaplan, *The Light Beyond*, pp. 146–148.

ISRAEL, PEOPLE OF – Regarding the peoplehood of Israel, the hasidic masters followed a trend that had been well developed among the kabbalists and Jewish philosophers. God's purpose in creation was to bestow good, and therefore the very first conceptual ingredient of creation had to be a recipient of that good. The recipient was to be the people of Israel, who would accept the Torah and live by it. The peoplehood of Israel was therefore seen as the very first conceptual ingredient of creation.

Even though the Jews were among the most downtrodden people of the eighteenth century, the hasidic masters taught that they were by far the most important in God's eyes. The Besht said that this is the reason why Israel is likened to the stars: both appear very small but in reality are very great.

The Besht also taught that if not for the people Israel, the world could not endure. It was in order that the universe be able to exist that God created the concept of Israel. The holy sparks that fell with the breaking of vessels (q.v.) could be elevated only by the people Israel, and it is through that elevation that the purpose of creation is fulfilled. This is likened to a king who deliberately loses his signet ring so as to afford his only son the opportunity of finding it. Since the people Israel have the task of elevating the fallen sparks, especially through eating, they alone have the obligation of reciting blessings over food.

Another important teaching of the Besht is that all blessing flows to the world only through the souls of Israel. Israel is thus like a rope bound to God, connecting Him with the physical world. Before the people Israel can be punished, God must first hide His face from them, since He cannot bear to see their suffering.

R. Dov Baer, the Maggid of Mezhirech, followed the same thread, saying that since there can be no king without subjects, God created the people Israel to be His subjects. In any activity, the "first thought is the final deed." When one builds a house, one's first thought is of having a place to live, and that thought permeates all of the building efforts. Similarly, the thought of creating the people Israel permeates all creation, and therefore Israel is rooted in all spiritual worlds. God Himself identifies with the people Israel, and the manner in which He reveals Himself reflects the status of Israel at the time.

The Maggid explains that for God, past, present, and future are exactly the same, and therefore He experienced delight in Israel even before creation. It was that delight that resulted in the original constriction (*tzimtzum*).

R. Israel, the Maggid of Kozienic, teaches that God is so completely transcendental that if He had not created an Attribute through which He could be worshiped, it would be impossible to pray to Him. This attribute is called Kingship (*Malkhut*) and is closely identified with the people Israel, who reflect His glory. It is for that reason that Israel sets its calendar by the moon, since the moon also shines only by reflected light.

In the writings of R. Abraham Joshua Heschel of Opatov, the most basic hidden point of creation was God's initial desire to do good, and only Israel can reach this point. In obeying God's will, Israel fulfills His purpose and thereby enhances the entire fabric of creation. Since they are so intimately bound to the body of His purpose, the people Israel are likened to God's *tefillin*, which are closely bound to the body.

While the *Habad* system echoed the Besht's doctrines, it laid great stress on the earlier kabbalistic teaching that, alone of all humanity, the people Israel posses a special soul that is a "portion of God from on high." The people Israel are called "God's children," since like a son they partake of the most intimate essence of their Father.

With the exception of R. Nahman of Bratzlav, none of the hasidic masters delved into the question about why the people Israel were chosen by God. R. Nahman does not answer this question but merely states that the solution lies in the realm of the incomprehensible. God knew that He would choose the Patriarchs even though they had free choice, but the issue involves one of the most basic unanswerable paradoxes in Jewish philosophy.

In another important teaching, R. Nahman states that God had absolutely no need to create the world, and nothing in His essence compelled Him to do so. It was only after the creation of the souls of Israel that He committed Himself to such creation, and only then was He compelled to complete it.

Of all the hasidic masters, none extolled the virtues of Israel more than did R. Levi Yitzhak of Berdichov, the original "lover of Israel." Making use of the talmudic adage "More than the calf wants to suckle, the cow wants to give milk," he taught that God's greatest pleasure was to bestow good to His people Israel. Israel is higher than all spiritual universes, even above the place where the initial constriction took place. It was only for the sake of Israel that God constricted His essence into Attributes that can be comprehended by humanity.

R. Levi Yitzhak of Berdichev writes that the Passover is called a sabbath, since it was with the inception of the people Israel at the Exodus from Egypt that the creation of the universe was actually completed. On Rosh Hashanah, God judges the world to see if it loves Him, but on Passover He judges the world to see if it loves His people Israel. Although Abraham had a mortal father, his real "father" was God's original thought, which was the creation of the people Israel.

Ar.K.

ISRAEL OF POLTUSK (d. ca. 1785) – Son of R. Peretz, he was a disciple of R. Dov Baer, the Maggid of Mezhirech. In *Adar* 1773, he together with R. Menahem Mendel of Vitebsk emigrated to the Holy Land. It was not long after that R. Menahem Mendel sent him back to Eastern Europe to raise funds. He was particularly suited to that role, since, in the early part of his life, he had made the rounds of the villages, preaching Hasidism, at the behest of R. Dov Baer.

His eloquence won many converts, and his pen was as persuasive as his preaching: "It is your responsibility," he wrote, "to rebuild the House of God, and it is incumbent upon you to support the settlers of the Holy Land." He was very hesitant to leave the Holy Land, and R. Menahem Mendel stressed his reluctance. "Even if I were to give him a thousand changes of garments a month, he would not have left of his own free will. He did this for my own sake."

R. Israel was successful in his mission and made contact with R. Shneur Zalman of Liady. He instituted the system of *maamadot* (collection of funds for the *Old Yishuv*).

He died in Fastov.

I. Halpern, *HaAliyot HaRishonim shel HaHasidim LeEretz Yisrael*, pp. 20–37.

ISRAEL OF RUZHYN (3 *Tishri* 1797–3 *Heshvan* 1851) – Son of R. Shalom Shakhnah and grandson of R. Abraham HaMalakh, Israel was born in Probrodzice, Kiev, South Russia. He was but six years old when his father died, and he was brought up by his elder brother, R. Abraham, who succeeded his father. At thirteen, he married Sarah, the daughter of R. Mosheh Halevi Efrati, head of the *yeshivah* of Berdichev and later rabbi of Butchan.

When his brother died childless in 1813, the sixteen-year-old Israel was his heir. He settled first in Squira and then in Ruzhyn, where he established his court. His new home was a departure from the pristine life of the early rebbes. Ruzhyn oozed royalty, and the rabbi was virtually the exilarch of Hasidism. His contemporary Dr. S. Rubin describes him: "He sat upon his throne, dressed in immaculate and expensive garments like one of the Russian nobles, and his hat was embroidered in gold. From the tip of his toes to his head there was an elegance about his costly clothes." Another contemporary, Prof. B. Mayer in his book *The Jews of Our Times* wrote that the rabbi's coach was drawn by four horses and that he employed a large retinue of servants. In Brama Fakuta, a non-Jewish writer, Pakula Braniecki, informs us that "the greatest architects, painters, and decorators came especially from Paris and Italy to the little town of Ruzhyn in order to build and decorate the rabbi's house."

ISRAEL BAAL SHEM TOV

On July 13, 1866 the London *Jewish Chronicle* reported, "The luxury of the palace is truly royal. . . . The apartments contain [the] most splendid Turkish and Persian carpets as well as the most heavy damask hangings." In spite of this external splendor, the rebbe led an extremely ascetic life. He justified his life-style by saying, "What can I do? It is not my choice. I am forced from above to take the road of honor and glory, and it is impossible for me to deviate from it."

Such were the claims on his time that the rebbe slept only a few hours each day. "One must not waste the time of the kingdom." He would rise at dawn and would spend many hours at prayer and study. He possessed a charismatic personality, and an extremely acute mind. His remarks were known for their brevity and deep meaning. In prayer R. Israel preferred the "still small voice." To a hasid, praying loudly and violently, he once whispered, "My friend, try first the quiet way." He urged his followers to pray at the times prescribed by the Codes. He identified himself with the problems of each hasid, and the doors of his hospitable home were never shut. The rebbe was often visited by members of the Russian gentry who sought his counsel.

There was unanimity among the rabbis in their affection for him. R. Abraham Joshua Heschel of Opatov bound R. Israel's girdle around his *kapote* with the words: "Heaven has honored me with *Gelilah*." Even R. Samson Raphael Hirsch, the leader of Jewish Orthodoxy in Germany, after meeting R. Israel, stated, "It is difficult to perceive how such a man could be born of a woman, for the light of the *Shekhinah* shines in his face."

The rabbi was imprisoned following the assassination of two Jewish informers, Isaac Oksman and Samuel Schwartzman. It was alleged that the followers of the rabbi were responsible for their deaths. For twenty-two months the rabbi languished in the prisons of Kiev and Kamenetz-Podolsk. In 1840, on the day after Purim, he was released and allowed to return to Ruzhyn. He was, however, under strict surveillance and, in order to forestall banishment to Siberia, R. Israel escaped to Romania, where he stayed first in Jassy, the Kombling and Skola.

The Russian government demanded his extradition. To save their leader from imprisonment, the hasidim alleged that he was an Austrian citizen. Eight people, both Jewish and non-Jewish, corroborated the claim while the Russian government produced documentary evidence to counter it. R. Yitzhak Noah Mannheimer (1793–1865), a member of the Austrian parliament, and Salomon Mayer Rothschild (1774–1855) intervened with Count Metternich and Ferdinand I of Austria to refuse the Russian demands.

R. Israel acquired an estate (Zolotoi-Potok) in Sadgora four miles from Czernowitz, where the glory of Ruzhyn was revived. His family joined him in 1842, and when his wife died on the first day of Passover 1847, he subsequently married the widow of R. Tzvi Hirsch of Rymanov.

R. Israel became a Turkish citizen, and on his passport was stamped "Native of Jerusalem." His hasid Israel Bak, a pioneer of Hebrew printing in the Holy Land, visited him and was sent to London to urge Sir Moses Montefiore to persuade the Czarist government to permit fund-raising for the Holy Land in Russia. R. Israel also helped Bak acquire a strategic piece of land in the Old City, on which to build a synagogue, which was eventually named *Tiferet Yisrael* in his honor.

"Everyone leaves behind books," he mused. "I leave sons." His six sons, whom he called his "six wings" and who all established hasidic dynasties, were R. Shalom Joseph of Sadgora, R. Abraham Jacob, R. Menahem Nahum of Stefanesti, R. Dov of Leove, R. David Moses of Chortkov, and R. Mordecai Shragai of Husyatin. There were also three daughters: Leah, Hayyah Malkah, and Miriam Mannie.

His discourses are to be found in *Irin Kadishin* (Warsaw, 1885), *Yeshuot Yisrael* (Podgorze, 1904), *Kenesset Yisrael* (Warsaw, 1906), *Peer Yisrael* (Jerusalem, 1921), *Kerem Yisrael* (Lublin, 1930), *Nahlat Yisrael* (New York, 1951), *Orot Yisrael* (Jerusalem, 1973), and *Ner Yisrael* (Bene Berak, 1973).

A. Y. Bromberg, *Migdolei HaHasidut*, vol. 6., *R. Israel Friedman MiRuzhyn*.

A. Marcus, *HaHasidut*, pp. 207–222.

A. D. Twersky, *Sefer HaYahas MiChernobyl VeRuzhyn*.

ISRAEL BAAL SHEM TOV (17 *Elul* ca. 1700–6 *Sivan* 1760), founder of Hasidism—Israel was born in either 1698 or 1700 in Okopy, a small village near Kamenetz on the border of Podolia and Moldavia. Hasidic tradition records that R.

ISRAEL BAAL SHEM TOV

Israel's father, Eliezer, lived in captivity for many years. Throughout his exile he remained loyal to his father and true to his wife, Sarah. He died when his son was still very young. Outwardly, Israel lived an unremarkable life. He was *behelfer* (assistant teacher) in Horodenka, near Brody, and then worked as a synagogue beadle and as a ritual slaughterer. At the age of eighteen he married, but his young wife died shortly afterward. While busy with everyday chores, Israel applied himself to mystical studies, particularly to practical Kabbalah. The writings of R. Yitzhak Luria and R. Hayyim Vital became his guides. It was believed that Israel had access to the writings of a mysterious kabbalist, R. Adam, whose identity has eluded historians.

It was in the course of an arbitration that Israel met R. Efraim of Brody, who happened to pass through Horodenka. A shrewd judge of character, the rabbi offered the youthful adjudicator his daughter in marriage. The rabbi died before he reached home, and the bride's brother, R. Gershon of Kuty, could not persuade his sister to annul the betrothal.

After his marriage, Israel spent a number of years in seclusion, in study and meditation in the forest and by the banks of the river Prut. The young thinker viewed the vast and solitary grandeur of the Carpathian Mountains as a reflection of the power and the glory of the Creator. He also acquired a useful knowledge of the healing qualities of various herbs.

His disciple R. Jacob Joseph of Polonnoye stated that Israel's instructor had been none other than the legendary prophet Ahiyah of Shilo. There is no evidence that Israel ever received rabbinic ordination, but there is abundant evidence he was endowed with remarkable attributes that compensated for the lack of formal qualifications. He followed the pattern of the wandering wonder-workers who wrote *kamayot* (amulets), exorcised demons and *dybukkim*, and prescribed *segulot* (healing aids). He healed the sick, not through magic but through prayer. By 1736 he became known as the Baal Shem Tov—master of the good name—or by the abbreviation Besht. He could communicate on equal terms with R. Dov Baer, the learned Maggid of Mezhirech, and with the scholarly R. Jacob Joseph of Polonnoye. He was equally at home with unlettered cobblers or farmers. It was not his habit to castigate. He had no desire to make sinners feel sad or overwhelmed with feelings of guilt or unworthiness. He sought instead to raise their spirit and redeem them with joy.

After a short stay at Tlust (eastern Galicia), he settled in Medziborz, near Brody. The Besht was said to be one of the three scholars who participated in the public disputation between the Frankists and the rabbis, held in Kamenetz-Podolsk in 1753. His presence there is disputed by many scholars.

His fame spread far and wide; even his brother-in-law, R. Gershon, formerly so hostile, became his devoted follower. Writing to his brother-in-law, then living in the Holy Land, he made this startling revelation: "On Rosh Hashanah 1747, I experienced an uplifting of the soul, and I asked the Messiah: 'Let me know, my Master, when will you appear on earth?' and the reply was: 'This shall be a sign unto you, when your teachings shall become known.' I have come into the world to show men how to live by three precepts: Love of God, Love of Israel, and Love of the Torah."

He exerted great influence on his followers. No one could meet him without falling under the spell of his unique personality. His methods were novel. The anecdote, the parable, the metaphor, and the aphorism played a great part, appealing to the heart as well as to the mind. He was the most approachable of men, and he won the hearts of the poor and the humble. His disciples loved him, revered him, and all but worshiped him. "If he had lived in the time of the prophets, he would have become a prophet," noted R. Leib Sarah's, a contemporary of R. Israel.

He died on the second day of Pentecost in the presence of his family and disciples. "I do not lament my fate," he remarked comfortingly to the bystanders. "I know full well that I shall leave through one door and enter through another. Let not the foot of pride overtake me." With this verse from Psalm 36:12 he was gathered to his fathers and was buried in Medziborz.

Historical Baal Shem

Fable and fact about the Besht are so interwoven that modern biographers find it difficult to distinguish between them. The earliest of the literary sources are dated half a century after his death. The *Shivhei HaBesht* was published in Kopys in 1815. Only one letter can be reasonably authenticated: a letter the Besht wrote to his brother-in-law and that was later published by his disciple R. Jacob Joseph of Polonnoye. Other letters have been attributed to him but are of doubtful authenticity. He did not write any books, but his teachings are recorded by this disciple in *Toldot Yaakov Yosef*, *Ben Porat Yosef*, *Tzofnat Paneah*, and *Ketonet Passim*. The Besht's sayings can also be found in *Tzavaat HaRibash*, the Testament of the Besht, printed in 1793, and *Keter Shem Tov* (Zolkiev, 1794).

Recently, Mosheh (Murray) Roseman in documents preserved in *Bibliotek Czartoryski* in Cracow has found taxpayers lists and the correspondence of local administrators dealing with Medziborz that was owned by the Czartoryski family. R. Israel is referred to as "Kabbaliste," "Balsem," or "Balzem Doctor." It is clear that the Besht lived, tax free, in a house belonging to the Jewish community. Unlike Ben Zion Dinur, who defined the crisis of eighteenth-century Polish Jewish society as essentially a crisis of leadership, the documents reveal that the Besht, far from being antiestablishment, was a staunch upholder of the community.

A number of individuals, such as Hershel the Scribe, Wolf Kuces, and David Porkes, all mentioned in the *Shivhei HaBesht*, appear in the Polish documents. In another document the Besht is recorded to have been instrumental in preventing the apostasy of a Jewish woman who had formed relationships with Poles.

Doctrines

The Besht has often been described as a pantheist. However, the pantheism of the Besht has little in common with the pantheism of Benedict Spinoza (1632–1677). Spinoza died about twenty-two years before the birth of the Besht, and the Besht was probably unaware of his existence. Whereas Spinoza's God is the Absolute, working exclusively through the laws of nature, which derive with geometric certainty from His Being, the Besht's God is personal and concerned with every individual. The Besht's pantheism might be better designated as *panentheism*, that is, a belief that all things and events are in God. To the Besht, God is both immanent and transcending. Spinoza sees a world without a purpose. The Besht sees a world created to fulfill God's purpose.

The Kabbalah had become the jealously guarded province of the intellectual elite, which reveled in mind-intoxicating and illuminating profundities. This was the rich inheritance the Besht wished to share with the masses. He believed that all the children of Israel were entitled to enter the spiritual kingdom, and he threw wide open the heavy gates. For it was not enough that this knowledge should be available. It had to be intelligible. The privilege of the few had to become the prerogative of the many.

The Besht applied the teachings of Kabbalah to everyday life. Whereas R. Isaac Luria revealed the divinity of the upper realms, the Besht revealed the divinity of things here on earth. Indeed, the Besht was an ardent student of Kabbalah, especially of the *Zohar*, a book that lay open on his desk at all times, and he believed "that the hidden light of creation was concealed in the *Zohar*."

Though a child of Kabbalah, the Besht rejected its asceticism. The body must be strong for the worship of the Lord. Therefore, one must not weaken the body. Not through fasting is the ire of God averted, but through joy. Joy was the keynote of the Besht's philosophy. He wrote, "Our Father in heaven hates sadness and rejoices when His children are joyful. And when are His children joyful? When they carry out His Commandments." This immediate, worldly joy is the true reward, the greatest reward, for the performance of a good deed and the fulfillment of a commandment. Rewards to be received in the world to come are incidental, for a *mitzvah* should be performed for its own sake. Tears of joy are permitted and are even desirable. In contrast, we should subdue sadness and raise ourselves to the higher realms of joy. Should we err, we are urged not to brood over the transgression, lest we sink further into a morass of melancholy. We should demonstrate sincerity of repentance by returning instantly, and with renewed ardor, to the service of God. We should understand that the evil impulse and the good impulse were created at the same time. God can be served by the evil impulse if the flame is directed toward Him.

ISRAEL BAAL SHEM TOV

One must pour one's very essence into every word, every God-directed thought. But how can we divest ourselves of the distracting influences and desires that constantly assail us? Song and dance are potent aids. When the Besht prayed, it seemed that all creation listened in awe. The verse "All my bones say, 'Lord, who is like unto Thee?' " (Psalm 35:10) was taken literally. And when he communed with his heavenly Father, it seemed as if every rib and every fiber of his body were included. In every single Jew, the Besht perceived a spark, sometimes dormant, of holiness. With boundless love and compassion the Besht looked upon his people.

For the Besht, evil did not exist. "What shall I do with my son? He is so wicked!" asked a despairing father. "Love him all the more," was the characteristic counsel of the Besht. Reprimands were not the way of the Besht. "God does not look on the evil side," he explained. "How dare *I* do so?" He believed that the Torah, the living words of the Most High, should transform the student; for one "must study the Torah to become a Torah." In the words of the Mishnah, it should "clothe [one] in meekness and reverence; it fits [one] to become just, pious, upright and faithful." *Kavvanah* and *hitlahavut* were as essential in study as in prayer. Humility was also important, and the scholar must guard against intellectual pride.

Evil is a chair for the good is the recurrent theme of the Besht. Not that evil is either rare or illusiory: it is powerful and subtle, drenching the world in blood and lying in wait to trip the unwary. The followers of the Besht needed no complex kabbalistic formulas to drive away demons; faith alone was sufficient—confident, joyous, triumphant faith. It was sinful to allow oneself to sink into depression or to be troubled by anxiety. Wherever God dwells, there joy prevails, and a hasid must always be joyous.

The Besht showed a way out of the messianic dilemma—through individual redemption. Let each pietist redeem himself, and only then the Messiah will come. He maintained that the *tzaddik* is guided by the Holy Spirit (*Ruah HaKodesh*), the lowest level of prophecy. Not only did the power of the *tzaddik* extend to the salvation of his living followers, but also he was engaged in redeeming the souls of persons who had died in previous eras and who were presumed to wander disconsolately, being transmigrated in stones, plants, animals, and other human beings.

The divine flow of blessings descends into the world through the *tzaddikim*. Different *tzaddikim* correspond to different people. The *tzaddik* cannot fulfill his role adequately if he is aloof from or out of touch with the people. The *tzaddik* has to fall from his high level of "adherence" to God, in order that he might establish some contact with the common people. "The secret of 'seven times does the *tzaddik* fall and ascend' is in order that he might associate with the sons of this world and thus be enabled to uplift them." He sweetens the laws, weighting the divine decree with compassion rather than with severity, turning the policy of strictness (*Midat HaDin*) into the policy of compassion (*Midat HaRahamim*).

The most revolutionary aspect of the Besht's teachings was the assertion that God desires to be served in all ways. There are no divisions between the sacred and the secular. God is everywhere and no place is free of Him. Torah study and prayer are important, but every action of our daily routine can be endowed with religious fervor and turned into a sacrament. All persons should serve the Almighty with all their power, for they should think that whatever happens is from God and they should be forever ready to do what the Lord thinks is good for them.

The Besht taught that it is possible for a person to be fully attached to God even while attending to the ordinary necessities of life. It is the task of the pious Israelite to redeem the Holy Sparks that are scattered through all creation. One cannot simply withdraw from the hurly-burly of life and busy oneself with the salvation of one's own soul. Instead, it is an obligation to combine sustained attachment to God with active participation in the affairs of the marketplace.

This attachment (*devekut*) is not merely a matter of thought but also one of total devotion and love. We should cling to the Creator with a perfect love, knowing that He is Absolute Goodness and that all that is good flows from Him. At times, the Besht employs the symbolism of love, and even of sex, to suggest the passion for the attachment.

In the time set aside for regular prayers, the ideal of *devekut* reaches its supreme climax. Worshipers should adhere to the letters and to the words that they articulate. For we must pour our very essence into every word and into every God-directed thought. Prayer is part of the *Shekhinah*, which may be why the *Shekhinah* is called prayer. Through *Bittul HaYesh* (negation of existence), we can rise above ourselves. Worshiping with spontaneity is more important than worshiping at prescribed times. *Hitlahavut* (enthusiasm) and ecstasy replace formalism. If strange thoughts intrude in the course of prayers, one should know that such thoughts derive from the mystery of "the breaking of the vessels" and the fall of the 288 sparks into the power of the shells. It is our task to separate the sparks and uplift them to their source. To the Besht the letters of the Torah were like infinite chains, with the visible, concrete end at one pole while the inner essence of the letters rises through the many worlds and culminates in God Himself. The Besht attributed his mystical achievements to the intensity and devotion of his prayers.

It is a popular misconception that the Besht disapproved of study. The fact is that he put a different emphasis on study. It was not simply an intellectual exercise. He believed that the Torah—the living words of the Most High—should transform students, for they "must study the Torah to become a Torah."

Gershom Scholem maintains that the historic significance of the Besht's movement was the substitution of personal redemption for preoccupation with messianism. It was the Besht's belief that he had opened a new chapter in Jewish worship that would hasten the coming of the Messiah. In his opinion every *tzaddik* is a living anticipation of the messianic era, when all evil (*klipot*) will be metamorphosed into goodness. The *tzaddik* was living proof of their faith that the Messiah was close at hand. "In every true *tzaddik* there is the revelation of the Messiah," wrote his great-grandson in *Likkutei MaHaran* (79). In this way the messianic hope was intensified while its personal focus was blurred. Every *tzaddik* was a companion of the Messiah, but none could claim with any assurance the ultimate dignity.

True, all the ideas we encounter in the teachings attributed to the Besht can be found in the earlier pietistic movements, especially in the Lurianic works of Kabbalah, and yet a new synthesis was effected by the Besht. Rapturous prayer; mystical meditation; immersion in the *mikveh*; intensification of the communal spirit through regular visits to the *tzaddik's* court, where food and drink were shared; a new surge of hope and faith in redemption; a deepened appreciation of the piety of the unlearned—all these aspects of Hasidism are the legacy of the Besht. His enduring contribution was to create the nucleus of an organized body of Hasidism that expanded with remarkable speed, capturing the loyalty of many.

M. E. Gutman, *R. Israel Baal Shem Tov*.

Y. L. Maimon, ed., *Sefer HaBesht*.

M. J. Rosman, "Jewish Perceptions of Insecurity and Powerlessness in 16th to 18th Century Poland," pp. 19–28.

E. Steinman, *R. Israel Baal Shem Tov*.

Ed. and J.B.A.

ISRAEL HARIF of Sanatov (d.1781)—This eighteenth-century kabbalist was one of the first scholars to associate himself with the Besht. He was the author of *Tiferet Yisrael* (Lvov, 1865) and is mentioned in the *Shivhei HaBesht*.

ISSACHAR BAER of Lubavitch (d. 1787)—A contemporary of the Besht, he was a disciple of R. Dov Baer, the Maggid of Mezhirech. In 1785, he settled in Lubavitch and was the teacher of R. Shneur Zalman of Liady. Though himself a rebbe, he regarded himself as a disciple of R. Menahem Mendel of Vitebsk. R. Shneur Zalman called him the "pure one."

ISSACHAR DOV BAER of Zloczov (d. 7 Av 1810)—Son of R. Aryeh Leib and a grandson of R. Naftali Yitzhak HaKohen of Frankfurt, he was a disciple of R. Dov Baer, the Maggid of Mezhirech. He was an outstanding scholar whose halakhic rulings were accepted by R. Hayyim Hakohen Rapoport of Lvov and R. Tzvi Hirsch of Zamosc.

He was the author of *Bat Eyni* (Dubno, 1781) and *Mevasser Tzeddek* (Lvov, 1850), in which he quotes the Besht, the Maggid, R. Elimelekh of Lejask, and R. Yehiel Michael of Zloczov. In what seems to be a prediction of the Nazi Holocaust, he wrote, "The Almighty will set up a ruler whose decrees will be harsher than those of Haman."

Despite ill health and failing eyesight, he undertook the journey to the Holy Land. He died in Safed, where he was buried next to the grave of R. Moses Alshekh. His son-in-law, R. Abraham Hayyim, succeeded him.

Y. Raphael, *HaHasidut VeEretz Yisrael*, pp. 139–141.

J

JACOB JOSEPH HAKOHEN of Polonnoye (d. 24 *Tishri* 1782) – Son of R. Tzvi Hakohen Katz, he was a descendant of R. Samson ben Pesah of Ostropol, R. Yomtov Lipman Heller, and R. Joseph Katz, the author of *Yesod Yosef* (Minkowce, 1803). He was a diligent student. "Each day," records *Shivhei HaBesht*, "he used to study in *tallit* and *tefillin*. Before eating, he would master seven pages of the Talmud, and even while he ate, between each piece of food, his mouth did not cease to recite the holy words. . . . Not one night passed – whether winter or summer, weekday, Sabbath, or holiday – that he did not rise at midnight to study. His study of Torah, his prayer, and all the holy acts he performed with such vigor that his very flesh trembled from him."

He was an ascetic. "He used to fast each day until nightfall, and once every month he would fast from Sabbath to Sabbath." At first he resisted the growing influence of the Besht but he was finally converted to Hasidism. He may have been influenced also by R. Aryeh Leib Gliner, preacher of Polonnoye. He then suffered persecution and indignities from the *Mitnaggedim*, and he was probably driven out of Shargorod in 1748. He was rabbi in Rashkov (1748–1752) and Nemirov (1752–1770) before finally settling in Polonnoye.

The Besht was aware of his new adherent's great potential. "The blessed one will thank me that I have found for Him 'a Yossele' such as this one," said the Besht. The "Yossele" to whom he referred was naturally R. Jacob Joseph. On another occasion he remarked, "All Jacob Joseph's works are pleasing to the Creator, and all his actions are in the name of God." The Besht was worried about his asceticism, and he urged him to desist. "I order you not to bring yourself into this danger, for this way is dark and bitter and leads to depression and melancholy. . . . God forbids fasting more than one is obliged to."

R. Jacob Joseph devoted himself to writing down and disseminating his master's ideas. He was the author of four monumental works, the most important being *Toldot Yaakov Yosef*, a commentary on the Torah and an analysis of the 613 commandments, which appeared in Medziborz and in Koretz in 1780. In it the expression "I heard from my teacher" occurs 249 times. This book was burned in Vilna, in Cracow, and in Brody. His second work, *Ben Porat Yosef*, was printed in Koretz in 1781. It is divided into two sections: the first part is a commentary on Genesis, and the second part contains a number of responsa and discourses, delivered on *Shabbat Shuvah* and *Shabbat HaGadol*. It also contains the letter that the Besht wrote to his brother-in-law, R. Gershon Kitover. *Tzofnat Paneah*, a commentary on Exodus, was printed in Lvov in 1782, and *Ketonet Passim*, published posthumously in Lvov in 1866, is, despite the assertion of Dubnow, authentic.

When the Besht died, R. Jacob Joseph did not succeed him but gave his allegiance to R. Dov Baer, the Maggid of Mezhirech.

In his works, R. Jacob Joseph criticized the rabbis for their pride and haughtiness. "For they study not for the sake of heaven, but personal aggrandizement." The teachers and ritual slaughterers, too, were castigated, for their lack of dedication. He had no sympathy for the rich who fail to respect either the genuine student and the teacher of the Torah, for whose material needs the rich do not adequately provide.

Only the *tzaddik* stands between heaven and earth. He is the channel or the means of heaven's reaching earth. He accomplishes this task by means of *devekut*. He must, however, be worthy of the people's trust. He must be willing to suffer for his people, and he must be concerned for the poverty of the people. He has to be among the people but always in the presence of God. His feet must be firmly rooted in reality, but like Jacob's ladder, his thoughts must be near to the heights. The *tzaddik* must be like Abraham, who pleaded for the doomed cities of Sodom and Gomorrah, and not like Noah, who was totally indifferent to the fate of his generation.

S. Dresner, *The Zaddik.*

JACOB JOSEPH (YEIVI) of Ostrog (1738-*Hol HaMo'ed* Sukkot 1791)–Born in Ostrog, the son of R. Judah Leib, the preacher of Ostrog, he was a disciple of R. Efraim of Brody and R. Dov Baer, the Maggid of Mezhirech. In 1766, he succeeded his father as preacher of Ostrog. R. Zusya of Annopol frequently visited him, and he was friendly with R. Barukh of Medziborz.

He was the author of *Mora Mikdash* (Koretz, 1782), an anthology of kabbalistic works and a polemic against those who talk during synagogue services. His work *Ein Mishpat* (Koretz, 1782) censured rabbis who bought their position. More important was his work *Rav Yeivi* (Slavuta, 1792)–discourses on the Torah–stressing the sanctity of Jerusalem. He pointed out that only those who observe the Sabbath in the Diaspora will share the sanctity of the Holy Land. *Tzaddikim* suffer all their lives until the day of their death, when they have a glimpse of the rewards awaiting them in the Garden of Eden.

He was succeeded by his son, R. Eliakim Getz (d. 26 *Elul* 1845), who deliberately chose to live in cramped quarters because he did not wish to have a permanent or comfortable home outside the Land of Israel.

R. Eliakim's son, R. Alter Mordecai, or R. Alternui, as he was called (d. 17 *Tishri* 1935), was rebbe for well over half a century. He was celebrated for his hospitality, especially to Jewish soldiers.

Y. Raphael, *Sefer HaHasidut*, p. 31.

JACOB KOPPEL (d. ca. 1740), kabbalist–Son of R. Moses of Mezhirech, Jacob was a noted kabbalist. His works *Shaarei Gan Eden* (Koretz, 1803) and *HaKol Kol Yaakov* (Slavuta, 1804) greatly influenced the development of hasidic liturgy.

JACOB KOPPEL of Vishnitz/Kosov (d. 15 *Elul* 1767)–Son of R. Nehemiah Feivish, Jacob–or "Koppel Hasid," as he was called–was a descendant of R. Ovadiah Yare Bertinoro and of R. David ben Samuel Halevi, known as the *Taz*.

Jacob and his family originated from Moravia. He married Hayya, the daughter of R. Zalman of Kolomyja. The Besht, when he visited the town, sensed the presence of a sage, whom he identified as Jacob Koppel. Jacob Koppel became a devoted follower of the Besht, and as he had a melodious voice, he acted as a reader in his *Bet HaMidrash*. He became known as a *shivisinik*, because the Hebrew verse *Shivisi Adonai* ("I have always placed the Lord before me") was the keynote of his life.

The Besht declared that Jacob's prayers ascended directly to the Throne of Glory, causing rejoicing in the celestial spheres. As a legacy, the Besht made him responsible for the spiritual welfare of the Jews in Marmaros and the Carpathian region. "I am giving you a beautiful garden," the Besht told him. "Tend it carefully."

He died in Tysmenitsa, near Stanislav. He had two sons, R. Mendel of Kosov and R. Yitzhak of Kolomyja, and a daughter, Bluma.

Y. Alfasi, *Tiferet SheBeMalkhut*, pp. 13–21.

JACOB SAMSON of Shepetova (d. 3 *Sivan* 1801)–Son of R. Yitzhak, the rabbi of Slavuta, he was a descendant of R. Samson of Ostropole. He was a disciple of the Maggid of Mezhirech and a close friend of R. Barukh of Medziborz.

He was a great halakhic authority whose considerable erudition earned him respect and recognition in rabbinic circles. He is quoted in *Zera Efraim* by R. Efraim Zalman Margulies. He was assigned the formidable task of expounding hasidic doctrines to such rabbinical authorities as R. Ezekiel Landau of Prague, R. Isaiah ben Judah Loeb Berlin and R. Efraim Zalman Margulies of Brody.

He succeeded his father as rabbi in Shepetova, but, in 1799, he settled in Tiberias where he met R. Nahman of Bratzlav. He traveled as an emissary on behalf of the hasidic settlers. His only son, R. Joshua died in his lifetime.

He died in Tiberias, where he was buried.

Y. Raphael, *Sefer HaHasidut*, pp. 28–29.

JACOB YITZHAK HAHOZEH Mi'Lublin (1745–9 *Av* 1815)—The father of Polish Hasidism, Jacob Isaac Horowitz, known as HaHozeh MiLublin (the Seer of Lublin), was the son of R. Eliezer Halevi, the rabbi of Yosefov. His mother, Meitel, was the daughter of R. Koppel of Lukov, near Tarnogrod, where he was born. He studied under R. Moses Tzvi Hirsch Meisels, the rabbi of Zulkov, and at the *yeshivah* in Sianiawa under R. Shmuel Shmelke Horowitz, who held him in high esteem. "When Jacob Yitzhak recites the benedictions," remarked his teacher, "the entire Heavenly Court responds 'Amen.' " Later he made his way to the Maggid of Mezhirech. "Such a soul has not made its appearance since the time of the prophets," the discerning Maggid declared. There he became friends with R. Levi Yitzhak of Berdichev and R. Israel the Maggid of Kozienice.

He subsequently became attached to R. Elimelekh of Lejask, who took a paternal interest in the newcomer, stating emphatically, "He is my equal." In the lifetime of his teacher, he established his own court in Lancut and in 1808 in Lublin. Lublin under him became the training ground for hasidic leaders. Gifted young men flocked there. The founders of the most illustrious hasidic dynasties in Poland and Galicia, such as Przysucha, Kotzk, Ger, Ropczyce, and Dynov, were all greatly influenced by the life and teachings of R. Jacob Yitzhak.

R. Menahem Mendel of Kotzk referred to him as the *Urim VeTumim*, and R. Uri of Strelisk declared, "Lublin is *Eretz Yisrael*. The courtyard of the *Bet HaMidrash* is Jerusalem, and the *Bet HaMidrash* is the Temple. The study of the Seer is the Holy of Holies. And the *Shekhinah* speaks from his mouth." Both disciples and followers left his presence comforted and hopeful. The rebbe, however, was full of humility. "There can be no man less worthy than I am," he sighed. "Woe to the generation that looks to me for leadership." Diligently and devotedly he served his community and arranged the marriages of forty orphans.

In Lublin, he faced opposition from the *mitnaggedim*, especially from R. Azriel Halevi Horowitz (d. 1890), known as the *eizener kopp* (head of iron). From his second marriage to Tehilah Sprinza, daughter of R. Tzvi Hirsch of Lancut, the Seer had four sons (R. Israel, R. Yosef, R. Abraham, and R. Tzvi Hirsch) and two daughters.

On the night of Simhat Torah 1815, after the *hakkafot*, he left his *Bet HaMidrash* and retired to his room on the first floor of his house. The room had only one small window. At midnight hasidim saw a body lying on the ground in the courtyard. He was seriously injured and died. This "mysterious" fall has puzzled hasidim ever since.

He developed the concept of the *tzaddik*. He maintained that it is the role of a great *tzaddik* to hasten the coming of the Messiah. Every *tzaddik* has already overcome the power of the "other side" within his personality. It remains his task to subdue the "shells" in the whole world and to usher in the era of redemption. The *tzaddik* must not adopt the role of the prophet who rebukes the people for their sins; rather, he must love the people and pray for miraculous help on their behalf. Like God, he is first of all the "Good" who is "beneficent to the evil as well as to the good." Once the sinner has been saved from troubles, the sinner repents from sins (*vayehi*). The *tzaddik* who really helps people is not the one who attains a high level of saintliness but the one who is continually engaged in attaining holiness.

He recognizes his sinfulness, and the higher he rises, the more self-critical he becomes. At the same time he feels at one with the sinners of this world. Therefore, his prayers are helpful to the common people (*behar*).

In his novel *For the Sake of Heaven*, Martin Buber focuses attention on the dispute between the Seer and his former disciple the "Yehudi." The latter believed that individual redemption must precede that of the community. The former believed that a concerted effort by the great *tzaddikim* can overcome the power of Satan.

He was the author of *Divrei Emet*, homilies on the weekly Torah readings, and novellas on the talmudical tractates *Shabbat* and *Hullin* (Zolkiev, 1808). This has now been reprinted eighteen times. His discourses can also be found in *Zot Zikaron*, first printed in Lvov in 1851 and since reprinted twelve times, and *Zikoron Zot* (Warsaw, 1869).

I. Alfasi, *HaHozeh MiLublin*.

A. I. Bromberg, *Migdolei HaHasidut*, vol. 19, *HaHozeh MiLublin*.

R. Elior, "Between Yesh and Ayin: The Doctrine of the Zaddik in the Works of Jacob Isaac, the Seer of Lublin," pp. 393–455.

JACOBS, Louis (b. 1920) – Born in Manchester, England, and educated at Gateshead Yeshivah, England, and the University of London, Louis Jacobs is now rabbi of the New London Synagogue and professor of Talmud at London's Leo Baeck College. He has been an important contributor to the study of Hasidism in the English-speaking world.

A prolific author, his major contributions to the study of Jewish mysticism and especially of Hasidism include an English translation with commentary of Moses Cordovero's *Palm Tree of Deborah* (1960), an English translation with commentary of Dov Baer Schneersohn of Lubavitch's *Tract on Ecstacy* (1963), a monograph on Aaron of Starosselje entitled *Seeker of Unity* (1966), and a book entitled *Hasidic Prayer* (1973). In addition, he has contributed important articles and essays on hasidic themes to the *Encyclopaedia Judaica* and to a wide variety of Jewish journals and has analyzed hasidic views in the context of his broader discussions of Jewish theology in his surveys of Jewish thought *Principles of the Jewish Faith* (1964), *A Jewish Theology* (1973), *Saints and Saintliness in Judaism* (1990), and *Turn Aside from Evil and Do Good,* by Tzvi Hirsch Eichenstein (1994).

In addition to the value of making original hasidic sources available to the English-speaking world through his excellent translations, Jacobs's importance as a student of Hasidism lies in his attempt to approach the subject topically and synthetically. He has tried to range over the entire corpus of hasidic materials, both anecdotal and theoretical, to distill from them their basic teachings on a wide variety of subjects, and, further, to erect on the basis of those studies an understanding of the more general hasidic weltanschauung. This process can be seen, for example, in his comprehensive article, "Hasidism," in the *Encyclopaedia Judaica* and in his treatment of the hasidic understanding of such concepts as "The Unity of God," "God's Transcendence and Immanence," and "The Love of God" in his more general discussion of those themes in his *Jewish Theology*.

Of Jacobs's longer studies, the two most valuable are his monograph on Aaron of Starosselje (1766–1828) and his detailed treatment of hasidic prayer. In the former, Jacobs not only traces the career of his subject but also presents a broad analysis of the basic kabbalistic-hasidic concepts, such as that of the ten *Sefirot* (divine emanations) and *tzimtzum* (divine withdrawal). In so doing, he gives a fine introductory account of the general religious-mystical theology of Hasidism. Moreover, insofar as Aaron of Starosselje was a contemplative hasidic master, the material presented helps to balance the overly worldly and activist image of Hasidism made famous by Buber and his disciples. Again, because of Aaron's close links with Shneur Zalman of Liady, whose greatest disciple he was, the work, both directly and indirectly, sheds light on the history and ideas of the *Habad* dynasty.

In *Hasidic Prayer*, the same qualities are in evidence, for Jacobs not only gives us the most detailed discussion of this subject available but also sheds light on the entire fabric of hasidic life. This study is especially valuable because its close attention to detail and firsthand acquaintance with the original sources helps to give proper emphasis to the theoretical, ritual, and halakhic aspects of Hasidism, which have been neglected by other, more popular treatments of the movement. As a result of Jacob's study of hasidic prayer (as of all of his hasidic works), one can gain a much truer image of hasidic life and a better appreciation of its authentic shape and character.

A. Sherman, *Commentary* 38:10 (1964): 60–64.

S.K.

JEHIEL MICHAEL (MICHEL) of Zloczov (ca. 1731–25 *Elul* 1786) – Son of R. Isaac of Drohobycz, he was born in Brody and traced his descent to Rashi. His father, who was at first an opponent of the Besht, became a devoted follower. He encouraged his son to become the Besht's disciple. Jehiel Michael married Rachel, the daughter of R. Mosheh of Nowe Maesta. After the death of the Besht, he studied under the Maggid of Mezhirech and R. Shmelke of Nikolsburg.

He served as preacher and teacher in Brody, Yampol, and Zloczov. He was rebbe for twenty-two years and lived in great luxury, wearing fine apparel and eating sumptuous meals. He justified his regal way of life by saying, "We are told in the Talmud (*Berakhot* 57) that a fine dwelling, fine clothes, and a beautiful wife broaden a man's understanding." He set himself high standards and urged his followers to pray even for their enemies that it may be well with them. "This is even more important than praying for your friends." His code of conduct was demanding: "One must be most careful not to take financial advantage of either a Jew or a gentile. Enslavement to money is a form of idol worship. It forms a barrier between man and God."

Despite his palatial residence, he believed in seclusion. After his marriage he isolated himself for a period of one thousand days. Among his disciples were R. Mordecai of Neshkhitz, R. Abraham Joshua Heschel of Opatov, R. Abraham Mordecai of Pinczov, and R. Mosheh Leib of Sasov.

He was the author of *Yeshuot Malko* on the Torah and Festivals (Jerusalem, 1978).

His five sons, whom he called the "Five Books of Moses," disseminated Hasidism in the Ukraine and Galicia. His eldest son, R. Joseph, or "Yossele" (d. 1824), married the daughter of R. Menahem of Vitkov. His second son, R. Yitzhak of Radzvillov (1744–1825), married the daughter of Mosheh Shoham of Dolina; he served as rabbi in Nadvorna, Opoczna, and Rymanov; and he was the author of *Or Yitzhak* on Torah and the *Ethics of the Fathers* (Jerusalem, 1961). His third son, R. Tzvi Benjamin Zeev (d. 3 *Nisan* 1822), was the rabbi of Zbaraz and the author of *Tiferet Tzvi Zeev* (Lvov, 1896) and *Rozin D'Oraita* (Warsaw, 1903). His fourth son, R. Mosheh (d. 10 *Iyyar* 1831), was rabbi of Zevil; he married the daughter of R. David, rabbi of Grabovitch. His fifth son, R. Mordecai of Kremenets (1746–13 *Tammuz* 1801), was the joint president with R. Abraham Joshua Heschel of Opatov of the *kollel* of the Holy Land. Among his disciples were R. Meir of Przemyslany and R. Yeshaya Shur of Iasi.

JERUSALEM – For the mystics there is only one eternal city, and that is Jerusalem. No other city in the world has a comparable claim on the allegiance of the Jewish people. "The prayers of all Israel," wrote R. Isaiah Horowitz, "rise to heaven via Jerusalem." Hasidic teachers agreed with these sentiments. "By our services to God," wrote R. Naftali of Ropczyce, "we rebuild Jerusalem daily, brick by brick, row by row. When the building is complete, the redemption will come" (*Ohel Naftali*).

Today, the Holy City is a thriving center of Hasidism, yet, until recently, few hasidic rebbes resided there. The early hasidic pioneers lived in either Safed or Tiberias. R. Nahman of Bratzlav did not even visit Jerusalem.

An early hasidic pioneer who settled in the Holy City was R. Moses (1776–1850) of Lelov. The descendants of R. Moses left their impact on the *Yishuv*. For thirty-two years, his son Eliezer Menahem Mendel lived there. He was followed by his son, R. David Tzvi Solomon (d. 1918).

A nineteenth-century hasidic establishment was the synagogue *Tiferet Yisrael*, or *Bet HaKnesset Nisan Bak*, which was built by Nisan Bak.

Today, Jerusalem is the home of the rebbes of Ger, Belz, Talnoyye, Rotmistrovka, Amshinov, *Toldot Aaron*, Karlin, Stropkov, Zevil, Nodvorna, Biala, and Biala-Przysucha.

Apart from the rebbes, Jerusalem is the home of many hasidic yeshivot: *Or Aneelam* Bratzlav, established in 1937; *Bet Imrei Yosef*, Spinka, 1940; *Bet Avraham* of Slonim, 1918; *Sefat Emet* of Ger, 1925; *Tiferet Yisrael* of Ruzhyn; Karlin and Stolin, established in 1939; *Bet Mordecai* of Zevil, 1948; and Belz, 1950.

There are also many hasidic *shtieblech* in Jerusalem and in its new suburbs.

Lubavitch has developed a *Shikun Habad* in Givat Shaul, and the Satmar *yeshivah Yitav Lev* has also opened a *kollel* and a Talmud Torah, which is not part of the *Hinukh Atzmai*.

There are many hasidim now living in Mattersdorf, Har Nof, and Katamon.

JEWISH CHRONICLE – To the *Jewish Chronicle* of London in the nineteenth century especially, Hasidism and hasidim were distasteful subjects. The paper, founded in 1841 (and thus today the oldest Jewish newspaper in the world), had a number of scholastic editors and contributors during the period, but their thinking and attitudes reflected largely those of the Sephardic and West European (German) Jewish elements that then dominated the Anglo-Jewish community and that were, if not ignorant of, then rather contemptuous of, their less civilized brethren of Eastern Europe.

In its review of the year 5605 (October 6, 1845, p. 249), the paper is almost complacent about Anglo-Jewry's quiescence, contrary to the European extremes of intellectualism among the *maskilim* on the one hand and "the imbecilities of a Besht" on the other.

The first special reference to the hasidim occurs on August 25, 1848 (p. 651), in an article, "The Sect of the Hasidim," by the writer Hollawdaerski. In a brief history, reference is made to the legend Shivhei ha-Besht, printed in 1814, by R. Baer, which went through five editions in four years, and to the Besht's *Ethical Wills*. The article is slightly cynical about the Besht's alleged "miracles" and describes how his disciples dispersed themselves all over Poland after his death, each "assuming for himself the title of *tzaddik*," having "acquired from him this sort of professional quackery."

As a pattern this served for the next thirty years at least, in any reference to hasidim, except that the derogatory language if anything grew stronger.

A dissertation on July 21, 1854 on the cruelties and megalomania of the czar, "The Jews in Russia under Nicholas I," while admitting the superior literacy and civilization of the Jews compared with the Russians, nevertheless takes a sideswipe at the "host of abuses and superstitions" of "the pernicious chassidim," "a real disgrace of the Mosaic religion."

A series of articles in 1859, beginning May 13 (p. 6), gives a lengthy synopsis-review of a pamphlet, *Beleuchtung eines ministeriellen Gutachtens über die Lage der Juden im Konigreich Polen* (Hamburg: Hoffman, 1859), which is highly critical of Hasidism. The June 3 installment (p. 6) opens with a quotation including the "prophecy": "this monstrous birth of Judaism—Mysticism, or as it is here called Hasidism, will gradually waste away, if it be deprived of its mainstays, oppression, and ignorance." More a wish than a prophecy!

Later, in 1880, another series of articles, "Religious Pilgrimages," devotes some space to the hasidim in Russia and Palestine, and the paper seized the occasion to print a leading article of nearly three-quarters of a page on "The Chassidim" (September 24, 1880), self-evident proof of Anglo-Jewry's ignorance on the subject. The paper was then newly owned by Asher Myers, Sydney Samuel, and Israel Davis; Myers was manager-cum-editor, Samuel a lawyer/litterateur/traveler, and Davis a scholar, the presumption being that Samuel wrote the articles and Davis the leader. In the lead article, the hasidic *tzaddikim* were most bitterly criticized not only for allegedly acquiring enormous wealth for themselves from their credulous followers but also for perpetuating a system of "gross superstition and impostures."

After the entry of many thousands of East European Jewish refugees from the devilish Russian pogroms in the next few years, a less dramatic view was taken of the movement, partly no doubt because of direct contact when hasidic *shtieblech* were opened by the newcomers in London's East End, some of which even joined the founders' list in 1887 of the Federation of Synagogues, considered more "Orthodox" than the old established English synagogues that formed the United Synagogue in 1870.

The hasidim became an accepted item of "news" value, but a certain hostility was transferred or masked under the disfavor with which the *Jewish Chronicle* regarded the later established "ultra-Orthodox" Adat Yisroel group in the early 1900s with which some hasidic congregations were merged, especially as the Adat at that time was avowedly anti-Zionist and the paper had become an out-and-out exponent of Zionism.

Toleration with, but not active sympathy for, the hasidim gradually came—despite hasidic reserve, to put it mildly—it may be observed as a sort of parallel that the editor at the time of the establishment of the state of Israel and in the 1950s actually gave space for a main feature article by their much-reviled "near-cousins" the Neturei Karta, to explain their anti-Israel views, something no other paper had ever done. The Satmaner Rebbe was well featured in some of his trans-Atlantic pilgrimages, among other signs of relaxation, Hasidism being by now a "curiosity" rather than an uncouth diversion from the path of ordinary Judaism.

During the 1960s and 1970s, the Lubavitch organization, by its dynamism, forced itself into public notice, reflected in news stories. In an issue as late as July 16, 1976 (p. 5) the *Jewish Chronicle*—which had for more than fifteen years favored something like an equivalent of American Jewish Conservatism in England and given considerable space to self-styled "progressive" Judaism—printed as a run-of-the-mill news picture one of prize-winning pupils and some hasidic teachers at the Lubavitch House junior school in London.

In 1982, the editor, Geoffrey Paul (1977–1990), was amazed by the volume of mail that followed an article by Rabbi Dr. Norman Solomon that criticized the hasidim of Lubavitch (April 16, 1982, p. 21).

The *Jewish Chronicle* estimated that 25,000 hasidim are living in the boroughs of Hackney and Harringay in North London, basing this information on the study *British Jewry in the Eighties—A Statistical and Geographical Study* (London, 1986, p. 23) by Stanley Waterman and Barry Kosmin.

D. Cesarani, *The Jewish Chronicle*, pp. 229, 240.

J.M.S.

JEWISH NATIONAL AND UNIVERSITY LIBRARY, Jerusalem—This library has one of the largest collections of books on Hasidism. The manuscript section has a number of manuscripts on *Habad* and Hasidism.

The library also holds the archives of R. Elijah Gutmacher and autographed letters by R. Jacob Aryeh Guterman of Radzymin, R. Hayyim Israel Morgenstern of Pulawy, and other hasidic rebbes.

Its bibliographical quarterly, *Kiryat Sefer* (founded in 1924), not only records hasidic works, published in Israel and abroad but also has many articles on hasidic printing and bibliographical subjects.

JEWISH THEOLOGICAL SEMINARY LIBRARY, New York—This library contains more than 273,900 printed volumes and more than 11,100 manuscripts. It has an extensive collection of hasidic works and works about Hasidism, including first editions and reprints. Practically all of the literature relevant to the study of Hasidism can be found in the library. Among the author entries are R. Levi Yitzhak of Berdichev, R. Elimelekh of Lejask, R. Shneur Zalman of Liady, and R. Nahman of Bratzlav. The literature of the opponents of Hasidism is also well represented, by such as the first edition of *Shever Poshim* and *Zemir Aritzim*. In addition, the library contains an excellent collection of kabbalistic literature.

In a separate group are about 200 titles arranged according to the geographic identifications of their authors or members of renowned hasidic dynasties, such as Alexander and Zydaczov.

In the area of manuscripts, the collection is fairly small, with a preponderance of material being of *Habad* literature from the nineteenth and early twentieth centuries. The manuscripts include homilies and commentaries on the Pentateuch, letters by hasidim, and many polemical anti-hasidic tracts. Two important non-*Habad* manuscripts in the collection are the *Herem* (ban) against R. Hayyim Halberstam of Zanz issued by the hasidim of Sadgora in Tiberias, and a hasidic manuscript written by Abraham Jacob Friedman of Sadgora, which has been identified by the late Prof. A. J. Heschel.

There is not as yet a printed catalog of the manuscript collection. Nonetheless, the library is an important research center for students of Hasidism.

M.M.F. and S.F.

JOEL of Nemirov (eighteenth century)—R. Joel was the rabbi of Nemirov until 1782, when he was succeeded by R. Jacob Joseph of Polonnoye.

There is no foundation whatsoever for the theory propagated by Isaac Schipper ("The Image of R. Israel Baal Shem Tov in Early Hasidic Literature," pp. 252–253, 551–552) that R. Joel was considered by the disciples of the Maggid to be the founder of Hasidism. Schipper confuses R. Joel with R. Joel Baal Shem, who is referred to in Maimon's autobiography (London, 1954, p. 70).

JOSEPH MOSES of Zalocze (ca. 1733–23 *Elul* 1815)—Although frail and ailing, he practiced a rigorous form of asceticism. An impassioned speaker, he served as preacher in Zborov and Zalocze. He was the author of *Brit Avraham* (Brody, 1875), a commentary on the Pentateuch, and *Beer Mayyim* (Medziborz, 1817) on the Passover *Haggadah*.

His works were published by his son, R. Joseph Elkanah, and by his son-in-law, R. Israel Halevi. Among those who gave encomiums were R. Abraham Joshua Heschel of Opatov, R. Tzvi Hirsch of Zydaczov, and R. Abraham Jacob of Sadgora.

Y. Raphael, *Sefer HaHasidut*, p. 61.

JOY (*simhah*)–Joy is a key concept in Hasidism; its opposite, *atzvut* (melancholia), is held to be, as a well-known hasidic maxim has it, not a sin in itself but the main cause of sin. As in other areas, the hasidic teachings on joy are not original but based on statements in the earlier Jewish moralistic and religious literature.

The contribution of Hasidism was to place such emphasis on *simhah* as to elevate it to the highest rank of spiritual values. This emphasis stems from hasidic views on the omnipresence of God. It is impossible for the believer to be really unhappy in a world that, for all its woes, reflects only the divine goodness, the very evils of human existence being no more than the obverse side of that goodness, the essential means of encouraging us to rise above our material circumstances to enjoy for all eternity the nearness of the Creator. Even to grieve over one's sins is unhealthy.

The psalmist's admonition to turn from evil and do good is interpreted as a total rejection of morbid introspection. The saying of the rabbis (*Mishnah Abot* 4:1)–"Who is rich? The one who rejoices in his portion"–is said to refer even to our spiritual portion. The hasidim are content to be themselves as God has made them.

Some hasidic masters, however, draw a distinction between *atzvut* (despairing sadness) and *merirut* (bitterness), a keen awareness of life's tragic dimensions and the angst that results from our recognition of how remote we are from God. The former is lifeless whereas the latter is symptomatic of the vitality that shows that our soul is not dead to spiritual realities. Even on the days of mourning in the Jewish calendar the hasidim are paradoxically expected to fulfill this *mitzvah* of mourning, as they do all others, with joy in God's service.

A typical hasidic pun succeeds in turning the talmudic saying about mourning on its head to yield the thought that when the month of *Adar* comes in, merits are to be increased by means of joy and even during the month of *Av*–the period of mourning for the destruction of the Temple–there must be joy, and by this means Israel's accusers will be diminished. Dubnow is unfair to Hasidism when he sees this stress on joy as mere escapism and mindless optimism.

Among many of the hasidic masters the doctrine of *simhah* was fully compatible with the need to take practical steps to alleviate suffering in this life. Yet the Mitnaggedic rabbis, too, speak disparagingly of the hasidim who, in their pursuit of *simhah*, "spend all their days as if at a feast." The hasid sings aloud in delight at being a Jew, a hasid, a follower of a particular rebbe, and above all, a servant of God. The hasidic dance is another means of awakening and giving expression to *simhah*.

A. Shochat, "On Joy in Hasidism" (Heb.), in *Zion* (1951): 30–43.

L.J.

JUDAH HASID (SEGAL) HALEVI of Szydlowiec (1660–1700)–A native of Dubno, he was the fiery Maggid of Szydlowiec, whom many suspected of being a secret follower of Shabbetai Tzvi. He formed a holy society whose members wore shrouds and traveled through Altona, Frankfurt, and Vienna, on a pilgrimage to the Holy Land.

Some then headed for Constantinople. R. Judah Hasid and his party went to Venice. The wealthy Samuel Oppenheimer of Vienna hired two boats for the pilgrims, but many did not survive the journey. Those who did reached the Holy Land on October 14, 1700. R. Judah died five days later. His followers purchased a site on which they erected a synagogue named *Judah HeHasid* in his memory, as well as forty homes for the poor.

The new settlers borrowed heavily from the Arabs who, in November 1701, attacked them, destroying the synagogue and driving most of them to Safed and Hebron. Only a few remained in the Old City.

In 1756, Feivish Ashkenazi was sent to Amsterdam, Mainz, and London to collect funds for the rebuilding of this synagogue. The rebuilt synagogue became known as the *Hurvah R. Judah HeHasid* (the ruin of R. Judah the Pious). It was destroyed by the Jordanians in 1948.

JUDAH LOEW BEN BEZALEL (MAHARAL) of Prague (1525–1609)–Known as the *Maharal MiPrague* (the Maharal of Prague, or *Der Hohe Rabbi Loew*, or the *Sublime Rabbi Loew*), he studied for some time under R. Solomon Luria in Przemysl, Poland. He began his rabbinical career as rabbi of Nikolsburg in 1553 and stayed in Nikolsburg for twenty years.

In 1573, he moved to Prague. On February 23, 1592, he was invited to a private audience with the Emperor Rudolph II, and in 1597, he became chief rabbi of Prague.

The many-faceted sage was an astronomer and alchemist, as well as a scholar of note. According to legend, he created the fabled *golem*, a wonder-working robot, which rescued the community from a fearful fate.

He was a prolific writer, and R. Simhah Bunem of Przysucha regarded him with awe, referring to him as "my teacher in the heavenly spheres." He devoted regular study sessions to the works of the *Maharal*, and many of the *Maharal's* teachings are echoed in those of Przysucha.

Writers and dramatists throughout the ages have been inspired by the mystical and science-fictional activities of the *Maharal*.

G. Winkler, *The Golem of Prague*.

JUNGREIS, Asher Anshel (1806–5 *Kislev* 1873)–Son of R. Samuel Pope (i.e., Papa, his place of birth), he was born in Csecse, a village in the western Carpathians. His poverty was such that when no wooden logs were available, father and sons had to stay in bed to keep warm while studying.

R. Asher studied in the *yeshivah* of R. Meir Eisenstadt at Balassa-Gyarmat, where he remained for two years. He then studied in the *yeshivah* of R. Koppel Harif in Vrbove.

He married the daughter of R. Meir Popper, who introduced him to Hasidism, and subsequently became rabbi in Mattersdorf in western Hungary. Asher Anshel was an ascetic and, from time to time, would fast three days at a stretch. He would regularly spend the whole of Thursday night in study.

It was R. Moses Sofer who recommended him to become the rabbi of Csenger, where he established a small *yeshivah* and gathered many hasidim around him. His prescriptions were dispensed by the local apothecary. He never changed from the Ashkenazic rite of prayer to the hasidic liturgy. However, he used the manuscript *Siddur HaAri*, which was presented to him by R. Meir of Przemyshlan.

He left a voluminous literary legacy. *Menuhat Asher* was published in two parts (Sighet, 1876, and Munkacz, 1905) by his son and son-in-law, respectively. More recently, a further volume–a commentary to *Ketubot* and some responsa–was printed in New York in 1958 and in Jerusalem in 1974.

He left three sons: R. Abraham Halevi (d. 1904), R. Moses Nata Halevi (d. 1889), and R. Samuel Zeev Halevi (d. 1909). None of his immediate descendants were hasidic rebbes, but we find many rabbis in the family.

R. H. L. Braun, *Toldot Anshei Mophet*.

A.S.

JUSTMAN, Hanokh Gad, of Pilica (1884–*Tishri* 1942)–Younger son of R. Pinhas Menahem Mendel Justman, brother-in-law of R. Judah Aryeh, the *Sefat Emet*, he was born in Ger. When the *Sefat Emet* died, his father become rebbe in Pilica, near Kielce, and R. Hanokh Gad became the rabbi.

He suffered indignities during the First World War when the Cossacks cut off his beard. When his father died in 1921, he succeeded him as rebbe and lived in Czestochowa, where he established a *yeshivah*, *Shifsei Tzaddik*. In 1932 he became rabbi of Wielun. He was active in the Aguda and a member of the *Mo'etzet Gedolei HaTorah*.

He lived for a time in the Warsaw ghetto, where he, together with his sons R. Joshua Heschel Yeheskiyahu, R. Abraham Bunem, and R. David Elijah and his three sons-in-law, was murdered in Treblinka. His son Aryeh Leib died at the beginning of the war.

JUSTMAN, Moses Bunem (1889–1942), Yiddish journalist–Born in Warsaw into a hasidic family, he worked at the Yiddish daily *Der Moment* from 1910 to 1925 and then at *Der Haynt* under the pseudonym Jeuschson or Itchele. He was the author of *In Rebben's Hoif* and *Fun Inzer Alten Oitzer* (Warsaw, 1932), an anthology of popular hasidic comments on the Pentateuch, five Scrolls, and Festivals.

He settled in the Holy Land in 1940.

JUSTMAN, Pinhas Menahem Eliezer, of Pilica (1849–11 *Kislev* 1921)–Son of R. Benjamin Eliezer, he married Hendel Leah, daughter of R. Abraham Mordecai Alter. When his wife died, he married *Hayyah* Yutta, the daughter of R. Nehemiah Rothenberg.

He was a hasid of R. Heinokh of Alexander and of R. Judah Leib of Ger. In 1905, he settled first in Pilica and then in Virshov and Czestochowa̧. He was the author of a five-volume work *Sifsei Zaddik* on the Pentateuch (Warsaw, 1936–1939).

He stressed that the Sabbath should be dedicated to study, and that one should study every day at least one page of the Talmud with the commentaries of Rashi and of R. Asher ben Yehiel. In the course of seven years, the study of the entire Talmud would be completed.

He himself would rise at 6 A.M. and with the exception of the ninety minutes he set aside for receiving hasidim (from 9:30 to 11 A.M.), he would spend the whole day in study.

In his will and testament he asked the forgiveness of those who had come to see him regularly and those who had given him gifts. He was succeeded by his son, R. Hanokh Gad.

K

KABBALAH—Although a number of the hasidic masters—the Maggid of Kozienice, Barukh of Kossov, Tzvi Hirsch of Zydaczov, Yitzhak Eizig of Komarno and his son Elazer Tzvi, the *tzaddikim* of Munkacs, and all the *Habad* leaders—were expert in the Kabbalah, Hasidism generally places far more emphasis on direct mystical experience than on kabbalistic gnosis.

Meshullam Feivish of Zbaraz quotes in the name of Menahem Mendel of Pzremyshlan, a disciple of the Besht, this definition of *nistar* (secret), the name usually given to the Kabbalah:

> *Nistar* refers to something it is impossible to communicate to another, the taste of food, for example, which cannot be conveyed to someone who has never tasted that particular food. So it is with regard to the love and fear of the Creator, blessed be He. It is impossible to convey to another how this love is in the heart. This is called *nistar*. But how can it be correct to call the kabbalistic science *nistar*? Whoever wishes to study has the book open for him. If he cannot understand the book he is simply an ignoramous for whom the Talmud and the Tosafists would be *nistar*. But the meaning of *nistarot* in the whole of the *Zohar* and the writings of the Ari of blessed memory is that all these are constructed on the idea of attachment (*devekut*) to the Creator. (*Derekh Emet*, n.p.n.d., *Kuntres* I, no. 22, p. 27)

Nevertheless, all the kabbalistic teachings were accepted as revealed truth by the hasidic masters, and the kabbalistic vocabulary is widely used by them. But in Hasidism, even when there is much concern with the "upper worlds" of the Kabbalah, the main thrust is on the way these are mirrored in the soul of man. A favorite quotation in hasidic literature is the kabbalistic interpretation of Job 19:26, which is read as: "From my own flesh I shall see God" (i.e., the divine nature as taught by the Kabbalah can be known through man reflecting on his own psychic nature). Typical is the saying of Hayyim Heikel of Amdur that this world is only a parable by means of which God can be seen, quoting the verse from Job (*Hayyim VaHesed* [Jerusalem, 1970], p. 19b). Similarly, R. Solomon of Lutzk, in his introduction to the Maggid of Mezhirech's *Maggid Devarav LeYaakov* (Jerusalem, 1962, pp. 9–11), describes how the sefirotic processes (see SEFIROT) operate in the human soul and how the hasid, aware of this, can elevate every thought and emotion to its requisite place in the sefirotic realm.

Hasidic thought is selective in its use of the kabbalistic terminology. The following are the main kabbalistic concepts as found in the writings of the hasidic masters and expressed in hasidic life.

Ein Sof (the Limitless)—God as He is in Himself before He becomes manifest in creation—desires to have creatures who can be the recipients of His bounty since it is the nature of the All-Good to bestow His goodness on others. In order that the finite emerge from the infinite, *Ein Sof* is required to "withdraw from Himself into Himself" so that room is left for the emergence of all worlds and time and space as we know them. This withdrawal (*tzimtzum*) produces an "empty space," which is penetrated by a thin ray of the infinite light known as *Adam Kadmon* (Primordial Man).

From the ears, nose, and mouth of *Adam Kadmon*, lights (*orot*) proceed wherewith the vessels or containers (*kelim*) are constituted so as to receive the light of the ten *Sefirot* (see SEFIROT). All of the divine creativity is described in terms of illuminations. Thus there are lights that are direct (*or yashar*) and others that are reflected (*or hozer*), that is, beaming back, as it were, to the infinite; there are lights that are surrounds (*or makif*) and others that are internal (*or penimi*).

In *Habad* thought especially, much use is made of the concepts of surrounds and internals to describe, respectively, God's transcendence and immanence. Phinehas of Koretz (*Midrash Pinehas* [Jerusalem, 1971], no. 9, p. 6) sees all disinterested giving on earth (e.g., the love of parents for their children, the lending of money without interest) in terms of direct light, and all compensatory giving (e.g., a child's gratitude to parents, the repayment of a loan) in terms of reflected light.

The vessels of the *Sefirot*, having been made ready, now require to be filled with the lights of the *Sefirot* themselves. For this purpose more subtle lights proceed from the eyes of *Adam Kadmon*. But as these pour into the vessels of the seven lower *Sefirot*, from *Hesed* to *Malkhut*, the vessels cannot contain the full power of the light and there takes place the breaking of the vessels (*shevirat hakelim*).

These are later reconstituted as *partzufim* (configurations) (i.e., combinations of *Sefirot*, which help one another to contain the light). There are five *partzufim*: *arikh* (long suffering, corresponding to the *Sefirah Keter*), *abba* (father, corresponding to *Hokhmah), imma* (mother, corresponding to *Binah*), *zeer* (impatient one, corresponding to the six *Sefirot* from *Hesed* to *Yesod*), and *nukvah* (female, corresponding to *Malkhut*).

The process of reconstitution is not a once-and-for-all matter but takes place all the time assisted by the deeds of human beings, in whose being the *sefirotic* realm is mirrored, who is created in the image of God. There is a great chain of being reaching back to *Ein Sof* and down to the material world. Human beings, at the bottom of the chain, can set the whole chain in motion. When they are virtuous, they send on high the impulses from below, in the language of the *Zohar*, and these promote in turn the impulses from above.

Since, as a result of the breaking of the vessels, all is in a state of disarray, a constant harmonizing process must take place in which humanity has the most important role to play, all depending on its deeds. When people are virtuous, the illuminations they send on high assist the sefirotic processes, and the divine grace can then flow freely through all worlds. People's evil deeds cause disharmony to reign on high, and then the flow of divine grace is arrested. Thus every one of our deeds has cosmic significance: our good deeds and thoughts promote some rectification (*tikkun*) on high, whereas our evil deeds and thoughts produce a flaw (*pegam*) on high.

All creation occurs by means of various divine names. We too can assist in the creative processes by meditating on these names, combining them in our mind and so both repeating, as it were, the creative acts of God and also influencing those acts, creation being conceived of as taking place all the time.

The combination of the divine names causes the diversity and multiplicity evident in the universe to be transcended by the divine unity, which is the ultimate reality. Unifications (*yihudim*) can be carried out by holy persons, though the task is fraught with danger, touching as it does on the most intense form of relationship between humanity and the full power of God. The simplest of these unifications—and there appears to be no objection to even ordinary worshipers' engaging in this—is the combination of the tetragrammaton with the the name *Adonai* (i.e., the letters of these two names are thought of as interwined). The tetragrammaton represents the divine mercy, *Adonai* divine judgment and sternness. By combining the two names, the worshiper causes the divine mercy to permeate the divine judgment, and the judgments are sweetened (*hamtakat hadinim*) at their source. In times of trouble and danger for the Jewish people, there are many references in hasidic legends to the *tzaddikim*'s performing some act or meditating on some divine name in order to sweeten the judgments at the source and so soften or completely remove their rigors.

In the famous letter by the Besht to his brother-in-law, Gershom of Kitov (printed at the end of Jacob Joseph's *Ben Porat Yosef* [Koretz, 1781]), the Besht tells how he had an ascent of the soul and met the Messiah in heaven. When the Besht asked the Messiah when he will come, the Messiah replied, "You will know of it in this way: it will be when your teaching becomes famous and revealed to the world, and when that which I have taught you spreads abroad so that others, too, will be capable of performing *yihudim* and having soul ascents as you do. Then will all the *klippot* [see *KLIPPOT*] be consumed and it will be a time of grace and salvation."

More specifically, the harmonization process is required because when the breaking of the vessels took place, 286 holy sparks (*nitzotzot*) were scattered through all creation, providing the spiritual energy by which all things are nourished and kept in being. But the sparks are imprisoned in material things, ready to be attacked by the demonic forces, the *klippot*. The holy sparks have to be rescued or redeemed for the sacred, which is achieved, according to the hasidic teaching, when we use worldly things in a spirit of holiness for the sake of God.

There is constant stress in hasidic literature on the need for humanity so to use the world and its delights that it succeeds not in gratifying the self but in releasing the holy sparks. This is the hasidic doctrine of *avodah begashmiyut* (serving God through the corporeal). Moreover, there is a tendency in hasidic thought to teach that each one of us has our own personal role to play, the sparks that only we can rescue being presented to us for the purpose.

Hasidic legend frequently speaks of a particular man's being guided by God into a strange, unusual situation because there are holy sparks that belong to the root of his soul, which only he can redeem.

The *Sefirah Malkhut* is conceived of as the *Shekhinah*, as a kind of female element in the Godhead. The rabbinic references to the exile of the *Shekhinah* are made to yield the thought that although disharmony is present in the sefirotic realm, a part of God is, as it were, exiled from God. The harmonization process is described in terms of the sacred marriage between the Holy One, blessed be He; the *Sefirah Tiferet*, the male principle; and the *Shekhinah*, the female principle (represented in the Lurianic scheme of the *partzufim* as the unification of *Zeer* and *Nukvah*). For her marriage the *Shekhinah* requires the female waters (*mayyin nukvin*) so as to bestir the male waters (*mayyin dikhrin*). These are provided by the deeds of the righteous, which is why the hasidim adopted the kabbalistic formula, to be recited before the performance of every good deed: "For the sake of the unification of the Holy One, blessed be He, and His *Shekhinah*" (*leShem yihud*).

According to the *Zohar*, the sacred marriage gives birth to the souls of the righteous. The human sex act is a reflection of the marriage on high and must, therefore, be engaged in only for the sake of heaven and in a spirit of holiness. The more a man consecrates himself during the sex act, the greater his chance of bringing down to the child born of it a specially elevated soul. This is the main reason why, in Hasidism, the *tzaddikim* are succeeded by their sons, resulting in dynasties of *tzaddikim*. The *tzaddik*, by his holy thoughts when he is with his wife, endows his sons with a special degree of sanctity.

The sefirotic realm is known as the world of emanation (*olam ha'atzilut*). Beneath that is the world of creation (*olam haberiah*). Beneath that is the world of formation (*olam hayetzirah*). And, finally, there is the fourth world, the world of action (*olam ha'asiyah*), which includes our material universe. All human souls come from one or another of these worlds – the loftiest souls, of which there are very few, from the world of emanation. Hasidic thought frequently speaks of the ascent of the soul from world to world during prayer (*Maggid Devarav LeYaakov* [Jerusalem, 1962], p. 35).

These are the four main worlds but there are, in addition, worlds without number, each the source of some special quality. Hasidic legend tells, for instance, of the Baal Shem Tov's enabling a man who could not sing to become a prayer leader by bringing down song from the world of melody. Because each soul has its root on high, people with the same soul root are attracted to one another and people are attracted to subjects of study that are in accord with their particular soul root. This is why each hasid finds a rebbe especially suited to him and why each has his own special task in life.

Hasidism accepts the kabbalistic doctrine of reincarnation (*gilgul*). Among the wonder tales the hasidim tell, many have *gilgul* for their theme. Of the rebbe of Apt, for instance, it is told that he was one of the few people who knew what they were in their precious existence and when leading the prayers on the Day of Atonement would say, when relating the words of the High Priest in the Temple, not "And thus did *he* say" but "Thus did *I* say," since in his previous existence he was a High Priest. Souls would come to the *tzaddik* to obtain a *tikkun*, a rectification.

G. Scholem, *Major Trends in Jewish Mysticism*.

L.J.

KAFKA, Franz (1883–1924) – Kafka came from an assimilated Czech Jewish family that regarded the "old Judaism" as a set of anachronistic rituals. In 1911 he discovered the East European Yiddish Actors Troupe, which for him represented the warmth and authenticity of Jewishness. His first real contact with Eastern Europe and with Hasidism, however, came through a friend, George Mordecai (or Jiri) Langer, who journeyed to East Galicia and became for many years a disciple of the rabbi of Belz. The mystical ideas and stories he encountered there he discussed with Kafka. Although this was not in itself sufficient to be a substantial influence upon the writer, in the hasidic vision, Kafka found chords of affinity with a simple yet mysterious folktale quality already present in his own imagings.

In 1912 Kafka read Pines' *Histoire de la Littérature Judéo-Allemande* (Paris, 1911) and noted that the Besht had been a vegetable gardener in the Carpathians and his brother-in-law's coachman before he became famous as the founder of the hasidic movement. It was in his solitary mountain walks that his early visions came to him.

In his *Diaries*, Kafka lingers over the whole hasidic conception of the *tzaddik*, as explained to him by Langer. In some mysterious sense, the *tzaddik* is a holy leader to be obeyed more than God is. Indeed the Besht was known to have commanded a favorite disciple to be baptized so that what before had presented itself as an irresistible temptation had now become the express command of his spiritual leader, and thus had the sting of sin removed from it. Kafka reflects on the idea of a supreme *tzaddik* who appears every generation, one who is not necessarily a miracle worker but in righteousness is supreme. In that category the Besht was not included. It was an obscure merchant and not he who was the *tzaddik* of their day, yet the girl who recognized the hidden excellence of the trader by the brightness around and asked him to marry her on the strength of this was told that she was destined for one even greater than he, so that there was a sense in which the Besht was even higher than a *tzaddik Hador*.

In Marienbad in 1916, Langer and Kafka studied the noble yet simple rituals played out between the Belzer rebbe and his hasidim. According to his biographer Max Brod, Kafka's attitude was a blend of sophisticated skepticism and wistful romanticism about hasidic pathos.

At the end of his life Kafka fell in love with Dora Dymant, daughter of a Gerer hasid. As she was herself in a state of rebellion against the constraints of her father's religion, the two began an affair, which became so serious for Kafka that he wrote to her father asking to marry Dora and stating that, although he had not been brought up to be a "practicing" Jew, he was nevertheless a "repentant one, seeking 'to return.' " Dora's father immediately took Kafka's letter to his spiritual authority, the Gerer Rebbe, who read it and uttered a single syllable: no. Within a few weeks, Kafka had died of tuberculosis.

F.G.

KAHAN, Israel Meir, of Radun (1838–1933) – Popularly known as the *Hafetz Hayyim*, after the title of his book, published in 1873, which was based on verses 13 and 14 of Psalm 34: "He who desires life."

Unassuming and unassertive, he lived in the remote hamlet of Radun, absorbed in his studies. He was the author of *Mishnah Berurah* (Lucid Learning), unabridged and authoritative codes of Jewish Law, which was printed between 1884 and 1907.

When religious Jewry of Eastern Europe turned to him for guidance, he responded readily. He was the keynote speaker at the Aguda *Knessiyah HaGedolah* in Vienna in August 1923, and in 1930 he led a delegation consisting of the rebbes of Ger, Belz, and Alexander to Dr. Bartel, the Polish prime minister, in order to secure support for Orthodox education. He also helped to establish the *Vaad HaYeshivot*.

M. M. Yosher, "R. Israel Meir HaKohon, the Hafez Hayyim," pp. 459–473.

KAHANA, David (1838–1916), historian – Born in Odessa, he was a grandson of R. Yitzhak Rabinowicz of Odessa. He received a traditional Jewish education. He was active in communal affairs and was instrumental in the appointment of Shalom Jacob Abramowitz (Mendele Mocher Seforim) as director of the *Talmud Torah*.

He was a prolific writer whose interests embraced many branches of history and literature. He contributed articles on Kabbalah, Frankism, and Hasidism to the monthly journals *HaShahar*, *Kenesset Yisrael*, and *HaShiloah*.

His rational and negative approach somewhat marred his otherwise balanced appreciation of the founders of the hasidic movement. No doubt, this was due to the relevant *Haskalah* tendencies of his age. He viewed Hasidism as a movement subjected to beliefs in miracles and the *tzaddik* cult, yet neglecting its high moral and ethical concepts and its humanism.

He was a pioneer in the study of the hasidic movement. He was the author of the two-volume *Toldot HaMekubbalim HaShabbetaim VeHaHasidim* (1913).

M.S.

KAISER, Alter Noah (1848–8 *Elul* 1920) – Alter Noah HaKohen Michalenski, the first hasidic rebbe to live in England, was born in Nesvizh, the son of R. Aryeh Meir. When his father died in the prime of his life, he was brought up by R. Yitzhak of Nesvizh. From 1870 he lived in the Holy Land for five years, studying in Safed and Hebron under the kabbalist R. Mordecai Abadi. In 1877 he became rabbi at Remet, near Sighet, where he styled himself as a hasidic rebbe.

In 1879, in collaboration with R. Abadi, he published the kabbalistic books *Hen Mordecai* and *Darkhei Hen* (Przemysl, 1879). He then spent some time in Bulgaria and Triest and was imprisoned on alleged charges of espionage. In 1890 he settled in Yardanov, near Cracow, where he was known as the Yardanover rebbe. Here, too, he was imprisoned for two and a half years. In January 1895 he came to London, where he published a seventy-six-page kabbalistic work, *Netivot Hen* (London, 1899).

After seven years in London he returned to the Holy Land, and during World War One he took refuge in Cairo and Alexandria. He died in Jerusalem and was buried on the Mount of Olives.

His son Shlomoh wrote a biography on him, *Toldot Hen* (London, 1979). His other son, Arnold Meir (1896–1967), was the general secretary of the Federation of Jewish Relief Organizations, London.

Y. Alfasi, *Sinai*, vol. 46, pp. 336–338.

KALEV, Yitzhak Eizig, of Nagyszollos (1751–7 *Adar* 1821) – Son of R. Ezekiel, Yitzhak was born in Szerencs. His father died when he was very young, and hasidic legend has it that it was R. Leib Sarah's who discovered this shepherd boy and led him to R. Shmuel (Shmelke) of Nikolsburg. "I have brought you a little soul from the Temple of Music," said R. Leib Sarah's. Yitzhak is reputed to have studied also under R. Elimelekh of Lejask for five years.

He married his first cousin, Feiga, the daughter of R. Enzil Kohn of Tarczal, and became rabbi of Nagy-Kallo, where he lived for forty years. His rabbinate extended to some 200 small communities, and among his followers was R. Ezekiel Panet.

In 1794, he appealed to the leaders of the community to make him a bigger weekly allowance. He cited his failing health and that he had been advised to take the waters of the spas. His wages were doubled, and he was called upon to rule on difficult *agunah* problems. He could communicate with people at every level and in many different ways.

Often, he would intersperse Hungarian words in his dialogue with the Almighty. Thousands of hasidim chanted his song *Szol a kakas mar . . . , Sirnak rinak a baranyok* (The cock is already crowing, it will soon be dawn). In the green forest, in the open field, a bird is walking, but what a bird? With yellow legs and wings of blue. It is waiting for me there. Wait, my rose, wait, always wait. If God willed me for you, I shall be yours. But when will this come to pass? *Yibaneh HaMikdash Ir Tziyon Temale* (When the Temple will be rebuilt, and Zion repopulated.) His melodies expressed the grief of the *Shekhinah* in exile and the yearnings of the House of Israel for redemption. His melodies were sung by hasidim and nonhasidim of Hungarian origin on happy occasions.

He was in the habit of wandering through the fields and listening to the melodies sung by the shepherds. It was one of those tunes that he adapted to Psalms 137:1 (By the waters of Babylon), after hearing it from the lips of a shepherd. He used to say, "Many a melody, once chanted by the Levites in the Holy Temple, is now in exile among the people."

He was tireless in mustering support for the poor in the Holy Land. He was president of the *kollel Eretz Yisrael*, and he transferred to the Holy Land the money collected by R. Moses Teitelbaum. He was venerated not only by his hasidim but also by R. Moses Schreiber and R. Hayyim Tyrer of Czernowitz.

On 3 *Nisan* 1817, his wife died, and he followed her about five years later. He asked that only the words "*er hat gikennt lernen und is geven an erlicher Yid*" (he could study and was an honest Jew) should appear on his gravestone. His burial place in Nagyszollos became the "Meron" of Hungary, and many made the pilgrimage. "All around the synagogue, right to the cemetery where the *tzaddik* is buried," said R. Naftali of Ropczyce, "one senses the sanctity of Jerusalem."

He left three sons. The eldest, R. Moses Hayyim, married the daughter of R. Yitzhak of Zydaczov and settled in Rozdol. His grandson R. Pinhas Hayyim Taub lived for many years in Margitta and later returned to Galicia; he died on 11 *Tishri* 1936.

L. Szilagyi-Windt, *A Kalloi Cadik*.

A.S.

KALISH, Abraham, of Amshinov (d. 1942) – Son of R. Abraham Menahem, he married the daughter of R. Solomon Hanokh HaKohen of Radomsk. He was renowned for his charitable works. He could not sleep until he had distributed his daily charity allocation.

KALISH, Dov Baer (d. 1943) – Youngest son of R. Shimon Kalish of Skierniewice, he married the daughter of R. Abraham, a descendant of Sasov. In 1927, when his father died and was succeeded by his elder brother, he gave him his allegiance. It was only in 1929, on the death of his brother, that he became rebbe of Lowicz, where he established a *yeshivah*, *Shem MiShimon* and produced a periodical in which his discourses were recorded.

During the Second World War, he lived in Warsaw together with his cousin R. Abraham Kalish of Radomsk. He and his family perished in the Holocaust.

KALISH, Isaiah, of Przysucha (1870–1943) – Son of R. Jacob David, he was known as "R. Isaiah of Przysucha." When his father died, his elder brother, R. Menahem, brought him up. He married the daughter of R. Meir of Przysucha, a descendant of the "Holy Jew."

At first he was reluctant to become a rebbe and earned his living as a wine merchant. He was so devout that he observed the Day of Atonement for two consecutive days. He rebuilt the *Bet HaMidrash* of the "Holy Jew" and traveled throughout Poland, collecting money for this purpose.

During the Second World War, he hid for two years in a wine cellar. He was arrested by the Nazis and died a few days later.

KALISH, Jacob David, of Amshinov (1814–4 *Kislev* 1878) – Son of R. Yitzhak of Warka, he was born in Zarek. He was fifteen years old when his father moved to Warka. He was a disciple of R. Menahem Mendel of Kotzk, who held him in high esteem. "If only I had ten more followers like you," R. Mendele told him, "I would never have shut myself up." He married Sarah Leah, the daughter of R. Samuel of Parczew. His life was beset with personal tragedies. All but one of his children died in infancy; a daughter, *Hayyah* Feiga, survived until the age of thirty, as did his wife. He subsequently married *Hayyah*, the daughter of R. Jacob of Yarnowice.

For a time he lived in Ger and in Przysucha; in 1840 he became rebbe and settled in Amshinov. "To be a rebbe," R. Jacob David said, "one has to be aware of three things: one must feel as if one sits on a chair full of nails; one should be able to read a petition; and [one must] regard the trouble of one's petitioner as one's own." He fought vehemently against Russian proposals to change the traditional hasidic garments and the wearing of beards.

He was survived by three sons from his second marriage: R. Menahem Mendel, who succeeded him; R. Isaiah; and R. Jeremiah.

A. Y. Bromberg, *Migdolei HaHasidut*, vol. 3. *Admorim LeBet Warka VeAmshinov*, pp. 92–109.

KALISH, Jeremiah, of Opole (1873–1942)–Son of R. Jacob David, who died when he was five years old. He was brought up by his brother, R. Menahem Mendel. He was ordained by R. Hayyim Soloveitchik of Brest-Litovsk, and he married the daughter of R. Abraham Eger of Lublin, where he lived for two years, then becoming the rabbi in Opole.

During World War I he was arrested first by the Austrians for alleged spying for Russia and subsequently by the Russians for spying for Austria. After languishing in prison for several months, he made his home in Warsaw, where he was known as the "Polish Levi Yitzhak of Berdichev." He died in the Warsaw ghetto and was buried in the courtyard of his home on Pavia Street.

KALISH, Joseph, of Amshinov (1878–3 *Heshvan* 1936)–Son of R. Menahem, Joseph was born in Amshinov and studied under his father. He married the daughter of R. Hayyim Eliezer Waks, the rabbi of Kalish. He became rabbi in Ostrov, near Lomza, and succeeded his father as rebbe of Amshinov.

He died in Otwock and was buried in Warsaw.

Toldot Anshei Shem, p. 110.

KALISH, Joseph Tzvi, of Bene Berak (1885–1 *Adar* 1957)–Son of R. Simon of Skierniewice, he married Yitta, the daughter of R. Yitzhak Jacob of Biala. At first he served as rabbi in Kurszov, near Otwock, and succeeded his father as rebbe of Skierniewice in 1927. In 1934, at the invitation of Yitzhak Gerstenkorn, he settled in Bene Berak. A tall, handsome man, with a luxuriant white beard, he endeared himself to hasidim of all sections. One of his customs was to kindle two lights on the eve of the Sabbath, a duty most relegate to their wives.

He was buried in Tiberias. His only daughter, Deborah Gitel, married R. Nahum Twersky, author of *MiDor El Dor* (Tel Aviv, 1967).

KALISH, Menahem Mendel, of Amshinov (1860–16 *Kislev* 1918)–Third son of R. Jacob David, he was born in Amshinov. Even as a youth he was renowned for his hospitality and for the care with which he supervised the accommodation of his father's many visitors. In 1874, he married Esther Golda, the daughter of R. Samuel Moses Alberstein of Biala, who won first prize in the state lottery.

On his father's death in 1878 he became rebbe but continued to visit other rebbes, such as R. David Moses Friedman of Chortkov, R. Tzaddok Hakohen Rabinowicz of Lublin, and R. Abraham Bornstein of Sochaczev. Like his father, he was very public spirited. He was a frequent visitor in Warsaw, where he interceded with the civil and military authorities on a variety of problems. He was particularly concerned with the plight of the religious Jews who were serving in the czarist armies. He endeavored to ensure the release of as many as possible, regarding this work as *pidyon shevuim*, the ransoming of captives.

He also tried to enhance Sabbath observance among Jewish merchants. He was disturbed by the desecration of the Sabbath by shopkeepers in Warsaw, and he personally pleaded with the malefactors. He tried to improve the situation of the helpless Jews who were arbitrarily and often brutally expelled from frontier areas during the First World War.

His prayers were lengthy, and he rarely finished morning prayers until late in the afternoon.

He died and was buried in Warsaw. He had one daughter, Rachel, who married R. Jacob Aryeh Morgenstern of Lamaz, and three sons–R. Joseph; R. Abraham, the son-in-law of the rabbi of Radomsk; and R. Simon Shalom of Otwock, who later emigrated to New York (d. 1957).

KALISH, Menahem Mendel, of Skierniewice (d. 18 *Adar* 1929)–Son of R. Simon, he was at first engaged in business and was, in 1925, elected one of the seven *parnassim* of the Warsaw Jewish community.

In the spirit of the Warka tradition, he was very hospitable, and no one who knocked on his door left empty-handed. On the Day of Atonement, he would himself prepare refreshments, so that they would be ready for the worshipers the moment the fast was over.

In his "ethical will" he asked his family to notify his ancestors of his death, so that they might intercede for him. He was buried in Warsaw.

KALISH, Menahem Mendel, of Warka (1819–16 *Sivan* 1868) – Son of R. Yitzhak, he was born in Zarek. His mother, Rachel, was the daughter of R. Tzvi Aryeh of Zarik. He was a disciple of R. Menahem Mendel of Kotzk, and he married the daughter of R. Tzvi Aryeh of Warka.

After his father's death in 1848, he was reluctant to become rebbe, and his father's hasid R. Shragai Feivel of Makov took over. It was only after R. Shragai Feivel died on *Shemini Atzeret* 1849 that he became rebbe.

He believed in the mishnaic adage "Silence serves as a fence to wisdom" (*Abot* 3:17) and the talmudic saying "Talk is worth a ducat, but silence is worth two" (*Megillah* 18a). He spoke with great conciseness, weighing every word. He rarely delivered a discourse. He would spend a whole evening with his followers without uttering a syllable. "The night of silence," as the hasidim called it, left an awesome impression on all who participated. "In Warka," remarked R. Dov Berish of Biala, "we serve God by thought."

He died in Warsaw, and his son R. Simhah Bunem succeeded him.

A. Y. Bromberg, *Migdolei HaHasidut*, vol. 3, *Hadmorei LeBet Warka VeAmshinov*, pp. 110–140.

KALISH, Mordecai Menahem Mendel, of Warka (1817–16 *Sivan* 1868) – Youngest son of R. Yitzhak of Warka, he was at first reluctant to become rebbe, and it was only thanks to the persuasion of R. Menahem Mendel Morgenstern of Kotzk and R. Benjamin Lubliner that he became rebbe of Warka, where he served for twenty years. One of his disciples was R. Berish of Biala.

He died at the age of forty-nine and was succeeded by his son, R. Simhah Bunem.

KALISH, Simhah Bunem, of Otwock (1851–2 *Shevat* 1907) – Son of R. Menahem Mendel, he was born in Warka. He was an ailing child who could hardly stand. Later he had to use a special orthopedic chair to get some comfort. He married Rehumah *Hayyah* Goldah, the daughter of Elijah Hertz, a hasid of the rebbe of Alexander. After his wedding he remained in Warka, and when his father died in 1868, many of the hasidim gave their allegiance to R. Dov Berish of Biala. It was only through the persuasion of R. Jacob Aryeh Guterman of Radzymin that he became rebbe.

He became renowned for his enthusiastic dancing, especially on Shemini Atzeret and Simhat Torah. Despite his malformed and diseased leg, which caused him continuous pain, he remained on his feet for many hours, dancing with his hasidim, oblivious of his physical disability.

The visit of R. Eliezer Waks and R. Joshua Trunk of Kutno to the Holy Land in 1887 encouraged R. Simhah Bunem to follow suit. There were some difficulties for him to overcome first. His father-in-law was opposed to the idea, and his son's wife was expecting a baby; above all, his hasidim were reluctant to let him go. In the winter of 1887, accompanied by his wife, three sons, two daughters, and two attendants (his elder son, R. Mendele, remained behind), he set out via Odessa for the Holy Land.

Like all Russian tourists, the party was given permission to stay for thirty days. Overstaying this period, the rebbe was arrested and imprisoned in Acre for five days. He was freed on medical grounds and allowed to remain in Tiberias, where he campaigned vigorously against the activities of the missionaries and their free medical and educational facilities.

After three months, the rabbi returned to Poland, where his sixteen-year-old daughter Rachel died when they reached Warsaw. He returned to Kurszev and then settled in Otwock. Meticulous and somewhat extreme in his observances, he would wait twenty-four hours between meat and dairy dishes, and a *shohet* would accompany him on every journey, for he would not eat in any of the homes he visited, not even in the homes of other rebbes.

He kept a special apartment for use during Passover. He would not tolerate modern dress and fought against the innovations of the *maskilim*. He was vehement against the employment of non-Jewish wet nurses and gentile domestics. Once he told a *baal korei* (a reader of the Law), "Do not read the Law grammatically. The *maskilim* have taken over the study of grammar, and we must show them that we are completely indifferent to them." He would shake hands with a visitor on arrival, but not on departure. This, he held, was a gentile custom.

Although nineteen years had elapsed since his visit to the Holy Land, his longing for it did not diminish. "There, in the Land of Israel, I see everything," he sighed. "Here I see nothing." In 1905, against the advice of his doctor, H. Soloveitchik, and without his family, he returned to the Holy Land, where he arrived just after Purim. At first he stayed with his relative, R. David Biderman of Lelov. Then he made his home in the *Deutsche* Quarter in Jerusalem. He then moved to Tiberias and lived close to the seashore. He kept in contact with the rebbes of Kobrin and Slonim and often visited the *yeshivah Or Torah*, near the grave of R. Meir Baal HaNess. He refused to be a rebbe. "When I crossed the ocean, I threw the rebbe's hat overboard."

The Sephardim bathed his body (*taharah*) in the lake of Kinneret. His grave is in Tiberias next to that of R. Menahem Mendel of Vitebsk.

He was survived in Poland by one daughter and four sons – R. Menahem Mendel, R. Yisrael Yehiel, R. Abraham Mosheh, and R. Jacob David of Otwock.

A. Y. Bromberg, *Migdolei HaHasidut*, vol. 3, *Admorim LeBet Warka VeAmshinov*, pp. 162–196.
Hamelitz, Odessa (16 *Shevat* 1888).

KALISH, Simon, of Skierniewice

(1858–20 *Tishri* 1927) – Son of R. Mordecai Menahem Mendel of Warka, he was named after his grandfather, who was known as "Simon the Merciful." He was ten years old when his father died. He married the daughter of David Elijah Bennet, a hasid of Warka. He himself was a hasid of R. Jacob Yehudah of Nadarzyn.

His path to the rabbinate was far from smooth. His father was first succeeded by R. Berish of Biala, and it was not until 1887, after R. Jacob Yehudah and R. Berish of Biala had died, that he became rebbe, first in Nadarzyn, then in Torchin and Skierniewice.

During the First World War he lived in Warsaw, where he looked after the welfare of the soldiers.

He was buried in Skierniewice, where he had lived for forty years. He was survived by five sons. After his death, a number of his followers joined R. Hayyim Tenenbaum of Nadarzyn.

His son R. Joseph Tzvi became rabbi of Bene Berak.

KALISH, Simon Shalom

(1883–19 *Av* 1954) – Son of R. Menahem, he was born in Amshinov. He married his cousin Brachah Feiga, the daughter of R. Isaiah of Przysucha. From 1914, he lived first in Warsaw and then in Otwock. His Friday evening *tish* would last until dawn.

He was active in the work of the Aguda and participated in the *Kenessiyah HaGedolah*.

In 1933, he visited the Holy Land and stayed there for over a year. His plans for settling there were disrupted by the outbreak of World War Two. His wanderings during the war took him to Vilna, Kovno, Shanghai, Japan, and, finally, Brooklyn, New York.

He was buried in Tiberias.

Toldot Anshei Shem, p. 11.

KALISH, Yerahmiel Judah Meir

(1901–27 *Iyyar* 1976) – Son of R. Simon Shalom, he was born in Przysucha. On his mother's side, he was a descendant of the "Holy Jew."

During the Second World War, he escaped to Vilna, then to Shanghai, and, after the war, to New York. He then emigrated to Israel in 1958, and after living for some time in Holon, established a *yeshivah*, *Shem Olam*, in Jerusalem. He printed his father's works.

His personal sufferings were masked by a smiling face and pleasant manner. He was buried on *Har HaMenuhot* in Jerusalem.

His son-in-law, R. Hayyim Malikovsky, is the head of the *yeshivah*.

KALISH, Yitzhak, of Warka

(1779–22 *Nisan* 1848) – Son of R. Simon of Zlushin, known as "Simon the Merciful," he was a descendant of R. Mordecai Jaffe (1530–1615). His mother, Yuta, first gave birth to seven daughters, and Yitzhak was the only son.

It was R. David Biderman of Lelov who introduced Yitzhak to the "Seer" of Lublin. He also became attached to the Yehudi, R. Simhah Bunem of Przysucha, and to his son R. Abraham Moses. After working for a time for Tamarel Bergson of Warsaw, a devoted follower of the Maggid of Kozienice, he served as rabbi first in Gowarczov and then in Ruda. He married Rachel, the daughter of R. Meir of Zarki. After the death of R. Abraham Moses in 1879, R. Yitzhak settled in Warka.

Among his great disciples were R. Jacob Aryeh Guterman of Radzymin, R. Dov Berish of Biala, and R. Shragai Feivish of Grice. He was one of the most communally minded of Polish hasidic rebbes. He was concerned with every facet of Jewish life, as well as with the economic plight of the Jews in the Holy Land, for whom he assiduously collected funds.

He traveled widely to urge the hasidic rebbes to fight against conscription. It was R. Israel of Ruzhyn who advised him to send Yisrael Birenfeld of Cracow to London to enlist the support of Sir Moses Montefiore. When Sir Moses visited Warsaw in May 1846, R. Yitzhak, together with R. Yitzhak Meir Alter, called upon him. The *ukase* by which the Jews were to be expelled from the western frontier zone of Russia was abrogated through R. Yitzhak's intervention.

The Cantonists were not R. Yitzhak's only problem. R. Yitzhak Meir Alter, R. Hayyim Dawidsohn, and R. Yitzhak were signatories to a manifesto dated 14 *Tevet* 1847, urging the Jews to settle on the land.

Together with the rabbi of Ger he barred secular subjects from the *heder* curriculum. "It is impossible for the words of the Torah to enter the hearts of the children, when their minds are full of other things." He took a firm stand on the issue of distinctive clothes worn by the hasidim. He urged his fellow Jews to be charitable and established societies in every town to provide the needy with their Sabbath necessities.

On one occasion, a boat full of hasidim traveling to Warka capsized, resulting in many casualties. As an atonement, the rabbi went into "exile" and lived for a time in Nadrazin.

His discourses are to be found in *Ohel Yitzhak* (Piotrokov, 1914). He was survived by two sons, R. Jacob David of Amshinov and R. Menahem Mendel of Warka, and four daughters – Hannah, Devorah, Zipporah, and Blumah.

A. Y. Bromberg, *Admorim LeBet Warka VeAmshinov*, pp. 10–91.

KAMELHAR, Yekutiel Aryeh (1871–1937), author – Son of R. Gershon, he was born in Kolaczyce, Galicia, and in 1904, he became the head of the *yeshivah Or Torah* in Stanislav. In 1926, he became the rabbi of the Rzeszov-Kurshin congregation in New York.

He emigrated to the Holy Land in 1933.

He was the author of a biography of R. Tzvi Hirsch of Rymanov (1909), and he wrote *Dor De'ah* or *Arba Tekufot HaHasidut HaBeshtit* (Bilgorayj, 1933), biographies of hasidic rebbes.

KAMENKA, Tzvi Hirsch (d. 7 *Tevet* 1781) – Son of R. David of Kamenka, he and his seven brothers were followers of the Besht. R. Tzvi Hirsch was extremely poor and could not afford to make the journey to the Holy Land. One day, a peasant left a pair of cobbler boots with the rabbi. A year passed and the peasant did not claim his property. While the rabbi was scarching for leaven on the eve of Passover, he found the boots, which were full of coins. "This treasure trove," he told his wife, "will enable us to settle in the Holy Land."

There, his wife saved the life of the wife of a Turkish official in a difficult childbirth. The grateful father responded by obtaining permission for R. Tzvi Hirsch to visit the cave of Machpelah.

He was the author of *Shenei HaMeorot* (Kishinev, 1896). His son, R. Shmuel II, the author of *Shem MiShmuel*, emigrated to the United States. His grandson, R. Abraham David, was the rabbi of Miropol (d. 29 *Heshvan* 1911).

KAPLAN, Aryeh (1940–1983) – Born in the Bronx, he studied in American and Israeli *yeshivot* and for a brief period worked as a physicist. For a time he was editor of the New York magazine *Jewish Life*. He was the author of more than fifty books, including *Meditation* and *Kabbalah*, *Meditation and the Bible*, and *The Bahir* (1990), and *Immortality, Resurrection, and the Age of the Universe* (1993).

He was a prolific and creative writer, who abandoned a career in physics and devoted himself to the dissemination of Torah. He contributed much to the revitalization of traditional Judaism in the United States. He not only was a talmudical scholar but also had a grasp of mysticism and hasidic thought.

KAPUST, Dynasty – The second son of R. Menahem Mendel Schneersohn of Lubavich, R. Judah Leib, born in 1811, established the hasidic dynasty of Kapust. His manner of prayer, his joy, and his inspiring teaching attracted many followers. He died at the age of fifty-six on 3 *Heshvan* 1867.

He was succeeded by his son, R. Shlomoh Zalman, who was born in 1820. After his marriage, he lived in Lepoli for ten years. He then returned to Lubavitch, studying under his grandfather.

On his father's death he went to live in Kapust, where he acted as rebbe for thirty-four years. He supported the *kollel Ramban*, an organization that sustained many hasidic families who had settled in the Holy Land. The Zionist leader M. M. Ussishkin (1863–1941), secretary of the Druzkieniki Conference of the *Hovevei Zion*, met him in 1887. The rebbe was in favor of Jews settling in the Holy Land, but he never became an active participant of the *Hovevei Zion* movement.

He died on 27 *Iyyar* 1900. He was the author of a classical work, *Magen Avot* (Berdichev, 1902), a collection of discourses on the weekly portions of the Law, the Holy Days, the Scroll of Esther, and the Song of Songs.

Z.T.

KARF, Jacob Israel (1883–19 *Tishri* 1952)—Son of R. Mottel, he was born in Medziborz and was ordained by R. Rafael of Bobruisk. He married Gitel, the daughter of R. Yehiel Meir of Zevil (Vladamir Volynsky) in 1907. She was murdered by the Bolsheviks on 2 *Elul* 1919. He then married her sister Yutta and became rabbi of Zevil.

In 1924, he emigrated to the United States and settled in Boston. He was the author of *Mikveh Yisrael* on the Pentateuch and *Netzah Yisrael* on *halakhah*.

Toldot Anshei Shem, p. 115.

KARLIN—Hasidic dynasty founded by R. Aaron the Great (d. 1772), when a small hasidic *minyan* was established in Karlin, a suburb of Pinsk, in 1770. There were soon hasidim of Karlin even in Vilna and other Lithuanian towns.

Solomon Maimon recorded in his autobiography, "These people [the hasidim] used to make pilgrimages to K[arlin] and M[ezhirech] and other 'holy' places where the leaders and teachers and the great lights of this sect lived."

From Karlin, the dynasty extended to Stolin under the guidance of R. Asher I (d. 1827), R. Aaron II (d. 1872), and R. Israel *HaYanukkah* ("the child") (d. 1921).

W. Rabinowitsch, *Lithuanian Hasidism*, pp. 8–106.

KASHER, Menahem (1895–1982)—A native of Warsaw, he was ordained by R. Meir Dan Plotzki in 1915. He was appointed as head of the *yeshivah Sefat Emet* by R. Abraham Mordecai Alter. A versatile rabbinic scholar, he was best known as the author of *Torah Shelemah*, an encyclopedic compilation of commentaries to the Pentateuch. By 1971, twenty-five volumes had appeared, covering Genesis and Exodus only. An English edition of this work under title *An Encyclopedia of Biblical Interpretations* has also appeared.

He was also the author of a Passover *Haggadah* (1956) with voluminous commentaries and an English translation. Another important work was his *Sarei HaElef* (New York, 1959), a complete bibliographic compendium of Hebraica by rabbinic authors between the years 500 C.E. and 1500 C.E.

KAVVANAH—Intention, or concentration, especially during prayer. The concept of *kavvanah* (lit., directing, i.e., the mind) has had a long and complicated history. The Talmud frequently urges the worshiper to maintain *kavvanah* during prayers, where the meaning of *kavvanah* is twofold: having God in mind and dwelling on the meaning of the words of the prayers. The concept was deepened by the medieval thinkers. The saying of Bahya Ibn Pakudah is often quoted: "Prayer without *kavvanah* is like a body without a soul." In the Kabbalah, especially in its Lurianic version, *kavvanah* assumes an entirely different meaning, for which the plural form, *kavvanot*, is generally used. The *kavvanot* (intentions) are the kabbalistic mysteries, the map of the sefirotic realm, which the adept is to have in mind when reciting the words of the standard prayers, each word hinting at one or another of the divine names and configurations on high.

Hasidism does not dispense entirely with the kabbalistic *kavvanot* and certainly believes that the kabbalistic unifications depend on the words of the prayers, which is why the hasidim used the Lurianic prayer book, in which these *kavvanot* are set forth to accord with the special words hinting at the mysteries. However, it appears from reliable sources that the Besht developed a new technique of *kavvanah*, furthered in the school of his disciple, the Maggid of Mezhirech, in which the worshipers "attached themselves to the letters" of the prayers. This idea is based on the notion that the letters of the prayers represent spiritual ability. *Kavvanah*, in this scheme, means that the worshipers are hardly conscious at all of the plain meaning of the words they utter, but instead, they allow their mind and heart to soar aloft, the combination of the letters into words representing for them the unification process on high, which they repeat and assist, as if it were here on earth. The early hasidic text, *Keter Shem Tov* (Jerusalem, 1968, pp. 48a–48b), describes the technique as:

> When he prays a man should put all his strength into the utterances and so he should proceed from letter to letter until he has forgotten his corporeal nature. He should reflect on the idea that the letters become combined and joined one to the other and this is great delight. For if in the material world unification is attended by delight, how much more in the spiritual realms! This is the stage of the world of formation. Afterwards he should reach the stage of having the letters in his thoughts alone so that he no longer hears that which he speaks. At this stage he enters the world of creation. Afterwards he should reach the quality of nothingness at which his physical powers are annihilated. This is the stage of the world of emanation, the quality of wisdom.

The *Habad* movement in Hasidism is an exception. In *Habad* there is a different form of *kavvanah*. This involves profound contemplation on the whole kabbalistic scheme, the mind dwelling on the full details of how all worlds proceed from *Ein Sof*. This is different from the Lurianic *kavvanot* in which each particular word represents some aspect of the sefirotic realm, whereas in *Habad* the worshiper's mind is on the process as a whole.

L. Jacobs, *Hasidic Prayer*, pp. 70–92.

L.J.

KEFAR HABAD–A hasidic colony near the Lydda-Tel Aviv railway, founded in 1949 by R. Joseph Yitzhak Schneersohn, on the site of the former Arab village of Safariya. The settlement began with seventy-four refugees from Russia, who were soon joined by fifteen families from Morocco. The Jewish National Fund allotted them 600 acres.

The pride of the settlement is the *yeshivah Tomhei Teminim*, established in 1954. Attached to it is a *kollel* for advanced students of rabbinics. It also offers vocational training. With the help of *Joint* and *Ort*, a printing press was set up, and much of the machinery was provided by the Jewish Master Printers and the Jewish Aid Committee in London. There are also an agricultural school, carpentry, locksmith and tool shops, and facilities for training in electronics and motor mechanics.

Girls attend the *Bet Rivkah* school, set up in 1959, and the teachers' training seminary. The comprehensive curriculum provides the students with a broad education according to the requirements of the ministry of education. The latest addition to the settlement is a youth center known as *Bet Shazar* (the House of Shazar), in honor of the late president Zalman Shazar, who was named after the first rabbi of *Habad*.

On 2 *Iyyar* 1955, five students and one teacher were murdered by Arab terrorists. A special institute, called *Yad HaHamishah* (Memorial of the Five) school of printing and graphic arts was established in their memory.

A satellite settlement, *Habad Bet*, was also established.

KEFAR HASIDIM–A religious *moshav*, seven and a half miles southeast of Haifa in the Zevulun Valley. This hasidic settlement was the result of an affiliation of *Nahalat Yaakov*, established in 1925 by R. Ezekiel Taub of Yablona, with the *Avodat Yisrael*, established by R. Isaiah Shapira. It was due to the suggestion by R. Menahem Mendel Ussishkin, chairman of the executive committee of the Jewish National Fund, that these two bodies amalgamated. In 1927, they were joined by a group of *Poalei Mizrachi*.

Though *Kefar Hasidim* was founded by hasidim, it has lost its hasidic character and only the name perpetuates its origin. The atmosphere changed when both the founders, R. Ezekiel Taub and R. Shapira, left the settlement.

KEHAL YITEV LEV D'SATMAR–This hasidic community in Williamsburg, Brooklyn, is a self-sufficient and cohesive entity, a testimony to the late R. Joel Teitelbaum's remarkable flair for organization.

By the 1990s, more than 40,000 hasidim were living in the area in renovated tenements along Lee and Division avenues.

Satmar issues a weekly newspaper (*Der Yid*). It has its own welfare network, including a holiday fund for orphaned children, insurance and pension plans, an emergency ambulance service, a burial society, butcher shops, *mikvaot*, *shatnes* laboratories, kindergartens, *Bet Rachel* schools for girls, *yeshivot*, *kollelim*, and bakeries.

The Satmar community is responsible for the education of nearly 5,000 children in fifteen schools. To become a member of this elite community, a man must undertake to observe the Sabbath and to bring up his children according to Orthodox traditions. A committee of three interviewers investigates every applicant.

Population shifts caused many hasidim to abandon Williamsburg. In 1962, Satmar tried to establish a colony in Mount Olive Township in New Jersey, but it was unable to receive a zoning permit. However, in 1976, *Kiryat Yoel*, a village of 340 acres, was set up near Monroe in Orange County, New York.

I. Rubin, *Satmar: An Island in the City*.

KETER SHEM TOV–An anthology of the teachings of the Besht, collected from the works of R. Jacob Joseph of Polonnoye and edited by R. Aaron ben Tzvi Hakohen of Opatov. It was first printed in two volumes in Zolkiev in 1794.

KIERKEGAARD, Soren Aaby (1813–1855)–One of the greatest Danish thinkers, who wrote a thesis on the "concept of irony" (1841). Not to burden his fiancée with his inherited pietist melancholy and to remove the "stake in the flesh," he broke off his engagement, a step he defended in *Either-Or* (1843), a book followed by an astonishing number of writings. His endeavor to "think existentially" led him to the use of literary pseudonyms. After 1848 he became more and more hostile to official Christianity. Ridiculed by "The Corsair" and in conflict with the state-church, he died at the age of forty-two.

His philosophy is the expression of an individual existence. In his theology, the Christian conduct of life with its paradox (its "ontological determination"), though objectively absurd (we cannot get beyond the eternal striving after truth), is seen as an object of passion for the faithful, as it was for the primitive Christians. What matters is the "how" and not the "what". Truth is here subjectivity, a daring deed; objectively, a paradox.

Abraham (a representative of the transition from the aesthetic to the ethical) is either a murderer (cf. the Sixth Commandment) or the model of the man to whom alone the divine commandment is addressed. Kierkegaard thus opposes Hegel's philosophy of objective thought with its optimistic pantheism of culture. To exist means to be an individual, irrational in the mathematical sense. Man then goes through three stages: the aesthetic (i.e., a sophisticated and romantic hedonism in abstracto), ethical (the reality proper of the individual), and religious.

A postulated system of existence could be comprehended only by God. Not intellectual acceptance, but only the leap of faith can in our volcanic existence lead to the "paradox of the religious." After this "leap," we become fundamentally different from the world around us.

A revelation given at a certain moment in history must of necessity be polemic. In the strangely ambiguous kind of anxiety we experience lies the possibility of freedom. To lead a religious life means to be dedicated to suffering and the abandonment of self (not resolving an aspect of fatalism!). Only through our own existential development can true religion thus be acquired. The insight thus achieved must be reduplicated in our lives.

A tendency parallel to that of Kierkegaard in its melancholy and uncompromising search is found on the part of R. Menahem Mendel of Kotzk (d. 1859). In order to achieve truth (*emet*), he was ready to sacrifice everything else. Though not negating this-worldliness, humanity, that is, the select, has to go against itself and society. R. Mendel's disciples would leave behind their studies, their homes, and even their wives. According to R. Mendel, the true worship of

God lies in the search for truth through the study of the Torah.

P. Z. Gliksman, *Der Kotzker Rebbe*.

A. J. Heschel, *A Passion for Truth*, pp. 216–221, 248–249.

U.L.

KINSHIP AND MARRIAGE–

Kinship has always played an important part in the organization and integration of hasidic communities. Functionally, it provides the basis for membership of the group, acts as a mechanism of social control, and, in the case of the charismatic leadership by the rebbe, legitimates this power. Even today, after the disruption caused by the Second World War, hasidic genealogies, dynastic and otherwise, are fervently remembered and brought into play whenever the occasion demands.

Although there was no officially prescribed form of marriage, cross-cousin marriage often took place within the dynasties themselves, and the rest of the community engaged in relative endogamy.

The degree to which hasidic communities today are organized in terms of kinship varies. Among hasidim Lubavitch, for example, kinship, except for the dynasty itself, plays a relatively minor part in group organization: affiliation to the group (which is distinguished by being the only hasidic group that actively "proselytizes") is largely voluntary, whereas in other groups today it is largely through birth or marriage. Also, the influence of the Rebbe of Lubavitch, which is considerable, provides "charismatic integration," which may be lacking in other groups, where kinship may provide that function.

On the other hand, kinship played an important part in the reestablishment of certain hasidic communities after the decimation of World War II. For example, among the hasidim of Belz in Antwerp, a new community was built up through the interplay between the existing kinship networks of a few nuclear families, who were united through marriage alliances. In the wake of the Holocaust, widely scattered hasidim of Belz of both Hungarian and Polish origin joined together to form new kinship networks, which provided the basis for a new community in Antwerp. Ties were established, too, by these kinship alliances between the two moieties (Hungarian and Polish), which provided further links with the wider society as all grades of Jew were represented in these networks, which were also closely related to the economic structure.

Because of the breakdown and scattering of the old kin-based communities, kinship ties were broadened to embrace hasidim in far-flung communities. Improved communications also played their part in facilitating marriages between hasidim in the various capitals of the world.

Traditionally, marriage would take place at seventeen or eighteen. This was determined partly by the great emphasis on premarital chastity and partly by the high status attached to being married, with correspondingly low status being attached to being unmarried. As the bridegroom would generally still be completing his studies at *yeshivah*, it would be incumbent upon the father-in-law to support him and his bride, until he could earn his own living and set up a separate household.

Thus, traditionally, residence after marriage was matrilocal, and the normal pattern of residence in Europe before World War II consisted of extended families, with several generations of a family living in the same house or nearby. With the decimation, uprooting, and scattering of families caused by both the Holocaust and the immigration to new centers in America, Israel, Belgium, and Great Britain, a major change occurred: there were less "dependent" elderly people in the family; housing was often on a modest scale; and families were now broken into nuclear units.

In that setting the marriage broker (*shadhan*) had a more important role than ever to play, as matchmaking entailed finding someone not only from a suitable ethnic and economic background but also of the right degree of piety in an increasingly secularized community. Marriage thus became not only a question of aligning two family groups, but of consolidating and reaffirming Orthodox Jewish values as a whole.

In very few hasidic families is the selecting of a mate left to the young couple themselves, although not all hasidic groups use an official *shadhan*. Lubavitch say "Everyone can be a *shadhan* if he has a good *shidah*"; likewise, the Belzer in Antwerp rarely use *shadhanim*–the family arranges the marriage. Romantic love plays a very minimal role in the selection of a mate, love being said to come afterward. Likewise dating and courtship in the popular sense are unknown, although the young couple are allowed to meet on a strictly chaperoned basis, in a suitable environment, on occasion before the marriage. Lubavitch, for example, allow an occasional visit to the cinema, whereas among other groups this would be unheard-of.

The rigid division of the sexes and strict laws of premarital chastity preclude the possibility of any physical contact whatsoever. Before the marriage, the young couple is instructed, separately, on each one's religious duties in marriage. The two are instructed on the holiness of the sexual act, and they are warned against letting it ever serve as an "abominable deed of passion and lust." Girls are instructed in the laws of family purity, which are regarded as the cornerstone of the sanctity of Jewish family life.

The division of the sexes carries over into the family after marriage, with a strict division of labor between husband and wife. The husband is generally expected to be the breadwinner and overall supervisor of religious matters; the woman is the housekeeper and mother and has fewer religious duties. Some hasidic women manage to fulfill roles outside the home (e.g., as teachers or by helping their husband in business), but it is still in the domestic sphere that they are expected to do valiantly, and they have to devote, for example, much time to cooking special dishes for Festivals, regardless of other commitments. Since most families are very large—birth control rarely being practiced—hasidic women have to spend a proportionately longer period engaged in child rearing than do other women.

The female's role, then, is strictly defined, as is that of the male. With the division of the sexes too, "togetherness" is not a feature of the husband-wife relationship. Since romantic love is not aspired to, personal attractiveness is less important than modesty, virtue, and domestic capability. Among some hasidic groups, however (especially those at a higher socioeconomic level), the woman takes great care of her appearance, wearing expensive, high-fashion wigs and custom-made clothes.

Traditionally, there were strong negative community sanctions against the divorced or separated, and the hasidim were noted for their low rate of divorce. Recently, however, in common with the wider Jewish community, divorce has been on the increase, with the woman less hesitant to instigate proceedings. In those cases, however, community sanctions in the form of gossip or disapproval are more likely to be applied to the woman than to the man, regardless of the facts of the case.

Hasidic family life is religiously determined. It is within the family that hasidic norms are perpetuated. The family must observe hasidic norms under every circumstance. In this sense, hasidic family life and kinship play an important part in reinforcing the structure of hasidic society.

J. Kupfermann, "The Lubavitch Community of Stamford Hill."

J.Ku.

KIRYAT BOBOV—The *kiryah* was founded by R. Solomon Halberstam of Bobov in Bat Yam, to the south of Tel Aviv. The foundation stone was laid on 20 *Kislev* 1958.

Today there are over a hundred families living in the *kiryah*'s modern apartments. The *yeshivah Kedushat Zion* and the synagogue *Bet Yehoshua*—the gifts of the rabbi's brother-in-law, Osias Freshwater—were founded in 1963. The *Talmud Torah Kol Aryeh* is named after R. Aryeh Leib Rubin, rabbi of Tomashov, the martyred father of the rabbi's wife. Forty-eight elderly people live in a pleasant and comfortable home called *Segulah*, which was opened in 1963.

The *kiryah*'s development has been hindered by technical and financial problems, as it is difficult to create a new *kiryah* by remote control from New York.

KIRYAT KALEV—Near Rishon LeZion is *Kiryat Kalev*, established on 7 *Adar* 1967 by R. Menahem Mendel Taub.

The *kiryah* has one of the most beautiful synagogues in the State of Israel. The five chandeliers are made up of 613 lamps, equivalent to the 613 commandments found in the Pentateuch. The four walls of the synagogue present a pictorial history of Judaism. On the Western Wall are scenes showing the life of Jonah, the Prophet Elijah, the exploits of Samson, the parting of the Red Sea, the crossing of the river Jordan, and the sun standing still at Gibeon.

As a visible reminder of the glory that was Kalev, two bricks of the original synagogue in Hungary have been placed in a prominent position on the Eastern Wall.

See TAUB, MENAHEM MENDEL.

KIRYAT VISHNITZ–The *kiryah* is in Bene Berak, and it is the largest autonomous hasidic settlement. *Kiryat Vishnitz*, named after the townlet of Vizhnitza (Vijnita, in Romanian) was the home of the rabbis of Vishnitz.

The foundation stone was laid on 2 *Sivan* 1950. The *shikkun* grew rapidly and now has a population of 4,000. The street names tell the story of the dynasty of Kosov and Vishnitz: *Rehov Torat Hayyim*, *Rehov Imrei Barukh*, *Rehov Ahavat Shalom*, *Rehov Tzemah Tzeddeh*.

Predictably, the chief building is the *yeshivah Bet Yisrael VeDamesek Eliezer*. There is also a *kollel Damesek Eliezer*. The *kiryah* is virtually self-sufficient with regard to its educational facilities. There are *yeshivot ketanot*, *Bet Yaakov* schools, and a teachers' seminary–*Zikhron Meir*. It is well equipped with social and welfare organizations.

Bet Shalom houses a hundred elderly people, the *Gemilat Hesed* fund grants interest-free loans to the needy, and *Ezrat Nashim* provides financial aid for indigent students. The *Bikkur Holim* takes care of the ailing, and a permanent building fund enables people to acquire apartments relatively cheaply. In the central banqueting hall, residents and nonresidents celebrate their festivities, and a sixty-eight-room hotel caters to visitors to the *kiryah*.

The settlement has its own diamond factory, bakery, and printing press as well as a special bakery where unleavened bread is produced by hand. Its twelve ritual baths are visited by more than 1,500 people each day. The *kiryah* has its own generator, the maintenance of which does not require a Jew to supervise it on the Sabbath.

The *kiryah* is proud of its high birth rate. The average family has six or seven children, ten or twelve not being unusual.

KIRYAT YISMAH MOSHEH–A hasidic settlement near Ramat Gan and *Kiryat Ono*, five miles east of Tel Aviv. It was founded by R. Hananniah Yom Tov Lippa Teitelbaum in *Adar* 1963, when the foundation stone was laid. After the death of the founder in 1966, the *kiryah* was faced with tremendous financial problems. In August 1972, the rabbi's wife sold 200 dunams of its land.

Today, there is no hasidic *yeshivah* there, because the *yeshivah* in the *kiryah* has been lent to a Lithuanian group. There are four houses of worship, two kindergartens, and a *Bet Yaakov* school.

KIRYAT YOEL–This hasidic settlement in the town of Monroe, in Orange County, in New York State, was established in 1974 by R. Joel Teitelbaum. The village became incorporated and grew at the rate of a hundred families a year. When R. Joel died, his successor, R. Moses, appointed his elder son, R. Aaron, as rabbi and head of the *yeshivah* there. By 1990, the population of the *kiryah* had grown to over 8,000. The size of the average family is 6.6, and children constitute 65 percent of its population.

To avoid the use of buses driven by women, the *kiryah* finances its own transport.

It is not, however, free from friction. About fifty families, in defiance of the rebbe, have established their own *Bene Yoel Independent School*, under Joseph Waldman.

J. R. Mintz, *Hasidic People–a Place in the New World*, pp. 90–91, 309–327.

KIRYAT ZANZ–Twenty minutes' walk from Netanya stands *Kiryat Zanz*, the largest hasidic settlement in Israel outside Bene Berak and Jerusalem. It was founded by R. Yekutiel Judah Halberstam of Klausenburg.

The foundation stone was laid on March 4, 1956, and the settlement was built according to Jewish Law. The most impressive building is the Great Synagogue, which seats 500 people and whose centerpiece is a 300-year-old Italian ark. Facing the Great Synagogue stands a small *Bet HaMidrash*. Diverse Torah institutions cater to every age group. The pride of the community is the main *yeshivah*.

The rebbe's efforts were not confined to his hasidim. For oriental Jews he established *Yeshivat Maharshad*, named in memory of his father-in-law, R. Samuel David Unger. There is also an orphanage for Sefardic children.

Fifty people live in a *bet avot* (home of the fathers). There are a diamond factory, a shopping center, a post office, a bank, a *mikveh*, and a 100-room hotel, *Galei Zanz*, where bathing facilities for men and women are provided on the beach on different days.

The most interesting building in the *kiryah* is the *Laniado Hospital*, which was the first religious hospital to be built for eighty years. The U.S. government contributed money toward the project. A school of nursing is attached to it.

Although R. Halberstam now lives in New York, he maintained close links with the *kiryah*.

KISLINTZ, Mordecai (Mottel) Hayyim, of Slonim (*Rosh Hodesh Tammuz* 1866–10 *Tevet* 1954)–Born in Slonim, he was seven years old when he emigrated with his father to the Holy Land. He married the daughter of R. Eliezer Katz of Safed. He was a follower of R. Abraham Weinberg of Slonim, who visited the Holy Land in 1929 and 1933.

In 1937, R. Mottel settled in Jerusalem and reluctantly consented to become rebbe. He did not deliver discourses but simply told hasidic stories.

KITOV, Eliyahu (1912–1976)–A native of Warsaw, he emigrated to the Holy Land in 1936. Apart from his educational activities, he edited *Hakol*, an organ of the *Po'alei Agudat Yisrael*, and was the author of works on Hasidism under the title *Hasidim VeAnshei Maasei* (Jerusalem, 1955) and *Behesed Elyon* on R. Moses Leib of Sasov (Jerusalem, 1955).

KLAPHOLZ, Israel Jacob (1910–1988), author–Born in Nowy Sanz, he studied in the *yeshivot* of Belz and Baranowicze under R. Elhanan Wasserman. He was the personal attendant of R. Aaron of Belz, and until 1964, he was the head of the Belz *yeshivah* of Bene Berak.

When R. Berele Rokeah became rebbe, he left the service of Belz and devoted himself to writing books on hasidic rebbes. He is the author of *Tales of the Baal Shem Tov* and *The Rebbes of Belz* (*Admorei Belz* [Bene Berak, 1972]) and *Maggid MiMezhirech* (Bene Berak, 1972).

KLIERS, Moses, of Tiberias (7 *Adar* 1874–23 *Shevat* 1934)–Son of R. Meir, he was born in Tiberias. He studied under R. Mordecai Hayyim of Slonim and married Dubra, the daughter of R. Yehudah Leib Kestilnitz. When she died in the prime of her life in 1903, he married his cousin Debrah, the daughter of R. Elishah. In 1909 he became rabbi of Tiberias.

He visited R. Samuel of Slonim in 1899 and on his return established a *yeshivah*, *Or Torah*, in Tiberias. "The rebbe gave me good advice," he would say. "Always do exactly the opposite to what your body urges you to do." Himself a rebbe, he remained a devoted hasid of Slonim and welcomed his rebbe in the Holy Land in 1929 and 1933.

He was the author of *Tabor HaAretz* (Jerusalem, 1906) and *Torat HaAretz* (Jerusalem, 1925).

KLINBERG, Shem, of Zaloczyce (1870–25 *Nisan* 1943)–Son of R. Abraham Mordecai of Zaloczyce, a descendant of R. Yitzhak Eizig of Komarno. He was a disciple of the rebbe of Komarno, whom he succeeded. He made his home in Cracow, where he was at home to his followers for two hours every day. He was murdered by the Nazis in the labor camp of Plaszov. His wife, Shlomtze, was killed on 24 *Adar* 1943. His son R. Menahem Mendel, who was active in the Aguda in Cracow, was murdered on 12 *Tishri* 1943.

He was survived by two sons, R. Yitzhak Eizig, in the United States, and R. Moses, in Israel.

His work *Ohelei Shem* on the Pentateuch and Festivals was published in Jerusalem in 1951.

Elleh Ezkerah, vol. 7, pp. 266–270.

KLIPPOT–*Klippot* are shells or husks, the name given in the Kabbalah to the demonic forces. The *klippot* are nourished by the good and holy but seek to destroy them or, at least, to encroach on their domain. The *Shekhinah* is especially prone to attack by the *klippot* (*Zohar* I, 1a), and it is the task of the *Shekhinah*'s devotees to defend her by living a holy life and thus frustrating the evil designs of the denizens of hell. There are, in the main, three impure *klippot* and one–*Nogah* (brightness, Venus, derived from Ezekiel 1:4)–that contains an admixture of good and evil.

In hasidic thought, this, together with other kabbalistic ideas, tends to be interiorized (i.e., the chief conflict with the *klippot* takes place in one's soul). According to *Habad* thought, the Jew has two souls: the divine soul, being the portion of God deep in the recesses of one's psyche, and the natural, or animal, soul, which is derived from *Nogah*. The task of Jews is to refine their natural soul and in this way reclaim even the *klippah* for the holy (*Tanya*, chap. 1 and 2).

The seven lean cows that swallowed up the seven fat cows in Pharaoh's dream (Genesis 41:4) are the seven potencies of the *klippot*, which, in those who have surrendered to evil, devour entirely all those people's good qualities (R. Israel of Kozienic, *Avodat Yisrael* [Lemberg, 1858], *miketz*, pp. 19b–20a). The purpose of the numerous journeys of the children of Israel through the wilderness was in order to reclaim the holy sparks (Abraham Joshua Heschel of Apt, *Ohev Yisrael* [Jerusalem, 1962], *behaalotekha*, p. 177).

The lord of the *klippot* is Samael, referred to as the *samekh mem*, the devil. Many of the hasidic legends have as their motif the overcoming of the *samekh mem* by the hasidic saints. Similarly, there are many tales of the saints' becoming sensitive to places in which evil deeds had been committed and so had become the home of the *klippot*.

In a responsum on table-rapping, R. Solomon Kluger of Brody (1785–1869) quotes (*Tuv Taam VaDaat*, 3rd series, Part II [Podgorze, 1900], no. 48) the hasidic master R. Shalom of Belz that the manifestations of table-rapping are produced by the *klippot*. Certain religious ceremonies, such as the burning of leaven on the eve of Passover, are understood as directed especially toward the destruction of the *klippot*. The hasidic masters who were opposed to the conquests of Napoleon and who prayed for his downfall did so because they thought of him as influenced by the *klippot*.

I. Tishby, *Torat HaRa VeHaKlippah BeKabbalat HaAri*.

L.J.

KOBRIN, Moses Polier (1784–29 *Nisan* 1858), hasidic rabbi—Son of R. Israel Polier, a baker, Moses was born in Piesk, near Slonim. He studied for two years under R. Moses of Sherszov, a disciple of R. Hayyim Heikel of Amdur. He subsequently became a hasid of R. Mordecai of Lachowicze. After the death of R. Mordecai, R. Moses followed the rabbi's son, R. Noah, for seventeen years. It was only after R. Noah's death that he reluctantly accepted the position of rabbi of Kobrin.

He regularly communicated with his followers by sending them letters of encouragement. "Each one of us must do his utmost to fully concentrate on our prayers, to pray joyfully and gladly. . . . Conduct yourselves with joy and gladness and the Lord will surely help you to succeed and prosper in all your physical and spiritual doings."

R. Moses was no author of books but once said, "My books are written in the hearts of Israel." After his death his hasidim collected and published his teachings under the title *Amarot Tehorot* (Warsaw, 1910).

R. Moses lived very modestly. When his silk kaftan became worn with age, he refused to have a new one made. "I will not waste Jewish money," he said. He was very modest by nature as well. When a hasid from Poland came to see him, he asked him, "Why have you come to me, when you have already been to your own rebbe? Your rebbe is a veritable *tzaddik* [and] the son of a *tzaddik*, whereas my father was just a simple villager." He forbade his hasidim to call him a *tzaddik*. Throughout his life he was filled with a constant desire for repentance. Before the blowing of the *shofar* on the New Year, he told his hasidim, "Fellow Jews, do not place your trust in me. Let each one of you do what is required of him."

The hasidim of Kobrin would chant the words of the rebbe in Yiddish. "Angel, Angel, it is no wonder that you are an angel. You sit in the heavenly spheres where you are not obliged to eat or drink or to beget children and support them. Pray, come down to us on earth, where you will have to eat and drink and procreate. Then we shall see, if you will still remain an angel. Then you will have the right to be proud of yourself, but not now."

Among his disciples were R. Meir Meirim (d. 1873), the author of a commentary of *Yerushalmi*, and R. Yitzhak Mattathias Weinberg, the founder of the Slonim dynasty. R. Moses was succeeded by his grandson, R. Noah Naftali.

KOENIG, Gedaliah Aharon (1921–1980)—Son of Eliezer Mordecai, he was born in Katamon, Jerusalem. He was a leading disciple of R. Abraham Sternhartz. He transcribed *Tovot Zihronot* (Jerusalem, 1951) and was the author of many unpublished manuscripts on Bratzlav *Hasidut*.

KOLLEL–In the eighteenth century, the term *kollel* was part of the *Halukkah* organization. Today the term denotes a graduate institution that subsidizes the studies of married *yeshivah* students. Supporting a student son-in-law was customary in Eastern Europe.

The past three decades have seen the extensive growth of *kollelim* in Israel and in the Diaspora. There are very few hasidic rebbes who do not sponsor a *kollel*.

Conditions vary from *kollel* to *kollel*. To maintain their large families, a number of students attend two *kollelim*–one in the morning and another in the afternoon or evening. Apart from monthly stipends, students in Israel receive a family allowance from the state, which is usually augmented by parents or by the salaries that the young wives earn as teachers.

KOLOMYJA (German, Kolomea; Polish, Kolomyja)–A city in the Ukraine, which the Besht often visited and lived in for some time. His home was later converted into a *Bet HaMidrash* and the ritual bath was called the *Besht's Mikveh*. The Besht first revealed himself to R. David, the Maggid of Kolomyja (d. 1759).

In his *Toldot Yaakov Yosef*, R. Jacob Joseph of Polonnoye quotes R. Leib Pistiner, who lived there. Other hasidic rebbes who resided there were R. Jacob Koppel; R. Eliezer of Dolina, known as "Eliezer the Great" (d. 1868); and R. Gershon, the author of *Avodat HaGershuni* (Vilna, 1925).

In 1939, the Jewish population was over 15,000, and there were *shtieblech* of Boyan, Vishnitz, Zydaczov, and Chortkov. On March 29, 1944, when the city was liberated, only several dozen Jews came out of their hiding places.

KOOK, Abraham Yitzhak (1865–1935), chief rabbi of the Holy Land–His father, R. Solomon Zalman Hakohen, was associated with the mitnaggedic tradition. His mother, however, was the daughter of R. Rafael, a hasid of *Habad*. She is said to have sewn a button from the coat of a hasidic rebbe onto her infant son's jacket. His education was nonhasidic.

Though not personally drawn to any particular hasidic court or rebbe, R. Kook was thoroughly conversant with hasidic literature. There appears to have been a kinship between his ideas and those of R. Nahman of Bratzlav.

An even closer relationship may have existed between his writings and the teachings of the *Habad* school. While living in England, R. Kook wrote a brief mystical treatise on the Hebrew alphabet, which he called *Rosh Milim*. The book discusses the mystical powers of the Hebrew letters, vowels, and musical trope–a theme found in the chapter "*Shaar HaYihud*" in R. Shneur Zalman's work the *Tanya*. R. Kook's frequent use of the term "lights" as an appellation for wisdom has its parallel in R. Shneur Zalman's writings.

Terms like *Memalei kol ha'olamim* and *soveiv kol ha'olamim*, referring to the immanence of God, can also be found both in R. Kook's writings and in *Habad* literature.

R. Kook was in frequent touch with hasidic rebbes, in both Israel and other countries. "It seems," he wrote on one occasion, "that even Hasidism, which came into the world to shine rich divine light and dazzling rays into heart and brain, has changed its character and now takes a path of ordinary strict observance [that] is difficult to distinguish from that of the *mitnaggedim*."

H.W.

KORETZ, Pinhas, of Korzec (1726–10 *Elul* 1791)–Son of R. Abraham Abba, a learned Lithuanian rabbi, he was born in Shklov. Pinhas not only studied rabbinics but also applied himself to mystical studies. The *Zohar* became the light of his life. "The *Zohar*," stated R. Pinhas, "has kept me alive. . . . Be heedful," he urged his followers, "not to allow three days to pass without studying the *Zohar*."

Apart from the *Zohar*, he diligently studied the works of R. Moses Cordovero and R. Isaac Luria, as well as the *Maggid Meisharim* on Torah, by R. Joseph Caro, containing the secrets divulged to him by his heavenly mentor on 135 occasions. R. Pinhas was reluctant to accept rabbinical posts and suffered great privations. To earn a minimal livelihood he taught children near Polonnoye. Eventually he settled in Korzec. There he came under the influence of R. Yitzhak Hakohen, the author of the kabbalistic work *Brit Kehunat Olam* (Lvov, 1848). Although R. Pinhas later moved to Ostrog and Sheptovka, he remained known as "Pinhas of Koretz."

He met the Besht three times. These meetings changed his life. He favored R. Jacob Joseph of Polonnoye as successor to the Besht. He greeted his writings as "Torah from Gan Eden." R. Pinhas's disciples were R. Jacob Shimshon of Shepetovka, R. Zeev Wolf of Zhitomir, and R. Rafael of Bershad.

His discourses were published in various collections: *Midrash Pinhas* (Bilgoraj, 1931), *Peer LaYesharim* (Jerusalem, 1921), *Nofes Zufim* (Lvov, 1864), *Geulat Yisrael* (Lvov, 1864), and *Likkutei Shoshanim* (Czernowitz, 1857). Many of his unpublished works can be found in private and public collections in Jerusalem.

His wife, Treina, gave birth to two sons, Meir and Mosheh. When she died, he married Yutta, who had two sons and one daughter (Yaakov Shimshon, Yehezkel, and Reizel Sheindel). At that time (1708–1770), the Haidamacks disrupted Jewish life, and many Jews fled from the lawless Ukraine. R. Pinhas urged them to remain in their homes. "Were it not for me," he later asserted, "not one Jew would have remained here."

He followed political developments closely and grieved over the disintegration of the Polish state. He always spoke in high praise of music and song. He collected money for the poor in the Holy Land. In 1791 he set out on a pilgrimage to the Holy Land but died during the journey, at the Russian frontier at Sheptovka.

His teachings reveal a firm belief in the reality of a miraculous order of events. In his view, the people of Israel are the vital nucleus of the world. Even the winds that blow in the various seasons of the year are determined by the way Jews shake and tremble when they say their prayers. One must pray for one's needs and believe staunchly that one's prayers will be answered. The *tzaddik's* words are effective when he rises to the level of a "tree of life." He used to say that he feared that his wisdom might prevail over his piety. In the event of sickness one must not resort to the help of the folk remedies of women but must believe in prayer and in the help of *tzaddikim*.

A. J. Heschel, "A Biographical Note on R. Phinehas of Koretz," pp. 213–214.

Yivo Bletter, vol. 33 (1949), pp. 9–48; vol. 35 (1952), pp. 124–125.

KOTZK, Menahem Mendel, of Kotzk (1787–22 *Shevat* 1859) – Menahem Mendel Morgenstern, one of the greatest hasidic personalities, was born in Bilgoraj, near Lublin. His father, Leibish, was a poor glazier. From infancy Menahem Mendel was headstrong, cold, reserved, and unwilling to confide in anyone. He studied rabbinics in the *yeshivah* of Zamosc under R. Yosef Hochgelerenter. In 1807 he married Gluckel, the daughter of Eliezer Nei of Tomaszov. Afterward he made his way to Lublin to the "Seer." He subsequently became a devoted disciple of the "Yehudi," after whose death he transferred his allegiance to R. Simhah Bunem of Przysucha.

After the birth of a son, David (who later succeeded his father), Gluckel died. A year later R. Menahem married *Hayyah* Halfan, the sister-in-law of R. Yitzhak Meir Alter. Two sons (R. Benjamin and R. Mosheh Yeruham) and two daughters (Sarah Zinah and Berachah) were born of this marriage.

After the death of R. Simhah Bunem, he settled in Tomaszov, where he became a legend in his lifetime. "A fire is burning in Tomaszov," hasidim used to sing. Toward that new light streamed hasidim of all kinds, both the erudite and the unlearned. In the plain and austere *Bet HaMidrash* they led a materially comfortless existence, but their hunger for knowledge was satisfied. Regularly, the rebbe delivered discourses on the Talmud and Maimonides.

The rebbe supported the Polish revolt of 1830–1831. He exhorted wealthy hasidim to aid Polish rebels. After the Russian army's suppression of the revolt, he lived for a time in Galicia, changing his name – Halprin – to Morgenstern, to deflect Russian retaliation.

From 1840 until his death in 1859 the rabbi of Kotzk remained secluded in his study. Through an opening in his door he listened to the reading of the Torah. The vast majority of his many disciples remained loyal to their rebbe. Among the faithful were R. Yitzhak Meir Alter of Ger, R. Abraham Bornstein of Sochaczev, R. Yehiel Meir of

Gostynin, and R. Hanokh of Alexander. The nineteen years of his isolation did not deter his hasidim. They clustered in the *Bet Ha-Midrash*, hoping against hope to behold the countenance of their great master, for they believed that their rebbe, in his self-imposed isolation, was fighting a great and fearful battle against the massed forces of evil.

He destroyed all his writings. His teachings, however, left a permanent imprint on the hasidic courts of Sochaczev, Ger, and Alexander. His discourses are to be found in numerous works by his disciples: in *Emet VeEmunah*, by R. Israel Yaakov Arton (Jerusalem, 1940), and in *Ohel Torah* (Lublin, 1909).

J. Fox, *R. Menahem Mendel MiKotzk*.

Ed.

KOTZK, TEACHINGS OF–The aspect of piety that R. Menahem Mendel stressed most was the quest for total truthfulness. As an Orthodox believer, he naturally regarded the entire sacred heritage, Bible, Talmud, Midrashim, and Kabbalah as true. But he insisted that those teachings must be internalized and made part of one's being. Only God is truth in Himself; human beings can be only searchers for truth. And as they seek the nearness of God, they must be forever on guard, lest pride or egocentricity pervert the purity of their quest.

This teaching must be viewed within its historical-cultural context: The Kotzker hasidim were not allowed to pursue their search outside the approved ways of isolationist Orthodoxy; they were not permitted to pursue secular studies. The truth was for them crystallized in the talmudic-kabbalistic literature. Any attempt to venture outside the circle of Orthodoxy was sinful. The hasidim were encouraged to pursue their search through the approved pathways of talmudic study, *Mussar* books, and the works of "Maharal," R. Loew of Prague. In those books, the kabbalistic worldview is presented in lucid, nonkabbalistic language.

Within those limitations, the Kotzker hasidim were allowed to question and to search. They were encouraged to examine their own conscience and the firmness of their faith by constant self-questioning (*sich iberfregen*). Those hasidim who felt troubled by questions concerning the existence of God were told they needed not to fear for their Orthodoxy, so long as they believed that without God, life was not worth living. To "find God" means to be caught up in the zeal of searching for Him, ever more deeply.

The Oral Law, in its fullness, was never yet written down. All of us must rediscover it in ourself, for the Talmud and Midrashim provide us only with hints. But if one comes to feel that one has already attained the fullness of understanding, then that person is totally on the wrong track (i.e., one's heart is impure). The *tzaddik* would tell his disciples that he expected them to refrain from sinning, simply because they had no time for it, by being so totally preoccupied with their quest.

Individual disciples were expected to discover their own way of serving God–not to imitate others, not even to imitate themselves. "He who studies Torah literally, or sins and forgives himself, or prays today because he prayed yesterday–a complete sinner is better than he."

Kotzker hasidim would spend a lot of time meditating, before actually reciting the traditional prayers. Accordingly, they would pray at a later hour and in appearance, at least, be in violation of the prescribed regimen in the *Shulhan Arukh*.

The type of piety favored at Kotzk was essentially unstable. It did not reflect the traditional practice of Torah study as a way of fulfilling God's command but as a way of achieving divine nearness. The *tzaddik* would "see" the tetragrammaton in letters of fire either before or after learning. The longing for originality and freshness and the constant self-questioning, "in fear and trembling," made the hasidim feel they were walking on a razor's edge, suspended over a burning fire. It is perhaps this contradictory demand for breaking all barriers while remaining within the bounds of rigid dogmas and laws that precipitated R. Menahem Mendel's mysterious psychical breakdown, when he withdrew to his own room and when a large portion of his followers withdrew from him to follow R. Mordecai Joseph, his trusted disciple.

Exactly what happened on that occasion can only be surmised, because the hasidim who knew would not tell, and those who told did not have firsthand knowledge. It is certain that R. Menahem Mendel fell into a state of melancholia, living in total isolation and wearing the same clothes, whether asleep or awake. His food would be given to him through special apertures, and he would listen to services through similar holes in the door. Only at rare moments would he receive some of his oldest and most trusted friends. The leadership of Kotzk was thereafter actually assumed by R. Yitzhak Meir of Ger, who led the fight against wearing "gentile" clothes, though R. Menahem Mendel himself did not altogether approve of that campaign.

It cannot be ascertained whether the isolation of the *tzaddik* in the last twenty-two years of his life was voluntary or not. His followers believed that the *tzaddik* lived behind closed doors on account of their sins, especially since "the gates of wisdom and knowledge," heralding the messianic era, were due to open in 1840 but instead were shut with a bang, as it were. So the closed doors of the *tzaddik* corresponded to the closing of the gates in heaven.

Heschel compared R. Menahem Mendel to Kierkegaard. Both were seekers of God, in "fear and trembling"; both were convinced that truth could be reached only by individuals' probing their own being with relentless ardor; both were engaged in combating conventional pieties; both insisted that rationality was self-deception when ultimate questions were at stake, since the divine is inescapably paradoxical; and both would brook no compromises and insist that we face up to the "either-or" of the meaning of life. This comparison is certainly meaningful, provided we recognize that it is limited to the psychological attitudes of the two pietists. Philosophically and dogmatically, they were worlds apart. It should be added that the psychic breakdown of the two extremists in middle age was not without significance for the ultimate meaning of their doctrines. Also, like the Danish philosopher, R. Menahem Mendel was convinced that the love of woman was incompatible with the love of God, save that a Jew was obligated to have children.

The Kotzker pattern of piety was bitterly opposed by some hasidic groups as well as by the growing camp of the "enlightened" (*maskilim*). Seen in the perspective of history, we cannot doubt that the extremist ardor of Kotzk served to widen the horizons of Jewish piety.

J.B.A.

KOVALENKO, Elimelekh (1883–27 *Tishri* 1964) – Son of R. Mordecai (d. 1891), the rabbi of Varnikov, near Kiev, and a descendant of R. Israel of Ruzhyn, Elimelekh was known as an outstanding Torah scholar. In 1902 he succeeded his maternal grandfather, R. Simhah Stienpress, as rabbi of Ostropol. During the Communist revolution, he did much to strengthen Jewish religious observance in Russia.

In 1928 he moved to Riga, Latvia, and two years later settled in New York, where he founded the *Anshei Sfard* congregation in Williamsburg. He was an authority on circumcision and acted as a *mohel*.

A.Sh.

KOZIENICE, Israel Hofstein (1733–14 *Tishri* 1815), the Maggid of Kozienice – One of the earliest leaders of Polish Hasidism was the Maggid of Kozienice. He was born in Opatov near Sandormiersz to Shabbetai, a poor bookbinder. The boy received his early talmudic education from the rabbi of Opatov, R. Dov Berish Katz. Later he studied in Ostrowiec under R. Yehezkel and in Horochov, Volhynia, under R. Mordecai Tzvi Horowitz. After the death of his father on 25 *Shevat* 1761, he settled in Przysucha, where he came under the influence of R. Abraham of Przysucha, from who he acquired knowledge not only of the Talmud and Kabbalah but also of the art of *maggidut* (preaching). He became a teacher, eventually making his way to Mezhirech. "I had studied 800 books on Kabbalah," the newcomer remarked with humility. "But when I arrived in the presence of the Maggid, I realized that I had not even begun to study."

After the death of the Maggid, he came under the influence of R. Elimelekh of Lejask. In 1765 he became Maggid of Kozienice, a small town northeast of Radom. To supplement his meager stipend, he also preached in the neighboring towns of Magnuszov and Grice.

He wrote prolifically. Among his published works are *Avodat Yisrael*, discourses on the Torah and the Ethics of the Fathers (Josefov, 1842); *Or Yisrael* (Czernowitz, 1862); *Nezer Yisrael* (Vilna, 1822); and *Bet Yisrael* on tractates *Pesahim*, *Betzah*, *Hagigah*, and *Mo'ed Katan* (Warsaw, 1864).

His writings and responsa demonstrate his mastery of Halakhah and earned him the respect of his contemporaries. His literary productivity and manifold communal commitments are the more astonishing when one considers that all his life he was frail in physique and beset by many ailments. Often he was too weak to rise from his bed and needed many blankets to warm him. Every day he had to be carried to the *Bet HaMidrash*. He never forgot the poverty of his early youth. He was a father to many orphans and brought up a number of them in his own house. When, in 1778, a fire ravaged the Jewish quarter of Kozienice, he financed the rebuilding of a whole street, which became known as the Maggid's street, and he allocated the houses to the poor. He himself lived in austere surroundings, for he had no desire for material comforts. His fame spread beyond the Jewish community, and he was visited by such Polish nobles as Adam Czartoryski, Josef Poniatowski, and Prince Radziwill.

He was deeply concerned with the welfare of Jewry as a whole. He urged the Russian government to abolish the tax on *shehitah*. In common with most hasidic rabbis, he opposed Napoleon. He attracted a number of magnates to his court, such as Shmuel Zbitkower, the "Rothschild of Polish Jewry." His son Berek Dov Bergson and his wife, Tamarel, were devoted followers of the Maggid. A number of the Maggid's disciples were employees of the benevolent Bergsons.

A passionate bibliophile, he rejoiced in a fine collection of early prints. He was instrumental in having hitherto unobtainable volumes printed, and it was also thanks to him that a number of kabbalistic manuscripts first appeared in print.

His son Mottel died in his father's lifetime, so it was his second son, R. Mosheh Elikum Beria, who succeeded him.

A father to his followers, and a statesman as well as a scholar, he was one of the most powerful pillars of Polish Hasidism.

A. Y. Bromberg, *Bet Kozienice*, pp. 11–52.

KRANZLER, Gershon (b. 1916)–Educated at the Julius-Maximilian University of Wuerzburg, Germany, and at Columbia University, New York, he graduated with a master's degree in 1943 and a doctorate in sociology in 1954. From 1967 to 1984 he was an instructor of sociology at the John Hopkins University, Baltimore.

At one time he was principal of the Jewish Day and High Schools of the Talmudical Academy of Baltimore.

Among his publications are *Williamsburg, a Jewish Community in transition* (New York, 1961), which won a prize as the best study of Jewish life in the United States and Canada in 1967, *The Face of Faith: An American Hasidic Community* (Ktav, 1973), and *Williamsburg Memories* (C.I.S., Lakewood, NJ, 1991).

KROCHMAL, Nahman (1785–1840), historian and philosopher–Born in Brody, son of a rich merchant, he became known as the "Mendelssohn of Galicia." At the age of fourteen he married and lived in Zalkiev, where he later became the head of the community. He was, for a time, the collector of a tax on the distilling of liquor. His main work, *Moreh Nevukhei HaZeman*, was published posthumously by L. Zunz (Lvov, 1851). In its seventeen chapters he traces the evolution of Judaism from the beginning of the Babylonian captivity to the expulsion from Spain.

In his lifetime, the hasidim of Galicia considered him their great opponent. They attacked him particularly because of his friendly exchange of letters with a neighboring Karaite scholar. In reply, Krochmal issued a circular letter, decrying the fanaticism of his enemies and calling for a more tolerant attitude toward that ancient Jewish sect. He attacked Hasidism, especially the dynasty of R. Tzvi Hirsch of Zydaczov. He maintained that Hasidism prospered only in lands of ignorance, that the rebbes were concerned mainly with their own material comforts, and that they encouraged superstition and drunkenness.

His ideas, however, have many affinities with the teachings of Kabbalah. He appreciated the hasidic emphasis on naive faith, and he pointed out that piety is generally perverted by the believers, veering toward either one or the other extreme–either toward skepticism or superstition or toward mysticism or materialism. His notion that the "spirit of the people" is reflected in all facets of public life parallels the Besht's idea that the Holy One, blessed be He, is served in all ways.

Krochmal's assertion about the uniqueness of the Jewish people not only in their ideal but also in terms of their collective being also has its roots in hasidic thought, as does his idea that the Jewish soul clings to the absolute spirit (*HaRuhani HaMuhlot*), Hasidism maintaining that the wisdom of the nations derives from the "shell of radiance" (*klippot nogah*), whereas the wisdom of Israel proceeds from the Lord Himself.

N. Rotenstreich, *Jewish Philosophy in Modern Times*, pp. 136–148.

M. Waxman, *A History of Jewish Literature*, vol. 3, pp. 451ff. and 456.

J.B.A.

KVITTEL (lit., slip, short note)—The *kvittel* is the name given to the petition (small note) presented by a hasid to the rebbe.

The *kvittel* originates from the time of the Besht. There is no trace of it in the works of R. Yitzhak Luria. Some writers, however, such as R. Yekutiel Kamelhar (*Dor De'ah* [Bilgoraj, 1933], p. 36) and M. Justman (*Fun unzer alten Otzar* [Warsaw, 1932]) find an allusion to it in the commentary of Nahmanides (Numbers 1:45). In the course of time, the *kvittel* assumed great importance.

The text would normally read:

> To his honored holiness, our lord, our teacher, and our master, may he live for many days:
>
> Please do rouse the mercies from the fount of true mercies and graces on [name and the mother's name], who is suffering from [nature of illness or problem].

The *kvittel* is accompanied by a contribution, *pidyon nefesh* (redemption of the soul), indicating that by this charitable offering the hasidim would redeem themselves. The hasidim may write their own *kvittel*, though normally the rebbe's *gabbai* writes it.

The rebbe reads the *kvittel* once. If he prayed at his ancestors' graveside, he would read the *kvittel* there again, and also before the sounding of the *shofar* on *Rosh Hashanah*.

R. Abraham Joshua Heschel of Opatov took all the *kvittlech* and said, "I bless all the people who are included in these petitions." In an emergency, a *kvittel* may be given in absentia. The rebbe would be especially delighted if he received a *Baal Shemesque Kvittel*. This is what the Apter rebbe called a *kvittel* that requested advice and a blessing in the service of God. At one time, R. Shneur Zalman of Liady refused to accept any other type of *kvittel*, making it clear that his function was not to be a procurer of material blessings. Similarly, R. Menahem Mendel of Kotzk refused to grant his hasidim such blessings, concerning himself only with spiritual matters.

Occasionally, a number of hasidim banded together and presented a comprehensive *kvittel*. It was regarded as a bad omen to drop a *kvittel*. *Kvittlech* would sometimes be placed at the graves of *tzaddikim* and at the *Kotel Maravi* in Jerusalem. There were fixed times when a hasid presented a *kvittel*. It was called in Yiddish *praven*, and Lubavitch hasidim call it *Yehidut*. Sometimes, hasidim would inscribe their names on the margins of their rebbe's prayer book, so that he would be reminded of them when praying.

The hasidim believed that their rebbes were endowed with the Holy Spirit (*Ruah HaKodesh*) and hence that they belonged to the general category of prophets. The prayer of the prophet is singularly effective. At the time of the prophet Samuel, it was customary to give a gift to the prophet in exchange for his theurgic help (1 Samuel 9:8).

Some even permitted a non-Jew to ride to the rebbe on a Sabbath to deliver a *kvittel*.

In the words of R. Elimelekh of Lejask, "It follows that through [the] giving of money to the rebbe, the power of the 'shells' (*klippot*) is broken; a powerful bond with the *tzaddik* is established, preventing the hasid from committing a grave sin and helping [hasidim] to be sanctified through the rebbe" (*Noam Elimelekh*, *Korah*).

Z. M. Schachter, *The Yehidut*, p. 187f.

J.B.A. and Z.M.S

L

LACHOWICZE, Mordecai, of Lachowicze (1742–17 *Shevat* 1810)–Son of R. Noah of Nesvizh, he was a disciple of R. Solomon of Karlin. After the martyr's death of his master, he studied under R. Barukh of Medziborz. He settled in Lachowicze, near Slutsk, where he became the target of the antihasidic polemics of Israel Loebel. He nonetheless gained many followers in Slutsk and Vilna and carried hasidic doctrines to northeastern Lithuania.

In 1798, he and R. Asher of Stolin were arrested at the instigation of mitnaggedic informers. His liberation, on the fifth day of Hanukkah, was celebrated as a holiday among the hasidim of Lachowicze.

He supported R. Abraham of Kalisk in his dispute against R. Shneur Zalman of Liady. He maintained that the *tzaddikim* did not come into this world to help satisfy the worldly needs of the hasidim but to instill into Jewish hearts the belief in the divine name and the fear of heaven.

He was in charge of funds for the Holy Land. Every day, without fail, when he got up in the morning, before each meal, and before and after study, he would set aside a small sum of money for the Holy Land. Among his disciples were R. Michael of Lachowicze, R. Moses of Kobrin, and R. Asher I of Stolin.

He died while on a visit to Stolin and was buried there. His son and successor was R. Noah.

W. Z. Rabinowitsch, *Lithuanian Hasidism*, pp. 150–156.

LACHOWICZE, Noah (1774–8 *Tishri* 1832)–Son of R. Mordecai, he succeeded his father as rebbe in 1810. In 1821, he issued the following appeal: "Throughout his life, my revered father not only preached but also performed the *mitzvah* of supporting the Jewish settlers in the Holy Land. . . . Therefore, my beloved brethren, do not neglect this precept, but look after it as the apple of your eye."

Some of his discourses can be found in *Torat Avot*. Among his disciples were R. Moses of Kobrin and R. Abraham Weinberg of Slonim.

R. Noah had no sons, and after his death the hasidim were divided in their allegiance: one group followed his son-in-law, R. Mordecai II; another joined R. Solomon Hayyim, the grandson of R. Mordecai I, who settled in Koidanov.

W. Z. Rabinowitsch, *Lithuanian Hasidism*, pp. 156–160.

LAG BAOMER–The thirty-third day of the *Omer*, corresponding to the eighteenth day of the month of *Iyyar*. This day has a great significance for the kabbalists, for it is the anniversary of the death of R. Simon Bar Yohai, to whom tradition has ascribed the authorship of the *Zohar* and who is regarded as the spiritual father of Hasidism.

R. Yitzhak Luria, according to the testimony of his disciple R. Hayyim Vital, would visit Meron with his family and stay there for three days. In Israel today, hasidim and pietists still converge on the white-domed tomb at Meron on *Lag BaOmer*. Psalms are recited and passages from the *Zohar* are quoted. At the stroke of twelve midnight, the *hadlakah* (bonfire) is lit. By tradition, the honor of kindling the fire belongs to the rabbi of Boyan.

Hasidic rebbes, especially the rebbes of Ruzhyn, would have special gatherings on that day. R. Barukh of Medziborz would dance with the *Zohar* in his hands. To R. Levi Yitzhak of Berdichev, the day was a foretaste of the Festival of Pentecost. R.

Samuel Heller regarded Meron as a very holy place.

In the Diaspora, visits would be paid to the graves of rebbes, especially to the grave of R. Tzvi Hirsch of Zydaczov, the "prince of the *Zohar*," and to the grave of R. Israel, the Maggid of Kozienice, who, according to hasidic legend, was the incarnation of R. Simon Bar Yohai.

Y. Alfasi, *Bisdei HaHasidut*, p. 356.

LAMED VAV TZADDIKIM–The concept of hidden *tzaddikim* (*Lamed Vavniks*) is already found in talmudic literature. Abaye, a Babylonian teacher of the fourth century, is the first to refer to the number thirty-six (*Sanhedrin* 97b and *Sukkah* 45b). The *Tikkunei Zohar* (ch. 21) maintained that there are two groups of thirty-six *tzaddikim*: one in the Land of Israel, and the other in the Diaspora. The idea of thirty-six secret saints became very popular in the Middle Ages.

In hasidic doctrine, the *tzaddik* who is a *nister* (concealed) ranks higher than the one who is *mefursam* (revealed), and a number of hasidic rebbes, such as R. Aryeh Leib Sarah's, were considered to be among the *Lamed Vav*. In the *Shivhei HaBesht*, a hosemaker was regarded by the Besht as one of the thirty-six righteous people upon whom the existence of the world depends (Tale 87).

Great significance was attached to the number thirty-six. The Besht did not reveal himself until his thirty-sixth year. Andre Schwartz-Bart in his novel *Le Dernier des Justes* (*The Last of the Just*) (1959) utilizes this theme.

G. Scholem, *Jewish Chronicle* (London) April, 21 1961, p. 23.

LANDAU, Aaron Tzvi, of Biala (d. 7 *Sivan* 1910)–Son of R. Berish Landau, he was a disciple of R. Yehiel Danziger and of his son, R. Yerahmiel Israel Yitzhak of Alexander. He declined to become rebbe and was engaged in business.

It was only after the death of the rebbe of Alexander in 1910 and for the last year of his own life that he became rebbe and settled in Biala. He died in Otwock. He was survived by his son and successor, R. Menahem Mendel (d. 1938).

Some of his discourses are to be found in *Shemesh U'Magen* (Tel Aviv, 1953).

LANDAU, Abraham (b. 1920)–Son of R. Jacob Yitzhak Don and a grandson of R. Zeev of Strykov, Abraham studied in the *Yeshivat Hakhmei Lublin* under R. Meir Shapira and R. Zeev Soloveitchik of Brest-Litovsk.

He became rebbe in 1946 and made his home in Tel Aviv. He is renowned for his scholarship and has established a *kollel*.

LANDAU, Alter Joseph David, of Oleczyce (d. 29 Av 1942)–Son of R. Simon Shlomoh of Oleczyce, he married the daughter of R. Hayyim Hager of Ottynia. On the death of his wife, he married the daughter of R. Shmuel Weinberg of Slonim. He became rebbe in 1897. He attended every poor wedding to gladden the hearts of the bride and bridegroom.

Together with his son R. Tzvi Aryeh, he was murdered by the Nazis.

LANDAU, Bezalel (b. 1924), author–Born in Jerusalem, he studied in the *yeshivah Etz Hayyim* and in *Mea Shearim*. He was the editor of *Hamodia* and is the author of *Baal Shem Tov U'Benei Heikhalah* (1961), *Tiferet Avot* on Biala (Jerusalem, 1967), and a biography of R. Elimelekh of Lejask. He is the author of many popular articles on Hasidism.

LANDAU, Dov Berish, of Biala (1820–25 *Nisan* 1876)–Second son of R. Abraham Landau of Ciechanov, who had five sons. He studied under his father and under R. Yitzhak of Warka and his son R. Menahem Mendel of Warka. He visited R. Menahem Mendel of Kotzk. He married Rachel, the daughter of R. Itche Meir of Biala, where he settled.

He declined rabbinical posts, and his wife opened a whiskey distillery. When that venture failed, she opened a small inn. After the death of R. Menahem Mendel of Kotzk, R. Dov Berish was regarded by many hasidim as his true heir. He attracted many followers and was known as a miracle worker. He was an ascetic and fasted regularly. He used a stone as a pillow and requested that that stone be used for his gravestone. He conducted *tish* and delivered discourses even on weekdays.

Among his disciples were R. Yehiel of Alexander and R. Simon Kalish of Skierniewice. He was survived by his sons R. Jacob Yitzhak, R. Aaron Tzvi, and R. Menahem Mendel. His son R. Simhah Bunem succeeded him.

His discourses are to be found in *Shemesh U'Magen Zikhron Menahem* (Tel Aviv, 1953) and *Kuntres Maggid Devarav LeYaakov* (Warsaw, 1930).

LANDAU, Ezekiel, of Prague (1713–1793) – A halakhic authority of universal recognition, Landau was a determined opponent of Hasidism, considering the claim made for the hasidic *tzaddik* as a "seer" (*ro'eh*) gifted with prophetic powers to be a serious departure from the rabbinic norm. His particular opposition was expressed in his objection to the hasidic adoption of the mystical formula coined by the kabbalists to be recited before the performance of the *mitzvot*: "for the sake of the unification of the Holy One, blessed be He, and His Shekhinah" (*leshem yihud*). It is probable that Landau's suspicion of the formula, containing ideas used by the Shabbateans for their heretical views, arose because crypto-Shabbateans were known to be active in Prague at that time. It is not without significance that no objection to the formula is found in other anti-hasidic polemics.

In Responsa *Noda bi-yhudah* (Zolkiew, 1823, *Yoreh De'ah*, no. 93), Landau writes:

> To the generations before ours, who did not know of this formula and never recited it but labored all their days in the Torah and the precepts, all in accordance with the Talmud and Codes whose words flow from the spring of living waters, the verse can be applied: "The integrity of the upright shall guide them" (Prov. 11:3). They are the ones who produced fruit on high and whose love was higher than the heavens. But in this generation they have forsaken the spring of living waters, namely, the two Talmuds, Babylonian and Palestinian, to hew out for themselves broken cisterns. They exalt themselves in their arrogant heart, each of them saying: "I am the seer. To me are the gates of Heaven open. Through my merit does the world endure." These are the destroyers of the generation. To this orphaned generation I apply the verse: "The ways of the Lord are right, and the just do walk in them, but the hasidim [substitution for "transgressors" in the verse] do stumble therein" (Hosea 14:10).

The hasidic reply in defense of the formula is found in the work *Shaar HaTefillah* ([Sudzilkov, 1813] responsum at beg., pp. 3–10), by R. Hayyim of Czernowitz (d. 1813). With deference to Landau's erudition and authority, Hayyim accuses him, nevertheless, of arrogance in dismissing the formula and the implied need for inwardness in religion, which it seeks to inculcate.

Although in his youth Landau had studied the Kabbalah in the *klaus* at Brody, he differs, too, from the hasidim by refusing to believe that we in this life can attain to any real understanding of this science and claiming we should concentrate all our intellectual efforts on the study of the Talmud and the Codes – the knowledge of the Kabbalah being merely the alphabet learned by children so they can later converse with others – and that only in the hereafter will we be capable of grasping the kabbalistic mysteries (*Tzion LeNefesh Hayyah*, *Berakhot* [Prague, 1791], Introduction).

It is said that when Landau received a copy of the work *Toldot Yaakov Yosef*, by R. Jacob Joseph of Polonnoye, he trampled it underfoot and ordered it to be publicly burned as a heretical work. According to the legend, this led R. Jacob Samson of Sheptovka, a disciple of the Great Maggid, to engage in a debate in defense of hasidic doctrine. The debate has frequently been published, but Dubnow claims there is no evidence of its being other than apocryphal.

L. Jacobs, *Hasidic Prayer*, pp. 140–153.

L.J.

LANDAU, Jacob Bene Berak (1893–1986) – A native of Russia, he studied in the *yeshivah Tomhei Temimim* and was ordained by R. Mendel Zak and R. Joseph Rozin. A hasid of R. Shlomoh Dov Baer of Lubavitch, he served as rabbi in Libau, Latvia, and was befriended by R. Joseph Yitzhak Schneersohn of Lubavitch.

In 1923 he emigrated to the Holy Land and a year later was appointed rabbi of Bene Berak, where he served for nearly half a century.

LANDAU, Jacob, of Ciechanov (1834–19 *Tevet* 1898) – Youngest son of R.

Abraham, he married the daughter of R. Aaron of Biala. He was a devoted disciple of R. Menahem Mendel of Kotzk and of R. Yitzhak Meir Alter of Ger. He became rabbi first in Nasielsk and then in Ciechanov.

In 1890, he emigrated to the Holy Land. He later returned to Poland and became rabbi in Yezuv, near Lodz. He was known as "R. Yankele Yezuver."

He died and was buried in Warsaw.

He left many manuscripts, among them a commentary on the Pentateuch and some novellae on the Talmud and *Yoreh De'ah*.

LANDAU, Jacob Yitzhak Don, of Strykov (1882–Heshvan 1942) – Son of R. Elimelekh Menahem Mendel, he was born in Zalszyn. He became known as the rebbe of Kinov, which was his first rabbinical post. He succeeded his father in 1936 and was reluctant to leave Kinov because it was close to Ostrowiec, the home of R. Meir Yehiel Halevi. However, when Kinov was burned down, he moved to Zegierz, where he established a *yeshivah Bet Aaron* and started to publish a rabbinical periodical *Bet Aaron*.

He was active in the Aguda and participated in the third *Knessiyyah HaGedolah* in Marienbad. During the Second World War he lived in Warsaw, where he worked for a time in the Shultz factory and was active in the *Ezrat Torah*, which helped refugee rabbis.

Together with his son R. Tuviah and son-in-law, R. Abraham Weinberg of Slonim, he was murdered in Treblinka. Another son, R. Abraham, is the rebbe of Strykov in Israel.

LANDAU, Menahem Mendel (d. 2 *Elul* 1938) – Son of R. Aaron and a grandson of R. Berish of Biala, his mother, Esther, was the daughter of R. Nathan Tennenbaum, a hasid of Izbice. In 1914, he succeeded his father, first living in Biala, then in Szydlowiec and, during the First World War, in Warsaw.

In 1925, he emigrated to the United States, settling in New York. He was the author of *Shemesh U'Magen*, which was edited by his son, R. Yehiel Landau of Tel Aviv in 1953.

LANDAU, Menahem Mendel Hayyim (1861–7 *Adar* 1935) – Son of R. Jacob, he was brought up by his grandfather R. Abraham Landau of Ciechanov and was ordained by R. Joshua Trunk of Kutno and R. Hayyim Eliezer Waks of Kalish. A nonconformist, he studied modern Hebrew and Jewish history, subjects outside the *yeshivah* curriculum. He married the daughter of R. Solomon Zalman. His wife opened a small shop to support them.

He was rabbi in Vaidova from 1886, and in 1896, he succeeded his father as rabbi of Novy Dvor.

In his controversial work *Mekitz Nirdamim* (Piotrokov, 1904), he urged religious Jews to combine secular and religious studies, to reorganize the *heder* system, and to provide education for girls.

He was a member of the Polish rabbinical association and one of the few hasidic rebbes to join the Mizrachi.

After the Balfour Declaration, he appealed in the *HaZafirah*, the Hebrew paper appearing in Warsaw, for support of the Mizrachi. He participated in the Mizrachi conference in Amsterdam in 1920, at which he was elected honorary president.

He visited London in 1921 and for eight years lived in Brooklyn and Detroit in the United States. He then returned to Poland and died in Otwock. He was buried in Warsaw.

He was the author of *Ateret Zekeinim* (Piotrokov, 1912), *Meir Einei Hakhamim* (Lodz, 1937), and a commentary on the *Haggadah* (Lodz, 1939).

Encyclopedia shel HaZionit HaDatit, vol. 3, pp. 222–226.

LANDAU, Tzvi Aryeh (1890–1966) Son of R. Simon Solomon of Olyka, a descendant of R. Moses Savran and the Maggid of Chernobyl. His father died when he was seven years old, and he was brought up by his brother. On the advice of R. David Moses of Chortkov, he became rebbe.

In 1914, he married the daughter of R. Jacob Leib of Turisk, and when she died, he married Sarah Feige, the daughter of R. Pinhas of Lachowicze, a son-in-law of R. Pinhas of Karlin.

In 1924, he emigrated to the United States, where he established a community *Ateret Tzvi Ben Shimon Shlomoh*. He was a member of the rabbinical association and was very active in education.

Toldot Anshei Shem, p. 70.

LANDAU, Zeev Wolf, of Strykov (1807–11 *Elul* 1891)–Elder son of R. Abraham Landau of Ciechanov, he married the daughter of R. Zanvil Weiner of Strykov. He was a disciple of R. Menahem Mendel of Kotzk and R. Yitzhak Meir Alter of Ger.

The rebbe of Kotzk made a great impression on him. "I am not surprised," said his friend R. Meir Yehiel Lipshitz of Gostynin, "that he remembers the discourses of R. Mendel better than I do. But what amazes me is that he has not forgotten even a letter or a gesture."

He succeeded his father as rebbe in 1875, when he was sixty-eight years old. He was the author of *Zeer Zahav Keter Torah*–comments on Torah and Festivals–which was printed in Warsaw in 1901. It also has an appendix, *Amarot Tehorot*.

His grandson published his *Mikhtavim*, an anthology of letters, discourses, and poems (Lodz, 1926). He was an elegant stylist who advocated the study of Hebrew as a spoken language.

Two of his sons, R. Mosheh Hayyim and R. Yehiel Michael, died in his lifetime. His surviving sons, R. Mordecai Mottel of Strykov and R. Menahem Mendel of Gombyn, maintained the dynasty of Strykov.

LANGER, Abraham, of Knihynice (1863–28 *Tammuz* 1918)–Son of R. Yehudah Tzvi of Stretyn, he became rabbi of Knihynice, Galicia, at the age of eighteen. In 1907 he succeeded his father as rebbe and became known as a miracle worker.

During the First World War, he took refuge in Budapest, where he died. His son R. Moses succeeded him as rebbe.

LANGER, George Mordecai (Jiri) (1894–1943)–He was part of a circle of Prague Jewish writers that included Kafka. In 1913 this "Western sophisticate" made a journey to the East, "inspired by a secret longing." His goal was the hasidic village of Belz in eastern Galicia. Although he was much attracted by a community that was living in a "state of unending ecstasy entirely beyond time, space, and matter" and was entirely willing to give up Western notions of success and career motivation, Langer found it difficult to surrender the more spiritual fruits of Western culture such as poetry and classical music.

He writes that when he was tired of learning, the marshes were his only means of "*spiritual* refreshment in all this wilderness." Moreover, his Western preconceptions of hygiene were appalled by the fact that dirt and insects seemed to be necessary preconditions of sainthood. Hard, too, was it for him to gain complete acceptance in his new society. The distant politeness of his fellow hasidim thawed when, through undernourishment, lack of exercise and air, and a suitable transformation of vestments, he came to look more like them. Conflict, however, was never quite eradicated from Jiri's soul, and while trying vainly to achieve hasidic joy, he was still revolted by what he termed "puritanism," "isolation," "ignorance," and "backwardness."

When he returned to his family, he had to contend with friction there too. In his Foreword to his brother's hasidic anthology *Nine Gates to the Hasidic Mysteries*, the poet Frantisek Langer makes it plain he regarded Jiri's religious foibles as a "case of belated adolescent psychopathy" on the strength of which he got him discharged from the army. Jiri, however, insisted on viewing this exemption as a direct intervention by the Belzer rebbe, and he spent the rest of the war with the hasidim. In the latter part of his life, however, he became again outwardly Europeanized.

For him Hasidism was "the Kabbalah made accessible to the people." The hasidim were notable for having elevated the occult above everything, and perhaps their most beautiful doctrine, according to Langer, is their stress on the ultimate fusion of the holy with all things. The heroic human being can release the sparks of godliness imprisoned in all matter.

J. Langer, *Nine Gates to the Hasidic Mysteries*.

F.G.

LANGER, Moses, of Toronto (1878–13 *Adar* 1945)–Son of R. Judah Tzvi of Stretyn, he was born in Brutchin. His mother, Gittel Leah, was the daughter of R. Solomon of Rozdol. He married Fruma, the daughter of R. Shalom Babad and from 1907 was rebbe in Stretyn, near Lvov.

In 1920, he settled in Toronto, where he established his *Bet HaMidrash*. He was survived by his sons–R. Mordecai, R. Shlomoh, and R. Yitzhak Eizig–and two daughters.

LANGER, Uri, of New York (5 *Elul* 1896–4 *Elul* 1970)–Son of Abraham of Stretyn, he was born in Knihynicze. He married his cousin the daughter of R. Israel of Arad. From 1918 to 1921, he was rabbi in Knihynicze, and in 1924, he emigrated to the United States.

He lived on East 4th Street, in New York, and was the rabbi of the *Hesed LeAvraham* community.

He was a prolific writer and was the author of *Nehmad VeNa'im* on the Torah (New York, 1934), *Or HaAggadah* on the *Aggadot* of the Talmud (Brooklyn, 1942), *Or HaDe'ah* (Brooklyn, 1958), and *Or HaHaggim* (Brooklyn, 1955).

LANGER, Uri, of Rohatyn (1820–18 *Iyyar* 1889)–Son of R. Yitzhak Langer, the rabbi of Tartakov, he married Sarah, the daughter of R. Abraham of Stretyn. He was a disciple of R. Israel of Ruzhyn and R. Yitzhak Isaac of Zydaczov. His discourses and customs are recorded in *Hillulei DeRabbi* (Kolomyja, 1890).

He was survived by his sons–R. Yehudah Tzvi, R. Yitzhak Aaron, and R. Yisrael.

A. Shu.

LAWAT, Abraham David, of Nikolayev (1835–1890), *Habad* scholar–Son of R. Yehudah Leib, he was a disciple of R. Menahem Mendel Schneersohn and of his son, R. Samuel. In 1875 he became rabbi in Nikolayev, where he established a *yeshivah*.

He was the author of *Kav Naki* (Warsaw, 1868), on the laws of divorce, and *Bet Aharon VeTosafot* (Vilna, 1881).

H. M. Heilman, *Bet Rebbe*, vol. 3, p. 21.

LEBOVITCH, Barukh Yehudah, of New York (1909–6 *Adar* II 1951)–Son of R. Michael, he was born in Hungary and was a descendant of R. Samuel (Shmelke) of Nikolsburg.

In 1927, he married Yentel, the daughter of R. Shmelke Schnitzler. He acted as *dayan* at Kish. He spent the war years in Nazi labor camps.

After the war, he emigrated to New York, where he died.

His son, R. Menahem Mendel (b. 1930), is the head of *Bet Birkhat Yehudah Bet HaMidrash* in London.

LECZNA, Solomon Leib, of Leczna (1778–19 *Nisan* 1843)–Son of R. Barukh of Rszeszov, he was a disciple of R. Mendel of Rymanov and of R. Jacob Yitzhak, the "Seer" of Lublin and the "Holy Jew" of Przysucha. "Each time he comes to my room," said the "Holy Jew," "I feel a sense of holiness."

His first rabbinical post was in Bokovsk, near Sanok, and later he succeeded R. Eizig as the rebbe of Leczna, in the Lublin province.

Apart from delivering discourses, he would refrain from speaking on the Sabbath. Every detail of the Sabbath was precious to him. He even kissed the twelve loaves on the table. He greeted each visitor affectionately, calling him "my son" or "my brother." Unlike many hasidic rebbes, he recited *yotzerot* (liturgical poems).

Among his disciples were R. Samuel of Sianiawa, R. Mattathias of Kosov, and R. Mottel of Neustadt. Many of his discourses are found in *Toldot Adam* (Yosefov, 1878), published by his son and successor, R. Joshua of Ostrova. His other son was R. Abraham, who married the daughter of R. Samuel of Slonim. His daughter Esther married R. Moses Leib Kligsberg, who settled in the Holy Land. His second daughter, Lieba, married R. Leibish of Leczna.

Tiferet Avot, pp. 78–79.

LEIB SARAH'S (1730–1791)–Aryeh Leib ben Sarah was one of the early figures of Hasidism. He is known by his mother's name, a feature not uncommon in those days. In his case a fanciful reason has been given: His mother, Sarah, fell victim to the glances of the son of the local potentate (*poretz*, in the Hebrew-Yiddish phrase). She was at that time a young unmarried girl, and in order to avoid his advances, she married very suddenly and of her free will an elderly widower who was the local *melamed* (teacher) and who was known for his extreme piety. As a reward for her modesty, she gave birth to a son who became a great and pious man. His father claimed descent from the famous R. Judah Loew, Maharal of Prague, after whom the boy was named–Loew being a form of Leib.

At the age of fifteen the lad is said to have visited the Besht. The boy displayed his devotions by means of certain ecstatic pranks and was warned by the master that such behavior involved danger. The master advised him to go cautiously in the path of godliness. Leib Sarah's inherited from the Besht the task of seeking out the thirty-six righteous men who exist unnoticed in each generation (*Sanhedrin* 97b). He would help these by supporting them from his funds.

Leib founded no dynasty of *tzaddikim* and held no court but was what one might call an itinerant *tzaddik*. The Maggid of Mezhirech received a visit from Leib, who boasted that his purpose in visiting R. Baer was in order to watch him don and remove his slippers. R. Baer gave him a letter commending Leib as a man of unsullied character and asking all to support him in his collections for the poor and pious.

Leib Sarah's name has become associated with that of the Austrian emperor Joseph II. The latter had planned secular education for the Jews of his realm as a compulsory measure, but many detected an ulterior motive behind it–that of ultimate assimilation. The emperor received a series of visits from an invisible elder who troubled him; this was Reb Leib.

By his own injunction, Leib was buried in a modest grave without any imposing tombstone but with a simple stone bearing only his name. It was eventually encircled by a simple enclosure with a thatched covering. Every effort to erect a more handsome building over the tomb brought tragic results to the builder. It was only when a descendant of Reb Leib tried to build a permanent roof over the hut that the builder fell without injury and the project was abandoned.

It is possible that the family name Baharal, given to some of Leib's descendants, is an abbrevation of Ben HaRav Leib.

Y. Raphael, *Sefer HaHasidut*, p. 30.

S. A. Horodetzky, *HaHasidut VeHaHasidim*, vol. 1, p. 84.

A.T.

LEIFER, Aaron Aryeh Leib (1740–2 *Adar* I 1813)–Son of R. Meir of Przemyshlan, he regularly visited R. Levi Yitzhak of Berdichev and R. Menahem Mendel of Rymanov. He was renowned for his scholarship. He served as a teacher in a small village near Lvov.

On becoming rebbe, he attracted disciples of the caliber of R. Mordecai of Neshizh and R. Menahem Mendel of Kosov.

He was succeeded by his son, R. Yitzhak of Kalusz.

LEIFER, Aaron Aryeh Leib, of Nadvorna (1817–14 *Shevat* 1897)–Son of R. Issachar Dov Bertshe of Nadvorna, he succeeded his father as rebbe. He was the author of *Yad Aaron* (Lvov, 1904).

He was survived by his sons, R. Moses and by R. Yitzhak.

LEIFER, Aaron Moses, of Huszt (19 *Kislev* 1906–1991)–Son of R. Shmuel Shmelke of Huszt, he was brought up by his grandfather R. Israel Yaakov, whom he succeeded. He married Perl, the daughter of the rabbi of Skola. At the outbreak of the Second World War, he stayed in Budapest and miraculously survived the Holocaust. He settled in the Williamsburg section of Brooklyn, New York, where his home was a refuge for new immigrants.

He was interred on the Mount of Olives. He was survived by his son R. Shmuel Shmelke, who is the head of *Yeshivah Torat Hesed* in Borough Park in Brooklyn. His other son, R. Barukh Pinhas, is the head of the *yeshivah* of Ger in Borough Park.

LEIFER, Aaron Moses, of Zolinia (1855–7 *Heshvan* 1923)–Son of R. Mordecai of Nadvorna, he married Perel Rosa, the daughter of Elijah Reich of Rzeszov. He became rebbe in Zolinia, and though he moved to Berutshin and to Lancut, he always remained the "rebbe of Zolinia."

He was known for his medical knowledge, and people came to him for prescriptions. He was an ascetic and fasted the whole week. On Saturday night he would play the violin.

His son, R. Tzvi Elimelekh, died in his lifetime. He was survived by two daughters, Gitel and Rebeccah.

LEIFER, Abraham Abba, of Pittsburgh/Ashdod (18 *Kislev* 1918–1990)–He was born in Nagykaroly, the son of R. Joseph, who had, in 1926, emigrated to Pittsburgh, Pennsylvania, where he acted as rebbe. His wife and children (five sons and daughters) joined him in 1927. Four years later, Abraham and two of his brothers returned to Europe to study under R. Shlomoh Zalman Friedman in Rahov, Romania, and under R. Yehudah Siegel Rosner. In 1939 he married his cousin Rachel, the daughter of R. Ittamar Rosenbaum of Czernowitz.

After spending the war years in labor camps, he became rabbi in Czernowitz. In 1947 he emigrated to the United States, where, after staying for a time with his father in Pittsburgh, he settled in Newark, New Jersey, where he established a *yeshivah Beer Mayim Hayyim*.

In 1966, on the death of his father, he succeeded him as rebbe of Pittsburgh. Four years later he made his home in Ashdod, Israel, where he established *Shikkun Pittsburgh* for 250 families. He founded a *kollel Tzidkat Yosef*, a Talmud Torah, *Yad Ittamar*, and other educational institutions.

He was survived by his second son, R. Mordecai Issachar Beer, who is the head of the *yeshivah* in Ashdod, his elder son, R. Yaakov Yitzhak Eizig Yehiel, having died at the age of twenty-two.

LEIFER, Issachar Dov Bertshe

(1845–2 *Elul* 1906) – Second son of R. Mordecai of Nadvorna. After serving as rabbi in Nagyszollos for five years, he became rabbi in Satmar in 1900. He married the daughter of R. Eliezer Brandwein of Jezupol.

His son, R. Meir, who originally served as rabbi in Strzyzov and Budapest, emigrated to the United States, where he lived first in Cleveland and then in the Williamsburg section of Brooklyn. R. Meir died on 12 *Nisan* 1941 and was succeeded by his son-in-law, R. Asher Mordecai, founder of the *yeshivah Bene Mordecai* and the *kollel Yad Ittamar*.

LEIFER, Issachar Dov Bertshe, of Nadvorna

(1790–3 *Elul* 1831) – Son of R. Itzikel of Kalusz, he was a disciple of R. Yitzhak of Radziwillov and of R. Uri of Strelisk. He also visited R. Abraham Joshua Heschel of Opatov and R. Israel of Ruzhyn. He married Rachel, the daughter of R. Abraham Leib of Nadvorna.

His son, R. Aron Leib, succeeded him.

LEIFER, Joseph, of Pittsburgh

(1891–5 *Adar* 1966) – Born in Bochnia, son of R. Issachar Dov Bertshe of Nadvorna. He studied in Satmar under R. Yehudah Greenwald, who ordained him. In 1916 he married Sarah Tauba, the daughter of R. Abraham Abba Wolf, the rabbi of Hodorov, and from 1920 to 1925 he was rebbe in Nagykaroly.

He frequently visited the United States and, in 1926, settled in Pittsburgh, as rabbi of the congregation *Ahavat Yisrael*. He was interred in Jerusalem.

He was the author of *Tzidkat Yosef*, published in Bene Berak in 1986.

Two of his sons, who were studying in Europe, perished in the Holocaust. He was survived by his son R. Abraham Abba, who succeeded him in Pittsburgh.

Toldot Anshei Shem, p. 76.

LEIFER, Levi Yitzhak, of Arad, Romania/Haifa

(1875–21 *Tammuz* 1962) – Son of R. Yehiel, he was ordained by R. Meir of Sianiawa. He married in 1914 the daughter of R. Meir Weisblum, and he was rabbi of Arad. He eventually settled in Haifa and was buried on *Har HaMenuhot*.

His sons were R. Joseph Meir of Brooklyn, R. Yehiel of Jerusalem, and R. David Elimelekh of Jerusalem.

LEIFER, Meir, of Craciunesti

(1848–30 *Sivan* 1908) – Third son of R. Mordecai of Nadvorna, he changed his name to Rosenbaum. He married Shifra, the daughter of R. Yehiel of Dorohoi. He became rabbi first in Iasi and then, in 1896, in Craciunesti, near Sighet. He was a perfectionist who never smiled except on Purim and Simhat Torah.

He was survived by R. Eliezer Zeev, who succeeded him.

LEIFER, Mordecai, of Nadvorna

(19 *Iyyar* 1835–1st day Sukkot 1894) – Son of R. Issachar Dov Bertzi. When his father died in the prime of his life, he was brought up by his uncle R. Meir of Przemyshlany, who loved him dearly and applied to him a verse from the Book of Esther: "*Ish Yehudi hayah . . . ushemo Mordecai*" (There was a certain Jew in Shushan, the castle, whose name was Mordecai).

R. Mordecai first settled in Nadvorna and in 1865 moved to Huszt, where the rabbi was R. Moses Schick. He then moved to Bustino. He was completely oblivious to the concept of time. *Shaharit* might finish in time for *Minhah*, or *Maariv* almost in time for *Shaharit*. The windows in his study were boarded up to exclude all daylight. He ate only once a day and lived the life of an ascetic. He asserted that he had been the High Priest in an earlier existence.

Much of his time was spent traveling, visiting the towns and villages of Marmaros. His wife, Hayyah, the daughter of R. Samuel (Shmelke) Taubes, the rabbi of Iasi, was renowned for her piety. The only piece of jewelry she possessed was a *shterentichel* (a kind of tiara), which was either pawned or pledged, but never available for her to wear. The rebbe's following came mainly from the lower classes – villagers, shopkeepers, arendars, tailors, cobblers, and tree-fellers. He could and did reach their level and their hearts.

His homilies were simple and reflected the life of the hasidim he cared for. They were published under the titles *Maamar Mordecai* (Marmaros Sightet, 1860), *Or Mordecai* (New York, 1956), *Gedulat Mordecai* (Sighet, 1895), and *Tiferet Mordecai* (Bergesacz, 1927). He was also the author of three prayers – two of them to be recited daily and one on the eve of the New Year. They are characterized by simple sincerity and true, deep feeling.

His son, R. Shmuel Shmelke succeeded him as rabbi in Huszt. The members of his family, who survived the Holocaust, carry on his traditions in Israel and in the United States. Some of the family members have changed their surname to Rosenbaum.

Y. Alfasi, *HaHasidut*, pp. 45-50.

S. Rosman, *Zihron Kedoshim*, pp. 100–110.

A.S.

LEIFER, Yitzhak, of Kalusz (1770–6 *Shevat* 1840) – Elder son of R. Aron Leib of Przemyshlan, he settled in Kalaszyce in 1873, where he served as a rabbi. He was highly esteemed by R. Israel of Ruzhyn, who called him the "good Jew." R. Mordecai of Nadvorna called him a "godly person" for he studied all day long clad in his *tallit* and *tefillin*.

He married Feige, the daughter of R. Ittamar HaKohen. He aroused the antagonism of the members of the *Haskalah*, who accused him of arson. His synagogue was closed until the actual culprit was found.

He had nine children, two daughters and seven sons. He was succeeded by his son R. Issachar Bertshe of Nadvorna. Another son, R. Solomon (d. 1868), lived in Hebron.

LEINER, Abraham Joshua Heschel, of Chelm (1843–27 *Shevat* 1930) – Son of R. Jacob of Izbice, he was brought up by his father and grandfather. After his brother's death in 1891, he became rebbe, first in Radzyn and a year later in Chelm. He left many manuscripts, one of which was published in *Kuntras Likkutei Divrei Torah Imrei Emet* in the Leviticus section of *Bet Yaakov* (Warsaw, 1937).

LEINER, Gershon Hanokh Heinokh, of Radzyn (1839–4 *Tevet* 1891) – Son of R. Jacob, he was born in Izbice. He was brought up by his grandfather R. Mordecai Joseph. He married Hadassah, the daughter of R. Joseph of Hurbiszov, near Lublin. He was a follower of R. Simhah Bunem for nine years and of R. Menahem Mendel of Kotzk for thirteen years. In 1861, at the age of twenty-two, he became rabbi of Radzyn (Radzyn Podolski). It was there that he prepared for publication his grandfather's manuscript *Mei HaShiloah*. At the age of thirty-three he began to work on a project that was to earn him a tremendous reputation. He succeeded his father as rebbe on 15 *Av* 1878.

Tohorot, the sixth and last order of the *Mishnah*, contains twelve tractates. Apart from the tractate *Niddah*, *Tohorot* has no *Gemara* in either the Palestinian or the Babylonian Talmud. R. Gershon produced a work called *Sidrei Tohorot* on tractate *Kelim*, commentaries and interpretations from rabbinic literature. He designed the work in the form of a pseudo-*Gemara* with a commentary in the format of Rashi on the left and *Tosafot* on the right, flanked with *Mesoret HaShas*, *Ein Mishpat*, and *Ner Mitzvah*. *Sidrei Tohorot* received accolades from many rabbinic authorities when it was first printed in Josefov in 1873. To placate his opponents who objected to the publication of a work in the format of a *Gemara*, the formula "collated from the words of the *Tanna'im* and *Amora'im*" was inserted in subsequent editions.

Jews are required by the Bible to wear ritual fringes. Each fringe originally consisted of seven white threads and one blue (*psil tekhelet*). The art of dying the blue thread was lost, but R. Gershon was determined to rediscover the source of the dye and thus restore the thread to its rightful place. This, he fervently believed, would hasten the redemption. In 1887 he wrote a thirty-eight-page booklet on the subject, entitled *Maamar Sefunei Temunei Hol* (Warsaw, 1887). Accompanied by his attendant, Israel Kotzker, he went to Naples, where he visited the aquarium four times; he also visited the Vatican museum, where he allegedly studied the garments reputed to have belonged to the High Priest.

On the eve of Shavuot 1888, he published a second treatise on the subject, a 208-page book entitled *Maamar Psil Tekhelet* (Warsaw, 1888), in which he claimed to have discovered *Hilazon* (*Sepia officinalis*), a member of the cephalop class, which includes the octopus and squid families.

On the first day of Hanukkah 1889, the rebbe and 12,000 of his hasidim began to wear the thread of blue. It was not accepted unanimously. Many scholars were opposed to it, among them R. Joshua of Kutna and R. E. Spector.

He was the author of *Ein HaTekhelet* (Warsaw, 1892); *Sefer Orhot Hayyim* (Warsaw, 1891) on the will of R. Eliezer HaGadol, which has been reprinted four times; *Sod Yesharim*, discourses on the Torah—part 1 (Warsaw, 1902), part 2 (Warsaw, 1903), and parts 3 and 4 (Lublin, 1908); *Tiferet HaHanohi*, a commentary on the *Zohar* (Warsaw, 1900); *Dalsot Shaarei HaIr* on *Tikkunei Eruvim* (Warsaw, 1902); and *Seder Tohorot* on *Oholot* (Piotrokov, 1903). Among his fifteen manuscripts that remained unpublished were novellae on the Palestinian and Babylonian Talmuds and responsa on the four parts of the *Shulhan Arukh*, responsa on *Agunot*, *Pri Etz Hayyim* on *Sefer HaMitzvot* of Maimonides, and on the letterings of the *Sefer Torah* according to the *Halakhah* and *Kabbalah*.

At circumcisions, he was both the *sandek* and the *mohel*. He would drink a fifth cup of wine on Passover, and he preferred the *etrogim* of Corfu to those of the Holy Land. His medical prescriptions were accepted by Warsaw chemists.

His son, R. Mordecai Joseph Eleazar, succeeded him. However, a number of hasidim gave their allegiance to R. Abraham Joshua Heschel of Chelm.

S. Z. Shragai, *BiNitivei Hasidut Izbica-Radzyn*.

LEINER, Jacob, of Radzyn (1828–15 *Av* 1878)—Son of R. Mordecai Jacob, he was known as the *Bet Yaakov* after his major work, a commentary on Genesis, printed in Warsaw in 1900. He was heir to his father's rabbinate but not to his father's fiery temperament. On 9 *Adar* 1844, he married Hannah, the daughter of the wealthy David Suchtevsky. After living in Izbice for thirty years, he settled in Radzyn. He gave discourses between each course at the Sabbath meal. His doors were always open wide to his followers, who were welcome to consult him at any time.

He was buried in Druzganiz.

His son R. Gedaliah was murdered by the Nazis. His eldest son, R. Abraham Joshua Heschel, was rabbi in Chelm, and his third son, R. Yeruham, lived for a time in London.

LEINER, Mordecai Joseph (1800–7 *Tevet* 1854)—The founder of the Izbice/Radzyn dynasty was born in Tomaszov-Lubelski. His father, R. Jacob, traced his ancestry to R. Meir of Padua. His father died when he was very young, and he was befriended by R. Menahem Mendel Morgenstern. He was a disciple of R. Simhah Bunem of Przysucha, where he spent nine years.

After R. Simhah Bunem's death, he became a disciple of R. Mendel of Kotzk. Even then he began to accept petitions from hasidim, and after the famous "Friday night incident" in 1839, he left Kotzk and settled first in Vengrov, then in Tomaszov, and finally in Izbice, where he lived for thirteen years.

He was the author of *Mei HaShiloah*, the first volume of which was printed in Vienna in 1860, and the second volume in Lublin in 1922; they were reprinted in Brooklyn in 1973. It is the only hasidic text published by a non-Jewish printer—Anton della Torre of Vienna. S. Z. Shragai maintains that it was actually printed in Yosefov, but the date and place were inserted to avoid Russian censorship. It was published without any approbations.

Among his disciples were R. Leibele Eger of Lublin and R. Tzaddok Hakohen.

He was probably the most original thinker of Hasidism. His teachings are based on the schools of Przysucha and Kotzk. He stressed that *mitzvot* performed mechanically are devoid of meaning. He opposed the "isolation" of the rabbi of Kotzk and stressed that the *tzaddik* was a spiritual guide rather than a miracle worker. He believed in informed faith rather than blind faith and that God should be served with intelligence as well as with devotion.

He maintained that the shortcomings of the biblical heroes were of minor importance, and he did not detract from their moral stature. He was of the opinions that in messianic times the commandments will not be obligatory and that the biblical figures based their actions on the belief that they were already living in the messianic era.

M. M. Faierstein, *All Is in the Hands of Heaven*.

LEINER, Mordecai Joseph Eleazar (1877–2 *Shevat* 1929), Radzyn–Son of R. Gershon Heinoch, he married Esther Duba and settled in Warsaw in 1914. He dedicated himself to the publication of his father's writings. In all nine texts were published, and fifteen remained in manuscript.

Active in communal affairs, he participated in the St. Petersburg rabbinical conference in 1914, conferring with the Russian minister of the interior, Peter Stolypin, and after the war with Josef Pilsudski as well as with the Jewish socialist leader, Herman Diamond. Twice he was arrested on charges of helping young men avoid military service.

He was vice president of the Aguda and participated in the *Knessiyah HaGedolah* held in Vienna in 1921.

He was violently opposed to the holding of autopsies, which had been proposed by the Polish government.

He was the author of *Tiferet Yosef*, a commentary on the Pentateuch (Warsaw, 1935).

He was buried in Warsaw.

He left four daughters: Havah, Tobah, *Hayyah*, and Zeldah, and one son, R. Samuel Solomon.

S. Z. Shragai, *BeNitivel Hasidut Izbica-Radzyn*, vol. 2, p. 181.

LEINER, Samuel Solomon, of Radzyn (18 *Shevat* 1909–29 *Iyyar* 1942)–Son of R. Mordecai Joseph, under whom he studied. In 1929 he married Shifra Michel, daughter of R. Joseph Kalish of Amshinov. He succeeded his father as rebbe in 1929. He left Warsaw and returned to Radzyn in 1935, where he established a *yeshivah Sod Yesharim*. With fatherly solicitude he cared for the students in his charge and put an end to the humiliating rota system whereby students ate in different homes each day. In his *yeshivah* the 200 students lived in comparative comfort. He opposed state schools and the teaching of secular subjects in Jewish schools. He was equally opposed to Zionism and to the Mizrachi.

During the Nazi occupation he left Radzyn and lived for a time in Parczev, Lublin, and Wlodowa. He denounced the *Judenrat* and those who collaborated with the Nazis. He warned: "Whoever crosses the threshold of the *Judenrat*, will forfeit both this world and the world to come, for they are aiding the Nazis in the extermination of the Jews." He advocated resistance: "Would that I had fifty people whom I could lead in a revolt." He was not deceived by the Nazi propaganda talk about "resettlement" and "labor camps." "Sobibor is no labor camp. It is an extermination camp!" he stormed.

His wife, his daughters, Yutah and Brachah, and his son, R. Mordecai Eleazar, were murdered in the Warsaw ghetto. The Yiddish poet Yitzhak Katzenelson (1886–1944) wrote a 1,200-line poem in tribute, called "The Song Concerning the Radziner," which movingly describes the heroism of the rebbe.

His son-in-law, R. Abraham Issachar Engelhardt, is rebbe in Bene Berak.

LEINER (Lainer), Yeruham (5 *Sivan* 1888–20 *Av* 1964), New York–Son of R. Abraham Joshua Heschel, he was born in Radzyn. In 1924 he was ordained by R. Moses HaKohen Adamashik of Chelm and married Rebecca, daughter of R. Tzvi Hirsch Halberstadt, a descendant of R. Abraham Abish of Frankfurt. Settling in North London in 1934, he established the *shtiebl Bet HaMidrash Kehal Yisrael* in Willesden, northwest London, in 1935. He strongly criticized Chief Rabbi J. H. Hertz for his controversial comments on sacrifices in his commentary in the *Authorised Daily Prayer Book*. A Torah scholar of great erudition, he corresponded with many leading contemporary rabbis. He wrote notes on the Palestinian Talmud, which were included in Grossman's edition of the *Yerushalmi* (New York, 1959), on the *Mishneh Torah* in the Pardes edition of *Maimonides Code* (Jerusalem, 1963), and cooperated with R. David Luria in *Kadmut HaZohar* (Tel Aviv, 1951), which tried to prove the antiquity of the *Zohar*. He was also the author of *Tiferet*

Yeruham on the Pentateuch, which was published by his son (Brooklyn, 1967).

He was a profound writer on *Halakhah*, *Aggadah* and Kabbalah, and eighty-one of his articles appeared in rabbinic periodicals: *Sinai*, *Hapardes*, *Hadarom*, *Kerem*, *Talpiyot*, and *Kol Torah*. He published a commentary on the Passover *Haggadah* (New York, 1956) and reprinted the works of his grandfather and uncle, to which he added long introductions.

In 1947 he settled in Borough Park, New York, where he died. He was survived by three daughters and a son, R. Mordecai Joseph (1918–3 *Shevat* 1991).

R. Mordecai Joseph studied at the *yeshivah* of Montreux and the *yeshivah* Etz Hayyim in London under R. Eliahu Lopian and R. Nahman Shlomoh Greenspan, and he married Rosa Hoffman, a descendant of R. David Hoffman, a rector of the Hildesheimer Seminary.

Succeeding his father in 1964, he devoted himself to the publication of the works of his father and his ancestors. In his edition of *Tiferet Yeruham*, he gives a bibliography of his father's manifold writings. He also published new editions of *Sefer HaZemanim* (New York, 1984), *Mei HaShiloah* (New York, 1984), and the *Izbica Haggadah*.

He was survived by a daughter, Rebecca, who married R. Mordecai Aaron Feinstein, and two sons, R. Moses, a student at the *yeshivah* of Brisk in Jerusalem, and R. Jacob, born in New York in 1962 and educated at the *yeshivot* of Lakewood and Mir. He was ordained by R. Zalman Nahman Goldberg. In 1992 he married Miriam Bookson and succeeded his father as rebbe of Radzyn in Borough Park.

T. Preschel, *Jewish Press*, February 15, 1991, p. 66a.

LELOV, David (1746–7 *Shevat* 1813)–Son of R. Solomon Tzvi and of Rebecca of Bielsko-Biala. Even as a boy he was known for his generosity. He would often take off his shirt and give it to a less fortunate playmate. He married Hannah, the daughter of R. Jacob of Negieven.

It was his habit to fast for days on end and to shun public gaze. He would hide himself in remote places where he could study undisturbed. He completed fourteen times the study of the Talmud. He visited R. Elimelekh of Lejask, R. Jacob Yitzhak, the "Holy Jew," R. Simhah Bunem, R. Yitzhak of Warka, and R. Shlomoh HaKohen of Radomsk.

He devoted his life to acts of practical loving-kindness, feeding the poor, visiting the sick, and redeeming captives. He greeted every visitor like a brother. No one was held at arm's length, not even sinners. In fact, he did not believe that sinners existed. "I love the good that is hidden in every Jew," he said. His benevolence extended to all creation. At fairs he made a point of feeding the horses that had been neglected by their owners.

Among his disciples were R. Yeshayah of Przedbort, R. Hayyim David Bernard of Piotrokov, and R. Dov Berish of Bendin. His eldest son, R. Mosheh, succeeded him. His other sons were R. Nehemyah and R. Avigdor. Some of his discourses can be found in *Migdal David* (Piotrokov, 1930), *Pri Kodesh Hillulim* (Lvov, 1932), and *Likkutei Divrei David* (Jerusalem, 1968).

A. Marcus, *Der Chassidismus*, pp. 49, 253, 363.

LETTERS–One of the basic ideas in early Hasidism is that of "clinging to the letters" in prayer (*devekut beotiot*). The implied notion is Neoplatonic. As Plato conceived of a realm of ideas, so in kabbalah, the letters of the alphabet constitute the inner essence of all creation–not the letters as we see them on paper but corresponding forms in the divine Pleroma. So, Nahmanides in his introduction to his commentary on Genesis speaks of the Torah in heaven as existing in the shape of so many "letters of black fire written on white fire," consisting of combinations and permutations of the various Names of God.

The kabbalistic worldview is dynamic in nature. The power of divine favor in the highest *Sefirot* (*Keter* and *Hakhmah*) is beyond all categorizations. When this power enters the *Sefirot* of the "Upper Mother" (*Binah, Ima illaa*), it begins to take on the shape of letters, ideas, and words. The counsel of the Besht was to pray with impassioned fervor, articulating every letter and sending it forth to the upper spheres–on the wings of "fear and love," as it were. Since the letters are like chains, hanging down from the highest *Sefirot*, the worshipers' feelings may reach to the realm of *Beriah* (creation = second realm) and possibly also to *Atzilut* (emanation = first realm). If the prayers are said unemotionally, they are relatively or completely ineffective. This method of prayer can be accepted by all–hence, one of the reasons for the mass appeal of Hasidism.

The concept of "clinging to the letters" is interpreted not as an automatic achievement by the worshiper, but as an act of grace, on the part of God, Who "contracts" His Being so as to approach those who endeavor to reach Him, with total concentration, transforming themselves into naught (*ayin*). God, Who is beyond all conception and articulation, bestows a touch of this quality of transcendence upon those who reach out to Him with all their being.

Another aspect of this conception occurs in the early writings of the movement. Since the heavenly letters emerge first, to be combined into words, it is possible for the *tzaddik* to recombine the letters into a favorable word, rather than into its opposite. So the letters of trouble (*z, r, ah*) may be recombined into words meaning an opening (*Zohar*) or acceptance (*ratzah*). The letters for a sore (*nega*) can be converted into a word meaning pleasure (*oneg*). Similarly, the letters of *amen* can be rearranged to read *maen*, meaning to refuse. In the Hebrew language, there are many such variations. Sometimes, a change in vocalization or accent will convert a curse into a blessing. This achievement by a *tzaddik* is called "the sweetening of the laws" (R. Jacob Joseph of Polonnoye, *Toldot Yaakov Yoseph* [ed. Warsaw, 1881], Noah, p. 31).

R. Schatz-Uffenheimer, *HaHasidut KeMistikah*, pp. 96, 98.

J.B.A.

LEVI YITZHAK of Berdichev

(1740–5 *Tishri* 1810)–Born in Husakov, near Przemysl, his mother, Soshe Sarah, was a descendant of R. Shmuel Eliezer Edels, and his father, R. Meir, was rabbi in Zamosz. From his early years, Levi Yitzhak showed a phenomenal aptitude for study. He was known as the "*Illui* of Yaroslav." When he married Peril, the daughter of Israel Peretz of Lubatov, he moved to the town of his father-in-law.

It was R. Shmelke Horowitz, later to become rabbi of Nikolsburg, who introduced him to Hasidism. He visited the Maggid of Mezhirech. When his father-in-law suffered severe financial setbacks and was imprisoned by the squire for falling in arrears with his payments, R. Levi Yitzhak set out to raise the redemption money for him.

In 1761 he succeeded R. Shmelke as rabbi of Rychwal. Four years later he became rabbi of Zelechov, and in 1772 in Pinsk. He took part in the disputation that took place in Praga, Warsaw, in 1781, and forcefully defended hasidic doctrines.

He faced fierce and mounting opposition by the *mitnaggedim*, but in 1785 he finally found peace in Berdichev, the "Jerusalem of Volhynia," where he lived for the last twenty-five years of his life. Here, he wrote his classical work *Kedushat Levi*, which was first printed in Slavuta in 1788. It contains discourses in his father's name on Hanukkah and Purim as well as selected discourses by his sons, R. Meir and R. Israel. A second edition was printed by his son in Berdichev in 1811. *Kedushat Levi HaShalem* (Jerusalem, 1964) contains 533 printed pages of discourses on the Pentateuch, on Festivals, on Talmud, on Midrash, and on the Ethics of the Fathers.

He encouraged Hebrew printing in the Ukraine. The printer Shmuel, son of Issachar Segal, printed twenty-eight books in thirteen years, and all received the *Haskamah* of either R. Levi Yitzhak or one of his sons. Apart from R. Abraham Joshua Heschel, no other hasidic rabbi gave as many *Haskamot* as he did.

He was one of the most lovable figures of Hasidism. He was a *Melitz Yosher*, a defender par excellence, and a mediator, who tempered justice with compassion. Suffering did not embitter this eternal optimist, who harbored a passionate belief in the inherent goodness of human beings. For good reason was he called "Darbarimdiger" (the merciful one). Many tales are told of his boundless compassion. Even the most blatant transgressor was given the benefit of the doubt. Many are the moving prayers that he composed. Among them is *Gott vun Avraham*, a touching farewell to the Sabbath, which Jewish women instantly took to their hearts. Equally famous is the song called "Duddele" (the "You" song).

His prayer was full of ecstasy. When he was about to pour out his prayers before the Almighty, he would tremble violently because of his love and awe of the glory of God. If he were praying in one corner of the room at the beginning of the service, he might well be at the other end of the room an hour later because of his enthusiasm. Fiercely, he defended the people against the itinerant Maggidim, who harangued and harrowed them.

A rare rapport seems to have existed between him and God, with Whom he communicated in terms of remarkable intimacy and warmth. It was said of him that "he loved God, and he loved Judaism, but his love of the Jews surpassed his love of God and Judaism."

His son, R. Meir, the author of *Keter Torah*–novellas on Talmud, Maimonides, Genesis (Mezirov, 1803), and Exodus (Zhitomir, 1803)–died on 29 *Tishri* 1806, in his father's lifetime. His second son, R. Israel, who succeeded him, died on 23 *Elul* 1818; he was the author of *Likkutei Maharan* and *Toldot Yitzhak ben Levi* (Berdichev, 1811). His third son, R. Dov Berish, who died in 1824, did not become a rebbe.

S. H. Dresner, *Levi Yitzhak of Berdichev*.

LEVIN, Hanokh Tzvi Hakohen, of Bendin (d. 19 *Adar* 1935) – Son of a wealthy ironmonger, Pinhas Jacob, he married Feigele, the daughter of R. Judah Aryeh Leib, the *Sefat Emet*. He wrote glosses on the Pentateuch, Talmud, Maimonides, and the Codes.

In 1921, he became rabbi of Bendin. He was particularly concerned with Sabbath observance: every Friday afternoon, he would make his rounds, urging shopkeepers to close their premises for the Sabbath.

In 1924, he accompanied R. Abraham Mordecai Alter on his second visit to the Holy Land. He was one of the three delegates sent to the Holy Land to heal the breach between R. A. J. Kook and R. J. H. Sonnenfeld.

LEVIN, Yitzhak Meir (1894–19 *Tishri* 1971), religious leader – Popularly known as "Itche Meir," he was the spokesman for the Aguda and one of the most colorful politicians to emerge in the interwar years in Poland. Son of R. Tzvi Hanokh HaKohen (later rabbi of Bendin), his mother was Feiga, the daughter of R. Judah Aryeh Leib Alter, the *Sefat Emet*. He married Mattel, the daughter of R. Abraham Mordecai Alter of Ger.

As a young man, he assisted his father-in-law in the work of the Aguda and supported Orthodox publications and the *Bet Yaakov* school movement. For half a century, he fought tirelessly to strengthen Torah Judaism, first as a member of the Warsaw Community Council and, after 1940, in Israel.

He was one of the signatories of the Declaration of Independence, became a member of the *Knesset*, and from 1948 to 1949 served in the Israeli provisional government as minister of social welfare. He was instrumental in creating a religious education system, which became the *Hinukh Atzmai*, and he campaigned for the exemption from military service of *yeshivah* students and observant young women.

At the insistence of the *Mo'etzet Gedolei HaTorah*, he left the government over the issue of the conscription of girls.

His eldest daughter perished in the Holocaust.

Kiryat HaRim Levin in North Tel Aviv is named after him.

Tidhar, 4 (1950), p. 1804.

LEVINSOHN, Yitzhak Baer (1788–1860), writer – A native of Kremenets, Volhynia, he was known as the "Mendelssohn of Russian Jewry." He was the author of antihasidic works, such as *Divrei Tzaddikim* (1830), *Teudah BeYisrael* (Vilna, 1828), and *Hefker Velt*, which was circulated in manuscript and not printed until 1904. He accuses the rebbes of fostering ignorance and the hasidim of idling away their time with lengthy visits to the rabbinic courts and neglecting their own families. He was equally critical of Yiddish, which he regarded as a mixture of degenerate words.

LEWIN, Aaron, of Rzeszov (14 *Heshvan* 1870–6 *Tammuz* 1941) – Son of Nathan, he was born in Przemysl, Galicia. In 1903 he married Doba, the daughter of Elijah Tzvi Friedman of Wieliczka, near Cracow. His first rabbinical post was in Sambor, where he was influenced by R. Uri Yolles. He devoted eight years to his work *Birkat Aaron* on tractate *Berakhot* (Drohobycz, 1913), a compendium of 310 essays on assorted subjects. In 1913, he was appointed crown councillor (*kaiserlicher rat*) by the emperor of Austria.

A dedicated Agudist, he was elected a member of the *Seym* in 1922; he also served as a deputy from 1931 to 1935. At the same time, he was president of the Aguda Central Council from 1923.

In 1926, he accepted the rabbinate of Rzeszov. In 1929, he was one of the delegates sent to London to discuss with Lord Winterton the issue of Jewish emigration.

His book *HaDrash VeHalyyun* on Genesis (Bilgoraj, 1927), on Exodus in 1931, on Leviticus in 1937, and on Numbers in 1939 became the preacher's vade mecum.

He was murdered by the Nazis at Lvov.

Elleh Ezkerah, vol. 1, pp. 401–462.

LEWIN, Menahem Mendel HaKohen (1899–1943) – Son of R. Hanokh Tzvi HaKohen of Bendin and Feigele, the daughter of R. Judah Aryeh Leib, the *Sefat Emet*, he married the daughter of R. David Weidenfeld of Warsaw.

His father, who died in 1935, stated in his will, "Let one of my sons succeed me, either Yitzhak Meir or Menahem Mendel." As his brother declined, R. Menahem Mendel succeeded him.

LIBERMAN, Hanokh (1900–13 *Adar* 1975), hasidic artist – Born in Lodz, he lived first in Poland and then in Russia. At the age of twenty-seven he won first prize in a national competition, enabling him to study at the Moscow Art Institute.

His wife and children were murdered by the Nazis. He left Russia in 1946 and lived for a time in Paris, London, and New York, where he died. A devoted hasid of Lubavitch, the rebbe encouraged him in his artistic work. One of his famous paintings is *Tashlikh*.

LIBERMAN, Hayyim (1892–1991) – Born in Pleschinetz, White Russia, he studied at the Lubavitch *yeshivah*, *Tomhei Te'mimim*, and at the Moscow University. In 1925 he became the personal secretary of R. Joseph Yitzhak Schneersohn, and two years later he was arrested together with the rebbe.

In 1928, he left the Soviet Union and lived for a time in Riga and Otwock, finally settling in the United States in 1940 and becoming the librarian of the Lubavitch Library, which he expanded and enriched. He was also on the editorial board of the *Great Dictionary of the Yiddish Language*, and he catalogued the *Strashun Rabbinic Collection* at the library of *Yivo*, New York.

Among his essays on Hasidism are *Vegen der Ausgabe fun Shivhei HaBesht* in Yiddish, *Yivo Bletter* 5 (1933), *Reb Nahman Brasslaver un di Umaner hasidim un maskilim* (New York), *Yivo Bletter* (1947), *Legendes und Emes vegen di Hasidische Drukerein* (New York), and *Yivo Bletter* (1950). He also wrote a series of articles entitled *Ketzad Hokrim Hasidut BeYisrael* (New York), *Bitzaron* (1953–1961), and *Ohel Rachel* in three volumes (New York, 1980).

Z.A.

LIBESHEI DYNASTY – This Lithuanian hasidic dynasty was founded by R. Shemaryahu (Weingarten) (d. 1846), a disciple of the Maggid of Mezhirech. He was succeeded by his son, R. Yehiel-Mikhal, whose son, Abraham Abba (d. 1861), followed him. The dynasty was continued by Hayyim Yitzhak (d. 1874) and R. Jacob Leib (d. 1922).

The dynasty was split when, in 1884, R. Abba (d. 1924), another son of R. Hayyim Yitzhak, became rebbe in Yanova.

This dynasty left no written work. Its rabbis were oppposed to fasting, and they stressed the importance of joyfulness. They had their own melodies. It is noteworthy that the rebbes of Libeshei combined the positions of rabbi and rebbe in the Lithuanian towns of Kobrin, Yanova, and Libeshei.

W. Z. Rabinowitsch, *Lithuanian Hasidism*, pp. 202–207.

LICHTENSTEIN, Hillel, of Kolomyja (1815–10 *Iyyar* 1891) – Son of R. Barukh Bendit, he was born in Vetsh, near Pressburg. He studied under R. Moses Sofer, who ordained him. In 1837, he married Reizel, the daughter of R. David of Galati. From 1850, he served as rabbi in Marghita, in Cluj, in Szikeze, and in Kolomyja. He participated in the rabbinical conference held in Nagymilhaly (Michalovce).

He was a devoted follower of R. Hayyim Halberstam of Zanz and was involved, with R. Menahem Mendel of Kosov, in a lengthy controversy over a ritual slaughterer.

He was the author of *Maskil El Dal* (Lvov, 1867), *Et Laasot* in Yiddish (Kolomyja, 1870), *Avkat Rachel* (Lvov, 1883), and *Teshuvat Bet Hillel* (Satmar, 1908).

He had nine children, five daughters and four sons. He was succeeded by his son, R. Solomon Zalman.

LILIT – A female evil spirit of the night, who occupies a prominent position in the *Zohar*, in later kabbalah and Hasidism, and in popular superstition.

The name is biblical, occurring in Isaiah 34:14, and is usually associated etymologically with *lailah* (night). The word is, however, possibly of Babylonian origin.

In the midrash it is said of her that she was Adam's first wife, before the creation of Eve or, alternatively, that she lay with Adam after he had separated from Eve. In both cases their union produced evil spirits (*shedim*), whose progeny continue to roam the world.

Lilit is particularly harmful to newly born male children and to women in childbirth. Amulets written to afford protection from Lilit are extremely common. She was also considered in kabbalah to continue to produce demons from her union with sleeping men.

She occupies in the world of *Sitra Ahra* the same position as the *Shekhinah* occupies in the world of the *Sefirot*.

D.G.

LIPSCHITZ, Aryeh Leib, of Vishnitz Nowy (1767–17 *Tevet* 1848) – Called after his famous work *Aryeh DeVei Illai*, he was born in Yaroslav, Galicia. He was the son of R. Hayyim Asher. He studied under R. Yitzhak Harif of Sambor, R. Aryeh Leib of Stryj, and R. Jacob Yitzhak Horowitz. After divorcing his first wife, he married Hannah, the only daughter of R. Moses Teitelbaum, who was then the rabbi in Sianiawa. He was a follower of the "Seer" of Lublin, the Maggid of Kozienice, and R. Naftali of Ropczyce. He served as rabbi first in Kreshov, in 1808 in Sianiawa, and in 1815 in Vishnitz, where he began his activities as rebbe. Owing to disputes in the community, he left the city in 1818 and settled in Brzesko, where he died.

He was eager to settle in the Holy Land, but ill health prevented him from so doing. He was very concerned with the problems of the *Agunot* – women separated from their husband who cannot provide evidence of their husband's death or whereabouts and who are thus unable to remarry. He believed, "He who enables an *Agunah* to remarry is as if he rebuilds the ruins of Jerusalem."

He often corresponded with R. Naftali Horowitz of Ropczyce, R. Hayyim Halberstam of Zanz, and R. Jacob Orenstein of Lvov. He was the author of *Ari SheBaHavurah* on tractate *Ketubot* (Lvov, 1852), *Hiddushei Aryeh DeVei Illai* on talmudical tractates (Przemysl, 1874), responsa *Aryeh DeVei Illai* on the four parts of the *Shulhan Arukh* (Przemysl, 1874), and *Ateret Zekenim* (Przemysl, 1891).

He was survived by three sons and three daughters. His son R. Meshullam Zalman Jonathan succeeded him as rabbi in Brzesko.

A. Surasky, *Marbitzei Torah U'Mussar MeOlam HaHasidut*, vol. 1, pp. 22–34.

LIPSCHITZ, Aryeh Leibish, of Opatov (1860–14 *Shevat* 1929) – Son of R. Joseph Zehariah Menahem of Selipo, he was a devoted follower of R. Abraham Twersky of Turiysk. He also visited the rabbi of Sianiawa. He was a staunch opponent of any change in hasidic dress. During the First World War he lived in Pressburg and eventually settled in Opatov. He married Hadassah, the daughter of R. Hayyim Meir Finkler of Pinczov.

In 1921, he emigrated to the Holy Land and lived in Jerusalem. He was the author of *Yismah Tzaddik* on Kabbalah (Piotrokov, 1911); *Yesod Likro*, prayers to be recited at the tomb of Rachel (Jerusalem, 1925); and *Shaagat HaAri* (Jerusalem, 1926).

He was buried on the Mount of Olives. He was survived by his sons R. Yissachar Dov and R. Jacob. His third son, R. Moses Solomon, died in his father's lifetime.

LIPSCHITZ, Issachar Dov, of Ungvar (1882–25 *Iyyar* 1944) – Elder son of R. Aryeh Leibish of Opatov, he was ordained by R. Samuel Engel. In 1900 he married Beila, the daughter of R. Abraham Shalom Halberstam of Sztrapko. For forty years he served as *dayan* of Ungvar, where he was strongly opposed by the Zionists, who controlled the community. During World War I, he transformed his *Bet HaMidrash* as a refuge for Jewish soldiers, and after the war he extended his *yeshivah*, appointing R. Abraham Tzvi Tzanzer as principal.

On the deaths of his wife, his eighteen-year-old daughter, Sarah, and his son

Joseph Zehariah, he married Esther, the daughter of R. Yehiel Nathan Halberstam of Bardiov, Hungary. He corresponded with R. Samuel Engel of Radomysl and with R. Moses Grunwald of Huszt.

He, his wife, his daughter Pesil Miriam, and his son R. Barukh Abraham were all murdered in Auschwitz. His surviving son, R. Yehezkel Shragai, was the rabbi of Sztrapko in Jerusalem. He published his father's writings, entitled *Divrei Yissachar Dov* (Jerusalem, 1954).

Elleh Ezkerah, vol. 7, pp. 108–111.

LIPSCHITZ, Moses, of Philadelphia (1898–29 *Tammuz* 1975)—Son of R. David Aryeh, he was born in Wielopole, Galicia. His parents settled in the Holy Land in 1900. Moses studied in the *yeshivah Hayyei Olam* under R. Jacob Orenstein. At the age of fifteen, he married *Hayyah*, the daughter of R. Asher Zelig Lichtman.

In 1913, he returned to Galicia to visit his grandfather in Vishnitz. The outbreak of the First World War prevented his return to the Holy Land, and he had to remain in Poland. After the war, he settled first in St. Louis and then in Philadelphia, where he established a community *Hevrat Mahzikei Hadaat*.

In 1958 he returned to the Holy Land. He was buried on *Har Hamenuhot*. He was survived by his eldest son, Asher Zelig, rabbi of *Geulat Yisrael*, in Philadelphia, and by another son, R. Hayyim Uri, the former editor of the *Jewish Press*.

U.L.

LIPSCHITZ, Yehiel Meir, of Gostynin (1810–21 *Shevat* 1888)—Born in Opoczna, Poland, son of R. Jacob Tzvi and his wife, Sarah, the daughter of R. Yehudah Leib ben Tzvi Hirsch. After the death of his parents when he was very young, he and his sister, *Hayyah* Sprinza, were brought up by their uncle R. Noah Samuel Lipschitz. He studied under R. Moses Yehudah Leib Silberberg of Kutno. He married the daughter of R. Leibish of Gostynin. He cherished the *mitzvah* of *hahnasat orkhim* (hospitality). He would not sit down to a meal without a guest.

He was a devoted follower of R. Menahem Mendel of Kotzk, R. Yitzhak Meir Alter of Ger, and R. Abraham Landau of Ciechanov. On the death of R. Landau in 1875, he became rebbe. He refused to take *pidyonot* from his hasidim but charged a fee for officiating at weddings. He differed with Kotzk in believing that prayers should be recited at the proper times. He was regarded as a miracle worker and was popularly known as the "good Jew of Gostynin" or the "*Tehillim Yid*." "*Tehillim* (Psalms)," he declared, "contain the whole music of the heart of man."

In his last will and testament he enjoins, "Study the Psalms many times. Let the Psalms be familiar to you, and recite at least five chapters of Psalms daily." What the *Zohar* was to R. Pinhas of Koretz, the Psalms were to R. Yehiel Meir. To some hasidim he allocated the recitation of ten chapters, to others the whole book. He signed a proclamation pleading that people should not read heretical literature. He also strongly deprecated the reading of secular works.

He was survived by two sons, R. Leibish and R. Israel Moses of Proskurov, and one daughter.

His teachings are to be found in *Meron HaRim* (Warsaw, 1892) and *Mei HaYam* (Lodz, 1910).

A. Y. Bromberg, *Migdolei HaHasidut*, vol. 2, *R. Yehiel Meir Lipshitz*.

LIPSCHITZ, Yitzhak, of Wielopole (1870–*Elul* 1943)—Son of R. Nathan Nata Dov of Wielopole, he acted as junior rabbi from 1912, and after that, as rebbe. He took refuge in Vienna during World War I, and in 1920 he settled in Brzesko.

He married Freida, the daughter of R. Jeshua, the *dayan* of Krasni.

After being discovered in a bunker in Bochnia, he was shot by the Nazis, who turned his synagogue in Brigel into a stable.

He was survived by his sons—R. Yehudah Zundel, R. Tzvi Hirsch, and R. Aryeh Leibush.

LITERATURE, HASIDIC—Hasidic literature in the English language falls into three distinctive categories, as follows.

1. Translations of various texts, such as works describing a given system of thought, commentaries on the weekly portion of scriptural readings, discourses, sermons, communications, fables, anecdotes, and incidental sayings by hasidic teachers.

LITERATURE, HASIDIC

2. Scholarly works about Hasidism or hasidic leaders, such as treatises on philosophy and mysticism, histories, biographies, studies in hasidic folklore, and sociological studies. Single titles are described briefly, in the comments that follow, as typical examples of these two groups.

3. Studies in essay or monographic format, usually published in learned journals or Festschriften, which deal with specific topics in the hasidic experience. Such essay materials, as well as works about Hasidism, usually include illustrations, either quoted and translated verbatim or reworked in a style suitable for the author's objectives.

Translations

The *Habad* branch of contemporary Hasidism leads in the field of translations, as attested by the number of texts available for educational and missionizing purposes, such as *Tanya*, by R. Shneur Zalman of Liady (founder of *Habad*), tr. and annot. by Nissan Mindel et al. (Brooklyn, NY: Kehot, 1973), and *Kuntres U'Mayon MiBais HaShem*, by R. Sholom Dov-Ber Schnersohn (leader of *Habad* in fifth generation), tr. by Zalman I. Posner (Brooklyn, New York: Kehot, 1969). There are also many other tracts written or compiled by *Habad* spokesmen.

Some works of the *Habad* school are of special interest to students of mysticism. The following two titles, both translated, annotated, and prefaced with introductions by Louis Jacobs, are typical: *Tract of Ecstasy*, by R. Dov-Ber Schneuri (leader of *Habad* in second generation) (London: Vallentine, 1963), elaborates in detail *Habad*'s theories concerning the Jewish soul in its divers components and functions. *Seeker of Unity: The Life and Works of Aaron of Starosselje* (London: Vallentine, 1966) suggests a unique solution to the difficult philosophic problem of how a finite, material universe could emerge from the creative processes of an infinite God.

Disciples of Bratzlaver Hasidism, apparently motivated by missionary zeal, recently brought out a selection of their master's teachings: *Rabbi Nahman's Wisdom: Shivhei HaRan, Sihos HaRan*, ed. Zvi Aryeh Rosenfeld (New York: Sefer-Hermon, 1973).

Two comprehensive anthologies are available that include materials representing the thought of nearly all hasidic schools: *The Hasidic Anthology*, by Louis I. Newman (New York: Bloch, 1944), is a large selection of didactic and homiletical data listed alphabetically according to specific themes, ranging from "After Life" through "*Tzaddik* and His Problems." These are grouped by subject headings, 205 in number, and identified in special indexes to author and source. *Tales of the Hasidim*, 2 vols., by Martin Buber (New York: Schocken, 1947–1948), is selected from approximately 650 anecdotal sources and arranged in chronological sequence of the listed hasidic masters. Primary interest is focused in this work on the ideological uniqueness of the various hasidic schools.

Major Works

Buber's works on Hasidism, for example, *For the Sake of Heaven* (a novel) (Philadelphia: Jewish Publication Society, 1953), *Hasidism and Modern Man* (New York: Horizon, 1958), *The Origin and Meaning of Hasidism* (New York: Horizon, 1960), and his numerous essays in periodicals, reflect his perception that the phenomena under discussion manifest an extraordinary process of religious and spiritual renaissance among East European Jewry. Though subject to the criticism that he weaves his own philosophic ideas into the described patterns of hasidic concepts (cf. G. Scholem's critique of Buber's methods in *Commentary*, vol. 32 [1961], pp. 305–316), his writings merit special attention for their depth and artistic formulations.

The World of Hasidism, by Harry M. Ra-binowicz (London: Vallentine, 1970), and *Hasidism: The Movement and Its Master* (Northvale, NJ: Jason Aronson, 1988) offe up-to-date, concise biobibliographic write-ups of leading personalities in the history o Hasidism. Trends of thought, associate with their respective names, are described i nontechnical language.

Lithuanian Hasidism, by Wolf Z. Ra-binowitsch (New York: Schocken, 1971) presents a comprehensive history of Hasidism in the land where it encountered it greatest opposition.

A Passion for Truth, by Abraham J. Hesche (New York: Farrar, 1973), is both a biogra-phy and a philosophic, analytical study of R

Menahem Mendel Morgenstern, the "Kotzker Rebbe," renowned in hasidic lore for his uncompromising striving for truth.

Rabbi Shneur Zalman of Liady, 2 vols., by Nissan Mindel (Brooklyn, NY: Kehot, 1974), is a detailed biography of the founder of *Habad* Hasidism. Volume two contains a description of *Habad* thought in its many ramifications.

Legends of the Hasidim, by Jerome B. Mintz (Chicago: University of Chicago Press, 1968), presents an analytical study of hasidic folklore, which is based upon the author's interviews with followers of some forty hasidic "courts" in the New York area.

A sociological study of a contemporary hasidic community in America is attempted by Israel Rubin in *Satmar: An Island in the City* (New York: Quadrangle, 1972). Though inconclusive, its findings are of particular interest with regard to the impact of an open pluralistic society upon the adherents of Satmar.

Studies in Essay Format

Hasidism represents an incomparable burst of creative energy, yet its treasure of new ideas is rather meager, except in the area of prayer, which is virtually its heart and core. Hasidic prayer, including its themes of contemplation, *kavvanah* (intent), ecstasy, *devekut* (cleaving to God), and *bitul hayesh* (self-annihilation), is the most frequently encountered subject of studies in learned journals. Issues are analyzed on many levels—as abstract concepts, as well as in their relatedness both to one another and to the totality of hasidic life. Scholars of renown (e.g., Martin Buber, Abraham J. Heschel, Louis Jacobs, Rivkah Schatz-Uffenheimer, Gershom Scholem, Joseph G. Weiss) devote much energy to the elucidation of those issues. Though further descriptions cannot be offered within this brief article, some general observations are called for.

Special research is pursued to define the ways hasidic mysticism differs from its predecessors'. Do any links exist between early Hasidism and the lingering Shabbatean heresy (cf. Weiss's "*Reshit tzemihata shel haderekh hahasidit*," in Zion, vol. 16 [1951], pp. 46–106)? Apropos of the Sabbatean tragedy, did a retrogression of the messianic doctrine actually take place in early Hasidism, as Scholem claims in *Major Trends in Jewish Mysticism* (New York: Schocken, 1941, p. 330f.)?

Louis Jacobs's monograph *Hasidic Prayer* (New York: Schocken, 1973) incorporates much of the creative research on the subject of the title in recent years.

Hasidic tales and legends are beautifully fictionalized in Meyer Levin's *Golden Mountain* (New York: Jonathan Cape, 1932) and Jiri Langer's *Nine Gates to the Hasidic Mysteries* (Northvale, NJ: Jason Aronson, 1993).

S.F.

LITHUANIA—In 1795, Lithuania was annexed to Russia. Between the two world wars, it was an independent state. On June 15, 1940, Russia took it over once again. A year later, it suffered German occupation. It again became independent in September 1991.

The situation in eighteenth-century Lithuania was different from that in Podolia. The *Vaad*—the council of the provinces of Lithuania—functioned well in the five provincial communities of Lithuania (Grodno, Brest-Litovsk, Pinsk, Vilna, and Slutsk), where Jews enjoyed a certain degree of internal autonomy. The Jews of Lithuania suffered very little from Cossack uprisings, and because they lived mainly in large concentrations, their economic situation was sounder than that of the Jews in the south.

Most of the rabbis and leading scholars of Eastern Europe were the products of the Lithuanian *yeshivot*. The cultural level of even the ordinary people was higher in Lithuania than in Poland. Kabbalah was also studied, but interest in it remained an individual matter in Lithuania. The pseudomessianic movements had no large following there. The Jewish community's cultural institutions and whole spiritual life were directed jointly by the *Kahal* and the rabbis.

At first, the Lithuanian rabbis there did not see anything threatening in the emergence of the hasidic movement. According to hasidic sources, Lithuanian Jews traveled great distances to listen to the Besht's teachings, though there is no indication in any of the sources that the Besht's emissaries visited Lithuania. The Besht himself did not venture there. Nor is there any historical truth that he influenced the appointment in 1746 of R. Yehiel Margalith as rabbi in Grodno. The Besht's son R. Tzvi, however, lived his whole adult life in Pinsk in the home of his father-in-law, R. Samuel Hasid, and is buried in the old cemetery there.

After the death of the Besht, R. Dov Baer, the Maggid of Mezhirech, extended his influence into Lithuania and White Russia. The pioneer of Hasidism in Lithuania was R. Aaron the Great of Karlin, and a number of hasidim in Karlin, Vilna, and other Lithuanian towns came under his influence. In fact, the term "Karliners" became a synonym for Hasidism.

R. Aaron's successors – R. Solomon, R. Asher, R. Aaron II, R. Asher II, and R. Israel the *Yanukkah* – all maintained the movement in Lithuania. Both lay and spiritual leaders issued excommunications against Hasidism in 1772 and 1781, which led to arrests of a number of important hasidic figures.

Apart from Karlin, there were the Amdur hasidim, led by R. Hayyim Heikel (or Heike), and by his son R. Samuel. His disciples R. Moses of Shershov and R. Samuel of Rosh (Rosi) also propagated Hasidism.

Important, too, was the dynasty of Lachowicze, founded by R. Mordecai and continued by his son R. Noah and his son-in-law R. Mordecai II. It spread hasidic doctrine in the northeastern part of Lithuania, as Karlin did in the southern parts.

A disciple of R. Moses of Kobrin – R. Abraham Weinberg – founded the Slonim dynasty, which was later maintained by R. Samuel and R. Abraham II.

There was also the Libeshei dynasty under R. Shemaryah Weingarten, and the Bereziner dynasty under R. Yehiel-Michal (d. 1848) and R. Yitzhak (d. 1863). After their deaths, the dynasty became divided between R. Yitzhak's son, R. Joseph (d. 1870), and his son-in-law, R. Hayyim Taubman, who died in 1907.

It was R. Wolf or "Wolfche" Ginsburg who founded the Horodok dynasty, which was carried on by his son, R. David, and later by R. Israel Joseph, who died in 1899.

Among those who perished in the Holocaust were R. Moses, the son of R. Israel of Stolin; R. Yohanan, the son of R. Noah; R. Moses Aaron, the son of R. David Solomon of Karlin; and R. Solomon II of Slonim.

The Jewish population at the outbreak of World War II was 175,000. After the liberation in 1944, only 8,000 Jews survived.

W. Z. Rabinowitsch, *Lithuanian Hasidism*.

W.Z.R.

LITURGY – Liturgy has always been the most convenient and significant vehicle by means of which sectarian religious groups have sought to give expression to their unique complexion, as well as to their independence from mainstream authority. It is not suprising therefore that Hasidism should have had early recourse to liturgical reform.

Immersed as it was in the spirit and doctrine of kabbalistic literature – and especially in the *Musar* literature derived from it by the sixteenth-century mystical school of Safed – Hasidism understandably chose to adopt the prayer rite of that school as the basis of its own liturgical reform. The Safed school had been founded by descendants of refugees from Spain; hence the (inaccurate) application of the term "*Nusah Sefarad*" (Sephardic rite) to describe the hasidic rite inspired by that school. Hasidism, in fact, chose for itself the specific rite initiated by Rabbi Yitzhak Luria (1534–1572), the most distinguished of the Safed mystics.

Luria was born of an Ashkenazic father and a Sephardic mother – a cross-fertilization that is also apparent in the prayer rite he introduced, being an amalgam of the Polish Ashkenazic rite and various innovations and changes based upon the Sephardic rite as followed in Palestine at that period. This was characterized by a trimming of the *piyyutim*, compensated for by the addition of a number of extra psalms, as well as various blessings and compositions woven around the esoteric traditions of the Kabbalah. The principle underlying these changes and innovations was that of providing a version that was an expression and representation of that essential mystical element without which prayer, according to the Lurianic system, could not be totally effective.

This was the element of *kavvanah*, the correct mystical intention. As part of the wider concept of *tikkun*, the correct *kavvanah*, involving particular reflection and meditation upon the various mystical combinations of the divine name, can result in an upward release of impulses that will accrue to the cause of sefirotic harmony. This in turn generates a reciprocal flow of blessing and grace to the world. In introducing his own liturgical adaptations, Luria was motivated by the desire to frame prayer formulas in such combinations as would not only promote the correct *kavvanah* but also facilitate their mystical objectives.

Luria's rite—the *Nusah HaAri* (rite of the divine Rabbi Isaac), after the initials of his popular cognomen—was initially adopted by individual mystics and hasidim. The Besht's circle in Medziborz used it in their private meetings, though in public they did not dare to recommend or introduce any departure from the standard Polish Ashkenazic rite.

It was R. Dov Baer, Maggid of Mezhirech (d. 1772), who gave the imprimatur to the *Nusah Ari* as the official prayer rite of the hasidic movement. The ensuing abandonment by the hasidim of the standard Ashkenazic rite and the establishment of a network of hasidic *shtieblech* (prayer rooms), played a major part in arousing violent reaction to the movement on the part of the authoritarian communal and rabbinic leadership of Poland and Russia. However, the dissolution in 1764 of the Council of Four Lands—the supreme synod of Polish Jewry—certainly emboldened the hasidim to pursue their independent policies without fear of effective and violent communal recriminations.

R. Dov Baer's authorization of the *Nusah HaAri* was later published, together with his other literary compositions, in a work entitled *Maggid Devarav LeYaakov*, by his disciple R. Solomon of Lutzk. This work defends the hasidic espousal of the Lurianic rite by emphasizing its unique superiority over other rites. To demonstrate this, R. Dov Baer drew attention to the mishnaic tradition (*Shekalim* vi, 1, 3) that there were thirteen prostrations in the Temple—one for each of the thirteen gates, there being one gate for each tribe and a thirteenth gate for those who were unaware of their tribal ancestry. This is to be linked to another popular rabbinic tradition (Jer. *Berakhot* iv, 5) that, corresponding to the earthly Temple, there is a celestial Temple, also containing gates for each tribe.

Prayer constitutes the vehicle that enables individuals to enter the heavenly Temple via their own tribal gate. The need for diverse liturgies arose because each gate has its own special combination. In times when all knew their tribal ancestry, it was naturally essential for them to follow the liturgical rite of their own tribe, which unlocked their own heavenly gate. However, once ignorance of tribal ancestry became rife, it was necessary to provide a liturgy that unlocked the thirteenth heavenly gate so that all Jews could gain entry. "Luria, through his familiarity with the paths of heaven, was enabled to create a liturgy that achieved this purpose, and it is better, therefore, to follow his rite, which is suitable for everybody" (*Maggid Devarav LeYaakov*, pp. 94–95).

Introductory formulas, recited in mystical circles before the performance of a mitzvah, were transmitted to Hasidism via the Lurianic system. These generally commence with the words *Leshem yihud kudsha' berikh hu ushekhintaeh* (In order to achieve the unification of the Holy One, blessed be He, and His *Shekhinah*) or *Hareini* (alt. *Hinneni*) *mukhan umezuman* (Behold, I am ready and spiritually prepared).

The effectiveness of these meditations as aids to concentration was recognized outside mystical and hasidic circles, and a number of them infiltrated into the Ashkenazic prayer book. Examples of the latter are the Meditations before putting on the *tallit* and *tefillin*, shaking the *lulav*, and counting the *Omer*.

R. Hayyim Joseph David Azulai (1724–1806), in his *Mahazik Berakhah* (489:3), inveighs against recitation of these kabbalistic meditations, which include references to holy names and celestial beings, by those who do not fully understand their profound significance. He also draws attention to the numerous errors that have crept into the formulas through the carelessness of copyists and printers. These are readily apparent, Azulai asserts, when one compares them with the authentic version as transcribed by Hayyim Vital and his son Samuel. Azulai therefore urges that no one should recite a meditation until one has personally cross-checked the authenticity of one's own version against the master copy by R. Hayyim Vital, which is kept in Egypt. "Laymen," warns Azulai, "are forbidden to recite the meditations, even from a correct version."

Azulai's strictures were widely noted, and many modern-day authorized editions incorporate a much abbreviated version of the meditations, omitting the recondite mystical references.

R. Shneur Zalman of Liady, concerned about the proliferation of rituals and compositions within the loose orbit of the Lurianic tradition, analyzed more than sixty versions of the ritual. His edited rite, garnished by many of his own meditations and supplied with a kabbalistic commentary, was published in 1800. This prayer book, known as *Dem Rebbin's Siddur*, is authoritative for *Habad* hasidim to the present day.

L. Jacobs, *Hasidic Prayer*.
Solomon of Lutzk, *Maggid Devarav LeYaakov*.

J.M.C.

LITURGY, HABAD–*Habad* liturgy is based on the prayer book by R. Shneur Zalman of Liady. Printed in Shklov in 1803, it was the very first prayer book to be published by Hasidism. More than sixty different texts were scrutinized by the author. It is based primarily on the Lurian liturgy (*Nusah Ari*). R. Shneur Zalman synthesizes a body of explicit rulings and prescriptions of the Talmud with the teachings and traditions of R. Isaac Luria. He omitted from his prayer book mystical devotions and other esoteric material that would be intelligible only to initiates of Kabbalah.

The prayer book consists of two parts. The first part contains a short, yet systematic guide to all the laws relating to the daily *mitzvot*: the laws concerning washing the hands in the morning; the size and manner of making the *tzitzit*; the use of phylacteries; the detailed study of sunrise, twilight, and sunset; the Grace after Meals; the various blessings; circumcision; *Pidyon HaBen* (where the exact amount of the weight of silver is designated); the *shofar*; Hanukkah and Purim; the procedures of the sale of *hametz* to a non-Jew; and the *Haggadah* for Passover, comprehensively annotated with all the customs of the *seder*.

The second part of the prayer book contains the text itself. He took great pains with both the grammar and the punctuation, carefully scrutinizing the printed editions and correcting any errors that had crept in through the centuries. The text includes all the prayers for the year. The following are the *Habad* innovations.

1. Psalm 107 is introduced prior to the *Minhah* service on a Friday, a custom attributed to the Besht.

2. The phrase *Or Hadash* (cause a new light to shine upon Zion) is omitted in the passage *Leel Barukh* in the morning service.

3. The phrase *Ahavat Olam* (with everlasting love) is recited both on weekdays and on the Sabbath.

4. An additional word is inserted in the *Musaf Amidah* of Shavuot, indicating that there were two he-goats (*Seirim*) on this day.

5. All preparatory prayers recited before the performance of the *mitzvot* are omitted.

6. The prayer *Veshameru* (i.e., the two biblical verses Exodus 31:16–17) before the *Amidah* on the Sabbath eve is retained, since it has been recited from Gaonic times. R. Shneur Zalman, however, questions their validity, and it is generally omitted by *Habad*.

7. The prayers before the blessing of the new month and the *zemirot* during the Sabbath and holiday meals are omitted.

8. The blessing for the *Hallel* on *Rosh Hodesh* is recited only by the reader.

9. The Ethics of the Fathers is included with substantial changes both in the text itself and in the distribution of the various *Mishnayot*.

10. The *piyyutim* are omitted.

N. Mindel, *My Prayer*.
A. Wertheim, *Halakhot VeHalikhot Battasidut*.

Z.T.

LITURGY, HASIDIC–The main changes introduced by the hasidim are as follows.

Morning Service: Omitting mention of the name of God in the benediction *Mekaddesh et shimha barabbim* and reciting *Barukh Sheamar* after *Hodu*, Psalm 130 before *Barekhu* on the Ten Days of Penitence, *Vidui* and *Shlosh Esreh Midot* before *Nefilat Apayyim*, and Psalm 86 before the special psalm of the day of the week (both are said before *Alenu*).

Afternoon service: Reciting Exodus 30:17–21, Numbers 28:1–8, and Exodus 30:34–36 (and some other verses) and adding some passages from *Keritot* 6a before *Ashrei* (as in the Morning Service). In the *Amidah*, *Sim Shalom* is said instead of *Shalom Rav*.

In the Morning Service on the Sabbath, Psalm 33 is recited after Psalm 19, and Psalms 98 and 121–124 are recited after Psalm 91.

In the Afternoon Service, the order of the three verses of *Tzidkatekha* are changed according to the Lurianic-Sephardi rite. *Hallel* is recited on both nights of Passover with benedictions after the *Maariv* service. On the Intermediate Days, no *tefillin* are put on–a change that sometimes gave rise to arguments in rabbinic circles.

Other customs adopted by the hasidim from Luria are the recital of the poem *Ahot Ketanah* after the *Minhah* service on the eve of Rosh Hashanah, the blowing of the *shofar* during the silent *Musaf Amidah* on Rosh Hashanah, the reading of the *Abodah Attah konanta* (instead of *Amitz Koah*) in the *Musaf* service on Yom Kippur and of *Hakkafot* on the night of the eighth day of Sukkot, omission of *Tahanun* in the week after Shavuot, and the recital of *Berikh Shemeh* (passage from the *Zohar*) before taking the Torah out of the ark. There were also some textual changes that had been adopted from Luria's ritual, (e.g., in the *Kedushah* and in the *Kaddish*).

H. Zimmels, *Ashkenazim and Sephardim*, pp. 120–121.

H.J.Z.

LODZ–City in Poland, about 75 miles (121 kilometers) southwest of Warsaw. Its growth in the middle of the nineteenth century was phenomenal. On the eve of World War II, 223,000 Jews were living there. One hundred and fifty factories, mostly textile mills, were owned by Jews. It became, next to Warsaw, the most important cosmopolitan community in Poland.

The hasidic influence was already discernible in the appointment of R. Ezekiel Nomberg, a hasid of Kotzk, who served as rabbi from 1832 to 1856. He was succeeded by another hasid, R. Moses Lipschitz, and the very last rabbi of Lodz was the hasid of Ger, R. Eliezer Elijah Treisman (d. 1920).

In the twentieth century, Lodz was the bastion of the hasidim of Alexander. Their *yeshivah*, *Bet Yisrael*, had an enrollment of 400 students. They even had their own political party and in the 1924 communal elections gained seven deputies.

Among the hasidic rabbis who lived in Lodz were R. Bezalel Yair (1863–1934), son of R. Yehiel of Alexander; R. Aaron Yehiel of Kozienice; R. Israel Elimelekh, son of R. Eleazar Beriah; R. David Bornstein (1878–1943); R. Immanuel Weltfried (d. 19 *Adar* 1939); R. Saadia Hanokh of Strykov; and R. Asher Anshel Gotschall.

On October 13, 1939 the Germans appointed a *Judenrat* under Mordecai Hayyim Rumkovski. A ghetto was established on April 13, 1940. The first deportations to the Chelmno and Auschwitz extermination camps were launched in December 1940, and they continued until June 1942.

A. W. Jasni, *Di Geschichte fun Jidn in Lodz*, 2 vols.

LOEBEL, Israel ben Judah Leib (late eighteenth century)–R. Israel Loebel of Slutzk was a maggid and *dayan* in several communities in White Russia and Lithuania and a zealous opponent of Beshtian Hasidism at the end of the eighteenth century.

R. Loebel was a prolific writer of homiletics, polemics against the hasidim, and one polemical essay against the *maskilim*, *Even Bohan* (Frankfort on the Oder, 1799).

Great importance is ascribed to his antihasidic works that constitute a significant source for the history of the controversy between the hasidim and *mitnaggedim*. They were used even by the *maskilim* in their fight against Hasidism.

In his *Sefer Viku'ah* (Warsaw, 1797), written in the form of a debate between a hasid and a *Mitnagged*, the author attacked vehemently the hasidic *tzaddikim*, complaining that they were devoid of Torah knowledge and greedy, as well as that their wonders were acts of chicanery. He threatened to summon them before non-Jewish courts. He vigorously attacked R. Shneur Zalman of Liady and did not spare criticizing even the Baal Shem Tov: "an empty pit devoid of the water of Torah" (*Sefer Viku'ah* 9, *Hasidim U'Mitnaggedim* II, 290).

R. Loebel strongly decried the changes that the hasidim had introduced into the liturgy from the Ashkenazic to the Lurianic rite. However, as a loyal adherent of R. Elijah, the Gaon of Vilna, he disregarded the change that the hasidim introduced concerning ritual slaughter with finely honed knives, since the hasidic *shehitah* did not violate Jewish Law. He cried out as well against the new sect's neglect of Torah study and its disrespect for scholars, and he viewed Hasidism as a continuation of the heretical sects that have arisen among the Jewish people over the generations.

Sefer Viku'ah was photocopied in 1965 and reprinted in 1970 (*Hasidim U'Mitnaggedim* II, 266–325).

Loebel's antihasidic composition in German—*Glaubwürdige Nachrichten von einer neuen und zahlreichen Sekte unter den Juden in Polen und Lithauen, die sich Chassidim nennt, und ihren die Menschheit empörenden Grundsätzen und Lehreh* (Frankfort on the Oder, 1799)—has been preserved only in a reprint by the German *maskilim* in *Shulamit* 2 (Dessau, 1807), 308–333. This composition also includes a debate between the author and a hasidic leader, entitled "Head of the Sect," who is almost certainly Rabbi Shneur Zalman of Liady. The cause of the debate was that the author's brother was ensnared by the hasidim. Several arguments in the exposition of R. Loebel's debate with the hasidic leader reflect *maskilic* thinking, and one may assume that these arguments are the fruits of their translators: This essay was translated into Hebrew by E. Deinard, *Herev Hadah* (Kearny, NJ, 1904) and M. Wilensky (*Hasidim U'Mitnaggedim* [Jerusalem, 1970], II, 326–338). Loebel's anti-hasidic work *Kivrot HaTaavah* (Warsaw, 1798) has not been preserved.

Loebel fought Hasidism not only with his pen. In 1798 he embarked on a propaganda tour throughout Poland and Galicia. Notwithstanding the persecutions and insults that he suffered at the hands of the hasidim, he was not discouraged in his war on them; he was even granted an audience with the Austrian emperor in Vienna.

It should be noted that a view has been offered by G. Scholem (*Zion* [1955]), that Loebel was inconsistent in his opposition to Hasidism, because in his homiletic works *Otzer Israel* (Shklov, 1786) and *Taavat Tzaddikim* (Warsaw, 1798), he speaks moderately about Hasidism and sees the positive aspects of the movement.

M. Wilensky, *Hasidim U'Mitnaggedim*.

M.W.

LONDON—The capital of the United Kingdom and the British Commonwealth of Nations.

Very few hasidim settled here in the nineteenth century, but by 1911, London's Jewish population had grown to 150,000. The influx resulted in the proliferation of small *hevrot*. Whether these *hevrot* included any hasidim is impossible to ascertain today. In 1896, a number of hasidim participated in the formation of the *Mahzikei Shomrei Shabbat*, which later became the *Mahzikei Hadat*, the Spitalfield Great Synagogue, one of the spiritual fortresses of Anglo-Jewry.

In the same year, the Austrian hasidim established a Dzikover *shtiebl* at 27 Fieldgate Street in the heart of London's East End. On May 13, 1913 the Austrian-Dzikover *shtiebl*, as it was then known, transferred to larger premises at 30 Dunk Street. A *shtiebl kehal hasidim* was established in Black Lion Yard to cater to hasidim on a nonsectarian basis. A Rizhyner *shtiebl*, too, was set up on Buxton Street in 1899, and one *Nusah Ari* on Old Castle Street in 1895. Meanwhile, individual hasidim were making a name for themselves, among them R. Moses Avigdor Chaikin, who became a member of the London *Bet Din*.

During the First World War, Belgian refugees founded *shtieblech* in northeast London, the *Schiff Bet HaMidrash*, by Moses Samuel Schiff, and the *Zelig Shemiah Shool*. In 1916, Leibish Rickel (d. 1929) from Galicia opened a *shtiebl* for his countrymen in Dalston.

In the 1920s, a number of hasidic rabbis came to London: R. Alter Noah HaKohen Michalensky Kaiser (1848–1920) spent some time in London; another rabbi of hasidic background was the controversial R. Joseph Shapotshnick (1882–1937).

Those who established hasidic roots in London were R. Aryeh Twersky, the rebbe of Turiysk, who arrived in 1923; R. Heinokh Dov Rubin of Sasov, who arrived in 1924; R. Shalom Moskovitch of Shatz; R. Israel Aryeh Margulies of Przemyshlan; R. Yehudah Schonfeld of Kielce; and R. Nathan David Rabinowicz of Biala. There were also small groups of hasidim in northwest London under R. Yeruham Leiner, R. B. Finkelstein, and R. S. Rubin of Sasov. In northwest London today, of the 1,500 ultra-Orthodox Jewish families, nearly 400 are hasidim. There are a Lubavitch grammar school and a *yeshivah gedolah*. There are two *Beis Yaakov* schools and a *Pardes* House school for boys. There are hasidic *batei midrash* under R. Chune Halpern and his two sons, R. David and R. Hayyim. Apart from a Gerer *shtiebl*, there is the Hager *Bet HaMidrash* and *kollel* under R. Gershon Hager.

The largest concentration of hasidim is to be found in Stamford Hill, North London. There are approximately 5,000 hasidim living around the Cazanove Road area. There are over forty *batei midrash*, *talmudei torah*, *yeshivot*, and *kollelim*, representing a colorful variety of different hasidic dynasties. There are the Vishnitz community under R. Shragai Feivil Schneebalg and the ever-increasing and wealthy Satmar community, which has three *batei midrash*. There are *shtieblech* such as *Vishnitz-Monsey*, Nadvorna, Ruzhyn, Skvare, Spinka, Klausenburg, Munkacs, and Biala. With the death of R. Shalom Schnitzler, of R. Hayyim Yitzhak Weingarten, the Lieger rav, and, in 1989, of R. Yudele Horowitz of Dzikov, the doyen of hasidic rebbes was R. Meshullam Ashkenazi. The Gerer dynasty was represented in London by R. Yaakov Heinokh Cymmerman (1885–1968), R. Pinhas Weitzman (1898–1960), and R. Simhah Bunem Lieberman. Ger has just completed the building of a large *yeshivah* in Lampard Grove.

The pioneer of hasidic educational establishments was R. Shmelke Pinter (d. 1994), who founded the *Yesodey Hatorah* schools. Most of the hasidim are affiliated with the Union of Orthodox Hebrew Congregations, set up in 1928 by R. Victor Schonfeld (1880–1930) and developed by his son R. Solomon Schonfeld. The hasidim operate their own educational network, which caters to all educational needs from kindergarten to *kollelim*.

There was no organized Lubavitch movement in England prior to the Second World War. R. Szemtov came to London in 1948 and soon established a network of educational establishments. There is hardly a facet of Jewish life that does not have the Lubavitch imprint.

LOWENSTEIN, Joseph (1837–1924) – Son of R. Abraham Abish, *dayan* in Lublin. He was ordained by R. Joshua Heschel Ashkenazi of Lublin. In 1860, at the age of twenty-three, he was appointed *dayan* in Horsel. Eight years later he became rabbi in Zolkiev, and in 1874, rabbi in Serock, near Warsaw. He declined offers of rabbinical positions in Opatov and Sochaczev, as he preferred to stay in a small community where he could devote himself to the study of the Torah.

He inherited a large number of manuscripts, which he edited and published. Among them were works by R. Abraham Abish of Lissa and the work *Bet Pinhas*, being novellas on a number of talmudical tractates by R. Pinhas Horowitz (Piotrokov, 1909), to which he contributed a detailed biography of the author and his brother R. Shmelke Horowitz, both leading personalities in Hasidism.

He also contributed to a number of Hebrew periodicals, for example, *HaPeles* in Poltava, *Shaarei Torah* in Warsaw, *Hameasef* in Jerusalem, and *Torah MiTzion* in Jerusalem. His knowledge of hasidic lore, biography, and genealogy was extensive.

His great work was *Dor Dor VeDorshav* (Warsaw, 1900), a book of days, comprising many thousands of dates. It is a pity, though, that the author did not cite his sources. A new edition was published in New York/Tel Aviv in 1949.

G. Kressel, *Leksicon HaSifrut HaIvrit BeDorot HaAharonim*, part 2, vol. 216/217.

A.S.

LUBAVITCH – Lubavitch, the important hasidic sect that is now a household word, is named after the Byelorussian village of Lyubavichi near Smolensk, which became the home of *Habad*, when R. Dov Baer settled there in 1813. A *yeshivah Tomhei Temimim* was opened there in 1879.

After the Russian Revolution, the town ceased to be a hasidic center, but the name "Lubavitch" was retained to designate the followers of *Habad* throughout the world.

R. Joseph Yitzhak Schneersohn arrived in New York in March 1940 and established Lubavitch headquarters in the Crown Heights section of Brooklyn, New York. He was joined in 1941 by his son-in-law, R. Menahem Mendel, who, in January 1950, succeeded him as rebbe and transformed a practically moribund branch of Hasidism (which had lost most of its followers in Eastern Europe) into a powerful and expanding national movement, deploying all the resources of modern communication and technology to spread its message. There are now over one hundred and eighty *Habad* houses in Israel and over thirteen hundred *Habad*/Lubavitch institutions worldwide. In the United States alone, there are more than 250 centers. In the Commonwealth of Independent States there are some sixty institutions of Jewish learning. Lubavitch emissaries have taken up residence to promote Jewish activities. The Lubavitch budget is over $100 million per year, and over 100,000 followers owe allegiance to it. Young men, nearly 2,000 emissaries newly graduated from Lubavitch *yeshivot*, were sent by the rebbe all over the world.

For two centuries, the rebbes of Lubavitch have perpetuated the teachings and traditions of Hasidism with its emphasis on the Divine presence in the world and the communion between man and his Creator. Lubavitch/*Habad* is a system of philosophy that teaches understanding and recognition of the Creator through wisdom, understanding, and knowledge. The initials of these three Hebrew words form the Hebrew word HaBaD. It is an outreach movement, reaching the alienated and the assimilated young Jews on university campuses, families in isolated communities, and Jews living under repressive regimes. All sections of the community are included, young and old, men and women, scholars and laymen. The Lubavitch Mitzvah and Holiday Campaigns have raised the awareness of Jewish life and Jewish practice among many Jews, motivating them to explore and to examine their identity.

In the educational field there are more than 40,000 pupils scattered in some hundreds of schools around the world. Employed are the latest educational aids from Hong Kong to Tel Aviv, Budapest to Chicago, in the many Lubavitch schools, youth centers, institutions, and agencies. These educational services serve a variety of functions for the entire spectrum of Jews regardless of affiliation or background.

A Lubavitch publishing house, Kehot Publication Society, is one of the largest Jewish publishing houses in the world. It publishes and distributes books, journals, pamphlets, cassettes, and educational materials designed for all ages in Hebrew, Yiddish, English, French, Spanish, Italian, Russian, Portuguese, Dutch, Swedish, and German. The central library and archive center in Brooklyn is a great repository of rare Jewish books and manuscripts.

See SCHNEERSOHN and HABAD.

E. Hoffman, *Despite All Odds*.

LUBLIN – City in eastern Poland, where Jews have lived since the fourteenth century. For several centuries it was the de facto capital of Polish Jewry, chiefly because of its being the principal meeting place of the Council of Four Lands (1580–1764), the autonomous governing body of the Jews in Poland. A further contributing factor was the talmudical college established by R. Jacob Pollak and his disciple R. Shalom Shakhna and continued by R. Solomon Luria, R. Meir ben Gedaliah, and R. Jacob and his son R. Heschel.

In the hasidic world, Lublin's fame rested on the "Seer": R. Jacob Yitzhak Horowitz, who has been called the "father of Polish Hasidism." His tradition was maintained by R. Judah Leib Eger, a grandson of R. Akiva Eger of Posen, and by his son R. Abraham (d. 1914), and by the great scholar R. Tzaddok HaKohen Rabinowitz, one of the most prolific writers of Hasidism.

Following the First World War, Lublin revived as a center of learning, with the establishment of the *yeshivah Hakhmei Lublin* by R. Meir Shapira, who, toward the end of his life, became the rabbi of Lublin. The *yeshivah* was guided by R. Simon Zelichover and R. Yehudah Aryeh Frumer.

Lublin was also the home of R. Mosheh Twersky of Turiysk, popularly known as "R. Moshele Trisker." He settled in Lublin in 1918 and his home at 29 Lubertovska was opposite the home of R. Abraham Joshua Heschel Rabinowicz of Biala (d. 8 *Tishri* 1933). There were many hasidic *shtieblech* on that street: the Radziner at number 18, the Kozinitzer at number 22, the Alexander at number 32, and the Umanover at number 34.

A ghetto was established at the end of March 1941, and deportations of the Jewish community to Belzec began on March 17, 1942. The *yeshivah* of Lublin shared the fate of Polish Jewry. The *Deutsche Jugendzeitung* in February 1940 gave a painfully vivid account of the wanton destruction of this great citadel of learning: "It was a matter of special pride to us," exults the Nazi narrator, "to destroy this talmudic academy, known as the greatest in Poland. We threw out of the building the large talmudic library and brought it to the marketplace. There we kindled a fire under the books. The conflagration lasted twenty hours. The Jews of Lublin stood about weeping bitterly. Their outcries rose above our own voices. We called up a military band and the cries of triumph of the soldiers drowned out the noise of the Jewish wailing."

Following the liberation of Lublin on July 24, 1944, the city became a temporary assembly point for a number of hasidim who had survived the Holocaust.

Dos Buch fun Lublin.

LUDMIR, Maid of (1805–1892)–Hannah Rachel, only child of R. Monish Verbermacher of Ludmir (Vladimir Volynski). Her mother died when Hannah was very young, and the lonely girl spent many hours at her mother's grave, praying and meditating. She maintained that "a new exalted soul was given to her." She donned *tzitzit* and wrapped herself in a *tallit* and put on *tefillin*. When her father died, she recited the *Kaddish* for him.

Financially well provided for by her father, she built a synagogue with an adjoining apartment for her. Every Sabbath, at the *seudah shlishit*, the door of her room would be opened and she would deliver erudite discourses.

At the age of forty, she was persuaded by R. Mordecai of Chernobyl to get married. The marriage did not last, and she emigrated to the Holy Land. There, in Jerusalem, she entered into a mystical partnership with a Kabbalist, and they resolved to hasten the coming of the Messiah.

She died in Jerusalem.

J. Twersky, *HaBetulah MiLudmir*.

A. Rapoport-Albert, "On Women in Hasidism: S. A. Horodezky and the Maid of Ludmir Tradition," pp. 495–529.

LURIA, Isaac ben Solomon (1534–1572)–Known as HaAri, "the Lion," from the initials of HaElohi Rabbi Yitzhak (the divine Rabbi Isaac). He is also referred to as Rabbi Isaac Ashkenazi Luria.

He was the most influential exponent of *kabbalah*. Very little is known about his early life, but he spent his youth in Egypt, where he devoted himself to the study of *halakhah*.

He then immersed himself in Kabbalah, making a profound study of the *Zohar* and other Jewish mystical works, including those of Cordovero, a contemporary of his.

He founded a school of Kabbalah in Safed. He himself committed very little to writing, most of his teachings being transmitted by his disciples. He did, however, leave a commentary to the *Sifra DiZeniuta* (Book of Concealment), a small but significant part of the Zoharic literature, short commentaries on a few other pieces of the *Zohar*, and three hymns for meals on the Sabbath.

After Cordovero's death in 1570, Luria's most distinguished student was R. Hayyim Vital (1543–1620), who with Joseph ibn Tabul is the main source of our knowledge of Lurianic teaching. The dissemination of the *kabbalah* outside Palestine was due chiefly to Israel Sarug, who was active in Italy at the end of the sixteenth century.

Luria taught his disciples how to communicate with the souls of the pious through devotion or concentration (*kavvanah*) in prayer. *Kavvanah* was one of the cornerstones of his approach because he believed that the concentrated intention of the practitioner–whether on the divine names in prayer or on the performance of the *mitzvot*–had a beneficial influence on the upper world and thus helped in the restoration (*tikkun*) of the lower world. This theory had a profound influence on the hasidic movement.

Luria did not favor any one particular liturgical usage, believing that each of the tribes of Israel had its own "entrance" to heaven. But since he himself used the Sephardi liturgy, this was adopted by the later hasidim, who combined it with their own Ashkenazi tradition, which explains their idiosyncratic form of prayer.

Other significant features of Lurianic Kabbalah are Luria's emphasis on the ideas of *tzimtzum* (the withdrawal or contraction of the divine), *gilgul* (the transmigration of the soul), and *shevirat hakelim* (the breaking of the vessels, an explanation of the origin of evil), as well as his belief in the imminent redemption of the world, for which *tikkun* (restoration by human agency) was a necessary prerequisite.

D.G.

LVOV (Polish, Lwow; German, Lemberg)–A city in eastern Galicia. From 1772 to 1918, it was under Austrian rule, and during the interwar period, it was the provincial capital of independent Poland. In 1939 the Jewish population numbered 110,000, the third-largest Jewish center in Poland.

Lvov became a center of Hasidism with the appointment of R. Meir Margulies (d. 1790). It also became a center of opposition to Hasidism. By the establishment of modern schools for secular instruction and by the literary parodies of Isaac Erter and Joseph Perl, every attempt was made to ridicule the movement and to stay its advances, but with little success.

Lvov was for a time the home of R. Uri of Strelisk (d. 1826); R. David Rokeah; R. Moses Langer; R. Leibish Efrati; R. Pinhas, the son-in-law of R. Yehiel Michael of Zevil; and R. Yehudah Michael of Sasov. The dynasties of Zanz and Bobov had many followers there.

Following the German invasion of Russia on June 22, 1941, about 10,000 Jews escaped from Lvov. On November 8, 1941, the Germans established a ghetto, and most of the community was deported to the Auschwitz extermination camp.

M

MAHLER, Raphael (1889–1977), historian – Born in Nowy Sanz, he received a traditional as well as a secular education at the rabbinical seminary in Vienna and at the University of Vienna. From 1923 to 1937 he lived in Warsaw, where he was deeply involved in the activities of Yivo.

In 1937, he emigrated to the United States. A prolific writer, his bibliography consists of 547 articles, books, and reviews. He was a frequent contributor to Yivo publications. He was the author of *The Struggle between Hasidism and the Enlightenment in Galicia during the First Half of the Nineteenth Century*, which was published in Yiddish, in Hebrew, and in English under the title *Hasidism and Jewish Enlightenment* (Philadelphia, 1985).

Influenced by Yitzhak Schipper, his work is a masterful sociological study drawn from a variety of sources. He stressed that Hasidism was a movement of the downtrodden petite bourgeoisie seeking liberation. He also noted that the Galician *maskilim* regularly acted as informers against the hasidim. Equally valuable is his essay on the controversy between Zanz and Sadgora in *Sefer Zanz* (Tel Aviv, 1970).

MAHZIKEI HADAS – One of the first Orthodox organizations to safeguard Jewish religious life in Galicia and Bukovina, it was founded by R. Joshua Rokeah of Belz and R. Simon Sofer (Schreiber) of Cracow on March 13, 1879. It published a bimonthly paper, *Mahzikei Hadas*, in Hebrew and in Yiddish, and its candidate, Simon Sofer, was elected as a member of the Austrian parliament.

In the interwar years, the *Mahzikei Hadas* was reorganized at a conference on Grodek Jagiellonski (Gorodek) on December 22, 1931, attended by delegates representing a hundred communities.

A. Bauminger, *Sefer Krako: Ir VeEm BeYisrael*, pp. 103–107.

MAIMON, Solomon (1753–1800), philosopher – His description of hasidic life and thought is important because it is the account of an eyewitness. However, it must be remembered that when he wrote his autobiography, he had already become a noted European philosopher. He viewed his early life in Poland from the Olympian heights of rationalistic enlightenment. Inevitably, some distortions of perspective may have affected his accounts.

Born in a village near Niesvizh, Lithuania, Maimon encountered at first only one or two hasidim. He became sufficiently interested, however, to travel to the court of R. Dov Baer of Mezhirech.

Some of the details in his report are characteristic of the early stages of the movement. He tells of hasidim walking about "with pipes in their mouths." He was disappointed with the frivolity and levity that he witnessed there.

He tells how a young emissary of the Maggid came to a small Lithuanian town and instructed the elders to do his bidding, as though he were endowed with absolute authority to establish a new order in the various communities. He describes some of the innovations of the hasidim, their falling into cataleptic states of ecstasy, and their resort to violent gestures in order to fend off "evil thoughts."

In general, his testimony is acceptable insofar as it relates to his personal experiences, but his interpretation of both Kabbalah and Hasidism is out of line. His identification of the ten *Sefirot* with the categories of Aristotle is, of course, untenable. Equally unacceptable is his interpretation of the hasidic movement as a secret order, dedicated to the total transformation of Jewish life, especially the deliverance of the people from the books of casuistic learning and the torments of penitence–then considered de rigueur.

He divided the rebbes into four categories: the wise, the cunning, the charismatic, and the naive, suggesting that an inner cabal manipulated the *tzaddikim* in order to attain its goal. He maintained that the objective of the hasidic sect was similar to that of the societies of the Illuminati in Bavaria and that it utilized approximately the same methods, its goal being to disseminate light to people dwelling in darkness, and in order to achieve this end, it made use, paradoxically, of superstitious beliefs.

Maimon was aware of the "healing light" that shone sporadically and intermittently upon the young who flocked to the new sect. He testified also to the social roots of the movement, but his view of it as a secret order, headed by philosophers, is no more than a reflection of the attitude and mentality of the Enlightenment.

S. Maimon, *Solomon Maimon: Autobiography*.

J.B.A.

MAIMON (FISHMAN), Judah Leib (1876–1962), religious Zionist leader–Born in Markuleshty, Bessarabia, he was educated in the Lithuanian *yeshivot*, where he was ordained. He served for a time as rabbi in Ungenci, Bessarabia. He joined the Mizrachi movement as a young man and attended its founding conference in Vilna in 1902. Throughout his life he participated in the Zionist congresses and eventually became the Mizrachi representative on the Zionist Executive.

After settling in Tel Aviv in 1913, he established *Mosad HaRav Kook*, the publishing house of the Mizrachi movement. He owned a collection of 40,000 volumes, which he later donated to the *Mosad* to become the nucleus of its present library facility.

After the establishment of Israel, he served for a number of years as minister of religion. He was a prolific writer, concentrating on hasidic and religious subjects. His works are replete with hasidic anecdotes.

Among his works are *Sarei HaMeah*, six vols. (1942–47); *Lemaan Tziyyon Lo Ehesheh*, two vols. (1954–55); *Middei Hodesh BeHodsho*, three vols. (1955–62); *Haggim U'Moadim* (1954–55); "R. Nahman of Bratzlav and His Journey to the Holy Land," in *HaTor* (second year); "Settlement of Hasidim in the Holy Land," in *HaTor* (vol. 6, pp. 11–12); "Kabbalah and Hasidism in the Holy Land," in *HaTor* (vol. 16); "R. Levi Yitzhak of Berdichev," in *Mishor* (vol. 1); and *Baal Shem Tov* (1960). He also edited the rabbinical journal *Sinai* and the series *Arim VeImahot BeYisrael* (Great Jewish Communities), commemorating the Jewish communities destroyed in the Holocaust.

Y.R.

MAIMONIDES, Moses (1135–1204) Hasidic thinkers may have accepted the view of some kabbalists that Maimonides, toward the end of his life, embraced mysticism, but they did not weary themselves to prove the point. Unlike the kabbalists, who, for apologetic reasons, found it necessary to seek the support of the Sage of Fostat by declaring that the divine wisdom of the Kabbalah coincides with philosophic teachings but simply employs only different terminology in order to justify the coexistence of these two currents in Judaism, Hasidism was not in need of these intellectual concessions. The development of Hasidism and its flourishing were not influenced by Maimonides–neither by his personality nor by his teachings. Maimonides did not serve for Hasidism as the authority to justify its teachings the way he did for Kabbalah. The famous Maimonidean controversy had already died a natural death. By the eighteenth century no one in hasidic circles took notice of the appearance of a new edition of Maimonides' *Guide for the Perplexed* (Yesnitz, 1742). The climate was overshadowed by the Eybeschütz-Emden controversy (when R. Emden accused R. Eybeschütz of being a follower of Shabbetai Tzvi).

The question before us is whether the attitude on the part of the hasidic masters toward Maimonides was a sort of indifference to the contents of the *Guide* and its metaphysical problems, or on the contrary, whether they found in its teachings an echo of their own theology. The evidence of the past 200 years proves to us that Hasidism did not find in Maimonides' teachings views opposed to its own; more so, it endeavored to search in the *Guide* for similarities and parallels to its teachings. True, admiration for the Sage was sometimes concealed; it did not always allow itself to cite the *Guide* by its name. Yet one cannot escape the fact that, except for R. Nahman of Bratzlav, Maimonides is referred to with warmth and reverence throughout the literature of the hasidic masters.

In the following chronological survey, specific references to the works of the masters are, for lack of space, omitted. They can be found in Jacob I. Dienstag's *Hamoreh Nevukim VeSefer HaMadda BeSifrut HaHasidut*. Numbers within parentheses at the end of each entry refer to the pages of that study.

R. Israel Baal Shem Tov, in his letter to his disciple R. Jacob Joseph of Polonnoye, refers with approval to Maimonides' reasons for the Divine Commandments in the third part of the *Guide*. He also leans on Maimonides' interpretation of the separate intelligences in that work (310–311).

R. Barukh of Kossov, though he does not accept the view that Maimonides turned afterward to Kabbalah, nevertheless is convinced that the Sage had acquired insights into the metaphysical realm no less than the kabbalistic masters (311).

R. Jacob Joseph of Polonnoye alludes not only to the philosophical section of the *Mishneh Torah*, *Yesodei HaTorah*, but also to the *Guide* (III, 49) and accepts the latter's reason for the rite of circumcision, whose "object is to limit sexual intercourse and to weaken the organ of generation" (311–312).

R. Menahem Mendel of Vitebsk defends Maimonides against the criticism of Nahmanides and attempts to equate the Sage's philosophic teachings with those of the kabbalists. He also accepts Maimonides' reasons for the rite of circumcision (312).

R. Menahem Nahum of Chernobyl accepts the views of the *Guide* (I, 17) on the subject of free will (313).

R. Abraham of Kalisk in a famous epistle has developed the mystical concept of communion with God and human beings and its relation to the problem of Divine Providence. "This subject," he writes, "is expounded by the Ancients." Undoubtedly, the *Guide* (III, 51) is the source for his analysis, though unlike his master, R. Menahem of Vitebsk, he hesitated to allude to the *Guide* by name (313–316).

R. Nahman of Bratzlav was perhaps the only hasidic master who opposed Maimonides in vehement tone and criticized the Sage for his reasons for the Divine Commandments: "May God forgive him." He nevertheless conceded that "in the messianic days the world will be compelled to study Maimonides' works, in particular *Bet HaBehirah* (Laws of the Temple), for he was the only codifier to include these laws in his halakhic code, the *Mishneh Torah*" (316–317).

R. Israel, Maggid of Kozienice, attempted to draw parallels between Maimonides and the *Zohar* on the reasons for the Divine Commandments. The reasons for the blowing of the *shofar* on Rosh Hashanah in the writings of the kabbalists R. Isaac Luria and R. Hayyim Vital reflect the views of Maimonides' *Teshubah* (III, 4). He also criticized R. Judah Loew (Maharal of Prague) for his attack on Maimonides (317–318).

R. Shneur Zalman of Liady in a way attempted to emulate Maimonides. Like the Sage, he compiled a code of law, and likewise he wrote a theological work, the *Tanya*, to parallel the *Guide*. During the bitter controversy against the hasidic movement, he compared it to the one leveled against the works of Maimonides during the thirteenth and fourteenth centuries. But apart from these external comparisons, there is a conceptual relationship between the Sage of Fostat and the *Tzaddik* of Liady. Maimonides' proposition in the *Guide* (I, 68) – that in God, the subject, action, and object of His knowledge are identical – is echoed by R. Shneur Zalman in his *Tanya* (ch. 42, 48). In discussing the attributes of God in his *Likkutei Torah* (*Pekudei*, p. 12), he leans on the *Guide* (318–320).

R. Tzvi Elimelech Spiro of Dinov, though a strong opponent of philosophic speculation, nevertheless expresses himself warmly about Maimonides, "who labored for the sake of heaven." He, too, accepted the thesis that the Sage eventually embraced kabbalistic teachings. R. Tzvi even composed a commentary on the metaphysical section of the *Mishneh Torah* (*Yesodei HaTorah*) and defended its author against criticism by the Rabad (320–321).

R. Moses Teitelbaum in his *Yismah Mosheh* often quotes with approval from the works of Maimonides in general and the *Guide* in particular. He does not hesitate to cite the latter's view on Aristotle: "Aristotle's intellect represents the extreme of human intellect, if we except those who have received divine inspiration." He cites lengthy sections from the metaphysical chapters of the *Guide* and the views of the master concerning the separate intelligences. Passages in the *Zohar* are explained by him with the help of this work (322).

R. Jacob ben Mordecai Joseph Leiner of Izbica equated the reasons for the Divine Commandments in the third part of the *Guide* with the views of the kabbalists (325–326).

R. Abraham of Slonim (Weinberg) in his *Yesod HaAvodah* attempted to draw parallels from the *Sefer HaMadda* and the *Guide* to hasidic teachings and copied entire chapters from the *Moreh* on the subject of Divine Providence. Although opposed to the study of philosophy, he justified Maimonides' approach, "for he composed the *Guide* in order to refute the heretics" (326–327).

R. Tzaddok HaKohen Rabinowitz of Lublin, though an opponent of philosophy, defended Maimonides, "whose sole purpose was for the sake of heaven." He particularly praised the master's role in combating the anthropomorphic conception of the Deity. R. Tzaddok is the author of *Otzar HaMelekh* on the *Mishneh Torah*, in which he also commented upon the metaphysical sections of this work (*Yesodei HaTorah*) usually ignored by most commentators (327–328).

R. Gershon Hanokh Leiner of Radzyn, too, accepted the view that Maimonides' teachings coincide with those of the kabbalists but are cloaked in philosophic garb in order to influence the perplexed. He criticized those who attacked the Sage for his views on Divine Providence. He likewise defends him for the manner in which he expounds the Divine Commandments and sees similarities on this theme in the *Zohar* and in the mystical writings of R. Isaac Luria. His opponents, he claims, "did not penetrate his profound views" (328–329).

J. I. Dienstag, "HaMoreh Nevukhim VeSefer HaMadda BeSifrut HaHasidut," pp. 307–330 (Hebrew section).

S. A. Horodezky, "HaRambam BeKabbalah U'VeHasidut," pp. 441–455.

T. M. Rabinowitz, "The Attitude of the Kabbalah and Hasidism to Maimonides," pp. 279–287 (Hebrew).

J.I.D.

MAN–In 1948, Martin Buber wrote a short and influential book that was translated into English as *The Way of Man according to the Teaching of Hasidism*. This book proved to be a seminal text, encouraging a renewed interest in hasidic thought among Western intellectuals. It has been ranked by Buber scholars with *I and Thou* as one of his most important works and was called by Gershom Scholem "a gem of literature." The main thrust of *The Way of Man* is that Hasidism is an existentialist teaching concerned with the concrete spirituality of the here and now. It is always in the here and now–where we stand–that we have to make the light of the hidden divine life shine. This is possible because each individual is unique with a unique task. Genuine persons, fulfilling their task, can transform themselves and by so doing transform the world. Making peace with ourselves enables us to make peace in the whole world.

Buber opens with the story of the dialogue between Shneur Zalman of Liady and his Russian jailer, the upshot of which is that the Bible addresses each individual in existential immediacy. The question God asks Adam–"Where are you?"–is thus not part of the problem of how much God actually knows of human beings' actions but an existential call to each of us, questioning us personally about our spiritual condition. For Buber the story not only illustrates a typically hasidic approach to text but also lays down the path along which we must journey. That path begins when someone responds to the divine question and recognizes how each person, like Adam of old, seeks to hide from God's question. Buber's understanding of Hasidism has been subjected to much scholarly criticism and has been dismissed as one-sided and historically false. Yet *The Way of Man* is a tour de force, which has not been surpassed as an introduction to the hasidic ethos.

At the base of the hasidic understanding of human beings are the images of the *Zohar* and Lurianism. What gave the hasidic movement its special character, however, was the way hasidic masters interpreted this classical kabbalistic imagery. It was psychologized and understood not only in cosmic terms but also as a map of the human soul in its service of God. A person was a microcosm, and the inner reaches of the divine were reflected in the different levels of the human soul, of which the great-souled *tzaddik* was possessed of higher levels than the ordinary Jew. Kabbalistic divine sparks were everywhere, sustaining all existence and representing the immanence of the Godhead in the everyday world. Elevating the divine sparks thus involved serving God via the physical world, a form of deconstructing the human ego and mundane reality, then reconstructing them anew in a transformed condition of cleaving to God (*devekut*).

Although Buber prefers to ignore the kabbalistic dimension of Hasidism, by laying emphasis on existentialism he reminds us that the lives of concrete individuals, rather than an abstract philosophy, are at issue in Hasidism. It is this existential dimension of Hasidism that underlies the recurrent tendency to antinomianism, a tendency that led to accusations of neo-Shabbateanism in the early days of the movement.

The Way of Man ends with the saying by R. Mendel of Kotzk that God is where we let Him in. Buber comments on this that we can let God in only to the place where we stand, to the little world entrusted to us, which we can make into a dwelling place for the *Shekhinah*. In a similar vein, we might say that a hasidic reply to the divine question with which Buber begins his book—"Where are you?"—might be, "You are where you let your true self in, often at the expense of your mundane self."

M. Buber, *Hasidism and Modern Man*.

A.U.

MANCHESTER—The Jewish community in Manchester, England, is the largest and most influential community outside London, with nearly 300 hasidic families living there. Manchester has two active Lubavitch centers, as well as *shtieblech* of Satmar, Belz, and Vishnitz.

The first hasidic rebbe to make a home in Manchester was R. Samuel Meshullam Zusya Golditch, popularly known as "R. Zusya" (d. 1940). He had a *shtiebl* in his home.

The appointment of R. Yitzhak Dubov (1887–1977) to the staff of the Manchester *yeshivah* in 1929 brought another hasidic leader to the town. A prominent personality at that time was *Dayan* I. Rivkin (d. 1947). On his death, R. Yitzhak Jacob Weiss (1902–1989) succeeded him as head of the *Bet Din*. He was the author of responsa *Minhah Yitzhak*.

MAPU, Abraham (1808–1867), novelist—Mapu, the founding father of the modern Hebrew novel, one of the pillars of the *Haskalah* and a harbinger of the *Hibbat Zion*, had an early encounter with Hasidism.

An only son, he was given a traditional Jewish education in *heder* and *yeshivah*. At the age of fifteen, he began to frequent a Lubavitch *shtiebl*. He was attracted by hasidic lore, which nourished his vivid imagination. There he met a practitioner of practical *Kabbalah* and was enthralled by the possibilities it offered. Despite his protestations, he was never permitted by his parents to visit a hasidic *shtiebl* again. Throughout his life, he remained sympathetic to the movement.

He was the first major Hebrew writer to create a new form of Hebrew literary expression. He was the author of *Ahavat Zion* (Vilna, 1853), *Ahavat Shomrom* (Vilna, 1865), *Ayit Tzavua* (Vilna, 1858), and a novel of the life and times of Shabbetai Tzvi, of which only a few chapters survive.

D. Patterson, *Abraham Mapu*.

S.J.G.

MARAGOWSKY, Jacob Samuel, of Radomysl (1856–1943), cantor and composer—Popularly known as "Zeidel Rovner," he was born in Radomysl and often appeared as a singer at hasidic gatherings. He was encouraged by R. Jacob Yitzhak Twersky of Makarev to devote his life to music and liturgical compositions. He occupied positions as cantor in Rovno, Kishinev, Berdichev, London, Lvov, and New York.

Many of his manuscripts are housed in the Yeshiva University, in New York.

MARCUS, Aaron (1843–1 *Adar* 1916) This Hebrew scholar, philosopher, linguist, and writer on Hasidism was a native of Old Hansa in Hamburg. He was a disciple of R. Yitzhak Bernays, whom he called "the gigantic *Hakham*." He also studied at *yeshivot* in Boscowitch, Moravia, and Galicia, as well as under R. Solomon Rabinowitz HaKohen of Radomsk. He was further influenced by R. Yitzhak Friedman of Bohusi, whom he met in Kattowice on September 4, 1882. He married into a hasidic family and declined the offer to become rabbi in Glasgow, Scotland, preferring to earn a living as a wine merchant.

In 1898, Marcus published an eleven-page pamphlet on Dr. Theodor Herzl's *Judenstaat*. "This Aaron Marcus of Podgorze has written to me a fine letter in which he places before me the possibility of having three million hasidim of Poland enter the movement. I answer him that the cooperation of the Orthodoxy is highly welcome – but a theocracy will not be created" (*Theodor Herzl's Tagebucher*, 1895–1904 [Berlin: Judischer Verlag, 1922], p. 297).

In another letter, dated May 7, 1896, Marcus gives Herzl an illuminating account of the state of Hasidism in Eastern Europe:

> The three million hasidim in the area of former Poland are distinguished from other Jews by the fact that they are not merely Jews by race, birth, habit, or confession, but self-conscious and – insofar as this is possible, under the pressure of circumstances – also, to some extent, politically organized Jews. . . . The masses are under the guidance of some fifty to sixty rabbis, on whom the propaganda would have to be concentrated. For six generations now, the house of the founder of this organization, the Friedman family in Bukovina, has acted as a real silent *negotiorum gestatorius* after the manner of the old exilarchs. The oldest and most venerable rabbi, David Moses Friedman in Chortkov, has not only taken a lively interest in the project, but has initiated negotiations with the *Hakham Bashi* . . . in order to obtain the sultan's permission for immigration to Palestine. His nephew, Isaac Friedman in Bohusi, whose hasidim founded the first settlement *Rosh Pina* near Safed in Palestine in 1881, is supportive. . . . Among the adherents who give blind devotion to these people are many millionaires. A certain Naftali Korretzer from Berdichev, who recently died, left 9½ million rubles, one million of it for charitable Jewish purposes, and seventy-two thousand to the aforementioned rabbi, and the rest to be divided among his eight children.

Marcus was eager to convene a conference of Orthodox leaders to negotiate with the Zionist executive. However, the conference did not take place, and Marcus expressed his disappointment in a letter to Herzl, dated March 23, 1900.

In all, the correspondence with Herzl covered forty-three letters on either side.

Marcus, whom Herzl called the "hasidische philosopher" and whom Max Nordau regarded as the "greatest living brain in the First Congress," was lost to Zionism. His interest faded, and he instead devoted himself to writing books on philosophy and on Hasidism (*Der Chassidismus* [Lvov, 1901]).

In Hartmann's philosophy he found allusions to *Habad*.

Marcus lived in Cracow until the outbreak of the First World War, when he fled to Frankfurt, where he died.

A. Willy, "The Western European Jew Who Turned Hasid." *Yivo Bletter* 39 (1947): 143–148.

MARGOLIOUTH, Meir, of Ostraha (1700–10 *Iyyar* 1790) – Son of R. Tzvi Hirsch, he served as rabbi in Jaslo, Horodenka, Lvov, and, from 1777, Ostraha. His appointment as rabbi of Ostraha in succession to R. Abraham Meshullam Ashkenazi was confirmed by the king of Poland, Stanislas II Augustus. R. Meir was a disciple of the Best and was the greatest talmudical authority of the eighteenth century to join the movement.

He married Hayyah, the daughter of R. Hayyim of Horodenka. He was the author of *Meir Netivim* (Polonnoye, 1791–1792), responsa and novellas; *Sod Yakhin U'Boaz* (Ostrog, 1794) on Kabbalah; *Derekh HaTov VeHaYashar* on the *Shulhan Arukh* (Polonnoye, 1795); and *Kotnot Or* (Berdichev, 1816).

He was survived by four sons: R. Joseph Nahman of Polonnoye, R. Bezalel, R. Saul, and R. Naftali Mordecai.

It was R. Meir's elder brother, R. Issachar Dov Baer, who represented the rabbinate in the disputation with the Frankists.

A. Walden, *Shem HaGedolim HeHadash*, p. 87.

MARGOSHES, Eliezer Joseph (1866–1955), Yiddish journalist – A native of Lvov, the son of R. Shlomoh, a descendant of R. Shlomoh Luria, he emigrated to the United States in 1903, where he wrote regularly for the Yiddish paper *Der Tog* and, from 1921, for the *Morning Journal*.

He had a great fascination for Hasidism. He was the author of *Groisse figuren in der velt fun Hasidus*. His contribution to the history of Hasidism, particularly to the dynasty of Belz, is considerable.

Tog/Morning Journal, April 11, 1955.

MARGULIES, Efraim Zalman, of Lanka (1865–16 *Nisan* 1922) – Son of the hasid of Belz Alexander Asher, he was born in Brody and married Eidel, the daughter of Yisrael Leib Frankel, the son-in-law of R. Meir of Przemyshlan. He became rabbi of Lanka and then of Drohobycz. In 1912 he took refuge in Kosice (Kaschau). He was greatly attached to the rabbi of Belz.

His son was R. Yisrael Aryeh, the rebbe of Przemyshlan in London.

MARGULIES, Yisrael Aryeh, of Przemyshlan/London (1892–24 *Tevet* 1957) – Son of R. Efraim Zalman, he was born in Przemyshlany and was ordained by R. David Menahem Monish Babad, the rabbi of Tarnopol, and R. Abraham Menahem Halevi Steinberg of Brody. He married Peshe (d. 1970), the daughter of R. Yitzhak Babad of Tartakov.

In 1927, he came to London and established a *shtiebl Kehillat Yisrael* at 14 Valance Road, in East London. In 1938, he moved to Cricklewood, northwest London. He was interested in education and helped in the establishement of the *Yesodey Hatorah* school and in the *North West London Jewish Day School*, which opened in 1945. He was active in the Aguda and was a member of the *Mo'etzet Gedolei HaTorah*.

In 1954, he moved to Hampstead Garden Suburb, where he established a *shtiebl*.

He was buried in Enfield Cemetery. He was survived by six daughters and three sons. Two of his sons-in-law were R. Abraham Moses Babad and R. Shmelke Pinter.

MATZAH (Unleavened bread) – Hasidim use *matzah shemurah* (unleavened bread), the production of which is overseen from the time the wheat is harvested. Most hasidim eat *matzah shemurah* throughout the Passover Festival, but the hasidim of *Habad* eat it only on the first night and not necessarily throughout Passover.

It is customary among the hasidim to bake the *matzot* on the eve of the Festival. The rebbes themselves participated in the baking, reciting *Hallel* and singing melodies as they baked. Some even recited the benediction over *Hallel*.

On 13 *Nisan* they would prepare the water (*mayyim shelanu*). On the first two nights of Passover, a number of hasidic rebbes would kiss the *matzah* and the bitter herbs. This was regarded as *hibbuv mitvah*, a custom already referred to by R. Isaiah Horowitz in his *Shnei Lukhot HaBrit* (2:45). The soaking of the *matzot* was forbidden.

In 1856, a machine for baking *matzot* was invented, and this was opposed by a number of hasidic rebbes, including R. Yitzhak Meir Alter, R. Hayyim Halberstam of Zanz, R. Abraham Landau of Ciechanov, R. Israel Joshua Trunk of Kutno, R. Ezekiel Halberstam of Sianiawa, R. Judah Leib of Ger, and R. Abraham Bornstein of Sochaczev (*Teshuvot Avnei Nezer, Orah Hayyim* 2:536). R. Shalom Mordecai Hakohen of Schwadron, on the other hand, permitted machine-baked *matzot*.

Y. Alfasi, *Bisdei HaHasidut*, pp. 349–365.

MEDZIBORZ (Yid Mezhibez), Podolia – A Jewish community existed in Medziborz from the beginning of the sixteenth century. Medziborz was owned by the Czartoryski family. It became the home of the Besht, which has recently been verified by M. J. Rosman's research in the Polish archives in Cracow, confirming many incidents recorded in the *Shivhei HaBesht*.

The records mention a number of the Besht's followers, such as Wolf Kotses and David Forkes, who were granted a weekly stipend by the community. The Besht himself is referred to as a kabbalist: "Balsem," "Balsam," or "Balsam Doctor." It is now confirmed that the Besht himself lived in a house belonging to the Jewish community, tax free, that he was supported by the establishment to the end of his days, and that such support was extended, after his death, to his son.

The Besht's grandson R. Barukh lived there for twelve years, as did his brother Moses Hayyim Efraim, later rabbi of Sudzilkov. It was also the home of R. Abraham Joshua Heschel of Opatov and of his son R. Shalom Joseph and his grandson R. Abraham Joshua Heschel.

A number of hasidic works were printed there from 1815 to 1827.

MEIR of Berdichev (d. 29 *Tishri* 1806) – Son of R. Levi Yitzhak, he married the daughter of R. Eliezer, the head of the *yeshivah* of Karlin. He was the author of *Keter Torah* on Genesis and novellas on the Talmud, Maimonides (Miezyrov, 1807), and Exodus (Zhitomir, 1803).

In his works he fully acknowledged his debt to his father: "All my life I have been reared in the presence of my Lord, my father." Conversely, R. Levi Yitzhak, too, quotes his son in his writings.

R. Meir died in his father's lifetime. He was survived by a son, R. Joseph, and three daughters.

MEIR of Przemyshlan (1780–29 *Iyyar* 1850) – Son of R. Aaron Leib (d. 1813) and a grandson of R. Meir the Great of Przemyshlan, who was a disciple of the Besht. It was, therefore, possible to confuse the grandson with his namesake and forebear, and most of the bons mots and stories associated with the name of R. Meir refer to the grandson.

He married, on the advice of R. Levi Yitzhak of Berdichev, the daughter of R. Ittamar HaKohen, a "hidden *tzaddik*."

The greater part of his career was spent in Przemyshlan, near Lvov, although he lived for a short time in other parts of the region, especially in Bessarabia. He was a disciple of R. Mordecai of Kremenitz. He began his career as a hasidic rebbe when he was thirty-three years old, after the death of his father.

Raphael Mahler records an official Austrian government document on R. Meir's activities. The report, which was originally inspired by malicious slanders put about by the *maskilim*, exonerates R. Meir completely on all charges of misconduct. He spent most of his income on "endowering the bride." On one occasion, he even sold his cow and gave the money to a poor bride.

Unlike most of his contemporary rebbes, he seemed to have had the approval of the nonhasidic scholars. R. Joseph Saul Nathanson of Lvov visited R. Meir, who told him that he would one day play an important role as the spiritual guide of an important community.

His chief fame lies in his wit and humor, and many of his sayings have become famous. He often used biblical passages as a basis for his themes. He was in the habit of dropping the first person when talking of himself and would begin his statements with: "Meir" or "Meirel says." He followed the pattern set by R. Levi Yitzhak of Berdichev and, at all times, attempted to vindicate the Jewish people by pointing out the meritorious aspects of their actions.

His sayings can be found in *Divrei Meir* (1909), *Or HaMeir* (1926), and *Marganita de R. Meir* (Lvov, 1926).

His son, R. Tzvi, succeded him.

R. Mahler, *Hasidut VeHaskalah*, pp. 412–415.

A.T.

MEIR BAAL HANES or KUPAT RABBI MEIR BAAL HANES (the fund of R. Meir the miracle worker) – It was the custom of the mistress of the house to drop a few coins into the *kupat* or *pishke* of R. Meir Baal Hanes before the kindling of the Sabbath candles. Even the poorest of the poor felt the need to make a contribution.

The first reference to "R. Meir the miracle worker" is found in the writings of R. Elijah ben Solomon HaKohen (d. 1729). In his *Midrash Talpiyot*, published in Amsterdam in 1698, he wrote, "He who loses something should contribute to R. Meir Baal Hanes and he will immediately recover the lost object." The Besht even composed a special prayer: "O Lord, our God, the God of our fathers, just as you have heard the prayers of Your servant R. Meir and performed miracles and wonders for him, so You may perform miracles for me and for all the children of Israel, who are in need of miracles."

Z. Vilnay, *Matzevot Kodesh BeEretz Yisrael*, pp. 315–324.

MEIR HALEVI of Opatov (d. 25 *Tammuz* 1831) – He was a disciple of R. Yitzhak Abraham of Pinczov and R. Jacob Yitzhak, the "Seer" of Lublin. He succeeded R. Yitzhak Abraham as rabbi in Stavnitz.

After the death of R. Jacob Yitzhak, many disciples accepted him as their spiritual leader. He violently opposed the doctrines of R. Simhah Bunem of Przysucha.

R. Meir called the Austrian government's attention to oppressive acts by the local police against the hasidim. He urged his followers to support the *tzaddikim* so that they should not be burdened with mundane problems.

He was the author of *Or LaShamayim* (Lublin, 1909).

He was survived by two sons, R. Pinhas and R. Israel.

Y. Raphael, *Sefer HaHasidut*, pp. 56–57.

MEISELS, Dov Berish, of Ujhely (1875–15 *Sivan* 1944) – Son of R. Mordecai Zeev, rabbi of Lask, he studied in Tarnov under R. Moses Apter and then in Zanz with R. Joseph Engel. He was reputed to have known a thousand pages of the Talmud by heart.

He married Rosa Blumah, the daughter of R. Moses Joseph, the rabbi of Ujhely, in 1897. From 1898 he was the *dayan* of the Sephardic community in Cluj.

He was the author of responsa *Binyan David* on the four parts of the *Shulhan Arukh* (Ujhely, 1932) and *Binyan David* on Torah (Ujhely, 1942).

He, his wife, and most of his children perished in Auschwitz.

His eldest son, R. Joseph Moses, was rabbi in Szamosuvjvas. His son R. Hayyim settled in the United States, and R. Joseph Zeev is rabbi of the Lieger *Bet HaMidrash*, in London.

Elleh Ezkerah, vol. 1, pp. 158–163.

MEISELS, Uzziel, of Neustadt (1744–28 *Kislev* 1786) – Elder son of R. Tzvi Hirsch, he visited the Besht in his youth and was a follower of R. Nahman of Kosov, R. Hayyim Heikel of Amdur, and R. Menahem Mendel of Przemyshlan. He married the daughter of the wealthy R. Shlomoh of Zelechov.

He served as a rabbi in Ostrowiec, in Ryczywal, and in Neustadt, near Cracow.

He died at the age of forty-two and was survived and succeeded by his son, R. Israel.

He was the author of *Tiferet HaTzvi* on the tractate *Betzah* (Zolkiev, 1803); *Etz HaDaat Tov*, novellas on tractate *Ketubot* (Warsaw, 1863); *Tiferet Uzziel* on Torah and the five *Megillot* (Warsaw, 1863); and *Menorah HaTehorah* on the laws of the Sabbath (Lvov, 1883).

A. Y. Bromberg, "R. Uzziel Meisels," pp. 200–211.

MELAVEH MALKAH – *Melaveh Malkah*, literally, "escorting the queen," refers to the festive meal held after *Havdalah* on Saturday night. Its origins can be traced in the Talmud to R. Hanina and R. Hika (*Shabbat* 117b and 119b). Tradition has it that King David, having been informed by God that his death would occur on the Sabbath, celebrated each time he survived that day. Hence, the meal is also called the "feast of King David" and commences with the words "*Da HeSeudata DeDavid Malkah*" (This is the feast of King David).

For the kabbalists and the hasidim the meal took on mystical dimensions. Escorting the queen served in effect to prolong the benefits she bestowed upon humanity. From R. Yitzhak Luria derives the notion that not until the Sabbath Queen has finally departed do souls return to purgatory from their Sabbath reprieve.

Hasidim who gather with their rebbe for the *Melaveh Malkah* bring their own delicacies: fish, herring, and borscht are the customary dishes. Toasting is done over vodka and brandy. Not all hasidim, however (e.g., the Munkaczer), celebrate with a meal.

The meal is celebrated with customary gaiety in song and dance.

A. Wertheim, *Halakhot VeHalikhot BaHasidut*, p. 153.

M.W.K.

MENAHEM MENDEL, of Przemyshlan (1728–21 *Tishri* 1771) – Menahem Mendel, or "R. Mendele," a disciple of the Besht, was a silent and self-effacing man who for twelve years did not utter a single word. Before his emigration, he visited Cekinowka, a small town near Soroki on the Dnieper, where he occupied himself with the redemption of captives.

"If we divert our thoughts from devotion to God and study excessively," he maintained, "we will forget the fear of heaven. Study should, therefore, be reduced, and one should always meditate on the greatness of the Creator."

He is referred to in the *Shivhei HaBesht*.

He was thirty-six years old when he accompanied R. Nahman of Horodenka to the Holy Land. He settled in Jerusalem. He urged his brother R. Tzvi of Zloczov to follow his example. "How long will you stay in the Diaspora?" he wrote. "And how long will you listen to those who speak in derogatory terms of the Holy Land?"

He yearned to meet the kabbalist R. Eliezer Rokeach, but the meeting never took place.

He was the author of *Darkei Yesharim VeHanagot Yesharot* (Zhitomir, 1805) and *Likkutei Yekarim* (Lvov, 1792). His disciple was R. Meshullam Feivish of Zbarazh.

He was buried in Tiberias.

A. Rubinstein, *Tarbiz*, vol. 35 (1965), pp. 174–191.

MENAHEM MENDEL of Vitebsk (1730–7 *Iyyar* 1788)–The founder of the Ashkenazic community in Safed was born in Vitebsk, the son of R. Moses, a disciple of the Besht. At the age of nine, he was taken by his father on a visit to the Besht. He then became a leading disciple of the Maggid of Mezhirech. He was first rabbi in Minsk and then in Horodok. His closest friend and colleague was R. Shneur Zalman of Liady. In 1775 he accompanied R. Shneur Zalman to Vilna to seek a personal interview with the Gaon. However, the Gaon would not consent to meet them.

In *Adar* 1777 he left Horodok–accompanied by R. Abraham Katz of Kalisk (Klyski), R. Israel ben Peretz of Plotsk, and 300 followers–for the Holy Land. The departure of the emigrants did not please the Polish authorities because it represented a loss of tax revenue. A law was immediately enacted decreeing that people leaving the country would require a special exit permit to be obtained after payment of a tax.

The travelers were warmly welcomed by the Jewish community in Istanbul, but their journey was not without tragedy. Some fifty lives were lost when one of the vessels capsized near the Crimean peninsula, and only thirty of that vessel's eighty passengers were rescued.

On 5 *Elul* 1777 he and the surviving pilgrims arrived in Acre and settled in Safed. He was welcomed by the Sephardim, and this pleasant relationship was cemented by the marriage of his son, R. Moses, to a Sephardic woman. The settlers soon exhausted their funds, and R. Menahem Mendel had to concern himself with their material needs. He began to enlist financial support from his followers in Russia.

As the appeal letters did not produce any immediate results, he sent R. Israel of Plotsk, R. Solomon Segal, and R. Israel Baer of Lubavitch to collect funds in Eastern Europe. He was in constant touch with R. Shneur Zalman of Liady. Not only did he fail to establish peace between the hasidim and the *mitnaggedim* in Eastern Europe, but disharmony followed him even to the Holy Land. To escape dissension he settled in Tiberias in 1781.

In his last will and testament, he instructed that his widow dispose of his household furniture and utilize the proceeds for the Ashkenazic *kollel* in the Holy Land. He was buried in Tiberias, and his grave is one of the very few that has been preserved intact.

His discourses can be found in *Pri Ha-Aretz* (Kopys, 1911) and *Maamarim Noraim* on the *Zohar* (Przemysl, 1885).

Ed.

Theology

The core of R. Menahem Mendel's teachings consists of the absolute unity of all existence in God, Who is the source of the universe. The unifying factor is *Hokhmah*, the divine mind. Through it all, the worlds are united and duality negated. Every occurrence in nature is a manifestation of this mind. There is no movement, great or small, without it. Human beings are meant to participate in this absolute unity, for God created everything for their presence. Humanity is truly a part of the Divinity, and we have to penetrate through the matter by contemplating the true inner nature of things. By *devekut* we become part of the celestial Divinity. The concentration of thought on a single concept leads to awe and to love.

R. Menahem Mendel also contributed to the development of many ideas commonly associated with *Habad*. One is the belief that people possess two souls: the *Nefesh Behemit*, or life force–the source of desire and of good and evil inclinations–and the *Nefesh Elohit*, or divine soul, which is a part of God above.

He felt fulfilled living in the Holy Land. "The Holy Spirit," he wrote, "may be expected to inspire persons in the Holy Land much more than in the Diaspora. Even in respect of charity there is a difference between its being done in the Diaspora and its happening in the Holy Land, for all the lands are governed by angels while the Land of Israel is watched over by the Lord Himself."

R. Schatz-Uffenheimer, *HaHasidut KeMistikah*.

S.L.B.

MERTZ, Ezekiel Shragai, of Kosice (1912–9 *Sivan* 1972)–Son of R. Yoel Sussman, Ezekiel immersed himself in Torah study. He had no interest in worldly affairs and lived a life marked by frequent fasts and abstinence. He married the daughter of R. Hayyim Zilberman. He was a follower of his grandfather R. Jacob Frankfurter. He studied under R. Menahem Pollak of Serencs and R. Saul Broch of Kosice.

During World War II, R. Ezekiel and his family lived in Budapest and then moved to Vienna. In 1956 he went to the United States and settled in Brooklyn in Williamsburg, where he became attached to R. Yoel Teitelbaum of Satmar and to R. Jacob Joseph Twersky of Skvira.

His congregation was called *Tolaat Yaakov*. His Torah discourses were published together with those of his father under the titles *Tiferet Yehezkel* and *Har Yir'eh* (Brooklyn, 1977).

A.Sh.

MESIVTA – A *yeshivah* set up in Warsaw in 1919 under R. Meir Dan Plotsky, R. Menahem Zemba, and R. Menahem Mendel Kasher.

Each candidate for admission to the *yeshivah* had to be older than thirteen and be able to master unaided one page of the Talmud and *Tosafot*. The *yeshivah*, which was administered by R. Solomon Yoskovitch and R. Solomon Klepfish, had the wholehearted support of R. Abraham Mordecai Alter of Ger.

In the course of five years, each student covered literally hundreds of pages of the Talmud. Time was allocated to the study of the Bible, with the commentary of Rashi, and moralistic works. The *yeshivah* also devoted two hours each day to Polish language, to mathematics, and to history. This revolutionary departure did not go unchallenged. R. Hayyim Elazar Shapira of Munkacs termed it "heresy."

MESSIAH – In his famous letter to his brother-in-law – Gershom of Kutov (printed at the end of Jacob Joseph of Polonnoye's *Ben Porat Yosef*) – the Besht describes a meeting he had with the Messiah during an ascent of soul. On the Besht's requesting the Messiah to tell him when he would come to redeem Israel, the Messiah replied it would be when the teachings of the Besht had spread abroad, whereupon the Besht expressed his dismay that it would take so long before redemption was nigh.

This authentic letter is somewhat ambiguous on the question of the role of messianism in early Hasidism. On one hand, as Tishby has observed, the advent of the Messiah is closely associated with the spreading of the Besht's doctrines, but on the other hand, as Scholem has pointed out, the Besht himself sees this as happening in the distant future. The historical background of the rise of Hasidism is similarly ambiguous on the question. It is true that messianism was in the air in the early eighteenth century, the Shabbatean and Frankist movements being still active in that period. Yet it would not be at all surprising to learn that in Hasidism a reaction set in against the excesses of these movements with a consequent suspicion of messianic fervor.

Scholem has noted further that the Lurianic doctrine of the reclamation of the holy sparks, as a prelude to the advent of the Messiah, receives in early hasidic thought (e.g., in the writings of R. Jacob Joseph) the novel interpretation that individuals have their own sparks to redeem in accordance with their soul-root, so that the concept of *geulah peratit* (individual redemption) is substituted for that of *geulah kelalit* (general redemption). Redemption is thus transferred to the individualistic plane to the extent that Scholem discerns in Hasidism a neutralization of the messianic element in Jewish thought.

The hasidic *tzaddik* takes over to some extent the role of the Messiah, his chief function being to aid his followers in achieving the redemption of their soul in the here and now, not the redemption of the whole community at the culmination of human history. It is certain that Hasidism never saw the Besht himself as occupying anything like a messianic role. Even the fact that some hasidic groups established themselves in Eretz Yisrael around 1788 is a marginal phenomenon, and in the letters written by their leaders there is no indication of any messianic intensity of feeling.

Yet, as Scholem also remarks, all this must not be construed as a real transformation or any kind of rejection of messianism by the early hasidim. After all, the hasidim were Orthodox Jews, and belief in the coming of the Messiah is one of the principles of the Jewish faith. The question is really one of emphasis. For all the stress on personal redemption in the present, the hasidic masters and their followers all looked forward with great longing to the coming of the Messiah.

It is well known that during the Napoleonic wars, the hasidic masters of Russia, Poland, and Hungary saw these events as the wars of Gog and Magog. R. Shneur Zalman of Liady, the "Seer" of Lublin, the Maggid of

Kozienice, and R. Mendel of Rymanov, especially, siding either with Napoleon or with the Russian czar, took steps, by means of prayer and magical acts—so the legends tell—in order to achieve the victory of one side or the other so that the way would be paved for the immediate coming of the messianic king and the establishment of the kingdom of heaven on earth.

Numerous are the tales of *tzaddikim* yearning daily for the Messiah. Hasidic legend tells of R. Moses Teitelbaum of Ujhely as being so diligent in his longing for the coming of the Messiah that he would always place his best walking stick beside his bed so that if the Messiah came while he was asleep, he would be ready to go out to welcome him. The prayers of R. Levi Yitzhak of Berdichev for the coming of the Messiah are a part of hasidic folklore, as are the Hungarian songs adapted by R. Yitzhak of Kalev to refer to the redemption. It is said that the wedding invitations to the marriages of the children of R. Levi Yitzhak were worded: "The wedding will, God willing, take place in the holy city of Jerusalem, but if, God forbid, the Messiah will not come, the wedding will take place in Berdichev."

There is a good deal of evidence that R. Nahman of Bratzlav saw himself in a messianic role, and legends tell of a similar role for R. Israel of Ruzhyn. It is rumored that on the gold-plated throne of R. David of Talno were inscribed the words "David King of Israel is alive."

Some of the hasidic masters were not averse to calculating the time when the Messiah was to come, generally in their own day. Two favorite dates in this connection were 1840 and 1941. The great synagogue at Belz had a special door that was never opened, waiting for the visit by the Messiah. The hasidim adopted the Lurianic Prayer Book, in which, following the Sephardic rite, the following words were added to the *Kaddish* prayer: *veyatzmah purkanei vekarev meshihei* (and let His redemption spring forth and His Messiah be nigh). Many of the words of the melodies to which the hasidim dance express an intense longing for the *Geulah*, the redemption.

The eschatological scheme as it is described in the tradition was, of course, accepted in its totality by the hasidim. The Messiah is a person. The hasidim never accept the notion of a messianic age apart from a personal Messiah. Similarly, the resurrection of the dead that will take place after the coming of the Messiah is conceived of in Hasidism in the most literal of terms. The supernatural elements in traditional messianism are given prominence in the thought of all the hasidic masters. In the messianic age, the third Temple will drop down from heaven, the priesthood will be reestablished, and the sacrificial system reintroduced. It should be realized, however, that in these attitudes the Hasidism did not differ very much from their mitnaggedic contemporaries.

Many of the hasidic leaders were opposed to Zionism on the grounds that the establishment of a secular state in the Holy Land before the advent of the Messiah was an impious denial of the divine intervention that will alone usher in the new era. Only a very few hasidic masters were prepared to adopt the compromise of other religious Jews who saw the establishment of the state of Israel not as the final redemption but as *athalta degeula* (the beginning of the redemption).

The most vehement opponents of Zionism among the hasidim were the Munkacser rebbe and the Satmarer rebbe. The former devoted many of his sermons to the total rejection not only of Zionism in general but also of the Mizrachi and even the Aggudat Yisrael for, as he saw it, qualifying the messianic dogma by accepting to a greater or lesser degree the idea that Jews can and should work for Jewish settlement in the land of Israel on a national basis and through normal political means.

During the First World War, when a number of prominent rabbis wished to have declared a public fast day on which prayers would be offered for peace, the Munkacser was strongly opposed to the idea, arguing that this would seem to imply that Jews wished to avoid the sufferings of the birth pangs of the Messiah, preferring to settle back into the old ways instead of repenting of their sins and longing for the new world that is to be brought into existence by God's direct action in sending His Messiah.

B. Z. Dinur, *BeMifneh HaDorot*, pp. 181–227.

I. Tishby, "The Messianic Idea and Messianic Trends in the Growth of Hasidism" (Hebrew), pp. 1–45.

L.J.

MESSIANIC MOVEMENTS–

Yearning to return to the promised land, the

Jews clung desperately to their conviction that the Messiah would redeem them and lead them back home. It was a conviction that rendered them pathetically vulnerable.

Like shooting stars, false messiahs flashed across the skies of Jewish history so that the flame of messianism glowed through the darkness of endless exile. But in the wake of each fallen star came disillusionment, despair, and disaster.

Again and again, pretenders arose to lift and then dash the hopes of the people. R. Akiva—one of Judaism's best loved sages—hailed as the Messiah Simeon Bar Kosiba, whom he renamed Bar Kochba, "son of a star."

Minor messiahs often appeared on the Jewish scene. Moses of Crete in the fifth century and Serenus of Syria and Abu Isa of Persia in the eighth century were the first of many. At least eight messianic movements were recorded during the first three Crusades. In 1172, the appearance of a "redeemer" in Yemen led Maimonides to warn the Jews of Yemen of the dangers of overcredulity. Among the most flamboyant was the twelfth-century's R. David Alroy of Kurdistan, who promised to liberate Persian Jews from the yoke of Islam.

In 1284, Abraham Abulafia of Messina proclaimed himself Messiah. In 1502, Asher Lamlein of Italy announced that the advent of the Messiah was imminent. Another aspirant to the Messiah's throne was David Reubeni, who claimed to be the plenipotentiary of his brother, King Joseph. Reubeni sought the endorsement of the pope and appealed to Emperor Charles I and King Manuel of Portugal for help against the Turks. Reubeni probably perished in a Spanish prison. Yet many believed in him, and he fired the imagination of Diego Pines (1500–1532), also calling himself Solomon Molkoh, and declared that the messianic age would commence in 1540. Unhappily, Molkoh did not live to see it. He was burned at the stake by the Inquisition in Mantua in 1532.

In 1648, Shabbetai Tzvi proclaimed himself Messiah but eventually converted to Islam. The most notorious of the pseudomessiahs was Jacob Leibovitch Frank (1726–1791). It was ironic that Jewry, for whom apostasy was anathema, sighed with relief when Jacob Frank and his followers embraced Christianity in February 1759.

A. H. Silver, *A History of Messianic Speculation in Israel*.

MICHELSON, Tzvi Ezekiel (1853–1942)—He was born in Bilgoraj, a descendant of a noted rabbinic family, counting among his ancestors the onetime chief rabbi of London, later of Berlin, R. Tzvi Hirsch Hirschel Lewin (Hart Lyon, 1721–1800). His father, R. Abraham Hayyim, a businessman, engaged private tutors for his son.

His father's fine library stimulated his natural interest in bibliography and history, especially the title pages, the introductions, the recommendatory epistles, and the subscription lists; all these held a particular fascination for him. The library also contained many manuscripts with autograph letters and texts with important marginalia.

His father died at an early age, and his mother with her three children stayed with her father, R. Samuel Eli, in Sokolov. He studied with R. Zeev Nahum of Biala. On 21 *Av* 1886, he married his cousin Hinda Sarah, the daughter of R. David Tevele Schwerdscharf. He was then attracted to the circle of R. Judah Aryeh Alter of Ger.

In 1880, he became rabbi in Karsinbrod, and then in 1893, he became rabbi in Plonsk, where he remained until the First World War. He spent the war years as a civilian prisoner of war in Karlsbad.

After the war, in 1922, he was appointed a member of the Warsaw rabbinate. He was a prolific author as well as an assiduous editor of the literary works of his ancestors and other rabbis. He annotated the works with exhaustive historical and biographical introductions, which are now indispensable tools for the student of the rabbinic history of Central Europe from the seventeenth to the twentieth centuries.

He was the author of more than twenty works. Among them were the three volumes of responsa *Bet Yehezkel* (Piotrokov, 1924), *Pinot Habayit* (1924), and *Tirosh VeYizhor* (Bilgoraj, 1936).

He made a great contribution to the biographies of hasidic personalities such as R. Simhah Bunem of Przysucha (e.g., R. J. Eibeschutz, *Hedwat Simhah* [Warsaw, 1930]), R. Pinhas of Koretz (*Midrash Pinhas* [Warsaw, 1930]), the rebbe of Radzymin (*Toafot Reem*

[Warsaw, 1936]), the Margulies family (*Bet Aharon* [Piotrokov, 1931]), and R. Alexander Ziskind HaKohen of Plotsk (*Torat Kohen* [Warsaw, 1939]), one of the last Hebrew books printed before the outbreak of the Second World War.

A number of hasidic biographies that are mainly his work were published under the name of his son, R. Abraham Simhah Bunem of Zgiersz. These include *Shemen HaTov* (Piotrokov, 1905), a biography of R. Shmelke Horowitz of Nikolsburg; *Ohel Elimelekh* (Warsaw, 1910), a biography of R. Elimelekh of Lejask; and *Dover Shalom* (Przemysl, 1910), a biography of R. Shalom Rokeah of Belz.

He perished in Treblinka. Three boxes of his unpublished manuscripts were lost in the Holocaust.

Elleh Ezkerah, vol. 2, pp. 195–203.

N. Shemen, *Di Biografia fun a Warshever Rav*.

MIKVAOT – The high spiritual value connected to frequent immersion in the ritual bath (*mikveh*) is stressed in Hasidism from its early beginnings and in every branch of the movement, though there is a hasidic tradition that, because of an infirmity, the Maggid of Mezhirech did not follow the practice. Had he done so, the Besht is reported as saying, he would have brought the Messiah, a saying that was later rationized to mean that by the power of his holy thoughts while in the *mikveh*, the Maggid would have been responsible for such penitential fervor among Jews that it would have succeeded in bringing the Messiah. Apart from this there is not a single instance of the hasidic masters' or their followers' neglecting the rite of immersion.

The Talmud speaks of Ezra's ordaining immersion after marital relations and forbidding the study of the Torah or the recital of prayers until the rite had taken place. The reason given for the enactment is that it would act as a check on overindulgence by the scholars. But the Talmud (*Ber.* 22a) finally records that "the immersion of Ezra" was eventually abolished, a rule recorded in the *Shulhan Arukh* (*Orah Hayyim* 88:1) as the established custom. However, there were still many in the post-talmudic period, including, it is said, Maimonides, who faithfully observed the immersion of Ezra.

Consequently, hasidic emphasis on this was no innovation and even had a semi-halakhic basis, which probably explains the paucity of attacks on hasidic ablutions in the anti-hasidic polemics, the *mitnaggedim* complaining, occasionally, only about the undue frequency of hasidic immersions. The hasidic master Kalonymus Kalman Epstein of Cracow (*Maor VaShemesh*, *emor*, beg. [Tel Aviv, 1964], p. 140) insists that the immersion of Ezra was abolished only for the masses. Those who wish to study the Torah and pray "in dread and fear" cannot afford to neglect it, and it is especially important for the study of the Kabbalah. Shabbetai Tzvi's study of the Kabbalah led to heresy because he and his followers did not observe the immersion of Ezra.

In addition to this semiobligatory immersion, Hasidism encouraged regular ablutions as an aid to purity of body and soul, as an essential means of attuning the mind to prayer, as a necessary rite to be performed before welcoming the Sabbath and the Festivals and before visting the rebbe (among some hasidic groups, such as in Chernobyl), before carrying out any *mitzvah*, and as an act of divine worship in itself.

A number of early hasidic texts (e.g., *Likkutim Yekarim*, [Jerusalem, 1974], no. 178, p. 56b, and *Keter Shem Tov* [Jerusalem, 1968], pp. 24b–25a) remark that the Besht attained to his lofty spiritual rank and received all his illuminations only because of his frequent ablutions and that these are far more spiritually helpful than fasting, which weakens the body. Attributed to Aaron of Karlin is the observation that the prophet Ezekiel had his prophetic vision beside the water and in the same way, whereas prophecy is impossible outside the Holy Land in normal circumstances. Yet, through immersion in the living waters of the *mikveh*, one can attain to the prophetic spirit even nowadays. A favorite motif in hasidic legend is the ability of the *tzaddik* to work miracles as a result of his immersion in the *mikveh*.

The alleged "*kavvanot* (mystical intentions) of the Besht for the *mikveh*" are quoted in a number of hasidic works (e.g., *Likkutim Yekarim*, *Yosher Divrei Emet*, no. 42, pp. 134–35; *Keter Shem Tov*, p. 2b; and *Siddur HaRav*, Appendix 5, pp. 629–630). The hasid, while in the *mikveh*, concentrates on various combinations of divine names, for example, the name "kna," which has the same numerical value as "*mikveh*." Significantly, these *kavvanot* differ in certain respects from the Lurianic *kavvanot* for the *mikveh*, a fact acknowledged by the hasidic masters, who seek to justify the Besht's new *kavvanot*, and which, no doubt, reflects the new emphasis given to the rite in Hasidism.

Hasidic theory has much to say about the mystical significance of the *mikveh*. The gathering of water represents the *Sefirah*, *Binah*, the world of the divine thought, of total unity in which there is neither multiplicity nor division. Water is transparent, symbolizing that stage in the divine creative process in which there is no color–the symbol of differentiation–but only the completely uncontrolled flow of divine grace.

Immersion in the *mikveh* brings about humanity's attachment to this stage, washes away the stain of sin and restores us to our source so that we emerge as a "new creature," reborn for a life of holiness. Just as at the beginning of creation water covered the earth, the water of the *mikveh* represents the "world of concealment," whereas human beings, created from the dust of the earth, represent the "world of revelation." When we immerse ourself in the *mikveh* we attach the revealed world to its hidden source and assist the unification process.

Immersion in the *mikveh* is part of the rite of conversion to Judaism. If, it is argued, immersion can change the status of a gentile to that of a Jew a fortiori, then it can bring an additional influx of sanctity to one already in a state of holiness. Thus the rite is no longer seen as a merely negative procedure whereby the taint of impurity gets removed. It is rather a positive means of increasing purity and holiness, of enabling one to ascend ever higher. The rite is also linked with the typical hasidic doctrine of self-annihilation–the loss of selfhood in the quest for the divine. The letters of *tevilah* (immersion) are virtually the same as those of *bittul* (annihilation). The whole body enters the waters of the *mikveh* to become, as it were, submerged in the divine. One's grasping ego transcended, one can now reach out to God in perfect freedom.

Hasidism developed its own rules regarding immersion and its own folklore on the subject. The usual practice was to dip under the water three times, but some hasidim considered it to be meritorious to add to these. As an atonement for sin, it was advised to dip fourteen times. Out of one's regard for the purifying effects of the *mikveh*, it is often the practice to leave some of the water on the beard and side-locks.

In the name of the Besht, R. Hanokh Heinokh of Alexander is reported to have issued a guarantee that even in the coldest weather, no harm would come from a visit to the *mikveh*. It was widely held that to bathe the eyes with *mikveh* water had a curative effect and that for a husband to bathe expressly for the purpose while his wife was in labor would ensure an easy birth. Hasidic tales tell of the *tzaddikim's* immersing in the ice-cold water of the *mikveh*, their holiness causing the water to come to the boil. Although there are halakhic objections to bathing the whole body on the Sabbath, the hasidim relied on the more lenient view because of the importance of ablutions in their scheme.

A. Wertheim, *Halakhot VeHalikhot BaHasidut*, pp. 66–68, 144–145.

L.J.

MILAN–Second-largest city of Italy, it has a Jewish population of 12,000.

Lubavitch activities started in December 1959, with the appointment of R. G. H. Garelik as the rabbi of the *Ohel Jacob* congregation. A kindergarten, a *Bet Hannah* day school, and a small *yeshivah* were established.

A number of families were sent to Milan by the rebbe of Lubavitch to foster the hasidic spirit and to stimulate activities.

The *Tanya* as well as *Talks and Tales* were published in Italian.

MINDEL, Nisan (b. 1912), author–A native of Rezekne, Latvia, he studied in *yeshivot* in Latvia, where he received his rabbinical ordination. He studied law and political science at the University of Manchester, in England, where he graduated with B.A. and M.A. degrees. He received his Ph.D. in 1962 from Columbia University.

He was foreign correspondent for the Jewish daily *Haint* in Riga and has been associated, since 1940, with the Lubavitch movement in which he served as director of publications.

He is the author of *Memoirs of R. Joseph Schneersohn*, *Rabbi Shneur Zalman of Liady* (New York, 1969) and has edited a bilingual edition of the *Tanya*. He is also the author of *My Prayer*, *Complete Festival Series*, and many other Lubavitch publications.

MINKIN, Jacob Samuel (1885-1962), author – Born in Swieciany, Poland, he emigrated to the United States and studied at Columbia University and at the Jewish Theological Seminary.

His work, *The Romance of Hasidism* (New York, 1935), was one of the first books on Hasidism to be written in English. It is scholarly, readable, informative, and sympathetic to Hasidism.

MINTZ, Benjamin (1903-1961) – A native of Lodz, he studied in the *shtiebl* of Ger and was an organizer for the *Tzeire Agudat Yisrael*. He emigrated to the Holy Land in 1923, becoming minister of posts in the new state of Israel and deputy speaker in the second *Knesset*. He was an active leader of the *Po'alei Aguda* and organized the exhibition of *Two Hundred Years of Hasidic Life in Eastern Europe*.

He was the author of a biography of R. Meir Shapira (1943), *HaRebbe MiGer* (Tel Aviv, 1950), and *Mevo LeShivhei HaBesht* (Tel Aviv, 1961).

M. Unger, *Tug Morgen Journal* (January 17, 1961).

MINZBERG, Abraham Eliezer, of Josefov (1831-4 *Shevat* 1904) – Son of R. Shlomoh Abraham Eliezer, a follower of the "Seer," he was born in Ostrowiec. He married Deborah Hannah, the daughter of R. Yitzhak David Biderman. He was a disciple of R. Jacob of Opoczna and R. Nathan David of Szydlowiec.

He became rabbi first in Teshpolo and then in Josefov. When, in 1879, a fire broke out in his home and destroyed his library and his unpublished writings, he regarded it as an omen that he should settle in the Holy Land, where he then lived for the rest of his life.

He was buried on the Mount of Olives. He was survived by two daughters and by two sons – R. Yerahmiel Yeshayah, the rabbi of Lukov, and R. Mosheh Tzvi of Jerusalem.

MINZBERG, David, of Ostrov (1903-21 *Elul* 1942) – Son of Yitzhak David Shalom, who died when David was three years old. He was brought up by his mother, *Hayyah*, who later married R. Moses Barukh of Radzymin. He married Sheine Golda, the daughter of R. Eliyahu Aryeh Lock, a hasid of Amshinov. He became attached to R. Meir Dan Plotzki and to the rebbe of Ger.

He wrote for the rabbinical periodicals *Diglenu*, *Haderekh*, and *Darkenu* under the pseudonyms *Bar Bar Rav* and *Rav Dimi*. He became the spiritual guide of the *yeshivah Hakhmei Lublin*. His wife, seven daughters, and one son took refuge in Siberia, but he and another son were killed by the Nazis in Lithuania.

MINZBERG, Leib (1887-1943), communal leader – Born in Radom, son of a hasid of Kozienice, he married the daughter of a hasid of Ger and was one of the founders of the branch of the Aguda in Lodz. He was a member of the Polish *Seym* from 1921 to 1928 and from 1930 to 1939.

A devoted hasid of Ger, he was, from 1930 to 1939, president of the Lodz Jewish community.

At the outbreak of the war, he escaped to Vilna. He was murdered by the Nazis in Bialystok.

Elleh Ezkerah, vol. 2, pp. 9-15.

MIRACLES – In every version of Hasidism it is believed that the *tzaddik*, as the channel through which the divine grace flows, has the power to perform miracles, the miracle (*mofet*) being conceived of as a supernatural intervention by means of which the laws of nature are suspended. Hasidic tales without number tell of miracles, chiefly in the realm of healing, wrought by the *tzaddikim*. Whether through his profound contemplation on the divine mysteries or by the force of his prayers, the *tzaddik* effects a cure for a person declared incurable by the doctors or enables barren women to conceive or brings about the sudden death of a brutal tyrant bent on destroying the innocent. Occasionally the tales make even more staggering claims such as the resurrection of the dead, levitation, or the capacity for the *tzaddik* to be in two places at once or to be surrounded by a miraculous light not of this world. The paradigms for all this are the biblical stories of Elijah and Elisha as well as Moses performing his wonders in Pharaoh's court and the miracle-working saints of talmudic times such as R. Haninah ben

Dose and Honi the Circle-Drawer. In hasidic thought the demarcation line between the natural and the supernatural is very finely drawn. Nature is only the garment that conceals the operations of the divine vitality through which all things are sustained. The *tzaddik*, through his attachment to God, can succeed in removing all barriers between God and His creation and so inhabits a world in which anything can happen. A favorite quote in this connection in hasidic literature is from the talmudic account of how R. Haninah ben Dose reassured his daughter, who had inadvertently used vinegar instead of oil for the Sabbath lamp: "He who said that oil should burn will say that vinegar will burn" (*Taanit* 25a). Opinions about the techniques by which miracles are wrought differ among the hasidic teachers. The early master R. Pinhas of Koretz (*Midrash Pinhas* [Jerusalem, 1971], no. 16, p. 5a) remarks that when a *tzaddik* sees a new idea during his study of the Torah, he releases the power of spiritual renewal inherent in the Torah and by so doing creates around him an aura of change, which produces miracles in the physical world.

In the thought of the Maggid of Mezhirech, the *tzaddik* can perform miracles through his severe contemplation whereby all things are reduced to their prior state of nonexistence only to reemerge having suffered a total change.

> The *tzaddik* may bring about change whenever he wishes and the High Priest could only do this on the Day of Atonement. The difference between Israel and the nations of the world is that they cannot bring about change but merely move objects from place to place, which does not apply to Israel, for they cleave to Him, blessed be His name, and they are thus able to return things to the Source of sources whence all things are formed. And He, blessed be He, on account of His love, alters things at all times from evil unto good even without prayer being offered. (*Or HaEmet* [Zhitomer, 1900], p. 55b)

But after the Maggid there can be discerned a move away from the idea of the inevitability of the miracle, through the semimagical art of contemplation, to the notion of the divine freedom influenced, as it were, but not coerced by the *tzaddik's* prayers. Thus Reuben HaLevi Hurwitz, a disciple of R. Elimelekh of Lejask, writes:

> Though we may find several *tzaddikim* who perform miracles and wonders (*nisim venifiaot*) nevertheless one should not err, heaven forbid, since truly there is none like unto our God . . . and if it puzzles you how it comes about that the *tzaddikim* perform miracles and marvels (*nisim umofetim*), indeed the truth is that the *tzaddikim* do nothing but pray to God the Creator, blessed be He, and He performs miracles for them, but the real action is done by the Creator, blessed be He. (*Dudaim BaSadeh*, [Israel, n.d.] p. 27a)

The possibility of the *tzaddik's* performing miracles was accepted unquestioningly by the hasidim, but not all of them were either content to see this as the chief function of the *tzaddik* or pleased with the emphasis on miracle-working instead of on the *tzaddik's* role as spiritual guide and mentor. The school of Prezysucha in particular tended to look upon the miracles of the *tzaddikim* as a kind of spiritual vulgarization. A maxim in this school was "signs and wonders in the land of the children of Ham" (i.e., only the spiritually unrefined, dwelling in the darkness of Egypt, are impressed by the performance of miracles).

The Kotzker rebbe interpreted the verse "Our fathers in Egypt gave no heed unto Thy wonders" (Psalms 106:7) not as a reproach but as high praise of our ancestors, who did not rely on miracles in order to have faith in God.

The Ruzhyner is reported to have said, "The more miracles are attributed to the *tzaddikim*, the more the ground is prepared for deception by clairvoyants, fortune-tellers and charlatan doctors. A *tzaddik* should merely offer prayer unto the Lord, and if he is a true *tzaddik*, his prayer will be heard."

R. Solomon of Karlin is reported as saying, "The greatest of all miracles is to bring into the heart of a Jew the holy influence whereby he may be enabled to pray properly unto his Creator."

Nevertheless a number of *tzaddikim* became especially renowned as *baalét mofet* (masters of marvels), that is, for their ability to perform miracles. It was in large measure the reputation of these men that made Hasidism attractive on the popular level and contributed to the spread of Hasidism among the masses, whereas the hasidic intellectuals set far greater store on their rebbe's degree of holiness and his spiritual attainments than on the claims made for him as a wonder worker.

J. G. Weiss, "The Great Maggid's Theory of Contemplative Magic," *HUCA*, vol. 31 (1960), pp. 137–147.

S. Y. Zevin, *Sippurei Hasidim*.

L.J.

MITNAGGEDIM–The term, which means "opponents," refers to Hasidism's adversaries from within the camp of traditional Judaism. Although criticism of the new movement already appears in print as early as the 1740s, the major, organized mitnaggedic activity begins in 1772, shortly after the death of R. Dov Baer, Maggid of Mezhirech and successor to the Besht. To a large extent, the Maggid is responsible for this opposition, for his emissaries were so successful in spreading out from their original areas in the Ukraine and Podolia to Jewish settlements that were far more advanced in Torah scholarship, such as White Russia and even Vilna, that they provoked organized opposition, led mostly by the heads of the Vilna community under the illustrious R. Elijah, the Gaon of Vilna.

Historians discern three distinct phases in the mitnaggedic efforts. The first was signaled by the ban of 1772, after hasidim had penetrated Vilna itself and organized a hasidic *minyan* there. Second was the ban of 1781, a year after the publication of the first hasidic tract, *Toldot Yaakov Yosef*, by R. Jacob Joseph of Polonnoye, disciple of the Besht, which bitterly criticized the rabbinic and communal establishment. The third and most rancorous attack by the *Mitnaggedim* came in 1797, when, during the Sukkot Festival, a day or two after the death of the Gaon, they decided to issue another ban. This excommunication was largely a reaction to the *Tanya* of R. Shneur Zalman, which had just appeared, and to the rumored rejoicing by hasidim at the news of the Gaon's demise. These developments led to the involvement of the Russian government (M. Wilensky has shown that, contrary to accepted opinion, it was the hasidim who first turned to gentile secular authorities) and the imprisonment of R. Shneur Zalman.

A considerable mitnaggedic polemical literature appeared during the decade of the 1790s, most of it by two *Maggidim*, R. David of Makow and R. Israel Loebel of Slutsk. The tone of most of these tracts is strident and militantly ad hominem; the tracts rarely face the basic issues objectively.

The mitnaggedic critique of Hasidism includes the following general items:

1. Most important: the charge concerning the neglect by hasidim of the study of Torah, both in practice and in theory (i.e., in the downgrading of *talmud torah* as the chief religious precept in Judaism). Hasidim were also accused of presumptuous irreverence toward the scholars of Torah.

2. Schismatic tendencies: hasidim abandoned the established synagogues and set up their own private *minyanim*; made changes in the liturgy; effected a new "style" in prayer–shaking, dancing, and praying loudly and with interjections in the vernacular; and introduced a new form of ritual slaughter with specially honed knives.

3. Accusations of heresy: *Mitnaggedim* averred that hasidim were guilty of residual Shabbateanism; "foreign grafts" (i.e., borrowing non-Jewish cultic forms and ideas); incipient antinomianism, such as ignoring the halakhic prescriptions for the set time of prayers; and meditating on the words of Torah in unclean places.

4. "Bizarre practices," which were not always defined: excessive merrymaking, pipe-smoking, and unconventional dress.

5. Charging the *tzaddikim* with financial exploitation of their naive hasidim, pretending to perform miracles, and illiteracy in Torah learning.

Especially important for the pivotal role he played was R. Hayyim of Volozhin (1749–1821), the most distinguished student of the Gaon. At one and the same time he is the most trenchant critic of the new movement in that, in his *Nefesh HaHayyim*, he exposes Hasidism's latent antinomianism, and he is the most moderate of the *mitnaggedim* in practice. Despite his boundless admiration for his teacher, he never joined in signing an anti-hasidic ban, and he never referred to the hasidim by the derisive epithet *kat* (sect), then in vogue.

His moderation stems largely from his tolerant and irenic personality; his theology, which allowed him to oppose Hasidism without rejecting hasidim; and his awareness of changing conditions: hasidic moderates had effectively triumphed over the radical wing, and the movement as a whole was rapidly becoming the majority. His *Nefesh HaHayyim*, published posthumously, was, in effect, a considered response to R. Shneur Zalman's opening to the rabbinic world. It made true dialogue possible for the first time, and it served to heal the breach during the first two decades of the nineteenth century.

R. Hayyim's critique of Hasidism may be briefly summarized as follows:

1. Hasidic overemphasis on *devekut* contained the potential for pneumatic anarchy and thus constituted a threat to the normative structure of prayer.

2. Hasidism devalued the role of *talmud torah* and wrongly gave precedence to prayer over Torah.

3. Hasidism's definition of the study of Torah *lishmah* (i.e., with the proper motivation, as implying *devekut*), constituted a danger to the whole enterprise of Torah study by substituting the experiential for the cognitive in the most important religious precept of Judaism.

4. Hasidism's penchant for devotional literature eclipsed, and led to neglect of the study of, halakhic texts.

5. While agreeing with R. Shneur Zalman's allegorical interpretation of the Lurianic doctrine of *tzimtzum* and accepting hasidic acosmism as well, R. Hayyim so modifies these doctrines as to undercut the immanentist foundation of hasidic thought and to reassert the transcendentalist quality of Jewish theology and experience, thus safeguarding the integrity of the *halakhah*.

In the course of time, the animosity between both camps largely disappeared, owing in part to the reconciliation initiated by R. Shneur Zalman and R. Hayyim and in part to the emergence of the *Haskalah* and other antireligious trends of modernity, which were considered by both as constituting far more serious threats to Judaism.

N. Lamm, *Torah Lishmah BeMishnat R. Hayyim MeVolozhin UVeMashevet HaDor*.

N.L.

MITZVOT – The biblical and rabbinic Commandments are the central topic of discussion in the Talmud and the Codes of Law. However, they provide relatively little information on what should take place in the mind of the person carrying out the *mitzvah*. Medieval philosophy and Kabbalah filled this breach. Maimonides' *Guide for the Perplexed* (III:51) describes spiritual reflection during the performance of the *mitzvot* as a supreme religious goal and derides those who simply carry them out "as if digging a hole in the ground."

According to R. Isaac Luria (sixteenth century), the *mitzvot* achieve a union between two aspects of the divine, termed "the Holy One" and the *Shekhinah*, with the ultimate purpose of rescuing the *Shekhinah* from exile. Due to the paradox of physical existence, sacred sparks of the divine are exiled and hence concealed within the negative, concealing realm of the *klippot* (lit., "shells"). Performance of the *mitzvot*, which almost all involve physical action, elevates the sparks to their source, releasing them from exile and resolving the paradox of physicality: the material world becomes an overt expression of the divine. This messianic goal is the purpose and function of the *mitzvot*.

Hasidism, with its quest for inwardness and meaning, emphasized this kabbalistic interpretation of the *mitzvot* and tended to demand awareness of it, at least in general terms, as part of the performance of the *mitzvah*. The kabbalistic formula "For the sake of unifying the Holy One and the *Shekhinah*" began to be said as a preparation for performing the action of the *mitzvah*, a practice criticized by R. Ezekiel Landau (1713–1793), rabbi of Prague.

The concept of preparation, with or without the verbal recitation of the formula, emphasized a further redemptive aspect of the *mitzvot*: by carrying out the *mitzvah*, the individual is *at that moment* unified with the divine. This is called *devekut* ("cleaving") to the divine. For the hasid, the simple act of, say, lighting a Hanukkah lamp can therefore become an opportunity for a deeply mystical experience. Elaboration of this theme produced some of the most remarkable texts of early Hasidism. Thus R. Menahem Mendel of Vitebsk (d. 1788) describes the *mitzvah* as a link with the *Ein Sof* through which the individual ascends to a level "higher than before the beginning of Creation," clearly an attempt to define an extraordinary ecstatic state.

Hasidic literature presents basic spiritual ideals concerning the *mitzvot*. There was strong criticism of the idea of a person's performing them not in a quest to be united with the divine but merely for the sake of social approval. A more subtle critique was the idea that one might be seeking a merely "selfish" spiritual reward rather than a higher, selfless goal. These concepts led to the idea of "hiding" one's good deeds, which is found in a number of schools, particularly that of Kotzk; R. Tzvi Elimelekh of Dinov (1783–1840) expounded the talmudic concept—"Greater a transgression for the sake of Heaven than a *mitzvah* for ulterior motives" (T.B. *Nazir* 23b)—in a subtle theory concerning the interplay of action and intention in his book *B'nei Issachar* (1846).

The performance of the *mitzvot* thus comes about not by way of a simple timetable of prescribed or prohibited actions but by way of an intimate and highly personal relationship with the divine. A variety of hasidic texts express this, such as the *Likkutei Halakhot* (Selected Laws), by R. Nathan Sternharz of Nemirov (d. 1845), a mystical commentary to the Code of Law, based on the teachings of R. Nahman of Bratzlav (d. 1810).

Some hasidic texts raise the question of the value of performance of the deed in a case when the spiritual intention is lacking, as well as the complementary issue concerning the power of an exceptional person to achieve the spiritual effect without the actual practical performance of the *mitzvah*. However, scholars generally agree on the conservatism of the hasidic movement in practice: *mitzvot* continued to be observed in daily life, with all the minutiae of practical detail expressed in the pages of the Code of Law, and a concern for *hiddur mitzvah* (careful and punctilious observance), which eventually led to full mitnaggedic acceptance of hasidic religious functionaries such as ritual slaughterers.

The hasidic halakhist R. Shneur Zalman of Liady (d. 1812) in his *Tanya* and other teachings drew the various kabbalistic and hasidic concepts about the *mitzvot* into a cohesive system, guiding the individual in the quest for conscious spirituality but also emphasizing the mystical power of the *mitzvah* even when it is not accompanied by *devekut*. Indeed, he states that conscious *devekut* reaches only the lower level of intimation of the divine. The higher level is described as an inscription engraved on a precious stone, so radiant that none can gaze at it. Only when a wax impression is made can the letters be discerned: thus brute action reveals the infinite; the highest level of contact with the divine is revealed on the lowest level—that of the simple practicalities of the *mitzvot*.

In the second half of the twentieth century, the outreach philosophy of the Lubavitch movement brought into play both the subtle relativistic hasidic perspective on the *mitzvot*, which was used to neutralize ultra-Orthodox condemnation of modern secular "transgressors" and the idea of the spiritual power of a single *mitzvah*. R. Menahem Mendel Schneerson (b. 1902) initiated a ten-point "Mitzvah Campaign," with "Mitzvah Tanks" staffed by *yeshivah* students, who invite nonobservant people to engage in *mitzvot* such as *tefillin* for men and Shabbat candlelighting for women. The intention was both to achieve a national or universal spiritual effect ("putting on *tefillin* in Manhattan aids Israeli security," "lighting Shabbat candles brings peace to the world") with messianic overtones and to help the participants discover their own practical point of entry or return to traditional Jewish life. The *mitzvot* in hasidic thought thus continue to represent not only commands that must simply be obeyed but also a mode of personal, national, and eschatological connection with the divine.

Shneur Zalman of Liady, *Likkutei Amarim Tanya*, bilingual ed., trans. N. Mindel et al. part I, chaps. 1, 23–25, 35–42; part III, chap. 5.

N.L.

MIZRACHI—A party within the World Zionist Organization.

"The Land of Israel and the People of Israel according to the Torah of Israel" is the motto of the Mizrachi, which was founded by R. Yitzhak Jacob Reines (1839–1915) in Vilna in 1902.

Few hasidic rebbes were involved in the work of the Mizrachi; however, notable exceptions were R. Barukh Hager (d. 1942) and R. Menahem Mendel Hager of Sosnowiec (d. 1954), a delegate to the Zionist congress and a worker for the *Keren Kayemet*.

Prominent among the Mizrachi leaders was R. Menahem Hayyim Landau (1861–1935), a grandson of R. Abraham Landau of Ciechanov. Other hasidim who inclined toward the Mizrachi were R. Judah Menahem Landau of Botosani and R. Judah Leib Kovalsky (1863–1925) of Wloclawek and R.

Yehiel Meir Blumfeld (1893–1943), disciples of R. Abraham Bornstein of Sochaczev.

R. Meir Bar Ilan (1880–1949), president of the Mizrachi movement, visited R. Abraham Mordecai Alter of Ger to enlist his support for the Mizrachi but did not succeed.

In his will and testament, R. Israel *Ha-Yanukkah* advised his followers not to support either the Zionists or the Mizrachists. He told R. Moses Lutzki, "If you want to study Hasidism, go to one of the Lubavitch *yeshivot*. If you want to go to a mitnaggedic *yeshivah*, go to the *yeshivah* of the *Hafetz Hayyim* in Radin. But if you go to Radin, do not stop at Lida," (a reference to R. Reines, who lived in Lida).

S. Federbusch, *Hazon Torah VeZion*, p. 212.

M'LOKHIM (angels) – A small hasidic group in the Williamsburg section of Brooklyn, New York, consisting of about 200 families. They are the first hasidic group to have originated in the United States.

They were followers of R. Hayyim Abraham Dov Baer Levine HaKohen (d. 1939), who was known as the *Malakh*. Before emigrating to the United States in 1923, he was the teacher of R. Joseph Yitzhak Schneersohn.

The *M'lokhim* consistute a separate and distinct community. Their relations with Lubavitch are strained. They study only the works of the second and third rebbe of Lubavitch, and not the works of the last two rebbes. They do not believe in decorative symbols, not even in adorning the cloth covering the holy ark.

The death of the *Malakh* left a void that has remained unfilled. When he died, the *M'lokhim* were guided by R. Jacob Schor, and when he died, in 1982, R. Meyer Weberman became their spiritual leader.

A thesis on the *M'lokhim*, entitled "Study of a Religious Community," as partial fulfillment for the degree of Master of Arts was submitted by Bernard Sober to the Faculty of Political and Social Science of the New School for Social Research, in New York, in June 1956.

J. R. Mintz, *Hasidic People*, pp. 21-26.

MODZITZ – A hasidic dynasty, founded by R. Israel Taub, and a city in Poland bearing that name. Located near Radom, in the province of Lublin, it was called Ivangorod by the hasidim, and today it is known as Demblin, but the hasidim still call it by its old Polish name, Modzitz.

The Modzitz hasidic dynasty was the first to place all of its emphasis on music and to bring music to the level of an art. They believed that music has the power to elevate the soul to the level of holiness. R. Ezekiel of Kazimierz, the progenitor of the Modzitz dynasty, stressed that music must spring from the heart, and he maintained that it is a source of strength, especially in times of stress. R. Samuel Elijah of Zwolin held that a melody had a soul and, like a human being, a complex chemistry. "The Law of God is perfect," he declared. "Therefore melody, too, must be perfect. Great responsibilities rest upon the singer. He has to prepare and purify himself most carefully. Nor should he deviate one iota from the song, lest he transgresses the precept, 'Do not add to the word which I command you, neither shall you diminish from it' " (Deuteronomy 4:2).

R. Israel Taub compared the seven notes of the scale to the seven days of creation. Just as the notes climb from the lowest to the highest and then return to the lowest, so, too, must humanity ascend and attain a high level.

Modzitzer music consists of marches, dances, and lengthy meditative works. The general pattern of the lengthy works is to start out on a low level and ascend to a final stage of ecstasy and the positive expression of hope and confidence. The most important Modzitzer composition is the *Ezkera, Elokhim, Veehemaya* (When I think thereon, O God, I must moan [Psalms 77:4]), composed by R. Israel during an operation in Berlin and consisting of thirty-two different movements. The song, which takes an hour and a half to recite, became a classic for the hasidim of Modzitz.

Modzitzer music has the power of attracting people to the Torah. R. Saul Taub, the second rebbe of Modzitz, once said that there are two phrases in our liturgy: " 'Lord of wonders, Who chooses song and Psalm' (*HaBoher BeShirah VeZimrah*) and 'King of the universe, Who has chosen us from all the nations and has given us Thy Law' (*HaBoher BaTorah*). I do not know which phrase is of greater significance." Likewise R. Israel says: "Everybody says that the Temple of song stands next to the Temple of repentance. But I say that the Temple of song is the Temple of repentance."

R. Saul developed the hasidic melodies and created many of these lengthy chants. He composed five long works called "operas," delineating the various stages of spiritual communion. Many of these chants were composed for High Holy Day services and Sabbath table gatherings. Each of the songs painted a vivid picture that left an indelible impression on the mind of the listener. The music was the only way of reaching the higher spheres. Every mood and scene in life was represented in the Modzitzer melodies.

Some of the famous Modzitzer creations are "*Niggun LeMehuserei Bayit*" (Song of the Homeless), adapted from Psalm 23 by R. Israel for those who were left homeless during World War I; the mystical *Yedid Nefesh*, sung at the Saturday afternoon meal; the expressive *Ashrenu*, a dance composed by R. Saul; the bold *Betzeit Yisrael*; *Barukh Elokeinu*; the enchanting *Shoshanat Yaakov*; and the majestic *Shir HaMaalot*. The vividly descriptive dance *Benei Betkha* was inspired by R. Saul's visit to Jerusalem.

Most of the Modzitzer music was composed by the three rabbis of the dynasty. However, some of their hasidim also composed a number of Modzitzer melodies. Among them were Idel Kaufman Idelsson (d. 1944) and Azriel David Fastag, who was a famous cantor in prewar Poland.

The noted authority on Modzitzer music today is Ben Zion Shenker (b. 1925). Residing in Brooklyn, New York, Shenker notated, preserved, and documented all of the Modzitzer melodies known today. Shenker has also produced seven phonograph records of Modzitzer music, thus popularizing them among Jews all over the world and arousing an interest in hasidic music in general. This paved the way for other hasidic groups to display their music. There is one record of Modzitzer music rendered by the New York Philharmonic.

Unlike other hasidic sects, Modzitz was not interested in copying secular tunes and using them in the service of God. Modzitzer music extends beyond hasidic circles. One can hear these melodies at all happy occasions throughout the Jewish world.

M. S. Geshuri, *LeHasidim Mizmor*.

A.Sch.

MONTEFIORE, Sir Moses (1784–1885)—In marked contrast to the attitude of both *maskilim* and *mitnaggedim* was that of Sir Moses Montefiore, who was perhaps the most outstanding Jewish personality of the nineteenth century. He devoted most of his life to fighting for the rights of Jews throughout the world. Though a Sephardi, he did not discriminate between his fellow Jews; Sephardim or Ashkenazim, hasidim or *mitnaggedim*, they were all his beloved brethren.

Montefiore's first visit to the Holy Land in 1827 fired the imagination of the hasidim. R. Simhah Bunem of Przysucha expressed surprise that Montefiore did not attempt to purchase the land of Israel from the Turks. One of his disciples asked, "What is the point of purchasing the land before the arrival of the Messiah?" "Let the Jews take it over, and the Messiah will follow," replied the pragmatic sage.

When Sir Moses visited Warsaw in May 1846, R. Yitzhak Meir Alter and R. Yitzhak of Warka called on him at the Angelski Hotel. On the same day, Dr. Louis Loewe, the secretary of Sir Moses, recorded the following:

> . . . a deputation of that preeminently conservative class of the Hebrew community, known by the appellation of Khassedim (*sic*), paid us a visit. They wore hats according to European fashion instead of the Polish "czapka" or the "mycka," which is similar to that of the Circassians. They were headed by Mr. Posener, a gentleman who had done much for the promotion of industry in Poland, and his son, and he informed Sir Moses that he would, though an old man, comply with the desire of the government and change the Polish for the German costume. Being a man held in high esteem by the Jews, and well spoken of by the prince, his example would have a most favorable effect upon others.

The hasidim in the Holy Land regarded him with great veneration. Dr. Loewe described the charismatic hasidic rebbe R. Dov Baer of Ovruch in these words: "One of the most rare sages I have ever met. Not only was he active without drawing any salary from communal funds, but he also distributes charity. From five to fifteen people would eat at his table every day."

Sir Moses also formed a close association with the Bak family, hasidim of Ruzhyn who became pioneers of Hebrew printing in the Holy Land. In 1843, Sir Moses sent them a new printing press, and the printer gratefully acknowledged the gift by inserting the sentence "The gift of Sir Moses and Lady Montefiore" in his publications. In 1845, Sir Moses sent Nisan Bak to Caterham, near Preston, England to study the art of weaving.

Emissaries from Hebron, Safed, and Tiberias often appealed to Sir Moses for help, and he always responded generously.

M. H. Rabinowicz, *Hasidism: The Movement and Its Masters*, pp. 230–231.

MONTREAL – Although a few hasidim resided in Montreal prior to the Second World War, their substantial influx to the city effectively began in the late 1940s and early 1950s. Because of both its proximity to New York, the center of hasidic life in North America, and an established infrastructure of hasidic institutions and economic opportunities in the Province of Quebec, there has been a substantial increase in numbers over the past two decades. The Montreal hasidic population, in 1994, numbered approximately 4,000 persons.

In 1970 the hasidic landscape in the city included followers of seven sects, the two largest of which were Lubavitch and Satmar, each claiming a membership of some one hundred families. The remaining hasidic population included followers of Belz, Bobov, Klausenburg, Tash, and Vishnitz. With the exception of Belz, which numbered some sixty families, the rest were considerably smaller and included few institutional facilities.

In 1941, a small group of nine students of the Lubavitch *yeshivah* in Warsaw, arriving via China, established a hasidic center, which developed successfully and by 1983 had a membership of 120 families.

After World War II the new immigrants, survivors of the Holocaust, gave a boost to Hasidism. Under the patronage of R. Yekutiel Halberstam of Klausenburg, a Zanz group was established in Montreal in 1949. R. Yoel Teitelbaum of Satmar visited Montreal frequently and established a *Talmud Torah*, a *Bet Esther*, and a *kollel Avrekhim*. These are now being maintained by R. Meisels, the son-in-law of R. Moses Teitelbaum, the rebbe of Satmar.

A Belzer *shtiebl* is situated about half way along the Rue Jeanne Mance. It was established in autumn 1952 under the name *Hasidei Belz U'Mahzikei Hadat*. Most of the Belz hasidim were of Hungarian origin.

The hasidic community today consists of ten sects. There are followers of Bobov, Munkacz, Papa, Skvira, Tash, and Vishnitz. The three most recently arrived groups – Munkacz, Papa and Skvira – number approximately thirty, twenty, and sixty families, respectively. While the Bobov and Klausenburger groups remain relatively small – approximately twenty-five and twenty families respectively – the Vishnitzer, who numbered some twenty families in the early 1970s, have grown today to approximately triple that size.

The largest hasidic sects today are Lubavitch, Satmar, Belz, and Tash. R. Meshullam Fish, the Tasher rebbe (derived from Nyiartash, Hungary), established a center some eighteen miles north of the city in the municipality of Boisbriand, in 1963, which, by 1994, numbered 120 families. Active, too, are the Papa hasidim, at first under R. Yoel Grunwald (d. 1984) and later under his successor, R. Jacob Ezekiel.

The Lubavitch sect, whose growth has resulted from the influx of Americans as well as their ability to attract Jews from the city's Sephardic population and some formerly unobservant Jews, is the largest, numbering about 250 families.

Among the rebbes who lived there were R. David Flaum (1896–1971), who arrived there in 1920; R. Eleazar Yolles (1904–1971) of Sambor, who lived there from 1948; R. Israel Aaron Unger, who was rebbe of Kosice in Montreal; R. David Rokeah (1898–11 *Sivan* 1971), the son-in-law of R. David Flaum; R. Yoel Moskovitch (1907–1980), who arrived in Montreal in 1949 and stayed there until 1966 – his son, R. Moses Meir, the rebbe of Schatz, still resides there; R. Yohanan Twersky of Talnoye lived there until 1934, when he emigrated to the Holy Land.

The hasidim have played their part in maintaining the religious standard of the community by supplying teachers, religious supervisors, and retailers of kosher provisions. In the light of their substantial numbers, each of the larger sects has established a series of educational institutions, including separate schools for boys and girls.

Despite their growing numbers, the hasidim's geographic location within the city has not changed radically since the mid 1960s.

With the exception of the Tasher sect, which left Montreal for the Boisbriand area, the majority live in the Fairmount-St. Viateur-Park Avenue area of Montreal; in lower Outremont, an adjoining municipality; and around Westbury Avenue and Queen Mary Road. Some hasidim reside in the poorer Jewish neighborhoods (Saint-Urbain and Jeanne Mance Street, between Avenue Bernard and Boulevard Saint Joseph).

However, two sects, the Klausenburger and the hasidim of Lubavitch reside outside this area; followers of the former live around the Wilderton area of the city while the latter reside in a section of the Snowdon district of Montreal. It is interesting to note that the increasing presence of hasidim in Outremont generated a series of hostile, if not anti-Semitic, reactions from some of their French-speaking middle-class Gentile neighbors, who found themselves "invaded."

Resulting from their numerical growth, the visibility of hasidic Jews has magnified. This has been accompanied by new hasidic-owned commercial and religious establishments catering to their specific needs.

The hasidim have successfully established a network of socializing institutions organized chiefly around the family. Defections are rare, the divorce and separation rates remain remarkably low, and the traditional male–female relations remain intact. Paradoxically, their high birth rate and negligible defections may ultimately endanger the community's future. When the present teenagers marry and have children in turn, there will be an urgent need for the provision of extra services. That, in turn, will require infusion of considerable financial resources and it might then become necessary to approach the provincial government as well as the mainstream Jewish community, two bodies with which the hasidim have so far carefully controlled their involvement.

In 1992 the Belzer hasidim permitted Garry Beitel to produce a fifty-two-minute documentary film entitled *Bonjour! Shalom! Les hassidim de Montreal au regard de leurs voisins Quebecois* in order to create a better understanding with their neighbors.

J. Gutwirth, "The Structure of a Hasidic Community in Montreal," pp. 43–62.

W.S. and J.G.

MORDECAI of Nesvizh (1748–8 *Nisan* 1800) – Son of R. Dov Baer, a scribe of the Council of Four Lands, he was a descendant of R. Nathan Nata Spira. He was a disciple of R. Yehiel Michael of Zloczov and a great friend of R. Aryeh Leib of Shpola. He married the daughter of R. Jacob, the rabbi of Ludmir.

He served as a rabbi in Leszniov (near Brody), Ludmir, and Nesvizh. After the death of R. Yehiel Michael in 1824, R. Mordecai became rebbe and was known as a miracle worker.

He was revered by his contemporaries and was visited by R. Jacob Yitzhak, the "Seer" of Lublin, and R. Hayyim of Czernowitz. R. Levi Yitzhak of Berdichev sent his son to study under him. Among his disciples were R. Uri of Strelisk and R. Kalonymus Epstein of Cracow.

He supported the hasidic settlements in the Holy Land and was president of the *Kollel Polin*. He was the author of *Rishpei Esh* (Warsaw, 1869). He maintained that the recitation of the Psalms would cause the annulment of harsh decrees. He was reluctant to deliver discourses. "It is forbidden to give discourses," he would say, "unless the prince of the Torah speaks with one."

He was survived by a daughter, Zartel, and three sons: R. Joseph of Ustilog, R. Jacob Aryeh of Kovel, and R. Yitzhak of Nesvizh.

A. Y. Bromberg, *Migdolei HaHasidut*, vol. 20, *Admorei Nesvizh Kaidanov Novominsk*, pp. 9–35.

MORGENSTERN, Abraham Pinhas, of Siedlice (1876–1943) – Son of R. Tzvi Hirsch of Lamaz, he succeeded his father as rebbe in 1926 and lived for a time in Biala, in Siedlice, and then at Zamenhof 7 in Warsaw. When his uncle R. Aaron Menahem Guterman died, many of his hasidim joined R. Abraham Pinhas.

He and his son, R. Joseph, perished in Auschwitz.

MORGENSTERN, Benjamin (1840–3 *Adar* 1866) – Son of R. Mendel of Kotzk, he married the daughter of R. Abraham Mordecai Alter of Ger. He died at the age of twenty-six. One of his sons, R. Abraham Mordecai, died young, and his other son, R. Israel Leib, had ten children.

MORGENSTERN, Benjamin Paltiel, of Stredin (1895–1944) – Son of R. Yitzhak Selig of Sokolov, he married the daughter of R. Joseph Kalish of Amshinov. He studied under his father and grandfather. From 1912, he lived for a time at the house of his father-in-law but soon returned to Sokolov, where he was principal of the *yeshivah*.

In 1932, he became rabbi of Stredin, near Sokolov, and on 3 *Heshvan* 1940 he succeeded his father as rebbe.

He worked in the Shultz shoe factory in the Warsaw ghetto and survived until the ghetto uprising. He was then deported to Auschwitz, where he died shortly before liberation.

He was succeeded by a nephew, R. Menahem Mendel of Tel Aviv.

MORGENSTERN, David, of Kotzk (1809–22 *Tammuz* 1873) – Elder son of R. Mendel of Kotzk, he was born in Tomaszov. He married Hayyah Toba, the daughter of R. Tzvi Hirsch Grunwald Diskes of Opoczno. He studied under his father and under R. Simhah Bunem of Przysucha. His wife kept a small shop earning a minimal livelihood.

On the death of his father, he succeeded him as rebbe. However, some of his father's hasidim, including his younger brothers, R. Benjamin and R. Moses, followed R. Yitzhak Meir Alter.

He was the author of *Ahavat David* (Warsaw, 1899), and some of his discourses are to be found in *Niflaot Hadashot* (Piotrokov, 1897).

He had four sons and seven daughters.

R. David's brother R. Mosheh Yeruham died in 1885, aged twenty-five.

MORGENSTERN, Hayyim Israel, of Pulawy (1840–12 *Sivan* 1905) – Son of R. David, he was born in Kotzk and was brought up by his grandfather. He studied under R. Noah of Wodzislov. At the age of seventeen, he married Yohebed, the daughter of R. Zelig Halevi Frankel.

When his father died in 1873, most of his hasidim followed him, with only a small number adhering to his younger brother, R. Tzvi Hirsch of Lamaz. After living in Kotzk for fifteen years, he moved to Pulawy, near Lublin, in 1888.

He believed it was the solemn duty of every Jew to take an active part in the rebuilding of the Holy Land. It was his ambition to establish an Orthodox agricultural settlement there. To enlist support, he sent copies of his work *Shalom Yerushalayim* to many rabbis. This was printed posthumously in Piotrokov in 1925.

Unhappily, he aroused the antagonism of a number of hasidim, and his plans to settle in the Holy Land were set back by a series of personal calamities. Within a brief period of time, his wife and his younger daughter (who was betrothed to R. David Bornstein of Sochaczev) died suddenly. He himself became seriously ill.

He delivered discourses not only on the Sabbath and on Festivals but also on the eve of the Sabbath before the services. He was survived by four sons: R. Tzvi, R. Moses Mordecai, R. Yitzhak Zelig, and R. Joseph, who, in 1929, became rabbi of Kotzk; he died on 14 *Tevet* 1939.

MORGENSTERN, Hayyim Jacob Aryeh, of Wyszkov (1875–1942) – Son of R. Tzvi Hirsch of Lamaz, he married the daughter of R. Menahem Mendel Kalish of Amshinov. In the lifetime of his father, he became rabbi of Vishkov, and after his father's death, in 1926, he succeeded him, although a number of followers adhered to his brother, R. Abraham Pinhas (1876–1942).

He participated in the *Shomer Shabbat V'Adat* Society. After the death of his uncle R. Aaron Menahem Mendel Guterman, in 1934, he moved to Radzymin and in 1939 settled in Warsaw.

He was murdered by the Nazis together with his nine sons. His only surviving child was his daughter, Gitah Tovah, the wife of R. Meir of Amshinov of Jerusalem.

His brother, R. Abraham Pinhas, was rabbi of Lamaz and Siedlice; he perished in the Holocaust, together with his son and son-in-law.

Elleh Ezkerah, vol. 7, pp. 47–53.

MORGENSTERN, Jacob Mendel, of Wenrov (d. 10 *Tishri* 1940) – Son of R. Yitzhak Zelig of Sokolov, he married Rachel, the daughter of R. Moses Tenenbaum, in 1902. His three children died young.

When the Nazis entered Wenrov, he was made to join a work crew responsible for clearing rubbish.

He set a shining example of faith and fortitude. "My afflictions and humiliations do not distress me," he told his hasidim. "My sufferings are easy to endure. But your sufferings, alas, are more than I can bear."

He was shot by the Nazis on the Day of Atonement.

MORGENSTERN, Joseph Aaron, of Lukov (1891–1942) – Eldest son of R. Tzvi Hirsch of Lamaz, he was born in Lamaz. He had six brothers and three sisters. He became rabbi in 1920. From 1933, he lived in Warsaw. He led a spartan existence, eating only one meal a day. He gave lengthy discourses, often quoting R. Judah Lowe ben Bezalel, the *Maharal*.

He was deeply distressed by the desecration of the Sabbath in Warsaw, and every Friday, before the Sabbath, he would walk through the streets, urging storekeepers to close their shops.

He, together with his wife and three children, perished in the Holocaust.

M. Unger, *Admorim SheNisfu BaShoa*, pp. 105–108.

MORGENSTERN, Moses Mordecai (1862–14 *Adar* 1929), Pulawy – Son of R. Israel, the rabbi of Pulawy, he studied under his father. He succeeded him as rebbe in 1906. In 1914, he moved to Warsaw.

He was preoccupied with publishing his works *Midrash Mosheh* (Warsaw, 1931) and *MiDarkei Mosheh* (Warsaw, 1935). He was a great bibliophile, and he possessed a library of rare books.

He died in Warsaw, where he was buried. He was succeeded as rabbi by his nephew R. Moses Barukh of Wlodowa.

MORGENSTERN, Shlomoh David, of London (1904–1962) – Son of R. Jacob Mendel of Wenrov, he married Havah, the daughter of R. Joshua Soroka. He came to London in 1932 and established a *shtiebl* in the East End of London. He was a stormy character and was involved in much litigation.

He emigrated to Chicago, where he died.

MORGENSTERN, Tzvi Hirsch, of Lamaz (1852–3 *Elul* 1926) – Third son of R. David of Kotzk, he was named after his grandfather, R. Hirsch Dishkes of Opoczno. His grandfather examined him on his week's study every Sabbath. In 1867 he married Yuta Henia, the daughter of R. Solomon of Radzymin, a granddaughter of R. Jacob Aryeh Guterman, in Kaluszyn. After his marriage he resided in Radzymin. His wife died in childbirth in 1886, and he subsequently married Sarah Menuhah, the daughter of R. Lipa Landberg of Warsaw. When she died he married once again. His third wife, Feigah Leah, was the daughter of R. David Goldman.

When his father died in 1873, he succeeded him as rebbe, living first in Radzymin, then in Lamaz, eventually settling in Praga, Warsaw, where he died. He was buried in Warsaw.

He had thirteen children and was succeeded by his son R. Jacob Aryeh. Another son, R. Abraham Pinhas, became rebbe in Siedlice. One daughter, Glicka, married R. Nehemiah Alter of Lodz. Another daughter, Elkah Berachah, married R. Abraham Weinberg of Slonim.

P. Z. Gliksman, *Der Kotzker Rebbe*, pp. 121–134.

MORGENSTERN, Yitzhak Zelig, of Sokolov (1866–3 *Heshvan* 1940) – Son of R. Hayyim Israel of Pulawy, he was born in Kotzk. At the age of sixteen he married Hayyah Hindah, the daughter of R. Mordecai Schonfeld of Pinczov, where he lived for a number of years. He studied in Sochaczev and was ordained by R. Hayyim of Brest-Litovsk. In 1899, he became rabbi of Sokolov-Podolski, near Siedlice. Dr. Zigmunt Bichowsky instructed him in medicine and taught him how to write prescriptions in Latin.

He was a delegate to the conference of communal leaders held in St. Peterburg in 1910, and he participated in the founding conference of the Aguda in Kattowitz in 1912. He was the main speaker of the *Tzeire Agudat Yisrael* foundation conference, held in Warsaw on 15 *Shevat* 1922. He attended the *Kenessiyah HaGedolah*, held in Vienna in 1923 and 1929, as well as the one held in Marienbad in 1937.

Like his father, he was deeply concerned with the state of the *Yishuv* and urged his followers to support the Holy Land. In 1924 he visited the Holy Land together with the rabbi of Ger and R. Tzvi Heinokh Levin of Bendin. On his return he urged Polish Jewry to settle there.

He wore a *tallit* even on Friday night and on the eve of the New Year. He fasted on the first four days of *Selihot* and never smoked on *Yom Tov*.

He lived for forty years in Sokolov, where, in 1900, he established a large *yeshivah Bet Yisrael*. He became one of the most prominent leaders of the Aguda, and their success was in no small measure due to his oratory and his publications. He also became one of the leaders of the *Agudat HaRabbanim* (rabbinical association) and traveled extensively on behalf of the movement.

He was blessed with an incisive Yiddish and Hebrew style and could inject wit and humor into his discourses. In a discourse entitled "*Elbono Shel Torah*," printed in 1920, the rebbe urged Orthodox Jewry to rally under the banner of the Aguda in order to uphold the honor of the Torah. He urged, during the interwar years, the formation of self-defense units to fight against pogroms.

In the last ten years of his life, he suffered from ill health, and at the outbreak of World War II, he was living in Otwock. One day, as he was sanctifying the Sabbath, the cup of wine fell from his hands. "They have killed my son," he cried. His premonition came true. His elder son, R. Mendel of Wenrov, was killed by the Nazis on the Day of Atonement.

The rebbe died in Otwock and was buried in Warsaw near the grave of R. Abraham Mordecai Alter, the son of R. Yitzhak Alter of Ger. He was succeeded by his son, R. Benjamin Paltiel. His daughter, Beila, married R. Nahum Mordecai Perlow, the rebbe of Novominsk in New York.

He wrote a number of articles for the *Degel HaTorah*, *Diglenu* (Warsaw, Shevat 1922), *HaBe'er*, and *Degel HaRabbanim*. All his other manuscripts perished in the Holocaust.

MOSAD HARAV KOOK, Jerusalem—"The Institute of R. Kook," founded in 1937, has a valuable hasidic library, which includes the books of R. Judah Leib Maimon (1875–1962) and those of Abba Bornstein of London. The guiding light of the institute is Yitzhak Raphael, a well-known writer on Hasidism.

In 1960, it published *Sefer R. Israel Baal Shem Tov—Studies on the History of Hasidism*, edited by J. L. Maimon; *Torot Baal HaToldot*, by G. Nigal (Jerusalem, 1974); and *Megillat Setarim*, by R. Yitzhak Yehiel Safrin of Komarno, edited by Naftali Ben Menahem.

In 1967, the Memorial Foundation of Jewish Culture contributed 10,000 Israeli pounds toward the publication of *Encyclopedia LeHasidut* (letters Alef to Tet), by Shalom Hayyim Porush (Jerusalem, 1980); *Encyclopedia LeHasidut Ishim* (letters Alef to Tet), edited by Yitzhak Alfasi (Jerusalem, 1986); and *Hasidut VeHasidim*, by Yitzhak Raphael (1991).

It also published the works of Wolf Rabinowitsch, *Lithuanian Hasidism* (1961); S. Federbusch, *Hasidut VeZion* (1963); M. Unger, *Admorim SheNisfu BeShoa* (1969); and Aaron Wertheim, *Halakhot VeHalikhot BaHasidut* (1989).

The *Mosad* has also published a number of biographies of hasidic leaders, such as R. Menahem Mendel of Kotzk, by Joseph Fox (1967); *The Seer of Lublin*, by Yitzhak Alfasi (1969); *R. Naftali of Ropczyce*, by Shlomoh Tal (1983); and *R. Abraham Joshua Heschel of Opatov*, by Leon J. Berle (1984).

In its periodicals *Sinai*, *Areshet*, and *Temirim* it published articles on Hasidism by A. Y. Bromberg, A. Bauminger, S. Z. Geshuri, Yeruham Leiner, G. Nigal, Abraham Ovadia, Z. M. Rabinowitz, Yitzhak Raphael, Abraham Rubinstein, S. Z. Shragai, and S. Y. Zevin.

The series *Arim VeImaot BeYisrael*, edited by J. L. Maimon, has many references to Hasidism.

MOSES of Przeworsk (d. 12 *Tevet* 1805)—A disciple of R. Elimelekh of Lejask, he was a scribe by profession. "I am neither a rebbe nor a rabbi," he would say. "I cannot be a rabbi, since I am no scholar. I cannot be a rebbe, since I do not know how to pray."

His work *Or Pnei Mosheh* on Torah and *Mishnah* was printed posthumously in Medziborz in 1810, and it received approval by R. Levi Yitzhak of Berdichev; R. Israel, the Maggid of Kozienice; R. Abraham Joshua Heschel of Opatov; and R. Efraim Zalman Margulies.

Among his disciples was R. Jacob Yitzhak, the "Seer" of Lublin. On one occasion, R. Elimelekh of Lejask spent the night at the home of R. Moses but could not fall asleep. "How could I sleep?" asked R. Elimelekh. "I am watching King David standing at the side of R. Moses while he is reciting Psalms."

Y. Raphael, *Sefer HaHasidut*, pp. 37–38.

MOSES of Shershov (d. 30 *Tishri* 1826) – A disciple of R. Hayyim Heikel of Amdur, he settled in Shershov (between Amdur and Kobrin). He spent his time studying, fasting, and mortifying his flesh. For two years, R. Moses of Kobrin was his devoted disciple.

W. Z. Rabinowitsch, *Lithuanian Hasidism*, pp. 141–142.

MOSES HAYYIM EFRAIM of Sudzilkov (1748–17 *Iyyar* 1800) – Son of R. Yehiel Michael Ashkenazi and Adel, the daughter of the Besht, he was the brother of R. Barukh of Medziborz. Until the age of twelve, he was brought up by the Besht, and thereafter by his brother-in-law, R. Abraham Gershon, who described him as a "prodigy."

He served as preacher of Sudzilkov, near Shepetovka. He was befriended by R. Dov Baer, the Maggid of Mezhirech, and by R. Jacob Joseph of Polonnoye. He lived a life of poverty. In the last year of his life, he settled in Medziborz, where he died and was buried next to the Besht.

His work *Degel Mahanei Efraim* (Banner of the Camp of Efraim), which was published by his son, R. Jacob Yehiel, in Korzec in 1810, is one of the classical works of Hasidism. It has been reprinted many times. The work not only contains discourses on the weekly portions of the Torah but also records his "visions" from 1780 to 1786. He quotes the discourses he heard from his father-in-law and from R. Menahem Mendel of Vitebsk.

His sons, R. Jacob Yehiel, R. Yitzhak, and R. Joseph, did not become rebbes.

Y. Raphael, *Sefer HaHasidut*, pp. 9–10.

MOSES LEIB of Sasov (1745–4 *Shevat* 1807) – Son of R. Jacob, he was born in Brody. His father was bitterly opposed to Hasidism, and he left home, without his father's permission, to spend thirteen years studying under R. Samuel (Shmelke) of Nikolsburg. "May the love of Israel enter your heart," was his teacher's blessing. And this blessing was fulfilled when R. Moses became known as a "lover of Israel."

He was also affectionately known as a "father of widows and orphans," and after morning services, he would regularly visit the homes of bereaved widows and comfort them. He was particularly concerned with the terrible plight of tenant farmers, who, when they fell behind in the payment of rent, were thrown into prisons by the Polish landowners. He was frequently instrumental in redeeming many of these prisoners.

All the money he received he distributed to the poor. He asked no questions of the recipients. Whoever asked was given help. On one occasion, when he was questioned for giving money to someone of ill repute, he replied, "Shall I be more concerned than God, Who gave it to me?"

He believed in *hitbodedut* (quiet meditation). He maintained that one should refrain from anger, which would be more pleasing in the sight of God than a thousand fast days.

After living for a number of years in Opatov, he settled in Sasov. Among his disciples were R. Jacob Yitzhak of Przysucha, R. Tzvi Hirsch of Zydaczov, and R. Menahem Mendel of Kosov.

He was the author of *Likkutei Ramal* (Czernowitz, 1856; Zhitomir, 1857), *Torat HaRamal HaShalem* (1903), and *Hiddushei Ramal* in three parts (Vienna, 1921).

He was succeeded by his only son, R. Yekutiel Shmelke (1800–18 *Kislev* 1869), who was seven years old when his father died.

Y. Raphael, *Sefer HaHasidut*, p. 38.

MOSES SHOAM of Dolina (eighteenth century) – Son of R. Dan, a devoted follower of the Besht, R. Moses was related by marriage to R. Yehiel Michael of Zloczov and R. Yitzhak of Radzvilov. He was rabbi in Dolina, eastern Galicia.

He was the author of *Divrei Mosheh* on Torah (Polonnoye, 1801), which had the approval of R. Hayyim Halberstam of Zanz, who stated that "he was great in *halakhah* and mysticism." He was also the author of *Imrei Sho'am* on tractates *Ketubot*, *Kiddushim*, and *Baba Metzia* (Kolomyja, 1880) and of *Seraf Pri Etz Hayyim*, a commentary on the work of R. Hayyim Vital (Czernowitz, 1864).

He was succeeded by his son, R. Samuel.

Y. Raphael, *Sefer HaHasidut*, pp. 11-12.

MOSKOWITZ, Bezalel Joshua, of Gliniany (1840–5 *Tammuz* 1914)–Son of R. Yehiel Michael, the son-in-law of R. Meir of Przemyshlan. In his youth, Bezalel was a follower of the rebbes of Chortkov and Husyatin. He married his cousin, the daughter of R. Abraham Hayyim Redlich of Nikolayev.

In 1867, he succeeded his father as rebbe of Gliniany. He lived a life of luxury in a stylish residence, employing many servants. On the Sabbath he spoke only Hebrew.

He was the president of the *kollel* of the Holy Land and financed the building of a synagogue in Safed, which was named after him. At the outbreak of World War I he lived for a time in Bolechov.

His son, R. Hayyim, who succeeded him as rebbe of Gliniany, died in 1921.

MOSKOWITZ, Ira (b. 1912), artist–Born in Galicia, his family emigrated to New York in 1927, where he studied in the Art Students League.

In 1972, he completed a portfolio, entitled *The Recluse*. It consisted of twelve colored etchings, with a text by Isaac Bashevis Singer. In 1973, he collaborated with Singer on a book entitled *The Hasidim*, which had seventy-five drawings and etchings. He also worked with Singer on *A Little Boy in Search of God or Mysticism in a Personal Light* (New York, 1976).

MOSKOWITZ, Israel Elimelekh, of New York (1877–18 *Adar* II 1954)–Son of R. Meir, a descendant of R. Joseph of Yampoli and R. Michael, the Maggid of Zloczov, he married Miriam, the daughter of R. Shalom Yolles, rabbi of Mosciska in 1899.

In 1908, he became rabbi of Turka, where he stayed until the outbreak of World War I. During the war he lived in Hungary and then in Prague.

His valuable library and all his manuscripts were burned.

In 1923, he emigrated to the United States and settled in the Bronx, New York, where he established a synagogue *Kerem Yisrael*.

He was the author of *Ner Yisrael*, homilies on Genesis and Exodus (New York, 1936).

MOSKOWITZ, Joel, of Shatz (1810–13 *Nisan* 1886)–Son of R. Hayyim of Satanov, he married Miriam Hayyah, the daughter of R. Meir of Przemyshlan. After living some years in the home of his father-in-law, he became rebbe in Wybranowka, near Lvov, and then lived in Sulica. He eventually settled in Shatz. He was one of the earliest rebbes to live in the Bukovina.

Like his father, he slept in a bed only on the Sabbath. A fifth of his income he distributed to the poor. His wife was renowned for her piety and wisdom, and for seventeen years following her husband's death she delivered discourses and accepted petitions from followers. She died on 25 *Adar* 1903.

On 6 *Av* 1978, the remains of the rebbe and his wife were reinterred on the Mount of Olives.

MOSKOWITZ, Joel, of Shatz (8 *Elul* 1907–17 *Tishri* 1980)–Son of R. Meir, he studied in Des and under R. Yeheskel of Sianiawa for many years. He was ordained by R. Samuel Engel of Radomysl and R. Meir Shapiro of Lublin.

In 1930, he came to London and married his cousin Miriam Hayyah, the daughter of R. Shalom Moskowitz.

In 1949, he emigrated to Canada and lived in Montreal until 1978, when he settled in Jerusalem. He dedicated his time to publishing the works of his grandfather.

He was succeeded by his sons, R. Moses Meir, who is the rabbi of Shatz in Montreal, and R. Jacob Yitzhak in Jerusalem.

MOSKOWITZ, Meir, of Shatz (1853–23 *Adar* I 1921)–Son of R. Joel, he was born near Lvov and succeeded his father as rebbe in 1886. He was a follower of the rebbe of Zydaczov.

He studied to be a scribe and lived a life of penury. He married Dinah, the daughter of R. Yitzhak Rubin of Brody, and when she died, he married the daughter of R. Jacob Yitzhak of Iasi.

He had ten children, five of them daughters; of his five sons, R. Yitzhak was rabbi of Radowicz, R. Moses Aryeh Leib was rabbi of Czernowitz, and R. Joel was rebbe of Montreal.

He died in Shatz and was reburied on the Mount of Olives in Jerusalem on 6 *Av* 1978.

MOSKOWITZ, Meir, of Zborov (1845–21 *Heshvan* 1915) – Son of R. Yehiel Michael of Gliniany, he married Sheindel, the daughter of R. Yisrael Elimelekh Unger of Zabno.

He was rebbe in Zborov. He neither delivered discourses nor officiated at the reader's desk but was renowned for the way he conducted a *melaveh malkah* after the termination of the Sabbath.

During World War I he lived for some time in Hungary. He died in Ujhely.

MOSKOWITZ, Moses Aryeh Leib, of Shatz/New York (1885–1953) – Son of R. Meir, he married Peshe Leah, the daughter of R. Nahum Brandwein of Bursztyn, in 1903. He lived in Czernowitz, and after the Holocaust he settled in New York.

His sons, R. Abraham Hayyim and R. Joel, perished in the Holocaust.

MOSKOWITZ, Schulim (17 *Kislev* 1878–22 *Tevet* 1958) – Son of R. Mordecai Joseph Moses of Sulitza, he was born in Wybranowka. He studied under his relative R. Elijah Samuel Schmerling of Bobruisk and under R. Shalom Mordecai Schwadron of Brzezany. He maintained that he received his rabbinical ordination from the rabbi of Belz. In 1897, he married his cousin Shlomtze, and they lived in Tarnov during the First World War.

From 1920 until 1927 he lived in Cologne, Germany, where he established his *shtiebl*. In 1929 he settled in London and opened a *Bet HaMidrash* in the East End, where he remained until the outbreak of World War II.

During the war he lived for a time in Leeds, later in Gateshead, and then in Stamford Hill, North London. He was renowned for his erudition. He was against television, which he called an "abomination."

He would dismiss with contempt any argument not based entirely on *halakhah*. He urged Chief Rabbi Israel Brodie to close down Jews' College, which he regarded as "an unclean house which defiles." He was a violent opponent of the establishment of day schools by the Zionist Federation.

He urged his children and grandchildren not to use perfume. He was opposed to the idea of female emancipation and strongly urged the retention of Yiddish as an everyday language.

His life was beset by personal tragedies. Except for one daughter, Miriam Hayyah, all his children died in his lifetime. His son Yitzhak died in 1931; his second son, Israel Jacob, in 1953; and his third son, Yehiel Michael, in 1956.

He was a prolific author and his work *Hagaot Daat Shalom* on *Orah Hayyim* was published in Jerusalem in 1958; *Vayomer Shalom* in New York in 1966, and *Daat Shalom* on Torah in Brooklyn in 1979. His commentary on *Pirkei Shirah* has not yet been published.

MOSKOWITZ, Yehiel Michael, of Gliniany (1818–26 *Kislev* 1867) – Son of R. Moses of Satanov, he married Frimet Rachel, the second daughter of R. Meir of Przemyshlan. In 1850, he became rebbe in Gliniany.

He was renowned for the exorcism of *dybbukim*. He was the author of *Kav Venoki* on Torah, Festivals, and liturgy, published in Munkacz in 1907.

He was succeeded by his son R. Bezalel Joshua. His other son, R. Meir, was rebbe in Zborov.

MOSKOWITZ, Yehiel Michael, of New York (1908–14 *Sivan* 1957) – Son of R. Shalom, the rebbe of Shatz in London, he was a disciple of R. Meir Shapiro.

During World War II he took refuge in Manchester, where he married Sosha, the daughter of R. Eliezer Horowitz of Mielec of New York. He died while visiting his father in London.

He was survived by six sons and two daughters.

MOSKOWITZ, Yitzhak, of Radowicz (1878–*Rosh Hodesh Adar* 1958) – Son of R. Meir of Shatz, he was a follower of R. Yehezkel of Sianiawa. He married Malkah the daughter of R. Joseph David of Sasov. He was rebbe in Radowicz.

After the Holocaust, he settled in New York, where he died.

His son R. Joseph David succeeded him as rebbe in New York. His other son, R. Shalom, was rebbe in Los Angeles.

MUNKACS (Russian, Mukachevo) – A city in the Ukraine, which was transferred from Czechoslovakia to Hungary in November 1938. With a prewar population of more than 15,000 Jews, it was the largest center of Hasidism in Hungary.

The growth of the hasidic movement in the town can be traced to the appointment of R. Tzvi Elimelekh Shapira as rabbi in 1825. He was rabbi for fourteen years and was succeeded by R. Azriel Green, who was also sympathetic toward Hasidism. One member of his *Bet Din* was R. Samuel Zeev Weiss (father of R. Joseph Meir Weiss).

In 1882, R. Solomon Shapira became rabbi there, and he was succeeded by his son, R. Tzvi Hirsch, who established a *kollel* there. He was also responsible for the setting up of *Batei Munkacs* in Jerusalem.

He was succeeded in 1914 by his son R. Hayyim Eleazar, who, after the war, established a *yeshivah Darkhei Teshuvah* in 1922 for 250 students.

He was opposed to Zionism, the Mizrachi, and even the Aguda. He alluded to the talmudic phrase that states that "the destruction of Jerusalem came about because of *Kamza* and Bar Kamza" (*Gittin* 55b). He implied that the Hebrew letters that make up the word "*Kamza*" stand for "Bundists, Revisionists, Communists, Mizrachists, Zionists, and Agudists." He violently opposed the establishment of a Hebrew high school (gymnasium) in Munkacs and Uzhorod. He was equally antagonistic toward the rabbi of Belz, R. Issachar Baer, who lived there for a time. He declared, "He and I cannot live in one town." Pamphlets such as *Maasei Rav*, *Maggid Mereshit* (Munkacs, 1927), and *Edut U'Mishpat* (Lvov, 1927) describe this controversy.

Munkacs was also the home of R. Issachar Dov Eichenstein, the rabbi of Zydaczov; R. Yitzhak Eisig Weiss of Spinka; and R. Pinhas Rokeach.

R. Shapira was succeeded by his son-in-law, R. Barukh Rabinowicz.

Munkacs was also a center of hasidic printing.

In 1944, Munkacs housed two ghettos, and transportation to concentration camps continued until May 24, 1944. Today there are barely a thousand Jews living there.

S. Weingarten, *Munkacz Arim VeImaot BeYisrael*, vol. 1, pp. 345–371.

M.S.

MUSAR – Hasidism and *Musar* represent historically the most recent manifestations of the flowering of religious genius in Judaism. The two movements have more in common than the personal names of their respective founders: R. Israel Baal Shem Tov and R. Israel Salanter (1810–1883).

Hasidism, it is generally recognized, emerged on the scene as a response to the spiritual crisis of the unsophisticated, impoverished masses in southeastern Poland of the eighteenth century. It reacted to the threat of debilitating helplessness with an infusion of spiritual vitality, rooted in the concept that God may be served through life's manifold experiences (e.g., prayer, study, earning a livelihood, partaking of food). However, He must be served with purity of heart and in a joyful mood, hasidic fellowships deriving inspiration and accepting guidance in these matters from their leaders and mentors (*tzaddikim*).

According to H. H. Ben Sasson in *Tenuat HaMusar BeLita* (World Congress of Jewish Studies, Jerusalem: Magnes Press, 1952), pp. 446–449, similar, if not identical, threats of spiritual disintegration became evident in the life of Lithuanian Jewry in the nineteenth century, a community skilled in talmudic studies but lacking in emotional commitment, at that point in history, to the values of Judaism. As a result of this situation, a breakdown was feared between "Torah" – abstract learning – and "Yira" – reverence for God's law. Hence Salanter's initial step in the organization of the *Musar* movement: his call to staid *baalei batim* to embark upon a process of self-evaluation.

In their aspirations and ultimate goals, both Hasidism and *Musar* converge on the attainment of the loftiest ideals in Judaism: inwardness in religious life, sense of serenity in the service of God, self-ennoblement in character and conduct, refined sensitivity to *mitzvot* concerning intrahuman relationships (*ben adam lehavero*), and expanding awareness of one's personal potential to improve the lot of the world and thereby contribute to the realization of the kingdom of God. Where the two diverge is in their methods.

Hasidism, which conquered the hearts of the masses within two or three generations since its founding, is essentially social and folksy, stimulating enthusiasm and mass participation, with the leader's (*tzaddik's*) court and the meeting hall (*shtiebl*) in the local community serving as focal points for sundry activities. As against these patterns of throbbing action, efforts at critical self-analysis and concentrated introspection predominate in the program of *Musar*. Such exercises–though systematically engaged in by groups in an emotion-laden atmosphere (e.g., meetings during twilight hours to the sound of soul-stirring plaintive melodies)–could not excite popular spontaneity of the hasidic style. The *shtiebl*, with its brotherliness and camaraderie, is not known among followers of *Musar*, though Salanter suggests in *Or Yisrael* ([Vilna, 1900], pp. 50, 58) the advisability of establishing local meeting rooms (*batei Musar*), to be available at all hours of the day for study and contemplation on *Musar* themes.

Musar's impact was largely confined to Lithuanian *yeshivot*. There its adepts–teachers and students–learned to blend the intellectualism of Talmud study with emotional fervor, classics on the ethics of Judaism, such as *Hovot HaLevavot*, by Bahya ibn Pakuda (1050–1120); *Mesillat Yesharim*, by Moses Hayyim Luzzatto (Ramhal, 1707-1747); and others having been incorporated into the curriculum. The position of the *mashgiah*, guide and supervisor in spiritual matters in that setting resembles that of a hasidic leader, as far as character training of students is concerned.

Few, if any, expressions against Hasidism are encountered in the writings of Salanter and his disciples. Indeed, many of their insights and comments sound like the utterances of hasidic teachers, just as many statements recorded in the names of the latter convey the impression that they hail from a background of *Musar*. However, there is no evidence in *Musar* literature to substantiate the claim advanced by Abraham E. Kaplan in *BeIkvot HaYira* ([Jerusalem: Mosad Harav Kook, 1960], pp. 26–27) that its founder attempted a synthesis between Lithuanian scholarship and hasidic ideology.

A notable exception with regard to the preceding statement is found in the remarks by the spiritual progenitor of *Musar*, the renowned R. Hayyim of Volozhin (1749-1821), in his *Nefesh HaHayyim* (Jerusalem, 1973), pp. 88–90, which is critical of prayer past the prescribed hour and exaggerated preparations for the fulfillment of a *mitzvah*. Hasidim are not mentioned by name, but their identity in these statements is beyond question. These remarks should be considered, however, within the context of R. Elijah Gaon's severe condemnation of Hasidism rather than as part of the framework of *Musar*.

Z. F. Ury, *Studies in Torah Judaism: The Musar Movement*.

S.F.

MUSHKAT, Isaiah, of Praga (1783-5 *Adar* 1868)–Popularly known as "R. Isaiah Harif," the son of the wealthy R. Jacob Moses, a hasid of the Maggid of Kozienice, he was born in Warsaw. It was through the effort of the Maggid of Kozienice that he married the daughter of R. Yitzhak of Radzvillov, who was the son of R. Michel of Zloczov.

He first served as rabbi of Szydlowiec and in 1840 in Praga. After the death of his father-in-law in 1832, he became rebbe. He was a hasid of the Maggid of Kozienice and of his son R. Moses Eliakum Beria.

He was closely associated with the hasidic rebbes: R. Yitzhak Meir Alter, who was then living in Warsaw, R. Yitzhak of Warka, and R. Yehiel Meir of Moglienice. He was among the signatories together with R. Hayyim Davidsohn and R. Yehiel Meir Alter on a number of manifestos. He contributed encomiums to many Hebrew books printed in Warsaw.

He was the author of *Atzei Besamim* on *Mishnah* and Codes (Warsaw, 1896).

For the last thirteen years of his life, he was bedridden. His only son, R. Abraham Meir, died in his lifetime. He was survived by two daughters, whose husbands were R. David of Chmielnik and R. Jacob Nata Rubin.

A. Y. Bromberg, *Migdolei HaHasidut*, vol. 23, *HaAdmorim MiPraga*, pp. 12–33.

MUSIC–Hasidism brought about a veritable renaissance of Jewish music. For the masters of mysticism, melody was rich with mystical meaning, and the *Zohar* often elaborates on this theme. "In the highest heavens," says the *Zohar*, "there is a certain temple with gates that can be opened only by the power of song."

The kabbalists of Safed, among them R. Yitzhak Luria, R. Solomon Alkabetz, and R. Israel Najara, created many notable melodies that have echoed through the ages.

"Serve the Lord with joy," was the vibrant theme that surged through Hasidism. "No child can be born except through joy. By the same token," reasoned the Besht, "if one wishes one's prayers to bear fruit, one must offer them with joy." The Besht applied the verse "Thou shalt be altogether joyful" (Deuteronomy 16:15) to our approach to everyday life, while the Torah applies it to the Festival of the Tabernacles.

The synagogue melodies were dear to the Besht, and he loved to officiate at the reader's desk. It was his custom to read the *Musaf* (the additional service) on the New Year, and on the Day of Atonement he would recite *Neilah* (the concluding service). Although the Maggid of Mezhirech did not act as reader, he, however, composed a number of melodies.

Hasidic music was unique in many ways. Songs were handed down from father to son. Often simple folk melodies became vehicles for awesome concepts.

Every dynasty had its own favorite tunes, and they became almost signature tunes. From a melody that a hasid hummed, it was often possible to identify the school to which he belonged. "Every Israelite has a portion in the world to come, and the main delight in the world to come will be derived from melody," declared R. Nahman of Bratzlav. "The only way to detach oneself from the world and to approach the Almighty is through song and praise." He maintained that "through songs, calamities can be averted. Music emanates from the prophetic spirit and has the power to elevate and to inspire."

R. Nahman interpreted the words of Jacob to his sons, "Take of the choice fruit of the land (*zimrat haaretz*) in your vessels and carry down to the man a present" (Genesis 43:11), to mean, "take of the songs of the land" because the word *zimrat* (fruit) can also be read as *zemirot* (songs). "Every branch of wisdom in the world has its own specific melody, says R. Nahman.

Habad established its own musical traditions. The founder of the dynasty, R. Shneur Zalman, was himself a gifted singer and believed that only step-by-step could one ascend to the highest of spiritual heights. There are certain stages: *Hishtapkhut Ha-Nefesh* (outpouring of the soul), *Hitorerut* (spiritual awakening), and *Hitpaalut* (ecstasy). At each stage, music could help. The first rabbi of Lubavitch composed what became known as the "Rabbi's Song" (*Den Rebben's Niggun*). This is the anthem of *Habad*, chanted only on special festive occasions, such as on 19 *Kislev* (the day when R. Shneur Zalman was released from prison).

In many cases, words were superfluous. R. Shneur Zalman once said to one of his followers, "I realize that you have not yet quite grasped the import of my discourse, so I will sing you a song." R. Shneur Zalman sang, and the hasid listened. "Now I understand what you wish to teach," responded the hasid with warmth and intelligence.

The choir of R. Dov Baer, the son of R. Shneur Zalman, won great renown, and his court was the training ground of many famous *hazanim*.

Although all hasidim agreed on the importance of melody, in the nineteenth century there were marked differences in attitude. The melody and dance were to the hasidim of Karlin on the same level as study and meditation.

In Przysucha, Kotzk, and Ger, however, music played a subsidiary role, and the emphasis was on study. Nevertheless, R. Yitzhak Meir Alter of Ger remarked, "Were I blessed with a sweet and beautiful voice, I would sing a new hymn to the Almighty every day. For the world is created anew every day, and new songs are created with it."

Different types of melodies were favored by the various groups of hasidim, for there was nothing stereotyped or regimented about hasidic life. Some liked sentimental lyrics; others preferred exuberant rollicking rhythms. Renowned in the history of hasidic musicology is the music of Kuzmir and Modzitz.

The dynasty of Bobov is renowned for its musical creativity. The composition of hasidic melodies was not confined to Poland. The melodies of Vishnitz echoed through Hungary, Romania, and Czechoslovakia.

Even in the Valley of the Shadow of Death, where a multitude of hasidim perished, even there, songs sustained them. It was then that R. Azriel Pastag composed a triumphant melody, "*Ani Maamin*" (I believe with a perfect faith in the coming of the Messiah), which was a passionate affirmation of undying faith.

Echoes of hasidic music are heard today. The most prominent of the nineteenth and twentieth centuries *hazanim*, such as Hershele Tolcyner, Yosele dem Rebben of Talnoye, Jacob Telechoner of Kaidonov, David Brod Shresliker (1882–1948), Nisan Spivak or Nissi Belzer (1824–1906), Jacob Samuel Maragowsky of Makarov (known as Zeidel Rovner), Josele Rosenblat, and Simon Hass, former cantor of the Central Synagogue, London, were all brought up in hasidic courts.

Hasidic music has influenced synagogue music, and the songs of modern Israel are greatly indebted to Hasidism. The steady output of long-playing albums and cassettes of hasidic songs in the United States and in Israel, as well as the regular hasidic song festivals held in Israel, are audible evidence of the timelessness of hasidic melodies, which poignantly express the strivings of the Jewish soul.

M. H. Rabinowicz, *Hasidism: The Movement and Its Masters*, pp. 329–341.

N

NADVORNA, Tzvi Hirsch (d. 20 *Sivan* 1801), hasidic rabbi – Son of R. Shalom Zelig, Tzvi Hirsch was a preacher first in Dolina, then in Nadvorna (Nadvornaya) in the Ivano-Frankovski part of the Ukraine. He was a disciple of R. Dov Baer, the Maggid of Mezhirech, and of R. Issachar Baer of Zloczov. R. Efraim Zalman Margulies of Brody commented that R. Tzvi Hirsch "turned many sinners to repentance."

Among his disciples were R. Menahem Mendel of Kosov, R. Tzvi Hirsch of Zydaczov, and R. Abraham David of Buczacz. A fine halakhist, he was the author of *Tzemah HaShem LeTzvi* on the Pentateuch (Berdichev, 1818), *Siftei Kedoshim* on the Psalms (Lvov, 1869), and *Mili D'Avot* on Ethics of the Fathers.

He was survived by two sons, R. David Aryeh and R. Moses Joshua Michael.

Y. Raphael, *HaHasidut*, pp. 40–41.

NAHMAN of Bratzlav (1772–18 *Tishri* 1810) – His grandfather was R. Nahman of Horodenka, an important disciple of the Besht. His mother, Feige, was the daughter of Adel, daughter of the Besht.

R. Nahman's early youth was given over to intense asceticism. He tells of an occasion when he fasted for a week. By Wednesday blood poured from his nose, but he continued to fast. His aim was to completely destroy the power of bodily desires. During his youthful learning of Bible, Talmud, and Midrash, he noted down the spiritual injunctions and teachings implicit in the text. These notes became the basis of *Sefer HaMidot*, his first literary work.

After his marriage he lived in Medvedovka. Little is known of this first period of his being a hasidic rebbe. In 1798 he went with his disciple R. Shimon to Israel. The journey had great mystical significance for R. Nahman. In Constantinople he concealed his identity and went about in ragged clothes, deliberately attracting the insults of other Jewish travelers. This was a "descent" that he felt necessary in order to achieve the immense spiritual ascent of entry into Israel.

Nearly all the known teachings of R. Nahman were written after this eventful journey. "The way to Eretz Yisrael" became an important motif, symbolizing a concealed level of Torah that is higher than the Decalogue and is the source of life for the world before the Giving of the Torah. "When the *tzaddik* falls to the level of an ignorant man, he keeps himself alive from 'the way to Eretz Yisrael.' "

In 1800 he moved to Zlatopol near Shpola. R. Aryeh Leib, who was called the Shpola "Zeide" (grandfather) and who was the *tzaddik* of the region, began to attack R. Nahman, and a bitter feud developed. The sources of it are obscure, but it seems that the Shpola Zeide objected to certain aspects of R. Nahman's path. R. Nahman was defended by the greatly respected leader R. Levi Yitzhak of Berditchev.

R. Nahman's teachings often refer to the rifts and feuds between *tzaddikim*. They relate to the concealment (*tzimtzum*) of the Divine Radiance, which is necessary for the creation of the world. Only with the advent of the Messiah will total unity be possible.

In 1802, R. Nahman moved to Bratzlav, where R. Nathan Sternharz of Nemirov became his devoted disciple and scribe. There now began the redaction of the first part of *Likkutei Moharan*, the collection of R. Nahman's teachings, which was published in 1808. The second part was published posthumously in 1811.

Apart from *Habad*, Bratzlav is the only school of Hasidism in which study of the written discourses of the rebbe became a central activity of the disciples. R. Nahman said he would like his hasidim to "advance with" each discourse for several months, that is, to strive to serve God and to progress spiritually in accordance with that teaching and then to move on to another.

Each discourse is like a world in itself. From all fields of experience and Torah study–Bible, Talmud, *Zohar*, philosophy, ethics, Kabbalah, and prophetic dreams–R. Nahman draws powerful images, which he connects together in an often totally unexpected way, revealing profound teachings concerning the striving of the Jew toward the true service of God. These discourses are viewed by Bratzlaver hasidim as near prophetic revelations and meaningful on many different levels. In recent years their free poetic quality and the existential questions they examine have excited much interest on the part of scholars, poets, and artists.

Some major themes from his teachings are described below.

The *tzaddik* has the nature and complexity of Moses. He is the leader of the generation, he rebukes it, and he apparently descends to its impure level in order to raise it and draw it near to the service of God. Close relationship with the *tzaddik* is essential for the individual; only through this can one be purified and thus break through the barriers that hem one in. R. Nahman enjoined all to pray in order to find the true *tzaddik*. There are many false *tzaddikim* who lead one astray.

Teshuvah (repentance) is a constant path of service to God. "It is impossible to serve God unless one begins each time anew. Sometimes one has to have several beginnings on a single day." "When one wants to go on the ways of *teshuvah*, one must be expert at advance and expert at retreat." Expert at advance means: not to rest, always to strive higher. Expert at retreat means: not to fall into despair.

One must conquer doubt and suffering, spiritual darkness, and despair. "As soon as one starts to walk on the true path, one is beset by opposing forces." They are to be overcome. R. Nahman once shouted out, "Despair does not exist at all!" Falling is in order to rise. Concerning suffering, he said, "When we know that all the events that happen to us are for our good, this is like the world to come." The way to achieve this is through connection with the *tzaddik*.

Simhah (joy) should be experienced, especially in the performance of the Commandments. *Simhah* is an end in itself, as an expression of faith in a situation of darkness. It is also a means toward the breaking down of barriers in the service of God. Through dancing and *simhah* one can ascend beyond reason to union with the *Ein Sof*.

Prayer is the pouring out of the soul. Through prayer with all one's strength one achieves rejuvenation and faith. "The main weapon of a Jew is prayer," to be used also in spiritual battles against evil desire. R. Nahman taught the practice of *Hitbodedut*, going out at night to a lonely place and calling directly to God. This remains an important custom of Bratzlaver hasidim.

Musar means ethics. There is a very strong ethical element throughout R. Nahman's teachings. He said, "For me the Kabbalah of R. Yitzhak Luria is all *Musar*." He thus brought exalted mystical teachings to the practical level of guarding one's senses and thoughts from evil.

R. Nahman advocated avoidance of philosophy. He warned against the study of works of Jewish philosophy such as *Guide for the Perplexed*, by Maimonides. The true method of religious inquiry, he maintained, is to be found in the *Zohar*, the teachings of R. Yitzhak Luria and the Besht. God is beyond reason, and therefore the only answer to the questions of the rationalists is simple *emunah*, faith. The *tzaddik* himself, however, should read philosophy books in order to rescue souls that may have been trapped in that realm.

In 1806, R. Nahman commanded R. Nathan to write *Likkutei Halakhot*, a literary expression of "advancing with" the discourses of his rebbe. Structured as a commentary to the *Shulhan Arukh*, each law is discussed in the light of particular discourses by R. Nahman. The intense radiance of *Likkutei Moharan* is thus applied to every aspect of Jewish observance and ethical conduct in daily life.

In that year too R. Nahman began writing *Megillat Setarim* (Scroll of Secrets), a still unrevealed work directly concerning the advent of the Messiah. He also disclosed to certain disciples what was later called *Sefe HaNisraf* (the Burnt Book). Although this wa considered an esoteric revelation even highe than *Likkutei Moharan*, R. Nahman commanded two of his disciples to travel aroun the villages and read to Jewish inhabitants certain sections from the book. This exceptional action has strong messianic overtones. R. Nahman felt that the revealing of this work was dangerous for him, and he interpreted the death of his young son in the summer of that year as due to his disclosure of such exalted teachings. Two years later, desperately ill while on a journey, he commanded it to be burned in order to save his own life. Its contents are therefore unknown.

Also in 1806 he began telling his famous *Sippurei Maasiyot*, remarkable stories of an almost surreal quality based on kabbalistic themes: a princess lost in an unholy realm, a diamond from which spring hostile creatures, escape to a fortress of water. These stories are regarded as bearing R. Nahman's most profound teachings, which only through this medium could be expressed.

For some years R. Nahman had been speaking of ten particular Psalms, which have a special purificatory effect. In 1809 he finally revealed them. They are called the *Tikkun K'lali*, (General Healing). The saying of these Psalms is today the most widespread manifestation of Bratzlaver teaching.

For the last few months of his life, R. Nahman moved to Uman, where thousands of Jewish martyrs were buried. He spoke of his task of *Tikkun Neshamot* (healing of souls). Uman was also noted for the Jewish free thinkers who lived there. R. Nahman encouraged them to visit him, engaged in discussions, and played chess with them. His own hasidim were startled by this activity, but R. Nahman said, "If one of them moves in the direction of repentance, the heavens move."

Although after the death of his rebbe during Sukkot 1810 R. Nathan assumed a vitally important organizational role, there was no real successor to R. Nahman, and he continues to be the rebbe to the Bratzlaver hasidim. When possible (ideally at Rosh Hashanah) they journey to his grave in Uman. The two major communities today are in Jerusalem, under the guidance of R. Gedaliah Koenig, and in New York, under the guidance of R. Rosenfeld. There is a *kollel* in Bene Berak and an incipient community in Safed.

Major works by R. Nahman and R. Nathan are *Likkutei Moharan*, Part I (Ostraho, 1808), Part II (Mohilov, 1811), *Sefer Ha-Midot* (Mohilev, 1811), *Sippurei Maasiyot* (Ostraho, 1816), *Shivhei HaRan* (Ostraho, 1816), *Sihot HaRan* (Ostraho, 1816), *Hayyei Moharan* (Lemberg, 1874), *Likkutei Halakhot* (Jerusalem, 1909), *Likkutei Tefillot* (Bratzlav, 1822), *Kitzur Likkutei Moharan* (Mohilev, 1811), *Likkutei Etzot* (Lemberg, 1858, 1841), *Yemei Maharanat* (Lemberg, 1876), and *Alim hi-Terufah* (Berdichev, 1896).

A. Green, *Tormented Master*.

N.L.

R. Nahman's Art of Storytelling

R. Nahman was by no means the first or the last hasidic rabbi to instruct his followers by telling them stories. Indeed, he himself is quoted as claiming to follow his great-grandfather's example in this respect, but he was undoubtedly alone in having his stories published, albeit posthumously, in book form.

In the preface to the first edition of *Sippurei Maasiyot* (1815) (there have been more than twenty since) R. Nathan of Nemirov reported the master's wish "to have a book of tales printed with the text in the Holy Tongue above and the vernacular text below," adding that the persistent popularity of these tales, corrupt versions of which were circulating in manuscript, had encouraged him to prepare the work for the press.

R. Nathan, who had apparently recorded selected tales from memory soon after hearing R. Nahman relate them, justified the literal Hebrew translation on the grounds that the slightest deviation from the author's deliberate choice of words and phrases was liable to distort or at least obscure the message, for the master, according to his faithful chronicler, meant to be understood on more than one level: simple people would be led by the sheer excitement of the narrative to draw the obvious moral from the climax, and the more learned would notice allusions to the profoundest of truths. The summaries of the narrator's remarks on arriving at the end of each tale amply support such a view. For instance, in interpreting the adventures of the prince who had been exchanged by a midwife soon after birth for the son of a palace slave as a reflection of the course and destiny of the universe, from Adam's sin to the coming of the Messiah, he commented that up to the time of R. Simon bar Yohai, the sacred mysteries were invariably discussed in this veiled manner. Equally indicative of his concern with metahistorical processes is a striking piece of negative evidence: the impossibility of identifying either his ingenious plots or their swiftly changing episodes in terms of time, space, or known sets of circumstances or conditions.

Here, in fact, was a talented storyteller who cloaked his insights into the interplay between heaven and earth in diverting fantasies in order to pursue and distribute truth. His expectation of being read on different levels continued to be fulfilled long after his death. In contrast to the commentaries emanating from his own circle, which teemed with discoveries of illuminating references to passages in the Talmud and the *Zohar*, secularizers hailed him as the forerunner of neo-Hebrew fiction.

E.M.

NAHMAN of Horodenka (d. c. 1780), disciple of the Besht–He was related by marriage to R. Moses Hayyim of Sudzilkov, a grandson of the Besht. Also, R. Nahman's son married Feige, the granddaughter of the Besht. R. Nahman accompanied the Besht on many journeys. "I have afflicted my soul and I have immersed myself in the ritual bath every day," said R. Nahman. "Even so, I could not rid myself of impure thoughts until I became attached to the Besht" (*Shivhei HaBesht* 112).

In 1764, together with R. Menahem Mendel of Przemyshlan, he set out for the Holy Land. By coincidence, R. Simhah of Zalocze, author of *Ahavat Zion* (Grodna, 1790), was on the same boat. The pilgrims left Galati on 27 *Iyyar* and waited in Constantinople for a boat until 18 *Elul*. On the voyage there was a violent storm, and R. Nahman, with a Scroll of the Law in his hands, cried out, "If, God forbid, it has been decreed that we perish, we do not accept this verdict."

On the eve of the New Year 1765, the party arrived in Jaffa. This must have been his second trip, because according to the *Shivhei HaBesht* (Tale 139), R. Eliezer Rokeah had traveled to the Holy Land to meet him there in June 1740. "If only we had been together in the Holy Land," said R. Nahman, "the Redeemer would have come." R. Eliezer died in Safed in 1741, shortly after his arrival in the Holy Land.

R. Nahman lived in Tiberias until his death. In one of his letters, he wrote, "Tradition maintains that the air of the Holy Land makes one wise. Before I came here, I hoped that I would learn to utter one prayer properly. Now that I am wise, would that I were able to utter one word properly."

Some of his discourses are quoted in *Toldot Yaakov Yosef*, by R. Jacob Joseph of Polonnoye, and in *Degel Mahanei Efraim*, by R. Moses Hayyim Efraim of Sudzilkov.

A. Rubinstein, "A Possible New Fragment of Shivhei HaBesht," pp. 174–191.

NAHMAN of Kosov (d. 1746), kabbalist–R. Nahman was one of the earliest adherents of the Besht. Data about his life and teachings can be found in the *Shivhei HaBesht* and in the works of R. Jacob Joseph of Polonnoye. Unlike the early hasidim who were poor, R. Nahman was a wealthy grain dealer. He was a member of the hasidic group in Kutov (Kuty) that included R. Moses, the rabbi of Kutov and R. Aryeh Leib Geliner, the preacher (*Mokhiah*) of Polonnoye. This group was active prior to the appearance of the Besht.

During a *seudah shlishit*, the group would study together. Most of them would later join the Besht, but it appears that for a long time R. Nahman did not acknowledge the Besht's writ. The Besht even told his disciples that R. Nahman wanted to kill him, meaning that during *Nefilat Apayim* (a prayer in which one prays for the downfall of one's enemies), R. Nahman prayed for the Besht's discomfiture.

R. Nahman had a follower in Vladimir Volynsky. He supported R. Jonathan Eibeschutz, and he was criticized by R. Jacob Emden, who called him "Nahman Kosover, the ignoramus of the Shabbatean sect" (Emden, *Petah Enayim* 14b, *Sefer Hitabbekut* 20b).

R. Nahman maintained that the dispute between the Besht and himself was not personal, but concerned the worship of God. It was a dispute similar to the ones between Saul and David and between Hillel and Shammai in ancient times. In contrast to the Besht, R. Nahman was unbending, a man who demanded much of himself and others. He practiced Lurian asceticism, fasting from Sabbath to Sabbath (he only ate on the Sabbath). He prayed with great fervor, according to the Lurian liturgy.

Though not a professional preacher, he castigated his listeners. He criticized those who found fault in others and not in themselves. "If you wish to praise, praise the Lord; if you wish to condemn, condemn yourself," was his motto. Like most of the *maggidim*, he utilized parables in his discourses, and many of them reflect his knowledge of art, drawing, painting, and silversmithing.

He called for perpetual *devekut*. "One can achieve *devekut* even by living a normal everyday life, by seeing the letters of God's name (tetragrammaton) constantly before one's eyes." To people who claimed that it was too difficult to practice such *devekut* while working as, say, a merchant, he said, "If you think of business while reciting the *Amidah*, why should you not be able to think of God while working in the market?"

A. J. Heschel, in *H. A. Wolfson Jubilee Volume*, pp. 113–141.

G.N.

NAHUM of Chernobyl (1730–11 *Heshvan* 1798)–Son of R. Tzvi Hirsch, he was born in either Nurinsk or Gurinsk, in the region between Berdichev and Kiev. His father died when he was a child, and he was brought up in the home of an uncle. He married Sarah, the granddaughter of R. Yitzhak Shapiro, rabbi of Kovno.

He studied Kabbalah diligently, and his way of life was ascetic in the extreme. To support his family he became a teacher, but his meager earnings were quite inadequate. He was attracted to the Besht and visited him twice. He is mentioned in the *Shivhei Ha-Besht*. He then became a disciple of R. Dov Baer, the Maggid of Mezhirech. Eventually he accepted a position as preacher at Chernobyl, but his financial position showed no improvement and his home in Chernobyl was marked by dire poverty. When his followers pleaded with him to move to more comfortable quarters, he refused. He denounced the love of money and luxury, and he criticized those *tzaddikim* who lived in great affluence. R. Shneur Zalman of Liady appealed to his followers to help R. Nahum.

Throughout the week he abstained from eating meat or drinking wine. It was his habit to recite *Tikkun Hatzot* at midnight, and he urged his followers to do likewise. He would travel regularly from town to town, not only to disseminate Hasidism, but to perform *pidyon shevuyim* (ransoming captives) for poor Jews who were unable to pay their dues to their landlord and were left to languish in prison. He became known as the "little Besht."

"Do many acts of loving-kindness," he told his hasidim. "Dower poor brides, visit the sick, give as much charity as you can, and fast one day each week. Do take care to speak as little as possible before morning prayers, and recite the *Shema* with awe and with love. Each word you recite in this way will help to bring life to your limbs. The 248 words of the *Shema* correspond to the number of limbs in the human body. Keep yourself from becoming angry. Let your speech be pleasant. If a person should come to praise you, do not let it lead you to self-importance."

He maintained that in every human being there are a Jacob and an Esau, that everyone is a compound of good and evil, and that the *tzaddik* bridges heaven and earth. Through good deeds, the *tzaddikim* give pleasure to God. He believed that simple faith is the foundation of the Torah and that prayer is more effective than anything else.

Many tales are told of his humility and his kindliness. He was the author of *Meor Einayim*, which was published in Slavuta in 1798, the year he died. It was acclaimed by the hasidim, and eleven more editions were printed in the nineteenth century. In 1966 a new edition was printed in Jerusalem. The work is divided into two parts: the first part contains discourses on the Torah, and the second part consists of comments on the *Aggadah*. He quotes the Besht twenty-eight times, and the Maggid of Mezhirech fourteen times.

His second major work, *Yismah Lev*, was published in Slavuta in 1791 and contains a collection of homilies on aggadic passages. In subsequent editions, both works appear together. *Hanhagot Yesharot* was printed in Zhitomir in 1868.

He was survived by one daughter and twin sons. His son R. Mordecai, who succeeded him as rebbe of Chernobyl, had eight sons.

R. Nahum, who was one of the earliest disseminators and pioneers of Hasidism in the Ukraine, was also the founder of a cluster of hasidic dynasties that still flourish today in the United States and Israel, where his name is perpetuated in a *yeshivah Meor Einayim* in Jerusalem.

Y. Raphael, *Sefer HaHasidut*, pp. 8–9.

NAPOLEON BONAPARTE (1769–1821), emperor of the French – The phenomenal exploits of Napoleon brought about a radical change in the status of European Jewry. As the Napoleonic armies marched through Italy, "the walls of the ghettos began to dance." The yellow badge gave way to the tricolor cockade, and the gates of the ghettos were torn off their hinges. In the Paris *Moniteur Universel* on 3 Prairial of the year VII (May 22, 1799), it was announced: "Bonaparte has published a proclamation in which he invites all the Jews of Asia and Africa to gather under his flag in order to reestablish the ancient Jerusalem."

Eight years later, on February 8, 1807, he summoned a *Sanhedrin* in Paris, commanding it "to reveal again to the people the true spirit of its laws and render proper interpretations of mistaken conceptions." The *Sanhedrin* obliged by releasing soldiers in the French army from their religious obligations. Although few Jews outside France and Italy accepted the pronouncements of the *Sanhedrin* as authoritative and binding, the emperor was for the moment satisfied with this experiment. "To me, at least, the *Sanhedrin* is useful," was his comment.

Although Napoleon was the hero of Polish Jewry, who regarded him as their liberator, Polish hasidic rabbis were divided on the issue. Among the staunch Napoleonic supporters was R. Menahem Mendel of Rymanov. While the rabbi baked *matzot* for the Festival of Passover, he would exclaim each time he put fresh dough into the oven: "Another Moscovite regiment goes into the fire."

On the other hand, R. Jacob Yitzhak of Lublin and R. Israel of Kozienice prayed for the victory of the czar. R. Naftali of Ropczyce also opposed French dominion, regarding Napoleon as a symbol of heresy and agnosticism.

Grateful for his relatively humane treatment in St. Petersburg, R. Shneur Zalman of Liady aligned himself with the anti-French faction. To R. Moses Meisels he wrote, "It was revealed to me during *Musaf* [the additional prayer on Rosh Hashanah] that if Bonaparte is victorious, there would be great material prosperity in Israel, but the Jews would become estranged from God. But should *Adoneinu* [our Lord] Alexander be victorious, even though they would suffer great poverty, the children of Israel would draw closer to their Father in heaven." According to a Lubavitch legend, Napoleon used to say, "Whenever I ride, that blond Jew rides before me." (R. Shneur Zalman was fair-haired.)

According to hasidic legend, the fate of Napoleon was decided not on the battlefields but in the courts of the hasidic rebbes. Legend has it that Napoleon came in disguise to plead with R. Israel, the Maggid of Kozienice, but his pleas were of no avail. For the rabbi interpreted the verse in Esther 6:13 (*Nofol Tipol*) "Thou shalt surely fall before him" to mean "Napoleon will surely be defeated."

S. Schwarzfuchs, *Napoleon, the Jews and the Sanhedrin*.

NATHANSON, Joseph Saul (1810–27 *Adar* I 1875), halakhic authority – R. Nathanson's grandfather, R. Dov Berish Heilprin, and his father-in-law, R. Yitzhak Aaron Ettinger, whose daughter Sarah was his wife, were hasidim. Although R. Joseph Saul himself was opposed to Hasidism, he had cordial relations with R. Shalom Rokeah of Belz and R. Hayyim Halberstam of Nowy Sacz, with whom he frequently corresponded.

He also wrote a commendation to *Daat Kedoshim* (1880), by R. Abraham David of Buczacz, and he highly esteemed R. Yitzhak Meir Alter of Ger. In his work *Divrei Shaul* on the Pentateuch, he quotes R. Levi Yitzhak of Berdichev. He opposed, however, the hasidic custom of reciting *Hallel* in the synagogue on Passover eve (*Shoel U'Meshiv* 2, part 4, no. 135) and the nondonning of *tefillin* on *Hol HaMo'ed* (*Shoel U'Meshiv* 2, part 3, no. 87).

From 1857 until his death, he was rabbi in Lvov and was recognized as one of the outstanding halakhists of his age. He was the author of *Shoel U'Meshiv* (1863–1890) on the *Shulhan Arukh*.

A. Y. Bromberg, *Migdolei HaHasidut*, vol. 15, *R. Joseph Saul Nathanson*.

NEO-HASIDIC SONG – During the 1960s, a new style of hasidic song developed in the United States. Because it did not adhere strictly to either the melodic or rhythmical characteristics of East European hasidic song,

NEO-HASIDIC SONG

many traditionalists were of the opinion that this type of music could, at very best, be labeled *shir dati* (religious song) or neo-hasidic song.

In the avant-garde of neo-hasidic music stood Shlomoh Carlebach, an ordained rabbi and composer of original melodies set to liturgical texts. Carlebach's first of many recordings–*Hanshomoh Lokh* (New York: Zimrani Records, 1961), featuring twelve songs–proved highly successful among a large segment of American Jewish youth. In addition to the contemporary sound of the melodies themselves, the choral and instrumental background had been arranged by Milt Okun, a well-known musician active in the field of popular American music. The resulting flavor was perceptibly different from that which had been considered traditional "Jewish" arrangements.

To Shlomoh Carlebach also belongs the distinction of being the first to take the *niggun* out of its usual habitats–the synagogue, the *farbrengen* (hasidic gatherings), *simhah* (wedding, bar mitzvah, etc.)–and to present it on stage in a concert performance accompanied by guitar and other musical instruments.

On the heels of Carlebach followed the Rabbis' Sons, a concertizing group of four observant young men trained in American *yeshivot*. The Rabbis' Sons appeared on stages in many major American cities during the late 1960s and early 1970s, and their exposure to contemporary American music was evident in most of their repertoire. An example of this influence can be heard in the opening tones of the Rabbis' Sons' *Mi Ho-ish* (New York: Emes Recording, 1967). Although the song initially shocked the hasidic ear, it nevertheless entered into and became part of the hasidic and *yeshivah* repertoires, where it has remained to this day.

Public performances by Shlomoh Carlebach and the Rabbis' Sons laid the groundwork for the appearance of a number of concertizing groups and a host of phonograph recordings, all featuring newly created songs set to liturgical texts. The music composed and performed by these various groups succeeded in satisfying the musical tastes of the younger generation, and it became their all-purpose as well as their religious music. As the recordings and concerts proliferated, older East European hasidic songs began to recede into the background and came to be looked upon by many Jewish youths as being out of tune with the times and belonging to a bygone era.

Perhaps the widest recognition of this newer music can be attributed to the first Hasidic Song Festival, presented in Israel during November 1969. Held as an open competition, the festival was performed in the major cities of Israel, and the recording of the event, issued under the Hed-Arzi label, became an instantaneous worldwide success. The subsequent yearly festivals and their recordings as well as the international concertizing of its troupe provided hasidic music with a completely new image. This type of music had an appeal to a large segment of the Jewish population as evidenced by Nurit Hirsh's (one of Israel's most popular song writers) "Ose Shalom" (Hasidic Festival, 1969). The song achieved highest standings on Israel's popular song charts and became familiar to millions of American Jews as the featured music on a series of television commercials.

To this day many hasidic music purists nurtured on the music of Modzitz, Bobov, Lubavitch, Ger, Vishnitz, and other dynasties have found great difficulty in considering neo-hasidic music an acceptable part of their musical repertoire. They passionately proclaim that many of these songs lack the depth, feeling, and intent of the more traditional *niggunim*. They point to the rather limited life span enjoyed by most of these melodies, which have become part of a sort of "Hasidic Hit Parade," to be discarded and forgotten, after a period of time, in favor of newer tunes. The death knell for true hasidic song, they feel, has been sounded by the crass commercialization of the material.

Hasidic music performed on a concert stage complete with orchestra, chorus, pop singers, costumes, and formations as an evening of entertainment has been criticized by nonhasidim as well as hasidim. Many neo-hasidic composers contend, however, that they are in keeping with strict hasidic tradition. European musical forms such as polkas, mazurkas, waltzes, marches, and shepherds' melodies have simply been replaced, they feel, with the melodic and rhythmical elements of American, Israeli, jazz, country, and rock music. In addition, they quote the hasidic masters, including R. Nahman of Bratzlav, who proclaimed that all music emanates from the heavenly spheres known as the *Hekhal HaNegginah* (Temple of Music). Because music is divinely inspired, it contains no "impurities," and therefore any and all music may be utilized.

One of the more striking departures of neo-hasidic song is its almost total disregard for the minor mode, the hallmark of most hasidic song as well as East European Jewish music in general. The brighter-sounding major scale seems to its composers more in keeping with ghetto-free contemporary Jews. The change in the rhythmic aspects of neo-hasidic song is also strongly evident. Syncopation is widely used and the influence of the rock beat that permeates Western culture is obvious.

In formal construction the neo-hasidic song is much like that of its forerunners. The melodies are primarily in two and three sections (A-B or A-B-A form), although with ever-increasing frequency, freer forms such as the ballad have begun to appear. Meter is by and large kept to the simple folk 2/4, 3/4, 4/4, and, occasionally, 6/8 time. Although most of the songs are within a narrow range melodically (distance from the lowest to the highest tone), more wide-ranging melodies are being heard. This may be attributed to the fact that many neo-hasidic composers are trained instrumentalists and think in terms of instrumental range.

Neo-hasidic song has been disseminated by means of phonograph recordings, instrumental bands, concerts, and music books.

Partial Listing of Recordings

R. Shlomoh Carlebach Recordings, Zimrani Records, New York.

Rabbis' Sons Recordings, Emes Records, New York.

Or Chodosh Recordings, Menorah Records, New York.

London Pirchei Recordings, Y&Y Records, New York.

New York Pirchei, Agudas Israel, New York.

Toronto Pirchei, Y&Y Recordings, New York.

Ruach Revival Recordings–Menorah Records, New York.

V.P.

NEO-HASIDISM–Martin Buber's desire to popularize the "message of Hasidism" did not go unsatisfied. Indeed, several generations have now come to know Hasidism in its Buberian guise, finding in his account of it something spiritually valid and vital for today. Outstanding among those who have been influenced by Buber's work and who have also tried to carry it on in various ways are A. J. Heschel, Maurice Friedman, Malcolm Diamond, Walter Kaufman, Elie Wiesel, and Lev Shestov.

Among this group of scholars, special attention should be paid to the work of A. J. Heschel, the scion of two great hasidic families, who knew Hasidism from the inside as Buber never did and who was also deeply influenced by Buber's existentialist rendering of the hasidic message. This is most clearly seen in Heschel's late work *A Passion for Truth* (1973), which is a comparative study of the Kotzker rebbe and the famous Protestant existentialist Soren Kierkegaard. In addition, Buber's influence can be seen in Heschel's many papers on hasidic themes, as well as in his larger corpus of Jewish and philosophical writings.

Buber's leading American disciple and translator, Maurice Friedman, has also been influenced by what he understands Buber's hasidic work to be about. He has written in detail on this aspect of Buber's corpus in his general study of Buber's thought, *Martin Buber: The Life of Dialogue* (1960), and has translated into English the early *Tales of Rabbi Nahman* (1956), *Hasidism and Modern Man* (1958), and *The Origin and Meaning of Hasidism* (1960). In addition, Friedman makes constant reference to Hasidism's influence on Buber in the scores of essays and monographs he has published on his master.

Another disciple who has written about Buber's form of neo-Hasidism is Malcolm Diamond, who treated the matter sympathetically, if simplistically, in his *Martin Buber: Jewish Existentialist* (1960). Walter Kaufman, a well-known American philosopher, has also been influenced by and in turn has tried to impress others with Buber's hasidic views. In his contribution to the *Philosophy of Martin Buber* (1967) volume in the Library of Living Philosophers series, he wrote, "What saves Buber's work (from objective scholarly criticism) is its perfection. He has given us one of the great religious books of all time, a work which invites comparison with the great scriptures of mankind–*Tales of the Hasidim*" (p. 681).

Another figure influenced by Buber both directly and indirectly, especially through the link supplied by A. J. Heschel, is the novelist Elie Wiesel. Wiesel's biographical roots are in the hasidic world of Eastern Europe, and hasidic characters and themes, understood largely in neo-hasidic categories, are central features of his stories. Moreover, Wiesel has authored a collection of hasidic tales retold in his own way, entitled *Souls on Fire* (1972), which owes much to Buber's work, especially to his retelling of the hasidic legends in *Tales of the Hasidim*. In passing, mention must also be made of the influence of Buber's writings on the eminent Russian émigré now working in France, Lev Shestov.

The influence of Buber's hasidic efforts has also been felt in non-Jewish circles. For example, Herman Hesse, in recommending Buber for the Nobel Prize in literature (which Buber failed to receive), wrote, "In *Tales of the Hasidim* Buber has enriched world literature with a genuine treasure as no other living author."

Among Christian scholars influenced by and sympathetic to Buber's neo-Hasidism, one should note especially Ronald Gregor Smith, the well-known Scottish theologian and first translator of Buber's *I and Thou* into English in 1937. Also influenced by Buber's hasidic work are Paul E. Pfeutze, author of *The Social Self in G. H. Mead and Martin Buber* (1954); J. A. Oldham, author of *Real Life Is Meeting* (1947); and Roy Oliver, author of *The Wanderer and the Way* (a study of Buber, 1968). Note should also be taken of G. Schaeder's *Hebrew Humanism of Martin Buber* (1973). In addition, scholarly as well as popular Christian journals often carry articles on or relating to this theme. (See, for example, *The Bridge* vol. I, 1955, and vol. III, 1958.)

Perhaps the surest indication of the vogue that Buber's neo-hasidic writings enjoyed was their discussion in the popular media, paradigmatically represented by a series of four short pieces entitled "Responses to Martin Buber's *Tales of the Hasidim*," which Norman Mailer, the influential American novelist, published in *Commentary* magazine between December 1962 and October 1963.

Scholars and hasidim alike have questioned Buber's presentation of neo-Hasidism, arguing that his image of hasidic life is more closely modeled after his own *I–Thou* philosophy than after authentic Hasidism. This charge of eisegesis has been forcefully made by three scholars especially: Gershom Scholem, the greatest academic authority on Jewish mysticism, in a paper entitled "Buber's Interpretation of Hasidism" (in *The Messianic Idea in Judaism* [1971]); Rivkah Shatz-Uffenheimer in a paper in *The Philosophy of Martin Buber* (ed. P. Schilpp and M. Friedman [1967]); and Steven T. Katz in his paper "Buber's Misuse of Hasidic Sources" (in *Proceedings of the XIII International Meeting of the IAHR*) and more fully in a monograph entitled *Martin Buber and Hasidism* (1978).

M. Friedman, *Martin Buber, the Life of a Dialogue*.

G. Scholem, "Martin Buber's Hasidism," pp. 218–225.

S.K.

NESHKHIZ, Yitzhak (1788–21 *Shevat* 1868), hasidic rebbe–He was the third and youngest son of R. Mordecai (d. 1800), the founder of the Neshkhiz (Nieusochojeze) dynasty. His father died when he was twelve years old, and his teacher was R. Mordecai Mardish of Paritch. In his youth, he visited R. Barukh of Medziborz. He married Gitel, the daughter of R. Meir (d. 1799), a granddaughter of R. Levi Yitzhak of Berdichev, where he stayed for some time after his marriage.

He was greatly influenced by the charismatic R. Levi Yitzhak. Each day, R. Yitzhak would devote time to the study of the *Kedushat Levi*. He was also a disciple of R. Jacob Yitzhak, the "Seer" of Lublin, and after his master's death, he became rabbi in Neshkhiz, near Baranowicze, where he lived for thirty-three years and became known as a miracle worker.

Among his many disciples were R. Barukh Shapira, R. Meir of Kobryn, and R. Yehoshua of Ostrog. Not only hasidic rabbis, but scholars, such as R. Shlomoh Kluger of Brody, R. Tzvi Hirsch Orenstein, and R. Yitzhak Eliyahu Landau, corresponded with him.

In 1864, he subsidized the publication of an edition of 6,000 copies of the Psalms with Rashi's commentary, so that they could be sold at a very low price. At first he declined to deliver discourses: "What can I add to the Torah?" he would say. But during the last year of his life, he would speak on the Sabbath. His discourses are to be found in *Toldot Yitzhak* (Piotrokov, 1868), published by Yitzhak Landau, and in *Zikhron Tov* (Piotrokov, 1892). He had no children.

A. Y. Bromberg, *Migdolei HaHasidut*, vol. 20, *Admorei Neshkhiz, Kaidanov, Novominsk*, pp. 51–75.

NETUREI KARTA – In the early 1940s, a group of Jerusalem Jews who had formed or, for the most part, inherited the view that Zionism was a spurious and idolatrous substitute for Judaism began to call themselves *Neturei Karta*. The adoption of this Aramaic equivalent of "guardians of the city" indicates their attachment to the attitudes and standards of the nineteenth-century European settlements in the Old City as perpetuated by the Orthodox community (*HaEdah HaHaredit*), which had been organized in 1921 in order to secure independence from Zionist control.

Since the campaign for the right to a separate communal existence had been backed by the Aguda, which, as a world movement, was in a better position to negotiate with the Mandates Commission of the League of Nations and the British Colonial Office, the community became virtually the Aguda's Jerusalem branch. However, the connection gradually weakened with the arrival of more central and eastern European Agudists whose circumstances rendered them less averse to collaborate with the Zionists, and it was finally severed in 1945 when the list headed by Amram Blau and Aaron Katzenellenbogen, former leaders of the Agudist youth movement, gained a sweeping victory in the communal elections to the surprise and the dismay of the Gerer Court, which then through I. M. Lewin, its chief representative in the political arena, played the dominant role in the formation of the Agudist policy of that time.

The *Neturei Karta* success was at least partly due to reinforcement of the hasidic element in the community both by R. Aaron Roth, author of *Shomrei Emunim* and guide of a closely knit band of disciples bearing the name of his book, who addressed an open letter to the electors, and, even more influentially, by the arrival, some six months before the elections, of the rabbi of Satmar.

Fifth in the direct line of descent from the eminent author of *Yismah Mosheh*, R. Joel Teitelbaum was known throughout the Hungarian cultural zone as a highly articulate and controversial figure of profound and acute learning, of uncompromising zeal, and with a remarkable power of leadership. His encouragement not only provided authoritative halakhic support for the *Neturei Karta* position, which he subsequently systematized in a massive volume entitled *Vayo'el Mosheh* (New York, 1959) but also—and particularly after his emigration to the United States (1947)—distributed it wherever survivors from his sphere of influence were making a fresh start. Nevertheless, *Neturei Karta* cannot be equated with Satmar or, for that matter, with any other section of Orthodox Jewry. As a rallying point for individual consciences, it transcends affiliations and backgrounds.

Faced with the prospect of partition, *Neturei Karta* stood firm. In 1948, Blau and Katzenellenbogen addressed a memorandum to the secretary-general of the United Nations in favor of the internationalization of Jerusalem; later in the year, while representatives of the Agudah were seated in the provisional legislature of the new state, both were escorted through the streets to prison on the charge of arranging an illegal procession. Subjection to Zionist rule reinvigorated the group, prompting it to interpret the situation in theological terms and to chart an appropriate course of conduct. An unambiguous conclusion was reached: Satan's work had been allowed to prosper in the form of a state entitled Israel but opposed in character and aims to the divine connotations of that sacred name; moreover, that state had been established in breach of the paths divinely imposed at the beginning of the dispersion, which forbade, under threat of the severest penalties, attempts to regain possession of the Holy Land by force (T. B. *Ketubot* 111); therefore, the inauguration of the state, which was tantamount to rebellion against the king in his royal palace and the erection of an idol in the sanctuary, heralded not the redemption but the start of a fresh and more grievous exile.

Accordingly, the faithful remnant had to defend the cause and honor of heaven by refusing to recognize the state, participate in its political system, share its emotions and expectations, or accept its bounty. Yet mere dissociation was not enough: in order to frustrate Satan's plan, the true Israel had to testify that the Covenant with heaven remained intact; that is to say, the protest had to be spectacular if it were to have the desired effect above.

Neturei Karta responded by developing a sacramental pattern of protest: debarred on principle from seeking police permission, its public gatherings–often in sackcloth and ashes–were exposed to violent methods of crowd dispersal; arrests led to trials at which the defendants, instead of pleading, challenged the validity of the state as well as its courts; the media, barely conscious of the metaphysical aspects but sensitive to the news value of such incidents, reported them; and sympathizers in the largest Jewish centers of America and Europe staged demonstrations of solidarity. Needless to say, this plan of campaign differs in approach as well as in style and manner from the series of protests raised on largely the same issues, that is, open transgression of the Commandments of the Torah, by the religious parties, which regard the state as at least a potential asset to Judaism.

Indeed, it is against religious "collaborators" with the state that *Neturei Karta* propaganda, as distinct from protest, is mainly directed. Writers in *HaHomah*, the group's internal periodical, tend to assume that their readers include devout Jews who have accepted the state, albeit unenthusiastically, and now judge it primarily by the extent of its support for their institutions and tolerance of their way of life. This assumption has inspired a variety of polemical material, often ingeniously handled and spiced with a pungent admixture of gallows humor that contrasts effectively with the homiletical tone and form in which most of the articles are couched.

The periodical acknowledges its descent from the anti-Zionist literature of the early days of the Zionist movement by quoting copiously from it–with a predilection for statements made by the ancestors of current leaders of Hasidism–and emulating its sharp scrutiny of the Zionist press. Yet however relentlessly it may expose the seamy side of secular life, its harshest criticism is reserved for religious politicians who claim to be saving what still remains to be saved for the faith.

Despite the group's intermittent bouts of self-criticism–chiefly to the effect that its members have adjusted too comfortably to the regime and the personal quarrels that have disturbed the harmony from time to time–*Neturei Karta* remains the center of religious opposition to Jewish nationalism in all its forms.

The appointment of R. Yitzhak Weiss as head of the *Bet Din* and the death of R. Yoel Teitelbaum in 1979 have not diminished the virulence of the *Neturei Karta*. R. Moses Hirsch, who arrived in Israel in the 1950s, married the daughter of R. Aaron Katzenellenbogen. He regards himself as the "foreign secretary" and contributes regularly to the East Jerusalem Arab paper *Al Fajr*. He is in correspondence with Palestine Liberation Organization chairman Yassir Arafat, to whom he wrote "that the temporary domination of Palestine by the Zionists has caused the desecration and impurity of the holy places." He visited Arafat in Tunis in September 1993.

At the Middle East Peace Conference in Madrid in 1991, an American member of the *Neturei Karta*, Hayyim Freiman, was present as an official member of the Palestinian Advisory Delegation.

The American *Neturei Karta* assured readers of the *New York Times* in 1985 that Zionism is the opposite of Judaism and that "the Zionist state is a complete falsification and caricature." Today, no more than 200 families belong to *Neturei Karta*.

E. Marmorstein, *Heaven at Bay: The Jewish Kulturkampf in the Holy Land*, pp. 89ff.

D. Landau, *Piety and Power*, pp. 150–156.

E.M. and T.R.

NEUFELD, Daniel (1814–1874), Jewish Polish historian–Editor of the Polish Jewish weekly *Jutrzenka* (Dawn) and of the *Encyklopedia Powszechna* (Common Encyclopedia), published in Warsaw in 1866. He believed that the function of history is "to make peace between the past and the present, and not to negate the past." Despite condemnation of the hasidic movement by all the "enlightened" Jews of his period, he saw in Hasidism the "working of a great idea" and believed that its adherents would slowly become modernized.

"The ideal Jew" was to him the one who synthesized within oneself "a conservative approach to religion, respect for historical tradition, and . . . acceptance of all that makes one educated and noble."

I. M. Biderman, *Mayer Balaban*, p. 20.

NEW MOON (Rosh Hodesh)–The beginning of the Hebrew month. During the period of the first Temple, the first day of every lunar month was a semi-festival. It was customary to pay visits of respect to the prophet (2 Kings 4:23) and to hold family feasts (1 Samuel 20:5).

In the Middle Ages, women were discouraged from working on that day. Many hasidic rebbes held *Tish* on *Rosh Hodesh*, sang melodies such as *Barekhi Nafshi* (Psalm 104), and delivered discourses. The Besht concluded the whole of the Psalms on the eve of *Rosh Hodesh*. In Munkacz, *tefillin* were removed before the *Musaf Amidah* was recited.

NEW SQUARE–Popularly known as New Square, two miles from Spring Valley along Route 45 is the hasidic village established in 1954 by the late R. Jacob Joseph Twersky, the rebbe of Square, who purchased one hundred and thirty acres of a dairy farm and named it after the Ukrainian town of Skvira, a town near Kiev.

In 1958, sixty-eight houses were completed and on November 6, 1961, the village was officially incorporated by the State Supreme Court of New York.

The rabbi died on 2 *Nisan* 1968 and was succeeded by his son R. David. In 1970, he purchased the Ramapo General Hospital, which was later converted into a *yeshivah*.

In 1979, the village received grants from the Federal Small Cities Program and Community Development to encourage the growth of industry.

In 1984, President Reagan designated the Jews of Rockland County as a disadvantaged minority.

By 1986, four hundred and fifty families constituted a population of two thousand one hundred. Many of the hasidim work in New York, a number of them in the diamond trade. They are taken back and forth in their own bus, fitted out as a synagogue with Torah and Ark, and they pray en route. It is a community of small modern houses with well-kept lawns and gardens.

It has educational facilities for boys and girls, and a *yeshivah*. It also has a chain at the entrance to keep out cars and trucks on the Sabbath and Holy Days.

The purpose of the community is to keep from exposing children to outside influences. There are no facilities for watching films or television, and the divorce rate is very low.

J. R. Mintz, *Hasidic People–A Place in the New World*, pp. 198-205.

NEW YORK–New York City, which is composed of five boroughs–Manhattan, Bronx, Brooklyn, Queens, and Staten Island–has the largest hasidic population in the United States and is the greatest hasidic center in the world.

Many hasidim arrived in New York with the wave of immigration from Eastern Europe in the nineteenth century, and they established a number of small *shtieblech*. Two such groups were the Shinover and Lizensker. One of the earliest hasidic pioneers was R. Eliezer Hayyim Rabinowitz of Skola, who arrived in New York in 1895. But after a short time, he returned to Poland. He was followed by R. David Mordecai Twersky (d. 1956) of Talnoye, who established the *Kehal Hasidim* congregation in 1913 on the Lower East Side of Manhattan. R. Eliezer Rubin (d. 1932) of Sasov, R. Barukh Joseph Zack (d. 1949), and the Kobriner rebbe arrived in 1917.

In the 1920s a steady stream of hasidic leaders began to settle in New York. Among these rebbes were R. Abraham Joshua Heschel Rabinowitz of Monastyrchina, R. Yehudah Aryeh Perlow (d. 1961) of Novominsk, R. Yitzhak Horowitz of Mielec, R. Mordecai Solomon Friedman (d. 1971) of Boyan, and R. Uri Langer of Knihinitch. The majority of these rebbes came from Poland, Galicia, and Russia. One Hungarian rebbe, R. Pinhas Shalom Rothenberg (d. 1968), arrived in 1926 and settled in the Bronx.

More hasidim as well as rebbes began to settle in New York during the 1930s. Prior to the Second World War, many rebbes found refuge in Vienna, of whom the most famous who came to America was R. Abraham Joshua Heschel of Kopyczynice, who settled in the Lower West Side of Manhattan. R. Joseph Yitzhak Schneersohn of Lubavitch and

R. Saul Taub of Modzitz arrived from Poland in 1940.

It was not until the end of the Second World War that the hasidim really began to exert an influence on the Jewish community. The rebbes of Satmar, Bobov, Klausenburg, and Skvira wielded tremendous power. In Brooklyn, Williamsburg became the center of the Hungarian hasidim; others settled in Crown Heights.

As the neighborhoods underwent population shifts, many hasidic rebbes moved to Borough Park and Flatbush. An estimated 250 hasidic *shtieblech* now exist in Borough Park. Among the rebbes who now live in Borough Park are R. Solomon Halberstam of Bobov; R. Jacob Perlow of Novominsk; R. Yisrael Shapiro of Blazova; the aged R. Hayyim Zanvil Abramowitz of Rubnitz, an immigrant from the Soviet Union; R. Hayyim Yitzhak Twersky of Rotmistrowka; R. Naftali Weisz of Spinka; R. Barukh Meir Jacob Shochet of Stolin; and R. Mosheh Leib Rabinowicz of Munkacs. Practically every hasidic group is represented by a *shtiebl* in Borough Park.

In alphabetical order, the following rebbes are active: the Bobover, the Bostoner, the Debreciner, the Desher, the Dinever, the Keresturer, the Klausenburger, the Kleinwardainer, the Kolbosover, the Kosover, the Kroler, the Kupitshinitzer, the Limster, the Lisker, the Lubavitcher, the Munkacser, the Popaner, the Ratzferder, the Sarmasher, the Satmarer, the Skulener, the Skvirer, the Spinker, the Stoliner, the Stropkover, the Vishnitzer, the Witzener, the Zanzer, and the Zelemer.

A number of rebbes have left New York and have founded their own hasidic communities elsewhere in New York State. New Square was established in 1956 by the rebbe of Sqvira; Kiryat Yoel, near Monroe, by the rebbe of Satmar; and Kiryat Kashan, near Bedford Hills, by R. Rafael Blum of Kashau.

Queens has never been a breeding ground of Hasidism. However, there are a few rebbes in Rego Park. In Far Rockaway is R. S. S. Rubin of Sulitza. Staten Island has become the home of R. Isaacson, a grandson of the rebbe of Nadvorna.

In Williamsburg, the most famous rebbes are R. Moses Teitelbaum of Satmar and R. Jacob Hezekiah Grunwald of Papa.

Hasidic trends began to pervade even the larger *yeshivot*, which follow the Lithuanian pattern, such as *Torah VeAvodah* in Brooklyn. Among the well-known hasidic *yeshivot* are *Hatam Sofer*, *Beer Shmuel*, *Lubavitch*, *Satmar*, *Bobov*, and *Stolin*. Almost all of these *yeshivot* have *kollelim* as well. In addition, several small, independent *kollelim* have been formed in various hasidic prayer houses.

The mass immigration of the hasidim to New York City aroused great interest among the Jewish community in general. Studies of the Williamsburg enclave have been made by such leading sociologists as George Kranzler, Solomon Poll, and Jeremy Mintz. The hasidim of Lubavitch have their own *Kehot* publishing company for the propagation of their literature. Innumerable hasidic classical works have been reprinted in New York. Sender Deutsch, a hasid of Satmar, established his own printing company. More *mikvaot*, kosher food stores, *glatt kosher* butchers, scribes, and religious goods stores proliferate in New York City. Hasidic music, too, has become popular by the production of phonograph records carrying the melodies of the various courts. The rebbes in New York City have their own union, called the *Agudat HaAdmorim*, which was originally set up in 1923.

Hasidim in America came into confrontation with an urban modern mass society, a heterogeneous population, secular orientation, and conflicts of roles. In this confrontation the hasidim could not blind themselves to the social conditions that enveloped them in America. At the same time, the American social system did not demand the abolishment of the hasidic way of life. Hasidim were able to survive "American incorporation" by adopting patterns of behavior that were complementary to the American system. The American society's enormous impact on Hasidism was mainly due to the following social conditions: high level of tolerance, religious freedom, and social diversity.

The fear of urban riots, crime, hippies, and drug users pushed the hasidim more toward forming hasidic associations, houses of worship, and educational establishments. They were not part of the American society and not even of the larger Jewish community.

When the uprooted hasidim arrived in the United States after World War Two, they found a spiritual wasteland, a strange cultural setting, and a language that they did not speak. They needed guidance, direction, and a new religious order. They were seeking a mystical fellowship through which they could relate to others with similar experience. Since American religious Judaism also was strange and unacceptable to them, they flocked to their own kindred groups from the same geographic origins and to those rebbes who more or less represented their religious thought patterns and the sentiments of their group.

They flocked to the hasidic rebbes for comfort, for moving words, for religious revitalization, and to return once again to the familiar and the traditional. Each hasidic rebbe is known for his particular specialization. One is known for exceptional piety, another for charity, a third for maintaining an open house, a fourth for lovely songs and merrymaking, a fifth for mysticism, a sixth for inspiration, a seventh for methodical advice and counseling, and an eighth for religious zealotry and militancy.

The hasidim in New York are represented by two basic schools of thought: one school, that of Satmar and its affiliated bodies, which numerically and materially represents the largest hasidic group in New York, advocates almost complete isolation, and the other, represented by Lubavitch, advocates full proselytization.

The hasidim under the Lubavitcher rebbe are engaged in a great variety of activities. They believe it is the responsibility of every Jew to be *mekarev*—embracers of other Jews "who have fallen by the wayside." One must go out into the larger Jewish world and bring *Yiddishkeit* (the Jewish way of life) to those who still have a Jewish *nitzutz* (spark) and rekindle "the flame of the soul." Through mechanization, public relations, extensive *Mitzvah* campaigns, and the dispatching of *shiluhim* (representatives) into various parts of the city, Lubavitch established a well-organized system of proselytization. They are setting up day schools in the form of religious parochial schools on both the primary and secondary levels for children of religious as well as nonreligious backgrounds.

The rebbe's sayings are taped and transmitted live through special telephone hookups to various parts of the world. They have also established a *yeshivah* for *baalei teshuvah*—a theological school for "repentants" who have returned to religion and to the hasidic way of life.

They operate an *etrog and lulav* (palm branch and citrus fruit) campaign; a *sukkah mobile*, a van set up as a *sukkah* (tabernacle); and a *tefillin* booth, a van equipped with prayer books, prayer shawls, and *tefillin*. And all this is controlled from 770 Eastern Parkway, in Brooklyn, the home of the rebbe of Lubavitch.

The isolationists, on the other hand, consisting of Satmar and affiliates, fear that any social contact with nonhasidim and nonreligious Jews will have an adverse effect on them. They insulate themselves within their own community and restrict social interaction mainly to hasidic Jews. These hasidim have set up countless restrictive institutional patterns, social norms, and community regulations, through which they guard, guide, and direct the behavior of the members of the community.

Despite hasidic attempts to isolate their community and despite all the restrictions and prohibitions that the leadership has placed on the members of the community, still, American opportunities, techniques, and skills have exerted an enormous impact on hasidic life.

A.Sh. and S.P.

NEW YORK PUBLIC LIBRARY

—Hasidic materials are among the strong points of the Jewish Division of the New York Public Library. Besides the usual classifications by author and title, the Jewish Division was a pioneer in the use of subject headings for various types of hasidic literature. Alongside the major headings of Hasidic Legends and Hasidic Works, there are subheadings under Hasidism for Apologetics, Biography, Drama, Ethics, Fiction, History, Philosophy, and Satires.

A number of rare first editions are also found here, including the first hasidic work ever published—*Toldot Yaakov Yosef* (Korzec, 1780). Jacob Joseph of Polonoye is also represented by the first editions of his *Ben Porat Yosef* (Korzec, 1781) and *Zofnat Paaneah* (Korzec, 1781). The writings of the Maggid, Dov Baer of Mezhirech, are highlighted by the first editions of the *Maggid Devarav LeYaakov* (Korzec, 1781) and *Or Torah* (Korzec, 1804). The collection includes a copy of the first edition of the work of the founder of the Lubavitch dynasty, the *Tanya* (Slavuta, 1795).

Menahem Nahum of Chernobyl is represented by his *Meor Einayim* (Slavuta, 1798) and *Yismah Lev* (Slavuta, 1798). The Jewish Division has a copy of the first edition of Nahman of Bratzlav's *Likkutei Moharan* (Ostrog, 1806), as well as two early versions of the *Shivhei HaBesht* (Berdichev, 1815, and Kapust, 1815).

Anti-hasidic works are highlighted by the first edition of Joseph Perl's *Megaleh Temirin* (Vienna, 1819). In another vein, the library possesses the rare *Habad* youth periodical *Heah*, which was published in Lubavitch, 1910–1914.

M.F.

NEWMAN, Louis Israel (1893–1972), rabbi, composer, editor, and author – Newman was born in Providence, Rhode Island. He is best known for his work *Jewish Influence on Christian Reform Movements* (New York, 1925) and his three English anthologies: *Hasidic Anthology* (New York, 1934), *Talmudic Anthology* (New York, 1947), and the supplementary work *Maggidim and Hasidim: Their Wisdom* ([New York, 1962] coeditor, S. Spitz).

Newman was a typical and brilliant personality of the New World, who combined within himself different, even paradoxical trends, for example, Wilsonian liberalism with Revisionist Zionism and the pioneering of a Jewish university in America. This tall, outwardly stern, slightly Victorian personality brought many social and dramatic ventures under the temple roof together with the popularization of mysticism in its hasidic form.

His widely read *Hasidic Anthology*, at its time the only sourcebook in English of hasidic literature, is preceded by a systematic introduction. It is derived from different sources and arranged alphabetically – though somewhat anachronistically – under 205 subjects ranging from "afterlife" to "the *tzaddik* and his problems."

Against Hillel's dictum "an ignorant man (*am ha'aretz*) cannot be a hasid" (*Avot* 2:5), the Besht expressed the opposite view: spiritual and moral perfection with a hasidic way of life are, on the contrary, open even to the humblest. The Maggid or folk preacher here proved more appealing than the interpreter of *halakhah*, going from simple parables all the way to "mystical ecstasy." The Besht's grandson R. Nahman of Bratzlav has been called "the greatest storyteller of the Jewish people." Here biblical texts are interpreted following the Maggid's own ethical and mystical inclinations. The genius of the local preachers is sometimes hidden under a strange garb of crudity and beauty. Newman has, therefore, limited himself to the "pristine and classic message of the *tzaddikim* and their adherents," "retouching" (i.e., modernizing) their style.

Out of the vast literature of profound hasidic sayings, if we had to choose one as most characteristic, it might be this one: "Faith is the portal to holiness" (R. Nahman of Bratzlav, p. 104). Or, from the book on Maggidim, which includes nineteenth- and twentieth-century authors: "If one truly believes that the Torah is perfect [i.e., through its various interpretations], it has the power to revive the soul and, at the same time, to grant contentment of spirit" (Hafetz Hayyim, d. 1933; p. 31). Or "The world is a chandelier. We are the candles; therefore let us give light" (M. J. Berdyczewski, d. 1921; p. 78). Or, from Newman's play *The Little Tzaddik* ([New York, 1961] p. 21): "Know that your soul is a golden ore which no one can crush!"

Newman's many creative talents explain the immense, even nationwide, appeal of his pulpit in New York.

Newman file, American Jewish Archives, Cincinnati.
CCAR Journal (1973).

I.O.L.

NIGAL, Gedaliah (b. 1927), writer – Born in Kassel, Germany, he emigrated to the Holy Land in 1939 and studied in *Kefar Noar Dati*, an agricultural high school, and then at the Hebrew University, where he earned a B.A. degree in Bible and Hebrew literature (1960), an M.A. in Hebrew literature (1966), and a Ph.D. in Hebrew literature (1972).

Since 1970, he has lectured at Haifa University and then at Bar-Ilan University. He is the author of many publications, among them *Mishnat HaHasidut BeKitvei R. Elimelekh MiLejask VeTalmidov*, *Torot Baal HaToldot* (1972), *Hasidic Sermons of R. Jacob Joseph of Polonnoye* (1975), *The Hasidic Tale, Its History and Topics* (Hebrew) (Jerusalem,

1981), and "Sources of *Devekut* in Early Hasidic Literature," in *Kiryat Sefer* 46 (1970). He also edited the *Noam Elimelekh* in two volumes (Jerusalem: Mosad Harav Kook, 1978) and has contributed many learned articles to *Tarbiz*, *Molad*, and *Sinai*.

NINTH OF AB (*Tishah BeAv*)–The day of mourning on which, according to tradition, both the first and second Temples were destroyed.

When *Tishah BeAv* occurred on a Saturday night, R. Naftali of Ropczyce would prolong the Sabbath meal, saying, "The Sabbath is a most precious guest. *Tishah BeAv* can surely wait. He is not a welcome guest." During the three weeks preceding the Ninth of Ab, he said, "It is not fitting that we should deplore the loss of the Holy Temple with all our hearts, for the Lord, Who endowed this edifice with holiness, is with us in exile. We should mingle mourning with joy, because our Lord is present among us" (*Ohel Naftali*, p. 114).

Similarly, R. Israel, the Maggid of Kozienice, said, "If the Lord dislikes the manner in which we observe the Ninth of Ab, He can surely abolish it." After reciting the Book of Lamentations, R. Moses Teitelbaum would discard the book, saying, "Let us hope that next year the Messiah will come and we shall no longer be lamenting."

During the three weeks from 17 *Tammuz* to 9 *Av*, hasidim would hold a *siyyum* to celebrate the conclusion of a talmudic tractate. The rebbe of Alexander gave this reason for the custom: "There was once a Temple in days gone by, and there will be another Temple in days to come. The celebration therefore is an expression of our faith."

NOTARIKON–*Notarikon*–using words as acronyms–is one way of finding hints of additional meaning. The Torah is interpreted in four ways–p.r.d.s.: *parades*, meaning *peshat* (literal), *remez* (hint), *derash* (homiletical), and *sod* (mystical sense). Using *Notarikon* as shorthand notes is mentioned in the *Mishnah* (*Shabbat* 12:5) and Midrashim (Mekhilta, Bo, 8; BT *Shabbat* 105a.) In the *Zohar*, deep thoughts are associated with such devices. God as nature (*Elohim*) is broken up into two words (*aileh* [these] and *mi* [who]) meaning plurality and personality (*Zohar*, *Hadkamah*).

Among the hasidim, the belief in the active role of the holy spirit (*ruah hakodesh*) led to the proliferation of this kind of interpretation. Only *tzaddikim* could give such teaching, and their ultimate source was believed to be the holy spirit. So, *notarikon*, like *gematriot*, were esteemed to be holy teaching, not simply a play on words or a mnemonic device (Zeev Wolf of Zbarazh, *Or Hameir*).

Some *notarikon* are especially characteristic: The *hasidim* would wear garments made of cloth called *atlas*. In *notarikon*, it represented the first letters of *ach tov leyisroel selah* (only goodness for Israel forever). *Yash* (*yod shin*), meaning, whiskey, had the same letters as "fear of God" (*Yire'at Shomayim*). *Tabak* (tobacco) was a reverse acronym of *kadosh berov tuvcho* ("Holy One, in the abundance of Your goodness"). As is well known, the Besht and some of the early *tzaddikim* considered smoking to be a form of prayer and meditation. *Notarikon* could also be used to attack opponents. So *hamor* (donkey) could mean hacham, mufleh, rav, wise, or distinguished rabbi.

E. Steinman, *Be'er HaHasidut*, pp. 371–381.

A.B.A.

OHEL (Hebrew, tent)–It is nowadays the custom among the hasidim to construct a sepulcher (*ohel*) on the grave of the *tzaddik* to enable the hasidim to pray there undisturbed, to place their petitions there, and to kindle lights there. The Besht, who is buried in Medziborz, and his disciples R. Menahem Mendel of Vitebsk and R. Abraham of Kalisk, who are buried in Tiberias, have no *ohel*. Nor has the "Seer" of Lublin.

In fact, a number of hasidic rabbis, such as the rebbes of Ostrova, Belz, and Biala, gave clear instructions that no *ohel* should be constructed over their grave.

OLESK, Hanokh Heinokh Dov, of Olesk (1800–1 *Elul* 1884)–Son of R. Samuel, Hanokh Heinokh as a young boy visited R. Jacob Yitzhak, the "Seer" of Lublin; R. Uri of Strelisk; R. Naftali Tzvi of Ropczyce; and R. Israel Friedman of Ruzhyn. He married Freidel, the daughter of R. Shalom Rokeah of Belz.

His first rabbinate was in Satanov; the next was in 1850 in Olesk, where he succeeded R. Dov Berish Flaum. When his father-in-law died in 1855, he became rebbe. He was renowned for his miracles and for exorcising *dybbukim*. Among his disciples were R. Ezekiel of Sianiawa, R. Hanania Yom Tov Lippa of Sighet, and R. Yitzhak Eizig of Zydaczov.

He was the author of *Lev Sameah*, a commentary on the prayer book (Lvov, 1862), which was reprinted in 1883 and in London in 1962; *Lev Sameah*, a commentary on the *Song of Songs* and on the Scroll of Esther (Lvov, 1868, reprinted in Zloczov in 1923); a commentary on Pentateuch (Przemysl, 1895); *Lev Sameah*, a commentary on the Passover *Haggadah* (Zloczov, 1923, and London, 1963); and *Lev Sameah HeHadash* (Arad, 1936, reprinted in Jerusalem, 1963).

One of his sons, R. Yoel, died in his youth. R. Hanokh Heinokh was succeeded by his son R. Yitzhak (1829–24 *Adar* 1904), who was the son-in-law of R. Joseph Yoska Gottesman. His third son, R. Solomon (1835–12 *Adar* 1919), married the daughter of R. Tzvi Aryeh Lisker and was rebbe in Sasov.

His sons-in-law were R. Asher Anshel Ashkenazi and R. Tzvi Hirsch Rokeah.

OLIPHANT, Laurence (1829–1888), British journalist and travel writer–A prolific and popular writer, wit, secret agent, war correspondent, mystic, entrepreneur, and traveler. This Victorian gentleman, described by East European Jews as a "second Cyrus," became a legend in the ghettos of Eastern Europe.

In the middle of May 1882, Oliphant expressed his desire to meet the rebbe of Sadgora, Abraham Jacob Friedman. The rebbe and his sons gave Oliphant a warm welcome. Oliphant wanted the rebbe's help to establish a national fund to purchase the Holy Land from the Turks. Later, he gave a graphic description of his momentous visit: "The rebbe sent his own carriage for us–a handsome barouche, drawn by a pair of valuable horses, with coachman and groom with caftan and curls. . . . The Rabbiner himself was a man with a white beard, apparently between sixty and seventy years of age who conversed intelligently on the subject of the conditions and projects of the Russian Jews" (*Blackwood* magazine [Edinburgh, 1883], vol. 130, pp. 641–643).

The rebbe was not particularly responsive to his visitor's ideas, however. "We are waiting for a miraculous deliverance," he told the Englishman, "and not for deliverance through a human agency."

Oliphant's enthusiasm was not shared by the *London Jewish Chronicle* either, which stated on October 19, 1883 (p. 11): "Mr. Oliphant seems to be much impressed by the sect of Hasidim which certainly does, at first sight, impress the observer with its strange mysticism."

P. Henderson, *The Life of Laurence Oliphant*.

OPATOSHU, Joseph (1886–1954), Yiddish writer – Born in Mlave, son of David, who came of hasidic background. After studying engineering at a polytechnic in Nancy, France, he returned to Russia. In 1907 he settled in New York, where he qualified as a civil engineer. From 1914 onward, he was a regular contributor to the Yiddish daily paper *Der Tog*, for which he worked until his death.

A prolific writer, one of his novels concerns hasidic life. His historical romance, *Poilishe Welder* (New York, 1921, and Warsaw, 1922), became a best-seller in the United States as well as in Poland. It sold over 17,000 copies and was translated into many languages. In it, the author portrays the conflict between the hasidim and the *maskilim*. It was set partly in the court of R. Menahem Mendel of Kotzk, and he took advantage of the enigmatic atmosphere of Kotzk to present the rebbe as torn by doubts and heretical thoughts and forced into seclusion by his family. His young hero starts his quest for religious identity amid the Polish peasants, and the author shows how little Kotzk was understood by the *maskilim* at the turn of the century.

Another novel, *Die Tentserin* (The Dancer, 1929), has its background among the hasidic immigrants of New York.

C. Madison, *Yiddish Literature*, pp. 326–347.

N.L.

OPATOV (Yiddish, Apt) – A town in the Kielce province of eastern Poland.

R. Nahman of Kosov, a follower of the Besht, visited it in 1740 to propagate Hasidism. Among the members of the "Holy Society of the Eternal Light for the Sabbath" was R. Zeev Wolf, known as *Siaps Introligator* (d. 1761), the father of R. Israel, the Maggid of Kozienice. The Maggid maintained his membership in the society even after he had moved to Kozienice.

R. Moses Yehudah Leib of Sasov came there in 1790 and established a *shtiebl*. It was he who converted R. Jacob Yitzhak, the "Holy Jew" of Przysucha, the head of the *yeshivah* there, to Hasidism.

It was also the home of R. Aaron ben Tzvi Hirsch, the editor of *Sefer Keter Shem Tov*, which was published in Zolkiev in 1794. Among his other works were *Oneg Shabbat* (Lvov, 1793), *Keter Nahorah* (Zhitomir, 1865), and *Or HaGanuz LaTzaddikim* (Zolkiev, 1800).

R. Meir Halevi (d. 1827); R. Yitzhak Simhah (d. 1937), the son of R. Tzemah of Szydlowiec; and R. Abraham Shalom of Ozarov (d. 1918) also lived there.

It was in 1800 that R. Abraham Joshua Heschel came to Opatov, where he stayed for nine years. Although he was rabbi in other places, he was known as the "Apter rebbe." It was he who said that Opatov was part of the land of Israel, and its Broad (Jewish) Street was Jerusalem.

There were many hasidic *shtieblech* there during the interwar years. The community was liquidated by the Nazis between October 20 and 22, 1942.

G. D. Hundert, *The Jews in a Polish Private Town: The Case of Opatov in the Eighteenth Century*, pp. 82–84.

ORENSTEIN, Mordecai Zeev, of Lvov (1735–2 *Tevet* 1787) – Son of R. Mosheh Ashkenazi, he was known as the "Great" to distinguish him from his grandson. At the age of nineteen, he became rabbi of Kaminka and later succeeded R. Ezekiel Landau as rabbi of Yampoli. He was very much influenced by R. Pinhas Horowitz. He visited the Maggid of Mezhirech. He then became rabbi of Lvov, where he served for the last nine years of his life.

His son R. Jacob Meshullam (1775–1839 was rabbi first in Yaroslav and then in Lvov R. Mordecai befriended the rabbi of Zydaczov and R. Uri of Strelisk.

He was the author of *Yeshuot Yaakov* o the *Shulhan Arukh* (Zolkiev, 1828) and o *Yeshuot Yaakov* on the Pentateuch (Warsaw 1907).

ORGAN – After the destruction of th Temple, the organ and other musical instru ments became forbidden in synagogal wo ship. In the nineteenth century, the orga was introduced in many Reform synagogue

Hasidim, however, followed the halakhic rulings of R. Moses Sofer and R. Akiba Eger, who forbade organ accompaniment not only during services but also during weddings. Organ music is regarded by the hasidim as *hukkat hagoyyim* (imitation of gentile customs).

ORLEAN, Yehudah Leib (1900–1943), educationist–Son of a hasid of Ger, he was born in Warsaw on February 21. He studied in the *shtiebl* of Ger. He wrote pamphlets in Yiddish and became the founder and ideologist of the *Po'alei Agudat Yisrael.*

For a time, he was the headmaster of the *Bet Yaakov* school in Warsaw at Twarda 37, and in 1935, with the approval of the rebbe of Ger, he became the head of the *Bet Yaakov* teachers' seminary in Cracow.

He was the author of the tracts *Die Zatte un die Hungerike* (The Satiated and the Hungry) (Warsaw, 1930) and *Gan Eden Havud* (Paradise Lost) (Warsaw, 1936).

During the Nazi occupation, when the seminary closed down, the rebbe of Boyan encouraged and supported him in other educational activities. He then moved to Wegrov and Warsaw, where, together with Eliezer Gershon Friedensohn, he organized the reestablishment of five *Bet Yaakov* schools in the Warsaw ghetto. He was then employed as an archivist for the Jewish community in Warsaw, where he looked after the Hebrew books left behind by the deportees.

He, his wife, and his five children were murdered by the Nazis.

Elleh Ezkerah, vol. 1, pp. 177–189.

OSTILOV, Joseph, of Ostilov (1764–18 *Elul* 1830)–Elder son of R. Mordecai of Neshkhitz, he married Trina, the daughter of R. Judah Meir, a descendant of R. Pinhas of Koretz and of R. Jacob Samson of Sheptovka. He became rabbi first in Ostilov (Ustilug), and, when his father died in 1800, he succeeded him as rebbe.

R. Joseph was a disciple of R. Jacob Yitzhak, the "Seer" of Lublin, whom he visited regularly. He had four sons: R. Pinhas, R. Mordecai, R. Barukh, and R. Levi Yitzhak. When Samuel Yehiel, the son of R. Don of Radzvillov, married the daughter of R. Joseph of Hubrieszov, in Ustilug, nearly 200 hasidic rebbes participated in the celebration.

This wedding became the scene of a famous confrontation concerning the controversial teachings of R. Simhah Bunem of Przysucha. Seeking to have him censored, and possibly excommunicated, came three opponents of Przysucha: R. Shimon Ashkenazi, R. Moses of Kozienice, and R. Meir of Opatov. To tell his side of the story, R. Simhah Bunem sent five articulate representatives: R. Yitzhak Meir Alter of Ger, R. Alexander Zusya of Sedlice, R. Issachar Baer Horowitz, R. Shragai Feivel Dancyger of Grice, and R. Eliezer Baer.

Sternly, the arbitrator, R. Abraham Joshua Heschel of Opatov, rebuked the anti-Przysucha section: "If you were living in a forest, you would quarrel even with the trees."

Y. Alfasi, *Bisdei HaHasidut*, pp. 483–485.

OSTROG (Hebrew, *Ostraha*), city in the Ukraine–This was the home of R. Jacob Joseph, author of *Yivi*; R. Asher Tzvi (d. 1817), a disciple of R. Dov Baer, the Maggid of Mezhirech; and R. Aaron Samuel ben Naftali Hirz Hakohen (d. 4 *Nisan* 1814).

Between 1794 and 1815, six printing presses, established by Abraham ben Yitzhak Eizig of Koretz, Aaron ben Yonah, Eliyahu ben Yitzhak, Zehariah ben Yehudah, and Eliezer Feivel Eisenberg, operated there. Among the hasidic works published there were *Maggid Devarav L'Yaakov*, *Shivhei Ari*, *Tikkunei Zohar*, *Likkutei Maharan*, *Sippurei Maasiyot* (1815), and *Shivhei HaBesht* (1815).

H. D. Friedberg, *History of Hebrew Typography in Poland*, pp. 115–118.

OSTROPOLER, Herschele, (late-eighteenth century), jester–Born in Balta, Podolia, he lived most of his life in Medziborz. For a time he served as a *shohet* in Ostropol. He was the court jester to R. Barukh of Medziborz. His witticisms were a form of wry social comment, sometimes sharp and sometimes subtle. "Why is the Day of Atonement called *Yom Kippurim* (i.e. like Purim)?" he once asked. And the answer he gave was: "It is because on both these days the Jews changed places. On Purim, Jews conducted themselves like gentiles (eating and making merry). While on the Day of Atonement, gentiles (i.e., nonobservant Jews) conduct themselves like Jews, visiting the synagogue, praying, and doing penance."

C. Bloch, *Hersch Ostropoler. Ein jüdischer Till-Eulenspiegel des 18. Jahrhunderts: seine Geschichten und Striche*.

OSTROPOLER, Samson (d. 1648), kabbalist–He was one of the greatest kabbalists of Polish Jewry. He served as a Maggid in Polonnoye. He was the author of *Dan Yadin*, a commentary on the kabbalistic work *Karnayim* (Zhitomir, 1806). He also wrote *Mahaneh Dan*, a commentary on the *Zohar*, in conformity with the kabbalistic system of R. Yitzhak Luria. But that work has not been preserved. He was also the author of *Aspaklaryah Meirah* (Furth, 1726). Some of his notes are preserved in the Bodleian Library, in Oxford, England.

He was murdered during the Chmielnicki massacres on July 22.

Hasidic legend has it that he predicted the actual year of the coming of the Messiah and foretold of the Russo-Japanese war.

G. Scholem, *Revue d'histoire des religions*, vol. 143, pp. 37–39.

OSTROV MAZOWIECKA, a town in central Poland–Among the hasidic rabbis who lived there was R. Gershon Heinokh Leiner of Radzyn, who established a *Talmud Torah* and societies for the visiting of the sick and the dowering of poor brides. In spite of his public-spirited qualities, he encountered violent antagonism from the *mitnaggedim*.

Ostrov was also the home of R. Joshua (d. 1873), the son of R. Shlomoh Leib of Leczna, and of R. Joseph Kalish, the son of R. Menahem Kalish, who lived there until 1918, when he moved to Amshinov.

The hasidic halakhist R. Meir Dan Plotski was the town's rabbi until 1928, when he moved to Warsaw to become the head of the *Mesifta*. On the advice of R. Joseph Kalish, R. Jacob Shragai Singer, a son-in-law of the rebbe of Alexander, was appointed rabbi in 1930.

Sefer HaZikkaron LeKehillat Ostrov.

OSTROW, Joshua (1819–28 *Sivan* 1873)–Son of R. Solomon Judah Leib of Leczna (d. 19 *Nisan* 1843), his father claimed that his son had the soul of R. Joshua ben Perachiah, a *tanna* of the second century B.C.E. and that his physiognomy was that of the Maggid of Mezhirech.

R. Joshua visited R. Mendel of Kotzk, R. Yitzhak of Warka, and R. Israel of Ruzhyn and was especially devoted to R. Moses of Kobryn. He married Gitel, the daughter of R. Tzvi Menahem Meisels, author of *Zikhron Tzvi Menahem*. In 1843 he succeeded his father as rebbe of Leczna, and then he moved to Sosnowiec. He finally settled in Ostrov in 1866.

At the instigation of the Austrian agitator Father Joseph Deckert, he was accused of ritual murder. It was claimed that he, together with his beadle Moses Beriches and Israel Frost, abducted a six-year-old Christian boy from the town of Lubartov and then murdered him before Passover. This allegation appeared in the Viennese newspaper *Vaterland* on May 11, 1893, twenty years after the rebbe's death. Joseph Samuel Bloch initiated proceedings against Deckert, who was found guilty of defamation of character, and he and his associates were fined.

He was the author of *Toldot Adam* on the Pentateuch and novellae on the Talmud, which were published by his grandson, R. Abraham Joshua Heschel Rabinowicz of Lublin (Josefov, 1874).

He was buried in Warsaw. In his will and testament he forbade the construction of an *ohel* over his grave and requested that no one be buried within four cubits of his grave. His only daughter, Rachel Leviah, married R. Jacob Yitzhak Rabinowicz, who succeeded him.

P

PALE OF SETTLEMENT – The Pale of Settlement determining the area in which the Jews of the Russian Empire could reside came into existence during the three partitions of Poland (1772, 1793, 1795). By these partitions, about a million Jews who had been living formerly under Polish rule came under Russian rule and were at once exposed to discriminatory treatment regarding residence rights. This was consistent with the already existing policy of prohibiting Jews from entering or trading in the Russian interior as practiced by the czars of Muscovy since the state came into existence in the fifteenth century.

In 1772 the Empress Catherine II specified that the territory within which Jews could exercise their former rights was restricted to their area of existing residence. In 1791 a decree further confirmed the right of residence of the Jews in the areas acquired by Russia by partition but permitted their settlement only in the provinces of Chernigov and Poltava and in the newly acquired territories to the north of the Black Sea. The Pale of Settlement was not fully defined until 1835, when it took into account the annexations of Bessarabia (1812) and the Kingdom of Poland (1815). It embraced an area from the Baltic to the Black Sea, consisting of Lithuania; the southwestern provinces of White Russia, Little Russia, and New Russia; the province of Kiev (except for its capital, Kharkov); and the Baltic provinces (old settlers only).

In the early years of the reign of Alexander II, a number of ministers and government officials recommended the abolition of the Pale of Settlement in the interests of the legal equality of all citizens of the empire. Some relaxations followed in the 1850s and early 1860s, when Jewish merchants of the first guild, Jewish graduates of higher institutions of learning, and Jewish artisans and their families were allowed to take up residence and trade outside the pale. But for the overwhelming majority of Russian Jews, the pale remained in existence until the February revolution of 1917 and was a dominating factor in their lives.

Within the pale, according to the census of 1897, there lived 4.8 million Jews – 11.5 percent of the total population and nearly 94 percent of all Russian Jewry. Two features marked the geographical distribution of the Jews in the pale: (1) in certain provinces (e.g. Grodno, 17.28 percent; Warsaw, 18.12 percent), their percentage exceeded their proportion in the general population, and (2) the overwhelming majority lived in towns (48.84 percent) and hamlets (*shtetl*) (33.05 percent). Only some 18 percent lived in villages. The pale very severely limited the economic opportunities open to the Jews, which, together with population growth, was a major factor in contributing to the pauperization of Russian Jewry. But it can also be argued that it helped to preserve their cohesion and identity and to counter assimilationist tendencies.

L. Greenberg, *The Jews in Russia*.

S.L.

PANET, Ezekiel (1870–22 *Kislev* 1929) – Second son of R. Moses, he was a follower of R. Ezekiel of Sianiawa. He married Hayyah Sarah, the daughter of R. Samuel Yehudah Pollack.

In 1895, he became rabbi of Marousujvar. After the death of his father in 1902, he succeeded him as rabbi of Des.

He was the author of *Knesset Yeheskel* in two parts on Torah (Des, 1931).

A.S.

PANET, Ezekiel, of Karlsburg (1783–20 *Nisan* 1845) – Son of R. Joseph, he was born in Bielitz, Silesia. At the age of thirteen he knew by heart the whole of Rashi's commentary on the Pentateuch. He spent two years at the *yeshivah* of R. Barukh Frankel Teumim of Leipnik, and from there he went to Prague, where he studied under R. Samuel Landau and R. Leib Fisheles. On 6 *Elul* 1802 he married *Hayyah* Rachel, the daughter of R. Moses Henig of Linsk. He stayed with his father-in-law for several years. There he studied with the rabbi of the town, R. Mendele, who aroused his interest in Hasidism.

In 1805 he visited the "Seer," the Maggid of Kozienice, and, above all, R. Menahem Mendel of Rymanov. In 1805 in a letter to his father, he takes issue with the accusations leveled against the hasidim. He skillfully refutes the anti-hasidic accusations.

In 1823 he accepted the rabbinate of Karlsburg (Alba Iulia), which effectively made him the chief rabbi of Transylvania. In the course of the twenty-three years of his rabbinate, he transformed Transylvania into a thriving Jewish area.

His main work was published posthumously under the title *Mareh Yehezkel U'Sheerit Zion* (Sighet, 1875). He was the author of a commentary on the Passover *Haggadah* (Sighet, 1879); *Mareh Yehezkel*, a homiletical commentary on the Pentateuch (Des, 1894); and a commentary on Psalms (Brooklyn, 1978). R. Ezekiel also recorded the homiletical interpretations of R. Mendel of Rymanov.

He left four sons and four daughters. Two of his sons became rabbis.

J. D. Friedmann, *Toldot Rabbenu Yehezkel*.

A.S.

PANET, Hayyim Bezalel, of Des

(23 *Sivan* 1803–19 *Nisan* 1874) – Elder son of R. Ezekiel, he studied under R. Moses Sofer of Pressburg. In 1823 he married Sarah Esther Bluma, the daughter of R. Leibish Neulaender of Alpar, where he stayed for ten years.

He became rabbi of Balkany, and later, in 1835, at Tasnad, where he served the community for thirty-one years. He suffered ill health throughout his life. Of his many manuscripts only his responsa were published.

R. Asher Samuel Panet, his son, edited *Derekh Yivhar* (Tasnad, 1895).

A.S.

PANET, Jacob Elimelekh, of Des

(1888–18 *Sivan* 1944) – Son of R. Ezekiel. In 1902, he became rabbi of Marousujvar, and in 1909, he married the daughter of R. Jacob Samson Kanner of Galicia. In 1926, he became junior rabbi of Des, and a year later, he succeeded his father as rebbe. He was very active in the Orthodox communities of Transylvania.

His son R. Hayyim Barukh was the son-in-law of R. Hayyim Halberstam, the head of the *Bet Din* of Satmar, and served under his father as the head of the *Bet Din* in Des.

R. Jacob Elimelekh was the author of *Zikhron Yaakov* on Torah (New York, 1953).

He, together with his five sons, one daughter, and their families, perished in Auschwitz.

PANET, Menahem Mendel, of Des

(1818–13 *Tishri* 1885) – Younger son of R. Ezekiel, he was born in Tarczal. Besides his father, he was taught by R. Moses Sofer. In 1839 he married Reizel, the daughter of R. Yehudah Leib Gross. He was an outstanding halakhic authority, who was first the rabbi of Alor (Orisor) and became in 1864 rabbi of Des, where his *yeshivah* attracted many students.

He edited his father's responsa. His own responsa were published under different names: *Shaarei Tzeddek* on *Orah Hayyim* (Munkacs, 1884), *Yoreh De'ah* (1883), *Mishpat Tzeddek* on the *Hoshen Mishpat* (Munkacs, 1884), and *Avnei Tzeddek* to *Even HaEzer* (Munkacs, 1885). These volumes are a testimony to his vast knowledge and to the high regard in which he was held by the great men of his generation. His homiletical commentary to the Pentateuch, *Maaglei Tzeddek* (Munkacs, 1884), contains many of his sermons.

He was succeeded by his son, Rabbi Moses.

A.S.

PANET, Moses, of Des

(1843–24 *Kislev* 1902) – Son of R. Menahem Mendel, he was a follower of R. Hayyim Halberstam of Zanz. His first rabbinate was in Alor, and later, in Nimozsa. On his father's death he settled in Des. He was the head of the *yeshivah* and had many hasidic followers.

He left no literary works, and only one of his discourses was printed in his son's work.

He was very active in organizing the charities destined for the Holy Land.

A.S.

PANTHEISM – The identification of the all with God. Hasidic thought has frequently been described as pantheistic in that it tends to see God as the only ultimate reality, so that He is "in" all things. However, Hasidism, for all its stress on the immanence of God, does not deny, as does pantheism, the transcendence of God. Indeed, hasidic thought, far from identifying God with the universe, suggests that without God there could be no universe, whereas without the universe there is no change in God, or, better, from God's point of view there is no universe at all. This is especially true of the *Habad* movement in Hasidism. A far better term for the hasidic view is, consequently, *panentheism*, "all is *in* God."

In the early hasidic text *Keter Shem Tov* ([edition Zolkiev, 1794–1795] I, pp. 5a–5b), the parable is given of a mighty king who sits on his throne, situated in a huge palace with many halls, all of them filled with priceless treasures. When the true servants of the king refuse to be distracted by the splendors of the palace and its treasures but press on in order to enter the king's presence, they discover to their astonishment that the palace and its halls do not really exist and that there is only the king in his glory and majesty.

In the same way, God hides Himself in the "garments" and barriers of the upper worlds and the cosmos. When we recognize that this is so, when we acknowledge that all is created out of God's essence – "like the snail whose shell is formed of itself" – that in reality there are no barriers between us and God, then "all the workers of iniquity" are dispersed. The same text (I, p. 8b) understands the verse "Know this day, and lay it to thy heart, that the Lord He is God in heaven above and in the earth beneath; *there is none else*" (Deuteronomy 4:39) to mean not alone that there are no other gods but that in reality there is nothing but God. Frequently in hasidic literature the Midrashic saying (Num. Rabbah 12:4) that there is no place empty of the *Shekhinah* is paraphrased in Aramaic as *let atar panui minnei* (no place is empty of Him).

The opponents of Hasidism were not slow to attack these ideas as heresy. It was claimed that hasidic panentheism would inevitably lead to "thinking on words of Torah in unclean places," meaning, to the erasing of the demarcation lines between the holy and the profane and between good and evil. Yet the disciple of the arch-opponent of Hasidism, the Gaon of Vilna, can write, "Apart from Him, blessed be He, there is nothing else whatsoever, in reality, in all the worlds, from the highest of the high to the lowest depths of the earth. So that one can say that there is no creature or world at all but all is filled with the essence of His pure unity, blessed be He" (Hayyim of Volozhyn, *Nefesh HaHayyim* [Vilna, 1837], *Shaar* 3, p. 67f.).

The only difference between R. Hayyim of Volozhyn and the hasidim, though it is an important difference, is that for the hasidim it is good to dwell on this thought at all times, whereas Hayyim of Volozhyn writes, "This tremendous matter is intended only for the sage, who can understand on his own the inner meaning of the idea by allowing his heart to run to and fro, for the sole purpose of inflaming the purity of his heart for God's service in prayer. But there is the greatest danger in too much contemplation of this theme." The hasidim seemed impervious to the danger. A hasidic tale tells of R. Shneur Zalman of Liady, who was once asked, "What is God?" He is reported to have held up a piece of bread, saying, "This is God."

L. Jacobs, *Seeker of Unity: The Life and Works of Aaron of Starosselje*.

E. Zweiful, *Shalom al Yisrael*, vol. 2, pp. 37–60.

L.J.

PARABLE – Hasidic preachers used parables and short stories to reach and teach the masses in a way that could easily be understood by them and would cause them no offense. Few of the parables were original. Some were taken from the *Musar* literature, such as *Hovot HaLevavot*, by R. Bahya Ibn Pakuda; others from commentaries on the Torah, such as *Akedat Yitzhak*, by R. Yitzhak Arama.

The Besht was very fond of telling parables and stories to make a point. It is said that he sometimes stopped people in the street to tell them stories. Some of his stories together with those of other members of his circle can be found in the books of his disciple R. Jacob Joseph of Polonnoye. At the end of his *Toldot Yaakov Yosef*, he records two short stories of the Besht's journey to Israel and the mystic events that then took place.

Generally the telling of short stories was regarded as an educational medium, a means of influencing the followers of the *tzaddik* in their religious observance and moral precepts. The Besht, however, conceived the idea that through the telling of worldly stories, one can worship God and conceive mystic unifications in the world of *Sefirot*. Thus, the telling of the story will cause purification, correction, and restoration of unity in the upper worlds, in the same way as is done by the study of the Torah, by prayer, and by observance of the commandments.

The first book of hasidic stories, *Shivhei HaBesht*, was published in Kopys in 1815–1816, fifty-five years after the death of the Besht. These stories about the Besht and his friends and disciples were gathered together by R. Dov Baer ben Samuel of Linitz, the son-in-law of R. Alexander, the scribe of the Besht. In his preface he stresses the authenticity of the stories, which he had been told by people who knew the Besht or who had heard them from others who had known him. The first publisher of *Shivhei HaBesht* was R. Israel Jaffe of Kopys, a follower of R. Shneur Zalman of Liady. In his preface he relates that he did not feel that the chronology of the events recounted was correct, and he had, therefore, changed the order to one he felt was more authentic. Thus, the book can be said to have been written by two authors: R. Dov Baer of Linitz, who describes what he had heard from his father-in-law, the Besht's scribe, about the miracles and wonders performed by the Besht and his circle, and R. Israel Jaffe, who told extraordinary tales about the Besht's father, the Besht's childhood, and mysterious scripts acquired by the Besht from the mysterious R. Adam.

Many researchers of Hasidism regard this book of stories, usually referring to S. A. Horodezky's edition of 1922, as a first-class historical source, because all the stories are regarded as being based on fact.

The book of tales by R. Nahman of Bratzlav, a great-grandson of the Besht, was published at the same time as the *Shivhei HaBesht*. R. Nahman, the greatest storyteller of Hasidism, while following the philosophical motives of his predecessors, adds other ideas that are peculiarly his own. He regards telling ordinary tales as a serious "descension" from the lofty spiritual position of the *tzaddik*, but, indirectly, such relaxation from the *tzaddik's* efforts and exertions in study and prayer is for the benefit of society. R. Nahman's stories are full of the belief in Divine Eminence in the world, but there is also evidence of a demonological consciousness, influenced by the Lurian Kabbalah. R. Nahman assumes that it is impossible to reveal lofty spiritual matters, unless these are clothed in worldly garments, namely, in stories.

R. Nahman's stories are divided into "tales in years" (*BeKerev Shanim*), which derive their vitality from the last seven *Sefirot*, and "tales of ancient years" (*Kadmoniyot*), which are based on *Binah* (intelligence), the last of the first three *Sefirot*. His stories allude to the personal status of the *tzaddik*-savior, who, due to the inferior position of the masses, must veil his own sublime position, which he does with the aid of stories.

Thirteen of R. Nahman's stories were put together by his scribe, R. Nathan Sternharz, and were first published in a Hebrew/Yiddish edition in 1815–1816. There now exists an extensive array of commentaries on and translations of these stories.

The nineteenth century saw the publication of numerous collections of hasidic tales, most of them containing nonauthentic material. Michael Levi Frumkin (Rodkinson), the author of *Shivhei HaRav*, *Adat Tzaddikim*, and *Pe'er MiKedoshim*, did a great deal in the field of story gathering and writing.

Jewish writers, especially I. L. Peretz, S. Y. Agnon, and S. J. Zevin, often used hasidic stories in their works. Several hasidic anthologies and many collections of hasidic stories have been and are still being published today.

G.N.

PASSOVER – First of the three Pilgrim Festivals, observed for eight days in the Diaspora and for seven days in Israel (14–22 *Nisan*).

One of the most beloved of the Jewish Festivals, Passover naturally occupies an important place in the lives of the hasidim. Many hasidic rebbes were actively engaged in *Maot Hitim* (literally, wheat money), which provided *matzot*, wine, and other

Passover essentials for the poor and the needy.

Because the first two days of Passover are celebrated with the family gathered around the *seder* table, hasidic rebbes (apart from the rebbe of Warka) discouraged hasidim from coming to them. All were, however, welcome at the hasidic courts on the last two days of the Festival. The rebbe of Warka, R. Bunem of Otwock, even had special apartments reserved for Passover, with a special kitchen and even different sets of books.

The rebbe and the hasidim would bake their own *matzot* on the eve of the Festival. They would recite *Hallel*, some even with a benediction, while baking. Most rebbes, with the exception of Lubavitch, wore a *kittel* for the *sedarim*. Rebbes would intersperse the recital of the *Haggadah* with illuminating commentaries, and many hasidic rebbes published commentaries on the Passover *Haggadah*. R. Isaac Taub of Nagy Kallo would explain the *seder* ritual in Hungarian. Most rebbes would eat the *afikoman* before midnight on the first night.

In the court of Dzikov, the *seder* table would be prepared on the previous Sabbath (*Shabbat HaGadol*), and the women and servants would share the table with the men. In other courts, such as Novominsk, there was a separate table for the women. In Ropczyce, all the children at the table—not merely the youngest—would ask the Four Questions. For *karpas* they would use potatoes and recite the benediction "Who createth the fruit of the earth." Throughout the year, however, they would recite the blessing "By Whose word all things exist" over potatoes.

In Belz, it was customary for the boy who asked the Four Questions to also open the door for the Prophet Elijah. In Lubavitch, when the festival occurred on a weekday, the prophet would be greeted with lighted candles. R. Menahem Mendel Morgenstern of Kotzk used five cups of wine at the *seder*, a custom also adopted by the hasidim of Radzyn.

Many hasidic rebbes would recite the blessing of the *Omer* at the end of the *seder*. *Habad* hasidim, however, recited it in the synagogue. On the last day of the Festival, many rebbes, especially those descended from the Besht, would hold a festive meal, which they called "the *seudah* of the Besht," to commemorate the deliverance of the Besht when his boat was captured by pirates en route to the Holy Land.

M. Unger, *Hasidut un Yomtov*, pp. 231–291.

PASTERNAK, Velvel (1933-27 *Tevet* 1982), musician—Born in Toronto, Ontario, Canada, Velvel graduated from Yeshiva University and Columbia University and was a student at the Juilliard School of Music.

His first experience with the music of Modzitz came at an early age, when he accompanied his father on visits to the home of R. Saul Taub of Modzitz in Toronto.

He was a faculty member of Yeshiva University, was on the staff of several leading day schools, and was a noted synagogue choir leader. He was the author of *Songs of the Chassidim* (New York, 1971), in which, for the first time, 210 of the most beloved hasidic songs were notated and appeared in print.

He participated in the recording of Modzitzer music in 1958 and recorded many Lubavitch and Bobov songs.

In 1963, he collaborated with Ben Zion Shenker and Valadimir Heifetz on *Modzitzer Favorite Melodies*.

PATASHNIK, Aaron (1889-1940), hasidic rebbe—Son of R. Yitzhak and a grandson of R. Abraham Samuel, R. Aaron predicted both that "a great storm was breaking over Poland" and that "he who would survive this tempest would see a great light."

R. Aaron lived in Rovno until 1937 and married the daughter of the rabbi of Sambor. He was an exceptionally fine musician. He and his family joined the partisans, and he urged other Jews to follow his lead. He died in the forest.

He was survived by his wife, Feige, and two daughters, who lived in Israel.

PATASHNIK, Nahum Joshua Halevi, of Dabrowice (d. 12 *Elul* 1942)—Son of R. Abraham Shmuel of Brzezany, a descendant of Chernobyl, and of R. David HaMaggid (d. 1809), R. Nahum married Hinde Perel, the daughter of R. Alter Mordecai Sefard of Ostrog. He was ordained by R. Hayyim Soloveitchik and spent fifteen years in the home of his father-in-law.

He became rabbi in Dabrowice but was always known as the "rebbe of Brzezany." He was very active in the Aguda, and in the

Rabbinical Association and even supported the *Keren HaKayemet*. He was in charge of eight neighboring communities.

In the Second World War, he advised the Jews to join the partisans. He, his wife, his son R. Yitzhak, his son's wife, Bathsheva, and their three children were shot by the Nazis together with a group of 16,000 Jews.

M. Unger, *Admorim SheNisfu BaShoa*, pp. 227–231.

PATASHNIK, Yitzhak (d. 15 *Elul* 1865) – Son of R. Michael (d. 15 *Kislev* 1848), he married Perel, the daughter of R. Aaron of Chernobyl and lived in Stolin with his father-in-law. In 1840, he settled in Brzezany and became rebbe after his father's death.

He was succeeded by his eldest son, R. Joseph (d. 1869). Some hasidim, however, followed his son-in-law, R. Hayyim Teibman.

R. Joseph's son, R. Abraham Moses, was only seven years old when his father died. He married the daughter of R. Issachar Dov Rokeah. He died on 11 *Tevet* 1917. He was survived by three sons: the eldest, R. Yitzhak, rabbi in Brzezany, died in 1939; R. Joseph, rebbe of Sarny, died in 1920; and R. Nahum Joshua was rebbe of Dabrowice.

M. Unger, *Admorim SheNisfu BaShoa*, pp. 227–231.

PAZNOWSKY, Abraham Tzvi (1777–7 *Adar* 1819) – Son of R. Eleazar, he married the daughter of R. Yehudah Leib Lipshitz, rabbi of Opoczno. He studied under his grandfather R. Shlomoh Zalman. At the age of twenty-one, he became rabbi of Pilice, and in 1812, he was appointed rabbi in Piotrokov.

All his children died in his lifetime, and he himself continuously suffered ill health. He died in Breslau at the age of forty-two. He was a devout disciple of the "Seer" of Lublin.

His book *Brit Avraham* was published in Dyrenfurt in 1819.

A. Y. Bromberg, *Migdolei HaHasidut*, vol. 19, *HaHozeh MiLublin*, pp. 126–132.

PEACE – A vibrant expectation in hasidic circles was the messianic vision of a perfect peace. Many stories are told of *tzaddikim* who believed that the advent of the Messiah was at hand. R. Levi Yitzhak of Berdichev used this idea when inviting guests to a wedding. He invited them to "Jerusalem Rebuilt," adding as an afterthought that "if the Messiah did not come, the wedding would take place in Berdichev." In the *Kedushah* and in the *Kaddish*, the hasidim inserted a reference to the Messiah.

It was natural for the hasidim to interpret every great war as the eschatological battle between the two mythical powers Gog and Magog that is supposed to culminate in the establishment of peace. R. Jacob Yitzhak of Lublin attempted, together with other *tzaddikim*, to turn the Napoleonic wars into a Gog-Magog confrontation.

The age of peace will dawn when the sparks of holiness, which are imprisoned in the shells, are liberated. Then Satan will be overcome, for Satan, too, is an angel who serves God by tempting the pietists. The Besht was wont to say that "evil is the chair for the good."

In the words of R. Nahman of Bratzlav, "The Sabbath candles increase peace, and the pursuance of peace brings honor in this world and a goodly share in the next." The pursuance of peace leads to trustfulness. Peace brings good tidings, and through education, peace is increased. Prayers are not heard when there is no peace, for peace is a sign of good life. The pursuance of peace saves one from death and exile, and blessings come through peace. Where there is peace there is no terror. Even the wicked who live in peace enjoy prosperity (*Sefer HaMidot*, pp. 152–153).

R. Shneur Zalman was instrumental in mollifying his opponents and establishing harmony within the Jewish community. Nonetheless, hasidim were in the forefront of the fight against every form of modernism, against secular learning, and against any change in the traditional ways of life. R. Yitzhak Meir Alter of Ger led the fight, in the middle of the nineteenth century, against the attempt by the Russian government to compel Jews to wear European garments.

As the hasidic movement spread, it was not uncommon for various hasidic groups to fight each other – the Shpoler against the Bratzlaver, Zanz against Sadgora. In all such cases, the hasidim believed there was a metaphysical reason for the disputes.

D. T. Hillman, ed., *Iggrot Baal HaTanya U'Benei Doro*.

J.B.A.

PEKIIN (Arab Baca) – A village in Upper Galilee, near Safed. According to legend, R.

Shimon Bar Yohai and his son Eleazer wrote the *Zohar* in one of the caves of Pekiin, where they spent thirteen years. R. Hayyim Attar lived there for two months. A number of hasidim settled there in 1783. In 1847, a small *yeshivah* was established there.

PERETZ, Isaac Leib (1852–1915), father of modern Yiddish literature – Peretz, who has been described as the "poet of Hasidism," was born in Zamosc and was brought up in a hasidic environment. He was employed as a bookkeeper by the Jewish community of Warsaw. His home was the meeting place of the Warsaw literati: the scholars, hasidim, and kabbalists.

Unlike his friends Smolenskin and Gottlober, who derided Hasidism, Peretz discovered in Hasidism an enchanted world of holiness and secret harmony. He was the first secular writer to explore the mystique of Hasidism. He preserved the pearls of Hasidism in their natural beauty. He discovered a rich folklore, tales, legends, and anecdotes. Each tale is told with great skill and verbal beauty.

In "Berl the Tailor," the all-knowing R. Levi Yitzhak of Berdichev learns of Berl's attitude. The rabbi agrees with the justice of the complaint, obtaining Berl's readiness to forgive God, and God's, in turn, to forgive Berl. In his story "If Not Higher," he tells of a hasidic rebbe who, during the Holy Days, disappeared for a time every morning. A man who followed him secretly saw the rebbe make his way to a forest, prepare firewood, and carry it to the hut of a sick old widow. There, posing as a peasant, he started the fire to keep the woman from leaving her sick bed.

Peretz's greatest work is the *Golden Chain*, a poetic drama of romantic imagination. In it he presents with crystal clarity the essential nature of Hasidism: its ecstasy and fanaticism. The dynamism of his style gives the breath of life to his characters. "For Peretz," stated A. A. Roback, "a character is always in movement."

He wrote, in turn, as a naturalist, a realist, and a romanticist, creating within each form an artistic pattern for younger Yiddish writers. Among the stories of Peretz, translated into English, are *The Book of Fire* (New York, 1960), *In This World and the Next* (New York, 1958), *The Three Canopies* (New York, 1958), and *Three Gifts and Other Stories* (New York, 1964).

C. A. Madison, *Yiddish Literature*, pp. 99–134.

PERL, Joseph (1773–1839), satirist – Born in Tarnov, he was an exponent of Galician *Haskalah* and he did all he could to further the cause of the *Haskalah* movement. In 1813, he founded the first *Haskalah* school in Tarnopol. He also established a synagogue, based on Reform ideas, and provided it with a choir.

Much of his time was spent in fighting against Hasidism. He encouraged the Austrian authorities to take measures against the hasidim. In 1816, he wrote a violently anti-hasidic tract, *Uber das Wesen der Sekte Chassidim*, in which he alleged that Hasidism jeopardized the welfare of the state. He is best known for his anti-hasidic satire *Megallei Temirim* (Revealer of Secrets), published under his pen name, Obadia ben Petahia (Vienna, 1819). It purports to contain 151 letters written by hasidic leaders in Galicia. The author pretends to be a hasid. Its hasidic discourses and homilies are distorted and misrepresented. A sequel, called *Bohen Tzaddik* (Test of the Righteous), written in 1825 but not published until 1838, presents agriculture as the panacea for the problems of the Jewish people.

Perl directed his weapon of satire particularly against R. Nahman of Bratzlav. He ridiculed his *Sippurei Maasiyot* and wrote imitations of these stories, claiming that they had been discovered after R. Nahman's demise. Perl's works remain a monument to the tragic obscurantism of the *Haskalah* movement.

I. L. Davidson, *Parody in Hebrew Literature*, pp. 61–74.

N.L.

PERLMUTTER, Abraham Tzvi (ca. 1844–1926), communal leader – Though of mitnaggedic background, he associated with hasidic rebbes, especially with R. Yehiel Meir Lipshitz, the "Psalm Jew" of Gostynin, who encouraged him to participate in communal affairs. After serving as rabbi in Leczna, Raciaz, and Radom, he became a member of the Warsaw rabbinate in 1909. In 1919, he was elected to the Aguda list, together with R. Moses Eliyahu Halpern, a member of the first Polish Seym. He was the ideal *shtadlan* of Polish Jewry.

PERLOW, Aaron, of Koidanov (1839–26 *Elul* 1897)–Son of R. Barukh Mordecai. He became rebbe in 1871, and while his father was still alive he drew up a public appeal in his father's name on behalf of the Koidanov *kollel* in Tiberias. He appealed to his followers: "Let no one of our followers change his contribution . . . from every couple one gold piece; let the poor not give less than that, apart from the regular yearly contributions to the Holy Land."

He wrote the introduction to the Koidanov prayer book *Ohel HaYashar*, which was printed in 1877. He further saw through the press R. Mosheh Cordovero's book *Or Ne'erav* with an appendix of his own, *Nireh Or*, published posthumously (Vilna, 1899). Printed together with the work of R. Mosheh Hagiz, *Sefat Emet* is a collection of writings by R. Aaron on the importance of the Holy Land (Vilna, 1866).

An eyewitness account described him as a man of short stature, who appeared before his hasidim only rarely. In the rabbi's house was an iron box, which served as a repository for the scant savings of the inhabitants of the town. Widows would deposit coin by coin to provide a dowry for their daughters. One time a rumor spread that the rebbe had gone bankrupt, and he was prosecuted by one of his creditors. He had to appear in the district court of Vilna, where the charges were dismissed.

His discourses are recorded in *Ateret Shalom* (Warsaw, 1895), *Zekher Tzaddik* (Vilna, 1905), and *Siah Avot* (Tel Aviv, 1963). He was succeeded by his son R. Joseph. His other sons were R. Shlomoh Hayyim and R. Nehemiah.

W. Z. Rabinowitsch, *Lithuanian Hasidism*, pp. 164–168.

PERLOW, Abraham Elimelekh, of Karlin (1891–14 *Heshvan* 1942)–Fifth son of R. Israel the *Yanukkah*, he married the daughter of R. Mordecai Joseph Twersky of Zlatopol. When his father died in 1921, he reluctantly became rebbe. He was well acquainted with modern Hebrew literature, especially with works related to Hasidism. He was even aware of the writings of Martin Buber.

He founded a *yeshivah* in Luninyets, a town situated between Pinsk and Stolin. Between 1922 and 1939, he visited his followers in the Holy Land four times and established a *yeshivah Bet Aaron* in Jerusalem. He returned to Poland in the summer of 1939, just before the outbreak of the Second World War.

During the Nazi occupation he lived in Pinsk and had to register for work as a night watchman. To save herself from a shameful death at the hands of the Nazis, his daughter Hannale took her own life by taking poison. The rabbi and his two sons were murdered by the Nazis a few days before the destruction of Karlin.

His brother R. Jacob had emigrated to the United States in 1923. He established four Stolin *shtieblech* in New York. He died in 1946 while visiting his followers in Detroit.

W. Z. Rabinowitsch, *Lithuanian Hasidism*, pp. 220–222.

PERLOW, Alter Yisrael Shimon, of Novominsk (1875–6 *Tevet* 1933)–Eldest son of R. Jacob, he and his twin sister, Reizel (the mother of the late Prof. Abraham Joshua Heschel), were born in Novominsk. In 1893 he married Feige Dinah, the daughter of R. Barukh Meir Twersky of Azarnitz. When his father died in 1902, he succeeded him as rebbe.

In 1916 he left Novominsk and settled in Warsaw. His home at Franczískanska 10 became one of the thriving centers of Hasidism. He knew by heart the whole of the *Mishnayot*. Toward the end of his life, he studied twenty-one chapters each day. On the Sabbath he spoke only Hebrew; a typical *seudah shlishit* would last three hours. On *Kol Nidre* night he recited aloud the entire book of Psalms.

He was associated with the Aguda and participated in many Aguda conventions held in Warsaw. He supported the daily newspaper *Yiddisher Togblatt* and was active in the *Mo'etzet Gedolei HaTorah*. From his famous forefathers he inherited a remarkable legacy: from R. Shlomoh Hayyim of Koidanov, prayerfulness; from R. Levi Yitzhak of Berdichev, love of humanity; from R. Pinhas of Korets, love of music; and from his father, diligence and a phenomenal memory. He ate only twice a day, at two o'clock in the afternoon and midnight. Often he refused to eat at all. "I am more than satiated with all troubles that I have heard the whole day long."

He died at the age of fifty-eight while studying *mishnayot* and was buried in Warsaw. He left volumes of writings, but most of the manuscripts perished in the Holocaust. However, in 1933 his commentary on the *Haggadah* was published in Warsaw and subsequently reprinted in New York in 1961 and 1992. His work *Tiferet Ish* on the Festivals was published in Jerusalem in 1969. A number of his discourses are to be found in *V'Yaan Yosef* (Jerusalem, 1972).

He was survived by twelve children. His wife, his daughter Malkah, and his son R. Jacob perished in Maidanek on 23 *Elul* 1943. His youngest son, R. Joseph, who succeeded him, died in Bergen-Belsen. His daughter Yentel, who married R. Judah Aryeh of Ostrog, and her children perished in the Holocaust. His other two sons were R. Aaron (d. 1963) and R. Nahum Mordecai, who was rabbi of Novominsk in New York. Other daughters were Sheindel Brachah (d. 1963), who married R. Nathan David Rabinowicz of London; Devorah (d. 1992), who married R. Yitzhak Eleazar Eichenstein (d. 1993); Shifhah (d. 1977), who married R. Abraham Yitzhak Twersky; and Nehamah (d. 1989), who married R. Yoel Teitelbaum; his daughter Sarah is married to R. Mosheh Eichenstein of Chicago.

A. Y. Bromberg, *Migdolei HaHasidut*, vol. 20, *Admorei Nezkhiz Kaidanov Novominsk*, pp. 140–168.

PERLOW, Barukh Mordecai, of Koidanov (1818–2 *Tishri* 1870)—Son of R. Shlomoh Hayyim, he married the daughter of R. Shalom of Azad. He succeeded his father as rebbe in 1866. He was the supervisor of funds for the Holy Land and was responsible for the *kollel* in Tiberias. His son R. Aaron left a graphic description of his father: "He studied the Torah in poverty and hardship, and he gave himself up entirely to the revealed lore and wisdom. He would study patiently, reading every word separately, like a man counting coins, and concentrating on it with all his might."

His discourses are to be found in the work of his son R. Shalom of Brahin. He was succeeded by his son R. Aaron.

S. Perlow, *Divrei Shalom*, p. 17.

PERLOW, Israel (*Kislev* 1868–2 *Tishri* 1922), *HaYanukkah*—the child rebbe—Son of R. Asher II, he was born in *Kislev* and named after the Besht. His father died in 1873, when he was only five years old. His mother, Deborah, and the hasidim decided to "crown" him rebbe, appointing R. Israel Benjamin Gloerman his guide and tutor. At his *bar mitzvah*, in 1881, he took over the leadership of the hasidim. He married Brachah Sheindel, the daughter of R. David Twersky of Zlatopol.

With his knowledge of Russian and German, he was able to deal effectively with the secular authorities on matters relating to the Jewish community. He sent special emissaries to collect funds for the *kollel* in the Holy Land. He did not deliver regular discourses. He prayed silently. However, his *Melaveh Malkah* was conducted to musical accompaniment. He and his three sons formed a quartet. Even *mitnaggedim* sought his guidance. He was an opponent of both the Aguda and the Mizrachi. He composed two testaments: one addressed to his family and the other to his followers.

In the testament to his family, he wrote as follows: "If my end comes while I am traveling, my body shall not be carried to my home, unless the place be only a few hours' distance from Mlynov [the burial place of R. Aaron the Great and R. Asher the First] or Drohobycz [the burial place of R. Asher the Second]. If it be the local custom to set up an *ohel* [structure over the grave], mine shall not be a large one but only medium-sized. If it be the custom to set up a tombstone, only my name and my father's name shall be inscribed on it, without any titles."

In a special letter dated 12 *Tammuz* 1921, he exhorted his followers to guard against dissension caused by flatterers and hypocrites. He urged his followers to form "one united band."

At the time when Sarah Schenierer was in the process of establishing a *Bet Yaakov* school in Cracow, he stressed the importance of religious education for girls. In his court were noted composers of music, the best known of whom were R. Jacob from Telekham and R. Yossele Talner. He was deeply concerned with the welfare of the settlers of the Old Yishuv, and he wrote thirty-six letters to his followers in the Holy Land.

He had six sons and four daughters. Accompanied by his two sons R. Asher and R. Hayyim, he went for medical advice to

Berlin and then to a convalescent home in Hamburg, Germany, where he died. He was buried in Frankfurt-am-Main. Hence, he is referred to by the hasidim as the "man of Frankfurt." His mother, Deborah, died on the very same day. He was succeeded by his eldest son, R. Abraham Elimelekh.

The *Yanukkah* more than fulfilled the hope and aspirations of his youth. He became a father to his people and a wise and erudite counselor, and he was unique even in Hasidism, a movement known for its innovation.

A. Ben Ezra, *HaYenukah MiStolin*.

PERLOW, Jacob, of Novominsk (1847–23 *Adar* 1902) – Son of R. Shimon of Zawichost, who died at the age of forty-three. He was brought up in the home of his grandfather R. Shlomoh Hayyim of Koidanov. In 1865 he married Havah Hayyah Perl, the daughter of R. Judah Leibish Liberson of Proskurov. In 1865 he became rabbi of Starosselje, near Kishinev.

After he had been married for fifteen years, with the marriage having produced a daughter, Gitel, and no sons, he consulted R. Yitzhak of Neshkhiz. "Change your place of residence," advised the sage. "Settle in Poland and there you will have sons." Accordingly, R. Jacob settled in Minsk Mazowieski in 1873, and two years later his wife gave birth to twins: a boy, Alter Israel Shimon, and a girl, Reizel.

With the help of a wealthy hasid, Shlomoh Fulman, he established the first hasidic *yeshivah* in Poland, in 1896. He was renowned for his erudition and his melodious rendering of the services. R. A. I. Kook described him as "unique in his generation."

He was succeeded by his son R. Alter Yisrael Shimon. His grandson R. Nahum Perlow of New York published his discourses, *Shufra D'Yaakov* (Jerusalem, 1964). His other sons were R. Yehudah Aryeh of Brooklyn and R. Shlomoh Hayyim of Bolechov. His daughter Reizel married R. Moses Mordecai Heschel, and his other daughter, Gitel, married R. David Moses of Koidanov.

A. Y. Bromberg, *Migdolei HaHasidut*, vol. 20, *Admorei Nezkhiz Kaidanov Novominsk*, pp. 128–139.

PERLOW, Jacob, of Novominsk/New York (b. 1930) – Son of R. Nahum Perlow, he was born in New York. He studied under his father and in the *Mesifta Hayyim Berlin*, in Brooklyn, under R. Yitzhak Hutner. In 1956, he married Yehudit, the eldest daughter of R. Abraham Eichenstein, the rebbe of Zydaczov in Chicago, and he continued to study in the *kollel Gur Aryeh* until 1962, when he assumed a teaching position in the *Bet HaMidrash LeTorah* in Chicago.

He held this post until 1970, when he became the head of the *yeshivah* of R. Samson Raphael Hirsch in Washington Heights, in New York, a post he occupied for eleven years. He became rebbe after the death of his father in 1976, and he joined the executive of the *Agudat Yisrael* of America. He is also a member of the Rabbinical Board of Torah Umesorah, an officer of the *Hinukh Atzmai*, and treasurer of the Russian Immigrant Aid Fund.

He developed his *Bet HaMidrash Adat Yaakov* in Borough Park, in Brooklyn, as a great center of Torah activities. He is a dynamic orator and frequently addresses meetings throughout the United States and abroad. He is the author of a 391-page work, *Adat Yaakov*, on talmudical topics (Jerusalem, 1982), which has the approval of R. Moses Feinstein.

His sons are R. Alter Israel Shimon and R. Joshua Heschel. His daughter, Feiga Dinah, married R. Elisha Hayyim Yitzhak Horowitz.

PERLOW, Johanan, of Lutsk-Karlin (1900–21 *Kislev* 1955) – Youngest son of R. Israel, he married the daughter of R. Simon Solomon Brandwein. During the Nazi occupation of Poland, he escaped to Russia with other partisans. His wife and elder daughter died there. He and his younger daughter, Zipporah, reached the Holy Land in 1946 and lived for a short time in Haifa.

In 1948 he made his home in New York, where he published *Siddur Bet Aaron Ve-Yisrael* (New York, 1952), a liturgical compendium on the rites and customs of Karlin. At the end of the book are letters written by the rebbes of Karlin. He urged his followers to live in unity and brotherhood, to study constantly, and to do everything with enthusiasm.

After his third visit to Israel in 1955, he died in New York and was reinterred on 18 *Adar* II in Tiberias. His sole male survivor is his grandson, R. Barukh Jacob Meir, born in

1954. Many of the hasidim of Karlin gave their allegiance to R. Moses Mordecai Biderman of Lelov on 15 *Av* 1962. A large section, however, remained loyal to the grandson.
Maariv, August 16, 1962.

PERLOW, Joseph, of Novominsk (1916–16 *Heshvan* 1945) – Son of R. Alter Israel Shimon, he married the daughter of R. Jacob Taub of Wolomin-Kuzmir. On his father's death in 1933, he succeeded him as rebbe.

He was deported first to Auschwitz and then to Bergen-Belsen. Survivors relate how the frail rabbi wandered around the camp, comforting the sick and regularly giving away his own meager allocation of food. The camp was liberated on April 15, 1945 by the British Second Army. R. Joseph died a few days later.

PERLOW, Moses, of Stolin (1891–29 *Elul* 1942) – Fourth son of R. Israel, the *Yanukkah*, he succeeded his father as rebbe of Stolin. A number of his father's followers, however, gave their allegiance to his brother, R. Abraham Elimelekh.

He married Deborah, the daughter of R. Pinhas of Kantikoziva. He studied secular subjects and was a man of general education. He was ordained by R. Elijah Hayyim Meisels of Lodz. He visited the Holy Land in 1933 and 1937 and established a *Bet HaMidrash* in Tel Aviv. "These young people," said R. Moses, referring to the pioneers of Tirat Tzvi, "sanctify God's name in public." He expressed himself in favor of the partition of the Holy Land between Jews and Arabs, as proposed by the Peel Commission, in order to make free immigration of Jews possible.

He established a *yeshivah* in Stolin, *Bet Yisrael*, which was a synthesis of Lithuanian talmudic scholarship with the spirit of Karlin. In 1939, when the Soviets occupied Stolin, he was evicted from his house.

When the Germans invaded Russia, he, his wife, his brother R. Asher, and his son R. Nahum Shlomoh were murdered when the Jewish community of Stolin was destroyed.
Elleh Ezkerah, vol. 5, pp. 46–49.

PERLOW, Nahum Mordecai, of Novominsk/New York (1897–9 *Elul* 1976) – Son of R. Alter Israel Shimon, he was born in Minsk Mazowiesk and was ordained by R. Eliezer Shalom of Parczev and R. Samuel of Wengrov. In 1916, he married Beila Rehuma (d. 1987), the daughter of R. Yitzhak Zelig Morgenstern of Sokolov. He visited the Holy Land in 1925. In 1927 he emigrated to the United States, settling first in the East New York neighborhood of Brooklyn, later moving to Crown Heights, and for the last six years of his life living in Borough Park, Brooklyn.

He was a member of the *Mo'etzet Gedolei HaTorah* and was active in the *Hinukh Atzmai* and the Russian immigrant rescue fund. He was a member of the presidium of the Aguda. He edited his grandfather's work *Shufrah D'Yaakov* (Jerusalem, 1964) and published his father's work *Tiferet Ish* on Festivals (Jerusalem, 1969). He gained ever increasing recognition in the United States in hasidic as well as in Torah circles due to his scholarship and the active role he played in communal affairs. He was widely acclaimed for his diligence in Torah study. Most of his discourses have not as yet been published.

He was succeeded by his son, R. Jacob. His second son, R. Barukh David (d. 1983), was rabbi in Chicago. Another son, Alter Israel Shimon, lives in New York and has recently reprinted his grandfather's *Haggadah Tiferet Ish* (New York, 1992).

PERLOW, Perele, of Koidanov (d. 1944) – Daughter of R. Yerahmiel Tzvi Rabinowicz of Siedlice. In 1930 she married R. Alter Perlow in Lodz and lived in Baranowicze. During the Second World War they lived in Vilna.

Perele organized a *Bet HaMidrash* for women. It met regularly at Bet Haholim Street 9, where, under her supervision, regular prayer and study sessions were held on the Ethics of the Fathers and the weekly portions of the Law with Rashi's commentary.

She occasionally invited male lecturers to deliver discourses. Her manuscript notes are to be found in the Jewish Historical Institute in Warsaw.

She died of typhus in a concentration camp near Danzig. She had no children.

PERLOW, Shalom, of Brahin (1850–26 *Heshvan* 1925) – Younger son of R. Barukh Mordecai, he lived in Lida. In 1884 he was appointed rabbi in Brzezany (Volhynia).

In 1890 he moved to Brahin, in the province of Minsk.

He distinguished himself by his literary works. He published *Divrei Shalom* (Vilna, 1882), which contains the teachings of Koidanov and biographical information about the dynasty; *Mishmeret Shalom* in two parts (Warsaw, 1912), dealing with the customs of his father and containing quotations by the rabbis of Karlin and Slonim; *Ateret Shalom* (Warsaw, 1895), a commentary on the liturgical poem "Lord, I Yearn for the Sabbath's Delight," by R. Aaron the Great of Karlin.

He was also the author of two booklets, *Midrash Pinhas HeHadash* (Warsaw, 1910) and *Shem Aaron* (Warsaw, 1910), which give the views of his ancestors on a variety of matters, including an instruction to teachers of young children not to strike their pupils.

In his last will and testament there is an appendix that discusses the exorcising of *dybbukim* and the transmigration of souls.

W. Z. Rabinowitsch, *Lithuanian Hasidism*, p. 167.

PERLOW, Shalom Alter, of Koidanov/Baranowicze (1904–1943) – Younger son of R. Nehemiah, who had settled in Baranowicze in 1921. He studied in the *yeshivah Ohel Torah* under R. Elhanan Bunim Wasserman at Baranowicze. In 1927 he succeeded his father as rebbe, and the following year he married Perele, the daughter of R. Yerahmiel Tzvi Rabinowicz of Siedlice.

During the Nazi occupation, he was "employed" by the Jewish community of Vilna to be an assistant to Reuben Kohen. He was murdered by the Nazis in Vilna.

Elleh Ezkerah, vol. 5, pp. 187–191.

PERLOW, Shlomoh Hayyim, of Bolechov (1880–11 *Tammuz* 1943) – Third son of R. Jacob Perlow, born in Novominsk. At the age of sixteen he wrote a work *Tosafot Hayyim* on the Minor Tractates, which received the approval of great halakhic authorities. The work, however, was not printed because his father felt that he was too young to be an author. At the age of seventeen he married his cousin Feige Devorah Miriam, the daughter of R. Joshua Heschel Padwa of Bolechov, whom he succeeded as rabbi in 1904.

He was one of the most erudite and prolific writers among the hasidic rebbes. He wrote learned responsa and corresponded with R. Elijah Hayyim Meisels. He was the head of a *yeshivah* of sixty students. On the High Holy Days he himself conducted all the services and even blew the *shofar*.

He was the author of a prayer book *Seder Tefillot L'Khol Hashanah*, which was printed in Sighet in 1907. It contained inter alia *Kehillat Shlomoh*, laws enacted by the codifiers; *Seder Zekhirot*, by his ancestor R. Levi Yitzhak of Berdichev; the Ethics of the Fathers, with comments by his ancestors; and the confession formula to be recited before *Kol Nidre*, composed by his ancestor R. Aaron the Great of Karlin.

In 1937 he published in Bilgoraj his 1,781-page anthology on the Psalms, *Mikdash Shlomoh*. It contained *Yalkut Shlomoh*, sayings culled from rabbinic literature on the Psalms; *Mekhor Hayyim* on the 613 commandments; and *Kerem Shlomoh* and *Bet Shlomoh* with comments based on R. Yitzhak Luria and the disciples of the Besht. In his introduction to this magnus opus, he traces his ancestry to King David, and in the last six pages, he gives a list of subscribers in Poland, New York, Toronto, and Tel Aviv.

He was killed by the Nazis in Stryj.

He had one son, Jacob Joshua Heschel, who had helped him in his work but who died as a youth, and five daughters: Alta Bat Zion, the wife of R. David Moses Shapira; Gitel, the wife of Elimelekh Shapira; Rachel, the wife of R. Yitzhak Hager; Reizel; and Sarah.

His wife was killed on 8 *Heshvan* 1942. His daughters, sons-in-law, and grandchildren were murdered by the Nazis. He was survived by a grandson, R. Yitzhak Mordecai Shapira, who reprinted his *Mikdash Shlomoh*.

Elleh Ezkerah, vol. 5, pp. 239–243.

PERLOW, Shlomoh Hayyim, of Koidanov (1797–17 *Av* 1862), founder of the Koidanov dynasty – He was son of R. Aaron, who died when Shlomoh was ten years old, and the grandson of R. Mordecai I of Lachowicze and of R. Asher of Stolin. He married the granddaughter of R. Shlomoh of Karlin and lived in the house of his grandfather in Stolin. He visited R. Barukh of Medziborz, R. Mordecai of Chernobyl, and R. Moses of Savran. He became rabbi of Turov, near Stolin.

When R. Noah of Lachowicze died without an heir in 1882, many of the hasidim chose his son-in-law, Mordecai II, as rebbe. The majority, however, followed his grandson R. Shlomoh Hayyim, who then settled in Koidanov, near Pinsk, where he lived for thirty years.

R. Shlomoh Hayyim did not write any books, but his grandson R. Shalom quotes sayings attributed to him. In the Koidanov prayer book *Or HaYashar Nusah R. Shlomoh Hayyim VeRabbi Asher MiStolin* (Vilna, 1928), which was published after his death, there is a special section describing his customs and giving details about his life-style, such as the white clothes he wore on the Sabbath, and the hasidic melodies that he sang. In his daily routine, printed on the title page of the prayer book, time is allocated to the study of the Talmud and the *Shulhan Arukh*, and he urged every Jew to guard against idle talk, gossip, levity, and slander. In his last will and testament he instructs his followers not to eulogize him as a saint. "Do not imagine," he wrote, "that I wanted to be *tzaddik*. All I wanted was to be a Jew." It is noteworthy that the family name Perlow is derived from the first name of R. Shlomoh's mother, Perl.

He was succeeded by his son, R. Barukh Mordecai.

S. E. Stam, *Zekher Tzaddik* p. 10.

PERLOW, Yehudah Aryeh Leib, of Novominsk/New York (1888–10 *Elul* 1961)—Second son of R. Jacob of Novominsk, he was ordained by R. Hayyim Soloveichik of Brest-Litovsk, R. Yoav Joshua of Kinsk, and R. Moses Nahum Yerushalimsky of Kielce. He married his cousin Esther Reizel, the daughter of R. David Twersky of Makarov. For a number of years he was rabbi in Wlodowa, near Brest-Litovsk, and in 1924 he settled in New York.

His *Bet HaMidrash*, on South Ninth Street, in Williamsburg, Brooklyn, was one of the first outposts of Hasidism in the New World. He was the author of *Lev Aryeh HaHadash* on Torah and novellas on Talmud (Jerusalem, 1933) and *Kol Yehudah* (New York, 1946). He was survived by a son, the philanthropist Jacob Yitzhak (d. 8 *Sivan* 1981) and three daughters.

A. Y. Bromberg, *Migdolei HaHasidut*, vol. 20, *Admorei Nezkhiz Kaidanov Novominsk*, pp. 160–161.

PEYOT (lit., corners, sidelocks)—The biblical injunction "Ye shall not round the corners of your head" (Leviticus 19:27) implies that some hair must be left on the side of the face. No obligatory measures are, however, laid down on the length of hair that is to remain. The kabbalists maintained that it was forbidden to remove any hair of the beard, or *peyot*. Such hairs are a representation in the human body of the channel on high, through which all the divine grace flows to all creation.

The *Zohar* admonishes Jews that they should not look like idol worshipers (Genesis 219b), and R. Yitzhak Luria computed that the numerical value of the Hebrew word "*peyah*" is equivalent to the divine name *Elohim* (eighty-six). Among many hasidim it is customary to leave the *peyot* completely uncut. In 1845, when Nicholas I made an attempt to abolish the wearing of *peyot* in Eastern Europe, the hasidim were ready to pay a fine in order to preserve their *peyot*.

A. Wertheim, *Halakhot VeHalikhot BaHasidut*, pp. 197–199.

PHILOSOPHY—The attitude of hasidic leaders toward philosophic inquiry and toward the use of human reason in matters of theological import was generally quite negative. Such rejection of rationalism is to be expected in a pietistic revival movement, particularly one that idealized the life of simple faith and that sought to view every occurrence, no matter how trivial and seemingly accidental, as a result of the will of God. In contrast to their rationalist forebears among medieval Jewry, hasidic thinkers generally saw the constructs of the human mind as inimical to true faith, except insofar as they were directly guided by revelation. No works that may be considered truly philosophical were created within the hasidic community.

Philosophy was, however, for postmedieval Jews, as much a matter of literary tradition as it was a method of inquiry. Through the influence of the Jewish philosophical and theological classics, the language of Neoplatonism and Aristotelianism had come to thoroughly permeate Jewish literature. Thus even the most doggedly antirational of hasidic authors spoke of emanations, of the separate intellects, or of the four elements, having no idea that such terms were part of a literary heritage ultimately derived from Greek philosophy. Aristotle himself might be referred to as "the leader of the deniers" or "the uncircumcised Philistine, may his name be blotted out!" but echoes of his philosophical terminology were to be found everywhere.

There were some hasidic writers who made conscious use of the medieval Jewish philosophical classics. Particularly in the *Habad* school, a certain degree of dependence on the rational tradition was encouraged. Thus the *Tanya* places great emphasis on the union of *intellectus*, *intelligens*, and intelligible object, a formula thought by the author to be Maimonidean, but that was actually derived directly from Aristotle's *Metaphysics*. R. Abraham of Kalisk, despite his opposition to the *Tanya* and his preachments on the life of simple faith, defends Maimonides' position on the relationship between an individual's willful adherence to God and the presence of Divine Providence in that individual's life. The grandson of the *Tanya*'s author, R. Menahem Mendel (Tzemah Tzedek) of Lubavitch, relies heavily on Maimonides' *Guide* in his explanations of the commandments.

Other hasidic authorities, particularly those from the Ukraine and Galicia, took a more uncompromising stand against the philosophical tradition. The most extreme of these was R. Nahman of Bratzlav, perhaps the most radical antirationalist in the history of Jewish theology. R. Nahman forbade the study of philosophic writings (though there are indications that he himself had some familiarity with them) and declared that anyone who studied the *Guide for the Perplexed* would diminish the [divine image] visible in every Jew. The list of proscribed books in Bratzlav included, in addition to the *Guide*, the philosophic section of Bahya's *Hovot HaLevavot*, Albo's *Ikkarim*, Arama's *Akeidat Yitzhak*, and the Bible commentaries of Abraham Ibn Ezra. (It is noteworthy that the publishing houses that were under hasidic influence rarely printed the classics of Jewish philosophy.) R. Nahman called for a life of faith, maintaining that "true faith is belief in God without any sign, proof, or reason" (Sihot *HaRaN* 106).

Maimonides presented a special problem for hasidic authors who sought to deny the validity of the philosophic enterprise. How could the greatest of the medieval rabbis have allowed himself to be misled into vain and forbidden pursuits? Some authors quoted the old legends that said Maimonides had toward the end of his days repented and acknowledged the truth of Kabbalah. Others used Maimonides' writings but sought to interpret them in mystical terms. Even R. Shneur Zalman of Liady, when quoting Maimonides' philosophic views in the *Tanya*, took pains to add the cautious phrase "and the sages of the Kabbalah agree with him" (*Tanya* 1:42; 2:7).

J. I. Dienstag, "HaMoreh Nevukhim VeSefer HaMada BeSifrut HaHasidut."

S. A. Horodezky, "HaRambam BeKabbalah U'VeHasidut," pp. 454 ff.

J. G. Weiss, *Mekharim BeHasidut Braslav*.

A.G.

PIDYON – Or *pidyon nefesh* (soul's ransom), a donation given to the rebbe. There were some hasidim who gave their rebbe a monthly or annual retainer besides the *pidyon*. But the *pidyon* had a sacramental aura about it. The term "*pidyon*" occurs in Exodus (21:30), where it connotes the ransom money paid by a guilty party. According to some historians, the Besht did not begin the custom of accepting *pidyonot* from his hasidim. *Pidyon* also refers to the redemption of the firstborn son. The Torah stipulates the sum of five *sela'im* as the *pidyon* amount for the child. One rebbe refused to accept any other money than that which he, a Kohen, received for his priestly services.

Many rabbis gave all their money to the poor and needy. There were times when the rebbe would not take a *pidyon*, or, if he took it, would not use it. The Belzer rebbe refused to use a gold watch that a hasid had brought him, because the hasid did not listen to his counsel. R. Shneur Zalman refused a gift sent to him by someone who had received it through robbery.

The *mitnaggedim* rebuked the hasidim, maintaining it encouraged the belief that one could purchase forgiveness from God by donations to the rebbe. It is argued that charitable donations are part of the ritual of repentance. If one cannot fast because of ill health, one is obliged to give money for charitable purposes. Since giving to an unworthy or ignoble cause would not serve the purpose of the *mitzvah*, a donation to a rebbe obviates that danger.

Pidyonot are defended on the grounds that they establish a concrete bond between the *tzaddik* and the hasid. The *tzaddik*, in the words of R. Elimelekh of Lejask, is the one who brings down to Israel three gifts: sons, life and livelihood. But he is generally so removed from the world so as to be unconcerned with it. Hence, it was necessary to draw his attention down to matters of this world (*Noam Elimelekh*, *VaYeira*).

The amount of *pidyon* money had to do with the intricacies of kabbalistic numerology, the name of the person, and that of his mother. It was usual to give a sum corresponding to the numerical value of the Hebrew word "*hai*" (life), that is, eighteen.

M. Wilensky, *Hasidim U'Mitnaggedim*, 2 vols.

A.B.A. and J.B.A.

PIEKARSKI, Israel Yitshak (1910–1991) – A disciple of R. Aryeh Tzvi Fromer and R. Abraham Weinberg, at the age of eighteen he became rabbi of Keshnev, Poland, where he also served as principal of the Radomsker *yeshivah*.

At the beginning of the Second World War, he lived for a time in London, where he was rabbi of the *Mahzikei Hadat* community. In March 1948 he emigrated to the United States, where he was the rabbi of the *Tzeirei Agudat Yisrael Bet Hamidrash* in the Bronx.

In 1950, he became principal of the Central Lubavitch *yeshivah* in Brooklyn.

He was survived by two daughters.

Jewish Tribune, September 24, 1992, p. 9.

PIEKARZ, Mendel (b. 1922–), writer – Born in Poltusk, Poland, he was educated in Polish *yeshivot* and for a time served in the Polish army. He arrived in the Holy Land on the *Exodus* and subsequently studied at Hebrew University.

Among his many writings on Hasidism were *Hasidut Bratzlav* (Mosad Bialik, 1972), *Bimei Tzemihat Hasidut* (Mosad Bialik, 1978), and *Hasidut Polin* (Mosad Bialik, 1990).

PILGRIMS – "It is a man's duty," says the Talmud (*Rosh Hashanah* 16b), "to pay his respects to his teacher on Festivals, on the New Moon, and on the Sabbath." A visit to the rebbe was a major event in the life of a hasid. "Those who travel to the rebbe," wrote R. Nahman of Bratzlav, "are recompensed. Although they may not receive Torah from him, they are nevertheless rewarded for their efforts" (*Midot* 24). R. Shlomoh of Karlin maintained that a visit to the rebbe would stand a hasid in good stead in the world to come (*Bet Aharon* 293). According to R. Uri of Strelisk, a hasid is obliged to travel to the rebbe, even though he would forgo a certain amount of Torah study and prayer in order to make the journey.

There were no fixed times for such a visit, any Sabbath or Festival was naturally an ideal time. But to visit the rebbe on the New Year and Yom Kippur and on Shavuot was the ambition of every hasid. "Court" affairs were governed by the *gabbai*, who acted as a liaison between the rebbe and his followers. The rebbe, at his *tish*, would recite *divrei Torah*, and the hasidim would sing joyous melodies in loving fellowship. Every gesture of the rebbe was observed and analyzed. It was the hasid's privilege to share *shirayim* of the rebbe's food.

The school of Przysucha encouraged young people, directly after their marriage, to travel to the rebbe for long periods of indoctrination.

A. Wertheim, *Halakhot VeHalikhot BaHasidut* pp. 159–161.

PINTER, Shmelke, of London (1919–11 *Tammuz* 1994) – Son of R. Hayyim (1881–1941), rabbi of Bukovsk, he was born in Vienna, where his parents had taken refuge during the First World War. After studying in Polish *yeshivot* for three years, he came to London in 1938, where, for a time, he was the head of a *yeshivah*, *Merkaz HaTorah*. In 1942 he married Gitel (Gertrude), the daughter of R. Israel Aryeh Margulies of Przemyshlan.

During the Second World War, he established the *Yesodei HaTorah* Schools, which now have over eleven hundred pupils and cater to all shades of the hasidic and even the nonhasidic community. He also had a *Bet HaMidrash Yeshuot Hayyim* and a *kollel*.

His wife died in 1983, and he subsequently married Babche, the widow of R. Abraham Eichenstein of Chicago.

He had four sons (R. Hayyim, R. Abraham, R. Issachar Meir Tzvi, and R. Yitzhak) and two daughters, one married to R. Yitzhak Dov Berger and the other to R. Azriel

Weinberg. R. Abraham, a past Labor Councillor of the Borough of Hackney, London, is now the principal of the schools.

PLOCK (Russian, Plotzk) – A town in the Warsaw province, sixty miles (ninety-six kilometers) northwest of Warsaw. In 1939, more than half of the Jewish population of 10,000 was hasidic.

R. Abraham Landau (1784–1875) married the daughter of R. Dan Landau of Plock and lived there until he moved to Ciechanov. His grandson Zusya Landau, also a native of Plock, dedicated one of his poems to him.

R. Alexander Zusya (1798–1837), a disciple of R. Jacob Yitzhak, the "Seer" of Lublin, and of R. Simhah Bunem of Przysucha, was rabbi in Plock in 1830. He was one of the four emissaries who defended the doctrines of Przysucha at the wedding at Ustilug.

Another hasidic rabbi in Plock was R. Hayyim Shapira, who was executed by the Poles on trumped-up charges of espionage in 1920.

A. Eisenberg, ed., *Plock, Toldot Kehillah Atikat Yamin BePolin*.

PLOTZKI, Meir Dan, of Ostrova (1866–6 *Nisan* 1928) – Son of R. Hayyim of Kutno, a hasid of Alexander. At the age of nine, Meir Dan joined the *yeshivah* of R. Hayyim Eleazar Waks of Piotrokov and subsequently studied in Sochaczev under R. Abraham Bornstein. At the age of fifteen he was betrothed to Zirel, the daughter of Mordecai of Warta.

He became a devoted hasid of the *Sefat Emet* and of R. Abraham Mordecai Alter of Ger. In 1891 he became rabbi of Warta. He was very communally minded. He participated in the Polish *Agudat HaRabbanim* and soon became the chairman of the executive committee. He was a great supporter of the Aguda and a member of the *Mo'etzet Gedolei HaTorah*. He was closely involved in the publishing of the Torah periodical *Degel HaTorah*.

His life was beset with many personal tragedies. His eldest son, Eliezer Yehudah, died at the age of eighteen, and his daughter died in the prime of her life. He himself was afflicted with a malignant tumor and had to undergo major surgery.

He published his first book, *Hemdat Yisrael* (Piotrokov, 1903), and in 1906 he printed the first part of his classical work *Kli Hemdah*, a pilpulistic commentary on the five Books of the Torah. It was printed in Piotrokov and Warsaw between 1906 and 1938.

When Solomon Judah Friedlander published *Sefer Kodashim* on the Jerusalem Talmud in 1907, R. Meir Dan immediately recognized it as being a forgery, and he printed a 112-page book, *Shaali Shelom Yerushalayim* (Bilgoraj, 1914), which proved conclusively the fallaciousness of Friedlander's claims.

He was chosen by a special rabbinical conference to visit the Holy Land in 1912 in support of the *Kollel Polin*.

After twenty-seven years in Warta, he became rabbi of Ostrova-Mazowiec in 1918. After the First World War he was a member of a rabbinical delegation to visit Belgium, England, and the United States. When the rabbi of Ger founded the *Mesifta* in 1919, R. Meir Dan became its spiritual leader.

I. Frenkel, *Yehidei Segullah*, pp. 161–165.

POALEI AGUDAT YISRAEL (PAI) – Religious labor movement, founded in Lodz in 1922. Originally designed to improve the social conditions of religious workers, it soon became involved in the training of members for agricultural work in the Holy Land. The PAI was founded in the Holy Land in 1933. In 1944, it established *Kibbutz Hafetz Hayyim*.

The overwhelming majority of PAI members were hasidim and were part of the Aguda. After the establishment of the state of Israel, PAI relations with the Aguda became strained. In 1949, the PAI joined the United Religious Front. In the elections of 1955 and 1959, it formed a united front with the Aguda. In 1961, it became a separate party, controlling fourteen settlements. It controls Youth Aliyah institutions, agricultural youth institutes for girls, and the Gedara Agricultural School for boys.

The PAI has 35,000 members, who are working in all the different branches of the Israeli economy, including fifteen agricultural settlements (*kibbutzim* and *moshavim*). The PAI is represented in the *Histadrut* as a trade union. According to the agreement of the affiliation, members participate in all the activities carried out by the trade union, and they benefit from its achievements, such as collective agreements, health insurance, and medical care (*kupat holim*). It has a youth movement–*Ezra*–and a paper–*She'arim*. Another enterprise is *Hydroponic Crops Ltd.*, an industrial organization for the cultivation of crops during the *Shemitah* year.

Among the members of the PAI who have served in the Israeli government were Benjamin Mintz, a hasid of Ger who was minister of posts from 1960 until his death in 1961, and R. Kalman Kahana, who was deputy minister of education in 1952 and again from 1961 to 1969. Dr. Yitzhak Breuer was the ideologist of the PAI, and the *Hazon Ish*, R. Yeshayahu Karelitz, was an ardent supporter of the movement.

G. Harpanes, *Mivhar Ketuvim*.

PODOLIA–A region in southwest Ukraine between the rivers Dniester and Bug.

East Podolia has been Russian since 1793. West Podolia became Austrian in 1772 and was part of Poland between 1918 and 1939.

The Jewish population of Podolia in 1765 was 38,365. Hasidism originated in the southern provinces of Podolia. In the middle of the eighteenth century, the Besht meditated in the Carpathian Mountains. He lived, died, and was buried in Medziborz. His disciple and successor, R. Dov Baer, the Maggid, lived in Mezhirech. R. Nahman of Bratzlav lived in Nemirov, R. Jacob Joseph in Shargorod, R. Rafael in Bershad, and R. Barukh in Tulchin. All of its towns and villages were centers of Hasidism.

Prevailing economic and social conditions made these southern provinces particularly favorable for the growth of the hasidic movement. Politically this was a period of lawlessness, bordering on anarchy, and the Jews who lived mainly in the villages and small towns suffered from the almost total collapse of law and order. The Jewish communities were both unstructured and at a low ebb spiritually.

During the Second World War, a greater part of Podolia became part of Romania, and after the liberation, only 60,000 Jews remained alive. Few of them, however, were hasidim.

M. N. Litinsky, *Korot Podolia VeKadmoniyot Sham*.

POLAND–The history of the Jews in Poland can be traced continuously, period by period, for over a thousand years. Jews began to settle there before Christianity had found general acceptance in Eastern Europe. At a time when Polish sovereignty extended from the Baltic to the Black Sea, the Jews were quick to explore the country's economic potential. Allied to these economic opportunities was an unusual degree of religious freedom. The Jews elected their own rabbis, who exercised wide-ranging spiritual jurisdiction. At the end of the sixteenth century, 300,000 Jews lived in 190 communities.

The *Kehillah*, or the Council of the Four Lands, embracing Little Poland (Cracow and Lublin), Great Poland (Poznan), Ruthenia (Brest and Grodno), and Volhynia, was established in 1551. It acted as the state's agent for Jewish taxation, dealt with questions of industry and commerce, and even approved school curricula.

"With fire and sword," the Cossack leader Chmielnicki (1593–1657) poured out his venom on the defenseless Jews. In the Ukraine, over 100,000 Jews were slain, and 774 communities were all but annihilated. In 1764, the Council of Four Lands was abolished, and for the next 120 years, the Jews shared the tribulations of Poland, which was now ruled by czarist Russia, Austria, and Prussia.

Between the two world wars, Poland was the greatest reservoir of European Jewry. Within the boundaries of the new Poland were 2.5 million of the 4.5 million Jews who lived in the old Russian empire.

By 1939, there were 3.3 million Jews, constituting 9.5 percent of the total population. The Jews were the second and largest minority, making up one-third of the total urban population. There were 300,000 Jews living in Warsaw, 194,000 in Lodz, and 55,000 in Lvov.

Despite the liberal constitution and the minority rights clauses of the Treaty of Versailles, Poland's newly acquired independence brought neither social security nor economic freedom to the Jewish community. Leading Polish statesmen preached virulent racist policies that anticipated the Nazi platform.

In 1926, Bogulav Miedzinski, deputy speaker of the Polish Seym, declared in the Diet, "Poland has room for 50,000 Jews. The remaining 3 million must leave Poland." The "cold pogrom" policy was officially endorsed by the state, which took over and monopolized key industries. The worst anti-Semites were the national democrats, the "Endeks." They planned to deprive Jews of their citizenship and even to deport them. The Jews had been able and eager to develop Polish industry and commerce, but the state adopted certain administrative measures that were specifically calculated to incapacitate the Jews, a policy diligently practiced by every Polish government during the interwar years.

Yet, this was in a sense a period of religious renaissance. It marked a reemphasis on Torah and the reemergence of a *Shulhan Arukh* Jew for whom the Torah was all-embracing and all-sufficient.

During this crucial interwar period, the power of Hasidism increased. One-third of Polish Jewry were hasidim. It was also a period of political awakening. No longer confined to the *shtiebl*, hasidim began to exert their considerable influence on every phase of Jewish life. Almost every town and almost every village had its own hasidic *shtiebl*. It is a fact that many a tiny far-flung Polish hamlet owes its immortality to a hasidic rebbe who lived there and adopted its name as his title, almost like a surname: so with Belz, Ger, Alexander, Bobov, Siedlce, Biala, Novominsk, Ozarov, Radzyn, and countless others.

Great personalities arose among the hasidim: men of vision and vitality, who molded and remade people's lives. Many of the rebbes in Poland maintained huge households, receiving and entertaining many visitors. They lived in a world of their own. They were known by the dress they wore, by the way they spoke, and by the melodies they hummed.

With the exception of the followers of Belz and Alexander, most of the hasidic rebbes were associated with the Aguda, participating in communal, municipal, and parliamentary elections. Nor was their interest confined to regional religious problems.

The rebbes established *shtieblech* in the various towns in which their followers resided. In Poland, most towns had both a Gerer *shtiebl* and an Alexander *shtiebl*. In Lodz there were thirty-five different *shtieblech*, each one catering to a different hasidic sect. Ger, a townlet on the Vistula, became the Jerusalem of one of the greatest hasidic dynasties of all time. For nearly a century, Alexandrov, or "Alexander," as the Jews called it, a little town near Lodz, occupied a unique position in Polish Jewry. No other dynasty, apart from Ger, attracted so vast a multitude. Similarly, there were the powerful dynasties of Bobov and Belz in Galicia.

Warsaw became the home of fifty hasidic rebbes. The rebbes were engaged in a strenuous fight against the anti-*shehitah* legislation, which was introduced by the deputy Janina Prystor, wife of the Senate speaker and former prime minister Alexander Prystor, on February 7, 1936. On January 31, 1938, deputy Dudzinski introduced a bill calling for the abolition of *shehitah*. Hasidic Jewry joined in protest demonstrations. At a meeting of 300 rabbis, "a fortnight without meat" was proclaimed. From March 14 to March 30, 1938, Jews were required to refrain from eating all meat (except poultry, which was not affected by the bill), even on the Sabbath, and to observe a day of fasting.

Poland had many bright stars. This was not a *dor yatom* (an orphaned generation). This was the birthplace of leaders, lay and religious, who made a tremendous contribution to Jewish culture. Among them was R. Israel Meir Kahan (1838–1933), known throughout the Jewish universe as the *Hafetz Hayyim*, which was also the title of his famous book, published in 1873, based on verses 13 and 14 of Psalm 34: "He who desires life . . . keep thy tongue from evil and thy lips from speaking guile."

Other personalities were R. Hayyim Ozer Grodzinski (1873–1940); R. Menahem Zemba (1882–1943); R. Meir Shapira (1887–1934), the rabbi-statesman; R. Aaron Levine (1879–1941); and Sarah Schenierer.

During the Nazi occupation, Poland became the graveyard of Polish Jewry, a central cemetery for the great Jewish communities of Europe. Extermination operations began after the invasion of the Soviet Union by the Nazis. On December 7, 1941, the first camp in which gas was used was put into operation at Chmelno, and this was followed by extermination camps at Belzec, Sobibor, and Treblinka. No more than 2,000–3,000 Jews, among them only a few hasidic rabbis, such as the rebbes of Ger, Bobov, Lubavitch, and Modzitz, were able to leave Poland legally. At the end of the war, 380,000 Polish Jews had survived.

The violent pogrom in Kielce in June 1946, when forty-two Jews were murdered, stimulated further emigration. Large-scale emigration followed the anti-Jewish policy adopted by the government under the guise of anti-Zionism. Today's Jewish population is estimated at between 6,000 and 8,000. There are small communities in Warsaw, Cracow, Bielsco Biala, Czestochova, Gliwice, Katowice, Lodz, Lublin, and Wroclaw. Today Poland is virtually *judenrein*, not only of Jews but of hasidim. In Warsaw, at the *Zydowsky Instytut Historycny* among the 820 Hebrew manuscripts, there are quite a number of hasidic items. Of the 60,000 Hebrew printed books, there are many volumes from the *Yeshivat Hakhmei Lublin*.

Countless Jewish burial grounds have now been totally eradicated. It is as if they had never existed. Others have been wantonly ravaged. What the Nazis failed to destroy during the war, Polish vandals devastated after the war, using the stones for building purposes or even reusing them for non-Jewish graves. Warsaw has what is probably the largest Jewish cemetery in the world, with some 360,000 graves. Only a few of the hasidic graves have been preserved. It is, indeed, an impenetrable jungle, an overgrowth of trees and bushes, the result of seventy years of neglect. In ruins stand the tombs of many hasidic rebbes, among them those of the Novominsker rebbe, R. Mordecai Heschel (father of the late Prof. Abraham Joshua Heschel), R. Yitzhak Jacob of Biala, and R. Meir Shlomoh Yehudah of Miedzyrzec. The same catastrophic conditions prevail in Minsk-Masowiecka.

Preserved only are the tombs of R. Elimelekh of Lejask, R. Hayyim Halberstam of Nowy Sacz, R. Ezekiel of Sianiawa, R. Naftali Horowitz of Lancut, and the "Seer" of Lublin. Everywhere else, there seem to be cemeteries without walls, and graves without stones.

Most of the hasidic places of worship have been destroyed.

M. H. Rabinowicz, *The Legacy of Polish Jewry*.

POLONNOYE – A town near Kamenets Podolsk in Podolia.

It was the home of R. Samson of Ostropol, who was killed in 1648; the residence of R. Aryeh Judah Leib, the *Mokhiah* of Polonnoye (d. 1770); and of R. Jacob Joseph Hakohen (d. 1782).

Between 1782 and 1820, many hasidic works were among the ninety books printed there by R. Samuel ben Issachar Baer and R. Joseph ben Tzvi Hakohen. During World War II, the Nazis exterminated Polonnoye's entire Jewish population.

H.D. Friedberg, *Toldot Hadfus HaIvri BePolania*, pp. 102–103.

PORTUGAL, Eliezer Zusya (*Rosh Hodesh Heshvan* 1898–eve of *Rosh Hodesh Elul* 1982), Skulner rebbe – Son of Israel Abraham (d. 1912), he was born in Romania. He studied under R. Hayyim Mordecai Roller, R. Bezalel Zeev Shafran, and R. Yehudah Leib Zirelson. He married Sheina Rachel, a descendant of the *Mokhiah* of Polonnoye.

He first served as rabbi in Skuleni, Moldavia. In the 1930s he moved to Czernowitz, where the Aguda appointed him director of *Kashrut*. He was also the principal of the *Beis Yaakov* Teachers' Seminary.

During and after the Second World War, he was active in rescuing Jewish children and providing them with an education. To that end, he traveled throughout Romania, setting up schools and orphanages for youthful survivors of the Holocaust. He continued his activities despite harassment by Communist authorities. In *Nisan* 1959, he and his son were jailed, and only pressure from abroad brought about their release. They were able to settle in the Crown Heights section of Brooklyn and then in Williamsburg, whence R. Eliezer Zusya continued his work for the Jews of Eastern Europe.

He organized a network of institutions in Israel, *Hesed LeAvraham*, which served the special needs of new immigrants from Russia.

He was the author of *Kedushat Eliezer* on Hanukkah (New York, 1983) and *Noam Eliezer* on Genesis (New York, 1983).

He was succeeded by his son, R. Israel Abraham.

A.Z.

PORUSH, Shalom Hayyim (b. 1933–), hasidic writer – Son of Mordecai, Porush was born in Jerusalem and was educated in the *yeshivot* of Ponevezh and Slabodka. He supervised the hasidic research centre of *Mosad HaRav Kook* and is the author of the *Encyclopedia of Hasidism*, volume 1, which deals with hasidic bibliography (Jerusalem, 1980).

He is a prolific contributor on Hasidism to daily, weekly, and monthly religious journals. His writings are highly specialized and his introductions, many of them unsigned, are models of their kind. His outstanding devotion to Hasidism is recognized by many authors and rebbes who entrust to him their manuscripts for editing.

POSNER, Shlomoh Zalman (1766–1848), industrialist – Though he was an opponent of hasidism, nonetheless he, together with R. Hayyim Dawidsohn, R. Yitzhak Meir Alter, and R. Yitzhak of Warka, issued, in 1841, a circular letter appealing to Jews to undertake agricultural work, citing a number of examples from the Talmud that the rabbis of the Talmud had owned fields and vineyards and did not disparage agriculture.

When Sir Moses Montefiore was in Warsaw between May 13 and 23, 1846, "a deputation of [the] preeminently conservative class of the Hebrew community paid us a visit," writes Dr. Louis Loewe. "They were headed by Mr. Posner, who had done so much for the promotion of industry in Poland, and his son."

L. Loewe, *Diaries of Sir Moses and Lady Montefiore*, vol. 1, pp. 354–355.

POTOK, Chaim (b. 1929–), rabbi and novelist – Born and educated in New York, he attended a *yeshivah* from the age of five to twenty-one and then studied at the Jewish Theological Seminary of New York, from which he graduated as rabbi. He earned a doctorate in philosophy at the University of Pennsylvania. He was a member of the faculty of the University of Judaism of Los Angeles and later was editor of *Conservative Judaism*. From 1965 until 1974 he was editor of the Jewish Publication Society of America. He was a chaplain of the U.S. armed forces in Korea from 1955 to 1957.

His mother's forebears were hasidim of Ruzhyn, and his father's of Belz. An ordained conservative rabbi turned novelist, his books reflect the complacent liberalism of pre-Vietnam Jewry. Discord is created by the influx of hasidic refugees from Nazi and Stalinist persecution. One Potok hero cries out that he dislikes the whole of the hasidic way of life and that "their presence destroyed [his] world." This is very much what second-generation American Jewry must have felt when it saw its middle-of-the-road institutions of learning swing to the right, under the forces of East European numbers.

In his novel *The Chosen* (1967), probably based on Lubavitch, David Malter gives a résumé of Hasidism to his son, Reuven, and while denying the exaggerated calumnies of the historian Graetz – drunkenness and the exploitation by the *tzaddikim* of their followers – still mirrors the author's distaste for many aspects of the movement. While understanding their zeal for building fences around a Judaism that has been decimated by the death camps, he still hates their lack of openness. Even the external trappings repel him – the dark clothes, the fringes, the beards and earlocks – as contrasted with the clean-cut modern American look.

Potok is offended by the inability of the hasidim to benefit from contemporary scholarship. He also shows that their introspection and self-discipline may be a bar to holiness.

There is no suggestion that the hasidim may possess a truth, as well as a joy, that the twentieth century does not know. Even though the *tzaddik* dances and sings, there are inward tears for the suffering of his people, and this is why hasidic melodies are often so sad.

In *My Name is Asher Lev* (1972), the contesting claims as modes of expressions of religion and of art are developed. According to the hasidic and Jewish view, the body is holy and must therefore be kept covered, but art wants to depict the beauty of the nude form, and yet the greatest art, like anything spiritual, is born from suffering.

Potok shows the romance and the beauty of spirituality while, perhaps, finding it unhealthy and the germinator of conflict.

F.G.

POVERTY – The pangs of poverty were more bearable in hasidic society than in the general Jewish community. When a hasid was faced with a special emergency, he could turn to the rebbe and receive some help. The hasidic rebbes were concerned with helping poor villagers and anyone in trouble.

Hasidim were taught to accept their fate without complaint and without questioning the will of God. As the Besht put it: "Whatever happens, it is all the same to me, since this is God's will." Such equanimity induced a quietistic mood, which follows the talmudic idea that poverty is a bright adornment of the Jewish people. It may be painful to bear but it is not a thing of shame.

Belief in the transmigration of souls (*gilgul*), which the hasidim accepted, helped them to feel that, in the long run, the gifts of fortune are evened out. Those who are poor now may have been rich in a previous incarnation, or they may be rich in a future incarnation.

R. Nahman of Bratzlav explains the strange reason why many *tzaddikim* in his day were rich, whereas they had been mainly poor in a previous age: "It is because," he said, "those *tzaddikim* had already lived in a previous incarnation and fulfilled the Torah in poverty. Therefore, they now deserve to be prosperous."

When the Besht was asked why the pious are poorer than the impious, he replied with the following allegory:

> A king desired to please his followers by announcing that each would be granted a particular wish. Thereupon some asked for honor, and others beseeched him for wealth, but only one said to him: "My sole wish is to speak to the king three times a day." Thus the pious prefer to communicate with the Lord three times a day, so that the Almighty may gratify their wishes. Since he does not have enough to eat, a poor man is in difficulty. He has to approach God each day and ask for food. The poor man is therefore worthy of speaking to God each day. God gives the rich man his needs all at once. He has been given wealth, so he has everything he needs for the rest of his life. He does not have to approach God every day to ask for his needs. (Rab Yivi, Psalm 13)

In hasidic society, the poor did not lose caste. They could get together in fellowship, in journeying to the court of the rebbe, and in observing the Festivals together. Celebrations were frequent in Hasidism; in fact, communal sharing prevailed at hasidic get-togethers and on pilgrimages. The poor may have suffered, but they did not suffer alone.

J.B.A.

PRAGER, Moses (1908–1984), writer–Originally named Moses Marks, he changed his name to Prager after his place of birth–Praga, part of Warsaw. For many years he worked on the *Yiddish Togblatt*. He emigrated to Israel, where he was editor of the *Bet Yaakov* journal for twenty-one years, contributing many articles on Hasidism.

He was the author of *R. Israel Baal Shem Tov* (Jerusalem, 1960) and *Haztzalat HaRebbe MiBelz* (Tel Aviv, 1950).

PRAYER–In the traditional rabbinic scheme, prayer, for all its significance, yields to the study of the Torah as the supreme religious obligation. In Hasidism, however, there is a marked tendency to give priority to prayer. The early hasidic text *Keter Shem Tov* (Jerusalem, 1968, p. 22b) remarks, in connection with the Baal Shem Tov's dialogue with his own soul:

> The soul declared to the rabbi, may his memory be for a blessing, that the reason why the supernal mysteries were revealed to him was not because he had studied many talmudic tractates and Codes of Law but because of his prayer, for at all times he recited his prayers with great concentration. It was as a result of this that he reached his elevated rank.

R. Kalonymus Kalman Epstein of Cracow (d. 1827), aware that the hasidic emphasis is untraditional, argues that the older teachings regarding study are still valid but they provide the means for the life of prayer (*Maor VaShemesh* [Tel Aviv, 1965], *VaYehi*, to Gen. 49:22, p. 56b):

> When the Jew draws near to the form of worship that is prayer, it is to the greatest thing in the whole world that he draw near. . . . In our generation, especially, the chief method by means of which one can refine one's character, so as to approach the divine and serve God, is prayer. From the time of his coming, the holy Baal Shem Tov, may the memory of the holy and saintly be for a blessing, caused the tremendous sanctity of prayer to illumine the world for whoever wishes to draw near to God's service. However, in order for one to attain to pure prayer it

> is necessary to engage in much service of the sages and to labor long, night and day, in the study of the Torah and in the performance of good deeds so that, as a result, one may learn how truly to pray with fear and great love, as those who have discernment know full well.

The reason for the hasidic preference is that in prayer, more than any other religious exercise, the hasidic ideal of *devekut* (attachment to God) can be realized. The hasidim lose themselves in prayer as their soul is raised on the wings of love and fear.

In Hasidism, prayer is to be recited with burning enthusiasm (*hitlahavut*) accompanied with violent movements and gestures and whereas the silent prayers are to be recited softly, the hymns and prayers of adoration are to be recited in a loud voice and with sweet melodies. These practices were severely criticized by the opponents of Hasidism, to whom the hasidim replied:

> R. Israel Baal Shem Tov, on whom be peace, said: When a man is drowning in a river and gesticulates while in the water that people should save him from the waters that threaten to sweep him away, the observers will surely not laugh at him and his gestures. So, too, one should not pour scorn on a man who makes gestures while he prays, for he is trying to save himself from the waters of presumption, namely, from the "shells" and strange thoughts that try to prevent him from having his mind on his prayers. (*Keter Shem Tov*, pp. 24a–24b)

Spontaneity was considered to be essential in prayer, and adequate preparations (*hakhanot*) had to be made before engaging in prayer–cleansing the body and reflecting on the august task the worshiper faced. In some versions of Hasidism it was held that these aims cannot be adequately achieved if the hasid is too much concerned with keeping to the statutory times of prayer as laid down in the Codes. Among such groups it became almost a duty to recite the afternoon prayer, for example, after the stars had appeared in the sky. One of the defenses offered was that the true worshiper, by way of prayers, reaches to a world beyond time. Another defense was that the lowliest beggar is admitted to the presence of the king, even when the time of the king's audience is over, provided the beggar's entreaty is not for himself but concerns a matter of urgency for the welfare of the king himself.

Generally, in hasidic thought, petitionary prayer, in its literal sense, is frowned upon as calling attention to the ego, the purpose of transcending, which is the true aim of prayer. Petitionary prayer is consequently seen as "prayer for the sake of the *Shekhinah*" (i.e., for the sake of God, Who suffers when people are in need).

It is somewhat curious that for all the hasidic emphasis on spontaneity in prayer, there are very few original hasidic prayers. This is no doubt to be explained on the basis of the hasidic belief that the standard prayers were divinely inspired and contained all the supernal mysteries so that it was heretical to imagine that they could be improved upon or supplemented by more recent compositions.

An important feature in hasidic prayer, one that was a source of great scandal to the *mitnaggedim*, was the intervention of the *tzaddik*. The prayers of the *tzaddik* for his followers can achieve that which could never be achieved by the puny efforts of the hasidim themselves. The *tzaddik*'s prayers for "life, children, and sustenance" help others to attain these. Through the prayers of the *tzaddik*, the sick are healed, the Jewish people are saved from persecution and oppression, they are able to earn their daily bread, and they are blessed with worthy sons and daughters.

The doctrine of the efficacy of the *tzaddik*'s prayers is taught in great detail in the work *Noam Elimelekh*, by R. Elimelekh of Lejask. Here the theological difficulties inherent in the doctrine are examined. The *tzaddik*'s intervention is effective because his soul can reach to worlds where all is sweetness and mercy and where there is no judgment whatsoever. Or, in another version, the *tzaddik*'s prayers create new worlds in which there has been no decree of suffering. God so desires the prayers of the *tzaddik* that He makes the fate of His world dependent on these prayers.

For the hasidim, only the most God fearing of men could act as prayer leaders. In many hasidic groups, this role was taken by the *tzaddik* himself. There was strong suspicion of the cantor and the choir–the normal officiants in nonhasidic synagogues–on the grounds that these preferred contrivance and mechanical art forms to the rush of soul demanded in true hasidic worship, to say nothing of the hasidic contention that cantor and choir were foreign importations.

The hasidim tended to congregate for prayer in special conventicles, where they would be free to pray in their own way and use the special prayer book of the great kabbalist Yitzhak Luria.

Hasidism also pays attention to correct dress for prayer. The Talmud (*Shabbat* 10a) advocates the wearing of a girdle around the loins during prayer, and although many later authorities argue that this does not apply in Western lands where trousers are worn, the hasidim still don a girdle (Hebrew, *avnet*; Yiddish, *gartel*) made of twined silk. The early hasidim avoided wearing garments of wool during their prayers on the grounds that woolen garments may contain an admixture of linen and there would thus be a barrier to the ascent of the prayers, since *shaatnez*, a mixture of wool and flax, is biblically forbidden (Deuteronomy 22:11). It is also not unknown for hasidim to smoke a pipe or cigarette before prayer on the analogy of the incense offered up in Temple times.

L. Jacobs, *Hasidic Prayer*.

A. Wertheim, *Halakhot VeHalikhot BaHasidut*, chap. 3, pp. 83–109.

L.J.

PRAYERS, TIMES OF – *Shaharit*, the morning prayer, has to be recited daily before the first quarter of the day has passed. *Minhah*, the second of the two statutory services, had to be recited until sunset. *Maariv* (*Arvit*) had to be recited after nightfall.

One of the major accusations leveled against the hasidim was that they did not adhere to the appointed prayer times. R. Abraham Katzenellenbogen makes this complaint in his letter to R. Levi Yitzhak of Berdichev. R. Yehiel Michael of Zloczov, the school of Przysucha, R. Levi Yitzhak of Berdichev, and the rebbes of Belz and Lelov all delayed their prayers.

A number of reasons have been advanced for this habit. The Besht maintained that this tactic confuses Satan. R. Israel of Ruzhyn stated that "the king had appointed an hour for those who would come to him with all their personal requests, and after this hour were barred from his presence. But those who come not on private business, but on matters of common welfare, require no special hour."

The hasidim believed that those who required more time to prepare themselves for worship were beloved by God, even if their worship were offered late. Preparations for prayer (*kavvanot*) were equivalent to prayer itself. Already in the Talmud do we find that the "early hasidim" used to go to the synagogue one hour before the morning service in order to direct their hearts to God. The hasidim would follow the example of *Tovelei Shaharit* (morning bathers), immersing themselves in the *mikveh* prior to prayer.

Other leading teachers were scrupulous in observing the regular times of prayer. "A man should not declare," said R. Naftali of Ropczyce, "that I cannot pray at this moment because my thoughts are far away. I shall wait until I can pray with proper *kavvanot*. We should pray at the appointed time to the best of our ability."

R. Eleazar of Tarnogrod rebuked his fellow hasidim for not praying at set hours. R. Abraham Mordecai Alter of Ger and R. Berele Rokeah of Belz broke with the traditions of Przysucha and prayed at the appointed times. Today, most hasidic rebbes adhere to the times prescribed by the Codes.

A. Wertheim, *Halakhot VeHalikhot BaHasidut*, pp. 83–110.

PREDESTINATION – Predestination is referred to in the Talmud. R. Akiva stated (*Abot* 3:19) "that all is foreseen, but choice is given." There is a rabbinic saying that a person's destiny is mapped out in all respects before birth. There is freedom to choose between righteousness and wickedness (*Berakhot* 33b).

By popularizing the kabbalistic dogma of "transmigration of souls" (*gilgul*), Hasidism enlarged the range of predetermination. It believed that people are born only for the purpose of righting a wrong committed in a previous incarnation or in order to perform one or more *mitzvot* left undone in a previous existence. In such cases their lives were certain to terminate as soon as their purpose was fulfilled (*Shivhei HaBesht*, pp. 100–141).

Hasidism also accepted the kabbalistic notion that souls differ greatly. A person endowed with a great soul is generally predestined to reach a high level of piety, and a person with a soul rooted in the lower realms is virtually condemned to a life of sin.

The hasidic theology assumes that a certain number of elevated souls capable of becoming *tzaddikim* are assigned to every generation. It is in respect of the role of the *tzaddikim* that Hasidism limited the range of predestination. The *tzaddikim* can alter the predestined course of events by means of their prayers.

Even when the divine will spells out the verdict, the rebbes can alter the arrangement of the letters and thereby change the course of Providence. Thus, the Hebrew letters z, r, h, spelling "trouble," can be changed to z, h, r, meaning "window"; the letters n, g, h, meaning "affliction," can be changed to the letters o, n, g, meaning "pleasure" (*Toldot Yaakov Yosef*, Noah, p. 31).

R. Schatz-Uppenheimer, *HaHasidut KeMistikah*.

J.B.A.

PRESS – At the beginning of the hasidic movement, links between its leaders and the people were through letters, which, upon arrival, were reproduced for distribution. Jewish Orthodox and hasidic circles generally viewed newspapers as media engaged in worldly vanities, resulting in the neglect of the study of the Torah. But because of the need to fight the Enlightenment, which had established a press of its own, the Orthodox and hasidic Jews also developed a press. Following is a review of newspapers, periodicals, etc., of a journalistic, public, social, and political nature, excluding theological and research types of literature.

In 1837, a collection of articles, *Haroeh*, directed against the Enlightenment and its organ *Kerem Hemed*, appeared in Lemberg, published by Jacob Bodek, Abram-Menachem Mendel Mohr, Jacob Mench, and Menachem Hacohen Fischman. An additional issue appeared in 1839.

During 1844–1845, three pamphlets of the quarterly *Yerushalayim Habenuyah*, with a more moderate stand toward the Enlightenment, appeared in Zolkiev, Lemberg, and Prague. During 1845–1855, *Shomer Ziyyon Hane'eman*, a monthly anti-Enlightenment paper, appeared in Altona (an addition to *Der Treue Zionswaechter*, in German, by Rabbi Ettlinger), possibly the first successful Orthodox Jewish organ. And in 1861–1862, the weekly *Tevunah*, with the same orientation, appeared in Memel.

In the years 1856–1859, *Yeshurun* appeared in Lemberg and was later transferred to Germany (Breslau, Furth, and, finally, in the period 1868–1878, to Bamberg, edited by R. Dr. Joseph Kabak [1829–1913]). *Yeshurun* appeared in Germany partly in German. Compared to *Haroeh* and *Yerushalayim Habenuyah*, *Yeshurun* dedicated itself more to positive subjects than to opposition to the Enlightenment.

A recognized publisher of all religious organs in Galicia for a quarter of a century was Joseph Kohen-Tzedek (1827–1903), active in Lemberg, Crakow, Frankfurt-am-Main, and London. He was friendly with intellectuals of the Enlightenment, wrote about talmudic problems, wrote poetry, and became known as an editor of leading articles and a debater. Toward the end of his life, he began to favor the Hibbat Zion movement and Zionism.

Kohen-Tzedek's journals were *HaMevasser* (the same title given a weekly edited by E. N. Amozeg, resembling Kohen-Tzedek's trend, which appeared in Livorno in 1861), *HaNesher*, *Meged Yerahim*, *Otzar Hokmah*, *Hayehudi Hanizhi*, and *Or Torah* – all journals that usually did not last long (e.g., in 1865, only two issues of *Meged Yerahim* appeared, and of *Otzar Hokhmah*, only three). But during 1860–1870, *HaMevasser* appeared as a weekly; *Hanesher* also appeared as a weekly during 1861–1872; and *Or Torah*, Kohen-Tzedek's last journal, began to appear as a monthly in Frankfurt in 1874, with its fifth and last issue published in Lemberg. In 1866, Kohen-Tzedek also published the following journals in Yiddish in Lemberg: *Der Juden Freind* and *Nayeste Nachrichten*, as compensation for the expenses on his Hebrew journals, which were less popular because the Jewish population understood Yiddish far better than Hebrew.

Kohen-Tzedek's papers usually dealt with information on Jewish problems at large, with Torah and Hebrew literature making an effort to exalt the Holy Torah without neglecting general studies and fighting the extremists among the Enlightenment intellectuals, the neologists, the reformers, the heretics, and those who published Jewish papers only to lead Jews away from the Torah and their ancestors' beliefs. This was the period when the hasidic periodical *Havazzelet* made its appearance in Palestine.

At the beginning of the Hibbat Ziyyon movement and Zionism, the Jewish press developed in various languages, followed by the anti-Zionist press. But while the reformers in Germany and the Bund in Eastern Europe had no use for the Hebrew language, Orthodox Jewry—alone among other organized non-Zionist bodies—also used Hebrew as the holy language, as did the hasidim and Agudat Israel. The Aguda contributed to the development of the Hebrew press as an instrument for nurturing the idea that Israel is a unique people that gets its essence of life from the Torah and whose existence does not therefore depend on secular material conditions.

During 1879–1914, the weekly *Mahzikei Hadat*, owned by hasidim and Orthodox, appeared in Galicia; in the years 1903–1906, the rabbinical Orthodox monthly *Hapeles* appeared in Poltawa (Ukraine), edited by the chief rabbi of the city, Elias-Akiva Rabinowitz (1862–1917), who was first a friend of Samuel Mohilewer and Zionism but who soon became a strong opponent of Zionism and radical movements and a leader of the Orthodox. Among the contributors to *Hapeles* were Jacob Lifschitz of Kovno, Elazar Atlas, and R. Yehudah-Loeb Zirelson.

In 1904, the quarterly *Haboneh* appeared in Lemberg, dealing with matters pertaining to religion and education in the Orthodox spirit; in 1907, the Orthodox weekly *Hakol* appeared in Warsaw; and in the period 1910–1914, Rabinowitz published the weekly *Hamodia*, in Poltawa—as a continuation to *Hapeles* and, encouraged by the Gerer and Lubavitcher rabbis, changed to Yiddish in October 1914 in order to reach a wider circle of readers.

After World War I, the worldwide Aguda founded the weekly *Haderekh* in Zurich, edited by R. Dr. Salomon Ehrmann; during 1920–1930, the monthly *Diglenu* (by Agudat Zeirei Emunei Israel [Society of Young Believers of Israel]); edited by R. Alexander Zusya Friedman, appeared in Warsaw; in 1926–1927, the weekly *Hashavua* and the monthly *Hane'eman*, of the Aguda, appeared in Telz (Lithuania); in 1928, the Orthodox in Lodz had a monthly, *Hakedem*, for a short time; in the years 1929–1932, the Aguda had a monthly, *Yavneh*, in Lemberg; from 1930 until World War II, the Aguda published the weekly *Darkenu*, in Warsaw, as a direct continuation of *Diglenu*, also edited by Friedman.

For about twenty years after 1947, the daily *Hakol* of *Pagi* appeared in Jerusalem. Also in Jerusalem, in 1948, the Aguda established the journal *Hayoman*, which, in 1949, was followed by *Hamevasser*. Since 1950, a daily newspaper, *Hamodia*, has been in existence in Jerusalem, serving as the official organ of the Aguda (the only Hebrew newspaper in Israel published in Jerusalem proper until the present day). The official organ of Po'alei Agudat Israel is *Shearim*, which has been appearing since 1951 as a daily. (Its predecessor appeared as a weekly from 1945 and before that, in 1936, had been the periodical *Hapoel Haharedi*.) *Shearim* has been transferred recently from Jerusalem to the Tel Aviv region.

So far the Orthodox and hasidic press in Hebrew have been reviewed (although for Kohen-Tzedek's press, his papers in Yiddish were mentioned; in addition, Orthodox organs in Hebrew in Transylvania and among survivors of the Holocaust are reviewed later). Following is an examination of the hasidic and Orthodox press in other languages as well, beginning with the Yiddish press in Poland.

After many Polish cities (Lodz, Warsaw, etc.) attempted to publish religious papers in Yiddish (e.g., *Der Yud* and *Dos Yidische Wort*), which were partly in the spirit of the Orthodox Jews in Germany, the daily influential Yiddish newspaper *Dos Yidische Togblatt*, which was inspired under the influence of Aguda, began to appear in Warsaw in 1929. Its initiator was M. Kaminer; the editor was David Flinker; its publication was encouraged by the Gerer rabbi. In those days Jewish newspapers in Poland used to publish erotic novels as serials; in contrast, the new Orthodox newspaper initiated the publication of a serialized novel, but with a Jewish historical background and a detective figure (as in the Beilis trial). Matters pertaining to Palestine were prominent in this newspaper, thanks to correspondence and descriptions sent directly from Palestine by Benjamin Minz.

Among the contributors and workers on the newspaper were outstanding hasidic and Orthodox Jews such as Isaac-Ber Akermann,

Dr. Nathan Birnbaum, Alexander-Zusya Friedman, Wolf Lipski, Mosche Marks (now known as Mosheh Prager), Dr. Levi Nimzowitz, Dr. Mordechai Rozner, Samuel Rotstein, Hillel Zeidmann, R. Shimshon Stockhammer, and Isaac Shapiro. The newspaper also served as a beginning for young people who later became famous in the Jewish press. *Dos Yidische Togblatt* was the greatest and most important among the hasidic and Orthodox newspapers in Yiddish and was financially successful.

In 1922, the Yiddish daily newspaper *Yidischer Lebn*, edited by Samuel Chereshevski, Dr. J. R. Holzberg (Ezyon), Yoel-Dov Zaks, and others, began to appear in Lithuania as an organ of the Aguda (known in Lithuania as Ahdut, Zeirei Israel, or Zeirei Agudat Israel). The newspaper later became a weekly and appeared with intervals until the annexation of Lithuania by the USSR. (It was the last Jewish newspaper in independent Lithuania to be discontinued by the Communists.)

At the end of the 1920s, the weekly *Yidische Zeitung*, edited by L. Kallus, and under the influence of R. Hayim-Eleazer Shapiro from Munkacs, began to appear in Germanized Yiddish. In the five years preceding World War II, the *Haint*, sponsored by the Habadnik Mordecai Dubin and edited by S. Witenberg and A. Chadakov, appeared in Latvia in two daily issues. In 1933, Nathan Birnbaum published periodical collections, *Der Ruf*, in Antwerp. And in 1934 *Dos Yidische Wort* was published by the Aguda in Czernowitz. (After the war, it appeared for a while in Transylvania, where *Bulletin Agudat Israel* also appeared in 1947 in Yiddish and Romanian.)

Besides Ettlinger's *Shomer Ziyyon Hane'eman*, there appeared in German a monthly, *Yeshurun*, in the years 1854–70, published by R. Samson Raphael Hirsch, and between 1914 and 1930, by the rabbinical school in Berlin, edited by Dr. J. Wohlgemuth. In the period 1862–1938, Dr. M. Lehmann's weekly, *Der Israelit*, appeared in Mainz. (He lived between 1831 and 1890; after his death, the editing was continued by his son.) During the Franco-Prussian War, *Halevanon*, edited by Yehiel Brill, began to appear in Hebrew along with *Der Israelit* (which had been founded in Jerusalem in 1863 and which between these two periods of Jerusalem and Mainz appeared in Paris). In 1873 and later, in 1877–1879, the Yiddish monthly *Hayisraeli* appeared, edited by Brill; in 1915–1921, *Blaetter*, of the Aguda youth, appeared in German along with *Der Israelit*.

In 1903–1923, *Frankfurter Israelitisches Familienblatt* appeared in Frankfurt; in the years 1913–1921, *Juedische Monatshefte* also appeared in Frankfurt; in the period 1915–1934, the weekly of the Aguda, *Die Juedische Presse*, appeared in Austria; during the years 1924–1930, *Ezra* appeared in Breslau and Frankfurt; in the period 1926–1927, *Arewus-Korrespondenz*, of the Aguda youth, appeared in Frankfurt; in 1927, *Der Bund*, of the Aguda, appeared in Frankfurt; and in 1929, *Adas Yisroel Blaetter*, also of the Aguda, appeared in Berlin.

It should be noted that the first Orthodox newspaper of Hungary, *Magyar Zsido*, appeared in Budapest in 1867–1870. Later, *Shevet Ahim*, in German with Hebrew lettering, appeared there. From 1888, and for the following thirty years, the Orthodox daily *Algemeine Judische Zeitung* appeared in Hungary—also in German with Hebrew lettering—followed by a weekly in Hungarian. At a certain period between the two world wars, the *Judische Presse* of the Aguda appeared in Bratislava (Slovakia).

A famous center of the Orthodox organs was in Transylvania. The following appeared in Hebrew: the weekly *Hator*, in 1876–1880 (in Sighet); the monthly *Bet Vaad Lahakhamim*, in 1880 (in Groswadein); *Kol Mevasser*, in 1898–1907; the weekly *Hashahar*, in 1908–1912; the weekly *Ha'emet*, in 1933–1940 (in Torda); the weekly *Degel Hatorah* (in Oberwisho); the monthly *Meged Yerahim* (in Satmar); and the weekly *Yeshurun*.

Besides those just mentioned, at the end of general information given about newspapers in Yiddish in Transylvania, there appeared in Sighet the *Sigheter Zeitung* in 1893, and the weeklies *Yidische Zeitung* and *Yidisches Blatt*, and, in Satmar, the *Ortodoxische Zeitung* (in Germanized Yiddish).

Finally, the organs of the Aguda, among survivors of the Holocaust, should be mentioned: *Dos Yidische Wort* was the second party's paper in chronological order. It had been founded as a weekly in the displaced persons camp of Feldafing in February 1946 as the central organ of the Aguda in Germany, appearing in Munich beginning with the eleventh issue, edited by R. Aviezer Burstein, Joseph Friedensohn, and Abraham Zemba, with an additional issue sponsored by Po'alei Agudat Israel in Germany, called *Baderech*, edited by David Adler. Only forty-seven issues of *Dos Yidische Wort* appeared, the last one in March 1949.

Dos Yidische Wort in Yiddish concentrated mainly on the Polish wing of the Aguda among survivors of the Holocaust. (Its first issues also contained articles in Hebrew.) The Hungarian Aguda had a biweekly of its own, *Kol Yisrael Bagolah*, which appeared in Munich; a bilingual (Hebrew and Yiddish) was edited by Meir Bram. Its last issue (no. 27) appeared Hanukkah 1948.

Kol Yisrael appeared for nearly thirty years in Jerusalem. It was founded in 1921 as a monthly by the Aguda, and the editorial of the first issue stated that "the absence of this organ of expression was felt for some time among the Orthodox in the Holy Land." It became a weekly in 1922 and existed until 1949. The editor of *Kol Yisrael* was R. Moses Blau, and, after his death, R. Moses Porush. In the years 1933–1938, a Yiddish supplement, *Die Yiddishe Stime*, was published for readers abroad.

On 2 *Adar Sheni* (February 12, 1948), when Jerusalem was at war, *Hayoman* began to appear as a daily but was discontinued on 1 *Shevat* 1949. *Hayoman* was followed by *Hakol*, edited by Uriel Zimmer of Pagi; it continued till 1967.

The Aguda founded the evening paper *Hamevasser*, edited by R. Menahem Porush, which began to appear on 2 *Kislev* 1948. After sixty issues, *Hamevasser* became a morning paper and later a weekly, until it was incorporated in *Elul* 1950.

On 19 *Elul* 1950, *Hamodia*, edited by Judah Leib Levin, began to appear. For some time *Hamodia* published an illustrated weekly, *Hapeles*, as well as a supplement for children.

The Po'alei Agudat published *Shearim*, which has been a daily since 1951.

Besides the dailies, mention should be made of the monthly *Bet Yaakov* (for education and literature), edited by Mosheh Prager, which has appeared in Jerusalem since 1949.

In England the Aguda publishes weekly *The Jewish Tribune*, in New York *Das Yiddishe Wort*. The hasidim of Satmar publish *Der Yid*, and in Israel, the hasidim of Belz publish *Mahneh HaHaredi*.

T.T.

PRIDE–Pride is a vice that is rejected with special fervor in Hasidism. It is regarded as a step to vanity. It ranks as a primary sin because of its metaphysical implications. Even when he was dying, the Besht explained, "Let not the foot of pride touch me" (Psalm 36:12). Hasidic rabbis never wearied of attacking pride and of praising humility. "Those who indulge in pride," they maintained, "isolate themselves in effect from the reality of the Supreme Being. They commit the ultimate sin of rejecting the all-pervasiveness of the Deity, for pride is a form of idolatry."

R. Nahman of Bratzlav maintained that the Messiah would not come until all haughtiness is eliminated from the world. Pride leads a person to drunkenness, and the giving of charity is a *segulah* for eliminating pride. A particularly propitious way to eliminate pride is to empathize with the suffering of the Jewish people. When we are haughty, our wisdom and foresight depart. Pride delays the coming of the Messiah and drives us from this world.

Similarly, R. Simhah Bunem of Przysucha says, "A 'Yud' that is too big [too proud] is no longer a 'Yud.' " This is a play on the words "Yud," or "Y" (the letter), and "Yud," the Jew.

The hasidic criticism of the attitude toward Torah learning held by some contemporary scholars centered on their pride. Thus R. Jacob Joseph of Polonnoye censored such scholars: "There are those who become proud when they study much Torah. . . . There are learned men whose very action is to show, who are the first to enter the synagogue and who study there only in order to display their prowess. Pride is most common among the learned, for there is a natural tendency toward pride through much study. The only antidote for this is humility."

For many of the rabbis of the time, the Torah had become "a means of display so that the people might remark, 'He is a wise man. . . . ' If scholars learned the traits of humility and modesty, then all would be well. But this is not at all the case, since it is well known to everyone that [the] more learned they are, the more vain they are" (*Tzaddik* 85-87). The hasidim maintained that an ideal hasid is one who is "humble, retiring, and ready to receive an abusive word without returning it" (*Tzaddik* 85).

J.B.A.

PRINTING – H. B. Friedberg in his *History of Hebrew Typography in Poland* (Tel Aviv, 1950) enumerates over fifty localities in the Ukraine, White Russia, and Lithuania where there were printing presses in the first half century of Hasidism. In all, less than a hundred hasidic books were printed up to 1836. As has been pointed out by H. Lieberman, only fourteen centers could be described as hasidic presses.

The very first hasidic work was *Toldot Yaakov Yosef*, printed by Tzvi Hirsch Margulics in Korzec in 1780. It is noteworthy that he printed also the first anti-hasidic pamphlet, *Zemir Aaritzim*, in Olexnitz. A number of hasidic books were printed in Berdichev (1807), Bratzlav (1821), Hrubiszov (1817), Kopys (1807), Medziborz (1817), Mogilev (1815), Ostrog (1793), Polonnoye (1791), Poritsk (1786), Sudzilkov (1817), Zaslav (1807), and Zhitomir (1804).

The Slavuta press was founded by R. Moses Shapira in 1792 and continued by his sons, first in Slavuta and then in Zhitomir. They printed three editions of the Talmud between 1800 and 1820 and the *Zohar*. In Berdichev, out of fifty-six Hebrew books printed between 1807 and 1821, only fourteen were of a hasidic nature.

In the second half of the nineteenth century and up to the outbreak of the Second World War, Warsaw, Piotrokov, Bilgoraj, Josefov, and Lublin had become important centers of hasidic printing. In the postwar years, many hasidic works were printed and reprinted in Israel and in the United States. In all, over 3,000 hasidic books have been printed. So far, only one volume–letters "aleph" to "tet"–of the bibliography of hasidic works (*Encyclopedia of Hasidism*), a 718-page work by the hasid R. Shalom Hayyim Porush, was printed by Mosad Harav Kook (Jerusalem, 1980).

H. Lieberman, "The Hasidic Printing Houses: Facts and Fiction," pp. 182–208.

PRISON – A number of hasidic rebbes spent some time in prison.

R. Shneur Zalman of Liady was arrested on 24 *Tishri* 1798 and released on 19 *Kislev* 1798. He was arrested a second time on October 26, 1800 and languished in prison for nine months and ten days until August 5, 1801. Like his father before him, R. Dov Baer was imprisoned by the Russian government in 1821 on charges of collecting money for the sultan of Turkey.

R. Israel of Ruzhyn (d. 1851) was imprisoned on flimsy charges in Kiev and in Kamenetz-Podolsk for twenty months. In winter 1887, R. Simhah Bunem Kalish was jailed by the Turkish authorities in the Holy Land for arriving there without a permit. R. David Tzvi Solomon Biderman was arrested in Jerusalem. R. David of Talnoye was kept in prison for a considerable time. R. Abraham Twersky of Turiysk was arrested for "subversive" activities. R. Mordecai Joseph Eliezer Leiner was arrested in 1883 for encouraging evasion of military service. R. Yitzhak Meir Alter of Ger was imprisoned in 1851. R. Samuel Abba of Zychlin was arrested by czarist authorities for supporting Polish independence for three weeks in 1854.

During the First World War, R. Meir Yehiel Halstock was arrested by Austrian authorities for anti-Austrian activities.

R. Jeremiah Kalish of Opole was arrested first by the Russians and then by the Austrians, who both charged him with espionage. R. Hayyim Shapira of Plock was executed by the Polish army on a similar and quite unsubstantiated charge. R. Joseph Yitzhak Schneersohn was arrested by the Soviets and freed only on 13 *Tammuz* 1927.

During the Nazi occupation of Poland, many hasidim were imprisoned in Pawiak, the main prison used by the Nazis in Warsaw. Sixty-five thousand prisoners passed through Pawiak during the war years.

PROVIDENCE – Hasidism teaches that Divine Providence is all-embracing. "The *Shekhinah* permeates all stages of life from the highest to the lowest," wrote the Besht. "Even when we commit a sin, the *Shekhinah* is in us, because otherwise we could not have carried out the act nor moved any organ" (*Keter Shem Tov* 22).

PRZEDBORZ, Isaiah (1758–4 *Elul* 1830), hasidic rebbe–Son of R. Meir, he was born in Lask. His father died when he was very young, and he was brought up by R. Pinehas Zelig, the rabbi of Lask. At the age of fourteen, he married the daughter of Dan Levenberg of Przedborz, a town near Kielce, and he studied in the *yeshivah* of R. David Tevele ben Nathan of Lissa, the rabbi of Przedborz. He was a companion of R. Jacob Yitzhak, the "Holy Jew" of Przysucha, and a disciple of the "Seer" of Lublin. In 1788 he became rabbi of Przedborz, and in 1815 he became rebbe.

His son R. Immanuel Weltfreid (1802–1865), who succeeded him, married the granddaughter of the "Seer" of Lublin. The dynasty was continued by his son R. Abraham Moses of Rozprze (d. 1918), who had three sons: R. Emmanuel of Lodz, R. Isaiah of Kalish, and R. Solomon of Tomaszov, who perished in the Holocaust.

T. M. Rabinowitz, *Rabbi Yaakov Yitzhak MiPrzysucha: HaYehudi HaKadosh*, pp. 125–126.

PRZYSUCHA, Jacob Yitzhak (1765–19 *Tishri* 1814), the "Holy Jew"–He was born in Przedborz, the son of R. Asher Rabinowicz (d. 1798), at one time rabbi of Grodzisk. At the age of fourteen he studied under R. Aryeh Leib Harif Heilprin and in Leszno under R. David Tevele. While he lived in Opatov with his parents-in-law, he acted for a while as *rosh yeshivah* of Opatov. He then became a teacher, wandering from place to place in search of pupils. He encountered R. David Biderman of Lelov, who brought him to the "Seer," who quickly recognized the qualities in his new disciple.

After the death of the "Seer," R. Jacob Yitzhak became known as the *Yehudi HaKadosh* (the "Holy Jew") or the *Yid HaKodesh*, as he was called with affection and with awe. Many explanations have been offered for this appellation. Some explained that it was to differentiate between him and his master, who was also named Jacob Yitzhak. Others maintained that the soul of R. Jacob Yitzhak was the incarnation of the soul of Mordecai, the hero of the Book of Esther, who is referred to as "Mordecai the Jew." According to a third theory, R. Jacob Yitzhak would scrupulously identify all authorities quoted in his discourses, and he would even attribute his own ideas to others, with the modest diclaimer: "I heard it from a Jew."

When his first wife, Feigele, died, he married her sister, Sheindel.

He died on the third day of *Hol HaMoed* Sukkot. He was survived by three sons: R. Yerahmiel, R. Nehemiah Yehiel, and R. Joshua Asher, and one daughter, Rebecca Rachel, who married R. Moses Biderman of Lelov. His discourses can be found in *Niflaot HaYehudi* (Piotrokov, 1908), *Torat HaYehudi* (Bilgoraj, 1911), *Tiferet HaYehudi* (Piotrokov, 1912), and *Keter HaYehudi* (Jerusalem, 1929).

The Doctrines of Przysucha

The Przysucha doctrines, like *Habad*, brought about a new orientation in Hasidism. What R. Shneur Zalman of Liady had done for White Russia and the Ukraine, R. Jacob Yitzhak did for Polish Jewry. "Ye shall not lie to one another" (Leviticus 19:11) enjoins the Torah, but it is equally essential for people not to lie to themselves. With all his strength, the Yehudi fought against superficiality, insisting on sincerity and total involvement in prayer, in study, and in every human relationship. Every deed should be performed only in the spirit of truth, for truth is the seal of God. Everything should be sacrificed for truth: oneself, one's time, and even part of the world to come.

In Przysucha, services were not always recited at their prescribed times; this was in order to allow time for one's fervor to reach a high pitch. The delay seemed to contradict a specific requirement of the *Shulhan Arukh*. But the Yehudi and his followers insisted that preparation for prayer was also prayer and that it is better to pray late than to pray without *kavvanah*. Regular hours are acceptable under normal conditions, but during an emergency, different methods must be used. For the hasid, life is always a battlefield, for there can be no armistice between those moral enemies–good and evil. The flame must burn privately, hidden within the individual, because an outward show of ardor is not essential. This practice was continued by R. Simhah Bunem and R. Mendel of Kotzk but was discontinued by the rebbe of Ger.

It appears that the "Holy Jew" and his followers downgraded the importance of the miracles that were said to take place at the courts of the various *tzaddikim*. As far as the *tzaddik* was concerned, his function in relation to his hasidim should, ideally, be limited to intellectual stewardship. His role as a charismatic personality, capable of evoking reverence of God through performance of supernatural feats (*moftim*), is deliberately de-emphasized by the Yehudi. Interestingly, little is recorded on behalf of the Yehudi about typical hasidic-kabbalistic suprarationalistic themes, such as restoration of the sparks or the *tzaddik*'s function as intermediary between the upper and lower realms.

The Przysucha hasidim selected new disciples with great care, searching out the brilliant talmudists. In Przysucha, the emphasis was on depth of feeling and intellectual reflection. Studies included works on philosophical piety such as R. Bachya Ibn Pakuda's *Duties of the Heart* and the books of R. Judah Low, the Maharal. They stressed the centrality of Talmud studies. Illustrative of their attitude is the interpretation–attributed to the "Holy Jew," of Leviticus 19:18: "Thou shalt love thy neighbor as thyself"–that our love of others should be like the love for our own self. A person should be more concerned with mind than with body. Above all we should revere the intellectual and spiritual leaders of the community who constitute its mind and heart.

The Yehudi postulates the ideal of *emet*–truth as absolute, pure, uncompromising, free of pretense, and self-critical–as the highest rung on the ladder of values. As Abraham Joshua Heschel put it, "The shift of emphasis from striving after mystical experience to reflective self-critical discipline was part of the revolution in Hasidism initiated by the 'Holy Jew.' " To Hasidism, the Yehudi applied the dialectic approach of the talmudists. Allied to his quick wit was a gentle disposition, for with humility he would expound his precepts to colleagues and disciples. He regarded pride as the source of all evil, and there was no trace of it in this unassuming *tzaddik*. "Why," he asked, "is the word 'justice' repeated twice in the injunction 'Justice, justice, shalt thou follow' [Deuteronomy, 16:20]? Because," he explained, "only just means should be used to secure justice." Moreover, one should never cease to pursue justice. "The main thing," said the Yehudi, "is not to mix good with bad. A hair of goodness is sufficient only if it is offered in truth and wholeheartedly without the slightest trace of evil. It is not a great effort to be a worker of miracles," maintained the Yehudi. "One who has reached a certain spiritual rung can shift heaven and earth. But to be a Jew, that is difficult. I would be glad to give up my share in this and the coming world for a single ounce of Jewishness."

The Przysucha school encouraged young people to leave their wives directly after their marriage and to travel to the rebbe for long periods of indoctrination. This practice was given special emphasis by the third rebbe of this school, R. Mendel of Kotzk, who demanded heroic piety from his followers. One must not compromise with the pleasures of life. Only if one rejects the world can one become a real hasid.

His disciple R. Simhah Bunem, too, stressed the need for hiding one's good deeds from the sight of others. This school agreed on the principles of elitism, intimacy among the members of the community, and a relentless drive for the quest of perfection in the service of God.

Martin Buber took the tension between the "Seer" of Lublin and the Yehudi to be paradigmatic of the struggle within the hasidic movement–between the magical-theurgic principle and that of deep, direct personal piety. In his novel *For the Sake of Heaven*, he describes the effort of the "Seer" to bring about the advent of the Messiah by means of kabbalistic devices. Eagerly, the "Holy Jew" awaited the arrival of the Messiah. He would practically hear the sound of the Messiah's *shofar* every day. But the Yehudi refused to overstep the clearly defined boundary between forcing God's hand and pleading for His redeeming grace.

The Przysucha school's approach to life and piety was at one time opposed by other hasidic rabbis. A *herem* (ban) against these doctrines was narrowly averted at the famous wedding of Ustilug. This school gave rise to several courts, which followed their own unique pathways. In addition to the main lines of Przysucha, Kotzk, and Ger, there were the courts of Izbica and Radoszyce. While the hasidim in Kotzk were taught to bring themselves closer to God, the *tzaddik* of Radoszyce, known as the "Holy

Grandfather," attempted to bring God closer to his people.

A. J. Heschel, *A Passion for Truth*, p. 45.

T. M. Rabinowitz, *Rabbi Yaakov Yitzhak MiPrzysucha HaYehudi HaKadosh*.

Ed. and S.F.

PSALMS – The reading of Psalms as a supplementary form of prayer was a common practice among the Jews long before Hasidism came into being. The emphasis on prayer by Hasidism implied the devotion of more time to both public and private recitations of the Psalms. Thc soul of the Besht was derived from the emanation (*Atzilut*) of King David, the reputed author of the Psalms.

Various hasidic dynasties such as those of Chernobyl and Kotzk differed in the emphasis they put on the work and manner of reciting Psalms. Some of the hasidic rebbes read the Book of Psalms every day. R. Pinhas of Koretz recited the Book of Psalms twice a week. Psalms were recited during the month of *Elul*, during the ten days of Penitence, on the eve of the Day of Atonement, and on *Hoshanah Rabba*. The Besht urged the recitation of certain Psalms at the graves of the *tzaddikim* on the New Year. He recommended the following Psalms: 4, 7, 11, 12, 13, 22, 23, 24, 38, 39, 40, 42, 43, 51, 86, 90, 91, 102, 103, 141, and 142. In Belz, a number of selected Psalms were recited every day from the first day of *Sehihot* until the Day of Atonement.

The Besht recited the whole Book of Psalms on the eve of the New Moon. R. Nahman of Bratzlav maintained that the Psalms were a true part of real repentance. He stated that "a chapter of Psalms well said is like a drink of punch." R. Issachar Dov Baer Hakohen of Wolbrum finished the whole Book of Psalms every Wednesday.

R. Yehiel Meir Lipschitz (d. 1888) of Gostynin was known as the "Psalm Jew" (*Tehillim Yid*). He used to say that by reading the Psalms, one can cure the sick and can be delivered from any trouble. He himself maintained that he was granted a precious gift from heaven, namely that whosoever he orders to recite Psalms would be saved.

When one of the sons of R. Yehudah Aryeh Leib Alter was ill, the rabbi of Gostynin advised the anxious father to recite a chapter of Psalms, and to an ignorant man he said, "Even if you do not understand either the meaning or the translation of the Psalms, you will still be saved." His Psalms were so highly regarded that the rabbi of Sochaczev, R. Abraham Bornstein, said, "The rabbi of Gostynin by his reciting of ten chapters of the Psalms is more effective than all my prayers." It is not surprising that Sholem Asch describes him, in the *Tehillim Yid*, as the ideal *tzaddik* who attains supreme heights of saintliness by reciting the Psalms with total and consuming passion.

R. Yehiel Joshua Rabinowicz of Biala recited five chapters of the Psalms at the conclusion of every Sabbath service. It is not surprising that many hasidic rebbes wrote commentaries and delivered discourses on the Psalms. The most outstanding work was by R. Shlomoh Hayyim Perlow, who wrote a monumental work on Psalms, *Mikdash Shelomoh*, published in Bilgoraj in 1937.

A. Wertheim, *Halakhot VeHalikhot BaHasidut*, pp. 179–180.

PURIM (Hebrew, lots) – A Festival commemorating the deliverance of the Jews of the Persian empire from extermination.

To hasidim, Purim was more than a "minor holiday." The rabbis would celebrate with their hasidim, donning their Sabbath garments and delivering discourses. In hasidic courts, the hasidim would elect one of their number as "Purim rabbi" or "Purim *Rosh Hakahal*" or "Purim beadle." Jesters would be employed to add to the merriment.

R. Moses of Kobryn asked his hasidim to give Purim gifts to one another and to give special donations to the poor of the Holy Land. "This is the best way to strike at Haman," he said.

Purim was considered an auspicious occasion. R. Aryeh Leib of Shpole and R. Noah of Lachowicze regarded it as an opportunity for great spiritual achievements. R. Issachar Dov Baer of Radoszyce invited barren women to his Purim celebrations and promised them that they would conceive worthy children. Purim was compared to the Day of Atonement, an ideal time for repentance. On the Day of Atonement one repents out of fear, whereas on Purim one repents out of love.

"On the Day of Atonement," said R. Levi Yitzhak of Berdichev, "we afflict our bodies. On Purim, however, we are asked to drink until we do not know *ad lo yada* (whether to curse Haman and bless Mordecai, or the reverse) (*Megillah* 7b). Can there be a greater affliction than 'not to know'?"

On the day after Purim, the rabbi of Parysov would distribute money among the poor, for "on Purim this *mitzvah* seems to be overlooked, and I deem it an excellent deed to perform a neglected *mitzvah*."

R. Shneur Zalman of Liady depicts Purim as the case of a classical *Kiddush HaShem* when the avenue of apostasy was open to the Jews but was defiantly rejected by them. R. Shneur Zalman maintained that if the Jews had changed their religion, Haman would not have attacked them. Similarly, his son R. Dov Baer, in his *Gates of Radiance*, asserted that "Purim is a classical example of self-sacrifice for Judaism." R. Nahman of Bratzlav stated that Purim is a preparation for Passover. Through the *mitzvah* of Purim we are protected from *hametz* on Passover (*Likkutei Moharan* 11:74).

Y. Alfasi, *Bisdei HaHasidut*, pp. 344–348.

R

RABINOWICZ, Abraham David Naftali Yerahmiel, of Parysov (1843–19 *Adar* 1912)–Son of R. Joshua Asher of Parysov, he was born in Zelechov. He was a disciple of R. Menachem Mendel of Kotzk and R. Yitzhak Meir of Ger. After serving as rabbi for many years in a number of communities, he succeeded his father as rebbe of Parysov. He made a point of not sleeping on the Sabbath because of the verse "The children of Israel shall 'guard' the Sabbath" (Exodus 31:16).

Some of his discourses are published in *Zekhuta D'Avraham* (Jerusalem, 1949) and *Shaarei Aryeh* (Jerusalem, 1958).

He was succeeded by his son, R. Joshua Asher.

RABINOWICZ, Abraham Issachar Baer, of Radomsk (22 *Heshvan* 1844–13 *Elul* 1892)–Youngest son of R. Solomon Hakohen of Radomsk, he studied under his father and married Rebecca, the daughter of R. Yitzhak Eizig. In 1866, at the age of twenty-two, he succeeded his father as rabbi of Radomsk in preference to his elder brothers.

He was concerned about the welfare of the soldiers conscripted into the czar's army. He regularly visited R. Hayyim of Zanz, the Maggid of Turiysk, and R. Abraham of Ciechanov. All his life he suffered acute diabetes. His discourses on the Torah, Festivals, and Bible *Hesed Le'Avraham* were printed in Piotrokov in 1897.

R. Hayyim Elazar Shapira of Munkacs eulogized him in *Maamar Zikhron Tzaddik* (Munkacz, 1905).

He was succeeded in Radomsk by his son, R. Ezekiel. His other sons were: R. Nathan Nahum (1873–1945), rabbi in Krimlov and Zawiercze, who died after the liberation of Buchenwald; R. Jacob Joseph; R. Moses Elimelekh; and R. Solomon.

His daughters married R. Menahem Mendel Alter of Pabianice, R. Abraham Kalish of Amshinov, and R. Mordecai Menahem Kalish of Otwock.

J. Silberberg, *Malkhut Bet Radomsk*, pp. 83–131.

RABINOWICZ, Abraham Joshua Heschel, of Lublin (1875–8 *Tishri* 1933)–Third son of R. Jacob Yitzhak of Biala, he was born in Ostrova and married Feiga Rebecca (d. 1934), the daughter of R. Shimon Alter, the brother of the *Sefat Emet*.

He was reluctant to become rabbi, and only when his brick factory burnt down in 1905 did he become rabbi, first in Chelmo and then in Lublin, where he devoted his life to publishing his father's writings.

He was the author of *Yeshuot Avraham*, a commentary on Genesis and Exodus, which was published in two parts, in Lublin, by his son and successor, R. Aaron Nathan David, in 1934 and in 1938.

He was survived by three sons–R. Aaron Nathan David, R. Shlomoh, and R. Tzvi–and six daughters–Dinah, Miriam, Yohebed, Naomi, Esther, and Devorah.

RABINOWICZ, Barukh, of Yampol (1811–29 *Sivan* 1859)–Son of R. Yitzhak of Yampol, he married Malkah *Hayyah*, the daughter of R. Shmuel Horowitz, the rabbi of Iasi. He suffered persecution by the *mitnaggedim* and lived for many years in Galicia, where he was befriended by R. Meir of Przemyshlan.

He died in Vienna and was survived by his sons, R. Eliezer Hayyim and R. Tzvi Hirsch.

RABINOWICZ, Barukh Pinhas, of Skole (27 *Tammuz* 1873–24 *Adar* 1920)–

Son of Eliezer Hayyim, he married *Hayyah* Adel Brakhah, the daughter of R. Asher Yeshayah Rubin of Kolbuszov, and settled in Brody, Galicia. He then became rabbi in Skole in succession to his father. Prior to World War I, after a short stay in Czechoslovakia, he relocated to Vienna, where he spent the remainder of his life.

He was the author of *Divrei Barukh* on the Ethics of the Fathers (Lvov, 1911); *Minhah Hadashah*, an array of seventy interpretations of the first verse of Genesis (Lvov, 1912); *Tal Orot* on the prayers for rain and dew together with a commentary on the hymn *Anim Zemirot* (Lvov, 1913); *Imrei Barukh* on Pentateuch (Vienna, 1916); *Parparot LaHokhmah* (Vienna, 1919); *Tosafot Hayyim* on Torah (Vienna, 1922); *Hamishah Sefarim Niftahim* (New York, 1984). He also compiled a prayer book, *Etz Hayyim*, according to the Skole ritual with his own commentary, but the manuscript was lost in Berdichev during World War One.

He was succeeded by his son R. David Yitzhak Eizig. His other son, R. Israel, a rabbi in Miami Beach, Florida, died on 29 *Elul* 1971.

A.Shu.

RABINOWICZ, Barukh Yerahmiel, of Petah Tikvah (b. 1913) – Son of R. Nathan David, he was born in Parczev. He was ordained by R. Ezekiel Michelson of Warsaw, R. Yehiel Meir Blumenfeld, and R. Joseph Elimelekh Grunwald of Ungvar. His marriage, in 1933, to Frimet, only daughter of R. Hayyim Eleazar Shapira of Munkacz, made him heir apparent of Munkacz. He succeeded his father-in-law in 1937 when he expanded the *yeshivah Darkhei Teshuvah*.

At the outbreak of the Second World War he was deported to Poland but miraculously was released and, through the intervention of the Mizrachi leader Hayyim Shapira, nine certificates were issued to him. He, his wife, and his children were allowed to emigrate to the Holy Land, where his wife died in a sanatorium in Hedera on 25 *Nisan* 1945.

He then married Yehudit, a marriage that caused great controversy among his hasidim. After spending some time in New York, he accepted a rabbinical post in Sao Paolo, Brazil, where he received the degree of master of philosophy. In 1963 he became chief rabbi of Holon, Israel, and in 1969 he founded *Darkei Teshuvah*, an institute for rabbinical education in Tel Aviv. He now lives in Petah Tikvah, where he has a *Bet HaMidrash*.

His two sons live in New York: R. Moses Yehudah Leib is rebbe of Munkacz, and R. Jacob, rebbe of Dinov. Both have spiritual affinity to Satmar.

RABINOWICZ, David Yitzhak Eizig, of Skola (1898–6 *Shevat* 1979) – Son of R. Barukh Pinhas, he was born in Brod, Czechoslovakia. He studied under his father and was considered a child prodigy. He was ordained by R. Meir Arak and R. Abraham Menahem Steinberg. During World War I he lived in Vienna, where he married Yoheved Esther Devorah, the daughter of R. Moses David Landau. In 1920 he succeeded his father as rabbi of Skola.

In 1939 he went to the United States, where he established his court in Williamsburg, Brooklyn, and later moved to Borough Park. He visited Israel in 1959 and 1977. One of his Torah scrolls was reputed to have belonged to the Besht. He died in London, where he had been receiving medical treatment, and was buried on the Mount of Olives in Jerusalem.

His children were R. Eliezer Hayyim, R. Meir, R. Joseph Barukh Pinhas, R. Abraham Moses, R. Israel Moses, and R. Asher Yeshayah. His grandson R. Abraham Moses (b. 1960), succeeded him.

R. David was a prolific author and wrote over twenty-five books. Among his publications are *Tzemah David* on Torah (Brooklyn, 1936); *Toldot Yitzhak* on the talmudical tractate *Berakhot* (New York, 1959); *Mekor HaBerakhah* on *Halakhah* and *Aggadah* (New York, 1967); *Or David*, discourses (Brooklyn, 1981); *Ner David* on Hanukkah (New York, 1984); *Imrei Yitzhak* (Brooklyn, 1989); and *Birkat Yeshurun* (Brooklyn, 1990). He was also a frequent contributor to the rabbinical journal *HaMaor*. There are many more manuscripts, which have so far not been published.

The Skoler rebbe had certain unique customs, such as praying in a separate room apart from the congregation, wearing a special *shtreimel* with a conical center on the Sabbath, reciting the hymn *Atkinu Seudata* before *Kiddush* on Friday night, and reciting *Nishmat Kol Hai* at the third meal on the

Sabbath afternoon. One revered custom of R. David's was having one of the hasidim choose at random a verse from the weekly Torah portion, then making this verse the basis of his discourse.

A.Shu.

RABINOWICZ, Eliezer Hayyim, of Skola (1845–5 *Iyyar* 1916) – Son of R. Barukh of Yampol, he married Mila Sarah, the daughter of R. Pinhas Rothenberg. He was rebbe in Yampol in Russia until 1870, when he moved to Skola in Galicia.

In 1893, he went to the United States, being the first hasidic rebbe to set foot on American soil. He gathered a few followers among the Russian immigrants. He was opposed by the socialist Yiddish paper, which mercilessly maligned him, viewing him as a detriment to the modern current in American Jewish settlement. He returned to Galicia.

Several years later, his son, R. Shmuel Abraham, successfully settled in the United States. Encouraged by his son, R. Eliezer returned and died there.

He was the author of *Siach Eliezer He-Hadash* on Genesis, Exodus, and Leviticus, printed in Munkacz in 1897; *Hibbat Kodesh Gorolo* (Kolomyja, 1892); and *Siach Hayyim* on Torah (Brooklyn, 1896).

A.Shu.

RABINOWICZ, Elimelekh Aryeh Hakohen, of Szydlov (d. 1943) – Son of R. Ezekiel Hakohen of Radomsk, he married Rachel, the only daughter of R. Jacob Biderman of Szydlov, whom he succeeded as rebbe. He was deported by the Nazis to Plaszov, and later, to Mauthausen, where he perished.

His son, R. Hayyim Ezekiel, the son-in-law of R. Yitzhak Jacob Elhanan Rothenberg of Czestochova, and his family also perished in the Holocaust.

RABINOWICZ, Elimelekh Jacob Yitzhak, of Suchedniow (1864–22 *Elul* 1939) – Son of R. Pinhas of Konskie, he was a grandson of R. Nathan David of Szydlowiec. In 1890, he married Frimet, the daughter of R. Hillel of Radoszyce. For a number of years he was rabbi of Suchendiov. In 1914 he settled in Kielce. He died on the anniversary of his father's death.

Of his fourteen children, twelve were murdered by the Nazis. His daughter Malkah Hannah had married R. Yehudah Hayyim Schonfeld, the rabbi of Kielce, who settled in London. Another daughter, Yehudit, married R. Israel Eliezer Ashkenazi; their son, Shlomoh Ashkenazi, is the well-known writer.

RABINOWICZ, Ezekiel, of Radomsk (1863–18 *Heshvan* 1911) – Third son of R. Abraham Issachar, he became rabbi in Neufeld in his father's lifetime. He wanted his brother, R. Jacob Joseph, to succeed his father as rebbe of Radomsk, but R. Hayyim Halberstam of Zanz persuaded him to accede to the wishes of his followers to become the rebbe, and at the age of twenty-nine he succeeded his father in 1892. He suffered ill health all of his short life.

He was renowned for his melodious rendering of the services. He was violently opposed to the *Bund*. He refused to take *pidyonot* and earned his living in the manufacture of bricks, managed at first by one of his hasidim, later by his son.

He was the author of *Knesset Yehezkel* on Torah and Festivals (Bendin, 1913). His elder son, R. Shlomoh Hanoch Hakohen, was murdered by the Nazis in Warsaw, and his other son, R. Elimelekh Aryeh, perished in Mauthausen.

He had four daughters.

J. Silberberg, *Malkhut Bet Radomsk*, pp. 111–131.

RABINOWICZ, Gedaliah Aaron, of Monasterzyska (1880–3 *Av* 1919) – Son of R. Joshua Heschel of Monasterzyska, he married the daughter of R. Barukh Meir Twersky of Azarnitz. He was rabbi in Kiev. His son, R. Yitzhak Yoel, was the rabbi of Monasterzyska in the United States.

RABINOWICZ, Israel, of Skola (1905–29 *Elul* 1971) – Son of R. Barukh Pinhas, he married the daughter of R. Mordecai Zusya Twersky of Turiysk. He settled in Kishinev, where he established a *yeshivah*. In 1939, he came to London and founded the Ohel Yisrael Congregation in Hendon.

After World War II he settled in the Upper West Side of Manhattan and then in Miami Beach, Florida. In 1970, he emigrated to Tel Aviv, where he died.

He was the author of *Yismah Yisrael* on the Pentateuch (New York, 1966) and also published several of his father's works.

A.Shu.

RABINOWICZ, Jacob, of Monasterzyska (1901-1972) – Son of R. Joshua Heschel, he became rabbi first in Monasterzyska and then in Uman. He published discourses in *Hazofeh* and *Hashiloah* and was the author of *Divrei Yehoshua* and *Yalkut Yehoshua*. He married Beila, daughter of R. Pinhas Rabinowicz.

In 1922, he emigrated to Philadelphia, where he became the president of the Union of American Rabbis. In 1955, he retired to Ramat Gan. His son, Prof. Pinhas Rabinowicz, a graduate of the University of Pennsylvania, is a noted mathematician.

RABINOWICZ, Jacob Yitzhak, of Biala (14 *Tevet* 1847-23 *Adar* 1905) – Son of R. Nathan David of Szydlowiec, he was born on the same date and day of the week that the medieval scholar R. Abraham Ibn Ezra completed his work *Iggeret Ha-Shabbat*. This is significant because the observance of the Sabbath, more than any other commandment, absorbed the rebbe. There is hardly a discourse in which he does not touch upon some aspect of the Sabbath. He studied under R. Leibish of Pinsk. He married Rachel Leviah, the only daughter of R. Joshua of Ostrov. He moved to Ostrov, where he was introduced by his father-in-law to the rebbes of Ruzhyn, Belz, Kobrin, and Zanz.

When the rebbe of Ostrov died, in 1873, R. Jacob Yitzhak was persuaded by R. David Morgenstern of Kotzk and the rebbe of Radzymin to assume rabbinic responsibilities. He moved to Biala Podolski, a town in the province of Lublin. He followed the doctrines of Przysucha. Protestations of piety were discouraged, and he was known far and wide for his open house. A special kitchen provided meals for visiting hasidim, and the rebbe himself regularly sampled the dishes to make sure that they were up to standard. He vehemently opposed the activities of the *maskilim*, whom he described as "little foxes destroying the vineyard of the Lord."

He left an "ethical will," in which he implored his children to cast aside jealously and enmity. He advised them to settle in different localities, should they decide to take up the rabbinate. "I would urge you," he wrote, "to announce by means of posters and through the newspapers that I ask forgiveness from those who pressed gifts into my hands. They regarded me as a *tzaddik*, but I am unworthy."

He died in Warsaw, where he was buried. He had three daughters: Matale, who married R. Menahem Mendel of Radzymin; Hannah, who married R. Joseph Tzvi Kalish of Skiernewice; and Rachel Gitel, who died in her youth.

His four sons branched off and established their own dynasties: R. Nathan David in Parzcev, R. Meir Shlomoh Yehudah in Miedzyrzec, R. Abraham Joshua Heschel in Lublin, and R. Yerahmiel Tzvi in Siedlice.

It was his son R. Abraham Joshua Heschel who published his father's works: *Yishrei Lev* on the Sabbath (Lublin, 1909) and *Divrei Binah* on Genesis (Lublin, 1909), on Exodus (Lublin, 1911), on Leviticus (Lublin, 1913), on Numbers (Lublin, 1914), on the Ethics of the Fathers (Lublin 1929), and on the Festivals (Lublin, 1931).

RABINOWICZ, Jacob Tzvi, of Parysov (d. 2 *Tevet* 1889) – Son of R. Joshua Asher, he was a disciple of R. Issachar Baer of Radoszyce and of R. Eleazar of Kozienice. He was ordained by R. Nehemiah of Bychova and R. Nathan David of Szydlowiec.

He married Sarah Yuttah, the daughter of R. Shlomoh Halperin of Pinczov, and it was through the influence of his father-in-law that he adopted the name Ashkenazi, the surname of his mother-in-law, who was a descendant of the Haham Tzvi Ashkenazi.

A renowned scholar, he was an ascetic. He would immerse himself in the ritual bath twice daily, as well as at midnight, and would, with the exception of the Sabbath, sleep on a hard bench without a pillow.

Many of the hasidim of R. Eleazar of Kozienice gave him their allegiance after the rebbe's death. He maintained that a Jew who does not rejoice in his Judaism shows ingratitude to the Almighty.

His discourses, edited by R. Israel Isaiah Halevi of Parysov, can be found in *Atarah L'Rosh Tzaddik* (Warsaw, 1895 and reprinted in Tel Aviv, 1965).

His twelve daughters all married rabbis.

He was buried in Parysov and his coffin was made out of the table at which he had studied. His widow, surviving him by twenty-six years, died in 1915. He was succeeded by his son, R. Uri Joshua Asher Elhanan.

RABINOWICZ, Jacob Tzvi, of Zelechov/Parysov (1804–25 *Iyyar* 1862)–Son of R. Joshua Asher, he was a disciple of R. Uri of Strelisk and R. Israel of Ruzhyn.

He was succeeded by his son, R. Jacob Tzvi (d. 2 *Tevet* 1889), the author of *Atarah LeRosh Tzaddik* (Warsaw, 1898), whose son, R. Joshua Asher Elhanan Ashkenazi (1870–1941), who died in the Warsaw ghetto, was the author of *Imrei Yehoshua* (Piotrokov, 1927).

RABINOWICZ, Joseph Benzion, of New York (1897–15 *Kislev* 1968)–Son of R. Meshullam Zusya, he was born in Herson, Russia. In 1922 he married the daughter of R. Pinhas Rabinowicz. After serving as rabbi, he emigrated in 1926 to the United States, where he established a *Bet HaMidrash Bet Shmuel* in Detroit. He also founded the Rabbinical Association of Detroit. He eventually settled in Givatayim, Israel, where he died.

RABINOWICZ, Joshua Asher Elhanan Ashkenazi, of Warsaw (1870–1941), hasidic rabbi–Son of R. Jacob Tzvi, he was born in Parysov. He was known for his concern for the poor.

During the First World War he lived in Warsaw. He later died in the Warsaw ghetto.

He was the author of *Imrei Yehoshua* (Piotrokov, 1927).

RABINOWICZ, Joshua Heschel, of Monasterzyska (21 *Adar* 1860–26 *Nisan* 1938)–Son of R. Yitzhak Yoel, he was born in Zinkov, Podolia. In 1886 he married Margala Rachel, the daughter of his uncle R. Pinhas of Skola. When his father died in 1885, he succeeded him as rebbe, settling in Monasterzyska a year later.

He was the author of *Divrei Yehoshua* (Berdichev, 1899).

In 1914 he settled in Uman and suffered many personal tragedies. Seven of his eleven children died in his lifetime. His eldest son, R. Gedaliah Aaron, was killed in the pogrom that took place in Uman on 3 *Av* 1919. He and his son Jacob were arrested by the communist authorities.

In 1924 he settled in Brownsville, Brooklyn. He was the author of *Torat Avot* on the Ethics of the Fathers (New York, 1926), *Yalkut Yehoshua* (Milwaukee, 1933), and *Nahlat Yehoshua* (New York, 1938). He wrote a *Sefer Torah* for his own use and corresponded with halakhic authorities such as R. Yitzhak Elhanan Spector and R. Hayyim Berlin.

RABINOWICZ, Meir Shalom, of Kaluszyn (d. 10 *Tevet* 1903)–Son of R. Joshua Asher of Parysov, he married his niece, the daughter of R. Jacob Tzvi of Parysov. He served as rabbi in Parysov and Kaluszyn. He became rebbe in 1899. He would spend the whole of Friday night in study.

He was the author of *Nehar Shalom* (Warsaw, 1908). His son, R. Joseph (d. 19 *Tishri* 1938), succeeded him.

RABINOWICZ, Meir Shlomoh Yehudah, of Miedzyrzec (1868–17 *Adar* 1942)–Second son of R. Jacob Yitzhak of Biala, he married Babcha, the daughter of R. Moses Yitzhak Eizig Barbash, a descendant of Berdichev. He first lived in Biala, then in Miedzyrzec, and from 1914 in Warsaw.

He died before the Warsaw ghetto was liquidated by the Nazis and was buried in Warsaw.

He had four sons and one daughter. His wife and two sons perished in the ghetto. One of the sons, R. Pinhas, was a cantor in Chicago.

RABINOWICZ, Moses (David) Hakohen, of Radomsk (1906–18 *Av* 1942)–Son of R. Nathan Nahum of Krimlov, Moses (or "Moishele," as he was popularly known) was born in Krimlov. He was a disciple of R. Dov Berish Weidenfeld of Trzebina. He married his cousin, Reizel, only daughter of the rabbi of Radomsk. His only son, Abraham Elimelekh Ezekiel Aaron, died in 1937 at the age of three.

In 1927, he became the head of the *yeshivah Keter Torah*. Three times each day he lectured to the 100 students of the *Kibbutz Gavoah* (Academy of Higher Studies) in Sosnowiec. He regularly visited the *yeshivot* of *Keter Torah* network and was regarded as one of the great Torah scholars of interwar Poland. In 1938, while on a business visit to Germany, he was arrested by the Nazis on a charge of nonpayment of taxes and was kept in prison for two months.

After staying for short periods in Krynica, Cracow, and Lodz, he took refuge in the home of his follower, Nathan Pinhas Erlich, in the Warsaw Ghetto at Novolipka 30. He worked for a time at the *Hesed Shel Emet* Burial Society and in Abraham Hendel's Shoe Factory. "I am sure," he stated, "that Amalek will eventually be defeated. But who knows whether we shall live to see it." He refused to leave the ghetto and asserted that he preferred to be killed in his own home. His burial place was recently discovered by R. Ezekiel Besser of New York in the Warsaw sepulcher of the rebbe of Novominsk.

His surviving disciples published some of his discourses in *Shivhei Kohen* (New York, 1943), *Birkhat Shlomoh* (New York, 1985), and *Torat HaOlot* (New York, 1989).

J. Silberberg, *Malkhut Bet Radomsk*, pp. 201–390.

RABINOWICZ, Moses Yehiel Elimelekh, of Labartov (1895–1942) – Son of R. Nathan David of Parysov and of Leah Reisl, the daughter of R. Yehiel Jacob of Kozienice. In 1912 he married *Hayyah* Miriam, the daughter of R. Israel Shapira of Grodzisk. For a time he was a wine merchant, but on the 7 Shevat 1930 he succeeded his father as rebbe and moved from Siedlce to Labartov.

He was a prolific author and wrote *Shemirat HaDaat* (Warsaw, 1927), *Avodat Halev* on prayer (Warsaw, 1927), *Emet VeShalom Elevo* (Warsaw, 1927), *VaYomer Mosheh* on Torah (Warsaw, 1927), *VaYedaber Mosheh* on Sabbath and Festivals (Warsaw, 1928–1930), *Maamar Hamidot* (Warsaw, 1928), and *Imrot Tal* (Warsaw, 1928).

He and his two sons, Yitzhak and Hayyim, and his daughter, Reizel, were murdered by the Nazis.

RABINOWICZ, Nathan David, of Biala/London (11 *Iyyar* 1899–29 *Tishri* 1947) – Son of R. Yerahmiel Tzvi of Siedlice, he was born in Ozarov. His father died when he was six years old, and he was brought up by his grandfather in Ozarov and by his uncle, the rabbi of Radzymin. Before he was ten years old he was reputed to know the Bible by heart. At the age of eighteen, on 15 *Kislev* 1918, he married Sheindel Brachah, the daughter of R. Alter Israel Shimon Perlow of Novominsk. He was ordained by R. Yehiel Meir Halevi Halstock of Ostrowiec and R. Tzvi Ezekiel Michelson of the Warsaw *Beth Din*.

On December 18, 1927 he arrived in London. His *shtiebl* at 6 Osborn Place, off Brick Lane, and subsequently, from 1932, at 10 St. Marks Rise, Dalston, attracted people from all walks of life. His passionate piety was combined with tolerance and warm humanity. He believed it was a positive duty to look for the good qualities that exist in every human being.

His literary output was considerable. These writings are as yet unpublished, but one small volume, his "ethical will" (*Divrei David* [London, 1948]), has seen the light of day. Urgently and affectionately, he implored his followers to live in fraternal harmony and to keep faith with God and humanity. "Make *Kiddush* over the Sabbath wine," the dying rabbi bade his wife, and he bequeathed to her in loving legacy an equal share in all the Torah that "I have learned and all the precepts, however few, that I have performed."

He was buried in Enfield, London.

He was survived by one son, R. Mordecai Yerahmiel Tzvi of London, and two daughters: Rachel Anne (d. 20 *Elul* 1987) was a contributor to the *Manchester Guardian* and the author of *Land and People of Israel* (1959) and *Feast of Freedom – Passover Haggadah* (New York, 1987). His other daughter, Miriam, is an artist working in plastics.

RABINOWICZ, Nathan David, of Parczev (1868–7 *Shevat* 1930) – Eldest son of R. Jacob Yitzhak of Biala, he married Leah Reizel, the daughter of R. Yehiel Jacob Hofstein of Kozienice, with whom he had three children. When his wife died he married Yutta, the daughter of R. Moses Leib Shapira of Strzyzov. During the First World War he lived in Russia, and from 1918 he lived in Siedlce, where he was known as the "Rebbe of Parczev." He was an opponent of *Haskalah* and of Zionism.

He was buried in Siedlce but was reinterred in Petah Tikva on 4 *Elul* 1977. He left an ethical will, which was published in Warsaw in 1930, in which he instructed his family to notify his ancestors who were buried in Warsaw, Lenczna, Szydlowiec, Przysucha, and Biala of his demise, so that they could intercede on his behalf. He also instructed that no one should be buried within "four cubits" of his grave and that his heirs should purchase a plot of land in Hebron to establish a study house there bearing his name.

His discourses were published by his grandsons, R. Joseph Yitzhak and Nathan David, in *VeElleh HaDevarim Shene'emru LeDavid* (Jerusalem, 1983).

He was survived by the eight children of his second marriage. His son R. Moses Yehiel Elimelekh, who succeeded him, and his daughter Feige Gitel were murdered by the Nazis. His son R. Barukh Joshua Yerahmiel is rabbi in Petah Tikvah, and his daughter Deborah Pearl married Jacob Landau (1900–1986), a descendant of Ciechanov who was a director of the *Po'alei Agudat Yisrael* and from 1948 to 1951 was the General Secretary of the Ministry of Social Welfare in Israel. Another daughter, Peska, who married Wolf Friedman, lives in New York. In her book *Going Forward* (New York, Mesorah Publications, 1994) she gives a moving account of her family.

RABINOWICZ, Nathan David, of Szydlowiec (1814–17 *Heshvan* 1866) – Son of R. Yerahmiel Tzvi, he studied under R. Issachar Baer of Radoszyce. He married Deborah Peril, daughter of R. Shmuel Wishlitzky. He frequently visited the rebbes of Zanz and Ruzhyn, and R. Yitzhak Meir Alter of Ger called him *Keter Shem Tov* (he who is crowned with a good name). He did not follow the practices of Przysucha but prayed in the prescribed hours as laid down by the Codes. He was known as a miracle worker.

He was succeeded by his son R. Jacob Yitzhak of Biala. His other sons were R. Tzemah Barukh (1836–1892) of Sydlowiec, R. Pinhas (d. 22 *Elul* 1901) of Konskie, and R. Shragai Yair (1839–1912), author of *Aron Edut* (Warsaw-Piotrokov, 1915–1922). His daughter, Sarah Yutta, married R. Efraim of Kazimierz.

RABINOWICZ, Nathan Nahum, of Krimlov (1873–eve of *Rosh Hodesh Iyyar* 1943) – Son of R. Abraham Issachar of Radomsk, he was a frequent visitor of R. David Moses Friedman of Chortkov and R. Ezekiel Halberstam of Sianiawa. At the age of twenty, he became rabbi of Krimlov. At the death of his father he settled in Zawiercze, where he established a *yeshivah Hesed L'Avraham*.

His children married into hasidic dynasties: R. Abraham Issachar Meir was the son-in-law of R. Shmuel Tzvi Danziger of Alexander, and his daughters married R. Isaiah Engelard of Sosnowiec, R. Isaiah Shapira of Grodzisk, and R. Dov Baer of Kalish.

At the outbreak of the Second World War, he lived first in Otwock and then in Warsaw. Like many of his contemporaries, he worked for a time in the Shultz shoe factory, which belonged to Abraham Hendel. He perished in Auschwitz.

RABINOWICZ, Nehemiah Yehiel, of Bychava (1808–19 *Tishri* 1853) – Son of R. Yitzhak Jacob of Przysucha and his second wife, Sheindel. His father died when he was six years old, and he was brought up by his half-brother, R. Yerahmiel. He married Reizel, the daughter of the wealthy Hayyim Moses of Wolodavka.

R. Nehemiah was a hasid of R. Israel of Ruzhyn and, at one time, stayed there for three months. He even spent Passover and the High Holy Days there. When his father-in-law died, he returned to Przysucha, and on the advice of R. Israel of Ruzhyn, he became rebbe of Bychava, near Lublin, at the age of twenty.

He studied eighteen chapters of the *Mishnah* and four pages of the Talmud daily, as well as the *Zohar* and Codes. He was renowned as a miracle worker, curing the sick and exorcising *dybbukim*. He immersed himself in the *mikveh* ten times daily. He himself, while wearing *tallit* and *tefillin*, would prepare the fish for the Sabbath. All the money he received from his followers he gave to the poor, and his family suffered great poverty.

He died on the anniversary of his father's death.

He was survived by his sons, R. Hayyim Gedaliah, R. Israel David, R. Bezalel, and R. Jacob Yitzhak of Bychava.

His discourses were published by his grandson, R. Menahem Mendel Rabinowicz of Yanova under the title *Maaseh Nehemiah* (1913) and were reprinted in Jerusalem by Tzvi Moskovitz in 1987.

D. Assaf, "The Expansion of Hasidism: the Case of R. Nehemiah Yehiel of Bychowa," pp. 269–299.

RABINOWICZ, Pinhas, of Konskie (d. 22 *Elul* 1901)–Son of R. Nathan David of Szydlowiec, he was known as a miracle worker. He lived in seclusion, far from worldly honors and pleasures.

His sons were R. Joseph Eliezer of Radomsk, who perished in the Holocaust; R. Jacob Yitzhak Elimelekh of Suchedniow, R. Nathan David of Konskie, and R. Hayyim Shragai.

RABINOWICZ, Solomon Hakohen, of Radomsk (1795–29 *Adar* 1866)–Son of R. Dov Tzvi Hakohen, a hasid of the "Seer" of Lublin and a descendant of R. Nathan Nata, the *Baal Amukkot*. He was born in Volshova, near Kielce. He accompanied his father on visits to the "Holy Jew" of Przysucha, the "Seer" of Lublin, and R. David of Lelov.

He studied first under the local rabbis, R. Reuben of Zavna and R. Aryeh Leib. Later, in Piotrokov, he continued his studies under R. Abraham Tzvi Hirsch (d. 1819), R. Moses Aaron of Kutno, and R. David Harif, author of *Bet David*. R. Shlomoh knew by heart the *Sefer Hashelah* by R. Isaiah Horowitz. He amassed a vast collection of rare books and manuscripts. He married Gitel, the daughter of R. Samuel (or Joseph) of Karzilov.

In 1834, on the advice of R. Issachar Dov Baer of Radoszyce, he became rabbi in Radomsk, where he spent thirty-two years of his life, and when the rebbe of Radoszyce died in 1843, he became rebbe. He gathered a small group of handpicked disciples but did not discourage a mass following. Among his followers were the historian Aaron Marcus, Dr. Hayyim David Bernard of Piotrokov, R. Nathan David of Szydlowiec, and R. Hillel of Radoszyce.

R. Shlomoh, renowned for his musical abilities, was a noted kabbalist and frequently visited R. Fishel of Strykov, R. Moses of Lelov, R. Ezekiel Taub of Kazimierz, and especially R. Meir of Opatov. His work *Tiferet Shlomoh* on Torah and Festivals (Warsaw, 1867) received the encomium of R. Dov Berish Meisels of Warsaw, R. Hayyim of Zanz, and R. Isaiah Muskat of Praga.

He had great respect for secular knowledge: "There are gentiles today," he said, "who understand the sciences that even King Solomon, with all his legendary wisdom, was unaware of."

He had three daughters and three sons. The eldest son was R. Aryeh Leibish (1823–1890), his second son was R. Tzvi Meir (1841–1902), and his youngest son and successor was R. Abraham Issachar Baer.

J. Silberberg, *Malkhut Bet Radomsk*, pp. 21–82.

RABINOWICZ, Shlomoh Hanoch Hakohen, of Radomsk (1882–18 *Av* 1941)–Elder son of R. Ezekiel, Shlomoh was born in Radomsk and studied under his father and his grandfather. He then continued his studies under R. Efraim Tzvi Einhorn (d. 1901) of Amstov and under R. Yitzhak Mordecai Hakohen Rabinowicz of Plavna. He married Esther, the daughter of R. Moses Elimelekh Hakohen.

In 1911, at the age of twenty-nine, he succeeded his father as rebbe. The outbreak of World War I prevented his return home from Hamburg, which he was visiting for medical reasons. He remained in Germany until the end of World War I. After the war he settled in Sosnowiec.

A man of substance, he owned glass and textile factories as well as properties in Sosnowiec, Berlin, Cracow, and Warsaw.

At a conference of hasidim of Radomsk, held in Cracow on the thirty-third day of the *Omer* 1926, it was decided to establish a network of *yeshivot Keter Torah*, which eventually included thirty-six *yeshivot* in Poland and western Galicia. These *yeshivot* were patterned after Lithuanian schools, and students were fully grounded in Talmud and Codes. The rabbi devoted a considerable portion of his income to the upkeep of these *yeshivot*, which catered to four thousand students. A *yeshivah Kibbutz Gavoa* for two hundred especially gifted students was established in Sosnowiec. In the 1930s the *yeshivah* published a periodical, *Keter Torah*. In Jerusalem, too, a *yeshivah* was established in 1937.

Though not politically oriented, he urged his hasidim to support the Aguda. As the Holocaust gathered momentum, he was urged to leave Poland, but refused. "I prefer to share the fate of my fellow Jews," he said. His successor-designate was his first cousin and son-in-law, R. Moses David Hakohen, under whose guidance the *yeshivot* reached high academic standards.

Together with his son-in-law, he worked in the Schultz shoe factory. He, his wife Esther, his daughter Reizel, and his son-in-law were killed at Novolipka 30 and were buried near the sepulcher of the rabbi of Novominsk.

Elleh Ezkerah, vol. 2, pp. 236–245.

RABINOWICZ, Tzaddok Hakohen, of Lublin (22 *Shevat* 1823–9 *Elul* 1900) – He was the son of a *mitnagged*, Jacob Hakohen, the rabbi of Kreutzburg, Latvia. His mother, Yetta, was the daughter of R. Tzaddok Halevi Horowitz, a descendant of the *Shelah*. Six years old when his father died, he was brought up by his uncle, R. Joseph ben Asher Hakohen Katz, author of *Karpas Zahav Shtayim* (Vilna-Horodno, 1836), who in 1836 became rabbi in Krinki, near Bialystok.

Tzaddok had an incisive mind and an astonishing grasp of *halakhah*. He became known as the *Illui* of Krynki. He was an extraordinary personality of phenomenal versatility. In fact, there are few areas of Jewish learning – biblical, talmudic, kabbalistic, halakhic, and homiletic – to which he did not make monumental and original contributions.

He married the daughter of the wine merchant, Samuel Hirsch of Wlodawka. Obtaining a *heter meah rabbanim* (the dispensation of one hundred rabbis, which is needed in certain circumstances to allow a man to remarry) was the task which, in 1847, brought him in touch with most of his great contemporaries, including R. Jacob Orenstein of Lvov, R. Yitzhak Meir Alter of Ger, and R. Shalom Rokeah of Belz.

After successfully accomplishing this mission, he married Havah Deborah (d. 1890), the daughter of R. Israel Jacob of Ciechanov. His wife earned a living selling secondhand clothes, which freed him to pursue his studies. Every day he would conclude a whole tractate of the Talmud, celebrating in the evening with a festive meal. He became a disciple of R. Mordecai Joseph Leiner of Izbice, whom he greatly venerated. "Had he lived in the time of the *Tanna'im*," said R. Tzaddok Hakohen, "he would have been one of them." When the rebbe of Izbice died in 1854, he transferred his allegiance to R. Judah Leib Eger, and then to the son, R. Abraham Eger.

Reluctantly, R. Tzaddok became rebbe. His first task was to begin the writing of a *Sefer Torah*, which took him twelve years to complete. He was a fervent bibliophile and wasted not a moment. All the monies he received from "the redemption of the firstborn" he devoted to the acquisition of books. Every book in his possession bore his elaborate glosses and annotations.

When his wife died, he married for the third time, to the widowed daughter of R. Fishel, a descendant of the "Holy Jew" of Przysucha. He died childless.

He was a prolific writer. Though none of his works was printed in his lifetime, over twenty were published posthumously, and an equal number of his manuscripts was destroyed during the Holocaust. Among his published works are *Pri Tzaddik* on Torah in five volumes (Lublin, 1901–1934); *Tzitkat Tzaddik* on Hasidism (Lublin, 1902); *Ressisei Lailah*, hasidic discourses with an appendix on dreams (Lublin, 1903); *Tiferet Tzvi*, responsa on *Yoreh De'ah* in two parts (Bilgoraj, 1909); *Dover Tzeddek* on Hasidism (Piotrokov, 1911); *Mahshavot Harutz*, discourses (Piotrokov, 1912); *Divrei Soferim*, hasidic thoughts (Lublin, 1913); *Meshiv Tzeddek* on the laws of *sukkah*, which includes his *bar mitzvah* discourse (Piotrokov, 1921); *Poked Akarim*, hasidic ideas (Piotrokov, 1922); *Tikkunat HaShovim* on repentance (Piotrokov, 1926); *Sihat Malakhei HaSharet* (Lublin, 1927); *Yisrael Kedoshim* on the sanctity of Israel (Lublin, 1928); *Or Zarua LaTzaddik* on the Hebrew language (Lublin, 1929); *Sefer HaZikhronot* on the Commandments (Warsaw, 1929); *Levushei Tzeddakah* (Lublin, 1929); *Otzar HaMelekh* on Maimonides (Lodz, 1929); *Zikhron LaRishonim* on prophecy with an appendix *Shemot BaAretz* on posttalmudic scholars, which *Sinai* published in Jerusalem in 1947.

Unpublished works include commentaries on Job and Jeremiah, on the Midrash, on the *Zohar*, and glosses on the Talmud and on the responsa of R. Akiva Eger.

An alphabetical index on his works has been published in two volumes by Hayyim Hirsch (Jerusalem, 1992).

A. Y. Bromberg, *Migdolei HaHasidut*, vol. 7, *R. Tzaddok Hakohen*.

RABINOWICZ, Tzvi Meir Hakohen (1902–1991), historian – Son of R. Yitzhak Mordecai, a descendant of Radomsk, he studied in the *yeshivah Torat Hayyim* in Warsaw, where he was ordained as a rabbi. He married the daughter of R. Israel Moses Schmidt of Cracow. In 1944, he settled in the Holy Land and studied in the Hebrew University, where, in 1962, he received a doctorate in philosophy.

He was a lecturer in Bar-Ilan University for many years. He was the author of biographies on R. Jacob Yitzhak of Przysucha (Piotrokov, 1932), on R. Simhah Bunem of Przysucha (Tel Aviv, 1944), and on the Maggid of Kozienice (Tel Aviv, 1947).

RABINOWICZ, Uri Joshua Asher Elhanan Ashkenazi, of Kolobiel (1870–1941) – Son of R. Jacob Tzvi of Parysov, he was encouraged by R. Shapira of Grodzisk to become rebbe in Kolobiel. He rarely delivered discourses. He sat quietly at the table, seen but not heard. During World War I he lived in Warsaw.

He was the author of *Imrei Yehoshua* (Piotrokov, 1927).

He died of a heart attack after the establishment of the Warsaw ghetto.

RABINOWICZ, Yehiel Joshua, of Jerusalem (7 *Tevet* 1901–22 *Shevat* 1984) – Son of R. Yerahmiel Tzvi of Siedlice, he was brought up by his grandfather, R. Leibish of Ozarov, and by his uncle, the rabbi of Radzymin. In 1919 he married Hannah (d. 1992), the daughter of the wealthy Eliezer Hakohen Barenholtz of Wlodowa. In 1924 he became rebbe in Siedlice.

In 1940 he was arrested by the Russians, but managed to escape to Baranowicze. After an arduous odyssey through Siberia and Kurdistan, he arrived in the Holy Land on *Lag BaOmer* 1947. For eight years he lived in Rehov Zevulun in Tel Aviv. On 15 *Tammuz* 1956 he moved to Jerusalem. His ardor was legendary, and he earned himself the title "Servant of the Lord." He recited *Alenu* after the *Shaharit* service on *Shabbat* morning, in addition to reciting it after *Musaf*. After the Sabbath service he recited five chapters of Psalms. In 1965 he established a *yeshivah Or Kedoshim* and a *Biala shtiebl* in Bene Berak.

He was the author of *Helkat Yehoshua* (Jerusalem, 1983).

He is survived by a daughter, Gilah, who is married to Hayyim Gothelf, and four sons, who all became rebbes: R. Yerahmiel Tzvi Judah, rebbe of Przysucha in Jerusalem; R. Jacob Yitzhak and R. David Mattathias in Bene Berak; and R. Benztion, the son-in-law of R. A. Babad of Sunderland, in Lugano, who also has a *shtiebl* in Jerusalem and Bene Berak.

M. E. Wiener, *HaRav HaKadosh MiBiala*.

RABINOWICZ, Yerahmiel Tzvi, of Przysucha (1784–8 *Iyyar* 1834) – Son of R. Jacob Yitzhak, the "Holy Jew," he married Golda, the daughter of R. David Dov of Bialobrzegi. After the death of his father, he was reluctant to succeed him. He earned his living as a watchmaker.

He was encouraged by R. Issachar Baer of Radoszyce to become rebbe. He was one of the staunch defenders of R. Simhah Bunem of Przysucha at the famous wedding of Ustilug.

He was survived by two sons: R. Nathan David of Szydlowiec and R. Jacob Yitzhak Elhanan of Przysucha. His daughter *Hayyah* married R. Elimelekh Shapira of Grodzisk. His other daughter, Brachah, married R. Tzvi Rapaport.

RABINOWICZ, Yerahmiel Tzvi, of Siedlice (1880–7 *Heshvan* 1906) – Son of R. Jacob Yitzhak of Biala, he married Havah, the daughter of R. Yehudah Aryeh Leib of Ozarov. He was a rabbi of rare artistic and intellectual gifts – an accomplished violinist and a painter of promise. His sketches reveal extraordinary insight.

He died at the age of twenty-six, having been rabbi for only six months, from 8 *Iyyar* to 7 *Heshvan*.

He left five children – three sons and two daughters: R. Nathan David of London; R. Hayyim, who died in his youth; R. Yehiel Joshua of Jerusalem; his daughter Alta, who married R. Zeev Pauker; and his other daughter, Perele, who married R. Alter Perlow of Koidanov.

RABINOWICZ, Yitzhak Yoel, of Monasterzyska/New York (1909–1 *Kislev* 1986) – Son of R. Gedaliah Aaron, who was killed in a pogrom on 3 *Av* 1919 at the age of thirty-nine, Yitzhak Yoel was brought up by his grandfather R. Joshua

Heschel. He was ordained by R. Samson Aaron Polanski and R. Moses Tzvi Rabinowicz.

In 1939, he married Leah (1914–15 *Tevet* 1993), the daughter of R. Joseph Teumim. He served as rabbi in the *Benei Yaakov* synagogue, in Brooklyn; was active in the support of *yeshivot* and the rehabilitation of refugees; and was chairman of the *Vaad HaRabbanim* of Flatbush.

He was succeeded by his son Gedaliah Aaron of Jerusalem. His other son, R. Nahum Tzvi, lives in Brooklyn. His sons-in-law are R. Yehudah Freeman and Dr. Moses Snad.

RABINOWITSCH, Wolf Zeev (1900–1991) – Born in Pinsk, Russia, he obtained his medical qualifications at the University of Koenigsberg in 1928. He worked in the surgical and neurological departments of the Jewish hospitals in Berlin and Cologne, and from 1939 at the Hadassah Hospital in Haifa. Side by side with his medical work, he devoted himself to research into Hasidism. The Gesellschaft zur Foerderung der Wissenschaft des Judentums published his monograph *Der Karliner Chassidismus* (1935).

His correspondence with his mentor, Simon Dubnow, appeared in *Essays and Letters, Simon Dubnow in Memoriam* (1954). In 1961, *Mosad Bialik* published his book *HaHasidut HaLitait*, which was awarded the L. Yaffe prize by the Jewish Agency. Thereafter, the book was published in English as *Lithuanian Hasidism*, by Vallentine Mitchell (London, 1970) and Schocken (New York, 1971). He published numerous articles in Hebrew, Yiddish, and German and is the author of many entries in the *Encyclopaedia Judaica*.

RADIO AND TELEVISION – Hasidim are opposed to television and believe both that it wastes time that can be put to better use in studying the Torah and that the depiction of crime, violence, and sex not only has a bad effect but also causes an increase in real-life violence. It corrupts our sensitivity of what is right, and it glorifies mindless violence, which mocks spiritual values.

In the hasidic settlements in Israel and the United States, the watching of television is forbidden, and most hasidic families do not own a television set.

Few hasidic groups other than Lubavitch use radio as a medium of communication. On several occasions, the rabbi of Lubavitch even permitted cable television and videotape cameras to film a *farbrengen*. In 1984, however, this was discontinued, and radio and telephone communications record the rebbe's broadcasts. Entertainment such as movies, theater, and concerts, is not permitted. Even videos are banned.

In a letter to his community dated December 21, 1990, R. H. Padwa of London wrote, "There is no estimating the danger caused to godliness and to the education of boys and girls by having a video recorder in the home. This is an opening for sinning and the destruction of humility and modesty."

He also forbade his followers to make video recordings of wedding parties.

J. R. Mintz, *Hasidic People – A Place in the New World*, pp. 182–183.

RADOM – A city in central Poland, sixty-two miles (100 kilometers) south of Warsaw.

In 1939, 30,000 Jews lived there, accounting for 33 percent of the population.

One of the first hasidic rebbes to settle in Radom was R. Shragai Yair Rabinowicz (1839–1921), the son of R. Nathan David of Szydlowiec. After his house in Bialobrzeg was burned down in 1907, he settled in Radom. When Czar Nicholas II succeeded his father, the rebbe predicted that the new ruler would exceed his father in wickedness.

His son-in-law, R. Joseph Eliezer (d. 1943), also lived in Radom. During the First World War, Radom was the home of R. Shmelke Horowitz (d. 1915), R. Moses Eliakim Briah (d. 1942), R. Jacob Yerahmiel of Zwolen (d. 1934), and R. Elimelekh of Kozienice (d. 1948).

The Nazis entered Radom on September 8, 1939, and on March 1, 1941, a ghetto was established. All of Radom's Jews perished in Treblinka, among them R. Joseph Eliezer of Kinski.

Sefer Radom.

RADOSZYCE, Issachar Baer (1775–18 *Sivan* 1843), hasidic rebbe – Son of R. Yitzhak, his mother, Miriam, was the sister of R. Zundel, *dayan* of Radoszyce. He married Beila, the daughter of R. Moses of Checiny, near Kielce. He lived for a time in Chmelnik, where he earned a living as a teacher. He visited R. Elimelekh of Lezajsk, R. Moses Leib of Sasov, and the "Seer" of Lublin. He became friendly with R. Abraham Joshua Heschel of Opatov and collated the latter's discourses under the title *Torat Emet*, which was printed in 1854.

In 1831, he succeeded R. Isaiah Weltfried as rabbi of Przedborz. He continued to reside in Radoszyce but stayed in Przedborz for a few months each year. He was known as a *baal mofet* (miracle worker). He would give petitioners *kamayot* (amulets, objects to ward off evil). He lived in great poverty and stated, "We are all visitors on this earth. We are just passing through it, and it is really not worth obtaining elaborate accommodation."

He was vehemently opposed to delaying the services beyond the hours prescribed by the *Shulhan Arukh*, as was the custom in the courts of Kotzk and Przysucha. He was equally opposed to the omission of *piyutim* and *tahanun*. He spent the whole of Friday night in prayer and study. On Friday night, before the recitation of the *Kiddush*, he would immerse himself in the *mikveh*. During the Festival of Tabernacles, he would set aside seven chairs in his *sukkah* for the *ushpizin*. He would leave his home on *Rosh Hodesh Elul* and spend the entire High Holy Day period, right through to Simhat Torah, in the *Bet HaMidrash*. He would light Hanukkah candles in the morning before the service throughout Hanukkah. Like the Maggid of Kozienice he often used Polish words in his melodies. He was a *tarnik* (i.e., he believed that 1840 would be the year of the redemption).

The rebbe left two sons, R. Israel Yitzhak Brown (1810–20 *Kislev* 1865) and R. Meir, and three daughters–Rebecca, Pearl, and Miriam. His son-in-law R. Hillel (d. 26 *Tevet* 1901) was an ascetic who spoke only Hebrew throughout his life. His grandson R. Kalmish and his three brothers–R. Yitzhak, R. Abraham, and R. Berel–joined the partisans and were killed by the Nazis.

Two months before the outbreak of World War II, on 18 *Sivan* 1939, the anniversary of the rebbe's *yahrzeit*, his *Bet HaMidrash* in Radoszyce was completely burned down.

Y. Alfasi, *HaSabah HaKadosh MiRadoszyce*.

RAKOVER, Mordecai (d. ca. 1820), jester–He was an employee of Tamarel Bergson and the jester (*badhan*) of R. Jacob Yitzhak of Lublin. Though domiciled in Rakov, he spent most of his time in the court of the "Seer" of Lublin. "He was created," said the "Seer," "in order to make us happy." Hasidim held him in high esteem, and R. Abraham Mordecai Alter of Ger always addressed him with deference as *Reb* Mordecai. He died in Radoszyce.

RAMAT VISHNITZ–A hasidic center on the heights of Mount Carmel, overlooking the Bay of Haifa. The settlement was established by R. Barukh Hager, the fourth son of R. Israel, on 3 *Tammuz* 1954.

The settlement includes a large synagogue, *Mekor Barukh*, seating some 500 worshipers. There are a *Talmud Torah*, an elementary school, a home for elderly people, and many social welfare organizations.

The rebbe died in 1962, and two of his sons maintain the *shikkun*: one of them, R. Eliezer, is the rebbe, and the other, R. Moses, is the head of the *yeshivah*. A publishing house has been established, and a new building, *Zeev Hesed VeEliezer David Halevi*, was consecrated in 1973. Ramat Vishnitz provides additional facilities for students of the *yeshivah* and for research into the history of the Vishnitz hasidic dynasty.

M. H. Rabinowicz, *Hasidism and the State of Israel*, pp. 128–129.

RAPAPORT, Shlomoh Yehudah (1790–1867)–Known as *Shir*, he was one of the greatest masters of Jewish historical research. He was a fine talmudical scholar, and at the age of twenty-one wrote glosses to the *Shulhan Arukh*. In 1824 he began to contribute articles to the journal *Bikkurei Ha-Ittim*. His biographies of medieval scholars were meticulously researched. He was elected rabbi in Tarnopol in 1834 and in Prague in 1840.

He bitterly opposed the Reform movement in Germany. He was equally opposed to the hasidic movement, chiefly on account of its disdain of secular learning. He condemned the *tzaddikim* for their fanatical intolerance of secular culture in all its manifestations. To the end of his life he kept up the struggle against Reform, Hasidism, and Romanticism.

S. Bernfeld, *Toldot Shir*.

RAPAPORT-ALBERT, Ada (b. October 26, 1945) – Lecturer in Jewish history in the Department of Hebrew and Jewish Studies of University College, in London. Born in Tel Aviv, she was awarded a B.A. degree by the University of London in 1968 and later, a Ph.D. Her dissertation was on "The Problem of Succession in the Hasidic Leadership with Special Reference to the Circle of R. Nahman of Bratzlav."

She is the author of various articles on the history of Hasidism and is currently editing a volume on Jewish historiography for *History and Theory*, writing a general history of the hasidic movement, and doing a study of R. Israel Baal Shem Tov and early Hasidism.

RAPHAEL, of Bershad (d. ca. 15 *Tevet* 1825) – Very few biographical data are available. He was a favorite disciple of R. Pinhas of Koretz. "The Almighty will view with favor the bringing of Raphael to His service," remarked R. Pinhas.

R. Raphael dressed with exceeding plainness. He bought his own vegetables in the marketplace and smiled at those who thought this undignified. He objected to the fact that the reader waited for him to finish the *Amidah* before repeating it.

He continuously stressed humility and truth. "One must beware of pride, since pride needs no foundation on which to build. One may be lying on one's bed, the house may be cold, and one may be covered with a torn blanket, and yet one may think in one's heart, 'I am great, I am great.' "

He often quoted his teacher: "Two things I learned from my master during my last visit to him: 'The less one talks, the nearer one is to holiness' and 'Only good deeds, of which no one knows, are valuable.' "

After his teacher's death, many hasidim followed him. He introduced a number of liturgical innovations, which were known as the "Bershad Liturgy." Many of his discourses are recorded in *Midrash Pinhas* (1873).

His son-in-law was R. Jacob Wertman.

S. A. Horodezky, *HaHasidut VeHaHasidim*, vol. 1, pp. 150, 155.

RAPHAEL (Werfel), Yitzhak (b. 1914), author and politician – Born in Sasov on July 5, son of Shmuel and Esther Werfel, he settled in the Holy Land in 1935 and married Geulah Maimon. He became a member of the Knesset and served as minister of religion and deputy minister of health from 1961.

He is chairman of the *Mosad HaRav Kook* and *Yad HaRav Maimon*. He is the author of *HaHasidut BeEretz Yisrael* (1940), *Sasov, My Home Town* (1946), *Hasidic Folklore* (1946), and *The Book of the Hasidim* (1947). He is also the editor of *Sinai* and of the *Entziklopediah shel HaTziyyonut HaDatit* in three volumes (1958–1965).

RAV'S NIGGUN (*Dem Rebben's Niggun*) – A melody without words attributed to R. Shneur Zalman of Liady. It is said to have been composed in 1799 while he was in prison in St. Peterburg. It is sung at solemn and festive occasions; on 19 *Kislev*, the anniversary of the rebbe's release from prison; at the beginning of the month of *Elul*; and at weddings and circumcisions.

The melody is divided into four parts: part one is called *Hishtapkhut HaNefesh*, the outpouring of the soul; part two, *Hitorerut*, spiritual awakening; part three, *Hitpaalut* and *Devekut*, feeling and communion; part four, *Hitpashtut HaGashmiyut*, disembodying of the soul. Some maintain that the melody corresponds to the four realms of the universe or to the four letters of the tetragrammaton.

M. Nulman, *Concise Encyclopedia of Jewish Music*, pp. 202–203.

REBBE – The title given from the earliest days of the movement to the hasidic master, probably in order to distinguish him from the *rav*, the traditional rabbinic leader. Although the term "*tzaddik*" is used in the hasidic literature for the holy guide and mentor, it is noteworthy that the hasidim refer to him as the rebbe, never as the *tzaddik*, possibly for reasons of humility so that the term used in this literature, implying the highest rank of spirituality, is not applied directly even to the foremost masters, though every hasid believes his own rebbe is, indeed, a *tzaddik*.

However, in referring to the masters in writing the term "*HaRav HaTzaddik*" is used. Moreover, the term "rebbe" denotes the intimate relationship between the master and his own followers. Even though a hasid may acknowledge there are many *tzaddikim*, there is, for each hasid, only one rebbe – the one to whom that hasid has chosen to give complete allegiance. Even when a *tzaddik* is known to have been the disciple of many *tzaddikim*, one of these is always said to have been the "main teacher" (*rabbo hamuvhak*).

There are very few instances of self-appointed hasidic masters. In the earlier period, the rebbe was ordained as such by his teacher; in the later period, he generally inherited the position from his father, though it is notorious that the rival contestants for the position of rebbe frequently led to a proliferation of hasidic dynasties.

Although one finds the term "*semikhah*" (ordination) used for the authority given to a man to serve as a rebbe, this has no connection with the traditional form of *semikhah* in which a disciple is declared to be competent in Jewish law. The hasidic "ordination" testifies rather to the candidate's fitness to lead a flock in the path of holiness. At the moment this kind of *semikhah* is bestowed, the recipient is also initiated into the secret of how to lead a community, that is, into the practical details of how a hasidic rebbe should conduct "court."

It was possible for a rebbe to be at the same time a traditional rabbi. All of the members of the Belzer dynasty were town rabbis of Belz. Masters such as R. Levi Yitzhak of Berditchev and R. Shneur Zalman of Liady were known as "Rov." But talmudic and halakhic learning were not considered to be essential to the rebbe and there have been instances of rebbes whose most ardent followers would make no claims as to their rebbe's prowess in learning. It was argued that in talmudic times, too, there were giants of saintliness such as R. Pinhas ben Yair and R. Haninah ben Dosa, who were masters of prayer and able to work miracles, but of whom not a single halakhic teaching has ever been found. However, historically considered, the rebbe and his function as a new type of mentor certainly represent a real innovation in Jewish life.

I. Berger, Introduction to *Eser Orot*, part of *Sefer Zekhut Yisrael*.

L.J.

REDEEMER – Many authors gave dates on which redemption was to have taken place. Nachmanides (1194–1270), basing his prediction on a verse in Daniel, predicted that the Messiah would come in 1356.

In his commentary on the Pentateuch, R. Yitzhak ben Judah Halevi (b. ca. 1250) of Sens, France, gives the date as 1405.

The *Zohar* characterizes the years 1300, 1306, and 1676 as "fateful years."

R. Yitzhak Abravanel (1447–1508) was certain that the Messiah had been born before the expulsion of the Jews from Spain.

R. Issachar Baer of Radoszyce was a *Tarnik* (i.e., he believed that 1840 was to be the year of redemption). R. Eliezer Horowitz of Dzikov maintained that the Messiah would not come that year. Feeling that the widely held belief among the people that the Messiah would come that year could have had harmful repercussions, R. Eliezer Horowitz declared, "If he does come, I do not mind that I will be called a liar."

As late as 1861, R. Meir Leibush, the *Malbim* (1809–1879), calculated that the redemption would begin in 1913 and that the process would take fourteen years.

Gershom Scholem maintains that after the collapse of Shabbatean movement, the hasidim adopted a neutral stance toward the messianic idea.

Although the Besht yearned for the Messiah, he did not spend time speculating on the exact moment of his arrival. In this respect he followed R. Yitzhak ben Moses Arama (1420–1494), who criticized such messianic speculations.

A similar attitude was adopted by authorities as diverse as R. Azaria dei Rossi, R. Judah Loew ben Bezalel, and R. Manasseh ben Israel (1604–1657).

Maimonides specifically stated, "It is a fundamental dogma to believe in the coming of the Messiah, even if he delays. But no one should attempt to guess or fix the time."

According to the Besht, "Exile from the Holy Land was the cause of Jewish spiritual degeneration." On one New Year's Day, the Besht pondered on the text "How we are undone! We are greatly confounded because we have forsaken the Land" (Jeremiah 9:18). "O, Prophet Elijah, when will you come and announce the advent of the Messiah? When will the Temple and the Altar be rebuilt?" (*Keter Shem Tov*).

The Besht believed that every individual could help hasten the advent of the Messiah and that national redemption would be achieved only by the totality of individual efforts. Fundamental to this philosophy was the belief that each human being had, within, a spark of the soul of the Messiah. By perfecting ourselves, we hasten the redemption. By engaging in dissension and disputes and causeless hatred, we delay it. "I asked the Messiah when he would come," he wrote in 1752 to his brother-in-law. "And the Messiah answered, 'Not until your teachings have spread throughout the world.' "

REDEMPTION – Two notions of redemption may be said to coexist in the religious literature of Hasidism. One is national/historical in scope, seeking the redemption of Israel and human history through the personage of the long-awaited Messiah. The other, a redemption on the personal/spiritual level, does not depend upon the messianic advent but may take place even within the situation of historical exile. The former notion is the inheritance of Hasidism from the long history of Jewish messianic anticipation, whereas the latter, though having some antecedents, is particular to the hasidic spiritualization of classical Jewish symbols and the new search for immediacy in religious life. Although certain hasidic authors, particularly in the school of Mezhirech, placed great emphasis on notions of personal and individual redemption, thus serving to "neutralize" the urgency of historical messianism, it would not be fair to say that the longings for Messiah are ever fully supplanted in Hasidism.

In a letter to R. Abraham Gershon Kitover discussing his famous "soul-ascent" of 1746, the Besht recalls a "conversation" he had with the Messiah. When asked by the Besht, "When will you come?" Messiah is said to have replied, "When your wellsprings [i.e., hasidic teachings] spread forth." The spread of Hasidism is thus seen as a part of the *tikkun* (restoration), which is needed in order to bring about the final redemption. Later tradition records that the Besht set out on a journey to the Land of Israel, only to be deterred along the way, and that he also at one time sought to redeem the soul of the messianic pretender Shabbatai Tzvi. While both of these acts may have to do with messianic theurgy, scholars are divided as to their historicity and meaning. A number of important personalities in the early hasidic movement did in fact settle in the Holy Land (R. Menahem Mendel of Przemyshlan, R. Nahman of Horodenka, R. Menahem Mendel of Vitebsk, etc.), but here too we have no clear evidence of messianic intentions, and the reasons for these journeys are a matter of scholarly debate.

The turn of the nineteenth century marked a sharp upturn in redemption-oriented activity and messianic speculations among hasidic leaders. R. Nahman of Bratzlav quietly proclaimed himself to be Messiah ben Joseph, thc forerunner of redemption, and hoped that his son, born in 1805, would be the final redeemer. The year 1810 (numerologically corresponding to "sound the great *shofar*") was thought by some to be the year when Messiah would make his appearance, while some two years later the masters of Lublin and Rymanov are reputed to have seen in the confrontation between the Napoleonic and czarist armies the final great premessianic battle.

The personal/spiritual reading of redemption also has its roots in the very beginnings of Hasidism. The Besht is quoted by his grandson as saying that "every man is obliged to redeem himself" (*Degel*, Balak). It was under the influence of the Maggid, however, that this tendency was most highly developed. R. Menahem Nahum of Chernobyl goes so far as to say that when an individual has realized God in one's own life, the promised "future" has arrived for that person (*Me'or Einayim, Shemot*). Here it does indeed seem that the personal goal of *devekut* has eclipsed collective historical messianism as a category of significance. Among other disciples of the Maggid, however, including R. Levi Isaac of Berdichev, anticipation of the Messiah was very much alive. Even open calculations as to the date of his arrival were not unknown (cf. *Or HaGanuz, Vayyehi*). A more moderate view, here expressed in the words of R. Shmelke of Nikolsburg, is perhaps most typical: "It is for this reason that we say, 'redeems Israel' and 'rebuilds Jerusalem' in the present tense (in the liturgy). In truth every day is Jerusalem rebuilt, bit by bit (*Divrei Shmuel, BeHukotai*). It is through the Jew's daily regimen of religious life that redemption is effected, and it is indeed on the present that our attention should be focused. The cumulative effect of Israel's merits, however, will be the long-anticipated redemption of the future.

In recent times, under the impact of the Holocaust and the renewal of Jewish statehood, questions of messianism and redemption have once again come to the fore in hasidic communities, though now cast in very different terms. The Hungarian hasidim in particular, largely under the leadership of the late R. Joel Teitelbaum of Satmar, have taken great pains to show that there is nothing of redemption to be seen in the state of Israel, led as it is by secular Jews. Some even claim that Messiah is delayed by this improper usurpation of a power that should be his alone. Other hasidim, notably those in the younger circles within *Habad*, seem to be caught up in a renewed messianic fervor, loudly proclaiming that Messiah will surely arrive within their present *rebbe's* lifetime, and others even proclaiming him quite openly as Messiah. These activities have led to significant conflict within the *Habad* community, as well as to denunciations of *Habad* from without.

A.G.

REFORM – As Orthodox Jews the hasidim were opposed to any idea that Judaism should or could be "reformed." Nor is it correct to see Hasidism itself, at least on the conscious level, as a "reformist" movement, despite the numerous innovations for which it was responsible. These latter were always held to be based on sound precedents in the classical Jewish sources.

Certainly all the hasidic masters believed in the doctrine of the immutability of the Torah in its Maimonidean formulation, which precludes any possibility not only of the Torah's ever being superseded but also of any of its laws ever being abrogated. In addition, the hasidim of Eastern Europe, where the movement arose and reached its zenith, were completely indifferent to the Reform movement in the West, about which they may have heard vague rumors, and for them the new tendency was so remote and irrelevant that they saw no need even to condemn it.

The Hungarian hasidim were an exception because Reform had made inroads into Hungarian Jewish life. But even here the vehement hasidic attacks by the Munkacser and others on the neologisms and the upholders of the status quo were not really hasidic at all in nature but simply part of the wider rabbinic opposition in the name of the Hatam Sofer's famous aphorism "Everything new is forbidden by the Torah."

There can be no doubt that Hasidism – especially with its kabbalistic doctrine that the wisdom of the gentiles is tainted and can taint the Jewish soul – was determined to reject the very notion that the Jew has anything to learn from Western civilization and still less any need to be influenced by its values when these differed from the old ways. But the attack by the *tzaddikim* in this matter was directed not against the German Reform of Holdheim and Geiger but against Hasidism's most powerful foe, the *Haskalah* movement. This Hasidism fought by banning the slightest change in dress and custom, by stern insistence on the use of the traditional methods in Jewish education, and even by the neglect of Bible teaching in favor of the Talmud and the espousal of an ungrammatical Hebrew style because the *maskilim* were well versed in grammar and knew their Bible and yet these had led them into heresy. Some of the *tzaddikim* devoted a major part of their activity to fighting the *Haskalah* heresy. Prominent in this sphere were the *tzaddikim* of Belz, the *Habad* teachers, the dynasties of Dynov and Munkacs, the Satmarer Rebbe, and R. Tzaddok Ha-Kohen of Lublin.

Of R. Tzvi Elimelekh of Dynov it is reported that he once prayed to God that even if Moses Mendelssohn is now in paradise because he was, after all, a pious Jew, he should be hurled down from there to the nethermost pit in hell because he has been the cause of Israel's defection from the Torah.

N. Urtner, *HaRav Tzvi Elimelekh MiDinov*, chap. 18, pp. 482–532.

L.J.

REPENTANCE – Hasidic teachings on repentance differ from earlier Jewish teachings only in mood and emphasis. The motive for repentance, according to the hasidic masters, should be far less the fear of punishment than the love and fear of God, the latter being generally understood in hasidic thought as a profound sense of the numinous, the awe and dread awakened by our reflection on the majesty of the Creator and on how sin creates a barrier between God and humanity.

The threat of hellfire is totally absent from the majority of hasidic treatments of repentance, though in *Habad* thought, our sufferings in this world are due to the divine mercy so that we may be freed from the far more terrible punishments of hell. The somewhat untypical hasidic master R. Arele Roth includes in his *Shomer Emunim* the full text of the medieval tractate *Gehinnom* as a means of encouragement for his followers to repent of their sins.

As part of its normal rejection of asceticism, Hasidism tends to frown on the older methods of self-torment as a panacea for sin. Especially nowadays, it was argued, when folk are so weak physically as well as spiritually, fasting is not enjoined, although some degree of mortification of the flesh is sometimes advised. But the more bizarre panacea, such as rolling in snow, were rarely practiced among the Hasidism and there is even to be detected a strong suspicion of such external acts.

There is a hasidic tradition that if one who has sinned recites the whole Book of Psalms with devotion three times in a single day, it is accounted to that individual as if the person had fasted for a whole week. For all that, sin is not to be treated lightly. While it is taught that it is in some respects easier to repent of severe sins than of lighter ones, since the holy sparks are most powerful in the lowliest stages of God's creation and these lead sinners back to their source, yet the *tzaddikim* were known to have imposed heavy penances on those of their hasidim who were guilty of really serious offenses against the Torah. But Hasidism believes that the way back to God is to refuse to dwell overall on the sins of the past, finding atonement for them in positive good in thought and deed. Repentance, moreover, is not for abject sinners alone. The *tzaddik* must be so conscious of his sins of omission as he ascends each day on the rungs of the ladder of holiness that he comes to feel he must repent for the unworthy nature of his worship until then.

It must not be thought that the citadel of repentance can be taken by storm. God led Israel out of Egypt gradually, and so, too, we can succeed in escaping from our bondage to evil inclination only step by step. If we try to achieve the sudden and total change of our nature in one great leap to rid ourself of sinfulness, we are bound to fall and then yield to total despair.

The role of the divine grace in repentance has been recognized. Were it not for God's help, no one could ever give up sinful conduct. A heavenly voice calls out to us all the time deep within the recesses of our heart, urging us to repent. Our task is to heed that voice. We can, however, take the initiative in repenting, and when we do, the divine response is with even greater compassion, the "male" principle on high: the rabbis tell us that when a woman "sows her seed first" in the connubial act, she will give birth to a male child.

Hasidism makes much of the rabbinic distinction between repentance out of love and repentance out of fear. Both are essential but the former brings us to a far higher spiritual stage than the latter. This is said to be the meaning of the way in which the three great autumnal Festivals are arranged in the Jewish calendar. On Rosh Ha-Shanah, with its terrifying *shofar* sounds, and on Yom Kippur, with its emphasis on remorse and fasting, we repent out of the fear of God. There follows the Festival of joy, Sukkot, when sin is abandoned because we turn back to our Maker in love.

Nahman of Tcherin, *Leshon Hasidim*, pp. 311–317.
Shneur Zalman of Liady, *Iggeret HaTeshuvah* in *Tanya*, pp. 180–202.

L.J.

RESPONSA (Hebrew, *She'elot U'Teshuvot*; lit., questions and answers) – Replies by halakhic authorities to problems on specific religious issues put to them by questioners. The responsa literature began in the Gaonic period and continues to the present day. It reflects the social, religious, economic, and political conditions of the Jews in many countries. In 1930, Boaz Cohen in his *Kuntres HaTeshuvot* (Books of Responsa), first published in Budapest, enumerated 1,791 volumes of responsa.

Among the hasidic rebbes who also were authors of authoritative responsa were R. Menahem Mendel Schneersohn, R. Abraham Bornstein of Sochaczev, R. Hayyim Halberstam of Nowy Sacz, R. Ezekiel of Sianiawa, R. Moses Teitelbaum, R. Yekutiel Judah Teitelbaum, R. Aryeh Leibish Lipshitz, R. Hayyim Tzvi Teitelbaum, R. Yitzhak Eizig Weiss of Spinka, R. Menahem

Mendel Panet of Des, R. Tzvi Hirsch Shapira, R. Hayyim Elazar Shapira, R. David Shapira, R. Menahem Monish Babad, R. Dov Berish Wiedenfeld, R. Yitzhak Jacob Weiss, R. Meir Shapira of Lublin, R. Shalom Mordecai Schwadron, and R. Shmuel Engel of Radomysl.

RIVLIN, Elijah Joseph (1805–12 *Tammuz* 1865), *Habad* scholar – Son of R. Aryeh Leib, he was a disciple of R. Aaron Horowitz of Starosselje and R. Dov Baer Schneersohn of Lubavitch. After the death of R. Dov Baer, R. Elijah Joseph did not follow his successor.

He occupied rabbinical positions in Drivin and Polutsk. In 1855, he emigrated to the Holy Land, where he became the leader of the *Habad* hasidim and the head of the *Habad kollel* in Jerusalem.

He was the author of *Oholei Yosef* on the laws of sanctifying the New Moon, which was published in Jerusalem in 1868.

RODKINSON (Frumkin), Michael Levi (1845–1904), writer – Born in Dubrovno, Belorussia, his mother, Rada Hayyah, was a daughter of R. Aaron Halevi Horowitz of Starosselje.

His earliest literary works were on the hasidic movement: *Shivhei HaRav* on the life of R. Shneur Zalman of Liady (Lvov, 1864), *Toldot Baalei HaShem* (Koenigsberg, 1876), and *Toldot Amudei Habad* (Koenigsberg, 1876). He also published a collection of hasidic stories, *Adat Tzaddikim* (Lvov, 1864) and *Sippurei Tzaddikim MeArba Netivei Lehet* and *Siftei Kedoshim MeArba Netivei Lehet*, dealing with R. Leib Sarah's, R. Leib of Shpole, R. Israel of Polutsk, and his disciple R. Azriel.

M.S. and G.N.

ROKEAH, Aaron, of Belz (17 *Tevet* 1880–21 *Av* 1957) – Son of R. Issachar Dov, he was born in Belz. When he was four years old, his mother died. He married his first cousin Malkah, the daughter of R. Shmuel of Sokal. On 22 *Heshvan* 1927, he succeeded his father as rebbe of Belz. Like his ancestors he was both rebbe and rabbi. On 3 *Tevet* 1928 he convened a conference in Lvov, in which 300 rabbis participated and established a rabbinical association.

In 1929, he participated in the delegation to Polish prime minister Bartel, seeking support for Orthodox Jewish education. When Hitler became chancellor in 1933, the rebbe declared, "Hitler is the very personification of the devil. He is worse than Amalek or Haman." When Prince Peter of Greece, a relative of the British royal family, visited the rebbe in 1937, the latter urged him to persuade Britain to suppress Arab terrorism in the Holy Land.

The rebbe supported a number of men known as *yoshevim*, who devoted their whole time to prayer and study. Every hasid who visited the rebbe was required to make a contribution toward maintenance of the *yoshevim*. Over 400 students studied in his *yeshivah*.

For four perilous years, 1940–1944, the rabbi lived precariously in Nazi Europe, traveling from Belz on Shemini Atzeret 1940 to Sakol and Przemysl and to the ghettos of Bochnia, Cracow, and Budapest. He withstood unspeakable hardship. He changed his name – first to "Aaron Singer," and then to "Aaron Twersky" – in order to confuse the Nazis, who pursued him relentlessly. A concerted effort to rescue him was set in motion by his hasid Berish Urtner. Chief Rabbi Herzog and R. Yitzhak Meir Levin supported these rescue efforts, and the certificates necessary to enter Palestine were issued. The rebbe left Nazi Europe via Romania, Bulgaria, Greece, and Turkey, and after one week in Istanbul, arrived in the Holy Land on 9 *Shevat* 1944. After a brief stay in Haifa, he settled in Tel Aviv at 63 Ahad HaAm, where he lived for thirteen and a half years.

He did not forget his fellow Jews in Europe. He declared 25 *Adar* and 14 *Sivan* 1944 to be fast days. He broke the tradition of Belz neutrality when he urged his followers to support the United Religious Front in the first elections of the Knesset in 1949.

In the Holocaust, the rebbe lost his wife, his three sons (R. Moses, R. Israel, and R. Judah Zundel), his four daughters (Rebecca Miriam, Eidel, Sarah Brachah, and Mirele), his brothers and sisters, and his twenty-six grandchildren.

In Israel, he married Gitel, the daughter of R. Barukh Goldstoff, but the marriage ended in divorce. His third wife was Hannah, the daughter of R. Yehiel Hayyim Labin of Makov, but there were no children.

He divided his time between Tel Aviv and Jerusalem, where he spent the summer months. He participated, on 10 *Av* 1953, in the rabbinical conference that convened in Jerusalem to protest against the proposed conscription of girls and, in 1956, he signed a manifesto supporting the aims of the Aguda. "These days, the Aguda does what the *Mahzikei Hadat* did in the time of my grandfather," said the rebbe.

He died at the age of seventy-seven in Shaare Tzeddek Hospital, in Jerusalem. Following the ruling of R. Dov Berish Wiedenfeld, he was interred on *Har HaMenuhot*, in Jerusalem, and not near his brother in Tiberias. His successor was his nephew R. Berele.

ROKEAH, David, of New York (1898–11 *Sivan* 1971) – Son of Abraham Jacob, he was born in Belz. He married his cousin the daughter of R. David Flaum. He served first as rabbi in Lvov, then moved to Montreal before finally settling in New York.

ROKEAH, Eliezer Elimelekh, of Kozienice/Radom (1860–1935) – Son of R. Shmuel Shmelke of Kozienice, he married the daughter of R. Meir Shalom Rabinowicz of Kaluszyn. When the Jews were expelled from Kozienice in the First World War, he lived in Radom, where, in 1915, he succeeded his father as rebbe.

ROKEAH, Issachar Dov, fifth rebbe of Belz (b. 8 *Shevat* 1948) – Son of R. Mordecai of Bilgoraj, he was born in Tel Aviv. His mother was Miriam, the daughter of R. Tzvi Hayyim of Huszt. When his father died in 1950, he was just one year old, and for the next eight years, his uncle R. Aaron took care of him. When his uncle died, his education was supervised by R. Joshua Feder and R. Shalom Brander. In Bene Berak, on 15 *Adar* 1965, he married Sarah, the daughter of R. Joshua Hager of Vishnitz and became rebbe. In 1975, his only son, R. Aaron Mordecai, was born. He was ordained by R. Dov Berish Weidenfeld and R. Moses Grunwald.

The rebbe has expanded the *yeshivah* established by his uncle, and in 1986 he established the *Mahzikei Hadat* community, which provides all the religious requirements of the expanding movement. On 10 *Sivan* 1980, he laid the foundation of the Great Synagogue, which is being built on the outskirts of Jerusalem in *Kiryat Belz*. He is an excellent organizer and has set up many educational institutions in Israel and the Diaspora. He is a member of the *Mo'etzet Gedolei HaTorah*.

His son, R. Aaron Mordecai, married the eighteen-year-old Sarah Leah Lemberg, a student of Bet Yaakov of Bene Berak and the daughter of R. Israel Eichler, the rabbi of Makov, Kiryat Ata. The marriage took place in Shikkun Belz, Jerusalem, on 16 *Av* 1993.

Jewish Tribune, July 29, 1993.

ROKEAH, Issachar Dov, of Belz (1854–22 *Heshvan* 1927) – Second son of R. Joshua, he was born in Belz. At an early age he married Batyah Rehumah, the daughter of R. Yeshayah Meshullam Zusya Twersky. For ten years he stayed in Chernobyl and was known as the "*Illui*" of Chernobyl. On the death of his wife in 1884, he married in 1886 *Hayyah* Devorah, the daughter of R. Abraham Shmuel Pitchnik of Brzezany.

He was gifted with a common touch. His manner was forceful and he favored the direct approach. He revived the *Mahzikei Hadat*, which was founded by his father. At the outbreak of the First World War, he moved first to Ratzford (Usfeherte) (1914–1918), then to Munkacs (1918–1921), and then, owing to the antagonism of R. Hayyim Elazar Shapira, to Halicz near Jaroslav.

In October 1922, Count Galecki, governor of Lvov, urged the rebbe of Belz to advise his followers to vote against the minority block. Unequivocally, the rabbi refused. In 1925, he returned to Belz, where he lived for the rest of his life.

He is quoted in the learned works of R. Yitzhak Shmelkes of Lvov, by R. Meir Shapira, and by R. Tzvi Ezekiel Michelson. He supported Sarah Schenierer, who founded the *Bet Yaakov* movement. The rebbe is described by Jiri Mordecai Langer (1894–1943), the Czech poet and author who visited him in 1913, 1914, and 1918, in his book *The Nine Gates*, which gives a vivid description of life in the rebbe's court.

His son R. Aaron succeeded him. His other sons were R. Yehoshua, R. Mordecai, and R. Shalom. He had five daughters: Hannah Rachel, Shevah, Heniah, Sarah, and

Yente. All his daughters married into the Chernobyl dynasty.

J. Langer, *Nine Gates to the Chasidic Mysteries*.

ROKEAH, Issachar Dov, of New York (1900–10 *Iyyar* 1965) – Son of R. Menahem Mendel, he was born in Dynov, Galicia. His mother, Rachel, was the daughter of R. Avi-Ezra Zelig of Kaluszyn. He married Hannah, the daughter of R. Shimon Horowitz. After serving as rabbi in Linsk, he emigrated to New York in 1930 and served as the rabbi of congregation *Bikkur Holim*.

In 1953, he published his grandfather's work, *Tzemah David*. His sons – R. Eliezer, R. Abraham Hayyim, R. Yehudah, and R. David – perished in the Holocaust. He was survived by his daughters, Esther Rivkah and Reizel; the latter married R. Menahem Shlomoh Taub, the rebbe of Kalev in Brooklyn.

ROKEAH, Joshua, of Belz (1825–23 *Shevat* 1894) – The fifth and youngest son of R. Shalom of Belz, he was born in Belz. He was renowned for his phenomenal knowl'edge and his worldly wisdom. He married Rebecca Miriam, the daughter of R. Shmuel Ashkenazi. On his wife's death, he married her niece Sarah Mirel, the daughter of R. Hayyim of Minkowitz.

On the death of his father in 1855, he became rebbe. He was one of the first hasidic rebbes to engage in politics. He formed the *Mahzikei Hadat* in 1878, opening branches in many cities. Through the intervention of Ignaz Deutsch of Vienna, the movement received government recognition. Two journals, *Mahzikei Hadat* and *Kol Mahzikei Hadat*, were published on alternative weeks. He was largely responsible for the election of R. Shimon Sofer to the Austrian parliament in 1879.

In 1882, the *Mahzikei Hadat* convened a conference, which was attended by 200 rabbis of different communities. The conference passed a resolution that only Jews observing meticulously the precepts of the *Shulhan Arukh* were to be granted full voting rights at Jewish communal elections. In his fight to preserve traditional Judaism, he enlisted the help of leading contemporary rabbinic authorities. He was also concerned with developments in Hungary. He was in sympathy with the convention held in 1865 in Michalovice, in northeast Slovakia, which decided on the secession of the Orthodox congregations and on the establishment of communities known as *status quo ante*. He was the unofficial spokesman of Galician Jewry, and virtually every appointment required his imprimatur.

Like his father he corresponded on halakhic matters with his contemporaries, and he also continued the building and extension of the *Bet HaMidrash* of Belz. He wore a *tallit* both for *Minhah* and *Maariv* on the Sabbath, even when not officiating at the reader's desk. He permitted *Hosafot* even for the Kohen and Levy portions of the reading of the Law.

He went to Vienna to undergo surgery and died on his return to Belz. He was survived by five sons: R. Shmuel, R. Aryeh Leibish, R. Yitzhak Meir, R. Naftali, and R. Issachar Dov, who succeeded him. He had three daughters: Freda, Mirel, and Reizel.

His discourses were published in *Ohel Yehoshua* as part of his father's work *Dover Sholem* (Przemysl, 1910).

A. Y. Bromberg, *Migdolei HaHasidut*, vol. 10, *Admorim LeBet Belz*.

ROKEAH, Joshua, of Jaroslav (1897–4 *Nisan* 1942) – Son of R. Issachar Dov, he married in 1913 Hannah Soshe, daughter of R. Joseph Meir Twersky of Machnovka. When he divorced his wife, he married in 1925 Hannah Shifra, the daughter of R. Moses Elikum Briah Goldberg.

When his father died in 1927, he became rebbe in Jaroslav, Galicia.

He, his wife, and his children – Israel, Yitzhak David, and Malkah – were murdered by the Nazis. His surviving son, R. Joshua, was the rebbe of Machnovka in Bene Berak.

ROKEAH, Meir, of New York (1871–5 *Tishri* 1942) – Son of R. Abraham Joshua Heschel, he was born in Karev. After being expelled from his native town in 1886, he lived in Przemysl, where he studied under R. Shmelkes. He married, in 1889, Reina, the daughter of R. Joseph Alter Epstein and became rabbi of Kozlov.

From 1914 to 1920 he lived in Budapest, and later in Tarnopol. In 1931 he settled on the East Side of New York, where, during the war years, he helped refugees.

His son, R. Moses, succeeded him in New York.

ROKEAH, Mordecai, of Bilgoraj (1903–25 *Heshvan* 1950) – Son of R. Issachar Dov by his second wife, he married, in 1922, Bathshevah, the daughter of R. Moses Aaron, the rebbe of Kobrin. In 1927 he became rebbe of Bilgoraj. Together with his brother he escaped the Nazi Holocaust, and in 1947, he married Miriam, the daughter of R. Tzvi Glick of Satmar.

He died at the age of forty-seven and was buried in Tiberias. He was survived by his only son, R. Issachar Dov, the rebbe of Belz.

ROKEAH, Moses, of Karev (1815–21 *Iyyar* 1882) – Son of R. Shalom of Belz, he married Sheindel, the daughter of R. Pinhas Horowitz of Iasi. All his sons became rebbes: R. Shmuel Shmelke in Kozienice, R. Abraham Joshua Heschel in Przemysl, R. Todres in Nemirov, R. Shalom in Greiding, and R. Issachar Dov in Libiczov.

His son-in-law, R. Naftali Goldberg, became rebbe in Sheltz, near Warsaw. He died on 18 *Tevet* 1907 and was succeeded by his younger son, R. Alter Shalom Elimelekh, who published his father's work *Kol Naftali* (Warsaw, 1932).

ROKEAH, Moses, of Kozlov/New York (1896–8 *Tishri* 1971) – Son of R. Meir, he was born in Strelisk and studied under the rabbi of Brzezany. He married Shlomtze, daughter of R. Aaron Halpern of Brzezany. He lived for a time in Tarnopol.

He emigrated together with his father from Lvov to the United States in 1931. When his father died in 1942, he succeeded him as rebbe in Crown Heights, Brooklyn.

He published his grandfather's works *Ginzei Yosef* and *Semihat Hahamim*. He was a great bibliophile and amassed a valuable library. His son, R. Meir, who married *Hayyah*, the daughter of R. Shimon Grunberger, succeeded him.

ROKEAH, Shalom, of Belz (1783–27 *Elul* 1855) – Son of R. Eleazar, who died at the age of thirty-two being survived by three sons and two daughters. Shalom's mother married again, and the boy was brought up by his uncle R. Issachar Baer of Sokal. He was known as the "*Illui*" of Rava. He married Malkah, the daughter of R. Issachar Baer of Sokol. Every day before daybreak, Malkah would wake her husband with the words "Shalom! Arise for the service of the Creator!" He consulted his wife on almost every problem, and his example was followed by his hasidim. "They seemed like Adam and Eve before they sinned, and their room is like the *Gan Eden*," said R. Hayyim of Zanz.

Through R. Shlomoh of Lutzk, Shalom was drawn to Hasidism. He visited many of the leading hasidic rebbes of the day. While he appreciated the rare qualities of all the *tzaddikim* he met, he remained an ardent devotee of the "Seer" of Lublin. It was at the suggestion of the rabbi of Lublin that he became rabbi of Belz, where he remained for his last forty years.

People came to him from Galicia, from Hungary, and from Poland. Among his outstanding visitors were R. Hayyim of Zanz and R. Tzaddok Hakohen of Lublin. He is quoted in the halakhic responsa of R. Shlomoh Kluger of Brody and of R. Joseph Saul Nathanson. The high incidence of apostasy among the *maskilim* convinced him that *Haskalah* represented a danger to Judaism.

Toward the end of his life he became blind. In conformity with his wishes, no *ohel* was built over his grave.

He was survived by seven children, two daughters, Eidel and Freidel, and five sons, R. Eleazar, R. Shmuel Shmelke, R. Moses, R. Yehudah Zundel, and R. Joshua, who succeeded him as rebbe.

His discourses were collated by R. Abraham Hayyim Simhah Bunem Michelson in *Dover Shalom* (Przemysl, 1910).

M. E. Gutman, *Migdolei HaHasidut: R. Shalom MeBelz.*

ROKEAH, Shalom, of Opatov (27 *Elul* 1907–1944) – Son of R. Issachar Dov of Belz. His mother, Hayyah Devorah, was his father's second wife. On 11 *Shevat* 1928 he married Hannah, the daughter of R. Israel Perlow of Stolin. In 1931 he became rebbe of Opatov. He was an ascetic who ate only once daily, late at night.

When his father died he became his brother's hasid. During the Nazi period he lived in Belz, Drohobicz, and Stryj. He died in the forest from exposure and starvation. His children–Israel, Issachar Dov, and Havah–perished in the Holocaust.

ROKEAH, Shmuel, of Sokal (1851-16 *Tishri* 1912)–Eldest son of R. Joshua of Belz, he married Sarah, the only daughter of R. Menahem Mendel Hager of Vishnitz. In 1887 he became rabbi of Sokal, and, when his father died in 1894, he became rebbe. In 1908 he established a *yeshivah*. He was succeeded by his only son, R. Shalom.

ROMANIA–Republic in southeastern Europe, bounded on the north and northeast by the Ukraine, on the west by Hungary, and on the east by the Black Sea. Under the 1947 peace treaty, Transylvania was restored to Russia, and Russia retained Bessarabia and Bukovina.

The Besht himself spent much time in the Carpathian Mountains of Romania, and peasants even today point to the valley where he stayed. Hasidism, however, was introduced in Romania at the end of the eighteenth century by R. Hayyim Tyrer (1760-1818), who was rabbi in Kishinev and then in Czernowitz.

In 1806, Iasi invited R. Aryeh Leib ben Shalom Segal (d. 1813) to be its rabbi. R. Aryeh was a disciple of R. Dov Baer, the Maggid of Mezhirech, and by marriage a relative of the "Seer" of Lublin. He declined the position, however, since he was more interested to settle in the Holy Land. R. Yoske (d. 1807) took his place.

The inscription on his tombstone describes R. Joseph as "the most distinguished rabbi of his generation." On his death in 1808, R. Abraham Joshua Heschel of Opatov succeeded him as rabbi of Iasi. "My eyes and my heart," said the rabbi of Opatov, "roam the country, and all the slaughterers are under my supervision." When R. Abraham Joshua left Iasi, he was succeeded by another hasid, R. David Hakohen (d. 21 *Iyyar* 1828) of Zawalov.

R. Yitzhak of Radzwillov, the son of R. Yehiel Michael, the Maggid of Zloczov, was rabbi in Botosani and Falticeni. The followers of R. Shneur Zalman of Liady established a group in Romania under R. Israel Mosheh (d. 1861), and small *Habad* groups were formed in other localities.

Several Romanian rabbis joined the hasidic movement. Among them were R. Aaron Moses Taubes (1781-1852), R. Joseph Landau (1791-1853), and R. Isaiah Shor (d. 1879). Other Romanian scholars who were sympathetic to the movement were R. Hayyim Yitzhak Isaacson of Harlau, R. Yom Tov Lipman Landau (d. 1870) of Galati, and Michael Daniel (d. 1828), the head of the Jewish community of Iasi.

By the middle of the nineteenth century the Ruzhyn dynasty dominated Romanian life. The founder of the dynasty, R. Israel Friedman, spent his youth in Botosani and later settled in Sadgora, Bukovina. His sons established courts in Romania: R. Nahum in Stefanesti; R. Dov Baer in Husi; and R. Yitzhak in Bohusi and his descendants R. Abraham Joshua Heschel (d. 1940) in Adjud, R. Moses Leib (d. 1947) in Pascani, R. Shalom Halpern (d. 1940) in Vaslui, and R. Mordecai Zusya Twersky (d. 1939) in Iasi.

The descendants of R. Yehiel Michael of Zloczov settled in many parts of the country: R. Shmuel Yehiel (d. 1862) in Botosani and R. Barukh Rabinowicz (d. 1890) in Iasi. A grandson of R. Abraham David of Buczacz, R. Jacob Yitzhak Warman (d. 1885), lived in Falticeni, and R. Aaron of Linitz (d. 1878) moved in 1868 to Podul-Illoaei, where he established his court.

R. Eliezer Zeev Rabin (d. 1852) made his home in Buczacz, near Botosani. His son, R. Joseph Aaron, was the author of *Yad Yosef* (Klausenburg, 1926). Another dynasty was that of R. Uri Landman (d. 1917), a descendant of R. Uri of Strelisk. He made his home in Podul-Illoaei.

Descendants of R. Meir of Przemyshlan also settled in Romania. R. Yoel Moskowitz (d. 1880) settled in Bukovina, R. Alter Aaron Moskowitz (d. 1911) in Podul-Illoaei, and R. Joseph Mordecai Joseph Moses (d. 1929) in Sulitza. After World War I, R. Meir Gutman was rabbi in Iasi, and R. Abraham Yoski and R. Eliezer Hakohen Yolles lived in Bucharest. Among the scholars who wrote prolifically on Hasidism were Israel Berger (d. 1919) and Shalom Gutman.

The absence of strong hasidic leadership in Romania made the path of the *Haskalah* easy. Even a number of hasidic descendants were influenced by the new trend. R. Menahem Nahum Friedman of Izkani wrote philosophical works, and R. David Twersky became a painter. The son of Abraham Heschel of Adjud was an author. "Hasidism in Romania," wrote Aaron Gutman in 1933, "is like a coin which has lost its shape and has no real influence on the religious life of the Jewish community."

After the Holocaust, the surviving hasidic rebbes left Romania for Israel and the United States. Today, not a single hasidic rabbi lives in Romania.

Y. Alfasi, *HaHasidut BeRumania*.

Y.A.

ROPCZYCE, Naftali Tzvi Horowitz (6 *Sivan* 1760–11 *Iyyar* 1827) – He was born in Lesniov, the son of R. Menahem Mendel Rubin. His mother, Beila, was the daughter of R. Yitzhak of Hamburg. At first, Naftali studied under his father, and later in the *yeshivah* of his uncle R. Meshullam Igra of Tysmenice. At the age of eighteen, Naftali married Rebecca, the daughter of R. Zeev Velvel Stokes of Brody. This marriage, however, ended in divorce. On the advice of the Maggid of Kozienice, he married the daughter of R. Tzvi Hirsch Goldhammer, a wine merchant of Dukla. Naftali quickly made a name for himself as a brilliant speaker and his bons mots spread far and wide.

He became a disciple of R. Elimelekh of Lejask, the Maggid of Zloczov, R. Menahem Mendel of Rymanov, and the "Seer" of Lublin. On R. Menahem Mendel's advice he became rabbi of Ropczyce, a town in the province of Rzeszov. Upon the death of his father on Simhat Torah 1814, he succeeded him as rabbi of Linsk. At the same time he also served as rabbi of Stryszov.

R. Naftali opposed the rise of Napoleon. He feared that the success of the French Revolution would be disastrous for the Jews of Poland, who would be conscripted into the army and forced to attend secular schools. A follower of the school of Przysucha, he nonetheless opposed unnecessary delay in the recitation of the statutory prayers. He set a high standard for his followers: "The main aim of a hasid," he said, "is to study Torah diligently, at least until the age of twenty-five. Only then should Hasidism be studied."

He also urged his followers to study the works of *Musar*. At *shalosh seudot* he started *Barukh HaShem yom yom* at the verse *Be Vo'o MeEdom* (when he came from Edom). He would sound the *shofar* on *Hoshanah Rabba*. On 8 *Tishri*, he would recite the Psalms twice. Women were permitted to eat in R. Naftali's *sukkah*, and they would sit in the same room at the Passover *seder*.

His discourses were recorded in *Zera Kodesh* – part one on the Torah and part two on the Festivals and the Aggada. *Zera Kodesh* was first published in Lvov in 1868. His second work, *Ayalah Sheluhah*, on Genesis and Exodus, was printed in Lvov in 1863. His third work, *Imrei Sheffer*, on the Torah, was printed in Lvov in 1884. *Ohel Naftali* (Lvov, 1911), edited by R. Abraham Hayyim Simhah Michelson, contains many of R. Naftali's stories.

He died and was buried in Lancut near Rzeszov. He was survived by three sons. His eldest son, R. Abraham Hayyim became rabbi of Linsk (d. 28 *Av* 1831). His second son, R. Jacob (d. 19 *Tevet* 1839), became rabbi of Mielec. His third son, R. Eliezer (d. 3 *Heshvan* 1860), became rabbi of Dzikov. His successor, however, was his son-in-law, R. Asher Yeshayahu Rubin, the author of *Or Yishai* (Lvov, 1876).

S. Tal, *R. Naftali Tzvi MiRopczyce*.

M.W.

ROSEN, Eliyahu Hayyim, of Jerusalem (1899–1984) – Born in Polutsk, he lived in Uman for twenty-two years. He was arrested by the Russians in November 1935. In 1937, he emigrated to Jerusalem, where he was involved in the construction of the Bratzlav synagogue in Jerusalem.

ROSENBAUM, David Moses, of Kretchnif (Crachunesti) (11 *Tishri* 1922–15 *Tammuz* 1969) – Son of R. Eliezer Zeev, he was born in Kretchnif. He survived the Holocaust. In Bucharest in 1946, he married Esther Rachel, the daughter of the rabbi of Nadvorna. He emigrated to the Holy Land, where, for a short time, he lived in Jerusalem. In 1948, he settled in Rehovot, where he established a *yeshivah Shaarei Eliezer* and a *kollel*, a home for senior citizens, and a *shikkun* for fifty religious families. In 1969, he went to visit his grandfather's grave in Romania. He died suddenly in Bucharest at the age of forty-seven and was buried in Rehovot.

He was survived by seven sons and seven daughters. His son R. Menahem Eliezer Zeev succeeded him in Rehovot, and another son, R. Israel Nissan, is rebbe in Kiryat Gat, and now in New York.

His biography, *HaRabbi BeYisrael*, was published in Rehovot in 1971. His discourses can be found in *Arba Arazim* (Bene Berak, 1967).

ROSENBAUM, Eliezer Zeev, of Karassonfalu (1882–28 *Iyyar* 1944)–Son of R. Meir, he married the daughter of R. Nissan of Husakov. For ten years he lived in Nadvorna. In 1908, he succeeded his father as rebbe of Kretchnif. He specialized in giving prescriptions, which were accepted by the pharmacists. After World War I he settled in Sighet. He was murdered by the Nazis.

His discourses are to be found *Raza D'Shabbat* (Jerusalem, 1967), *Arba Arazim* (Bene Berak, 1967), and *Raza D'Uvda* (Jerusalem, 1971).

All his children–R. Nissan Hayyim, R. Shmuel Shmelke, R. Meir, and R. Mordecai–became rebbes. His youngest son, R. David Moses, was rabbi of Kretshineff in Rehovot.

ROSENBAUM, Hayyim Mordecai, of Nadvorna/Bene Berak (24 *Iyyar* 1904–15 *Tevet* 1977)–Son of R. Ittamar, he was born in Czernowitz. He married his cousin, the daughter of R. Eliezer Zeev of Kretchnif. At the age of twenty-five, he became rebbe and settled in Seret, Bukovina.

During World War II he spent three years in Nazi concentration camps in Transnistra. In 1948 he emigrated to the Holy Land and lived in Jaffa for ten years. He then moved to Bene Berak, where he established a *yeshivah Maamar Mordecai*.

One of his sons, R. Yitzhak Yehudah Yehiel Eizig, was killed, in 1946, at the age of seventeen, when he tried to reach the Holy Land on the illegal ship *Knesset Yisrael*. The rebbe was succeeded by another son, R. Jacob Issachar Baer. He left a manuscript *Divrei Hayyim* on Torah.

His two sons-in-law are R. Tzvi Rosenbaum of *Kefar Ata* and R. Eliezer Zeev of *Ramat Gan*.

Der Yid, December 30, 1977.

ROSENBAUM, Issachar Baer, of New York (24 *Elul* 1904–1981)–Born in Czernowitz, he was the second son of R. Ittamar. At the age of nineteen, he married the daughter of R. Betzey of Satmar, and when she died, he married the daughter of R. Eliezer Weinberger.

In 1928, he became rebbe in Strosnitz, Bukowina.

After the war, he emigrated to the United States, where he first lived in the Bronx, then in Williamsburg, Brooklyn, and from 1960, in Borough Park, where he established a *Bet HaMidrash Shaar Hashamayim*. He was a diligent scholar who completed the Talmud seven times.

He was buried on the Mount of Olives. He was survived by four sons and was succeeded by the eldest, R. Asher Mordecai of Cleveland.

Der Yid, January 9, 1981.

ROSENBAUM, Ittamar, of Nadvorna/Tel Aviv (*Tammuz* 1886–22 *Sivan* 1973)–Son of R. Meir of Kretchnif (Crachunesti), he was born in Minhaileni, Romania. In 1900, he married Malkah, the daughter of R. Asher Yeshayahu of Kolbuszov. He studied under his father. When his father died in 1902, Ittamar's elder brother succeeded him.

After living in Vienna and Marmaros during the First World War, R. Ittamar settled in Czernowitz. After the Second World War, he went to live in Crown Heights, in Brooklyn, New York.

In 1969, he emigrated to Israel and made his home in Yad Eliyahu, Tel Aviv. His son R. Yitzhak Eizig, the Zutska rebbe, who had lived in Borough Park since 1962, took over his father's *Bet HaMidrash* in Tel Aviv, now in Bene Berak. His other sons are R. Hayyim Mordecai, rebbe of Nadvorna in Bene Berak; R. Issachar Baer of Strosnitz in New York (d. 1981), and R. Asher Yeshaya in Hadera. His son-in-law is R. Abraham Abba Leifer in Ashdod.

ROSENBAUM, Meir, of Kretchnif (1852–1 *Tammuz* 1908)–Son of R. Mordecai Leifer of Nadvorna. It was R. Meir who changed his surname to Rosenbaum. He married the daughter of R. Yehiel of Durohi and lived in Iasi for ten years. After his father's death in 1895, he established his court in Kretchnif, near Sighet. He was renowned for his miracles and his *kamayot*.

ROSENBAUM, Nissan Hayyim (1899–19 *Kislev* 1942)–The eldest son of R.

Eliezer Zeev. He married the daughter of R. Tzvi Hirsch Reiman, the rabbi of Kretchnif, where he lived for six years. He became rabbi of Bursztyn. His discourses on the Sabbath lasted four hours.

He was killed by the Nazis. His son R. Tzvi Hirsch miraculously escaped death in Auschwitz and Buchenwald and settled in Kefar Ata. He published his grandfather's book, *Raza DeShabbat* (Jerusalem, 1969). R. Nissan's discourses are printed in *Torat Hayyim VeEmunah* (Jerusalem, 1976) and in *Seder Hakkafot LeShmini Atzeret* (Jerusalem, 1988). His son R. Nissan is the son-in-law of R. Zusya Twersky, the rabbi of Chernobyl of Bene Berak.

ROSENBERG, Yehudah Yudil (1860–1939), author – Born in Radom into a well-known rabbinic family, he studied in Lublin and became *dayan* in Warsaw, then in Lodz. In 1912, he settled in Toronto.

He edited a rabbinical periodical, *Kol Torah*, and translated the *Zohar* into Hebrew (Montreal, 1924). This received the approval of many hasidic authorities. He edited a large collection of stories, *Tiferet Maharil* (Piotrokov, 1914), on R. Yehudah Leib of Shpole.

ROSENBLATT, Yosele (1882–1933), cantor and composer – Born in the Ukraine, his family lived for a time in Sadgora, where he was influenced by the hasidic court. His liturgical chants, records, and compositions show not only the unusual quality of his voice but also his hasidic *hitlahavut*. Many hasidim in Europe and the United States flocked to his concerts.

S. Rosenblatt, *Yosele Rosenblatt*.

ROSENFELD, Eleazar Halevi, of Auschwitz (10 *Nisan* 1862–7 *Av* 1942) – Son of R. Joshua, he was born in Kaminka. He married Fradel, the daughter of R. Hayyim Halberstam of Zanz, in 1878. In 1888, he became rabbi in Bochnia, then in Kaminka, and in 1897 in Auschwitz. He visited the Holy Land in 1936 and established a *Bet HaMidrash* in Mea Shearim, Jerusalem.

He returned to Poland before the outbreak of the Second World War and died in the ghetto of Chrzanov.

His sons were R. Hayyim Alexander, R. Shalom Reuven, and R. Naftali Shmuel Tzvi Hirsch.

ROSENFELD, Joshua, of Kaminka (1830–7 *Heshvan* 1897) – Only son of R. Shalom of Kaminka. He married Sheindel, the daughter of R. Shmuel Tzvi Hirsch. He was very stringent in his observances. When his daughter Yente became an *agunah*, it affected him so much that, for thirteen years from 1884, he never uttered a word. Only the recitation of *Kiddush* and the blessings of the Hanukkah candles were audible.

He was survived by his sons, R. Shalom and R. Eleazar. His daughter Rebecca Henie married R. Shlomoh Halberstam of Bobov.

ROSENFELD, Shalom, of Kaminka (1853–1930) – Son of R. Joshua, whom he succeeded as rebbe in 1897. He married Beila, the daughter of R. Abraham Horowitz.

His seven sons all became rebbes: R. Naftali Shmuel in Kaminka, R. Hayyim Jacob in Lvov, R. Yitzhak in Rzeszov, R. Menahem Mendel in Bystrzyca, R. Moses Aryeh in Moshciska, R. Reuven, *dayan* of Kaminka, and R. Aaron David in Borisov.

ROSENFELD, Shalom Halevi, of Kaminka (1800–20 *Heshvan* 1852) – Son of R. Jacob Joseph of Rawa, he was known as an "*Illui*." When he was very young, his father took him to meet the "Seer" of Lublin. He studied under R. Shlomoh Kluger. He married Hannah Goldah, the daughter of R. Naftali Tzvi Hirsch.

At the age of twenty-two he became rabbi in Jaryczov Nowy, and then, in 1837, in Kaminka. He was a great adherent of R. Naftali of Ropczyce and R. Shalom of Belz. He was the author of *Ohev Shalom* (Brooklyn, 1983).

His only surviving son, R. Joshua, succeeded him.

ROSENHEIM, Jacob (1870–1965), Orthodox leader – Born in Frankfurt-am-Main, he was apprenticed to a bank, then founded the Hermon publishing house and was responsible for the publication of the *Israelit*. He was active in Freie Vereinigung fuer die Interessen des orthodoxen Judentums, which was founded by R. Samson Raphael Hirsch in 1886. He was also the founder of the *Agudat Yisrael*, which was established in Kattowitz in 1912.

From 1940, he lived in the United States, spending the last years of his life in Israel. He worked in close harmony with the hasidic rebbes, especially R. Abraham Mordecai Alter and R. Israel Alter. In 1929 the title of "Morenu" was awarded to him by the second *Knessiah Gedolah* in Vienna.

Some of his essays were translated into English: *Tents of Jacob* (1957) and *Samson Raphael Hirsch's Cultural Ideals* (1951). A collection of his *Memoirs: Erinnerungen, 1870–1920* was published in 1970.

H. Schwab, *Jacob Rosenheim.*

ROSENZWEIG, Franz (1886–1929)– One of the most seminal of the Jewish philosophers of the twentieth century. Much to the scandal of his very assimilated secularized German Jewish parents, his desire to get to the spiritual roots of European culture with which, like them, he identified prompted him to go one step further than they had and to convert to Christianity–with one proviso, however: reluctant to reject his Jewish identity, he wanted to convert as a Jew.

In preparation for conversion, he attended a Yom Kippur service at the semi-hasidic Potsdammer Strasse synagogue in Berlin, where he felt the presence of a personal God. Ever after, he looked back to that particular Yom Kippur as the beginning of a personal self-transformation, for what was sin but a certain distancing from God, whereas Yom Kippur provided the opportunity of closing the gap.

In September 1914, Rosenzweig joined the Red Cross and worked in German-occupied Belgium as a nurse, volunteering in 1915 for the regular army. He wrote to a cousin that he had experienced so much in 1913 (the year of the fateful Yom Kippur) that the war meant little to him. His experience in the Balkans and on the Eastern Front afforded him the opportunity to come into contact with Sephardic and hasidic culture.

In his "letters from the trenches," he points to the smug snobbism on the part of those in German Jewry vis-à-vis their "primitive" Polish hasidic brethren as one of their most shameful traits. On May 23, 1918, he wrote to his mother that, although in Germany he had tended to see the negative aspects of being a member of a "stiff-necked" set of "degenerate parvenus," among the poor hasidic Jews of Eastern Europe for the first time he began to see being a Jew as a positive–"a unique nation on earth." Whereas the hasidim were the real Jews, German Jewry was only a pretentious imitation of their very bourgeois German neighbors. In the children in particular, as products of the *heder*'s educational system, he glimpsed what he called the "total Jew":

> The young Jewish boys are magnificent, and I felt something I rarely feel, pride in my race, in so much freshness and vivacity. Driving through the town, too, I was impressed by the masses of Jews. Their costume is really very attractive and so is their language (*van vannen kimmen zey*?). . . . I can well understand why the average German Jew no longer feels any kinship with these East European Jews: actually he has very little such kinship left: he has become philistine, bourgeois; but I, and people like me should still feel the kinship strongly.

Rosenzweig comments on the comprehensiveness of Yiddish education in the Polish *heder* system in contrast to the fragmented human being turned out by the West European model. "German city children are essentially proletarians without tradition, without substance, and hence without imagination. Here the five-year-olds already live in a context of three thousand years." Through the *heder* the Jewish nation constantly renewed itself and did not need war or crisis to make it feel its identity as a nation.

Rosenzweig's famous Lehrhaus–which he founded with the support some of the most illustrious members of the German Jewish intelligentsia of varying degrees of affiliation to Judaism, such as Martin Buber, Erich Fromm, Ernst Simon, R. N. Nobel, Gershom Scholem, and Nahum Glatzer–was an attempt to adapt this model to the German Jewish temperament. What he took from the Polish *heder* was the idea that instead of one pedagogue's lecturing "about" Judaism, people of all degrees of Jewish and secular learning simply study together the authentic Jewish sources.

On 28 May, 1918, Rosenzweig wrote to his mother that he had visited a hasidic *shteibel* on *Shabbat*. First, he was struck by the purely masculine character of the place. The singing during *seudah shlishit* (the third meal) impressed him most of all: "I have never heard anything like it. These people don't need an organ; with their surging enthusiasm, the voices of children and old men blended." His mother would find some of these songs analyzed in an academic journal, *Ost und West*. He certainly could not agree with the view of those sophisticates who regarded this style of worship as a decadent version of the Hasidism of 150 years before. Such prayer was eternal, and those who thought differently did not know what prayer was!

In 1918, he began to produce his major work, *The Star of Redemption*, which he wrote on postcards sent home to his mother from the various trenches, outposts, trains, and hospitals where he was posted. The *Star* was published in 1921.

As a soldier, Rosenzweig suffered the first twinges of the illness that killed him. In 1920 he married; in 1921 the disease was diagnosed; and by 1922 he was no longer able to talk or to get about. His physical confinement only helped him to become more observant. His colleagues and disciples formed a *minyan* (a quorum of ten) to pray and learn by his bedside, and R. Leo Baeck had him ordained as a rabbi. A machine was constructed that helped his wife to decipher his wishes and take down his thoughts as he continued his literary activities. On his sickbed Rosenzweig carried out many translations from Hebrew into German, including the poems of Yehudah Halevi and, with Martin Buber, a new translation of the Bible. In 1922, too, his son, Rafael Nehemiah, was ushered into the covenant of Israel.

In 1923, the disease was halted. Where before Rosenzweig had looked forward to a speedy death, he now had to adjust to life as a total paralytic. But about him there was a harmonious and creative atmosphere like that of a contemporary *tzaddik* (saint).

In December 1929 he was unable to finish a sentence to his wife: ". . . and now it comes, the point of all points which God had truly revealed to me in my sleep, the point of all points for which there. . . ." For Rosenzweig the moment of death was "the ultimate verification of life." And to his very last breath he was preoccupied with crystallizing the experience he was going through according to the hasidic mode!

At his request, there was no eulogy at his grave, but on his headstone was engraved Psalm 73:23: "Nevertheless, I am continually with Thee; Thou holdest my right hand."

Emotionally, the key experiences in Rosenzweig's spiritual life were Yom Kippur and death. Death prompted his philosophical revolution against idealism. For Rosenzweig, as for modern existentialism, death is at the crux of his philosophy. Unlike the idealists, Rosenzweig believed that being lost in some abstraction of the whole was no comfort. The worst thing of all was the fear that the "I" has of becoming an "it." Although only the single individual—the "I"—can die, at the stage of every emotion and every religious experience, as limited as they may be, only the single individual matters; for Rosenzweig as for Hasidism only through the lonely individual can revelation, redemption, and God enter in.

F. Rosenzweig, *The Star of Redemption*.

F.G.

ROSMAN, Murray J. (b. 1949), historian—Born in Chicago on July 4, he studied at the Jewish Theological Seminary, from which he received B.A., M.A., and Doctor of Philosophy degrees. He held academic positions at Bar-Ilan University, Hebrew University, and Tel Aviv University. He carried out archival research in Cracow, Warsaw, and Lublin.

He is the author of a number of learned articles on the history of Polish and Russian Jewry. In his study of *Medziborz* (in the *Shorter Encyclopedia Judaica* [Russian]), vol. 5; in "The Quest for the Historical *Ba'al Shem Tov*" (in *Tradition and Crisis Revisited* [Cambridge, MA: Harvard University Center for Jewish Studies]); and in "Social Conflicts in Medziborz in the Generation of the *Ba'al Shem Tov*" (in *Hasidism: A Reappraisal* [Oxford, Blackwell]), he proves that certain details in the accounts found in the *Shivhei HaBesht* are corroborated in Polish archival sources.

M. J. Rosman, "Medziborz and R. Israel Baal Shem Tov," pp. 177–189.

ROTH, Abraham Hayyim, of Bene Berak (b. 1924)—Son of R. Arele, he was born in Satmar and married Beila Hayyah, the daughter of R. Mordecai Goldman of Zevil. After the death of his father, he succeeded him and published many of his father's works. A man of immense compassion, he combines knowledge of human nature with a sense of humor.

He is planning a center in the Mea Shearim area of Jerusalem, where he intends to erect Torah institutions and apartments for his hasidim. Many of his father's followers, however, give their allegiance to his brother-in-law, and this has been a cause of friction between them.

The rabbi now lives in Bene Berak.

ROTH, Arele (1894–6 *Nisan* 1947), hasidic mystic – Son of R. Shmuel Jacob, he was born in Ungvar. At the age of nine, he was sent to study at the *yeshivah* of R. Joseph Rothenberg in Krasnoye. Later he attended *yeshivot* in Galicia, and for four years studied under R. Yeshayahu Zilberstein and R. Moses Forhand in Vaitzan in central Hungary.

During the First World War he lived in Hungary and befriended the rabbis who sought refuge in Budapest. Among them were R. Issachar Dov Rokeah of Belz, R. Israel Hager of Vishnitz, and, above all, R. Tzvi Elimelekh Spiro of Blazowa, who called R. Arele a "Good Jew" and urged him to become a rebbe.

After his marriage, at the age of twenty-two, to Sima, the daughter of R. Yitzhak Katz of Budapest, he lived for a time in Satmar and acquired a small group of followers. In 1925 he went to the Holy Land, where, in Jerusalem, he formed a hasidic group. In 1929, he returned for medical reasons to Satmar, where the "self-appointed rabbi" aroused much antagonism. He was forced to leave Satmar for Beregszaz (Beregovo), where he established a *yeshivah Shomrei Emunim*, which was supported by R. Hayyim Elazar Shapira of Munkacs, and in which eighty students studied.

In 1939, he returned to the Holy Land, where he established a close-knit community under the name *Toldot Aaron*. He was a strong opponent of Zionism. He stressed the importance of ecstatic prayer. He urged his followers to lead a disciplined life. He advocated asceticism and laid down meticulous rules governing the community's way of life: men were not allowed to shave their beard or trim their sidelocks; women were required to cut their hair after marriage and to keep their head covered with a kerchief.

He was a prolific writer and was the author of *Iggrot Shomrei Emunim* (Jerusalem, 1942); *Asifat Mikhtavim* (Des, 1943); fifty-two letters, *Derekh Tzaddikim* (Jerusalem, 1967); *Taharat HaKodesh* (Jerusalem, 1958); *Mevakesh Emunah* (Jerusalem, 1943); *Shomer Emunim* (Jerusalem, 1942); *Shulhan HaTohor* (Satmar, 1933, and Jerusalem, 1969); *Noam HaLevavot* (Satmar, 1934); and *Kuntres HaTzavaah* (Jerusalem, 1947).

He died in Jerusalem and was buried on the Mount of Olives. He was survived by his son, R. Abraham Hayyim, and by a daughter who married R. Abraham Yitzhak Kahan, who is his father-in-law's spiritual successor.

A. Roth, *Uvdah D'Aaron*.

ROTHENBERG, Asher Yeshayahu, of New York (d. 26 *Tishri* 1972) – Son of R. Moses Shmuel. He studied in the *yeshivah Torah VeYirah* of Satmar in Williamsburg, Brooklyn, and was the head of the *kollel Or Malei*. He married Sosha, the daughter of Issachar Berish Weiser. He was survived by his sons: R. Joseph Israel Tzvi, R. Mordecai, R. David Yehudah Leib, and R. Issachar Berish.

ROTHENBERG, Hayyim Shlomoh, of Maszokaszowy (1870–6 *Tevet* 1920) – Son of R. Joseph, he married Reiza, the daughter of R. Asher Yeshaya Rubin. From 1893 onward, he was rabbi of Nir Adani, Hungary, where he established a *yeshivah*. In 1906, when three of his children died, he moved to Debrecin, and in 1911 to Maszokaszowy.

Before his death he destroyed all his manuscripts except *Shemuah Tovah*, which was published in Brooklyn in 1943. He was succeeded by his son, R. Moses Shmuel, rabbi in New York and Bene Berak.

ROTHENBERG, Israel Tzvi Halevi, of Krasnoye (1890–3 *Sivan* 1944) – Son of R. Joseph, he was born on the fifth day of Sukkot. After the death of his brother, R. Hayyim Shlomoh, he became rebbe and head of the *yeshivah Ateret Yisrael*. He married Mindel, the daughter of R. Hayyim Shlomoh. His was a rigorously ascetic life, keyed to the rabbinic dictum "Take care of your soul, and the body will take care of itself."

When the Hungarian authorities began to organize labor battalions during the Second World War, he sheltered those who tried to evade conscription. He was sent to Auschwitz, where he and his son, Alter Hayyim Shlomoh, were murdered.

His discourses, which were discovered in Cracow after the war, are to be found in *Or Malei* (Brooklyn, 1957).

His wife, Mindel, his elder daughter, Alta Rechamah, and his daughter's husband, R. Yehudah Tzvi Eichenstein, together with their four small children, were murdered in Kamenetz-Podolsk in *Elul* 1941.

ROTHENBERG, Issachar Dov, of New York (d. 1986) – Son-in-law of R. Shalom Moskowitz of Shatz, whose daughter Malkah he married in London. He lived in London for a time and had a *Bet HaMidrash* in Stamford Hill. Later he settled in New York, where he became a leading figure in the Satmar community.

He published the works of his father-in-law – *Hagaot Daat Shalom* on *Orah Hayyim* (Jerusalem, 1958) and *Daat Shalom* on the Pentateuch (Brooklyn, 1979).

ROTHENBERG, Joseph Halevi, of Krasnoye (3 Av 1853–23 *Heshvan* 1912) – He was born in Halicz, the son of R. Tzvi Hirsch. He married Sarah Yitel, the daughter of R. Meshullam Feivish Halevi of Nyirtass. He was a follower of the rebbes of Belz, Zydaczov, Dynov, and Komarno. He was ordained by R. Joseph Benjamin Reich of Halicz.

After living in Debrecin for three years, he became, in 1898, rabbi of Krasnoye, where he established a hasidic dynasty.

He was the author of *Benei Shileshim* (Savalive, 1913), *Vayizbor Yosef* (Munkacs, 1915), a commentary on the Passover *Haggadah* (Brooklyn, 1978), and *Benei Shileshim* on Hanukkah (Brooklyn, 1979).

He was succeeded by his son, R. Hayyim Shlomoh.

ROTHENBERG, Meir Halevi, of Stavnitz/Opatov (d. 25 *Tammuz* 1827) – He was at first rabbi in Stavnitz, then in Opatov. He was a disciple of the "Seer" of Lublin. He was a great protagonist of the school of Przysucha. He married the daughter of R. Joseph David Zeidman and was the author of *Or LaShamayim* (Lvov, 1850).

ROTHENBERG, Pinhas Eliyahu, of Pilice (1820–1903) – Son of R. Joseph and a brother of R. Yitzhak Meir Alter of Ger. He was born in Yanova and married Deborah, the daughter of R. Elijah of Piotrokov. He was a disciple of R. Hanokh of Alexander, and when R. Yehiel Danziger left Pilice for Alexandrov in 1876, he succeeded the former as rebbe.

ROTSTEIN, Samuel (1900–1977), writer – Son of R. Mordecai Nissan, who died in the Warsaw ghetto in 1942, Samuel was, before World War II, editor of the *Yiddishe Togblatt*. He was the author of *The Kodesh of Tirna* (Lodz, 1925), *Malkhusdige Hasidut* (Warsaw, 1927), and biographies of *The "Seer" of Lublin* (Warsaw, 1939), *Ger* (Warsaw, 1936), and *Sarah Schenierer* (Tel Aviv, 1965).

RUBIN, Abraham Dov, of Lancut/New York (1887–21 *Elul* 1963) – Son of R. Eliezer Rubin, a descendant of R. Menahem Mendel of Linsk. Abraham Dov was born in Lancut, Galicia. His mother was descended from R. Tzvi Elimelekh Spiro. His father died when he was a young boy, and he was brought up by his grandfather R. Simhah Shapira, the rabbi of Lancut, and R. Abraham Mordecai of Mosciska.

In 1906, he married Toba Hayyah, the daughter of R. Shalom Rubin of Rzeszov. He was rebbe in Rzeszov until 1928, and in 1929, he emigrated to the United States and established a *Bet HaMidrash Bet HaKenesset Lancut* in New York.

His son, R. Shalom (b. 1927), is the rabbi of the *Young Israel* congregation in the Bronx.

RUBIN, Abraham Joshua Heschel, of Safed (1825–30 *Tishri* 1909) – Son of R. Elimelekh of Sokolov, he married the daughter of R. Shmuel Zanvil Bindiger. He served as rabbi in Sokolov; then in Yaslo, near Rzeszov; and finally settling in Safed in 1890 and becoming attached to the Zanz *Bet HaMidrash*.

It is noteworthy that he served each of these communities for a period of nineteen years. His son R. Yitzhak succeeded him in

Safed, and another son, R. Tzvi Joseph, in Jaslo.

RUBIN, Aryeh Leibish, of Cieszanov (1881–26 *Iyyar* 1942) – Son of R. Yitzhak Tuviah, he was born in Nowy Sacz. His mother was Nehamah, the daughter of R. Hayyim Halberstam. He was a disciple of R. Shlomoh Uri Keller of Zanz. At the age of seventeen, he married Hannah Rachel, the daughter of R. Simhah Issachar Baer of Cieszanov. He was ordained by R. Meir Arik and R. Shmuel Engel of Radomysl. In 1914 he succeeded his father-in-law as rabbi in Cieszanov, and during World War One he lived in Budapest for five years. He returned to Cieszanov in 1919, and in 1923 he moved to Tomaszov Lubelski.

During the Second World War, he and his son R. Meir escaped to Siberia, where they died. His widow and his other children settled in the United States after the war. His son R. Shalom Ezekiel is rabbi of Cieszanov in Brooklyn; another son, R. Simhah Issachar Baer, is rabbi of Tomaszov in Brooklyn; and his daughter, Freda, is the wife of R. Shlomoh Halberstam of Bobov.

RUBIN, Asher Yeshaya, of Tukoi (1919–29 *Tevet* 1945) – Born in Szaszregen, on the eve of Passover, the son of R. Jacob Israel Vishurun. In 1938 he married his cousin Hayyah Fria, the daughter of his uncle R. Meir Joseph Rubin, the rebbe of Bodragkeztur. He was ordained by R. Jonathan Steif of Budapest. He became rabbi in Tukoi.

He, his wife, his daughters, and his father-in-law were taken to Auschwitz by the Nazis. From there he was taken to a labor camp, but he died from exhaustion on the way. The other members of his family died in Auschwitz.

His discourses are to be found in *Sheerit Barukh* (New York, 1974) and in *Zera Kodesh Matzavto* (New York, 1974).

RUBIN, Asher Yeshaya, of Kolbuszov (1846–21 *Elul* 1914) – Son of R. Yehiel, rabbi of Kolbuszov. His father died when he was fourteen years old, and his mother insisted that no appointment be made before her son reached maturity. He was brought up by his grandfather R. Yitzhak Eizig of Komarno, and he married Hannah Shifrah, the eldest daughter of R. Alexander Safrin.

All his life was spent in controversy over the succession, but this did not disturb his way of life. He would rise at five o'clock in the morning and spend his entire day in prayer and study. His sons-in-law were R. Barukh Pinhas Rabinowicz of Skola, R. Menahem Mendel Rubin of Kolbuszov, R. Ittamar Rosenbaum of Nadvorna, and R. Hayyim Shlomoh Rothenberg of Maszokaszowy.

RUBIN, Asher Yeshaya, of Ropczyce (1775–14 *Nisan* 1845) – He was born in Warsaw, the son of a tailor, Eliezer Lipman. His mother was the daughter of R. Asher, the rabbi of Narol. He visited the "Seer," the Maggid of Kozienice, R. Mendele of Rymanov, and the rebbe of Opatov. On the advice of the "Seer," he married Reiza, the only daughter of R. Naftali of Ropczyce, whose surname he assumed.

Although R. Naftali had three sons, he chose his son-in-law as his successor, and for eighteen years, from 1827, R. Asher Yeshaya was rebbe of Ropczyce.

His work *Or Yisha* on Torah and Festivals was first printed in Lvov in 1876 and was subsequently reprinted many times. His son R. Manasseh succeeded him in Ropczyce. His other sons were R. Aaron, rabbi in Rymanov, R. Elimelekh, rabbi in Sokolov, R. Menahem Mendel, rabbi in Glogov, and R. Yehiel, rabbi in Kolbuszov.

RUBIN, Barukh, of Szamosujaar (8 *Adar* II 1864–30 *Kislev* 1936) – Son of R. Meir of Glogov, he was born in Dombrova, Galicia. He married Sarah Shlomze, the daughter of R. Menahem Mendel Eichenstein. He lived with his in-laws in Nikolayev. In 1894, he became rabbi of Brzozdowce, Galicia, and afterward lived in Kolomyja. During the First World War he moved to Gherla, Transylvania, where he lived for eighteen years.

He had a fine hasidic library and was a prolific writer, but all his manuscripts were destroyed in the Holocaust. He is, however, mentioned in the responsa of R. S. Engel and R. A. N. Steinberg. Only one volume survived: *She'erit Barukh* on the Pentateuch, printed in *Or Yishai* (New York, 1974).

His erudite wife settled in Mea Shearim, Jerusalem, prior to the outbreak of the Second World War, where she accepted *kvittlech* and delivered learned discourses to pious women. She was a frequent visitor to the grave of Rachel. She died on 20 *Tishri* 1946 and was buried on the Mount of Olives.

Their children were R. Jacob Israel Yeshurun of Szaszregen and R. Meir Joseph of Szamosujaar; the latter's daughter, Mirel Gala, married R. Tzvi Hirsch Kahana of Spinka.

RUBIN, Elimelekh, of Jaslo (1853–20 *Heshvan* 1905)–Son of R. Yitzhak of Brody, his mother was Edel Raza, the daughter of R. Shalom of Belz. As a very young boy he became blind, but the disability did not prevent him from gaining a thorough mastery of rabbinics or from leading a normal life. His activities were the talk of Galicia. He even officiated at the reader's desk on the High Holy Days.

When his father died, he became rebbe of Shebarshin, and in 1890, he settled in Bibrov, Galicia. He married Hannah, the daughter of R. Jacob Moses Feivish of Hivniv. Their son R. Shragai Feivish succeeded him. Another son, R. Yitzhak, settled in New York.

RUBIN, Hanokh Heinokh Dov, of Sasov/London (1889–13 *Tammuz* 1929)–Son of R. Eleazar, he was born in Sasov. His mother was the daughter of R. Shlomoh of Sasov. He married Devorah, the daughter of R. Menahem Eichenstein. He studied under R. Manasseh of Rzeszov.

During World War I he lived in Lvov, and in 1924 he settled in London. His genuine piety and true humility made him an object of veneration.

He died at the age of forty and was buried in Enfield, in London. He had three sons. His son R. Simhah succeeded him.

RUBIN, Hayyim Yehiel, of Dabrova (23 *Nisan* 1854–1918)–He was the son of R. Meir of Glogov. He married Devorah, the daughter of R. Alexander Sender Lippa Eichenstein. He was first rabbi of Limno; later he succeeded his grandfather as rebbe in Dabrova.

He died in Berlin. His sons became rebbes: R. Issachar Berish in Berlin and New York, R. Yitzhak Eizig in Sighet, and R. Eleazar in Drohobycz.

RUBIN, Hono Tzvi Hirsch, of Zanz (1894–1944)–Son of R. Naftali of Vishnitz, he married Echsa, the daughter of R. Yehiel Nathan Halberstam, but there were no children. He was rabbi in Satmar for many years, and in 1934, he settled in Old Zanz. He was murdered in Auschwitz.

RUBIN, Issachar Berish, of New York (1893–28 *Av* 1962)–He was born in Dabrova, the son of R. Hayyim Yehiel. He was ordained by R. Shmuel Furher, the rabbi of Krasni. In 1915, he settled in Berlin, where he lived for twenty-four years. Known as the rebbe of Dabrova, he was the spiritual guide of the Polish refugees. In 1919, he married Hayyah, the daughter of R. Naftali Bindiger-Weinberger. When she died, he married Hannah Sarah, the daughter of R. Issachar Baer Shapira.

In 1939, he emigrated to the United States, making his home in New York. He managed to rescue a number of his father's manuscripts. He had nine children: five daughters and four sons.

RUBIN, Jacob Israel Vishurun, of Szaszregen (1 *Tevet* 1884–15 *Sivan* 1944)–He was born in Zydaczov, the elder son of R. Barukh. He married Leah Rachel, the daughter of R. Mordecai Joseph Moses Moskowitz of Sulitza. He settled in Szaszregen in 1918 and became the head of the *Bet Din*. When his wife died in 1910, leaving him with one daughter, Hannah, he married, two years later, the daughter of R. Hayyim Dachner of Seret.

In 1916, he was held captive by the Russians. Through the intervention of the Emperor Franz Joseph, he was exchanged for a Romanian captive.

When the rabbi was taken to Auschwitz, he urged his fellow inmates to "eat to live, eat to survive." He himself perished there, but his son R. Menahem Mendel, now of Brooklyn, saved his father's notes in the margin of his *Shulhan Arukh*. These were published under the title *Sefer Gilyoni Yosher* (Jerusalem, 1973).

His other sons who survived the Holocaust were R. Shmuel Shmelke, the rabbi of Sulitza in Far Rockaway, New York, and R.

Mordecai David, the rebbe of Szaszregen in Brooklyn.

RUBIN, Joseph David, of Sasov/New York (1896–5 *Adar* 1983) – Son of R. Eleazar of Sasov, he was brought up in the home of his grandfather R. Shlomoh. He married Sosha, the daughter of R. Naftali Horowitz. From 1933 he was rebbe of Sasov of *Agudat Eleazar* congregation in New York.

He was the author of *Atzei Levanon* (Lvov, 1928) and *Ahavat Torah*, discourses in Yiddish on Torah and Festivals (New York, 1942).

He was survived by his son, R. Shalom Eleazar.

Der Yid, March 11, 1983, p. 50.

RUBIN, Joseph Meir, of Mihalyfalva (1914–21 *Sivan* 1945) – Son of R. Jacob Israel Vishurun, he married Esther, the daughter of R. Hayyim Moskowitz of Gliniany, and became rabbi of Mihalyfalva.

He died after being liberated from Teresienstadt. He was reburied in Tiberias on 6 *Heshvan* 1965. His wife and his two daughters, Hayyah Reiza and Menuhah, perished in the Holocaust.

RUBIN, Manasseh, of Ropczyce (1795–1861) – The eldest son of R. Asher Yeshaya of Ropczyce, whom he succeeded. He was a disciple of R. Tzvi Hirsch of Rymanov. He was the author of *Lehem Shemanoh* (Lvov, 1876). His daughter, Sarah, married R. Yitzhak Marilles, who succeeded him.

RUBIN, Meir, of Glogov (4 *Heshvan* 1830–30 *Tishri* 1898) – He was born in Ropczyce, the son of R. Menahem Mendel of Glogov. In 1848, he married Mirel Geula, the daughter of R. Joseph Ungar of Dabrova, where he succeeded his father-in-law. When fire destroyed his home, including many priceless books and manuscripts, he moved to Rzeszov, where he died.

His sons were R. Hayyim Yehiel, rabbi in Dabrova; R. Shalom, rabbi in Rzeszov; R. Yitzhak Tuviah, rabbi in Zanz; and R. Barukh, rabbi in Brzodowa.

RUBIN, Menahem Mendel, of Glogov (1806–30 *Elul* 1873) – Son of R. Asher Yeshaya of Ropczyce, he was brought up by his grandfather R. Naftali. He married Havah Esther, the daughter of R. Meir Rothenberg of Opatov. He became rabbi in Glogov in 1845.

He was highly esteemed by his contemporaries, and R. Hayyim of Zanz called him "the Holy Light of Israel." He would write copious notes on the books he was studying, and one such annotated volume is in the possession of R. Menahem Mendel Rubin of Brooklyn.

His work *Likkutei Maharam* was printed in *Or Yishai* (Lvov, 1869).

His children were R. Meir, R. Jakob Joseph, R. Asher Yeshaya, and R. Joshua.

RUBIN, Menahem Mendel, of New York (b. 1922) – Son of R. Jacob Israel Vishurun, he was born in Szaszregen, and in 1944 he married Hannah, the daughter of R. Hayyim Meir Yehiel Moses of Mielec. Both he and his wife were sent to Nazi death camps. The rabbi was liberated by the Americans and his wife by the Russians. After liberation, he established a *yeshivah* in Krumbach, Bavaria, with the help of the American general Lucius D. Clay.

In 1948 he settled in Brooklyn, where he established a community *Yaakov Yisrael Vishurun*. He devoted himself to educational activities, and for twenty years he was the head of the *Torah VeYirah D'Satmar* educational committee. He is also active in conserving the graves of his ancestors in Lancut and Ropczyce.

He is the author of *Minhat Yeshurun* (Brooklyn, 1968).

RUBIN, Shmuel Shmelke, of Sulitza/New York (b. 21 *Adar* 1925) – Son of R. Jacob Israel Vishurun, he was born in Szaszregen. During the Nazi era, he was incarcerated in many camps and was eventually liberated by the Russians in 1945. He was ordained by R. Hillel Lichtenstein, R. Yitzhak Zeev Sofer, and R. Nahman Kahana. After working in the liberated camp Fernwald under R. Amram Grunwald, he settled in 1949 in New York as the rabbi of Sulitza and married Shifrah, the daughter of R. Issachar Baer Rosenbaum of Stroznitz.

He established the congregation *Kehillat Yaakov* in Far Rockaway. He also established a *yeshivah Tiferet Kehillat Yaakov*, named in memory of his father, in Jerusalem. His son,

R. Jacob Israel Vishurun, is principal of the *Kollel Krastir* of New York.

RUBIN, Simhah, of Sasov (b. 1911)–Son of R. Hanokh Heinokh Dov, he married, in 1930, Havah, the daughter of R. Dov Heschel of Lvov. When she died in 1966, he married Osna, the daughter of Aryeh Ingolfeld. In 1973, he moved to Golders Green and is known for his charitable works.

He regularly offers advice on moral issues, not only to his hasidim but to Anglo-Jewry as a whole. He issues warnings against mixed bathing, cites the problems of having non-Jewish live-in helpers, and condemns the indiscriminate watching of television. He is one of the spiritual guides of the *Bet Yaakov* primary and grammar schools. His children are R. David Manasseh, Hanokh Dov, and Golda, who married Issachar Dov Rokeah.

RUBIN, Yitzhak, of Brody (1835–20 *Elul* 1874)–Son of R. Elimelekh of Sokolov, he married Eidele, the daughter of R. Shalom of Belz, who was renowned for her erudition and piety. Her father remarked that "all she was short of was a *spodek* [rabbinic hat]." After living for a time in Radziechov, R. Yitzhak moved to Brody and became rebbe.

After his death, his wife, who became known as "Eidele, the rebbe" accepted petitions and gave discourses. Their children were the blind R. Elimelekh and R. Naftali Tzvi, the rebbe of Radziechov.

RUBIN, Yitzhak, of Sosnowiec (1875–16 *Heshvan* 1930)–Son of R. Asher Yeshaya of Chrzanov, he was renowned as an "*Illui*." He married the daughter of R. Alter Rothenberg. From 1901 he was rabbi of Old Sosnowiec, and to avoid Russian expulsions he changed his surname to Glickman.

His son R. Joshua succeeded him in Sosnowiec. Another son, R. Naftali Tzvi, was rabbi in New York. Other sons–R. Shalom, R. Alter David, and R. Hanokh David–and his daughters–Golda Breindel, Rebecca, and Sheindel–all perished in the Holocaust.

RUBIN, Yitzhak Eizig, of Sighet (1875–5 *Heshvan* 1943)–He was born in Dabrova, son of R. Hayyim Yehiel. He became rebbe in Sighet. During the interwar years he lived in Marmarosz. In 1941, when he was expelled to Galicia, he lived in Dabrova.

He was shot in the cemetery on the eve of the Sabbath while digging his own grave. His son, R. Issachar Berish, is rebbe of Dolina in New York.

RUBIN, Yitzhak Tuviah, of Zanz (13 *Tammuz* 1858–21 *Sivan* 1927)–He was born in Dabrova, the son of R. Meir of Glogov. In 1873, he married Nehamah, the daughter of R. Hayyim Halberstam of Zanz. He was rebbe in Zanz and lived in the same house as R. Hayyim of Zanz. During the First World War, he lived in Budapest, where he later died.

His sons were R. Tzvi Hirsch Leib, R. Asher Yeshaya, R. Aryeh Leib, and R. Moses Elikum Bria. They all became rebbes.

RUBINSTEIN, Abraham Hayyim (1912–13 *Tevet* 1983), historian–Born in Tomaszov, Poland, he studied at and graduated from the rabbinical seminary *Tachkemoni*, in Warsaw. He emigrated to the Holy Land in 1935. He was awarded a doctorate by the Hebrew University in 1940, and was a lecturer and then professor at Bar-Ilan University, where he was also head of the hasidic department.

He edited Zweifel's work *Shalom al Yisrael* (Jerusalem, 1973) and was the author of *Perakim BeTorat HaHasidut U'VeToldoteha* (Jerusalem, 1978). Apart from many valuable articles he wrote on Hasidism, his critical and learned edition of the *Shivhei HaBesht* was published posthumously in Jerusalem in 1991.

RYMANOV, Tzvi Hirsch Hakohen (1778–13 *Heshvan* 1847), hasidic rebbe–Tzvi Hirsch of Przytyk, or "Hirsch Mesharet" (Hirsch the Beadle), was born in Dabrova. His father, Yehudah Leib, died when he was ten years old. Tzvi Hirsch was brought up by his uncle, who apprenticed him to a tailor. "I was careful not to ruin what was new and to repair what was old," was his comment on those early days. He came under the influence of R. Moses of Przeworsk, and became the "attendant" (beadle) of R. Menahem Mendel of Rymanov. "When he does the cleaning," observed his master, "he drives out all the demons, and the air grows pure and the house is fit for prayer."

After the death of his mentor, R. Tzvi Hirsch was, for twelve years, a disciple of R. Tzvi of Ropczyce, who styled him "rabbi." In 1827 he became rebbe and was renowned for his miracles. He imposed a tax (*kofer nefesh*) on his wealthy hasidim, using the proceeds for charitable purposes. All the *pidyonot* were promptly divided among the needy and among the residents in his *Bet HaMidrash*. "When Tzvi Hirsch died," remarked R. Meir of Przemyshlany, "the gates of charity were closed."

His discourses are to be found in *Be'erot HaMayim* (1894). His son, Joseph (d. 1913), succeeded him.

S. A. Horodetsky, *HaHasidut VeHaHasidim*, vol. 4, p. 12 (1954).

A.S.

RYMANOVER, Menahem Mendel (1745–19 *Iyyar* 1815), hasidic rebbe–Son of R. Joseph Harif, he was born in Neustadt. At the age of eleven, he visited R. Dov Baer, the Maggid of Mezhirech. He studied under R. Shmuel (Shmelke) of Nikolsburg and R. Elimelekh of Lejask, who called him "Joseph, the *tzaddik*." He made a special study of the works of R. Yitzhak Alfasi, who according to hasidic legend appeared to him in a dream and advised him to continue his studies in Lejask.

He married the daughter of a well-to-do man from Przytyk, who supported him during his studies. In 1796, he settled in Przytyk, a town in the Rzeszov province of Poland. It was not until 1801 that he made his home in Rymanov. He was a supporter of Napoleon and prayed for his victory.

He opposed the domiciling of Jews in small villages, fearing that this would foster assimilation. He urged women to dress in the traditional style, and he instituted regulations concerning weights and measures. On the last day of every month he would check the scales in every Jewish shop.

His life was beset with personal tragedies. His wife died, and he later lost his young daughter. "Lord of the universe," exclaimed the grieving rabbi, "when you took away my wife, I still had my daughter and could rejoice in her. Now you have taken her, too, and I have no one left to rejoice in except You alone."

Among his disciples were R. Naftali Tzvi of Ropczyce, R. Tzvi Hirsch of Zydaczov, and R. Ezekiel Panet. His discourses can be found in *Ilana deHayyei* (Piotrokov, 1908), *Menahem Zion* (Satmar, 1935), *Divrei Menahem* (Lvov, 1863), and *Torat Menahem* (Lvov, 1876). He had two sons, R. Nathan Yehudah Leib and R. Israel Jacob.

M. E. Gutman, *R. Mendel MiRymanov*.

S

SABBATH—Jewish day of rest, a covenant between Israel and God and one of the cornerstones of Judaism. To the hasidim, the Sabbath is greater than the world to come. "God wanted to give His people a taste of the spiritual delight of the world to come," said R. Levi Yitzhak of Berdichev. "Therefore He gave them the Sabbath." This is why the Sabbath is called "a good gift." When one keeps the Sabbath according to all its laws, the "gift" consists of forgiveness for all of one's sins. According to R. Elimelekh of Dynov, one of God's names was "Sabbath." "The Sabbath," said R. Yehudah Aryeh Leib Alter of Ger, "is called a 'testimony,' for on the Sabbath the natural laws are suspended."

To prepare oneself for the Sabbath's sanctity and purity, the rebbes and the hasidim would visit the *mikveh* on the eve of the day, in order to welcome the holy day in purity. "It is worthwhile walking a mile," said R. Aaron of Karlin, "in order to go to a *mikveh*." The rebbes would wear their finest garments on the Sabbath, usually a *kapote* made of silk or velvet. Many of them wore white garments. They would also wear a *shtreimel*, as R. Pinhas of Koretz said: "The Hebrew letters of *Shabbat* stand for *shtreimel* instead of *tefillin*." They were also diligent in arranging *eruvim* to enable people to carry and to walk beyond 2,000 cubits (two-thirds of a mile). In prewar Poland, both large and small towns all had their *eruvim*, which were looked after by the local communities and enabled the hasidim to bring food and drink to the rebbe's court.

At the evening service that ushers in the Sabbath, many rebbes, like the rebbes of Belz and Karlin, would don a *tallit*, even when they were not officiating at the reader's desk. They would recite Psalm 107, and apart from *Habad*, hasidim would recite the whole of the Book of Song of Songs. Some would pronounce a benediction over spices before the *Kiddush* on Friday nights, because the Talmud relates that on the eve of the Sabbath before sunset, R. Shimon bar Yohai and his son had encountered an old man bearing two bundles of myrtles: "What are these for?" they asked him. "They are in honor of the Sabbath," he replied (*Shabbat* 33b). On Friday night, only *Habad* hasidim omitted the *VeShamru* (Exodus 31:16–17) from the Friday night liturgy.

Following the Lurian tradition, they would have twelve plaited loaves to correspond to the twelve loaves of *Lehem Hapanim* (shewbread), which were placed in the Temple every week (Leviticus 24:5–6). Fish and meat as well as *tzimmes* were eaten. It is reported that the Besht settled in Medziborz because fish was easily obtainable there. During the reading of the Law, the most important *aliyah* apart from the Kohen and Levi portions was *Shishi* (the sixth portion), which corresponded to the kabbalistic symbol of *Yesod*. The *tzaddik* (the *Yesod* of the world) was customarily honored with *Shishi*.

The rebbes would on the Sabbath conduct what is known in Yiddish as a *firen tish* (festive meal), when food and drink would be supplemented by spiritual fare. The rebbe would give a *dvar Torah*, accompanied by songs and dancing. *Minhah*, the afternoon service, was followed by a *seudah shlishit*. In the gathering dusk, the rebbe gave discourses, his followers joined in the singing of mystical melodies such as *Atkinu Seudata* or Luria's *Benei HeKhalah*, and they would prolong the Sabbath as much as possible. Only bread and fish or herring were eaten, and no lights were lit. As the Besht said, "The hasidic custom of eating the third Sabbath meal in company with comrades rather than in the midst of one's own family is founded on the following reason: among good Jews, it is eminently desirable that a man offer up his soul in the presence of ten Jews. At the conclusion of the last Sabbath meal, we offer up our supersoul, received by us on the Sabbath. We desire to do this in congenial company." The hasidim, reluctant to let the honored guest depart, followed the timing of Rabbenu Tam, prolonging the Sabbath day as long as possible.

After *Havdalah* many rebbes chanted the poem of R. Levi Yitzhak of Berdichev "*Gott fun Avruhom*" (God of Abraham, Isaac, and Jacob, the holy Sabbath passes away; may the new week come to us, for health, life, and all good; and may it bring us sustenance, good tidings, deliverance, and consolation). The conclusion of the Sabbath they celebrated with a *melaveh malkah*, chanting hymns and relating hasidic stories, especially about the Besht.

R. Saadia Hanokh, at the end of the nineteenth century, organized in Lodz a *Shemirat Shabbat* society to persuade the textile manufacturers to close their factories in order to enable their workers to observe the Sabbath. R. Jacob Aaron Morgenstern organized a similar body in Warsaw. He himself would make the rounds of the stores and through gentle persuasion achieved much success.

Most Israeli municipalities today debar Sabbath traffic from predominantly hasidic areas.

SADGORA DYNASTY–After his imprisonment by the Russians, R. Israel Friedman of Ruzhyn settled, in 1845, in Sadgora, near Czernowitz, the capital of Bukovina, then under Austrian rule. He lived in a magnificent Moorish-style palace. The town became a center of Hasidism. R. Israel's six sons all established hasidic dynasties in different parts of Romania and Austria.

R. Israel's second son, R. Abraham Jacob Friedman (d. 1883), continued the life-style of his father. He lived in a style of *malkhut* as befits a direct descendant of King David. A pilgrimage to Sadgora was considered as *aliyah leregel*, similar to a pilgrimage to the Temple in Jerusalem. The rebbe believed in worshiping God in a garb of beauty and splendor. The spirit of gladness, nobility, and honor hovered there. Like his father, he, too, was arrested, in 1857, and spent fifteen months in the Czernowitz prison. He was released on 3 *Tammuz* 1858. Dr. Theodor Herzl endeavored to enlist his sympathies for Zionism: "Over there [in *Eretz Yisrael*] we will build a more beautiful Sadgora for the wonder-rabbi," wrote Herzl in his diary on June 16, 1896.

The rebbe was instrumental in completing the building of the *Tiferet Yisrael* synagogue in Jerusalem, which was destroyed by the Jordanians in 1948. The dynasty was maintained by R. Abraham Jacob's three sons–R. Shlomoh of Sadgora (d. 1880), R. Yitzhak of Boyan (d. 1917), and R. Israel of Sadgora (d. 1906)–as well as by his sons-in-law–R. Avi Ezra Zelig of Moglienice, R. Nahum Baer of Sadgora (d. 1883), R. Israel of Chortkov (d. 1934), and R. Shlomoh Yosef of Medziborz.

R. Israel of Sadgora had six sons–R. Aaron of Sadgora (d. 1912), R. Shalom Joseph of Czernowitz (d. 1935), R. Abraham Jacob of Tel Aviv (d. 1960), R. Shlomoh Hayyim of Sadgora (d. 1972), R. Yitzhak of Rymanov (d. 1924), and R. Yehudah Tzvi of Sadgora (d. 1951).

M. M. Brayer, "Admorei Romania VeUngaria VeEretz Yisrael," pp. 190–246.

M.M.B.

SAFED (Tzfat)–A town twelve miles northwest of Tiberias in Upper Galilee. Safed is one of the four holy cities that the kabbalists endowed with special mystical significance. In the sixteenth century, it became a center of the kabbalistic school under R. Moses Cordovero, R. Yitzhak Luria, and R. Hayyim Vital. In the eighteenth and early nineteenth centuries, several hasidic rabbis settled there. The kabbalist R. Hayyim Joseph Azulai maintained that the inhabitants of Safed were more fitted to fathom the depth of the Torah and to penetrate its secrets than were the inhabitants of any other city in the Holy Land. The numerical value of the Hebrew word "Safed" (750) was equivalent to the Hebrew word "*teka*" from the prayer "Sound the great horn for our freedom." It was here that R. Yitzhak Luria, the "holy Ari," lived and died.

In 1759 an earthquake destroyed the city's buildings and 190 Jews lost their lives. R. Simhah of Zalosce, who visited Safed in 1764, reported that after the earthquake, the number of Jews was reduced to "forty or fifty households." The hasidic *Aliyah* of

1777 revived the settlement. Over 300 hasidim under R. Menahem Mendel of Vitebsk settled there. It was also the home of R. Issachar Dov (d. 1794), a disciple of the Maggid of Mezhirech.

In 1837, the city was once again destroyed by an earthquake, and over 4,000 Jews lost their lives. The Hebrew printing press, established by Israel Bak in 1831, was transferred to *Kefar Tarmaq*. Two years later, a census ordered by Sir Moses Montefiore revealed that there were 237 hasidim living there under the spiritual guidance of R. Abraham Dov of Ovruch (d. 1851), a disciple of R. Nahum of Chernobyl. Notable hasidim were R. Gershon Margulies (d. 1839) and R. Kopul Horowitz, the son of the "Seer" of Lublin.

In the middle of the nineteenth century, a number of hasidic rebbes settled there. They were R. Uri Urenstein (d. 1879); R. Moses Krengel; R. Naftali Hayyim (d. 1895), son of R. Meir of Dzikov; and R. Joseph Alter (d. 1879), son of R. Hayyim of Kosov. However, at the end of the nineteenth century and at the beginning of the twentieth century, Safed did not attract hasidim in large numbers. Of the twenty-two old synagogues in the Old City, fewer than half are hasidic, including the *shtieblech* of Chortkov, Vishnitz, Chernobyl, Karlin, Kosov, *Habad*, Turiysk, and Zanz. Near the tomb of R. Shimon bar Yohai, there is a small *yeshivah*, which was under the spiritual guidance of R. Yohanan Twersky of Jerusalem.

Recently, a number of Bratzlav hasidim, inspired by the late Abraham Sternharz and his disciple Gedaliah Aaron Koenig (d. 23 *Tammuz* 1980), have begun establishing a hasidic settlement there. The movement is known as the Society for the Revival of the Religious Settlement in Upper Galilee. The members have already established a *Talmud Torah* and a *yeshivah Or Tzaddikim*, which particularly welcomes Russian immigrants.

A. M. Haberman, *Toldot HaDefus HaIvri BeZefat*.

SAFRIN, Abraham Mordecai, of Borislav (1860–8 *Kislev* 1942) – Second son of R. Eliezer Tzvi of Komarno, he married Feiga, the daughter of R. Hayyim Jacob Dominitz. He was rabbi in Neustadt and then in Zaslo. His sons R. Eliezer Tzvi and R. Hayyim Tzvi and their families perished in the Holocaust. His son R. Hayyim Jacob was the rebbe of Komarno in Ungvar, New York, and Jerusalem.

SAFRIN, Alexander Sender (1770–21 *Av* 1818) – Third son of R. Yitzhak Eizig, he married Hannah, the daughter of R. Yaakov Kopul of Lukov.

He was an ascetic and fasted every week from Sunday to Thursday. He served as rabbi in Zydaczov, Zvurno, and, from 1812, Komarno. Unlike his brothers, who dedicated their lives to mysticism, he concentrated on the Talmud. In the course of his life, he completed it seven times. For most of the day, he wore *tallit* and *tefillin*.

He died in Ujhely, where he was buried. He was the author of a homiletical work *Zikhron Devarim* (Lvov, 1871) and responsa (Przemysl, 1879). He adopted the surname of Safrin. His son, R. Yitzhak Eizig Yehudah Yehiel, succeeded him.

SAFRIN, Alter Issachar Dov, of Altstadt (1873–*Sivan* 1943) – Son of R. Mosheh Hayyim, he was rebbe of Stary Sambor during the interwar years. He married Leah, the daughter of R. Shmuel Shmelke Rubin of Seret. He and his brother and their families perished in the Holocaust.

SAFRIN, Barukh, of Komarno (1914–7 *Sivan* 1943) – Son of R. Shalom. His mother, Havah, was the daughter of R. Israel Perlow of Stolin, where he was brought up. In 1934 he married his first cousin Sheindel, the daughter of R. Elijah Bombach of Auschwitz.

At one time he was eager to settle in the Holy Land and tried to obtain a certificate to enable him to do this. In 1937, he succeeded his father and established in Komarno a *yeshivah Binyan Shalom*, in memory of his father. It was his custom to pray with two pairs of *tefillin* (Rashi and Rabbenu Tam), worn simultaneously, and afterward to don a third pair (*shimushei rabba*).

In 1939, he received a permit to enter Hungary, but he refused to leave his mother behind. He sold all his valuables to support the refugees. "If the world will survive," he said, "I will buy others. But if the world is going to be destroyed, why do I need them?"

In *Kislev* 1943, he was deported first to Rudik and then to Sambor. He was urged to escape but refused. "As long as there remains a Jew in the ghetto," he replied, "I will remain with him." He was shot by the Nazis in the cemetery of Sambor. His fate was shared by his wife and his sons, Shalom and Jacob Moses (aged five years and nine years, respectively).

B. Yasher, "Bet Komarno," pp. 167–173, 346–349.

SAFRIN, Eliezer Tzvi (1830–24 *Iyyar* 1898), kabbalist–Only son of R. Yitzhak Eizig Yehudah Yehiel, he was born in Zydaczov. He was stricken with paralysis in childhood. He studied under R. Yehudah Tzvi of Razdol, and he visited R. Shalom of Belz, R. Meir of Przemyshlan, and R. Horowitz of Dzikov. He married Hannah Sarah, the daughter of R. Joseph Shine.

In 1874, he succeeded his father as rebbe. He stressed that worshipers should dress in clean and fine garments. It would not be respectable to pray before the King of Kings in torn raiment. He insisted that the *Zohar* should be studied before each service, and that the Talmud and Midrash be studied after the service.

He was the author of *Or Einayim*, an encyclopedia on Kabbalah (Przemysl, 1882); *Ben Beiti* on Genesis (Przemysl, 1900); a commentary on Psalms (Ungvar, 1927); *Damesek Eliezer*, a commentary on the *Zohar* in seven volumes (published between 1902 and 1928, in Przemysl and Munkacs); *Sefer Megillat Setarim* (Jerusalem, 1965); and *Zekan Beito* on the Ethics of the Fathers (Jerusalem, 1973).

He had four sons–R. Menahem Monish, R. Pinhas Nathan, R. Abraham Mordecai, and R. Jacob Moses, who succeeded him–and two daughters–Zipa Hinda and Frimet.

SAFRIN, Hayyim Jacob, of Jerusalem (1892–5 *Sivan* 1969)–Son of R. Abraham Mordecai of Boryslav, he was born in Komarno. He married, in 1913, Hayyah, the daughter of R. Yitzhak Flaum. During World War I, he lived in Ungvar and served as rabbi there.

In 1938 he emigrated to the United States, where he lived until he settled in Jerusalem in 1962 and established a *yeshivah Hekhal HaBrakhah VeDamesek Eliezer*.

He left more than forty manuscripts. Those published were *Shabbat Shalom U'Mevorakh* (Jerusalem, 1970), *Bet Yaakov* (Jerusalem, 1964), and *Bet Avot* (Jerusalem, 1974).

His son R. Pinhas is rebbe of Komarno in Jerusalem, and his other son, R. Menahem Monish, is rebbe in Bene Berak.

SAFRIN, Issachar Berish, of Zydaczov (d. 2 *Shevat* 1932)–Son of R. Yitzhak Eizig of Safrin, he was a disciple of the "Seer" of Lublin. His son and successor, Yitzhak Eizig, was a prolific author.

SAFRIN, Jacob Moses, of Komarno (5 *Tammuz* 1861–15 *Tammuz* 1929)–Son of R. Eliezer Tzvi, he was born in Komarno. He married Alta Esther Feigtshe, a granddaughter of R. Abraham Mordecai of Pinczov.

He became rebbe in 1898 and was known for the passion with which he prayed, often fainting from emotion and overexertion. He would never use negative words, such as "darkness," preferring to say "no light" instead. On the New Year he would pray for the rebbes of Belz, Sasov, and Olesk. During the First World War, he lived in Sambor and Debrecin, Hungary.

He returned to Galicia in 1922 and lived for a time in Lvov. When his wife died in 1916, he married, in 1918, the widowed daughter of R. Yitzhak Eizig Weiss of Spinka.

He died while visiting a spa near Vienna, and he was buried in Komarno. All his manuscripts were lost in the Holocaust.

He had six daughters and one son, R. Shalom, who succeeded him.

SAFRIN, Menahem Monish, of Bene Berak (3 *Nisan* 1918–1990)–Son of R. Hayyim Jacob, he was born in Ungvar. He studied under R. Joshua Grunwald of Huszt. He emigrated to the Holy Land in 1939 and succeeded his father as rebbe in Bene Berak, where he established a *kollel* and a *Talmud Torah*. He married Freida *Hayyah*, the daughter of R. Shalom Wagshal. When she died, he married *Hayyah* Brachah, the daughter of R. Yehoshua Orenreich.

His son R. Yitzhak Shlomoh is the rebbe of Komarno in Givat Shaul, Jerusalem. His other son, R. Eliezer Tzvi, is rabbi in Bene Berak.

SAFRIN, Pinhas Nathan, of Rudki (1855–29 *Adar* 1932) – Son of R. Eliezer Tzvi of Komarno, he married the daughter of R. Naftali Hayyim Horowitz. As the marriage remained childless, he divorced his wife and married the daughter of R. Joshua Horowitz of Dzikov. He became rebbe in Rudki and was renowned for his melodious rendering of the prayers. During the First World War, he lived in Hungary. He was survived by one daughter.

SAFRIN, Shalom, of Komarno (1893–26 *Adar* 1937) – Only son of R. Jacob Moses, he was brought up by his grandfather and by his uncle R. Pinhas Nathan. In 1910, he married Havah, the daughter of R. Yisrael Perlow of Stolin.

In 1929, he became rebbe. His son R. Shlomoh and his wife perished in the Holocaust. He was succeeded by his son R. Barukh.

SAFRIN, Yitzhak (Eizig) Yehudah Yehiel, of Komarno (25 *Shevat* 1806–6 *Iyyar* 1874) – Son of R. Alexander Sender, he was born in Sambor. By the time he was seven, he already knew by heart three tractates of the Talmud – *Baba Kamma*, *Baba Metzia*, and *Baba Batra*. His father died before his *bar mitzvah*, and he was brought up by his uncle R. Tzvi Hirsch of Zydaczov. In 1825, he married Gitel, the daughter of R. Abraham Mordecai Horowitz of Pinczov.

He visited many rebbes, but the influence of his uncle was paramount. When his uncle died, he returned to Zydaczov, where he became *dayan*, and in 1831, he became rebbe in Komarno.

He was a unique and many-faceted personality. His secret diary, *Megillat Setarim*, was published in Jerusalem in 1944 by N. Ben-Menahem, based on a lithograph edition of the diary, which appeared in Warsaw in 1944. In this, he asserted that his soul was a reincarnation of those of R. Shimon ben Yohai and the Besht. He even implied that he was the Messiah, the son of Joseph. He stated that from the age of two until the age of five, he had marvelous visions. A holy spirit had filled him, enabling him to speak words of prophecy and to see from one end of the world to the other. The "strange thoughts," he insisted, are sent to us so that we might elevate them to their source in God. To deny that the strange thoughts were sent for a purpose is, in fact, to deny that God has control over all and that he sent them that they might be elevated.

He was the author of fifteen works. Among them are *Mitzvat Omer* (Lvov, 1858); *Derekh Emunah* on the thirteen articles of Faith (Lvov, 1850); *Penei Zaken* on tractate *Shekalim* (Lvov, 1851); *Notzer Hesed*, a commentary on the Ethics of the Fathers (Lvov, 1856); *Netiv Mitzvotekha* on Torah (Lvov, 1858); *Otzer Hayyim* (Przemysl, 1884); and *Zohar Hai* (Lvov, 1875).

He died in Uhjely and was survived by three children: Hinda Sarah, R. Alexander Sender, and R. Eliezer Tzvi, who succeeded him.

H. Y. Berl, *Reb Yitzhak Eizig MiKomarno*.

SANDAK (*sandek*) – The person who holds the baby during circumcision. The word is of Greek origin, derived from either *syndidcus* meaning "a patron," or *synteknos*, "a companion to the father." It was customary among the hasidim to give this honor to the rebbe, for it was regarded as *hibbuv mitzvah* (zealously performing the *mitzvah*).

Occasionally, a number of hasidic rebbes, such as R. Gershon Heinokh Leiner and R. Hayyim Elazar Shapira of Munkacs, combined the two offices of *sandek* and *mohel*.

SARAH (d. 1740), mother of the Besht – She was separated from her husband, Eliezer, by a group of vandals. During her husband's absence, she supported herself by being a midwife.

Contrary to the accepted view (Dubnow, *Toldot HaHasidut*, vol. 1, p. 44; Horodezky, *HaHasidut VeHaHasidim*, vol. 1, p. 2), she did not die shortly after her husband, Eliezer, who died in 1703. She lived with the Besht and his wife, Hannah. One source suggests that she remarried and that her second husband's son-in-law, R. Joseph Ashkenazi, was a friend of the Besht. This theory is corroborated by the inscription on her gravestone.

S. A. Horodezky, *HaHasidut VeHaHasidim*, vol. 2, pp. 67–71.

Y.E.

SATMAR – This hasidic community in Williamsburg, Brooklyn, was founded in 1948 by R. Yoel Teitelbaum. Other hasidim –

Hungarian and Romanian refugees—soon joined him, and by 1961, the community numbered 860 heads of households and is now one of the largest hasidic communities in the world. For some years until 1972, Israel Rubin, associate professor of sociology at Cleveland State University, lived with the Satmar hasidim and observed their patterns of life, thought, and culture. He is the author of *Satmar, an Island in the City* (Chicago, 1972), in which he describes in detail how children are raised in Satmar, what they study in school, how they earn a living, how they pray, and the almost blind faith they have in their spiritual leader, the *Rov*. He analyzes the stresses and changes within Satmar, as the influences of the outside world begin to touch the life of the community. He also finds that Satmar women have more authority today than formerly.

The very name of Satmar has become a focus of violent partisanship, because of its militancy and anti-Zionist elements. Most of the members of the *Neturei Karta* of Mea Shearim are closely aligned with Satmar.

The hasidim of Satmar take pride in their wanted otherness in garb and appearance and in their fervent devotion to customs and traditions. Intensive Jewish studies from a very early age are obligatory.

SAVRAN, Moses Tzvi (d. 25 *Tevet* 1838)—Son of R. Shimon Shlomoh, he was the founder of the hasidic dynasty bearing his name. He was the disciple of R. Barukh of Medziborz, R. Levi Yitzhak of Berdichev, and R. Abraham Joshua Heschel of Opatov.

He held rabbinic positions in Savran, Titshlinik, and Berdichev. Some of his discourses were published by his disciple R. Azriel Dov in *Likkutei Shoshanim* (Lvov, 1872) and *Yalkut Kitvei Kodesh* (Jerusalem, 1961). He was a violent opponent of the hasidim of Bratzlav, whom he called "sinners" who cause others to sin, and he warned his followers not to intermarry with them. "Moreover, a hasid of Bratzlav should not be employed to teach your children, nor should their slaughterers be used. Those who have pity on them deserve no pity."

In vain did R. Nathan of Nemirov urge him to cease his vendetta and pleaded, "I am fifty-five years old and for thirty-five years have been engaged in disseminating R. Nahman's teachings." He begged R. Tzvi not to listen to slander.

R. Moses established a dynasty that lasted for two generations. He was succeeded by his son, R. Shimon Shlomoh (d. 1848), and thereafter by his grandson, R. Moses (d. 1913). Incidents relating to R. Moses Tzvi's life are recorded in *Eser Atarot* by I. Berger (Brooklyn, 1954) and in *Shemuot Tovot*, by C. A. Deutschman (Warsaw, 1896).

S.F.

SCHACHTER, Zalman Meshullam (b. 1924), hasidic writer—Born in Zolkiev, Poland, and educated in Vienna, he was ordained in 1947 by Lubavitch. He was awarded an M.A. degree by Boston University and a doctorate of Hebrew letters by the Hebrew Union College, Cincinnati. He served the Jewish community as congregational rabbi, Hebrew school principal, and Hillel director. From 1956 to 1975, he was professor of religion at the University of Manitoba and from 1975 to 1987, professor of Jewish mysticism at Temple University, Philadelphia.

He is the author of *Spiritual Intimacy: A Study of Counseling in Hasidism*; *Fragments of a Future Scroll*; and *Paradigm Shift: From the Jewish Renewal Teachings of Reb Zalman Schachter-Shalomi* (1993).

SCHATZ-UFFENHEIMER, Rivkah (1927–19 *Adar* 1992)—She was born in Rio de Janeiro, Brazil, and emigrated to Israel in 1935. She received B.A., M.A., and Ph.D. from the Hebrew University.

She became a member of the department of Jewish thought, later serving as its chairman.

In 1967, she was promoted to Senior Lecturer, and in 1982, to Edmonton Professor of Jewish Mysticism.

She was known as an outstanding and original researcher in the fields of Hasidism, in Jewish messianism, and in the philosophy of R. Abraham Yitzhak Kook. She was particularly interested in the Maggid of Mezhirech, R. Elimelekh of Lejask, R. Shneur Zalman of Liady, and the doctrines of Izbica. Although a disciple of Gershom Scholem, she did not hesitate to deviate from a number of his ideas and was often critical of Martin Buber.

She was the author of *Quietistic Elements in Eighteenth-Century Hasidic Thought* (in Hebrew) (Jerusalem, 1968), she edited *Maggid Devarav LeYaakov laMaggid Dov Ber MiMezhirech* (Jerusalem, 1976), and she wrote many original and thought-provoking articles in *Tarbiz* and *Molad*.

In recent years, she headed a project for the scientific publication of the *Zohar*. She was awarded the "Kugel" prize by the city of Holon, as well as a citation by the Israel Council of Jewish Women's Organizations for her achievement in Jewish studies.

SCHECHTER, Solomon (1850-1915) – In common with many other proponents of the scientific approach to the study of Jewish literature, Solomon Schechter was reared in an environment dominated by typical East European Hasidism and, whatever his later cultural and intellectual development, could never be indifferent to that movement. Born in Focsani, Romania, to a *Habad* hasid and named after Shneur Zalman of Liady, the founder of the sect, he inherited an emotional and enthusiastic Judaism, to which he remained ever loyal.

As a young man, however, acquainted, at first clandestinely, with secular ideas, he became disillusioned with many of the outward aspects of Hasidism and was sufficiently attracted to the *Haskalah* to join the literary campaign against his former associates. In two anonymous contributions to Smolenskin's *HaShahar*, published in 1876–1877 under the titles "A Word as Sweet as Honey" and "Talks of those Golden Spouts," he followed earlier critics of Hasidism in parodying the notions and life-style of some of its adherents. Both articles are in epistolary form, the former purporting to be a letter from a hasid indignantly disclaiming any connection between the founder of the movement and systematic and original thought, and the latter consisting of six letters that make brilliant but merciless use of irony and satire to contrast the naïveté of a fresh convert with the cynical self-interest of the *tzaddik* and his retinue.

Schechter always remained opposed to what he regarded as the degeneracy of Hasidism in the excesses of the *tzaddik* cult, but his deep personal religiosity and the essentially nonrational nature of his individual commitment ensured that his relationship with the anti-Hasidism of the *Haskalah* was no more than a youthful flirtation. As he matured, he apparently regretted the one-sidedness of his early diatribes and felt the need to express his admiration for the sublime and noble in Hasidism. His papers "The Chassidim," delivered at Jews' College in 1887, and "Saints and Saintliness," read at the seminary in 1905 (both printed in his *Studies*), were designed to stress the value of the romantic, mystical, and saintly elements in Judaism and to rehabilitate these among Jews who had lost contact or sympathy with them. Acknowledging a love-hate relationship with Hasidism and including some criticisms of the pernicious aspects of the movement, he nevertheless succeeded in portraying, with great warmth, the movement's outstanding qualities and its commitment to humility, joy, and enthusiasm.

Schechter's lively and extroverted participation in communal prayer, his yearning for a group of disciples and followers, his ultimate exchange of the academic satisfaction of Cambridge for the challenge of heading a rabbinical seminary in a vibrant Jewish community, and the charismatic leadership he gave to that institution and to Conservative Judaism as a whole all seem to owe much to the hasidic influences of his early years.

A. S. Oko, *Solomon Schechter . . . a Bibliography*.
S. Schechter, *Studies in Judaism*, first and second series.

S.C.R.

SCHENIERER, Sarah (1873–7 *Heshvan* 1934), founder of *Bet Yaakov* – Daughter of Bezalel Hakohen of Tarnov, a devoted hasid of Belz, she learned sewing and embroidery and earned her living as a dressmaker. She spent the First World War years in Vienna and was greatly influenced by the teachings of R. Dr. Flesch of the Stumpergasse Synagogue.

After the war, she returned home to Cracow and with the blessing of the rabbi of Belz, R. Issachar Dov Rokeah, started a school for twenty-five girls at Catachina 1, in Cracow's Jewish quarter. This was followed by the establishment, in 1931, of a *Bet Yaakov* Seminary at Stanislava 10, which was funded by the *Bet Yaakov* Committee under Cyrus Adler of New York. She was helped by Dr. Leo Deutschlander and Yehudah Leib Orleans.

She died in Vienna after a short illness. By 1937–1938 there were, in Poland alone, 248 *Bet Yaakov* schools, providing education for 35,485 children.

J. Grunfeld-Rosmarin, "Sarah Schenierer," in *Jewish Leaders*, pp. 405–433.

SCHIPPER, Ignaz (Eizig) (1884–1943), Jewish-Polish historian – Born in Tarnov, Austria, he studied jurisprudence in Cracow and Vienna. He was a member of the *Po'alei LeZion* and in 1922 joined the General Zionists. He was from 1919 to 1927 a deputy in the Polish parliament, and he lectured at the Institute for Jewish Studies in Warsaw. He devoted most of his time to Jewish history, and he wrote on capitalism among Jews, the history of Jewish culture, the theater, and drama.

He was a master of the brief essay as well as the long narrative. He made a notable contribution to the history of Hasidism. "Even if the Besht did not possess a grain of reality," he wrote, "he was without doubt a force in history, and the legend of his life was a moving force that shaped the development of history."

I. Schipper, "The Image of Israel Baal Shem Tov in Early Hasidic Literature," in *HaDoar* 29 (1960), pp. 252ff., 551–552.

SCHNEERSOHN, Hayyim Tzvi (1824–1882), Lubavitch emissary – Son of R. Nahum Tzvi, and a great-grandson of R. Shneur Zalman of Liady, he began helping the Old Yishuv at the age of eighteen. His fund-raising activities took him to Damascus, Egypt, Persia, India, Amsterdam, Australia, and the United States.

SCHNEERSOHN, Joseph Yitzhak, of Lubavitch (12 *Tammuz* 1880–10 *Shevat* 1950) – Son of R. Shalom Dov Baer and Sterna Sarah, he was born in Lubavitch. At the age of fifteen he was appointed his father's personal secretary, and two years later, on 13 *Elul* 1897, he married Nehamah Dinah, the daughter of R. Abraham Schneersohn and a granddaughter of R. Menahem Mendel of Lubavitch.

With financial support from Yaakov and Eliezer Poliakoff, he opened a spinning and weaving mill in Dubrovno, Moghilev, and established a *yeshivah* in Bukhara. In 1895 and 1896, he participated in the conference of religious and lay leaders in Kovno. In 1904, he helped supply Passover food to Jewish soldiers in the Far East. Between 1903 and 1911, he was arrested four times in Moscow and St. Petersburg.

He succeeded his father as rebbe in 1920 and continued his campaign for the furtherance of Jewish education throughout Communist Russia. Neither the menace of the *Cheka* nor the machinations of the *Yevsektsiya* could discourage him. He was forced to leave Rostov and lived for a time in Leningrad.

On 15 *Sivan* 1927, he was arrested once again, accused of counterrevolutionary activities, and sentenced to death. Protests were orchestrated by world Jewry at the highest levels. Pleas for clemency came from the Republican presidential candidate, Herbert Hoover. His death sentence was commuted to exile in Kostroma in the Urals. He was released on 12 *Tammuz* 1928 and permitted to leave Russia. That year, he went to live in Riga, and a year later he visited the Holy Land. In 1934, he took up residence in Warsaw, moving to Otwock two years later.

The rebbe miraculously escaped the Nazi onslaught. He arrived in New York on March 19, 1940, and founded the Central *yeshivah Tomhei Temimim*. He set up both *Mahnei Yisrael* to strengthen Orthodoxy and *Merkaz LeInyanei Hinukh*, the central organization for Jewish education. Another enterprise was the *Kehot* publication society, which published a vast assortment of material, from textbooks to studies of hasidic philosophy. In 1945, he set up *Ezrat Pleitim VeSiduram*, the refugee relief and rehabilitation organization that brought material assistance to displaced persons. In 1948, he established *Kefar Habad* in Israel, on the site of a onetime Arab village, Safria.

He was survived by three daughters. His daughter *Hayyah* Mushka married R. Menahem Mendel Schneerson, who succeeded him.

His bibliography, which consists of discourses delivered on Sabbaths, Festivals, and special occasions from 1920 to 1950, covers thousands of pages and makes up fifty-four books. He also wrote his memoirs: *Sefer HaZikhronot* (Brooklyn, 1947).

A. H. Glitzenstein, *Sefer HaToldot Rav Yosef Yitzhak Schneersohn MiLubavitch*.

SCHNEERSOHN, Levi Yitzhak (1878–20 *Av* 1944) – Son of R. Barukh Shneur, a descendant of R. Dov Baer, he married Hannah (1879–1965), the daughter of R. Meir Shlomoh of Nikolayev. He was a disciple of R. Hayyim Soloveitchik of Brest-Litovsk and R. Elijah Hayyim Meisels of Lodz. He became rabbi in Yekaterinoslav.

He was imprisoned by the Communists and exiled to Siberia. In 1944, he was permitted to return to Alma Ata. His son was R. Menahem Mendel of Lubavitch.

SCHNEERSOHN, Menahem Mendel, of Lubavitch (29 *Elul* 1789–13 *Nisan* 1866), third rebbe of Lubavitch – He was the son of R. Shalom Shakhna. His mother, Devorah Leah, was the second daughter of R. Shneur Zalman of Liady. In 1806, he married *Hayyah* Mushka, the daughter of R. Dov Baer, and after the death of his father-in-law in 1827, he succeeded him. He actively encouraged the pursuit of farming by Jews, and in 1844, he bought from Prince Shezedrin 9,700 acres of land at Shezedrin, near Minsk, where he established a settlement for 300 Jewish families.

He set up a special council, *Hevrah Tehiat HaMetim*, to alleviate the sufferings of the Cantonists – the boy soldiers of Czar Nicholas – who were taken to distant villages. Special emissaries visited these groups, lessening the likelihood of conversion by the conscripts. He participated in the rabbinical conference convened in 1843 in St. Petersburg. Among the delegates were R. Yitzhak of Volozhyn; banker Israel Halpern of Berdichev; Bezalel Stern, director of the Jewish school in Odessa; and Aryeh Leib Mandelstam, official translator. The conference lasted from May 6 to August 27, but the delegates agreed on very few issues.

The rebbe fought the *Haskalah* movement both in private and in public. Passionately, he opposed the ideas of revising the liturgy and of editing the Scriptures. Between 1844 and 1845, practical steps were taken to expand the Lubavitch *yeshivot* in Dubrovno, Kalisk, and other centers that had an enrollment of 600 students.

He traveled widely, and his friendship with Prof. I. Berstenson, the court physician to the czar, often helped in delicate negotiations relating to the welfare of the community. He suffered, though, from the malevolence of informers like Hershel Hodesh, Benjamin the Apostate, and Lipman Feldman, who tried, unsuccessfully, to trap him.

He was survived by seven sons and two daughters. He was succeeded by his younger son R. Shmuel.

He was the author of forty-one works, among them, *Or HaTorah* (Berdichev, 1913) and *Tzemah Tzeddek* (Vilna, 1884).

A. H. Glitzenstein, *Sefer HaToldot Rav Yosef Yitzhak Schneersohn MiLubavitch*.

SCHNEERSOHN, Shalom Dov Baer, of Lubavitch (20 *Heshvan* 1860–2 *Nisan* 1920), fifth rebbe of Lubavitch – He was the second son of R. Shmuel. On 11 *Elul* 1875, he married Sterna Sarah, the daughter of R. Joseph Yitzhak of Ovruch. In 1880, he began his communal activities, helping his father. In 1882, he succeeded his father as rebbe of Lubavitch.

His life was a combination of intense intellectual activity and practical concern for the welfare of every Jew. He worried about the 100,000 "Mountain Jews" (*Berg Yidden*) who lived in the Caucasian Mountains, far from the centers of Jewish life. The rebbe directed R. Shmuel Halevi Levitin of Rakshik to travel there and set up educational institutions. In 1902, he established a large factory in Dubrovno, enabling many Jewish families to earn a living. That same year, he helped to organize *Hevrat Mahzikei Hadat*, a society aimed at strengthening Torah education and observance.

In 1897, he founded the *yeshivah Tomhei Temimim* in Lubavitch. Emphasis was placed on profound contemplation in prayer. He disapproved of the Zionist movement. In a letter dated 1909, addressed to the religious settlers in the Holy Land, he alludes to "reformers whose only goal is to destroy the Jewish faith and to deprive it of its sacred character." In 1912, he sent a group of hasidim to Hebron to set up a *yeshivah*, called *Torat Emet*. Another branch was opened in Jerusalem in 1960.

R. Shalom Dov Baer is called the "Maimonides of Hasidism" due to the breadth and clarity of his discourses on hasidic philosophy. Many of these remain in mimeographed editions. The most important of the printed collection of his discourses is *Festival of Rosh Hashanah 5666* (New York, 1971).

In 1915, he moved to Rostov, and when he died, he was succeeded by his only son, R. Joseph Yitzhak. He was the author of glosses on the prayer book (Brooklyn, 1941); *Hanokh LeNaar* (New York, 1943); *Kuntres U'Maayan MiBet Hashem*, translated by Zalman I. Posner (New York, 1969); and *Torat Shalom, Sefer HaSihot* (New York, 1946) on the *Tanya* and discourses covering the period from 1867 to 1920.

A. H. Glitzenstein, *Sefer HaToldot R. Shalom Dov Baer*

N.L.

SCHNEERSOHN, Shemaryah Noah, of Kopys (1846–1926) – Youngest son of R. Yehudah Leib Schneersohn of Kopys, he was educated by his father, grandfather, and uncle. In 1869, he was appointed rabbi of the *Habad* hasidic community in Bobruisk, White Russia, and remained there until his death. In 1901, he organized one of the first hasidic *yeshivot* in Bobruisk.

He was the author of *Shemen LaMaor*, a collection of discourses and homilies, which was published in Tel Aviv in 1964.

Following his death, most of the Kopys hasidim rejoined the Lubavitch branch of the *Habad* movement.

N.L.

SCHNEERSOHN, Shmuel, of Lubavitch (2 *Iyyar* 1834–13 *Tishri* 1882) – He was the seventh and youngest son of R. Menahem Mendel. At the age of twenty-one, he began his communal activities, necessitating his traveling extensively within Russia and abroad. He visited Germany, Italy, and France. Throughout his life he strove to organize public opinion abroad to put pressure on the czar so as to improve conditions for the Jews.

In 1866, he became the fourth rebbe of Lubavitch. Several of his brothers became hasidic rebbes, too – in Kopys, in Liady, and in Nieshin – but R. Shmuel inherited the main body. In 1880, he was placed under house arrest.

He combined communal activities with intellectual powers. He knew several languages, including Latin. Many of his discourses have been published, but a considerable number are still in manuscript form. He was very critical of superficial intellectualism.

He had four sons and two daughters. He was succeeded by his son R. Shalom Dov Baer.

He was the author of *Likkutei Torah* (Vilna, 1884). His work *Likkutei Torat Shmuel*, a collection of his discourses, was printed in New York from 1945 onward, and so far, twelve volumes have appeared.

A. H. Glitzenstein, *Sefer HaToldot R. Shmuel Admur Maharash*.

N.L.

SCHNEERSOHN, Yehudah Leib, of Kopys (1811–3 *Heshvan* 1866) – Second son of R. Menahem Mendel of Lubavitch, he settled in Kopys, where he established his own dynasty. He was known as *Maharil R. Yehudah Leib*. He studied under his grandfather the *Mittler* rebbe and under his father. His manner of prayer, his joy, and his inspired teaching of Hasidism made him very popular. He married the daughter of R. Shlomoh Freides of Shklov. He accompanied his father to the conference at St. Petersburg in 1843.

He died at the age of fifty-five and was survived by three sons. His son R. Shlomoh Zalman (1830–27 *Iyyar* 1900) married the daughter of R. Aryeh Leib Luria of Lepoli, where he lived for ten years. He then returned to Lubavitch, where he studied with R. Shmuel. In 1867, he became the second rebbe of Kopys. He was active in the *kollel Ramban*, the organization that sustained many hasidic families in the Holy Land. When Zionism emerged, the Zionist leader Menahem Mendel Ussishkin (1863–1941), born into a hasidic family, met the rebbe in 1887 to elicit his support for the movement. Although in favor of Jews settling in the Holy Land, the rebbe never participated in the movement.

He was the author of *Magen Avot* in two parts – discourses on the weekly portions of the Torah, Festivals, the Book of Esther, and the Song of Songs (Berdichev, 1902).

Z.T.

SCHNEERSON, Menahem Mendel (11 *Nisan* 1902–3 *Tammuz* 1994), seventh rebbe of Lubavitch – The late Rebbe americanized his name by deleting the second "h" (had been Schneersohn). The most phenomenal Jewish personality of the twentieth century was born in Nikolayev, Russia, to R. Levi Yitzhak, a noted kabbalist and a grandson of R. Menahem Mendel of Lubavitch. His mother was Hannah, the daughter of R. Meir Shlomoh of Nikolayev. He had two brothers, Yisrael Aryeh Leib and Dov Baer. At the age of five, he moved with his parents to the Ukrainian city of Yekaterinoslav (now Dnepropetrovsk).

In 1928, at the age of twenty-six, he married, in Warsaw, Hayyah Mushka (1901–1988), the second daughter of R. Joseph Yitzhak Schneersohn of Lubavitch. She was his second cousin once removed. He lived for a time in Berlin, where he took courses in mathematic and physics. In 1939, he continued his studies in engineering at the Sorbonne in Paris. With the Nazi occupation of France, he lived for a time in Nice in southern France, and, then on June 23, 1941, he settled in Crown Heights, Brooklyn, where he became chairman of *Merkaz L'Inyonei Hinukh*, the educational arm of the Lubavitch movement.

His younger brother, Dov Baer, and his wife's younger sister and her husband, R. Menahem Horenstein, were murdered by the Nazis. In 1947, he flew to Paris to greet his mother, Hannah, who had just been released from a displaced persons camp, and he returned with her to the United States.

After the death of his father-in-law on 10 *Shevat* 1950, he reluctantly assumed the leadership of Lubavitch. The keynote of *Ufaratzta*, found in the scriptural text (Genesis 28:14), "and thou shalt spread abroad to the west, to the east, and to the north, and to the south," was the motto of the rebbe. He excelled as an administrator of the Lubavitch empire no less than as a scholar.

While she was alive, he was very attached to his aged mother and would start the day by bringing her milk. He would then spend the rest of his day controlling and increasing the already far-flung and manifold activities of the movement. He extended its activities to north Africa, and now *Habad* brings hasidic teachings to Casablanca, Marrakesh, Serfou, and Meknes. His followers are expected to demonstrate to their fellow Jews the *mitzvot* of donning *tefillin*, kindling the Sabbath lights, pronouncing the benedictions of *etrog* and *lulav*, and sounding the *shofar* and eating *shemurah matzot*. In 1959, he set up in Israel *Kefar Habad* and *Nahlat Har Habad* to accommodate the Russian immigrants to Israel. He has organized a peace corps to bring Judaism to Jews in many out-of-the-way places. With fleets of vehicles, known as *mitzvah* tanks, the rabbi's adherents propagate Judaism.

His unique analytical style of thought resulted in a monumental contribution to Jewish scholarship. Many volumes have been published that contain the rabbi's talks and writings. Central among them are twenty-six volumes of *Likkutei Sihot* (collected talks). The *Iggrot Kodesh*, a chronological collection of the rebbe's correspondence and responsa, is now in the midst of publication and brings the total of letters published to more than 8,000. This includes only material written in Hebrew and Yiddish until 1959. The rebbe's correspondence in English is also being prepared for publication. The correspondence ranges from mysticism to Talmud and hasidic philosophy to science and world events. He was forthright in his views and criticized the various scientific theories concerning the age of the world. He maintains that the world is only 5754 years old and that the population explosion is God's will. Though nonpolitical, in the election campaign for the 1988 *Knesset*, he backed the *Agudat Yisrael*. It increased its representation from two to five members. An ardent supporter of a Greater Israel that would incorporate the West Bank, he opposed the 1979 Peace Treaty with President Sadat. In 1990 his supporters frustrated a Labor Party attempt to form a government. He was against the Peace Accord of Rabin and Peres with the Arabs and maintained that any sacrifice of territory would weaken Israel's defense position. He discouraged university education, which, he maintained, could endanger Judaism. In the past forty-four years he never left New York.

Despite the deterioration of the Crown Heights area, unlike the hasidim of Bobov, who moved to Borough Park, the rebbe urged his followers to remain in Crown Heights and to preserve it as a thriving Jewish community.

In his prime, nearly 5,000 people per year were received by him in audience, and hundreds of letters passed through the hands of his secretariat.

On the eve of Shemini Atzeret, in October 1977, he suffered a heart attack. He was distressed when Barry Gourary, the son of

SCHNEURI (SHNEERSOHN), DOV BAER

his brother-in-law, removed many valuable books from his library. This resulted in vexatious litigation in American courts in 1986–1987. He opposed the strategy of mass meetings and public protests against the Soviet authorities. His own approach was always based on *shtadlanut*, persuasion at the diplomatic level.

He never took a vacation or visited Israel, but his influence spread around the world in a way unparalleled by any other Jewish religious leader.

He never accepted the mantle of the Messiah, as some of his more zealous followers proclaimed by putting stickers on car bumpers, putting up all over Israel posters declaring that he was the Messiah, and using Madison Avenue-style advertising, though critics accused him of not denying these claims.

He suffered a stroke in 1992 and on March 2, 1994, a second one. He also underwent surgery on his bladder and for cataract. He died of heart failure at the Bet Israel Medical Center in Manhattan and was buried in the Old Montefiore Cemetery in Queens, next to his wife and father-in-law. He died childless, and his last will and testament did not name a successor.

He left an estate of $50,000 and bequeathed his library and his assets to the *Habad* movement. Rabbi Yehudah Krinsky was named executor, and senior members of the movement have so far refused to discuss the question of a successor.

E. Hoffman, *Despite all Odds*.

SCHNEURI (SHNEERSOHN), Dov Baer, of Lubavitch (9 *Kislev* 1773–9 *Kislev* 1828) – Eldest son of R. Shneur Zalman, he was called the *Mittler* rebbe because he was the middle one of the first three leaders of *Habad*. In 1788 he married Sheine, the daughter of a pious teacher. He was living and studying in Kremenchug, in Little Russia, when his father died in 1813. He then settled in Lubavitch (Lubavichi), a small town in the district of Smolensk. His accession was contested by his father's star disciple, R. Aaron Halevi of Starosselje. The consensus of the hasidim, however, was to accept the leadership of R. Dov Baer, who was staunchly supported by his younger brother, R. Hayyim Abraham (d. 1841).

Concerned about the economic and physical plight of the Jews, he set up in 1815 Jewish agricultural settlements in the Kherson region, which he visited in 1817. Like his father, he supported the *Yishuv* in the Holy Land and was responsible for the collection and distribution of financial aid from Russia. He recommended placing collection boxes in every Jewish home. He yearned to settle in Hebron and maintained that prayers recited there are particularly effective, for, according to tradition, this was the gateway to paradise. He encouraged *Habad* hasidim who were living in the Holy Land to move to Hebron in order to strengthen the community.

He would stand immobile in prayer for as long as three hours at a time, and at the end of his prayers, his hat and shirt would be soaked in perspiration. He emphasized the importance of study and contemplation in Hasidism, and he wrote a tract on the different kinds of emotion and ecstasy that can be experienced in prayer, pointing out the danger of sham emotion and self-deception. This was a point of argument with R. Aaron, who accorded some value even to sham ecstasy.

He was one of the most prolific authors. In 1826, he was unjustly imprisoned by the Russian government on a false charge that he had collected 200 or 300 rubles for the sultan of Turkey. He was ordered to appear in Vitebsk before Governor-General Chavanski, who was to conduct the investigation. Through the good offices of Dr. Heibenthal and Jan Lubormirsky, he was released, and to this day, the anniversary of his release, 10 *Kislev*, is celebrated by *Habad* hasidim.

He died on 9 *Kislev*, at the age of fifty-four, on the anniversary of his birth. He was survived by two sons – R. Menahem Nahum and R. Barukh – and seven daughters. R. Menahem Mendel, his sister's son and the husband of his elder daughter, succeeded him.

He was the author of several works, among them, *Shaar HaTeshuvah VeHatefillah* (Shklov, 1817); *Derekh Hayyim* (Kopys, 1819); *Ner Mitzvah VeTorah Or* (Kopys, 1820); *Ateret Rosh* (Kopys, 1821); *Imrei Binah* (Kopys, 1821); *Shaarei Orah* (Kopys, 1822); *Kuntres HaHitpaalut* (Shklov, 1817); *Torat Hayyim: Bereshit* (Kopys, 1826); *Shemot* (Shanghai, 1947); *Pokeah Ivrim* (Shklov, 1832); *Iyun*

Tefillah (Warsaw, 1871); *Inyan HaHishtatut* (Warsaw, 1871); *Maamarim Yekarim* (1864); *Perush HaMilot* (Warsaw, 1867); *Bad Kodesh* (Warsaw, 1871); *Shnei HaMe'orot* (Lvov, 1882); *Shaarei Teshuvah* and *Maamar Mizmor Shir LeYom HaShabbat* (Warsaw, 1898); *Piskei Dinim: Yoreh De'ah* (New York, 1959); *Maamar Atah Ehad VeShimkha Ehad* (New York, 1965); and *Maamar Pokeah Yam Lifnei Mosheh* (New York, 1967). His *Kuntres HaHitpaalut* was translated by Louis Jacobs under the title *Tract of Ecstasy* (Vallentine Mitchell, 1953). His correspondence *Iggrot Kodesh* was printed in New York in 1981.

A. H. Glitzenstein, *Sefer HaToldot R. Menahem Mendel Baal Tzemah Tzeddek*.

H. M. Heilman, *Bet Rebbe*.

N.L.

SCHOCHET, Jacob Immanuel (b. 1935), hasidic writer—Born in Basel, Switzerland, of Lithuanian rabbinic descent, he received his rabbinical training in the Central Lubavitch *yeshivah* in New York. He graduated with a Ph.D. in philosophy and since 1971 has served as professor of philosophy at Humber College, Toronto. He is also visiting professor in religious bioethics at the School of Medicine of the University of Toronto and professor of Jewish law, Hasidism, and Jewish mysticism at Maimonides College, Toronto.

He is an acknowledged authority on Jewish philosophy and Jewish mysticism. He has published many articles in scholarly and popular journals and is the author of more than thirty books. His works include biographies of the Besht (Toronto, 1961), the Maggid of Mezhirech (New York, 1974), *Tzava'at Harivash* (1975), the multivolume *Likkutei Sihot* (1980–1994), *Chassidic Dimensions* (1991), and *Mashiach—The Principle of Mashiach and the Messianic Era in Jewish Law and Tradition* (1991).

He is the rabbi of the Kielcer congregation.

SCHOLEM, GERSHOM (1897–1982)—The greatest academic authority on Jewish mysticism, he is almost single-handedly responsible for the creation of the academic investigation of this branch of Jewish creativity. Born in Berlin, Scholem studied at the German universities of Jena, Berne, and Munich. He received his Ph.D. in Oriental languages in 1923 for a scholarly edition and translation of the *Sefer Bahir*, the oldest extant kabbalistic text. He moved to the Hebrew University, in Jerusalem, in 1923, and his work there resulted in the steady production of articles and monographs on all aspects of the Jewish mystical tradition. His work has made the Jewish mystical tradition both accessible and intelligible to both the Jewish and the more general scholarly community.

His major publications are *Major Trends in Jewish Mysticism* (1941), *Jewish Gnosticism, Merkabah Mysticism and Talmudic Tradition* (1960), *On the Kabbalah and Its Symbolism* (1965), *Ursprung und Anfaenge der Kabbalah* (1962), *The Messianic Idea in Judaism* (1971), and *Shabbatai Tzvi VeHaTenuah HaSabbeta'it* (2 vols. [1957], English translation: *Sabbatai Tzvi* [1973] and *Kabbalah* [1974]). A full bibliography of his publications up to 1967, running to over 500 items, can be found in *Studies in Mysticism and Religion Presented to Gershom Scholem on his Seventieth Birthday* (1967).

Scholem's studies have transformed understanding of the Jewish mystical tradition, rescuing it from the misunderstanding and abuse it received in the hands of earlier scholars and making it at once a fascinating and respectable part of the Jewish tradition. Scholem stressed the variety of Jewish experience and the legitimate religious character of its mystical tradition. In so doing, he was especially concerned to present counterevidence against the monolithic, primarily *halakhic*-philosophical interpretation of Jewish history and creativity.

Scholem's studies centered primarily on the medieval tradition, with special concentration on the ideas and authorship of the *Zohar*, the school and theology of Isaac Luria, and the seventeenth-century pseudomessianic Shabbatean movement.

All the aforementioned studies throw light on the historical and intellectual background of Hasidism, especially Scholem's monumental researches into the Shabbatean movement, which was in large part responsible for the immediate historical milieu out of which Hasidism emerged. With regard to his direct studies on Hasidism, his most sustained and important discussion is to be found in the chapter on Hasidism in his book *Major Trends in Jewish Mysticism*. In that work he painstakingly searched out the deep religious-historical connections between the earlier pseudomystical Shabbatean movement and the Baal Shem Tov and his circle and clearly presented the basic ideas of the hasidic movement in the earliest phase.

In Scholem's view, Hasidism as a mature, independent movement is a "typical revivalist movement," which did not renounce the proselytizing mission of later Kabbalah. However, according to Scholem, what distinguishes Hasidism from earlier Jewish mystical movements is that it retained and spread those elements in the kabbalistic tradition "that were capable of evoking a popular response" while "neutralizing" the explosive eschatological messianic element, which had been central to Lurianism and Shabbateanism. Hasidism is thus seen to shift messianic concern to the periphery of its religious consciousness.

The corollary of that shift is a new concentration on the individual and on individual redemption and a new "psychologizing" of traditional mystical doctrines, which emphasized the emotional and ethical implications of those doctrines rather than their more traditional metaphysical connotation. Scholem saw this "psychological" revaluation clearly present in the hasidic interpretation of such traditional kabbalistic concepts as *tikkun*, *devekut*, and *kavvanah*, to name only three. In addition, Scholem emphasized that the most revolutionary and original contribution of Hasidism to the history of religion is its doctrine of the *tzaddik* through which "personality takes the place of doctrine." The *tzaddik* now becomes the living incarnation of Torah around which the hasidic community gathers and provides the organic center for the individual and communal life of the hasidic community.

More specialized, yet seminal studies of hasidic topics that have developed the general understanding set out in *Major Trends* include an important discussion—"The Neutralization of the Messianic Element in Early Hasidism" (reprinted in *The Messianic Idea in Judaism*), a profound explication of the doctrine of *devekut* (reprinted in *The Messianic Idea*), and a devastating critique—"Martin Buber's Interpretation of Hasidism" (in *The Messianic Idea*). Scholem also published several important papers on the *Mitnagged* polemic against Hasidism (see *Zion* 20 [1955], pp. 73–81, 153–162), among other studies.

Finally, Scholem also did pioneering work in the field of establishing a critical hasidic bibliography, beginning this work by listing hasidic sources in his *Bibliographica Kabbalistica* (1933) and by compiling a detailed bibliography for the literature of Bratzlaver Hasidism in a pamphlet entitled *Kuntres Elleh Shemot* (1928). All in all, Scholem's pioneering work laid the foundations for an objective-critical study of Hasidism, and some of his students, most notably, J. G. Weiss and Rivkah Schatz-Uffenheimer, began to work in this direction.

G. Scholem, *Major Trends in Jewish Mysticism.*

——, *Trends in Jewish Mysticism.*

E. Urbach and B. J. Werblowsky, eds., *Studies in Mysticism and Religion Presented to Gershom G. Scholem on His Seventieth Birthday.*

S.K.

SCHONFELD, Yehudah Hayyim, of Kielce/London (1892–13 *Elul* 1967)—Born in Wloclawek, a descendant of the "Holy Jew," he studied under his grandfather R. Elhanan Ungier in Piatek Piontke. In 1917, he married Malkah Hannah, the daughter of R. Elimelekh Jacob Yitzhak Rabinowicz.

In 1931, he came to London, where he established a *Bet HaMidrash* in the East End, and later in Golders Green. A gentle and kindly man, he devoted himself to fostering Jewish family purity. In 1966, he settled in Israel, where he died a year later.

He is survived by his son, R. Motel.

SCHWADRON, Shalom Mordecai Hakohen, of Brzezany (27 *Nisan* 1835–16 *Shevat* 1911)—Popularly known as the *Maharsham* (*Moreinu HaRav Shalom Mordecai*), a name based on his authoritative responsa, he was the son of R. Moses, a hasid of R. Meir of Przemyshlan. His mother, Esther Gitel, was a granddaughter of R. Yitzhak of Drohobycz. He married Yenta, the daughter of R. Abraham Yakir, a hasid of Stretyn.

He visited hasidic rabbis, such as R. Abraham of Stretyn, R. Yitzhak Eizig of Zydaczov, and R. Shalom Rokeah of Belz. On the recommendation of R. David Moses Friedman of Chortkov, he was appointed rabbi in Potok-Zloty. Later he served for two years in Buczacz, and for the last thirty years of his life was rabbi in Brzezany.

In addition to his twelve halakhic works, which cover 3,753 responsa, he was the author of a hasidic work *Tekhelet Mordecai* on the Pentateuch (Sighet, 1912). Throughout the month of *Elul*, he would spend the whole day in his *tallit* and *tefillin*, studying the writings of R. Yitzhak Luria and other kabbalistic works.

A. Y. Bromberg, "Shalom Mordecai of Brzezany," pp. 295–297.

SCHWARTZ-BART, ANDRÉ (b. 1928).—Born in Metz, André Schwartz-Bart joined the Resistance when he was fifteen. Captured by the Nazis, he managed to escape and take part in the final 1944–1945 campaign against the occupation.

Schwartz-Bart writes with such well-documented realism that it is hard to credit that he himself never participated physically in the agony of his family and his people. (Though he himself was never in a concentration camp, his parents and three of his brothers and sisters died there.)

Of a working-class background, Schwartz-Bart educated himself while earning his living in a factory, becoming a student at the Sorbonne.

Schwartz-Bart's novel, *The Last of the Just* (Paris, 1959), deals with the mystical hasidic notion of the *tzaddik*, or "Just," the saint who gives the entire creation its raison d'être. This theme is in line with hasidic thinking and has its roots in Kabbalah and in the Bible story itself. One thinks of Abraham pleading that God spare the city of Sodom: "Will You kill the just with the unjust? Will the Just One of the earth not do justice?" (Genesis 18:23–25). Apparently, the existence of a certain minority of good people ensures the continued existence of an undeserving majority. From this arises the hasidic notion that each generation depends for its right to exist on *Lamed Vav*, or thirty-six hidden, righteous people.

But Schwartz-Bart has mixed up the two different hasidic notions—that of the rebbe (possibly hereditary, although only in a later development of Hasidism) and that of the *Lamed Vav tzaddikim*, the hidden thirty-six righteous, who, far from belonging to a known dynasty, are so hidden that sometimes even the person involved is not aware of the essential function their piety plays in the preservation of human society.

However, Schwartz-Bart's version centers on a publicly acknowledged dynasty of "Just" who are deeply preoccupied with their singular destiny. Jewish persecution through the centuries is filtered through the racked sensibility of a family of *tzaddikim*, culminating in a hero who undergoes the final agony of the camps.

The author certainly allows himself a certain artistic license when he rolls into one not only the roles of rebbe and *tzaddik*, but also that of the Messiah.

The redemptive quality of the suffering just, of the *tzaddik* who bears the evil of his time, is an idea that has been taken over and emphasized by Christianity, and the central place that Schwartz-Bart gives it in his novel betrays a Western rather than a hasidic influence. Intentionally so, for Ernie—Schwartz-Bart's hero—is a figure who embodies the taunt the author hurls at Christianity. It is Jew rather than Gentile who is the Messiah, suffering "Just" rather than Super-Mensch. How can Christians continue to believe their Messiah has come when suffering continues? the author demands. More rational is the Jewish mystical (and hasidic) idea that there is a potential Messiah in every age, but that he will be revealed only when his contemporaries deserve it. From the Jews, to whom the prophets had originally assigned it, the Christians stole the role of "suffering Lamb of God," and Schwartz-Bart is only making restitution when his hero, Ernie, gathers specifically Jewish children around him to comfort them. From his murmurings to them we can almost hear the words: "Suffer the little children. . . ."! In his role of *Maggid* (storyteller), in which he regales these children with tales of Paradise when, as he well knows, it is the gas chambers that awaits them, Schwartz-Bart's hero reminds us of Janusz Korczak, the great teacher who followed his pupils to the crematoria.

Mythically, Ernie is a suffering "Just," a martyr, a Messiah without kingdom or the ability to save. Unlike the Christian hero, and more realistically, Schwartz-Bart's protagonist can only suffer with the others; he can change nothing. The question is asked in the novel: What happens to suffering if there is no God to intervene? Unless the Saint take all upon himself. . . . ?

The Hasidism of Schwartz-Bart, true to a certain skepticism felt by many contemporary Jews, survivors of recent history, is sadly truncated, lacking belief in God and the hasidic joy to which such spirit of affirmation through suffering brings. As an artist, however, Schwartz-Bart does succeed in showing the relationship of many Christian religious notions of saintliness both to the actual role of Jews throughout history and to the very derivation of those same notions from an ancient form of Jewish mysticism that in the Jewish world has found expression in the past few centuries in Hasidism.

Schwartz-Bart's novel, though in fact a unique concoction of various origins, as all works of art are, succeeds in conveying the hasidic and mystical resonance of Jewish destiny.

G. Scholem, "The Tradition of the 36 Hidden Just Men."

F.G.

SECLUSION (*hitbodedut*) – Hasidic rebbes stressed the value of seclusion as a means of achieving *devekut*. R. Yitzhak Luria advised that one should separate oneself from other people and be alone – just oneself and the Creator.

Both the Besht and his disciples R. Jacob Joseph of Polonnoye, R. Nahman of Bratzlav, and R. Aaron of Karlin practiced *hitbodedut*: "To be in solitude is of supreme advantage, the most important ideal," wrote R. Nahman (*Likkutei Moharan, Tinyana*, p. 147). "A man should set aside at least one hour or more during which he is alone in a room or in a field, so that he can commune with his Creator. He should take care to carry this out daily at a special time."

He maintained that the ideal time for *hitbodedut* is at night when one can seclude oneself and express oneself before the Almighty. This is the way to attain true joy and to subdue the power of fantasy, which is the source of all lust and desire.

R. Aaron of Karlin, too, stressed, "You should seclude yourself one day a week, if possible, in a special room devoted to spiritual practice, where you can fast and do *teshuvah* and study Torah. . . . During the whole day be especially careful not to engage in any idle talk – just involve yourself in Torah and fear of God all day" (*Hanhagot Tzaddikim*, no. 3, p. 3).

Y. Buxbaum, *Jewish Spiritual Practices*, p. 631.

SEFER YETZIRAH (Book of Creation) – One of the oldest books of Jewish mysticism. It originated between the third and fifth century C.E. L. Goldschmidt assigns it to the second century. According to Zunz, Graetz, Bacher, and Bloch, it was composed in the period of the Gaonim in the eighth century, probably in Palestine. It is mentioned in the Palestinian Talmud and has even been attributed to either R. Akiba or the patriarch Abraham. It was first printed in Mantua in 1562, and more than fifty commentaries have been written on it. It was translated into English, German, French, Italian, and Czech.

Though containing only six short chapters and less than 2,000 words, it is one of the most remarkable works in Jewish literature. The Talmud mentions that, by using it, two scholars created a three-year-old calf (*Sanhedrin* 65b and 67b). The subject of the book is the creation of the world or the formation of the world in "thirty-two ways of wisdom," represented by the twenty-two letters of the Hebrew alphabet and the ten *Sefirot*.

The book has two versions. One of them was found in the Cairo *Genizah*.

E. Muller, *History of Jewish Mysticism*, pp. 47–50.

SEFIROT – The *Sefirot* have been most aptly described as "emanations" from the divine, acting as intermediaries or graded links between the completely spiritual and unknowable Creator and the material sublunar world.

This was the kabbalists' solution to the problem of the completely spiritual – being able to make contact with the completely material sublunar world, a *Sefirot* ladder of spiritually graded emanations reaching from heaven to earth and from earth to heaven. The *Sefirot*, ten in number, were the ten rungs of the ladder, the ten manifestations of divine power, the ten sources of creation and blessing.

In answer to the threat to the belief in the unity of God that this doctrine implies, the *Zohar* assures us that God is an organic whole but with different manifestations of power – just as the life of the soul is one, though manifested variously in the eyes, hands, and other limbs.

Other kabbalists express "the many that are yet one," by using the human body to symbolize the ten *Sefirot*. "His limbs are many but he is one." Another favorite symbol indicating unity in multiplicity is the tree, with its central trunk and branches to the left and right.

The most usual names for the *Sefirot* are *Keter* (Crown), *Hokhmah* (Wisdom), *Hesed* (Kindness), *Gevurah* (Might), *Tiferet* (Beauty), *Netzah* (Victory), *Hod* (Splendor), *Yesod* (Foundation), and *Malkhut* (Kingdom or Sovereignty).

The first is also called *Ein Sof*, or Infinite, above human understanding. From the *Ein Sof* appeared a glimmer of light, which is the second *Sefirah Hokhmah*, the first perceptible to the human intellect. From thence, one emanates from the other like one candle's lighting the next. "Above even *Keter*," says the *Sefer Yetzirah*, "is the Cause of causes, which must not be numbered with them, for it is a hidden entity."

Such *mitzvot* as *tefillin* and *lulav*, which failed to appeal to those imbued with the spirit of rational philosophy of the Middle Ages, assumed new significance when regarded as symbols of the *Sefirot* themselves. Additionally, the all-important doctrine of reciprocal action was emphasized: "As the warrior carries the charm, the charm carries the warrior," that is to say, prayer, observance of the *mitzvot*, and ethical habits help to pour beneficial power into the *Sefirot*, which the *Sefirot* retransmit as a blessing to humankind. This doctrine of reciprocal action would obviously intensify the *hitlahavut*, or enthusiasm of mystical observance. Not only the *mitzvot* that were mystically connected with the *Sefirot*, but also words, ideas, and personalities from the Torah itself, in addition to their normal meaning, assumed a *Sefirot* symbolism or significance, thus providing infinite inspiration for the student searching for the "way of truth."

The actual term "*Sefirah*" is, according to the kabbalists, derived from the biblical connotations of the root S-F-R (cf. Exodus 24:10 and Psalms 19:2, 56:9, etc.). The book *Bahir* describes the *Sefirah* as "sapphirelike light flashes of God."

Sefer Yetzirah prefers the other shade of meaning–of "numbers," "*mispar*." Scholem translates the term as "spheres." There are many other names and synonyms used for the *Sefirot*.

Leading kabbalistic schools on the doctrine of the *Sefirot* began to flourish in southern France and Spain in particular, from the twelfth century onward, and included such personalities as Isaac the Blind, Azriel ben Solomon, Nahmanides, and Moses de Leon.

I. Tishby, "Kitvei HaMekubbalim R. Ezra VeR. Azriel MiGerona."

——, *Mishnat HaZohar*.

S.H.

SEGAL, Israel, of Zamosc (1710-1772)

–Son of R. Moses, Israel was born in Bobruisk, near Lvov, and was a contemporary of both the Besht and R. Dov Baer, the Maggid of Mezhirech.

In his ethical work *Nezed Hadema* (Dyhernfurth, 1773), a number of passages are interpreted as veiled attacks against Hasidism. Many of these allegations were later taken up by Joseph Perl.

H. Liberman, "Israel of Zamosz," pp. 113–120.

SEGULLAH (a charm)

–When the rebbe sees that the hasidim crave for something tangible as evidence of the potency of his blessing, he may give them a *segullah*.

Segullot vary in range from herbal medicines to *kamayot*. The rebbe generally gives items that are related to Jewish sacramental life: leftover *etrogim*, *matzah*, wine, oil from the Sabbath lamps, Sabbath foods, and *haroset*. Amulets are also used. The Besht stated that an amulet need not contain God's name or the name of an angel. It was sufficient if it contained the rebbe's own name.

In *Sefer HaHaum*, also called *Segullot Yisrael*, by R. Shabbetai Lipshitz of Orshava, many *segullot* are enumerated. There are *segullot* to counteract barrenness, to ensure male offspring, and for preventing difficult births.

See *Yehidut*.

Z. M. Schachter, *The Yehidut*, p. 459.

Z.M.S.

SELIHOT (penitential prayers)

–Penitential prayers, written by poets of medieval Spain, such as Solomon Ibn Gabirol, Judah Halevi, and Moses Ibn Ezra, are recited during the period preceding Rosh Hashanah (from 1 *Elul* among the Sephardim, and from the Sunday before Rosh Hashanah among the Ashkenazim).

Many hasidim, like Lubavitch, recited it at midnight in conformity with the idea of the psalmist's "At midnight I will rise to give thanks unto Thee" (Psalm 119:62). In Belz and many other Galician dynasties, they were recited at 4 A.M., before daybreak. In Ger, *selihot* were recited at night only on the first and last night prior to Rosh Hashanah.

In Belz, the rabbi himself officiated at the reader's desk and also recited the whole Book of Psalms. Before *selihot*, a hasid once said to R. Mordecai of Nadvorna, "I am in a great hurry. I have to look through the *selihot* liturgy." "Don't be in such a hurry," replied the rabbi. "The *selihot* have not changed since last year. You would do better to look at yourself and see whether you have changed."

SEPHARDIM–Jews of Spain, Portugal, and other countries located in the Mediterranean area are known as Sephardim or Sephardic Jews.

At first, the Sephardim of the Holy Land lived in harmony with the newly arrived hasidim. R. Abraham Gershon was welcomed by the Sephardim when he settled in Hebron, where he lived for six years. He was even invited to become their spiritual leader, an honor he was reluctant to accept. As more hasidim continued to arrive, however, the Sephardim began to have second thoughts about the influx. They were afraid that the new arrivals would become a financial liability, and they were reluctant to give them an equitable share of the funds collected in the Diaspora. As this became clear to the hasidim, they began to appeal directly to fellow Jews in Eastern Europe.

Conversely, R. Shalom Dov Baer of Lubavitch took a great interest in the *Berg Yidden*–the 100,000 Sephardic Jews who were living in the Caucasian Mountains in Russia. He set up an institute for the training of rabbis, teachers, *shohetim*, and cantors for the Sephardic community.

R. Joseph Yitzhak Schneersohn established a network of institutions in Morocco. *Yeshivot* were also established in Djerba, Tunisia. R. Yekutiel Judah Halberstam, the founder of *Kiryat Zanz*, Netanya, was particularly concerned with the status of Israel's Yemenite and North African citizens, and he became incensed when he heard of discrimination or intolerance toward the Sephardim. "How can we have anything but admiration," he declared, "for a community that produced the 'Golden Age' of Spain and [for] such luminaries as Yitzhak Alfasi, Moses Maimonides, Joseph Karo, Hayyim Ibn Attar, Shalom Sharabi, and the kabbalist Abraham Azulai (1570–1643)?" For the Oriental Jews he established *Yeshivat Maharshad*, named in memory of his father-in-law, R. Shmuel David Ungar.

Through his personal emissary in Europe–R. B. Goredezky–the rabbi of Lubavitch appointed R. Michael Lipsker to organize educational establishments for the Jews in Morocco and Tunisia. Today, *Habad* is the most important Jewish organization in Moslem countries.

SERPENT–From the story of the tempting of Eve in the Garden of Eden, the serpent (*nahash*) became in the *Midrash* a symbol of evil. It was identified variously with evil inclination, with Satan or Samael, and with the creature upon which Samael rode.

In Kabbalah, the primeval serpent (*nahash kadmoni*) represented the powers of evil and darkness (*Sitra Ahra*) and had its domain in the rivers and crevices of "the great abyss." The serpent had evil designs upon the *Shekhinah*, and its power to dominate the *Shekhinah* was increased by our sinful deeds.

D.G.

SEUDAH SHLISHIT (third [Sabbath] meal)–It is traditional to eat three meals on the Sabbath (based on the rabbinic exegesis (see *Shabbat* 118a) of Exodus 16:25. The third meal, known as the *seudah shlishit*, is traditionally eaten between *Minhah* and *Maariv* on Sabbath evening and in any case must not be started before the time for *Minhah* (*Shulhan Arukh*, *Orah Hayyim* 291:2).

The third meal is of particular importance in Hasidism and is the major event in the weekly hasidic calendar. During the third meal, the following specifically hasidic aspects are of significance and deserve special attention. The hasidim gather at the table (*der tish*) of the *tzaddik* in an environment of hushed excitement and expectation in order to re-create and renew their interdependence and their communal solidarity. The meal begins with the *tzaddik*'s making *motzi* (blessing over the *hallah*). After a few bites the *tzaddik* passes the rest of his portion among his followers, who eagerly compete for the remains, called *shirayim*.

The same procedure regarding *shirayim* is then followed through the remaining courses, usually including a fish dish symbolic of (1) good luck ("against the evil eye"); (2) the messianic age, which, according to tradition (*Baba Batra* 74b–75a), will be ushered in by the feast of the great fish leviathan; and (3) the special blessings of God. The reason the remains (*shirayim*) were so eagerly sought after was the belief that the *tzaddik* had, in kabbalistic terms, raised the "hidden sparks" (*nitzotzot*) present in the food, thereby elevating it to special sacramental status. Either between courses or after the meal the *tzaddik* gives his *divrei Torah* (Torah teaching) for the week. That teaching usually consists of reflections on the Torah portion for that week, though the theme and emphasis vary.

Another essential feature of the *seudah shlishit* is the special hasidic *niggunim* (melodies), which are associated with the occasion, music being highly valued as a means of religious expression and communion between God and man. The Besht and many later *tzaddikim* are credited not only with an appreciation of the power of music but also with the creation of specific *niggunim*. These *tish niggunim* (table melodies), which vary somewhat between hasidic dynasties, are presented without words or are applied to more traditional Sabbath *zemirot* (melodies). It is also customary to sing two songs credited to the great sixteenth-century mystic of Safed, Isaac Luria (the "Ari"), namely, "Atkinu Seudata" (I shall arrange the meal) and "Benei Hekhalah" (children of the palace). It is also customary in many hasidic dynasties for the hasidim to recite Psalm 23 and for the rebbe to chant Psalm 121 responsively with his hasidim, after which the rebbe makes *Havdalah*.

In addition to the concrete and procedural aspects cataloged previously there is also a more strictly kabbalistic-mystical aspect specifically associated with this third meal. Among the hasidim it is generally held that the occasion is symbolically comparable to death and that during this time hasidim are especially close to God. As the Sabbath is nearing its end (i.e., "dying"), so too the hasidim experience something of the profound meaning of death, and as a corollary they experience something of that unique closeness (*devekut*) to God, which is possible only on the far side of the grave.

Inseparable from these notions is also the further kabbalistic doctrine, held by the hasidim to be literally true, that on the Sabbath, Jews are blessed with an extra soul. With the departing of the Sabbath this extra soul likewise departs, and with its departure its spiritual power, which helps lift us nearer to God than is ordinarily possible, is lost. There is also the belief that on the Sabbath the suffering of those in Gehenna is suspended and that with Sabbath's passing, their torment begins again. Thus the end of the Sabbath is a cause for sadness. This is also one of the reasons why the hasidim seek to prolong the Sabbath in order to give these poor souls additional respite.

And again, the hasidim, drawing on early kabbalistic tradition (see *Zohar*, Exodus 88), see in this meal a symbol of "the complete harmonious perfection" of the upper worlds, from which "all the six days that are to come will receive blessing."

A. Wertheim, *Halakhot VeHalikhot BaHasidut*.

S.K.

SEX – Much of Hasidism's attitude toward sex is an adaptation of earlier kabbalistic ideas. In Kabbalah, sex is not seen as evil but as *razah deyihudah* – the secret of union. The very origins of the universe are to be found in a never-ceasing process of arousal, coupling, and gestation within the life of a God who is both male and female. The complex inner flow of divinity, described in graphic sexual terms, is the highest of mysteries. The revelation at Sinai is described as the "nuptials" between God and Israel; the Sabbath is a time when *Shekhinah* and the community of Israel meet in sexual embrace. To some, the union of male and female is the mystical symbol of life and love in the realm of *Sefirot*.

Hence, the sex impulse is not a shameful passion or one to be suppressed; rather it is a holy urge, natural and even noble, if expressed in loving union between husband and wife. Even the sex organs are not "pudenda" – a source of shame, but, just as the hand is noble when it writes a Sefer Torah but ignoble when it steals, thus the sex organ is noble when it expresses purity and love but ignoble when it is the instrument of lust, sensuality, or illicit sex. Nothing in creation is ugly; it is by humanity's folly that ugliness is ascribed to things beautiful in themselves.

Hasidism, then, inherited attitudes that (1) the world is good, being saturated with the very essence of God; (2) our physical needs, part of God's manifestation in the finite world, are thus in themselves worthy and good; (3) our actions have cosmic significance; and (4) our *kavvanah* gives our actions cosmic value. Accordingly ([1] and [2]), the sex organs are good, ([3] and [4]), cosmic benefits derive from loving and noble coitus, and evil influences are given dominance in the world by ugly and vulgar sex pleasures.

Thought alone–*kavvanah*–is sufficient to make all the difference. Hence, even *hirhurim*–erotic thoughts without sex–can do evil and can be worse than behavioristic sins, because thought is part of the spiritual world and because its effect on the *Sefirot* is therefore even more immediate. Illicit sex, vulgar speech, and erotic thoughts all are in the service of *Sitra Ahra*–the Universal Evil–and cause diminution of the power of God.

Thus Hasidism, the movement of joy, which preached, according to the Besht, spontaneity, joyousness, and fervor, still had firm ties to the mystic traditions–to the *Zohar*, to the Safed circle, and to the Kabbalah of R. Isaac Luria. The belt-tightening asceticism in terms of food and drink and joylessness in sex, which characterized the Safed circle, grew even more so in the latter part of the sixteenth century under R. Yitzhak Luria and his kabbalistic system.

Kabbalah suffered gross perversion in the seventeenth century under the pseudomessianism of Shabbetai Tzvi and Jacob Frank. Relief from external oppression became so urgent a need that a strange doctrine was propounded: sin can become the vehicle of redemption, and the breaking of law its fulfillment. The result was gross sexual immorality carried on with the express intention of bringing about redemption. The reaction to this antinomian episode was even more melancholy, in the form of a backlash into new austerities and mortifications, which continued even after the hasidic revolution in the eighteenth century.

The Besht had to overcome this negative tradition and even found it necessary to admonish one of his disciples who was given to self-affliction. One need have mercy on one's own body and even on its lusts and passions, he wrote to him, giving a homiletic twist to Isaiah's call (58:7) "that thou hide not thyself from thine own flesh." It is proper, he went on, to have lust for material things because through this, one can come to "lust" for Torah and worship.

What prompts us, he asked, to sin in sexual matters? Love–and love is a Godly attribute. But we dilute thereby its godly quality and render it profane. Even erotic love and sexual passion are instilled in us so that we may come thereby to love of God. The word *hesed* in Leviticus 20:17, ordinarily translated "loving-kindness," is, in this context, used to signify incest. The homonymous use of the same word for both concepts, indicates, the Besht wrote, that even this sinful passion is merely an unripe fruit of the higher virtue, or a distortion of that virtue of love of God.

The Besht even gave a new interpretation to the talmudic phrase according to which conjugal relations are to be carried out "as if possessed by a demon." Moralistic tracts circulating in his time endorsed the idea, but the Besht takes an opposite or happier view: the conjugal act should be executed with burning passion, with desire, and with joy. He goes so far as to set this up as a model for the spiritual life. The Kabbalah may have used sexual symbolism in expounding its doctrine, but the Besht used erotic desire itself. He wrote, for example, "Just as in physical union one cannot procreate except with a live organ, with joy and pleasure, so in spiritual union such as in speaking words of Torah and prayer, can one create only when alive with joy and pleasure."

The Besht had to combat the twin influences of *Zohar* and Kabbalah in one more area–that of anxieties associated with *keri*, or nocturnal emissions. The *Zohar* had traced these to incubi or to succubi (female demonic spirits that visit a man when he sleeps and that thus give birth to new evil spirits). This notion had a profound negative influence on attitudes toward sexuality generally and brought much sadness and melancholy into the hearts of the Jewish masses. Not so, says the Besht; banish this unnecessary anxiety. Actions and thoughts can be sinful, but if this physical reflex is not caused by preoccupation with sinful thought, it might even be good. Slight as this departure from the *Zohar* sounds, the Besht thus eased consciences and banished depression from many a tortured soul.

Soon after the Besht's death, however, this attitude and outlook went into eclipse. A new generation of hasidic teachers resumed the theme of the negation of sexual desire and the evil of nocturnal emission. And yet there were some hasidic leaders of that new generation who, like the Besht, were quite reassuring to their disciples. One such was R. Yaakov Yitzhak, the "Seer" of Lublin, who taught: Don't be sad about sin, because sadness caused by sin is worse than the sin itself, and is more harmful to the service of God. The "Seer" discounts, moreover, the view that would suppress sexual pleasure. More important, he says, is that one direct one's thoughts heavenward.

The "Seer" is also credited with the following qualification of another accepted moralistic principle. That principle taught, in the words of the Talmud, that one should "sanctify oneself at the time of cohabitation." How can this be, asks the "Seer," when the sex act involves one's total passions and feelings, leaving no mind for "sanctification"? What the principle means, he teaches, is that one should sanctify oneself *before* the act, intending it for the proper and holy purposes, and then surrender oneself to the totality of sexual passion.

In Kotzk, hasidim moved to the furthest extreme from the declared hasidic purpose of joyousness. Kotzk was the town in Poland where R. Menahem Mendel held sway, where he and his disciples reached new heights of self-abnegation and of "holy sadness." Severity, sacrifice, and Spartan discipline were the hallmarks of Kotzk. Newly married young men would come to Kotzk, not merely to spend a Sabbath or a holy day with their rebbe to return home spiritually uplifted, but to stay a year and longer. Kotzk would train them in the subjugation of passionate desire.

In contrast with the Besht, R. Mendel saw passion as an enemy, because it is so fiery and so strong that it tends to "crowd out" or improperly encroach upon the love of God. All the forces within us, he taught, should be harnessed to the service of God. God must be the master of the house within us, but instead, erotic passion intrudes, beginning to make its voice heard and to "spin webs." It becomes before long master of the house and assumes control of our inner life. Again, the polar opposite of the Besht, R. Mendel claimed that two yearnings cannot exist simultaneously—the yearning for God and that for sexual gratification. Lust, he went on to say, is not a psychological need of human nature; it is a passing confrontation. It is like lodging in an inn: one stays overnight and then resumes one's journey. Jealousy may be inborn, but lust comes with practice. Yet erotic passion can become a dominant force, affecting one's thoughts and achievements.

An external symbol of one of Hasidism's teachings about sex is the "gartel," the belt worn around the waist during prayer and study. Its purpose is to separate, as it were, the upper world from the lower, the spiritual from the physical. Although R. Mendel of Kotzk was opposed to externals, showing identical disdain for the condition of his clothing and for mere external piety, he nonetheless insisted that his followers wear the gartel.

Another moralistic principle coming from the Talmud is to "sanctify yourself even with the permitted." This became more than a way of life at Kotzk. R. Mendel pointed out that of several possible versions of the marriage formula to be recited by the groom in a marriage ceremony, the one chosen is "Behold thou art sanctified unto me." Why is this? In order, he explained, to remind the groom that his conjugal relations must be in sanctity and holiness—except that to him this meant the sanctity of reserve and suppression.

As was to be expected, a reaction set in against this way of thinking and acting. R. Isaac Meir took polite exception: "What are we without desire and passion? Our supremacy over the beasts consists in our recognition of our impulses and in our proper control over them." But the real break came with another of his disciples, R. Mordecai Joseph. This disciple removed himself from Kotzk to Izbica. R. Mordecai Joseph took polite but sharp issue with his former mentor, especially on the matter of attitudes toward erotic desire; it was this difference of opinion, according to A. J. Heschel, that caused the break between them. R. Mordecai Joseph preached against the holy sadness, the righteous anger, the extremism, the otherworldliness of Kotzk. It is wrong to reject fundamental human desires, he taught. The middle road of moderation in gratifying them is best, but even if one had to choose—"better a flood than a drought."

The very existence of passion is a kindness from God. To the question, How can a holy soul be created through an act of lust? he would respond, "This may indeed be a mystery, but what is clear is that some hidden power lies within a woman, from whom, in birth, holiness emanates. Birth," he says, "can come about only by spiritual obliviousness"—much like what was said earlier by the "Seer" of Lublin with regard to total involvement in sexual passion. For the moment, our awareness is suspended. If we tried to keep our mind on God, we would be incapable of the "suspension" needed to bring about conception and birth. Furthermore, God thus makes it manifest retroactively that our entire intent was for heaven's sake.

Another illustration of the differences between R. Mendel and R. Mordecai Joseph centers on the person of the biblical Pinhas, grandson of Aaron. Pinhas was a hero in Kotzk because of the "zealotry" he manifested in dramatically ending the brazen sexual immorality between Israelites and Midianites by slaying the culprit, Zimri. He thus became a model of zealotry for the hasidim of Kotzk. In a daring departure from this line of thinking, and in audacious exegesis of the biblical story, R. Mordecai Joseph sides with Zimri, the object of Pinhas's wrath. "Zimri," he writes, "knew what he was doing, while Pinhas, failing to understand Zimri's deeper motivation, acted childishly," with the foolish haste of zealots who take deeds at face value only. Nevertheless, Pinhas was granted "my covenant of peace" for acting according to his perception of things.

Another such example is the biblical verse concerning the "captive woman." Deuteronomy 21:10–11 reads, "When thou goest forth to battle . . . and takest its captivity; when thou seest among the captives a woman of beauty and thou desirest her and wouldest take her unto thee for wife." Conventional understanding of the verse has it that its aim is to counter the tendency, so common among conquering warriors, to visit rape upon their victims. Since obedience to an uncompromising prohibition to that effect is too much to expect (this point of view holds), the Torah temporizes, so to speak. It provides for a phased sequence of taking the foreign woman to wife, a sequence designed to help cool the conqueror's ardor and protect the woman's sensibilities. Accordingly, the Talmud declared, "The Torah speaks *k'neged* (in view of, against) the evil impulse." The evil impulse is so uncontrollably strong in this matter that the Torah meets it halfway, to ward off a greater evil. To R. Mendel of Kotzk, that interpretation is unthinkable. Since when does the Talmud make compromises with the evil impulse? The Torah itself declares, once and for all, "Ye shall not go astray after what your eyes see," meaning, says the Talmud, "not go astray after harlotry." One dare not yield to the desire that leads to sin! The objection becomes all the more pointed when the *Zohar*'s interpretation of this verse is remembered. "Battle against thine enemy," means, says the *Zohar*, "thine enemy the evil impulse." So how could the Talmud have suggested that we surrender before we even begin? R. Mendel therefore reinterprets the Talmudic passage: The Torah speaks *k'neged*—meaning not "in view of" but "against" the evil impulse. The Torah reveals what the evil impulse would have us do, but it also directs us to overcome it and not do it.

R. Mordecai Joseph now interprets this verse far differently, opposite to that of his mentor and different still from that of the conventional. The strong desire one has for the captive woman indicates that there is something valuable in her that one seeks to bring within the fold. The desire comes from God. Hence the Torah permitted such because often, when the impulse is so overbearing, it apparently comes from God in the way that the mating of Judah and Tamar was part of a divine plan for history. Such a view is daring enough, though hardly useful to moral decisions. Still, it was a view put forth by earlier mystics such as R. Hayyim Ibn Attar (d. 1743) in his Bible commentary. The opponents of Hasidism (*mitnaggedim*) were understandably intolerant of such notions.

The prime disciple of R. Mordecai Joseph was R. Tzaddok (d. 1900) of Lublin, with whom the joyous affirmations of the Besht come full circle. He wrote profoundly on all aspects of religious philosophy, including sex, and had some novel contributions to make: Those who seek to crush or uproot the evil impulse are doomed to disappointment. The attempt has charm and beauty, but, just as "Charm is deceitful and beauty is vain" (Proverbs 31:30), because they are superficial or transitory, so is this effort. So the Talmud itself teaches, in comparing the efforts of Palti ben Laiysh with that of Boaz.

We need to recognize these impulses and channel them properly with divine assistance: "But God fearing . . . is to be praised." Moreover, R. Tzaddok taught that "there is a compensatory mechanism," so to speak, in the economy of our psychic energy. "Who is free of the sins of sexual passion had better be on guard against tendencies to undue anger or murderousness."

D. M. Feldman, *Birth Control in Jewish Law*.

A. J. Heschel, "R. Nahman of Kosov."

D.M.F.

SHABBETAI of Rashkov (1655–1745)–A disciple of the Besht, he was the author of a prayer book (Korzec, 1794) based on the *kavvanot* of R. Yitzhak Luria and also of an anthology of Luria's writings *Sefer Kelolot Tikkun VeAliyot HaOlamot* (Lvov, 1778; Czernowitz, 1880).

His son R. Joseph (d. 5 *Adar* 1770) was a disciple of R. Pinhas of Koretz. He was succeeded by his son R. Shlomoh Zalmina (d. 13 *Nisan* 1852).

The dynasty was maintained by R. Shabbetai (d. 8 *Tevet* 1883), who was known as a great animal lover. Every morning, he himself fed the animals. He was succeeded by his son R. Yehiel Joseph, who died on 7 *Adar* 1896. His other son, R. Shlomoh Zalmina (d. 20 *Heshvan* 1916), was the son-in-law of R. Abraham Joshua Heschel of Medziborz.

SHABBETAI TZVI (9 *Av* 1626–1676), pseudo-Messiah–Son of a merchant, Mordecai Tzvi, he was born in Smyrna (Izmir) on the Sabbath. He studied in Smyrna under R. Joseph Eskapa, R. Samuel Primo, R. Yisrael Benjamin, and R. Moses Galante. At the age of eighteen, he was ordained as a *hakham*. He wandered through Greece and Thrace, where he stayed for two years, and he visited Salonika, Constantinople, Jerusalem, and Egypt.

Between 1642 and 1648, he lived in semi-seclusion and contracted two marriages in Smyrna, which ended in divorce. On March 31, 1664, he married Sarah, an orphan of the 1648 massacre. One year later, he met Nathan of Gaza, who became his "prophet." He suffered from manic-depressive psychosis, alternating between feelings of sublime happiness and ecstasy and moods of dejection and melancholy.

Claiming that the Messiah ben Joseph had preceded him in the guise of a Polish Jew–Abraham Alman, who was murdered by the Cossacks–Shabbetai Tzvi proclaimed himself the Messiah, the son of David. Although he was excommunicated by the *Bet Din* of Smyrna, his chief aide, Nathan of Gaza, continued to issue messianic manifestos proclaiming that he was the long-awaited redeemer of Israel about to inaugurate the kingdom of God in Jerusalem.

Shabbetai Tzvi made great efforts to enlist the sympathies of Polish Jewry, whose sufferings he vowed to avenge. The movement took root and spread. It captivated the Jews of the Levant, particularly the Marranos and their descendants. In far-off communities, from London to Morocco, hopes were stirred. Gluckel from Hamelin (1646–1724), the German writer of memoirs, living mainly in Hamburg, described the impact of Shabbetai Tzvi and spoke of the "joy" that cannot be expressed in words.

Shabbetai Tzvi left for Constantinople on December 30, 1665. He was arrested by the Turkish authorities on February 6, 1666 and charged as a rebel against the Ottoman Empire. He was imprisoned in Abydos in Gallipoli and was later moved to Adrianople. On September 16, 1666, he was offered the choice: convert to Islam or face execution. He preferred a Turkish turban to a martyr's death, and he became known as *Aziz Mehemed Effendi* or *Kapici Bashi* (keeper of the palace gate). He lived in Adrianople and Constantinople until 1672, when he was exiled to Dulcigo in Albania. In 1674, when his wife, Sarah, died, he married Esther, the daughter of Joseph Filosof of Salonika. He died on the Day of Atonement, on September 17, 1676.

In spite of his apostasy, Shabbetai Tzvi still retained many supporters. They rationalized his actions as necessary in order to achieve the ultimate goal of retrieving the imprisoned holy sparks from the realm of evil. They maintained that by converting to Islam, Shabbetai Tzvi was actually descending into that realm and personally reenacting a primal struggle.

After his death, several of his supporters claimed the messianic mantle. The most notorious was Jacob Leibovitch Frank (1726–1791) of Galicia, who proclaimed himself the Messiah. Orgies took the place of mystic speculations, and immoral rites were the order of the day. Jews sighed with relief when Frank and his followers embraced Christianity in February 1759.

Shabbetai Tzvi, the Besht maintained, had a "spark of holiness," but Satan caught him in his snares (*Shivhei HaBesht*, Tale 66). According to hasidic legend, the death of the Besht was the result of his spiritual fight against Shabbetai Tzvi. Legend also has it that Shabbetai Tzvi appeared to the Besht in a dream.

There is no evidence of any association whatsoever between Shabbeteanism and the hasidic movement. In fact, whenever his name is mentioned in the *Shivhei HaBesht*, the phrase "May his name be blotted out" follows (*Shivhei HaBesht*, Tale 41, 64, 66).

A *shohet* of Byshev was disqualified because he belonged to the sect of Shabbetai Tzvi (*Shivhei HaBesht*, Tale 177). The book *Hemdat HaYamim*, first printed in Izmir (1731–32), which had Shabbetean associations, was discarded by the Besht (Tale 64).

I. Tishby, "Between Shabbeteanism and Hasidism," pp. 268–338.

SHALOM, Shakhnah (1771–14 *Tishri* 1803) – Son of R. Abraham Hamalakh, his mother, Gitel, was the daughter of Meshullam Feivish Horowitz. He was six years old when his father died. His mother, who was then twenty-four years old, never remarried; she emigrated to the Holy Land and died in Tiberias.

R. Shalom was brought up in the home of R. Nahum of Chernobyl, and he married the daughter of R. Abraham of Korostyshev. He led an ascetic life, eating very little. He became rebbe in Pogrebisce and was known for his compassion even to the sinful. His maxim was that "the soul of every human being emanates from the divine."

He was survived by two sons, R. Israel of Ruzhyn and R. Abraham (1787–1813).

SHALOM, Shin (1904–1990), poet – Born in Parczew, Shalom (original name Shalom Joseph Shapira) was the son of R. A. J. Shapira, who was a hasidic rabbi as well as an artist of repute, the scion of the dynasties of Ruzhyn, Kozienice, and Sadgora and of R. Dov Baer, the Maggid of Mezhirech. The poet's mother, Esther Rabinowicz, came from the family of R. Jacob Yitzhak the "Seer" of Lublin and R. Aaron of Karlin.

S. Shalom's grandfather R. Hayyim Meir Yehiel was one of the founders of *Kefar Hasidim*. Shalom was a teacher at Rosh Pina, Hadera, and Jerusalem. He was awarded the Bialik prize (1941), Tchernichowsky prize (1945), Brenner prize (1950), and Israel prize (1973). He is the author of ten volumes of poetry, short stories, and plays. Although his poetry is basically secular in character, his hasidic origin and kabbalistic background deeply influenced his poetry.

Monotheistic pantheism – if such a term may be constructed – of the Kabbalah and the teachings of the Besht may still be regarded as the keystones in S. Shalom's conception of humanity. His poetry is permeated by a deep love of the people of Israel and their homeland. His *Shirei Kommemiyut Yisrael* (Songs of Israel Reestablished) celebrates the apogee of the Jewish state in the spirit of messianic faith. The same sentiment characterizes his great autobiographical poem *On Ben Pelek* and other more recent poems.

The most salient characteristics of hasidic thought flow together in S. Shalom's poetry and give them their special quality, a haunting refrain not always discernible on the surface. It is also noticeable in his prose works, especially in his autobiographical stories, such as *The Aliyah of My Grandfather*, *The Aliyah of the Hasidim*, and his autobiographical novel, *The Unextinguished Light*.

A pronounced hasidic character is found also in his play *Dan Hashomer* (Dan the Watchman), adapted by Max Brod as the libretto of the first Hebrew opera to the music of Mark Labri.

S. Shalom's book of poems *Or HaGanuz* (Hidden Light), published in 1976, represents a memorial prayer (*Kaddish*) to his whole family of hasidic rabbis, who perished in the Holocaust.

M. Ribalow, *The Flowering of Modern Hebrew Literature*, pp. 207–236.

Z.F.K.

SHAPIRA, Abraham Elimelekh, of Grodzisk (1894–23 *Kislev* 1967) – Son of R. Israel of Grodzisk, he married Malkah, the daughter of R. Yerahmiel Moses Hofstein of Kozienice. He was reluctant to become rebbe and emigrated to the Holy Land in 1926. But after the Holocaust, during which all his family perished, he became the rebbe of Grodzisk in Jerusalem.

He was the author of *Sefer Mishnat Hakhamim* (Jerusalem, 1934) and *Emunat Yisrael* (Jerusalem, 1965). His wife, Malkah, was a well-known author.

SHAPIRA, Abraham Jacob (1884–24 *Adar* II 1962), hasidic artist – Son of R. Hayyim Meir Yehiel of Drohobycz, his mother was Bathsheva, the daughter of R. Yitzhak of Bohush. He married Esther Golda, the daughter of R. Nathan David Rabinowicz of Parczev. After living with his father-in-law in Vienna during the First World War, he accompanied him to the Holy Land in 1922. For a time he worked in the *Kefar Hasidim* settlement. When his father died, he became rebbe and made his home in Jerusalem.

At the age of sixty, when his wife died, he began to paint pictures. He naturally chose those assignments that evoked his sympathy and challenged his craftsmanship. His subtle perception and concentration on the essentials rendered him a very talented artist. The director of the new Bezallel School of Arts and Crafts in Jerusalem, Jacob Steinhart, encouraged him to exhibit his work in Tel Aviv, New York, and Philadelphia.

His discourses are published in *Netivot Shalom* (Jerusalem, 1928). His son was Shin Shalom, one of the greatest poets of Israel.

Hazofeh, 24 *Adar* 1963.

SHAPIRA, Alter Reuven, of Bukovsk (1910–*Iyyar* 1942) – Son of R. David of Bukovsk, he married his cousin, the daughter of R. Pinhas Joseph Halevi Kanar. He was ordained by his uncle R. Tzvi Elimelekh of Blaszowa.

It was only through the persuasion of R. Meir Shapira, then rabbi of Sanok, that he succeeded his father as rebbe of Bukovsk. He was deported to Sambor, where he was imprisoned. He, his wife, and their children perished in the Holocaust.

SHAPIRA, Avi Ezra Zelig, of Moglienice (d. 19 *Av* 1885) – Son of R. Hayyim Meir Yehiel of Moglienice, he married the daughter of R. Abraham Jacob Friedman of Sadgora. When his father died in 1849, he did not become rebbe but lived with his father-in-law. Only in 1883 did he become rebbe and settle in Stryj.

His sons, R. Yitzhak Mordecai and R. Hayyim Meir Yehiel, became rebbes.

SHAPIRA, David, of Dynov (1822–19 *Adar* 1874) – Son of R. Tzvi Elimelekh of Dynov, he succeeded his father as rebbe in 1851, although a number of his father's adherents followed his brother, R. Eliezer of Lancut.

His discourses are to be found in *Tzemah David* on Torah (Przemysl, 1879).

One of his sons, R. Yeshayah Naftali Hirtz, succeeded him in Dynov. His other sons were R. Tzvi Elimelekh, rabbi in Blazova, and R. Meir Yehudah, rabbi in Bukovsk.

SHAPIRA, Eleazar, of Lancut (1808–12 *Elul* 1865) – Son of R. Tzvi Elimelekh of Dynov, he married the daughter of R. Joshua Heschel of Dukla. He visited R. Tzvi Hirsch of Zydaczov and R. Tzvi Hirsch of Rymanov. In 1829, he became rabbi in Rybotyce, in 1838 in Strzyzov, and then in Lancut. In 1841 he succeeded his father as rebbe.

He died in Vienna and was buried in Lancut.

His book *Yodei Binah* on Pentateuch was published posthumously in Przemysl in 1911.

His sons were R. Shlomoh of Munkacs, R. Tzvi Elimelekh of Bircza, R. Simhah Shapira of Lancut, and R. Menahem Pinhas.

SHAPIRA, Eleazar, of Lancut (1865–19 *Tammuz* 1938) – Son of R. Simhah, he married the daughter of R. Zeev Wolf of Uziran, where he became rabbi. In 1913, he moved to Lancut, and during the First World War, he lived in Vienna. In 1917, he then returned to Lancut.

His son-in-law, R. David Fuhrer, succeeded him in Lancut. His son, R. Hayyim, perished in the Holocaust.

SHAPIRA, Elimelekh, of Grodzisk (1826–1 *Nisan* 1892) – Son of R. Hayyim Meir Yehiel of Moglienice, he married the daughter of R. Yerahmiel of Przysucha.

Later in life, when his wife died, he married Hannah Brachah, the daughter of R. Hayyim Shmuel Horowitz of Checiny. After the death of his father in 1848, his father's adherents divided their allegiance between him and his four brothers.

He suffered many personal tragedies. In 1873, his son R. Hayyim Meir Yehiel died in the plague. His surviving children were R. Kalonymus Kalman of Piaseczno and R. Yeshayah, one of the founders of *Hapoel Hamizrachi*.

R. Elimelekh was the author of *Imrei Elimelekh* on Pentateuch and Festivals (Warsaw, 1876) and *Divrei Elimelekh* (Warsaw, 1890).

His son R. Yisrael succeeded him in Grodzisk. Many hasidim, however, followed R. Yehiel Meir Halstock of Ostrowiec.

SHAPIRA, Hayyim Elazar, of Munkacs (5 *Tevet* 1872–2 *Sivan* 1937)– Son of R. Tzvi Hirsch, he was born in Strzyzov. The family moved to Munkacs in 1882. He first married, in Trzebinia in 1897, the daughter of R. Shragai Yair of Bialobrzeg. The marriage remained childless. In 1907 he married the daughter of R. Jacob Moses Safrin of Komarno. In 1901, in the lifetime of his father, he became head of the *Bet Din* of Munkacs, and in 1914 he succeeded his father as rebbe. He was also the president of the *kollel Munkacs* in the Holy Land.

In 1920, when R. Issachar Dov Rokeah of Belz came to live temporarily in Munkacs, R. Hayyim Elazar became his great opponent. This hostility lasted until 1933.

In 1922, R. Shapira established the *yeshivah Darkhei Teshuvah*. To make the personal acquaintance of the kabbalist R. Shlomoh Eliezer Alfandari, the *Saba Kaddisha* (the holy sage), he visited the Holy Land in 1930 and stayed thirteen days.

He was a fiery antagonist not only of the Zionist movement but also of the Aguda. He opposed vehemently the establishment of the Hebrew Elementary School in Munkacs. He always made his position clear: if he opposed a course of action, he did not mince words. Yet, despite all his uncompromising political policies, his contact on a personal level was cordial, winning him friends in many quarters. His kindness and consideration for the underprivileged knew no bounds. He was one of the finest *mohelim* in the country. To perform the *mitzvah* of *milah* he would travel any distance.

His library, which incorporated those of his father and grandfather, was one of the finest rabbinic collections ever assembled, especially in the areas of responsa and Hasidism.

He was a prolific author, producing over thirty books. Much of his work was edited and published by himself, and many of his works appeared posthumously between 1938 and 1944. Among his published works were *Olat Tamid*, a commentary on the tractate *Tamid* (Bratislava, 1922); *Ot Hayyim VeShalom* (Beregszasz, 1921); *Shulhan Arukh Shaar Yissakhar*, commentary to the *Haggadah* (Munkacs, 1938); *Shaar Yissakhar* in three parts, based on the Jewish calendar (Munkacs, 1938–1940); *Hayyim VeShalom* in two parts (Marmaros Sighet, 1938–1940); *Darkhei Hayyim VeShalom* (Munkacs, 1940); and *Minhat Elazar*, responsa in five volumes (Munkacs, 1902–1930), which was widely acclaimed as one of the most important additions to the halakhic literature of modern times.

He was survived by an only daughter, Frimet, who married R. Barukh Rabinowicz, today living in Petah Tikvah.

D. Kahana, *Toldot Rabbenu*.

A.S.

SHAPIRA, Hayyim Meir Yehiel, of Drohobycz (1863–30 *Nisan* 1924)– Son of R. Avri Ezra Zelig and Hadassah Feiga, the daughter of R. Abraham Jacob of Sadgora. After the death of his father, he settled in Drohobycz. He was the first rebbe of the Ruzhyn dynasty to support Zionism.

At the outbreak of World War I, after living for a time in Hungary, he settled in Vienna, where, together with R. Shlomoh Friedman, he established the *Yishuv Eretz Yisrael* society, which supported Zionist endeavors. In the summer of 1922, he and his family settled in Jerusalem.

His son, R. Abraham Jacob, succeeded him.

Hozofeh, 28 *Nisan* 1944.

SHAPIRA, Hayyim Meir Yehiel, of Moglienice (1796–15 *Iyyar* 1849)– Son of R. Avi Ezra Zelig and Margalit, the daughter of R. Israel the Maggid of Kozienice, where he was brought up. He married the daughter of R. Eliezer, the granddaughter of R. Elimelekh of Lejask. He became rebbe first in Grice and then in Moglienice.

He did not support the Polish insurrection of 1831, since he felt that it would be easily suppressed by the Russians. "If only my hasidim emigrated to the Holy Land," he sighed, "I would gladly accompany them." Together with R. Yitzhak Kalish he appealed to the Polish hasidim to support the Old Yishuv.

He prayed with great intensity. For him, prayer was so devastating an experience that he regularly took the precaution of preparing his last will and testament before attending the synagogue. Hence, he was known as the *Seraph*.

His discourses are recorded in *Tiferet Hayyim* (Warsaw, 1900) and *Sihot Hayyim* (Warsaw, 1914). He had five sons and two daughters.

SHAPIRA, Isaiah (11 *Shevat* 1891–5 *Sivan* 1945) – Younger twin son of R. Elimelekh of Grodzisk, he married Hayyah Sarah, the daughter of R. Nathan Nahum Hakohen Rabinowicz of Krimlov. He was reluctant to become rabbi or rebbe.

For a time he had a license to sell liquor. He visited the Holy Land in 1914, and when he returned to Poland, he became one of the founders of the Mizrachi, in 1917, and worked with Zionist leader Yitzhak Nissenbaum.

Three years later, he settled in Jerusalem and became the head of the Mizrachi Immigration and Labor Department. In 1924, he visited Poland and urged the rabbis of Yablonov and Kozienice to follow his example. From 1933, he managed the cooperative bank *Zevulun* in Tel Aviv, and ten years later he settled in Kefar Pines.

He died in Jerusalem and was buried on the Mount of Olives.

Hazofeh, 8 *Sivan* 1945.

SHAPIRA, Israel (1874–*Elul* 1942) – Son of R. Hayyim Meir Yehiel, he was brought up by his grandfather. In 1892, he married his first cousin, Nehamah Feiga, the daughter of R. Asher Perlow of Stolin. After twenty years in Grodzisk, he settled in Warsaw during World War I.

During the Second World War, the aged rabbi was taken to Treblinka, where he sought to give comfort to his fellow prisoners. "Let us die like R. Akiva," he exhorted them. His daughters and his son were all murdered by the Nazis.

His only surviving son, R. Elimelekh, was rabbi in Jerusalem.

SHAPIRA, Israel (1890–2 *Heshvan* 1990) – He was born in Rybotycze, Galicia, the son of R. Joshua of Blazova. He was ordained by the rabbi of Brzezany and married the daughter of R. Moses of Rozwadov, a descendant of Ropczyce. He lived in Uczrik-Dolno (Istrik) and participated in the *Kenessiyah Gedolah* in Vienna in 1923. In 1931, he succeeded his father as rebbe of Dynov and Blazova.

He suffered five years in Nazi concentration camps, especially in the Janoweka Road Camp. His wife, his only daughter, his daughter's husband, and their children all perished in the Holocaust. Liberated from Bergen-Belsen, he lived for a while in Antwerp. In 1946, he settled in Williamsburg, Brooklyn, and then in Borough Park. He served on the presidium of the Aguda and was a member of the *Mo'etzet Gedolei HaTorah*.

He was interred on the Mount of Olives.

His son, R. Tzvi, succeeded him.

SHAPIRA, Issachar Baer (1900–11 *Adar* 1957) – Son of R. Pinhas, he married the daughter of R. Ittamar Rosenbaum of Nadvorno. He became rebbe in Novoselitz, Romania, in 1920, and in 1935 he settled in Jerusalem, where he lived until 1938.

He emigrated to the United States, where he became rabbi of congregation *Shaarei Tefillah* in the Bronx.

SHAPIRA, Joshua, of Blazova (10 *Sivan* 1862–12 *Adar* I, 1932) – Son of R. Tzvi Elimelekh, he succeeded his father as rebbe and married the daughter of R. Jacob of Dilatyn.

He was the author of *Keren Yehoshua* on Torah (Bilgoraj, 1933).

He had three sons: R. Meir of Blazova and R. Eliezer of Rybotycze, who were murdered by the Nazis, and R. Israel, who was rabbi of Blazova in New York.

SHAPIRA, Judah Meir (d. 29 *Nisan* 1829) – The eldest son of R. Pinhas Shapira of Koretz, he was a disciple of R. Hayyim of Krasni. He succeeded his father-in-law, R. Jacob Samson, as rabbi of Shepetovka. He was one of the first opponents of the luxurious life-style of R. Barukh of Medziborz.

His son R. Dov Baer (d. 26 *Adar* 1850), son-in-law of R. Naftali Hirtz of Zinkov, was rabbi in Skala, Volhynia, then succeeded his father as rebbe in Shepetovka. He later moved to Tluste in Galicia, where he was befriended by R. Moses Tzvi of Savran.

Another son of R. Judah Meir was R. Joseph (d. 23 *Adar* 1826), who lived in Shepetovka.

A.Sh.

SHAPIRA, Kalonymus Kalmish, of Piaseczno (19 *Iyyar* 1889–4 *Heshvan* 1944) – Son of R. Elimelekh of Grodzisk, he married *Hayyah* Miriam, the daughter of R. Yerahmiel Moses Hofstein of Kozienice, where he spent four years.

On 13 *Elul* 1909, his father-in-law died, and R. Shapira became rabbi of Piascecno, a small town near Warsaw. He also had a home in Warsaw and commuted between the two places. In 1923, he established a *yeshivah*, *Daat Mosheh*, which soon achieved great fame. He wrote a small tract, *Hovat HaTalmidim* (Warsaw, 1932), which became the guide for *yeshivah* students throughout Eastern Europe. In this work he showed himself a great pedagogue.

He tried to raise the morale of the students, many of whom suffered financial hardship. His students were encouraged to study the works of *Musar*. Though he never studied medicine, he often gave his followers medication that amazed the medical world.

In addition to his work for the *yeshivah*, he succeeded the rabbi of Radzymin as president of the *Shomer Shabbat* organization and was indefatigable in his endeavors to stamp out the desecration of the Sabbath in the business sections of Warsaw.

The Jewish community of Piaseczno was liquidated between January 22 and 27, 1941. The hasidim urged him to flee to Stolin, but the rabbi declined. "I am not one to desert my followers at a time like this. My place is surely with them." His only son, R. Elimelekh Benzion, was wounded in an air raid on Warsaw and subsequently died. His daughter-in-law, Gitel, was killed outside the hospital when visiting her husband.

In the Warsaw ghetto the rebbe worked in the Shultz shoe factory under Abraham Handel. He was deported to the Lublin area, where he was killed.

Some of his notes were recovered after the war and were printed in Jerusalem in 1960 under the title *Esh Kodesh*.

SHAPIRA, Malkah (1894–16 *Heshvan* 1971), writer – Daughter of R. Yerahmiel Moses of Kozienice, she married R. Abraham Elimelekh Shapira of Grodzisk. The couple settled in the Holy Land, where Malkah, mother of three children, attended courses under Joseph Klausner at the Hebrew University.

Her friend, the founder of the *Hopoel Hamizrahi*, Joshua Radler Feldman (better known as "Rabbi Binyamin"), without telling her, sent her first essay to the periodical *Doar HaYom* (ed., Ithamar ben Tzvi) and to *Davar* (ed., Berl Katznelson).

She wrote a number of hasidic stories such as *Shaninu BeMaginim* (Jerusalem, 1952), *BeLev HaMistorin* (Tel Aviv, 1955), and *Midin LeRahamim* (Jerusalem, 1969). "Wisdom lies not in knowing what to write," she used to say, "but in knowing how much to leave out."

SHAPIRA, Meir, of Blazova (d. 1942) – Son of R. Joshua, he married his cousin, the daughter of R. Joseph. He was rabbi in Blazova, and rebbe from 1932. During the Second World War, he entrusted the manuscripts of his grandfather to a gentile neighbor. "Keep them safe," he pleaded, "and after the war, you will be well recompensed."

He perished in unexplained circumstances. After the war, his sister, Hannah Halberstam, retrieved the manuscripts, and they were printed under the title *Tzvi LeTzaddik*.

SHAPIRA, Meir, of Lublin (7 *Adar* 1887–7 *Heshvan* 1934) – He was born in Zibenbergen, near Czernowitz, the son of R. Jacob Shimshon. At the age of nine, he was known as the "*Illui*" of Shatz. He was ordained by R. Yitzhak Shmelkes of Brody, R. Shmuel Yitzhak Schorr, and R. Meir Arak. He married the daughter of the wealthy merchant Jacob David Breitman of Tarnopol. At the age of twenty-three he published his first work *Imrei Daat* on Torah, but the work was destroyed in a fire at the bindery in Tarnopol in 1914.

In 1910, he became the rabbi of Gliniany, Galicia, where he spent ten years. Subsequently, in 1920, he became rabbi of Sanok (1920–1923), and later, of Piotrokov (1924–1930).

Active in the Central Council of the Rabbinical Association, he served as a member of the Polish parliament from 1922 to 1928. He was a great innovator. Among his far-reaching innovations was the *Daf Yomi* (daily page), which he proposed at the first *Kenessiyah Hagedolah* in Vienna on 3 *Elul* 1923. It required the study of one page of the Talmud each day, so that in seven years the entire Babylonian Talmud would be covered in a cycle of study, which would unite scattered world Jewry in an intellectual bond. The *Daf Yomi* caught the imagination of both scholar and layman and was inaugurated on Rosh Hashanah 1924. The first *siyyum* of the entire Talmud was celebrated on 15 Shevat 1931.

R. Shapira's second major achievement was the establishment of *yeshivat Hakhmei Lublin*. The foundation stone was laid at 37 Lubertovski Street, Lublin, on *Lag BaOmer* 1924. To raise funds for such a costly enterprise, he set out for the United States on 19 *Elul* 1927. He also visited England, France, Germany, and Switzerland. The new *yeshivah* building was consecrated on 29 *Sivan* 1930. It was one of the finest prewar buildings in Poland. It opened with 120 students. Only the most promising were admitted.

In 1933, he accepted an invitation to become rabbi of Lodz, but on 3 *Heshvan* 1934, he suddenly became ill, died four days later, and was buried in Lublin.

On 27 *Elul* 1958, his remains were reburied on *Har HaMenuhot* in Jerusalem.

He was the author of *Or HaMeir* (Piotrokov, 1926).

A. Surasky, *Rabbi Meir Shapira*, 2 vols.

SHAPIRA, Meir Yehudah, of Bukovsk (d. 19 *Tishri* 1909) – Son of R. David of Dynov, he married the daughter of R. Israel, the son-in-law of R. Hayyim of Kosov. He was rabbi in Medziborz and Bukovsk. He was the author of *Or L'Meir* on the Pentateuch (Przemysl, 1913).

He was succeeded by his son, R. David (1878–1924).

SHAPIRA, Moses, of Slavuta (d. 9 *Kislev* 1839) – Son of R. Pinhas of Koretz, he married the daughter of R. Yitzhak of Polonnoye and became rabbi of Slavuta, in Volhynia. He was endowed with artistic talents and taught himself graphics. In 1792, he opened a printing press in Slavuta. Out of Slavuta came editions of the Babylonian Talmud, Bibles, Codes, prayer books, and several hasidic works. Eventually, a controversy arose between the Slavuta printers and those of Vilna. After much litigation, and on the advice of R. Shlomoh Eger of Posen, the right for the publication of the Talmud was reserved for Vilna.

In 1825, R. Moses turned over the printing press to his two sons, R. Shmuel Abba (1784–5 *Iyyar* 1863) and R. Pinhas (1792–14 *Tammuz* 1872).

In *Iyyar* 1836, a gentile worker was found hanging in the Tailors' Synagogue. There was every indication that he had taken his own life; in fact, the widow declared that her late husband had suffered from melancholia and fits of depression. Yet the two brothers were arrested and sent to Kiev prison, where they languished for two years. Meanwhile, their father, Moses, died. On the eve of *Rosh Hodesh Elul* 1838, they were found guilty and were sentenced to pass through a gauntlet (*ckboz ctpoi*) of soldiers who whipped them. One of the brothers lost his *yarmulke*. He returned voluntarily to retrieve his cap and had to endure further blows. R. Pinhas was blinded in one eye.

They were sentenced to exile in Siberia, which was commuted to life imprisonment in Moscow. It was not until June 1856 that Czar Alexander II set them free. They both returned to Slavuta, where R. Shmuel Abba succeeded his father as rabbi; R. Pinhas spent his last years in Teplik.

A.Shu.

SHAPIRA, Perele (d. 1839), female rabbi – Eldest daughter of R. Israel Hofstein of Kozienice, she married R. Avi Ezra Zelig Shapira of Magnuszev. She wore ritual fringes and observed religious rites, fasting Mondays and Thursdays. She received petitions from her followers. "The *Shekhinah* rests upon her," acknowledged R. Elimelekh of Lejask. Her own father urged hasidim to visit her.

All her children died in infancy.

SHAPIRA, Pinhas (d. 3 *Sivan* 1944)–Son of R. Shalom, his father was rabbi in Blanatshin, Galicia. He married the daughter of R. Meir Rosenbaum of Karassonfalu. He settled in Kozakonyha, Marmaros, in 1905.

During World War I, the Hungarians deported him to Galicia, and he lived in Stryj. In 1918, he settled in Felsovisso. He perished in the Holocaust. His discourses are to be found in *Sefer Tzofnat Paneah* (Jerusalem, 1954).

His son, R. Issachar Baer (1900–11 *Adar* 1957), after living for some time in Jerusalem, settled in the Bronx. He was interred in Tiberias.

SHAPIRA, Shlomoh (1831–21 *Sivan* 1893), founder of the Munkacs dynasty–He was born on the seventh day of Hanukkah, the eldest son of R. Elazar of Lancut. In his youth, he was betrothed to Frimet Rivkah, daughter of R. Yekutiel Shmelke Rubin of Kolomyja, whom he married in Sasov in 1846. He lived there in the home of his father-in-law and eventually became *dayan* there in 1849. He was ordained by R. Joseph Saul Nathanson of Lvov and R. Mordecai Zeev Ettinger of Cracow. When R. Shlomoh's father accepted the position of rabbi of Lancut in 1857, R. Shlomoh succeeded him as rabbi of Strzyzov and was then rabbi in Munkacs.

He visited many hasidic rebbes but regarded himself as a disciple of R. Naftali of Ropczyce. During this time he corresponded with many of the great halakhists of Poland and Galicia.

He was concerned about the problems affecting Hungarian Jews, and he was active in the work of the *Orthodoxe Landes Kanzlei*, the headquarters of Hungarian Orthodox Jewry. On his frequent visits to Budapest, he was in close touch with the leading rabbis, such as R. Simhah Bunem Schreiner, and the lay leader Ignaz Reich. He would observe *Tikkun Hatzot* every night. He was a great bibliophile and diligently sought old manuscripts and early Hebrew books.

He wrote a number of books: *Shem Torah*; *Shem Shlomoh*, commentaries on the lesser tractates of the Talmud, and on Psalms; and many responsa on halakhic problems.

In his will, he expressed the wish that none of his works should be published. But his descendants reinterpreted his wishes. He was survived by two sons, R. Tzvi Hirsch and R. Moses Leib of Strzyzov.

A.S.

SHAPIRA, Tzvi Elimelekh, of Blazova (1841–5 *Nisan* 1924)–Son of R. David, he was a disciple of R. Hayyim Halberstam of Zanz. He married the daughter of R. Moses of Roswadov. He became rabbi of Rabotycze in East Galicia, and later in Blazova.

During the First World War he lived in Budapest, then in Przemysl, and eventually he returned to Blazova, where he remained for the rest of his life. He was renowned for his melodious voice, and he acted as reader on the High Holy Days. He possessed a remarkable memory. He prayed quietly, avoiding flamboyancy. He promulgated the concept of R. Levi Yitzhak of Berdichev about collective responsibility and mutualism, both in mode of behavior and in prayer, so that each should regard himself as a vital link in the chain of Judaism.

His literary works were published by his grandson R. Israel of New York under the title *Tzvi LeTzaddik*, commentaries on the Pentateuch (Cracow, 1935), and responsa on the four volumes of the *Shulhan Arukh* and on religious observances throughout the year (New York, 1955).

He was succeeded by his son R. Joshua.

A.S.

SHAPIRA, Tzvi Hirsch, of Munkacs (1850–16 *Tishri* 1913)–Son of R. Shlomoh, he was born in Strzyszov and married Esther, the daughter of R. Hannaniah Horowitz of Ulianov. He was known as an outstanding scholar and had an encyclopedic knowledge of rabbinics and mysticism. His youth was spent under the guidance of his father and grandfather. He accompanied them on their journeys to visit many hasidic rebbes.

His father put him in charge of the *Bet Din* of Munkacs. R. Shapira's wide reading is reflected in his main halakhic work, *Darkhei*

Teshuvah, in four parts (Vilna and Munkacs, 1892–1904). The fifth part was completed by his son and was printed in Szolyva in 1912. This erudite work is a summary of the vast responsa literature on *Yoreh De'ah*, the second part of the *Shulhan Arukh*. It has become an indispensable reference work of practical *halakhah* and is a vade mecum for every halakhist.

A selection of his responsa was published under the title *Tzvi Tiferet* (Munkacs, 1912); *Be'er LaHai Roi* is his commentary to the *Tikkunei HaZohar* (Munkacs/Beregszasz, 1903–1921). His hasidic works are to be found in his commentary to the Torah, *Tiferet Banim* (Bardiov, 1921), in his *Haggadah shel Pesah* (Munkacs, 1914), and in *Darkei Emunah* (Munkacs, 1914).

He was appointed rabbi of Munkacs on June 5, 1893. In addition to being a communal rabbi and rebbe of many hasidim, he also became the principal of a great *yeshivah* that produced many rabbis.

His only son was R. Hayyim Elazar.

D. Kahana, *Bet Shlomoh–Tzvi Tiferet*.

A.S.

SHAPIRA (SPIRA), Avigdor, of Czestochova (1880–18 *Adar* 1927)–Son of R. Shalom Shapira, a descendant of Moglienice and Kozienice, he settled in Czestochova in 1900 and was very active in the Aguda. He was succeeded by his son, R. Jacob Yitzhak. His daughter married R. Yoel Teitelbaum of Satmar.

SHAPIRA (SPIRA), David, of Bukovsk (1878–29 *Shevat* 1924)–Son of R. Meir Yehudah of Bukovsk, he was the son-in-law of R. Joshua Horowitz of Dzikov. When his wife died, he married the daughter of R. Hannaniah Yom Tov Lippa Teitelbaum of Sighet. He was rebbe in Bukovsk from 1909, and after the First World War he lived in Sanok. He refused to join the Aguda.

When he died, his son, R. Alter Reuven, succeeded him.

SHAPIRA (SPIRA), Jacob Joseph, of London (d. 20 *Av* 1946)–A descendant of Dynov, he came to London in 1926. A year later, he established a *shtiebl*, *Kehillat Yaakov*, in Stamford Hill and was rabbinical district supervisor of *Kashrut*.

He was the author of *Mili D'Hespeda*, a fifteen-page eulogy on R. Issachar Dov Rokeah of Belz, and a twenty-two-page treatise *Rishmei She'elah* (London, 1934).

His son, R. Melekh (1903–1983), was rabbi of the Willesden Synagogue, London.

SHAPIRA (SPIRA), Tzvi Elimelekh, of Dynov (1783–18 *Tevet* 1841)–Tzvi Elimelekh, or "Hersh Melekh," as he was popularly known, was born in Shklar, near Dynov, the son of Pesah, a humble villager of Jawornik, Galicia. His family name was originally Langsam but was changed to Spira. He was a disciple of the "Seer" of Lublin. He married the daughter of Shmuel of Zitsch. He visited many hasidic rebbes, especially R. Menahem Mendel of Rymanov, R. Abraham Joshua Heschel of Opatov, and R. Tzvi Hirsch of Zydaczov.

He began his rabbinical career acting as *dayan* on the *Bet Din* of R. Joshua of Dynov. He occupied rabbinical posts in Strzyzov, Rybotycze, and Halicz and then succeeded R. Tzvi Avigdor Ashkenazi as rabbi in Munkacs, where he stayed for four years from 1925. He founded the *Tamhin DeOraita Hevrah*, whose rules and regulations he drafted (Munkacs, 1896). There, he introduced sixteen *takkanot* (enactments). He also changed the order of service of the synagogue to the Sephardic rite.

His humility was proverbial. He maintained that every Jew should study Kabbalah: "Through mysticism, the Jews will achieve redemption even before the appointed time without suffering the pangs of the Messiah. No one is exempted from study." In his attitude toward the study of the Kabbalah, he followed in the footsteps of R. Tzvi Hirsch of Zydaczov.

The rebbe would kiss the *matzot* and the *maror* (bitter herbs) and the four cups of wine during the *seder*. He would recite *Sefirat HaOmer* (counting of the Omer) before the *seder*. He encouraged his sons to put on the *tefillin* of *Rabbenu Tam* immediately after their *bar mitzvah*. He would wear his *tefillin* while he acted as *sandek*. He himself began writing a *Sefer Torah* and had reached the section of *Massey* (Numbers 33) when he died. He also wrote phylacteries for members of his family.

He maintained that there was no knowledge in the realm of either science or philosophy that could not be found in the Torah. He considered philosophic speculation a waste of time. By word and deed, he fought *Haskalah*. "I am fully aware," he wrote of the presumptuousness of the assimilationists, "that they respect neither the prophets nor the *Tanna'im*. They are descended from the 'mixed multitude.' " He censored Moses Mendelssohn for "sinning and causing others to sin."

He urged his followers not to acquire any heretical works. In a house where heretical writings were found, it was forbidden to study the Torah. He stressed, however, the power of repentance. "How can those who are full of sin and transgression pray to God? Because at the very moment of prayer, they are transformed into a new being and are worthy of praying."

He died at the age of fifty-eight. He had four sons–R. Eleazar, R. David, R. Meshullam Zusya, and R. Shmuel–and three daughters. His son R. Meshullam Zusya and his daughter Rebecca predeceased him. The dynasty was maintained by R. Elazar and R. David.

Apart from R. Tzaddok Hakohen Rabinowicz of Lublin, no other hasidic rebbe was so prolific a writer. His writings were numerous and profound. They covered the whole realm of rabbinic literature. His work *Benei Yissakhar*, discourses on the Sabbath, New Moon, and Festivals, first published in Zolkiev in 1846, has since been reprinted nineteen times. It has been acclaimed as a monumental achievement, and it is an encyclopedic storehouse of thought. Each *sidrah* is explained according to *Pardes* (*Peshat*, *Remez*, *Derash*, and *Sod*).

He was the author of twenty-nine other works, some of which are *Agra deKalla* on the Pentateuch and Midrashim, which was first printed in Lvov in 1868 and went through six editions; *Agra de Pirka*, first printed in Lvov in 1858; *Mayein Ganim*, a commentary on the *Or HaHayyim* by R. Joseph Yaavitz, first printed in Zolkiev in 1848 and reprinted thirteen times; *Derekh Pikudekha* on the 613 commandments (Lvov, 1851), reprinted eighteen times; *Berakhah Meshuleshet* on the *Mishnah* and a number of tractates (Przemysl, 1897); *Veheye Berakhah* on *Mishnah Zera'im* and on the tractate *Shabbat* (Przemysl, 1888); and *Hiddushei Maharza* on the laws of Hanukkah (Przemysl, 1882).

N. Urtner, *HaRav Tzvi Elimelekh MiDinov*, 2 vols.

A.S. and U.L.

SHAPIRA (SPIRO), Abraham, of Tluste/New York (1890–1972)–Brother of R. Meir Shapiro of Lublin, he reprinted the works of his brother and grandfather. He emigrated to Israel and established a *Bet HaMidrash* in Bene Berak. He reinterred in Jerusalem the remains of his brother.

SHAPIRA (SPIRO), Nathan Nata (ca. 1585–1633), kabbalist–Born in Cracow, he was one of the great pathfinders of the Lurianic Kabbalah in Eastern Europe. His work *Megallei Amukkot*, published by his son in Cracow in 1637, was frequently reprinted. It offered 252 interpretations of one single passage of the prayer of Moses (Deuteronomy 3:23). He also interpreted the letter *alef* in the word *VaYikra* (Leviticus 1:1) in a thousand different ways.

His commentary on the Pentateuch was published in Lvov in 1785. He was greatly venerated by the hasidim and influenced hasidic thought.

SHAPOTSHNICK, Joseph, of London (1882–16 *Heshvan* 1937)–Born in Kishinev, son of R. Yehudah Aryeh, the Belzisze rebbe, he studied under R. Joseph Abelson and was ordained by R. S. M. Schwadron of Brzezany. In 1909, he married *Hayyah* Gitel and after a short stay in Berlin, moved to London in 1914.

He was one of the most controversial rabbis of his generation. He began to solve the problems of the *agunah*, thereby arousing the hostility of the rabbinic world. He established a rival board of *shehitah* and became a tool in the hands of unscrupulous butchers. He carried on a vendetta against Chief Rabbi J. H. Hertz. He was a prolific writer.

He was survived by a son, Louis Levi (1909–1982), minister of the Great Garden Street Synagogue, London.

SHAVUOT–Feast of Weeks (Pentecost), the second of the Pilgrim Festivals, the Festival that celebrates the conclusion of the grain harvest and is associated with the Revelation on Mount Sinai. "The season of the giving of the Law," which coincides with the *Yahrzeit* of the Besht, was an ideal time for hasidim to spend with their rebbe.

The rebbe of Kotzk explained why it is called the "time of the giving of the Law" and why it is not called the "time of the receiving of the Law": "The Torah," he said, "was given to us in the time of Moses. But we still continue to receive the Torah. Moreover, although the Torah was given to every Jew alike, it was not received by everyone in equal proportion, because the receiving depends on one's power of understanding and the intellectual capacity of each individual."

In Ger, a special melody was used for *Akdamut*, the hymn composed by R. Meir ben Yitzhak Nahorai of Worms in the eleventh century, and recited on the first day of the Festival prior to the Reading of the Law. The rebbe of Munkacs would even deliver a discourse before the recitation of *Akdamut*.

In Belz, it was customary to scatter branches on the floor of the *Bet HaMidrash* because Shavuot is a judgment day for the fruits of the trees (*Rosh Hashanah* 1:2). R. Asher Tzvi Ostrorer stated that we spread out herbs and grass to remind ourselves that we should devote our life to the Torah, even though we have nothing but edible herbs to keep us alive.

A number of hasidic rebbes suggested reasons for the tradition of eating dairy products on the Festival. R. Menahem Mendel of Rymanov said that "when the Jews received the Torah, they were like newborn infants, and infants normally eat dairy dishes." R. Israel, the Maggid of Kozienice, stated that "the Jews could no longer use their old dishes after the giving of the Torah; hence they had to make do with milk dishes." R. Pinhas of Koretz maintained that "we eat dairy food so that we can welcome with humility the day of the giving of the Torah."

R. Israel Friedman of Ruzhyn would not deliver a discourse on the Sabbath before the Festival. "I am like a farmer before the harvest," he said. "The old wheat is gone, and the new wheat has not yet come in."

When R. Lipman Radomsker returned home after spending Shavuot in Kotzk, his father-in-law asked him what he had learned. "I have learned the meaning of 'Thou shalt not steal.' I knew that it was forbidden to steal from others, [and] now I know that one must not steal from oneself."

SHAZAR (Rubashov), Shneur Zalman (1889–1974), third president of Israel – He was born in Mir, in the Minsk province, and named after the founder of the *Habad* dynasty. He received a traditional education and imbibed the *Habad* allegiance of his parents. Apart from Zionist activities, he was attracted to the Shabbatean movement and to mysticism. He recalled that months before his father died, he had taught him the Rav's melody. "During the darkest moments of my life," he remembered, "when I was submerged in anguish and perplexity, I called to mind that melody. It has always given me new strength and new courage and the assurance that I was doing the right thing."

Despite his devotion to Bible criticism, he regarded himself as a follower of *Habad*. He visited *Kefar Habad* on the anniversary of the rebbe's release and visited the rebbe in New York in 1966 and 1971.

He produced an annotated edition of *Shaalu Shelom Yerushalayim* by R. Gedaliah of Siemiatycze (Jerusalem, 1963), which describes the eighteenth-century journey by R. Judah HaHasid and his disciples to the Holy Land.

A. Manor, *Zalman Shazar: Yihido VeYetziroto*.

SHEDRUWSKI, Meir Shalom, of Bialystok (d. 22 *Heshvan* 1940) – Son of R. Dov, he married the daughter of R. Menahem Nahum Epstein of Bialystok (1846–1 *Av* 1918), who was a disciple of R. Abraham Weinberg of Slonim. For thirty years, "R. Meirke," as he was known, assisted his father-in-law in the rabbinate of Bialystok. In 1918, he became rebbe and kept in touch with the hasidim in Kobryn.

He was succeeded by his son, R. Shmuel Aaron, who was one of the leaders of the Aguda and who married the daughter of R. Pinhas Issachar of Sosnowiec.

SHEHITAH – According to the *Shivhei HaBesht*, one of the occupations the Besht followed before he became renowned was that of *shohet*. A legend tells of how the Besht, grieving over the fowl he was obliged to slaughter, would whet his knife not with water but with his tears. For the hasidim, in addition to the motif of *tzaar baalei hayyim* (causing unnecessary pain to any of God's creatures), the knife used for *shehitah* had to satisfy the strictest requirements of the law, because as the Kabbalah declares, a spirit of uncleanness rests upon the meat of a bird or animal that has not been killed in the proper manner, and to eat that meat is to contaminate the soul.

The hasidim were, consequently, dissatisfied with the type of knife made of coarse iron and that could not be adequately sharpened. Such knives were used everywhere in Russia and Poland, though not in Germany, at that time. The hasidim, following the German practice, introduced special, honed-steel knives (*sakkinin melutashot* [polished knives]). Eventually, this type of knife was used by *shohetim* everywhere, but in the early days of the movement, many of the *mitnaggedim* expressed their strong disapproval of the hasidic innovation both because it constituted a serious break with tradition and because, the *mitnaggedim* claimed, the new knives did not meet the requirements of the Law since, being too sharp, they could easily slip.

The issue of the knives figures prominently in anti-hasidic polemics, though the *mitnaggedim* were hard put to demonstrate the knives' inadequacy, and in the fierce polemics issuing from the school of the Gaon of Vilna, the issue is not raised at all.

Behind the whole controversy is clearly the attempt by the early hasidim to break with the hegemony of the *kahal*–the communal leadership–to whom the *shehitah* taxes were due. By having a separate *shehitah*, the hasidim were able to achieve a degree of financial security and to assert their independence. In a later period, too, there are numerous instances when hasidim preferred to have their own *shehitah* and their own *shohetim*, authorized by the *tzaddik* to whom they owed their allegience. Not infrequently was this the cause of severe communal dissension both between the hasidim and the non-hasidic rabbis and communal leaders and among the hasidim themselves, since each *tzaddik* preferred the *shohetim* he recognized as alone worthy.

Hasidic legend tells, too, that *tzaddikim*, including the Besht, discerned by means of the holy spirit whether or not an animal had been properly slaughtered. This was a source of offense to the mitnaggedic rabbis, who argued, "It is not in Heaven" (i.e., once the Torah has been given by God, it is His will that matters of *kashrut* should be determined by the normal canons of halakhic investigation by way of the processes of human reasoning and not by means of divine inspiration).

Ch. Shmeruk, "Social Significance of the Hasidic *Shehitah*," pp. 47–72.

A. Wertheim, *Halakhot VeHalikhot BaHasidut*, pp. 200–208.

L.J.

SHEITEL–Hasidic women wear a *sheitel*, a wig made of real or artificial hair. In many hasidic circles, especially in Hungary, they would wear a kerchief or a *sterntichel*. This is based on Jewish tradition, which requires married women to cover their hair so as not to attract the attention of men.

SHEKHINAH–A term derived from the Hebrew verb *shakhan* (to dwell), denoting the presence of God dwelling among people. The term in this sense was coined by the early rabbis in an attempt to avoid a direct reference to God.

It becomes particularly associated with the concept of divine light, as in the phrase "the radiance of the *Shekhinah*." The *Shekhinah* rests on particularly pious individuals, especially those who devote their time to the study of the Torah and the performance of the *mitzvot*.

At the time of the destruction of the Temple (*mishkan*), the *Shekhinah* went into exile, as it were, and was thought to accompany the Jewish people in their wanderings–sharing their sufferings and longing with them to be reunited once more with the Holy Land.

In Lurianic Kabbalah this exile was interpreted as a consequence of the disaster that overtook the world at the time of Adam's sin.

In Kabbalah, the *Shekhinah* is identified with *Malkhut*, the female element in the world of the *Sefirot*, and is the tenth and last one in the sefirotic hierarchy. This position makes the *Shekhinah* most vulnerable to assault from *sitra ahra* (the other side), for she has no light of her own, depending solely on reflected light from the other *Sefirot*, just as the moon depends for its light on the sun. This means also that the aspects of all the other *Sefirot* are united in her.

Being the last of the *Sefirot*, and therefore the nearest to the created world, the *She-*

khinah is that aspect of the Godhead with which the hasid can seek communion. In the view of the Kabbalah and of the hasidim, the purpose of the performance of the *mitzvot* is to help the *Shekhinah* to unite with *Tiferet*, the male principle. The sins of Israel hinder this union and prevent the "reunification of worlds," which is a necessary prerequisite for the coming of God's kingdom.

The hasidim, in accordance with this belief, adopted the formula (much deplored by their opponents), "For the sake of the unification of the Holy One, blessed be He, and His *Shekhinah*," which they recited before the performance of *mitzvot*.

D.G.

SHEMINI ATZERET (Hebrew, eighth day of the solemn assembly) – The last day of the Festival of Tabernacles.

R. Elijah, the Gaon of Vilna, ate and slept in a *sukkah*, even on Shemini Atzeret. The Besht, however, would not even enter the *sukkah* on that day. The disciples of the Maggid of Mezhirech, however, did eat in the *sukkah* on Shemini Atzeret. Subsequently, some hasidic rebbes, such as Lubavitch and Ruzhyn, followed the custom of the Maggid.

Others, like Belz, adhere to the usage of the Besht. Ger compromised by simply reciting *Kiddush* in the *sukkah*. In Belz, after the service on Shemini Atzeret, the ark was kept open, and hasidim would file by to kiss the Scrolls of the Law. Hasidim would hold *hakkafot* on the evening and morning of Shemini Atzeret.

SHENKER, Benzion (b. 1925), soloist – Born in Brooklyn, he is an alumnus of the *Mesivta Torah V'Daat* and of Brooklyn College. He has been collecting and notating the music of Modzitz since 1941. He has produced many recordings of the melodies of the rebbes of Modzitz.

SHEVER POSHIM – Also known as *Zimrat HaAretz* (Warsaw, 1795), and written by David of Makov.

It is an attack against the hasidic leaders, particularly against R. Levi Yitzhak of Berdichev; R. Hayyim Heikel of Amdur, R. Israel, the Maggid of Kozienice, and R. Jacob Yitzhak, the "Seer" of Lublin. In his bitter criticism of the movement, the author pinpoints the warnings of the Gaon of Vilna against hasidic tendencies.

He criticizes the innovations of the hasidim and their journeys to the courts of the rebbes, which added to the heavy burden of the impoverished masses. He appealed to the women not to allow their husbands to waste their time and money on hasidic pilgrimages. He stresses that the movement encourages contempt for Torah study. He disputes the basic belief of Hasidism that their rebbes were endowed with the spirit of holiness (*Ruah HaKodesh*). He states that to teach Kabbalah in public is in itself a violation of traditional safeguards against the vulgarization of esoteric mystical concepts.

The author saw parallels between the Quakers and the hasidim, in the emphasis that both groups put on the virtue of spontaneity and the need to wait for the light of inspiration.

A. Rubinstein, "Shever Poshim L'David Makov," pp. 240–249.

J.B.A.

SHIMON of Yaroslav (d. 16 *Tishri* 1850) – Son of R. Israel and a descendant of the kabbalist R. Jacob Kopel of Tarnogrod, Galicia. R. Shimon was a disciple of R. Elimelekh of Lejask and of his relative the "Seer" of Lublin. Among his disciples were R. Yitzhak Eizik Eichenstein and R. Joseph Babad of Tarnopol. He was the author of *Torat Shimon*, commentaries on the Psalms (Berlin, 1923).

He was succeeded by his son R. Bunem Menahem Mendel (d. 1890). The dynasty was maintained by R. Shimon of Yaroslav, known as R. Shimon the Second (d. 15 *Shevat* 1915). His son R. Eleazar, who was rebbe of Yaroslav and in Berlin, perished in the Holocaust.

SHIRAYIM – It was the hasid's privilege to share *shirayim* (remnants) of the rabbi's food. The rebbe would merely taste a dish and then pass it down the table. This custom can be traced back to talmudic times. "He who leaves no bread on the table [at the end of a meal] will never see a sign of blessing," warns the Talmud (*Sanhedrin* 92a). The Palestinian Talmud records that R. Yohanan bar Napaha would gather up the morsels left over from the previous night's meal and eat them, saying "Let my portion be among those who were here [in the synagogue] yesterday" (*Yerushalmi*, *Mo'ed Katan* 2:3).

The hasidim developed the kabbalistic and Lurian ideas further, maintaining that the rebbe sanctified the food he tasted and that he was setting free the imprisoned *nitzotzot* (sparks), restoring them to their original source.

Shirayim were regarded as an effective *segullot*.

A. Wertheim, *Halakhot VeHalikhot BaHasidut*, pp. 167–169.

SHISHI (sixth portion of the Sabbath Torah reading)—The *Zohar* regards *Shishi* as the most important *aliyah* (*Shelah Le-Kha*), and R. Yitzhak Luria, too, attaches a great significance to this portion. The number six has a mystical association. The sixth *Sefirah* is *Yesod*, and *Yesod* is identified with the *tzaddik*, for Proverbs 10:25 calls the *tzaddik* "the foundation of the world."

It has become customary among hasidim to honor the rebbe with *Shishi*, a custom already referred to by R. Aaron of Karlin in *Bet Aharon*. The dynasty of Ruzhyn, however, prefers the *aliyah* of *Shlishi*.

A. Wertheim, *Laws and Customs in Hasidism*, p. 151.

SHIVHEI HABESHT (in praise of the Baal Shem Tov), Kopys (1814)—*Shivhei HaBesht* is the first collection of the tales about the Besht. It contains biographical details about his parents, childhood, acquisition of mystical knowledge, travels, teachings, miracles, and death. Interspersed among these are stories about a few other hasidic leaders, followers of the Besht.

The material included in *Shivhei HaBesht* was circulated orally and in manuscript form, and it was subject to textual variations. The first edition was issued by Israel Yofeh of Kopys, who edited the manuscript and added tales that he had heard from others. The publication met with popular success despite rabbinical opposition to the printing of the book. Within the same year (1814–1815), two more Hebrew editions appeared in Laszcov and Berdichev, respectively. For the first time, the author's name appeared on the title page: he was a *shohet* from Ilnitsy—R. Dov Baer ben Shmuel, the son-in-law of Alexander, the Besht's scribe for eight years.

In the same year, an anonymous Yiddish translation appeared in Ostrog, which lacks 40 percent of the tales that are in the Hebrew edition but at the same time, contains four stories that are missing in the Hebrew edition. Moreover, the Yiddish version contains clear references to the Besht's journey to the Holy Land. The Hebrew version indicates the source from which the author learned the particular narrative. These credits are omitted in the Yiddish version.

From 1817 to 1848, the Austrian censor banned publication of hasidic works. Subsequently, the book appeared in more than fifty editions. It is a basic work of hasidic literature, serving as a source and model for subsequent collections of the tales. The latest publications are *In Praise of the Baal Shem Tov (Shivhei HaBesht): The Earliest Collection of Legends about the Founder of Hasidism* (Bloomington, IN: Indiana University Press, 1970); Joshua Mundstein, *Shivhei HaBaal Shem Tov*, a facsimile of a Unique Manuscript, Variant Versions and Appendices (Jerusalem, 1982); and *Shivhei HaBesht* with introduction and annotations by Avraham Rubinstein (Jerusalem, 1991).

A. Yaari, "Two Basic Recensions of Shivhe HaBesht," pp. 249–272, 394–408, 552–562.

D.B.

SHLOMOH of Karlin (1738–22 *Tammuz* 1792)—Son of R. Meir Halevi of Karlin, he was a disciple of R. Aaron the Great and R. Dov Baer, the Maggid of Mezhirech. On the death of R. Aaron, he succeeded him and brought up his son, R. Asher, as well as R. Shalom of Prohobicz.

It was said of him that he could move mountains with the power of his prayers. He devoted his whole life to the service of the Almighty. He believed that prayer was of the utmost importance and that to teach Jews how to pour out their heart to the Almighty was the greatest miracle. The Karliner rebbe put special emphasis on praying with the utmost intellectual intensity. He believed that a rebbe not only was a spiritual leader but could also help his followers in material matters. He said, "I am ready to be the Messiah, the son of Joseph, provided that the Messiah, the son of David, comes at last."

He was persecuted by the *mitnaggedim*, who forced him to leave Karlin and to move to Ludomir. During the conflict between Russia and Poland, a Cossack shot him while he was standing at the table and reciting the *Kiddush*. He died and was buried in Ludomir.

His discourses are recorded in *Imrei Kaddosh HaShalom* (Lvov, n.d.), *Bet Aharon* (Brody, 1875), and *Shema Shlomoh* (Piotrokov, 1928).

W. Z. Rabinowitsch, *Lithuanian Hasidism*, pp. 40–42.

SHLOMOH of Lutzk (d. 10 *Shevat* 1813)–A disciple of the Maggid, R. Dov Baer of Mezhirech, R. Shlomoh served successively as preacher at Sokal and Koretz. He faithfully wrote down the sayings and discourses of the Maggid, which were published in *Maggid DeVarav LeYaakov* (Koretz, 1874). He aroused the antagonism of R. Yehiel Michael of Zloczov, but R. Moses Leib of Sasov tried to defend him because he had served in the holy of holies of the Maggid.

His work *Divrat Shlomoh* (Lvov, 1859) received the approval of the "Seer" of Lublin, who wrote, "It is right that his works should be widely known." R. Shlomoh anticipated Eliezer ben Yehudah (1858–1922), one of the pioneers of the modern Hebrew renaissance. "It is essential," he wrote, "that the people living in the Holy Land should use the holy tongue, the language in which the universe was created. If they do not speak the holy tongue, the land does not really belong to them, and they can easily be banished. It is only our country if we speak the holy tongue" (*Divrat*, *Shelakh*). "Only through true repentance will redemption come, and it is with the help of the *tzaddikim* that this can be achieved" (*Tazria*).

His son, R. Dov Berish (d. 21 *Elul* 1850) of Olesko, was a disciple of R. Mordecai of Neshkhiz and R. Uri of Strelisk.

Y. Raphael, *Sefer HaHasidut*, p. 22.

SHLOMOH ZALMAN of Wielipoli (1804–17 *Kislev* 1858)–Son of R. Abraham of Patshanov, he was a disciple of R. Meir of Opatov and R. Naftali of Ropczyce. He was an ascetic, suffered ill health, and was confined to his bed. He had to be carried to the synagogue on the Day of Atonement.

He wrote glosses on R. Moses Cordovero, *Tomer Devorah*, but instructed that this manuscript be buried with him. He died in Cracow.

His son R. Abraham (d. 4 *Shevat* 1906) lived in Tarnov. R. Abraham had two sons: R. Shlomoh Zalman (1857–19 *Tevet* 1938), who was rebbe first in Wielipoli, and R. Joseph Hayyim, who was the son-in-law of R. Alter of Strzyszov. R. Joseph Hayyim was murdered by the Nazis on 6 *Av* 1942.

SHMUEL of Amdur (d. 1799)–He was the son of R. Hayyim Heikel of Amdur.

R. Israel Leibel, the virulent hasidic writer, recorded, "I therefore issue a challenge to all the rabbis of the above-mentioned sect to [participate in] a public debate with me: to R. Shmuel of Amdur, to R. Mordecai of Lachowicze, and to R. Mottel of Chernobyl" (*Sefer HaVikuah* [1798], Dubnow, *Toldot*, p. 459).

Only one letter by R. Shmuel has survived. Writing to his brother, R. Dov, he states, "My beloved brother, since I am not a man of words, and particularly since a high wall has come between us, I am therefore writing . . . to remove every obstacle between us . . . and also forgiveness is greater than wisdom."

He had two sons–R. Moses Aaron, the son-in-law of R. Mordecai of Lachowicze, and R. Hayyim Heikel (the Second), the son-in-law of R. Moses of Shershov. Neither of his sons became a rebbe.

W. Z. Rabinowitsch, *Lithuanian Hasidism*, p. 141.

SHNEUR ZALMAN (18 *Elul* 1745–24 *Tevet* 1813), founder of *Habad*–Son of Barukh and Rivkah, he was born in Liozna, Belorussia, and is known as the *Rav* or the *Alter Rebbe* (old rebbe). He was a descendant of R. Yehudah Loeb ben Bezalel, the *Maharal* of Prague. At thirteen he became a member of the *Hevrah Kaddisha*, and at fifteen he married Sterna, the daughter of businessman Yehudah Leib Segel of Vitebsk. He studied under R. Issachar Baer of Lubavitch. At the age of twenty, he left Vitebsk for Mezhirech. For three years he studied under R. Dov Baer, following him from Mezhirech to Annopol. There he met colleagues of the caliber of R. Elimelekh of Lejask, R. Levi Yitzhak of Berdichev, and R. Nahum of Chernobyl. He was a companion and tutor of R. Abraham HaMalakh (Abraham "the Angel"), the son of the Maggid.

Although one of the youngest and newest of the disciples, R. Shneur Zalman was encouraged by the Maggid to compile a new *Shulhan Arukh*. This "*Shulhan Arukh* of the Rav" won high praise from his contemporaries. It provided weighty evidence that the hasidim were not attempting to lighten the yoke of the *mitzvot*. This work was published in two parts: *Hilkhot Talmud Torah*, in Shklov (1814), and *Yoreh De'ah*, in Kopys (1814).

In general he followed the Ashkenazic scholars, just as he opted for the halakhic authorities in preference to the mystics. After the death of the Maggid in 1772 and the departure in 1777 of R. Menahem Mendel of Vitebsk and R. Abraham of Kalisk for the Holy Land, R. Shneur Zalman was the acknowledged head of the hasidic communities in White Russia.

He was accused by the *mitnaggedim* of activities that were detrimental to the state, such as sending money to Turkey every year. In October 1798, he was arrested and imprisoned in the Peter and Paul fortress. A special committee of the Secret Council (*Tainy Soviet*) investigated the matter. The rebbe submitted an appeal in Hebrew and was released on 19 *Kislev* (November 23) of that year. This day is still celebrated among the hasidim today as a "holiday of deliverance."

Two years later, on November 9, 1800, he was once again arrested, this time confined in the Secret Department of the Senate. After spending four months and ten days there, he was finally released in March 1801, when Alexander succeeded as the czar of Russia. The rebbe then took up residence in Liady, on the estate of Prince Lubomirski, where he arrived on 14 *Av* 1801.

Ceaselessly, he worked for peace and reconciliation with his opponents. Vindictiveness was alien to him. In order to convince his opponents of the baselessness of their accusations, he himself visited a number of rabbinic scholars, especially mitnaggedic scholars. He devoted much energy to the rallying of support for the hasidim in the Holy Land, undertaking an extensive fund-raising journey throughout Russia. He engaged in a bitter controversy with R. Abraham (Katz) of Kalisk–then in the Holy Land–and with R. Barukh of Medziborz, the grandson of the Besht. They objected not only to his interpretation of Hasidism but also to his method of collecting and distributing funds for the Holy Land.

He was not destined to enjoy tranquillity. He lived through the Franco-Russian war, he being on the side of Russia. "I would die rather than live under him [Napoleon]," wrote R. Shneur Zalman. He feared that a victory by Napoleon would bring emancipation to the Jews but would be detrimental to the maintenance of traditional Judaism.

He was a gifted composer of hasidic melodies. He himself composed ten *niggunim*. The classic of *Habad* melodies is the *niggun* of the *Alter* rebbe. He represented the synthesis of Lithuanian intellectualism with hasidic fervor. No other hasidic rabbi left such a distinctive imprint on the movement. He established a dynasty, and he formulated a philosophy, known as *Habad*–an acrostic of the kabbalistic terms *Hokhmah*, *Binah*, and *Daat* (wisdom, understanding, and knowledge). He was the author of *Likkutei Amarim*, known as the *Tanya*, after the first word of the treatise, printed in Slavuta in 1796.

He devoted twenty years of his life to the composition of the work. It consists of five parts: Part 1, *Likkutei Amarim*, or *Tanya*, or *Sefer shel Benonim*, comprising a foreword and fifty-three chapters; Part 2, *Shaar HaYihud VeHaEmunah* (Portal of Unity and Belief), with a foreword and twelve chapters; Part 3, *Iggeret HaTeshuvah* (Epistle of Repentance), with twelve chapters; Part 4, *Iggeret HaKodesh* (Sacred Epistle), with thirty-two sections; and Part 5, *Kuntres Aharon* (Latest Treatise). The concluding section contains the rabbi's passionate pleas to his followers: He urges them not only to devote more time to the reciting of the prayers but also to recite them in unison. He urges the study of the whole Talmud every year by each community, arranging for the apportionment of various tractates among its members. They should read at least once a week Psalm 119, which is dedicated to the greatness of the Torah. Above all, they should be strict in their observance of the Sabbath.

Emotion and *hitlahavut*, the legacies of the Besht, are fused with intellectualism. He examined the various facets and components of the soul, differentiating in the kabbalistic tradition between the divine soul (*Nefesh Eloihoit*)–which is centered in the mind as well as in the heart, the vital center of thought, speech, and deed–and the animal soul (*Nefesh HaBahamit*)–which resides in the blood. That animal soul is the core and sustenance of our vitality and of our character, both good and bad. He examined humanity's role in the cosmic order, the purpose of human existence, the concept of the messianic era, the resurrection, and the qualities of fear and love in relationship to God.

He left a vast literary treasure house. Many of his works were published posthumously. His published works include *Beurei HaZohar* (Commentaries on the *Zohar*), edited by his son R. Dov Baer (Kopys, 1816; New York, 1955); *Torah Or* (Torah Light), discourses on the first two books of the Pentateuch and of the Book of Esther, edited by his brother, R. Yehudah Leib (Kopys, 1837; New York, 1975); *Likkutei Torah* (Torah Gleanings) in two volumes, on the remainder of the Pentateuch and on the Book of the Song of Songs, edited by his grandson, R. Menahem Mendel of Lubavitch (Zhitomir, 1888; New York, 1965); *Seder Tefillot MiKol HaShanah al Pi Nusah HaArizal* (New York, 1965); and *Shulhan Arukh* (New York, 1960).

He died in Piena (Kursk district) and was buried in Hadich (Poltava district). He left three sons and three daughters. He was succeeded by his eldest son, R. Dov Baer.

R. A. Foxbrunner, *The Hasidism of R. Shneur Zalman of Liady*.
N. Mindel, *Rabbi Shneur Zalman*.

SHNEUR ZALMAN (Zalkind) (1887–1959), Hebrew and Yiddish poet and novelist–A native of Shklov, Belorussia, his father, Yitzhak Eizik, was a descendant of R. Shneur Zalman of Liady. He was named after the founder of *Habad*. He lived in Poland, Switzerland, France, the United States, and Israel. He was a nonconformist and a restless spirit who hurled defiance at the forces of social injustice.

His vivid imagery, his lively imagination, and his ability to breathe life into a multitude of characters made him a great novelist. He was a great poet and an eminent writer in both Hebrew and Yiddish. Much of his writing concerns his native Shklov. In his *HaTzaddik Ba* (The *Tzaddik* Comes), he depicts, in idyllic terms, the Sabbath meal and the arrival of a hasidic rebbe in a small town. His novel *The Rebbe and the Emperor* is about the life of Napoleon and R. Shneur Zalman of Liady.

M. Spiegel, *Restless Spirit*.

SHOHAM, Moses, of Dolina (eighteenth century)–Son of R. Dan, a close associate of the Besht, whom R. Moses visited in his youth. He married the daughter of R. Yehiel Michael, the Maggid of Zloczov. He was renowned as a great kabbalist. R. Abraham Joshua Heschel of Opatov testified that he was "a master of Kabbalah and *Halakhah*" and that "he never deviated from the tenets of the Torah."

He was the author of *Divrei Mosheh*, which was published in Medziborz in 1801. His grandson R. Shimshon Shlomoh Schwartz of Marmaros published his commentary on the *Etz Hayyim* by R. Hayyim Vital under the title *Seraf Peri Etz Hayyim* (Czernowitz, 1864).

He was succeeded by his son, R. Shmuel.

Y. Raphael, *Sefer HaHasidut*, pp. 12–13.

SHOHET, Barukh Meir Jacob, of Stolin (b. 1954)–The only son of Ezra and Feiga Shohet. His mother was the only surviving daughter of R. Yohanan Perlow, who died in 1955, The hasidim then remained leaderless, as his son-in-law, Ezra Shohet, did not succeed him. Some followed R. Joshua Heschel Halitovsky. Others, in 1962, gave their allegiance to R. Moses Mordecai Biderman of Lelov.

Many hasidim in the United States and in Israel decided, however, to accept the late rebbe's grandson, who was then eight years old, as their rebbe. In March 1975, he married his first cousin, Rivkah Shohet, and officially became the rebbe of Karlin and Stolin. The marriage ended in divorce in 1977. He remarried a year later *Hayyah* Miriam Steinwurzel, the daughter of R. Moses David, the principal of the *yeshivah* of Bobov.

He had one son, David Joshua, from his first marriage and ten children from the second.

He has collected a very fine library and worked for Russian Jews now living in Israel. One of his emissaries is the rabbi in Kiev.

He currently spends the year half in Israel and half in the United States.

J. R. Mintz, *Hasidic People—a Place in the New World*, pp. 112–120.

A.T.

SHRAGAI, Shlomoh Zalman (b. 1899), religious Zionist leader—Born in Gorzkowice, Russian Poland, on December 31, son of Mosheh and Frumet Weingarten, he attended the *yeshivah* in Radomsk (1912–1913). He settled in the Holy Land in 1924 and served as mayor of Jerusalem (1950–1954). He became a member of the World Zionist Executive and head of the *Aliya* Department of the Jewish Agency.

He is an adherent of the Radzyn dynasty and among his works are *BeMaayanei Hasidut Izbica-Radzyn* (Jerusalem, 1960); "Hasidut HaBaal Shem Tov BeTefisut Izbica-Radzyn," in *Sefer HaBesht*, pp. 153–201 (Jerusalem, 1960); *Peamei HaGeula* (1963); *Benetivei Hasidut Izbica-Radzyn*, Part 1 (Jerusalem, 1972) and Part 2 (Jerusalem, 1974); and *Di Rabbayim fun Izbice, Radzyner Heder* (Paris, 1972).

SHTIEBL (Yiddish, meaning "little room.")—A place of worship of the hasidim. The adoption by the hasidim of the Lurian liturgy compelled them to establish their own places of worship. The *shtiebl* was not merely a place of worship, but was also a house of study, a refuge, and a shelter. Here, in a congenial atmosphere, the hasidim would gather to pray, talk and relax, and hold their *seudah shlishit* accompanied by song and dance. It is comparatively easy to establish a *shtiebl*—any room can be converted by adding an ark, some tables, and some benches.

Long after the hasidim had achieved legitimacy and acceptance, the trend toward homely and unadorned prayer rooms continued. "Better to pray with a few people, so long as friendship prevails among them, than to pray in a large congregation with an unfriendly atmosphere," said R. Aaron of Karlin. Eventually, each group of hasidim would establish its own *shtiebl*. In Warsaw alone, there were over a hundred hasidic *shtieblech* of Ger, and every hasidic rabbi would have his own *shtiebl* in different localities.

A. Wertheim, *Halakhot VeHalikhot BaHasidut*, pp. 68–71.

SHULHAN ARUKH—Hasidism did, of course, give primacy to the study and knowledge of the Torah, but it is nevertheless true that Hasidism also gave much special emphasis to the devotions of the heart, even when such devotion was not accompanied by Torah knowledge or Torah training. The Besht elaborated on the "*heart of fire*," that sincere thirst for God and devotion to Him by the simple folk. "The Holy One, blessed be He, asked for the heart" (*Sanhedrin* 116), yet, this emphasis on "service of the heart" was never meant to detract from the primacy of the central place or the basic obligation of the Jew to study and to know Torah.

R. Aaron of Zhitomir, a disciple of R. Levi Yitzhak of Berdichev, pointed out "that it is impossible to have a true fear of God without first delving deeply into the Torah." Similarly, R. Shlomoh of Karlin wrote that "to prepare for prayer, one does not need a book of *Musar* but only the study of the Talmud. The holiness of the Talmud is very great. . . . It destroys all the 'shells' that separate us from our Creator." From the first generation of the hasidic movement until today, Hasidism has produced among the hasidic masters great Torah scholars.

Apart from the hasidic contribution to *halakhah*, Hasidism produced the *Shulhan Arukh HaRav*, by R. Shneur Zalman of Liady, which covers the sections of *Orah Hayyim* and *Yoreh De'ah*. Almost 200 years have elapsed since R. Joseph Karo wrote his *Shulhan Arukh*. Much halakhic material has accumulated. It was R. Karo's task to examine and sift all the new material. The essential novelty of R. Shneur Zalman's work can be summarized as follows: to present the Law in an orderly form, in language that is at once precise and readable; not merely to present the final decisions of the Laws, but rather to present them within the context of the halakhic background; and third, when the *halakhah* includes various differing opinions, R. Shneur Zalman gives us the final practical decision.

The first part of R. Shneur Zalman's work was *Hilkhot Talmud Torah* (a treatise on the laws of Torah study), which was printed anonymously in Shklov in 1794 with the approval of R. Heinokh Schik, the rabbi of Shklov. Shklov at that time was a mitnaggedic stronghold, and the fact that this treatise was published there gives the publication special significance. The entire *Shulhan Arukh*, including forty-three responsa, was published in Kopys in 1816.

With the exception of the first section, his entire work was published posthumously. The Vilna edition of 1908 has become the prototype of many subsequent reprints. The latest edition was published by Kehot Publications in New York in 1960. In later editions, this part was published as part of the Rav's *Shulhan Arukh*, which demonstrates his astounding erudition and profound analysis. His work was studied and expounded by R. Shneur Zalman's brother, R. Yehudah Leib, and by his grandson, R. Menahem Mendel, the author of *Tzemah Tzeddek*.

Since its publication, the Rav's *Shulhan Arukh* has remained a classic and a basic halakhic text, quoted and studied by all scholars. The *Hafetz Hayyim* in his *Mishnah Berurah* often refers to the *Rav's Shulhan Arukh*.

A. D. Lavut, *Shaar HaKollel* (Hebrew).

S.R.

SILBERFARB, Hanokh Heinokh Dov (1890–8 *Av* 1978), Tel Aviv – He was the son of R. Meshullam Zalman Joseph, his mother being the daughter of R. Aaron of Koidanov. He was born in Sztrapko and studied under his grandfather and father. He married Esther Dinah, the daughter of R. Moses of Sulitza. In 1920 he became rabbi in Urial, Bessarabia, and in 1929, he succeeded his father-in-law as rebbe in Buczacz.

After surviving the Second World War, he settled in Tel Aviv in 1948, where he was the rebbe of Koidanov and Buczasz. Toward the end of his life, almost blind, he spent the whole day in prayer and study.

He had three sons: R. Yoel; R. Shalom, one of the leading members of the *HaPoal Mizrachi*; and R. Aaron (1914–23 *Adar* 1994), who succeeded him. R. Aaron established a *Bet HaMidrash* in Bene Berak, but lived all his life in Rehov Dizengoff, Tel Aviv. He was buried in *Zikhron Meir* cemetery, Bene Berak, and was succeeded as rebbe by his nephew, R. Jacob Erlich.

Hamodiah, 10 *Elul* 1978.

SILBERFARB, Meshullam Zalman Joseph (1868–1944) – Son of R. Moses Silberfarb, he was born in Rovno. His mother was the only daughter of R. Hanokh Heinokh of Olesko. He was noted for his warm hospitality, and his house had four doors so that guests could enter on any side.

He married the daughter of R. Aaron of Koidanov, and in 1896 he became rebbe in Sztrapko. He recited the entire Book of Psalms every Friday night. He was murdered by the Nazis.

SILENCE – How does the infinite diversity of the cosmos derive from one God? Since this derivation is continuous, it cannot adequately be accounted for in one act of creation. In Kabbalah, the unfathomable wisdom of God descends into understanding (*Binah*) whence it comes down into words. In Hasidism, the problem is to ascend heavenward from words into pure thought. It is necessary to serve the Almighty with one's soul only, that is, in thought (*Tzavaat HaRibash*).

The Maggid, the successor of the Besht, taught: "It is best to serve God by silence" (*Maggid Devarav LeYaakov*, 4). In graphic imagery we are told that thought is called the father of speech. In all these cases, the term "thought" (*mahshavah*) is not a rational weighing of alternatives, but a kind of trance in which the *tzaddik* becomes the recipient of divine power. The Besht asserted that when one clings to the Creator, and thought of something comes to one's mind, this is probably part of the holy spirit (*Ruah HaKodesh*).

The world of speech (*Olam HaDibur*) is lower than the realm of holiness, which is reached through silence. Some *tzaddikim* were extremely careful not to give expression to any unpleasant thoughts, on the grounds that it could be changed so long as it did not acquire the reality of speech (*Midrash Pinhas*). In the school of *Habad*, the attainment of an ecstatic trance of total devotion and silence was assiduously cultivated (*Kuntres HaHitpaalut*).

R. Israel of Ruzhyn, citing the verse "An altar of earth shalt thou make unto Me" (Exodus 20:21), interprets it to mean "an altar of silence," which is more pleasant to God than anything else.

J.B.A.

SILVERMAN, Naftali Herzka Halevi, of Ujfeherto (d. 9 *Tishri* 1897) – A disciple of R. Hayyim Halberstam, he was known as a miracle worker. Even members of the Hungarian nobility came to him for advice and guidance. He was the author of *Zikhron Naftali* (Kleinwardein, 1938; reprinted in Brooklyn, 1962).

SIMHAH BEN JOSHUA, of Zalozce (1711–1768) – A preacher in Zalozce, near Brody, he was a disciple of R. Nahman of Kossov. Leaving Constantinople on September 26, 1764, he met R. Nahman of Horodenka and R. Mendel of Przemyshlany, who were also traveling to the Holy Land.

After seven months he returned home and wrote an account of his journey, *Sippurei Eretz HaGalil* (Tales of Galilee). He was also the author of *Ahavat Tziyyon* (Grodno, 1790), *Lev Simhah* (Zolkiev, 1753), and *Netiah shel Simhah* (Zolkiev, 1757).

A. Yaari, *Masot Eretz Yisrael*, pp. 382–423, 773–775.

SIMHAT TORAH, Festival of the Rejoicing of the Torah – On that day the annual cycle of the public reading of the Torah is both concluded and recommenced. In the Diaspora, the Festival is celebrated on the morrow of Shemini Atzeret (23 *Tishri*).

Naturally, the warmhearted hasidim regarded Simhat Torah as a great spiritual Festival. In the presence of their rebbe, there was no frivolity, irreverence, or unseemliness. The joy they experienced and radiated was the outcome of piety. The *Shivhei HaBesht* tells of the exuberance, dancing, and singing with which the disciples of the Besht celebrated Simhat Torah.

The custom of seven *Hakkafot* has its origin in the kabbalistic circle of R. Yitzhak Luria. Some of the hasidic rebbes, such as those of Ropczyce, Zanz, and Vishnitz, had their own rituals (*Seder Hakkafot*) printed. Some composed special liturgical hymns. Some recited *Eshet Hayyil* and passages from the Psalms. They also observed *Hakkafot* on Shemini Atzeret (22 *Tishri*). This custom is derived from *Hemdat Yamim*, a work composed in the first quarter of the eighteenth century, which recommends that *hakkafot* be conducted on the night of Shemini Atzeret in honor of the Land of Israel, where Simhat Torah is celebrated on that day.

The Maggid of Kozienice sang and danced with a small scroll of the Torah for two hours without interruption. R. Hayyim Halberstam of Zanz used to throw apples to his hasidim, and the hasidim treasured the apples as *segulot* (lucky charms).

It was on Simhat Torah night 1815 that the "mysterious fall" took place. R. Jacob Yitzhak of Lublin, who had retired to his room on the first floor of his house after the *hakkafot*, was found, late at night, lying on the ground outside the house. "The evil powers pursued me," he told his disciples.

M. Unger, *Hasidut un Yom Tov*, pp. 142–182.

T.P.

SINGER, Israel Joshua (1893–1944) – Born in Bilgoraj, the grandson of a rabbi, he studied in a hasidic *yeshivah*. He lived in Warsaw and Kiev and settled in the United States in 1934. He wrote short stories about Polish Jews and their hasidic milieu. His novel *Yoshe Kalb* (1932) was printed in an English translation under the title *The Sinner* and was dramatized by Maurice Schwartz.

He was also the author of the novel *Die Brider Ashkenazy* (The Brothers Ashkenazy) (1936), in which he chronicles the rise and fall of a hasidic middle-class family in the textile industry of Lodz. He captures the mood of Hasidism and its ecstasy, warmth, and many dimensions.

C. Madison, *Yiddish Literature*, pp. 452–478.

SINGER, Yitzhak Meir, of Alexandrov (1893–16 *Tammuz* 1942) – Son of R. Elijah, who was, at one time, rebbe in Przysucha and for the last thirty years of his life in Kalish. At an early age, he married Malkah Perel, the daughter of R. Shmuel Tzvi Danciger of Alexandrov. After his marriage, he stayed with his father-in-law, and in 1914, he became rabbi of Alexandrov. During the Nazi era, he lived in Lodz and was murdered in Tomaszov-Mazowiecka.

His son R. Jacob Feivel married Yutta, the daughter of R. Joseph Kalish of Amshinov, and was rabbi in Ostrov-Mazowiecka. He, his wife, and his seven children were killed by the Nazis in Slonim. His daughter, Rosa Mindel, and her five children also perished in the Holocaust.

Elleh Ezkerah, vol. 7, pp. 91–97.

SOCIOLOGY – With the exception of some sketchy endeavors, there were no really significant socioscientific studies on Hasidism until the 1960s. In his book *Williamsburg, a Jewish Community in Transition* (New York, 1961), George Kranzler gives a sociohistorical view of the development of Williamsburg, Brooklyn, since 1920. After 1945, those already in the neighborhood were joined by Orthodox survivors of the Holocaust–mostly of Carpathian, Russian, and Hungarian origin. He examines their class structure, family pattern, and synagogal organization.

Solomon Poll, in his book *Hasidic Community of Williamsburg* (New York, 1962), describes the economic activities of the hasidim after World War II. Many hasidim earn their living in the manufacture of kosher food and religious articles.

In *The Legends of the Hasidim* (Chicago, 1968), Jerome Mintz chronicles hasidic life in Brooklyn through 383 well-documented case histories. He explores the relationship between hasidic legend and hasidic law and between ritual values and customs. He discusses the function of the rebbe, the upbringing of the children, the role of the women, the relevance of magic and mysticism, and the social interactions of the various courts with each other and the outside world.

Jacques Gutwirth's *Vie juive traditionnelle* (Paris, 1970) is the only such work that deals with Western Europe. Concentrating on Antwerp, Belgium, after the Second World War, it analyzes the economic activities, the diamond industry, demographic factors, religious behavior, and the social system.

In *Satmar, an Island in the City* (Chicago, 1972), Israel Rubin, formerly professor of sociology at Cleveland State University, deals dispassionately with the Williamsburg Satmar community, a group often attacked for its social exclusiveness. Rubin, who over a period of years lived with the Satmar hasidim, observed their patterns of life, thought, and culture.

In *Life in a Religious Community: The Lubavitch Hasidim in Montreal* (Toronto, 1974), William Shafir studies the Lubavitch community from a psychological point of view. For these hasidim, their relationship with their rebbe in Montreal is a fundamental factor of common identity. The author makes some shrewd comments on their missionary activities: results that are below their expectations.

These books and the study of the *Lubavitch Community of Stamford Hill, London*, by Jeanette Kupfermann (an unpublished thesis for the University of London, 1975), is a contribution toward the better understanding of Hasidism.

Egon Mayer in *From Suburb to Shtetl–the Jews of Borough Park* (Philadelphia: Temple University Press, 1979) investigated the standing of the 50,000 hasidic Jews who live in this middle-class area and who are followers of different rebbes: hasidim of Belz, Munkacs, Papa, Stolin, Zanz, and Vishnitz.

Lisa Harris, in her book *Holy Days: The World of a Hasidic Family* (New York, 1985), gives a graphic description of the lifestyle of a hasidic family in New York.

J. Gutwirth, *Vie juive traditionnelle: ethnologie d'une communité hassidique*.

J.G.

SOKOLOV, Nahum (1859–1936), Zionist leader–Born in Wyszogrod, near Plock, into a family rooted in tradition, his father being a descendant of the kabbalist Nathan Shapira, he was a prodigy in talmudic studies. After his marriage he lived in Makov and was a pioneer in modern Hebrew journalism, later becoming president of the World Zionist Organization. In his work *LeMaranan U'LeRabbanan* (1901), he tried to bring Orthodox circles closer to Zionism. He visited R. Yehudah Aryeh Alter of Ger and tried to enlist hasidic support for the Zionist movement.

In an address on Hasidism, delivered in London on February 5, 1928, he expressed his admiration of the hasidic movement. He maintained that Hasidism was like a melody that cannot be translated and cannot be interpreted. He was critical of Graetz and of Yitzhak Erter, who criticized the movement (*Die Zeit*, February 7, 1928, p. 2).

Toward the end of his life he started a series of articles called "Leaders of Hasidism," but he managed to complete only an essay on R. Nahman of Bratzlav.

S. Kling, *Nachum Sokolov: Servant of His People*.

SOLITUDE–R. Nahman of Bratzlav instructed his disciples to seek daily solitude in the fields and forests. He himself, when he returned after a period of solitude, "saw a new world, and it seemed as if it had taken on an altogether different appearance."

R. Elimelekh of Lejask regarded solitude as a means whereby the soul might cling to the Creator of the world. R. Yitzhak Taub urged his followers to go to the forest every day, "Put your ears to the tree and to the earth, and hear how every tree and every blade of grass sings praises to the Creator."

The rabbi of Chortkov did not give discourses for a long time. When asked for the reason, he replied, "There are seventy ways of reciting Torah, and one of them is through solitude and silence."

R. Menahem Mendel of Kotzk, for the last twenty-two years of his life, lived a life of solitude.

Nahman ben Simhah of Bratzlav, *Likkutei Moharan*, pp. 95–96.

SONNENBERG-ZBITKOVER, Temerel

SONNENBERG-ZBITKOVER, Temerel (d. 1830) – Daughter of R. Aryeh Leibush Halevi Horowitz, rabbi of Stanislav and Tysmenice, who married Berek, son of Shmuel Zbitkover, a contractor to the Russian and Polish armies. Berek was able to obtain, from Stanislas Augustus, the last king of Poland, land in Praga, where he built a synagogue and a cemetery at his own expense.

Temerel was a devoted follower of Hasidism and a great adherent of the hasidic rebbes. The rebbes of Warka and R. Simhah Bunem of Przysucha were employed by her for a time. She would not tolerate the publication of books by the *Haskalah*, which she regarded as heretical. Legend has it that she paid three gold coins for every copy of Joseph Perl's *Megalei Temirin* (Vienna, 1819), a parody of Hasidism, which she then destroyed.

When her only daughter married, the Maggid of Kozienice attended the wedding in Warsaw. She left 300,000 gulden for charity. One of her descendants was the philosopher Henri Bergson.

J. Shatzky, *The History of the Jews in Warsaw*, vols. 1 and 2.

M.S.

SONNENFELD, Joseph Hayyim

SONNENFELD, Joseph Hayyim (1849–1932), Agudist leader – Born in Verbo, Slovakia, he was orphaned at the age of four. He studied in the *yeshivah* of Pressburg under R. Abraham Shmuel Benjamin Sofer. In 1873, he settled in the Old City of Jerusalem, where he was closely associated with R. J. L. Diskin. He was the head of the *kollel Shomrei Hahomot* (Guardians of the Walls). He believed in complete separation of the Orthodox from the secularists.

In 1920, he was elected rabbi of the separate Orthodox community. He appeared before many of the commissions that were investigating conditions in the Holy Land. He had an unbounded love for the land. When a member of the Royal Commission asked him whether Palestine was big enough to absorb new immigrants, he replied, "When children return from exile to their mother's home, the mother never says that there is no room for them."

M. Blau, *Amudei Dinhora*.

SOULS

SOULS – The *Zohar* states that "when one is born, one is given a soul, corresponding to the animal. . . . Those who are more worthy are given a spirit [*ruah*] corresponding to the living angels [*hayyot*]. Those who are even more worthy are given a soul corresponding to the divine throne" (*Zohar* 2:94b).

The Besht taught that in the lowliest of persons there dwells a soul, a sacred mystery, the garment of the Living God. It therefore behooves us to keep our garment spotless, in order that we may return it whenever bidden, without blemish. "Do not," the Besht said, "consider the time you spend on eating and sleeping wasted. The soul within you is rested during these intervals and is enabled to renew its holy work with fresh enthusiasm" (*Keter Shem Tov*, p. 4a).

The first part of the *Tanya* is devoted to the theme of two souls. R. Shneur Zalman maintains there are two souls: the animal soul and the divine soul, which is clothed with *Hokhmah* (the highest attribute of the ten *Sefirot*). The lower, or animal, soul is called *Nefesh HaBehomit* or *Nefesh HaHiyyunit*. Only the Jew is endowed with the divine soul. This idea is already to be found in Yehudah Halevi (*Kuzari*, p. 127) and in R. Judah Loeb of Prague (*Tiferet Yisrael*, end of chap. one).

"Every Jew," said R. Shneur Zalman, "whether righteous or wicked, has two souls. These souls are alluded to in the verse 'The souls that I have made' (Isaiah 57:16). This is true even though there are thousands of different levels of souls, one above the other without end. The souls of the Patriarchs and Moses are greater than the souls of our generation" (*Tanya* 1–2, 5b).

R. Dov Baer in his *Tract on Ecstasy* speaks of five levels of the divine soul: *Nefesh*, *Ruah*, *Neshamah*, *Hayyah*, and *Yehidut*.

L. Jacobs, "The Doctrine of the 'Divine Spark' in Man in Jewish Sources," in *Studies in Rationalism, Judaism and Universalism, in Memory of Leon Roth*.

SOUTH AFRICA—There were hasidim living there in the first decade of the twentieth century. On October 16, 1909, fifty-seven men met at the Palmerston Hotel, in Johannesburg, to discuss the establishment of a hasidic *Bet HaMidrash*. Only three years later, in 1912, a three-story house situated at the corner of Main and Ferreira streets was purchased for £1575, then worth about $7,800, and the *Bet HaMidrash* was opened on June 1, 1912.

In 1928, with the shift of the Jewish population to the new suburb of Doornfontein, the congregation purchased a site at the corner of Harrow and Siemert roads. In 1930, the first services were held there. This synagogue remained active for more than thirty years, when a new *Bet HaMidrash* was opened in Yeoville in 1963.

The arrival of R. Mendel Lipsker in 1942, the emissary of the rebbe of Lubavitch, gave the movement a new impetus. Among his achievements is the founding of *Habad* House as a center for young people. Apart from the increasing activities of *Habad* in different parts of South Africa, no other hasidic group has had any noticeable representation. This is probably due to the fact that the main South African Jewish community emanates from Lithuania.

In Capetown, a hasidic *Bet HaMidrash* existed on Buitenkant Street. When Sea Point grew into a popular residential area, the synagogue was transferred to premises on Arthur's Road, where it continued to function until 1970.

J.A.

SPARKS, HOLY—Among the ideas expounded by Lurian kabbalists and the Besht was the concept of *nitzotzot*—holy sparks. They believed that the roots and the source of the tree of knowledge consist of 248 sparks, which fell when the vessels were broken. As a result of Adam's disobedience, those sparks descended lower and lower, until they were clothed with a combination of good and evil. There was *Shevirat HaKelim*—the breaking of the vessels—the fragmentation that took place. The particles are called *nitzotzot*.

By way of the principle that whatever was "higher falls lower," the fact is that our world contains many fragments. Humanity's main task in this world is to "transform darkness into light" (*Zohar* 1:4a). One, therefore, must separate these sparks and elevate them (step by step) from the inanimate to the domain of plants, animals, and humans, raising them higher and higher until they return to their root and source. This is the purpose of the observance of the Torah and Commandments.

Whenever we eat anything or make use of a utensil, even when we do so for the sake of our own body, at the same time, we rectify the sparks and elevate them to their source. By using the physical for a holy purpose, we release the sparks contained within it and cause the elevation of this spark to its source. By wearing *tzitzit* and *tefillin*, we liberate these sparks from their imprisonment. Just as the soul constantly yearns to be free, so the sparks yearn for the act that will liberate them from their place of internment.

Only true repentance and remorse can restore the sparks. Every Jew is given a certain number of sparks to retrieve. They may be scattered in many parts of the world. This is the reason for our dispersal.

A. Kaplan, *The Light Beyond*, pp. 234–240.

Z.T.

SPERBER, David (1875–25 *Adar* II 1962)—Son of R. Barukh Kalonymus, he was born in Zablotov and was brought up in Marmaros. He studied under R. Meir Arak. He married the daughter of R. Moses Stern, the rabbi of Havasmezo, and served there as *dayan* for twenty years, becoming rabbi in Brasov in 1925.

After the Second World War, he settled in Jerusalem, where he was a member of the *Mo'etzet Gedolei HaTorah*. Throughout his life, he was a devoted hasid of R. Moses Hager of Kosov.

He was the author of responsa *Afraksta D'Aniya* (Satmar, 1940); *Mikhtav LeDavid*, novellas on the Torah (Jerusalem, 1977); and *Sefer Higayon Levavi* of R. Moses of Sasov (Jerusalem, 1970).

SPIEGEL, Moses Menahem, of Ostrova/New York (1898–17 *Tevet* 1982)—

Son of R. Naftali Aryeh, his mother was the daughter of R. Jacob Yitzhak of Kaluszyn. Together with his father (who died in 1949), he emigrated to the United States in 1926. He himself lived in Brownsville, in Brooklyn, and then moved to Williamsburg, where he was the rabbi in the *Polisher shtiebl*.

He had two daughters and two sons: R. Jacob Yitzhak and R. Abraham Elhanan. His brother, R. Pinhas Eli, is the rebbe of Ostrov in Long Beach, New York.

SPIEGEL, Naftali Aryeh, of Ostrova (1869–20 *Tishri* 1949)–Son of R. Moses, he was born in Lublin and married the daughter of R. Yitzhak Kalish. He was rabbi in Czechov, near Lublin, and when his father-in-law died, he succeeded him as rebbe in Ostrova.

He emigrated to the United States in 1926.

SPIEGELGLASS, Nathan (1882–1942)–Son of R. Ezekiel, a hasid of Zwolen, he was born in Warsaw and studied under R. Meir Yehiel Halevi Halstock of Ostrowiec. He married Perel, the daughter of the wealthy Mordecai Shmuel Klein, one of the leaders of the Warsaw community. He was head of the *yeshivah Emek Habakhah*, which had an enrollment of 500 students.

Although he prayed in the *Radzmyner shtiebl*, he was regarded as a rebbe by many followers. He and his three married sons, their wives, their children, his youngest son, who was barely twenty, and his youngest daughter, Freidele, aged fourteen, all perished in the Holocaust.

SPIRITUALISM–Hasidism, in common with Orthodox Jewish practice, forbids communication with the dead. The incident of Saul and the witch of En Dor (1 Samuel 28:7–19) and the esoteric experiences of a number of talmudic sages (*Berakhot* 18b, *Gittin* 56b) are isolated instances.

Hasidism believes implicitly in the existence of spirits but rigorously opposes spiritualism–the attempt to contact those spirits. The dead should not be disturbed. Such practices are regarded as evil and undesirable. Only on rare occasions do we find in hasidic legends, as in the case of the *dybbuk*, that the dead are summoned to a court of law on earth.

STEINBERG, Yehudah (1863–1908), Hebrew writer–Born in Lipkany, Bessarabia, he grew up in a hasidic home, as his father was a hasid of Sadgora. After his marriage, he came under the influence of the *Haskalah*. He lived in Yedintze, where he earned his living as a teacher.

He wrote numerous short stories, dealing mostly with Jewish life in Russia. Two collections of short stories, *Sippurei Hasidim* and *Sihot Hasidim*, both printed in Warsaw in 1904, were devoted entirely to Hasidism. He was one of the first Hebrew writers to write about Hasidism with warmth and sympathy. Only a few of his stories deal with the leaders of the movement. For the most part, he depicts the lives and ways of ordinary hasidim, describing their piety, simplicity, optimism, and devotion to their families and fellow Jews.

Y. Fischman, *Introduction to Kol Kitvei Yehudah Steinberg*.

T.P.

STEINER, Isaiah, of Kreszteer (1851–3 *Iyyar* 1925)–Popularly known as "R. Shayele," he was born in Zborov. His father died when he was three years old. He studied in the *yeshivah* of R. Hershele Liszker and subsequently for a short time in Budszentmihlay, but he soon returned to Liszka, where R. Hershele, in 1870, made him his *shamash*. He soon became known as "*Shayele Shamash*." The aging rebbe advised some of his hasidim to give their *kvittlech* to R. Shayele, and he groomed R. Shayele to be his successor.

On the death of R. Hershele, R. Hayyim Halberstam and R. Mordecai Rosenbaum of Nadvorno proclaimed R. Shayele the leader of the Liszker hasidim. At first, R. Shayele stayed in Olasz-Liszka, but out of deference to R. Hershele's family, he moved to the nearby town of Bodrog Keresztur (Kreszteer in Yiddish), where he lived for the next five decades. His Hasidism was unsophisticated, primarily one of simplicity and popular appeal.

His understanding of human nature made him a most sought-after arbitrator in disputes. Even non-Jews came to him for guidance. He died at the age of seventy-four and was succeeded by his only son, R. Abraham Steiner, who survived his father by only three years.

Both sons-in-law of R. Shayele were noted scholars: R. Israel Abraham Alter Landau, the rabbi of Edeleny, was the author of responsa *Bet Yisrael*, of which only a small part was printed in Miskolcz in 1942. A complete edition appeared in Buenos Aires in 1954. His other son-in-law, R. Reuben Hayyim Klein, rabbi of Snina, perished in Auschwitz. His commentary to *Yoreh De'ah*, *Mateh Reuben*, was printed in Vranov in 1938.

A.S.

STEINMAN, Eliezer (1892–1970), Hebrew writer and essayist – Born in Obodovka, he was active in Hebrew and Yiddish journalism and contributed articles to *HaZefirah* and *Der Moment*. In attempting to find a synthesis between Jewish culture and world literature, he compared the thoughts of R. Nahman of Bratzlav with those of St. Francis of Assisi and Ibsen.

In 1924, he settled in Tel Aviv, worked for *Haaretz*, and published many stories. His writing on Hasidism *Be'er HaHasidut* (Tel Aviv, 1951) was followed by a series of nine books on Hasidism (1958–1962) and a collection of hasidic stories *Kankan HaKesef* in four volumes (Ramat Gan, 1969). He writes like a hasid speaking to hasidim, but he does not cite his sources, and his works are lacking in historical and critical perspective.

M. Waxman, *A History of Jewish Literature*, vol. 4, p. 196f.

STEINSALTZ, Adin (b. 1937), scholar – Born in Jerusalem into a secular family, he studied mathematics at the Hebrew University in Jerusalem. He is the head of the Israel Institute for Talmudic Publications. He is currently working on his monumental translation and commentary of the Babylonian Talmud into modern Hebrew, of which more than a million copies have already been sold.

Through his extensive writing and teaching, he has made a notable contribution to hasidic thought. His book *The Long Shorter Way* (Jason Aronson, 1988), based on lectures on *Habad* philosophy delivered from 1977 to 1980 to a small group in Jerusalem, has fifty-three chapters, corresponding to the number of chapters in the *Tanya*. It focuses on the profound dilemma of the *Benoni*, the intermediate person, who, neither purely wicked nor purely good, must struggle with evil and temptation throughout his or her life.

He is also the author of the provocative book *The Thirteen Petalled Rose* (Jason Aronson, 1992), which presents an eloquent and profound statement of Jewish theology based on kabbalistic structures. He is author of dozens of books in Hebrew and English, including *The Sustaining Utterance* (1989), *In the Beginning* (1992), *The Strife of the Spirit* (1988), *On Being Free* (1995), and *The Tales of Rabbi Nachman of Bratslav* (1993), all published by Jason Aronson Inc.

STEINSCHNEIDER, Moritz (1816–1907), bibliographer – Born in Prossnitz, Moravia, he was one of the founders of modern Jewish scholarship and the father of Jewish bibliography. Apart from his monumental catalogs, much of his work was devoted to the unearthing of information about the contribution of Jews to medieval science.

He regarded all forms of mysticism as a variation on superstitions borrowed by Judaism from the surrounding nations. He describes Hasidism in very negative terms, calling it "a malady of Judaism." However, he did admit that he was not fully knowledgeable about the movement and was unfamiliar with much of its literature (J.B.G.W. 6, 27f, 41).

A. Herzberg and L. A. Feldman, eds. *History and Jewish Historians*: Essays by S. W. Baron, p. 285.

STEMPEL, Shragai Feivish (1880–1945) – A native of Cracow, he was active in the Aguda and a member of the municipal authorities and the Jewish community. In 1922, he was elected as a member of the Polish parliament, and he participated in Aguda conferences. He, his wife, and members of his family perished in Auschwitz.

His son, R. Moses (1910–*Av* 1941), studied in the *yeshivah* of Bobov, and in 1930 married Nehamah Golda, the daughter of R. Benzion Halberstam of Bobov. R. Moses, too, perished together with his father-in-law in Lvov on 1 *Av* 1941. His wife and his two children, R. Shmuel Yehudah Leibel and Shoshanah, survived.

His widow remarried Joshua Meir Freshwater of London.

STERNFELD (Horowitz), Joshua Asher, of Parysov (1867–1941) – Son of

R. Mordecai Zeev Horowitz, a follower of the "Seer" of Lublin, Joshua was born in Warsaw and was a disciple of R. Joshua Asher of Parysov and R. Jacob Meir Shalom of Kaluszyn. He was a diligent student of the *Zohar*, which he knew by heart. He declined, however, to give discourses on mysticism, which he regarded as "hidden Torah."

After the death of his rebbe in 1924, many hasidim followed his brother, R. Mordecai of Pabianice. When R. Mordecai died a year later, R. Joshua became rebbe. He would not accept *pidyonot* and regarded himself as a guide rather than a rebbe.

He died as a result of suffering inflicted by the Nazis.

Elleh Ezkerah, vol. 6, pp. 235–238.

STERNHARZ, Nathan, of Nemirov (15 *Shevat* 1780–1845), disciple of R. Nahman of Bratzlav – Born in Nemirov, Podolia, to a nonhasidic and relatively well-to-do family. At an early age, he married Esther Sheindel, the daughter of R. David Tzvi of Mogilev, the rabbi in Shargorod, an active opponent of Hasidism. For the following two years, he lived with his father-in-law and was supported by him, pursuing traditional talmudic studies. It was only when he returned with his wife to his parental home in Nemirov in 1796 that R. Nathan was first drawn to Hasidism. He visited a number of the *tzaddikim* of the time, including R. Zusya of Annopol, R. Levi Yitzhak of Berdichev, and R. Barukh of Medziborz.

In 1802, shortly after R. Nahman's own arrival in the town, R. Nathan joined the circle of R. Nahman's followers and soon became attached to him. Before long, R. Nahman discovered R. Nathan's literary talents and employed him as his secretary. Until R. Nahman's physical condition deteriorated drastically in 1808, he dictated his teachings to R. Nathan or let him copy his original notes. After 1808, R. Nathan began to record these from memory, after hearing R. Nahman address the gatherings of disciples at his court. In this manner he wrote down and edited for R. Nahman the books *Likkutei Moharan*, *Sippurei Maasiyot*, and *Sefer HaMidot* as well as the manuscript of a book that R. Nahman subsequently ordered to be burned.

In addition to this, R. Nathan, a compulsive writer, recorded continually and in great detail many of R. Nahman's more casual discourses, thus compiling the material that later served as the basis for his biographical works – *Shivhei HaRan*, *Sihot HaRan*, and *Hayyei Moharan* – and for his autobiography, *Yemei Moharan*. Following R. Nahman's instructions, he also began to note down his own "innovations" – elaborations on the teachings of R. Nahman – which appeared many years later as the books *Likkutei Tefillot*, *Likkutei Etzot*, and *Likkutei Halakhot*.

The bulk of this literature bears the distinct marks of R. Nathan's personal sensitivities and idiosyncrasies, of which the most outstanding are his esoteric tendencies and the discreet but consistent suppression of evidence relating to prominent members of the Bratzlav circle whom he might have considered as his rivals. Notably, during R. Nahman's lifetime, though he was acknowledged as a skillful and dedicated scribe, R. Nathan did not occupy a central position in the Bratzlav circle. Whereas later Bratzlav traditions depict him as the closest disciple of R. Nahman and the natural candidate for the role of chief organizer, though not as a *tzaddik* in his own right, of the circle after the death of R. Nahman, in reality he never penetrated the inner circle of R. Nahman's oldest disciples. However, after the death of R. Nahman and inspired by a new sense of mission, R. Nathan practically rescued the Bratzlav circle from total dissolution by reviving its collapsing institutions and recruiting new adherents to the teachings of R. Nahman.

He outlived his master for thirty-five years and was the most prolific writer in Hasidism. In his endeavor to spread his master's teachings, R. Nathan, in 1821, secretly set up a printing press in his own house in Bratzlav, where, bypassing state censorship regulations, he published a number of R. Nahman's and his own works. Through a denunciation to the authorities, the press was discovered and put out of operation in 1824.

In 1822, R. Nathan visited the Holy Land, returning in 1823. Although R. Nathan alienated the Bratzlav old guard, and despite the bitter controversy led against him by R. Moses Tzvi of Savran, the new generation of Bratzlaver hasidim accepted R. Nathan's leadership while continuing, at his own insistence, to worship R. Nahman as their only true *tzaddik*. It was largely due to R. Nathan's commitment to this cause and due to his literary and organizational skills that the Bratzlav literature and the circle's cohesiveness have been preserved to the present day.

M. Piekarz, *Hasidut Braslav*, pp. 203–211.
J. G. Weiss, *Mehkarim BeHasidut Bratzlav*, pp. 66–86.

A.Ra.

STOLIN GENIZAH – Stolin, a city near Pinsk, in Belorussia. During the nineteenth century, Hasidism flourished in the courts of the Stolin and Karlin rebbes. The archives of the rebbes, which were housed in the cellars of the rebbe's residence in Stolin, were composed of correspondence between rebbes, public appeals, *pinkasim*, other documents, and a manuscript of *Sefer HaTzoref* by Joshua Heshel ben Joseph Zoref (1633–1700), who was suspected of Shabbatean tendencies.

These archives were utilized by Dr. W. Z. Rabinowitsch in his study of the history of Hasidism in Lithuania.

W. Z. Rabinowitsch, "Min HaGenizah HaStolinit," pp. 125–132.

STORY, HASIDIC – There are two kinds of hasidic stories (*maasiyot*). The first of these is the tale told by the *tzaddik* himself either in the form of a *mashal* (parable) or in the form of an apparently trivial account of mundane affairs but containing, in reality, so the hasidim believed, supernal profundities so that in the telling, unifications (*yihudim*) were performed. The grandson of the Besht (*Degel Mahanei Efrayim*, *VaYeshev* [Jerusalem, 1963], p. 54) remarks, "I have myself heard and seen my grandfather, of blessed memory, tell stories and speak of external matters, and yet in these very things he used to serve God with his pure and refined intellect."

According to hasidic legend, when the Maggid of Mezhirech visited the Besht, of whose fame as a holy man he had heard, he was at first repelled by the banal tales Besht told about his horses.

The second and more usual type of hasidic tale consists of hagiographical narrative, the hero of which is not the *tzaddik*. These tales (*sippurim*) are generally of a miraculous nature or such as to convey the saintly conduct of the *tzaddik*.

To tell such stories was considered to be a high religious duty. The word for "story" is *maaseh* – the term used in *maaseh merkavah* (the account of the Heavenly chariot seen by the prophet Ezekiel) – and a well-known hasidic aphorism has it that to relate the deeds of the *tzaddikim* is akin to studying the deepest kabbalistic mysteries and with the same effect achieved. At other times also but especially after the termination of the Sabbath at the *melaveh malkah* repast, the hasidim gather around an elder or the *tzaddik* to be regaled in a mood of mystic exaltation with the mighty deeds and wonders performed by the *tzaddikim* and the way in which these served God.

The hasidic tale is told with an artlessness that conceals its significant contribution as a new, highly imaginative Jewish art form. Much is made of accurate reporting (e.g., "A heard it from B, a completely trustworthy man who would not lie for all the money in the world and who was an eyewitness to it"). Not unaware of the astonishing claims made in these tales in which nothing is impossible for the *tzaddik*, the hasidim justify the miracles on various grounds, for example, that in exile, God wishes to show that He has not abandoned His people; that the saints are really earlier teachers whose souls have become reincarnated in their bodies so that there is now the double merit of the ancients and of present-day *tzaddikim*; or because just before the advent of the Messiah there is bound to be a great outpouring of spiritual power.

The hasidic story serves multiple functions. For instance, it encourages the hasidim to believe in the reality of the spiritual universe; it comforts them to know that God still cares for His people; it inspires them to become more closely attached to the hasidic way and to their rebbe; and it removes doubts and strengthens faith in God and His Torah. The very telling of the tale has, moreover, a kind of magical effect, re-creating the original bursting forth of the divine grace that took place when the marvel first happened. In addition, many of the hasidic stories, as well as the sayings of the *tzaddikim* and their maxims that belong to the same genre, have a strong religious and ethical content, showing how the hasidic life at its best is to be lived.

The telling and retelling of the behavior, the wisdom, and the spiritual counsel of the *tzaddikim* urges the hasid, if not to emulate the conduct of the saints, at least to approximate it insofar as it is possible for a mere mortal to mirror forth in his poor life the deeds of "angels on high," the hasidic term by which the *tzaddikim* are frequently known in the tales.

Another not unimportant function of the hasidic stories is historical. Through the numerous anecdotes, related with precision and detail, the hasidim come to know who is who in the hasidic chain of tradition and the place of their own rebbe and his court in the scheme. They are also informed of the rules of discipleship, how each *tzaddik* went searching for the master to whom he could alone be attracted by the root of his soul.

Nor should the sheer entertainment value of the tales be overlooked, a value required in an atmosphere of total dedication to the rigorous demands of hasidic life.

Finally, the hasidic storytellers were genuinely engaged, whether or not they knew it, in literary creativity. Even a rationalist like Ahad Ha-Am could say that in modern times there is little to touch the inventiveness and rich color and drama of the hasidic tale.

J. Dan, *The Hasidic Novella*.

L.J.

STORYTELLERS – Storytelling is the oldest of human arts. Before people could read or write they told one another stories. Customs and manners change, but stories survive the passing of time. The tales of the Bible have called forth the admiration of mankind. A third of the Talmud is replete with picturesque legends, allegories, anecdotes, and stories. Compilation of the nonlegal sections of the Talmud by Jacob Ibn Habib in the fifteenth century became one of the most popular Jewish books. Posttalmudic literature, too, is a veritable treasure house of Jewish legendary material.

Around no other figure in Jewish history, ancient or medieval, have evolved so many stories as around the Besht. He spoke to his followers in a language they could all understand. He rightly felt that to reach the less well educated one has to explain matters to them by the use of a story. Hence, to speak of Hasidism is to tell a story. The air was literally buzzing with miracles, tales of tormented souls and evil spirits. The tales of the hasidim had a generative power and were also a great medium of popularizing the movement.

R. Nahman of Bratzlav, the great-grandson of the Besht, was a master of the parablelike tale and a spinner of fantastic fables. It was his opinion that "Hasidic tales purify the mind. Through these narratives, the heart is aroused and enraptured with the most powerful longings for God."

Not since the development of the *Haggadah* and the Midrash in the early centuries of the common era has the story been given such importance and status as in Hasidism. It was believed that relating stories of hasidic rebbes was equivalent to reciting prayers. Hasidic ideas were explained by a parable and not by philosophy.

The *Shivhei HaBesht* (Kopys, 1815) was the first popular hasidic book. A year after its publication, in 1816, Joseph Perl, an opponent of Hasidism, in his *Das Wesen der Sekte Chassidim* (Dubnow, I, 278–279) stated, "There was a time when the sect merely whispered the miraculous deeds of the Besht from ear to ear, until, in the years 1814 and 1815, they determined to assemble these oral traditions and to bring them to the public through the printing press."

Shivhei HaBesht has gone through many editions, and they were followed by the tales of R. Nahman, which were printed in innumerable editions in both Hebrew and Yiddish, for he is regarded as one of the greatest storytellers of the Jewish people.

It is noteworthy that very little else was published until the mid-nineteenth century. The dominant figure in the revival of the hasidic story was Michael Levi Frumkin, also known as Michael Rodkinson. He published *Kehal Hasidim*, *Adat Tzaddikim*, *Sippurei Tzaddikim MeArba Meitivei Lehet*–all stories of *tzaddikim* and all published in Lvov from 1864 to 1865. The four *tzaddikim* were R. Leib Sarah's, R. Leib of Shpole, R. Israel of Polutsk, and his disciple R. Azriel. Frumkin also wrote *Shivhei HaRav* (Lvov, 1864), a short biography of R. Shneur Zalman of Liady.

Pe'er MiKdoshim, of which the date and place of printing is unknown, was written in ornate language and consists of stories of both hasidic rebbes and of a number of nonhasidic personalities, such as "A Rabbi in Cracow," "R. Moses Isserles," and "R. Eliezer Edels, the *Maharsha*."

Yehudah Yudil Rosenberg, a prolific writer who described himself as a descendant of the *Maharal* of Prague, wrote a book entitled *Niflaot Maharal* (Piotrokov, 1909), dealing with the golem of Prague. He also edited a large collection of stories under the title *Tiferet Maharal* (Piotrokov, 1914), about R. Aryeh Leib of Shpole. Although he uses authentic stories, he embellished the facts. Like Frumkin, Rosenberg was no hasid, and he regarded Hasidism as a unified movement, whereas hasidic writers were inclined, as a rule, to write about one particular hasidic rebbe, generally the one to whose group they belonged. Examples of this are *Ohel Elimelekh* (Przemysl, 1910), by Abraham Hayyim Michelson, on R. Elimelekh of Lejask, and *Ohel Naftali* (Lvov, 1911), about R. Naftali of Ropczyce.

Of great importance is the work *Zekhut Yisrael* (Piotrokov, 1910), by Israel Berger, published in four volumes, which deals with the biographies and stories of forty hasidic rebbes.

Most of the hasidic storybooks were published between the 1850s and 1914. In the twentieth century, R. Nahman's tales have been edited by S. A. Horodezky, David Kahana, Eliezer Steinman, and Arthur Green. In 1906, Martin Buber was the first to introduce R. Nahman to the Western world. He translated the *Tales* into German, which were then translated into English by Maurice Friedmann. Some of the stories of R. Nahman are found in Meyer Levin's *Golden Mountain*, and a number of verbatim translations have recently been published by Arnold J. Band, *Nahman of Bratslav, the Tales* (New York: Paulist Press, 1978), and by Esther and Gedaliah Koenig, *The Thirteen Stories of R. Nahman of Bratzlav*.

J. Dan, *The Hasidic Story: Its History and Development*.

G.N.

STRANGE THOUGHTS (Mahshavot zarot)

STRANGE THOUGHTS (Mahshavot zarot) – The curious doctrine of the elevation of strange thoughts occupied, to the dismay of the *mitnaggedim*, a prominent place in early hasidic life and thought, though it was generally abandoned in the third generation as suitable only for the greatest of saints. The doctrine holds that when strange thoughts such as of pride, lust, idolatry, and violence, invade the mind during prayer or at other times, they should not be rejected out of hand but should be elevated by being raised in the mind to their source on high in the spiritual world.

Every thought should be seen as sent by God for the purpose of rectification (*tikkun*), the holy sparks that nourish that thought being thus reclaimed for the sacred and rescued from the demonic forces. R. Jacob Joseph of Polonnoye (*Toldot Yaakov Yosef, VaYakhel*) writes:

> I have heard from my master how to rectify strange thoughts. If it is a thought about women he should elevate it by attaching it to its root in loving-kindness, according to the mystery of "And if a man shall take his sister . . . it is *Hesed* (Loving-kindness)" Leviticus 20:17). And thoughts of idolatry produce a flaw in Beauty (*Tiferet*). Enough has been said.

J. G. Weiss has put forward as a distinct possibility the view that the doctrine owes much to the principle of the descent of the *tzaddik* into evil for the purpose of rescuing the holy sparks found there. The early hasidim applied this not in action but in thought, especially during prayer.

The "mystery" to which R. Jacob Joseph alludes was strenuously attacked by the *mitnaggedim*, who roundly denied that any such "mystery" can be found in the kabbalistic writings (David of Makov, *Shever Poshim*). "How dare they bring filthy alien thoughts into the innermost precincts of the Temple! 'The spider taketh hold with her hands and is in the king's palace' " (Proverbs 30:28).

Eventually the whole doctrine was disregarded by the hasidim as a dangerous playing with fire. R. Shneur Zalman of Liady argues that the practice is stupid except for the great *tzaddikim* whose "alien thoughts" are not their own but come into their mind by a kind of telepathy from the minds of others (*Tanya*, ch. 28). R. Nahman of Bratzlav, the great-grandson of the Besht, discourages the practice for the ordinary hasid but advocates it for the *tzaddik* (*Likkutei Moharan*, nos. 96 and 233). R. Tzvi Elimelekh of Dynov permits the practice even for the ordinary hasid, provided the strange thought is not about a sin to which he is prone.

The only later hasidic master to accept uncompromisingly the older doctrine is R. Yitzhak Eizik of Komarno, who goes so far as to declare it to be heretical to reject the doctrine because that would imply a denial of God's Providence (i.e., that God is even *in* the strange thought). Apart from this there are hardly any references in later hasidic literature to what was at one time an essential ingredient in the life of religion as understood by Hasidism.

J. G. Weiss, "Reshit HaHasidut," pp. 46–106.

L.J.

STRELISK, Uri (1757–23 *Elul* 1826), HaSeraf – Son of R. Pinhas, a poor, humble workman, he was born near Yanova and married the daughter of R. Kopel Hasid of Kolomyja, a disciple of the Besht. He studied in Lvov. He visited hasidic rebbes such as R. Elimelekh of Lejask, R. Jacob Joseph of Ostrog, R. Pinhas of Koretz, and R. Zusya of Annopol. He became, however, the most devoted disciple of R. Shlomoh of Karlin. After the murder of his rebbe in 1792, he became rebbe in Lvov and later settled in Strelisk.

He did not adhere to the kabbalistic doctrines of either Zydaczov or *Habad*. His hasidim were mainly very poor, and when he was once asked the reason for their poverty, he replied, "When they pray, they pray that they may be blessed with true faith and true fervor. They do not pray for worldly goods." He hated fame or renown. "It is better for a person to jump into the heat of a fiery furnace than to become famous." Hasidim maintained that he had various facial expressions, depending on whether he was praying, learning, eating, or receiving visitors. Hence, he was known as the *Seraf* (a heavenly being), for *serafim* are described as six-winged creatures who sing praises to the Lord (Isaiah 6:2).

His discourses, recorded by his disciple R. Zeev Wolf, were published under the titles *Imrei Kodesh* (Lvov, 1871) and *Sefer Imrei Kodesh HeHadash* (London, 1944) and have so far been reprinted ten times. In 1928, R. Reuven Margulies published an enlarged edition under the title *Or Olam*.

R. Uri's favorite disciple was R. Yehudah Tzvi of Stretyn. "When the Messiah will come," said R. Uri, "all the *tzaddikim* will go to meet him. I shall go with R. Yehudah Tzvi Hirsch. I shall have no reason to be ashamed of him."

His son R. Shlomoh succeeded him but died a few months after his father, on 22 *Tevet* 1827, saying, "How can I survive without such a father?" His son R. Levi Yitzhak succeeded him.

Y. Raphael, *Sefer HaHasidut*, pp. 51–52.

STRYKOW, Fischel, of Strykov (1773–17 *Tevet* 1822), hasidic rebbe – Son of R. Joseph Tzvi of Bielozierka, he was a disciple of R. Elimelekh of Lejask and R. Zeev Wolf of Zhitomir. He was an ascetic, praying until late at night and eating minimal meals. He settled in Strykov, a town near Lodz, in central Poland. Legend has it that Napoleon asked for his blessing.

His only son, R. Jacob, refused to succeed him, and many of R. Fischel's hasidim transferred their allegiance to his disciple R. Shmuel Abba of Zychlin (1810–1879).

STUDY – The *mitnaggedim* accused the hasidim of being indifferent to the study of the Torah and of despising talmudic scholars, but the revolutionary nature of hasidic attitudes toward study consisted far more in difference of aim and emphasis than in any neglect of study itself.

The hasidic stress on purity of motive in study (*Torah lishmah*) and on constant attachment to God (see DEVEKUT) tended to encourage the hasidim to see Torah study not as the supreme end of the religious life (the view of the *mitnaggedim*) but as the best means, apart from prayer, of attaining to the love and fear of God (see HALAKHAH). On prayer, and contrary to the traditional scale of values, the hasidic attitude reversed the order, seeing devotional prayer as higher, because it is more conducive to *devekut* than is even Torah study. Very revealing in this connection are two passages that aroused the ire of the *mitnaggedim* in the early hasidic work *Tzavaat Ribash*.

> The soul declared to the rabbi (the Besht) that the reason why the supernal matters were revealed to him was not because he had studied much Talmud and Codes but only because of his prayers, which he used to recite at all times with powerful concentration. It was as a result of this that he attained to such an elevated spiritual rank. (No. 41)
>
> When he studies (the Torah) he should pause from time to time in order to attach himself to God. Nevertheless he must engage in study even though it is impossible for him to attach himself to God

> during the time of study. Yet study he must, for the Torah polishes the soul and is a tree of life to those who hold fast to it so that if he will not study he will cease (in any event) from his attachment to God. He should think to himself that he is unable to be attached to God during the time he sleeps or at a time of smallness of soul and [that] the time spent in study is surely not worse than these times. For all that, it is essential for him to settle himself at every hour and every moment so as to have an attachment to the Creator, blessed be He, as stated above. (no. 29)

The denuciations by the scholars in the early hasidic works are based on the alleged unworthy motives of those who, the hasidim declared, studied only in order to win a reputation for scholarship or in order to acquire wealth and fame in the community. In its intense stress on absolute purity of motive, Hasidism decried all self-seeking; even the study of the Torah for the sake of meriting eternal bliss was held to be ultimately unworthy (*shelo lishmah*; see, e.g., Jacob Joseph of Polonnoye's *Toldot Yaakov Yosef, Shelah*, p. 141c).

R. Meshullam Feivish of Zbarazh ("*Yosher Divrei Emet*," no. 9, in *Likkutim Yekarim* [Jerusalem, 1974], pp. 113b–114a) goes so far as to say that even though students of the Torah are bound to obtain intense pleasure from their studies (since the Torah is truly sweeter than honey), yet scholars who study with the pleasure in mind instead of attachment to God commit spiritual prostitution. The same author (in no. 3, p. 111a) takes the term "*Torah lishmah*" (Torah for its own sake) to mean rather "Torah as its name implies," the word "Torah" meaning "to show" and the aim of Torah study being to become attached to God, Who is "shown forth" in the Torah, the garment of God.

Although the Talmud (*Pesahim* 50b) advocates that the Torah be studied even when one's motives are unworthy (because it will eventually lead to study for its own sake), the hasidic masters discouraged such half-measures. The true hasid is expected to study *lishmah* right from the beginning. In fact, the hasidic stress was not, at least in the earliest period, on the meaning of the texts but on attachment to the sacred letters of the Torah, which are, according to the Kabbalah, the form assumed on earth by the spiritual powers on high. Attachment to the letters of the Torah is thus attachment to God. We have the eyewitness account of Meir of Ostrog, disciple of the Besht, that this is how the Besht used to study the Torah (*Sod Yakhin U'Voaz* [London, 1955], p. 6).

The mitnaggedic opposition to the hasidic view was mainly on the grounds that the hasidic view was bound to hinder serious study. How could the texts be mastered or even grasped at all with any degree of understanding if the student's mind was concentrated not on the texts but on God? The disciple of the Gaon of Vilna R. Hayyim of Volozhin wrote his *Nefesh HaHayyim* as a counterblast to the hasidic understanding of *Torah lishmah*. R. Hayyim is critical both of the hasidic denunciations of Torah study when the motives are unworthy and of the hasidic interpretation of *lishmah* as *devekut*.

Hayyim continues: Study out of impure motives will lead eventually, as the Talmud says, to study of the Torah for its own sake, whereas it is sheer delusion to imagine that the majority of us are capable of rising to the heights of pure motivation right from the beginning. The sole result of hasidic strictness in this matter is for Torah study to be neglected. In any event, those who have studied much Torah, whatever their motives, are scholars and are entitled to the respect due a student of the Torah. To despise them is to despise the Torah. As for *Torah lishmah*, this, remarks Hayyim, means exactly what it says: study of the Torah for its own sake, for the sake of the Torah as the word of God, not with the aim of having God always in the mind.

Eventually, the hasidic masters appear to have acknowledged the justice of the mitnaggedic critique. R. Yitzhak Eizik of Komarno (*Notzer Hesed*, Commentary to the *Mishnah*, on *Avot* 1:13) ridicules those hasidim who refuse to study because they cannot attain to the stage of *Torah lishmah*. It is far better, says this *tzaddik*, to study out of unworthy motives than not to study at all.

Among the hasidim of Kotzk, Ger, Sochaczev, Belz, Komarno, and many other places, study of the Torah was understood in its traditional connotation. Even as early as the disciples of the Great Maggid, we find a compromise position adopted by the founder of the *Habad* movement in Hasidism–R.

Shneur Zalman of Liady. For that teacher, study of the Torah in its conventional sense is the highest form of *devekut* not because the mind is on God during study but because the Torah gives expression to the thought of God, and when we are attached in our mind to that thought, we are wondrously attached to God Himself. R. Shneur Zalman (*Tanya*, chap. 5, pp. 17–19) writes:

> Behold, with regard to every kind of intellectual perception, when one understands and grasps an idea in one's mind, the mind seizes the idea and encompasses it in thought so that the idea is held, surrounded, and enclosed in the mind in which it is comprehended. Conversely, the mind is clothed by an idea it has grasped. For instance, when one understands fully a rule in the *Mishnah* or the *Gemara*, one's mind seizes the idea and encompasses it, and, at the same time, one's mind is encompassed by the rule. Now, behold, this rule is the wisdom and will of the Holy One, blessed be He, for it arose in His will that, for instance, when A pleads thus and B thus, the rule will be thus. And even if, in fact, a case of this kind never comes before the courts, nonetheless, because it arose in the will and wisdom of the Holy One, blessed be He, that this is the rule, it follows that when one knows and grasps this rule in one's mind in accordance with the decision laid down in the *Mishnah* or the *Gemara* or the Codes, one also grasps, seizes hold of, and encompasses in the mind the will and wisdom of the Holy One, blessed be He, of whom no thought can conceive.

Like the majority of East European Jews, the hasidim studied mainly Talmud and the Codes. With the exception of the Pentateuch, the Bible was not studied in depth. The hasidim had a special fondness for study of the Midrash. The method of biblical exegesis as found in hasidic works bears a close resemblance to the fanciful, imaginative, and striking method of the Midrash, with its conscious distortion of the plain meaning of the text in order to yield a startling and novel idea.

Naturally, much time was given over by the hasidim to the study of the hasidic classics as well as to other devotional works, especially those of a mystical character, such as Elijah de Vidas's *Reshit Hokhmah*, Eleazar Azikri's *Sefer Haredim*, Isaiah Horowitz's *Shenei Luhot HaBerit*, Alexander Zusskind of Grodno's *Yesod VeShoresh HaAvodah*, and the Commentaries to the Torah of R. Moses Alsheikh and R. Hayyim Ibn Attar.

Many of the hasidic groups encouraged the study of the Kabbalah, but others tended to leave such study for the chosen few. Only a very few hasidic masters such as R. Hayyim of Zanz and R. Menahem Mendel of Lubavitch studied the works of the medieval Jewish philosophers. Hebrew grammar was not studied at all by the hasidim. All of the hasidim were strongly opposed to secular studies both as a waste of valuable time that should be spent in Torah study and because of the belief that the "wisdom of the gentiles" is spiritually tainted.

It was rare in the nineteenth century for the hasidim to study in *yeshivot*. The way generally adopted was study among fellows in the *Bet HaMidrash* of their hometown. The rabbinic injunctions for a man to leave his home in order to study the Torah were applied to the hasid's journeys to the court of his rebbe. A number of hasidic *yeshivot* were, however, established in the twentieth century, perhaps under the challenge of the famous Lithuanian *yeshivot* (e.g., the Tomhei Temimim *Yeshivot* of Lubavitch and the *yeshivah* in Lublin established by Rabbi Meir Shapira, a hasid of Chortkov).

J. G. Weiss, "The Study of the Torah According to the Theory of Rabbi Israel Baal Shem Tov" (Hebrew), pp. 151–169.

L.J.

SZPETMAN, Joshua, of London

(1887–7 *Nisan* 1964) – A native of Lublin, he lived in Warsaw, where he was befriended by Hillel Zeitlin. He emigrated to England and served as a rabbi of the Nelson Street Sephardische Synagogue in the East End of London.

He was a prolific writer and a regular contributor to the Yiddish press. He wrote many tracts, replete with hasidic ideas, on the Festivals.

T

TABERNACLES – The third of the Pilgrim Festivals, Sukkot, in Hebrew, originally a harvest Festival, it is described as *Zeman Simhatenu* (the time of our rejoicing). It begins on 15 *Tishri*.

"The feast of Tabernacles is the only *mitzvah*," said R. Simhah Bunem of Przysucha, "which we fulfill with all our body." R. Moses Horowitz decorated his *sukkah* with the seven products of the Holy Land. In Ropczyce, apples were hung among the foliage, and after the Festival, each hasid received an apple from the hands of the rebbe. R. Hayyim Halberstam would borrow a great number of coins and distribute them among the poor. When asked why he had made such a special point about being charitable on Sukkot, he replied, "We are commanded to adorn the *sukkah*. And what better adornment can there be than the distribution of charity among those who lack the means with which to rejoice in this season of rejoicing."

Not only were celebrations held on the "Water-drawing Festival" (*Simhat Bet HaShaevah*) – of which a vivid description is given in the Talmud (*Sukkah* 53a) – which begins at nightfall of the first day of Sukkot, but also rebbes would make a special banquet on that night, when celebrated visitors *ushpizim* (Aramaic: guests) were expected by tradition to grace the *sukkah*. This is based on the tradition, already mentioned by the *Zohar* (*Emor* 103b–104a), that on each of the seven days of the Festival of Sukkot, one of the seven patriarchs, or biblical heroes (Abraham, Yitzhak, Jacob, Joseph, Moses, Aaron, and David), is welcomed into the *sukkah*. In Belz, the rebbe lit seven candles in their honor. In other dynasties, the guests are welcomed in a different order.

Although halakhically, women were exempted from eating in the *sukkah*, in Ropczyce, however, women ate in the *sukkah*. R. Fischel of Strykov would eat in the *sukkah* even in the rain despite the ruling given in *Orah Hayyim* 539.

See ETROG, SHEMINI ATZERET, and SIMHAT TORAH.

TANYA – A fundamental exposition of hasidic thought, written by R. Shneur Zalman of Liady (1747–1812), founder of *Habad Hasidut*. *Tanya* (so named after the initial word of the book, lit., "It was taught") was first published in Slavuta, in 1796, and again in Zolkiev, in 1798. It is alternatively titled *Likkutei Amarim* (Collected Discourses) and *Sefer shel Beinonim* (Book of the Intermediates). The latter title is descriptive of the first section of the work, which analyzes the religious situation of the "intermediate man" (*benoni*), his inner struggles, and the path to their resolution. In addition, *Tanya* contains four other sections: *Shaar HaYihud VeHaEmunah* (Gate of Unity and Faith), *Iggeret HaTeshuvah* (Epistle of Repentance), *Iggeret HaKodesh* (Holy Epistle), and *Kuntres Aharon* (Final Treatise). Of these, the last two were included only in later editions of the work.

The highly original starting point of the book is its dedication to the spiritual problems of the "intermediate man." In his use of that term, R. Shneur Zalman makes a major departure from its conventional sense. The *benoni*, as he defines him, is not a man whose actions are partly virtuous, partly sinful; indeed, he never sins in thought, speech, or deed. What distinguishes him from the *tzaddik* – the wholly righteous man – is that *inwardly* he experiences a conflict between his recognition of the divine will and his physical and self-centered desires. Thus the distinction between the *benoni* and the *tzaddik* does not lie at the level of overt behavior but at the deeper level of the state of the soul. In a sense, therefore, *Tanya* is a study of spiritual psychology. The ideal to which it outlines the path is the transformation of the entire personality of the *benoni* from one marked by inner conflict to one of single-hearted unity.

The source of the conflict, the author explains, lies in the fact that the Jew possesses two souls, or centers of consciousness. The *nefesh habehamit* (animal soul) belongs to the Jew as part of the created world. Just as the very creation of a finite and physical world involved concealment of the divine infinity, so does the *nefesh habehamit* share this concealment, which expresses itself in a sense of the individual's separateness from God – his feeling of existing in and for himself. R. Shneur Zalman expresses this by saying that the animal soul is a product of the *klippot*, the shells that conceal God's infinity. The *nefesh elohit* (godly soul) is, on the other hand, "truly a part of God above," an awareness the Jew has, consciously or unconsciously, of being wholly one with God. This is the innermost core of the Jews' religious personality, so that however far they distance themselves from their faith, they remain essentially bound to God in unconscious, "hidden" love, and awe.

This division in the soul is the key to the Jew's spiritual problems. The *nefesh habehamit* is the source of evil, for evil is the assertion of our independence from God, the pursuit of our physical desires for their own sake. So long as the Jews allow this part of their soul to express itself, they experience a tension, a pull contrary to their innate love and awe of God. They can combat this in two ways: by suppressing (*itkafya*) or by sublimating (*ithafcha*) the animal soul. Suppression is the way taken by the *benoni*, who must constantly assert the godly over the animal part of his nature. Sublimation is the way of the *tzaddik*, who so transforms his *nefesh habehamit* that its thoughts and passions are entirely animated by the will of God.

The remainder of this section of *Tanya* is devoted to outlining the means by which this transformation is to be achieved. Of particular importance are study of the Torah, meditation, and prayer; restraining all promptings of the animal soul; and joy in performance of the precepts. Practical guidance is given for the avoidance of despair and the achievement of joy. Throughout, the emphasis is placed on reflection and contemplation as the instructors of emotional life. Two points may be singled out: in the section dealing with the love of Israel (chap. 32), the author develops the idea that because the root of each Jewish soul is contained in God Himself, the community of Jewish souls possesses a real metaphysical unity, and in the passage on *kavvanah*, "direction of the mind" (chaps. 38–41), he explains how the individual can, by prayer and study and with the proper mental preparation, reach to the most exalted spiritual universes. These dimensions are therefore not remote in space and time but are accessible in the present to the soul that opens itself to them.

The first part of *Tanya* is thus devoted to the individual, to the analysis of the soul. The second part, "Gate of Unity and Faith," concerns the cosmos as a whole and the relationship of God to the created world. Its central theme is the idea of the unity of God. In this it moves far beyond a bare restatement of monotheism, that there is only one God. Its affirmation is that there is *only* God: nothing else besides Him has reality. The universe and God are not two things, for all that exists is One. This unity has two aspects: The "lower unity" is the continual dependence of the world on God's creative activity. To imagine that creation was a single event, confined to the beginning of history, is an error induced by seeing it in terms of human creation. A craftsman shapes raw materials into new artifacts. But the creation of the world was ex nihilo – not only the forms but the materials themselves were created out of nothing. The result is that whereas an artifact exists independently of its maker, the world is continually dependent on God and is, in fact, perpetually re-created. Without the sustaining power of God, expressed in the letters of the divine speech, it would immediately lapse into nonexistence.

The "higher unity" goes beyond even this. Lurianic Kabbalah faced the problem of how a finite world could have issued from an infinite God. If infinity fills every dimension, how is there room, as it were, for physical objects to exist? The answer it provided was the doctrine of *tzimtzum*, literally, the "contraction" by which God withdrew into Himself, leaving room for a finite world to emerge by an endless series of limitations of the divine light. R. Shneur Zalman refused to interpret this literally, as some of his predecessors had done. For if it were true in any simple sense, it would create the very problem it set out to solve. It would imply a limitation, albeit self-willed, in the all-presence of the *Ein Sof*, the infinite God. Instead, he writes, *tzimtzum* is a screening rather than a withdrawal of the divine light. God is not absent, but hidden from our physical senses. Thus we, who see through the veil of the senses, perceive the physical world as real, *yesh*, and the spirituality of God as remote and intangible, *ayin*. But from the point of view of God, the opposite is true: the infinite is real, and the physical is as if it did not exist. In this radical reading of Luria's doctrine, the unity of God is absolute. There is no world apart from Him. We only *believe* the world is real, and this is the meaning of God's concealment.

This doctrine is intimately connected with the psychology of the individual as expounded in the first section. The individual thinks of himself as an independently existing person, a *yesh*. By true contemplation he will see that this is not so; this will lead to an abandonment of self, *bittul hayesh*, which in turn will result in an inner attitude of total love and awe of God.

The third section, "Epistle of Repentance," explains the centrality of repentance to the Jew. *Teshuvah* is understood here not in its limited sense of repenting for actual sins but in a deeper and more inclusive meaning of the "returning" of the soul. Not only sin but also any failure of absolute unity between the Jew and God represents a concealment, an "exile." By the "higher repentance" of complete love and awe, the soul is restored to its source. This too is an important innovation, for it makes *teshuvah* a continual concern of every Jew, not only when one has acted wrongly, and it sees the drama of exile and redemption of the divine presence as an individual as well as a cosmic process.

The remaining two sections of *Tanya* consist of letters and discourses on a variety of mystical concepts.

The importance of *Tanya* lies in three directions. First, it was the first work of hasidic literature to systematize the theology of the movement and to chart the relationship between the cosmogony of the earlier Kabbalah and the orientation—typical of hasidic thought—on humanity and its religious situation. Second, it laid the foundation for *Habad* Hasidism, the movement of which R. Shneur Zalman was the initiator, and it remains today the cornerstone of its thinking. Third, it was a precursor of a general change in Jewish thinking that spread far beyond the hasidic world. In its location of the spiritual universe within the reach of the individual soul and in its emphasis on self-discovery as the path of religious truth, it foreshadowed what has become the dominant orientation of Jewish thought as a whole in the twentieth century.

Shneur Zalman of Liady, *Tanya*.

A. Yidasin, *HaLekach VeHaLibuv*.

J.S.

TAUB, Abraham Mordecai Shalom, of Sasov (1875–24 *Adar* 1937)—Son of R. Yehudah Tzvi of Rozdol, he married Gitel, daughter of R. Shlomoh Meir of Sasov. He became rabbi in 1906, and then, during the First World War, stayed with his father-in-law in Lvov. On the death of his father-in-law, he succeeded him as rebbe of Sasov in 1919. He was renowned for his hasidic melodies.

He was succeeded by his son R. Yehudah. His other sons—R. Eliezer Zeev, R. Hanokh, and daughter, Hannah—all perished in the Holocaust.

TAUB, Eliezer Shlomoh, of Wolomin (1870–23 *Tammuz* 1938)—Son of R. Efraim of Kazimierz, he married the daughter of R. Nathan David Rabinowicz of Szydlowiec. He succeeded his father as rebbe of Wolomin in 1904. During the First World War, he settled in Warsaw, where he was renowned for his melodies. He was buried in Praga.

His daughter Reizel married R. Emanuel Weltfreid of Lodz, and his other daughter married R. Joseph Perlow of Novominsk. He had five sons—R. Aryeh Leib, R. Efraim, R. Yitzhak, R. Abraham, and R. David Tzvi, who succeeded him.

TAUB, Ezekiel, of Kazimierz (1812–17 *Shevat* 1856)—Both Kuzmir (Kazimierz) and Modzitz occupy high places in the history of hasidic musicology. The founder of the dynasty, R. Ezekiel, was born in Plonsk, the son of R. Tzvi Hirsch, one of the disciples of the Besht. He was probably murdered by the Cossacks when the Russian army under Suvorov fought against the Polish patriot Kosciuszko in 1792. R. Ezekiel had three brothers–R. Leib, R. Beer, and R. Wolf–and together they were all called the "four holy *hayyot*," based on Ezekiel 1:5, which reads, "Four living creatures." The rabbis adapted it for their own use and called themselves "four holy creatures (*hayyot*)."

R. Ezekiel lived for a time in Warka and visited a number of hasidic leaders. The "Seer" of Lublin said of him that "his face resembled the face of Abraham, our father." R. Ezekiel became the patron of hasidic music in Poland. Like his master, the "Seer," he employed a *badhan* and a choir. Commenting on the verse "Thou shalt surely help to lift him up again" (Deuteronomy 22:4), which refers to an animal that has fallen by the wayside, R. Ezekiel explained that one was duty bound to help the singer by joining in the song. He would say, "I do not feel any delight in the Sabbath unless it brings forth a new melody."

He was the author of a commentary on the Pentateuch *Nehmad MiZahav* (Piotrokov, 1909), which contains many references to song and dance.

Among his sayings were "One *niggun* explains more than a thousand words." "*Niggunim* composed according to the rules of music are not truthful. They are songs that do not emanate from the heart."

He left four sons.

TAUB, Ezekiel, of Yablonov (1886–13 *Iyyar* 1986)–He was the only son of R. Jacob (1861–7 *Av* 1920) of Yablonov and a descendant of R. Ezekiel of Kazimierz. "I would rather be a laborer in the Land of Israel," his father, R. Jacob, had remarked, "than a rabbi in the Diaspora."

R. Ezekiel succeeded his father as rebbe and married Pearl, a descendant of Piaseczno. Together with R. Isaiah (d. 1967), the son of R. Elimelekh Shapira of Grodzisk (d. 1945), and R. Israel Eliezer Hofstein of Kozienice, R. Ezekiel formed a society called *Nahlat Yaakov* in memory of his father, to enable people to buy land in the Holy Land by spreading payments over five years. Later, *Nahlat Yaakov* merged with a similar association, *Avodat Israel*, founded by the rebbe of Kozienice.

R. Ezekiel journeyed to the Holy Land and bought twenty-six thousand dunams, and in *Adar* 1924, R. Ezekiel and twenty-five families landed in Haifa, rather than Jaffa, for he was afraid that his followers would be attracted to Tel Aviv. "Two thousand years ago," declared R. Ezekiel, "Cyrus, King of Persia, proclaimed, 'Whosoever there is among you of all His people–the Lord, his God be with him–let him go up' (2 Chronicles 36:23). These days, too, we hear such a proclamation, which calls upon the Jews to rebuild Zion and Jerusalem."

Lack of experience in agriculture and the hardships of the malaria-infected lands led to the departure of a number of the settlers.

In his autobiography, Dr. Chaim Weizmann describes with astonishment and approval a visit to these unusual pioneers. "Balfour [Lord Arthur James, 1848–1930] alighted from his car and went into the barracks to receive the blessing of the rabbi" (*Trial and Error*, pp. 398–399). The Jewish National Fund allotted to these hasidim 1,800 dunams of land near Nahalal, and soon there were 110 families living there.

In 1928 R. Ezekiel left the Holy Land, but he returned in 1936. He departed once again, this time for the United States, and worked in a variety of professions. He studied psychology at the University of San Fernando. His wife, who visited Poland in 1939, perished in the Holocaust.

In 1982, R. Ezekiel returned to *Kefar Hasidim*, where he died four years later.

TAUB, Hayyim Yerahmiel, of Zwolen (1879–1942)–Son of R. Moses Aaron, he married *Hayyah* Alta, the daughter of R. Pinhas Rabinowicz of Konskie, where he stayed for five years. He studied under R. Joab Joshua Weingarten and under his father, who was also his musical mentor. His father would say that throughout the year, he was sustained by the pleasure he had derived from his son's prayers on the Days of Awe. R. Hayyim Yerahmiel lived for a time also in Zychlin and Mlawa.

On the New Year, R. Hayyim Yerahmiel would enter the *Bet HaMidrash* with seven *shofrot*, inherited from the rebbes of Kazimierz, Zwolen, Konskie, Szydlowiec, and Przysucha.

On the death of his father-in-law in 1914, he returned to his father's home in Zwolyn, where he became rebbe. His father subsequently moved to Warsaw, where he, too, settled after the death of his father. He had *shtieblech* in Praga, Pulutsk, and Radom. He was noted for his musical compositions.

Before the outbreak of the Second World War, he told his followers that "heavy clouds were gathering." The Nazis deported his wife, his younger brother, R. Naftali Jacob of Nowydwor, his elder son, R. Shmuel Yitzhak, his younger son, R. Pinhas Eliyahu, and his sons-in-law, R. Benzion Sokolower and R. Elimelekh Lipshitz, to Treblinka. He himself worked for a time in the Shultz shoe factory in Warsaw, before he, too, joined them in Treblinka, where they all met their death.

M. Unger, *Admorim SheNisfu BaShoa*, pp. 92–94.

TAUB, Israel, of Modzitz (1849–19 *Kislev* 1921) – Son of R. Shmuel Eliyahu, he was born in Racionz. At an early age, he married the daughter of one of the most outstanding *baalei tefillot* (cantors) in Poland, Hayyim Saul Freedman of Ozarov. For thirteen years he lived with his parents-in-law, devoting himself exclusively to intense study. He was influenced by the work *Menatzeah Binginot* (Vilna, 1884), by Tzvi Nissan Golomb. In his own work, *Divrei Yisrael*, he devotes a lengthy excursus to music. He likened the seven tones of the scale to the seven spheres in the kabbalistic theory of creation and to the seven days of the week.

When his father died, in 1888, he settled in Demblin, known by the hasidim as Modzitz. His court became a center for melody. His first composition was an arrangement of Psalm 114:1: "When Israel went forth from Egypt." If a morning passed without bringing forth a new melody, he would sigh, "I have lost a morning." In addition to being a very prolific composer, he enjoyed the role of reader, and he delighted his hasidim with his innovative renditions. For every Festival he produced an appropriate musical melody.

The rebbe himself did not read music, and his melodies were not written down. Nonetheless, literally, by word of mouth, they were carried far and wide. Some of his melodies were without words; others were taken from the Sabbath eve *Zemirot* and the liturgy. The highlight of his work consisted of melodies for the *seudah shlishit*. He composed melodies for *Benei Hekhalah*, *Yedid Nefesh*, and *Mizmor l'David*, the *niggun* of the homeless, written when he was forced to leave Modzitz. *Mitnaggedim* and even gentiles would crowd outside his *Bet HaMidrash*, enthralled by the melodies of this untutored genius.

In 1913, he became dangerously ill with diabetes, and in the same year, one of his legs had to be amputated in Berlin by Professor Israels. Pain did not extinguish his spirit. The rabbi refused to undergo the operation with the help of anesthetics, and on the operating table he composed a song, *Ezkerah Elokim VeEhemayah* (Psalm 77:3): "When I remember this, O God, I moan, when I see each town on its site." This piece consists of thirty-two short movements and takes half an hour to sing.

A year later, he settled in Warsaw, where he died. His sepulcher is one of the few that survived intact in the otherwise vandalized Warsaw cemetery.

He was the author of *Divrei Yisrael* on Genesis (Lublin, 1901), Exodus (Warsaw, 1912), Leviticus (Piotrokov, 1930), and *Ishei Yisrael*; a commentary on the Passover *Haggadah* (Warsaw, 1938); and six tracts, published in Warsaw between 1936 and 1938 under the title *Tiferet Yisrael*.

M. S. Geshuri, *Negginah VeHasidut*, pp. 69–78.

TAUB, Menahem Mendel, of Kiryat Kalev, Rishon-le-Zion (b. 1918) – Born in Marghita, Romania, the son of R. Yehudah Yehiel of Rozdol. Two weeks before the outbreak of World War Two, he married Hannah Sarah Shifra, the daughter of R. Pinhas Shapira, the rabbi of Kochnia. During the war, he was imprisoned in several concentration camps, including Belsen. He was liberated on the last day of the war. His wife had been sent to different concentration camps, but the two were eventually reunited. His father-in-law, however, perished on 3 *Sivan* 1944.

The intervention of his brother-in-law enabled him to emigrate to the United States. He settled in Cleveland, Ohio, where he set up a *yeshivah*. He later moved to New York.

After seventeen years in the United States, he emigrated to Israel, where he established *Kiryat Kalev* in Rishon-le-Zion. He launched a number of educational activities and was zealous in organizing the scheme of *Bar B'rav d'had Yoma* (one-day-scholar scheme) to provide every area with facilities for adult Torah education.

He has a center *Mishkan Kalev* in Tiberias (near *Kiryat Shmuel*), a *yeshivah Or Kalev* in Bene Berak, a *kollel* in Rishon-le-Zion and in Jerusalem, and a *Bet HaMidrash* in Bene Berak. His success lies in his individual approach and his creativity. Almost every day he comes up with new ideas for strengthening religion in the State of Israel.

TAUB, Menahem David, of Praga (1873–*Av* 1942) – Son of R. Efraim of Kazimierz, he married, at the age of nineteen, Miriam Breina, daughter of R. Jacob Moses Teumim, the rabbi of Nowydwor, where he continued his studies. When his father died in Praga in 1904, he succeeded him as rebbe. But because his brother, R. Yerahmiel Tzvi, also lived in Praga, he settled in a village near Warsaw. It was only when his brother moved to Warsaw in 1906 that he made his residence in Praga, where he lived for thirty years.

On Friday afternoon before the advent of the Sabbath, he would walk through the busy streets of Warsaw, crying, "The Sabbath is coming, Jews!" He was tireless in his work for the *Shomer Shabbat* society and for *Taharat HaMishpahah*. He died in the Warsaw ghetto.

His successor was his only son, R. Levi Yitzhak, a disciple of R. Menahem Zemba and the author of *Mahshevet Levi*, novellas on the Talmud, and other works, which were destroyed in the Holocaust. He was among the founders of the religious youth movement *Bene Torah*, which later became known as the *Tzeire Agudat Yisrael* and had the support of the rebbe of Ger. He was still alive during the Warsaw ghetto uprising but died near Buchenwald in 1944.

Elleh Ezkerah, vol. 4, pp. 250–257.

TAUB, Pinhas Hayyim, of Rozdol (22 *Tishri* 1867–11 *Tishri* 1935) – He was born in Komarno, the son of R. Yehudah Tzvi, the rabbi of Rozdol. He studied under his uncle R. Eliezer Tzvi Safrin of Komarno. In 1884, he married Feiga, the daughter of R. Abraham Hayyim Horowitz of Linsk, where he went to live. When the house of his father-in-law was burned down in 1886, he returned to Rozdol, where he became rebbe.

For fifty years he was in charge of collecting funds for the Holy Land. He was renowned for his diligence and rarely concluded his morning prayers before four o'clock in the afternoon. He would wear a *tallit* on Friday evening, when he recited *Shalom Aleikhem*. He requested his son to recite *Kaddish* after him for twelve months (not for eleven months, as is customary).

Every three years he concluded the study of the whole Talmud. At the outbreak of World War One, he lived in Marghita, and it was only in 1923 that he returned to Rozdol.

He was the author of a 1,681-page manuscript *Torat Hesed* on the Torah, of *Ohel Mo'ed* on the Festivals, and of *Alufei Yehudah* on the *Pri Etz Hayyim* by R. Hayyim Vital. All of his writings perished in the Holocaust. His grandson, however, R. Menahem Mendel Taub, published his *Sefer Ohel Mo'ed* on Hanukkah (Kiryat Kalev, 1977).

His son R. Yehudah Yehiel succeeded him. His other sons – R. Naftali Bezalel, R. David Shlomoh, and R. Moses Ezra – and his daughter, Miriam Yocheved, all perished in the Holocaust.

TAUB, Saul Yedidyah Eleazar, of Modzitz (1882–16 *Kislev* 1947) – Born in Ozarov, the son of R. Israel, he received no formal grounding in the rudiments of musical theory, yet there was music in his veins. He was a tenor of great dramatic power. What other rabbis achieved through scholarship, he achieved through music, drawing many to Hasidism.

After living in Rakov and Karszev, he moved to Otwock, near Warsaw, in 1929. Sholem Asch and Hillel Zeitlin were among his frequent visitors. His discourses appeared in *Kuntres Maamarim*, a periodical published between 1936 and 1938.

He visited the Holy Land in 1925, 1935, and 1938. During his first visit, he was received by British High Commissioner Herbert (later Lord) Samuel. He strongly condemned the British White Paper of 1939.

He established a *yeshivah Tiferet Yisrael* in memory of his father. When the Second World War broke out, he fled to Vilna, narrowly escaping the Nazi clutches. He journeyed via Siberia and Japan and in 1940, reached the United States, where his brother, R. Israel Tzvi lived. He settled in Williamsburg, Brooklyn, and resumed publication of his father's commentary of Leviticus.

In the summer of 1947, he settled in Tel Aviv. He died on November 29, 1947, the day the United Nations recommended the establishment of a Jewish state. He was the last person to be buried on the Mount of Olives before it was taken over by the Jordanians. There was not even time to put a tombstone on his grave, and this was not done until after the Six-Day War, when the Old City was captured by the Israelis.

He was succeeded by his son, R. Shmuel Eliyahu, who published his book *Imrei Shaul* on High Holy Days and Festivals (Tel Aviv, 1960).

B. Kagan, ed., *Zwolen Yizkor Book.*

TAUB, Shmuel Eliyahu, of Tel Aviv

(1906–4 *Iyyar* 1984) – Son of R. Saul Yedidyah Eliezer, he was born on April 5 in Lublin. His mother was Keila Nehamah, the daughter of R. Abraham Eger of Lublin. He was ordained by R. Tzvi Ezekiel Michelson. In 1926, he married Rebecca Zlata, the daughter of R. Hayyim Moses Kohn and a granddaughter of the rabbi of Ciechanov and Rotmistrovka.

In 1935, while accompanying his father on a visit to the Holy Land, he decided to settle there and became a member of the Tel Aviv rabbinate. When his father died in 1947, he succeeded him as rebbe.

He was the author of many melodies. He composed twelve new melodies every year. He collected the discourses of his father and published them under the title *Imrei Shaul*. He was a member of the Aguda and of the *Mo'etzet Gedolei HaTorah*. Among his noted compositions was *Ki BeSimhah* (1955) and *Hodu LaShem* (1955). He also established a *yeshivah Imrei Shaul* and *shtieblech* in Tel Aviv.

Though an Israeli, the rabbi observed some of the customs of the Diaspora, such as the *hakkafot* (circuits) on the night of Shemini Atzeret. "If our fellow Jews outside the Holy Land are celebrating," said the rabbi, "we should, nay, we must, participate in their joy." He dedicated the sixth circuit of the *hakkafot* (*Ozer Dalim* [Who supports the poor]) to the memory of the six million Jews murdered by the Nazis. The lights of the synagogue were dimmed, and mournful melodies were chanted. The rabbi refused to despair over the state of religion in Israel. "Conditions today," he said, "are much better than they used to be."

He visited London in *Kislev* 1984. He died shortly afterward and was buried on the Mount of Olives.

He was succeeded by his son R. Israel Don, who was born in 1948. He had two sons and two daughters.

D. Shtockfish, ed., *Sefer Demblin-Modrzyc*, pp. 227–233.

TAUB, Shmuel Eliyahu, of Zwolen

(1828–26 *Iyyar* 1888) – Son of R. Ezekiel, he was gifted with a fine baritone voice, as well as a fine mind. "The love of God is perfect," he reasoned, "therefore, melody, too, must be perfect. Great responsibility rests with the cantor. He must prepare himself most carefully. Nor should he deviate one iota from the melody, lest he transgress the precept 'Thou shalt not add unto the word which I command you, neither shalt ye diminish it' (Deuteronomy 4:2)."

After a fire that destroyed his home in Zwolen, he settled in Warsaw.

All his five sons – R. Moses Aaron, R. Israel, R. Jacob, R. Ovadiah, and R. Hayyim Benjamin – were music lovers.

TAUB, Yehudah Tzvi, of Rozdol

(1849–1 *Sivan* 1886) – Son of R. Shlomoh, he married Zippa Hinda, the daughter of R. Eliezer Tzvi Safrin of Komarno. He succeeded his father in 1886 but died in the same year.

One of his sons, R. Moses, who died on 19 *Iyyar* 1936, was rebbe, first in Nemirov, then in Kalev and Sighet. R. Moses had a son, R. Menahem Mendel Shlomoh, who was born in 1903. He married Reizel, the daughter of R. Issachar Dov Rokeah of Linsk and is the rebbe of Kalev in New York. He published his father's book *Et Razon* on Genesis (Brooklyn, 1951).

TAUB, Yehudah Yehiel, of Rozdol

(28 *Shevat* 1887–19 *Av* 1937) – Son of R. Pinhas Hayyim, the rabbi of Rozdol, he was born in Linsk. He married Brachah Freida, the daughter of R. Moses David Ashkenazi of Stanislav. In 1912, he settled in Marghita in Transylvania, and after the death of his father in 1936, he succeeded him as rebbe in Rozdol. He had always suffered ill health,

and he died, at the age of fifty, in Grosswardein but was buried in Marghita.

He was the author of *Lev Sameah HeHadash* (Arad, 1936). His eldest son, R. Hanokh Heinokh Dov, died young, in 1935. His other sons, R. Eliezer Tzvi and R. Shalom, perished in the Holocaust.

TEFILLIN–The hasidim, like all other Orthodox Jews, attach great significance to the wearing of *tefillin*, but the special hasidic emphasis on this *mitzvah* is seen in the mystical intentions, based on the Kabbalah, that hasidim have in mind when wearing *tefillin* and more especially with regard to the following details of their observance. In hasidic thought, much is made of the Talmudic saying (*Berakhot* 6a) that God wears *tefillin*, the contents of which are the praises of Israel as His chosen people. Levi Yitzhak of Berdichev is depicted in hasidic legend as demanding of God that He pardon Israel, or otherwise, His *tefillin* would be invalid.

Much is made, too, in hasidic circles, of famous *tzaddikim's* descendants who wear the *tefillin* of their forebears and so acquire mystic power. In the debate between R. Shneur Zalman of Liady and R. Barukh of Medziborz, great-grandson of the Besht, the latter is said to have sought to silence his opponent by reminding him that he was wearing the *tefillin* of his saintly grandfather and was thus the true interpreter of his doctrines.

Concerning the order in which the four sections of the *tefillin* are to be arranged, there is a well-known debate between the medieval authorities Rashi and Rabbenu Tam (see *Menahot* 32b and commentaries). The normal practice is to follow *Rashi*, but the custom developed in some circles of donning, in addition, a pair of *tefillin* according to the arrangement of Rabbenu Tam. The *Shulhan Arukh* (*Orah Hayyim* 34:4) rules, however, that to wear the *tefillin* of Rabbenu Tam in addition to those of Rashi is only permissible for those who are renowned for great piety; otherwise, it betokens priggishness. Nevertheless, the hasidim do wear both pairs of *tefillin*, since the *Zohar* refers to both pairs and the movement seems to encourage in its followers attitudes of extreme mystical piety. For hasidim to wear the *tefillin* of Rabbenu Tam is, in fact, to fulfill the requirements of the Law, not simply to engage in an act of dubious piety.

Similarly, there is a debate as to whether *tefillin*, which are not worn on Sabbath or the Festivals, have to be worn on *Hol HaMo'ed*, the intermediate days of Festivals (see *Tosafot Menahot* 36b). The *Shulhan Arukh* (*Orah Hayyim* 31:2) rules that it is forbidden to wear *tefillin* on *Hol HaMo'ed*, since to do so suggests an attitude of disrespect to the day by treating it as an ordinary weekday rather than as a Festival. But R. Moses Isserles, recording the Ashkenazic custom, states that "in these lands" the *tefillin* are worn on *Hol HaMo'ed*. Normally the hasidim, as Ashkenazim, follow R. Moses Isserles but here depart from his ruling because, again, the *Zohar* is strict in saying the *tefillin* are not to be worn.

When a circumcision takes place in the synagogue, the older custom is to keep the *tefillin* on during the ceremony (*Magen Avraham* to *Orah Hayyim* 25, n. 28, and *Siftei Kohen* to *Yoreh De'ah* 265:24). Against this established custom the hasidic leader and halakhic authority R. Shmelke of Nicolsburg argued that it is disrespectful to the "sign" provided by circumcision for the congregation to wear at the same time the "sign" provided by the *tefillin*. His disciples the "Seer" of Lublin and Moses Leib of Sassov adopted this ruling; from them it spread among many groups of hasidim.

See HALAKHAH.

A. Y. Sperling-Danzig, *Taamei HaMinhagim*, pp. 11–19.

L.J.

TEITELBAUM, Aaron, of Volovo (1881–3 *Sivan* 1944)–Youngest son of R. Israel Jacob Yukel, he married Hayyah, the daughter of R. Shmuel Babad. In 1905, his father appointed him rabbi of Volovo, and in 1924, he succeeded his father as rebbe. He was the head of a *yeshivah*. He fought against Zionism and even against the Aguda.

In the summer of 1941, he and most of his community were deported beyond the Dniester, from whence he escaped to Budapest. He buried all his manuscripts, but they could not be found after the war. He and all his family were murdered in Auschwitz.

His commentary, *Toldot Aharon* on Psalms, was published together with *Tefillah L'Mosheh* (New York, 1972).

His only surviving son was R. Hannaniah Yom Tov Lippa, the rebbe of Volovo in New York.

TEITELBAUM, Abraham Aaron, of Kolboszov (1834–12 *Elul* 1910) – Son of R. Yekutiel Yehudah, he was ordained by R. Nahum Reuven Plasker. He married Ritza, the daughter of R. Yehiel Rubin of Kolboszov. After the death of his father-in-law, in 1860, he succeeded him but was subjected to a controversy, since his mother-in-law wanted to secure the succession for her young son, Asher Yeshayah.

A eulogy and his ethical will *Hesped Mar* was printed in Lvov in 1911. He was succeeded by his son, R. Yehiel.

TEITELBAUM, Alexander Shmuel, of New York (1888–1970) – Son of R. Aryeh Leibish, he was born in Rzeszov. He studied in the *yeshivah* under R. Joseph Reich of Rzeszov and R. Nathan Levin. In 1934, he married the daughter of R. David Horowitz, a descendant of Ropczyce.

When he arrived in the United States, he studied in the *yeshivah* of R. Yitzhak Elhanan and R. Moses Soloveitchik. He was one of the founders of the *yeshivah Ahavat Torah* in the Bronx and was the rebbe of Kolboszov in the Bronx. In 1951, he reprinted his grandfather's book *Yismah Mosheh*.

He was survived by two daughters and one son, R. Leibish David.

Toldot Anshei Shem, p. 29.

TEITELBAUM, Aryeh Leibish, of New York (1888–29 *Shevat* 1941) – Son of R. Yehiel, the rebbe of Kolboszov, he was born in Mosziski. He studied under his father and grandfather. In 1908, he was ordained by R. Moses Babad of Lvov and R. Nathan Levin of Rzeszov. In 1906, he married Deborah, the daughter of R. Hayyim Yonah Halpern of Rzeszov, where he continued his studies with his brother-in-law, R. Eliezer Reisher. From 1911 to 1920, he was rabbi in Kolboszov.

In 1921, he emigrated to the United States and established a community *Bet HaMidrash Kahal Yeraim* in the Bronx. He was a renowned preacher and cantor and was one of the founders of the *yeshivah Ahavat Torah*.

His son, R. Alexander Shmuel, succeeded him.

Toldot Anshei Shem, p. 38.

TEITELBAUM, David, of Etshed (1870–1944) – Son of R. Abraham Aaron of Kolboszov, he married the daughter of R. Shimon Mireles of Yaroslav, where he officiated as a *dayan*. In 1903, he became rabbi in Etshed in Hungary, where he established a *yeshivah*.

He and his family perished in the Holocaust, with the exception of one son, R. Naftali, who survived and lived in Paris, then in New York.

He was the author of *Divrei David*, homilies on the Torah, published in Miskolc in 1943.

TEITELBAUM, Eliyahu Bezalel, of Teczso (1850–29 *Av* 1918) – Son of R. Yekutiel Yehudah, he was born in Gorlice. In 1875, he was appointed rabbi of Havasmezo, and then in Tecszo, where he served from 1883 to 1918. Although a follower of his brother, R. Hayyim Tzvi, he, too, served as rebbe.

TEITELBAUM, Elazor Nissan, of Drohobycz (1786–8 *Tishri* 1854) – Only son of R. Moses Teitelbaum, he was born in Sianiawa. In 1802, he married Reiza Bluma, the daughter of R. Aaron, the rabbi of Hodorov. She was scholarly, well versed in talmudic law, and reputed to know the whole Bible by heart. For some time he lived in Drohobycz, where his wife's father was rabbi.

In 1834, they moved to Ujhely, his parental home. On the suggestion of R. Moses Teitelbaum, he became rabbi of Sighet, but life was made difficult for him by factional divisions among the hasidim. In 1840, he became rabbi in Drohobycz, where he spent most of his day in *tallit* and *tefillin* in prayer and study. He died on *Shabbat Shuvah*. His wife died a year later, on the Fast of Gedaliah 1855.

They had three sons and one daughter: R. Yekutiel Yehudah of Sighet, R. Shmuel of Gorlice, R. Nahum Tzvi of Drohobycz, and Hannah Rachel, who married R. Israel Rappoport, the rabbi of Tarnov.

His discourses are recorded in *Zikhron Elozor* (Brooklyn, 1983).

A. Y. Bromberg, *Migdolei HaHasidut*, vol. 8, *R. Mosheh Teitelbaum*, pp. 136–152.

A.S.

TEITELBAUM, Hannaniah Yom Tov Lippa, of Brooklyn (d. 10 *Tevet*

1983)–Son of R. Aaron, he was born in Volovo, Czechoslovakia, where he studied in his father's *yeshivah*. He married Zipporah Yentel, the daughter of R. Israel Tzvi Halevi Rothenberg, the rabbi of Krasnoye, where he became a *dayan* and the head of a *yeshivah Ateret Tzvi*, and when she died, he married Feiga, the daughter of R. Nahum Efraim Halberstam of Tarnov.

In 1947, he emigrated to the United States and was rebbe of Volovo in Brooklyn, where he established a community *Yismah Mosheh*.

He was survived by his sons–R. Joseph, R. Nahum Efraim, and R. Aaron.

Toldot Anshei Shem, p. 58.

TEITELBAUM, Hannaniah Yom Tov Lippa, of Sasov (1904–11 *Adar* 1966)–Son of R. Hanokh Heinokh of Sasov, he married, in 1924, his cousin Hayyah Rosa, the daughter of R. Yoel Teitelbaum of Satmar, and he became the head of the *Bet Din* of Satmar. Later, he became rabbi in Samiah, where he was also principal of the *yeshivah*. During the Second World War, disguised as a beggar and sometimes as a soldier, he escaped to Romania. From 1944 to 1947, he lived in Jerusalem, where he established a *yeshivah Yitav Lev* and a girls' school *Or HaHayyim* in Bene Berak. In 1948, he moved to New York but visited Israel frequently.

His wife died in 1954, and he remarried in Israel. In *Adar* 1963, he laid the foundation stone of a new sixty-dunam *Kiryat Yismah Mosheh*. Unlike his kinsman R. Yoel, the rabbi sought the support of David Ben-Gurion and Mizrachi leader Shlomoh Zalman Shragai for his new project. He was a perfectionist and amazed the architect with his knowledge of technical detail.

In 1963, he became very ill and was forced to spend the next eighteen months hospitalized. He died and was buried in Tiberias.

He left one daughter and four young sons. His eldest son, R. Joseph David, born in 1954, was proclaimed rebbe. He continued his studies at the *yeshivah* of the rabbi of Klausenburg.

TEITELBAUM, Hannaniah Yom Tov Lippa, of Sighet (6 *Sivan* 1836–29 *Shevat* 1904)–Son of R. Yekutiel Yehudah Teitelbaum, he was born in Sztropkov. He studied in his father's *yeshivah* and together with his father visited many hasidic rabbis, especially R. Hayyim Halberstam.

His first marriage, to the daughter of R. Manasseh Rubin of Ropczyce, remained childless. In 1878, after obtaining a *Heter Meah Rabbanim*, he married his cousin Hannah, the daughter of R. Yoel Ashkenazi of Zloczov.

At the age of twenty-eight he became rabbi of Tecszo, where he remained until 1883, when he succeeded his father as rabbi in Sighet. He was a fiery speaker and a fearless fighter for the maintenance of Hungarian Orthodoxy. The Sighet *Kehillah* joined the *Landeskanzlei*, and "Rab Lippele," as he was known, took an active part in the deliberations of the organization. He convened a rabbinical convention of fifty rabbis, at which he was elected president.

He was known by the name of his book *Kedushat Yom Tov*, a two-part homiletical commentary of the Pentateuch, printed in Marmaros Sighet in 1905 and reprinted in Brooklyn in 1947.

His sons were R. Hayyim Tzvi, who succeeded him in Sighet, and R. Yoel Teitelbaum of New York.

Marmaros Book, pp. 9, 262.

TEITELBAUM, Hanokh Heinokh, of Karecska (1884–7 *Heshvan* 1943)–Son of R. Joseph David Meir of Sasov, he married the daughter of R. Hannaniah Yom Tov Lippa of Sighet. In 1923, he became rabbi of Karecska, and his inaugural discourse was published in Munkacs.

He was a prolific author, but only one single manuscript of his survived the Holocaust: *Sefer Midrash Rabba* with a commentary *Ein Hanokh* was published by his son, R. Hannaniah Yom Tov Lippa, in New York in 1957.

TEITELBAUM, Hayyim Tzvi, of Sighet (1880–6 *Shevat* 1926)–Son of R. Hannaniah Yom Tov Lippa, he succeeded his father as rebbe at the age of twenty-three, in 1904. He was the third Teitelbaum to occupy the rabbinate in Sighet. He visited the rabbis of Sianiawa, Gorlice, and Belz. He was no innovator but one who maintained the traditions of his family. During his tenure of office, a split occurred in Sighet. A faction seceded from the main body and set up a separate community, the *Sephardic Kehillah*. They joined the national organization of the status quo ante and thus dissociated themselves from the Orthodox congregations of Hungary. R. Teitelbaum was also involved in a controversy with the rabbi of Vishnitz regarding responsibility for the charitable collections intended for the Rabbi Meir Baal Hanes fund.

He traveled often and over long distances to visit his followers. It was on a visit to Kisvarda when he suffered the stroke that led to his death at the early age of forty-five. He died in Kleinwardein and was buried in Sighet.

He was the author of *Atzei Hayyim*, homilies on the Torah in two parts (Sighet, 1927); on the Festivals (Sighet, 1934); responsa (Sighet, 1939); on *Mikvaot* (Sighet, 1939); and on *Gittin* (Sighet, 1939). Other works known to exist before World War Two appear to have been irretrievably lost. He was survived by his wife, Simah Brachah, the daughter of R. Shalom Eliezer Halberstam of Ujfeherto.

His son R. Yekutiel Yehudah succeeded him at the age of fourteen, in Sighet. His other son, R. Mosheh, is now the rabbi of Satmar in New York.

Marmaros Book, pp. 9–11.

TEITELBAUM, Israel Jacob Yukel, of Volovo (1840–1924)—Son of R. Shmuel, rabbi of Gorlice, he was brought up by his grandfather in Drohobycz. He studied under his grandfather and R. Hayyim Halberstam. In 1854, he married his cousin Hendel, the daughter of R. Yekutiel Yehudah. In 1858, he moved to Sighet and in 1862, became rabbi in Badfalva, a community of 400 families, where he served for twenty-seven years.

There he prepared for publication his grandfather's work *Heshiv Mosheh*. In 1889, he became rabbi in Gorlice, where he stayed for five years and where he became involved in a bitter controversy with his brother-in-law, R. Barukh Halberstam, who claimed the right to be rabbi there.

In 1894, he accepted a position in Volovo, which included ministering to thirty-two neighboring villages as well. In his thirty years there, he established a *yeshivah*.

His wife, to whom he was married for seventy years, died on 3 *Elul*, and he followed her twelve days later. Like his grandfather R. Moses Teitelbaum, he lived for eighty-four years.

He had seven sons and three daughters. His son R. Aaron succeeded him.

TEITELBAUM, Mordecai (1882–ca. 1930), author—Very little biographical data on him are available. He was encouraged by his brother-in-law, R. Joseph Schneersohn of Lodz, a descendant of R. Shneur Zalman, and also by Shemaryah ben Levi Yitzhak of Warsaw to pursue his research on *Habad*.

He published his work *HaRav MiLadi U'Mifleget Habad* in two parts (Warsaw, 1910–1913). He wrote articles on "Lack of Tolerance," which appeared in the Hebrew periodical *HaMelitz* (1901) under the pseudonym *Aviezer*. He mastered several languages and possessed considerable knowledge of history, philosophy, literature, and related subjects.

S.F.

TEITELBAUM, Moses (1759–28 *Tammuz* 1841), the *Yismah Mosheh*—Born in Przemysl, the son of R. Tzvi Hirsch of Zborov, he traced his ancestry to R. Moses Isserles and R. Abraham Joshua Jacob Heschel (d. 1664) of Lublin. His father, Tzvi Hirsch, was a merchant whose business commitments often kept him away from his home for extended periods. His mother, Hannah, was famed for her piety. Later, R. Moses referred to her as *Baalat Ruah HaKodesh* (one who possessed the powers of prophecy). Her brother, R. Yehudah Halevi, rabbi of Strzyszov, guided him. After the death of his uncle, he continued his studies under his cousin R. Aryeh Leib Halevi, principal of the *yeshivah* of Strzyszov, who instructed him in the rudiments of Kabbalah.

R. Moses married Hayyah Sarah, the daughter of R. Nisan, a prominent member of Przemysl. They had one daughter and one son, R. Eliezer Nisan. After the untimely death of his father-in-law, he became, in 1782, rabbi in Sianiawa in succession to R. Barukh Teumim Frankel. At that time, he was still a *mitnagged* and had never visited R. Elimelekh of Lejask.

He was reputed to have known 800 pages of the Talmud by heart. He studied diligently both rabbinics and medieval Jewish philosophy, such as the *Moreh Nevukhim*, *Ikkarim*, and *Akedat Yitzhak*.

His daughter, Miriam Hannah, married R. Aryeh Leibish Lipshitz, the author of *Aryeh Debe Ilai*, who was an adherent of R. Jacob Yitzhak, the "Seer" of Lublin. It was due to the influence of his son-in-law that R. Moses visited the "Seer." The doyen of Hasidism made an immediate impact on him; he became a hasid and visited him three times. To widen his hasidic experience he visited R. Yisrael, the Maggid of Kozienice, and R. Menahem Mendel of Rymanov.

In 1807, he became rabbi of Satoralja Ujhely in Hungary, and on the death of the "Seer," in 1815, he became rebbe. His fame as a rebbe and *tzaddik* spread. Hasidim from neighboring Galicia came by the hundreds to spend the Festivals with him. He was also highly regarded by R. Moses Sofer Schreiber.

He established a *yeshivah* that attracted many gifted young men, among them R. Hershele Lisker and R. Aaron Meir Friedlander, and it was due to him that Hasidism spread in Hungary. It was with the cooperation of R. Moses Sofer Schreiber that an amicable agreement was reached about administration of the collection for the Rabbi Meir Baal Hanes fund.

He was a mystic to whom religious secrets were revealed in dreams, and he recorded the dreams he felt to be significant. Once, in a dream, he was taken to the Garden of Eden, where he saw *Tanna'im* studying the Talmud. "Is this all there is in paradise?" the rabbi exclaimed in astonishment. He was told, "You are wrong in believing that the *Tanna'im* are in paradise. Paradise is in the *Tanna'im*."

He lived in daily expectation of the coming of the Messiah. Each night, before he went to sleep, he would prepare his Sabbath clothes and remind the beadle to wake him the moment the Messiah arrived. Whenever the rabbi heard a noise, he would ask, "Has he come?" Once, on the eve of Atonement, when he was eighty-two, he exclaimed, "Master of the universe! Had I known in my youth that I would grow old before the coming of the Messiah, I would not have been able to survive all these years. I would have died in anguish. Only faith and hope have kept me alive to this day."

Even gentiles sought the rabbi's blessing. The mother of Louis Kossuth (1802–1894) who later headed the struggle for Hungarian independence from Austria, came to the rebbe when her child was very ill. The rabbi opposed mixed dancing and forbade Jews to hire gentiles to work for them on the Sabbath. Every Sabbath from *Rosh Hodesh Elul* to *Hoshanah Rabba*, he delivered a discourse in the synagogue. He wore a *shtreimel* even on weekdays. He would rise at 5 A.M. and rarely completed the morning service before two or three in the afternoon. The evening service would take place when it was almost midnight. He fasted on the Fast of the Firstborn and would not take advantage of the *siyyum* in order to forgo the fast. His only daily meal was at midnight.

He never smoked or wore glasses; nor did he ever ask for medical advice. Although he stressed the need for humility, he insisted that we should also glory in being the creation of God.

He lived in an old, decrepit house and refused to let his hasidim provide him with a more suitable home. "Why should I build a house here, in the land of the gentiles? Surely, the Messiah will come soon, and I will return to the land of my fathers."

His wife died on the eve of *Rosh Hodesh Nisan* 1840, and he died a year later. He asked the leaders of the community to appoint as his successor his son, R. Eleazar Nisan. His grave survived the Holocaust and continues to be a place of pilgrimage.

His works were published posthumously by his descendants. *Yismah Mosheh*, the name by which he is commonly called, was edited by his grandson R. Yekutiel Yehudah and was published in five parts on the Pentateuch (Lvov, 1849–1861); *Yismah Mosheh* on the prophets and five *Megillot*, edited by R. David Moses, was printed in Marmaros Sighet in 1906; *Yismah Mosheh* on the Aggadic parts of the Talmud (Sighet, 1908); *Tefillah LeMosheh*, a commentary on the Psalms (Cracow, 1880); and responsa *Heshiv Mosheh* (Lvov, 1866). All of his works have been reprinted several times.

His first and most reliable biography was written by his great-grandson R. Moses David Teitelbaum in his *Tehillah LeMosheh*.

A. Y. Bromberg, *Migdolei HaHasidut*, vol. 8, *R. Mosheh Teitelbaum*, pp. 22–119.

A.S.

TEITELBAUM, Moses, of Satmar (b. 1915) – Son of R. Hayyim Tzvi, he was born in Sighet. His parents died when he was eleven years old, and he was brought up by R. Nahum Tzvi Kahana, his uncle R. Yoel Teitelbaum, and his grandfather R. Shalom Eliezer Halberstam. In 1936, he married his cousin Leah, the daughter of R. Hanokh Heinokh Meir, the rabbi of Karecska, where R. Moses became the head of a *yeshivah*. In 1939, he became rabbi in Zenta, in Yugoslavia, which was then part of Hungary. During the Nazi period, he was in Auschwitz and then in Theresienstadt, from whence he was liberated. His wife perished in Auschwitz.

After the war, he married the daughter of R. Aaron Teitelbaum, the rabbi of Volovo, and lived for a time in Sighet. But owing to communist persecution, he emigrated to the United States, where he established a *Bet HaMidrash, Atzei Hayyim*, first in Williamsburg, Brooklyn, then in Borough Park, and was known as the rabbi of Sighet. After the death of his uncle in 1979, he succeeded him as rebbe of Satmar and also became the head of the *Edah HaHaredit* in Jerusalem.

His eldest son, R. Aaron, who married Sosha, the daughter of R. Moses Joshua Hager of Vishnitz, is the *rosh yeshivah* and rabbi of *Kiryat Yoel*. His second son, R. Zalman, is the rabbi of Sighet in Borough Park. His third son, R. Shalom Leizer, works in the Satmar office. He also has four daughters.

TEITELBAUM, Moses David, of Lapus (1856–21 *Adar* II 1935)—Son of R. Israel Jacob Yukel, he was born in Drohobycz and was brought up by his grandfather. He married Hayyah, the daughter of R. Leibish Halberstam of Dukla. He was appointed rabbi in Lapus, near Des, where he served for more than fifty years.

He published the works of his grandfather and established a *yeshivah* for more than a hundred students.

He was survived by his sons—R. Abraham Hayyim, rabbi of Krenice; R. Yitzhak Shmuel; and R. Yekutiel Yehudah, who survived the Holocaust and was rabbi of the *Bikkur Holim Anshei Sefard* in the Bronx.

He edited *Tefillah LeMosheh* (Lvov, 1885) and *Yitav Lev* (Sighet, 1875).

TEITELBAUM, Naftali, of New York (1895–6 *Tishri* 1971)—Son of R. David, the rabbi of Eshed, near Munkacs. He succeeded his father as rebbe. During the Second World War, he lived in Budapest, where he helped refugees. After the war, he settled in New York and was known as the "rabbi Kolboszov and Eshed." He married Rebecca, the daughter of R. Yitzhak Reuven Lipshitz.

He was survived by a son—R. Yitzhak Reuven David—and three daughters.

TEITELBAUM, Yekutiel Yehudah, of Sighet (1808–6 *Elul* 1883)—Yekutiel Yehudah, or "R. Zalman Leib," as he was known, son of R. Elazar Nisan, was born in Drohobycz. At the age of ten, his parents entrusted him to his grandfather R. Mosheh, whom he regarded as his teacher par excellence. In his youth he made friends with R. Herschele Lisker, the Lisker rebbe. He accompanied his grandfather to R. Jacob Yitzhak, the "Seer" of Lublin, when he was only four years old. He married Rachel, the daughter of R. Moses David Ashkenazi, rabbi of Tolcsva, Hungary, who later emigrated to the Holy Land, where he died in Safed on 17 *Tammuz* 1856.

In 1833, he became rabbi of Stropkov, and then, in 1841, of Satoralja Ujhely in succession to his grandfather. He remained there for six years. In 1846, he accepted a position in Gorlice, where he stayed until the death of his father in 1855, when he succeeded him as rabbi in Drohobycz. There he faced much antagonism, another rabbi—R. Elijah Horoshovski—being appointed in opposition. Four years later, on 18 *Tammuz* 1858, he became rabbi of Marmaros Sighet.

He established a *yeshivah* and became involved in communal life. In 1866, he supported the formation of the *Hevrah Mahzikei Hadat* in Michalovce, where the "Michalovce ruling" was drafted and adopted. He also supported the formation of an independent Orthodox communal organization and signed a number of their circulars. His own community did not join the organization because of internal strife when some 100 families organized themselves into a Sephardic community.

He was also engaged in a fiery controversy with the rabbi of Vishnitz over responsibility for charitable collections for the Holy Land. A court of five rabbis under R. Moses Grunwald, the rabbi of Huszt, decided to divide the contributions into two parts: one part under the rabbi of Vishnitz, and the other under the rabbi of Sighet.

Despite R. Teitelbaum's many commitments, he found time to write important works. In his younger days, he had edited his grandfather's work *Yismah Yisrael* and also his responsa *Heshiv Mosheh*, to which he added his glosses with the signature *Yitev*. His own homiletical work on the Pentateuch, *Yitev Lev*, he published anonymously in Marmaros Sighet in 1875 (and reprinted in Brooklyn in 1963). His second work, *Yitev Panim*, homilies on Festivals, was edited by his grandson R. Moses David Teitelbaum (Lvov, 1882, reprinted in Munkacs in 1883, in Huszt in 1912, and in New York in 1948). Another work, *Rav Tuv LeBet Yisrael* on Torah, was printed in Lvov in 1889 and reprinted in Brooklyn in 1973. His responsa *Avnei Tzeddek*, part one on *Orah Hayyim*, and *Yoreh De'ah* were published by his grandson posthumously (Lvov, 1885). His commentary on the Passover *Haggadah* was published in New York in 1947.

His son R. Hannaniah Yom Tov Lippa succeeded him. His other sons were R. Abraham Aaron, rabbi of Kolboszov; R. Moses Joseph, rabbi in Ujhely; and R. Eliyahu Bezalel, rabbi of Tesch. One of his sons-in-law, married to his daughter Pessil, was Barukh Halberstam of Rudnik, the son of R. Hayyim Halberstam of Zanz.

Marmaros, pp. 1–28.

A.S.

TEITELBAUM, Yekutiel Yehudah of Sighet (1912–25 *Iyyar* 1944) – Son of R. Hayyim Tzvi, the rabbi of Sighet. His father, whom he succeeded as rabbi, died when he was fourteen years old, and six months later, his mother, too, died.

He studied under his relative R. Yekutiel Yehudah Gross, who, until he reached maturity, acted as rabbi on his behalf. In 1930, he married his cousin, the daughter of R. Yoel Teitelbaum, and when she died in pregnancy in 1931, he married another cousin, Gitel Yehudit, the daughter of R. Meshullam Zusya Halberstam.

During World War II, his home was a refuge for fugitives from Poland and Slovakia. He was deported to Auschwitz, where he, his wife, and his children – Zusya and Yehiel Michael – were murdered.

Most of his writings were lost in the Holocaust. Just a few of his discourses survived and are recorded in *Atzei Hayyim* (Brooklyn, 1957).

TEITELBAUM, Yoel, of Satmar (18 *Tevet* 1887–26 *Av* 1979) – Perhaps no hasidic rabbi of the twentieth century provoked so much veneration and as much antagonism as R. Yoel. Idolized by some and vilified by others, his entire career was engulfed in fierce controversy.

He was born in Sighet, the son of R. Hannaniah Yom Tov Lippa. His mother, Hannah, was the daughter of R. Yoel Ashkenazi of Zloczov. Yoel studied under his father and R. Jacob Hirsch Turner. He was ordained by R. Moses Grunwald. In *Shevat* 1904, he married Havah, the daughter of R. Abraham Hayyim Horowitz, a descendant of Ropczyce.

He first lived privately in Satmar, where he had his own *Bet HaMidrash* and *yeshivah*. His father died a few days after his wedding, and R. Yoel's elder brother, R. Hayyim Tzvi, was appointed rabbi in Sighet, an appointment opposed by R. Yoel.

In *Elul* 1911, he moved to Orshove, in the Hungarian district of Ugoca. In *Adar* 1926, he became rabbi in Karoly (or Nagy Karoly) in Transylvania. When his brother died in Kleinwardein at the age of forty-five, after being rabbi in Sighet for twenty-two years, R. Yoel, at first, would not permit his brother's son, R. Zalman Leib, to succeed to his father's post. Eventually peace was made, and R. Zalman Leib became both the rabbi of Sighet and R. Yoel's son-in-law.

R. Yoel was continually embroiled in controversies. He urged the appointment of R. Shmuel Gross as his successor in Karoly while others favored R. Abraham Abish Horowitz. The community was divided, and even the civil authorities were involved in this unseemly quarrel. After the death of R. Eliezer David Grunwald, R. Yoel became rabbi of Satmar (Satu Mare). His appointment, however, started a bitter quarrel, lasting nearly four years. Hebrew tracts were published by supporters of R. Yoel's candidacy, as well as by his opponents. This controversy ended in a decisive victory for R. Yoel, who became the rabbi of Satmar in *Adar* 1934. Until 1939, he devoted himself, single-mindedly, to transforming Satmar into a stronghold of Orthodoxy.

Nearly 300 students studied in his *yeshivah*. He established *Bet Tavshil* (soup kitchen), popularly known as *Minza*, to provide hot midday meals. In addition, each student received one kilo of bread every morning. The *Tomhei Dal* (Supporters of the Poor) committee was set up to supervise these activities. The rabbi would not permit a wedding to take place unless he was assured that no non-Orthodox practices, such as mixed dancing, would be allowed. The *mikveh* in Satmar was constructed according to his detailed specifications. The supervisor kept a register to make sure that no one evaded this religious duty.

His personal life was beset with tragedy. Of his three daughters, Esther died in 1922, Rachel in 1931, and the third, *Hayyah* Rosa, after World War II. His wife died in Satmar in 1936. A year later, he married Alta Feiga, the daughter of R. Avigdor Shapira, the rebbe of Czestochova, a descendant of Zanz and Kozienice.

During the Second World War, he, his wife, and his beadle, Joseph Ashkenazi, escaped to Klausenburg, in a Red Cross ambulance. On May 3, 1944, they were arrested and taken to the ghetto of Klausenburg, and then, in *Tammuz* 1944, to Bergen-Belsen, where they remained until December of that year. One potato per day was their only source of sustenance. Through the intervention of Dr. R. R. Kasztner, vice president of the Zionist organization in Budapest, and his assistant Joel Brand, the rebbe was among the 1,368 people permitted to leave for a neutral country. The train left Budapest on June 29 and reached Bergen-Belsen on July 8, where R. Yoel joined them. He arrived at the Swiss border on December 7, 1944 (21 *Kislev*), a day celebrated by Satmar hasidim as a day of deliverance.

Through the efforts of Chief Rabbi Yitzhak Herzog, he was allowed to enter the Holy Land, where he arrived in 1945. During his one-year stay, he established a *yeshivah Yitev Lev D'Satmar*. However, he decided to emigrate to the United States, and in *Tammuz* 1946 he made his home in Williamsburg, Brooklyn.

The Satmar community *Kehal Yitev Lev D'Satmar* flourished and became a self-sufficient entity, a testimony to his remarkable flair for organization. By the 1990s over 50,000 hasidim were living in the area. Satmar publishes periodicals and a weekly newspaper, *Der Yid*. It has its own welfare network, including a holiday fund for orphan children, insurance and pension plans, an emergency ambulance service, a burial society, and large synagogues. It operates its own butcher shops and supervises the production of a variety of processed foods. It maintains *mikvaot*, a *shatnes* laboratory, a kindergarten, *Bet Rachel* schools for girls, and bakeries where *matzot* are baked by hand on the eve of Passover.

The *yeshivah* building is one of the largest in the world, with nearly 1,000 students, and dormitory facilities. It is not unusual to find, on a weekday, 700 worshipers in the large synagogue. The Satmar community is responsible for the education of some 10,000 children in many schools, and buses transport them to and from their homes. After finishing the Talmud Torah, they continue their studies in the *yeshivah* and eventually graduate to the *kollel*.

The girls can choose between commercial courses and studying for a teaching diploma. With the exception of the Yeshiva University, Satmar is the largest Jewish educational organization in the Western world. To become a member of this elite community, a man must undertake to observe the Sabbath and to bring up his children in the Orthodox tradition. A committee investigates the religious and moral suitability of every applicant.

He was the author of polemical works: *VaYoel Mosheh* (Brooklyn, 1959), which went through five editions, and *Kuntres al HaGeulah VeAl HaTemurah* (Brooklyn, 1967) and *Sefer Gahalei Esh* (edited by Alter Moses Menahem Goldberger) (Kiryat Yoel, 1984). He was also the author of very learned works: *Divrei Yoel*, an eight-volume commentary on the Torah (*Hiddushei Torah*) parts one to nine (Jerusalem, 1963); responsa *She'elot U'Teshuvot*, part one on *Orah Hayyim* and *Yore De'ah* and part two on *Even HaEzer* and *Hoshen Mishpat* (Brooklyn, 1967); *Sefer Tehillim* (Brooklyn, 1974); and a commentary on the Passover *Haggadah* (Brooklyn, 1974).

R. Yoel was regarded as the senior rabbi of his generation. Rabbis and rebbes gathered around his Sabbath table. It was not unusual for a hundred people to seek his counsel in the course of a single day. He had a complex personality, uncompromising in the realm of religion, yet kindly, considerate, and generous, with a keen sense of humor. Many Satmar hasidim owed their financial success to monetary gifts from the rabbi. At one time he officiated at Sabbath services and on Sabbath *Rosh Hodesh*. He would also read the *Megillah* in public. He insisted that his hasidim should work for a living and exhorted them to be honest in their business dealings.

In 1968, he suffered a stroke and lived either in Belle Harbor, New York City, or in Monroe, New York, in semiseclusion.

In 1976, *Kiryat Yoel*, a village of 340 acres, was set up near Monroe in Orange County, New York, and by 1990, the population of the *kiryah* numbered more than 8,000.

The years did not diminish R. Yoel's implacable antagonism to the "secularist state of Israel." To him, Zionism was an evil creed, and to cooperate with the Zionists was a major sin. Nationalism was an imitation of the gentiles. He referred to the talmudic tractate *Ketubot* 111a, which states that the people of Israel were bound by an oath not to revolt against the nations where they were held captive and not to try to hasten the end.

The precept of *Yishuv HaAretz* (settling in the Holy Land) applied only to the period of the Temple and was not binding today. He claimed that Jewish destiny was to pray for the coming of the Messiah, who would bring redemption and the restoration of the Jewish homeland. His hasidim demonstrated in public against the state of Israel, even picketing the United Nations building in New York and carrying anti-Israel placards. His followers were not permitted to visit the Western Wall.

After the death of R. Selig Reuben Bengis (1864–1953), the rebbe, in 1953, became the spiritual head of the *Eda HaHaredit*, which encompasses the extremist *Neturei Karta*. His opposition to the State of Israel was not incompatible with his commitment to the Land of Israel, which he visited in 1932, 1947, 1952, 1955, and 1959. He objected to the use of Hebrew as an everyday language, but as Israel was no worse than any other country, he did not oppose individual hasidim's settling there. He even founded two settlements there, in Bene Berak and Jerusalem. He also visited England in June 1955, June 1959, and August 1965.

In 1968, Vice President of the United States Hubert Humphrey called on him to discuss the tension that prevailed between the black militant and Jewish communities.

He died in Mount Sinai Hospital in New York on Sunday, 26 *Av* 1979. More than 100,000 people attended his funeral in Monroe, where he was buried in a privately consecrated cemetery.

His successor was his nephew R. Moses Teitelbaum of Sighet.

A. Fuchs, *HaAdmor MiSatmar*.

A. Rosmarin, *Der Satmarer Rebbe*.

TEKHELET (Hebrew: blue) – A thread of blue was included in the veil of the tent of meeting (Exodus 26:31), in the *ephod* (Exodus 28:6), in the garments of the princes and nobles (Ezekiel 23:6), and, above all, in the fringes (Numbers 15:38). According to the Talmud, the blue dye was obtained from *hillazon* – a snail found in the sea. Its color was between green and blue. It is noteworthy that dyed *tzitzit* were discovered in the Bar Kokhba caves. The Midrash, (Numbers *Rabba* 17:5) states, however, that "nowadays we possess only white *tzitzit*, the *tekhelet* having been concealed." Reference to it is made by Natronai Gaon of Pumbedita in the early eighth century. Maimonides, too, in his commentary to the *Mishnah*, maintained that it had been lost, for the art of dying the blue thread had been the secret of a few families that lived on the coast of Palestine.

"The redemption will begin," wrote R. Gershon Heinokh Leiner (1839–1891), "when we are permitted to rebuild the Temple. If we are worthy, permission will be granted, even before the ingathering of the exiles." He was determined to rediscover the source of the dye and to restore the thread to its rightful place. He fervently believed that such restoration would hasten the redemption. Hasidim believed that R. Samson of Ostropol in his work *Mahaneh Dan* predicted that the *tekhelet* would be rediscovered in the nineteenth century.

In 1887, R. Gershon Heinokh wrote a thirty-eight-page booklet entitled *Maamar Sefunei Temunei Hol* (Warsaw, 1887) on the subject. In it, he lists the conflicting views on the number of *tzitzit* that should be dyed. Rashi maintains that four of the eight threads should be colored. R. Abraham ben David of Posquieres believed that only two should be dyed. R. Gershon Heinokh endorses the view of Maimonides that one is sufficient.

Accompanied by his attendant Israel Kotsker, he went to Naples in 1887 and again in 1888, where he visited the Aquarium four times. He studied the Italian seashore and became an expert on marine life. According to Dr. Aaron Marcus, the rebbe even visited the Vatican Museum, where he allegedly studied the garments reputed to have belonged to the High Priest, especially the *tzitz* (a plate or crown of pure gold, described in Exodus 28:36). According to the Bible, the gold plate was held in position on the forehead of the High Priest by a blue thread.

In 1888, he published a second treatise on the subject, entitled *Maamar Petil Tekhelet*, in which he claimed to have discovered *hillazon*, a member of the *Cephalopod* family, which is related to the octopus and squid families.

A factory was established in Radzyn, Poland, and soon 12,000 hasidim were wearing the thread of blue. At the recommendation of R. Abraham Bratzlaver (d. 1918), the practice was adopted by the hasidim of Bratzlav with a slight variation. While the hasidim of Radzyn are content to include one blue thread among the eight prescribed by the Torah, the hasidim of Bratzlav favored two blue threads together with the six white ones.

Many scholars, however, opposed the restoration of the blue thread. Among them were R. Joshua of Kutno, R. Meir Arak, R. Elhanan Spector, and R. Hillel Moses ben Tzvi, who decried the practice in his book *Mishkanot L'Avir Yaakov* (Jerusalem, 1875). In addition, hasidic rebbes, like R. Aryeh Leib Alter of Ger, R. Abraham Bornstein of Sochaczev, and R. Tzaddok Rabinowicz of Lublin, did not support him. Among his few supporters was R. Akiva Joseph Schlesinger (1837–1922), author of *Lev Ivri*, published in 1865. To win over his detractors, R. Leiner wrote a third 250-page work, *Ein Tekhelet* (Warsaw, 1891), which was published posthumously.

It is noteworthy that R. Isaac Herzog, in an unpublished dissertation entitled "The Dying of Purple in Ancient Israel" (1919), which was a study of *Tekhelet*, maintained that it was extracted from the snails *Janthina pallida* and *Janthina bicolor*.

M. M. Kasher, "Tekhelet BiZman HaZeh," pp. 241–258.

TEL AVIV, largest city in Israel–Tel Aviv has more than 700 synagogues, and there are few hasidic dynasties that are not represented by a *shtiebl* in Tel Aviv. Before the outbreak of World War II, Tel Aviv became the refuge of the descendants of Ruzhyn, many of whom had been living in Vienna during the interwar years. R. Shlomoh Friedman settled in Tel Aviv in 1938, and R. Israel of Husyatin arrived there with his son-in-law in 1937. North Tel Aviv was the home of R. Mordecai (Mottle) Shalom Joseph Friedman of Sadgora/Przemysl, who settled there in 1939. Today, there are few rabbis of Ruzhyn left in Israel.

Ahad Ha-Am was the pen name of Asher Ginsberg, the essayist, and the street in Tel Aviv named after him has become the "street of the rabbis." Here lived R. Aaron Rokeah, the rabbi of Belz, R. Mordecai Shalom Friedman, R. Abraham Jacob, R. Shlomoh, and R. Nahum Mordecai Friedman. Here, too, lived the son-in-law of R. Israel of Chortkov–R. Tzvi Aryeh Twersky, or "Herschele," as he was popularly known. On his release from the Nazi camps he settled in Tel Aviv in 1939. He died in 1968, and a *kollel Chortkov Zlatopole* has been established in his memory by his son-in-law. R. Yitzhak Friedman of Bohusi, too, moved to Tel Aviv in 1959. He was known as the "people's rebbe," and he maintained a *kollel* there. The most prolific writer of the hasidic rebbes in Tel Aviv was R. Moses Yehiel Epstein (d. 1971), the rabbi of Ozarov. Today the dynasty is maintained by his grandson R. Tanhum Becker.

Modzitz, too, was represented in Tel Aviv by R. Saul Yedidyah Eliezer, whose son R. Shmuel Eliyahu Taub lived in Tel Aviv, and his tradition is being maintained by his son R. Israel Dan. The Karlin/Koidanov dynasty was represented by R. Hanokh Heinokh Dov Zilberfarb of Koidanov, who died in 1978 and was succeeded by his son R. Aaron. An interesting personality was R. Yehudah Tzvi Brandwein of Stretyn (d. 1969), who worked for the religious department of the *Histadrut*.

It was also the home of R. Ittamar Rosenbaum of Nadvorna, who lived in Yad Eliyahu, and for some time the abode of R. Yehiel Joshua Rabinowicz of Biala. Tel Aviv has many hasidic *yeshivot*, among them *Yeshivah Hiddushei Harim* of Ger and that of Belz.

Today, only three rebbes reside in Tel Aviv: Ozarov, Modzitz, and Sadgora, who are also planning to move to Bene Berak.

TENNENBAUM, Jacob Yehudah of Warka/Naradzin (1816–5 *Kislev* 1886) – Son of R. Nathan Nata, he married the daughter of R. Menahem Mendel of Warka. After the death of R. Berish Landau of Biala, he became rabbi first in Warka, and then in Naradzin. Unlike the rebbes of Warka who were immersed in community affairs, he lived a secluded and ascetic life. He allowed twenty-four hours to elapse between partaking of meat and dairy dishes. He ate only once a day.

His son R. Hayyim (d. 7 *Iyyar* 1931) was brought up by his grandfather, the rabbi of Warka. He married the daughter of R. Mendel Blustein. He had five sons and three daughters, who all married rebbes.

The other son of R. Jacob Yehudah, R. Yerahmiel Joshua Moses (d. 12 *Adar* 1914), married the daughter of the wealthy R. Joseph Mintz of Siedlice. He was renowned for his long *peyot*, which almost reached his legs.

TEOMIM, Aryeh Leib, of Lejask/Brody (d. 1831), Galician rabbi – Rabbi of Lejask, he was a strong opponent of Hasidism. In 1815, he was appointed rabbi in Brody. The hasidim opposed the secular school that was opened by the Austrian authorities in 1818. R. Teomim, however, welcomed it, since "the Torah has to be combined with general knowledge."

He was the author of commentaries on the Torah and of novellas on talmudical tractates *Yaalat Hen* and *Ayyelet Ahavim*, both published in Zolkiev in 1802.

Y. A. Kamelhar, *Dor Deah* 2, pp. 159–161.

TETRAGRAMMATON – The four-letter, ineffable name of God (YHVH). It represents the total world of the divine, and it can also be analyzed into the various parts of the sefirotic world. For example, YHVH can be seen as a symbol of the way in which the emanation of the *Sefirot* took place: the tip of the first letter, *yod*, represents *ayin*, the inconceivable nothingness, which is the origin of all (*yod* itself represents *Hokhmah*); the first *heh* represents *Binah*; the *vav*, because of its numerical value, represents the six *Sefirot* below *Binah*; the last *heh* represents *Malkhut*.

Conversely, in their prayers, worshiping mystics are required to concentrate on the last letter of the tetragrammaton (representing *Malkhut*, or the *Shekhinah*) and then ascend through the other letters until they reach contemplation of the first letter, *yod*. In so doing they effect a unification (*yihud*) of the divine name, since in the parlance of the *Zohar*, they unite *heh* to *vav*, *vav* to *heh*, and *heh* to *yod*.

The *vav* of the tetragrammaton is also considered to represent *Tiferet*, the summation of the six *Sefirot* below *Binah*. *Tiferet* is also called *HaKadosh Barukh Hu* (the Holy One, blessed be He). Consequently, meditation upon, and unification of, the last two letters of the tetragrammaton stimulate union between the Holy One, blessed be He, and His *Shekhinah*, an aim that is embodied in the hasidic formula recited before prayer and in the performance of other *mitzvot*.

Each of the ten different names of God is associated with one of the ten *Sefirot*. YHVH represents *Tiferet*. When it is vocalized, like *Elohim*, it represents *Binah*. In combination with *Tzeva'ot*, it represents *Netzah*.

D.G.

TIBERIAS – Tiberias, a town on the western shore of the Sea of Galilee, is one of the four holy cities of Israel. "From Tiberias," says the Talmud (*Rosh Hashanah* 31b), "the Israelites will be redeemed." "The king Messiah," predicts the *Zohar*, "will appear in Tiberias." The city, with its surroundings, was granted for Jewish settlement to Don Joseph Nasi by Sultan Sulliman I in the sixteenth century. R. Isaiah Horowitz lived in Tiberias and was buried near the graves of R. Yohanan ben Zakkai and Moses Maimonides.

Tiberias had been resettled by R. Hayyim Abulafia (1660–1744), who had come from Izmir in Turkey at the invitation of Sheik Zahir al-Amr. "Arise, and come up," Abulafia wrote. "Inherit the land of Tiberias, which is the land of your fathers." In the eighteenth century it attracted hasidic leaders: R. Menahem Mendel of Przemyshlan (d. 13 *Tishri* 1770) together with R. Nahman of Horodenka settled there in 1765. R. Nahman lived there until his death five years later. He yearned to meet the kabbalist R. Eleazar ben

Samuel Rokeah (1665–1742), but the meeting never took place.

Soon after, in 1781, R. Menahem Mendel of Vitebsk (1730–1788) and R. Abraham Hakohen of Kalisk (d. 1810) settled there. In 1782, R. Menahem Mendel built a three-story edifice, which consisted of a *Bet HaMidrash* and accommodation for him on the first floor. R. Barukh of Medziborz sent him an ark cover from Poland. The synagogue, destroyed in an earthquake in 1837, was partially rebuilt two years later and is now used by the hasidim of Karlin. In May 1839, Moses Montefiore and his wife worshiped there.

In the 1880s it was taken over by the hasidim of Stolin under the guidance of R. Yohanan Perlow. R. Meir ben Jacob (d. 1806) of Bychowa visited Russia four times—in 1789, 1791, 1801, and 1803—to try to resolve the dispute between R. Shneur Zalman of Liady and R. Abraham of Kalisk. R. Nahman of Bratzlav stayed in Tiberias from Sukkot to *Adar* 1799. It was from Tiberias that men such as R. Shlomoh Zalman Hakohen (d. 20 *Adar* 1799), who styled himself "chief rabbi," sent emissaries to Russia. At the same time, R. Zeev Wolf, the son of Naftali Tzvi of Ostrog, a disciple of Dov Baer of Mezhirech, settled there in 1798. He established a *Bet HaMidrash* called *Bet HaMidrash shel Rab Zeev*. In all, between 1774 and 1938, 165 emissaries were sent out from Tiberias.

In 1812, a traveler, Johann Ludwig Burckhardt (1784–1817), found a thousand Jews living there. R. Dov Baer Schneersohn, in 1823, urged his followers to support the community. The hasidim then established a synagogue *Hasidei Reisin*, which was destroyed by the earthquake in 1837. It was rebuilt, in 1855, by Shmuel Leib of Pinsk and was again destroyed by flood in 1934. In 1837, a thousand Jews lost their lives in the violent earthquake, which destroyed most of the sixteenth-century city, but two years later, 600 Jews were living there.

By the mid-nineteenth century there were already a number of *kollelim*: *Estreich*, *Vishnitz*, *Karlin*, *Kosov*, *Bukovina*, *Zhitomir*, and *Koidanov*. In 1866, R. Barukh Mordecai of Karlin wrote, "We have received several letters from the Holy Land, and from our *kollel* in the holy city of Tiberias, informing us of their hardships. The [cholera] epidemic is steadily getting worse."

Tiberias was then the home of R. Naftali Tzvi Hirsch (d. 27 *Elul* 1865), son of R. Aaron of Kitov, a grandson of the Besht, who was known as "Tzvi Hirsch Besht," and of R. Moses Joseph Wahrman (d. 10 *Kislev* 1858), son of R. Abraham David of Buczacz.

It was in Tiberias that R. Moses Kliers, rabbi of the Ashkenazic community, married the daughter of R. Yehudah Leib, a hasid of Slonim, and together with the followers of R. Noah Weinberg, son of Abraham of Slonim, founded soup kitchens for the needy and established, in 1899, the *Or Torah Yeshivah*, near the tomb of R. Meir Baal Hanes. From the *halukkah*, which was divided into twenty-eight parts, Tiberias received four parts.

An inventory made on behalf of Sir Moses Montefiore in 1875 points out that in 1855 the *Habad* community consisted of 140 persons, among them 44 men, who congregated in two synagogues. The first, known as the Large Synagogue, was bought by R. Ezekiel Manasse. The second, known as the Small Synagogue, was situated close to the Sephardic synagogue and had been purchased by the *Mittler Rebbe*. In 1866, the community consisted of 228 persons. There was then a *yeshivah* attached to the Small Synagogue. There was also a *Bet HaMidrash*, which was situated next to the Large Synagogue and was known as *Das Mosheh VeYehudit*.

There were four societies of the *Habad* community: the *Bikkur Holim*, to cater to the needs of and to provide assistance for the sick; *Hevrah Kaddisha*, to deal with matters pertaining to the burial of the dead; *Hakhnasat Kallah*, to assist the poor and orphans in their marriage preparations, including the provision of dowries; *Olei Regalim*, to ensure that ten members of the community go to Jerusalem each *Yom Tov* to pray there for peace on behalf of their brethren in the Diaspora (each of the ten was given funds toward his traveling expenses); and *Hahnassat Orkhim*, to offer hospitality to all who came from afar to pray at the holy resting places of their forefathers.

In the 1890s, hasidim of Boyan and Chortkov under Joseph Heizler built a hasidic *Bet HaMidrash* on the seashore—near the *Senyor* synagogue—which was later destroyed by floods. On 6 Av 1929, R. Joseph Yitzhak Schneersohn, the rebbe of Lubavitch, visited

Tiberias, which greatly encouraged the hasidic settlement.

Many hasidic rebbes are buried in the cemetery of Tiberias. Today Tiberias is a flourishing Jewish city with relatively few hasidim. R. Hirsch Leib Brandwein (1889–1958) and R. Abraham Weinberg were the founders of *Kiryat Shmuel*, where, in 1930, the hasidim of Slonim erected a *Bet HaMidrash Or Torah* and R. Menahem Mendel Taub of Kalev established *Mishkan Kalev*.

O. Avissar, *Sefer Tevariah*, pp. 454–457.

TIEBERG, Judah Moses, of Bene Berak (1898–23 *Adar* II 1977) – Born in Plavno, Poland, he married the daughter of R. Bezalel Yair of Lodz (1865–1934). He received his rabbinical diploma from R. Meir Yehiel Halevi Halstock of Ostrowiec, who described him as a "great talmudist, well versed in the law." He was known as the "*Illui*" of Lodz. His work *Hashavah LeTovah* (Piotrokov, 1933) was acclaimed by his colleagues, and R. A. I. Kook praised his reasoning and understanding.

In 1934, with the blessing of R. Yitzhak Menahem Dancyger (d. 1943), the rebbe of Alexander, he settled in Jerusalem. It was not, however, until 1947 that he assumed leadership of the hasidim of Alexander. He settled in Bene Berak and traveled widely to raise funds for his educational institutions.

Considerable rivalry had existed in Poland between the followers of Ger and the followers of Alexander, but as the rabbi phrased it, "After the Holocaust, dissension disappeared."

He established *shtieblech* in Rehovot, Tel Aviv, and Jerusalem. He was succeeded by his son, R. Abraham Menahem Mendel.

TIFERET YISRAEL (or BET HAKNESSET NISAN BAK) – It was R. Israel Friedman of Ruzhyn who raised money to enable Nisan Bak (1815–1889) to acquire a strategic piece of land near the Western Wall in Jerusalem, but difficulties were many. The grave of Sheik Abu Shush was discovered, and it took delicate diplomacy, including the intervention of the Austrian consul, to have the remains reinterred in another locality.

Meanwhile, the *Hurvah* Synagogue of Judah Hasid, which had stood in ruins for nearly 150 years, was being rebuilt. The foundation stone was laid on 17 *Nisan* 1857, the synagogue was dedicated on 24 *Elul* 1864, and it became the foremost synagogue of Jerusalem.

The completion of that synagogue inspired Bak to persevere in his efforts to erect the hasidic synagogue. In a public proclamation, he pleaded for additional funds, pointing out, "It is already twelve years since we acquired the site to erect a magnificent structure." He was supported by R. Abraham Jacob of Sadgora and by the family of Ezekiel Reubin Sassoon. The beautiful synagogue, with thirty windows facing the Temple Mount, and a twelve-windowed dome, designed by a Russian architect, was consecrated on *Shabbat Nahamu* 1870. It was known as *Tiferet Yisrael* (in honor of R. Israel of Ruzhyn) or *Bet Haknesset Nisan Bak* (*Nisan*'s *Shul*), for Nisan was its first *gabbai*. Together with many other historic synagogues, it was destroyed by the Jordanians in 1948.

TIKKUN (Hebrew, repair) – After the breakup of primeval creative formations, the Almighty released another radiation of lights. This new creation is called by R. Yitzhak Luria *Olam HaTikkun* – the world of remedy, of reconstruction – in contrast to the earlier universe, to which he refers as *Olam HaTohu* – the world of confusion.

On one hand, human beings, by their righteous thoughts and deeds, have it in their power to stimulate and increase the flow of the divine bounty to the world. On the other hand, by wrongful actions, they constrict and may even block the channels for its descent. The key to heavenly power is held by humanity.

The kabbalists believed that by acts of loving-kindness one can atone for the cosmic catastrophe (*Shevirat Kelim*). This act of atonement was called *Tikkun* (lit., ordering, repairing, to make restitution). Among the hasidim, *Tikkun* is also used as a term for providing whiskey and light refreshments on the occasion of a *yahrzeit*, on the welcoming of an important visitor, on the return from a journey, on an engagement, and on other celebrations. It is an opportunity for the hasidim to wish one another *LeHayyim Tovim U'LeShalom*.

This *minhag* was endorsed by R. Uri of Strelisk, who stated that the numerical value of the Hebrew expression *LeHayyim* is equivalent to that of the Hebrew word *minhag*, namely, ninety-eight. R. Menahem Mendel of Vitebsk, however, in his ethical will forbade his son to drink any intoxicating liquor during the week.

TIKKUN HATZOT (Hebrew, midnight prayer) – This service originated in the kabbalistic school of Safed. It consists of the recitation of Psalms 79, 102, and 137; the *Viddui* (confessional); the thirteen articles of the divine attributes; and dirges. There are two orders of service: *Tikkun Rachel* – mourning for the exile of the *Shekhinah*, recited during the days when *Tahanun* is read – and *Tikkun Leah* – recited on the Sabbath and Festivals and on days when *Tahanun* is not recited.

The Besht would recite *Tikkun Hatzot* (*Shivhei HaBesht* 23), as did R. Elimelekh of Lejask. R. Aaron of Karlin, in his *Bet Aharon*, maintains that a person should observe *Tikkun Hatzot* both in the summer and in the winter, even if one has no time for study. R. Shneur Zalman of Liady revised the service and recommended that it be recited not in solitude but in the synagogue with a *minyan*.

In the course of time, it became the exception rather than the rule to recite *Tikkun Hatzot*. R. Mordecai of Chernobyl explained the lapse by saying that *Tikkun Hatzot* was tantamount to the pangs of the Messiah. "We have already reached that stage; hence the recitation is no longer mandatory."

G. Scholem, *On the Kabbalah and Its Symbolism*.

TISH (Yiddish; table; in hasidic parlance: the rebbe's table or meal) – The hasidim considered it mandatory to be present whenever the rebbe held a *Tish* (i.e., ate a meal in public). There they heard the rebbe's Torah, watched the rebbe sing and dance; and sang and danced with him. They followed the rebbe's bearing and movements, each of which they considered of special significance because such movements had been inspired by the rebbe's devotion and holy thoughts.

The hasidic leaders in general held their *Tish* on Sabbaths and Festivals. The hasidim would rush home after synagogue services (on the eves of Sabbaths and Festivals and on Sabbath and holiday mornings), eat their own meal, and then go to the rebbe, who would start his meal at a later hour so as to give his hasidim time to assemble.

The most honored of the rebbe's followers would sit with the rebbe at the table. Some of them would eat with him as his guests, particularly so if they had come from out of town. The rest of the hasidim would crowd around the table.

At hasidic courts that had many followers, some hasidim, especially the younger ones, would try, long before the start of the meal, to find places from which they could observe the rebbe closely.

Some rebbes would break bread at the Sabbath meals with twelve *hallot* (Sabbath loaves), in accordance with a custom of R. Yitzhak Luria, to commemorate the twelve show breads of the sanctuary. Hasidim would take pieces and treasure them as a *segullah* (charm).

After the rebbe had partaken of some of the food, the leftovers (*shirayim*) would be taken and eaten by the hasidim, for food from which the rebbe had eaten was regarded as holy and benedictive. At tables where there were a great number of hasidim, each hasid would naturally try to get ahead of the others in obtaining the leftovers.

Toward the end of the meal, the rebbe would "say Torah" (i.e., deliver a discourse based on the biblical portion of the week or on a subject germane to that Festival). Some rebbes did not "say Torah" but sang instead. Some rebbes sang melodies, or even songs, of their own composition.

There was a good deal of singing at the *tish*. At some *tishen* there was also dancing. The hasidim might dance while the rebbe remained in his seat, or the rebbe might dance with the hasidim.

Many hasidim would not complete their meal at home but would partake of a little additional food at the rebbe's table and say the grace after meals together with him.

The third meal of the Sabbath (*shalosh se'udot*) was eaten by the hasidim together with the rebbe. According to the Talmud, it was mandatory to eat three meals on the Sabbath, and it was one of the innovations of Hasidism that the third meal should be eaten not in private but in company, amid singing and the saying of Torah. It was at this meal, which was eaten on the Sabbath toward evening and which lasted into the night, that some rebbes would say their main Torah. At that meal only *hallah* and fish were eaten. Some rebbes ate fish with their fingers only, insisting on not using a fork. They based this custom on a homiletical interpretation of Genesis 9:2.

The remaining contents of the cup of wine over which the rebbe had said grace (the cup of blessing), would be drunk by hasidim, mixed with other wine. The wine from the cup of blessing was regarded as benedictive (cf. Babylonian Talmud *Berakhot* 51b).

A special feature at some hasidic courts was the *stellen Wein* (putting of wine). The rebbe's *gabbai* (major domo) would have near the rebbe's *Tish* cases filled with bottles of wine. Individual hasidim would each order a bottle for themselves from these cases. The gabbai would put the ordered bottles on the table and announce the names of those who had ordered them. Later the rebbe would take these bottles and hand them to the persons who had ordered them. Each of these would pour himself a cup and go up to the rebbe, who then wished him *LeHayyim* (to life). Afterward the man would pour the remaining contents of his bottle into the cups of those hasidim who had not ordered bottles of their own. They in turn would then go up to the rebbe to receive his *LeHayyim*.

The *melaveh malkah* meal, which was eaten after the end of the Sabbath to escort the departing Sabbath Queen, was also eaten by hasidim in company and amid singing. At this meal the rebbe as a rule did not say Torah. Some rebbes told stories of the Besht.

A *tish* could last for several hours. At some courts there were, especially on Friday nights, second *tishen*. Some of the hasidim would have left by that time because of the lateness of the hour, but those who remained–the younger people as a rule–would talk with the rebbe on hasidic subjects. They would be served fruit and would sing and dance. This was the second *tish*.

In addition to Sabbaths and Festivals there were other occasions when a rebbe would hold *tish*, such as the yahrzeit of a great hasidic leader or of a *tzaddik* of the dynasty to which that particular rebbe belonged.

The pattern and frequency of the *tish* would, of course, vary from dynasty to dynasty and even from rebbe to rebbe. A rebbe might change the pattern and frequency of his *tish* during his lifetime due to a change in general or personal circumstances.

Habad hasidim do not use the expression *tish* (Lubavitch hasidim generally have their own idioms for many hasidic practices). Their closest equivalent to the practice of the *tish* was the *farbrengen*. Lubavitch hasidim do not practice *shirayim*.

M. Unger, *HaHasidut un Leben*, pp. 79–93.

A. Wertheim, *Halakhot VeHalikhot BaHasidut*, pp. 150–153, 165, 169.

T.P.

TISHBY, Isaiah (1908–1992), scholar of Jewish mysticism–Born in Sanislo, Hungary, he received a traditional Jewish education. At the age of eighteen, he moved to Grosswardein and later to Budapest and Vienna. He emigrated to the Holy Land in 1933 and began studying at the Hebrew University in the following year. He studied Jewish philosophy, Kabbalah, and Jewish literature, receiving a Ph.D. in 1943 under the supervision of Gershom Scholem.

He excelled in providing intellectual explanations and modern translations of medieval texts in Hebrew and Aramaic and was the first scholar in the early 1940s to edit and publish a work on the writings of the sixteenth-century Lurianic Kabbalah of Safed (*Torat HaRa VeHaKelippah BeKabbalat HaAri*) (second ed., 1943).

Tishby was appointed to be a senior lecturer at the Hebrew University in 1951 and rose to the rank of full professor of Jewish mysticism and ethical literature in 1959. His greatest contribution was his three-volume work *Mishnat HaZohar* (Wisdom of the *Zohar*), which has been translated into English and published by the Littman Library at Oxford University Press. Another of his achievements was his entry in the *Hebrew Encyclopedia* on "Major Trends of Hasidic Thought."

In 1979, he received the prestigious Israel Prize for Jewish Studies. He was a visiting professor at several American universities and a visiting fellow at the Oxford Centre for Post-Graduate Hebrew Studies.

D.G.

TOBACCO–The legends told about the Besht speak of his long pipe, the *lulke*, over which, it is said by some sources, he would even recite a benediction. Many of the hasidic masters similarly were tobacco smokers. The hasidic fondness for this weed is based mainly on two ideas: the first is that smoking before prayers assists the bowel movements so that the body can be thoroughly cleansed before the devotions are uttered; the second is that smoking is an aid to contemplation on the significance of prayer.

In the anti-hasidic polemics there are many references to the early hasidim's spending wasteful hours, so their opponents declared, in smoking before prayer. The hasidim retorted that prayer is like incense ascending to God and that the fragrance of tobacco is a symbol of this. Second, tobacco smoking was held to be of high significance because of the doctrine of the elevation of holy sparks (see KABBALAH). It was also argued by the hasidim that there are specially subtle sparks in tobacco, which have to be released and rescued for the holy by the hasid's smoking of a pipe or cigarette in a spirit of devotion.

Further advantages of tobacco are stated in later hasidic works. Thus David Moses of Chortkov observed that tobacco was used by pagan savages before it was brought to Europe. Its use by the hasidim raises the weed from the profane to the holy in that no one is ashamed to accept from another a peck of snuff or a cigarette, and so acts of benevolence are carried out all the time (*Divrei David*, Husiatyn [1904], p. 66).

Another idea is that the smoke of the pipe acts as a screen for us, hiding us from evil inclinations, which seek to lead us into sin. On the other hand, it is reported that R. Shalom of Belz used to smoke a pipe in his youth but once saw a hasid take so long in making his pipe ready that Shalom was able, in the interval, to read a whole page of *Gemara*, and thereupon he made a firm resolve that he would never smoke again.

M. Wilensky, *Hasidim U'Mitnaggedim.*

L.J.

TOLDOT YAAKOV YOSEF – A commentary on the Torah by R. Jacob Joseph of Polonnoye (d. 1784), it is the first hasidic work ever to be published. In the book the author uses the expression "I have heard from my teacher (the Besht) . . ." 249 times. It was printed in Korzec in 1780. Ben Yaakov in his *Otzar HaSefarim* also refers to a Medziborz edition.

The work appeared without the customary encomium. R. Abraham Shimshon Katz, head of the *Bet Din* in Rashkov, and R. Abraham Dov Baer, head of the *Bet Din* of Chmelnik (sons-in-law of R. Jacob Joseph) wrote, "Because of our preoccupation with the printing we have not been able to acquire encomiums from the great scholars of the land. But we are certain that all of them would give their assent to this precious book."

The preface of the Korzec edition was omitted from later editions.

S. H. Dresner, *The Tzaddik.*

TORAH – In explaining the concept of the Torah, hasidic masters built largely on the systematic framework developed by earlier Jewish teachers and kabbalists. God's purpose in creation has been to bestow goodness on the world. But in order that this goodness be perfect, it could not be given as a free gift. Rather, it would have to be earned.

In the teachings of the Besht, the visible Torah is only the body, whereas the soul of the Torah permeates the entire structure of the spiritual cosmos. The true Torah is hidden and clothed in stories and commandments, but in the world to come, its intrinsic nature will be revealed. The Torah served as a blueprint for all creation. The Torah is tantamount to God's palace, and through it one can explore His treasures. The Besht told the following parable.

> A king once sent his son to a faraway land in order that he would later have all the more enjoyment from him. With the passage of time, the royal prince forgot all the delights of the palace. When the king sent for him, he did not want to return.
>
> The king sent many nobles to try to convince his son to come back, but it was to no avail. Finally, a wise man undertook the task. He changed his speech and clothing and brought himself down to the son's present level. He was thus able to meet the son on his own level, and he eventually brought him back to his father, the king. It is for this reason that the Torah is clothed in physical concepts and stories. (*Keter Shem Tov*, 144)

In his *Degel Mahaneh Efraim*, the Besht's grandson states:

> Just as human beings have 248 limbs and 365 veins and nerves, so the Torah has 248 positive commandments and 365

negative commandments (*Makkot* 24a). Every commandment thus parallels a particular limb in the body. The life force of each limb comes from the source of that particular commandment. The life force of a person as a whole, therefore, comes from the Torah as a whole. (*HaAzinu* 77c)

R. Dov Baer, the Maggid of Mezhirech, taught that it is only through the physical letters of the Torah that God can be comprehended by humanity. As a whole, the Torah is greater than the entire universe. And even the stories found in the Torah are eternal (*Imrei Tzaddikim* 75).

R. Jacob Yitzhak, the "Seer" of Lublin, quotes the Maggid as saying that there are two kinds of evil urges: the first one fires us to sin, and the other cools us and prevents us from doing good. The Torah is likened both to a fire, which inspires us to do good, and to water, which quenches the flames of sin (*Zikhron Zot* 60).

In the writings of R. Levi Yitzhak of Berdichev, we find that the Oral (or Unwritten) Torah contains all the expressions (of the written Torah). The main concept of the Unwritten Torah is that it was given through that which the righteous of each generation expound in the Torah. Through these innovations in Torah, all universes are directed. Our sages thus teach that "God makes a decree and a righteous person can nullify it" (*Kedushat Levi*, p. 134).

R. Menahem Mendel of Vitebsk taught that the Torah is the ultimate concept of freedom. It is written that the tablets were the work of God, and the writing was the writing of God, engraved on the tablets (*Exodus* 32:16). Our sages say, "Do not read 'engraved' (*harut*), but 'free' " (*herut*) (*Erubin* 54a). The Torah implies two types of freedom: "freedom from the Angel of Death and freedom from the subjugation of government" (*Likkutei Amarim* 5b).

According to *Habad* the Torah is the garment of the soul. Even though these are called garments for the soul, they are really infinitely higher than the soul. The *Zohar* teaches us that "the Torah and God are both one." The Torah is the wisdom and the will of God (*Tanya* 4).

A similar concept is found in the writings of R. Elimelekh of Lejask. All of God's attributes are placed in the Torah, and, therefore, the *tzaddikim* can make use of the Torah to achieve these attributes and to perform miracles. When a righteous one studies the Torah for its own sake, that individual brings the Creator into the letters of the Torah just as He was at the time of creation (*Noam Elimelekh, VaYera* 8a).

But if the world was created for the sake of the Torah, why was it not given to the Patriarchs or other early generations? R. Abraham Joshua Heschel of Opatov explains that it could not have been given to earlier generations, because they were not ready for it (*Ohev Yisrael* 36b).

R. Menahem Mendel of Kotzk summed up a basic philosophy in these words: there are many paths to God, but the path of the Torah is the safest (*Emet VeEmunah* 12). His disciple R. Yitzhak Meir of Ger declared that the Torah is Israel's lifeline, and if you let it go, Israel will be drowned in the frivolities of this world (*Siah Sarfei Kodesh* 3:40).

A. Kaplan, *The Light Beyond*, pp. 158–172.

A.K.

TORNHEIM, Issachar Dov Hakohen, Walborz (1801–2 *Heshvan* 1887)– Son of R. Abraham Tzvi, who died when Issachar was ten years old. He married Esther Malkah, the daughter of R. Abraham Tzvi of Walborz. He was a disciple of R. Uri of Strelisk, R. Issachar Dov of Radoszyce, and R. Eliezer Hofstein of Kozienice. He became rebbe on 26 *Kislev* 1862 and settled in Piotrokov.

He officiated at the reader's desk at every service on weekdays and on the Sabbath. On Friday night, he studied twenty-four chapters of the *Mishnah Shabbat* before reciting *Kiddush* at midnight. His Sabbath table was set with silver utensils: "Just as one honors the Sabbath in this world, so will one be honored in the hereafter."

He was the author of a commentary on the Pentateuch, *Avodat Yissakhar* (Lodz, 1912). He also wrote a commentary on the tractate *Niddah*, which was lost.

He was succeeded by his son R. Jacob Moses, who died on 14 *Kislev* 1918. His other son, R. Akiba Meir (1843–1 *Heshvan* 1909), became rebbe in 1897.

TREBLINKA–Nazi extermination camp, situated sixty-two miles (ninety-nine kilometers) northeast of Warsaw. Between 1942 and October 1943, a total of 870,000

Jews were gassed there. Mass expulsion of the Jews from Warsaw began on June 22, 1942.

Among the hasidic rabbis who perished there were R. Yitzhak Menahem Dancyger of Alexander together with his seven sons-in-law; R. Moses Bezalel Alter, the brother of the rabbi of Ger; R. Hayyim Yerahmiel Taub, rabbi of Zwolen; R. Israel Shapira of Grodzisk; R. Nathan Nahum Rabinowicz of Krimlov; R. Jacob Dan of Strykov; and R. Hanokh Gad Justman of Pilice.

TROKENHEIM, Jacob (1888–1943), communal worker – Son of R. Feivel, a devoted hasid of Ger, he was born in Warsaw. He married the daughter of Israel Kesztenbaum of Lublin. He was an active Aguda worker, a member of the municipality of Warsaw from 1919 to 1939, a senator from 1935 to 1937, and a member of the Polish Seym from 1937. During World War II, he escaped to Vilna but returned to Warsaw, whence he was deported to Maidanek.

Elleh Ezkerah, vol. 1, pp. 268–277.

TRUNK, Israel Joshua (1820–1893), halakhist – "R. Yoshuale," as he was popularly known, was born in Plock, Poland, and served as a rabbi of Szrensk, Gabin, Warka, Pultusk, and, from 1861, Kutno. He was in close touch with R. Yitzhak Meir of Ger and R. Abraham Bornstein of Sochaczev. He was opposed to R. Gershon Leiner's reintroduction of *Tekhelet*: "If the majority do not accept it," he said, "I follow the majority."

Hasidic rabbis such as R. Jacob Aryeh Guterman of Radzymin and R. Yehiel Dancyger of Alexander consulted with him on halakhic matters. He permitted agricultural work during the Sabbatical year in the Holy Land. He supported the *Hibbat Zion* movement and visited the Holy Land in 1885. He refused to become a rebbe, referring the petitioners to R. Yehiel Meir Lipshitz of Gostynin.

He was the author of *Yeshuot Yisrael* on the *Shulhan Arukh Hoshen Mishpat* (1870) and *Yeshuot Malko* (1927–1939).

His son, R. Moses Pinhas, married a granddaughter of R. Yitzhak Kalish of Warka.

A. Y. Bromberg, *HaGeonim Mikutno Berzan VeChebin*, vol. 21.

TRUTH – Truth (*emet*) in hasidic thought is more a moral than an intellectual virtue, denoting especially self-knowledge; lack of sham and hypocrisy in religious life; and complete sincerity in the service of God without any ulterior motives (*piniyot*, lit., "turnings aside," i.e., of the heart, from God). The cultivation of this virtue is demanded by the hasidic emphasis on *Torah lishmah* (Torah for its own sake), the ideal of directing the mind solely to God when studying the Torah and practicing the *mitzvot*. To do these things with the aim of winning a reputation for piety and learning is for Hasidism a gross caricature and a species of idolatry that sets up a barrier between the human and the divine and so encourages the heretcal view that we and the world can enjoy an existence independent of God.

When the letter *alef*, the first letter of the alphabet, representing the One, states R. Jacob Joseph of Polonnoye, is added to the word *met* (dead), the new word formed is *emet*. Falsehood is spiritual death, but God is present when truth is present (*Toldot*, *Va-Yehi*). Only through the unqualified pursuit of truth can we attain to *hokhmah* (wisdom) (*Degel Mahaneh Efraim*, *Bereshit*). The letters of the word *kahash* (lies) are the same as those of *hoshekh* (darkness), but whoever is attached to truth in the innermost parts is attached to the light through which we see light (*Toldot*, *Bo*).

If one is honest and true in business affairs, one draws down into these activities the "seal of the Holy One, blessed be He," namely, truth, and by so doing one rescues the holy sparks inherent in all worldly things and restores them to their source (*Ma'or VaShemesh*, *VaYetzei*). The worst of all evil traits is falsehood, because falsehood pollutes the good and produces an imbalance, whereas the teller of truth automatically realizes the good and becomes a chariot for the *Shekhinah* (*Noam Elimelekh*, *Terumah*). Truth is the gateway to faith. It is impossible for us to have real and strong faith in God if we are guilty of insincerity whether in thought or in emotions or even through a sham posture (*Maor VaShemesh*, *Sukkot*).

A number of hasidic masters were noted for their ruthless pursuit after total integrity. The early master R. Pinhas of Koretz was renowned for this quality. When we worship God in sincerity, said R. Pinhas, everyone knows of it, hide it though we may, just as the insincere are eventually exposed to ridicule (*Midrash Pinhas* [Jerusalem, 1971], no. 33, p. 19b).

If we fool others, we are aware of our fault, but how can we avoid fooling ourselves that we are righteous when our attempts to overcome the falsehood within us are themselves tainted? R. Pinhas replies that when we really try to lead a life of integrity, God endows us with the power to acknowledge the truth (*Midrash Pinhas*, no. 4, p. 37a).

R. Nahman of Bratzlav was another master famed for his constant quest for truth. Among this teacher's sayings on truth (*Sefer HaMiddot* [Warsaw, 1912], s.v. *emet*, pp. 13–16) are "It is better to die than to live a lie," "Where there is truth there is peace," "He that is far from truth is far from charity," and "Through falsehood God is forgotten."

Of all the hasidic masters, R. Menahem Mendel of Kotzk stressed the need for truth so that he is known among the hasidim as "the pillar of truth." The hasidim of Kotzk in their concern to eradicate every trace of self-esteem and in their complete disregard of public opinion, both of which they saw as obstacles to the attainment of religious sincerity, would speak curtly to one another and to strangers and tended to view all respectability as bogus. It is said that whereas normally, people do good openly and practice their vices in secret, the hasidim of Kotzk would parade their sins and do good in stealth. R. Menahem Mendel of Kotzk said, It is written: "You shall therefore lay up these words of Mine *upon* your heart" (Deuteronomy 11:18). The verse does not say "*in* your heart," for how could truth penetrate hearts that were blocked and ossified? The truth, observed Menahem Mendel, should be like a stone *upon* the heart, and then eventually, the truth would enter. Interpreting a well-known Midrash about God's casting down truth to the earth, Menahem Mendel believed that from the moment humankind was created, truth got buried in the grave.

The human situation is itself a condition of falsehood, yet deep in every human soul there is a longing to embrace the truth. We must live with this tension but never surrender our quest for truth. Even religious people, even many of the *tzaddikim*, taught Menahem Mendel, prefer to live in a world of illusion, cushioned from truth by religious palliatives and religious promises of reward and comfort. Constant self-scrutiny is essential if the prayer of the psalmist is to be answered: "Create in me a clean heart, O God; put a new and right spirit within me (Psalm 51:12).

A. J. Heschel, *A Passion for Truth: Reflections on the Founder of Hasidism, the Kotzker and Kierkegaard.*

L.J.

TWELVE HALLOT (twelve Sabbath loaves)—It was customary among hasidim, especially among rebbes, to have twelve *hallot* at the Sabbath meal. The *hallot* were arranged in a certain order. The custom was derived from a practice by R. Isaac Luria, which in turn had its roots in the *Tikkunei Zohar*. In some localities it was customary to bake one big *hallah*, which consisted of twelve sections.

The obvious explanation for the custom is that that it commemorated the twelve show breads that were set before the Lord in the sanctuary every Sabbath (Leviticus 24:5–8). However, there are also kabbalistic explanations.

At the *tish*, after having broken the *hallah*, the rebbe would distribute pieces among his hasidim, who treasured them as *segullot* (good luck charms). In the rabbinic responsa literature, the question was discussed whether, at Passover time, *hallot* that were kept as charms were to be regarded as outright *hametz* and therefore had to be destroyed or whether it was sufficient to sell them for the Passover period.

A. Wertheim, *Halakhot VeHalikhot BaHasidut*, pp. 150–151.

T.P.

TWERSKY, Aaron, of Chernobyl (1787–1 *Kislev* 1871)—Eldest son of R. Mordecai of Chernobyl, he was renowned from his youth for his piety. He was brought up by his grandfather R. Nahum. In 1839, he succeeded his father as rebbe. He was also *gabbai* for collection of funds for the Holy Land and was involved in a controversy with his brother, R. Jacob Israel of Cherkassy, concerning the presidency of the *kollel*, which ended in his favor. He married the daughter of R. Gedaliah of Linitz, and when she died, he married Simah Husha, the daughter of R. Aaron of Kitov, a descendant of the Besht.

He based his discourses on his grandfather's teachings and on the commentary *Or HaHayyim* by R. Hayyim ben Moses Attar. He once wrote in a letter, "Even if they [his hasidim] live as long as Methuselah, they will never realize even a thousandth part of the good I—with God's help—have bestowed on them."

His sons were R. Zusya of Chernobyl, R. Menahem Nahum of Leove, and R. Barukh Asher of Azarnitz. He had two daughters: Sarah, who married R. Israel, the grandson of R. Nahman of Bratzlav, and Feigel, who married R. David Moses of Chortkov.

Sefer Besht, pp. 369–380.

TWERSKY, Aaron Elimelekh Shneur Zalman, of Krasnoye (23 *Tishri* 1884–19 *Heshvan* 1924)—Son of R. Mordecai Dov of Hornistopol, he married Rosa, the daughter of R. Moses Horowitz of Rozvadov. He was rebbe for twenty-seven years in Igentruvka, and from 1908 in Krasnoye, in Galicia.

He died in Cracow and was succeeded by his son, R. Moses.

TWERSKY, Abraham, of Turiysk (1806–2 *Tammuz* 1889) the Maggid of Turiysk—Son of R. Mordecai of Chernobyl, he was known as the "Maggid of Trisk." He married Rikel, the daughter of R. Jacob Aryeh of Kowel (d. 27 *Elul* 1837).

R. Abraham lived in a sumptuous manner. Among his many followers were R. Jacob Tzvi of Parysov, R. Elimelekh of Grodzisk, R. Yehiel of Alexander, and R. Jacob Yitzhak of Biala. He regarded all his visitors as his guests and entertained them at his own expense.

He was the author of *Magen Avraham* on the Pentateuch (Zhitomir, 1887), which was reprinted in Warsaw in 1903 and in Jerusalem in 1964 and 1974. In this commentary on the Pentateuch and Festivals, he shows the influence of R. Samson ben Pesah of Ostropol, and he quotes R. Nathan Nata Shapira and R. Pinhas of Korets. He was fascinated by *gematria* and numerology.

During the reign of Nicholas I, he was imprisoned for a short time on a charge of sedition. He was an implacable opponent of *Haskalah*, especially of Abraham Kupernik (1821–1892), the founder of the Society for Promotion of Culture among the Jews of Russia.

He had six daughters and three sons: R. Menahem Nahum of Brest-Litovsk, who died in his father's lifetime, on 4 *Shevat* 1887; R. Mordecai of Kaziemierz; and R. Jacob Aryeh of Trisk.

A. D. Twerski, *Sefer HaYahas MiChernobyl VeRuzhin*, chaps. 10 and 12.

TWERSKY, Abraham Joshua Heschel, of Skvira (1826–3 *Kislev* 1886)—Son of R. Yitzhak of Skvira, he married Havah, the daughter of R. Yitzhak Meir of Zinkov. When she died, he married the daughter of R. Joseph Zilberfarb of Toporov. He became rebbe while his father was still alive.

His sons were R. Joseph Meir, R. Jacob, R. Moses Dan, and R. David. His daughters were Malkah, who married R. Mordecai Joseph of Zlatapol, and Shifra, who married R. David Twersky of Rotmistrovka.

TWERSKY, Abraham Joshua Heschel, of Tel Aviv (1894–10 *Tishri* 1987)—Son of R. Joseph Meir (1857–1917), he was born in Skvira and married Havah, the daughter of R. David Aaron Twersky. The family was persecuted by the *Yevsektsiya* (the Jewish branch of the Communist Party). He was exiled and spent several years in Siberian labor camps. From 1958 to 1968 he lived in Moscow.

He was one of the last rebbes to leave the Soviet Union. He claimed to have a Torah scroll that had belonged to the Besht. Unlike most hasidim, the rebbe did not chant *Lekhah Dodi* but merely recited it. He was deeply concerned with the plight of the new immigrants from Eastern Europe, many of whom would visit him in Bene Berak, where he was known not only as the rebbe of Makhanovka but also as the "rebbe of the proletariat."

He was succeeded by his sister's grandson, R. Joshua Rokeah.

TWERSKY, Abraham Yitzhak, (b. 1903) of London/New York—Son of R. Moses Mordecai, he was born in Turiysk. In 1924, he married Shifra, the daughter of R. Alter Israel Shimon Perlow of Novominsk. He became attached to R. Meir Shapira and undertook, on his behalf, fund-raising missions in France and England. While on a visit to London, he was appointed rabbi of the Sphardishe Synagogue in the East End of London.

He was active in the *Keren HaTorah* and the Federation of Jewish Relief Organizations. He was also the editor of *Jewish Weekly* (*Die Wochenzeitung*) and was deeply involved in the work of the Aguda and the Union of Orthodox Hebrew Congregations.

After World War II, he settled in the United States, where he was joined by his brother, R. Barukh Meir (1913–1981), who had spent the war years in London and later became public relations officer of the Rabbinical Council of America.

TWERSKY, Barukh Asher (d. 22 *Sivan* 1905)–Third son of R. Aaron of Chernobyl, he married the daughter of R. Moses Twersky of Korostychev. He was a great Torah scholar and corresponded with many rabbis, including R. Mordecai Dov Twersky of Hornistopol.

His son R. Shlomoh Shmuel (1856–29 *Adar* 1935) married his cousin, the daughter of R. Isaiah Meshullam Zusya Twersky, the rabbi of Chernobyl. In 1934, he went to the United States and settled in Borough Park, Brooklyn.

He was succeeded by his son R. Jacob Israel Twersky (1902–8 *Kislev* 1983).

A.Shu.

TWERSKY, Barukh Benzion (1870–22 *Elul* 1945)–Son of R. Aaron, he married the daughter of R. Eliezer Ingerleib of Ustilug. He was persecuted by the Communist authorities, settled in the United States in 1924, and established a congregation *Bet Aharon* in Pittsburgh. A few years later, he moved to Brownsville, Brooklyn.

His son, R. Menahem Nahum Joseph (1889–8 *Sivan* 1973), succeeded his father-in-law, R. Abraham David Kaufman of Miropol, in his father's lifetime. In 1928, R. Menahem went to the United States and became the Loyev-Miropoler rebbe in Chelsea, Massachusetts. He went to Israel in 1963 and lived in Jerusalem for one year. He then returned to Chelsea.

A.Shu.

TWERSKY, Barukh Meir, of Azarnitz (d. 5 *Iyyar* 1911)–Son of R. Menahem Nahum of Leove, he married the daughter of R. Abraham Joshua Heschel of Lutschinez. He had three sons–R. Aaron of Kishinev, R. Mordecai Israel of Hotin, Romania, and R. Yitzhak of Bielynitz–and three daughters–Feigele, who married R. Alter Israel Shimon Perlow of Novominsk, Malkah, who married R. Moses Mordecai Twersky of Lublin, and Perl, who married R. Gedaliah of Monastyrhchina.

TWERSKY, Benzion Judah Leib, of Hornistopol (1867–28 *Tevet* 1951)–Third son of R. Mordecai Dov, Benzion married the daughter of R. Yitzhak Yoel Rabinowitz of Kantikoziva. He first lived in Hornistopol, then in Kiev. Following both the communist revolution and the typhus epidemic in 1920, he left Russia and settled in Cracow. In 1925, he moved to Antwerp and established his court on Provincie Straat.

In 1934, he emigrated to Israel and lived in Tel Aviv. He was always a lover of the Land of Israel and had previously visited it in 1914 with the intention of establishing a hasidic settlement there, but as a Russian citizen, he had been forced to return to Russia.

While visiting Jerusalem in 1936, he published his father's work *Turei Zahav*. Caught up in Europe at the outbreak of World War Two, he managed to escape to the United States and founded a congregation *Bene Yehudah* in Chicago.

A.Shu.

TWERSKY, David, of Kiev (d. 15 *Kislev* 1919)–Son of R. Yitzhak of Skvira, he married the daughter of R. Shlomoh Wertheim of Savran. When she died, he married the daughter of R. Elikum Getz of Ostrog. He was known as a diligent student, and once a month he would conclude the six orders of the *Mishnah*.

His sons were R. Mordecai of Skvira, R. Moses, R. Aaron, R. Shlomoh, R. Yitzhak, and R. Nahum and R. Jacob Joseph, who were rabbis of Skvira in New York.

TWERSKY, David, of Talnoye (1808–10 *Iyyar* 1882)–Son of R. Mordecai, he was born in Chernobyl. He lived first in Wasilkov for fifteen years, where he suffered much from his opponents. He later moved to Talnoye. When his father died, unlike his brothers he did not become a rebbe, but in deference to his mother, gave his allegiance to his elder brother at first. He married the daughter of R. Israel Abraham, a descendant of R. Zusya of Annopol.

Like all rebbes of Ruzhyn and Sadgora, he lived in luxury, with many servants to attend him in his palatial residence. He even owned a golden throne, inscribed with the words *David Melekh Yisrael Hai VeKayom* (David King of Israel lives forever).

At one time he was briefly imprisoned by the Russian authorities, having been accused of sedition. He loved music and encouraged musicians to become part of his entourage. He especially befriended the cantor Nisan Belzer. He was tolerant and long-suffering. Once, an opponent hurled a stone at him; the rabbi kept the stone among his treasures.

He was the author of *Birkat David* (Zhitomir, 1862, reprinted in Jerusalem in 1967), *Magen David* (Zhitomir, 1852; Lublin, 1873; Lvov, 1880; Tel Aviv, 1960; Jerusalem, 1974), and *Kehillat David* on Torah and Festivals (Lublin, 1881; Jerusalem, 1974).

He was succeeded by his only son, R. Mordecai.

A. D. Twerski, *Sefer HaYahas MiChernobyl VeRuzhyn*, p. 62.

TWERSKY, David Mordecai, of Talnoye/New York (1888–17 *Tishri* 1956)—Son of R. Menahem Nahum, his mother, Simah, was the daughter of R. Moses of Savran. He was ordained by R. Yitzhak Yeruhem Diskin of Talnoye. He married, in 1903, Havah, the daughter of R. Shlomoh Zelmina Zuckerman of Rashkov, a descendant of R. Abraham Joshua Heschel of Opatov.

He became rabbi in Tulchin. In 1913, he emigrated to the United States and set up a congregation *Kehal hasidim* on the Lower East Side of Manhattan. He was active in the *Agudat HaAdmorim*, the Mizrachi, and the Central Relief Organization.

He was succeeded by his son R. Yohanan, who was rebbe in Jerusalem.

Toldot Anshei Shem, p. 27.

A.Shu.

TWERSKY, Eleazar, of New York (25 *Tishri* 1893–1 *Tammuz* 1976)—Son of R. Shlomoh of Skvira, he was born in Belz. His mother, Feiga, was the daughter of R. Aryeh Leib Rokeah. In 1910, he married Rifka Rachel, the daughter of R. Meir Moskovitz of Shatz (Sulitza). In 1920, he became rebbe of Skvira in Palatshin, Romania. After spending the Second World War in Bucharest, he emigrated, in 1949, to the United States and settled in Borough Park, Brooklyn.

He visited the Holy Land in 1961. He was the author of a tract *Tiferet Eleazar* (Brooklyn, 1984). He left a will that said he should not be eulogized, nor should the title "Righteous" (*tzaddik*) be inscribed on his gravestone. No *ohel* was erected over his grave.

His son, R. Abraham, succeeded him (1912–13 *Shevat* 1984). He, in turn, was succeeded by his son, R. Shalom Meir.

TWERSKY, Gedaliah, of Malin (1828–22 *Nisan* 1909)—Son of R. Israel, he was only one year old when his father died. He was raised and tutored by his maternal grandfather, R. Aaron of Chernobyl, and he adopted the surname Twersky. He became rabbi in Malin.

His son, R. Shalom (1891–6 *Iyyar* 1970), was rebbe in Kiev. He spent the war years in Siberia. His wife and family perished in Babi Yar. He came to the United States in 1946 and lived in Los Angeles. In 1963, he relocated to Haifa, Israel.

His son R. Abraham Joshua Heschel married the daughter of R. Tzvi Rokeah of Olesko and became rabbi in Radomysl. He was murdered on 25 *Iyyar* 1919, during the Petlura pogroms, which were then rampant throughout the Ukraine. Another of R. Gedaliah's sons was R. Mordecai Israel (d. 22 *Elul* 1911). He succeeded his father-in-law, R. Yitzhak Kuten of Stanislav.

A.Shu.

TWERSKY, Hannah Havah (Nineteenth century)—Daughter of R. Mordecai Twersky of Chernobyl (1770–1837). Her father testified that she was endowed with a holy spirit from the womb and from birth. He deemed her equal in piety to his sons, the "eight candles of the *menorah*."

Her aphorisms and parables spread her fame throughout Poland. She dealt tenderly and tirelessly with the women who flocked to her for guidance. She emphasized the importance of correct and careful education and urged her followers to be charitable in every way.

TWERSKY, Hanokh Heinokh Dov, of Chicago (1886–22 *Elul* 1971) – Son of R. Abraham Joshua Heschel of Radomysl, he was born in Olesko, Galicia. He married, in 1911, Havah Hannah, the daughter of R. Joseph Jerusalimsky, the rebbe of Koretz, who lived in Kishinev. From 1914 to 1918 he was rabbi in Radomysl, and when his father was murdered in 1919, he became rabbi in Malin.

In 1924, he went to the United States and established a congregation *Lev Someah* in Chicago. He published his grandfather's prayer book *Lev Someah*.

In 1967, he settled in Bayit V'Gan, Jerusalem.

Toldot Anshei Shem, p. 54.

A.Shu.

TWERSKY, Hayyim Yitzhak (1866–24 *Nisan* 1943) – Son of R. Abraham Joshua Heschel, he was born in Leove. He married Rachel Devorah, the eldest daughter of R. Yitzhak Yeshayah Halberstam. In 1897, he succeeded his father. From 1923 he lived in Kiev.

His religious activities caused him to be exiled to Siberia in 1937. There he died as a result of going on hunger strike, having refused to eat *hametz* throughout Passover.

His son, R. Meshullam Zusya, was rabbi of Chernobyl in Bene Berak.

TWERSKY, Isadore (b. 1930) – Son of R. Meshullam Zusya (d. 1972), he was born in Boston and was educated at the Rabbi Isaac Elhanan Theological Seminary Yeshiva University), where he received a rabbinical diploma, and at Harvard University, where he studied under Prof. Harry Woolfson. From 1956, he was professor of Hebrew literature and philosophy.

He is the author of *Rabad of Posquieres, a 12th-Century Talmudist* (1962) and *Maimonides Reader* (1969).

In his father's lifetime, he served as assistant rabbi of the *Talner Bet Hamidrash Tzemah David*. Without actually becoming a rebbe, he performed the functions of a rebbe. He married the daughter of the late R. Joseph B. Soloveichik.

Z.A.

TWERSKY, Isaiah Meshullam Zusya (d. 28 *Tammuz* 1881) – Second son of R. Aaron, he married the daughter of R. Tzvi of Titov and was rebbe in Chernobyl. His son, R. Shlomoh Benzion (1870–8 *Tishri* 1939), married the daughter of R. Zalman Choderov and became rebbe at the age of thirteen. He was called the *Yanukkah* (child) of Chernobyl.

After World War One, he visited the United States but, discouraged by its lack of Orthodoxy, returned to the Soviet Union and spent the remainder of his life in Kiev.

A.Shu.

TWERSKY, Israel, of Kozienice/ Brooklyn (1900–9 *Shevat* 1954) – Son of R. Shlomoh Hakohen Schwartz, he served as a *gabbai* to the rebbe of Kozienice. He arrived in the United States in 1924 and became Kozienicer rebbe in congregation *Kerem Yisrael* in Crown Heights, Brooklyn. He was the author of kabbalistic sermons, *Einei Yisrael* (New York, 1936).

A.Shu.

TWERSKY, Jacob Aryeh, of London (9 *Av* 1895–21 *Tishri* 1979) – Son of R. Mordecai Zusya (d. 1937), rabbi of Iasi, he was born in Turiysk. Between 1917 and 1923, he lived under Soviet rule in Odessa and then in Kamenetz-Podolsk. He befriended a Russian general who helped him to escape first to Husyatin and then to Lvov.

After living in Warsaw, Berlin, Vienna, and Antwerp, he was, in 1923, the first hasidic rebbe to settle in London. He made his home first in the East End of London and then in North-East London. He welcomed everyone with warmth and affection. His melodious voice attracted even nonhasidim to his *Bet HaMidrash*.

He refused to send his children to non-Jewish schools – an attitude that encouraged Dr. Avigdor Schonfeld to establish a Jewish day school in London.

In 1964, he emigrated to Bene Berak, Israel. He had three sons and two daughters. His son R. Yitzhak is rebbe in Bene Berak.

TWERSKY, Jacob Aryeh, of Turiysk (d. 28 *Iyyar* 1918) – Son of R. Abraham of Turiysk, he married Feiga, the daughter of R. Yohanan of Rotmistrovka. He inherited from his father a unique collection of ritual objects made of silver and gold. The most cherished of all of these items was a golden

Hanukkah *menorah*: more than 100,000 rubles had to be melted down to make it. Out of the base, an ingenious mechanism brought forth miniature Russian soldiers to chant the hymn *Ma'oz Tzur*. At one time, armed robbers came to Turiysk and stole much of the silver and gold. The *menorah* remained because it was simply too massive to be carried away. It was sent to a central bank in Kiev for safekeeping. Ironically, when the Communists seized power in 1917, the *menorah* was confiscated, eventually disappearing without a trace.

Some time after the robbery, R. Jacob Aryeh left his native Turiysk and moved to Kovel. During the First World War, he wandered from place to place in search of refuge. He lived for a short period of time in Zevil (Novogrod Volinsk) and Rovno.

He died after immersing himself in the ritual bath one Friday and was buried in Hrubieszov. He had four sons and three daughters.

His son R. David (d. 1943) married the daughter of R. Yitzhak Friedman of Bohusi. In 1906, he settled in Zwirk, near Bohusi, where he was known as a miracle worker.

A. D. Twerski, *Sefer HaYahas MiChernobyl VeRuzhyn*, chap. 18.

TWERSKY, Jacob Israel, of Brooklyn (1902–1939) – Son of R. Shlomoh Shmuel, his mother was the daughter of R. Meshullam Zusya of Chernobyl. In 1925, he married a descendant of R. Yeeve. In 1937, he emigrated to the Holy Land, where he lived for two years. When his father died, he returned to live in Brooklyn.

He was succeeded by his son, Shlomoh.

TWERSKY, Jacob Israel, of Cherkassy (1794–13 *Elul* 1876) – Son of R. Mordecai of Chernobyl, his mother, Sarah, was the daughter of R. Aaron of Karlin. His mother died when he was five years old. He married Deborah Leah, the daughter of R. Dov Baer Schneersohn of Liady, where he lived for two years. When his father died in 1828, he returned to Chernobyl.

In 1834, he became rebbe in Hornistopol. He established a *maamadot* (regular contributions to be paid by his hasidim) and gave *kamayot*. He was the president of the *kollel* of Volhynia. He was greatly influenced by *Habad* teachings, and this is reflected in his work *Shoshanat HaAmakim* (Lublin, 1884), which is in two parts: *Emek Tefillah* and *Emek HaHokhmah*.

He had no sons and was succeeded by the son of his daughter, R. Mordecai Dov of Hornistopol.

A. D. Twerski, *Sefer HaYahas MiChernobyl VeRuzhyn*, chap. 26.

TWERSKY, Jacob Israel, of Milwaukee (1905–10 *Av* 1973) – Fifth son of R. Benzion Yehudah Leib, he was born in Hornistopol. In 1922, he married, in Bobov, Devorah Leah, the eldest daughter of R. Benzion Halberstam. After staying some time in Bobov and in Cracow, he emigrated to the United States in 1925, and after serving in a number of congregations in New York, he became the rabbi of congregation *Anshei Sefard* in Milwaukee, Wisconsin. In 1939, he established his own congregation, *Bet Yehudah*. A warmhearted personality, R. Jacob Israel always had his house open to anyone who needed help. He often visited Montreal.

All of his five sons graduated with academic degrees from universities and are, at the same time, rabbinical scholars following hasidic tradition. The eldest son, R. Shlomoh Meshullam Zalman (b. 1923), is a research scholar in Talmud in Denver, where he is also a rebbe. R. Mottel (Mordecai Dov) is a certified public accountant in Brooklyn, New York. R. Abraham Joshua Heschel graduated from medical school in Milwaukee and is now clinical director at St. Francis Psychiatric Hospital in Pittsburgh. R. Aaron David served as a law professor at Hofstra University in Hempstead, New York.

R. Yehiel Michel Twersky (b. 1939) succeeded his father as rabbi in Milwaukee. An alumnus of Lakewood Yeshivah, he studied under R. Aaron Kotler. He married Feiga, the daughter of R. Israel Abraham Stein. He is an active member of the Aguda. He is also a gifted musician and has composed several hasidic songs, one of which – a recording with the title *A Voice on High* – was released in Milwaukee in 1967.

New York Times, July 23, 1978, p. 38.

A.Shu.

TWERSKY, Jacob Joseph, of Skvira (1899–2 *Nisan* 1968) – Born in Skvira, near Kiev, he studied under his father. He married Treine, the daughter of R. Pinhas Twersky, the rebbe of Ustilug, a son-in-law of the rebbe of Belz. He remained in Belz for the first two years of his marriage. His first rabbinic position was in Calarasi, in Bessarabia. He later moved to Iasi, where he remained until 1944. He then stayed in Bucharest until 1948, when he emigrated to the United States.

He arrived in New York on May 10, 1948. In 1961, he founded the townlet of New Square, in Rockland County, New York. He was buried there.

He was succeeded by his only son, R. David Twersky, who is the son-in-law of R. Moses Hager, the rebbe of Vishnitz. He was survived by two daughters—one married to the son of the rebbe of Vishnitz and the other to the son of the Rotmistrovka rebbe.

Jewish Tribune, April 5, 1968.

TWERSKY, Jacob Joseph, of Stanislav (1870–13 *Iyyar* 1931)—Third son of R. Menahem Nahum of Rotmistrovka. He first married the daughter of R. Israel Shalom Joseph of Bohusi. Next he married the daughter of R. Nahum Mordecai Friedman. Last he married Freidel, the daughter of R. Mattathias, the rebbe of Stanislav.

After the death of his father-in-law, he succeeded him as rebbe. During the First World War, he lived in Vienna, was one of the signatories of the *Hevrat Yishuv Eretz Yisrael*, and was associated with the Mizrachi.

He is survived by a son, R. Yohanan.

TWERSKY, Jacob Yitzhak, of New York (1896–2 *Sivan* 1945)—Son of R. Isaiah, a descendant of Chernobyl, he was born in Makarov. His mother was a descendant of R. Hayyim of Zinkov and of R. Abraham Joshua Heschel of Opatov.

In 1923, he married, in Uman, the daughter of R. Joshua Heschel of Monastyrhchina. He succeeded his father as rebbe in Kiev in 1919.

In 1924, he emigrated to the United States and settled in Chicago.

Toldot Anshei Shem, p. 54.

TWERSKY, Judah Leib, of Hornistopol (1868–28 *Tevet* 1951)—Third son of R. Mordecai Dov, he married Rachel, the daughter of R. Yitzhak Yoel, the rebbe of Kowtikozova. He succeeded his father as rebbe on 22 *Elul* 1903. In 1914, he visited the Holy Land and returned two days before the outbreak of the First World War.

After the Russian Revolution, he lived in Kiev, then in Cracow, and eventually in Antwerp. In 1934, he once again visited the Holy Land, where he printed his father's book *Turei Zahav*. He left Belgium just before the Nazi occupation and settled in New York.

His son was R. Nahum Twersky.

TWERSKY, Menahem Nahum (1810–27 *Tevet* 1870)—Elder son of R. Aaron, he married the daughter of R. Israel of Linchinitz. He studied under his father and became rebbe in Leove during his father's lifetime, though he died one year before his father. He was succeeded in Leove by his son R. Mordecai (1845–14 *Kislev* 1910), the son-in-law of R. Shmuel Ashkenazi. Like his father, he studied under R. Aaron.

R. Menahem Nahum's second son, R. Barukh Meir Twersky (d. 5 *Iyyar* 1911), was the son-in-law of R. Abraham Joshua Heschel of Linchinitz. He became rabbi of Azarnitz (Nazarinitz).

R. Menahem Nahum was succeeded by his son R. Yitzhak (d. 4 *Kislev* 1940). He served as a rebbe in Beltsy in Bessarabia. During the Second World War, R. Yitzhak was taken to Abadovka, a village in Transnistria, where he perished. His son R. Aaron (d. 1941) was rebbe in Kishinev. His other son, R. Mordecai Israel (1880–1941), became rebbe in Mohilev. He married Batsheva, the daughter of R. Abraham Joshua Heschel of Hodorov. In 1920, he moved to Hotin in Bessarabia. He was murdered on 15 *Tammuz* 1941. His son, R. Jacob Twersky, survived the Holocaust; married Pearl, the daughter of R. Heschel, the Kopyczynicer rebbe in New York; and is now rabbi in Park East Jewish Center in the Bronx. He has two sons and one daughter.

R. Mordecai Israel's daughter, Malkale (d. 1983), married R. Aaron (d. 5 *Tevet* 1963), the son of R. Alter Israel Shimon Perlow of Novominsk.

A.Shu.

TWERSKY, Meshullam Zusya (1893–25 *Iyyar* 1972)—Son of R. Menahem Nahum, he married the daughter of R. Isaiah Bronstein, a rabbi in Bessarabia. He settled in the United States in 1924 and was the rabbi of congregation *Bet David*, in Roxbury, Massachusetts. He then moved to nearby Brookline.

After his death, his son, Isadore Twersky, continued the leadership of the congregation.

A.Shu.

TWERSKY, Meshullam Zusya, of Bene Berak (1917–17 *Heshvan* 1988)–Born in Musir, near Kiev, the son of R. Hayyim Yitzhak of Leove. Most of his early studies were done secretly at the Lubavitch *yeshivah* in Russia. In 1934, he emigrated to the Holy Land, where he was befriended by R. Menahem Nahum of Rotmistrovka and his brother, R. Zeev.

In 1936, he returned to Poland to study under his grandfather R. Yitzhak Yeshayah of Czechov. In 1939, he returned to the Holy Land. He married the daughter of R. Jacob Mordecai Brandwein, a descendant of Zloczov. His father died in Siberia on 24 *Nisan* 1943, and his mother was killed by the Nazis.

For eighteen years (1941–1959) he lived in Jerusalem and then settled in Bene Berak. He established a *kollel*, *Zikhron Kedoshim*; a Talmud Torah, *Bene Aharaon*; and a *yeshivah*.

He was buried in Bene Berak. His son, R. Menahem Nahum, succeeded him.

TWERSKY, Mordecai, of Chernobyl (1770–20 *Iyyar* 1837)–Known as "Reb Mottele," he was the son of R. Nahum of Chernobyl. He married *Hayyah* Sarah, the daughter of R. Aaron the Great of Karlin. When she died, he married the daughter of R. David Leikis, a disciple of the Besht.

R. Mottel lived in regal style, *maamadot* (financial contributions) were leveled on his hasidim to maintain his court, and emissaries were dispatched at regular intervals to collect the dues. He studied under his father.

He was the author of *Likkutei Torah* (Lvov, 1862), which was endorsed by R. Abraham Jacob of Sadgora and R. Hayyim Halberstam of Zanz. "A man, wearing his *tallit* and *tefillin*, should study this book every day," wrote R. Hayyim.

He was in favor of a comprehensive curriculum that included Bible, *Mishnah*, Talmud, *Zohar*, *Reshit Hokhmah*, *Ein Yaakov*, and *Shulhan Arukh*.

He died in Annotovka, near Kiev. Each one of his eight sons established a separate court in Russia: R. Aaron in Chernobyl, R. Moses in Korostyshev, R. Jacob Israel in Cherkassy, R. Nahum in Makarov, R. Abraham in Turiysk, R. David in Talnoye, R. Yitzhak in Skvira, and R. Yohanan in Rotmistrovka.

A. D. Twerski, *Sefer HaYahas MiChernobyl VeRuzhyn*.

TWERSKY, Mordecai, of Rotmistrovka (1840–17 *Iyyar* 1920)–Second son of R. Yohanan, he married the daughter of R. David of Talnoye. In 1905, he settled in Jerusalem. He was interested in art, and his home was a treasure trove of art objects.

On *Hol HaMo'ed* Passover, he was attacked by Arabs on his way to the Western Wall and died two months later.

TWERSKY, Mordecai Dov, of Hornistopol (29 *Kislev* 1840–22 *Elul* 1903)–He was born in Hornistopol, the son R. Meshullam Zusya. His mother, Sterna Rachel, the daughter of R. Jacob Israel of Cherkassy, died when he was six years old. He and his two sisters were sent by his father (who had remarried) to live with their maternal grandfather.

A child prodigy, he became a master of Talmud and Kabbalah. In 1855, in Husyatin, he married Reiza, the daughter of R. Hayyim Halberstam. He studied there with R. Naftali Halberstam, the grandson of his father-in-law, and with his brother-in-law, R. Joseph of Linitz. In 1860, when R. Jacob Israel left Hornistopol for Cherkassy after twenty-six years of service in that town, R. Mordecai Dov, in 1873, assumed the position of rebbe there. He also traveled to various other communities to visit his hasidim.

He was the president of the *kollel Volhynia*, a position previously held by his grandfather. He corresponded with many halakhic authorities, such as R. Joseph Saul Nathanson of Lvov; R. Yitzhak Aaron Ettinger of Przemysl; R. Hayyim Berlin; R. Rafael Shapira of Volozhin; R. Hayyim Halberstam, his father-in-law; R. Rafael Shapira; and R. Joshua Leib Diskin of Jerusalem.

His responsa, which total about 184, were published posthumously under the title *Emek*

She'elah (Piotrokov, 1906; Tel Aviv, 1961; New York, 1975). They deal with problems on the four codes of the *Shulhan Arukh*. He was also the author of *Hibur LeTaharah* (Berdichev, 1898; New York, 1975) on the laws of ritual washing and on *mikvaot*. His *Turei Zahav* (Jerusalem, 1936 and 1969) is a commentary on the laws of interest as codified in the *Shulkhan Arukh, Yoreh De'ah*. He also wrote *Pele Yoetz* (Tel Aviv, 1970)–discourses on Genesis, Exodus, Hanukkah, and Purim. Another book, *Emek HaHokhmah*–on the weekly portions of the Torah, discourses on the completion of the Talmud, dedication of a *Bet HaMidrash*, and eulogies–was published together with those of R. Jacob Israel *Emek HaTefillah* under the title *Shoshanat HaAmakim* (Lublin, 1884; Satmar, 1928; Jerusalem, 1928).

The manuscripts of two of his unpublished works–*Kad HaZahav* on Kabbalah and a treatise on the laws pertaining to the names of divorce bills–were destroyed. The first one was lost in a fire that burned down his house and *Bet HaMidrash* on 7 *Sivan* 1882, and the second one in a pogrom in 1918–1919.

All of his sons became hasidic rebbes in different cities: R. Aaron Elimelekh Shneur Zalman in Krasnoe, Galicia; R. Hayyim Moses Tzvi (9 *Adar* 1866–20 *Kislev* 1934), who succeeded his father-in-law in Rotmistrovka; and the youngest son, R. Barukh David (1875–26 *Kislev* 1926), who was rebbe in Kalinkovichi in White Russia and whose discourses were published in *Ve-Yevarekh David*.

A. Y. Bromberg, *Admorim L'Bet Zanz*, vol. 9, pp. 86–149.

A. Surasky, *Marbitzei Torah M'Olam HaHasidut*, vol. 2, pp. 21–62.

A.Shu.

TWERSKY, Moses (1895–1943)–Son of R. Aaron Elimelekh Shneur Zalman, the rebbe of Krasnoe, whom he succeeded in 1924. He married Freida, the daughter of R. Ezekiel Hakohen Rabinowitz of Radomsk.

In 1942, he was living in Lvov, where he and his family were murdered.

TWERSKY, Moses Meshullam Zusya (1892–5 *Shevat* 1920)–Son of R. Benzion Yehudah Leib, he married the daughter of R. Simhah Issachar Dov Halberstam of Ciechanov. He was rebbe in Leove, Volhynia, and Kiev. He was an outstanding talmudical scholar. He was involved in communal work and assisted in the burial of victims of the tragic typhus epidemic that eventually claimed his own life.

His brother, R. Hayyim Aaron (d. 1956), married the daughter of R. Yitzhak Jacob David Hager of Storojineti-Vishnitz. He lived in Tel Aviv, where he set up a *shtiebl Bet Yehudah* in memory of his father. He was a communal leader and offered assistance to postwar Jewish refugees.

A.Shu.

TWERSKY, Moses Mordecai, of Lublin (1877–8 *Iyyar* 1943)–Son of R. Jacob Aryeh of Turiysk, he married Malkah, the daughter of R. Barukh Meir Twersky of Azarnitz (Nazarinitz). Thus, he became the brother-in-law of R. Alter Israel Shimon Perlow of Novominsk. He lived first in Turiysk and Kovel and on 28 *Iyyar* 1918, settled in Lublin.

His life-style was austere. He would rise at 2:30 A.M. and recite the entire Book of Psalms, which he knew by heart. He would then repeat also from memory the substance of all the *kvittlech* (petitions) that had been presented to him the previous day. After a brief rest, he would go to the *mikveh* and by 9 A.M. would conclude his morning prayer. He had a light lunch, his only meal of the day. On Sukkot he devoted four hours to the ritual waving of the *arba minim*.

An active president of the *Shomrei Shabbat V'Hadas* society, the rebbe succeeded in persuading many firms to close on the Sabbath. In 1925, he supported the hasidic delegation, led by Aaron Kirschenbloom, to establish *Nahalat Lublin* in the Holy Land. He was closely associated with R. Meir Shapira. He would travel to different localities to meet his hasidim. However, he rarely visited Warsaw, since he did not want to infringe on the territory of his brother, R. Nahum, who lived on Mila Street and was also known as the Trisker rebbe.

His discourses are appended to the *Sefer HaYahas MiChernobyl* (Lublin, 1938).

At the outbreak of the Second World War, he declined a visa to Switzerland. "A captain must be the last to leave the old ship," he said. Together with his wife and daughter Gitel, who had married R. Aaron Twersky, he perished in Kempnitz forest, near Lublin. His eldest son, R. Yohanan, the rabbi of Radziejov, born in 1906 and the son-in-law of R. Issachar Dov Rokeah of Belz, also perished in the Holocaust. His second son, R. Aaron David, rabbi in Gorzkov, near Lublin, was the author of *Sefer HaYahas MiChernobyl* (Lublin, 1932), a valuable genealogy, which was later expanded to *Sefer HaYahas MiChernobyl VeRuzhyn* (Lublin, 1938; reprinted in Jerusalem, 1960). He married the daughter of R. Zeev of Kovel. He was survived by his sons—R. Abraham Yitzhak and R. Barukh Meir—and his daughter, Rikel, who, in 1933, married R. Menahem Tzvi Eichenstein, the rabbi of St. Louis.

Jewish Press, June 14, 1985, p. 88.

TWERSKY, Moses Tzvi, of Philadelphia (1890–25 *Sivan* 1972)—Son of R. Menahem Nahum, his mother, Simah, was the daughter of R. Moses of Savran. In 1905, he married Rifkah Miriam, the daughter of R. Meshullam Zusya Heschel. He was, for a time, the rabbi in Tulchin.

He then emigrated to the United States and settled in Philadelphia. He was very active in the Mizrachi.

TWERSKY, Nahum (1903–19 *Kislev* 1972)—Son of R. Benzion Leib of Hornistopol and of Rachel, the daughter of R. Yitzhak Yoel, the rebbe of Kantikoziva. He was brought up in the home of his grandfather R. Mordecai Dov. During the First World War, his father moved to Kiev with the family.

In Warsaw, in 1923, R. Nahum married Devorah Perel Gitel (d. 1984), the daughter of R. Joseph Kalish of Skierniewice. Ten years later, he emigrated to the Holy Land and worked for a bank. On Sabbaths and Festivals he reverted to the role of rebbe at the *shtiebl Bet Yehudah* at Rehov Nahmani 49, in Tel Aviv, where he officiated as reader and gave discourses.

He was the author of *MiDor el Dor* (Tel Aviv, 1967), a valuable work on hasidic dynasties, and also published his grandfather's work *Pele Yoetz* (Tel Aviv, 1970). He was buried in *Nahalat Yitzhak*, near Tel Aviv.

He was survived by one son and one daughter, Raya, who married the biblical scholar Prof. Menahem Haran of the Hebrew University.

TWERSKY, Nahum, of Warsaw (1874–1942)—Third son of R. Jacob Aryeh, his grandfather R. Abraham, the Maggid of Turiysk, died before his *bar mitzvah*. R. Nahum married the daughter of R. Mordecai of Spikov. He was an itinerant rabbi, traveling from town to town and visiting remote villages. He divorced his wife, who emigrated to the United States with their two children.

He then married the daughter of R. Issachar Dov of Hoderov and settled in Warsaw. Though nonpolitical, he urged his hasidim to vote for the Aguda.

At the outbreak of the Second World War, he took refuge in Turiysk, where he was murdered by the Nazis.

Elleh Ezkerah, vol. 5, pp. 87–91.

TWERSKY, Pinhas, of Ustilug (1880–19 *Iyyar* 1943)—Popularly known as "R. Pinyale," he was the eldest son of R. Mordecai of Rotmistrovka. In 1900, he married Hannah Rachel, the daughter of R. Issachar Dov Rokeah of Belz, where he lived for thirty years. In the work *Or HaMeir*, by R. Meir Shapira of Lublin, one of his responsa is mentioned.

During the First World War, he lived first in Ujfeherto, then in Munkacz. When his father-in-law died in 1926, he lived first in Ustilug for about five years, and then in Przemysl, from 1932.

During the Nazi occupation, he lived in Sambor for two and a half years. He, his wife, and their six children were murdered by the Nazis. He is survived by one daughter, Treina, the wife of R. Jacob Joseph Twersky of Skvira.

Elleh Ezkerah, vol. 1, pp. 181–189.

TWERSKY, Shlomoh, of Skvira (1873–7 *Adar* 1921)—Third son of R. David of Chernobyl, he married Feiga, the daughter of R. Rokeah in Belz in 1891, and he stayed there until 1894. He then became rabbi in Gorov, but a short time after his father's death, he was murdered in Kiev at the age of forty-seven.

His scholarly wife escaped to Poland, where she married R. Yitzhak Meir Kahal, head of the Warsaw rabbinate. She perished in the ghetto on 4 *Av* 1941.

He was survived by a son, R. Eleazar.

TWERSKY, Tzvi Aryeh, of Zlatopol (1890–18 *Av* 1968) – Son of R. Mordecai Joseph of Zlatopol, R. Tzvi – or "R. Hershele," as he was popularly known – studied under his father. He married Havah, the daughter of R. Israel Friedman of Chortkov. At the outbreak of the First World War he moved to Vienna and became rebbe in 1929. He was interned in the Dachau concentration camp and on his release settled in Tel Aviv in 1938.

He was the author of *Hatov VeHaTakhlit* (Vienna, 1933) and *Emunah VeDaat* (Vienna, 1933). He was interested in philosophy and ascribed to Hasidism a significant place in mystical speculations.

He was buried on the Mount of Olives in Jerusalem, and a *kollel*, *Chortkov/Zlatopol* was established in his memory by his son-in-law, R. Pinhas Biberfeld (b. 1915). A native of Berlin and the son of a physician, R. Pinhas studied in the Berlin rabbinical seminary under R. Yehiel Jacob Weinberg and subsequently in the Hebron *yeshivah* in Israel.

TWERSKY, Yitzhak, of Azarnitz (d. 1941) – Son of R. Barukh Meir, he married the daughter of R. Israel Ashkenazi of Olesko, who lived in Romania. He was known for his *kamayot* and his Latin medical prescriptions. He was transported to Transnistria, where he was shot. His wife and two children died of starvation and typhus.

His son R. Shimon and his daughter Rebecca were murdered. His son R. Aaron survived and subsequently studied in the Rabbi Isaac Elhanan Theological Seminary in New York. His daughter Hannah, whose husband, Dr. Shimon Stein, perished in Romania, survived and married R. Efraim Asher Halevi Rothenberg, rabbi of *Kehillat Ner Yisrael* in Los Angeles.

M. Unger, *Admorim SheNisfu BeShoa*, pp. 158–160.

TWERSKY, Yitzhak, of Tel Aviv (1886–28 *Adar* 1978) – Son of R. Moses Dan of Skvira, he married the daughter of R. Abraham Joshua Heschel Twersky. When she died, he married the daughter of R. Mordecai of Staro Konstantinov, Podolia, a descendant of Zloczov. After the Russian Revolution, he organized the *Agudat HaHayyim* society to strengthen religious life in the Ukraine.

In 1926, he emigrated to the United States, living first in Harlem, New York, and subsequently in the Bronx, where he established *Bet HaMidrash Ohel Mosheh Mahaneh Dan Hasidei Skvira*. He settled in Tel Aviv in 1953.

He is survived by two sons, R. Abraham Joshua Heschel and R. Aaron, who reside in the United States.

Toldot Anshei Shem, p. 55.

TWERSKY, Yitzhak (Menahem) Nahum, of Rava-Ruska (1888–1942) – Son of R. Mordecai of Shpikov, Podolia, in 1904 he married Sheva, the daughter of R. Issachar Dov Rokeah of Belz. During the First World War, he lived in Munkacz, Halicz, and Belz. He succeeded his father in 1919. In 1927, he became rabbi of Rava-Ruska. He traveled to various towns to collect money for charitable purposes.

When the Nazis invaded Poland, he was sent to Belzec, where he, his wife, and their children perished.

Elleh Ezkerah, vol. 4, pp. 132–136.

TWERSKY, Yohanan (1900–1967), writer – Born in Shpikov, Ukraine, on May 24, son of R. Nahum. His mother was *Hayyah*, the daughter of R. Mottel of Shpikov. He studied in Odessa, where he was befriended by Hayyim Nahman Bialik. Later, he lived in Kishinev and Berlin. In 1926, he emigrated to the United States, where he taught for twenty years at Hebrew College in Boston.

In 1947, he settled in Israel. His historical romance *Halev VeHaHerev* (Tel Aviv, 1955) is based on R. Nathan's account of R. Nahman's pilgrimage to the Holy Land. Other writings deal with the Besht and R. Levi Yitzhak of Berdichev. *HaBetulah MiLudmir* is a fictional biography of the hasidic "Maid of Ludomir" (Jerusalem: Mosad Bialik, 1950).

Who's Who in Israel (1952), p. 670.

TWERSKY, Yohanan, of Talnoye (1906–20 *Kislev* 1981) – Son of R. David Mordecai, he was born in Tulchin, Podolia. His mother, Havah, was a descendant of Ruzhyn and Zloczov. He studied for five years in Rabbi Isaac Elhanan Theological Seminary in New York.

In 1924, when he moved to Jerusalem, he studied in the *Yeshivah Ohel Mosheh* under R. Joseph Hayyim Sonnenfeld. In 1929, he married Zipporah, the daughter of R. Moses Langer of Stretyn, Toronto. In 1934, he moved to Montreal, where he was rebbe until his return to Israel in 1953.

He settled in Jerusalem, living first in Rehavia, then in Bayit Vegan. He established a *yeshivah* in East Jerusalem, near the grave of Simon the Just (Shimon HaTzaddik), and a *kollel*, *Meor Einayim*. He published his father's work, *Magen David* (Tel Aviv, 1960), a photoreprint of the Zhitomir 1853 edition.

His son, R. Israel Mordecai, succeeded him in Jerusalem. His other son, R. Hai Yitzhak, lives in the United States of America.

Jewish Tribune, December 16, 1981.

A.Shu.

TWERSKY, Zeev, of Rotmistrovka (d. 20 *Sivan* 1937) – Son of R. Yohanan of Rotmistrovka, he married the daughter of R. Meshullam Zusya of Chernobyl. He was renowned for his scholarship and left a manuscript dealing with *halakhah*. He emigrated to the Holy Land in 1935.

One of his responsa is mentioned by R. Abraham Yitzhak Kook, who greatly venerated him. It was published in *Kol Torah* (Jerusalem, 1936).

He was survived by his sons, R. Nahum Moses and R. David. His daughter married R. Hayyim Meir Hager of Vishnitz.

TZANZER, Hayyim (1720–6 *Shevat* 1783) – Son of R. Menahem Nahum of Zanz, hence known as "Tzanzer." He married the daughter of R. Joseph Halpern of Brody.

He supported R. Jacob Emden in his controversy with R. Jonathan Eybeschutz. He is mentioned in the responsa of R. Ezekiel Landau (*Yoreh De'ah* 141) and in the writings of R. Jacob Joseph of Polonnoye.

The Besht greatly esteemed him, saying that he had "a spark" of the Tanna of the first century, R. Yohanan ben Zakkai. The Maggid of Mezhirech asserted that he actually looked like R. Yohanan ben Zakkai (*Shivhei HaBesht*, Tale 241). He was one of the scholars who lived in Brody and actually opposed the activities of the Besht.

His discourses are recorded in *Ne'edar BaKodesh* on *Avot* (Lvov, 1862). He also wrote glosses on the *Shulhan Arukh, Yoreh De'ah* (Slavuta, 1861).

In *Shivhei HaBesht*, however, the Besht was actually censored for neglecting to eulogize him (no. 16), thus the assumption that he died in the lifetime of the Besht. Horodetsky identified him with R. Hayyim Tzanzer of Brody, who died in 1783, twenty-three years after the death of the Besht.

He had one son, R. Shmuel Aaron, and two daughters.

N. Gelber, *The History of the Jews in Brody*, pp. 63, 109, 330–331, 334.

TZAVAOT HARIBASH (Testimony of R. Israel Baal Shem Tov and Upright Rules of Conduct) – First published in Zolkiev in 1793, it is attributed to the Besht. R. Shneur Zalman of Liady writes, "The truth is that this is not his ethical will, and that he made no such will before he departed this life. It is rather a collection of his sayings, compiled by others. Although these were insufficiently skilled in translation, the authentic meaning is conveyed" (Tanya, *Iggeret HaKodesh*, no. 25).

The work contains the basic ideals of Hasidism and the idea of *devekut*, attachment to God in the mind at all times. One should cultivate an attitude of equanimity, being indifferent to both the praise and the blame of others and be so devoid of any desire for physical pleasure that it makes no difference to one whether one eats delicacies or coarse, unpalatable food. God wishes to be served in many different ways, and even when we converse with others, our mind can be on God and perform "unifications" (*Yihudim*). Weeping is very bad, for one must worship in joy. Only if weeping is because of joy is it permissible, and then it is very good.

This was one of the first hasidic works. It was banned in Cracow, but it was published elsewhere in thirty-four editions. It has been translated into English by Stanford D. Shanblatt, a graduate of the Jewish Theological Seminary.

Y. I. Schochet, *Tzavaat HaRibash*.

S. D. Shanblatt, "The Testament of the Baal Shem Tov," pp. 282–285.

L.J.

TZIMTZUM (Heb., contraction, withdrawal, concentration) – A term used in Lurianic Kabbalah for the process whereby the

Godhead initially withdraws into itself, so that space can be made wherein emanation or creation may occur. This concept serves to explain both how creation can take place in an area that would otherwise be full of God's presence and how evil could enter a world in which God existed.

In late Kabbalah, including hasidic circles, there were various views concerning the correct interpretation of *tzimtzum*. Some thought of it literally. Others considered it to be merely a symbolic representation of an occurrence within the Godhead that was beyond human perception.

Generally speaking, in hasidic thought, and particularly in *Habad, tzimtzum* was considered essential in order to prevent humanity from being overwhelmed by the divine effulgence. God withdraws, as it were, and then covers Himself with a garment, which is the universe itself. The task of the hasid is to penetrate this garment in order to uncover the divine truth.

R. Menahem Mendel of Vitebsk, following his teacher the Maggid of Mezhirech, regarded *tzimtzum* as a necessary prerequisite of revelation, since only a limited aspect of the divine could be communicated to the finite mind. God had to conceal Himself, so to speak, before He could reveal Himself.

The Besht's chief disciple, R. Shneur Zalman of Liady, discussed *tzimtzum* at some length in his *Tanya*, and he was closely followed in this by R. Aaron HaLevi of Starosselje. According to the latter's *Avodat HaLevi*, there were two acts of *tzimtzum*: the first enabled the *Ein Sof* in general to be revealed, and the second allowed the light of *Ein Sof* to appear in a more finite form.

For R. Nahman of Bratzlav, *tzimtzum* was a continuous process within the Godhead and was most significant because of the "empty space" it created. It is this that leads to doubts in the human mind about the very existence of God.

D.G.

TZITZIT (Hebrew; fringes) – In ancient times, all garments with four corners that were worn during the day had *tzitzit* on their four corners. It was to keep alive one's consciousness of the special relationship the Jew has with God. "And ye may look upon it, and remember all the commandments of the Lord and do them" (Numbers 15:39). The rabbis believed that "seeing leads to remembering and remembering leads to doing."

Tzitzit were worn by men only, because of the general rule that women are exempted from "precepts that have to be performed at a specific time." Up to the second century there was also a blue cord (*tekhelet*) included in the fringes. R. Gershon Heinokh Leiner was the pioneer in the revival of *tekhelet* in 1889.

Nowadays, the use of fringes in an outer garment is limited to the *tallit*, worn by men (who are or have been married) for morning prayers (except on the Eve of Atonement, when it is put on before nightfall). Today, the *tallit katan* (small *tallit*), also known as *arba kanfot* or just *tzitzit* (a rectangular piece of cloth with an aperture in the center sufficient to let it pass over the head) is worn all day, usually under the shirt or beneath an outer garment. Most hasidim, however, display the fringes openly, for they regard the fringes as of equal weight to all the commandments of the Torah (*Sifre* on *Shelah* [Zulzbach, 1802], p. 23a). They regard it as an external identifying mark of a pious Jew.

A number of very pious hasidic women such as the Maid of Ludomir wore *tzitzit* despite the objections of the medieval scholar R. Jacob ben Moses Halevi Mollin (known as the *Maharil*) (1361–1427).

The kabbalists signified that the total number of windings in a fringe was thirty-nine, and this is also the numerical value of the Hebrew letters in the last two words of the *Shema*: "*Adonai Ehad*" (the Lord is One). R. Nahman of Bratzlav maintains that the *tzitzit* are a safeguard against immorality. He points out that when Noah became drunk and uncovered himself, his sons Shem and Japhet covered their father's nakedness (Genesis 9:23). The *Tikkunei Zohar* (18:37a) points out that this refers to *tzitzit*; hence "they did not see their father's nakedness," for *tzitzit* cover all nakedness (*Likkutei Moharan* 7:4). R. Nahman further believes that through the observance of *tzitzit*, a man is protected against the snares of Satan. The serpent made use of "evil marriage" (in seducing Eve), and therefore his concept is sexual immorality (*Likkutei Moharan* 7:4).

R. Levi Yitzhak of Berdichev in his work *Kedushat Levi* (p. 157b) states that through the observance of the commandment of *tzitzit*, we mitigate the blue (*tekhelet*), which alludes to darkness, for *tekhelet* shares the Hebrew root with *tikhlah* (ending or destruction). God looks upon us in the same manner and through the same color with which we look on Him, and the white *tzitzit* transform it into a brilliant light.

A. Kaplan, *The Light Beyond*, pp. 250–253.

TZVI HIRSCH (1735–c. 1780)—Only son of the Besht. As a child he was playful, did not enjoy studying, and had difficulty with writing. R. Abraham Gershon of Kutov tried to teach him, but it seems that he was unsuccessful. In a letter from Hebron dated 1748, R. Gershon urged his former pupil to apply himself to study. When the Besht lay dying, his only son was asleep. When he finally awakened, his father spoke to him and he replied, "I do not understand what you are saying."

He did not inherit his father's mantle of leadership, but he did inherit his father's manuscript *Sefer HaTzoref* and took it with him when he moved to Pinsk. He left it in the possession of his son R. Aaron of Titov (d. 1829). His other sons were R. Israel, "the Silent One," and R. Dov Baer of Olianov.

Tzvi Hirsch lived in Pinsk during the persecution of the hasidim. Very little is known about his life, except that he lived in the house of his father-in-law, R. Shmuel Hasid, who supported him.

He died and was buried in Pinsk. He played no part in the hasidic movement.

D. Ben-Amos and J. R. Mintz, *In Praise of the Baal Shem Tov*, pp. 179, 181–182, 186, 258.

Y.E.

TZVI HIRSCH of Tomaszov (1800–7 *Heshvan* 1870)—Son of R. Israel Leibel, he was born in Bilgoraj, near Lublin, and he studied in the *yeshivah* of Tarnogrod. After his marriage, he settled in Tomaszov and was a hasid of R. Simhah Bunem of Przysucha.

On the death of his teacher in 1827, he became closely associated with R. Menahem Mendel of Kotzk and served him as personal attendant and scribe. While R. Mendele lived a life of "seclusion," R. Tzvi was his only contact with the hasidim, who flocked to see the "invisible rebbe."

After R. Mendele's death, R. Tzvi Hirsch became an adherent of R. Yitzhak Meir Alter, R. Heinokh of Alexander, and R. Aryeh Leib Alter. He refused to become a rebbe or to receive *kvittlech*. He was buried in Kotzk next to his master.

Y. Alfasi, *Bisdei HaHasidut*, p. 435.

U

UMAN (in Polish, Human), city near Kiev–In 1749 the Haidamacks massacred many Jews and burned down part of the town. Other massacres took place in 1765 and on June 19, 1768, when peasant revolutionary Maxim Zhelesnyak attacked the city with Cossack commander Ivan Gonta, killing over 20,000 Jews. This pogrom, on 5th *Tammuz*, is known as "the day of the Evil Decree of Uman."

R. Nahman of Bratzlav had been to Uman, on his return from the Holy Land, as early as 1799. In 1802 he told R. Nathan, "It would be a good place to be buried in. The souls of the martyrs await me." R. Nahman settled there in 1810, four months before he died, on the fourth day of Sukkot, 18 *Tishri* (15 October). "Come to visit my grave on Rosh Hashanah," R. Nahman exhorted his followers. "On Rosh Hashanah everyone must be here. . . . Nothing is greater than to be with me for Rosh Hashanah." The rebbe made a formal promise: "When my days are ended and I leave this world, I will intercede for anyone who comes to my grave. If someone were to come to my graveside after my death, give charity, and recite ten Psalms, as prescribed (Psalms 16, 32, 41, 42, 59, 77, 90, 105, 137, 150), I will span the length and breadth of the universe to save him. I will pull him out of hell by his side curls. It makes no difference who it is or how gravely he has sinned. All he has to do is to take upon himself not to return to his folly" (*Yemei Moharan*, 72). He was buried in the old cemetery in Uman among the martyrs murdered by the Haidamacks.

By 1834 a Bratzlav synagogue or *kloyz* had been erected in Uman, and in 1866 a hasid of Bratzlav settled there.

Since R. Nahman's death in 1810 until Nazi Germany's invasion of the Ukraine in 1941, his hasidim, known as the *Toite hasidim*, regularly visited Uman on Rosh Hashanah. Until the closing of the Russian border in 1917, hasidim would come from Poland and the Holy Land. When Uman became inaccessible, R. Nahman's hasidim in Poland gathered in the *yeshivat Hakhmei Lublin* for Rosh Hashanah. They were encouraged by R. Meir Shapira, who said to them, "I am a rebbe without hasidim. You are hasidim without a rebbe. Let us, therefore, join forces." In 1937 the Soviet authorities closed the Bratzlav synagogue, converting it to a metal factory. In the Holy Land, a Bratzlav *kibbutz* was formed in Jerusalem, and, in 1940, R. Abraham Sternhartz began another one at the graveside of R. Shimon Bar Yochai in Meron.

During the Second World War, the Nazis exterminated 17,000 Jews of Uman and greatly damaged the cemetery. In 1959, there were 2,000 Jews living there, and the only remaining synagogue was closed. The Soviets had built houses over the cemetery. The plot containing R. Nahman's grave was acquired by Daniel, a hasid of Bratzlav who designed his house in such a way that the exterior wall ran alongside the rebbe's grave. However, the house is now occupied by a non-Jew. In 1967 Michael Dorfman of Moscow visited Uman, and a year later R. Tzvi Aryeh Rosenfeld, accompanied by eleven people from the United States of America, revived the pilgrimage to Uman.

In 1988 Russian authorities authorized visits to Uman, and two hundred and fifty hasidim took advantage of this. In 1989 a thousand hasidim gathered there for Rosh Hashanah, and the numbers have since doubled and trebled.

A large factory site was acquired a short distance from the gravesite. To make Rosh Hashanah in Uman as successful as possible, the Bratzlav community has established an international committee to help coordinate the arrangements. An advance team of hasidic workers travel to Uman weeks before Rosh Hashanah to prepare accommodations and arrange field kitchens. Ukraine declared its independence in January 1992 and issued its own currency; it very much welcomes the revival of the pilgrimage.

Bratzlav hasidim were horrified when, in January 1993, President Hayyim Herzog asked Ukrainian president Leonid Kravchuk to allow the remains of R. Nahman to be reinterred in Israel.

Uman! Uman! Rosh Hashanah! A Guide to Rebbe Nahman's Rosh Hashanah in Uman.

UNGER, Eleazar, of Tarnov (1890–2 *Elul* 1943)—Eldest son of R. Shalom David, he married the daughter of R. Naftali Rokeah of Nawarja, who was the son of R. Joshua of Belz. In 1919, he became rabbi of Zabno, and in 1923, he succeeded his father as rebbe in Tarnov. When his wife died, he married Adel, the daughter of R. Aaron Elimelekh Shneur Zalman Twersky, the rebbe of Krasnoe.

At the outbreak of the Second World War, he was deported. He, his wife, and three of their children were murdered. Only two daughters, Malkah and Gitah, survived.

M. Unger, *Admorim SheNisfu BaShoa*, pp. 36–39.

UNGER, Israel Elimelekh, of Zabno (1820–7 *Elul* 1867)—Son of R. Joseph of Dabrova, he married Mattel, the daughter of R. Yehiel, who was the son-in-law of the "Seer" of Lublin. He was befriended by R. Hayyim Halberstam, who persuaded him to become a rebbe and to establish his court in Zabno. He did not survive his father for long.

He was succeeded by his son R. Jacob Yitzhak. His other sons were R. Moses Elikum Briah of Dabrova and R. Mordecai David of Zanz.

UNGER, Israel Joseph, of Tarnov (1868–1 *Tammuz* 1942)—Youngest son of R. Jacob Yitzhak, a descendant of R. Elimelekh of Lejask, he was born in Zabno. He married Brakhah, the daughter of R. Reuben Horowitz of Dembice. He studied under his uncle R. Joshua Horowitz of Dzikov. When his uncle died in 1913, he became rebbe in Tarnov, where he lived for thirty years.

He composed many melodies that were transcribed by Shlomoh Blum, cantor of the synagogue *Bikkur Holim*. During the Nazi occupation, he and his sons R. Meir Eliyahu of Pikeliai and R. Reuben of Kazimierz were murdered. One son, R. Jacob, and one daughter, Beila Shula, survived.

The rabbi's most cherished possessions—manuscripts by his grandfather R. Eliezer of Dzikov and by his father; letters from R. Hayyim Halberstam, from R. Meir of Dzikov, and from his uncle R. Naftali Hayyim Horowitz of Jerusalem—were destroyed by the Nazis.

M. Unger, *Admorim SheNisfu BaShoa*, pp. 179–182.

UNGER, Manasseh (10 *Kislev* 1900–21 *Tammuz* 1969), writer—Son of R. Shalom David, the rabbi of Zabno, he lived for a time in Warsaw, and then in the Holy Land, eventually settling in the United States. He wrote extensively in Yiddish on the martyrdom of hasidic rebbes during the Nazi Holocaust.

He is the author of *Hasidut and Leben* (New York, 1946), *Pshisha and Kotzk* (Buenos Aires, 1949), *Good Yomtov, Kinder* (New York, 1950), *Moadim LeSimhah* (Tel Aviv, 1953), *De Hasidishe Welt* (New York, 1955), *Hasidus un Yomtov* (New York, 1958), *Reb Israel Baal Shem Tov* (New York, 1963), and *Admorim SheNisfu BeShoa* (Jerusalem: Mosad Harav Kook, 1959).

UNGER, Mordecai David, of Dabrova (1770–7 *Shevat* 1843)—Son of R. Tzvi Hirsch, he was a disciple of R. Elimelekh of Lejask and the "Seer" of Lublin. He was renowned for his scholarship. He corresponded with many halakhic authorities of his day.

He established his court at Dabrova. He was survived by his sons: R. Joseph, R. Menahem Mendel, R. Abraham Elhanan of Opoczno, R. Moses, R. Yehiel Tzvi Hirsch, and R. Naftali.

UNGER, Mordecai David, of Zanz (1858–15 *Elul* 1916)—Son of R. Israel Elimelekh of Zabno, he married the daughter of R. Moses Unger, the son-in-law of R. Hayyim Halberstam of Zanz. From 1872 to 1876 he lived with his in-laws.

His son R. Benzion and all but one of his family perished in the massacre of Zanz on 15 *Elul* 1943. His son R. Jacob Yitzhak, who escaped to Siberia, later lived in Paris for a time and eventually, in 1951, became rebbe of *Dabrova* in Borough Park, Brooklyn, where he established a *Bet HaMidrash, Bet Yosef*.

UNGER, Naftali Tzvi, of Dabrova

(1880–16 *Av* 1942)–He was born in Dabrova, the eldest son of R. Moses Elikum Briah. In 1897, he married Sarah, the daughter of R. Moses Halberstam of Bardiev. He established a *yeshivah* in Stary Sacz.

He was deported by the Nazis to Zolinia Miasteczko, where he was murdered. His son R. Yitzhak of Gorlice was murdered in Auschwitz. Two other sons, R. Barukh Abraham and R. Zalman Leib, survived and live in Brooklyn.

UNGER, Shalom David, of Zabno

(1860–2 *Elul* 1923)–Son of R. Jacob Yitzhak, he was born in Zabno and married the daughter of R. Menahem Mendel Shapira of Lancut. As the marriage proved childless, he married Bluma Hannah, the daughter of R. Moses of Rozwadov. He was rabbi in Rakova. He succeeded his father as rebbe in Zabno in 1892. He corresponded with R. Ezekiel Halberstam, R. Issachar Shalom Teichtel, and R. Shlomoh Auerbach.

He spent the years of the First World War in Vienna, settling in Tarnov in 1919. He was the author of responsa *Yad Shalom* on the four parts of the *Shulhan Arukh*, which were published in Talshava in 1911; a second edition was published in New York 1967.

He died in Vienna but was buried in Zabno.

His sons were the author Manasseh, R. Eleazar, and R. Israel; his daughter, Perel, was the wife of R. Israel Shapira of Blazowa.

UNGER, Shlomoh David, of Nitra

(1886–8 *Adar* 1945)–Only son of R. Joseph Moses, he was born in Piestany, Slovakia. His father died on *Hol HaMo'ed Sukkot* 1897 at the age of forty-two. Shlomoh David studied in the *yeshivah* of R. Noah Barukh Fisher and then under R. Shmuel Rosenberg of Unsdorf. He married his cousin Miriam Leah, the daughter of R. Noah Barukh Fisher. At the age of twenty, he became *dayan* in Krompachy and for thirty-nine years was the head of the *yeshivah* in Nitra, which had 300 students. He is mentioned in the responsa of R. Shmuel Engel of Radomysl.

He was active in the Aguda, and in 1935, he visited the Holy Land with an Aguda delegation. In *Elul* 1937, he opened the *Knessiyah Gedolah* in Marienbad by reciting Psalm 10:1 with the verse: "Why standest Thou afar off, O Lord? Why hidest Thou Thyself in times of trouble?" This made a tremendous impact on the assembly. In the words of one delegate, "If I had come here only to listen to this recitation, it would have been enough."

He encouraged his son-in-law, R. Michael Dov Weissmandel (1903–1956), to travel to London to obtain travel permits for 200 families from Slovakia. In 1942, he was appointed chief rabbi of the Jews of Slovakia, and his home had, for a time, diplomatic immunity.

He was murdered in Auschwitz. His manuscript (*Haggadah shel Pesah* [New York, 1954]) was preserved by a gentile woman and were published by his son, R. Shalom Moses, and by his son-in-law. His daughter, who survived, married R. Yekutiel Yehudah Halberstam of Klausenburg. His son-in-law, R. Michael Dov Weissmandel, was one of the leaders of the *Pracovna Skupina* (working group) for the rescue of Jews under the Nazis. His book *Min HaMetzar* (From the Depth), containing his memoirs and his activities during the Nazi period, was published posthumously in 1960.

Elleh Ezkerah, vol. 2, pp. 251–265.

UNGER, Yehudah, of Sokolov

(1862–17 *Sivan* 1939)–Son of R. Jacob Yitzhak of Zabno. In 1880, he became rabbi in Sokolov. In 1895, he was rebbe in Rzeszov, and then in Neumarkt. He was succeeded by his only son, R. Naftali, who, together with his sister, was murdered by the Nazis.

In 1906, R. Naftali published in Yaroslav the second part of his grandfather's work *Imrei Noam*.

UNITED STATES OF AMERICA

–The most important fact about Hasidism in the United States today is its very survival and functionality as a vital movement on the American Jewish scene nearly three centuries after its founding in Eastern Europe.

Contrary to the predictions of the experts who had long ago assumed that Hasidism would never be able to take root in the materialist climate of the *Goldene Medineh*, numerous smaller or larger hasidic communities evolved concurrent with the spreading of centers of Orthodox Jewish immigrants from New York to Los Angeles in this century. Hasidism's survival amazed even the most sympathetic scholars, such as Gershom Scholem, who had declared it a victim of the Holocaust, buried in the mass graves of the six million. The movement also belied the prognosis of the cognoscenti who since the middle of this century foretold its ultimate doom with the death of the last generation of the survivors who had attempted to revive some of the glorious past of this Jewish religious folk renaissance around a few scions of the famous dynasties who had come to these shores in search of former followers of their movements, who had preceded them.

Now at the waning of the twentieth century, Hasidism is a strong and growing phenomenon on the broader Jewish scene in America, as well as in Israel, England, Belgium, and other centers of renewed Orthodox Jewish life in the world. Contrary to the doomsday sayers who had written off as an anachronism these attempts at its revival, Hasidism in this country is vital, vibrant, and expanding into new realms in spite of ever-mounting extrinsic and intrinsic problems and threats to its survival. Even in the face of the severe economic crisis of the early 1990s, its leaders and adherents look forward to its survival and a solid future not only in Williamsburg, Crown Heights, and Borough Park, Brooklyn, and Monsey, New York.

The major reason for this optimistic attitude is not only the unswerving loyalty of the followers of the famous hasidic rebbes who survived the harrowing experiences of the Holocaust and who succeeded in reestablishing their communities in this country. More important is the fact that the bulk of those rebbes' hasidim are no longer just the survivors, but a large and growing number of second- and third-generation American-born hasidim. These so-called *avreikhim* are increasingly assuming a large share of the burden of initiating the growth of and running large networks of organizations and institutions designed to meet the multiple needs of the hasidic communities in this country and the rest of the Jewish world. From a purely demographic perspective, it is equally important that a typical hasidic family in such neighborhoods as Williamsburg or Borough Park or in the suburban and exurban centers in upstate New York and elsewhere has between seven and nine children. This veritable population explosion, which undoubtedly causes some economic and corollary psychological problems, forces the leaders of the hasidic communities to search for ever new means of creating avenues of economic and other support for the needs of their people.

It would, of course, be wrong to limit discussion of the development of Hasidism in this country to the rise of the major hasidic communities in Williamsburg, Crown Heights, Borough Park, Flatbush, and their suburban branches, such as Monsey, Monroe, and New Square, New York. Isolated smaller or larger congregations of hasidim existed in the United States even before the beginning of this century, especially in such cities as Los Angeles and Chicago, outside New York. The voluminous correspondence of the former rebbe of Lubavitch R. Joseph Yitzchak Schneersohn and the glowing newspaper reports of his visits to the United States as the emissary of his father before and after World War I, for example, indicate the presence of numerous congregations that followed the Nusah Ari, headed by former students of the *Habad Yeshivot*. R. Schneersohn's reception by large masses of religious Jews—not only hasidim—and the public receptions by political dignitaries, mayors, and members of the U.S. Congress and the presidential cabinets speak of the not inconsiderable power and political clout of the then still very limited hasidic elements in this country. The visits of the rebbe were instrumental in creating a more or less cohesive movement that prepared the groundwork for the future explosive growth that evolved after his escape to this country, after his settling in Crown Heights, and after his building of the network of his organizations and institutions that reached out to the broader masses of the American Jewish community.

R. Schneersohn's vision and work were taken up and further expanded and broadened far beyond even the keenest expectations of his ardent followers by his successor and son-in-law. During the past four decades, R. Menahem Mendel Schneerson, a superior scholar, organizer, and administrator, built Lubavitch into a large empire of educational, religious, and Jewish and general political structures unlike any that had previously been known in the contemporary Jewish world, not only in the United States.

But it would be a mistake to focus only on Lubavitch or the equally large and powerful empire that the Old Rebbe of Satmar—the late R. Yoel Teitelbaum—developed in this country after his escape from the concentration camp. After a short stay in the Holy Land, he settled in Williamsburg in 1947 and rebuilt his community in cultural isolation from both Jewish and non-Jewish society—a job that was further consolidated and expanded by his nephew and successor, R. Moses Teitelbaum.

Long before the arrival of these two giants, however, hasidic communities were organized by pockets of followers of various schools, especially after World War I, not only in Brooklyn, on the Lower East Side, in the Bronx, and in other parts of Jewish New York. They were established by lay hasidim or by *Einikleh*—distant relatives of the heads of the various dynasties of the Polish, Russian, and Hungarian major and minor hasidic movements in such cities as Boston, Philadelphia, Pittsburgh, Milwaukee, Los Angeles, Chicago, and Baltimore—centers of Orthodox Jewish life. Some of them were of shorter duration. Others, such as Boyan, Novomiusk, and Stolyn, continue to exist and exert not inconsiderable impact on the broader Jewish community about them, especially if they were headed by dynamic leaders who reached out and who attracted especially the younger elements by the intensity of their hasidic life-style and their educational and intellectual efforts. Generally, however, Hasidism in the United States received its major boost by the impact of the major figures, such as the rebbes of Lubavitch, Satmar, Bobov, Klausenberg, Sighet, Blazova, and Poppa, as well as other survivors of the Holocaust who were able to attract hundreds and thousands of followers by their charismatic leadership and by their ability to translate their personal following into well-structured, large communities with effective administrations and support systems. They have had a major share in what has become the acknowledged renaissance of Orthodox Judaism in this country and in the rest of the contemporary Jewish world. They did achieve it, often linking their efforts with those of the Jewish day school, the *yeshivah* movements, and the educational innovations wrought by the surviving heads of the great *yeshivot gedolot* from Eastern Europe who came to America during and after World War II. Foremost among them were the great of Torah scholarship such as R. Aaron Kotler, R. Moses Feinstein, and the other founders of the outstanding academies of talmudic and rabbinic research in the United States, such as Telshe in Cleveland, Mir in Brooklyn, and Ner Israel in Baltimore.

This historical development has taken decades of consistent efforts and the confluence of significant sociopolitical and socioeconomic factors that made it possible for Hasidism to become an intrinsic part of the fabric of American Jewish life and of the broader pluralist society of the United States.

Foremost among the factors that effected the strong loyalty of the younger generations of mostly American-born hasidim to the lifestyle and underlying ideology of their elders in the midst of the most powerful mediablitzed society are the intensive, independent educational system for boys and girls established by their rebbes soon after their arrival in this country. Both the old Lubavitcher and the Satmar rebbe did not want their youth to blend into the Orthodox Jewish day schools as had the boys and girls of the earlier smaller hasidic groups, except for the Tzelemer Rav—R. Levi Yitzchok Gruenwald—who in many critical areas had prepared the ground for the rebbe of Satmar and the other Hungarian rebbes. Disregarding the tremendous costs and efforts involved, they set up their own independent school systems, which ranged from nursery schools to institutes of advanced talmudic studies. In the spirit of their insistence on total independence in all realms, particularly as far as their Jewish and general political stances were concerned, they spurned the financial help of the major American Jewish fundraising organizations that provide the essential sources and resources for the broad spectrum of most institutional and organizational life. At the cost of tremendous sacrifices, they chose to go their own way. They trained their own teachers and insisted on the approach and methodology that had characterized their intensive *chinukh* in Eastern Europe. Satmar, in particular, wrought its own system and style of education, which in a number of critical aspects differed even from the flourishing Jewish day schools.

All teaching was to be conducted in Yiddish rather than in English or modern Hebrew, consonant with the anti-Zionist political stance of the rebbe. Whereas the boys' schools concentrated on the classic *yeshivah* education, starting text study at a much earlier age plus study of hasidic literature, the Satmar and other Hungarian hasidic girls' schools were taught mostly orally by their women teachers until a growing body of appropriate texts and supplementary materials were created.

Even more crucial was the difference between the curricula of Satmar and similar hasidic schools and that of the Orthodox Jewish day schools: whereas the latter took great pride in offering their students an excellent secular education–paralleling that of the public schools–in addition to offering religious education, Satmar and similar schools for boys limited secular education to the required minimum and for all practical purposes stopped it after *bar mitzvah*. The inevitable consequence that had a serious bearing on the economic future of the hasidic masses was the radical shift away from overwhelming emphasis on higher secular education for the vast majority of American Jewish youth, who do concentrate on higher professional academic and other career goals. In contrast, hasidic youth–following the pattern created by the nonhasidic *yeshivot gedolot*, concentrate on intensive talmudic and halakhic studies long past high school age and even after marriage. The hasidic girls' schools developed mostly vocational high schools that enable their students to find work in such relatively desirable fields as bookkeeping, computer programming, and secretarial or sales jobs, not only in teaching. Oriented toward early marriage and having vitally needed earning power, not only to help their parents and save up for the high costs of a wedding and setting up a home, they are thus able to help their future spouse to spend at least a year or more in advanced rabbinic study in a *kollel*–after marriage.

More important was the fact that besides those graduates of the hasidic *yeshivot* who sought a career in teaching or in rabbinic and related fields, the vast majority were forced to concentrate on learning a trade or finding work on some level of business. In contrast to concentration on the professions, like their other Jewish contemporaries, young and middle-aged hasidim have not spurned the menial jobs and trades. It became quite common to see hasidim work as truck drivers, bus drivers, auto mechanics, locksmiths, electricians, or refrigeration experts. They learned to handle sophisticated mechanical devices, high-tech electronic equipment, and heavy machinery. Unabashed they wear work uniforms, handling forklifts and other heavy construction equipment, their long *peyot* and *tzitzit* dangling from their caps and pants. Still more important for their career was the fact that many hasidic *yeshivah* graduates have turned to business in spite of their insistence on retaining their hasidic garb and other limitations on the usual social conventions that are part of American business life.

Until the recent serious economic crisis, a good many of the middle-aged and young hasidim who turned to business and established enterprises of their own in retail, wholesale, international trade, export, import, and manufacturing proved quite successful. They were helped tremendously by the federal designation of hasidim as a disadvantaged minority in 1984, after a ten-year struggle and heavy political pressure. They used the political clout they had developed over the decades by their ability to produce large blocs of votes for their candidates. Certain outstanding hasidic entrepreneurs, such as the owners of 47th Street Photo Co., gained national reputations.

At the same time, political activism and the constantly growing need for jobs, housing, and funds induced leaders of hasidic communities to turn to the newly opened channels–federal, state, and local programs–that had been made available to the members of other racial and ethnic minorities since the mid 1960s and the war on poverty. As a result, the general economic situation of the hasidic communities in the United States improved steadily, though as many as 50 percent of the members earned incomes below the poverty level, even if both husband and wife were able to earn a halfway decent income. Their large families and the heavy burden of buying expensive kosher food and providing their private education, clothing,

UNLEARNED AND THE IGNORANT, THE

and other needs limited their ability to afford them more than the bare minimum. Except in some communities, such as Borough Park, Flatbush, and Monsey, which sported a good measure of conspicuous consumption in terms of their housing and life-style, the majority of the hasidim were limited to the life-style of the lower-income classes. Naturally, the severe economic downturn of the early 1990s had a serious impact on the hasidic working masses as well as on the roughly 10 percent who had worked their way up as entrepreneurs in such areas as insurance, financial management, and real estate.

One aspect of the hasidic life-style and attitude that became a characteristic of hasidic communities and their efforts to cope with the constant problems and threats to their survival is the insistence of the hasidim on self-help. Not only were they able to confront the constant exposure to personal attacks, theft, crime, and discrimination, but their initiative and readiness to innovate new solutions to their pressing problems led to the development of such by now famous organizations as *Hatzoloh*, the largest such medical volunteer corps in New York State; *Bikkur Holim*; *Tomkhei Shabbos*; and numerous others that have made their mark on Jewish life in America, not only on the hasidic community. They have been imitated in other communities and countries, such as Canada and Israel. The general emphasis on self-help and on meeting the needs of their population since the 1940s has resulted in the constant proliferation of institutions and organizations that indicate the sensitivity of the hasidim to the problems of others and to a general dedication to *hesed*—caring for their needy.

In general, though still beset by ever new problems and crises, the hasidic communities have succeeded in blending into the mainstream of American business while retaining their independence, and, by initiative and use of their strengths, in meeting the constant challenges to their survival in this country.

G.K.

UNLEARNED AND THE IGNORANT, THE—Hasidism has a marked tendency to treat with greater sympathy and understanding than was usual on the part of the older tradition the religious strivings of the unlearned and ignorant Jew. Three main factors are at work in this hasidic reassessment. First there is the hasidic suspicion of mere learning without profound religious motivation. The hasidic attacks on self-seeking rabbis gave much encouragement, intentionally or otherwise, to those who did not belong to the learned establishment.

Second, Hasidism emphasizes attachment to God (*devekut*) as the ultimate aim. Obviously, that aim in its fullest reaches was attainable only by the saints, but insofar as ordinary Jews could approximate it, they could be as successful as a rabbinic scholar; possibly they could be even more successful in that their mind was not distracted by the additional and difficult task of mastering the talmudic dialectics.

Third, the hasidic teachings regarding the lofty soul of every Jew prevented any disparagement of either Jews who were not intellectually gifted or Jews who had financial worries that did not permit them to engage in scholarship. Furthermore, as the institution of *tzaddik*ism developed, all of the followers of a particular rebbe—both learned followers and unlearned followers—were in some respects on an equal footing, united in common aims and loyalties, and members of the same joyous brotherhood, whom it ill suited to despise one another.

The hasidic concern with ordinary Jews even though they may be ignorant expresses itself in numerous hasidic tales. In some of them, the Besht himself pretends at first to be an *am ha-aretz*—the old rabbinic name for the ignorant—and he is accused of being such by his opponents. And there are the delightful stories of simple folk whose naive prayers, uttered in complete devotion, had a far greater appeal than the prayers of the rabbis, as in the famous tale of the boy without any knowledge of Hebrew who played his flute to the glory of God, or that of the hardworking tailor who, on the eve of Yom Kippur, promised to forgive God if God agreed to forgive him. Even in the halakhic sphere, the hasidic master R. Yekutiel Judah Teitelbaum (responsa *Avnei Tzeddek* [Lemberg, 1888], *Even HaEzer*, no. 8) states that "nowadays," despite talmudic opposition, an ordinary Israelite may marry the daughter of a *kohen* because the old type of *am haaretz* no longer exists.

Yet those who make too much of hasidic regard for the common people are mistaken.

The appeal of early Hasidism was to the spiritual elite, and even in later Hasidism, with its mass appeal, the complaint is frequently voiced by hasidic writers that there are both a watering down of hasidic standards and too much pandering to the demands of the vulgar herd. Among some hasidic groups, for instance, *Habad*, Kotzk, and Ger, the unlearned, though not entirely excluded, certainly did not belong in the mainstream of hasidic activity.

And while there were undoubtedly popular *tzaddikim* whose reputation was acquired through the ability to work miracles, these *baalei mofet* were not infrequently seen by other *tzaddikim* as a somewhat inferior class. The majority of the *tzaddikim* saw their function to be that of spiritual guide for the sophisticated rather than that of comforter of the masses. The involved techniques advocated in prayer and worship in the hasidic books were hardly suited to the ordinary hasid who was content to be a mere hanger-on in the rebbe's court.

L. Jacobs, *Hasidic Prayer*, pp. 26–35.

L.J.

UPPER AND LOWER WORLDS

– A basic theory of Kabbalah is that of two worlds – the celestial world (i.e., the world of the Godhead and the *Sefirot*) and the terrestrial world, in which mankind lives. They are called respectively the *elyonim* and the *tahtonim*. There is a constant exchange of influence between them, the central channel of the exchange being the lowest *Sefirah*, *Malkhut*, which symbolizes the *Shekhinah*.

One of the central ideas is that creation in the terrestrial world is modeled on the pattern of the upper world. For example, the *Zohar* speaks of a Tabernacle and a Temple in the celestial world, which match those constructed on earth. Consequently, events in the lower world have repercussions in the relevant areas in the upper world.

Kabbalah, developing an earlier rabbinic idea, speaks also of four worlds: the world of emanation (*atzilut*), consisting of the ten *Sefirot*; the world of creation (*briyah*), consisting of the throne of glory and the heavenly chariot; the world of formation (*yetzira*) (i.e., the world of the angels); and the world of making, or human activity (*asiya*) (i.e., the physical world). The last three were derived exegetically from Isaiah 43:7: "I have created it, formed it, made it." The four worlds are also designated together by their first letters – *Abiyah*.

D.G.

URI FEIVEL of Krasnopole (d. 22 *Tammuz* 1808)

– Son of R. Aaron, a disciple of the Besht, and a colleague of both R. Leib Sarah's and the "Seer" of Lublin. Many of his manuscripts on the Pentateuch, on the five *Megillot*, on the *Tikkunei Zohar*, and on the *Sefer Yetzirah* and *Sifra* were destroyed in a fire in Krasnopole, where he lived most of his life.

After the fire, he moved to Tulchin, then to Duvank. His work *Or HaHokhmah* on Torah and Festivals in two parts was published in Zloczov in 1815, with the encomiums of R. Jacob Orenstein of Lvov, R. Efraim Zalman Margulies, and the "Seer" of Lublin. It was reprinted in Jerusalem in 1970.

He was survived by a son, R. Menahem Mendel, and a son-in-law, R. Jacob.

USSISHKIN, Abraham Menahem Mendel (1863–1941), Zionist leader

– Born in Dubrovno, in the Mogilev district, his father was Moses Tzvi, a hasid of *Habad*. He received a traditional Jewish upbringing. In 1881, he established a youth group whose aim was to settle people in the Holy Land. Three years later, he founded, in Moscow, the *Bene Zion* society and was chosen, in 1885, to be secretary of all of the *Hovevei Zion* groups in Moscow.

In 1886, he asked the rebbe of Kopys, the leader of *Habad*, for an interview in order to discuss the settlement of Jews in the Holy Land. The rebbe received him very graciously, and for an hour and a half, young Ussishkin outlined the material and spiritual foundations of the *Hibbat Zion* movement. The rebbe said that he appreciated the *Hibbat Zion*, which "tends to unite all hearts" and that he would therefore be prepared to do as much as possible for the movement.

S. Kling, *The Mighty Warrior: The Life and Story of Menahem Ussishkin*.

USTILUG WEDDING

– Many hasidic rebbes, including R. Abraham Joshua Heschel of Opatov, and a great number of hasidim attended the wedding in Ustilug,

USTILUG WEDDING

known as the "Great Wedding," of R. Samuel, the son of R. Dan of Radziwillov (a grandson of R. Michael of Zloczov), and the daughter of R. Joseph of Hrubieszov (the son of R. Mordecai of Nesvizh).

The wedding became renowned because many opponents of R. Simhah Bunem of Przysucha, such as R. Simon Ashkenazi, R. Moses of Kozienice, R. Meir of Opatov, and R. Kalonymus Shapira of Cracow, who strongly disapproved of the Przysucha doctrines, especially their disregard of the prescribed times of prayer, wished to denounce and even to "excommunicate" R. Simhah Bunem of Przysucha in the presence of the Apter rebbe, who was then regarded as the "senior rebbe."

R. Simhah Bunem, who had been invited to the wedding, was prevented by his disciples, especially R. Menahem Mendel of Kotzk, from attending. He was, however, staunchly defended by a delegation consisting of five of his disciples: R. Yitzhak Meir of Ger, R. Eliezer Hakohen of Polutsk, R. Feivel of Grice, R. Zusya of Siedlice, and R. Issachar Baer Horowitz (son-in-law of Temarel Bergson), who appeared specially to defend their master. As a result of their intervention and with the support of R. Yerahmiel Tzvi of Przysucha (son of the "Yehudi"), the rebbe of Opatov – impressed by the erudition of the delegation – not only refused to take note of the opponents of Przysucha but also censured them by saying, "If you were living in a forest, you would quarrel even with the trees."

L. J. Berle, *R. Abraham Yehoshua Heschel HaRav MeApta*, pp. 46–50.

V

VIENNA, capital city of Austria–Until 1916, it was the capital of the Austro-Hungarian empire. By 1923, the Jews of Vienna numbered 201,313, making it the third-largest Jewish population in any European city.

Vienna had few hasidim as permanent residents before the First World War. The devastation of Galicia wrought by the Russians in the early years of the war, however, resulted in many hasidic rebbes' and their followers' settling there. Jews represented 77,000 of the 130,000 who took refuge in Vienna.

Hasidic courts were set up by the rabbi of Chortkov R. Israel Friedman, R. Mordecai Shragai Friedman of Husyatin, R. Yitzhak Meir Heschel of Kopyczynice, R. Abraham Jacob Friedman of Sadgora, R. Mordecai Shlomoh Friedman of Boyan, R. Mordecai Joseph Friedman of Sadgora, R. Yitzhak Eizig of Zablotov, R. Naftali of Mielec, R. Ittamar Rosenbaum of Nadvorna, R. Hayyim Meir Yehiel of Drohobycz, R. Tzvi Ashkenazi, and R. Moses Leib of Strzyzov, to name but a few of the sixty rebbes who lived there.

All of these hasidic courts became centers of many "converts" to Hasidism. The hasidic rebbes were concentrated mainly in the Leopoldstadt district, nicknamed "Matzah Island," which is located on the island formed by the Danube Canal and the Danube River. Leopoldstadt housed almost half of Vienna's Jewry during the interwar years. Some also lived in the third and the ninth districts.

The hasidim remained outside the *Kultusgemeinde*. The Aguda held its *Knessiyah Gedolah* there in 1923 and 1928. It had, in the interwar years, 104 Jewish houses of worship, which received official recognition of the *Kultusgemeinde*, 85 of which were hasidic.

After the collapse of the Austro-Hungarian empire, half of the hasidic rebbes and refugees returned to Poland and Galicia; the other half remained in Vienna.

After the *Anschluss*–the annexation of Austria by Germany–the remaining rebbes left for the Holy Land and the United States. By 1936, the Jewish population was reduced to 176,034. On *Kristallnacht*, forty-nine synagogues were destroyed. Jews were deported to Lodz, Izbice, Kielce, Buchenwald, Dachau, Mauthausen, Auschwitz, and Bergen-Belsen.

In 1993 there were about 10,000 Jews living in Vienna, including only about 1,000 hasidim. They have several *shtieblech*: *Bet HaMidrash Torah Etz Hayyim*, *Shomrei HaDat*, *Agudat Yisrael*, and *Mahzikei HaDat*.

H. P. Freidenreich, *Jewish Politics in Vienna, 1918–1938*, pp. 117, 119, 120, 122, 129, 132.

M.S.

VINAVER, Chemjo (1900–1974), musicologist–Born in Warsaw, a descendant of R. Mendel of Warka, from whom he inherited his love of Jewish music. He studied music in Berlin, where he lived until 1938.

He emigrated to New York, where he founded the *Vinaver Choir*. He wrote a magnum opus, *Hasidic Cantata for Orchestra, Chorus and Solo*, and an *Anthology of Jewish Music* (1955).

VITAL, Hayyim (1542–1620), kabbalist–Also called Hayyim Calabrese, he was the son of R. Joseph, a native of Italy, where he worked as a scribe. Hayyim studied in Safed under R. Moses Alshekh (1508–1600)–the author of *Torat Mosheh*, a homiletical commentary on the Bible–who ordained him, and for twenty-two months he was the disciple of R. Yitzhak Luria. He propagated his teachings at length in voluminous writings. He also devoted two and a half years to the study of alchemy, astrology, and astronomy.

After he moved from Safed to Damascus, he was the rabbi of the Sicilian Jews of the city. He regarded his teacher, the Ari, as a celestial being. After the death of the Ari, he saw him frequently in his dreams. If it had not been for him, very little would have been known of R. Luria's teachings.

His works *Etz HaHayyim* (Tree of Life) (Korzec, 1782), *Otzerot Hayyim* (Korzec, 1783), and *Tikkunei Avonot* (Korzec, 1783) contain his comments on his teacher's system. In his reincarnation book (*Sefer HaGilgulim*) (Frankfurt-am-Main, 1684), he revealed a list of Jewish sages who had recently returned to this world. In his *Sefer HaHezyonot* (Book of Visions), he records his dreams and visions.

His *Shaarei Kedushah* (Gates of Holiness), published in 1734, is a textbook of kabbalistic meditations. He describes the elements of Luria's system, the Ten *Sefirot*, the Four Universes, and the Five Levels of the Soul. The fourth section of the work was never published, but it exists in a number of manuscripts. It advocates the methods of R. Abraham Abulafia and R. Yitzhak of Acco. R. Vital discusses meditations involving *yihudim* (unifications), and he spells out in detail its technique: initiates are to spend the entire day in preparation, immersed in Torah study, not speaking any unnecessary word, and concluding with actual immersion in the *mikveh*. They are then to seclude themselves, wear white garments, and divest themselves of all physical sensation. Mentally, they then ascend from one firmament to the next until they reach the highest one.

R. Vital believed that one can attain sanctity through torment, flagellation, fasting, mastery over the passions, renunciation of pleasures, and ritual baths. He claimed to be the Messiah of the House of David, who is to precede the Messiah, the Son of David.

R. Ezekiel Halberstam of Sianiawa reprinted R. Vital's book *Sefer HaGilgulim* in 1875. R. Vital's works were held in high regard by all the hasidic rebbes.

A. Kaplan, *Meditation and Kabbalah*, pp. 187–190.

A.K.

VITEBSK, city in northeastern region of Belorussia—R. Shneur Zalman of Liady married the daughter of R. Leib Segal of Vitebsk and lived there for four years. Even after leaving Vitebsk, he frequently went back to visit.

The town was also the home of R. Menahem Mendel of Vitebsk, prior to his departure to the Holy Land, and of R. Aaron Moses Halevi of Starosselje.

Vitebsk was dominated by the hasidim of Lubavitch. Many rabbis of Vitebsk, such as R. Gershon Rivlin and R. Yitzhak Eizig Behard, were hasidim of Lubavitch.

Before World War Two, there were about 50,000 Jews living there. When Vitebsk was liberated by the Soviet army on June 26, 1944, there were no Jews there. Today, the Jewish population numbers about 20,000, with very few hasidim.

WAHRMAN, Abraham David, of Buczacz (6 *Adar* 1771–29 *Tishri* 1841)—Son of R. Asher Anshel, rabbi of Buczacz, he was born in Nadvorna. He studied under his father and under his uncle R. Joshua Haref of Sasov. He married the daughter of R. Tzvi Hirsch Kro, author of the responsa *Neta Shaashuim* (Zolkiev, 1829). At the age of twenty, in 1791, he became rabbi in Jaslowice. When his wife died, he married the daughter of R. Mordecai of Ungvar. It was there that he became attracted to Hasidism and was influenced by R. Levi Yitzhak of Berdichev, as well as by R. Moses Leib of Sasov and R. Tzvi Hirsch of Nadvorna. In 1819, after twenty-four years as rabbi, he succeeded his father-in-law as rebbe in Buczasz, where he was befriended by R. Hayyim of Czernowitz.

He never consulted doctors and discouraged others from doing so. He believed that sin caused ill health and disease. He was wont to prolong the services. His *seudot shlishit* would not end before dawn. He thought that the Messiah would come in 1840.

He was a prolific author and among his twenty-two publications were *Amarot Tehorot* on the laws on immersion on the Sabbath (Lvov, 1879); *Eshel Avraham* on the Passover *Haggadah* (Lvov, 1887); *Eshel Avraham* on *Shulhan Arukh, Orah Hayyim* (Lvov, 1886); *Birkhat David* on the Pentateuch (Lvov, 1848); *Divrei Avot* on the Ethics of the Fathers (Lvov, 1879); *Mahzeh Avraham* on Torah (Lvov, 1876); *Daat Kedoshim* on the laws of *shehitah* (Lvov, 1871); *Tehillah LeDavid*, a commentary on the Psalms (Lvov, 1872); and *Mili D'Hasidutah* (Kolomyja, 1850).

He was succeeded by his son R. Israel Aryeh Leib, who married the daughter of R. Isaiah Schorr of Iasi. He, in turn, was succeeded by his son, R. Abraham David, whose grandson, R. Meshullam Feivish (d. 17 *Heshvan* 1968), miraculously escaped the Holocaust.

The other sons of R. Abraham David of Buczacz were R. Jacob and R. Moses Joseph, who settled in Tiberias and died on 10 *Kislev* 1858.

M. Wunder, *Meorei Galicia*, vol. 2, pp. 944–960.

WAHRMAN, Jacob Yitzhak, of Iasi (1890–29 *Tishri* 1972)—Born in Iasi, son of R. Meshullam Feivish. After the Second World War, he settled in Tel Aviv, where he lived until his death on the anniversary of his grandfather's death.

He was twice married: first to Feiga, the daughter of R. Issachar Saul Teichman, and when she perished in the Holocaust, he married Miriam Rosa, a descendant of Rozwadov.

His brother and six sisters perished in the Holocaust.

WAKS, Hayyim Eleazar (1822–1 *Tammuz* 1889)—Born in Tarnogrod, son of R. Abraham Yehudah Leibish. His mother, Tobah, was a descendant of R. Yehiel Michael of Nemirov. He studied under R. Shmuel Zeinvil Heller of Przemysl. He married Bluma, the daughter of R. Moses Halberstam of Zborov (an elder brother of R. Hayyim Halberstam). For twenty-two years, he was rabbi in Tarnogrod and then, in 1862, became rabbi in Kalish. When his wife died in 1866, he married Shifra Mirel, the daughter of R. Israel Joshua Trunk of Kutno.

He visited R. Ezekiel Taub of Kazimierz, R. Abraham Bornstein of Sochaczev, and R. Elimelekh of Grodzisk. He became a rebbe and accepted *kvittlech*. He supported R. Leib Eger of Lublin when R. Leib was criticized by his opponents for his tardiness in attending circumcisions. He always consulted R. Hayyim Halberstam on halakhic and communal matters.

In 1869, he assumed the presidency of *Kollel Polin Kupat R. Meir Baal HaNes*. On 22 *Sivan* 1878, there was a pogrom in Kalish, and he subsequently lived in Warsaw for four years. In 1885, he became rabbi in Piotrokov. In *Sivan* 1886, together with his father-in-law, he visited the Holy Land. He urged the purchase of *etrogim* from the Land of Israel in preference to those from Corfu. He strongly opposed emigration to the United States.

He was the author of responsa *Nefesh Hayyah* on the Codes (Piotrokov, 1876), *Nefesh Hayyah* on the Pentateuch (Warsaw, 1933), on Festivals (1934), and *Shem U'She-erit LeNefesh Hayyah* (Jerusalem, 1961).

His son-in-law was R. Joseph Kalish of Amshinov.

A. Surasky, *Marbitzei Torah MiOlam HaHasidut*, vol. 1, pp. 232–247.

WALDEN, Aaron (8 *Shevat* 1838–23 *Tammuz* 1912), author – Son of Isaiah Nathan, he was born in Warsaw and was a hasid of R. Menahem Mendel of Kotzk, of R. Yitzhak Meir Alter of Ger, and of R. Hanokh Heinokh of Alexander.

He was the author of bibliographical works: *Shem HaGedolim HeHadash* (Warsaw, 1865) lists 1,500 rabbis and it saw three editions in his lifetime. He also published works on Hasidism: *Ohel HaRabbi* (1913) on the "Seer" of Lublin, *Niflaot Yitzhak* (1914) on R. Mordecai Menahem and R. Jacob David of Kalish, *Niflaot HaRabbi* (1911) on the "Seer" of Lublin, and *Mikdash Me'at* on Psalms (Warsaw, 1889).

WARSAW (Polish, Warszawa), capital city of Poland – In 1596 it succeeded Cracow as the capital of Poland. According to the 1792 census, only 6,750 Jews were living there. By the end of the eighteenth century, a number of hasidim were living in Praga, a suburb of Warsaw. David Friedlander (1750–1834), a friend of Moses Mendelssohn, who visited Warsaw in the first decade of the nineteenth century, records that the hasidim were increasing in number.

The wealthy Sonnenberg-Zbitkower family encouraged the growth of Hasidism. The marriage of Issachar Horowitz to the daughter of Tamarel with the participation of R. Israel Hofstein, the Maggid of Kozienice, gave to the hasidic community additional status. According to many authorities, the disputation between the hasidim, led by Stanislas Hoga, and the *mitnaggedim* took place in Warsaw on July 18, 1824. A hasidic work, *Yesod Emunah*, by R. Hanokh Cohen, was printed in Warsaw in 1821.

R. Yitzhak Kalish of Warka (d. 1848) frequently visited Warsaw for a variety of communal affairs. It was there that in 1846, he met Sir Moses Montefiore. The foremost of the hasidic pioneers was, however, R. Yitzhak Meir Alter, who settled in Warsaw in 1826. One hundred and thirty householders signed a petition proposing that R. Yitzhak Meir be appointed *dayan*. In 1864, out of a population of 243,000, 77,000 were Jews.

In 1870, the city had sixty hasidic *shtieblech*. A fee of ten rubles was required to open a *shtiebl*. By 1880, there were 300 places of worship, two-thirds of them hasidic.

Some of the leading Warsaw rabbis of the time were, however, *mitnaggedim*. Among them were R. Shlomoh Zalman Lipshitz (1819–1839), R. Hayyim Dawidsohn (1839–1854), R. Dov Berush Meisels (1854–1870), and R. Jacob Gesundheit (1870–1873).

Until the First World War there were no hasidic rabbis in Warsaw, for the rebbes tended to avoid big cities. They preferred remote hamlets where they could sequester themselves with their hasidim. With the advent of World War One, however, that situation changed, and the capital soon became the home of fifty rebbes. Prominent among them were R. Abraham Moses Kalish of Pabianice, R. Moses Mordecai of Kotzk, R. Joseph Aaron Morgenstern of Lukov, R. Mordecai Joseph Eliezer Leiner of Radzyn, R. Hayyim Yerahmiel Taub of Zwolen, and R. Alter Israel Shimon Perlow of Novominsk.

The hasidic community began to take an active part in communal affairs, and voting for the *kehillah* took place in frenzied excitement. In Warsaw, in the election of July 1, 1926, the Aguda received fifteen seats, and on May 20, 1931, when there were no fewer than thirty different parties, the Aguda obtained nineteen out of fifty seats. It was headed by Elijah Mazur and devoted 200,000 zlotys to religious affairs.

Many *hadarim* and *Talmud Torah* centers were combined into the *Horev* school system. There were many *yeshivot*, *Bet Yaakov* schools, and newpapers. In the 1936 elections, the balance was redressed in favor of the secularists. Warsaw then contained the largest Jewish community of twentieth-century Europe, and the second-largest in the world, next to New York. On the eve of World War II, the Jews in Warsaw numbered 368,400 (29.1 percent) of the total population.

Between October 1939 and January 1940, the Germans ordered anti-Jewish measures: Jews had to wear a white armband with a blue Star of David. A Jewish ghetto was established in mid-November 1940, and the Jews became confined to a small area. Of Warsaw's 1,800 streets, 73 were assigned to the ghetto.

Many hasidic rebbes were deported to the ghetto. "Hasidim," noted Hayyim A. Kaplan in his *Scroll of Agony*, "were even dancing, as is their pious custom on Sukkot." In the *Judenrat*, the Jewish community council set up by the Nazis under the chairmanship of Adam Czerniakov, hasidic leaders were represented. Among them were Yitzhak Meir Levine, Dov Shapira, Shimon Stockmacher, and Eizig Ackerman. A decree issued by the council on January 20, 1941 recognized the Sabbath as an official day of rest. To the end, Meshullam Kaminer and Alexander Zusya Friedman organized an underground network of schools and study courses for young and old so that "the Torah should not be forgotten in Israel."

On July 22, 1942, on the eve of the Fast of Av, the deathly deportations began. The daily number of Jews transported from the ghetto to Treblinka had reached 10,000 by October 1942. Within fifty-five days, 350,000 Jews had been transported to such demonic death factories as Treblinka, Maidanek, Auschwitz, Sobibor, and Chelmno; there were a dozen other such infamous destinations as well.

In the Shultz shoe factory at 44-46 Novolipki Street, the hasidic manager, Abraham Handel, sheltered many rebbes. Among the illustrious employees were R. Shalom Rabinowitz, the son of R. Hayyim Meir of Neustadt; R. Moses Bezalel Alter, R. Abraham Alter, R. David Halberstam, R. Kalonymus Shapira of Piascezno, and R. Joseph Perlow of Novominsk.

'A survivor has drawn a poignant picture of this strange workshop:

> Here you see sitting at the wood blocks [and] mending shoes [the work consisted mostly of pulling out nails with pliers] the Koziglower rebbe, R. Aryeh Frummer. . . . From time to time he addresses a word to the rabbi of Piascezno. . . . *Gemarot* [talmudical passages] and biblical texts are quoted, and the names of Maimonides and R. Jacob Ben Asher are mentioned. And who cares about the SS, about the *volksdeutsch* supervisor, or about hunger and misery and persecution and fear of death. (Hillel Zeidman, *Togbuch fur Varshaver Ghetto* [Buenos Aires, 1947], p. 147)

A number of hasidic rabbis, such as R. Moses David Rabinowicz, son-in-law of the rabbi of Radomsk, worked for a time at the *Hesed shel Emet* burial society. Others were active in *Toz* (the society for the protection of health among the Jews) or in the *Judenrat*. The rebbes of Ger, Bobov, and Lubavitch as well as a few others escaped the Holocaust. But most of the rebbes together with their families and followers perished there.

The historian Emanuel Ringelblum records, "Most of the rebbes were shot during the raids. The long beards and the sidelocks aroused the hatred of the Germans, and many a rabbi paid with his life for his awesome courage for sticking to his beard and sidelocks."

Another eyewitness, A. A. Kaplan, writes,

> On the night of Sukkot, I met a large group of zealous hasidim on Mila Street, and they sang festive songs in chorus and in public, followed by a large crowd of curious people and sightseers. Joy and revelry in poverty-stricken Mila Street! When they sang, they reached such a state of ecstasy that they could not stop until some heretic approached them, shouting: "Jews, to safeguard your lives is a positive biblical command. It is a time of danger for us. Stop this commotion." Only then did they become quiet. But some of them replied in their ecstasy: "We are not afraid of the murderers." (*Scroll of Agony*, ed. A. I. Katsh, [London, 1965], pp. 194–195).

Soon the streets of Warsaw, once citadels of Hasidism, were a pile of rubble, nearly a quarter square mile in area.

Y. Greenbaum, ed., *Varshau*.

J. Shatzky, *The History of the Jews in Warsaw*.

WEALTH—Hasidism arose chiefly among the lower classes and its rapid growth has been regarded, with some justification, as due, in part at least, to the resentment felt by the impoverished against the domination of their communities by the wealthy, a resentment that found expression in early hasidic denigration of wealth and material prosperity as hindrances to the pursuit of spirituality. Possessions tended to be considered by the majority of the early masters as the cause of self-aggrandizement and as a barrier to realization of the divine will.

Yet a complete doctrine on the poverty ideal was not allowed to emerge, largely because typical hasidic doctrine regarding the reclaiming of the holy sparks inherent in all things demanded that wealth, too, be embraced willingly when God had given it. Again, the sorry financial plight of the masses of East European Jewry brought with it the need that the hasidim turn to the *tzaddik* to pray on their behalf for "life and sustenance." And some degree of material prosperity was seen to be essential if the hasidim were to be able to afford the cost of their religious duties and their obligation to help the poor.

Attributed to R. Israel of Ruzhyn is the saying that whereas, as the rabbis remark, poverty is as becoming to Israel as a red rose is on a white horse, since Israel in exile has lost so much of its glory, it can afford to lose that "glory" (i.e., poverty) as well. To give liberally of one's wealth was expected of the hasid. Both R. Shneur Zalman of Liady and R. Tzvi Elimelekh of Dinov argue that the old talmudic rule that no more than a fifth of one's wealth be given to charity does not obtain when the poor are starving and have no one to turn to other than their wealthy brethren.

Although most of the early leaders of Hasidism were poor, some of the later masters such as R. Mordecai of Chernobyl and R. Israel Ruzhyn and his sons conducted their "courts" in lordly fashion—residing in fine homes fitted with opulent furnishings, driving about in a horse and carriage, and generally behaving like contemporary Polish counts. The rationale for that mode, of great offense and scandal especially to the *maskilim*, was that meanness or restriction in the *tzaddik's* path would arrest the flow of the divine grace for which he was responsible.

A degree of extravagance was required, it was maintained, in order for the *tzaddik* to mirror forth the sheer abundance of the divine blessing. It was not unknown for some of the later hasidic masters to become "sleeping partners" in the businesses of their hasidim, contributing the merit and the blessings to bring success to the enterprises. But basically, there were no real class distinctions in the courts of the *tzaddikim*, the distinctions between rich and poor tending to become transcended through the equality of the hasidim in the pursuit of a common goal.

Nahman of Tcherin, *Leshon Hasidim*.

L.J.

WEIDENFELD, Dov Berish, of Trzebinia (5 *Shevat* 1881–10 *Heshvan* 1966)—Son of R. Jacob, he was born in Grymalov. His father died before he reached the age of *bar mitzvah*, and he was brought up by his elder brothers. In 1900, he married Yakht, the daughter of Israel Joseph Kluger of Trzebinia, where he lived for some time. He was a hasid of the rabbi of Husyatin and of R. David Moses of Chortkov. He was very devoted to R. Hayyim Halberstam of Zanz.

In 1918, he became *dayan* of Trzebinia and rabbi in 1923. There he established a *yeshivah*, *Kokhov MiYaakov*.

During the Second World War, after taking refuge in Lvov, he was deported to Siberia in 1940 and lived for a time in Bukharia. In 1946, he settled in Israel, where his wife died in 1947. He then married Reizel, the daughter of R. Moses Lieberman of Kosice. He became the head of the *yeshivah Hayyei Olam* and then established his own *yeshivah Kokhov MiYaakov*.

He was the author of responsa *Dovev Meisharim* (Trzebinia, 1937).

Panim El Panim 391, pp. 13, 16.

WEIDENFELD, Jacob, of Grymalov (1840–21 *Shevat* 1894)—Son of R. Eliezer, R. Jacob—or "R. Yankele," as he was popularly known—was born in Stanislav. His father took him, when quite young, to visit R. Israel of Ruzhyn and R. Hayyim Halberstam. He studied in the *yeshivah* under R. Meshullam Issachar Halevi Horowitz of Stanislav. He married Rachel, the daughter of R. Shapsai Rapaport of Dabrova, where he lived for two years.

In 1865, at the age of twenty-five, he became rabbi of the city of Grymalov, near Tarnopol. He established a *yeshivah* and regularly visited the successors of R. Israel of Ruzhyn–the rebbes of Sadgora, Chortkov, and Husyatin.

He was the author of responsa *Kokhob Mi-Yaakov* (Bilgoraj, 1933), which were printed thirty-nine years after his death and reprinted in New York in 1958.

He had six children. His son R. Yitzhak Hayyim succeeded him in Grymalov.

A. Surasky, *Marbitzei Torah M'Olam HaHasidut*, vol. 1, pp. 246–247.

WEIDENFELD, Nahum, of Dabrova (1874–2 *Kislev* 1940)–Son of R. Jacob, he was born in Grymalov. His mother was Rachel, the daughter of R. Shapsai Hakohen Rapaport. He was ordained at the age of twenty by R. Yitzhak Shmelke of Lvov. In 1896, he married Tobah, the daughter of R. Abraham Pauker of Iasi. In 1897, he succeeded his grandfather as rebbe of Dabrova, where he lived for forty-three years. He established a *yeshivah* for sixty students.

In 1907, he was delegated by R. Shalom Mordecai of Brzezany to investigate the financial position of the *Kollel Galicia* in the Holy Land. He was active in the Aguda and participated in the Kattowitz conference of 1912.

When the Nazis captured Dabrova, he lived for a time in Sianiawa, where he died. His eldest son, R. Jacob, died in Antwerp in 1930, at the age of thirty-two. All of his other children perished in the Holocaust.

He was the author of responsa *Hazon Nahum* on *Orah Hayyim* and *Yoreh De'ah* (Bilgoraj, 1939) and a tract on *Tosafot Sheviit* on the problem of *shemitah* (Jerusalem, 1909). His manuscripts on the Talmud were lost in the war.

WEIKSELBAUM, Shlomoh Aryeh, of Tyczyn (1849–10 *Tammuz* 1927)–Born on *Rosh Hodesh Heshvan*, he was the son of R. Zeev Wolf (d. 1905), a brother of R. Shlomoh Leib of Leczna. He was a disciple of R. Jacob Moses of Komarno; above all, of R. Hayyim Halberstam, with whom he stayed for nearly six years; and of R. Halberstam's son, R. Ezekiel of Sianiawa, who encouraged him to become rebbe.

He married Havah Alta, the daughter of R. Judah Hayyim Ginsberg. He remained in Tyczyn during the First World War. He was violently opposed to czarist Russia and stated, "I have a tradition emanating from the rebbe of Ropczyce that the Russian Empire will be split up before the coming of the Messiah."

He was the author of *Birkhat Shlomoh*, *Hakhanat Lev LiTefillah* (Bilgoraj, 1927), and an anthology of hasidic ideas, published in Warsaw in 1927.

Der Yid, July 31, 1987.

WEINBERG, Abraham, of Baranowicze (1884–1 *Iyyar* 1933)–The son of R. Shmuel Weinberg of Slonim, he married the daughter of R. Tzvi Morgenstern of Lamazy. After the death of his father, in 1916, most of his father's hasidim followed R. Abraham, and, because his elder brother, R. Issachar Leib, remained in Slonim, R. Abraham settled in Baranowicze, where in 1918, he established a *yeshivah*, *Torat Hesed*.

He was in close contact with his hasidim in the Holy Land, whom he visited in 1929 and 1939. His son, R. Shlomoh David Joshua, succeeded him.

He was the author of tracts entitled *Bet Avraham* (Jerusalem, 1950–53) and *Bet Avraham* (Jerusalem, 1958), which contain discourses on the Pentateuch and Festivals and include letters that he wrote to his followers in the Holy Land.

WEINBERG, Abraham, of Slonim (1804–11 *Heshvan* 1884)–Son of R. Yitzhak Mattathias, *dayan* of Pinsk/Karlin and hasid of R. Asher of Stolin, he was born in Pinsk. He was a disciple of R. Noah of Lachowicze and R. Moses of Kobrin. He married Esther Dvosha, the daughter of R. David Zeltzer, a hasid of Lachowicze, and when she died, he married his niece Esther, the daughter of R. Hillel, and became the principal of the *yeshivah* in Slonim. On the death of R. Moses of Kobrin on 28 *Nisan* 1858, many of R. Moses' followers chose R. Abraham as his successor. He established a *yeshivah*.

He was the author of *Hesed Le'Avraham* in two parts (Josefov, 1886, and Jerusalem, 1974), containing a commentary on the Torah; *Yesod HaAvodah* in two parts (Warsaw, 1892 and Shanghai, 1946; reprinted in

Jerusalem, 1974); an allegorical commentary on the *Mekhiltah* entitled *Be'er Avraham* (Warsaw, 1927; reprinted in Jerusalem, 1970); *Maamarim* on the Sabbath (Jerusalem, 1957); and *Torat Avot* on Torah and Festivals (Jerusalem, 1961).

The rebbe corresponded frequently with his hasidim in Tiberias. He dealt with spiritual matters, the holiness of the Land of Israel, the sanctity of the Sabbath, and the importance of unity. He stressed that the Torah should be studied for its own sake and emphasized the supreme importance of prayers, love and awe of the Creator, humility, and faith.

He advised his followers to keep away from melancholy, for this causes one to fall into the power of the evil impulse. He regarded the *tzaddik* as the foundation of the world. The *tzaddik* had the power to uplift the people of his generation by repentance and worship. He is the unifying agent who binds his adherents into a single, harmonious society.

"Beware of discourtesy to the poor," he used to say. "If you turn them out of your house, you are guilty of rejecting the Lord Himself, 'for He standeth at the right hand of the needy' " (Psalm 109:31).

Among his "Ten Rules on Happiness" were: "Happy is the one who studies the Torah, who fears God, who sanctifies the name of God, who withstands temptation, who ends his days in repentance and holy service, and dies with a clear conscience." Commenting on Psalm 85:12, "Truth springeth out of the earth," he said, "Truth is near to me on the ground, but you do not wish to bend down to reach for it."

He was the president of the *Kollel Reisin*. His love for the Land of Israel was so great that he sent his three young grandsons to settle there.

He was succeeded by his grandson R. Shmuel.

W. Z. Rabinowitsch, *Lithuanian Hasidism*, pp. 188–191.

WEINBERG, Abraham, of Slonim/Jerusalem (1889–12 *Sivan* 1981) – The son of R. Noah, he was born on *Rosh Hodesh Tammuz* in Tiberias, where he studied. He was ordained by R. Moses Kliers. He visited Poland in 1906 and studied in Slonim with his uncle R. Shmuel, who sent him on many important missions.

He married in Tiberias the daughter of a hasid of Slonim and participated in the civic life of the town. He was elected first a member of the municipality, and in 1938, mayor. In 1929, one of his four sons was killed by Arab terrorists in Tiberias.

When R. Shlomoh David Joshua, the last rebbe of Slonim, died, he refused to succeed him. He regarded himself as a follower of R. Mordecai (Mottel) Hayyim Kislints (1864–1954), who had emigrated to the Holy Land in 1935. R. Mottel found it irksome to wield authority. "If you call me a rebbe," he told his adherents, "I will not forgive you in this world or in the next." He did not deliver discourses but simply told hasidic stories. It was not until the Second World War, in which all his relatives perished, and after the death of R. Mottel, in 1954, that R. Abraham reluctantly assumed the leadership of the hasidim of Slonim and moved to Jerusalem.

The unpretentious rebbe was highly respected for his diligence and his scholarship. He spent his days in the study of the Talmud, completing the entire Talmud twice each year, on the anniversary of his father's death in *Elul* and on his mother's death in *Adar*. He was active in the Aguda and was a member of the *Mo'etzet Gedolei HaTorah*. His *yeshivah*, *Bet Avraham*, established in 1942, is very large. There is a *kollel* attached to it.

He was succeeded by his son-in-law, R. Shalom Noah Brazovsky (b. 1911). However, a small portion of his hasidim followed his relative R. Abraham Weinberg, who lived in Bene Berak.

WEINBERG, Abraham, of Warsaw (1872–20 *Elul* 1942) – Son of R. Israel Nissan, a hasid of Ger, he was born in Stuczin. He studied at the *yeshivah* of R. Abraham Bornstein of Sochaczev. After his marriage, he lived in Warsaw, where he presented talmudic discourses to selected students. He was appointed a member of the Warsaw rabbinate and worked closely with R. Jacob Meir Biderman and R. Menahem Zemba.

He was the author of *Reshit Bikkurim* on *Behorot* (Piotrokov, 1930).

Elleh Ezkerah, vol. 3, pp. 9–16.

WEINBERG, Abraham Joshua Heschel (1898–24 *Nisan* 1978) – Son of R. Issachar Leib of Slonim, he was brought up by his grandfather R. Shmuel of Slonim. He married the daughter of R. David Weidenfeld of Warsaw. In 1928, he refused to succeed his father as rebbe, and it was only in 1933, after the death of his uncle, that he became rebbe. In 1935, he emigrated to the Holy Land and settled in Tel Aviv.

He was the author of *Otzar Orkhei HaTorah BeOholei Yissachar*, Part One of which appeared in Tel Aviv in 1973, and other parts of which appeared between 1974 and 1984.

One son, R. Shmuel Weinberg, was deputy mayor of Bene Berak, and his other son, R. Aryeh, is head of the *yeshivah Shuvu Banim*.

WEINBERG, David, of Ger (1860–19 *Heshvan* 1924) – Son of R. Israel, a grandson of R. Isaiah of Przedborz, and a hasid of Belz. After serving as rabbi in Sokal, he became in 1906 the rabbi of Ger. He became a devoted follower of R. Abraham Mordecai Alter of Ger.

WEINBERG, Dov Berish, of Przedborz (d. 23 *Av* 1873) – Son of R. Tzvi Hirsch, he traced his descent to Rabbenu Asher Ben Yehiel (1250–1327). He married the daughter of R. Isaiah of Przedborz. He was the devoted disciple of R. Issachar Dov of Radoszyce. After serving in a number of communities in which he suffered from dissension, he became the *dayan* of Przedborz.

Some of his discourses can be found in his son's book *Kuntres Halokh Devash* (Piotrokov, 1908).

He was survived by five sons and one daughter.

WEINBERG, Shlomoh David Joshua, of Baranowicze (1913–6 *Heshvan* 1943) – Only son and successor of R. Abraham II of Slonim. His mother was the daughter of R. Tzvi Hirsch of Lamazy. He married the daughter of R. Yitzhak Menahem Dancyger and lived in Alexander for two years. He was deeply involved with the upkeep of the *yeshivot Torat Emet* in Slonim and *Bet Avraham* in Jerusalem. He was deported to Baranowicze, where he was closely associated with R. Elhanan Wasserman.

His discourses can be found in *Bet Avraham*, tract no. 3 (Jerusalem, 1958) and in *Zikhron Kodesh* (Jerusalem, 1967).

He was murdered in a labor camp near Baranowicze and was buried in a mass grave.

W. Z. Rabinowitsch, *Lithuanian Hasidism*, p. 225.

WEINBERG, Shmuel, of Slonim (1850–19 *Shevat* 1916) – Son of R. Michael Aaron, R. Shmuel succeeded his grandfather R. Abraham as rabbi of Slonim. He was greatly influenced by R. Hayyim Halberstam of Zanz and R. Abraham Landau of Ciechanov. He was associated with the *Mahzikei Hadat* and encouraged the establishment of *mikvaot*, Torah centers, *yeshivot Torat Hesed* in Baranowicze and *Or Torah* at the tomb of R. Meir Baal Hanes in Tiberias.

A collection of his discourses can be found in *Bet Avraham*, tract no. 3 (Jerusalem, 1951).

He was succeeded by his son, R. Abraham II of Baranowicze.

W. Z. Rabinowitsch, *Lithuanian Hasidism*, pp. 192–193.

WEINBERGER, Joshua, of Belz (27 *Shevat* 1894–20 *Heshvan* 1966) – Son of R. Mordecai, the rabbi of Belz. He emigrated to the United States and served as rabbi of Dynov in the Bronx, New York.

He was survived by his sons – R. Shlomoh, a rabbi in New Jersey; R. Dov Zeev, rabbi of Young Israel in Williamsburg, Brooklyn; and R. Petahiah Meir in New Rochelle.

WEINGARTEN, Abraham Abba, of Libeshei (d. 1861) – Son of Yehiel-Mikhal, he was rabbi of Yanova, near Pinsk, and also in Libeshei. His synagogue existed until the Holocaust and was known as the "prayer house of R. Abele."

The dynasty was continued by his son, R. Hayyim Yitzhak (d. 1879), and by his grandson, R. Jacob Leib (d. 1922).

W. Z. Rabinowitsch, *Lithuanian Hasidism*, pp. 204–207.

WEINGARTEN, Joab Joshua, of Konskie (1847–1 *Heshvan* 1922) – Son of R. Nathan Nata, he married the daughter of R. Jacob Handelsman of Radom. He studied under R. Zeev Nahum Bornstein of Biala and under R. Abraham Bornstein of Sochaczev, who called him "my bookcase." After the death of R. Abraham, he followed R. Abraham's son, R. Shmuel.

He first lived in Radom, then in Nasielsk, where he shared a house with his rebbe. He was rabbi first in Lutomiersk, and from 1889 in Gostynin, where he was befriended by R. Yehiel Meir. In 1894, he became rabbi in Konskie, becoming known as the "Konskie rabbi."

He was the author of *Helkat Yoav* on the four parts of the *Shulhan Arukh*; the first part was printed in Piotrokov in 1903, and the second part in 1905.

His son R. Meir, who succeeded him, perished together with his wife, Yutta, and his son R. Dov Berish, his wife, and their two children in Treblinka.

A. Surasky, *Marbitzei Torah M'Olam HaHasidut*, vol. 2, pp. 266–281.

WEINGARTEN, Shemaryahu, of Libeshei (d. 1847) – Son of R. Abraham Abba Joseph of Soroka in Bessarabia, he was a disciple of R. Dov Baer, the Maggid of Mezhirech. He married the daughter of R. David Halevi of Stepan. In 1802, he became rabbi in Libeshei. He had the authority to appoint hasidim as *dayanim* and as ritual slaughterers.

In his memoirs *Ayarati Motele* (Tel Aviv, 1951; pp. 67ff.), Hayyim Chemerinski wrote, "The old *tzaddik* had wide powers, with rabbinical authority over all the surrounding small towns. . . . His followers were ignorant commoners, from the lowest classes, the dregs of society."

He was succeeded by his son, R. Yehiel-Mikhal, followed by R. Abraham Abba. The Libeshei rebbes left no written works. They were opposed to fasting, and they stressed the importance of joyfulness. They had their own hasidic melodies.

W. Z. Rabinowitsch, *Lithuanian Hasidism*, pp. 202–204.

WEINRYB, Bernard Dov Sucher (1900–1982), social historian – Born in Turobin, Poland, he studied in Breslau at the Jewish Theological Seminary. In 1934, he emigrated to the Holy Land, and in 1939, he settled in the United States, where he taught at Jewish Teachers' Seminary, Brooklyn College, Columbia University, and Yeshiva University.

He was the author of *The Jews in Poland: A Social and Economic History of the Jewish Community in Poland from 1100 to 1800* (Philadelphia, 1973), in which he deals with the origin of the hasidic movement; "East European Jewry Since the Polish Partition" in the *Jews, Their History*, edited by Louis Finkelstein (New York, 1970); and of *Texts and Studies in the Communal History of Polish Jews* (New York, 1950).

WEINSTOCK, Israel (1909–1980), author and scholar – A native of Brody, he was a descendant of Ruzhyn. He studied in Poland and Vienna and was the rabbi of Hampstead Garden Synagogue, in London, during the Second World War. In 1949, he emigrated to Israel.

He was the author of *Studies in Jewish Philosophy and Mysticism* (*BeMaagelei HaNiglah VeHaNistar*), which was published by Mosad HaRav Kook in 1969. He was also the editor of the Hebrew periodical *Temirim*, of textbooks, and of studies in Kabbalah and mysticism.

Contrary to the prevailing notion that the *Bahir* was compiled in the West at the end of the twelfth century, Dr. Weinstock cites conclusive evidence that that mystical textbook was already known several centuries earlier in Babylon and in the Holy Land.

Jewish Chronicle, November 7, 1986, p. 2.

WEINSTOCK, Moses Yair (d. 1982) – He was a descendant of R. David Biderman of Lelov and a disciple of R. Judah Ashlag. He married his cousin Hadass Devorah, the daughter of R. Joseph Levi Weinstock.

He lived in the United States for twelve years and then settled in the Holy Land. In 1958, he lost the power of speech and devoted the rest of his life to writing books on mysticism. Among his works were *Kodesh Hillulim* and *Pri Hillulim*.

WEISBLUM, Abraham Yitzhak, of Staszov (d. 1991) – A descendant of R. Moses Biderman of Lelov, he settled in the United States after the Second World War, living first on the East Side of Manhattan, then in Williamsburg, Brooklyn, for the rest of his life. All his family perished in the Holocaust.

He was buried on *Har HaMenuhot*, Jerusalem.

WEISBLUM, Eleazar, of Lejask (1741–28 *Tammuz* 1807)—The elder son of R. Elimelekh of Lejask, he was a follower of R. Mordecai of Neshkhiz; R. Israel, the Maggid of Kozienice; and R. Pinhas of Koretz. He edited his father's works and prepared *Noam Elimelekh* for the press.

After his father's death, most of his followers adhered to his disciples, Eleazar being left with a very small following. He suffered much poverty.

He first married the daughter of R. Israel Tzvi Hirsch Lipiner of Grodzisk, who died in childbirth. He then married the daughter of a wealthy man from Sianiawa. He was succeeded by his son, R. Naftali.

WEISBLUM, Eleazar, of Rzeszov (1838–15 *Tammuz* 1910)—He was the only son of R. Elimelekh of Rudnik, a descendant of Lejask. He married Brendel, the daughter of R. David Halberstam of Chrzanov. He was ordained by R. Hayyim Eleazar Waks of Piotrokov. In 1876, he became rabbi of Bukovsk; two years later, in Przeworsk; and subsequently, rebbe in Rzeszov.

He was renowned for his medical prescriptions, which were accepted by pharmacists. In 1900, when he was sixty-two years old, he divorced his wife and married Hayyah, the daughter of R. Hayyim Jonah Halpern, the rabbi of Rzeszov. In 1905, she gave birth to his only daughter, Kreindel Finkel, who married R. Shlomoh Horowitz of Rozwadov, who succeeded him.

His discourses, on Torah and Festivals, can be found in *Mishnah LaMelekh*, published anonymously in Przemysl in 1902. The work was reprinted in Brooklyn in 1952.

WEISBLUM, Eliezer Lipa, of Chmelnik (1743–26 *Adar* 1813)—Son of R. Elimelekh of Lejask, he married the daughter of R. Shmuel, a teacher in Sianiawa. He settled in Chmelnik, where he became rebbe. His prayers were so fiery that R. Jacob Yitzhak, the "Seer" of Lublin, said, "He needs nine angels to make up his *minyan*."

He was the author of *Orakh LeTzaddik* on the Pentateuch (Warsaw, 1893).

He was survived by two sons—R. Aryeh Leib and R. Elimelekh—and one daughter.

WEISBLUM, Elimelekh, of Rudnik (1788–19 *Tevet* 1849)—The son of R. Menahem Issachar Dov of Przeworsk, he became attached to R. Menahem Mendel of Rymanov and R. Naftali Tzvi of Ropczyce, who testified that "this young man is capable of welcoming the Prophet Elijah without preparation."

In 1824, after the death of R. Naftali, he became rebbe of Rudnik, a town where his brother-in-law, R. Tzvi Joseph Rubin, was rabbi. He then settled in Lancut and often traveled as far as Hungary to meet his followers. Every Thursday he would check the weights and scales of the Jewish merchants in the marketplace.

Some of his discourses are recorded in his son's book *Mishnah LaMelekh*.

WEISBROD, David (1912–1991), writer and journalist—Born in Poland, he studied in the *Yeshivat Hakhmei Lublin*. In 1936, he emigrated to the Holy Land. He was the author of popular works on Hasidism, such as *Arzei HaLevanon*, *HaBaal Shem Tov VeTalmidav*, and *Hakhmei Yisrael* (Tel Aviv, 1947). He also wrote under the pseudonym *HaLahmi*.

WEISS, Jacob Joseph, of Spinka (Szaplonca)/Bene Berak (1916–19 *Nisan* 1988)—Son of R. Israel Hayyim, he was born in Spinka. His mother died while giving birth to him, and he was brought up in the home of his grandfather. During the Second World War, he was taken from camp to camp, narrowly missing death. His wife, Alta, and his three children perished. His father, too, was murdered.

After the war, he returned to Borsa and to Selische, where he found one of his father's manuscripts, which he published in 1954 under the name *Hakal Yitzhak*. After living for a time in Borsa, Transylvania, he emigrated to the United States, where he lived in Crown Heights, Brooklyn. He established a *Bet HaMidrash* and a *yeshivah*.

In 1955, he settled in Bene Berak, where he maintained a *yeshivah* and set up a number of welfare agencies. To perpetuate the memory of his son, R. Abraham Abish, who had died in 1972, at the age of twenty-five, he established a *kollel*, *Ner Avraham*. He also planned the building of a *kiryah* in Petah Tikvah.

Jewish Tribune, April 14, 1988.

WEISS, Joseph G. (1918-1969) – Born in Budapest, he attended the university there. He then studied at the Hebrew University and at the University of London, where he earned B.A. and Ph.D. degrees.

He was a lecturer at University College, London; director of the Institute of Jewish Studies; and editor of the *Journal of Jewish Studies*. He contributed many learned articles to *Hadoar* (1965), *Journal of Jewish Studies* (1953, 1957, 1960, 1965), *Zion* (1951), *Kiryat Sepher* (1969), *Alei Ayin* (1952), *Hebrew Union College Annual* (1960), and *Tarbiz* (1958).

Published posthumously were *Studies in Bratslav Hasidism*, edited by M. Piekharz (Jerusalem, 1974), and *Studies in Eastern European Jewish Mysticism*, edited by D. Goldstein (1983).

His works on Hasidism were marked by meticulousness and sensitivity. He fully explored the writings of R. Nahman of Bratzlav, whom he regarded as an extraordinary and paradoxical thinker and poet who believed that "the hasid is like any other Jew, but does everything with passion." He maintained that Hasidism, like any other revivalist movement, always aims at the total mobilization of emotions and that Hasidism, wherever it spread, left in its wake emotional intensification of Jewish life, somewhat akin to the religious upheaval in seventeenth-century England.

WEISS, Joseph Meir, of Spinka (18 *Adar* 1838–6 *Sivan* 1909) – Born in Munkacs, the son of R. Shmuel Tzvi, a *dayan* of Munkacs and a hasid of R. Tzvi Elimelekh of Dynov. His mother was the daughter of R. Tzvi Hirsch of Drohobycz. As a child, Joseph Meir became known as an "*Illui*." He studied under his uncle R. Yitzhak Eizig of Svalyava. He also visited R. Shalom Rokeah of Belz. In 1852, he was sent to Ungvar to study under R. Meir ben Judah Leib Eisenstadt. He then continued his studies under R. Eisenstadt's son, R. Menahem, and under R. Shmelke Klein of Nagyszollos.

In 1854, he married Pearl, the daughter of R. Mordecai of Borsa, a descendant of R. Meir of Przemyshlan, where he lived for a number of years and established a *yeshivah*.

Apart from R. Shalom Rokeah of Belz, whom he called "my master, my teacher, and my guide," he also visited R. Mendel Hager of Vishnitz and R. Yitzhak Eizig of Zydaczov, who encouraged him to become a rebbe. He corresponded with the leading rabbinical authorities of his time, among them, R. Yitzhak Elhanan Spector of Kovno and R. Shalom Mordecai Hakohen Schwadron of Brzezany.

In the summer of 1857, his young wife died suddenly. A year later, he remarried. After Purim 1868, his second wife died in Munkacz, leaving him with two young daughters. In 1870, he married the widowed daughter of R. Ezra Jacob Bash of Spinka, a hasid of Zanz.

In *Sivan* 1873, he became rebbe in Spinka. Thousands of hasidim from Hungary and Galicia thronged to him. like all Hungarian Jews, he was deeply concerned about the Tisza-Eszlar blood accusation of 1882.

Apart from his regular *yoshvim*, all were welcome in his house. "Eat, dear children, eat!" the rabbi exhorted his indigent guests. Every day he distributed eighteen gulden – one-third to the poor, one-third to his *yoshvim*, and one-third to the poor of the Holy Land.

His works were published posthumously: *Imrei Yosef* on Genesis (Sighet, 1910); on Exodus (Munkacs, 1911); on Leviticus and Numbers (Sighet, 1913); on Deuteronomy (Seini, 1922); on Festivals, part one (Varanov, 1929); part two (Varanov, 1931); *Hakdamot Likkutei Torah VeHaShas* (Munkacs, 1911); *Kuntres Berakhot VeHodaot* (Sighet, 1912); *Zemirot Shabbat* (Brooklyn, 1974); and *Sefer Minhagei Spinka* (Bene Berak, 1981).

He was succeeded by his son, R. Yitzhak Eizig. In *Elul* 1974, his remains were brought from Romania and reinterred, in Petah Tikvah.

Y. J. Cohen, *Sages of Transylvania, 1630–1944*, pt. 2, pp. 91–92.

WEISS, Yitzhak Eizig, of Spinka (1875–13 *Sivan* 1944) – Son of R. Joseph Meir, he married Miriam, the daughter of R. Yisrael Baer Eichenstein of Verecke. From 1904, when his father became ill, he guided the hasidim. In 1909 he succeeded his father as rebbe. He was known as a student of outstanding diligence. The Talmud was his constant companion.

His love of learning was an all-consuming passion. "Holy Creator," the rebbe would exclaim, "have compassion on me. I only desire to serve you." He was renowned for his kindliness and concern for the poor and especially for his students. Every Tuesday, he was at home to all his students, who had their evening meal with him.

He would not begin his morning prayers unless he had first distributed money among the needy. When he had no money of his own, he would borrow money for the purpose.

His Hasidism was an amalgam of Kabbalah and *Halakhah*. He was influenced by Zydaczov, Novy Sacz, and Belz. He corresponded with many halakhic authorities, such as R. Tzvi Hirsch Shapira of Munkacs; his son, R. Hayyim Elazar; and R. Aryeh Leibish Horowitz of Strij.

He gave daily *shiurim* to his students, even on Saturday nights. He urged them to study the Torah with love, regarding it as a pleasure. He discouraged them from reading the newspapers and pressed them to devote every minute of their time to study.

He wrote to King George V of England during the king's illness, asking for help for his *yeshivah*. He also congratulated the president of the United States on his election.

During the First World War, he moved to Munkacs, where he stayed for twelve years. To avoid the antagonism of R. Shapira, he moved to Nagyszollos in 1930, where he established a large *yeshivah*. He did not sever his links with Spinka. Twice each year, on the *yahrzeits* of his parents, he would make a pilgrimage to his hometown to renew his ties with the Spinka hasidim. He had many opportunities to leave Eastern Europe, but he could not bear to abandon his hasidim.

On *Rosh Hodesh Sivan* 1943, the rebbe together with his eldest son, R. Israel Hayyim, was taken to Auschwitz. A Jew implored him: "Rabbi, pray for a miracle. We are traveling to our death." "Do not be afraid," the rabbi comforted him. "We are going to welcome the King Messiah. Surely, the Messiah is in chains, and it is our duty to redeem him." Throughout the fearful journey, he sang, over and over again, the phrase "Purify our hearts, to serve Thee with love." With the words from Leviticus 6:6, "Fire shall be kept burning upon the Altar continually," he met his Maker. Thirty members of his family perished in the Holocaust.

His son R. Jacob Joseph was the only member of the family to survive the war. After the liberation, he returned to Selische, where he found one of his father's manuscripts. He named it *Hakal Yitzhak*, since the Hebrew word *hakal* is numerically equivalent to 138, the numerical value of the name *Yitzhak*. That work, *Hakal Yitzhak*, was published in two parts: part one on Genesis and Exodus (New York, 1952), and part two on Leviticus, Numbers, and Deuteronomy (New York, 1954). He also published responsa, *Hakal Yitzhak* (New York, 1966).

S. Y. Gross and Y. Cohen, *Marmoros Book*, p. 42.

WEISS, Yitzhak Jacob (8 *Adar* 1902–11 *Sivan* 1989)–Son of R. Joseph Yehudah, he was born in Dolina, Poland. His mother was Yoheved Batshi, the daughter of R. Israel Meisels of Dolina. At the outbreak of World War I, the family moved to Munkacz, then Czechoslovakia, where the rabbi of Belz was living at that time.

He was ordained by R. Meir Arak and R. Shmuel Engel. From 1922 to 1929 he was the head of the Belz *yeshivah* in Munkacs. In 1928 he married Alta Rebecca Leah, the daughter of R. Pinhas Zimmebaum, the rabbi of Grosswardein. He later became a *dayan* in Grosswardein. During World War II, when a ghetto was established in Grosswardein, he escaped to Romania and lived in Arad and Bucharest.

In volume one of his responsa under the heading *Pirsumei Nisa* (London, 1955, pp. 26ff.), he gives a moving account of his life in Nazi-dominated Hungary, where his wife died in 1945. While waiting in Prague for an American visa, he accepted the position of senior *dayan* in Manchester, where he served for twenty-one years. He married Malkah, the daughter of R. Hayyim Dov Halpern, the rabbi of Vaslui, and when she died in 1973, he married thirdly Hannah Miriam (d. 1990), the daughter of R. Hayyim Meir Hager of Vishnitz.

On the advice of R. Yoel Teitelbaum of Satmar, he joined the *Bet Din* of the *Eidah Haredit* in Jerusalem in 1970 and became *Rosh Bet Din* nine years later.

He was the author of monumental works. His book *Divrei Yitzhak* on *Orah Hayyim* and *Yoreh De'ah* was published in Grosswardein as early as 1941 with the encomium of R. Dov Berish Weidenfeld of Trzebinia. His magnum opus, however, was responsa *Minhat Yitzhak* on the four Codes of the *Shulhan Arukh* in nine parts, of which the first four parts were published in London in 1955, 1958, 1962, and 1967, and parts five to nine of which were published in Jerusalem in 1972, 1976, 1980, 1983, and 1985. He also wrote *Minhat Yitzhak* on the weekly portions of the Torah (Jerusalem, 1975).

Y. J. Cohen, *Sages of Transylvania*, pp. 93–95.

WELTFRIED, Immanuel, of Pabianice (d. 19 *Adar* 1939) – Elder son of R. Abraham Moses of Rozprza, he first lived in Pabianice, and after the First World War, in Lodz. He married the daughter of R. Joshua Horowitz of Dzikov, and when his wife died, he married Havah, the daughter of R. Yehudah Aryeh Leib Epstein of Ozarov and the widow of R. Yerahmiel Tzvi Rabinowicz of Siedlce (d. 1906).

He was buried in Lodz, near the grave of the rabbi of Radoszyce.

WELTFRIED, Immanuel, of Przedborz (1802–27 *Shevat* 1865) – Son of R. Isaiah of Przedborz, he married the daughter of R. Israel Horowitz, son of R. Jacob Yitzhak, the "Seer" of Lublin. He was a disciple of R. Issachar Baer of Radoszyce and became known as a miracle worker.

His son R. Abraham Moses (1850–20 *Elul* 1918) was a disciple of R. Hayyim Halberstam. After living in Rozprza, near Piotrokov, he settled in Przedborz in 1910. His melodies were renowned, and he was endowed with great worldly wisdom.

Three of his five sons were R. Immanuel of Pabianice, R. Shlomoh Zalman of Tomaczov, and R. Isaiah (b. 12 *Av* 1939) of Kalish.

Elleh Ezkerah, vol. 5, pp. 229–230.

WELTFRIED, Shlomoh Zalman, of Tomaszov (1870–1943) – Son of R. Abraham Moses, a descendant of the Holy Jew of Przysucha. He was a hasid of Chortkov and became rebbe in the lifetime of his father. After his father's death, he lived in Tomaszov. He practiced *hitbodedut* (seclusion). He would pray and study in seclusion for hours every day. Not even his children were allowed to disturb him during his devotions.

In 1935, he settled in Lodz, which, because of its geographical position, was more accessible to the hasidim. Even hasidim who followed other rebbes would regularly visit him for his guidance and to listen to his thought-provoking discourses.

During the Second World War, he lived in Warsaw. He, his seven sons, and one daughter were all murdered by the Nazis.

Elleh Ezkerah, vol. 5, pp. 229–233.

WERDYGER, David (b. 1910), cantor – Born in Cracow, the son of a prominent hasid of Ger, he sang as a soloist with the leading cantors of Cracow. During World War II, he spent two years in Nazi concentration camps.

After the war, he settled in America, winning acclaim for his cantorial talents. As a singer and composer, he produced many hasidic melodies. He was cantor at congregation *Talmud Torah* in Flatbush, Brooklyn.

WERTHEIM, Aaron (1882–9 *Iyyar* 1988) – Born in Romania, son of R. Joseph, a descendant of R. Aaron of Chernobyl and R. Aryeh Leib Wertheim of Benderi. He studied under R. Moses Soloveitchik of Brest-Litovsk and was ordained by R. Judah Leib Zirelson of Kishinev and R. Moses Feinstein.

He emigrated to the United States, where he received a doctorate from Dropsie University and served, for fifty years, as rabbi of *Bene Yisrael* congregation, in Linden Heights, Brooklyn. He was active in the Mizrachi and the Rabbinical Association.

He was the author of *Halakhot VeHalikhot BaHasidut* (Laws and Customs in Hasidism) (Jerusalem, 1960; reprinted, 1989), which was translated into English by Shmuel Himelstein (Ktav, 1992). It deals with many religious topics in a refreshing and original manner.

WERTHEIM, Aryeh Leib, of Benderi (d. 3 *Tammuz* 1854) – Son of R. Shimon Shlomoh of Savran (d. ca. 1790), he married the daughter of R. Abraham of Korostyshev. When his wife died, he married the daughter of R. Judah Meir of Shepetovka. In 1814, he settled in Benderi.

The dynasty was maintained by his son, R. Yitzhak (d. 3 *Sivan* 1911) and then by R.

Shimon Shlomoh (1865–18 *Shevat* 1925), who was rabbi in Bessarabia.

Y. Alfasi, *HaHasidut*, pp. 82–83.

WESSELY, Naftali Herz (1725-1805), writer – Born in Hamburg, he spent his youth in Copenhagen. He studied in the *yeshivah* of R. Jonathan Eybeschuetz and settled in Berlin, where he was associated and collaborated with Moses Mendelssohn's translation of the Torah.

He was a prolific author, and in his work *Divrei Shalom VeEmet* (Berlin, 1782), he advocated secular instruction for the Jews. He insisted that a true knowledge of Judaism was impossible without secular culture. He aroused the bitter enmity of the hasidim.

J. S. Raisin, *The Haskalah Movement in Russia*.

WIDEREWITZ, Hayyim Jacob (1836–1911) – Born in Dobromilsi, White Russia, he received a traditional *Habad* education and studied under R. Menahem Mendel Schneersohn of Lubavitch, who ordained him.

From 1877, he was a rabbi in Moscow, where he served for sixteen years. He edited and published the responsa of his rebbe.

After being expelled from Russia in 1893, he settled in New York, where he was the rabbi of a small hasidic synagogue. He was one of the first hasidic rabbis to emigrate to the United States.

Z.A.

WIENER, Herbert (b. 1916), author and scholar – Born in Boston, he graduated in 1942 from the University of Massachusetts. He is well-known for his writings in the field of Jewish mysticism, Hasidism, and religious problems in the state of Israel.

His series on the Lubavitch movement was published in *Commentary*, vol. 23 (1957, pp. 231–241 and 316–327). His book *9 ½ Mystics* (New York, 1969) records "a treasure hunt for the life secrets of the mystical tradition known as the Kabbalah."

WIESEL, Elie (b. 1928) – Literary personality and leading literary figure dealing with the Holocaust of European Jewry. Born in Sighet, Romania, Wiesel was raised in a strictly Orthodox–hasidic environment.

In 1944, along with his entire family and village, he was sent first to Birkenau, then to the Auschwitz, Buna, and Buchenwald concentration camps, from which he emerged the sole survivor of his family. After the war, Wiesel settled in Paris and then moved on to New York, where, in addition to his literary and journalistic work, he has been active in Zionist activities and in alerting the world to the cause of Soviet Jewry (see his *Jews of Silence*, 1968). He has been a professor at City College of New York, and he is currently Distinguished University Professor at Boston University. He was the recipient of the Nobel Peace Prize in 1986.

Writing in French but drawing his literary imagination largely from the hasidic world of his youth, Wiesel has explored the nature of the Holocaust and its implications for post-Holocaust Jewry in a series of moving and penetrating novels, the most famous of which is *La Nuit* (1958; *Night*, 1960), which records through the medium of literary imagination his autobiographical experiences in the death camps. Other novels of his that deal with similar and related themes are *L'Aube* (1960; *Dawn*, 1961); *Le Jour* (1961; *The Accident*, 1962); *La Ville de la Chance* (1962; *The Town beyond the Walls*, 1964); *Les Portes de la Forêt* (1964; *The Gates of the Forest*, 1966); *Les Chants des Morts* (1966; *Legends of Our Time*, 1968); *Zalmen, ou la Folie de Dieu* (1968; *Zalman, or the Madness of God*, 1975); *Le Mendiant de Jerusalem* (1968; *Beggar in Jerusalem*, 1970); *Le Serment de Kolvillag* (1973; *The Oath*, 1973); and *Ani Ma'amim* (1974).

Wiesel's response to the Holocaust, as expressed in these novels, draws most heavily on hasidic inspiration. In the face of the unfathomable tragic experience of the modern Jew, Wiesel, rather than search for a new theodicy to vindicate God, prefers to tell a hasidic tale and to exhort the Jews not to lose their faith in God or their way in the world. Thus the hero in *The Gates of the Forest* says, "There is joy as well as fury in the hasid's dancing. It's his way of proclaiming, 'You don't want me to dance; too bad, I'll dance anyhow. You've taken away every reason for singing, but I shall sing. . . . You didn't expect my joy, but here it is; yes, my joy will rise up; it will submerge you' " (p. 198).

Wiesel's literary work reveals the penetrating imprint of hasidic thought and life in many ways. Among the more important are the following.

1. Wiesel uses aphoristic style to convey in compact fashion a profound spiritual insight. For example, in *The Gates of the Forest*, the following aphorism is placed in the mouth of the hero: "What, then is man? . . . Hope turned to dust . . . but the opposite is equally true. What is man? Dust turned to hope."

2. The author emphasizes the centrality of the moral struggle and the need to make hard moral decisions. Thus we see that the main issue for the hero of *Dawn*, and, again, of *The Accident*, *The Town beyond the Walls*, and *The Gates of the Forest* centers on our freedom to act or not to act, the latter also being a choice.

3. Inseparably related to the importance of existential decision in his novels is Wiesel's free literary use of the seminal kabbalistic-hasidic doctrine of *Tikkun*. That is, that it is we who must prepare the way for the Messiah; that it is we who must be active in history, rather than passive; that it is human activity that is an essential ingredient in the redemption of mankind and history. This theme is especially pronounced in Wiesel's later work, *The Gates of the Forest*, which comes as close to being a definitive statement of his views on the Holocaust as one is likely to find. In that work he argues that humanity must take on what amounts to divine responsibility for history: "Whether or not the Messiah comes doesn't matter; we'll manage without him. It is because it is too late that we are commanded to hope. We shall be honest and humble and strong, and then he will come, he will come every day, thousands of times every day" (p. 225).

4. The theme of the importance of having a teacher—which pervades Wiesel's novels—a teacher in the sense of a living guide, giving organic-dynamic expression to an existentially authentic confrontation with people, world, and God, is unmistakably drawn after the image of the hasidic *tzaddik* and his relation to his hasidim. This theme of intense interpersonal communication out of which grows the most meaningful of concrete truths is a key element in Wiesel's work and is very much influenced by Martin Buber's and A. J. Heschel's emphasis on that aspect of hasidic community.

Of Wiesel's direct writings on Hasidism, one particular title calls for notice—his retelling of hasidic tales in *Souls on Fire* (1972). That volume, which grew out of lectures on Hasidism originally presented in New York, sums up his deep love for his hasidic roots and the powerful sway they still exercise over him. The tales are retold in a moving, indeed, beautiful, fashion, conveying much of the authentic flavor of the original. In some respects Wiesel's tales and comments reflect more the influence of Buber's dialogical pansacramentalist version of Hasidism and of Heschel's somewhat existentialized version of Hasidism than the authentic original message. Overall, however, *Souls on Fire* is an important collection of hasidic tales, which enriches the literature on Hasidism available in English and which conveys something of the warmth and meaning of hasidic life to those personally unacquainted with it.

Wiesel is also the author of *Ecstasy and Sadness: Further Tales of the Hasidic Masters* (1982).

M. Friedman, "Elie Wiesel: The Modern Job," pp. 48–52.

S.T.K.

WILENSKY, Mordecai (b. 1914), author—Born in Kobryn, he studied in the *yeshivah* of Kobryn, in the Hebrew gymnasium in Brest-Litovsk, and at the Hebrew University. He was professor of Jewish history at the Hebrew College, Boston. He was awarded a grant by the Council of Learned Societies and by the American Philosophical Society to study in Leningrad in 1967.

He is the author of the Hebrew work *Hasidim and Mitnaggedim—a Study of the Controversy between Them in the Years 1772–1815* (Jerusalem: Mosad Harav Kook, 1970). He utilized unpublished tracts, unpublished letters from the archives of Dr. Israel Klausner, the Jewish collection in St. Petersburg, and the Dubnow archives at Yivo.

He is also the author of many learned articles such as "The Polemic of R. David of Makow against Hasidism" (*Proceedings of the American Academy of Jewish Research*, vol. 25 [New York, 1956]), "Some Notes on R. Israel Loebel's Polemic against Hasidism" (*Proceedings of the American Academy of Jewish Research*, vol. 30 [New York, 1962]), "The Burning of Anti-Hasidic Pamphlets in the Eighteenth century" (*Tarbiz*, 1958), and "The Testimony against the Hasidim in the Polemical Literature of the Mitnaggedim," in the Jubilee Volume of Prof. Y. Baer (1960).

WOMEN–There have been no women kabbalists in Judaism. The Kabbalah, however, contains some elements of feminine theology. The *Shekhinah*, the divine presence, is described in feminine terms.

In Hasidism, the woman, the *hasidah*, as she was called, occupied an honored position. The Besht never forgot the devotion of his own wife, Hannah. R. Israel loved her deeply and did not remarry after she died. "Heaven has departed with her," he grieved. "I thought that a storm would sweep me up to heaven, like the Prophet Elijah, but now that I am only half a body, this is no longer possible." In his last will and testament he urged his hasidim to honor their wives.

The Besht taught his followers to regard feminine beauty as a reflected radiance of the Divine Being. "If you encounter a beautiful woman," he said, "pause and reflect on the infinite source of all that is beautiful. In this way, you will be moved to love God more intensely."

He adored his only daughter, Adel, and he applied to her the verse "At his right hand was a fiery law unto them" (Deuteronomy 33:2). The first letters of the Hebrew words *Esh*, *Dat*, *Lamo*, make up the name Adel.

When one of his followers, Jonah Spravedliver, complained to the Besht about the strange behavior of his wife, Yente, the master reassured him: "She has seeing eyes and hearing ears," and bestowed upon her the title "prophetess."

R. Nahman of Bratzlav often urged his followers to honor and respect their wives. "Women," he said, "have much anguish from their children. They suffer in pregnancy and in childbirth and then have the trouble of raising the children. This is in addition to the many other areas where they suffer. you should take this into consideration, honoring and respecting your wives" (*Sihot HaRan* 264).

R. Leib Sarah's was the only hasidic rebbe whose name was always associated with that of his mother. She had married an elderly scholar in order to escape the unwelcome attentions of the local squire's son.

Feige, the daughter of Adel, was said to be endowed with "divine spirit." Merish, the daughter of R. Elimelekh of Lejask, was renowned for her scholarship. Freida, eldest daughter of R. Shneur Zalman of Liady, collected her father's aphorisms and was honored by the hasidim. Her father instructed her in hasidic lore. His other daughter, Devorah Leah, mother of the *Tzemah Tzeddek*, is said to have given her life to her father in a mystical transaction, enabling him to live.

Perele, eldest daughter of R. Israel of Kozienice, wore *tzitzit* (ritual fringes), fasted on Mondays and Thursdays, and received petitions from her followers. "The *Shekhinah* rests upon her," acknowledged R. Eimelekh. Rachel, daughter of R. Abraham Joshua Heschel of Opatov, was equally renowned. Her father stated that she "has a holy spark." Rebecca, the wife of R. Simhah Bunem, was known for her acts of loving-kindness.

The daughter of the rabbi of Belz, Eidele, who married R. Yitzhak Rubin of Sokolov (d. 1876), delivered discourses, distributed *shirayim*, and conducted herself like a rebbe. "All Eidele needs is a rabbi's hat," remarked her father fondly. Similarly, Sarah, the daughter of R. Joshua Heschel Teumim Frankel, made a name for herself. When her husband died in 1916, she more or less took his place. She fasted regularly, and asceticism became her way of life. Yet it proved to be no barrier to longevity. She died in 1937, at the age of ninety-nine.

In the same way, "Malkale, the Triskerin," the daughter of R. Abraham Twersky of Turiysk, distributed *shirayim* and received petitions twice daily from the hasidim. Another woman of rabbinic learning was Hannah Havah, the daughter of R. Mordecai Twersky of Chernobyl (d. 1837), who, according to her father's testimony, was endowed "with the holy spirit from the womb and from birth." He deemed her equal in piety to his sons, "the eight candles of the *menorah*."

Highly regarded, too, were Hayyah Moskowitz, the daughter of R. Meir of Przemyshlan; Sarah, mother of R. Joshua Heschel of Olkusz and wife of R. Hayyim Shmuel of Checiny; Nehamah, the daughter of R. Hayyim of Zanz; and Sarah Shlomtze, the daughter of R. Menahem Mendel of Zydaczov. The most famous of all hasidic women was Hannah Rachel, the only child of R. Monesh Werbermacher, who became known as the Maid of Ludomir.

Although the majority of hasidic women were themselves unlettered, they were still often the ones largely responsible for the eruditon of their husbands and sons. They maintained and sustained the family, relieving their husbands of material cares so as to allow them to devote themselves exclusively to matters of the mind and soul. The lives of these wives were difficult.

Feige, the wife of R. Yitzhak Meir Alter of Ger, was a vendor of cloth. Yoheved, the wife of R. Judah Leib Alter of Ger, became a sugar merchant. The wife of R. Jacob Guterman of Radzymin turned peddler. Hannah Devorah, the wife of R. Tzaddok Hakohen Rabinowitz of Lublin, dealt in clothes.

There is no justification for the accusations leveled by the *Haskalah* writers that Hasidism undermined Jewish family life when young men (especially those of Kotzk) stayed away from their homes at the courts of their rebbes for lengthy periods. Most hasidic rebbes permitted women to visit and consult them. It was to the rebbe that women turned to unburden their hearts. One exception to this practice was R. Yitzhak ben Mordecai of Nezkhis, who discouraged such visits.

An important part was played by Tamarel Bergson, wife of Baer Shmulovitch. She supported a number of young men who later became rebbes. She herself was a devoted hasidah of R. Yitzhak Kalish of Warka, R. Mendel Morgenstern of Kotzk, and R. Yitzhak Meir Alter of Ger.

To meet the needs of women who could not read Hebrew, the *Shivhei HaBesht* was translated into Yiddish, as were the collections and stories of R. Nahman of Bratzlav, who wished his stories to be printed in bilingual editions so that "a woman who is barren could read one of the stories and by this she would be blessed with children" (*Hayyei Moharan*, p. 16). R. Dov Baer of Lubavitch, too, wrote *Pokeah Ivrim* in Yiddish, so that it could be read by women.

From the beginning of the twentieth century, a number of hasidic parents encouraged their daughters to study. Private tutors were in great demand. A secular education, especially study of the Polish or Russian language, was of more than academic use, for women, often the breadwinners, needed to deal intelligently with the non-Jewish world.

To counteract the *Tarbut* (under the auspices of the Zionists) and the *Cysho* (central Yiddish school organizations), the *Bet Yaakov* movement was established by Sarah Schenierer. She describes the scene:

> As we pass through the *Elul* days, the trains which run to the little *shtetlekh* where the rebbes live are crowded. Thousands of hasidim are on their way to them, to spend the solemn High Holy Days with their rebbes . . . and we [the women] stay at home, the wives, the daughters and the little ones. We have an empty *Yom Tov*. It is bare of intellectual Jewish content.

The first *Bet Yaakov* school was established in Cracow in 1917. Its success was phenomenal. The *Keren Hatorah* (the special Aguda fund established by German Jewish Orthodoxy for Torah institutions) gave them financial support. Moral support came from the rabbi of Belz and the rabbi of Ger. "It is our duty nowadays," the rabbi of Ger said, "to work for the *Bet Yaakov* movement, where the future mothers of Israel are being educated in the true traditional spirit of the Torah, and are receiving sound, all-round schooling."

Even Satmar, which originally opposed the *Bet Yaakov* movement because of its affiliation with the Aguda, has now established a *Bet Rachel* school system, whereby girls are taught Bible stories, moral teachings, and simplified laws and customs.

In the schools of the Lubavitch movement, girls are encouraged to study *Tanya*, Hebrew discourses of hasidic rebbes, and *sihot* by the rebbe.

The new rapidly expanding Jewish feminist movement or Jewish liberalism has so far not touched the hasidic community. Hasidic women do not regard themselves as second-class citizens. The fact that they cannot constitute a *minyan*, be called up to the Torah, or write or authorize a divorce, as well as the fact that they are shut off from the source of power and decision making does not worry them in the least.

A woman who dressed immodestly is regarded as transgressing *Daat Yehudit*, the norm of Jewish behavior. Hasidic women pray in a segregated part of the *shtiebl* or behind heavy curtains, where they cannot be seen. This is not regarded as the mores of a bygone age. The segregation of the sexes at the synagogue and at social gatherings, weddings, and other festivities, as well as the prohibition against mixed dancing, is based on traditional Judaism. Hasidism does not subscribe to the notion that "families that pray together stay together," for hasidic family life is generally more stable than that of their non-Orthodox counterparts.

The hasidim adhere to the concept of the woman as being "all glorious within." They regard the home and childbearing as women's main preoccupations. Marriage is not considered by the hasidim, as it is by some church fathers, as a compromise with the flesh, but rather as a sanctification.

Courting is not encouraged, and marriages are arranged through go-betweens (*shadhan*). A woman is expected to procreate, large families being the norm. Birth control is utterly forbidden, and divorce is comparatively rare. Abortion is forbidden, and *taharat hamishpahah* is observed rigidly.

The hasidim preserve the practice of shaving or cutting off a woman's hair prior to or after the wedding ceremony. The *sheitel* (wig) or the kerchief is part of the normal attire of the hasidic woman.

The hasidim are against *bat mitzvah* celebration for girls on the ground that it is a Reform innovation.

R. Joseph Yitzhak Schneersohn of Lubavitch set up the Women's Association for the purity of the family, and in a letter written in 1936, he stated, "It is the duty of the wives and daughters of the hasidim to stand in the forefront of any enterprise for the strengthening of religion and of Judaism in general" (*Iggrot Kodesh*, vol. 4 [Brooklyn, 1983], pp. 12 and 13). Similarly, the late rebbe, R. Menahem Mendel Schneerson, founded the Lubavitch Women's Organization and wrote letters to *Neshei U'Bnos Chabad* (Brooklyn, 1981, pp. 31–32). The Lubavitch foundation of Great Britain has issued many publications for women, among them, *A Woman of Valour–an Anthology for the Thinking Jewess* (London, 1976).

It is noteworthy that a number of women, such as Rivkah Schatz Uffenheimer and Rachel Elior of Jerusalem, Jaffe Eliach of New York, and Ada Rapoport-Albert of London, have made notable contributions to the study of Hasidism and mysticism.

Openly and appreciatively, hasidic writers and rebbes acknowledge the vital part played by women in Jewish life. No wonder many women responded with such instant warmth to Hasidism.

H. M. Rabinowicz, *Hasidism: The Movement and Its Masters*, pp. 341–350.

A. Rapoport-Albert, "On Women in Hasidism: S. A. Horodecky and the Maid of Ludmir Tradition," pp. 495–524.

WOOL–Hasidim avoided woolen garments, thereby lessening the risk of wearing apparel with the admixture of flax (*shatnes*), which is prohibited by the Torah (Deuteronomy 22:11). R. Hayyim Joseph David Azulai noted that the hasidim in the Holy Land, like R. Menahem Mendel of Vitebsk and R. Abraham of Kalisk, wore silk and not wool (*Birhei Yosef*, *Yoreh De'ah* 299). R. Moses Teitelbaum stated that, "he who is imbued with the fear of God should not wear wool" (*Heshiv Moshe*, *Orah Hayyim* 7).

A. Wertheim, *Halakhot VeHalikhot BaHasidut*, pp. 193–195.

WUNDER, Meir (b. 1934), author–Born in Haifa, he studied in the *yeshivah* of Ponevezh and graduated with an M.A. from the Hebrew University. He is the author of *Meorei Galicia*, *Entziklopediyah L'Hakhmei Galicia*, published in Jerusalem in four volumes (1978–1992), in which he deals with many hasidic rebbes. The work received the prize of the World Federation of Polish Jews.

He is also the author of many learned articles on Hasidism, such as *R. Zehariah Mendel of Yaroslav* (Sinai, vol. 73 [1973], pp. 79–87), *Torat Shimon* on R. Shimon of Yaroslav (Jerusalem, 1974), and *Elef Margaliot* (A Thousand Pearls), biographies of one thousand ancestors (Jerusalem, 1993).

Y

YAHRZEIT (lit., year time, i.e., anniversary of a death) – The anniversary of the death of a deceased relative is commemorated on the *yahrzeit*. In talmudic times, many refrained from drinking wine or eating meat on that day, and some fasted (*Nedarim* 12a). Manasseh ben Israel, in his *Nishmat Hayyim* (chap. 27) gives a reason for the fast: "The soul," he said, "ascends to a higher sphere, and this is a source of grief to the living."

The Besht fasted on a *yahrzeit*. The hasidim, however, followed the tradition of R. Dov Baer, the Maggid of Mezhirech, who advised his hasidim "not to fast, but to make a *seudah* and to distribute money to charity." It is customary among the hasidim to sing and even to dance at such a *seudah* and to say that "the soul should have an *aliyah*." (May the soul of the deceased be raised to a still higher level of purity.)

Mishnayot are studied. R. Israel Friedman of Ruzhyn studied chap. 24 of *Kelim*, for all the seventeen *mishnayot* concluded with the Hebrew word *Tahor Miklum* (clear). Others studied the *Mishnah Mikvaot* chap. 7. No *Tahanun* (a group of elegies) is recited in the morning service on Mondays and Thursdays, and daily petitions for grace and pardon are said in the morning and afternoon. It was customary for the rebbe to officiate at the *Musaf Amidah* and at Saturday night services prior to the *yahrzeit*.

In Belz, the rebbe would also officiate at the Friday evening service prior to the *yahrzeit*. To R. David Moses Friedman of Chortkov the *yahrzeit* was a festive day, for the soul is elevated to a higher sphere. In this way Hasidism follows the kabbalists, by whom the day of *yahrzeit* was regarded as a "marriage," a blissful reunion of the soul with the *Shekhinah* (divine presence).

One outstanding celebration is the *yahrzeit* of the *Tanna* and mystic R. Shimon Bar Yohai (ca. 130–160). On Lag BaOmer his tomb is visited and a bonfire is lit. R. Yitzhak Luria recorded, "In these last eight years my teacher, his wife and family have gone there, and they stayed there for three days" (*Etz Hayyim* 22).

A. Wertheim, *Halakhot VeHalikhot BaHasidut*, pp. 225–228.

YARMULKA (Polish origin, the name of a skullcap; Hebrew, *kippah*) – The concept of men's constantly wearing some head covering is well developed in the Talmud and Codes and is most strictly observed by hasidim. Hasidim wear a *yarmulka* at all times, even while sleeping; the only time one is not worn is while bathing. Even when a hat is worn, a *yarmulka* is worn underneath.

The Talmud states that wearing a head covering is supposed to lead to reverence, and in hasidic lore, the analogy of the word *yarmulka* is equivalent to *yara malkah*, literally, "fear of the king." In the *Shulhan Arukh*, R. Shneur Zalman of Liady gives another reason, namely, that the head is part of the body, usually covered by Jews, and therefore uncovering the head is revealing one's nakedness before God.

With the exception of young children, hasidim do not worship while wearing only a *yarmulka*. They either wear a hat over it or cover their head with their *tallit*. It is also a custom among many hasidim not to go outdoors without a hat to cover their *yarmulka*. Some hasidim, especially scribes, wore a second *yarmulka*, instead of a hat, when they worked.

Most hasidim prefer a velvet *yarmulka*, making the observance as rich and beautiful as possible. The Belzer hasidim do not wear unlined *yarmulkot*. On the High Holy Days many hasidim wear special, tassled, white crocheted *yarmulkot*.

The Significance of the Skullcap.

A.K.

YAROSLAV, Shimon (1759–15 *Tishri* 1849) – Son of R. Israel Abraham Marilles, a *mitnaggid*, who strongly objected to his son's adherence to Hasidism. R. Marilles even summoned his son to a court of law, conducted by R. Jacob Orenstein, and stated that, if his son remained a hasid, he did not wish him to recite the *Mourner's Kaddish* for him after his death.

R. Shimon married Beila of Yaroslav. He was a disciple of R. Elimelekh of Lejask; R. Jacob Yitzhak, the "Seer" of Lublin; R. Menahem Mendel of Rymanov; R. Tzvi Hirsch of Rymanov; and, above all, R. Tzvi Hirsch of Zydaczov. "If you wish to live a long life," maintained R. Shimon, "study at the feet of every *tzaddik*." He asserted that he himself had visited 250 *tzaddikim*.

His wife had a small shop that sold leather shoes. "From afar, they call me the 'great rabbi, R. Shimon,' " said the rabbi. "In my own area, I am known simply as 'R. Shimon.' In my own house I am just 'Shimon.' "

He himself never ate meat unless he celebrated a *siyyum*, yet he permitted the eating of meat at a circumcision *seudah* during the Nine Days. Unlike his teacher R. Elimelekh of Lejask, he was meticulous in observing the *melaveh malkah*.

Among his disciples were R. Shlomoh Zalman Frankel, R. Shalom Rosenfeld, R. Hayyim Halberstam, and R. Yitzhak Eizig Safrin. He had five daughters and four sons: R. Eliezer Zeev (1800–3 *Shevat* 1852), who lived in Germany; R. Naftali Baer, who was rabbi of Litovsk; and R. Yitzhak, the rebbe of Ropczyce. He was succeeded by his son R. Bunem Menahem Mendel (d. 1890), who, in 1880, established a branch of the *Mahzikei Hadat* in Yaroslav.

R. Shimon was the author of *Torat Shimon*, which was published in 1908 in Yaroslav by R. Hayyim Teitelbaum on the urging of the rabbi of Belz.

He was succeeded by R. Shimon II (d. 15 *Shevat* 1915), who married Nehamah, the daughter R. David Teitelbaum of Kolbuszovo. He spent the first year of World War I in Vienna, where he died. He was survived by three sons: R. David, who married the daughter of R. Menahem Mendel Eichenstein of Zydaczov and died in 1935; R. Eliezer, who lived for some years in Berlin, where he published, in 1923, the second edition of R. Shimon Yaroslav's work *Torat Shimon*; and R. Israel Aryeh, his younger son, who married Simah, the daughter of R. Asher Yeshayah Rubin of Zolkiev; R. Israel perished in the Holocaust.

M. Wunder, "R. Shimon MiYaroslav," pp. 59–67.

M.Wu.

YEHIDUT (counseling in Hasidism) – In *Habad* language, the interview between a rebbe and a hasid is called *yehidut*. It may include a blessing, an intercession, or the prescribing of *kamayot*. The rebbe has no obligation to motivate the hasid to follow his advice. This he takes for granted. The rebbe's counsel is not subject to repeal or revision. The hasid who comes to the rebbe has a reason for doing so. The rebbe has something the hasid needs such as an *etzah* (counsel or advice) or an exhortation. To help his hasid, the rebbe is motivated by love and by his awareness of the cosmic significance of his role in earth. The rebbe is aware of the needs of his hasid. His task is to help the hasid not only with spiritual concern but also with more mundane problems.

When a hasid comes to the rebbe about a particular ill, it is generally hoped that the rebbe's blessing alone will provide the cure. The hasid would usually feel more reassured of the potency of the blessing if the rabbi bestowed an amulet. At times, the rebbe would prescribe medicinal cures. Those ranged from the herb cures of the Besht to the highly sophisticated medicinal prescriptions of the Piotrokover Rebbe-Doctor, known as the "Zalushiner rebbe," R. Dr. David Bernard, to a prescription by the rebbe of Piaseczno.

The problem of poverty, too, was within the domain of the rebbe. Although some rebbes had a reputation for not wanting to help hasidim escape poverty, generally the rebbe showed great concern for the welfare of the hasidim.

Husbands and wives, parents and children, and partners in business all came to seek equitable settlement and reconciliation before the rebbe. Occasionally, gentiles, too, came to seek the rabbi's help. Rebbes were sought by hasidim to adjudicate in cases of social and economic problems and in cases of *hasagat gevul* (removing of boundaries, interference with somebody else's business). Hasidim also came to the rebbe in the hope that his miraculous intervention might help them to escape being drafted by imperial decrees. Childless widows, bound by leviratic law, came to the rebbe to help them locate their brothers-in-law.

Sometimes a hasid would come to the rebbe to relate dreams. If the dream had troubled him, he needed the rebbe's reassurance of its innocuous nature, or, if the dream were a foreshadowing of events to come, the hasid would need the rebbe's help in taking countermeasures. Erotic dreams necessitate *teshuvah* (repentance). Very little is done about an erotic dream in itself; the rebbe's primary concern lies in the hasid's preoccupation with the dream and the fantasy material. There are times when good dreams are encouraged. A hasid is not to neglect dreams, but rather to pay attention to what they have to teach.

The hasid also gives the *pidyon nefesh* (soul's ransom). This is generally a cash donation given for the maintenance of the rebbe's household or for his charities.

The counseling process, which occurs in the *yehidut*, is very intense; yet the *yehidut* itself may be of short duration. The depth at which rebbe and hasid are involved with one another and the assumption of mutual love and trust indicate that once the hasid's defenses have been reinforced, there is almost no length to which both would not go to work through the life problem of the hasid. The *etzah* represents the climax of the *yehidut*. The *etzah* is considered to be more valuable than prophecy. For the prophet can foretell only that which is already destined to come to pass, whereas the rebbe is capable of giving an *etzah* and can also make it come to pass. The rebbe's *etzah* carries with itself the power of a fiat. The hasid's trust in the rebbe usually means that he will not question even a seemingly impossible counsel, once the rebbe has given his *etzah*. The rebbe himself does not take credit for the *etzah*, because he normally operates within the halakhic frame of reference. By taking the rebbe's advice, even though he may not have understood its application, the hasid helped to prepare the way for the working of a miracle.

The practice of charity is another *etzah*, counseled to prepare the hasid to receive a miracle. The more heroic and selfless the charity, the greater and more powerful is the hasid's merit. The rebbe often advises the hasid to recite Psalms: "He who wants to soften the decree of God, let him tell His praises" (i.e., recite all the Psalms).

For the hasid the problem of physical illness is no less a problem to bring to the rebbe than is any other problem. In dealing with health, the rebbe's advice often included a *segullah* – a charm that acted as a panacea and whose power is derived from forces higher than itself. There are times when the rebbe may see himself as powerless in the face of heaven's decree against his hasid.

The *segullot* ranged from herbal medicines and symptomatic palliatives to the occasional use of coprophiliac abominations that are sure to help because they are so horrible. Generally, rebbes employed substances that were related to Jewish sacramental life: leftover *etrog*, *matzah*, wine, oil from the Sabbath lamps, Sabbath foods, and *haroset* were the main ingredients in the rebbe's "pharmacopoeia."

The rebbe is the healing agent in his own *segullot*. He uses charms, *kamayot*, and amulets. Following the example of the Besht, rebbes felt that a charm or amulet need not contain God's name or the names of angels. It was sufficient that it contained the rebbe's own name.

The rebbe is involved not only in acting as an attorney for patients but also in negotiating a new deal for them. There are some rebbes who felt that the use of medicines was unnecessary. Instead of referring a hasid directly to a particular physician, the rebbe may tell the hasid only the place where medical help can be sought.

The rebbe's task extends up to and even beyond the grave. The rebbe served as a model for the confrontation with death. An entire section of the hagiography of the rebbes deals solely with their demise. Often, hasidim who were facing death were reassured by the rebbe's promise to help them even after their demise. The patient who was brought to the rebbe because he was thought to be possessed by demons was a sight that attracted much attention. A public exorcism was an impressive occasion.

The rebbe healed the halt, the lame, and the blind. He gave back speech to the mute. He was also called upon to minister to many ills that were hysterical manifestations.

From the time of the Besht, the rebbe served as a *shadkhan*. It was the custom of the father of the bride or the groom to come to the rebbe to inquire about the suitability of a particular match.

The rebbe was also consulted in cases of difficult births, and he would be approached for intercession, which would assist the mother to complete the birth process. Cases of abandoned wives were numerous. These unfortunate women came to the rebbe in the hope that he would help them find their missing mates. Rather than describing the specific place where the husband might be found, the rebbe would send the woman to the general vicinity and assure her that there she would find the husband.

Once the hasid has received the partial blessing, it is obvious that the *yehidut* is finished. In most cases, the formulas of the blessings followed the formulas of the liturgical devices. However, each rebbe used a different formula. Most of them began with "*Der Oybershter zull helfen* . . ." (May God help). Some rebbes recited the formula while holding the hasid's hand. Others placed their hands on the hasid' head. Some rebbes rose to their feet when they bestowed the blessing.

Thus, since the appearance of Hasidism, the rebbe has continued to serve as a helper. Despite the fact that today a variety of helpers are available, the rebbe still has a part to play. He possesses the art of "listening" with all his faculties and absorbing all the cues a hasid brings with him. It is a quality that is all too seldom exhibited by the professionals.

Hasidim come to the rebbe with every sort of problem. The rebbe may help by changing the hasid's external or internal environment or by changing only the hasid's attitude toward his environment and his problems.

Z. M. Schachter, *The Yehidut–A Study of Counseling in Hasidism*.

Z.M.S.

YESHIVAT BET EL–Situated near the synagogue of R. Yohanan ben Zakkai in Jerusalem, it was founded in 1753 by the kabbalist R. Gedaliah Hayon and his son-in-law, R. Shalom Mizrahi Yedidiah Sharabi (1720–1777), known as the *HaReshash* or *HeShemesh*.

R. Sharabi was regarded by many as the spiritual heir, and even the physical incarnation, of R. Yitzhak Luria. He was the author of the kabbalistic prayer book *Nehar Shalom* (Salonica, 1806) and *Rehovot HaNahar* (Salonica, 1866)–works very much venerated by the hasidim.

Yeshivat Bet El had a fraternal association called *Ahavat Shalom*, whose members pledged to come to one another's aid "in temporal and spiritual matters in this world and in the hereafter."

A. L. Frumkin, *Toldot Hakhmei Yerushalayim*, pp. 116–119.

YESHIVAT HAKHMEI LUBLIN–"In these days, *yeshivah* students should not be required to live in shacks and, like beggars, eat every day in different houses, nor should students spend their nights as watchmen in warehouses," stated R. Meir Shapira. "I have a dream of a great *yeshivah* more beautiful and larger than any before. I will build for them a royal palace." His idea was wholeheartedly endorsed by the *Knessiyah Gedolah* in Vienna on 10 *Elul* 1923.

In Lublin, onetime seat of the medieval Council of Four Lands and the home of R. Shlomoh ben Yehiel Luria, the Maharshal; R. Jacob Pollack; and the "Seer" of Lublin, R. Shapira erected his "palace" under very heavy verbal fire. "Wasteful" and "untimely" were the terms used by his opponents.

A fifty-five-acre site at Lubartovski 57 was donated by R. Shmuel Eichenbaum, and the foundation stone of the *yeshivah* was laid on Lag BaOmer (18 *Iyyar*) 1924 in the presence of 30,000 people, including the rebbes of Ger and Chortkov, R. Shlomoh Eger, and R. Aaron Lewin of Rzeszov. Shapira went on a fund-raising mission to England, France, Germany, Holland, Denmark, Switzerland, and the United States, where he arrived on 17 *Elul* 1927, delivered 242 addresses, and collected $50,000.

The new *yeshivah* was consecrated on 28 *Sivan* 1930 in the presence of the rebbes of Ger and Chortkov. The Aguda daily paper, *Dos Yiddishe Togblat*, published a special edition for the occasion. At a cost of one million zlotys, it was one of the finest buildings in prewar Poland. Six stories high, with 120 rooms, a huge auditorium, stately lecture halls, a dining room, a library of some 40,000 books, and even a model temple, designed by Hanokh Weintrop, to aid students in the study of *Kodashim*, the fifth order of the Mishnah, dealing with sacrifices in the temple services.

The *yeshivah* was designed to accommodate 500 resident students and up to 1,000 day students.

Only the most outstanding students were admitted. Candidates were required to know by heart at least 200 pages of the Talmud. The *yeshivah* opened with 70 students, and within five months, it had 120; by 1932, 200.

R. Shapira died at the age of forty-six in 1934, and rabbis such as R. Shimon Engel, known as "Shimon Zelechover"; R. David Minzberg; and R. Aryeh Leib Landau maintained the high standard of scholarship set by the founder. The *yeshivah's* spiritual guides were R. Menahem Zemba, R. Moses of Boyan-Cracow, and R. Tzvi Frummer, who visited frequently.

The *yeshivah* shared the general fate of Polish Jewry. The following account appeared in the *Deutsche Jugendzeitung* in February 1940: "We threw out of the building the large talmudic library and brought it to the marketplace. There we kindled a fire under the books. The conflagration lasted twenty hours."

During the war it was first used as Gestapo headquarters, then as a hospital for German troops. It is now occupied by the medical academy of Lublin. In June 1985, a plaque in Hebrew, Polish, and Yiddish was affixed: "In this building was the *Yeshivat Hakhmei Lublin* in the years 1930–1939."

Today, there are *yeshivot* perpetuating *Hakhmei Lublin* in Montreal, Canada, in Detroit, Michigan, and in Bene Berak, Israel.

A. Surasky, *Rabbi Meir Shapira*.

YESHIVOT, institutions of talmudic learning – Strangely enough, Poland, the home of the Torah, was not, at first, the home of great *yeshivot*. During the nineteenth century, mitnaggedic Lithuania had the monopoly. The voice of the Torah went out from Mir, and the word of the Lord from Slabodka. The great *yeshivot*, usually situated in tiny towns, became the Cambridges, the Oxfords, the Harvards, and the Yales of the entire Jewish world.

The renowned academy of Mir, established in 1817, was the foremost Torah academy of Eastern Europe. Three hundred students attended the *yeshivah* at Radin, the hometown of R. Israel Meir HaKohen, the *Hafetz Hayyim*. Lomza, established in 1853, although of mitnaggedic tradition, welcomed youngsters from hasidic backgrounds. The *yeshivah* at Klezk, headed by R. Nathan Tzvi Finkel, was the home of 260 youngsters. R. Elhanan Wasserman (1875–1941) was the principal of the *yeshivah* at Baranowicze, near the Russian border. Once the voice of the Torah became suppressed throughout the Soviet Union, Baranowicze became a haven for students escaping *Yevsektsiya* (the Jewish branch of the Communist Party).

In addition to these celebrated *yeshivot*, there were the *yeshivot* of Bialystok, Kamenets, Vilna, Brest-Litovsk, Nowogrodek, and Grodno. There were also Navardiker *yeshivot*, whose concept of Judaism was influenced by the mystic trends in which emphasis was laid on spiritual life, rather than on mastery of the Talmud.

The lack of hasidic *yeshivot* forced hasidic *bahurim* (young men) to study in the *shtieblech* and *batei midrashim* of the rebbes. At the beginning of the twentieth century, 3,500 youths were studying in the *shtieblech*, and more than 2,000 studied at the *shtieblech* of Ger. Prominent among these *shtieblech* in Warsaw were those at 30 Moranowska, 4 Nalewky, 47 Stawki, and 32 Nowolipki. The trend toward hasidic *yeshivot* developed gradually. Young men were spared the difficult choice between inadequate study in the home atmosphere of the *shtiebl* and a thorough talmudic grounding in the alien setting of a Lithuanian or mitnaggedic *yeshivah*.

In 1896, R. Jacob Perlow of Novominsk established a *yeshivah* in Minsk Mazowieck, and R. Eliezer Halstock in Ostrowiec. That trend toward hasidic *yeshivot* intensified during the interwar years, when rebbes, one after another, began to establish their own academies. R. Shalom Dov Baer Schneersohn of Lubavitch, who had a *yeshivah Tomhei Temimim* with several branches in Russia as early as 1892, founded *yeshivot Tomhei Temimim* in Lodz, Vilna, and Kaluszyn during his residence in Otwock from 1927 to 1938. Similarly, R. Menahem Mendel Alter Kalish of Pabianice, near Lodz, established *Yeshivat Darkhei Noam* (rays of pleasantness). R. David Bornstein of Sochaczev established *Bet Avraham*, and R.

Hanokh Justman established *Sifsei Tzaddik* in Czestochova.

Equally successful was R. Shlomoh Hanokh Hakohen Rabinowitz of Radomsk. His *yeshivah Keter Torah* (crown of the Torah) had thirty-six branches in Poland and Galicia. The Radomsk successor-designate was his first cousin and son-in-law, R. Moses David Hakohen Rabinowitz. Three times a day, he lectured the 150 students in the *Kibbutz Gavoah* (higher study academy) in Sosnowiec. Under his guidance, the *yeshivot* of Radomsk achieved high standards of learning, particularly at the famous centers in Lodz, Sosnowiec, Bendin, Radomsk, Kielce, Kattowitz, Auschwitz, Piotrokov, and Czestochova. The rebbe himself, who was a man of substance, supplied half the budget of the *yeshivot*, and the remainder was subscribed by his hasidim. No provision was made for rabbinical diplomas. Emphasis was on study and not on certification. *Gemara* (Talmud) and *Tosafot* (critical and explanatory notes on the Talmud by French and German scholars) were the main objects of this concentrated curriculum.

Under the influence of R. Israel Meir HaKohen, the *Hafetz Hayyim*, much time was devoted to the study of *Kodashim* (fifth order of the *Mishnah*). Students and teachers were not necessarily hasidim of Radomsk. In Sosnowiec, the principal of the *yeshivah* was R. Joseph Lask, a hasid of Ger.

In addition to the newly established hasidic *yeshivot*, a *yeshivah* was established at 18 Swietojerska in Warsaw. This was the *Mesivta*, established in 1919 under R. Meir Dan Plotzki, rabbi of Ostrowiec. No candidate under the age of thirteen was admitted, and no one was accepted without being able to master unaided one page of the Talmud and *Tosafot*. During their first year, students studied 245 pages of the Talmud. The number progressively increased, so that the number of pages rose to 305, 345, 404, and 430, in the second, third, fourth, and fifth years, respectively. In all, a student mastered 1,729 pages of the Talmud in the course of his studies.

Unlike other *yeshivot*, which concentrated wholly on talmudical studies, the *Mesivta* devoted two hours each day to Polish language, mathematics, and history. This "revolutionary" departure did not go unchallenged and was condemned as heresy by R. Hayyim Elazar Shapira of Munkacs. Among the spiritual guides at the *yeshivah* were R. Menahem Zemba, R. Meir Hakohen Warshavsky, rabbi of Mokotov, and R. Menahem Mendel Kasher, author of *Torah Shelemah*.

Like the rabbi of Ger, R. Benzion Halberstam of Bobov was also actively engaged in the education of Jewish youth. He established a *yeshivah Etz Hayyim* (tree of life), which eventually had forty-six branches throughout Galicia. A special society, *Tomhei Temimim* (upholders of the perfect), looked after the physical needs of the students.

During the interwar years, the *yeshivot* in Congress Poland (the frontiers established by the Congress of Vienna in 1815) and Galicia were under the wings of the *Horev* movement, and those of the eastern provinces were linked by the *Vaad Hayeshivot*. This was established at a three-day conference held in Vilna in 1925 (2–5 *Tammuz*) with the participation of R. Israel Meir HaKohen. Particularly active in the *Vaad* were R. Hayyim Ozer Grodzinski and R. Joseph Schorr of Vilna.

The *Horev* organization reported, in 1937, to have under its wing 136 great *yeshivot*, 500 teachers, and 11,957 students. It was helped by the American Joint Distribution Committee and by the Foundation of Prof. Waldemar Mordecai Wolff Haffkine (1860–1930), discoverer of a serum against cholera and bubonic plague, who, in 1896, became director in chief of the government plague research laboratory, now known as the Haffkine Institute in Bombay. Professor Haffkine bequeathed an annual subsidy of £2,750 sterling, the income from an investment of £45,225, deposited in the Banque Cantonale Vandoise in Lausanne for *yeshivot* in Eastern Europe. This fund was administered by the Hilfsverein der Deutschen Juden (German Jews' Aid Society) and during the period 1931–1938. About £6,835 was allocated to Polish *yeshivot*.

In Hungary, too, there were a number of hasidic *yeshivot*. In Sighet, a *yeshivah* was under R. Zalman Leib Teitelbaum and under R. Moses Teitelbaum. In Nagyszollos there was the *yeshivah* of R. Yitzhak Eizig of Kalev, and in Satmar, of the four *yeshivot*, two were hasidic and attracted large numbers of students, especially under the dynamic leadership of R. Yoel Teitelbaum. There were also great *yeshivot* established by the rebbe of Spinka.

In Romania, there were a number of hasidic *yeshivot*. *Bet Yisrael* in Bohusi was under the guidance of R. Menahem Mendel Friedman and R. David Twersky. The *yeshivah Bet Avraham* was established in 1933 in Stefanesti in memory of R. Abraham Mattathias Friedman. In Bessarabia, there was a *yeshivah* in Kishinev under R. Moses Hirsch Heilprin. In Czernowitz the *yeshivah Beh'er Mayim Hayyim* was established in 1923 under the guidance of R. Alexander Zusya Portugal. In Czechoslovakia, during the interwar years, flourished the great *yeshivah* of R. Hayyim Elazar Shapira.

The Vishnitz dynasty, too, established *yeshivot*. A *yeshivah Bet Yisrael V'Damesek Eliezer* was founded before World War I under R. Israel Hager of Vishnitz and under his son, R. Menahem Mendel. It closed in 1918 but was revived between 1923 and 1940 under R. Eliezer Hager and under R. David Schneebalg. In Seret, Bukovina, was the *Yeshivah Bet Yisrael B'Tamkhin D'Oraita*, where half of each day was devoted to Torah; the other half was devoted to vocational training.

In the Holy Land, the very first hasidic *yeshivah*, *Hayyei Olam*, was established in 1876. In 1925, R. Abraham Mordecai Alter of Ger established the *Sefat Emet yeshivah* in Jerusalem and later, the *Hiddushei HaRim yeshivah* in Tel Aviv, with branches in many parts of Israel. In Bene Berak, in *Kiryat Vishnitz*, R. Hayyim Meir Hager founded the *Bet Yisrael V'Damesek Eliezer yeshivah*. R. Aaron Rokeah of Belz had his *yeshivah* in Rehov Agrippa, in Jerusalem. The network of the Belz Torah institutions has been expanded by his successor, R. Berele.

Today, *Yeshiva Mesivta Tiferet Yisrael* of Ruzhin in Jerusalem attracts students from the United States and England. Among its supporters in Israel was R. Israel Friedman, the rabbi of Kopyczynice. R. Shlomoh Friedman of Tel Aviv even formed an association to support the *yeshivah*, and an appeal signed by nine rabbis of the Ruzhyn dynasty was launched. Also active is R. Abraham Yitzhak Kahan, the *Toldot Aharon*, who has established a large *yeshivah* in Jerusalem. Satmar, too, has many Torah institutions. The *yeshivah* in Jerusalem has over 300 students, and sites have been acquired for additional constructions. Dormitories are provided for the students. Lubavitch has been very active in the *yeshivah* world, with its *Tomhei Temimim yeshivot* in many parts of the country.

The growth of *yeshivot* in the Holy Land has been phenomenal. From 1929 to 1930, there were sixteen large *yeshivot* with 2,873 students. By 1937, there were seventy-eight *yeshivot*. In Israel, the establishment of *yeshivot* is part of the hasidic way of life. Almost every rebbe has, or wishes to have, his own academy.

In 1971, there were 300 different *yeshivot*, with 20,000 students. Of the 120 educational institutions enumerated in the directory of recognized agencies (published by the Ministry of Social Welfare, 1970–1971), nearly one-third were hasidic. Of the 158 Israeli *yeshivot*, many are associated with the *Vaad HaYeshivot*, which provides food and clothing for students and their dependents. The Ministry of Education exercises no supervision over the *yeshivot*, but the Ministry of Religious Affairs provides subsidies for them and their students. The ultra-Orthodox have their *Ihud HaYeshivot* (union of the *yeshivot*), which supports many institutions in Jerusalem.

The hasidic *yeshivot* in Israel, like their forerunners in Eastern Europe, are not training schools for professional rabbis, and students have no immediate vocational objective. Yiddish is still the primary language of the *yeshivot*, and the overriding concern is to produce learned laypersons rather than spiritual leaders. Apart from Lubavitch, the hasidic *yeshivot* frown upon *yeshivah*-cum-technical-college institutions.

The state of Israel has permitted full-time *yeshivah* students—whose number has today increased to nearly 40,000—to defer military service.

A remarkable expansion of *yeshivot* has occurred in the United States. In New York, more than 100,000 youngsters attend *yeshivot*. The largest *yeshivah* is probably that of Satmar, primarily in Williamsburg and Borough Park, Brooklyn. R. Joseph Yitzhak Schneersohn, in 1940, founded the *yeshivah Tomhei Temimim* under R. Gurarye, which now has many branches throughout North America.

In England, there is a Lubavitch *yeshivah* in Hampstead Garden Suburb. There is the

Mesivta yeshivah in North London, as well as *yeshivot* of Belz and Bobov. Ger has just opened a £2-million building in North East London.

There are also hasidic establishments under the auspices of Lubavitch in Melbourne, Australia, in Milan, Italy, and in other parts of the world.

A. Fuchs, *Hungarian Yeshivot: From Grandeur to Holocaust*.

W. B. Helmreich, *The World of the Yeshiva: An Intimate Portrait of Orthodox Jewry*.

Ed. and J.N.

YIDDISH – Yiddish has been the language of Ashkenazi Jews for a thousand years, and before the Holocaust almost 11 million were Yiddish speaking. The exodus from Eastern Europe in the nineteenth and early twentieth centuries carried Yiddish to the four corners of the earth.

In the eighteenth century, at the time of the rise of Hasidism, the kingdoms of Poland and Lithuania were dismembered by Russia, Austria, and Prussia. In Russia, the Jews were confined to the formerly Polish Prussia. In Russia, the Jews were confined to the formerly Polish territories – the Pale of Settlement, the Ukraine, and Belorussia, where the majority of the Jews did not speak the state language but where all spoke Yiddish. Because the hasidic movement had set out to champion the common people, it helped to raise the status of the Yiddish language. Yiddish was no longer the speech of the ignorant and of women. Hasidic rebbes wrote their learned works in Hebrew, but they spoke and preached and told their stories in Yiddish.

Yitzhak Leibish Peretz, who started the neo-hasidic trend in Yiddish, wrote, "Two elements played a great role in the development of the Yiddish language: the Jewish woman and Hasidism." Similarly, Shmuel Nigal (1883–1955) stressed that "Yiddish grew in importance and esteem thanks to Hasidism. The common Jew acquired self-assurance and forcefulness." These views have been endorsed by Dov Sadan, who declared that "a proper appreciation of Hebrew literature cannot be undertaken without simultaneously reevaluating the significant role Yiddish played as a popular living tongue and important conveyor of hasidic teachings. A light perusal of the literature of that era makes plain that Hebrew texts had their origin in Yiddish. Never had this language been put to such multifaceted use, as by the hasidic movement."

The sayings of the Besht are occasionally reported in Yiddish. The *Shivhei HaBesht* was printed in two Yiddish editions. Yiddish phrases abound. Reporting on what he saw on one of his journeys to heaven, the Besht referred to his scribe and said, "*Oich du, Senderal, bist geblieben hinterstelig*" (You, too, little Sender, remained behind) (*Shivhei HaBesht*, p. 53).

R. Nahman of Bratzlav spoke in Yiddish to his followers, advising them to pray in Yiddish. His stories were in idiomatic Yiddish. R. Nathan of Nemirov, who wrote a fluent Hebrew, quotes R. Nahman as saying, "*Gott iz mit dir, bei dir, leben dir; shrek dich nit; kein yiush is gor nit faranen*" (God is with you, in you, and next to you; do not be afraid; do not despair) (I. Zinberg, *Die Geschichte vun der Literatur bei Yiden*, vol. 7, p. 205).

The hasidim of R. Nahman of Bratzlav were careful to quote their master's words in the original Yiddish. The greatest contribution to the revival of Yiddish was due to the inspired art of storytelling by the hasidic rebbes. Since it was a great *mitzvah* to elaborate wondrous tales concerning *tzaddikim*, the popular imagination was greatly stimulated. As a result, a massive collection to fascinating folktales was produced, which needed only artistic polish to achieve the power and permanence of great literature. This was achieved in the twentieth century by J. L. Peretz, M. J. Berdyczewski, and M. Buber.

R. Levi Yitzhak of Berdichev is known for interspersing his prayers with invocations in Yiddish. While praying or studying, he would cry out, "*Darbarmdiger*" (All-Merciful). Among the famous compositions attributed to him are songs composed in a mixture of Hebrew and Yiddish, such as the *Reb Levi Yitzhak Berdichever's Kaddish* (or the *Rebbe's Kaddish*), *Dudule* (also known as *Du-Du*), and *Got fun Avrohom*. R. Elimelekh of Lejask, in his *Tzetel Katan* (small epistle), urges his followers to accustom themselves even to rendering thanks to God in Yiddish.

R. Meir of Przemyshlan, known for his witty homilies, found spiritual meaning in Hebrew words, which he interpreted as if they were in Yiddish. So, the verse "*VeHeim lo yade'u derakhai*" (They do not know my ways [Psalm 95:10]) he interpreted as "When people stay at home they do not know my ways" (Horodezky, *HaHasidut*, p. 114). R. Dov Baer Schneersohn of Lubavitch wrote a book in Yiddish, *Opening the Eyes* (*Pokeah Ivrim* [1817, reprinted Brooklyn, 1973]), in which he states, "While many ethical tracts are available for the scholar who knows Hebrew, for those who do not know Hebrew, it is difficult to find ethical books that are written in Yiddish. So they remain without any counsel about how to repent. Consequently, my heart stirred me to write the paths of repentance in Yiddish." The frontispiece of the Shklov 1932 edition states, "Now [R. Dov Baer] also gave guidance to ordinary people [*gemayne layt*] who want to repent, as to how they should conduct themselves. So, he wrote this book in Yiddish" (N. Loewenthal, *Communicating the Infinite*, p. 293, n. 60).

Hitler and Stalin destroyed Yiddish culture in Europe. In addition, their extermination of one-third of the world's Jewish population, the great majority of whom were Yiddish speaking, dealt a great blow to the prospective continuity of Yiddish. The sources of Jewish culture – Yiddish folk schools, the Yiddish press, Yiddish literature, and Yiddish theater – were destroyed to a large extent. It is a miracle that Yiddish has survived.

In some present-day hasidic educational establishments, Hebrew texts are translated into Yiddish, which continues to be the daily language of Hasidism. Yiddish hasidic papers are still published in New York (*Der Yid*) and in London (*Jewish Tribune*).

In the past, Yiddish was denigrated by assimilationists. In 1876, Elias Ackord (*Die Juden oder die nothwendige Reformation des Juden in der Republik Polen* [Warsaw, 1786]) even advocated that Yiddish be banned. The *maskilim*, the followers of the Enlightenment, and Moses Mendelssohn waged an uncompromising onslaught on Yiddish, because they regarded it as a corrupt jargon and a lingering ghetto ailment. They stressed the necessity of displacing Yiddish with German as the vernacular of the Jews, so as to bring about cultural alignment with the German people.

Historian H. Graetz referred to Yiddish as a "despised language." Early Zionists classified it as the language of the *galut* (exile). The hasidim, however, regarded it as *Mame loshen* – the language of the cradle and of the home.

Yiddish is still used by the hasidic rebbes living in Israel and in the Diaspora. It is the language of the Aguda and of the Belz- and Satmar-oriented schools. It is also the language of the *yeshivot* and the *kollelim*. The hasidim say, "*A Yid red Yiddish*" (A Jew speaks Yiddish). "Though Yiddish is not a holy language it should be perpetuated as the language of the martyrs."

U. Weinreich and B. Weinreich, *Yiddish Language and Folklore: A Selective Bibliography for Research*.

YIVO – The Yivo Institute for Jewish Research was originally founded in 1925, with Vilna, then Poland, as its headquarters. After the occupation of Vilna by the Nazis, the central headquarters were transferred to New York, where a branch had existed previously.

At present, Yivo's holdings of scholarly materials are divided into two sections: the Library, containing books, monographs, and periodicals, and whose total now numbers over 300,000 volumes, and the Archives, housing manuscripts, documents, and photographs, among other things, and whose total amount of archival material constitutes 7,500 linear feet.

Yivo's Library has a relatively strong collection of hasidic materials, especially considering the fact that the purpose of Yivo is study of the Jewish social sciences, rather than the Jewish religion. The so-called Vilna rabbinic collection, which was rescued from the prewar Vilna Yivo and Strashun libraries, contains a strong hasidic section, which is well organized and cataloged due to the efforts of R. Haim Liberman, personal secretary to the sixth Lubavitcher rebbe, R. Joseph Yitzhak Schneersohn, and the librarian of the rebbe's rich personal collection. Liberman cataloged not only the hasidic section but the whole rabbinical collection as well.

The collection is particularly strong on *Habad*-Lubavitch materials, containing many rare and important editions of *Habad* works, such as the Zolkiev 1805 and Shklov 1806 editions of R. Shneur Zalman of Liady's *Likkutei Amorim*, popularly known as the *Tanya*.

Other rare and important *Habad* works in the library are *Torah Or* (Kopys, 1836) (1st ed.) and *Siddur HaRav* (Kopys, 1816), both written by R. Shneur Zalman of Liady, the founder of *Habad* Hasidism. However, not only is the Yivo collection strong on *Habad* materials, but it also contains a great many works on the general hasidic movement, most of which were published in the mid-nineteenth century. Especially interesting is the *Keter Shem Tov*, containing the teaching of the Besht, founder of Hasiduth, which was published in Zolkiev in 1794 and 1795 (1st ed.).

The general Yivo Library is particularly strong in the Maseh-Book genre of hasidic tales in Yiddish. The materials contain wonderful tales about various hasidic masters and were published for the simple folk, mainly in Poland, in the late nineteenth and early twentieth centuries. The library also contains some hasidic texts that were published in displaced persons camps after the Holocaust, such as *Osef Mikhtavim*, printed in Landesburg in 1947 by the Gerer hasidim there. *Ohel Elimelekh*, a book of tales about the famous Elimelekh of Lejask, was reprinted in Landesburg in 1948 by several hasidim there.

Needless to say, Yivo has most of the scholarly contributions to research, such as Horodezky, Marcus, and Dubnow.

The Library also contains most hasidic periodicals ever published. Among these are *Ho-Ach*, a children's magazine published by the Lubavitcher *yeshivah* in Russia in the early twentieth century; *HaTomin*, a scholarly periodical published by the Lubavitcher rebbe in Otwock, near Warsaw, during the 1930s; and other such periodicals subsequently published in the United States and Israel.

The Yivo Archives contain many resources regarding hasidim. The Dubnow Collection, assembled by eminent Jewish historian Simon Dubnow and part of the Elias Tcherikower Collection at Yivo, contains many manuscripts dealing with hasidim. Included are letters by Lubavitcher rebbes, handwritten copies of several of R. Nahman Bratzlaver's works (mid-eighteenth-century manuscripts), and replies from rabbis and scholars to Dubnow's inquiries on hasidic thought and history.

Another interesting collection is that of R. Ezekiel Shragah Rubin-Halberstam, the Chesinover rebbe. R. Rubin-Halberstam, a descendant of the well-known Zanzer hasidic dynasty, currently resides in Brooklyn and periodically donates sections of his personal archives to the Yivo Archives. There are now almost ten boxes of materials. Among them are hasidic wedding invitations, photos, letters to and from R. Rubin-Halberstam including some from living hasidic leaders, greeting cards, *teshuvot* on halakhic problems, posters, clippings, and some pictures. This might possibly be the only collection of its type in the United States (open to the public) and will certainly aid future scholars in their study of the emergent hasidic community in the United States after World War II.

Another interesting collection is the one containing *kvittlekh* and correspondence (supplications) given to the Greiditzer rav—R. Elijah Guttmacher (1795–1874). Although not a hasid, he achieved fame as a wonder-worker, and thousands of Jews, both hasidic and nonhasidic, streamed to him to appeal for his aid. The Archives contain about thirteen boxes with these *kvittlekh*.

The Archives are admittedly weak in the areas of original manuscripts on hasidic life and hasidic texts. However, they do have several such items, for example, a handwritten pamphlet by R. Gershon Henokh Leiner of Radzyn on the laws of Passover; a handwritten message by the fourth Lubavitcher rebbe, R. Shmuel Schneersohn (d. 1882); plus other documents and letters written by *Habad* hasidim. The Archives also have a small collection of photocopied manuscripts, which includes Torah discourses and letters of various hasidic leaders.

A.P.

YIZKOR BOOKS—Books commemorating Jewish communities in eastern Europe, many of which were destroyed in the Holocaust. The very first book published in New York, as early as 1943, was *Lodzer Yizkor Buch*, by the *Fareynikter Rettungskomitet* (United Rescue Committee).

In an exhibition of *Yizkor* books held in Tel Aviv in 1961, over 100 *Yizkor* books were displayed. Listings on *Yizkor* books were published by Philip Friedman, Jacob Shatzky, Dina Abramowicz, Shalom Shunami, and Beryl Mark. These books were published in Austria, France, Germany, Israel,

South America, and the United States. The Dubnov Foundation published two volumes about Polish Jewry in 1963.

The *Encyclopedia of the Jewish Diaspora* published a volume on Warsaw Jewry, edited by Yitzhak Greenbaum (Tel Aviv, 1953). Outside Israel most of the books are in Yiddish; in the United States they normally contain English summaries.

So far, some 900 *Yizkor* books have been published by *landsmannschaften* and by individuals. Among the editors are Isaiah Trunk, Nahman Blumenthal, N. Michael Gelber (1881–1966), Raphael Mahler, Philip Friedman, Jacob Shatzky, and Joshua Goldberg. Mosad HaRav Kook published a series of books under the title *Arim VeIma'ot BeYisrael* on a number of Jewish communities in eastern Europe.

Though the professional historian will find many of them nostalgic and romanticized, nevertheless they contain a great deal of useful information, especially on Hasidism, hasidic rebbes, and religious leaders. Particularly valuable are the contributions of Meir Shimon Geshuri on hasidic music.

A. Wein, "Yizkor Books," pp. 1694–1695.

YOLLES, Efraim Eliezer Hakohen, of Philadelphia (5 *Shevat* 1891–25 *Heshvan* 1989) – Son of R. Shalom, the rabbi of Stryj. In 1912, he married his cousin Bina, the daughter of R. Yehudah Tzvi Yolles, the rabbi of Sambor. He studied under R. David Horowitz of Stanislav, R. Nathan Levine of Rzeszov, and R. Kopel Reich of Budapest.

In 1916, he became a member of the *Bet Din* of Stryj and an assistant to his father. He became a military chaplain to the Austrian army. In 1921, he went to the United States and became rabbi of the Stryer congregation on the Lower East Side of New York for one year. He then settled in Philadelphia, where he was rabbi of Congregation *Kerem Yisrael* of the Strawberry Mansion section of the city. He then became the head of the *Bet Din* and one of the founders of the *yeshivah* of Philadelphia. He was also an active member and honorary president of the *Agudat Harabbanim* of the United States and Canada.

He helped R. Meir Shapira in his fundraising for the *Yeshivat Hakhmei Lublin*, and he regularly visited the rebbe of Lubavitch.

He was the author of *Divrei Efraim Eliezer*, responsa published in New York in 1983. A number of his responsa were also printed in *Shemen HaRosh* (Strij, 1933) by his brother, R. Israel Asher. He also republished, with his own annotations, the medieval law code *Orhot Hayyim* of R. Aaron Hakohen of Lunel (New York, 1959). Many of his Torah essays appeared in the rabbinic journal *Tiferet Bahurim–Magen Giborim* (Zaleshchyki, 1909) and in the American *Hamaor* and *Hapardes*.

He had two daughters, Esther and Sheindel Shoshanah.

He was buried on the Mount of Olives.

Toldot Anshei Shem, pp. 62–63.

A.Shu.

YOLLES, Eleazar, of Montreal (1904–11 *Av* 1976) – Son of R. Yehudah Tzvi, the rabbi of Sambor, Eleazar was ordained by R. David Horowitz, the rabbi of Stanislav. During World War I, he lived in Romania. In 1928, he married Zipporah, the daughter of R. Jacob Shimshon Kanar, the rabbi of Klausenburg. He lived in Bucharest for a time.

In 1948, he settled in Montreal, Canada, where he lived for the next twenty-eight years. In 1954, he was a delegate to the *Knessiyah HaGedolah* in Jerusalem.

He died in Montreal but was buried in Tiberias. His daughter, Leah, married R. Pinhas Menahem Rokeah.

YOLLES, Isaiah Asher Hakohen, of Stryj (1893–2 *Tevet* 1944) – Son of R. Shalom, he was born in Neustadt and brought up by his grandfather R. Uri of Sambor. He studied in Stryj for eight years and married the daughter of R. Manasseh Eichenstein of Rzeszov. When she died, he married Mirele, the daughter of R. Yisrael Rokeah of Boryslav.

During the First World War, he lived in Bohemia, and after the war, he returned to Stryj. In 1926, he established a *yeshivah Neve Shalom* in memory of his father. He encouraged development of the *Tzeire Aguda* and wrote articles for the Aguda papers. He corresponded with halakhic authorities such as R. Abraham Menahem Mendel Steinberg of Brody and R. Menahem Munish Babad.

"I do not know whether we will survive the Holocaust," wrote the rebbe during the war. "But I believe wholeheartedly that our enemies will come to a bitter end." During the war, he was at first protected by Polish gentiles but was discovered. He perished in a forest together with the Jews of Stryj.

He was the author of *Shemen HaRosh* on the Pentateuch, talmudic discourses, and responsa, including some of his father's responsa (Stryj, 1933).

His five sons were R. Meshullam Uri, a student at the *Yeshivat Hakhmei Lublin*; R. Alter Yitzhak of Belz; R. Moses Elijah of Drohobicz; R. Shalom; and R. Eliezer Dov. His brother, R. Efraim, lived in Philadelphia.

Elleh Ezkerah, vol. 4, pp. 172–177.

A.Shu.

YOLLES, Jacob Tzvi (1778–9 *Sivan* 1825), hasidic scholar – Son of R. Naftali, he was usually known as "Reb Yankele Przemysl," where he was born. He was brought up by his grandfather, and he served as rabbi first in Dynov, then in Glogov and in Hussakov. He was a disciple of R. Jacob Yitzhak, the "Seer" of Lublin, and he visited R. Tzvi Hirsch of Zydaczov and R. Naftali of Ropczyce.

He was the author of twenty-seven works on all branches of rabbinics. He was renowned for his work *Melo HaRoim* (Zolkiev, 1838), as well as encyclopedic work on the Talmud, arranged alphabetically, which went through many editions. In his work *Kehillat Yaakov* (Przemysl, 1909), he quotes the hasidic rebbes R. Jacob Yitzhak, the "Seer" of Lublin; R. Yisrael, the Maggid of Kozienice; R. Menahem Mendel of Rymanov; R. Abraham Joshua Heschel of Opatov; and R. Tzvi Hirsch of Zydaczov. His work *Hinukh Bet Yehudah* (Warsaw, 1869) received the approval of R. Jacob Aryeh of Radzymin, R. Joshua of Ostrova, R. Yehudah Leib Eger, and R. Jacob Tzvi of Parysov.

M. Yari-Wold, ed. *Kehillat Raysha. Sefer Zikkaron*, p. 80.

YOLLES, Judah Tzvi, of Sambor (12 *Tammuz* 1852–11 *Shevat* 1919) – Eldest son of R. Uri, he was ordained by R. Yitzhak of Ottynia. He was rabbi in Sokolov, Galicia, and when his father died, he succeeded him in Sambor. He married the daughter of R. David Wolkenfeld, a descendant of Lejask.

His sons were R. Moses, R. Nahum, R. Elijah, R. Eleazar (later of Montreal), and R. Naftali. He was succeeded by his son-in-law, R. Yoel Moskovitch (1888–2 Av 1941), the husband of Frieda and the son of R. Mordecai Joseph Moses of Sulitza, a descendant of Zloczov.

A.Shu.

YOLLES, Nahum, of Przemysl (1861–9 *Tevet* 1919) – Third son of R. Uri of Sambor, he married the daughter of R. Israel, a descendant of R. Epstein of Neustadt. He served as rabbi in Czehov, near Przemysl. He succeeded his father as rebbe in Sambor in 1915.

His son R. Elijah, the son-in-law of R. Shalom Yolles, succeeded him in Przemysl. R. Elijah later moved to Istrik. He was a great Torah scholar and was a follower of the rebbe of Husyatin.

The other two sons of R. Nahum were R. Abraham Jacob, rebbe of Sambor, and R. Kalonymus Kalman, the son-in-law of R. Samson Gottesman of Lachowicze and rabbi in Sambor. The latter later moved to Turka.

They all perished in the Holocaust.

A.Shu.

YOLLES, Shalom, of Stryj (24 *Adar* 1856–10 *Av* 1925) – Son of R. Uri Hakohen of Sambor, he was brought up in the home of R. Abraham Jacob Friedman of Sadgora and studied together with R. Yitzhak of Boyan. He also studied under R. Joseph Saul Nathanson and R. Yitzhak Shmelkes. He married Esther Sheindel, the daughter of R. Eliezer Yitzhak Teicher, the rabbi of Sarnosc. When she died in 1920, he married Hannah, the widow of R. Meir Moskovitch of Zborov.

In 1884, he became rabbi in Neustadt, Galicia, and in 1896, in Moszisk. He was persuaded by R. Yitzhak Friedman of Boyan to become rebbe. He dreamed of emigrating to the Holy Land. "In the Diaspora," said the rabbi, "it is forbidden to criticize the Holy Land. How can one criticize a country that the Almighty Himself has described as desirable?"

At the outbreak of World War I, he had to leave Stryj and on his return appointed his two sons, R. Israel and R. Efraim, to be in charge of communal affairs. After Passover 1925, he settled in the Holy Land and on Lag BaOmer was invited to light the *hadlakah* (bonfire) in Meron. After three months' stay in Jerusalem, he died and was buried on the Mount of Olives.

His son R. Isaiah succeeded him as rabbi of Stryj. His son R. Efraim Eliezer was rabbi in Philadelphia. Two other sons–R. Uri Aaron of Kalusz and R. Moses, the rebbe of Stanislav–and his daughters–Hannah and her twelve children, and Havah–were murdered in the Holocaust.

A.Shu.

YOLLES, Uri, of Sambor (24 *Iyyar* 1833–1 *Adar* II 1910)–Son of the kabbalist R. Efraim Tzvi, known as "Efraim Hirsch Hasid," a follower of R. Uri, the "Seraph" of Strelisk (1757–1826). Uri was born in Lvov. He was a disciple of R. Joseph Saul Nathanson and R. Yitzhak Shmelkes, who ordained him. In 1851, he married Sarah Yente, the daughter of R. Shimshon Tene, the *dayan* of Komarno, where he lived for some time. His wife repaired sacks and supported him out of her earnings. He was a close follower of R. Shalom Rokeah of Belz, where he stayed as one of the *yoshevim* from 1849 to 1851.

After the death of R. Shalom, in 1855, he became attached to R. Abraham Brandwein of Stretyn, who encouraged him to become rebbe. He settled in Sambor and then in Komarno. He completed the whole of the Talmud seven times. He set up several funds to support the needy in the Holy Land and in Sambor, especially Jewish, and even non-Jewish, orphanages.

He established a *Sandek* society to help poor pregnant women. He participated in the rabbinical conference in Cracow in 1903. On the Day of Atonement he would stand on his feet for twenty-six hours, and throughout the night he studied the tractate *Yoma*. His prayers were similar to and as fiery as those of R. Uri, the "Seraph" of Strelisk. Despite his manifold problems, he was always full of joy and happiness. He himself would help with preparations for the Sabbath, and on the Sabbath he would say, "I feel the taste of the Garden of Eden."

He was succeeded by his son R. Yehudah Tzvi. His other sons were R. Shalom, who died in Jerusalem, and R. Nahum, who was rebbe in Przemysl.

R. Uri's Torah discourses were published under the title *Amarot Tehorot* together with the eulogy of R. Zeev Wolf Singer, *Misped Tamrurim* (Lvov, 1911), as well as in *Shulhan HaTahor* (Lvov, 1909), a collection of ninety-one hasidic comments on the Passover *Haggadah*, published by R. Ben Zion Halevi.

M. Unger, *Admorim SheNisfu BaShoa*, pp. 171–178.

A.Shu.

YSANDER, Torsten (1893–1960)–Swedish theologian and scholar of Hasidism. Ysander, a bishop in the Church of Sweden from 1936 to 1959, was appointed chaplain to the Swedish king in 1939. In 1922, he traveled to the Ukraine to meet Russian sectarians and to Poland to observe the hasidic community. Under the guidance of Jewish friends, he visited the hasidic communities of Warsaw and Cracow. The trip strengthened his theory on the strong similarity between Beshtian Hasidism and Russian sectarianism, especially the Khlysty, Skoptsy, Molokane, and Dukhabors.

His views on the Hasidism of the Besht, founder of the movement, are summarized in his *Studien zum Besht'schen Hasidismus in seiner religionsgeschichtlichen Sonderart* (1933). According to Ysander, certain hasidic characteristics–its dances, its songs, behavior during prayer, and the institution of the *tzaddik*–closely resemble Russian sectarian practices. As Hasidism became established, it ceased to be a revolutionary sect, its similarity to the sectarians diminished. Contemporary Hasidism only slightly resembles its origins.

Beyond the similarities, Ysander did not establish an actual contact between the founder of Hasidism and Russian sectarianism.

Y. Eliach in *Proceedings of the American Academy of Jewish Research*, vol. 36 (1968), pp. 57–83.

Y.E.

Z

ZAK, Barukh Joseph (1887–16 *Sivan* 1949) – Born in Krasilov, Russia, the son of R. Israel Zak, the Krasilover rebbe, a descendant of R. Yehiel Michel of Zloczov and of the Besht. At an early age, he married the daughter of R. David Shlomoh Rabinowicz, the Kobriner rebbe, and pursued his studies under his father-in-law.

In 1913, he emigrated to the Holy Land with the aim of establishing a hasidic agricultural settlement. During World War I, he was exiled to Egypt by the Turkish authorities. In 1916, he arrived in New York and at the request of the Kobriner hasidim, became their rebbe. He was active in many organizations, including the Agudat Israel of America.

Zak was a prolific writer, publishing several books. Among his publications are *Birkhat Yosef* on Torah and Festivals (New York, 1919), *Midrash Pliah* (New York, 1923), *Sekhel Tov* (New York, 1925), and *Sekhel Tov HaShalem* (New York, 1941). He also published many articles in the *Yiddishe Licht*, a New York-based periodical, between 1923 and 1926.

Z.A.

ZANGWILL, Israel (1864–1926), Anglo-Jewish writer – Zangwill, Anglo-Jewry's most celebrated novelist and dramatist, was also a man of action, participating in the efforts to procure a home for his homeless fellow Jews of eastern Europe.

A son of Yiddish-speaking immigrants, his father ended his years in Jerusalem "not because," said Zangwill, "he was a Zionist but because it was Zion." Zangwill was brought up in an atmosphere of *shtetl* Orthodoxy and Hasidism. His father, Moses Zangwill, a poor peddler of Whitechapel, was, his son said, "always praying and studying, something of a saint." He used to take Israel as a boy to a *shtiebl* at a very early hour every morning, and the son said afterward that the poetry of it made a great impression on him. The *shtiebl* was depicted by Zangwill in *Children of the Ghetto* (1892) in the chapter "The Sons of the Covenant" and in the chapter "Shmendrik": "Mekish was a hasid who was a member of the hasidic sect, founded by the Besht." He speaks of the Besht and the wonder-working rabbi of Sadgora.

Under the influence of Solomon Schechter, whose essay "Hasidism" made a big impact at the time, Zangwill, who called himself Schechter's pupil, wrote a study on the Besht in his *Dreamers of the Ghetto* (1898), with an acknowledgment to "my indebtedness to my friend Dr. Schechter." Zangwill was certainly the first writer to introduce the Besht's Hasidism to English imaginative literature. In *Dreamers of the Ghetto*, he portrayed a follower of the Besht, who on his deathbed wrote down his memories of the Besht, "my revered master, the ever-glorious and luminous Israel Baal Shem." Unfortunately, Zangwill followed Schechter too closely in repeating Schechter's strictures against the cult of the *tzaddik*.

> Now that he (the Baal Shem) is dead, and these extravagances are no longer to be checked by his living example, so monstrous are the deeds wrought and the things taught in his name, that though the Chasidim he founded are become – despite every persecution by the Orthodox Jews, despite the scourging of their bodies and the setting of them in the stocks, despite the excommunication of our order and the closing of our synagogues, and despite the burning of our books – a mighty sect throughout the length and breadth of Central Europe. (p. 250)

In another place in the work, Zangwill states:

> And I weep the more over this spoliation of my Chasidim, because there is so

> much perverted goodness among them, so much self-sacrifice for one another in distress, and such faithful obedience to the *tzaddik*, who everywhere monopolises the service and the worship which should be given to God. Alas! that a movement which began with such pure aspiration, which was to the souls of me and so many other young students as the shadow of a great rock in a weary land, that a doctrine which opened out to young Israel such spiritual vistas and transcendent splendours of the Godhead, should end in such delusions and distortions. (p. 256)

In "Bethulah," Zangwill relates the story of an encounter between a modern American Jew and the beautiful daughter of an East European hasidic rebbe. At first attracted by the picturesque hasidim, the American decides to remain in the town for some time. But when he learns that the girl, the rebbe's only child, is being held in seclusion because of her father's "kabbalistic mystifications," the Westernized narrator is horrified, for "Bethula was not a being to be employed as a sort of supernatural advocate, but a sad, tender creature needing love and protection. . . . And for some fantastic shadow-myth a beautiful young life was to be immolated" (*They That Walk in Darkness* [London: William Heinemann, 1899], p. 143).

Many years later, Zangwill used the same method he had used in his study of the Besht for an unfinished but still unpublished kabbalistic romance. Supposedly it is a contemporary account of Jacob Frank, the post-Sabbatean Messiah, whose degeneration had been one of the reasons that brought about the hasidic revival.

Of the general type of *Meah Shearim* Jews of Jerusalem, including many hasidim of whom his father was one, Zangwill wrote, "I cannot share the intolerance for the Jews of the old type who live in Jerusalem. I feel that in these grey beards pouring over the Talmud, we have a finer type of humanity than the Prussian Junker. It pays a people better to keep up such a standing army of mystics and students than to nourish a military caste."

J. Leftwich, *Israel Zangwill*.

J. H. Undelson, *Dreamer of the Ghetto*, pp. 115–116, 136, 138, 254.

J.L.

ZEDERBAUM, Alexander (1816–1893)–Born in Zamosc, Poland, he lived in Odessa and St. Petersburg. He was one of the leading figures of the Russian Jewish Enlightenment. He edited the Hebrew periodicals *HaMelitz* and *Kol Mevasser*, as well as a Russian weekly, *Vestnik Russkikh Yevreyev* (Russian Jewish Herald), and a Yiddish newspaper, *Yiddishes Folksblat*.

Throughout his life he fought Hasidism, which he regarded as a retrogressive movement. He wrote a work *Keter Kehunah* (Odessa, 1868), which was an anti-hasidic polemic.

J. Raisin, *The Haskalah Movement in Russia*, pp. 169–171.

ZEEV TZVI BENJAMIN of Zbarazh (d. 3 *Nisan* 1822)–He was the third son of R. Yehiel Michel of Zloczov and was known as Zeev Tzvi, Tzvi Zeev, and Benjamin Wolf. His discourses can be found in *Razin D'Oraita* (Warsaw, 1903), *Tiferet Tzvi Zeev* (Lvov, 1896), and *Kitvei Kodesh* by his disciple R. Aaron ben Shmuel of Ropczyce in his work *Yeshuot Malko* (Jerusalem, 1974).

ZEEV WOLF of Stary Ostrog (d. 8 *Adar* 1823)–Son of R. Naftali Tzvi, he was a disciple of R. Dov Baer, the Maggid of Mezhirech. He served as rabbi in Stary Ostrog, and R. Zusya of Annopol was his in-law. In 1798, he emigrated to the Holy Land, where he met R. Nahman of Bratzlav. He first settled in Haifa, and then in Tiberias.

He was a close associate of his disciple R. Menahem Mendel of Kosov. Among his other disciples were R. David Shlomoh of Serock and R. Joshua of Kosov.

His wife died on 3 *Heshvan* 1839. His daughter, Zizi Hannah, after the death of her husband, R. Israel Abraham of Ostrog, who had succeeded his father-in-law, emigrated to the Holy Land, where she died in the earthquake on 24 *Tevet* 1837. R. Zeev Wolf's son, R. Abraham Naftali, and his son's wife, Sarah, too, died in the earthquake.

A few of the discourses of R. Zeev Wolf are published in *Or Tzaddikim, Menorat Zahav* (Warsaw, 1902), and *Bet Aharon* (Brody, 1875).

Y. Alfasi, *Tiferet ShebeMalkhut*, pp. 24–26.

ZEEV WOLF of Zhitomir (d. 14 *Adar* 1798)–He was a disciple of R. Dov Baer, the Maggid of Mezhirech, and was associated with R. Jacob Joseph of Polonnoye and R. Nahum of Chernobyl. He looked after R. Nahum when the latter was in prison. Among his own followers were R. Eliezer of Zhitomir and R. Shakhna Tzvi of Nemirov.

He was the author of *Or HaMeir* on the Pentateuch, *Megillot*, and Festivals, which was published in Korzec in 1798 and has been reprinted sixteen times. A classic of hasidic literature, it contained the encomiums of R. Levi Yitzhak of Berdichev and R. Mordecai of Korzec. He was critical of the *tzaddikim* who entirely rejected the ideal of solitude and who were always on the move, journeying from place to place for the purpose of obtaining financial assistance. He did not, however, deny either the *tzaddik's* power to help his followers materially as well as spiritually or his ability to awaken the holy spark through his travels.

R. Zeev Wolf regarded the government decrees of compulsory military service as a divine punishment for the sins of assimilation, and he deplored Israel's mingling with the gentiles and learning their ways (Balak). He pleaded for a higher standard in human relationships and urged people to be kind to each other. "Angry people fill their mouth with live coals, with needles, sharp and hard. For each harsh word, they deserve to be banished from holiness and to suffer shame and disgrace until their soul is purified. Each of us must be master of his mouth."

He disapproved of noisy prayers. "So many people think that they must raise their voices and clap their hands and shake their limbs and make noises with their feet. They imagine that in this lies the essence of prayer. Such people are ignorant."

He was survived by his sons, R. Israel Dov and R. Moses.

Y. Raphael, *Sefer HaHasidut*, p. 66.

ZEEV WOLF KOTSES of Medziborz (d. ca. 1765) – A colleague and close associate of the Besht, at first R. Zeev opposed the Besht. He particularly objected to the Besht's styling himself *Besht*, but he soon became one of his closest adherents. He accompanied the master on many of his journeys. He is mentioned eight times in the *Shivhei HaBesht* (nos. 34, 41, 123, 128, 159, 173, 200, and 203).

He adopted an orphan whom he raised as his son, and the Besht arranged his marriage to a girl whom the Besht had adopted and raised (Tale 123). R. Barukh of Medziborz described R. Zeev Wolf as a "famous and saintly hasid."

ZEIDMAN, Hillel (b. 1915–), author – Born in Skalat, Galicia, the son of R. Abraham, a hasid of the rebbe of Husiatyn. He received a Ph.D. degree from Warsaw University. He contributed articles to the Aguda paper *Das Yiddish Togblat* (1930–1939) and *Moment* (1938–1939), and from 1937 he worked as an archivist in the Jewish community in Warsaw.

Miraculously escaping the Holocaust, he emigrated to the United States in 1946, where he contributed a number of articles on hasidic rebbes in *Elleh Ezkerah* ("These will I remember!" being biographies of leaders of religious Jewry in Europe who perished during the years 1939–1945), edited by Dr. Isaac Lewin (New York, 1959).

He also wrote articles for *Di Yiddishe Woch* (New York), *Hamodia* (Jerusalem), *HaBoker* (Tel Aviv), and *Hadoar* (New York) and was the author of *Tog Buch fun Varshaver Ghetto*, a diary from July 12, 1942, to April 1943 (Buenos Aires, 1947).

Who's Who in World Jewry, p. 246.

ZEITLIN, Hillel (1871–1942), religious thinker – Son of R. Aaron, a hasid of *Habad*, he was born in Korma, White Russia, and lived for a time in Homel. An ardent Zionist, he supported the Jewish Territorial Organization, which aimed at finding a suitable site, not necessarily in Palestine, for a Jewish settlement on an autonomous basis. For a time he lived in Vilna, and then, in 1906, this "Litvak" made his home in Warsaw.

At ease in both Hebrew and Yiddish, he wrote many monographs, which were both learned and lucid. His controversial articles in the Warsaw Yiddish papers *Haynt* and *Der Moment*, for which he worked for thirty-six years, ranged from ones on the *Tanya* of R. Shneur Zalman of Liady to ones on the stories of R. Nahman of Bratzlav and from the Seym elections to anti-Semitism. He often foretold the approaching end of European Jewry.

He wrote learned articles entitled "*Al Gevul Shenei Olamot*" (*Hatekufah* 4 [1919], pp. 501–545) and on mysticism. He even translated the *Zohar* into Hebrew and wrote a commentary on it, of which only the introduction was published. He was the author of *Rabbi Nahman Bratslaver* (Warsaw, 1910), *Rabbi Israel Baal Shem Tov* (Warsaw, 1911), *Hasidus* (Warsaw, 1922), *Torah Licht, Aggadah, Kabbalah, Hasidut Habad* (Warsaw, 1937–1938), and *Shmusen iber di Habadishe Welt Bavegung* (Warsaw, 1938).

His Yiddish articles together with a few translated from the Hebrew were edited by his son Aaron and were published under the title *Rab Nahman Bratslaver der Zeer fun Podolie* (New York, 1952). His work *Be-Pardes HaHasidut VeHakabbalah* was published in Tel Aviv in 1960.

To his home at 60 Slizka Street, Warsaw, flocked hasidim, *mitnaggedim*, writers, politicians, Agudists, Bundists, and Zionists. For a time he lived in the Jewish Hospital, until on September 12, 1942, the institution was liquidated.

On the road to Treblinka, Zeitlin heard the footsteps of the Messiah. He went to meet him wearing his *tallit* and *tefillin* on the eve of the New Year. He was shot to death on the *Umschlagsplatz* in Warsaw.

A. Holtz, "Hillel Zeitlin, Publicist and Martyr," pp. 141–146.

ZEMBA, Menahem (1883–19 *Nisan* 1943), religious writer–He was born in August, in Praga, a suburb of Warsaw. After the death of his father, Eliezer Lippa, when Zemba was nine, he was brought up by his grandfather R. Abraham Zemba, a disciple of R. Yitzhak Meir Alter of Ger. A frail and ailing child, he possessed a most incisive mind and a phenomenal memory. Married at eighteen to Mindele, the daughter of Hayyim Isaiah Zederbaum, a wealthy iron merchant, he was relieved of financial problems.

He threw himself wholeheartedly into his studies, to which he devoted twenty hours each day. For five or six hours a day, he shared his talmudical "discoveries" with a small group of students. He did not believe that the master should prepare in advance his daily lectures, because he felt that it was more profitable if the students participated in the actual preparations. He did not work in a vacuum but kept in close touch with R. Meir Simhah Hakohen of Dvinsk.

The death of his father-in-law compelled him to spend some time attending to business, but this did not distract him from his studies.

In 1935, he became a member of the Warsaw rabbinate and worked together with R. David Shapira, R. Samson Stockhammer, R. David Kahana, and R. Ezekiel Michelson.

He was the author of *Zera Avraham* (Warsaw, 1920), responsa bearing the name of his grandfather; *Gur Aryeh Yehudah* (Warsaw, 1928), responsa in memory of his middle son, Judah, who died at the age of eighteen; *Totzaot Hayyim* (Warsaw, 1921), a compendium on the thirty-nine categories of labor prohibited on the Sabbath; and *Mahazeh LaMelekh*, novellas on Maimonides' code *Yad HaHazakah*, for which he was awarded a literary prize by the Warsaw community.

He also wrote *Otiot Porhot*, select sayings; *Menahem Yerushalayim*, novellas on the *Talmud Yerushalmi*; and novellas on the *Talmud Bavli* and on the *Shulhan Arukh* in four parts, which were destroyed in the Warsaw ghetto fire. His contributions also appeared in the periodical *Degel HaTorah* (Banner of the Torah), edited by R. Menahem Kasher, director of the *Mesivta yeshivah* in Warsaw. When R. Kasher left for the United States, R. Zemba published the last two issues himself. When R. Joseph Hayyim Sonnenfeld died, R. Moses Blau was delegated to offer R. Zemba a rabbinical post in Jerusalem, but R. Zemba refused to leave.

To the end he regarded himself as a devoted disciple of Ger, and the rebbe of Ger–R. Abraham Mordecai Alter–loved him dearly. "Come, let us consult our Menahem," the rabbi of Ger would say.

During the Nazi occupation, R. Zemba exhorted and inspired the fighters of the Warsaw ghetto uprising. He stated:

> Of necessity, we must resist the enemy on all fronts. . . . We shall no longer heed his instructions. Henceforth, we must refuse to wend our way to the *Umschlagplatz*, which is but a blind and a snare–a veritable stepping-stone on the road to mass annihilation. . . . Had we lived up to our presumed status of a "people endowed with wisdom and understanding," we would have discerned ab initio the enemy's plot to destroy us as a whole, root and branch, and would have put into oper-

ation all media of information in order to arouse the conscience of the world. As it is now, we have no choice but to resist.

He lived for a time at Nalevka 37. He was murdered on 19 *Nisan*, on the sixth day of the Warsaw Uprising, while crossing Kupietzka Street, and was buried at 4 Kupietzka Street. He was reinterred in Jerusalem in 1958.

Many of his unpublished manuscripts were burned in the Warsaw ghetto.

His wife, Mindele, and their two unmarried daughters, Leah and Debbie Rachel, together with their married daughter, Hannah, her husband, R. Shmuel Leib Baer, and their two children, Yankele and Sarah, died in the gas chambers. Their unmarried son, Aaron Naftali, and other members of the family perished in Maidanek.

I. Elfenbein, "Menahem Zemba of Praga," pp. 603–617.

ZEN – The resemblance of the two mysticisms was first pointed out by Martin Buber in terms of Zen's *kōan* and Hasidism's stories. Both have similar ideas but express them differently.

Introduced to China in the fifth century, Zen (*Ch'an* in Chinese, from the Sanskrit *dhyāna*, which means "meditative position") flourished, with its peak during the eighth to the eleventh century, with establishment of most of its present doctrines and methods, and, finally, with its transplantation into Japan around 1200.

Despite its strictly monastic discipline, Zen has widely attracted millions of people and penetrated into the depth of their religious and cultural life. The goal of Zen is to reproduce the same content of enlightenment (*satori*) achieved by Shakyamuni, the founder of Buddhism, by means of *zazen* (meditative sitting). *Zazen* is the primary means that disciplines one to be qualified for enlightenment, though the enlightenment may not come to one in time of séance but through other incident. *Zazen*-like prayer in *devekut* needs intensive concentration to nullify alien thoughts, demanding thereby a state of *muga* (annihilation of the self) for its practice.

Whereas the hasidic system of *haalaat hamahshavot hazarot* consists of reversion of corporeal desires into their primordial root in holiness by way of contemplation, the liquidation of corporeality in Zen intends the reduction of diversity to uniformity by way of the calmness of mind called *mushin* (no-mind-ness). The state of *mushin* does not mean loss of consciousness, unlike the peak of *devekut*, which keeps one in a trance without self-consciousness. *Mushin* is the harmony between man and environment without dichotomy, as the moon reflects itself wherever there is a body of water.

Mu (nothingness) is the *essence* of reality according to Zen, and being is a merely transitive phenomenon generated on the surface of nothingness like waves of the sea. The idea of *mu* was a synthesis of the primal nothingness of Taoism and the Buddhist negativism of the void. Lin-Chi (d. 867) taught, "There is no substance at all in the universe; only names which are tentative and void we have. What is truly absolute is nothingness!" Zen has resolved beingness as void in contrast with Western philosophy, which has been so constantly attached with the solidness of material that it cannot conceive of the steadfastness of the naught.

The universe fills with *mu*, a sort of *pleroma* out of which all phases of being emanate. In Hasidism too, nothingness (*ayin*) was considered as *hyle* of which creation was made. But *ayin* could never be identical with the absolute, though it might be a highest source of reality. Hasidism believes that God, Who is infinite, is finally responsible for the creation and management of all hosts of being, and therefore there is a possibility that we can intercede with Him for changing the Providence if necessary. Compared with that, Zen, which is atheist by nature, has no details of knowledge about the creation, and it contents itself with the interchanging relationship of being and nothing, with taking little care of history. Life in Buddhism is cursed under the chain of causation, and salvation will not come unless we renounce ourself and take the world as it is.

Enlightenment in Zen consists of two levels: first, luminous enlightenment itself, which takes place in unutterable ecstasy, and second, intellectual reflection, which followingly conceptualizes the content of enlightenment, in most cases, at review with a Zen master. This seems to be equivalent to *bittul hayesh* (total extinction of corporeality) in Hasidism. The flash of enlightenment destroys all preconceptions in one's mind all at once so as to open a new dimension of right understanding.

Passing the gate of *satori*, we realize that all including ourselves are void and nothing and that nothingness is the absolute; therefore we too are absolute. When that understanding is once *incarnated* on us, it consequently frees us from the attachment of illusion, and we become the master to ourselves. It is this unconditioned subjectivity of *prajñā* (wisdom) that has characterized unparalleled insight in the arts of Zen.

On the other hand, standing in prayer before God, hasidim are often struck with the *mysterium tremendum* that what is an "I" to them is essentially an "it" to God. God is the only solid self. This is the discovery, a sort of *satori* in Hasidism, that eventually opens a way to the ultimate dialogue between man and God. The encounter to the eternal You is still deficient to attain the level of true wisdom unless one abases oneself. Hasidic exegeses of Torah as well as legends instruct us in the significance of such *bittul ha-yesh*. The deductive approach of Hasidism presupposes the entity of God and commands us to obey Him. But the approach of Zen is inductive; no one knows what *mu* is until one experiences it oneself. Thus the 1,700 items of *kōan* (public case) in Zen are enigmatic; they are brief stories—primarily questions and answers of paradox and negation.

The rationalism of irrationalism was indispensable to Zen to break through the inadequacy of language in order to bring believers to the immediacy of the inexplicable truth. The paradoxy of *kōan* is totally incompatible with the straightness of hasidic tales.

F. Blofeld, *The Zen Teaching of Huang Po on the Transmission of Mind.*

J.Y.T.

ZEVIN, Shlomoh Joseph (1890–1988), scholar—Son of R. Aaron Mordecai, a native of Kazimirov, Belorussia, he studied in the *yeshivah* of Mir and later under R. Shemaryah Noah Schneersohn. He helped R. Joseph Yitzhak Schneersohn to establish secret *hadarim* in Soviet Russia. He served as a rabbi in several Russian cities and emigrated to Eretz Yisrael in 1934.

He was the editor of the *Entziklopedyah Talmudit* (Talmudic Encyclopedia), and he received the Israel prize for religious literature in 1949. He was the author of *Ha-Mo'adim BeHalakhah* (Tel Aviv, 1955), which has gone through three editions, and *Sippurei Hasidim*, 443 hasidic stories, published in Tel Aviv in 1955 and 1959. His life was a synthesis of the scholarship of Lithuania with the fervor of Hasidism.

Leksikon fun der Nayer Yiddisher Literatur, vol. 3, p. 659.

ZHITOMIR, Ukraine—The home of R. Zeev Wolf of Zhitomir.

The first Hebrew printing press was established there in 1804 by Tzvi Hirsch of Zolkiew, and a number of hasidic and kabbalistic works were published there, among them, *Sefer R. Israel Besht* (1805) and *Keter Torah* (1806).

In *Kislev* 1847, the three Shapira brothers—R. Haninah Lippa, R. Aryeh Leib, and R. Joshua Heschel—the sons of R. Shmuel Abraham Abba of Slavuta, established another printing press there. Seven years later, one of the brothers, R. Aryeh Leib, set up his own. Between 1858 and 1864, the other two brothers published a new edition of the Babylonian Talmud; R. Aryeh Leib published a new edition of the Jerusalem Talmud.

H. D. Friedberg, *Toldot Hadfus HaIvri BePolania*, pp. 134–135.

ZINBERG, Israel (1873–1939), literary historian—Born in Volhynia, he studied in Karlsruhe and in Basel, where he qualified as a chemist and also received a doctorate in philosophy. In 1898, he settled in St. Petersburg, where he worked in a chemical laboratory. He began to specialize in Jewish literary history and contributed many articles to the Russian Jewish Encyclopedia (1907–1914), to Russian Jewish periodicals, and to Yiddish publications. In 1938, he was exiled to Vladivostok, where he died.

His monumental work *Geshikhte fun der Literatur bay Yidn*—a study of Jewish literary history from the Spanish period to the end of the Russian *Haskalah*—was published in eight volumes (1929–1937) and was reprinted in ten volumes in Buenos Aires in 1970. Mysticism was his favorite subject, and one-third of this work is devoted to it. He devotes an entire volume to the rise and development of Hasidism. He describes the Besht, his disciples, and the struggle against the *mitnaggedim*.

He follows in the footsteps of Dubnow and maintains that the Besht wished to remove the veil of melancholy hanging over the Jewish quarters and to dispel the dark spirit of fear and dread. He regards the Besht as lenient in ritual matters. He gives a balanced view of R. Nahman's stories and characterizes R. Nahman as a mystic with a poetic soul, but adds that one has to dig through sand to find the sparkle of a pearl.

M. Waxman, *A History of Jewish Literature*, vol. 4, pp. 825ff.

ZIRELSON, Judah Leib (1860–1941), chief rabbi of Bessarabia – Born in Kolzelets, Ukraine, he was, at the age of eighteen, appointed rabbi of Priluki and in 1908, elected rabbi of Kishinev. As early as 1891, he criticized many rabbis for not supporting the *Hovevei Zion* movement and for not purchasing *etrogim* from the Holy Land.

At first, he was an active Zionist, but in 1908, he dissociated himself from Zionism. He became one of the founders of the Aguda, but he welcomed the Balfour Declaration when he stated that "out of thick darkness a light begins to break through." He became a member of the *Mo'ezet Gedolei HaTorah* and presided over the *Knessiyah HaGedolah*, held in Vienna (1923 and 1929) and in Marienbad (1927).

He strongly opposed the Malcolm MacDonald White Paper of May 1939, which limited Jew immigration to Palestine to 75,000 during the next five years. He made his views public in the presence of British statesman and supporter of Zionism Josiah Clement (later Lord) Wedgwood (1872–1943), who at that time visited Kishinev. Zirelson, however, supported the report of the Royal Commission on Palestine under the chairmanship of Earl Peel, who, in 1937, recommended the partitioning of the Holy Land into a Jewish state, an Arab state, and a British mandatory enclave.

Following the incorporation of Kishinev into Romania, Zirelson played an active role in the affairs of Romanian Jewry. In 1922, he was elected to the Romanian parliament and to the Kishinev city council. In 1926, he became the only Jewish member of the Romanian senate.

He was the author of many rabbinic works. He was a *Habad* hasid of the Kopys branch and from time to time delivered public discourses on hasidic themes.

He was killed by the Germans in Kishinev.

Elleh Ezkerah, vol. 1, pp. 164–176.

Z.A.

ZLOCZOV, Abraham Hayyim (ca. 1750–26 *Tevet* 1816), hasidic rebbe – Son of R. Gedaliah, rabbi of Zolkiev, Abraham Hayyim was a disciple of R. Dov Baer, the Maggid of Mezhirech, and R. Yehiel Michael of Zloczov. He studied under R. Shmuel Shmelke Horowitz of Nikolsburg. He married and divorced the daughter of R. Pinhas Horowitz of Frankfurt. After his divorce, he married the daughter of R. Issachar Baer of Zloczov. There were no children.

He became rabbi in Zborov, and when his father-in-law emigrated to the Holy Land in 1793, he succeeded him as rabbi in Zloczov. He was renowned for his mastery of *Halakhah*. R. Efraim Zalman Margulies of Brody described him as "one to whom the secrets of the Torah have been revealed."

He was the author of *Orah LeHayyim* on the Pentateuch, which was published by his stepson, R. Joseph Azriel (Berdichev, 1817) and which received the approbation of R. Levi Yitzhak of Berdichev, R. Israel, the Maggid of Kozienice, the "Seer" of Lublin, R. Abraham Joshua Heschel of Opatov, and R. Jacob Orenstein of Lvov. It was reprinted in Lvov in 1838 and in Jerusalem in 1960. He also wrote a commentary *Pri Hayyim* on *Avot* (Lvov, 1873; Jerusalem, 1962) and a commentary on the Passover *Haggadah*, *Pri Hayyim* (Lvov, 1873; Vienna, 1921).

Y. Raphael, *Sefer HaHasidut*, p. 331.

ZOHAR – The major work of Jewish mysticism, exercising a profound influence on all subsequent mystical movements, and providing the foundation for Lurianic Kabbalah and *Hasidut*.

Its full title is *Sefer HaZohar* (Book of Splendor). But it is also referred to as *Mekhiltah* (or Midrash) *de-R. Shimon ben Yohai*. Its authorship was, in fact, attributed by kabbalists to the second-century *tanna* of this name, who, while hiding with his son from the Romans, received revelations of the divine mysteries in a cave.

The *Zohar* first appeared at the end of the thirteenth century in Spain, where it was circulated by R. Moses de Léon. This has been the subject of much debate among scholars. The traditional school maintains that R. Moses simply disseminated the texts that contained the insights of Rabbi Shimon, while the more critical school believes that the Zohar is in the main R. Moses' own work, albeit based on earlier source material.

The *Zohar* is really a collection of books more than a unified, systematic work. The main part is a *midrash* on the Torah, arranged according to the order of the *sidrot*, including the portion Pinhas but it covers only a small part of Deuteronomy, only *VaEthanan*, a little of *Vayyelekh*, and *Haazinu*. Printed editions are usually to be found in five volumes, the first three consisting of the exposition of the Torah, the fourth being *Tikkunei HaZohar*, and the fifth, *Zohar Hadash*. Other smaller works are to be found interspersed among these major sections.

The *Zohar* deals with the whole range of Jewish religious experience from a mystical, theosophic point of view. Its view of existence is determined by the relationship between the two worlds, the upper world and the lower world. The upper world is the domain of the Godhead, and the divine attributes are systematized there through the structure of the *Sefirot*, a celestial hierarchy through which divinity is emanated from the highest realms of *Ein Sof* (the Unknowable Infinite) to the lowest *Sefirah, Malkhut*, which is also identified with the *Shekhinah*. The plurality of the *Sefirot* is, however, only apparent, not real, for they all make up the divine unity.

The *Sefirot*, separately and together, have an influence upon the lower physical world in which man lives. But it is an essential part of the *Zohar*'s philosophy that man also has an influence upon the upper world. If he falls a prey to *sitra ahra* (the other side, i.e., the demonic power of evil), which seeks to disrupt the unity of the *Sefirot* and to gain control of both worlds; then he weakens the force of good in the divine realm. The *mitzvot* of the Torah were given to Israel to help the people to work for the unification of all of the powers in the upper world and to frustrate the designs of *sitra ahra*. Thus, even the minutiae of *halakhah* have an important bearing on humanity's role in the divine scheme of things.

The *Zohar* is written in its own characteristic admixture of Hebrew and Aramaic, and it contains stories and legends about R. Shimon and his companions and their journeys and discussions. And there are also to be found beautiful allegories concerning the Torah and the human soul, the future world of paradise, and the exalted progress of the mystical mind, which tries to perceive the mysteries of the divine.

It was the approach of the *Zohar* to the profoundest preoccupations of the human mind – the problems of creation, the purpose of human existence, the origin of evil, the suffering of the righteous, the role of the Jewish people, and the "end of days" – that evoked an immediate response in the Jewish soul, and the *Zohar* soon became an object of study, third in importance only after the Torah and the Talmud. Indeed, some kabbalists set it higher than the Talmud.

Its reputation was even further enhanced after its views had been interpreted and expanded by the school of Lurianic Kabbalah in Safed in the sixteenth century. And it was in this form that the *Zohar* exercised such a decisive influence on the hasidic movement.

Great controversy surrounded proposals to print the *Zohar*. Two editions finally were published contemporaneously, in Mantua (1558–1560) and Cremona (1559–1560). The *Tikkunei Zohar* was published separately in Mantua (1558).

There is a great wealth of commentary published (and unpublished) on the *Zohar*. The most outstanding aids to comprehension of the *Zohar* are:

R. Tzvi Hirsch Horowitz: *Sefer Ispeklaryah HaMe'irah* (Amsterdam, 1750)

R. Issachar Baer Hakohen of Szczebrzescin: *Sefer Mareh Cohen* (Cracow, 1589)

R. Aaron Selig of Zolkiew: *Hibbur Amudei Sheva* (Cracow, 1635–1636)

R. Joseph ben Shraga: *Sefer Yesha Yah* (Venice, 1637)

R. Issachar Baer of Kremnitz: *Sefer Imrei Binah* (Prague, 1611)

R. Isaiah Menahem Mendel of Lodz: *Yalkut HaZohar* (Piotrokov, 1912)

R. Isaac Eisig of Komarno: *Zohar Hai* (1875–1881)

R. Jacob Moses Safrin: *Damesek Eliezer* (1902–1928)

In addition, commentaries were written by the following hasidim: R. Israel Hofstein, the Maggid of Kozienice; R. Dov Baer Schneersohn; R. Mordecai Joseph Leiner;

R. Tzaddok Hakohen Rabinowicz; and R. Tzvi Hirsch Shapira.

D. C. Matt, *Zohar, The Book of Enlightenment.*

D.G.

ZOREF, Joshua Heshel (1633–1700), pseudoprophet – Born in Vilna, he sought refuge in Amsterdam during the persecutions that ensued in the wake of the Polish-Swedish war in 1656. Returning to Vilna, he began his mystical studies. He was an ascetic, and during the messianic excitement of 1656, he had visions that he described in five volumes corresponding to the Pentateuch. These writings delved into the mystical meanings of the *Shema* and were based on numerological manipulations of his own. His disciples considered him to be a prophet or the Messiah, the son of Joseph.

He went to Cracow, where he married the daughter of R. Jacob Eleazar Fischhof, a follower of R. Judah Hasid. Hasidic masters such as the Besht, R. Dov Baer, the Maggid of Mezhirech, R. Levi Yitzhak of Berdichev, R. Nahum of Chernobyl, and R. Aaron of Karlin had copies of Zoref's works. It is patently clear that the hasidic leaders were not familiar with Zoref's secret role as a Shabbatean adherent.

The Besht highly praised his works and wanted to have them published, as he, too, was completely unaware of their Shabbatean character. In the *Shivhei HaBesht* the personage of Zoref seems to have merged with the mysterious figure of R. Adam Baal Shem. Copies of Zoref's works seem to have been available, but R. Efraim Zalman Margulies (1760–1828) of Brody, who was aware of their Shabbatean origin, vetoed their publication.

The view that Zoref was transformed into R. Adam Baal Shem is advocated by Gershom Scholem.

G. G. Scholem, *Kabbalah*, pp. 452–453.

S.T.

ZUCKERMAN, Shalom, of Rashkov (1883–21 *Iyyar* 1930) – Son of R. Shlomoh Zalmina of Rashkov, he married the daughter of R. Yitzhak Pechenick of Brzezany and settled in Calarasi in Bessarabia. Following the traditions of Ruzhyn, R. Shalom lived in a well-decorated and palatial residence. A talmudist and a warmhearted leader, he had a large following.

During the winter months, he traveled to neighboring towns to meet his hasidim. In 1923, he visited the United States; two years later, he settled in the Bronx and established congregation *Anshei Rashkov*.

His son-in-law, R. Aaron Pechenick of Jerusalem, carried on as rabbi of the congregation for several years, but he did not act in the capacity of a rebbe. He was an active member of the Mizrachi movement and the author of several articles on Hasidism.

A.Shu.

ZUSYA (Meshullam Zusya) of Annopol (d. 2 *Shevat* 1800) – Born in Lupochova, near Titkin, he was the son of R. Eliezer Lippa and the brother of R. Elimelekh of Lejask. He studied under R. Shmelke Horowitz, who told him, "You are wise enough to do your own studying." He was a devoted follower of R. Dov Baer, the Maggid of Mezhirech. It was through his influence that his brother also became a hasid.

In his youth, he and his brother decided to go into "exile" to atone for their "misdeeds." Traveling incognito for three years, they suffered the rigors of the road. They traveled from town to town, from village to village, and reached as far as Oswiecim (Auschwitz). Legend has it that R. Zusya would not sleep the night there. "I can smell," he is reputed to have said, "Jewish bodies being burned."

He was a remarkable man in an age of remarkable men. He would travel across the country, raising money to ransom prisoners. He befriended R. Shneur Zalman of Liady, and together with R. Israel of Polotsk and R. Nahum of Chernobyl, supported R. Shneur Zalman of Liady in his controversy with R. Abraham of Kalisk.

After the death of R. Dov Baer, the Maggid of Mezhirech, he settled in Annopol (Hanipoli). He gave approbations to R. Shabsai of Rashkov's prayer book *Seder Tefillah MiKol HaShanah*, printed in 1788 and to the *Tanya*, printed in Slavuta in 1796. Although he lived in unmitigated penury, he would say, "I have never experienced any suffering." His wife, Hendel, found it hard to suffer deprivation and even asked him for a divorce. "In the Talmud (*Sanhedrin* 22)," he told her, "it is written that if a man puts away his first wife, the altar will shed tears for him. My pillow is wet with these tears."

His humility was equaled by his kind-heartedness and his total devotion to serve God and people. "No matter when I lift my soul up to heaven," remarked R. Nathan Adler (1741–1800), the German kabbalist of Frankfurt, "R. Zusya is always ahead of me." R. Zusya was never content with his spiritual achievements, and he strove ceaselessly to improve and perfect his way of life. His favorite saying was "In the world to come they will not ask me, 'Why were you not like Moses?' but they will ask me, 'Why were you not Zusya?' "

He maintained that there are five verses in the Bible that constitute the essence of Judaism: "You shall be wholehearted with the Lord your God" (Deuteronomy 18:13); "I have set the Lord always before me" (Psalm 16:8); "You shall love your neighbor as yourself" (Leviticus 19:18); "In all your ways acknowledge Him" (Proverbs 3:6); and "To walk humbly with your God" (Micah 6:8). These verses begin in Hebrew with one of the letters *Tav, Shin, Vav, Bet,* or *Heh*, which spell the Hebrew word for repentance (*teshuvah*).

R. Zusya survived his brother by fifteen years. For the last seven years of his life he was bedridden and in pain. On his gravestone, these words are inscribed: "Here lies a man who served God in love, who rejoiced in suffering, and turned many away from sin."

His aphorisms and discourses can be found in *Menorat Zahav* (Warsaw, 1902). His son, R. Tzvi Menahem Mendel (d. 1814), succeeded him in Annopol. Another son, R. Israel Abraham Abba (1772–1814), served as a rabbi in Czernigov.

Y. Raphael, *Sefer HaHasidut*, p. 18.

A.T.

ZWEIFEL, Eliezer (1815–1888), author – Born in Mogilev, the son of a hasid of R. Menahem Mendel of Lubavitch, he served for twenty years as an instructor of religion and Talmud in the rabbinical seminary in Zhitomir. His work *Shalom al Yisrael* (Peace to Israel) was printed in four parts in Zhitomir and Vilna between 1868 and 1873. It was only through the endorsement of Abraham Krochmal and Adolf Jellinek that H. Z. Slominsky, censor of Zhitomir, permitted the book to be published.

Zweifel tried to create harmony between the *mitnaggedim* and the hasidim. He was one of the first Hebrew writers to view Hasidism with sympathy and understanding. He believed that the movement had a sound religious basis and that its teachings could be traced back to ancient Jewish sources. He defended Hasidism against many false charges and vindicated the movement from charges of imposture.

In his book, he quotes copious extracts from hasidic and rabbinic sources. He considers the Besht to belong to the great spiritual triumvirate: the Vilna Gaon, Mendelssohn, and the Besht. He stated, "Hasidim love and honor their wives, and they spend more money to adorn and beautify them than the *mitnaggedim*" (part 3, vol. 2, p. 31). He expressed the opinion that prolonged stay at the court of the *tzaddikim* offered the hasidim temporary relief from their domestic troubles and liberated them from their obligations to their wives and children (part 3, vol. 2, p. 32).

As a forerunner of neo-Hasidism, Zweifel was a great influence on S. Dubnow, M. J. Berdyczewski, S. A. Horodezky, and M. Buber. A new edition of his work in two volumes was published by A. H. Rubinstein (Jerusalem, 1973).

M. Waxman, *A History of Jewish Literature*, vol. 3, pp. 315–319.

ZYCHLINSKI, Hanokh Saadiah, of Strykov (1885–1942) – Second son of R. Moses Nethanel (d. 1912), he was twenty-seven years old when his father died. During the First World War, he lived in Lodz. He was an ascetic and wasted little time in sleep. He would never remove his clothes throughout the week except on the Sabbath. He ate little. He was a noted kabbalist, and his discourses were interwoven with lengthy quotations from the *Zohar* and the works of R. Yitzhak Luria.

On the New Year, before the blowing of the *shofar*, he would read passages from *Pri Etz Hayyim*, by R. Hayyim Vital. He would often visit Wloclawek to see his hasidim. He organized a society *Shmirat Shabbat* for observance of the Sabbath. In 1931, he participated in the world conference for the observance of the Sabbath, held in Berlin. He was a staunch supporter of the Aguda and participated in its national conventions. He supported the *Bet Yaakov* journal *Kindergarten* and the *Yiddishe Togblat*. He was among the signatories of a proclamation exhorting hasidim not to read the heretical press.

At the outbreak of the Second World War, he lived in Warsaw at Nalevka 55. The rebbe together with his sons, R. Moses Nethanel and R. Meir, his wife, his only daughter, Sarah, and her husband, R. Reuben, and his brother Joshua were all murdered by the Nazis.

Elleh Ezkerah, vol. 2, pp. 164–168.

ZYCHLINSKI, Samuel Abba, of Zychlin (19 *Kislev* 1809–26 *Elul* 1879) – Son of R. Yitzhak Zelig, a hasid of R. Fishel of Strykov. He studied briefly under R. Simhah Bunem of Przysucha, and later under R. Leibish Harif of Plotsk. He married Golda Ratza, the daughter of R. Mordecai of Bodzan. In 1844, he became rebbe in Zychlin, where he was known as a miracle worker.

He gave public discourses not only on the Sabbath and Festivals but also daily, between *Minhah* and *Maariv*, on the *Midrash Rabba*. On the Sabbath he spoke only Hebrew. He observed nightly *Tikkun Hatzot* and served as reader at every single service.

He was a great Polish patriot and believed that the salvation of Israel was bound up with the fate of the Polish nation. He regarded Russia as the enemy and oppressor of both peoples. Betrayed by mitnaggedic informers, he was imprisoned by the Russian authorities and held in Luniniec prison for three weeks in 1845.

He was succeeded by his only son, R. Moses Nethanel (d. 1912). R. Moses had two sons, R. Hanokh Saadiah and R. Menahem Yedidiah (1870–1940), who was the son-in-law of R. Isaiah Shapira.

R. Samuel Abba (1893–1942), the son of R. Menahem Yedidiah, was the son-in-law of R. Eliezer Weisblum. He and his three sons – R. Mordecai Efraim, R. Avigdor Barukh, and R. Asher – perished in the Holocaust on the Fast of Esther 1942. Only one daughter, Esther Leah, survived.

Bibliography

Agus, Jacob B. *Modern Philosophies of Judaism*. New York: Behrman Jewish Book House, 1941.

Alfasi, Yitzhak. "Admor Bizkhut Atzmo." *Sinai* 23 (1969): 336–338.

——. *Bet Kosov U'Vishnitz*. Tel Aviv, 1974.

——. *Bisdei HaHasidut*. Tel Aviv: Ariel, 1986.

——. *Enziklopedyah LeHasidut* (Hebrew), letter Aleph to Tet. Jerusalem: Mosad Harav Kook, 1986.

——. *Gur*. Tel Aviv: Sinai, 1954.

——. *HaHasidut*. Tel Aviv: Zion, 1969.

——. *HaHasidut*. Tel Aviv: Sifrit Maariv, 1974, 1979.

——. *HaHasidut BeRomania*. Tel Aviv: Segullah, 1973.

——. *HaHasidut VeShivat Zion*. Tel Aviv: Sifrut Maariv, 1986.

——. *HaHozeh MiLublin*. Jerusalem: Mosad Harav Kook, 1969.

——. *HaRav MiApta*. Jerusalem: Makhon Siftei Zaddikim, 1981.

——. *HaSabah HaKadosh MiRadozyce*. Tel Aviv: Sinai, 1957.

——. *Kiryat Sefer*, vol. 49. 1974.

——. *MiPrizdor LeTraklin*. Tel Aviv: Hazaot M'Or, n.d.

——. *Sefer HaAdmorim*. Tel Aviv: Hotzaat Zion, 1961.

——. *Tiferet SheBeMalkhut*. Tel Aviv: Ariel, 1961.

——. *Toldot HaHasidut*. Tel Aviv: Zion, 1959.

Allentuck, Marcia, ed. *The Achievement of Isaac Bashevis Singer*. Southern Illinois University Press, 1969.

Anshei Shem. Cracow: Josef Fischer, 1895.

Ariel, David. *The Mystic Quest: An Introduction to Jewish Mysticism*. Northvale, NJ: Jason Aronson, 1988.

Assaf, David. "The Expanion of Hasidism: The Case of R. Nehemiah Yehiel of Bychowa," in *Studies in Jewish Culture in Honour of Chone Shmeruk*, ed. Israel Bartel. Jerusalem: Zalman Shazar Center, 1993, pp. 243–269.

Avissar, Oded. *Sefer Tevariah*. Jerusalem: Keter, 1973.

Avtichi, Aryeh, and Avtichi, Ben Zakai, eds. *Stolin: Sefer Zikaron*. Israel: Irgun Yoze Stolin Vehasevivah BeYisrael, 1952.

Bacher, W. *Exegetische Terminologie der Judischen Tradition und Literatur*. 2 vols. Leipzig: J. G. Hinrichsche Buchhandlung, 1899–1905.

Band, Arnold J. *Nahman of Bratslav*. New York: Paulist Press, 1978.

——. *Nahman of Bratslav: The Tales*, ed. and trans. from Hebrew and Yiddish. London: S.P.C.K., 1979.

Baranowicze: Sefer Zikharon. Tel Aviv: Association of Former Residents of Baranowicze in Israel, 1953.

Baron, Salo W. *History and Historians*, compiled by A. Hertzberg and Leon A. Feldman. Philadelphia: Jewish Publication Society of America, 1964.

——. *The Jewish Community*. 3 vols. Philadelphia: Jewish Publications Society of America, 1948.

Barzilay, Isaac. *Shir and Contemporaries*. Israel: Masada Press, 1969.

Bauminger, Aryeh, ed. *Sefer Krako: Ir VeEm BeYisrael*. Jerusalem: Mosad Harav Kook, 1959.

Bechtel, Dalphine. *Der Nister, Sortilèges Contes*. Paris: Juilliard, 1992.

——. *Der Nister's Work 1907–1929: A Study of a Yiddish Symbolist*. Berne: Peter Lang, 1990.

Ben-Amos, Dan, and Mintz, Jerome R. *In Praise of the Baal Shem Tov*. Northvale, NJ: Jason Aronson, 1991.

Benayahu, M. "The Printing Press of R. Israel Bak in Safed," in *Areshet*, vol. 4. Jerusalem: Mosad Harav Kook, 1986, pp. 271–295.

Ben Ezra, A. *HaYanukkah MiStolin*. New York: Shulsinger, 1951.

Ben Menahem, Naftali. "Yahason shel Gedolei HaHasidut el Abraham Ibn Ezra," in *Sefer HaBesht*. Jerusalem: Mosad Harav Kook, 1961.

Berger, Abraham. "Approaches to Rabbi Nahman and His Tales," in *Studies in Jewish Bibliography, History and Literature: In Honor of I. Edward Kiev*, ed. Charles Berlin. New York: Ktav, 1971, pp. 11–19.

Berger, Israel. Introduction to *Eser Orot*, part of *Sefer Sehut Yisrael*. Jerusalem: Hebrew Bookstore, 1954.

Berl, Hayyim Y. *Reb Yitzhak Eizig MiKomarno*. Jerusalem: Mosad Harav Kook, 1965.

Berle, Leon J. *R. Avraham Yehoshua Heschel HaRav MeApta*. Jerusalem: Mosad Harav Kook, 1984.

Bernfeld, Simon. *Toldot Shir* (Shlomoh Yehudah Rapaport). Berlin: Ahiasof, 1899.

Biala-Podlasko. Ed. M. I. Faigenbaum. Tel Aviv: Kupat Gemilat Hesed of the Community of Biala-Podlasko, 1961.

Biale, David. *Gershom Scholem: Kabbalah and Counter-History*. Cambridge, MA: Harvard University Press, 1979.

Biderman, Israel Mordecai. *Mayer Balaban*. New York: Dr. I. M. Biderman Book Committee, 1976.

Birnbaum, Salomon. *The Life and Sayings of the Baal Shem*. New York: Hebrew Publishing Company, 1933.

——. "Nathan Birnbaum," in *Men of the Spirit*, ed. Leo Jung. New York: Kymson, 1964, pp. 517–551.

Blau, A. *Amudei Dinhora*. Jerusalem: Kol Yisrael, 1932.

Blau, Ludwig. *Das altjudische Zauberwesen*. Budapest, 1898.

Bloch, Chaim. *The Golem*, trans. Harry Schneiderman. Vienna, 1925.

——. *Hersch Ostropoler. Ein jüdischer Till-Eulenspiegel des 18. Jahrhunderts: seine Geschichten und Streiche*. Berlin/Vienna: B. Harz, 1921.

——. *Der Prager Golem*. 1920.

Blofeld, F. *The Zen Teaching of Huang Po on the Transmission of Mind*. London, 1958.

Blumenthal, David R. *Understanding Jewish Mysticism: A Source Reader*, vol. 2. New York: Ktav, 1982.

Blumenthal, Nahman, and Korzen, Meyer, eds. *Lublin*, vol. 5 of *Enziklopediya shel Galuyot*, 7 vols. Jerusalem/Tel Aviv: Enziklopedia shel Galuyot, 1956.

Bornstein, Aaron Yisrael. *Neos Deshe*. Tel Aviv: pub. by the author, vol. 1, 1974; vol. 2, 1978.

Bornstein, Aviezer. *HaAdmor HaRofeh*. Tel Aviv: L'Aleph Hotzaot Sefarim, 1970.

Braun, R. H. L. *Toldot Anshei Mofet*. Grosswardein, 1944.

Brawer, Abraham. *Galicia VeYehudeya*. Jerusalem: Mosad Bialik, 1965.

Brayer, Menahem. "Admorei Romania VeUngaria VeEretz Yisrael" ("The Hasidic Rebbes of Romania, Hungary, and Their Relationship to Eretz Yisrael"), in *Hasidut VeZion*, ed. S. Federbush. Jerusalem: Mosad Harav Kook and Moriah, 1963, pp. 190–246.

Brod, Menahem M., ed. *HaRabbi MiLubavitch*. Kefar Habad: Mosdot Habad, 1986.

Bromberg, Abraham Yitzhak. *Migdolei HaHasidut*, a series. Jerusalem: Hatzaot Hamakhon L'Hasidut.

——. Vol. 1: *R. Hayyim Halberstamm of Zanz*, 1949.

——. Vol. 2: *R. Yehudah Leib Alter MiGur, the Sefat Emet*. 3rd ed., 1966.

——. Vol. 3: *Admorim LeBet Vorka VeAmshinov*, 2nd ed., 1954.

——. Vol. 4: *Admorei Alexander*, 2nd ed., 1954.

——. Vol. 5: *R. Abraham Bornstein MiSochaczev*, 2nd ed., 1955.

——. Vol. 6: *R. Israel Friedman MiRuzhyn*, 2nd ed., 1955.

——. Vol. 7: *R. Tzaddok HaKohen*, 2nd ed., 1956.

——. Vol. 8: *R. Mosheh Teitelbaum*, 1954.

——. Vol. 9: *Admorim LeBet Zanz*, 1956.

——. Vol. 10: *Admorim LeBet Belz*, 1955.

——. Vol. 11: *R. Yehiel Meir Lipshitz*, 1956.

——. Vol. 13: *Mishpahat Eiger*, 1958.

——. Vol. 14: *R. Hanokh Heinokh HaKohen Levin*, 1958.

——. Vol. 15: *R. Joseph Saul Nathanson*, 1960.

——. Vol. 18: *Bet Kozienice*, 1961.

——. Vol. 19: *HaHozeh MiLublin*, 1962.

——. Vol. 20: *Admorei Nesvizh Kaidanov Novominsk*, 1963.

——. Vol. 21: *HaGeonim MiKutno Berzan VeChebin*, 1965.

——. Vol. 22: *R. Abraham Mordecai Alter MiGer*, 1966.

——. Vol. 23: *HaAdmorim MiPraga*, 1966.
——. Vol. 24: *R. Eliyahu Guttmacher*, 1969.
——. *HaRav Eliyahu Guttmacher*. Jerusalem, 1961.
——. "R. Uzziel Meisels." *Sinai* 32 (1969): 200–211.
——. "Shalom Mordecai of Brzezany." *Sinai* 32 (1952–1953): 295–297.
Brauminger, Aryeh, Bosk, Meir, and Gelber, N.M. *Sefer Krako* (Hebrew). Jerusalem: Mosad Harav Kook, 1959.
Buber, Martin. *A Bibliography of His Writings, 1897–1978*, compiled by Margot Cohen and Rafael Buber. Jerusalem: Magnus Press, 1980.
——. *For the Sake of Heaven*. Philadelphia: Jewish Publication Society of America, 1953.
——. *Die Geschichte des Rabbi Nachman*. Frankfurt am Main: Rutter & Loening, 1906.
——. *Hasidism and Modern Man*, ed. and trans. Maurice Friedman. New York: Horizon Press, 1958.
——. *I and Thou*, trans. Walter Kaufman. New York: Charles Scribner, 1970.
——. *Die Legende des Baal Schem*. Frankfurt-am-Main: Rutter & Loening, 1907.
——. *The Legends of the Baal Shem Tov*, trans. Maurice Friedman. New York: Harper, 1955.
——. *The Origin and Meaning of Hasidism*, ed. Maurice Friedman. New York: Horizon Press, 1960.
——. *Tales of the Hasidim*, trans. Olga Marx, 2 vols. New York: Schocken Books, 1947–1948.
——. *Tales of the Hasidim: Early Masters*. New York: Schocken, 1961.
——. *Tales of the Hasidim: Later Masters*. New York: Schocken, 1961.
——. *The Tales of R. Nahman*, trans. Maurice Friedman. New York: Horizon Press, 1956; Harper & Row, 1965.
——. *The Way of Man According to the Teachings of Hasidism*. London: Vincent Stuart, 1963.
Burstin, Aviezer. *Tzidkat HaHaham*. Haifa: Ohel, 1966.
Buxbaum, Yitzhak. *Jewish Spiritual Practice*. Northvale, NJ: Jason Aronson, 1990.
Cesarani, David. *The Jewish Chronicle*. Cambridge, UK: Cambridge University Press, 1994.
Chagall, Marc. *The Hasidim*. New York: Crown Publishers, 1970.
Challenge: An Encounter with the Lubavitch-Chabad. London: Lubavitch Foundation of Great Britain, 1973.
Cohen, Arthur. *A People Apart: Hasidism in America*. New York: E. P. Dutton, 1970.
Cohen, Yitzhak Yosef. *Sages of Transylvania* (Hebrew). Jerusalem: Hungarian Sages Memorial Project Machon Yerushalayim, 1989.
Dan, Joseph. *The Hasidic Novella* (Hebrew). Jerusalem, 1966.
——, ed. *The Hasidic Story*. Jerusalem: Keter, 1975.
——. *The Hasidic Story: Its History and Development*. Jerusalem, 1977.
——. *The Teachings of Hasidism*. New York: Behrman House, 1983.
Davidson, Israel. *Parody in Jewish Literature*. New York: Columbia University Press, 1907.
Dawidowicz, Lucy S., ed. *The Golden Tradition: Jewish Life and Thought in Eastern Europe*. Boston: Beacon Press, 1968.
Demblin-Modrzyc Book, ed. David Sztockfisz. Israel: Argoni Demblin, 1969.
Dienstag, Jacob I. "HaMoreh Nevukhim VeSefer HaMadda BeSifrut HaHasidut" ("Maimonides' Guide and the Sefer HaMadda in Hasidic Literature"), in *Abraham Weiss Jubilee Volume*. New York: Abraham Weiss Jubilee Committee, 1964, pp. 307–331.
Dinur (Dinabourg), Ben Zion. *BeMifneh HaDoot (At the Turning Point of the Generation)*. Jerusalem, 1956.
——. "Reshitah shel HaHasidut ViyoSodotekha HaSozialiyim, VeHaMeshihiyim." *Zion* Z (January 1943): 107–115; 3 (April 1943): 117–134; 8:2–3 (January–April 1944): 89–108; 9:4 (July 1944): 186–197; 10:1–2 (November 1944–February 1945): 67–77.
——. *Toldot Yisrael*. Tel Aviv: Dvir; Jerusalem: Mosad Bialik, 1971.
Domb, I. I. *The Transformation: The Case of the Neturei Karta*. London: Domb, 1958.
Dresner, Samuel H. *Levi Yitzhak of Berdichev*. Northvale, NJ: Jason Aronson, 1994.
——. *The Zaddik*. Northvale, NJ: Jason Aronson, 1994.
Dubnow, Simon. *Dubnow, Simon: 1860–1960 – The Man and His Works*, ed. Aaron

Steinberg. Paris: French Section of World Jewish Congress, 1963.

——. *Geschichte des Chassidismus*, trans. A. Steinberg, 2 vols. Berlin: Judischer Verlag, 1931.

——. *History of the Jews*, trans. into English by Mosheh Spiegel, 5 vols. South Brunswick, NJ: Thomas Yoseloff, 1967.

——. *A History of the Jews in Russia and Poland*, trans. I. Friedlaender, 3 vols. Philadelphia: Jewish Publication Society of America, 1916–1920.

——. *Toldot HaHasidut*. Tel Aviv: Dvir, 1967.

Ehrmann, Salomon. "Tobias Lewenstein," in *Guardians of our Heritage*, ed. Leo Jung. New York: Bloch, 1958, pp. 471–483.

Ehrmann, Naftali Hertz. *HaRav*. Jerusalem/New York: Feldheim, 1977.

Eidelbaum, Meir. *R. Israel Baal Shem Tov*. Tel Aviv: Sifraita, 1986.

Eisenberg, E., ed. *Plotz: Toldot Kehillah Atikat Yamin BePolin*. Tel Aviv: Committee for the Plotzk Memorial Book, 1967.

Eisenstein, Miriam. *Jewish Schools in Poland: 1919–1939*. New York: King's Crown Press, Columbia University, 1950.

Elfenbein, Israel. "Menahem Zemba of Praga," in *Guardians of Our Heritage*, ed. L. Jung. New York: Bloch Publishing Company, 1958, pp. 603–617.

Eliach, Yaffa. *Hasidic Tales of the Holocaust*. New York: Vintage Books, 1982.

——. "The Russian Dissenting Sects and Their Influence on Israel Baal Shem Tov, Founder of Hasidism." *Proceedings of the American Academy for Jewish Research* 36 (1968): 57–83.

Elior, Rachel. "Between Yesh and Ayin: The Doctrine of the Zaddik in the Works of Jacob Isaac, the Seer of Lublin," in *Jewish History: Essays in Honor of Chimen Abramsky*, eds. Ada Rapoport-Albert and Steven J. Zipperstein. London: Peter Halban, 1988, pp. 393–455.

——. *The Paradoxical Ascent to God: The Kabbalistic Theosophy of Habad*. New York: State University of New York, 1992.

——. *The Theory of Divinity of Habad Hasidism: Second Generation*. Jerusalem: Magnes Press, 1982.

——. *Torat HaElohut BaDor HaSheni shel Hasidut Habad*. Jerusalem: Magnes Press, 1982.

Elleh Ezkerah: Osef Toldot Kedoshei Tash-Tash-Heh (Hebrew), biographies of leaders of religious Jewry in Europe who perished during 1939–1945, 7 vols. New York: Research Institute of Religious Jewry, 1956–1965.

Enziklopediyah LeHaluzei HaYishuv U'Vonav (Hebrew), ed. David Tidhar. Tel Aviv: Hotzaat Sifrit Rishonim, 1949.

Encyclopedia of Religious Zionism (Hebrew), eds. Yitzhak Raphael and Geulah Yehudah Bath. 5 vols. Jerusalem: Mosad Harav Kook, 1958–1983.

Encyclopedia of the Holocaust, ed. Israel Gutman, 4 vols. New York/London: Macmillan, 1990.

Encyclopedia of Zionism and Israel, ed. Raphael Patai, 2 vols. New York: Herzl Press/McGraw-Hill, 1971.

Engel, Shmuel. *Shem Shmuel*. Munkacs: Meficei Thoras Meharasch, 1940.

Ettinger, Shmuel. "The Hasidic Movement—Reality and Ideals," in *Essential Papers on Hasidism*, ed. G. D. Hundert, pp. 226–244.

——. "The Jews in Russia and the Outbreak of the Revolution," in *The Jews in Soviet Russia since 1917*, ed. L. Kochan. Oxford: Oxford University Press, 1970.

Faierstein, Morris M. *All Is in the Hands of Heaven—the Teachings of Rabbi Mordecai Joseph Leiner of Izbica*. Hoboken, NJ: Ktav, 1989.

Federbush, Simon, ed. "Admorei Romania VeUngaria VeEretz Yisrael," in *Hasidut VeZion*, ed. S. Federbush. New York: Moriah, 1963, pp. 190–246.

——. *HaHasidut VeZion* (Hebrew). New York: Moriah, 1963.

——. *HaRambam: Torato VeIsriyuto*. New York: Cultural Department of the World Jewish Congress and the Torah Department of the Jewish Agency, 1956.

——, ed. *Hazon Torah VeZion*. Jerusalem: Mosad Harav Kook, 1963.

——. "Talmud Torah LeShitat R. Yisrael Besht," in *Essays Presented to R. Israel Brodie*, ed. H. J. Zimmels et al. London: Soncino, 1967, pp. 151–171.

Feldman, David M. *Birth Control in Jewish Law*. New York: New York University Press, 1968.

Fishman, Judah Loeb, ed. *Sefer HaBesht* (Hebrew). Jerusalem: Mosad Harav Kook, 1960.

Fishman, Y. *Introduction to Kol Kitvei Yehudah Steinberg*. Tel Aviv, 1959.
Fleer, Gedaliah. *Rabbi Nahman's Fire*. New York: Hermon Press, 1972.
Fox, Joseph. *R. Menahem Mendel MiKotsk* (Hebrew). Jerusalem: Mosad Harav Kook, 1985.
Foxbrunner, Roman A. *The Hasidism of R. Shneur Zalman of Liady*. Tuscaloosa/London: University of Alabama Press, 1992.
Fraenkel, Josef, ed. *The Jews of Austria*. London: Vallentine Mitchell, 1967; 2nd ed., 1970.
Frankel, J. *Prophets and Prophecy*. Cambridge, UK: Cambridge University Press, 1984.
Freidenreich, Harriet Pass. *Jewish Politics in Vienna, 1918–1938*. Bloomington and Indianapolis: Indiana University Press, 1991.
Frenkel, Isar. *R. Meir MiLublin* (Hebrew). Tel Aviv: Beitan Hasefer, 1952.
——. *Rabbi Meir Yehiel MiOstrovezh*. Tel Aviv: Netzah, 1953.
——. *Yehidei Segullah*. Tel Aviv: Sinai, 1969.
Frenkel, K. L. *BeOholei Tzaddikim*. Tel Aviv: Hotzaot Vaad Hasidei Skernewicze, 1967.
Friedberg, Hayyim Dov. *Toldot HaDefus HaIvri BePolania* (*History of Hebrew Typography in Poland*). Tel Aviv: Baruch Friedberg, 1950.
Friedman, J. D. *Toldot Rabbenu Yehezkel*. Munkacz, 1894.
Friedman, Maurice. *Abraham Joshua Heschel and Elie Wiesel*. New York: Farrar, Straus & Giroux, 1987.
——. "Elie Wiesel: The Modern Job." *Commonweal* 85 (October 14, 1966): 48–52.
——. *Martin Buber's Life and Work, 1945–1965*. New York: E. P. Dutton, 1983.
——. *Martin Buber, the Life of a Dialogue*. London: Routledge, 1955.
Frischman, David. *Kol Kitvei D. Frischman*. Warsaw: Toshiya, 1913.
Frumkin, A. L. *Toldot Hakhmei Yerushalayim*. Jerusalem, 1929.
Fuchs, Abraham. *HaAdmor MiSatmar*. Jerusalem: Abraham Fuchs, 1980.
——. *Hungarian Yeshivot* (Hebrew). Jerusalem: Abraham Fuchs, 1978.
Fuenn (Finn), Shlomoh Joseph. *Kiryah Ne'emanah Vilna*. Vilna: R. M. Rom, 1850.
Gaon, Moses David. *Yehudei HaMizrach BeEretz Yisrael*. Jerusalem: Azriel, 1938–1948.
Gelber, N. M. *History of the Jews of Brody* (Hebrew). Jerusalem: Mosad Harav Kook, 1956.
——. Toldot Yehudit Brodie," in *Arim VeAmohot BeYisrael*. Jerusalem: Mosad Harav Kook, 1959.
Gellerman, Jill. "The Ecstatic Dance of Prayer as Exemplified in the Oral Traditions of Hasidism." *Journal of the Ohio Folklore Society* (December 13, 1972): 1–24.
Gershuri, Meir Simon. *HaNiggun VeHaRikud BeHasidut* (Hebrew), 3 vols. Tel Aviv: Netzah, 1954–1955.
——. *LeHasidim Mizmor*. Jerusalem, 1936.
——. "LeTorat HaNiggun BaHasidut" (Hebrew), in *Sefer Krako*, ed. A. Bauminger. Jerusalem: Mosad Harav Kook, 1959.
——. *Negginah VeHasidut*. Jerusalem, 1972.
Glatzer, N. M. "Franz Kafka and the Tree of Knowledge," in *Arguments and Doctrines*, ed. Arthur A. Cohen. Philadelphia: Jewish Publication Society, 1970.
——. "Franz Rosenzweig," in *Yivo Annual of Jewish Social Science* 1 (1946): 107–133.
——. *Franz Rosenzweig, His Life and Thought*. New York: Farrar, Straus & Young, 1953.
——. "Was Franz Rosenzweig a Mystic?" in *Studies in Jewish Religion*, presented to A. Alexander. Tuscaloosa, AL: Alabama University Press, 1979, pp. 121–132.
Gliksman, Pinhas Zelig. *Der Kotzker Rebbe*. Piotrokov: 1938; reprinted in Israel, 1972.
Glitzenstein, Avraham Hanokh. *The Arrest and Liberation of Rabbi Shneur Zalman of Liady*, trans. Jacob Immanuel Schochet. Brooklyn, NY: Kehot, 1964.
——. *Or HaHasidut*. New York: Kehot, 1965.
——. *Sefer HaToldot Menahem Mendel Baal Tzemah Tzeddek*. New York: Otzar HaHasidut, 1976.
——. *Sefer HaToldot Rav Yosef Yitzhak Schneersohn MiLubavitch*. New York: Otzar Hahasidut, 1976.
——. *Sefer HaToldot R. Shalom Dov Baer Admor Maharash*. Israel: Kefar Habad, 1969.
Gold, Hugo. *Geschichte der Juden in Bukovina*, 2 vols. Tel Aviv: Olamenu, 1956.

Gold, Y. M. *Darkhei Hayyim VeShalom* (The Customs and Observances of Rabbi Hayyim Elozar of Munkacs). Jerusalem, 1974.

Gollancz, H. *Sefer Mafteah Shlomoh*. Oxford, 1914.

Graetz, Heinrich (Hirsch). *Geschichte der Juden von den Altesten Zeiten bis auf die Gegenwart*. Leipzig: Oskar Leiner, 1868.

——. *History of the Jews*. Philadelphia: Jewish Publication Society of America, 1891.

Green, Arthur. *Menahem Nahum of Chernobyl: Upright Practices, the Light of the Eyes*. Ramsey, NJ: Paulist Press, 1982.

——. *Tormented Master*. Tuscaloosa, AL: University of Alabama Press, 1979.

Greenbaum, Yitzhak, ed. *Varshau*, vol. 1, part 1, of *Enziklopediya shel Galuyot*, 7 vols. Jerusalem/Tel Aviv: Enziklopedia shel Galuyot Company, 1953.

Greenberg, Louis. *The Jews in Russia*. New Haven/London: Yale University Press, 1944.

Greenwald (Grunwald), Leopold (Yekutiel Yehudah). *LeKorot HaHasidut B'Ungaria*. Budapest: Katzburg, 1921.

——. *Toisand Yor Yiddish Leben in Ungarn*. New York: Feldheim, 1945.

Gross, S. Y., and Cohen, Y. *Marmoros Book*. Tel Aviv, 1983.

Grunwald, J. J. "Lekorot HaHasidut BeHungaria," in *HaZofeh LeHohmat Yisrael*, vol. 5, part 4. Budapest, 1921.

Grunfeld-Rosenbaum, Judith. "Sarah Schenierer," in *Jewish Leaders*, ed. Leo Jung. New York: Bloch, 1953, pp. 405–433.

Gurfinkel, Michel. "Les Lubavitcher." *L'Arche* (Paris) 205:58–63.

Gutman, Mattityahu Ezekiel. *Migdolei HaHasidut: R. Nahum MiChernobyl*. Tel Aviv: Mosad Harav Kook, 1953.

——. *Migdolei HaHasidut: Rabbi Shalom MeBelz* (Hebrew). Bilgoraj: N. Kroneberg, 1935.

——. *R. Dov of Leove*. Cluj, 1926.

——. *R. Dov Baer MiLeove*. Tel Aviv: Sifriyah Netzah, 1952.

——. *R. Israel Baal Shem Tov*. 1922.

Gutwirth, Jacques. "Antwerp Jewry Today." *Jewish Journal of Sociology* 10 (1968): 14–137.

——. "The Structure of a Hasidic Community in Montreal." *Jewish Journal of Sociology* 14 (1972): 43–63.

——. *Vie Juive Traditionnelle: Ethnologie d'une Communauté Hasidique*. Paris: de Minuit, 1970.

Haberman, A. M. *Toldot HaDefus HaIvri BiTzefat*. Tel Aviv: Hotze'at HaMuseum Leimnut, 1963.

Hager, Barukh. *Malkhut Hasidim* (Yiddish). Buenos Aires: Union Central Israelita Polaca en la Argentina, 1955.

Halachmi, David Weisbrod. *Arzei HaLevanon*. Tel Aviv: Alter Bergman, 1956.

Halpern, Israel. *HaAliyot HaRishonim shel HaHasidim LeEretz Yisrael*. 1946.

——. *The Hasidic Immigration to Palestine during the 18th Century* (Hebrew). Jerusalem/Tel Aviv: Studies and Texts in Jewish Mysticism, Schocken, 1946.

——. *Iggorot Hassidim M'Eretz Yisrael*. Jerusalem: Yad Yitzhak Ben Tzvi, 1980.

——. *Yehudim VeYehadat BeMizrach Eiropa*. Jerusalem: Magnus Press, 1968.

Handler, Andrew. *Rabbi Eizik: Hasidic Stories about the Zaddik of Kallo*. Cranbury, NJ: Associated University Presses, 1978.

Hannover, Nathan. *Yeven Metzulah* (*Abyss of Despair*). Luvov, 1851; trans. A. J. Mesch, New Brunswick, NJ, 1983.

Harparnes, Gershon. *Mivhar Ketuvim*. Tel Aviv: Po'alei Agudat Israel, 1977.

Harris, Lis. *Holy Days: The World of a Hasidic Family*. New York: Summit Press, 1985.

Hayman, Ronald. *Kafka: A Biography*. New York: Oxford University Press, 1942.

Heilman, Hayyim Meir. *Bet Rabbe*. Tel Aviv, 1902.

Heilman, Samuel. *Defenders of the Faith*. New York: Schocken, 1992.

Helmreich, William B. *The World of the Yeshiva: An Intimate Portrait of Orthodox Jewry*. New York: Free Press, 1982.

Henderson, Philip. *The Life of Laurence Oliphant*. London: Robert Hale, 1956.

Hertzberg, A., and Feldman, Leon A., eds. *History and Jewish Historians: Essays by S. W. Baron*. Philadelphia: Jewish Publication Society of America, 1964.

Herzl Year Book, ed. Raphael Patai, vols. 1–6. New York: Herzl Press, 1958–1965.

Heschel, Abraham Joshua. "A Biographical Note on Phinehas of Koretz," in *Alei Ayin*, pp. 213–214. Jerusalem, 1948–1952.

——. *The Circle of the Baal Shem Tov: Studies in Hasidism*, ed. S. H. Dresner. Chicago: University of Chicago Press, 1985.

——. *A Passion for Truth: Reflections on the Founder of Hasidism, the Kotzker and Kierkegaard*. London: Secker & Warburg, 1973.

——. "Rabbi Gershon Kitover, Parshat Hayav VeAliyato L'Eretz Yisrael" (Hebrew). *Hebrew Union College Annual* 23:2 (1950–1951).

——. "Rabbi Nahman of Kosov, Companion of the Baal Shem Tov." In *The Harry A. Wolfson Jubilee Volume*, pp. 113–141, ed. Saul Lieberman. New York: American Academy for Jewish Research, 1965.

——. "Rabbi Yitzhak of Drohobycz," in *The Circle of the Baal Shem Tov*, ed. S. H. Dresner. Chicago: University of Chicago Press, 1988, pp. 152–153.

——. *Umbekannte Dokumenten zu der Geschichte fun Chassidus* (Yiddish), pp. 113–135. New York: Yivo Bletter 36, 1952.

Hess, Moses. *Rom und Jerusalem*. Leipzig: M. W. Kaufman, 1899; trans. M. J. Bloom. New York: Philosophical Library, 1955.

Hillman, David Tzvi, ed. *Iggrot Baal HaTanya U'Venei Doro*. Jerusalem: HaMesorah Publishing Company, 1953.

Hoffman, Edward. *Despite All Odds*. New York: Simon & Schuster, 1991.

Hollaenderski, Leon. *Les Israelites de Pologne*. Paris: Degetau, 1846.

Holtz, A. "Hillel Zeitlin, Publicist and Martyr." *Jewish Book Annual* 28 (1970): 141–146.

Horodezky, Samuel Abba. "The Genealogy of Simon Dubnow," in *Yivo Annual of Jewish Social Science* 6 (1951): 9–18.

——. *HaHasidut VeHaHasidim*, 2 vols., 3rd ed. Tel Aviv: Dvir, 1951.

——. *HaHasidut VeToratah*. Tel Aviv: Dvir, 1944.

——. "HaRambam BeKabbalah U'VeHasidut." *Moznayim* 3 (1935): 454 ff.

——. *Leaders of Hasidism*. London: Hasefer Agency for Literature, 1928.

——. *Olei Zion*. Tel Aviv: Mahlaka L'Inyoni Hanoar, 1947.

——. *Religiose Stromungen im Judentum*. Bern/Leipzig: Ernest Bircher, 1920.

——. *Shivhei HaBesht*. Tel Aviv: Dvir, 1947.

——. *Torat HaKabbalah shel Mosheh Cordovero*. Berlin: Eshkol, 1924; reprinted Jerusalem: Mosad Harav Kook, 1951.

——. *Torat HaKabbalah shel Yitzhak Ashkenazi VeHayyim Vital*. Jerusalem: Mosad Harav Kook, 1947.

Huberman, Hugo. "Hasidism in Bessarabia," in *Yivo Bletter* 39 (1955): 278–283.

Hundert, Gershon David, ed. *Essential Papers on Hasidism*. New York: New York University Press, 1991.

——. *The Jews in a Polish Private Town: The Case of Opatov in the Eighteenth Century*. Baltimore, MD: John Hopkins University Press, 1992.

Idel, Moshe. "Differing Conceptions of Kabbalah in the Early Seventeenth Century," in *Jewish Thought in the Seventeenth Century*, eds. Isadore Twersky and Bernard D. Septimus. Cambridge, MA: Harvard University Press, 1987.

——. *Hasidism: Between Ecstasy and Magic*. New York: State University of New York, 1993.

——. *Kabbalah: New Perspectives*. New Haven, CT: Yale University Press, 1988.

——. *The Mystical Experience in Abraham Abulafia*. Albany, NY: State University of New York at Albany, 1987.

Idel, Moshe, and McGinn, Bernard. *Mystical Union and Monotheistic Faith: An Ecumenical Dialogue*. New York: MacMillan, 1989.

Israel ben Eliezer. *Keter Shem Tov*. Zolkiev, 1780.

Jacobs, Louis. "The Concept of Hasid in the Biblical and Rabbinic Literature." In *Journal of Jewish Studies* 8 (1957): 143–154.

——. "The Doctrine of the 'Divine Spark' in Man in Jewish Sources," in *Studies in Rationalism, Judaism, and Universalism in Memory of Leon Roth*, ed. Raphael Loewe. London: Routledge & Kegan Paul, 1966, pp. 87–115.

——. *Faith*. London: Vallentine Mitchell, 1968.

——. *Hasidic Prayer*. New York: Schocken, 1973.

——. *Holy Living: Saints and Saintliness in Judaism*. Northvale, NJ: Jason Aronson, 1990.

——. *Jewish Mystical Testimonies*. New York: Schocken, 1976.

——. *Jewish Teachings of the Hasidic Masters*. New York, 1976.

——. *Rabbi Moses Cordovero: The Palm Tree of Deborah*. London: Vallentine Mitchell, 1960.

——. *Seeker of Unity: The Life and Works of Aaron of Starosselje*. London: Vallentine Mitchell, 1966.

——. *Tract on Ecstasy: Dob Baer of Lubavitch*. London: Vallentine Mitchell, 1963.

Jasni, A. Wolf. *Di Geshichte fun Jidn in Lodz*, 2 vols. Tel Aviv: HaMenora, 1966.

Kahana, Abraham. *Sefer HaHasidut*, 2nd ed. Warsaw: L. Levin-Epstein, 1922.

——. *Sippurei Maasiyot*. Warsaw: Maamakim, 1922.

Kahana, David. *Bet Shlomoh–Tzvi Tiferet*. Irsava, 1928.

——. *Toldot Rabbenu*. Munkacz, 1938.

Kahana, I. Z. *Mehkarim BeSifrut HaTeshuvot*. Jerusalem, 1973.

Kaiser, D. *Sefer Toldot Hen*. London: Hebrew Books and Gift Centre, 1979.

Kamelhar, Yekutiel Aryeh. *Dor De'ah*. Bilgoraj: Kamelhar, 1933.

Kaplan, Aryeh. *Gems of Rabbi Nahman*. Jerusalem: Aryeh Kaplan, 1980.

——. *Hasidic Masters*. New York: Moznaim, 1984.

——. *Immortality, Resurrection and the Age of the Universe: A Kabbalistic View*. Hoboken, NJ: Ktav, 1993.

——. *Jewish Meditations*. New York: Schocken, 1985.

——. *The Light Beyond*. New York/Jerusalem: Feldheim/Moznaim Publicity, 1981.

——. *Meditation and Kabbalah*. Northvale, NJ: Jason Aronson, 1995.

——. *Rabbi Nahman's Wisdom*. Brooklyn, NY: Breslov Research Institute, 1973.

Kaplan, Hayyim Aaron. *Megillat Yissurin: Yoman Ghetto Warsha*. Tel Aviv: Am-Oved, 1966.

——. *Scroll of Agony: The Warsaw Diary of Chaim A. Kaplan*, trans. and ed. Abraham I. Katsh. New York: Macmillan, 1965.

Kasher, Menahem Mendel. "Tekhelet BaZman HaZeh," in *The Leo Jung Jubilee Volume*, ed. M. M. Kasher, Norman Lamm, and Leonard Rosenfeld. New York: Jewish Center, 1962, pp. 241–248.

Kasher, Shlomoh. *Perakim BeTorat HaHasidut*. Jerusalem: Makhon Torah Shlomoh, 1968.

Katz, Steven. *Martin Buber and Hasidism: A Critique*. London: Routledge & Kegan Paul, 1978.

——, ed. *Mysticism and Philosophical Analysis*. New York: Oxford University Press, 1978.

——. *Mysticism and Religious Traditions*. New York: Oxford University Press, 1983.

Kitov, Eliyahu. *Hasidim VeAnshei Maaseh* (Hebrew). Jerusalem: Yad Eliyahu Kitov, 1977.

Kiapholtz, Israel. *Bet Ruzhyn*. Bene Berak: Mishmor, 1987.

——. *HaHozeh MiLublin*. Bene Berak: Peer HaSefer, 1985.

——. *HaMaggid MiMezhirech*. Bene Berak: Peer HaSefer, 1972.

Klausner, Israel. *Toldot HaKehillah HaIvrit BeVilna*. Vilna: Hakehillah HaIvrit, 1935.

Klausner, Joseph. *Vilna BiTekufat HaGaon*. Jerusalem: Reuven Mass, 1942.

Kleinman, M. H. *Sefer Mazkeret Shem HaGedolim*. Piotrokov: 1907; Bene Berak: Bina, 1987.

——. *Zikhron LaRishonim*. Piotrokov, 1914.

Kling, Simcha. *The Mighty Warrior: The Life Story of Menahem Ussishkin*. New York: Jonathan David, 1965.

——. *Nachum Sokolov: Servant of His People*. New York: Herzl Press, 1960.

Koenig, Esther. *The Thirteen Stories of Rebbe Nahman of Bratslav*. Jerusalem: Hillel Press, 1978.

Kramer, Chaim. *Crossing the Narrow Bridge*, ed. Moshe Mykoff. Jerusalem/New York: Breslov Research Institute, 1989.

Kranzler, George (Gershon). "Chasid from the Left Bank," in *Orthodox Jewish Life* 22. New York: 1955.

——. *Williamsburg: A Jewish Community in Transition*. New York: P. Feldheim, 1961.

Kressel, G. *Leksikon HaSifrut HaIvrit BeDorot HaAharonim*, 2 vols. Merhaviah: Sifrat Poalim, 1952.

Krochmal, Nahman. *Moreh Nebukhei HaZeman*. Lvov, 1863.

Kupferman, Jeanette Ann. "The Lubavitch Hasidim of Stamford Hill." M. Phil. dissertation. London: University College, 1975.

Kurzweil, B. *Essays on the Fiction of S. Y. Agnon*. Jerusalem: Schocken, 1976.

Lachower, F. *Rishonim VeAharonim*. Jerusalem: Dvir, 1966.

Lamm, Norman. "The Ideology of the Neturei Karta according to the Satmar Version." *Tradition* 13 (1971): 38–53.

——. *Torah Lishmah BeMishnat R. Hayyim MeVolozhin U'VeMashevet HaDor*. Hoboken, NJ: Ktav, 1989.

——. *Torah Umadda: The Encounter of Religious Learning and Worldly Knowledge in the Jewish Tradition*. Northvale, NJ: Jason Aronson, 1990.

Landau, Bezalel. *HaGaon HeHasid MiVilna* (Hebrew). Jerusalem: Usha, 1965.
——. R. Elimelekh Milejansk. 1963.
Landau, Bezalel, and Ortner, Nathan. *HaRab HaKadosh MiBelz*. Jerusalem: Or Hasidim, 1967.
Landau, David. *Piety and Power*. London: Secker & Warburg, 1993.
Langer, Jiri. *Nine Gates to the Chasidic Mysteries*. Northvale, NJ: Jason Aronson, 1993.
Lavut, Abraham David. *Shaar HaKollel*. Vilna, 1914.
Leftwich, Joseph. "Hasidic Influence in Imaginative English Literature." *Jewish Book Annual* 17 (1959): 3–12.
——. *Israel Zangwill*. New York: Thomas Yoseloff, 1957.
Leksikon fun der Nayer Yiddisher Literatur (Yiddish), ed. Samuel Niger and Jacob Shatzky, 7 vols. New York: Congress for Jewish Culture, 1956–1968.
Leshon Hasidim. Bene Berak. n.d.
Levin, Myer. *The Golden Mountain*. New York: Berhman House, 1951.
Levin, Sholem Dov Baer. *Toldot Habad bi-Rusiya HaSovyetit 5678–5710*. Brooklyn, NY: Otzar Hasidim, 1989.
Levin, Y. I. "The Holy Rabbi, R. Eliezer of Tarnogrod." *HaModia* (14 *Nisan* 1959).
Levin, Yehudah Leib. *HaAdmorim MiIzbica*. Bene Berak: Hotzaot Yehudit, n.d.
——. *Sefer Alexander Admor R. Hanokh Heinokh Hakohen*. Jerusalem: Daat, 1969.
Lieberman, Hayyim. "The Hasidic Printing Houses: Fact and Fiction." *Yivo Bletter* 34 (1950): 182–208.
——. "Israel of Zamocz." *Bitzaron* 16 (1955): 113–120.
——. "*Keitzad Hokrim Hasidut BeYisrael.*" *Bitzaron* 16 (1955): 113–120.
——. *Ohel Rachel*, 3 vols. Brooklyn, NY: Empire Press, 1980.
Litinsky, Menahem Nahum. *Korot Podolia VeKadmoniyot Shem*. Odessa: 1895.
Loewe, Louis. *Diaries of Sir Moses and Lady Montefiore*, 2 vols. London: Griffith, Farrow, Okeden & Welch, 1890 (facsimile edition published by Jewish Historical Society, London, 1983).
Loewenthal, Naftali. *Communicating the Infinite: The Emergence of the Habad School*. Chicago: University of Chicago Press, 1990.
——. "The Concept of Mesirat Nefesh (Self-Sacrifice) in the Teachings of R. Dov Baer of Lubavitch, 1773–1827." Ph.D. thesis. London: University of London, 1981.
Lowenkopf, Anne N. *The Hasidim*. Los Angeles: Shelbourne Press, 1973.
Lublin–Encyclopedia of the Jewish Diaspora–Poland Series, vol. 5, ed. Nahman Blumenthal and Meir Korzen. Jerusalem/Tel Aviv: Encyclopedia of Jewish Diaspora Company, 1957.
Madison, Charles. *Yiddish Literature: Its Scope and Major Writers*. New York: André Ungar, 1968.
Mahler, Raphael. *HaHasidut VeHaskalah* (Hebrew). Merhavya: Sifriat Poalim, 1961.
——. *Hasidism and the Jewish Enlightenment*. Philadelphia: Jewish Publication Society of America, 1985.
Maimon, Solomon. *Solomon Maimon: Autobiography*, trans. J. C. Murray. London: East and West Library, 1954.
Maimon, Yehudah Leib, ed. *Arim VeImahot BeYisrael*, 6 vols. (vol. 1, 1946; vol. 4, 1950; vol. 5, 1952; vol. 6, 1955). Jerusalem: Mosad Harav Kook, published between 1946 and 1955.
——. *Sarei HaMeah*, 5 vols. Jerusalem: Mosad Harav Kook, 1953.
——, ed. *Sefer HaYovel Shimon Federbusch*. Jerusalem: Mosad Harav Kook, 1961.
——, ed. *Sefer HaBesht*. Jerusalem: Mosad Harav Kook, 1960.
——, ed. *Sefer Yovel Shimon Federbush*. Jerusalem: Mosad Harav Kook, 1960.
Malachi, A. R. *Jubilee Volume of Hadoar*. 1952.
——. "LeToldot Bet HaArigah shel Montefiore BiYerushalayim," in *Abraham Weiss Jubilee Volume*. New York: The Abraham Weiss Jubilee Committee, 1964, pp. 441–459.
Manor, Alexander. *Zalman Shazar: Yehido VeYetziroto*. Tel Aviv: Aleph, Hatoza Ve-Hatzaot Sefarim, 1961.
Mantel, Martin. "The Tales of Rabbi Nachman of Bratzlav: A Translation with Annotation and Comparative Source Studies," 2 vols. Ph.D. dissertation. Princeton, NJ: Princeton University Press, 1977.
Marcus Ahron (Pseudo Verus). *Der Chassidismus*, 3rd ed. Hamburg: S. Marcus, 1927.
Marmaros Book in Memory of a Hundred and Sixty Jewish Communities, ed. S. Y. Gross and Y. Yosef Cohen. Tel Aviv: Beith Marmaros, 1983.

Marmorstein, Emile. *Heaven at Bay: the Jewish Kulturkampf in the Holy Land*. New York: Oxford University Press, 1948.

Matt, D. C. *Zohar, the Book of Enlightenment*. London, 1983.

Mayer, Egon. *From Suburbia to Shtetl: The Jews of Boro Park*. Philadelphia: Temple University Press, 1979.

Meckler, David L. *Fun Chernobyl bis Talna*. New York, 1931.

——. *Miracle Men: Tales of the Baal Shem and His Chassidim*. New York: Bloch Publishing Company, 1964.

Megillat Ger, ed. Gershon Sapazshinkov. Buenos Aires: Residentes des Guer en Argentine, 1975.

Melitzei Esh, see Stern.

Menahem Mendel of Vitebski. *Pri HaAretz*. Jerusalem, 1965.

Michelson, A. H. S. *Ohel Elimelekh*. Piotrokov, 1910.

Mindel, Nissan. *My Prayer*. New York: Kehot, 1974.

——. *The Philosophy of Chabad*. New York: Kehot, 1973.

——. *Rabbi Shneur Zalman of Liady*. Brooklyn, NY: Kehot, 1980.

Minkin, Jacob. *The Romance of Hassidism*. New York: Macmillan, 1935.

Mintz, Benjamin. *Shivhei HaBesht*. Jerusalem: Talpiot Publications, 1961.

Mintz, Jerome R. *Hasidic People—a Place in the New World*. Cambridge, MA: Harvard University Press, 1992.

——. *Legends of the Hasidim*. Northvale, NJ: Jason Aronson, 1995.

Mondschein, Joshua, ed. *Shivhei HaBesht*. Jerusalem: Hanabal, 1928.

Moskovitz, Tzvi. *Kol HaKatuv LeHayyim on Rabbi Hayyim Halberstam*, ed. Rafael Halevi Zimetbaum, with an appendix on *Divrei Yehezkel Shragrai*. Jerusalem: Moskovitz, 1962.

Muller, Ernst. *History of Jewish Mysticism*. Oxford: East and West Library, 1946.

Nadler, Allan L. "Piety and Politics: The Case of the Satmar Rebbe." *Judaism* 31 (1982): 135–152.

Nahman ben Simhah of Bratzlav. *Likkutei Moharan*. Jerusalem: 1963.

——. *Sefer HaMidot*. Bene Berak: 1966.

Nahman of Tcherin. *Leshon Hasidim*. Tel Aviv, 1961.

Nathan (Sternharz) of Nemirov. *Alim LiTerufah*. Jerusalem: 1968.

——. *Hayyei Moharan*. Lvov, 1875.

——. *Yemei Maharnat*. Jerusalem, 1961.

Newman, Eugene. *Life and Teachings of Isaiah Horowitz*. London: E. Newman, 1972.

Newman, Louis I., ed. *The Hasidic Anthology*. Northvale, NJ: Jason Aronson, 1987.

Newman file. American Jewish Archives, Cincinnati, OH.

Nigal, Gedaliah. *The Hasidic Tales: History and Themes*. Jerusalem: Markus, 1981.

——. "Moro VeRabbo shel R. Israel Baal Shem Tov." *Sinai* 71 (1972): 150–159.

——. *Noam Elimelekh*, 2 vols. Jerusalem: Mosad Harav Kook, 1978.

——. "R. Eliezer MiTarnogrod VeSefarav." *Sinai* 73 (1973): 72–78.

Nulman, Macy. *Concise Encyclopedia of Jewish Music*. New York: McGraw-Hill, 1975.

Oholei Shem. Pinsk: M. M. Glauberman, 1912.

Oko, Adolph S. *Solomon Schechter: A Bibliography*. Cambridge, UK: Cambridge University Press, 1930.

Opatoshu, Joseph. *In Polisher Welder*. Buenos Aires: Literary Society of Yivo, 1965.

Ortner, Nathan. *HaRav Tzvi Elimelekh MiDynov*, 2 vols. Bene Berak: Makhon L'Enazahat Hasidut Galicia, 1972.

Oryan, Meir. *Sneh Boer BeKotzk*. Jerusalem: Reuben Mass, 1980.

Patterson, David. *Abraham Mapu*. New York: Thomas Yoseloff, 1965.

Peretz, J. L. *HaHasidut*. Tel Aviv: Dvir, 1952.

——. *In This World and the Next*, trans. M. Spiegel. New York: Thomas Yoseloff, 1958.

Perl, Joseph. *Magaleh Temirin*. Vienna: Anton Strauss, 1819.

Perlow, Shlomoh. *Divrei Shalom*. Vilna, 1882.

Piekarz, Mendel. *Hasidut Braslav* (Hebrew). Jerusalem: Mosad Bialik, 1972.

——. *Ideological Trends of Hasidism in Poland during the Interwar Period and the Holocaust* (Hebrew). Jerusalem: Bialik Institute, 1990.

——. *Studies in Bratzlav Hasidim* (Hebrew). Jerusalem, 1972.

"Pinkas HaKehillot" (Hebrew). *Encyclopedia of Jewish Communities in Romania*, vol. 1. Jerusalem: Yad Vashem, 1969.

"Pinkas HaKehillot" (Hebrew). *Encyclopedia of Jewish Communities in Hungary*, Jerusalem: Yad Vashem, 1976.

Pinkas HaKehillot Romania, vol. 2. Jerusalem, 1980.
Plotzk, see Eisenberg, E.
Poll, Solomon. *The Hasidic Community of Williamsburgh*. Glencoe, IL: Free Press, 1962; New York: Schocken, 1969.
Porush, Shalom Hayyim. "BiNsivei Hasidut Izbice Radzyn." *Sinai* 77 (1975): 94–96.
——. *Encyclopedia of Hasidism* (Hebrew), vol. 1, *Works* (letters aleph to tet), ed. Yitzhak Raphael. Jerusalem: Mosad Harav Kook, 1980.
Prager, Mosheh. *Eleh shelo Nikhnu Korot Tnuat Meri Hasidut BeGeta'ot* (Hebrew), 2 vols. Bene Berak: Netzah, 1963.
Rabinowich, I. *Major Trends of Modern Hebrew Fiction*. Chicago: University of Chicago Press, 1968.
Rabinowicz, Mordka Harry (Tzvi). *A Guide to Hasidism*. London/New York: Thomas Yoseloff, 1960.
——. *Hasidic Rebbes*. Jerusalem: Targum/Feldheim, 1989.
——. *Hasidism: The Movement and Its Masters*. Northvale, NJ: Jason Aronson, 1988.
——. *Hasidism and the State of Israel*. London/Toronto: Littman Library of Jewish Civilization, Associated University Press, 1982.
——. *The Legacy of Polish Jewry*. New York: Thomas Yoseloff, 1965.
——. *The World of Hasidism*. London: Vallentine Mitchell, 1970; New York: Hartmore Press, 1970.
Rabinowitsch, Wolf Zeev. *Hasidut Halitait*. Jerusalem: Bialik Institute, 1961.
——. "Karlin Hasidism." *Yivo Annual of Jewish Social Science* 5 (1950): 123–151.
——. *Lithuanian Hasidism*. London: Vallentine Mitchell, 1970.
——. "Min HaGenizah HaStolinit." *Zion* 5, Jerusalem (1940): 125–132.
Rabinowitz, David. *Tiferet Avot* (Hebrew). Jerusalem: Main Hahokhmah, 1961.
Rabinowitz, Tzvi Meir. "The Attitude of the Kabbalah and Hasidism to Maimonides," in *Maimonides Jubilee Volume*, ed. J. L. Fishman. Jerusalem: Mosad Harav Kook, 1935.
——. *R. Simhah Bunem MiPrzysucha*. Tel Aviv: Tevunah, 1945.
——. *HaYehudi HaKadosh*. Piotrokov: 1932.
Raisin, J. S. *The Haskalah Movement in Russia*. Philadelphia: Jewish Publication Society of America, 1913.
Raphael, Yitzhak. *Al Hasidut VeHasidim*. Jerusalem: Mosad Harav Kook, 1991.
——. *HaHasidut VeEretz Yisrael*. Jerusalem: Hatzaot Sefarim, 1940.
——. *MiMayenot HaFolklor HaHasid*. Jerusalem: Ahiasaf, 1945–1946.
——. *Sefer HaHasidut*. Tel Aviv: Z. Leinman, 1947.
——. *Sefer HaHasidut*. Tel Aviv: Abraham Ziyyoni, 1955.
Rapoport, J. "A Letter from Dr. Herzl to the Rabbi of Chortkov." *Zion* 78 (1930): 351–352.
Rapoport-Albert, Ada. "Confession in the Circle of R. Nachman of Braslav." *Bulletin of the Institute of Jewish Studies* 1 (1973): 65–97.
——. "On Women in Hasidism, S. A. Horodezky and the Maid of Ludmir Tradition," in *Jewish History, Essays in Honour of Chimen Abramsky*, ed. Ada Rapoport-Albert and Steven Z. Zipperstein. London: Peter Halban, 1988, pp. 495–525.
——. "The Problem of Succession in the Hasidic Leadership, with Special Reference to the Circle of R. Nahman of Bratslav." Ph.D. thesis. London: University of London, 1974.
Reisin, Zalman. *Leksikon fun der Yiddisher Literatur, Presse und Filologie*, 4 vols. Vilna, 1926–1929.
Ribalow, Menahem. *The Flowering of Modern Hebrew Literature*. London: Vision, 1959, pp. 207–236.
Ringleblum, E. *Notes from the Warsaw Ghetto*. 1974.
Rosenblatt, Samuel. *Yossele Rosenblatt*. New York: Farrar, Straus & Young, 1954.
Rosenheim, Jacob. *Agudistische Schriften*. Frankfurt-am-Main: Der Israelit und Hermon, 1931.
Rosman, Murray J. "Jewish Perceptions of Insecurity and Powerlessness in 16th to 18th Century Poland." *Polin* 1:19–28.
——. "Miedzyboz and R. Israel Baal Shem Tov (Besht)." *Zion* 52:2 (1987): 177–189; also in *Essential Papers on Hasidism*, ed. G. D. Hundert, pp. 209–226.
Rosman, Shlomoh. *Zikhron Kedoshim*. Rehovot, 1969.
——. *Sefer Rashei Golat Ariel*. Brooklyn, NY: Mifal HaNetzahat Zikhron Kedoshim, 1975.
Rosmarin, Aaron. *Der Satmarer Rebbe*. New York, 1967.

Roth, A. *Shulhan HaTahor*. Jerusalem, 1966.
Roth, Aaron. *Uvda D'Aaron*. Jerusalem, 1948.
Roth, Cecil. *Essays and Portraits in Anglo-Jewish History*. Philadelphia: Jewish Publication Society of America, 1962.
——. *Ritual Murder Libel and the Jews*. London: Woburn Press, 1935.
Rothschild, M. M. *HaHalukah*. Jerusalem: Reuben Mass, 1969.
Rothstein, Shmuel. *Rabbi Menahem Zemba: Hayav U'Feulotav*. Tel Aviv: Nezah, 1948.
Rozenzweig, Franz. *The Star of Redemption*, trans. William Hallo. London: Routledge, 1971; New York: Holt, Rinehart & Winston, 1970.
Ruben, A. *A History of Jewish Customs*. 1967.
Rubin, Israel. *Satmar: An Island in the City*. Chicago: Quadrangle, 1972.
Rubinstein, Abraham. "Al HaKuntres Zimrat HaAretz BiKetav Yad." In *Areshet*, vol. 3, ed. Ben Menahem and Yitzhak Raphael. Jerusalem: Mosad Harav Kook, 1961.
——, ed. *Joseph Perl's Uber des Wesens der Sekte Chassidismus*. Jerusalem: Israel Academy of Science and Humanaities, 1977.
——. "A Possible New Fragment of Shivhei HaBesht." *Tarbiz* 35:2 (1965): 174–192.
——. "Shever Poshim LeDavid Makov." *Kiryat Sefer* 35 (1959–1960): 240–249.
Samuel, M. *Blood Accusation: The Strange History of the Beiliss Case*. London: Weindenfeld & Nicolson, 1967.
Sapazshnikov, Gershon, ed. *Megillat Ger*. Buenos Aires: Residenta de Guer en Argentina, 1975.
Schachter, Zalman M., *Spiritual Intimacy: A Study of Counselling in Hasidism*. Northvale, NJ: Jason Aronson, 1993.
——. *The Yehidut–A Study of Counselling in Hasidism*. Doctoral dissertation. Cincinnati, Ohio: Hebrew Union College, 1968.
Schatz-Uffenheimer, Rivka. *HaHasidut KeMistikah*. Jerusalem: Magnes Press, Hebrew University, 1968.
——, ed. *Maggid Devarim LeYaakov*. Jerusalem: Hebrew University, 1976.
Schechter, Solomon. "The Chassidim," in *Studies in Judaism*. London: Adam & Charles Black, 1896.
Schindler, Pesach. *Hasidic Responsa to the Holocaust in the Light of Hasidic Thought*. Hoboken, NJ: Ktav, 1990.
——. "The Holocaust and Kiddush Hashem in Hassidic Thought." *Tradition* 13:4–14:1 (1973): 88–104.
——. "Responses of Hasidic Leaders and Hasidim during the Holocaust in Europe, 1939–1945." Doctoral dissertation, New York University, 1972.
Schipper, Ignaz. "The Image of Israel Baal Shem Tov in Early Hasidic Literature." *Hadoar* (1960): 252 ff., 551 ff.
Schmelzer, A. "Toldot Yehudei Bukovina," in *Al Yehudei Romania*. Tel Aviv.
Schmulewitz, I. *The Bialystoker Memorial Book*. New York: Bialystok Association, 1982.
Schneebalg, A. Z. *Rosh Even Yisrael*. New York, 1989.
Schneersohn, Joseph I. *Iggrot Kodesh Mahariis*, 12 vols. Brooklyn, NY: Otzar Hasidim, 1982–1985.
——. *Lubavitcher Rabbi's Memoirs*, vol. 1. Brooklyn, NY: Otzar Hasidim, 1956.
Schochet, Yaakov Immanuel. *Mystical Concepts in Chassidism*. Brooklyn, NY: Kehot, 1979.
——. *Rabbi Israel Baal Shem Tov*. Toronto: Liebermans, 1961.
——. *Tzavaot HaRibash*. New York: Kehot, 1982.
Scholem, Gershom (Gerhard) G. *Das Buch Bahir*. Darmstadt: Wissenschaftliche Buchgesellschaft, 1980.
——. *Jewish Gnosticism: Merkabah Mysticism and Talmudic Tradition*. New York: Jewish Theological Seminary of America, 1960.
——. *Kabbalah*. Jerusalem: Keter, 1974.
——. *Major Trends in Jewish Mysticism*. London: Thames & Hudson, 1955.
——. "Martin Buber's Hasidism." *Commentary* 32 (1961): 218–225.
——. "The Neutralization of the Messianic Element in Early Hasidism," in *The Messianic Idea in Judaism*. New York: Schocken, 1971.
——. *On the Kabbalah and Its Symbolism*. New York: Schocken, 1965.
——. *Origins of the Kabbalah*. Philadelphia: Jewish Publication Society, 1987.
——. "Samson Ostropoler." *Revue d'histoire des religions* 143 (1953): 33–37.
——. *Shabbetai Tzvi*, 2 vols. Tel Aviv: Am Oved, 1956–1957.
——. "The Tradition of the 36 Hidden Just Men," in *The Messianic Idea in Judaism*. New York: Schocken, 1971.
Schrire, T. *Hebrew Amulets*. London: Routledge Kegan Paul, 1968.

Schwab, Hermann. *The History of Orthodox Jewry in Germany*. London: Mitre, 1950.

——. *Jacob Rosenheim*. Berlin: Louis Lamm, 1924.

Schwartz, Pinhas Zelig HaKohen. *Shem HaGedolim*. New York: I. Grossman, 1959.

——. *Shem HaGedolim MeEretz Hagar*. Jerusalem, 1969.

Schwartzman, Meir. *Esh HaTamid*. Tel Aviv: Aviv Publishing, 1962.

——. *HaMaor HaGadol*. Israel: Netzah, 1966.

——. *HaRabbi HaRishon MiGur*. Jerusalem: Hozaot Kitvei Kodesh, 1958.

Schwarzfuchs, Simon. *Napoleon, the Jews and the Sanhedrin*. London: Littman Series, Routledge & Kegan Paul, 1979.

Sefer Besht, ed. L. J. Maimon. Jerusalem: Mosad Harav Kook, 1977.

Sefer Cracow, Ir VaEm BeYisrael. Jerusalem: Mosad Harav Kook, 1959.

Sefer Dinuburg (Ben Zion Dinur), ed. Yitzhak Fritz Baer, Joshua Gutman, and Moses Shur. Jerusalem: Kiryat Sefer, 1949.

Sefer Emunat Tzaddikim. Warsaw, 1880.

Sefer HaZikkaron LiKehillat Ostrov, ed. A. Margalit. Tel Aviv: Association of Former Residents of Ostrov, 1960.

Sefer Kielce, ed. Pinhas Zitrin. Tel Aviv: Irgun Olei Kielce B'Yisrael, 1957.

Sefer Marmoros. Tel Aviv: Beit Marmoros, 1983.

Sefer Radom, ed. Yitzhak Perlow. Tel Aviv: Irgun Yotzer Radom B'Yisrael, 1961.

Sefer Rohatyn–Kehillat Rohatyn, ed. M. Amihai. Tel Aviv: Former Residents of Rohatyn in Israel, 1962.

Sefer Sandz, ed. Raphael Mahler. New York: Sandzer Society of New York, 1970.

Sefer Shimon Dubnow, ed. S. Rawidowicz. Paris, 1954.

Sefer Toldot Rabbenu, ed. David Kahana. Munkacz: Grafia, 1938.

Shachar, I. "Catalogue of Amulets," in *Osat Feuchtwanger* (Hebrew). Jerusalem: Israel Museum, 1971, pp. 227–304.

Shaffir, William. "Separation of the Mainstream in Canada: The Hasidic Community of Tash." *Jewish Journal of Sociology* 29. London, 1974.

Shanblatt, Sanford D. "Tzavaat HaRibash" ("The Testament of the Baal Shem Tov"). *Judaism* 9:3 (New York, 1960): 282–284.

Shatzky, Jacob. *The History of the Jews in Warsaw*, 2 vols. New York: Yiddish Scientific Institute–Yivo, 1953.

Shemen, Nahman. *Di Biografia fun a Warshever Rav*. Montreal, 1949.

——. *Das Gezang fun Hasidut*, 2 vols. Buenos Aires: Centre Farband for Polish Jews in Argentina, 1959.

——. *Lublin*. Toronto: Gershon Pomeranz Essay Library, 1951.

Shimon Menahem Mendel of Garvatshov, *Sefer Baal Shem Tov*, vol. 2, *Mishpatim*. Satmar, 1943.

Shmeruk, Chone. "Social Significance of the Hasidic Shechitah." *Zion* 20 (Jerusalem, 1955): 47–72.

——. "Tales about R. Adam Baal Shem in the version of 'Shivhei HaBesht.' " *Zion* 28 (1963): 86–105.

Shneur Zalman of Liady. "Iggeret HaTeshuvah," in *Tanya*, pp. 180–202. Vilna, 1930.

——. *Tanya (Likkutei Amarim)*. Trans. Nisan Mindel. New York: Kehot, 1969.

Shragai, S. Z. *Beikhal Izbice-Lublin*. Jerusalem: Mosad Harav Kook, 1977.

——. *BeNitivei Hasidut Izbica-Radzyn*. Jerusalem: published by the author; vol. 1, 1972; vol. 2, 1974.

Shragai, S. Z., and Bik, A. *Izbitz-Lublin*. Jerusalem: Mosad Harav Kook, 1983.

Shtockfish, David, ed. *Sefer Demblin-Modrzyc*. Tel Aviv: Association of Former Residents, 1969.

Shuchatowitz, Avrom. "The Modzitz Hasidic Dynasty and Its Contribution to Jewish Culture." Ph.D. thesis. New York: Touro College, 1974.

The Significance of the Skullcap. New York: Kehot, 1957.

Silberberg, J. *Malkut Bet Radomsk*. Bene Berak: J. Silberberg, 1993.

Silver, Abba Hillel. *A History of Messianic Speculation in Israel from the First through the Seventeenth Centuries*. New York: Macmillan, 1927.

Simon, Leon. *Ahad Ha'Am: A Biography*. 1960.

——. "Tehiyat HaRuah," in *Parshat Derakhim*, vol. 2 in *Kol Kitvei*. Tel Aviv: Dvir, 1947.

Sochachewsky, B. A. *Joseph Shapotchnick: A Biography*. London, 1927.

Solomon of Lutzk. *Maggid Devarav LeYaakov*. Jerusalem, 1962.

Spector, Sheila L. *Jewish Mysticism: An Annotated Bibliography on the Kabbalah in English*. New York: Garland, 1984.
Sperling-Danzig, Abraham Yitzhak. *Taamei HaMinhagim*. Lvov, 1896; reprinted Tel Aviv, 1957.
Spiegel, Moshe. *Restless Spirit*. New York: Thomas Yoseloff, 1963.
Spiro, Kalmish Kalonymus. *Esh Kodesh*. Jerusalem: Vaad Hasidei Piazesno, 1960.
Stam, Shalom Eli. *Zekher Tzaddik*. Vilna: Yitzhak Moses Aranov, 1905.
Steinberg, Yehudah. *The Garden of Hassidism*, trans. Haim Schachter. Jerusalem: World Zionist Organization, 1961.
——. *Kol Kitvei Yehudah Steinberg*. Tel Aviv: Dvir, 1959.
Steinhartz, Nathan. *Y'Mei Moharnat*. Bene Berak: Keren Hadfass, 1956.
Steinman, Eliezer. *Be'er HaHasidut, Sefer Al Admorei Polin*. Tel Aviv: Knesset, n.d.
——. *Kitvei Rabbi Nahman*. Tel Aviv: Knesset, 1956.
——. *R. Israel Baal Shem Tov*. 1960.
——. *Sefer Be'er HaHasidut*, 10 vols. Tel Aviv: Knesset, n.d.
——. *Sefer Mishnat Habad*, 2 vols. Tel Aviv: Knesset, 1957.
——. *Shaar HaHasidut*. Tel Aviv: Knesset, 1957.
Steinsaltz, Adin. *In the Beginning: Discourses on Chasidic Thought*. Northvale, NJ: Jason Aronson, 1992.
——. *The Long Shorter Way: Discourses on Chasidic Thought*, ed. and trans. from the Hebrew by Yehudah Hanegbi. Northvale, NJ: Jason Aronson, 1988.
——. *The Sustaining Utterance*. Northvale, NJ: Jason Aronson, 1989.
Stern, Abraham, *Melitzei Esh*, 3 vols. New York: Grossman, 1962.
Stern, J. P. *The World of Franz Kafka*. New York: Holt, Rinehart & Winston, 1980.
Sternharz, N. *Alim Literufah–Mikhtevei Moharanat*. Jerusalem, 1930.
Surasky, Aaron. *BeLahavat Esh* (Mosheh Yehiel Halevi Epstein), 2 vols. Tel Aviv: Esh Dat Rabbinical Seminary, 1985.
——. *Demuyot Hod* (Hebrew). Jerusalem: Netzah, 1978.
——. *Marbitzei Torah U'Mussar Me'Olam HaHasidut*, 6 vols.: vol. 1, 1986; vol. 2, 1986; vol. 3, 1987; vol. 4, 1987; vol. 5, 1988; vol. 6, 1988. Bene Berak: A. Surasky.
——. *Rabbi Meir Shapira*, 2 vols. Bene Berak: Netzah, 1967.
Szilagyi-Windt, L. *A Kalloi Cadik*. Tel Aviv, 1960.
Tal, Shlomo. *R. Naftali Tzvi MiRopcyce*. Jerusalem: Mosad Harav Kook, 1983.
Tanya (*Likkutei Amarim*), Shneur Zalman of Liady, trans. Nisan Mindel. New York: Kehot, 1969.
Taylor, Anne. *Laurence Oliphant, 1829–1888*. Oxford, UK: Oxford University Press, 1982.
Teichthal, Yissahar Shlomo. *Em Habanim Semehah*. Budapest: Zalman Katz, Katzburg, 1943.
Teitelbaum, Yoel. *Kuntres Al HaGeulah VeAl HaTemurah*. Brooklyn, NY: Jerusalem Publishing, 1967.
——. *VaYoel Mosheh*. Brooklyn, NY: Jerusalem Publishing, 1978.
Teitelbaum, Mordecai. *HaRav MiLadi Umfleget Habad*, 2 vols. Warsaw: Tosiah, 1910–1913.
Teller, Hanokh. *The Bostoner*. Jerusalem/New York: Feldheim, 1990.
Teshima, Jacob Yuroh. "Self-Extinction in Zen and Hasidism," in *Zen and Hasidism*, pp. 108–117. Wheaton, IL; London: Madras Publishing House, 1978.
Tidhar, David. *Encyclopedia LeHalutzei HaYishuv*. Tel Aviv: Sifrit Rishonim, 1947.
Tiferet Banim Avotem. See Weinstock, Mosheh Yair.
Tishby, Isaiah. "Between Shabbetainism and Hasidism" ("Beyn Shabbatit LeHasidut"). *Knesset* 9 (1945): 238–266.
——. "Kitvei HaMekubbalim R. Ezra VeR. Azriel MiGerona." *Sinai* 16 (1945).
——. "The Messianic Idea and Messianic Trends in the Growth of Hasidism." *Zion* 32 (1967): 1–45.
——. *Mishnat HaZohar*. Jerusalem: Bialik Institute, 1961.
——. *Torat HaRa VeHaKlippah BeKabbalat HaAri*. Jerusalem, 1960.
——. *The Wisdom of the Zohar: An Anthology of Texts*, trans. David Goldstein, 3 vols. Oxford, UK: Oxford University Press, Littman Library, 1989.
Tishby, Isaiah, and Dan, Joseph. "*Torat HaHasidut VeSifrutah*," in *Hebrew Encyclopedia*, vol. 17, pp. 769–822. Jerusalem/Tel Aviv, 1965.

Toldot Anshei Shem, vol. 1, eds. Oscar Z. Rand and Aaron Moses Grynblat. New York: Toldot Anshei Shem, 1950.

Tsamriyon, Tzemach Mosheh. *Haitonot Sheerit HaPeletah B'Germania*. Tel Aviv: Jubilee Committee of the 25th Anniversary of Bergen-Belsen, 1976.

——. *Die Hebraische Presse in Europa*, 2 vols. Haifa: published privately, 1976.

Twerski, Abraham J. *Generation to Generation*. New York: Traditional Press, 1985.

Twersky, Aaron David. *Sefer HaYahas MiChernobyl VeRuzhin (The Genealogy of Chernobyl and Ruzhyn)* (Hebrew). Lublin: Tzveke, 1930; reprinted Jerusalem, n.d.

Twersky, Johanan. *HaBetulah MiLudmir*. Jerusalem: Mosad Bialik, 1949.

Uman, Uman, Rosh Hashanah: A Guide to R. Nahman's Rosh Hashanah in Uman. Jerusalem and New York: Bratslav Research Institute, 1991.

Undelson, Joseph H. *Dreamers of the Ghetto*. Tuscaloosa, AL: University of Alabama Press, 1990.

Unger, Manasseh. *Admorim SheNisfu BaShoah*. Jerusalem: Mosad Harav Kook, 1969.

——. *HaHasidut un Lebn*. New York, 1946.

——. *Die Hasidische Velt*. New York: Hasidut, 1955.

——. *Hasidut un Yom Tov*. New York: Hasidut, 1963.

——. *Pshische un Kotsk*. Buenos Aires: Farband of Polish Jews in Argentina, 1949.

——. *Reb Israel Baal Shem Tov*. New York: Hasidut, 1963.

——. *Sefer Kedoshim*. New York: Shulsinger Bros., 1967.

Unna, Josef. "Nathan HaCohen Adler," in *Guardians of our Heritage*, ed. Leo Jung. New York: Bloch, 1958.

Urbach, Ephraim, and Werblowsky, B. J., eds. *Studies in Mysticism and Religion Presented to Gershom G. Scholem on His Seventieth Birthday*. Jerusalem: Magnus Press, 1967.

Urtner, Nahman. See Ortner, Nathan.

Ury, Zalman F. *Studies in Torah Judaism: The Musar Movement*. New York: Yeshiva University Press, 1970.

Vasher, Barukh. "Bet Komarno" (Hebrew). *Sinai* 53 (1963): 167–173, 346–349.

Vilnay, Zeev. *Matzevet Kodesh BeEretz Yisrael*. Jerusalem: Mosad Harav Kook, 1956.

Walden, Aaron. *Shem HaGedolim HeHadash*. Warsaw, 1879.

Warsaw, ed. Yitzhak Greenbaum, vol. 1. Jerusalem/Tel Aviv; Encyclopedia of the Jewish Diaspora Company, 1953.

Waxman, Meyer. *A History of Jewish Literature*, 2nd rev. ed. New York: Bloch, 1936–1960.

Wein, Abraham. "Yizkor Books," in *Encyclopedia of the Holocaust*, vol. 4, ed. Gutman, Israel. New York: Macmillan, 1990, pp. 1694–1695.

Weiner, Herbert. "The Lubavitcher Movement." *I Commentary* 23 (1957): 231–241.

——. "The Lubavitcher Movement." *II Commentary* 23 (1957): 316–317.

——. *9½ Mystics*. New York: Collier, 1971.

Weingarten, Shmuel. *Munkacz Arim VeImaot BeYisrael*, vol. 1, ed. J. L. Fishman. Jerusalem: Mosad Harav Kook, 1946.

Weinreich, Uriel, and Weinreich, Beatrice. *Yiddish Language and Folklore: A Selective Bibliography for Research*. New York: Yivo, 1959.

Weinryb, B. *The Jews of Poland*. Philadelphia: Jewish Publication Society of America, 1972.

Weinstock, Israel. *Studies in Jewish Philosophy and Mysticism* (Hebrew). Jerusalem: Mosad Harav Kook, 1969.

Weinstock, Mosheh Yair. *Kodesh Hillulim*. New York: Ateret, 1978.

——. *Tiferet Banim Avotam*. Jerusalem: M. Y. Weinstock, 1976.

——. *Tiferet Bet David*. Jerusalem: M. Y. Weinstock, 1968.

Weiss, Joseph George. "Reshit HaHasidut" ("The Beginnings of Hasidism"). *Zion* 15 (1951–1952): 46–106.

——. "A Circle of Pre-Hasidic Pneumatica." *Journal of Jewish Studies* 8 (1957): 199–213.

——. "Contemplative Mysticism and 'Faith' in Hasidic Piety." *Journal of Jewish Studies* 4 (1953): 19–29.

——. "The Great Maggid's Theory of Contemplative Magic." *Hebrew Union College Annual* 31 (1960): 137–147.

——. "The Kavvanot of Prayer in Early Hasidism." *Journal of Jewish Studies* 9 (1958): 163–192.

——. *Mahkarim BeHasidut Bratzlav* (Hebrew). Jerusalem: Mosad Bialik, 1974.

——. "Some Aspects of R. Nahman of Braslav's Allegorical Self-Interpretation." *Tarbiz* 27: 2–3 (January 1958): 358–372.

——. *Studies in Eastern Jewish Mysticism*, ed. David Goldstein. Oxford, UK: Littman Library, 1985.

——. "The Study of the Torah according to the Theory of Rabbi Israel Baal Shem Tov" (Hebrew), in *Tiferet Yisrael*, Festschrift for Israel Brodie. London, 1967.

——. "Via Passiva in Early Hasidism." *Journal of Jewish Studies* 11 (1960): 137–155.

Werner, A. *Tzaddik Yesod Olam*, 2 vols. Jerusalem: Makhon L'Erot Daat, 1986.

Wertheim, Aaron. *Halakhot VeHalikhot BaHasidut*. Jerusalem: Mosad Harav Kook, 1960.

——. *Laws and Customs in Hasidism*, trans. Shmuel Himelstein. Hoboken, NJ: Ktav, 1992.

Wertheim, Jack, ed. *The Uses of Tradition*. New York/Jerusalem: Jewish Theological Seminary of America, 1992.

Who's Who in Israel. Tel Aviv: Mamut Limud, 1952(?).

Who's Who in World Jewry. New York: Who's Who in World Jewry, Inc., 1955.

Wiener, Meir Yehezkel. *HaRav HaKadosh MiBiala*. Bene Berak: Gize Maharitz, n.d.

Wiesel, Elie. *Somewhere a Master*. New York: Summit, 1982.

——. *The Trial of God*. New York: Random House, 1979.

Wilensky, Mordecai. "HaIm Hozer Agru BeMilhamto BaHasidut." In *Bizaron*, pp. 396–404. New York: 1968.

——. *Hasidim U'Mitnaggedim* (Hebrew), 2 vols. Jerusalem: Mosad Bialik, 1970.

——. *HaYishuv HaHasidi BeTvaria*. Jerusalem: Mosad Bialik, 1988.

Willy, Aaron. "The Western European Jew Who Turned Hasid." *Yivo Bletter* 39 (1947): 143–148.

Winkler, Gershon. *The Golem of Prague*. New York: Judaica Press, 1980.

Wohlgelernter, Maurice. *Israel Zangwill*. New York: Columbia University Press, 1964.

Wunder, Meir. *Elef Margulies*. Jerusalem: HaMakhon LeInatzeah Yehudit Galicia, 1993.

——. *Meorei Galicia–Enzyklopediya LeHakhmei Galicia*, 4 vols. Jerusalem: Institute for the Commemoration of Galician Jewry, vol. 1, 1978; vol. 2, 1982; vol. 3, 1986; vol. 4, 1990.

——. "R. Shimon MiYaroslav." *Hamayon* (1973): 59–67.

——. "R. Zechariah Mendel of Yaroslav." *Sinai* 73 (1973): 79–86.

Yaakov Rosenheim Memorial Anthology, ed. Joseph Friedenson. New York: Orthodox Library, 1968.

Yaari, Avraham. *Masaot Eretz Yisrael*. Tel Aviv: Abraham Ziyyoni, 1946.

——. *Shluhei Eretz Yisrael*. Jerusalem: Mosad Harav Kook, 1951.

——. "Two Basic Recensions of Shivhei HaBesht" (Hebrew). *Kiryat Sefer* 39 (1964): 249–272, 394–408, 552–563.

Yaari, Yehudah. *Sippurei Maasiyot MiShanim Kadmoniyot*. Jerusalem: Mosad Harav Kook, 1971.

Yari-Wold, M., ed. *Kehillat Raysha. Sefer Zikkaron*. Tel Aviv: Former Residents of Rzeszov, 1967.

Yehezkeli, Mosheh. *Hatzalat HaRabbi MiBelz Migai HaHarigah BePolin*. Jerusalem: Yeshurun, 1962.

——. *Nes HaHatzalah shel HaRabbi MiGur*. Jerusalem: Yeshurun, 1959.

Yidasin, A. *HaLekah VeHaLibur*. Tel Aviv, 1968.

Yoshar, Moses M. *The Chafetz Chaim*, 2 vols. Brooklyn: Mesorah Publications, 1984.

——. "R. Israel Meir Ha-Kohen the Hafets Hayyim," in *Jewish Leaders*, ed. Leo Jung. New York: Bloch, 1953.

Zadok HaKohen of Lublin. *Kunteros Et HaOkhel in Pri Tzaddok*. Israel, 1960.

Zeitlin, Hillel. *BePardes HaHasidut VeHaKabbalah*. Tel Aviv: Yavneh, 1960.

——. "HaHavayah HaHasidut" (Hebrew), in *Gevul Shnei Olamot*. Tel Aviv: Yavneh, 1965, pp. 225–374.

Zekher Tzaddik LiVrakhah: Yehudah Horowitz MiDzikov. London: printed by his disciples, 1990.

Zevin, Shlomoh Yosef. *HaMoadim BeHalakhah* (Hebrew), 6th ed. Tel Aviv: Abraham Ziyoni, 1957.

——. *Sippurei Hasidim*. Tel Aviv: Avraham Ziyoni, 1963.

Zilberberg, Joshua Uzziel. *Malkhut Bet David* (Hebrew). Bene Berak: J. U. Zilberberg, 1991.

Zimer, Uriel. *Rabbi Israel Baal Shem Tov*. New York: Kehot, 1960.

Zimmels, H. J. *Ashkenazim and Sephardim*, Jews' College Publications, New Series No. 2. London: Oxford University Press, 1958.

Zinberg, Israel. *A History of Jewish Literature* (*Di Geschichte fun Literatur bei Yi-*

den, Buenos Aires, Jewish Culture Congress, 1964), 12 vols., trans. B. Martin. Cleveland and London: The Press of Case Western University, 1972.

Zipperstein, Steven J. *Elusive Prophet: Ahad Ha'Am and the Origins of Zionism*. London: Peter Halban, 1993.

Zupnik, J. H. *Hamaor*. New York, *Tishri* and *Kislev* 1955.

Zweifel, Eliezer Tzvi. *Shalom al Yisrael*. Zhitomir: Shmaduv, 1873.

Zwolen, Yiskor Book, ed. Berl Kagan. New York: New York Independent Zvoliner Benevolent Society, 1982.

ABOUT THE EDITOR

Rabbi Tzvi Rabinowicz, a descendant of famous hasidic and rabbinic families in Poland, was the regional rabbi of Cricklewood, Willesden, and Brondesbury synagogues in London. A noted historian and writer, Dr. Rabinowicz obtained his rabbinical diploma from Jews' College of London and received his Ph.D. in 1948 from the University of London. He is the author of many books, including *A Guide to Life: Jewish Laws and Customs of Mourning*, *Treasures of Judaica*, *Hasidism and the State of Israel*, *Hasidism: The Movement and Its Masters*, and *The Prince Who Turned into a Rooster: One Hundred Tales from Hasidic Tradition.*